W9-ASE-853

FIFTH EDITION

Why Stop?

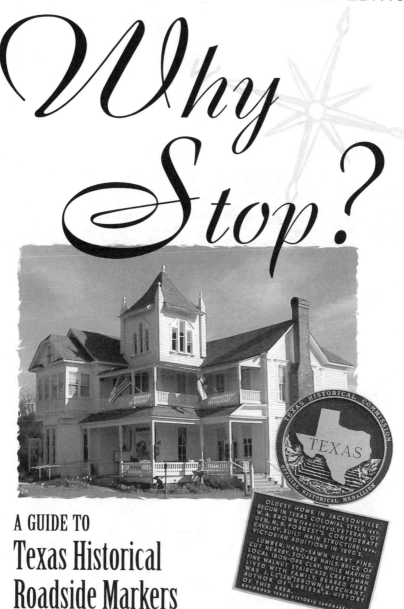

A GUIDE TO

Texas Historical Roadside Markers

BETTY DOOLEY AWBREY AND CLAUDE DOOLEY
AND THE TEXAS HISTORICAL COMMISSION

Published by Taylor Trade Publishing
An imprint of The Rowman & Littlefield Publishing Group, Inc.
4501 Forbes Boulevard, Suite 200, Lanham, Maryland 20706

Distributed by NATIONAL BOOK NETWORK

Library of Congress Cataloging-in-Publication Data

Dooley-Awbrey, Betty.
    Why stop? : a guide to Texas historical roadside markers / Betty
Dooley Awbrey and Claude Dooley.—1st Taylor Trade Pub. ed.
        p. cm.
    Includes bibliographical references and index.
    ISBN 1-58979-243-2 (pbk. : alk. paper)
    1. Historical markers—Texas—Guidebooks. 2. Texas—History, Local.
    3. Legends—Texas. 4. Texas—Guidebooks. I. Dooley, Claude W. II.
Title.
        F387.D68 2005
        917.64'04'6—dc22

The paper used in this publication meets the minimum requirements of American
National Standard for Information Sciences—Permanence of Paper for Printed
Library Materials, ANSI/NISO Z39.48-1992.

Manufactured in the United States of America.

Contents

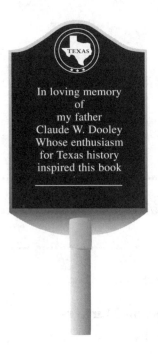

In loving memory
of
my father
Claude W. Dooley
Whose enthusiasm
for Texas history
inspired this book

Dedicated to
The Texas Historical Commission
and all other organizations whose research
and recordings have enriched
our knowledge of the history of Texas

Acknowledgments

We wish to express our appreciation to the Texas Historical Commission for making its files available and for the courtesy and assistance of its members in compiling this book, especially—

Larry Oaks, Executive Director, Texas Historical Commission
Cynthia Beeman, Director, History Programs Division
Dan Utley, Chief Historian
Linda Henderson, Historian
and
the staff of the Texas Historical Commission

We also thank the members of the Texas Historical Commission in each of the counties. The Commission maintains an excellent web site at: www.thc.state.tx.us/ and has a database of all historical markers at: http://atlas.thc.state.tx.us/

Special thanks to my husband, Stuart Awbrey, for his many hours of work on document conversion and compilation.

About Texas Historical Markers . . .

The markers you will encounter are designated Official Texas Historical Markers by the Texas Historical Commission. Markers are erected to commemorate historical sites, buildings, and events; institutions such as churches, businesses, and organizations; and individuals whose achievements have been recognized.

The most common types of markers are those pictured. Many of the earlier markers are made of stone, usually granite, featuring either engraved lettering or a metal plate with inscription. The familiar aluminum marker with raised lettering on a black background is more commonly used now. Also, there is the round medallion, which identifies a structure as a Recorded Texas Historic Landmark. An interpretive plate offering historical background of the building often accompanies the medallion.

Preface

From the Panhandle to the Gulf Coast, from Texarkana to El Paso, this vast area that once was a sovereign nation holds an enviable history that intrigues all who are fascinated by its legends. Much of this history endures through the inscriptions on historical markers that recount an array of interesting facts about people, places, and events that shaped the history of this state.

The purpose of this book was to include the text of markers located along highways and country roads so that hurried travelers could "meet" the fascinating individuals, "experience" the dramatic events, and see the historical places of Texas without having to stop to read the markers. That purpose continues with this fifth edition.

When the first edition of *Why Stop?* was published in 1978, there were more than 6,000 recorded historical markers in Texas. By the time the second edition was published in 1985, that number had increased to 10,000. In 1999, at the publication of the fourth edition, there were more than 11,000 markers. To date the Texas Historical Commission has approximately 12,800 markers.

More than one hundred seventy new marker texts were added to the fifth edition of *Why Stop?* Since a book this size can only accommodate a fixed number of inscriptions, it was necessary to delete markers. With each new edition the decision of selecting which markers to delete becomes an increasingly difficult task. The decision was made to feature markers located on U.S. and state highways, based on the assumption that travelers of rural roads have more time to stop and read the markers.

While the purpose of *Why Stop?* is to give readers the pleasure of learning about the colorful history of Texas without having to delay a trip, I believe that these inscriptions about the great, near-great, and not-so-great events and people that made this legendary state what it is will inspire you to learn more and maybe even stop awhile. When there is time to stop and read the markers, you will want to go to the courthouse squares, often the location of several historical markers. Also, be advised that the historical commissions of some counties publish brochures that include the locations of the markers in their counties.

Inscriptions on roadside markers are written by the Texas Historical Commission staff, based upon research done by county historical commissions. To the best of my knowledge the inscriptions are quoted as they appear on the markers. Any errors are unintentional, and corrections reported to me will be considered in future editions of *Why Stop?*

Please note that indicated locations of some markers may be inaccurate. Some markers have been relocated due to highway construction, and others, unfortunately, have been vandalized. I will appreciate your informing me of relocated markers.

Betty Dooley Awbrey
San Antonio, Texas

How To Use This Guide

The marker inscriptions selected for this book have been compiled for the convenience and enjoyment of both the traveler and the history enthusiast. They occur in the order of the alphabetized cities or towns nearest them. By locating the name of the town you are approaching, you can determine the location of nearby markers by the information in italics. Indicated distances are measured from the nearest town within the county in which the marker is located. Of course, the index includes towns, counties, and key persons and events responsible for the markers.

ABBOTT (Hill Co.)   *IH 35 Access Road*
Czech Settlers in Hill County
One of the most influential and numerous national groups to settle in Hill County, Czechs came to this area from Fayette County and the Province of Moravia in Austria-Hungary. Many sought greater freedom due to barriers to attaining national status in the old country, political restraints, introduction of German into the schools, and compulsory military service.

Land agents painted a rosy picture of opportunities awaiting those who purchased cheap state university lands in this region. The first immigrants arrived in the 1870s and found the soil so fertile that they induced many others to join them. Building of the Texas Central and "Katy" Railroads boosted immigration.

Capital of Czech settlement in the area is Abbott, named for Jo Abbott (1840–1908), judge, legislator, and lawyer. Surrounding towns are Zee Vee (so called for the local ZV cattle brand), Penelope, and Aquilia.

Neighbors admired the Czechs for their neat, well-managed farms and their thrift and industry. For many years they retained a strong group spirit, speaking their own language and observing old world customs. In recent decades they have mixed more with other groups and today fill many public and professional offices as well as continuing to farm.   (1970)

ABERNATHY (Hale Co.)   *US 87, at City Hall*
Town of Abernathy
Founded when Santa Fe Railroad was extended from Plainview to Lubbock, 1909. Named for Monroe G. Abernathy (1868–1962), treasurer of South Plains Investment Company, firm which promoted townsite.

Community prospered, becoming a major railhead for shipping of cattle. Several buildings from the defunct town of Bartonsite were moved here and new ones built. Center of civic activities was the "Old Tabernacle" (1918–1947), located on city square. In early days, before roads were built, broad plowed furrows marked way to house of town doctor.

Economy is agriculture-based.   (1973)

ABILENE (Taylor Co.)   *US 83/84, 12 mi. S in roadside park*
Taylor County
Created 1858. Named for Edward, James and George Taylor, 18, 20, and 22, Tennesseans who came to Texas in 1833 and died at the Alamo, March 6, 1836. Organized 1878, with county seat at Buffalo Gap, through which went the Fort Concho to Fort Belknap stagecoach and longhorns on western trail up to Kansas. County seat was moved to Abilene in 1883. Of the 254 Texas counties, 42 bear Indian, French or Spanish names. 10 honor such colonizers as Stephen F. Austin, "Father of Texas". 12 were named for Washington, Clay and other American patriots. 96 were named for men like the Taylors who fought in the Texas War for Independence (15 dying at the Alamo), signed the Declaration of Independence, or served as statesmen in the Republic of Texas. 23 have the names of frontiersmen and pioneers. 11 honor American statesmen who worked for the annexation of Texas; 10, leaders in Texas since statehood, including jurists, ministers, educators, historians, statesmen; and 36, men prominent in the Confederacy during the Civil War. El Paso and 8 others have geographical names, San Jacinto and Val Verde were named for battles; Live Oak and Orange, for trees; and Mason for a fort.   (1964)

ABILENE (Taylor Co.)   *US 83 at SH 36, 2.3 mi. E of intersection*
Lindbergh in West Texas
(September 26, 1927)
Four months after his record-setting trans-Atlantic solo flight, Charles Augustus Lindbergh (1902–1974) landed here for one hour and thirty-six minutes during a nationwide publicity tour. Touching down at Kinsolving Field (now the site of Abilene Zoo) after an almost nine-hour flight from Santa Fe, "Lucky Lindy" was given a hero's welcome by thousands of West Texans. His famous Ryan monoplane, "Spirit of St. Louis," was taxied into a fenced area and surrounded by National Guard troops for protection. An escort plane landed later.

Heading a parade into Abilene were seventy-one mayors and countless officials. Lindbergh was escorted by Mrs. Mildred Moody (1897–1983), wife of Gov. Dan Moody and an Abilene native; Mayor Thomas Edward Hayden (1891–1949); and Chamber of Commerce President

Charles William Bacon (1871–1947). The young pilot reportedly balked at a "throne" rigged for him in an open Nash automobile, and rode with Mrs. Moody through the town to Federal Lawn.

Lindbergh delivered a brief speech over loud speakers praising the ideal terrain and weather in Texas for developing civil and military aviation. He was escorted back to his plane and flew two hours and forty-two minutes to his next stop in Fort Worth.   (Texas Sesquicentennial 1836–1986)

ABILENE (Taylor Co.)   *IH 20, ¼ mi. W of Tye*
Butterfield Mail and Stage Line
One of major horse-drawn transportation projects of history. Was authorized by act of Congress on March 3, 1857. Contract for semi-weekly service overland to San Francisco, Calif., was awarded to company headed by John Butterfield; another stockholder in the $2,000,000 venture was express pioneer Wm. G. Fargo. The line employed some 2,000 people and used hundreds of stagecoaches and thousands of animals. In addition to receipts from freight and passengers it had a $600,000 annual subsidy for carrying U.S. mail.

Company operated from Sept. 1858 to Feb. 1861 with a 25-day schedule for the 2,795-mile trip (8 to 9 days were allowed for crossing Texas). Route began in Tipton, Mo., and Memphis, Tenn., uniting at Fort Smith, Ark., entering Texas near Sherman, thence westward through the Comanche-held frontier, leaving the state at El Paso.

Stage stations were located about every 20 miles, and the best known in this vicinity were Fort Belknap, Fort Phantom Hill, Mountain Pass and Fort Chadbourne. Between Fort Belknap and Tucson, Arizona mules were used to pull the coaches as they were less appealing to Indians. Each coach accommodated four to ten passengers at an average fare of $200 each; mail and freight charges were ten cents per one-half ounce.   (1969)

ABILENE (Taylor Co.)   *US 277, near site, at juncture*
w/FM 2928, 15 mi. SW
In Vicinity of Coronado's Camp
In 1541, the Spanish explorer Coronado is thought to have passed this way en route from New Mexico to the fabled Indian village of "Quivira," though his path across vast Texas plains is now difficult to determine.

Upon finding that his Indian guide, "The Turk," had taken him too far south, Coronado halted at a small canyon or barranca.

Here he conferred with his captains and decided to follow the compass directly north.

When they reached "Quivira" (possibly in Kansas), no gold was found—only the poor, grass huts of a Wichita village.   (1968)

ABILENE (Taylor Co.)   *US 277, at site, about 8 mi. SW*
Camp Barkeley
(February 15, 1941–March 21, 1945)
Site of main entrance to Camp Barkeley, one of the nation's largest military camps of World War II. At peak, 60,000 men were in training here. Named for Pvt. David B. Barkeley of the 89th Division, who died on a secret scouting expedition behind German lines during the Meuse-Argonne Battle of World War I. Among famous units trained here were the 45th and 90th Infantry Divisions and the 11th and 12th Armored.

A medical replacement training center, the largest in the country, was also established here, with 15 battalions. In May, 1942, the Medical Administrative Corps Officer Candidate School was activated and graduated about 12,500 candidates.

Camp Barkeley eventually grew to be a complete city unit twice the size of Abilene in the 1940s. It had a 2,300-bed hospital, 2 cold storage plants, a bakery, 4 theaters, 2 service clubs for enlisted men, 15 chapels, and 35 post exchange buildings.

The military personnel were housed in hutments, except for some 4,000 in barracks. Part of the post was also a German prisoner-of-war camp. Once some of the prisoners escaped, to the alarm of Abilene citizens, and others attempted to tunnel under the fences. Camp Barkeley was declared surplus in 1945.   (1969)

ACTON (Hood Co.)
FM 1190, Acton Cemetery
Grave of Elizabeth Crockett
Three miles south to the grave of Elizabeth Crockett, wife of David Crockett, hero of the Alamo. Died March 2, 1860 age 74.

ADAMSVILLE (Lampasas Co.)
US 281
John Patterson Home
Built 1879–1880 by John Patterson, first man to cultivate (in 1854) land in county, and a minuteman during Civil War. (1965)

ADAMSVILLE (Lampasas Co.)
US 281 at N city limits
Joseph Leeland Straley Ranch
House built by Lee Straley who settled near Adamsville in 1856. He first had a log cabin on the river then built this house of walnut which was cut at Townsen sawmill. The furniture in the house was also made by a fine cabinet maker at the mill.

AGUA DULCE (Nueces Co.)
SH 44, 2 mi. E
Battle of Agua Dulce
During the Texas Revolution, Dr. James Grant (1793–1836), a Scottish-born physician, and Francis W. Johnson (1799–1884) recruited an army of volunteers to invade Mexico and capture the town of Matamoros. After Sam Houston expressed disapproval of the poorly-organized venture, many recruits left the expedition before it reached the settlement of San Patricio along the Nueces River in January 1836.

Mexican General Santa Anna, who was organizing an army to attack Texan forces at the Alamo in San Antonio, discovered the Matamoros plan and dispatched General Jose Urrea to stop the advancing expedition. Urrea's cavalry, reinforced with 300 infantrymen, crossed the Rio Grande on February 16. Meanwhile, Grant and Johnson divided their troops to hunt for horses. Johnson's men were camped at San Patricio when Urrea attacked on the morning of February 27. Johnson and 4 others escaped, while 18 Texans were killed and 32 captured. On March 2, Urrea's soldiers surprised Grant's company at Aqua Dulce Creek (3.25 Mi. NW). Grant was among the 12 Texans killed; 6 were taken prisoner, and 6 escaped. The brief skirmish occurred on the same day the Texas Declaration of Independence was signed at Washington-on-the-Brazos. (1976)

ALAMO (Hidalgo Co.)
1341 W US 83 Bus.
Camp Ebenezer
From 1902 to 1909, Peter Ebenezer Blalock and George L. Hawkins bought 32,000 acres of land here. By 1908 they had built shipping pens at this site and named the railroad depot Ebenezer. Their ranching plans ended in 1909 when the tract was sold to the Alamo Land and Sugar Company. Under the direction of C. H. Swallow (1868–1957), the company colonized the land after 1914. Excursion trains brought prospective farmers, housed here at "Camp Ebenezer." The depot was moved one mile east in 1919 to serve the new town of Alamo. The camp served until the 1930s as temporary housing for land buyers. (Texas Sesquicentennial 1836–1986)

ALBANY (Shackelford Co.)
US 180 at US 283, Albany City Park
Shackelford County
First inhabited by Nomadic Indian tribes, Shackelford County was created in 1858 and named for Dr. John Shackelford (1790–1857). The first permanent Anglo-American settlers in this area included J. C. Lynch (1828–1912), a native of Ireland who moved here in 1858; W. H. Ledbetter (1833–1884), who arrived in 1859 and later started the Ledbetter Salt Works; T. E. Jackson (b. 1820), a merchant who settled in the northern part of the county before 1860; and G. W. Greer (1812–1893), who operated a stage station on Hubbard Creek after 1861.

During the Civil War (1861–1865), settlers took refuge at "family forts" such as Fort Mugginsville and Fort Hubbard. They gained military protection from frontier perils when the U.S. Army established Fort Griffin in 1867. Griffin, the lawless settlement that grew up around the fort, attracted buffalo hide hunters and cattlemen driving herds up the western cattle trail.

Shackelford County was organized Sept. 12, 1874, with Fort Griffin as temporary county seat. Albany was chosen permanent county seat in Nov. 1874. The county's population increased sharply after the arrival of the Texas Central Railroad in 1881. Petroleum production generated an economic boom, 1910–1930. Chief industries today (1976) are petroleum and ranching.   (1976)

ALBANY (Shackelford Co.)   *SH 180, 14 mi. W*
Bud Matthews Switch of the Texas Central Railway
In 1900, the Texas Central Railway extended a line northwest from Albany across this portion of Rose Ella (Matthews) Conrad's cattle ranch. Ella and her Brother John A. "Budi" Matthews, for whom this site is named, promptly constructed cattle pens and a loading chute at this location. Surrounding ranchers soon were shipping their cattle from this switch to markets in Fort Worth. As many as 105,000 head of cattle were shipped annually until the railroad ceased operations in 1967. Since that year local ranchers have continued to load cattle onto trucks from this site.   (1993)

ALBANY (Shackelford Co.)   *US 283, Fort Griffin State Park*
Family Forts
C.S.A.
Few in numbers and with little protection from the military but refusing to abandon their country, certain families of courageous and determined people on the Texas frontier during the Civil War gathered together in hastily constructed stockades and held out against the threats of hostile Indians and renegade whites known as "forting up." This plan was encouraged by the military for this part of the state. Most of the men 18 to 45 were away in Confederate service, and those 17 and over 45 were subject to periodic militia duty for frontier protection. Family forts gave settlers way to protect stock, farms and provide some schooling for their children.

Best-known family fort in this sector was Fort Davis, located 8 miles east on bank Clear Fork of Brazos in Stephens County, where some 120 people lived during last year of Civil War. Named for Confederate President Jefferson Davis, it was laid off in lots. Log houses with dirt roofs, mud in cracks, dirt floors, were connected by pickets driven into ground. A blockhouse was used by women and children during raids. There were no luxuries, little food; all clothes, soap, soda, candles were made. Nearest supplies were 100 miles away, doctor 65 miles. Yet, there were dances, candy pulls, weddings, "feasts," Sunday school, occasional sermons and blue-backed spellers. Other family forts near were Lynch and Green ranches, Shackelford County; Blair's Fort, Allen's ranch, Eastland County; Buffalo Springs, Clay County; Bragg's, Murray's, Young County; Picketville, Mugginsville, Owls Head, Stephens County.   (1963)

ALBANY (Shackelford Co.)   *US 180 at US 283, Albany City Park*
The Cook Ranch Oil Field
(5 mi. NW on FM 1084)
William Ivy Cook (1857–1923) and his wife Matilda moved to this county in 1895. With a brother-in-law, J. H. Nail, Cook purchased a 27.75 section ranch. The Cooks bought out Nail in 1898, and have owned the ranch ever since. During the 1918 Breckenridge and Ranger booms, Cook sold leases but prophesied he could drink from his hat all of the oil under his land. In 1925 his widow leased all open acreage to Charles Roeser, Tol Pendleton, and Marshall R. Young, of Roeser & Pendleton, Inc. This firm's second well in 1926 struck oil at 1241 feet and flowed at 1,000 barrels a day. This prolific flow of oil at such a shallow depth has been one of Cook ranch field's remarkable features. Commercial low pressure gas injection was started on the ranch in 1927 and helped elevate recovery standards internationally.

With the oil wealth, Mrs. Cook founded the W. I. Cook Memorial Hospital in Fort Worth in 1929.

Cook field enriched Albany and its trade area by expanding petroleum-related business activities. Of the 1087 wells drilled on the ranch, 825 yielded oil and four gas. Production has now exceeded thirty million barrels. Marshall R. Young remains owner of the oil firm.   (1976)

ALBANY (Shackelford Co.)   *US 180, 12.5 mi. W*
Butterfield Overland Mail Trail
The trail of the Butterfield Overland mail passed this point 1858.

ALICE (Jim Wells Co.)   US 281 at SH 44
Jim Wells County
Formed from Nueces County, created March 11, 1911; organized May 6, 1911; named for Judge James B. Wells, an able lawyer, born near Aransas Pass, Texas July 12, 1854. Died at Brownsville December 21, 1923. Alice, the county seat.

ALICE (Jim Wells Co.)   FM 1931, near intersection of FM 359,
                                                          on outskirts of town
Archelaus Bynum Dodson
(December 31, 1807–March 10, 1898)
Texas patriot famed as man who introduced the Lone Star flag during the Texas Revolution.

Born in North Carolina, Dodson came to Texas with his parents in 1827. He served as a delegate to the 1832 convention seeking governmental reforms.

On May 17, 1835, he married Sarah Rudolph Bradley. Later in the year 1835, Dodson was first lieutenant in Texas defense unit under Capt. Andrew Robinson.

To Robinson's company his bride presented her handiwork—a red, white and blue flag with a single star, launching tradition of Lone Star Flag of Texas. This banner flew at Washington-on-the Brazos when Declaration of Independence was signed March 2, 1836.

Dodson continued to fight in the Texas Revolution until after victory at San Jacinto. He located his headright of land Grimes County, moving family there in 1844. Mrs. Sarah Bradley Dodson, flag maker and mother of six children, died in 1848. Her grave is in Bethel cemetery, near Bedias, Grimes County.

Dodson in 1850 married Louisa McWhorter, a widow. In 1860 he moved his family west to another Texas frontier, on the Nueces River. In this vicinity he lived to a respected old age. At death he was buried in Collins cemetery, a half-mile south of here.   (1969)

ALICE (Jim Wells Co.)   US 281, 14.4 mi. N
Vicinity of Texas Rangers'
Battle of May 29, 1850
A gallant fight in an era after the Mexican War, while the Federals and Texans were ridding Nueces to Rio Grande area of marauders.

Texas Rangers under Capt. John S. "Rip" Ford surprised a camp of Comanches near this site on May 29, 1850. In numbers, Rangers and Indians were about equal. Seven Comanches were wounded, four slain; one ranger was killed and two were wounded. Comanche Chief Otto Cuero was wounded by Capt. Ford and slain by a bullet from the gun of Ranger David Steele, who sent Chief's regalia to Governor P. H. Bell, an ex-Texas Ranger.   (1969)

ALLEN (Collin Co.)   Exchange Parkway, Allen Station Park
Allen
Fertile land and plentiful water drew settlers to this area from as early as the 1840s. This part of Collin County was well populated by 1876 when the Houston and Texas Central Railroad built a water supply stop on Cottonwood Creek near this site. The railroad stop and newly created town lots established a center of commerce for local farmers and their families and provided better equipment and broader markets for agricultural production. The surrounding open prairie soon was developed into small family farms.

The Houston and Texas Central Railroad filed documents to create the town of Allen from the James L. Read survey in 1876. The village was named for Ebenezer Allen, a former Republic and State of Texas attorney general and a founder of the Houston and Texas Central Railroad. A dry goods store, barber shop, and school soon opened in the rapidly growing town. Sam Bass reportedly led an outlaw gang that robbed the Allen Depot on February 22, 1878. This was probably the first successful train robbery in Texas.

By 1884, the town of Allen had three churches, a flour mill, and a population of 350. In 1908, the Texas Traction Company built an electric railway through town, calling it the Interurban, the citizenry numbered 550 by 1915. Allen was incorporated in 1953 with 400 residents. Electric railway service ended in 1948, but railway freight service continued. Strong economic growth in the Dallas-Fort Worth area helped the town's population grow to include more than 19,000 citizens in the 1990s.   (1998)

ALPINE (Brewster Co.)   *US Hwy. 67/90, 8 mi. E*
Brewster County
Formed from Presidio County, created February 2, 1887, organized February 14, 1887. In 1897 the territory of Buchel and Foley Counties was added to Brewster. Named for Henry Percy Brewster, 1816–1884 soldier and statesman, a hero of San Jacinto.

Murphyville, county seat, 1887, name changed to Alpine, 1889. Largest county in area in the state.

ALPINE (Brewster Co.)   *US 67/90, 2.3 mi. E*
Alpine
Original name Osborne. Central gateway to Big Bend National Park. Largest city in largest county in Texas. Center for mining, livestock, travel.

Named for its mountainous setting. Site well known for its spring during Indian days. First settled in 1882 as a Southern Pacific railroad stop. Called Murphyville, 1883–1887, for owner of the waterhole.

Originally in Presidio County. Was made county seat 1887 when Brewster County was created.

Historic sites marked. Western lore displayed at museum, Sul Ross State College.   (1965)

ALPINE (Brewster Co.)   *US 90 at US 67, 8 mi. E, at roadside park*
Ancient Rocks Boundary
The mountains toward the east are limestone reef beds deposited in the Cretaceous and Permian Seas about 135 million years and 250 million years ago, respectively. The limestone reefs overlie deformed rocks in the Ouachita Fold Belt, which is visible along the highway to the east, near Marathon. To the south are younger limestone beds deposited about 125 to 135 million years ago. They also rest above the Ouachita Fold Belt (so named for the Ouachita Mountains of Arkansas-Oklahoma, where the formation was first studied by geologists).

Toward the west, northwest, and southwest are layers of lava and associated volcanic rocks 25 to 35 million years old. These were thrust upward, into, and over most of the older sedimentary rock layers. Many of the molten rock masses cooled and hardened underneath, while vast quantities poured over the surface in the form of lava flows and volcanic debris up to a mile in thickness. Subsequent erosion has sculptured these highlands by removing much of the younger volcanic rock, and cutting deeply into the older sea deposits. Out of the lower, igneous hills grow yucca and other cacti, contrasting with juniper and piñon on the higher elevations.   (1970)

ALTO (Cherokee Co.)   *SH 294, 9 mi. W*
Box's Fort
John M. and Sally Box, along with John's brother Stephen F. and his wife Keziah Box and their families, came to Texas from Alabama in1834. John and Sally's son, Roland W. Box, and his wife Mary Hallmark Box purchased ⅓ of the Stephen Burnham land grant and built a log fort on a hill near its northern boundary. Within the enclosure they built a log house and a dugout, and Box's Fort became the center of a settlement as the extended Box families made their own homes in and near the fort. John A. Stillwell, Thomas G., and Nelson Box and their cousins Samuel C. and James E. Box fought in the Texas Revolution. The home of John A. and Letty T. Box was a post office called Box's Creek from 1851 to 1866. Over time, several churches and stores operated in the vicinity, but by 1900 Box's Fort no longer appeared on area maps.   (2000)

ALTO (Cherokee Co.)   *US 69 to CR 2405, 2 mi. N*
Chief Bowles' Last Homesite
In 1836, General Sam Houston negotiated a treaty with the Cherokees in Texas allowing possession of the lands they occupied in East Texas. The leading figure among the Cherokees at that time was Duwali (also known as Bowl, Chief Bowles and Bold Hunter). After the Texas Revolution, the Senate of the Republic of Texas declared the treaty invalid. Near this site in 1839, Chief Bowles learned of Texas President Mirabeau B. Lamar's orders to remove the Cherokee from Texas. Bowl mobilized his people to resist the expulsion, but they were defeated and the chief was killed at the Battle of the Neches on July 16, 1839, in what is now Van Zandt County.   (2001)

ALTO (Cherokee Co.) *US 69 & FM 1911, 10.5 mi. S*
Homer-Alto Road
As the population increased in Angelina and Cherokee counties in the 1860s, a formal system of roads began to take shape. Until that time, roads were usually forged by farmers and other pioneers carrying goods to market or traveling to new homes, as in other areas of Texas. Construction of a road from Homer (at that time Angelina County seat) to Alto began in 1860. The survey crew followed buffalo and Indian trails to determine the best route for the new road. Once open, it was the official mail route from Homer to Alto, and then on to Rusk, the Cherokee County seat. It led through a community known as Denman Springs until 1882 when Lufkin was created there and the road became Denman Avenue. The main part of the Homer-Alto Road became State Highway 40 in the 1930s and later U. S. Highway 69.   (1999)

ALTO (Cherokee Co.) *US 69, 1 mi. S, then 1 mi. E*
Cherokee Home of Grand Xinesi
In the present county of Cherokee was the home of the Grand Xinesi, chief priest and custodian of the sacred fire of the Hasinai Confederacy of Indians.

If fire was allowed to die out, it was his duty to carry more fire with proper ceremony to their homes to be rekindled. It was to the Hasinai, the principal tribe of this Confederacy, that the word "Texas" was generally applied.

ALTO (Cherokee Co.) *SH 21, 1 mi. SW*
Site of Delaware Indian Village
Noted as interpreters and messengers of peace, the Delaware were chiefly instrumental in bringing the other tribes to the general treaty at Bird's Fort (in the present county of Tarrant) in 1843.

ALTO (Cherokee Co.) *SH 21, 2 mi. SW*
Site of Lacy's Fort
Built before 1835 as a home and trading post by Martin Lacy, Indian agent for the Mexican government.

Used as a place of refuge after the massacre of the Killough family, October 5, 1838.

ALTO (Cherokee Co.) *SH 21, 5 mi. SW*
Site of Neches Indian Village
Here at the opening of the 18th century stood a village of the Neches Indians. Their name was given to the river and later a mission, San Francisco de los Neches, established near by. With the Cherokees, the Neches Indians were expelled from Texas, 1839.

ALTO (Cherokee Co.) *SH 21, 5 mi. SW*
Mound Prairie
Bulging out of the earth a few yards from this point, three prehistoric Indian mounds interrupt the prevailing flat terrain. Long overgrown with grass, the mounds and adjacent village (covering about 11 acres) constitute one of the major aboriginal sites in North America. From about 500 to 1100 A.D., Caddoan Indians inhabited the village, which lay near the southwest edge of a great mound-building culture. Called "Mississippian," this culture once flourished throughout the present Eastern United States.

Excavations during 1939–1941 and 1968–1969 showed two of the mounds to have had ceremonial purposes. One may have been capped with bright yellow clay and both apparently supported temples. The tallest mound (about 20 feet) revealed several major burials.

The village surrounding the mounds but settled before they were built, contained many round houses that probably resembled giant beehives. Thousands of pot fragments, some pipes, charred corncobs and nuts, and flint points were found in the area.

Centuries after its abandonment by the Indians, this region was again a center of civilization when, in 1690, the first Spanish mission in East Texas was built nearby to minister to the Tejas Indians.   (1970)

ALTO (Cherokee Co.)   *SH 21 at CR 2610, 2 mi. E*

Ellis P. Bean
June 8, 1783–October 3, 1846

Born in Tennessee, Ellis P. Bean came to Texas with Philip Nolan's mustang hunters in 1800. He was captured by Spanish troops in 1801, and taken to Mexico as a prisoner. In 1810 he was freed in exchange for service to the Royalist Army, but he quickly deserted to the rebels under Morelos. Fifteen years later, Bean returned to the U. S. as a Mexican colonel to seek aid for the rebel cause. He joined Andrew Jackson's army at the Battle of New Orleans, but returned to Mexico within the year. In 1816 he barely escaped the Royalists by leaving his wife to flee to the U. S. He married a Tennessean in 1818. They moved to Texas in 1823, where Bean served Mexico as an Indian agent. After Texas independence, Bean made his home near this site. He disappeared in 1843 to return to Mexico, dying in the home of his first wife in 1846.   (1999)

ALTO (Cherokee Co.)   *SH 21, 7 mi. E at Angelina River*

Angelina River

Early Texas artery of travel and transportation. Ran through land of civilized Indians whose word "Tejas," for friend, gave name to northern part of New Spain, then to the Republic and State of Texas.

Here in 1690, Spanish explorers and missionaries found a young girl eager to learn Christianity. For her sweet disposition, she was called Angelina. Her name soon was used for the river where she lived. Though French and Spaniards were enemies, Angelina befriended all, and for years acted as interpreter.

Angelina River by 1779 was route for settlers to come from the coast to East Texas. It was crossed by El Camino Real (King's Highway to Mexico) and by Smugglers' Road, for those dodging tax collectors. In the 1830s, John Durst promoted on the Angelina, just south of here, a port for shipping cotton to New Orleans and receiving merchandise in return.

Other Texas Rivers named by Spaniards include the Blanco, Brazos (River of the Arms of God), Colorado, Concho, Comal (a pan), Frio, Guadalupe, Lavaca, Llano, Medina, Navidad, Navasota, Neches, Nueces, Pedernales, Pecos Rio Grande, San Antonio, San Gabriel, Trinity and San Jacinto. Anglo-American names for streams include Canadian, Pease, Red and Devil's River.   (1965)

ALTO (Cherokee Co.)   *SH 21, 7 mi. E*

Site of Linwood

On land inherited by Delilah Dill Durst from Helena Kimble Dill, whose daughter born in 1804 was thought to be first white child native to Texas.

Built about 1830 by Delilah's husband, Joseph Durst, who settled in Texas in early 1800's and rose by 1826 to office of alcalde in Nacogdoches.

During troubles of 1832, the Battle of Nacogdoches ended here with surrender of Colonel Piedras' army to 17 Texans.

Later was home of Geo. Whitfield Terrell (1802–1846), who served Republic of Texas as attorney-general and as minister to England, France, and Spain.

Birthplace of Geo. B. Terrell (1862–1947), state representative, commissioner of agriculture, and congressman-at-large.   (1965)

ALTO (Cherokee Co.)   *Caddoan Mound State Historic Site, 6 mi. SW*

Zebulon Pike Campsite

In 1807, under commission from Gen. James Wilkinson, Governor of the Louisiana Territory, Lt. Zebulon Pike led an expedition to explore the headwaters of the Arkansas and Red Rivers and to report on Spanish settlements in the New Mexico area. Heading south from present Colorado, where the party saw the mountain later named Pike's Peak for the expedition's leader, they were arrested by Spanish authorities. Under escort back to the United States, the party camped near this site on June 23, 1807. The Pike Expedition furnished an important account of Spanish Texas and New Mexico.   (1982)

ALVARADO (Johnson Co.)   *6921 US 67 at IH-35*

Site of Norman Springs & Norman Grove

William Balch (1804–1870) claimed land around this site as a member of the Peters Colony in 1849. When he returned with his family in 1851, they found a group of Caddo Indians camping on one side of the springs. The Balch family built their cabin on the other side and lived peaceably with their neighbors. Other Caddo were living in the area that became Alvarado. Like the new settlers, they were attracted by the abundance of fresh water. The springs were located on the road from Birdville and Fort Worth to Hillsboro, Waco, Ft. Graham and other destinations. William Balch founded the town of Alvarado in 1854 and the family moved into town. Joe (1798–1882) and Sarah (1797–1897) Shaw and their family settled here and farmed the land. Joe Shaw was a three-term county sheriff. With settlers coming in increasing numbers, the Caddo Indians moved to the Oklahoma territory or further west, and by 1860 the area was dominated by new settlers. Tennessee native Lafayette Norman (1826–1904), veteran of the U. S. war with Mexico and later the Confederate Army, purchased 245 acres around this site with his third wife Julia in 1872. The Normans supplied thirsty and weary travelers with access to their spring; the site became known as Norman Springs and Norman Grove. A seven-year drought in the 1930s and a five-year drought in the 1950s significantly reduced the water table in this region. Norman Springs slowly became little more than a muddy patch. By the dawn of the 21st century, the once free-flowing spring that provided priceless fresh water to the early Indians and pioneer settlers of the Johnson County frontier was marked only by a willow tree.   (2000)

ALVIN (Brazoria Co.)   *SH 35, 6 mi. S in roadside park*
Vicinity of Oyster Creek and Chocolate Bayou
Most early Texas homes and towns were built along streams that provided water for people and livestock, and travel for boats said to be capable of "floating on a heavy dew."

Oyster Creek served, 1822–1861, as such a homesite-highway. Its boat landings were piled high with sugar, cotton, cane and other products of some of America's richest plantations.

Chocolate Bayou was an area of early-day cattle raising.

These were 2 of 50 streams and 10 bays that made this coast a network of useful waterways.
                                                                (1968)

ALVORD (Wise Co.)   *US 287 near N city limit*
NE at 606 Washington Street, Is Birthplace of
General Ernest O. Thompson
(1892–1966)
Acknowledged world leader in petroleum conservation.

A third generation Texan, born here in Alvord. Left college to enter service in World War I, earning a battlefield commission as lieutenant colonel—at the time the youngest in American Army. In 1930, he gained national acclaim as crusading mayor of Amarillo.

Appointed (1932) to Texas Railroad Commission; served by election until 1966. From prior career of lawyer-hotel owner, he stepped into public duty which sent him at once into East Texas during the world's greatest oil boom, to enforce proration. At peril of his life, he shut off noncomplying wells and made the petroleum industry respect Texas laws. He became a pioneer in conservation practices. With promptings from President Franklin Roosevelt, he led in 1934 in founding of the Interstate Oil Compact Commission. In Paris in 1937, he represented the United States at the World Petroleum Congress. By presidential order he was returned to Texas by the army in World War II, to ensure oil supplies for allied military forces.

He was awarded American Petroleum Institute Gold Medal for distinguished achievement, in 1951. As an international authority on oil—a key to world trade—he had great influence on the course of history.   (1972)

ALVORD (Wise Co.)   *US 287 in Alvord*
City of Alvord
By 1882, when the Fort Worth & Denver Railroad built a line to this area, a small agricultural community had developed here on an old Indian trail. First known as Nina, the town was renamed Alvord in 1883, probably in honor of J. B. Alvord, president of the railroad. Early businesses here included mercantile stores, a drugstore, a variety store, a bank, hotels, and a saloon with a second floor opera house. The first school was established at Briar Branch in 1890. Alvord has continued to develop as a center of farming, ranching, and oil production.   (1982)

AMARILLO (Potter Co.)   *Located on highways leading into Amarillo*
Amarillo
County seat, Potter County; founded in 1887. Incorporated 1892. Named for Arroyo Amarillo Spanish name of nearby creek. Transportation, financial, cultural and medical center. Gateway to Alibates Flint Quarry National Monument, Lake Meredith, Palo Duro State Park, Panhandle-Plains Historical Museum, Boys Ranch.   (1965)

AMARILLO (Potter Co.)   *US 66, 3 mi. W in front of plant main office*
Amarillo Helium Plant
This plant, operated by the United States Bureau of Mines, was the first to produce helium from the extensive helium resources in the Texas Panhandle. From 1929 until 1943, it furnished almost all of the world's supply of helium.

Operating around the clock, the plant extracts helium by liquifying the natural gas and separating helium from it at temperatures 300 degrees below zero.

The natural reserves in these fields and in extensions into adjacent states contain more than 95 percent of the world's known supply of helium.

This is also the site of the world renowned research center which provides fundamental data on the production and uses of helium.

Helium is used for a variety of purposes: lighter-than-air craft, low-temperature research, shielded-arc welding; and in national defense, nuclear energy programs and space exploration.
                                                                            (1965)

AMARILLO (Potter Co.)   *2 locations: US 87/287, 15 mi. N;*
34 mi. NE on Alibates Rd.
The Canadian River
A travel route and dwelling site for over 12,000 years, the Canadian River supported stone and adobe Indian villages from the 12th to the 14th centuries.

This waterway was also one of the first interior rivers of the U.S. known to early explorers. Coronado, coming from Mexico, crossed the Canadian in 1541 in his search for the famed city of Quivira. Juan de Onate, also seeking Quivira, saw the river in 1601. The Canadian traders, Pierre and Paul Mallet, followed it in 1741. Josiah Gregg, famous Missouri trader, took $25,000 worth of goods to Santa Fe along the river trails in 1839. Gold seekers bound for California were escorted along the trails in 1849 by army captain R. B. Marcy.

During its history, the river has borne many names. The origin of the word "Canadian" is disputed. A possible source is the caddo word "Kanohotino," which means "Red River." Some think it was named by the French-Canadians who traveled it in the 1700s, while others believe the river is called "Canadian" because it rises in a "canyon" (from the Spanish word meaning "boxed-in").

Beginning near the Colorado-New Mexico line in the Sangre de Cristo mountains, the Canadian flows 900 miles. Its course runs southeast, then east until it finally joins the Arkansas 36 miles from Fort Smith.   (1967)

AMARILLO (Potter Co.)   *SH 136, 7.5 mi. NE*
Canadian River Municipal Water Authority
Canadian River Project
The Canadian River Municipal Water Authority was authorized by a Texas constitutional amendment on May 27, 1953. It was approved, by vote of citizens of eleven West Texas cities, for purpose of supplying municipal and industrial water to Amarillo, Borger, Brownfield, Lamesa, Leveland, Lubbock, O'Donnell, Pampa, Plainview, Slaton and Tahoka.

Construction was supervised by the United States Bureau of Reclamation. Sanford Dam (located 34 mi. NE of here) is the impounding structure for Lake Meredith. The aqueduct system consists of 322 miles of concrete pressure pipe—the longest pipeline supervised by the Reclamation Bureau to this date. Construction costs ($83,799,000) covered the following items: municipal and industrial water, $76,975,000; flood control, $2,833,000; fish and wildlife, $2,891,000; recreation $1,100,000. Water cost will be repaid to Federal government, with interest, over a 50-year period. This is largest repayment contract ever made between a water authority and the U.S. government.

This section of pipe is identical to that utilized in segment of the aqueduct two miles west of this marker. This pipe section is 78 inches in diameter, 22 feet in length and weighs 36,000 pounds.   (1968)

AMARILLO (Potter Co.)   *SH 136, about 30 mi. NE*
(Overlooking Lake Meredith)
Pioneer in Texas Geology and Paleontology
Dr. Charles Newton Gould (1868–1949)

One of early scientists to use geology in search for oil and gas. This region's rapid economic growth in 1920s and '30s was result of Gould's selection of drill site for Hapgood No. 1-Masterson, discovery well of the vast Panhandle-Hugoton gas field, the world's largest known source for helium.

Gould was born in Ohio; grew up in Kansas, where he began teaching; gained scientific background in summer schools and in covered wagon and horseback field trips; by 25 was a widely-known paleontologist; became a professor at the University of Oklahoma.

In 1903–1905 he made studies of Texas Panhandle water resources, for the United States geological survey. A geological structure he observed (1904) and named Alibates Dolomite in 1907 led him to suggest to Amarillo merchants and ranchmen the drilling site in 1918 for Hapgood No. 1-Masterson Well. In 1919 he set the location for Gulf No. 2, first oil well in the Texas Panhandle and high plains region.

Gould was the scientist who first identified these quarries (now Alibates National Monument) as source for flint artifacts made by ice age Folsom man—a major North American anthropological discovery.   (1967)

AMARILLO (Potter Co.)   *US 287, 30 mi. N*
First Gas Well in the Panhandle of Texas

The discovery well in the vast Panhandle-Hugoton Gas Field, largest known gas field in the world, is located one mile east of this point on the east slope of John Ray Butte.

The geological structure was discovered by Dr. Charles N. Gould in 1905 while in the employ of the United States Geological Survey, and the well was located by him in 1917.

This well, the Hapgood-Masterson No. 1, was started December 1, 1917, and completed at a cost of $70,000 as a gas well December 7, 1918, at a depth of 2,605 feet. It produced about 5,000,000 cubic feet of gas per day. This discovery initiated the development of this great gas field and of the Panhandle oil fields.

The gas field now extends 275 miles from the Texas Panhandle north into Kansas, with a width in places of more than 90 miles. Pipelines from this field transmit gas to Denver, Kansas City, St. Louis, Chicago, Detroit, and to most of the cities and towns of the Mid-West. Lines also carry gas to Los Angeles and to other cities and towns on the West Coast.   (1965)

AMARILLO (Potter Co.)   *SH 136, 20 mi. NE*
The Fort Smith-Santa Fe Trail
Marcy Route, 1849

Clearly visible to the northeast and southwest are ruts of the old Fort Smith-Santa Fe Trail, the overland route connecting river ports of Fort Smith and Van Buren, Arkansas, with Santa Fe, New Mexico. Route gained national fame when Col. R. B. Marcy, U.S. Army, escorted party of 500 Arkansans—professional and business men and families—over this road in June 1849, on the way to California's gold fields. Scores of goldseekers in smaller groups also used the route that year.

Old trail became proposed route in 1853 for first Transcontinental Railroad as surveyed by Lt. A. W. Whipple. Prior to the Civil War, this route had won congressional support, but the war shifted sentiment so that Union Pacific, to the northward, actually was built first. During the war, a mail line left the old Butterfield stage route in eastern Oklahoma and went by way of this point over to Las Vegas and Santa Fe. In 1878 began usage of this link of road for a mail-stage line from the Federal fort at Mobeetie, in the Texas Panhandle, to Las Vegas, New Mexico. The trail has not been used since 1888.   (1965)

AMARILLO (Potter Co.)   *SH 136, 12 mi. NE*
Fort Smith-Santa Fe Trail
Gregg Route, 1840

This marks the site of the nationally known Overland Trail that connected the river ports of Fort Smith and Van Buren, Arkansas, with Santa Fe, center of travel and trade since 1609.

11

This road was pioneered by Josiah Gregg, a Santa Fe trader who first passed this point on March 15, 1840. Many goldseekers later used his route, beginning in the summer of 1849, after gold was found in California.

Before barbed wire fences, regular travelers here were military parties and traders.   (1964)

AMARILLO (Potter Co.)   *US 87, 16 mi. N at Canadian River Bridge*
Great Spanish Road
Near course of the Canadian River, early as days of the American Revolution, men from Santa Fe went past this spot on trips to meet traders from San Augustine, Nacogdoches and other Spanish towns of East Texas. In 1786, Pedro Vial was commissioned by the Spanish governor at Santa Fe to establish this route, and secure direct connection from Santa Fe to San Antonio, Texas with access to East Texas towns. The great Spanish road served well colonial Texas and fore-shadowed 20th century usage of the route for a segment of a great international highway.

First Ranch in Potter County
Established 1877 at point 1½ miles east of this site, by Bates and Beals, northern investors. Ran the LX brand, and once had a cowboy named Will Rogers, later internationally famous as a humorist.

First Store in Potter County
Opened 1878 a few hundred feet west of this marker, by William Pitcher, whose name was given to nearby creek, and who figured in a desperate robbery from which LX cowhands "rescued him."   (1964)

AMARILLO (Potter Co.)   *US 87/287, 19 mi. N*
The LX
First Ranch in Potter County
Established by W. H. Bates and D. T. Beals, Colorado merchants and ranchers on the Arkansas River since 1870. "Crowded conditions" there resulted in moving herd and brand to the Panhandle of Texas in 1877—three years after Indians were expelled from this region. LX cattle were being driven to Dodge City for shipment to market or to ranges in Montana and Wyoming as the Buffalo were being exterminated in the area.

The ranch extended from present cities of Dumas (30 mi. N) to Amarillo (20 mi. S), and was 20 miles wide—1,000 square miles of open range. The ranch was sold in 1884 to the American Pastoral Company, LTD., London. Ownership included 210,597 acres of land, 45,000 cattle, and 1,000 horses. Famous LX cowboys included Allie Bates and John Ray, whose names are on geological maps, and Charles Siringo, author of *Western Americana* and *Cattle Rustler Detective*.

Potter County was organized on Aug. 30, 1887, by 53 qualified electors. By unanimous vote of the 38 LX Cowboys Amarillo was elected the county seat.

In 1906 the Pastoral Company began liquidating. Heirs of large purchasers now own the properties.   (1971)

AMARILLO (Potter Co.)   *US 87/287 right of way, 19 mi. N*
The United States
Topographical Engineers in the High Plains of Texas
This region and much of Western America was mapped under adversity, as territory held by hostile Indians. With the dual aims of compiling scientific data and opening the way for settlers, U.S. Army topographers covered ground earlier traversed by conquistadors and mountain men. Earlier travelers mentioned their experiences. The topographers mapped the terrain.

The United States Army Topographical Corp. from 1838 to 1863 consisted of 36 officers. Barometer, compass, sextant, and pencil were their instruments for handling data on climate, geographical features, soil, feasible routes for wagons or railroads, and sites for towns and industrial developments.

Three topographical parties investigated the land that is now Potter County: Lt. James W. Abert invaded this Indian region in 1845 to survey environs of the Canadian and other rivers; Lt. James H. Simpson in 1849 reconnoitered a proposed railroad route from Fort Smith to Santa Fe; Lt.

Amiel W. Whipple in 1853 mapped another railroad route from the Mississippi to the Pacific. The United States owes great honor to these and other topographers. (1973)

ANAHUAC (Chambers Co.) *SH 61 at SH 10, 5 mi. NE*
Site—Mission Nuestra Señora de la Luz
Established in 1757 by Franciscan missionaries with the purpose of civilizing and Christianizing the Orcoquiza and Bidai Indians. Abandoned in 1772.

ANAHUAC (Chambers Co.) *IH 10, 8 mi. NW at Trinity River Bridge*
Taylor White Ranch
On this ranch, a part of the grant of James Taylor White who came to Texas in 1828, the Texas force camped before Anahuac and the colonists drew up the Turtle Bayou Resolutions, June 13, 1832.

ANAHUAC (Chambers Co.) *IH 10, ¼ mi. E of the Trinity River Bridge*
Missión Nuestra Señora de la Luz Del Orcoquisac
and Presidio San Agustín de Ahumada
Two of the most misfortune-ridden outposts of Spain in Texas, "Our Lady of the Light" Mission and its auxiliary fort, were founded near here in 1756 to guard against French encroachment from the east.

The two friars who were to minister to members of the Orcoquisac tribe arrived shortly after the 30 soldiers who were to man the fort. Soon, however, the elder friar died. The younger, asking to be relieved of his duties, complained vividly of biting insects, extremes of heat and cold, and the thick and stinking water in the lake near the lonely mission.

The 50 families who were to establish a town at the site never arrived, and although valiant efforts were made at improvement, conditions instead became worse. A woeful lack of training among the soldiers sparked unrest among the Indians. Meager supplies of food, clothing, and ammunition were the rule, and some commanders treated their men with great cruelty.

In 1767, an official inspector reported that due to the terrain, discord among the staff, and failure to convert the Indians, the presidio and mission should be closed. In 1771, fearing an invasion of Apaches, the authorities withdrew the personnel, and these two remote outposts of Spain were totally abandoned. (1970)

ANAHUAC (Chambers Co.) *IH 10, 6 mi. NE in White Ranch Park*
Near Site of the Signing of
Turtle Bayou Resolutions
Drafted and signed at Turtle Bayou on June 13, 1832; this first formal protest of Texas colonists against Mexican tyranny formed an early step in events that led eventually to the Texas Revolution of 1836.

The settlers were protesting recent restrictive laws of Mexico designed to limit immigration and trade between the United States and Texas, passed because Mexico feared losing Texas to the U.S.

In particular, citizens of Anahuac were enraged by unreasonable acts of Col. Juan Davis Bradburn, a local agent of the Mexican government. Alarm spread after Bradburn unjustly imprisoned several Texans, one of whom was the later Alamo hero, William B. Travis.

Fighting broke out on June 9 and 12, 1832, between citizens and Bradburn's militia. Following this, the Texans met at Turtle Bayou to plan future action. Here they drew up resolutions censuring violations of Mexico's constitution of President Bustamante, encouraging resistance to his regime, and inviting all Texans to uphold the cause of civil liberty.

Signers of the document, most of whom later served with valor in the 1835 revolution and in the Texas Republic, were John Austin, W. H. Jack, Hugh B. Johnson, Luke Lesassier, Wylie Martin, and R. M. Williamson.

ANAHUAC (Chambers Co.) *Fort Anahuac Park*
Fort Anahuac
Known as Perry's Point until 1825, Anahuac was a port of entry for early Texas colonists. In 1830 the Mexican government established a military post here to collect customs duties and to enforce the law of April 6, 1830, which curtailed further Anglo-American colonization. Situated

on a high bluff at the mouth of the Trinity River, Fort Anahuac controlled access to East Texas settlements. Two 18-pound guns topped the 7-foot-thick brick walls of the bastion. 4-foot-thick walls protected the adjacent barracks, and an underground tunnel led to a nearby powder magazine.

Col. Juan Davis Bradburn, commander of the Anahuac garrison, angered Texas colonists by conscripting labor and supplies to construct the fort and by failing to control his disorderly troops. In 1832 he unjustly imprisoned William B. Travis, Patrick C. Jack, and other settlers here. When he refused to release the men, armed conflict erupted between Texas and Mexican forces. The confrontation here, which also sparked fighting at Velasco and adoption of the Turtle Bayou Resolutions, resulted in Bradburn's dismissal and the removal of Mexican troops from the post. Today the ruins of Fort Anahuac are a physical reminder of events that kindled the drive for Texas Independence. (1976)

ANAHUAC (Chambers Co.) — SH 61 and FM 1724 exits, 9 mi. NE
James Taylor White
A veteran of the War of 1812, James Taylor White (b. 1789) migrated to this area from Louisiana in 1828. As a rancher, he developed one of the largest herds of longhorn cattle in Southeast Texas.

On White's ranch in June 1832, area colonists signed the Turtle Bayou Resolutions. Written to protest the actions of Captain Juan Davis Bradburn, commander of Mexican troops at Anahuac (9 mi. SW), the resolutions were an early sign of the growing dissatisfaction with Mexican governmental policies which limited the rights of colonists. Four years later, during the Texas Revolution, White provided aid and shelter for settlers fleeing the advancing Mexican forces under General Santa Anna. He also helped the Republic of Texas by supplying cattle for the Texas army.

Following the revolution, White began driving his cattle overland to markets in New Orleans. His early cattle drives, utilizing sections of the Opelousas Trail, preceded development of post-Civil War routes, including the Dodge City and Chisholm Trails.

White died in 1852 and was buried near his home (200 yds. S). His cattle brand, the "Crossed W," inherited from his father in 1806, is still used by members of the White family. (1980)

ANDERSON (Grimes Co.) — FM 3090, ½ mi. W of old Piedmont community, or about 7 mi. NW of Anderson, at site
Site of Piedmont Springs Resort
In operation as early as 1850 as health spa and resort because of three nearby sulphur springs (varying in taste from mild to strong). Numerous drinking places and bathhouses allowed guests to move freely about grounds.

Grand four-story hotel with 100 rooms, built about 1860, was social center for area, where guests enjoyed billiards, poker, horse races, and Gen. Sam Houston once danced the minuet.

In 1865, hotel became hospital, headquarters for John G. Walker's "Greyhound Division" Confederate Army. Owner closed the building after losing money in panic, 1870s. (1967)

ANDERSON (Grimes Co.) — 2 blks. S of Main St. at SH 90 Intersection
Steinhagen Log Cabin
Built before 1860. Log walls are unspliced. Slaves hand-hewed the timbers, stones; made doors, window shutters. (1965)

ANDERSON (Grimes Co.) — 579 S. Main, Fanthorp Inn State Historic Park
Fanthorp Inn
Built in 1834 by Henry Fanthorp as a home for his bride, Rachel Kennard. Enlarged for hotel purpose. Served as first mercantile establishment and first post office (1835) in the region. Here Kenneth Lewis Anderson, Vice-President of the Republic of Texas, died July 3, 1845. Stage lines from Houston to Old Springfield and Nacogdoches to Austin crossed here. (1936)

ANDREWS (Andrews Co.)   *SH 176, 15 mi. W in roadside park*

Andrews County
Created August 21, 1876
Organized May 11, 1910
Named for
Richard Andrews
Killed at the Battle of
Concepcion, October 28, 1835
The first man to fall in
The Texas Revolution
County Seat, Andrews

ANDREWS (Andrews Co.)   *US 385, Courthouse grounds*

Billionth Barrel

On May 25, 1965 from one of 7,400 producing oil wells in the county's 196 fields, came the billionth barrel of Andrews County crude oil.

In the 35 years and 5 months since oil flowed from the county's discovery well, C. E. Ogden No. 1 in Dec. 1929, Andrews has attained a new place in history.

In 1929, the county had about 400 people. Its wealth mostly in land and livestock, amounted to $8,109,399. Five persons in the county filed income tax returns. There were fewer than 100 children in school. Highway bonds in the amount of $200,000 were about to be issued, as a measure of county improvement.

By 1956, Andrews County produced more than 60,000,000 barrels of oil annually—gaining recognition as number one in Texas and the United States.

Of great significance is the fact that presently proven reserves underlying the county total more than one billion barrels, without any consideration for additional recoveries by secondary methods.

Andrews is more than a product of the billion barrels of crude oil it has produced, more than the gasoline plants working through the night, more than modern highways, paved streets, homes, schools, dreams. Its destiny is great in human resources and oil.   (1965)

ANDREWS (Andrews Co.)   *SH 176, at original town square*

**Early Settlers
of Andrews County**

One of last frontiers of Texas. Anglo settlement here lagged 60 years behind rest of state due to Indians and scarcity of water.

In 1886 O. B. Holt became first man to file for county land. First settlers included the Cowden brothers and Peter Von Holebeke.

In 1900 county had 87 people; it was finally organized in 1910. With windmill pumps and drift fences, ranching became feasible, although soil was so dry that a grazing cow crashed through a dugout roof into a bed one day.

In 1930 the discovery of oil brought wealth and rewarded the tenacity of first pioneers.   (1970)

ANDREWS (Andrews Co.)   *US 385, 3 mi. N, then 3 mi.*
                                             E on Florey Park Rd.-Rec. Bldg.

Florey Park

Named for old town of Florey, established as a post office 7 miles to the northeast in 1909, prior to the organization of Andrews County, June 1910.

In heart of the Means oil field, opened 1930, this park is at site of a 1934–1958 camp of Humble Oil & Refining Company. In the 24 years of the camp's history, its many residents developed an oasis here. The recreation area, with its lush grass and tall trees, attracted visitors from all parts of the county.

On September 22, 1958, Humble Company donated the land to be used as a county park.

                                             (1965)

ANDREWS (Andrews Co.)

Whalen Lake School
(2 mi. S)

One of the first schools in Andrews County, opened in 1907 near the north edge of Whalen Lake, on land donated by Mrs. M. B. Dillard. The one-room school, built by Joe and Jake Mathis, with materials purchased by Will Gates, served the children of homesteaders "proving up" their claims by living on the property 3 years. Teachers were Miss Grace Stanford, a Mr. Taylor, Miss Mary Lewis, and Earl Lontz, each remaining one year.

The school closed in 1910, and the building was moved as most of the settlers fulfilled their claim agreements and left.   (1974)

ANDREWS (Andrews Co.)   SH 176, 6 mi. W

Andrews County Discovery Well (½ mi. S & ½ mi. W)

C. E. Ogden No. 1, producing 200 barrels a day from San Andrew lime formation was brought in Dec. 1929 by Deep Rock Oil Co.—the Andrews County Discovery Well and first of 730 wells in Fuhrman-Masco Oil Field.

Bought Feb. 1932, by Tripplehorn Brothers, of Fort Worth. Has now pumped for more than 35 years.

Since 1956, Andrews has been top producing county in Texas and U.S. Fuhrman-Masco Field has produced 55 million barrels of oil—its contribution to total of more than a billion barrels for Andrews County in May, 1965.   (1965)

ANDREWS (Andrews Co.)   SH 176 at FM 181, 16 mi. W

Frankel City

In 1941, the Fullerton Oil Company of California struck oil near this site, and by 1945 more than 100 drilling rigs were in operation. The discovery brought great numbers of workers into the area, resulting in the establishment of the town of Fullerton.

Located approximately one mile north, Fullerton provided newcomers with two churches, two cafes, two filling stations, a grocery store, delicatessen, beauty shop, and Andrews Telephone Exchange. Buses transported children to and from school in Andrews (16 mi. SE). By the end of World War II, the boom town also boasted supply stores, oil field service companies, welding shops, and an electric plant.

Fullerton's name was changed to Frankel City when the U.S. Post Office was established in 1948. At one time the post office served as many as 500 area families. By 1976, however, most of the oil had been taken from the ground, and workers in the field were laid off or transferred to other jobs. The town was abandoned as the post office and other businesses closed.

The old Prairie Schooner Cafe, moved to this site from its original location, is all that is left of Frankel City. The ghost town, however, remains an important part of West Texas history.   (1984)

ANDREWS (Andrews Co.)   SH 115, 2.5 mi. NE

The J. S. Means Ranch House

Built in 1900, this is one of the oldest houses in Andrews County. S. H. Purcell, his wife, and two relatives each filed on a section of public land, building this home where section-corners met, so that each individual could fulfill the legal requirement to live on his claim. Soon after proving their claims, they sold out to Mr. and Mrs. J. S. Means, who then (1904) owned 14 sections. Adding much more land, the Means family established a very successful working ranch. It continues to run cattle, even though the range has contained oil fields since the 1920s.   (1974)

ANHALT (Comal Co.)   SH 46, 23 mi. NW

Joseph Scheel House

A typical home of German settlers, built late 1860s by Bernhard Joseph Scheel (1815–1879) and wife Anna Barbara (Link).

Hand-cut, faced local stone; native cedar timber; and cypress shingles were used. Son Hermann and grandson John later owned the place.   (1972)

ANNA (Collin Co.)   FM 455, 2 mi. W, then US 75 frontage road .6 mi. S

Coffman Cemetery

This cemetery, which dates to the mid-19th century, is on land donated by early settler John Coffman (1804–1880). His son, George W. Coffman (1840–1913), owned and operated a homestead one mile west of this site. The oldest marked grave dates to 1876. Descendants of many of the families represented in the graveyard still reside in this part of Collin County. The primary burial ground for the community of Coffman for over a century, this cemetery serves as a reminder of the area's past. (Texas Sesquicentennial 1836–1986)

ANNA (Collin Co.) *SH 5, 2 mi. N*
Site of Collin McKinney Homestead
Collin McKinney, a delegate to the General Convention at Washington-on-the-Brazos who helped draft the Texas Declaration of Independence from Mexico and later the Constitution of the Republic of Texas, settled in this area about 1846. On July 10, 1848, McKinney bought the Rob Whitaker survey around this site from Anna Whitaker, paying $500 for 640 acres. The McKinney family was active in the region: They were instrumental in building the Mantua Road and the organization of the town of Mantua and the Van Alstyne Christian Church. Collin McKinney divided his land among his heirs in 1857. He died in 1861. The McKinney family gave his house to the city of McKinney in 1936. The structure burned in 1980. Collin McKinney's legacy continues to influence the history of North Texas. (2000)

ANSON (Jones Co.) *Courthouse Anson*
Anson Jones
Born in Massachusetts January 20, 1798, was licensed to practice medicine in 1820. Came to Texas in 1833. Doctor Jones participated in the Battle of San Jacinto 1836 while a surgeon in the Army of Texas. He was a member of the Congress of the Republic 1837–1841. Minister to the United States 1838. Secretary of State 1841–1844. He was the last president of the Republic of Texas 1844–1845. Died in Houston, Texas January 9, 1858. (1936)

ANSON (Jones Co.) *11th St. and Commercial (US 277/83)*
Jones County Courthouse
The Seventh Texas Legislature created Jones County in 1858 and named it for Anson Jones, the last president of the Republic of Texas. The Civil War, Reconstruction, and the area's untamed wilderness combined to postpone the county's formal organization until 1881. Voters selected Jones City, later renamed Anson, as permanent county seat. The first permanent courthouse was a small frame building, which served until the county purchased a hotel in 1884 for use as a courthouse. An 1886 brick courthouse served the county for the next 24 years. In late 1909, the Jones County Commissioners Court, led by County Judge J. R. Stinson, determined that the growth of the county called for a larger courthouse. They selected Elmer G. Withers of Stamford (15 mi. N) and the Texas Building Company of Fort Worth as architect and contractor, respectively. Completed in 1910, the Jones County courthouse is an excellent example of Beaux Arts styling, with influences from the Arts and Crafts movement found in the decorative painting uncovered during 1990s rehabilitation on the ceiling of the district courtroom. Other notable features include the statue of Lady Justice atop the domed clock tower and the pedimented porticoes with flanking pairs of Ionic columns on each façade. Constructed of brick and Pecos red sandstone, the Jones County courthouse continues to stand as an important part of Anson's architectural heritage and a center of politics and government for the citizens of the county. (2000)

ANSON (Jones Co.) *US 277 and 180 at courthouse*
Fort Phantom Hill, CSA
Located 10 miles east, 9 miles south on Old Butterfield Stageline. Upon secession, company of First Regiment Texas Mounted Rifles used it as an outpost to give protection against Indians. Stopover on way west for some Union sympathizers and people wanting to avoid conflict of war. In 1862 the frontier defense line was pulled back more than 30 miles east. However, scouting parties and patrols of Confederate and state troops intermittently visited the post in aggressive warfare to keep Indians near their camps and away from settlements and to check on invasion by Union forces. Usually supplying their own mounts, guns and sustenance, these men guarded the frontier until war's end. Texas Civil War Frontier Defense Texas had 2000 miles of coastline and frontier to defend from Union attack, Indian raids, marauders. Defense lines were set to give maximum protection with the few men left in the state. One line stretched from El Paso to Brownsville. Another had posts set a day's horseback ride apart from Red River to the Rio Grande. Phantom Hill and other U. S. forts used by scouting parties lay in a line between. Behind

these lines and to the east organized militia, citizens' posses from nearby settlements backed the Confederate and state troops to curb Indian raids. A memorial to Texans who served the Confederacy. (1963)

ANSON (Jones Co.) *FM 600, 10 mi. N of Abilene*
Fort Phantom Hill
Established Nov. 14, 1851, as unit in chain of forts from Red River to Rio Grande, to defend frontier settlers and west-bound 49ers. Officially "Post on Clear Fork of the Brazos" everyday name became "Phantom Hill," either from prevalent mirages or sighting of ghostly Indian in moonlight.

Abandoned by U.S. Army on April 6, 1854, fort served in 1858–1861 as stage stand for Southern Overland Mail. In 1871–1872, the army again used this as a sub-post of Fort Griffin, 40 miles northeast. The adjacent village was temporary county seat when Jones County was organized in 1881. (1970)

ANSON (Jones Co.) *US 83, N of Taylor-Jones Co. Line*
Butterfield Trail Marker
Butterfield Trail, US Mail Route, St. Louis to San Francisco. Crossed here 1858–1861.

ANTELOPE (Jack Co.) *SH 281*
Town of Antelope
Named for Springs where herds of antelope watered and Kiowa Indians had a campsite. In 1875, Walter S. Jones platted townsite on Henrietta-Graham mail route. By 1887, place had 400 people, a general store, post office, a school, doctors, hotel, and spa built around its mineral wells.

Town was overnight stop and supply point for cattle trails leading north. The G. R. Christian camp No. 703, United Confederate Veterans, active 1895–1941, served as city's park association.

Economy is based on ranch and oil income; area is known for its churches and hospitality. (1970)

APPLE SPRINGS (Trinity Co.) *FM 2501 4 mi. N*
Benjamin Burke
(1793–1863)
Pioneer farmer Benjamin Burke migrated to Texas about 1829 and received an 1834 land grant from Mexican government in what is now Tyler County. He served in the Texas army in 1836 during the War for Independence. About 1859 he moved to the Centralia community in Trinity County.

He married Susan (Ogden) Burke (1808–1870) and had nine children. Two of his sons fought in the Confederate Army during the Civil War (1861–1865).

AQUILLA (Hill Co.) *FM 3370 and 1133, in Aquilla*
Town of Aquilla
Named for Aquilla (from the Spanish word for "eagle") Creek. The townsite was surveyed, 1879, when the Texas Central Railroad was built through Hill County.

As businessmen and citizens moved here, Aquilla grew to be a main shipping point. At one time, it had 13 retail stores, 3 hotels, a health spa, 4 churches, a school, and other businesses. One of the earliest chartered state banks in Texas opened here in 1905. At the town's peak (1910–1920), ranchers, farmers, and drummers (traveling salesmen) filled the streets. Presently, a sound farming economy prevails. (1968)

ARANSAS PASS (San Patricio Co.) *SH 361 (Goodnight Ave.)*
Terminal Railroad
Built in 1892, the Aransas Harbor Terminal Railroad ("Old Terminal Railroad") provided a means for transporting rock from mainland quarries to jetties under construction in the pass. In 1909, the Aransas Pass Channel and Dock Company was chartered to build a channel from the first South Texas deep water port at Harbor Island to Aransas Pass. As the channel was dredged, the displaced sediment was piled along one side and became the basis for a railroad bed.

Opened in 1912, the new terminal railroad extended along the roadbed and a series of eight trestles. It connected with the San Antonio and Aransas Pass Railroad in Aransas Pass, and was an important cotton shipping tool. Passenger service was inaugurated with the "Toonerville Trolley," passenger coaches pulled by a converted Model T Ford truck which transported workers from the mainland to a new shipyard on Harbor Island during World War I.

After Corpus Christi was designated a deep water port in 1922, business declined for Harbor Island and the railroad. In 1931, the rail line was converted to a road for automobiles, which was in turn replaced by a new highway in 1960. Hurricanes in 1961 and 1970 left few visible remnants of the terminal railroad. (1989)

ARANSAS PASS (Aransas Co.)
SH 35 Bus., 0.9 mi. N
Cementerio San Antonio de Padua
According to local lore, George Lewis (1859–1895) donated one-half acre of land at this site to the Hispanic citizens of the area for use as a cemetery, provided that he be buried in the center of the land. Handmade stones indicate burials dating from the 19th century; the first recorded deed was signed in 1933. Years of wind and rain have rendered many stones illegible. A number of children who died in an influenza epidemic in 1940 and many veterans of U S. and international conflicts are interred here. A statue of San Antonio holding a child, crafted in Mexico, was brought across the border by the local priest for placement in an open chapel on the cemetery grounds. It is revered by the families of those interred here. (1998)

ARCHER CITY (Archer Co.)
SH 79, 8 mi. S
Extinct Town of Anarene
Landowner Charles E. Graham (1872–1937) in 1908 granted the Wichita Falls and Southern Railroad a route across his property and platted a town at this site. Anarene was named for his wife Annie Lawrene Graham, daughter of pioneer cattleman J. Marion Keen. Graham built a hotel and obtained a post office, cattle pens, dipping vat and other facilities. The town schoolhouse was used for religious services. In 1921 oil was discovered nearby. A refinery was built in 1938. When oil production ceased and the trains stopped running in 1954, Anarene quickly declined. (1976)

ARCHER CITY (Archer Co.)
SH 79, 6 mi. S
Archer County
A part of Peter's grant 1841, created January 22, 1858. Organized July 27, 1880. Named in honor of Dr. Branch Tanner Archer 1790–1856.

Texas Commissioner to the United States, 1835, member of Congress, Secretary of War of the Republic of Texas. First permanent settlement, 1874, first railroad 1890.

Archer City, the county seat.

ARCHER CITY (Archer Co.)
SH 25, 4.5 mi. NW
Archer County Copper Mines
(¼ mi. NE and 5 mi. SSE)
The civilized world first heard of copper in this area from Texas Rangers after an 1860 campaign against Comanches on the Pease River, about 100 miles to the northwest. The Ranger captain, Lawrence S. ("Sul") Ross, later to serve Texas as Governor, had nuggets picked off the surface of the ground and hauled to Austin. In 1861, assistant state geologist, S. B. Buckley, charted the mineral site. The Rangers' ore haul was processed and used in gun caps for Confederate forces during the Civil War. To get more of the needed metal, the Texas Copper Mining & Manufacturing Company was founded on May 28, 1864, but wartime shortage of men apparently prevented recovery of copper at the time. The T.C.M. & M. Co., based in Dallas, sent W. F. Cummings to Archer County in 1880 to open mining sites. Although the Texas Commissioner of Agriculture and Statistics reported in 1882 that no mining had commenced, ore eventually was hauled out and shipped to smelters in the East. No central vein or deposit could be found.

The Boston & Texas Copper Company of Tucson, Ariz., leased the mine site here in 1899. It produced some copper ore which was processed in El Paso, but again the project failed to meet expectations. (1971)

ARCHER CITY (Archer Co.)
SH 25 at FM 210, 2 mi. W at roadside park
Battle of the Little Wichita
In reaction to an Indian attack on a mail stage, Capt. Curwen B. McLellan set out on July 6, 1870, from Fort Richardson with 56 men of the 6th Cavalry. On July 12, McLellan's command

encountered a war party of 250 Kiowas led by "Kicking Bird" near the north fork of the Little Wichita (6 miles NW). After a brief skirmish, McLellan ordered his troops into retreat, fighting a defensive battle across the middle and south forks of the Little Wichita. The Indians gave up the chase on the 13th. Corporal John Given and Private George Blume were killed. 13 medals of honor were awarded for heroism. (1974)

ARCHER CITY (Archer Co.) US 281, 5 mi. S of Windthorst in roadside park
Bridwell Park
Donated to his countrymen by conservationist-philanthropist Joseph Sterling Bridwell (1885–1966) Missourian who moved to Texas in 1909. Drilling his first well in 1921 on W. T. Waggoner estate, in 1927 he formed Bridwell Oil Co., which ultimately produced 50 million barrels of petroleum.

In 1932 he bought local ranch (with headquarters 5 mi. to NW), where he bred famous herd sire Larry Domino and other fine Herefords.

A founder and president (1940) West Texas Chamber of Commerce, Bridwell gave nation the site for Sheppard Air Force Base.

He and wife had 2 daughters. (1972)

ARCHER CITY (Archer Co.) SH 199, adjacent to city park, Megargel
On Route of The Comanche Exodus
After living 1854–1958 on the reservation set aside by State of Texas near camp Cooper (30 mi. SW), the Comanche Indians with their goods were removed to Oklahoma. Near this spot on a head branch of Kickapoo Creek (so named, 1830) the Exodus camped on Aug. 3, 1859, with its escort, a company of 1st United States Infantry under Capt. C. C. Gilbert, along with the Indian agent Matthew Leeper. At same time (25 mi. E), Maj. George H. Thomas escorted the supervising Indian agent, Maj. R. S. Neighbors, and 1059 lower Brazos reserve Indians to Oklahoma Reservation.

Megargel was founded here, 1910. (1971)

ARCHER CITY (Archer Co.) SH 25 at FM 210, 2 mi. W at roadside park
In Vicinity of French Trading Area
(4.5 mi. W)
In the mid-1700s, Indians of this region met at a trading ground near this site with Frenchmen who brought them manufactured goods, sometimes including guns and ammunition—products denied them by the Spanish who held sovereignty, but could not prevent intrusions from Louisiana. The Spanish explorer Jose Mares on a road-mapping expedition here in 1787 saw evidences of the French. Among noted early-day visitors were Captain R. B. Marcy of the U.S. Army and Indian agent R. S. Neighbors, who camped nearby in 1854 while seeking a good site for an Indian reservation. (1974)

ARCHER CITY (Archer Co.) SH 79, 15 mi. NE
Old Buffalo Road
Named for traffic in buffalo hides and bones, road from plains hunting grounds crossed this site. Hunters hauled thousands of hides to market in 1870s. The first settlers in late 1870s–1880s sold bones for fertilizer and bought supplies to sustain life during hard times. (1973)

ARLINGTON (Tarrant Co.) FM 157, 1 mi. N of Trinity River
Site of Bird's Fort (1 mi. E)
In an effort to attract settlers to the region and to provide protection from Indian raids, Gen. Edward H. Tarrant of the Republic of Texas Militia authorized Jonathan Bird to establish a settlement and military post in the area. Bird's Fort, built near a crescent-shaped lake one mile east in 1841, was the first attempt at Anglo-American colonization in present Tarrant County. The settlers, from the Red River area, suffered from hunger and Indian problems and soon returned home or joined other settlements.

In August 1843, troops of the Jacob Snively Expedition disbanded at the abandoned fort, which consisted of a few log structures. Organized to capture Mexican gold wagons on the Santa Fe Trail in retaliation for raids on San Antonio, the outfit had been disarmed by United States forces.

About the same time, negotiations began at the fort between Republic of Texas officials Gen. Tarrant and Gen. George W. Terrell and the leaders of nine Indian tribes. The meetings ended on September 29, 1843, with the signing of the Bird's Fort Treaty. Terms of the agreement called for an end to existing conflicts and the establishment of a line separating Indian lands from territory open for colonization. (1980)

ARLINGTON (Tarrant Co.)   *FM 157, ¾ mi. N of Trinity River Bridge*
Sloan-Journey Expedition of 1838
In the spring of 1838, Captains Robert Sloan and Nathaniel T. Journey led a group of about 90 Northeast Texas frontiersmen on a punitive expedition against the Indians who had raided their homes in present-day Fannin County. The trail led them to the vicinity of present-day Euless and Arlington, where they attacked a small Indian village, killed several Indians, and recovered a few horses. The Sloan-Journey Expedition is among the first known Anglo-American activities in what is now Tarrant County that helped to open North Texas to white settlement. (1984)

ARLINGTON (Tarrant Co.)   *3001 W. Division (US 80)*
Top O' Hill Terrace
Beulah Adams Marshall bought land here along the Bankhead highway in the early 1920s and opened a tea room, hosting teas and serving dinners to Dallas and Fort Worth patrons. In 1926, Fred and Mary Browning purchased the property and shortly began converting the facilities into a casino, adding an escape tunnel and secret room for hiding the gambling paraphernalia during raids. Known as Top O' Hill Terrace, the popular spot attracted gamblers as well as visitors who were often unaware of the gaming activities. The restaurant, along with the tea garden that exists today, was a legitimate business, operating alongside a brothel as well as the casino, which benefited from the nearby Arlington Downs Racetrack. Top O' Hill Terrace facilities included a horse barn and a private stable for Browning's prized stud, Royal Ford, purchased from oilman and Arlington Downs owner W.T. Waggoner.

Contemporary to the Top O' Hill heyday was the outspoken Dr. J. Frank Norris (d. 1952), longtime pastor of first Baptist Church of Fort Worth. The conservative Norris, co-founder of fundamental Baptist Bible Institute, later known as Bible Baptist Seminary and later as the Arlington Baptist College, was an ardent proponent of prohibition and gambling reform. One of his targets was Top O' Hill Terrace, which he reportedly vowed one day to own. In 1947, Texas Ranger Captain M.T. "Lone Wolf" Gonzaullas led a raid on Top O' Hill, catching the gambling operation in full swing. In late 1956, under the leadership of Earl K. Oldham, the Bible Baptist Seminary bought the property and relocated here, fulfilling Norris' promise, although neither he nor Browning (d. 1953) had lived to see it. Today, the Arlington Baptist College continues to use the site, which retains many of its original structures and features a statue of Norris by noted sculptor Pompeo Coppini. (2003)

ART (Mason Co.)   *SH 29, 7 mi. E Mason, ½ mi. W*
Art Methodist Church
Organized 1856 by the Rev. C. A. Grote, first minister to preach here. First building was erected in 1858. The present structure was built 1890 on land donated by Ernst Jordan, Sr., charter member.

Until 1927, all worship was held in German language.

The two Methodist churches in Art united in 1939. At that time frame building was moved beside this rock building and equipped for Sunday school classes.

ASPERMONT (Stonewall Co.)   *US 380, 7.5 mi. E*
Site of the Courthouse at Rayner
First county seat of Stonewall County. Erected in 1888. County seat removed to Aspermont in 1898.

ASPERMONT (Stonewall Co.)   *US 83 at US 380*
Stonewall County
Explored 1541 on behalf of Spain by Francisco de Coronado. Visited by Texans early as the 1840s. Mapped by U.S. Army expedition of Capt. Randolph Marcy 1849.

Yielded salt for use of early settlers and hunters. Was site of buffalo hunters' capital, Rath City, 1876–1879.

County created in 1876; organized 1888. Named in honor of Confederate General Thomas Jonathan "Stonewall" Jackson (1824–1863), whose courage and fighting skill inspired Texas soldiers in the Civil War.

First county seat, Rayner, replaced 1898 by Aspermont, named for high location. (1965)

ASPERMONT (Stonewall Co.) $\qquad$ *US 83 at US 380*
County Named for Confederate Hero General "Stonewall" Jackson
1824–1863
Gen. Barnard E. Bee, a Texan, gave him the famous sobriquet in first battle of Manassas. Jackson was rallying his men for a charge as other units retreated. Bee, seeing him, cried to his men, "There is Jackson standing like a stone wall. Let us determine to die here, and we will conquer." In battles of Gaines Mill and Malvern Hill, Hood's famous Texas Brigade fought under his command. After Gaines Mill when Jackson saw the strong Union fortified position which the Texans had overrun, he—not known to give praise—said, "The men that took this position were soldiers indeed."

Texas in the Civil War
Texas made an all-out effort for the Confederacy after a 3 to 1 popular vote for secession. 90,000 troops, famed for mobility and daring, fought on every battlefront. A 2,000-mile frontier and coast were successfully defended from Union troop invasion and savage Indians. Texas was the storehouse of western Confederacy. Wagon trains laden with cotton—life blood of the South—crossed the state to Mexico to trade for medical supplies. State and private industry produced guns, ammunition, wagons, pots, kettles, leather goods, salt, hospital supplies. Wives, sons, daughters, slaves provided corn, cotton, cloth, cattle, hogs, cured meats to the army, giving much, keeping little for themselves. $\qquad$ (1963)

ASPERMONT (Stonewall Co.) $\qquad$ *US 83, 10 mi. S in roadside park*
Rath City (4 mi. SW)
In 1876, during an international demand for buffalo hides, Charles Rath (1836–1902) founded this town. He opened the Rath, Lee & Reynolds Mercantile Store. He sold supplies and bought the hides from the buffalo hunters. On one occasion in 1877, there were 1,100,000 hides at his trading post. The town, also known as "Reynolds City," boasted a corral, hide yard, saloon, and restaurant. Skins stretched across poles sheltered the hunters. A tower beside the corral was used as a lookout to ward off Indian attacks. By 1879, the buffalo disappeared and the town vanished. $\qquad$ (1979)

ATHENS (Henderson Co.) $\qquad$ *SH 19, 1 mi. S in roadside park*
Henderson County
Formed from Houston and Nacogdoches Counties.

Created April 27, 1846. Organized August 4, 1846. Named in honor of James Pinckney Henderson (1808–1858).

First Governor of the State of Texas. Buffalo, Centerville and Athens since 1850 have served as county seats.

ATHENS (Henderson Co.) $\qquad$ *SH 19, 1 mi. S in roadside park*
Athens
Founded 1850. Named for Athens, Greece.

Supply and military training headquarters during Civil War. Sent army about 1,000 men.

Center for manufacturing and agriculture. Home of annual Old Fiddlers' Contest and of Henderson County Junior College. Black-eyed peas capital of the world.

ATHENS (Henderson Co.) $\qquad$ *SH 19, 1 mi. S in roadside park*
Henderson, C.S.A.
Voted 400–49 for secession. Sent about 1,000 into Confederate Army with one detachment of 150 having only 13 live to return. Caldwell's farm three miles northeast and Fincastle 19 miles southeast of Athens, had camps of instruction. Confederate supply depot, Fincastle had stores of grain, meat in charge of Captain Thomas F. Murchison, who also was county enrolling officer. Wartime manufactures included earthenware, jugs and dishes. Other products for C.S.A. were cotton, corn beef, pork, timber. Cynthia Ann Parker, delivered from Indian captivity 1860 by Sul Ross Ranger Unit lived during war at Athens. Postmaster General of Confederacy was John H. Reagan, who had been surveyor and first probate judge in Henderson.

ATHENS (Henderson Co.)   *1601 Patterson Rd. (US 175)*
at East Texas Arboretum & Botanical Society
Bushrod W. J. Wofford
Bushrod William John "Bush" Wofford was born in February 1832 to William M. and Mariah Frances Johnston Wofford in Madison County, Alabama. He grew up an only child in Tippah County, Mississippi. His parents died when he was a young man, and he came to Texas in the early 1850s. In 1852, Wofford married Martha A. Miller of Anderson County, Texas. The following year, he bought 320 acres of the Matthew Goliher Survey near Fincastle (25 mi. SE). He built a house, using hand-hewn logs, handmade bricks and, perhaps, an existing cabin structure. His first son, George M. Wofford, was born in February; Martha died a few months later. Wofford remarried to Frances Eliza Ayres of Tippah County in 1855, bringing her to his Fincastle home. It is believed she initiated additions to the cabin, including a long, front gallery porch, two log rooms and a dog run, and clapboard siding. Between 1855 and 1878, Bush and Eliza had nine children, many of whom lived to become successful residents of Henderson County. During his long life, Wofford worked as a farmer and owned a Fincastle mercantile business, called Wofford & Son. He also served as a lieutenant in a reserve unit from Fincastle during the Civil War. Eliza and Bush moved to Athens in 1890. He died in 1891, and he is buried with Eliza at the Athens City Cemetery. The house remained in Fincastle until 2001, when the family donated it for relocation to this site. Wofford descendants provided funds for the restoration of the house and its use as a museum.   (2002)

ATHENS (Henderson Co.)   *204 W. Corsicana St. (US 175)*
Site of Hawn Lumber Company
As the geographic center of the newly redrawn Henderson County lines, Athens became the county seat in 1850. Charles H. and Lillian (Barksdale) Hawn arrived with a load of lumber on the first train to stop in Athens in 1881. Charles Hawn quickly established a role for himself and his family in the village. Called "adept as an architect and master builder" by the Athens Register, Hawn built a new county courthouse in 1885. He also is credited with the design and construction of many early houses in and around Athens, including the residence of Senator J. J. Faulk and his wife in 1882. In December 1886 Charles and Lillian Hawn purchased two acres on this site in order to establish the Hawn Lumber Company. Hawn continued to provide lumber and labor for many of the buildings around the town square as well as settlers' homes. He is credited with constructing the Faulk-Gaunt building and the Gaunt Brothers buildings in downtown Athens, as well as the home of Joseph Thomas La Rue. Charles and Lillian Hawn's second son, William A. Hawn, became president of the company. He inherited family holdings including Charles' several sawmills upon his father's death in 1922. W. A. Hawn served as city commissioner and mayor, postmaster and school board member for the city of Athens. Under his direction, the Hawn Lumber Company remained a strong fixture in the city's building trade. William A. Hawn died in 1960; the company remained in the family until it closed in 1997. From the early development of Athens to the end of the 20th century, the Hawn Lumber Company was instrumental in the city's growth.   (1999)

ATHENS (Henderson Co.)   *US 175 right-of-way, 6 mi. NW*
William Richardson
(Dec. 6, 1805–May 30, 1864)
Born in South Carolina, William Richardson moved to Pickens County, Alabama in 1830. There he married Mary "Polly" Kilpatrick (1813–1889) on Feb. 13, 1834. Children born to them were John K., James J., Sara F., Margaret C., Martha E., William A., Peter M., Andrew J., Franklin P., Ann, Allen, Texana, Mary M., and Judeth. Richardson moved his family, slaves, and the families of his brothers, Steven Madison and Matthias, to Texas by wagon train, arriving at this location on Dec. 12, 1855.

Richardson built a home (1 mi. NE) and became a successful planter. His "Three Circles" cattle brand was recorded in 1855. He was appointed to lay out one of the first roads between Athens and Kaufman. Highway 175 follows much of his original route. He and his brothers helped found the First Baptist Church in Athens.

The slaves he brought to Texas were Dinah, Charles, Gin, Rachel, Washington, Henry, Tom, Harrison, Kate, Easter, Til, Carolina, Jane, Sam, Congo, Marion, Mimm, and Jube. All took the

Richardson name, and most stayed on with the family after being freed. Later they and their descendants established the Sand Flat community (1 mi. NNE).

William Richardson is buried in the family cemetery (1 mi. NE) along with his wife, two sons, and two grandchildren. Some of the slaves are buried there also.   (1984)

ATLANTA (Cass Co.)   *101 N. East St., off Main St. (SH 249)*
Bessie Coleman
(1892–1926)
The tenth of 13 children born to tenant farmers Susan and George Coleman, famed aviatrix Bessie Coleman was a native of Atlanta, Texas. The family moved to Waxahachie when Bessie was two years old. She followed her brothers to Chicago in 1915 and developed an interest in flying. Because she could find no one in the United States who would teach an African-American woman, Coleman learned to fly in France and obtained her international pilot's license in 1921. Upon her return to the United States, she was hailed as the first black woman to pilot an airplane. Bessie Coleman died in an air accident in Jacksonville, Florida, in 1926 and is buried near Chicago.   (2002)

AUGUSTA (Houston County)   *FM 227, 10 mi. E of Grapeland, in Hayes Park*
Daniel McLean
(1784–May 10, 1837)
John Sheridan
(April 5, 1796–May 10, 1837)
This area's earliest settlers; from North Carolina. McLean came to Texas in 1813 with Gutierrez-Magee Expedition, seeking to free Mexico from Spain. Returning when Austin opened Texas to Anglo-American colonization, he took up land in 1824 on San Pedro Creek (E of here); his brother-in-law, John Sheridan settled on Silver Creek (300 yds. N) near site of present Slocum (12 mi. NW). They were both killed by Indians while pursuing stolen horses. Mrs. Sheridan, with help of a boy, brought back the bodies. Each man was buried on his own land.   (1971)

AUSTIN (Travis Co.)   *FM 969, 8 mi. E*
Site of the Home of Reuben Hornsby
Built in 1832 by Reuben Hornsby (1793–1879) and his wife, Sarah Morrison Hornsby (1796–1862).

Second built in "Austin's Little Colony." First in the present county of Travis. Famed for Christian hospitality. Here Josiah Wilbarger recovered after being scalped in 1833.

Mr. Hornsby and his sons fought in many Indian battles and served as scouts in Capt. John J. Tumlinson's company of Rangers, which was organized here in 1836.

AUSTIN (Travis Co.)   *Loop 1, Under MoPac Bridge*
Travis County
Created January 25, 1840. Organized April 8, 1843. Named in honor of William Barrett Travis. Born Edgefield district South Carolina, August 1, 1809. Came to Texas in 1831. Commander at the Alamo where he was killed March 6, 1836.

Austin, the county seat, selected as the capital of the Republic of Texas in 1839 and by a vote of the people in 1850 made the permanent capital of the State of Texas.

AUSTIN (Travis Co.)   *1st St. W, W bank of Waller Creek,*
                                                    at Town Lake in Austin City Park area
The Grinninger Fence
First known use of barbed wire in Texas (1857), by John Grinninger, immigrant from Europe, worker in an early Austin iron foundry. Grinninger, who lived on Waller Creek (NE of here) grew fruit, vegetables and flowers. To protect garden, he ran homemade barbed wire along top of his fence. Noted peace officer and sometime outlaw Ben Thompson is said to have recalled years later that in youth he tore jeans on that fence. Grinninger was murdered in 1862. In 1867 first U.S. patent on barbed wire was issued.

Expansion of the cattle industry in 1870s led to business for wire-makers, for Midwest and Western America lacked timber for fences. John Warne "Bet-A-Million" Gates created a sensation in the 70s in San Antonio by penning wild cattle with barbed wire.

Joseph F. Glidden and Isaac L. Ellwood, of Illinois, were most successful barbed wire manufacturers in the United States. Their Texas manager, H. B. Sanborn, erected "model" fences in 1870s–1880s in Grayson and Potter Counties, showing ranchers the practicality of enclosing vast acreages. Barbed wire is said to have saved ranching from extinction; it gave each landowner control of cattle breeding and property.

Wire's many styles are now prized by collectors. (1969)

AUSTIN (Travis Co.)

FM 1431, 1.3 mi. N from road,
at Nameless Church and Cemetery

Site of Community of Nameless

First surveyed in the 1850s, this area attracted numerous settlers by 1868. A community grew up, and in 1880 townspeople applied for a post office. After postal authorities rejected six names, the citizens replied in disgust, "Let the post office be Nameless and be d—d." The implied "name" was accepted.

Besides the post office (1880–1890), town had store, meat market, and school, which also served as a church. The present school was erected in 1909; classes were discontinued in 1945. Today only school, cemetery, and ruins mark site of once active community. (1970)

AUSTIN (Travis Co.)

Capitol grounds

Texas and the Civil War Secession Convention

The election of Abraham Lincoln in 1860 caused unrest and drastic action all over the South and in many Texas counties. Despite petitions, editorials and political pressure, Gov. Sam Houston refused to call a special legislative session to consider the position Texas should take. On Dec. 3, 1860, a group of secession leaders took matters into their own hands and called on the people to elect delegates to a convention to meet in Austin on Jan. 28, 1861. Counties sent 177 delegates, and the convention met in the capitol from Jan. 28 to Feb. 4 and March 2 to March 25. A committee on public safety, with broad powers, acted for the convention between sessions.

By vote of 166 to 7, the convention adopted the ordinance of secession and called for a statewide election—the first state in the Confederacy to let voters have a direct voice. 108 of the 122 counties favored secession by a vote of 46,129 to 14, 697.

The convention voted to join the Confederacy, send delegates to its congress, gear for war and raise troops to protect the frontier. When Gov. Sam Houston refused to take the oath supporting the Confederacy, the convention replaced him with the Lieutenant Governor Edward Clark. (1965)

AUSTIN (Travis Co.)

Capitol grounds

The Texas Capitol

Austin became the capital of Texas Jan. 19, 1840, and this hill was platted as Capitol Square. A modest statehouse built here in the 1850s soon developed structural flaws. The Constitutional Convention of 1876 set aside about 3,000,000 acres of public land to finance another building. This was authorized after the 1850s capitol burned on Nov. 9, 1881.

Architect E. E. Myers of Detroit won a national competition with his plans for this capitol. The contractor was Mattheas Schnell of Rock Island, Ill. Basement excavation began early in 1882. Railroads built especially for this project hauled limestone from the Oatmanville quarries in Travis County as well as stone donated by the owners of the Granite Mountain in Burnet County. The 900 workmen on the project included 86 granite cutters brought from Scotland. Charles B. and John V. Farwell, Chicago bankers, funded the construction and were repaid in land in ten Panhandle counties, on which they founded the famous XIT ranch. At dedication ceremonies on May 18, 1888, the capitol was accepted on behalf of the people by State Senator Temple Houston, son of Texas hero Sam Houston. He called it "A structure that shall stand as a sentinel of eternity." (1976)

AUSTIN (Travis Co.)

Capitol grounds

Moses Austin
(October 4, 1761–June 10, 1821)

The initiator of Anglo-American settlement in Texas, Moses Austin was a native of Durham, Connecticut. After his marriage to Mary Brown in 1785, Austin became a leading figure in the development of the American lead industry. His business took him to Virginia and then west to the Mississippi Valley. A colonizer and pioneer as well, Austin helped establish several frontier communities.

Moses Austin's decision to venture into a colonization enterprise in the Spanish territory of Texas led him to San Antonio de Bexar in 1820. With the help of Felipe Neri, Baron de Bastrop, Austin requested permission from the Spanish governor, Antonio Martinez, to settle a colony of 300 Anglo-American families in his province. Austin returned to Missouri, where he learned in March 1821 that his petition had been granted. Although ill from the effects of his journey, he began making plans to raise a colony. Three months later, Moses Austin died in the Hazel Run settlement, where he was buried. He was later reinterred in Potosi, Missouri.

In response to his father's dying wish, Stephen F. Austin continued the colonization project and led the first of the "Old 300" colonists into Texas in late 1821.

(Texas Sesquicentennial 1836–1986)

AUSTIN (Travis Co.)   *1201 Brazos, at front of State Archives and Library*
The Archive War
In 1839, Austin became the capital of the Republic of Texas. The national archives—state papers and land titles—were housed on Congress Avenue. In 1842, after Mexican armies seized San Antonio and seemed likely to capture Austin, many residents fled in what was called "the breakup." From his home in Galveston, President Sam Houston ordered removal of the government papers. A local "Archive Committee" responded by burying them. The President then tried unsuccessfully to have Congress create a new capital near the coast. Later his men came secretly to haul the papers to the interim capital, Washington-on-the-Brazos, loading them before dawn on Dec. 30, 1842.

Mrs. Angelina Eberly, a noted innkeeper and one of the few women in Austin during the breakup, found the men loading the archives in darkness. Running to the city cannon on Congress Avenue at Pecan (6th) Street, she fired at the wagons. The 26 men departed with the records. About 68 citizens rode after them, hauling along the city cannon. Some 20 miles from Austin they retrieved the archives without bloodshed.

Because the archives remained here, the President and the Congress returned in 1845, preserving Austin as the capital of the Republic and (later) the state.   (1978)

AUSTIN (Travis Co.)   *1010 Colorado St.*
The Governor's Mansion
Official residence of the Governor of Texas. By law, each chief executive must live here during his term of office. Before the erection of this structure in 1855–1856, the only official executive home had been the rough, two-story frame "President's House" at present Seventh and San Jacinto Streets.

Within these walls, many decisions of statewide import have taken place. Here in 1861 Gov. Sam Houston decided not to support the Confederacy. Also, like numerous 19th-century houses, the mansion acquired a ghost story after the nephew of Gov. Pendleton Murrah (1863–1865) committed suicide here.

Built some thirty years before the pink granite capitol, this structure was first occupied by Gov. Elisha M. Pease, who selected the site and design. Pioneer architect-contractor Abner Cook supervised the construction of the stately residence in Greek Revival style. Austin-made bricks were used, and huge pine logs were hauled from Bastrop, then adzed to form the six massive pillars with Ionic capitals.

Distinguished visitors have included U.S. Presidents and heads of state from other countries. More than perhaps any other residence in Texas, the Governor's mansion is a repository of Texas history.   (1969)

AUSTIN (Travis Co.)   *N. Congress at W 1st*
Austin, C.S.A.
An active place during the Civil War, Austin was the site of the Secession Convention, March 2, 1861, and legislative sessions which lasted until June 1865. City visitors during the early 1860s included lobbyists, cotton speculators, military leaders, and businessmen seeking to aid the war effort. Five stage lines and a pony express to the railhead at Brenham provided commu-

nications. Also located here was the Texas Military Board, an agency created to obtain arms and munitions for 33 militia districts.

A city arsenal was set up on Waller Creek in southeast Austin. A gun cap factory in the old land office on 11th Street made 14,000 shells a day, and a foundry produced guns and cannon. Factories for shoes and gunpowder, and a sewing room in the basement of the capitol, furnished goods for the Confederate Army. The city also maintained a military fort.

During the war citizens endured Indian raids, epidemics of fever and diphtheria, rumors of slave uprisings, and a scarcity of food. Hotels refused room and board, even to state legislators, unless payment was made in gold, silver, or goods such as nails and tobacco. As a result, some lawmakers lived in their wagons and cooked over open fires.   (1965)

AUSTIN (Travis Co.)   *601 N. Congress*
Littlefield Building
George Washington Littlefield (1842–1920) came to Texas from Mississippi in 1850. After serving in Terry's Texas Rangers in the Civil War, he made his fortune ranching and driving cattle. He moved to Austin in 1883 and, in 1890, established the American National Bank, which included a ladies' banking department. He hired architect C. H. Page, Jr., to design this Beaux Arts Classical building, which opened in 1912 with a rooftop garden. His bank was on the ground floor. For the corner entrance, he commissioned Tiffany's of New York to cast bronze, Bas Relief doors by sculptor Daniel Webster. These were later donated to the University of Texas, of which Littlefield was a major benefactor.   (2002)

AUSTIN (Travis Co.)   *US 183 at FM 1625, 5 mi. S*
Pilot Knob
Pilot Knob, the only example of an exposed submarine volcano in Texas, appears today as a prominent hill one mile northwest. It was formed some 80 million years ago on the bottom of a warm, shallow sea which covered much of the continent during the Cretaceous Period. The molten rock which it spewed forth rose to the surface from deep within the earth's crust, following a channel opened by a belt of fractures known as the Balcones Fault Zone.

Reef organisms were attracted to the irregularity on the sea floor. Seeking food and protection on its slopes they multiplied rapidly, not unlike coral reefs form now in the South Pacific Ocean. As corals, starfish, oysters, and other marine life died, their shells and skeletons were fossilized around the volcano. Outcroppings of the small reefs which they formed can be seen today along the banks of Onion Creek, immediately north of Pilot Knob.

As the Cretaceous sea receded, the volcano was exposed in its entirety. The long weathering to which it was subjected eroded much of the mass, leaving only the central portion or vent. Today, it rises 710 feet above sea level, 180 feet above the surrounding valley. Diameter of its rim is 1.5 miles.

The Pilot Knob area, 29 square miles around the volcano, is probably the best known igneous (volcanic) rock locality in the entire Balcones zone. Principal component of both the central knob and the several smaller knolls on its south and east is basalt, a dark gray to black volcanic rock. Weathered volcanic ash, similar in composition to basalt, underlies the valley around Pilot Knob and makes the land rich for farming.

AUSTIN (Travis Co.)   *Main entrance to Barton Pool, Zilker Park*
Barton Springs
Clear and icy, these springs over the years have drawn Indians, pioneers, and tourists to this spot. The waters are brought from limestone strata to the surface by the Balcones Fault, which bisects Central Texas. Average flow is 27,000,000 gallons daily.

During 1730–1731, Spanish friars located three missions here (see marker, SE side of pool). Colorful settler William "Uncle Billy" Barton patented the land about 1837, naming two of the springs for his daughters Parthenia and Eliza. His two tame baby buffaloes soon began to attract sight-seers to his place, in spite of constant danger from Indian attacks.

As the place gained in popularity, one astute Austin merchant installed a merry-go-round here and rented bathing suits to swimmers. In 1871, he and several others built ice-making machines at the springs. In addition, flour mills, sawmills, and a quarry appeared along the creek banks.

About 1875, the riverboat "Sunbeam" ran excursions to Barton's at 50 cents a round trip. At one period a ferry was located here on a main road to Austin.

Between 1901 and 1913 A. J. Zilker, leading merchant, bought this land and in 1918 and 1931 deeded it to the people of Austin for use as a park. (1970)

AUSTIN (Travis Co.) *2100 Barton Springs Rd.*
Andrew Jackson Zilker
Voted Austin's most worthy citizen twice, Indiana native Andrew Jackson Zilker (1858–1934) grew up with a strong respect for the laborers along the Ohio River. He came to Austin penniless in 1876 but quickly became a businessman and bank director. He contributed to his community at the neighborhood, city and county levels. Believing in the importance of "practical" education, he indirectly funded school industrial programs when he sold 366 acres of parkland, including Barton Springs, to the city. The payments on the land were required to go to the school district. A gift of 32 additional acres in 1934 added to the city's most cherished recreation area, Zilker Park. (2003)

AUSTIN (Travis Co.) *900 block of Comal St., cemetery entrance*
State Cemetery of Texas
Burial ground for the honored dead of Texas, this cemetery contains the remains of Stephen F. Austin, the "Father of Texas"; nine governors of Texas (as of 1968); and representatives of every period of state history and every department of state government.

Statuary at the graves includes a marble figure of Albert Sidney Johnston by Elisabet Ney and bronzes of Austin and Joanna Troutman by Pompeo Coppini.

The cemetery was founded in 1851 when Gen. Edward Burleson, hero of the Texas Revolution, was interred on this tract. In 1854, the state purchased the land, which had once belonged to Andrew Jackson Hamilton, provisional Governor of Texas from 1865 to 1866.

The cemetery was seldom used, however, until the 1860s, when some officers of the Confederate Army of Texas were buried here. Today small, white marble headstones mark the graves of about 1,583 soldiers and 515 graves of members of their families.

Through the untiring efforts of Louis W. Kemp, a state official (1881–1956), the remains of over 100 prominent persons were reinterred here after 1930.

Since 1951, those eligible for burial here include designated state officials, Confederate veterans, and certain others. In 1968 there were 2,389 graves. (1968)

AUSTIN (Travis Co.) *100 N Interregional (IH 35),*
on NW corner of intersection with E 1st St.
Palm School
When Edwin Waller platted Austin in 1839, he set aside this site for construction of an armory that would offer protection for the new capital of the Republic of Texas. In 1845, Texas joined the United States and the armory became a federal installation. By 1888, it was no longer in use and the United States government donated the land to the city of Austin as the site for a new public school.

The Tenth Ward school building was completed here in 1892. One of the first Austin schools built after legislative authorization of city-operated school systems, Tenth Ward opened under the leadership of Principal Florence Ralston Brooke (1858–1944), a native of England. The name of the school was changed in 1902 to honor Swante Palm (1815–1899), Sweden's former Consul to the State of Texas and a prominent Austin resident and University of Texas benefactor. Miss Brooke remained as principal until 1912 when she was transferred to Austin High School.

In 1976, after 84 years of operation, Palm School was closed. Former students here include many of Austin's business, civic, and professional leaders, and reflect the school's dramatic impact on the city's development. (1982)

AUSTIN (Travis Co.) *IH 35 east frontage road, between 15th & 16th Sts.*
Swedish Hill
Residential development of this area began in the 1870s when a number of Swedish immigrants erected homes near their downtown businesses. Initially bounded by Red River, 14th, 18th, and Navasota Streets, the neighborhood became known as Svenska Kullen (Swedish Hill). A Swedish Methodist and other Swedish churches were built in the area, which was later divided by the interstate highway. A number of historic houses remain in the section of Swedish Hill that is east of the interstate. The neighborhood was listed in the National Register of Historic Places in 1986. (1990)

AUSTIN (Travis Co.) *Loop 360 off US 183*
Balcones Fault Aids Colonization of Texas
Curving through the center of Texas from Hill County south and west to Uvalde County is the rugged escarpment-fault called Balcones. The abundance of natural resources associated with this geologic formation affected the pattern of colonization in Texas. The numerous springs and wooded hills of the escarpment and adjacent fertile prairies attracted Indian tribes and Spanish colonists before the area was permanently settled by Anglo-American pioneers.

Spanish explorer Bernardo de Miranda in 1756 named the formation "Los Balcones," meaning "balconies." Part of El Camino Real, the "King's Highway," it skirted the fault line. Spanish missions and presidios were located at springs near San Antonio, Austin, and elsewhere, but many Spanish settlements disappeared before 1800.

Anglo-Americans led by Stephen F. Austin began to settle near the Balcones Escarpment before 1830. Through their courage and determination, early pioneer settlements grew into the towns and cities that today dot the fault line. The town of Austin, with its combination of beauty and natural resources, was chosen capital of the independent Republic of Texas, which became the 28th state of the United States. (1976)

AUSTIN (Travis Co.) *903 S Capitol of Texas Hwy. (Loop 360)*
Eanes-Marshall Ranch
Alexander Eanes (1806–1888) moved to Texas from Mississippi in 1845 and acquired this ranch by 1857. In 1873, he sold the property to his brother, Robert Eanes (1805–1895), who had moved to the area following the Civil War. A log cabin built on the Eanes Ranch was the first Eanes school, and the community also assumed the Eanes name. Robert Eanes sold the ranch to his son-in-law, Hudson Boatner Marshall (1862–1951) in 1883. Marshall dismantled the ranch house and moved it to a site adjacent to the nearby creek. (Texas Sesquicentennial 1836–1986)

AUSTIN (Travis Co.) *US 183, 11693 Research Blvd.*
Aynesworth-Wright House
Isaiah Hezekiah Aynesworth (b. 1797), a Baptist preacher and cabinetmaker, constructed this Greek Revival residence about 1852. Originally located at 4507 East Avenue, it was a two-room house with an enclosed dog-run hallway. Additional rooms were later attached to the back porch. Dr. Joseph Wright (1798–1898) purchased the property from Aynesworth in 1855. A physician and surveyor, Wright practiced medicine in a log building near his home. The house was moved to this location and restored in 1978 by the Franklin Savings Association. (1980)

AUSTIN (Travis Co.) *43rd St. at Speedway, NE corner*
Hyde Park
Advertised in 1892 as "the most fashionable part of the wealthiest and most aristocratic ward in the city," Hyde Park was Austin's first planned suburb. Encompassing an area bordered by the present streets of Guadalupe, 38th, Duval, and 45th, it was promoted by Monroe M. Shipe (1847–1924), president of the Austin Rapid Transit Railway Co. and the M.K.&T. Land and Town Co.

Shipe arranged for an electric streetcar line to run from Congress Avenue to Hyde Park. He built a lake and pavilion for recreation and had the city's first moonlight tower erected at the corner of Speedway and 41st Street. He also built the first Hyde Park School, and by 1893 forty homes had been built in the neighborhood.

Among the area's illustrious early residents, whose homes still remain, were sculptress Elisabet Ney; Swiss woodcarver Peter Mansbendel; and horticulturist F. T. Ramsey. By the early 1900s the large Victorian homes in the neighborhood were being joined by smaller bungalows. The lake was drained and the pavilion was razed. Hyde Park was within the city limits of Austin by the 1930s and the streetcar ceased operation in the 1940s. Renewed interest in the 1970s resulted in revitalization of the neighborhood. (1989)

AUSTIN (Travis Co.) *6266 SH 290 W*
Old Rock Store
Influenced by the style of early German rock buildings in Central Texas, James Andrew Patton (1853–1944) supervised the construction of this building in 1898. A German mason laid the stone. Patton fought Comanches as a Texas Ranger and was a civic leader and local postmaster. He was known affectionately as "The Mayor of Oak Hill." He and his family, followed by others, operated

a general store here for many years. The building also housed a local Woodmen of the World lodge hall on the second floor. (1970)

AUSTONIO (Houston Co.) *SH 21, .3 mi. W*
The Homesite of Samuel Cartmill Hiroms
One of this community's pioneer settlers, Samuel Cartmill Hiroms (1836–1920) was born in Polk County. His parents were among Stephen F. Austin's "Old three hundred" colonists. Hiroms taught school and served as Polk County surveyor. He served in the Confederate Army during the Civil War (1861–1865). After his first wife died, he married Emily Ann Johnston (1853–1948) in 1869 and moved his family to Houston County. In 1878, Hiroms settled here in the Creek community, which later became Austonio. He received land for his teaching services and was an early leader in the Methodist Church. (1978)

AZLE (Tarrant Co.) *FM 730, .6 mi. N of SH 199*
Kiowa Raid on Walnut Creek
In April 1867, a band of about sixty Kiowa Indians, led by Chiefs Satank and Satanta, raided the home of William Hamleton on Walnut Creek. Hamleton was away when the Kiowas killed his wife, Sally, and captured two children, Lavina and Mary. Lavina was released from captivity after six months, but Mary was given to an Indian family and grew to adulthood among the Kiowas. Called To-goam-gat-ty, she became an accepted tribal member and married another captive, Calisay. The site of the 1867 Kiowa raid is now under the waters of Eagle Mountain Reservoir. (1983)

BAIRD (Callahan Co.) *Old US 80, 7 mi. E*
The United States Military Telegraph Line
Established in 1874–1875 from Fort Griffin to Fort Concho, crossed here.

BAIRD (Callahan Co.) *US 80, within city limits*
The Dr. John Collier Residence
This home was constructed in the early 1880's soon after Baird was selected as the county seat of Callahan Co. It was first the home of Elias Norton, an early merchant of Callahan Co. It later became the home of Dr. John Collier, prominent educator in the early days of the county and founder of the Baird College and its president for a number of years.

BALLINGER (Runnels Co.) *US 83, 7 mi. S*
San Clemente Mission
(Site 10 mi. SE)
The first mission known to have been established in Texas east of the Pecos River, San Clemente was a hastily built, two-room structure located on a hill about 17 mi. S of present Ballinger. (Some historians place the site farther south, near Junction.) Although earlier than the great Spanish mission movement, this was one of the first (1684) in Texas and was founded by Juan Dominguez de Mendoza and Fray Nicolas Lopez.

Named for the San Clemente River (actually the Colorado), the mission was founded at the request of the Jumano Indians, who desired Christianity and the friendship of the Spanish. The building was probably constructed of logs, its lower story serving as a chapel and its upper story as a lookout post. Though they stayed only from March 15 to May 1, awaiting envoys from 48 tribes (bands), the Spaniards baptized many of their several thousand Indian allies.

Finally, being attacked by hostile Apaches, Mendoza returned with his men to El Paso six months after he had left. Although Mendoza did not know it, French explorer La Salle had landed on the Gulf Coast, 1684. This fact, plus Mendoza's report of seeing a French flag among the Indians, quickly led to other Spanish expeditions being sent to chart the Texas wilderness. (1968)

BALLINGER (Runnels Co.) *US 67 at US 83, .8 mi. E of intersection*
Site of Picketteville
First civilian settlement in Runnels County. Founded 1862 by frontiersmen whose picket houses and corrals gave place its name. Original settlers included Mr. and Mrs. John W. Guest and three sons; Henry and R. K. Wylie, their cowboys and Negro servant; Mrs. Felicia Gordon and five sons. In 1862 "Rich" Coffey's family also moved here. Indian hostilities of Civil Wars years (1861–1865) caused these ranchers to band together for protection. In 1866 they left with cattle

for open range. Their picket corral later penned the trail herds of John Hittson, John and Joseph Henderson, and others. (1973)

BALLINGER (Runnels Co.) *Courthouse lawn*
Charles H. Noyes (1896–1917)
Charles H. Noyes, 21, died when his horse fell while rounding up cattle on the Noyes' ranch. His father and mother, Gus and Lula Noyes, erected monument in 1919 as a tribute to their son and all Texas cowboys.

Pompeo Coppini of Chicago studied horses two years before sculpturing the statue. (1966)

BALLINGER (Runnels Co.) *US 83 in the city*
Abilene & Southern Depot
Morgan Jones (1840–1926), a Welsh-born railroad builder, and his nephews Morgan C. (1876–1964) and Percy Jones (1885–1951) built the Abilene & Southern Rail Line in 1909 between Abilene and Ballinger. This stone structure was finished soon after the first train arrived, Sept. 9, 1909. The design, with octagonal twin towers, was unusual for depots of that era. The railroad did a flourishing passenger and freight business. Passenger service ended in 1941 and freight service in 1966. (1978)

BANDERA (Bandera Co.) *SH 16, .8 mi. W.; also SH 16, 1 mi. E*
Bandera County
A strategic Indian point in early days. Rangers and Comanches struggled here in 1843. In 1854 Elder Lyman Wight settled Mormon Colony. In 1855 Poles settled here. From early days a part of Bexar County, created and organized in 1856.

Bandera, the county seat founded by John James, Charles de Montel and John Herndon in 1853.

BANDERA (Bandera Co.) *FM 689, 10 mi. N*
Bandera Pass
Celebrated Indian pass known from the earliest days of Spanish settlement. Identified with many a frontier fight and many a hostile inroad. Old Ranger trail from the Medina to the Guadalupe River and the United States Army route between frontier posts followed this route through the mountains.

BANDERA (Bandera Co.) *SH 16, on public square across the street from the Courthouse*
Old Texas Ranger Trail
This winding, 100-mile trail from San Antonio to Kerrville was, during the 19th century, a strategic patrol road traveled by Texas Rangers to protect the surrounding area from hostile Indian attacks.

During uneasy pioneer days roads such as this, regularly scouted by Rangers, helped promote early white settlement by strengthening frontier defense.

Because Bandera was located midway on the trail and because Bandera Pass, 10 miles north, frequently harbored Indian ambushers, the town became a focal point for Ranger activities along the road.

Perhaps the best-known battle to occur on the old route happened in Bandera Pass in the spring of 1841. At that time a company of 40 Texas Rangers under intrepid Indian fighter Capt. "Jack" Hays was on a scouting mission in the Guadalupe Mountains. Halfway through pass, they were suddenly attacked by several hundred wild Comanches who lay hidden in the brush and behind boulders in the narrow gorge.

A bloody fight ensued, much of it hand-to-hand combat with Bowie knives; but after their chief was slain, the Indians withdrew and finally escaped.

Thus the Rangers and this trail helped remove the Indian menace and open the frontier across Texas. (1968)

BANDERA (Bandera Co.) *SH 16 (Cypress St.)*
Schmidtke-Callahan House
This home was constructed in the 1870s by Georgia stonemason James Henry White for Charles F. Schmidtke (1839–1884). A native of Germany, Schmidtke was an early Bandera merchant, grist

31

miller, and lumber mill operator. White's grandson J. Calvin Callahan (d. 1958), the owner of a feed store and poultry business, purchased the property in 1927. The limestone house, with influences of Greek revival styling, remained in the Callahan family until the 1970s.   (1981)

BANQUETE (Nueces Co.)

Fort Lipantitlan Park Rd. off FM 3088,
20.1 mi. NW of Corpus Christi;
12 mi. NW of FM 70

Fort Lipantitlan

In 1728 a Spanish fort was built at this site near a Lipan Apache village with the Aztec name "Lipantitlan." The post was later abandoned, and the village was deserted after many Indians died with the Gutierrez-Magee Expedition at the Battle of Medina, Aug. 18, 1813.

Garrisoned again about 1831 by Mexican troops as a deterrent to further Anglo-American colonization, Fort Lipantitlan was then a simple earthen embankment surrounding unfinished barracks. In 1835 the soldiers borrowed a cannon from the settlers in nearby San Patricio, foreshadowing a similar incident at Gonzales which led to the skirmish of Oct. 2, 1835, and sparked the Texas Revolution. Late in Oct. 1835, Capt. Philip Dimitt, commander of Texas forces at Goliad, dispatched a company under Ira Westover to take Fort Lipantitlan. Westover captured the fortification on Nov. 3 and the next day stopped a Mexican counterattack led by Capt. Nicolas Rodriguez. Although not decisive, the battle boosted the Texans' morale.

On June 7, 1843, Fort Lipantitlan was successfully defended by an army of volunteers under Gen. James Davis against an attack by Gen. Antonio Canales and his "Republic of the Rio Grande" forces. After that battle, the post was abandoned and soon crumbled into ruin.   (1976)

BANQUETE (Nueces Co.)

SH 44 at FM 666

Banquete, C.S.A.

In the critical Civil War years, Banquete meant water, supplies, repairs and defenses to thousands on arid trips along the Cotton Road to Mexico.

The Cotton Road was well known, for it followed a segment of the historic "King's Highway" of early explorers. Yet its vital role for 4 years in supplying the Confederacy earned it undying fame.

It was the way to Mexico's border towns of Bagdad and Matamoros, where 20,000 speculators clamored for cotton, using valuable European goods to make attractive bargains. To get guns, ammunition, shoes, clothing, medicines—necessities scarce at home—the Confederacy sent to neutral Mexico long trains of 5 to 15 wagons or ox carts that lumbered for many weeks over the desert. Sometimes to lighten a load for an exhausted team, cotton bales might be hidden in roadside brush. The traffic left signs in the wilds. Often the landscape would whiten with the lint thrown off passing loads.

Banquete's water made possible the long hauls to Mexico and back to the goods-hungry Confederate population. Thus the town named for an 1832 fiesta honoring Texas colonists served a strategic role in the history of the Civil War, 1861–1865.

BARKER (Harris Co.)

211 Baker Rd. (IH 10)

Barker Post Office

The settlement that became Barker developed on the Missouri-Kansas-Texas railroad in the late 1890s. G. T. Miller applied for a post office in 1898. It occupied a corner of his store, which also was used as a saloon. The structure was damaged in the 1900 storm, and postmaster Miller moved it to the east side of the Barker-Clodine Road and rebuilt it. He remained postmaster until 1911. Moved to a new location on the Katy Freeway (Interstate Highway 10) in 1967, it was designated a third-class post office in 1969 and a second-class office in 1977. In 1978 the postal service considered closing it, but residents rallied and saved it. Designated first class in 1981, the post office moved to Baker Road in 1984.   (2001)

BARKSDALE (Edwards Co.)

SH 55 in Barksdale

The Pioneer Coalsons
(Cedar Creek Ranch and Graves about 9 mi.)

Indians attacked goat camp of Nick Coalson on June 1, 1877; son Arthur, 10, was killed; Johnny, l4 wounded. Coalson escaped after 3 hours of hard fighting. One year later he lost his wife Alice, a daughter, Etta Elizabeth (twin of Arthur), and infant stepson in another Indian raid. Captains Pat Dolan and Dan Roberts with Texas Ranger units, S. D. Coalson (Nick's son), U.S.

Army scout Jim Hill, Jim and John Welch, and Henry and Sam Wells pursued but failed to find the Indians. The victims' graves are near old homesite, on Half-Moon Prairie. Coalson descendants are prominent in Texas history. (1972)

BARKSDALE (Edwards Co.)
SH 55 in Barksdale
Dixie Settlement
(Forerunner of Barksdale)
Named for Camp Dixie, a Texas Ranger post near military road to Fort Inge (42 mi. SE). First civilian settler was Jerusha Sanchez, midwife for Nueces Canyon area widowed by Indians in the 1870s. Next came Elizabeth Hill, whose eldest son Jim was a military scout. Lewis Barksdale, a veteran of Republic of Texas wars, opened a ranch on his 1876 land grant. The J. R. (Bob) Sweeten family established a store that became the focus for the expanding community. When a post office was created in 1882 and named for Lewis Barksdale, the name Dixie disappeared from use. (1974)

BARKSDALE (Edwards Co.)
SH 55 in Barksdale
Site of Nix Mill
(1885–1926)
Built by John L. Nix (1842–1915) to cut rawhide lumber, grind corn and wheat, and gin cotton. Upper floor housed gin; lower, grist mill. On east side was sawmill with wood furnace and boiler to furnish steam power. Furnace was fed cedar and oak wood. Spanish oaks, white oaks, and elms from Nueces River watercourse were sawed into the rawhide lumber from which were built town's wagon yard feed stalls, a dance hall, and other structures.

After Nix, successive owners were J. L. Jackson, W. D. Hutcherson, Edward Miller, Matthew Taylor, and O. C. Henderson. (1972)

BARNHART (Irion Co.)
US 67
Barnhart
Named for William F. Barnhart, an agent of the Kansas City, Mexico & Orient Railroad, this community was founded in 1910. During the 1920s and 1930s it was a major freighting center and considered by many the largest inland livestock shipping point. The Ozona-Barnhart Trap Co. set up cattle holding pens (traps) along the trails into town to protect area ranches. Barnhart declined with decreased rail traffic. It was once the site of a school, post office, newspaper, drugstore, theater, bank, four cafes, two hotels, three groceries, and a variety of other businesses. (1981)

BARSTOW (Ward Co.)
Grounds of Community House
(Old Ward Courthouse)
Vicinity of Early Public Library
The Republic of Texas set a cultural example by legislation for a state library in 1839. In 1874 cities were authorized to establish public libraries, but most were privately financed.

A library near here about 1890 was gift of Miss Ana Gould, a daughter of railroad magnate Jay Gould, when she was visiting the stone quarry 4.5 mi. east. She established the library—the first in Ward County, which was not organized until 1892—for families near the quarry.

Most Texas counties now have free public libraries, since a 1919 law granted this privilege. (1967)

BARTLETT (Bell Co.)
SH 95, 1 mi. N
St. John Lutheran Church
The first Lutheran worship services in this area were held at the home of early German settler J. E. Pietzsch, who had moved from Austin County. In 1880, a small school and church building was erected on land donated by John Bartlett, for whom the nearby town of Bartlett was named.

St. John Lutheran Church was formally organized on December 16, 1883. A year later the Rev. Immanuel Glatzle arrived to become the first resident pastor. By 1896 the congregation had acquired more land and erected a small white frame sanctuary. All written records were destroyed in a 1922 fire which burned the parsonage and two outbuildings. Larger facilities were needed by 1931, so a new church structure was built that year. Dedication services were held January 10, 1932. On August 12, 1951, the congregation dedicated its new pipe organ, which at the time was the largest in any Texas Lutheran church.

33

From its beginning St. John Lutheran Church has served the spiritual and educational needs of the surrounding communities. Although the last German service was conducted in 1942, the church continues to reflect the ideals and traditions of its founders. (1983)

BARTLETT (Bell Co.) *SH 95, 1 mi. N*
Site of German-English School
(50 yds. W)
Established by German immigrants in 1880, the German-English School was an early school in the Bartlett area. First called Indian Creek School, the name was changed due to popular usage and the nature of instruction, which was in English during the winter and German during the summer. Closely associated with St. John's Lutheran Church, the school shared facilities with the church until 1896, when a church sanctuary was built. The school was closed in 1948, but the building remained in use for community functions until the early 1960s. (1988)

BARTLETT (Bell Co.) *SH 317 (506 N Main)*
First Baptist Church of Belton
The First Baptist Church of Belton was organized in the summer of 1853 under the leadership of the Rev. Solomon G. O'Bryan and the Rev. David Fisher. There were eight charter members, and the congregation met in a small frame building on Pearl Street on the north side of Nolan Creek. Early visiting preachers included John Clabaugh and Judge R. E. B. Baylor.

Clabaugh was called as permanent pastor of the church in 1856 and held services once a month until the beginning of the Civil War. Visiting ministers served the congregation during the war. A revival held in 1864 at the courthouse by the Rev. W. W. Harris resulted in many new members for the church.

The Rev. M. V. Smith began an eighteen-year pastorate in Belton in January 1875. The congregation, which had been meeting in other churches, built a stone structure on the east side of Main Street, south of the present church buildings. After the stone church was destroyed by fire in 1947, construction began on the present structure at 506 N. Main. The facilities have been enlarged over the years to serve the growing congregation.

With service to its congregation and the community, the church has contributed to Belton's history. (Texas Sesquicentennial 1836–1986)

BARTLETT (Bell Co.) *Old US 281 (Old Austin-Belton Rd.), 2 mi. S*
Lampasas River Bridge
Erected to replace an 1875 toll bridge at this site, this was one of several bridges authorized by the Bell County Commissioners Court in 1889. Built by the Penn Bridge Company of Beaver Falls, Pennsylvania, it is a rare surviving example of a double-intersection Pratt Truss Bridge (also known as Whipple Truss Bridge, after the engineer who patented the design in the 19th century). Measuring over 196 feet in length, the bridge consists of eleven pin-connected panels. Large pieces of native rock were used to form the abutments, and the floor is made of heavy timber planking. (Recorded Texas Historic Landmark—1990)

BASTROP (Bastrop Co.) *SH 71, 1.5 mi. E*
Bastrop County
A part of Austin's grant in 1821 created the Municipality of Mina 1834, became the County of Mina in the Republic of Texas 1836.

Name changed to "Bastrop" December 18, 1837, in honor of Felipe Enrique Neri Baron de Bastrop, 1770–1829 land commissioner of Austin's colony, member of the Congress of Coahuila and Texas.

Bastrop, the county seat.

BASTROP (Bastrop Co.) *SH 21, 1 mi. NE (Bastrop State Park)*
Erected in Recognition of the
Distinguished Service to Texas of
Felipe Enrique Neri,
Baron de Bastrop
1770–1829
Pioneer Red River empresario. Land commissioner of Austin's colony. Member of the Congress of Coahuila and Texas. In his honor this county and county seat have been named.

BASTROP (Bastrop Co.) *SH 71 W, 2 mi. E in roadside park*
Mrs. R. T. P. Allen
Resident of Bastrop County, 1857–1863. Wife of Col. Robert Thomas Pritchard Allen (1812–1888), graduate of West Point, civil engineer, mathematics professor, Methodist preacher, U.S. mail agent and co-publisher "Pacific News," San Francisco, 1849–1850; founder and commandant of Kentucky Military Institute and of Bastrop Military Institute. Their family visitors from time to time in Bastrop included Governor Sam Houston, whose son, Sam Junior, was a B. M. I. cadet.

Mrs. Allen, during the Civil War, was an angel of mercy to prisoners at Camp Ford, Tyler, where her husband, at that time colonel of the 17th Texas Infantry, was commandant, 1863–1864. She nursed the ill, consoled the homesick, cheered the despondent, attended church services with the prisoners. She was so much esteemed and loved that one of the Federals wrote a poem in her honor.

After the war, returned with her husband to state of Kentucky. There Col. Allen resumed operation of Kentucky Military Institute. His brother-in-law, Jay Cooke, of Philadelphia, who had won international fame as the United States' financier for the Civil War, backed Allen and K.M.I. until his 1873 business failure known as the Jay Cooke money panic. (1965)

BASTROP (Bastrop Co.) *SH 71, about 2 mi. W, then 1 mi. S on SH 304, on house*
Aldridge-Fitzwilliam Home
Built 1852 on part of league granted in 1831 by the Mexican government to Mozea Rousseau, a member of Austin's second colony.

First portion was erected by John Aldridge, farmer, whose family lived here until about 1865. The 2-story part was built about 1872 by J. W. Fitzwilliam, captain in Confederate Army and plantation owner. House is called "Wexford" after town in Ireland where he was born. Home is still owned by the Fitzwilliam family. (1968)

BASTROP (Bastrop Co.) *SH 71 at Loop 150*
Early History of the
City of Bastrop
Long before white men arrived, this region was inhabited by Tonkawa and Comanche Indians. In 1691 the first Spanish explorers crossed this territory en route to East Texas. From their route, parts of "El Camino Real" (The King's Highway) were blazed, thus placing Bastrop on a major early travel artery.

Because El Camino Real crossed the Colorado River here, this was a strategic spot. In 1805 the fort "Puesta de Colorado" and accompanying community were founded here to protect commerce on the road.

In 1825 this area became "Mina," one of the first settlements in the Colony of Stephen F. Austin. It was named for revolutionary leader Xavier Mina.

In the years that followed, many members of its first 100 families served in the Texas Revolution (1836), the Mexican War (1846–1848), and were active in political life in the Republic and State of Texas.

In 1837 when the town incorporated, the name was changed to "Bastrop" to honor the Baron de Bastrop, influential early land agent and statesman. The city was also designated county seat in 1837. From 1851–1870, this was seat of Bastrop Military Academy, an important Texas school. First courthouse was built in 1853; present one in 1883 on same spot. (1968)

BASTROP (Bastrop Co.) *SH 21, 1 mi. NE (Bastrop State Park)*
The Gotier Trace
Originated in 1820s. Crossed the present counties of Austin, Washington, Fayette, Lee, Bastrop; joined San Felipe, capital of Stephen F. Austin's colony, with Bastrop. Marked by James Gotier, a settler who (with several in his family) died in Indian massacre near this site in 1837.

Like most early Texas roads, this was only a marked route which travelers could follow—dusty in droughts, boggy in rains.

From such traces, wagon roads and cattle trails, Texas has developed over 67,000 miles of fine paved highways—a system recognized as nation's finest. (1967)

BASTROP (Bastrop Co.) *SH 21, 1 mi. NE (Bastrop State Park), at entrance*
Lost Pines of Texas
Located 80 miles west of the main pine belt of Texas, these trees probably were once part of vast prehistoric pine forests. As land areas gradually rose, possibly due to glacier activity, most of the forests moved east. Ideal local conditions have kept the "lost pines" intact.

One of the first records of the trees was made in 1807 by Zebulon Pike, explorer for whom Pike's Peak was named. In the 19th century, these loblolly pines supported the county's main industry. Local lumber was shipped by riverboat and ox-wagon to points all over Texas. (1969)

BASTROP (Bastrop Co.) *SH 21 at Loop 150, 2 mi. E,*
at Bastrop State Park Refectory
The CCC at Bastrop State Park
President Franklin D. Roosevelt and the U.S. Congress, as part of the "New Deal" efforts to offer unemployed workers jobs on public projects, created the Civilian Conservation Corps (CCC) in March 1933. Due to decades of lumbering activities, Bastrop County's "Lost Pines" forest was a prime candidate for the CCC's reforestation program and a logical site for the establishment of a park, and two hundred recruits of the CCC's company #1805 arrived in Bastrop in November 1933. With the help of Austin architect Arthur Fehr and a group of "local experienced men" or L.E.M.s, the men worked to create a state recreational park in the forest. Built of native materials in the "NPS rustic" style promoted by the National Park Service, the park structures, particularly the central refectory, reflect the expert craftsmanship of the CCC.

A second CCC company, #1811, arrived in November 1934 to assist with reforestation work and development of nearby Buescher State Park. Additional activities included making native wood furniture for this and other Texas state parks, and building roads, trails, bridges, and small lakes. CCC work at Bastrop ended with the park substantially complete in 1939. (1991)

BASTROP (Bastrop Co.) *SH 304, 5 mi. S*
Hubbard-Trigg House
Has colonial "widow's walk." Built 1890 by Robt. W. Hubbard. Still in his family. Enlarged by K. M. Trigg, father of Mrs. F. H. Birmingham, present owner. (1964)

BASTROP (Bastrop Co.) *SH 21, 12 mi. NE*
King's Highway
Camino Real
Old San Antonio Road marked by the Daughters of the American Revolution and the State of Texas; A.D. 1918.

BATESVILLE (Zavala Co.) *Batesville Plaza*
Site of First Zavala County Courthouse
Zavala County was created in 1858 from Maverick and Uvalde Counties. Named for Lorenzo de Zavala, a veteran of the Battle of San Jacinto, the county was not organized for judicial purposes until 1884. In that year citizens elected county officials and selected Batesville as the county seat.

Batesville originally was known as the Bates Ditch Community or Bates City. Elijah A. and Ellen J. Bates are credited with its founding. They came to the area in the late 1860s and became a prominent ranching family. Bates, who is credited with the first irrigation project in the area, began selling two-acre plots of the irrigated farmland, and a settlement grew up near his home.

After the selection of Batesville as the Zavala County seat, Bates conveyed a portion of his land for use as a courthouse square. The first county courthouse and jail were constructed at this site in 1885. Built of burnt bricks made from Leona River soil, the two-story courthouse featured offices downstairs and a courtroom upstairs. The structure was used as the county courthouse until 1928, when the seat of government was moved to Crystal City. The old courthouse then was used for a variety of purposes until it was torn down in 1947. (1984)

BAY CITY (Matagorda Co.) *SH 35, .7 mi. E*
Matagorda County
Organized March 6, 1834, into the Mexican municipality of Matagorda. Created a county of the same name in 1836.

Organized in 1837. Named of the bay on which it fronts.

County seat, Matagorda 1837. 1894 Bay City, since.

BAY CITY (Matagorda Co.)　　　　　　*SH 35, east side of Colorado River bridge*
Elliott's Ferry

During the early days of Anglo-American colonization in Texas, the Matagorda Bay prairie area was an important route for people traveling between settlements. A convenient river crossing was a necessity, and a ferry was established on the Thomas Cayce league of land near this site. Known as Cayce's Ferry, the site was garrisoned by a small army post.

In January 1839, George Elliott (1806–1862) purchased land on the west bank of the Colorado River from Thomas Cayce, and from that time the ferry crossing was known as Elliott's Ferry. George Elliott was assisted in his endeavors by two nephews, William Elliott and John Elliott, who continued the ferry business after George Elliott's death.

By 1863, a small settlement had grown up around Elliott's Ferry. A small mercantile business and a post office known as Elliott's Ferry, Texas, were in operation in 1872. In 1893, the post office name was changed to Elliott, Texas, and a year later was moved to Bay City.

In 1902, a bridge was built over the Colorado River two miles northwest of Bay City. Known as the "Old River Bridge," its completion resulted in the demise of Elliott's Ferry.

(Texas Sesquicentennial 1836–1986)

BAY CITY (Matagorda Co.)　　　　　　　*SH 60, 18 mi. S, then 3.4 mi. E*
Selkirk Island

William Selkirk (1792–1830), one of Stephen F. Austin's original "Old Three Hundred" settlers, came to Texas from New York in 1822. Selkirk was a surveyor for the Austin colony and served in the colonial militia. He was part of a group sent (1824) by Austin to make a treaty with the Waco and Tawakoni Indians. His grant of land, known as Selkirk Island, was among the first issued by the Mexican government to American colonists in 1824. Ownership of the property has remained in his family since that time. Selkirk's descendants have been prominent civic and business leaders in Matagorda and Galveston Counties.

Originally Selkirk's land grant consisted of several islands formed by the branches and channels of the Colorado River. When the grant was surveyed in 1824, a log raft (fallen trees) blocked the river near Selkirk's property. This raft hindered navigation inland for many years. Recent dredging closed the channels so that the land is no longer divided into islands. In the 19th century a sawmill stood where Mill Creek once emptied into the now dry east bed of the Colorado River. According to legend, one of Jean Lafitte's pirates hid a treasure at the northern end of Selkirk Island.　　　　　　　　　　　　　　　　　　　　　　　　　(1974)

BAYTOWN (Harris Co.)　　　　　　*5 mi. E of Crosby-Lynchburg highway*
Oakland

One mile south to the site of Oakland home of David G. Burnet (1788–1870), first president of the Republic of Texas. To Oakland he brought his bride in 1831, and there they and their son William wrested a livelihood from the soil.

BAYTOWN (Harris Co.)　　　　　　　　　*SH 146, E of Hartman Bridge*
Bayland Orphanage
(Site ½ mi. SE)

Established in 1866 by Texas Confederate veterans for children of deceased soldiers. Had capacity for 250. Rev. Henry F. Gillette was first superintendent. C.S.A. Col. Ashbel Smith, diplomat, soldier, and statesman, was staff doctor. Trustees included leading citizens.

Donations from Harris and Galveston Counties started the home, but later gifts came from as far away as New Orleans.

After the Confederate children grew up, home and school were opened to others. Bayland was forerunner of the De Pelchin Faith Home of Houston.　　　　　　　　　　(1964)

BAYTOWN (Harris Co.)　　　　　　*SH 146, 1.8 mi. E of Hartman Bridge*
Ashbel Smith, M.D. (1805–1886)

Born in Hartford, Connecticut, this prominent physician, statesman, soldier, and educator received his degree from Yale Medical College in 1828. After a period of study in France, Smith returned to the United States to practice medicine in the state of North Carolina.

He determined to go to Texas upon hearing news of the events of the mid-1830s and arrived in 1837, too late to participate in the Revolution. He soon, however, was appointed Surgeon-General of the Texas Army and established a home, known as Evergreen Plantation, one mile east of this site. Smith later served the Republic of Texas as Secretary of State and as Minister to Great Britain, France, Belgium, and Spain. After Texas attained statehood, Smith served several terms in the state legislature. A Civil War veteran, he was elected Captain of the Bayland Guards and Colonel of the 2nd Texas Infantry of the Confederate Army.

Also noted for his work in higher education, Ashbel Smith served as president of the first Board of Regents of the University of Texas and led support for establishment of its medical branch in Galveston.

A significant leader during Texas' formative years, Ashbel Smith died at his home on Evergreen Plantation and is buried in the State Cemetery in Austin.   (1984)

BAYTOWN (Harris Co.)   *Bay Oaks Harbor, 2000-½ Tri Cities Beach Rd.*
Bell Prairie

Once located southwest of this site was the home of Henry Falvel Gillette (1816–1896). A native of Connecticut, Gillette came to Texas in 1840 at the urging of his cousin, Ashbel Smith. He became a noted educator in Harris, Washington, and Polk counties. He married Lucinda Maxey (1826–1901) of Washington County in 1842.

The Gillette family lived on the plantation of Lucinda's father, William Maxey, in present San Jacinto County from about 1848 until 1859, when Henry bought property on Galveston Bay. He named his plantation home Bell Prairie. The plantation included a two-story brick home, matching carriage house, and slave quarters. A wharf on the property was used for the importation of cattle from England.

In addition to operating his plantation, Gillette was superintendent of the Bayland Orphan's Home on nearby Goose Creek and was a founding member and worthy master of the Cedar Bayou Masonic Lodge.

Following Henry Gillette's death, Bell Prairie remained in the family until the mid-20th century. The plantation home was severely damaged in the 1900 hurricane and burned to the ground after being struck by lightning in the 1915 storm.   (1989)

BEAUMONT (Jefferson Co.)   *University St. between Florida St. and*
US 287/US 96/US 69
The Lucas Gusher

Discovery well of the Spindletop Oil Field and the first important well on the Gulf Coast. It blew in on Jan. 10, 1901, flowing 100,000 barrels of oil a day from a depth of 1020 feet. The oil production which resulted made Beaumont a city and the Sabine District a major oil refining and exporting center of the world. The Lucas Gusher was drilled by the Hamill Brothers, contractors, under the direct supervision of Captain Anthony F. Lucas for Guffey and Galey of Pittsburgh, on the McFaddin, Weiss and Kyle lease.   (1936)

BEAUMONT (Jefferson Co.)   *Old N Port Arthur Rd. at FM 365, 7 mi. S*
Early Texas Oil Pipelines

This marks route of Texas first oil pipeline to Tidewater, constructed 1901 to transport oil from famed Spindletop gusher (7 mi. North), which came in on Jan. 10 and flowed at rate of 75,000 barrels a day.

A group later to become the Gulf Pipeline Company laid 11 miles of line in 1902 to Port Arthur; by 1904 the area had 513.5 miles of pipelines.

Earlier lines had been built in Nacogdoches, 1889, and Corsicana, 1898. Pipelines were made necessary by heavy production, meager storage facilities, and poor roads for freight wagons hauling out the oil.

Mountains are ripped open, river beds tunneled, and continents spanned by pipelines. The "Big Inch" line laid from Texas to the Atlantic in World War II was a decisive factor in victory for the allies.

Pipeline still increases daily; the work employs thousands. Besides interstate lines, oil fields use miles of pipes leading to railroad and barge docks, refineries and processing plants.

Within Texas today are more than 146,000 miles of pipelines transporting petroleum and its products, enabling the natural resources of the state to be shared by other people of the world.

BEAUMONT (Jefferson Co.)

SH 124, 12 mi. SW
in the Village of Fannett

Dugat-Hamshire House

Built by Alcad Dugat (1847–1921), an Acadian farmer, sheep-raiser, and furniture-maker. The house, of traditional Acadian plantation architecture with Victorian detail, was erected in two stages. The smaller wing was built in 1876, and the main house completed in 1888. The Dugat home served as an inn for travelers on the old Beaumont-Galveston road.

The property was purchased in 1924, by Josephine Hamshire, whose heirs owned the house until 1959. (1974)

BEDIAS (Grimes Co.)

Bedias Civil Center on FM 1696

Town of Bedias

Named for North and South Bedias Creeks, which in turn were named for the Bidai Indians, an agricultural people reputed to have been the oldest inhabitants of the area. "Bidai" means "brushwood," which may refer to the building material used in their dwellings.

The first white settlement in this vicinity was founded 1835 by Thomas P. Plaster, and for a while it was called Plasterville. In 1903, the community of "Old" Bedias surrendered most of its population to "New" Bedias after a branch of the International & Great Northern Railroad was built to the northeast.

Townspeople from Pankey and Cotton also moved here. The name "Bedias" was retained, but only after a heated struggle in which determined citizens refused to have the town named for a railroad official.

A famous, early resident of the Bedias area was Sarah Dodson, who in 1835 made the first "Lone Star" flag in Texas. She lived here from 1844 to 1848 and is buried in old Bethel cemetery, seven miles west.

One of the most unique features of this region is the large number of Tektites (also called Bediasites) found here. These are beautiful, glassy, meteor-like stones which fell to earth 34 million years ago. Amazingly, Indians called them "jewels of the moon." (1968)

BEDIAS (Grimes Co.)

SH 90, 4.1 mi. N at roadside park

Sarah Bradley Dodson

Born in Kentucky in 1812, eleven-year-old Sarah Bradley and her parents arrived in Texas in 1823 with Stephen F. Austin's Old Three Hundred colonists, settling near Brazoria. Sarah married Archelaus Bynum Dodson of nearby Harrisburg on May 17, 1835.

As tensions mounted between Mexico and the Texian colonists, a call for military volunteers was circulated in September 1835, and Archelaus Dodson became First Lt. in Captain Andrew Robinson's Harrisburg Volunteers. Sarah offered to design and make a flag for her husband's company. Using blue, white, and red calico, she fashioned a flag of three equal squares, with a five pointed white star in the center of the blue square. Reportedly the first Lone Star flag, the banner was displayed in the town of Gonzales in October 1835, and in December flew during the siege of Bexar. When the Declaration of Independence was signed, two flags were seen flying over Convention Hall. One was described as a Lone Star flag and is believed to have been the one made by Sarah Dodson.

Following the Texan victory at San Jacinto, the Dodsons lived in Fort Bend County, then moved in 1844 to Grimes County. They donated the land for Bethel Cemetery (5 mi. N) where Sarah was buried in 1848. (Texas Sesquicentennial 1836–1986)

BEEVILLE (Bee Co.)

US 181, about 9 mi. S, near intersection of Aransas Creek

Aransas Creek Settlers

Earliest known residents were Karankawa Indians who named creek. On this stream was one of the most famous ranches in early Texas, occupied in 1805 by Don Martin De Leon, who in 1824 founded Victoria.

In 1830s Irish colonists came by way of Copano Bay, settling downcreek. Anglo-Americans from older settlements, came by road and trail, stopping mainly upcreek. Stockraising, trucking and freighting provided livelihoods in the rich, new prairie land.

In 1850 Patrick Fadden sold to Ft. Merrill corn and vegetables from 1835 land grant of his uncle, Father John Thomas Malloy. Fadden and W. R. Hayes freighted supplies to settlers in 1860s. Hayes had early post office in his home, 1870; was county judge 1876–1892.

John Wilson, an 1850s upcreek settler, brought first Durham cattle to country; built one of first wooden fences, enclosing 600 acres of homesite with rough heart pine plank.

On creek's north bank stood ranch of Frank O. Skidmore, founder of Skidmore, who gained fame for building first barbed wire fence and windmill in county. He promoted breeding of registered Herefords and in 1886 gave much of right-of-way to the San Antonio and Aransas Pass Railroad. (1967)

BEEVILLE (Bee Co.)   105 W. Corpus St. (US 59)
Bee County Courthouse
Bee County was created in 1857 from parts of five neighboring counties. The first county seat was located seven miles east of this site, and the first commissioners court was held on the banks of Medio Creek in February 1858. The city's earliest courthouse consisted of a box frame structure. In 1912, local architect W. C. Stephenson designed this, the county's fourth courthouse. A native of Buffalo, New York, Stephenson aided in the design of the death mask of President William McKinley. He was the architect of several Beeville buildings, including the Rialto Theater, two churches and several houses, and later designed the Classical Revival McMullen County courthouse. W. C. Whitney, builder of three other Texas courthouses, contracted to build the Bee County courthouse for $72,050. Whitney died during construction and W. C. Stephenson's partner, Fritz Heldenfels, completed the project. Stephenson drew upon the strong contemporary influence of the French Beaux Arts School with a level of grandeur previously nonexistent in Bee County. Some original Beaux Arts features such as the cast stone balustrade originally outlining the roof were later removed, and the 1943 addition partially obscured the symmetrical plan and façade of the edifice. The Bee County courthouse is a fine example of the Classical Revival style. Of particular significance are the grand portico and projecting pediment entry with Corinthian columns and dentils along the roofline. The Chicago-style windows, comprised of one glass pane flanked by two narrower ones, with transoms above, are noteworthy. Also unusual is Stephenson's Lady of Justice; unlike most such symbols, she is not depicted as blind. (2002)

BEEVILLE (Bee Co.)   US 59, 4 mi. NE
Medio Creek
Named by the Spaniards about 1800 because of its midway position between the San Antonio and Nueces Rivers. Rises in Karnes County; empties into Mission River. Crossed by explorers, padres, soldiers, settlers who traveled on three early ox-cart roads that led from Mexico to Mission Le Bahia at Goliad.

The Cart War of 1857, between Texas and Mexican teamsters on the freight route between San Antonio and Gulf ports, originated along San Patricio Road, southernmost of the three roads. The Mexican cart drivers used mesquite beans as feed for their teams, starting the mesquite brush which thrives along creek.

Settlers were attracted here by the tall grass, and many veterans of the Texas Revolution were given bounty lands in the area. First post office in Bee County was established in 1857 at Medio Hill pioneer community, once a down-creek settlement.

In 1909, the town of Candlish was founded within 50 feet of here, with a hotel, general store, school. The store closed; Candlish became a ghost town.

In 1938–1939 on Medio and Blanco Creeks, fossil beds yielded 1,000,000-year-old fossils of a new mastodon species (named Buckner's Mastodon), rhinoceros, elephants, alligators, camels and three-toed horses. (1967)

BEEVILLE (Bee Co.)   US 181, 3.6 mi. N in roadside park
Early Trails in Bee County
From pack trails and wagon roads that marked this area at least 300 years have developed such modern roads as US Highway 181. The old trails of Indians, wild cattle, and mustang horses formed highways for 17th-, 18th-, and 19th-century expeditions coming from Mexico to claim sovereignty for Spain over land of Texas. When pioneers established land grants in this section, they also found Indian trails useful, placing towns along them. Beeville, the county seat, was situated at the natural intersection of San Patricio-Helena Road with Goliad-Laredo Road.

About 20 miles south, the Matamoros-Goliad Road ("Camino Real" to old-timers) was probably the most historic road in this area. In the years 1861–1865, the "Cotton Road"—called

"Lifeline of the Southern Confederacy"—crossed Bee County. A later route of great value was a cattle trail that channeled thousands of Longhorns north from the Rio Grande to the Red River and up the Dodge City Trail or the Chisholm Trail to northern markets. In this area were also La Para (or Grapevine) Road; the Indianola-Papalote Road; and a road to now-vanished St. Mary's, a port on Copano Bay, off the Gulf of Mexico. (1968)

BEEVILLE (Bee Co.)   *SH 202, E 10 mi., W of Refugio*
Blanconia (Old N2) Church
The first Baptist church in Refugio County was organized on April 22, 1855, and met in the Doughty schoolhouse near Refugio. In 1865, the first sanctuary was erected (5 mi. W) and named for the cattle brand of member and benefactor N. R. McDaniel. The Blanco Baptist Association was organized at the "N2" Church in 1873. In 1888, the fellowship moved to Blanconia where the first sanctuary on this site was built in 1891. One of the oldest Baptist churches in South Texas, Blanconia Church served as a nucleus for growth of area churches and has ordained several pastors. (1985)

BELLAIRE (Harris Co.)   *7008 S Rice Ave. at City Hall*
Bellaire
William Wright Baldwin, president of the South End Land Company, founded Bellaire in 1908 on part of the 9,449-acre ranch once owned by William Marsh Rice, benefactor of Rice Institute (now Rice University). Baldwin surveyed the eastern 1,000 acres of the ranch into small truck farms, which he named Westmoreland Farms. He platted Bellaire in the middle of the farms to serve as an exclusive residential neighborhood and agricultural trading center. The project was separated from Houston by approximately six miles of prairie.

South End Land Company advertisements, targeted to midwestern farmers, noted that Bellaire ("Good Air") was named for the area's gulf breezes. The original townsite was bounded by Palmetto, First, Jessamine, and Sixth (now Ferris) Streets. Bellaire Boulevard and an electric streetcar line connected Bellaire to Houston. The town was incorporated in 1918, and C. P. Younts served as first mayor.

The post-war building boom in the late 1940s and early 1950s resulted in rapid population growth. Completely surrounded by the expanding city of Houston by 1949, Bellaire nevertheless retained its independence and its own city government. (1990)

BELLAIRE (Harris Co.)   *Bellaire Blvd. at Second St.*
Texan Capture of Mexican Dispatches
The San Jacinto Campaign in Southwest Harris County
After the fall of the Alamo on March 6, 1836, Gen. Sam Houston led the Texan Army in retreat from Gonzales. The Mexican Army under Gen. Santa Anna followed eastward from San Antonio. On April 14, while Houston's army was north of him, Santa Anna led a division of his army from the Brazos River near present Richmond to Harrisburg. He crossed present southwest Harris County, then an uninhabited prairie, and reached Harrisburg (12 mi. E of this site) on April 15. The Mexicans burned Harrisburg on April 17 and continued marching east.

Houston's army, arriving at Buffalo Bayou opposite Harrisburg on April 18, found the town in ruins, but did not know the whereabouts of the Mexican Army. That day, Texan scouts led by Erastus "Deaf" Smith captured three Mexicans, including Capt. Miguel Bachiller, a courier, and a guide in this vicinity. The prisoners and their dispatches revealed the location, size, and plans of the Mexican Army. With this vital intelligence, Houston intercepted Santa Anna's march on April 20 and defeated his division with a surprise attack on April 21 at the San Jacinto River. The Battle of San Jacinto ended the Texas Revolution and secured the Independent Republic of Texas. (1989)

BELLVILLE (Austin Co.)   *SH 36/159, .5 mi. NW*
Austin County
A part of the grant to Stephen F. Austin in 1821. Created a municipality under the Mexican government in 1828. Became a county of the Republic of Texas, March 17, 1836.

Named in honor of Stephen Fuller Austin, 1793–1836, pioneer empresario founder of Anglo-American Texas. San Felipe De Austin, Capital of Austin's colony, 1824–1836. Seat of provisional government of Texas, 1835–1836. County seat, 1837–1848, Beeville, since.

BELLVILLE (Austin Co.)   *30 S. Holland St., off SH 36*
Bellville
Brothers Thomas and James Bell came to this area from Florida in 1822 with Stephen F. Austin's colony and acquired about 2,000 acres of land in 1837. Thomas Bell offered a portion of his land at this site for a new townsite to replace San Felipe as the county seat; his offer was accepted by voters in 1846. Pioneers from such faraway places as England, Germany, Connecticut, Maryland and Georgia were drawn to the new town, which was platted in 1848 and soon called Bellville by popular vote. A courthouse and jail were erected in 1848 and Bellville's first hotel opened in 1849. Within ten years, the booming town boasted about fifteen businesses. The Civil War left the town nearly deserted, and as in many similar Texas towns it was difficult to rebuild during the Reconstruction era. Positive growth began about 1877 as new business ventures took root. In 1880 the Gulf, Colorado and Santa Fe Railway arrived in Bellville, and the population doubled rapidly. The Episcopal and German Methodist churches organized about 1881, and the Bellville Standard newspaper was established in 1882. A telephone company began operations and a library was established by 1886. Cotton production rose in the late 1890s and more than 10,000 bales were shipped each growing season. By the turn of the century Bellville was thriving both culturally and economically. Oil replaced cotton as the area's major industry in 1915 when black gold was discovered around Bellville. Development of local oil fields further spurred the town's growth and continued to help support Bellville throughout the 20th century.   (1999)

BELTON (Bell Co.)   *US 81, 4 mi. S in roadside park*
Bell County
Settlement began on Lampasas River, 1847. Created Jan. 22, organized Aug. 1, 1850. Named for Peter Hansbrough Bell (1812–1898), native of Virginia; veteran of Battle of San Jacinto; served in Somervell expedition to stop Mexico's raids into Texas; officer in Mexican War; Governor of Texas 1849–1853; U.S. Congressman, 1853–1857.

First county seat Nolanville, moved Dec. 16, 1851, to Belton. By 1860 population was 4,799. Sent 12 troop companies into Civil War. Furnished goods from flour mills, hat factory, tanyard, leather works, blacksmith shops, cabinet shop, beef slaughter pens.   (1965)

BELTON (Bell Co.)   *6870 S. IH-35*
Gulf, Colorado and Santa Fe Railway Planing Mill
Built in 1912 at the Santa Fe rail yards in Temple, this planing mill was part of a complex of buildings that housed repair facilities for the railroad. Workers at the mill manufactured replacement parts for wooden elements of the Santa Fe's boxcars and early wooden passenger cars. Heavy timbers used in the building's construction were assembled in such a manner to handle the pounding of heavy machinery inside. In use until the late 1940s, the mill was moved to this location in 1989 to save it from demolition. Although no longer sited along the railroad route, it still serves as a reminder of the significant role the Santa Fe played in the industrial development of Bell County.   (2001)

BELTON (Bell Co.)   *IH 35, 2 mi. N*
Little River Fort
Site of a picket fort on Little River commonly called Fort Griffin. Also known as Fort Smith and Little River Fort. Erected by Geo. B. Erath and 20 Texas Rangers in November, 1836 as a protection against Indians. Abandoned as a military post before the Santa Fe Expedition camped here, June 24–29, 1841, but used by settlers many years as a place of defense against the Indians.

BELTON (Bell Co.)   *5 mi. W on old Killeen Hwy.*
Sanderford Log Cabin
One of earliest homes in Nolan Valley community. Built when he moved to Texas in 1867 by John Rice Sanderford (1841–1923), a veteran of the Civil War.

Birthplace, 1895, of John Roy Sanderford, state senator from this district from 1933 to 1937.

Settler John Rice Sanderford was father of 12 children: First wife, Elvira Keith, for whom he built this cabin of hand-hewn oak logs, died in 1884; his second wife was Emily Viola Lacy. The descendants are area leaders in civic and business life.

Cabin restored by youngest son, Judge T. E. Sanderford, 1964.   (1967)

BEN FRANKLIN (Delta Co.)   *FM 128, 3 mi. SW*
Giles Academy
Early settlers, who came to this area from Giles County, Tenn., founded an academy at this site in 1859, hired fellow-Tennessean Thomas Hart Benton Hockaday (1835–1918) as the first teacher, and named the new school in memory or their Southern Tennessee homeland. Hockaday taught at Giles until his enlistment in the Confederate Army in 1862, and after the Civil War for several years before moving to Franklin County in 1870s. He presented a curriculum emphasizing arithmetic, reading the classics, and use of the English language. His daughter, Ela Hockaday (1876–1956), founded the well known Hockaday school for girls in Dallas in 1913. School expenses, including teachers' salaries, were paid by parents of the students.

A small community center, with a blacksmith shop, general merchandise store, and church, grew up around the large log schoolhouse. After the organization of common school districts in Texas in 1883, the academy became Giles School, District No. 4. The old log house was replaced with a frame structure in 1886. A more modern building, erected on this site in 1924, was badly damaged by a tornado in 1936. The Giles School never reopened, and its students were distributed between the Ben Franklin and Pecan Gap Schools.   (1973)

BEN FRANKLIN (Delta Co.)   *FM 128, 1½ mi. SW on South Side of Camp Site*

Site of Old Camp Rusk
(Southern Boundary, 1861)
A training camp of Texas 9th Infantry Regiment, Confederate States of America. Named for Gen. Thomas Rusk, early Texas leader. Activated, 1861, when Texas state senator, Sam Bell Maxey, resigned office, raised militia known as Lamar Rifles of Light Infantry. Other local militia combined with Maxey's to form 9th Regiment.

Regiment left here, Dec. 1861; fought many battles including famous ones at Shiloh, Corinth, Mobile, Chickamauga, Atlanta, New Hope Church, Missionary Ridge, Murfreesboro and Perryville.   (1967)

BEN WHEELER (Van Zandt Co.)   *SH 64, 2 mi. W*
Prairie Springs Cemetery
Associated for many years with the Prairie Springs Methodist Episcopal Church, South, this cemetery dates to 1866, when the infant grandson of R. W. Berry was buried here. Berry formally deeded land for the graveyard in 1880, although several other burials took place here before that time. The Prairie Springs Church moved to the town of Ben Wheeler (2 mi. SE) in 1893, but title to the cemetery was not formally transferred to the Prairie Springs Cemetery Association until 1949. The large graveyard is the burial ground for many of the area's pioneers and their descendants.   (1985)

BENCHLEY (Robertson Co.)   *SH 6 at Old San Antonio Rd., FM 2339, FM 279*
El Camino Real
(Also Known as Old San Antonio Road and Old Spanish Trail)
A trail of adventure, hardships, opportunity and freedom, over which history stalked into Texas. To the Spanish, El Camino Real was a road traveled for the King—to colonize, Christianize, seek adventure or look for riches. This road became the most famous.

Its many parts were made, discovered or known hundreds of years before 1691, when Domingo Teran de los Rios, first Governor of Texas, joined and marked the different trails for the king. It was the route from Monclova (crossing the Rio Grande near Eagle Pass) to the Missions of East Texas. Probably its trailblazers were buffalo and Indians, or Aztecs on trading expeditions. It was also possibly traveled, described and changed in part by French explorer La Salle; by Alonso de Leon and Father Damian Massanet planting missions in East Texas; and by the French nobleman St. Denis seeking trade along the Rio Grande.

As the years wore on, it was traveled in 1820 by Moses Austin, as well as by thousands of settlers who followed him. San Augustine, Nacogdoches and San Antonio were its principal cities; inns sprang up along the way. Soldiers and supply trains used it during the Texas Revolution, Mexican War and Civil War. It is still followed in part by this highway.

43

BENCHLEY (Robertson Co.)

SH 6, 1 mi. E

Staggers Point

Earliest large community in Robertson's colony. Settled by Irishmen who came to America in 1821; lived in South Carolina and then in Alabama; and in 1829 sent west an emissary, Robert Henry, to find a permanent location. In 1833, their ox-wagon train arrived, and log cabins were built. By 1836, kinsmen had joined early arrivals, to strengthen settlement.

Community name, meaning "Strivers' Point" in dialect, was probably given for rugged zeal of settlers in face of hardships. James Dunn built a fort, to give neighborhood a refuge during Indian raids. In War for Independence, 1835–1836, Staggers Point men fought in major actions, including the April 21, 1836, Battle of San Jacinto, which freed Texas from Mexico.

In 1830s and '40s, the Irish were compelled to keep up their defenses against the Indians. Women as well as men earned respect for skill with "long guns." In time their village had a church, stores, cotton gin, race track, and taverns, and was invaded by gamblers and ruffians drawn to the races. Until the settlers subdued the lawless, duels and gunplay were common.

This remained a progressive community until 1868, when Houston & Texas Central Railway bypassed it, and business waned. Descendants still honor the settlers.   (1973)

BEND (San Saba Co.)

FM 580

Dr. Edward D. Doss

Edward D. Doss (1849–1928) beloved pioneer doctor in this area for 40 years; served as pharmacist, general practitioner, obstetrician, dentist & on occasion surgeon & nurse. Traveled horse back, two wheel cart, horse & buggy ('Old Ross' in picture). Crossed river by ferry boat. Wore out 3 Ford cars. Came to Bend with wife Arebell Tomblinson, 1882. Owned & operated general merchandise store with son, Lawrence. "No night too dark or road too long to serve his fellow man." Erected by those who loved him—July 1965.

*Picture of doctor at hitched buggy is posted on granite marker.

BENJAMIN (Knox Co.)

US 82, 4.5 mi. E

Texas Business Pioneer
Pleasant C. Sams
(1845–1921)

In 1850s came to Texas from Arkansas. At 16, on outbreak of Civil War, was left in charge of family mills, instructed by his father to give entire flour output to widows of Confederates.

In 1862, captured in Missouri, as he went through enemy lines to get his bride; escaped from Federal who also admired bride. Wedding trip was horseback ride to Texas. He served 1864–65 in Confederate Frontier Regiment.

Pioneer cattleman; business and financial leader. Founder and president, Benjamin Commercial Company, president and director, First National Bank, Benjamin.   (1965)

BENJAMIN (Knox Co.)

US 82, E 6 mi.

The Narrows

This crest separates the drainage basins of the Wichita River, whose waters flow into the Mississippi, and the Brazos River, which winds through Texas to the Gulf of Mexico.

Known as good hunting grounds because of buffalo grass, fresh springs and herds of mustangs from which to get mounts, the narrows were crossed by the Comanche, Wichita, Kiowa, Apache, Seminole and Tonkawa Indians. Evidences of battles and camps are still being found. Later, settlers used the well-worn paths. Today its canyons and ravines are used for ranching.   (1965)

BENNETT (Parker Co.)

IH 20, 15 mi. W of Weatherford in rest area

Original Plant of Acme Brick Company
(4.3 mi. NW)

First manufacturer in Texas to make high-grade pressed brick.

Founded 1891 by industrial pioneer George Bennett (1852–1907), developer of coal mining and other natural resources.

Located here because of large deposits of shale near Brazos River. Bennett community grew up around plant, with dormitory and store. The kilns were fired with local fuel: coal, then wood.

Brick were shipped out by mule-drawn wagons or nearby Texas & Pacific Railroad. Before 75th anniversary in 1966, Acme became the largest maker of face brick in the United States.   (1966)

BENNETT (Parker Co.) *US 80 at FM 113*
First Plant of ACME Brick Co.
One of earliest North Texas brick factories. Built in 1891 by George Bennett. Plant site located here because of large deposits of quality shale near Brazos River. Kilns were fired with locally mined coal; later with wood; then gas. Plant used mule-drawn wagons for short deliveries; the nearby T. & P. Railway for statewide sales.

By 1966, its 75th Anniversary, Acme is the largest maker of face brick in the United States.
(1966)

BERTRAM (Burnet Co.) *SH 243, 6 mi. NE*
Mount Horeb Lodge
Chartered Jan. 21, 1854; met in log schoolhouse.

Erected own lodge hall 1856 on land given by grant master Sam Mather and B. K. Stewart. First floor used as church and school. A fire in 1915 razed hall. Lodge rebuilt here 1916 on and given by G. T. and W. J. Williams.   (1967)

BERTRAM (Burnet Co.) *SH 29 West, Vaughan Highway Park*
Bertram
The town of Bertram was founded in 1882 when the Austin and Northwestern Railroad established a route through the area. The community was named for Rudolph Bertram, an Austin merchant who was instrumental in the development of the rail line. Many early residents were from the settlement of South Gabriel (2 mi. SE). Homes and commercial buildings of the pioneer settlers were moved here by brothers L. R. and J. W. Gray. The first store, also relocated from South Gabriel, was run by James D. Riley and Capt. Tom D. Vaughan.

Bertram developed as a marketing center for the area's diversified agricultural production. Continued growth came during World War I when the demand for farm and ranch products increased. By the 1920s, it was the site of auto dealerships, four banks, a newspaper, a hotel and a variety of other businesses.

The economic depression of the 1930s, World War II and improved methods of transportation combined to limit Bertram's growth. Incorporated in the 1970s, the town remains an agricultural center. It serves as a reminder of the pioneers who settled here over a century ago. Many of their descendants still live in the area and serve as leaders of the community.   (1982)

BIG LAKE (Reagan Co.) *US 67, 3 mi. W in roadside park*
Reagan County
Formed from Tom Green County. Created March 7, 1903, organized April 20, 1903. Named in honor of John H. Reagan (1818–1905).

Indian fighter and surveyor, member of Texas Legislature and United States Congress. Postmaster General of the Southern Confederacy. County seat, Stiles, 1903–1925 Big Lake since.
(1925)

BIG LAKE (Reagan Co.) *US 67, 1 mi. W*
City of Big Lake
The land on which the original townsite of Big Lake was located was owned in 1903 by T. H. Taylor, who sold 320 acres to the Orient Land Company, which agreed to build a railroad station and lay out a town to be called Big Lake.

The city took its name from a lake created by rain which gathers in a natural land depression about one and one half miles from here. Once filled by spring-fed water, it is now the largest dry lake in Texas. In pioneer days it was the only known fresh water between the Concho River and springs at Fort Stockton and was a campsite for Indians, Mexican traders and cattle drivers. Oldest house in Reagan County, the John Gardner house, is located near its banks.

The town was established in 1911. Its first economic activity was a stockpen built by the Kansas City, Mexico & Orient Railroad, a hotel, and a grocery store. It grew up around the line of the railroad and by 1915 had about fifty families.

Big Lake was incorporated on May 28, 1923, and in 1925 became the seat of Reagan County. Land additions were made in 1914 and 1925. Today the city is a center for the oil and gas industry.   (1967)

BIG LAKE (Reagan Co.)   *US 67, 14 mi. W*
Santa Rita No. 1
Discovery well for Big Lake Oil Field. First gusher in Permian Basin; first University of Texas producer. On land once thought almost worthless. Fruit of the faith of Big Lake lawyer Rupert Ricker. Though in 1919 no oil had been found within 100 miles, Ricker got leases on 431,360 acres of University of Texas land in Crockett, Irion, Reagan and Upton Counties. Soon working with him were P. G. Stokes, Big Spring; Frank Pickrell and Hyman Krupp, El Paso; and others.

Their wildcat well, ½ mile south of this site, on Ollie Parker's ranch, was drilled by Carl Cromwell. Dee Locklin was tooldresser. Slow and hard drilling made crew name well for Santa Rita, patronness of the impossible. 4 years, 2 months and a day after permit was filed, and at 3,055 feet, well pressure tossed the rig's bucket high into the air. Santa Rita was a producer! The date was May 28, 1923.

This day the Permian Basin, since acclaimed one of the greatest oil regions in the world, had its first big find. Other spectacular fields were to follow.

Multi-millions in royalty dollars have since made the University of Texas one of the world's most heavily endowed schools. Original rig that brought in Santa Rita now is on the university campus.   (1965)

BIG LAKE (Reagan Co.)   *SH 137 right of way, 18 mi. NW*
Stiles Cemetery
(1 mi. W)
Established about 1903. Site is on land then owned by early settlers G. W. and Lizzie Stiles.

Plot summarizes much frontier history, as it holds graves of cowboys who died in accidents of cattle range; one Spanish-American War veteran; victims of shootings, rattlesnake bites, epidemic dysentery. Most were pioneers of steady habits and quiet lives.

Already in use for many years, the 3-acre plot was deeded to county in 1920 by J. D. Wagner, an adventuring man, who lived for years alternately in Texas and in South America.   (1970)

BIG LAKE (Reagan Co.)   *US 67, 2 mi. E in roadside park*
This County Named in 1903 for John H. Reagan
(First Chairman of Railroad Commission of Texas)
As Congressman, 1876–1887, sponsored bill creating Interstate Commerce Commission; resigned 1891 from United States Senate to head newly-formed Railroad Commission, modeled after I.C.C., and created to regulate shipping rates and practices.

In his term, 1891–1903, railway transportation of petroleum became important in Texas. The Commission was given jurisdiction in 1917 over pipelines. This led to formation of the oil and gas division.

The legislature made the Commission responsible in 1919 for oil and gas conservation. Proration began in 1920s. Complete regulation came in the 1930s with 1,700,000-barrel-a-day production in East Texas.

Commission policies were acclaimed when in World War II Texas was able to supply the Allies with great stores of oil necessary for victory.

The Commission's goal is to prevent waste and protect oil and gas reserves by orderly regulation of exploration, production and transportation.

Such men as Chairman Reagan have set high ethical standards that have continued in the Commission, causing it to merit the confidence of the people and of the petroleum industry.   (1966)

BIG SANDY (Upshur Co.)   *SH 155, 1 mi. SW*
Walters' Bluff Ferry
(Site Located 1.3 mi. SE)
Located at a noted early-day crossing on Sabine River, this pioneer ferry carried settlers traveling north or south into Upshur or Smith Counties. It was begun before 1849 by Robt. Walters, a Texas Revolutionary veteran, and used until a bridge was built, 1903. Town of Florence was once situated near ferry on south bank of the Sabine.

Ferriage rates in 1860 were 50¢ for a wagon drawn by two horses or oxen; 75¢ for a wagon and more than two animals. A pleasure carriage was charged 40¢; a man and horse, 10¢; loose livestock, 5¢ per head.   (1968)

BIG SPRING (Howard Co.) *US 87, 5 mi. S in roadside park*
Howard County
Formed from Young and Bexar Territories. Created August 21, 1876, organized June 15, 1882. Named in honor of Volney Erskine Howard (1809–1889). Came to Texas in 1844, delegate to the First State Constitutional Convention. Member of the Texas legislature. Member of the United States Congress. Big Spring, the county seat.

BIG SPRING (Howard Co.) *Big Spring State Park (off Bus. 20)*
Big Spring State Park on Route of
Old Comanche War Trail
For Comanche war parties, about 1750 to 1875, the Big Spring was an oasis. Here paths from northeast, north and northwest twined into the war trail that led to San Antonio and other Texas points, and down into Mexico. At the Big Spring, parties from far away as the Arkansas Valley could rest their horses. At this point on return trips northward, their weary captives might find water, rest, and possibly food.

The Comanches harassed settlements, robbing and burning stores, mills, farms, ranches; killing men and capturing women and children to be held for ransom, slavery, or adoption into the tribe.

The war trail was well marked, for warriors took on their long expeditions numerous pack and riding horses, hordes of dogs, and their women and children to wait upon the men and assist in the looting.

Indians in the Civil War years, 1861–1865, had much freedom to invade Texas. By 1866 they were selling to New Mexico traders thousands of cattle stolen from Texas ranchmen. Most of the Comanches were put on reservations in 1875. Afterward their old trails were used by white settlers and by hunting parties on special leave. In 1881 a hunting party attacked builders of the T. & P. Railroad working near here. (1966)

BIG SPRING (Howard Co.) *US 87 at FM 821, 8 mi. S*
First Commercial Oil Well
in Howard County
On Nov. 9, 1925, this wildcat well No. 1 H. R. Clay, drilled by Fred Hyer, began pumping oil in a venture that hinted at vast oil resources in West Texas.

The well on Clay's land hit pay dirt at 1,508 feet. Soon oil land speculators developed a great interest in this formerly "worthless" territory and other wildcatters flocked to the area.

As a result of efforts here, the Permian Basin—one of the richest oil repositories in the state— was developed. Since 1925 Howard County has produced more than 300 million barrels. (1968)

BIGFOOT (Frio Co.) *FM 472*
William Alexander A. Wallace
Known as Big Foot Wallace. Defender of Texas and Texans. As soldier ranger and mailrider he protected the advancing frontier. Died January 7, 1899. (1965)

BIROME (Hill Co.) *FM 308, in front of the Birome Community Center*
Birome
Founded 1910. One of five International and Great Northern Railway stations in southern Hill County.

Important agricultural market. Named for Bickham and Jerome Cartwright, descendants of settler Matthew Cartwright, whose 1856 land patent included this townsite. (1967)

BISHOP (Nueces Co.) *FM 665 at FM 666, 5 mi. W of Driscoll*
Cattle Drives from South Texas
By 1840 tens of thousands of wild cattle roamed this vast South Texas region between the Rio Grande and the Gulf of Mexico. The longhorns were almost worthless to Texans, so in 1842 extended cattle drives began with small herds driven to New Orleans and Missouri. Edward Piper, in 1846, drove 1,000 head to Ohio; by 1850 drives began to California; and in 1856 a herd was driven to Chicago. During the same period bovines were shipped by boat to New Orleans and Havana, Cuba, but with little or no profit. The number of cattle driven out of South Texas did not diminish the growing cattle population, as over 3.5 million head were present in 1860.

Several thousand cattle were delivered to the Confederacy during the early years of the Civil War, but not until the conflict ended did cattle drives become profitable. Industrialization and urbanization of the Northern U.S. created a huge market, and the westward expansion of railroads provided the means of transportation. In this vicinity several "feeder" trails led north to connect with the Chisholm and Dodge City trails to the Kansas railheads.

By 1880, 4 million head had been driven to market, and Texas cattle had spread throughout the West. (1973)

BLANCO (Blanco Co.) US 281 at Little Blanco Rd., 6 mi. S
Saint Mary's Help on Christians
Catholic Church

In 1850s when first Catholic families came to Blanco County, worship was in homes and halls. Land was purchased in 1887. By efforts of Father Virgilius Draessel and people of Twin Sisters, this church was built and dedicated in 1889.

Stone for foundation came from quarry about a mile from site. Other building materials came by wagon over 30 miles of rough roads and trails.

BLANCO (Blanco Co.) US 281, Main and 3rd St.
Old Blanco County Courthouse

Designed in Victorian style by architect F. D. Ruffini. Erected in 1886 as first permanent county courthouse. Building served only four years—until 1890. County seat then moved to Johnson City.

Purchased by Chas. E. Crist, the structure entered varied career as school, Blanco National Bank, office of "Blanco County News," opera house, Farmers Union Hall, and hospital (1936–1970). Now houses Blanco Museum of Early West. (Recorded Texas Historic Landmark—1972)

BLANCO (Blanco Co.) FM 165, 8 mi. NE in roadside park
Peyton Colony Lime Kiln

Peyton Colony was a freedmen's community established in the 1860s under the leadership of former slave Peyton Roberts. In addition to homes, the community included a local school and Mt. Horeb Baptist Church. This lime kiln was built by Peyton Roberts and his neighbors to provide high-quality materials with which to make mortar for buildings in Blanco County, some of which remain today. The kiln was restored in the 1960s in conjunction with the construction of a roadside park at the site. It stands as a reminder of the efforts of ex-slaves to begin new lives. (1988)

BLEAKWOOD (Newton Co.) SH 87, 9.1 mi. S
Swift Cemetery
(2.7 Mi. E)

The trading village of Salem was founded in 1835 by Seth Swift. A quaker and whaling merchant, Swift had moved to this area from Massachusetts with his wife, Lydia, and six children. When Lydia died about 1852, Swift set aside an acre of land for a cemetery. Upon his death in 1869, Swift was buried beside his wife in a pink marble casket he had brought from Massachusetts. Several other members of the community are believed to be interred in the cemetery, as well. Lost to forest overgrowth for many years, the graveyard has been restored. (1988)

BLEAKWOOD (Newton Co.) SH 87, 1.5 mi. S
Watson Chapel Methodist Church

On 5-acre site given by George Adams (1842–1906). This church has been in continuous use since its construction in 1883 by men of community. Accoring to tradition, a man named Watson financed the project. Square nails were used. Heart pine lumber for structure was shipped by steamboat on the Sabine River from Orange to town of Salem, then hauled by ox-teams to this site. Belfry and Sunday school rooms were added later. (1972)

BLEDSOE (Cochran Co.) SH 125 at FM 595
Town of Bledsoe

Promoted and founded in July 1925 by South Plains & Santa Fe Railroads. Named for railroad president S. T. Bledsoe. In later 1920s became important cattle shipping point. It was also county's largest town. Population hit 750. Began decline after rail freight traffic decreased in 1930s. (1970)

BLESSING (Matagorda Co.)   *SH 35, 1 mi. from cemetery and 3 mi. N of Blessing*
Old Hawley Cemetery
Known 1838–1899 as Demin's Bridge Cemetery. Second post office in Matagorda County was located nearby in 1858.

Two acres donated by Emelius Savage and his son Norman for the cemetery and Tres Palacios Baptist Church, founded 1852. More land given by Jonathan E. Pierce, who in 1900 named area Hawley, honoring United States Senator Robert Bradley Hawley.

Buried here are the brothers Johnathan E. and Abel H. ("Shanghai") Pierce and many other famous early cattlemen; also, more than 50 veterans of Civil War and all U.S. wars since 1865. (1967)

BLUM (Hill Co.)   *SH 174 at Brazos Bridge*
Site of Early Cattle Trail
Often called Chisholm Trail, since it connected with that famous route lying to the north.

At Kimball Crossing (1.3 mi. SW) this trail entered Hill County. Drovers rested and reshod horses at Towash and Fort Graham, and then forded the Nolan River into Johnson County.

(1967)

BLUM (Hill Co.)   *SH 174, 3 mi. N*
Erected
In Memory of Phillip Nolan
Born in Ireland. First came to Texas and established residence at Nacogdoches in 1791. When killed was a resident of Natchez, Miss. Was killed near this site March 21, 1801 by the Spaniards. Was buried there by Negro slaves Ceasar and Robert. Nolan's death aroused a wave of indignation that led to the independence of Texas.

BOERNE (Kendall Co.)   *US 87, 6 mi. S*
Kendall County
Created January 10, 1862. Organized February 18, 1862.

Named in honor of George Wilkins Kendall, 1809–1867, poet, journalist, author and farmer. One of the founders of the "New Orleans Picayune." Member of the Santa Fe Expedition. Most successful sheep raiser in the Southwest.

Boerne, the county seat.   (1936)

BOERNE (Kendall Co.)   *US 87 county line*
Confederate Army Chaplain
Andrew Jackson Potter
(1830–1895)
Born in Missouri. Orphaned at age 10, was a jockey, gambler, ruffian. Fought in Mexican War, 1846–1847. Was a Texas Ranger later. Converted in a camp meeting, he learned to write and became a Methodist minister.

Served 4 years in the Confederate Army. Like any chaplain, had pay and rations of a private. In camp he conducted regular religious services, counseled, taught men to read and write, handled mail, visited the sick. Once whipped an editor for libeling the army. In battle line, until firing order came, he had Bible in hand, preaching to his men "on the brink of eternity." Fought to end of battle, then took down from lips of dying men words of family or friends; prayed for the passing soul; aided the wounded.

After war, with Bible in left hand, pistol in right, preached 30 years on Texas frontiers. Gave many a wild town its first sermon, sometimes preaching in a settlement's only public building— a saloon. Founded several churches. From enforcing respect for his work with fists and guns, was called "the fighting parson." At home he owned on this site, 1868–1883, several of his 15 children were born. He died in his pulpit, and was buried in Caldwell County.   (1965)

BOERNE (Kendall Co.)   *US 87 on Main*
Ye Kendall Inn
The center section of Kendall Inn is the old Reed house, built by Erastus Reed and his wife, Sarah Conning Reed, who purchased the land April 23, 1859, and later leased to Henry Chipman. After 1869 its fame grew as the "King Place" under ownership of Colonel & Senator Henry C. King.

By 1878 the Boerne climate had attracted large numbers of health seekers to find relief from asthma, sinus, etc. To accommodate them, C. J. Roundtree & N. L. Wadsworth extended the old building to its present size and adopted the new name the Boerne Hotel.

This was the stagecoach stop during the early 1880s. In 1909 Dr. H. D. Barnitz changed the name to "Ye Kendall Inn."

BOERNE (Kendall Co.)   *3.3 mi. S, at entrance to cavern on Cascade Cavern Road*
Cascade Cavern

Probably formed during the Pleistocene epoch by the underground passage of the Cibolo River, Cascade Cavern presents an interesting mix of geological, archeological, and historical features. It exhibits a combination of the joint and the dip and strike types of caverns, and is the home of a number of unusual animals, including cliff and leopard frogs, Mexican brown bats, and Cascade Cavern salamanders.

Archeological evidence uncovered near the cave indicates the presence of two Indian sites. It is probable that the Indians used the cave for shelter, and soot found on the side of a natural chimney suggests that they had fires.

Commercial development of the cave, known earlier as Hester's Cave, began in the 1930s. The current name, taken from the seven waterfalls at the entrance to the cathedral room, officially was adopted in a 1932 ceremony led by State Attorney General, and later Governor of Texas, James V. Allred.

Over the years, Cascade Cavern has provided visitors and Boerne area residents with many opportunities for recreation and exploration, and it remains one of the state's important geological sites. (1984)

BOERNE (Kendall Co.)   *334 S. Main St. (US 87)*
Staffel Family and the Staffel Store

German immigrant August Staffel arrived in Texas in 1852 and in due course made his way to Boerne, where he purchased property at this site in 1854. When Boerne was granted a postal station in 1856, Staffel served as first postmaster and housed the post office on his property. Staffel's other businesses included the Staffel store, stagecoach office, saloon, livery stable and wagon yard. After August's death in 1870, his wife, Bertha, operated the post office out of the Staffel store until 1881 and sold the property in 1905. Reminders of early economic development in Boerne, the Staffel store and the Staffel family played a significant role in that heritage. (2001)

BOERNE (Kendall Co.)   *IH-10 Welfare exit, 8 mi. N, then*
1.5 mi. S of Welfare community
Nicolaus Zink

In 1844, Bavarian-born civil engineer Nicolaus Zink (1812–1887) was selected to lead a group of German immigrants overseas to establish settlements on a Texas land grant. This colonization effort was headed by Prince Carl of Solms-Braunfels and financed by a German corporation known as the Mainzer Adelsverein.

Upon arrival in Texas in late 1844, Zink realized that the grant the colonists were to settle was in the heart of Comanche Indian territory. He persuaded Prince Solms to settle at an alternate site, which became the town of New Braunfels. Zink's leadership in the face of unrest, disease, starvation, and monetary problems was vital to the survival of the colony. He eventually was responsible for the supervision of about one-half of the German immigrants bound for New Braunfels.

After 1847, Zink lived in a variety of places, including Sisterdale, Comfort, and an area south of Fredericksburg. In 1868, he acquired this property and built the central portion of the limestone house at this site. He later gave land for and helped engineer the San Antonio and Aransas Pass Railroad bed to Kerrville. Zink lived here until his death and is buried in an unmarked grave near his home. (1984)

BOLIVAR (Denton Co.)   *FM 2450 at FM 455*
Townsite of Bolivar

Named indirectly for Simon Bolivar, South American statesman, general and patriot. It might have been called "New Prospect," but for a mug of rum. When town was founded in 1852, a man who had settled here from Bolivar, Tenn., wanted to name the community in honor of his hometown. But a preacher-doctor insisted that it be named New Prospect. An election was called to settle the matter and the Tennessean exchanged mugs of rum for votes; Bolivar won.

During the 1800s, Bolivar was the westernmost fort in Denton County and the first settlement west of Collin County. Two stagecoach lines changed horses here. The town thrived and could count three hotels, several stores, a gin, a flour mill, a sawmill, a blacksmith shop, a saloon, a church and a school.

It was here that the Texas cattle trail joined the Jesse Chisholm Trail, but it was John Chisum, Texas cattle baron, who had herds here and furnished beef to the Confederacy during the Civil War.

Bolivar and the surrounding area were havens for Sam Bass and his men. Two Bolivar men were jailed in 1890 for harboring notorious marauders.

Many early settlers (whose descendants still live here) played important roles in development of county. (1970)

BOMARTON (Baylor Co.) *SH 277, on access road*
St. John Catholic Church (of Bomarton)
Established in 1908, when services and masses were held in Mary's Creek schoolhouse or in home of Matt Marak. First church edifice was built 1909, with John Cocek, Marak, Leopold, Skrehot, and Alois Sykora, trustees. Father Paul Mosler was installed as first pastor in 1910. Brick church was built in 1936. (1970)

BONHAM (Fannin Co.) *US 82, 4 mi. E at rest area*
Fannin County
This area was first settled by Anglo-Americans who traveled up the Red River by steamboat in 1836. Fannin County was created in 1837, organized 1838, and named for James W. Fannin (1805–1836), who was massacred with his soldiers at Goliad (March 27, 1836) after surrendering to the Mexican Army.

County officials first met at Jacob Black's cabin on the Red River. The county seat was moved in 1840 to Warren and in 1843 to Bois D'Arc, which was renamed in 1844 in honor of James Butler Bonham (1807–1836), a hero of the siege of the Alamo. (1975)

BONHAM (Fannin Co.) *US 82, 1.5 mi. W*
Congressman Sam Rayburn
Born in Tennessee on Jan. 6, 1882, Samuel Taliaferro Rayburn came to North Texas with his parents in 1887. His political career began in 1906 with his election to the Texas House of Representatives, where he was Speaker of the 1911–1913 session.

Rayburn was elected to the U.S. Congress from the 4th District in 1912, the first of his 25 consecutive terms there. Rising quickly to a leadership position, he was chairman of the Democratic party caucus in 1921. As head of the House Interstate and Foreign Commerce Committee (1931–1937) and then Majority Leader (1937–1940), Rayburn sponsored much of President Franklin D. Roosevelt's New Deal legislation.

On Sept. 16, 1940 Rayburn was elected Speaker of the House of Representatives. Except for the 80th (1947–1949) and 83rd (1953–1955) Congresses, when he was Minority Leader, Rayburn held the speakership until 1961, longer than anyone in the nation's history. A party leader as well, he was chairman of the Democratic National Conventions of 1948, 1952, and 1956.

Rayburn died on Nov. 16, 1961, and Presidents Harry S. Truman, Dwight Eisenhower, and John F. Kennedy, along with Lyndon B. Johnson, were among national figures at his funeral. He is buried in Willow Wild Cemetery. (1975)

BONHAM (Fannin Co.) *US 82, 1.5 mi. W*
Sam Rayburn House
In 1916, three years after he began his career in the U.S. Congress, Sam Rayburn built this home for his parents, who had left their farm at Windom. The 2-story house had a front porch on each floor. In 1934 architect W. B. Yarborough enlarged "the home place," turning the porches into 2-story portico. When not in Washington, Rayburn lived here with other members of the family. Deeded to the Texas Historical Commission in 1972, the house is now (1974) a museum. (1965)

BONHAM (Fannin Co.)   *SH 78 at FM 274, 10.5 mi. N*
Joseph Sowell
In September 1836, Joseph Sowell (1804–1841) came to Texas shortly after the Republic was established. Settling on his 1280-acre land grant just south of the Red River, Sowell made his home about 1.5 miles northwest of this site. In the short time he lived in Texas, Sowell was closely involved with the creation and development of Fannin County and with the protection of the frontier settlers. Upon the creation of Fannin County in 1837 and its organization the following year, Sowell was appointed to the county board of land commissioners and served as county treasurer. He and fellow pioneer J.S. Scott built a tavern at Warren, the first county seat, where Sowell had served as postmaster. As leader of his militia company to defend the frontier and its settlers, Sowell led several attacks against the region's Native Americans. Additionally, he served as quartermaster for the Army of the Republic of Texas. On October 31, 1841, a band of Indians raided the horse stable at the tavern in Warren. In the ensuing struggle, which involved the guests and proprietors of the tavern as well, Joseph Sowell was killed, leaving behind a widow and four children. He was buried near his homesite. As an early settler in northeast Texas whose interest and concern for his duty as a citizen was realized in the positions he held and his active involvement in local affairs, Joseph Sowell played a significant role in Fannin County's early development.   (2003)

BONHAM (Fannin Co.)   *SH 78, 4.5 mi. S*
Arledge Ridge Cemetery
Among the early settlers of this area were Joseph and William Arledge, brothers who arrived from Alabama in the 1850s. Both established successful farms in the area, and the growing settlement became known as Arledge Ridge. Joseph Arledge operated one of the earliest freight lines in Fannin County, with regular routes to the port city of Jefferson. William Arledge established a cotton gin in the central part of the county and later sold an acre of land to be used for a community school and church.

A tract of land, deeded by William Arledge in 1876, was designated as a community burial ground. According to local tradition, burials may have taken place in the cemetery as early as the 1840s, but the oldest documented grave is that of Joseph Arledge, who died in 1855.

Interred in the Arledge Ridge Cemetery are many early settlers, as well as a number of Civil War veterans. Additional land acquisitions in 1893, 1948, and 1965 enlarged the cemetery tract. The Arledge Ridge Cemetery Association, organized in 1948, maintains the historic graveyard and sponsors an annual homecoming event.   (1988)

BONHAM (Fannin Co.)   *US 82 W at Chinner St.*
Bailey Inglish
(ca. 1797–1867)
In 1837, Bailey Inglish moved his family to this area from western Arkansas, where he had been an influential leader of pioneer settlers. Here he was active in the formation of Fannin County, serving on the land board and later as Chief Justice. To guard against repeated Indian raids, he built a fort on his land for area residents. The settlement that developed, first known as Bois d'Arc, became Bonham. Inglish was instrumental in its early growth through active public service and donations of land for town lots, a cemetery, and a female seminary.
(Texas Sesquicentennial 1836–1986)

BONHAM (Fannin Co.)   *SH 78 to US 82; also at E 9th and Liscomb Dr.*
Vicinity of Fort Inglish
Spot where settlement of town of Bonham began. On 1250 acre land grant of Texas Republic to Bailey Inglish (1797–1867) former Miller County, Ark., sheriff who led train of settlers by ox cart to this state in 1837.

Here they built a log stockade and block-house with gun ports in community defense. In a typical fight (1841), the Indians were repulsed but captured two young boys hunting cows near the fort. (The boys returned later.)

Called Bois d'Arc in 1840, town was renamed (1843) to honor Texas War for Independence hero, Col. James Butler Bonham (1807–1836).

BONHAM (Fannin Co.)   *US 82 (Sam Rayburn Dr.) at Katy Blvd.*
Site of Booker T. Washington School
According to local tradition, the Bonham Colored School began in a one-room structure in northwest Bonham in the early 1890s. Enrollment in the 4-teacher school grew from 40 pupils in 1904 to 216 in 1911. By 1920, the school offered 11 grades and was called Booker T. Washington. A new school complex, funded in part by the Rosenwald Foundation, was built on 10 acres here in 1928; Ray Seay served as principal. School expanded to 12 grades in 1940. Until 1966, when it closed due to school integration, the school served as a focal point for Bonham's entire African American community.   (Sesquicentennial of Texas Statehood 1845–1995)

BONHAM (Fannin Co.)   *SH 78 and FM 274, 17 mi. NW*
Site of the Smith Plantation
Gideon Smith (b. 1815), a native of Alabama, moved to Fannin County in 1851 and purchased a 3,000-acre tract. He deeded half of the property to his brother John C. Smith, who joined him in 1855. Gideon Smith served one term in the Texas Legislature (1857–1858) and participated in the Civil War as a colonel in the Confederate Army. John Smith became a doctor and practiced medicine in the area. Both men were successful planters. Part of the plantation, one of the earliest in the area, has been continuously in production of grain and cattle since 1851.   (1980)

BON WIER (Newton Co.)   *FM 1416, 5 mi. W*
Francis Wilson
(1790–1867)
A central figure in the early days of Texas Methodism, Virginia native Francis Wilson was the son of a Scot-Irish immigrant and a native Marylander. After a brief period of military service in the War of 1812, he became a Methodist minister, preaching his first sermon on Dec. 25, 1815. He rode the circuits in West Virginia and Ohio until 1839, when he moved to the Republic of Texas over the objections of family, friends, and his bishop.

Stationed first at Shelbyville and then at San Augustine, Wilson traveled over all of East Texas, holding camp meetings and organizing churches. Noted for his lectures and stirring sermons, he was respected throughout the area. In 1846, Wilson was appointed as a delegate to the first convention of the Methodist Episcopal Church, South. He was instrumental in the establishment of Wesleyan Male and Female College in San Augustine. In 1847, Wilson and his wife Elizabeth settled near Belgrade on the Sabine River.

Francis Wilson's last official sermon was in 1851 as a missionary to the black communities on the Austin circuit. Shortly after, he retired in poor health to his home in Newton County, but continued to preach locally until 1864. He died three years later and is buried in the old Belgrade cemetery (2 mi. SE).   (1983)

BOOKER (Lipscomb Co.)   *SH 15 at SH 23*
Booker
Platted 1917 by Thomas C. Spearman, Santa Fe Railway official. Named for railroad locating engineer, B. F. Booker, town of La Kemp, Okla., (6 mi. North) moved here 1919. First train arrived July 4, 1919, official birthdate of Booker. Economy based on farming, cattle and (since 1956) oil and gas production.   (1969)

BOOKER (Lipscomb Co.)   *SH 15 at SH 23*
Route of
Jones and Plummer Trail
Established about 1874, when used by the freighting firm of Ed Jones and Joe Plummer to haul tons of buffalo hides from their general store in Lipscomb County to Dodge City, Kansas.

Also in its early days, this trail carried crucial supplies to Generals Nelson Miles and Philip Sheridan during their famous 1874 Indian campaign.

Materials for building Fort Elliott, at Mobeetie, also came over trail. The fort then became southern terminus for the route, Dodge City, Northern.

In its later years (until 1885), it became a cattle trail.   (1968)

BORGER (Hutchison Co.)

SH 136, 2.5 mi. W

The Marcy Trail

Captain R. B. Marcy was commissioned in 1849 by the Federal government to establish a less hazardous route with good water supply, on an even terrain, to be more direct from Fort Smith thru Santa Fe to the gold fields of California.

This historical marker was dedicated on the path by the Rotary Club of Borger, Texas, 19 June, 1956.

BORGER (Hutchinson Co.)

SH 136, 6 mi. N in roadside park

Bents Creek
(About 15 mi. E)

Named for Charles (1799–1847) and William Bent (1809–1869), famed for frontier trading with mountain men and "wild" Indians. As early as 1835 they came from their headquarters near present La Junta, Colo., to trade with the Kiowas and Comanches along the Canadian River, in this vicinity. They built at least three posts along the river and tributary creeks; most permanent post was Fort Adobe, built 1843–1844. In the ruins of this fort (NE of here) Kit Carson fought his last big Indian battle (1864), and buffalo hunters and Indians fought the battle of Adobe Walls in 1874.

(1971)

BOVINA (Parmer Co.)

US 60, 50 ft. N near Sands Motel

Bovina (Elevation: 4070 ft.)

Early in the 20th century, this was one of largest cattle shipping points in the United States.

Originated as the Hay Hook line camp of the XIT—famed ranch that received over 3,000,000 acres of land in payment for building Texas State Capitol, 1882–1888. One of the earliest structures in Parmer County, division number eight headquarters of XIT, stood 400 yards northeast of site of this marker. The shipping pasture, 640 acres in area, was 1 mile east. The Pecos & Northern Texas Railroad built to this point in 1898, and cattle for eastern markets were loaded here. Train crews called the place "Bull Town," but the community chose the name "Bovina" when establishing the post office in 1899.

This was the first post office in Parmer County, created 1876, named for Martin Parmer (1778–1850), patriot and signer of Texas Declaration of Independence. Although known to explorers early as 18th century, county had few inhabitants before 1907, when it was organized, with Bovina one of its leading towns.

By 1915, Bovina had 200 people, 2 churches, a bank, a school, and a hotel for prospective settlers. It is now market and supply center for rich area of irrigated farms, and still produces fine cattle.

(1968)

BOVINA (Parmer Co.)

US 60, 5.5 mi. NE

Site of Parmerton (Elevation 4,202 Feet)

Founded as Parmer Switch on Pecos & Northern Texas Railroad in 1898. In 1906, became site of a model farm, using Campbell dry farming method, run by Capitol Freehold Land & Investment Co.

In 1907 Parmerton Townsite Co. bought 200 acres of the farm and laid out a town, which was designated first county seat that same year. A post office was soon established.

When, in late 1907, Farwell was elected new county seat, Parmerton's citizens departed, taking homes and other buildings with them. Only the railroad switch marks the site today.   (1971)

BOWIE (Montague Co.)

US 287, 4 mi. NW

Bushy Mound

From this lookout on whose summit an Indian chief lies buried, Kiowas and Comanches spied on early settlers before launching unexpected attacks.

BOWIE (Montague Co.)

US 81, .5 mi. NW

Montague County

Created December 24, 1857. Organized August 2, 1858. Named in honor of Daniel Montague, 1798–1876. Pioneer Texas surveyor and Indian fighter, commander of a company in the Mexican War.

BOWIE (Montague Co.)

US 81, 5 mi. N on Queen's Peak

Queen's Peak Indian Lookout

Discovered by white men in 1848. Permanent white settlement began in this region in 1858. Its early history is a long story of Indian raids. In memory of pioneer women, who, in the midst of such dangers, daily risked their lives for others, this monument is erected.

BOWIE (Montague Co.)

US 287 at US 81

Home County of Governor James V. Allred
(March 29, 1899–Sept. 24, 1959)

Vigorous, forthright and humane chief executive of Texas in years 1935–1939.

Born in Bowie, one of nine children of Renne and Mary Henson Allred. Worked in youth as a soda pop bottler, shoeshine boy, newsboy. Attended local schools, Rice University, Cumberland Law School; was in U.S. Navy during World War I.

Admitted to the bar in 1921, his early law practice was with firm of Bernard Martin and Ben G. ONeal, Wichita Falls. After experience as assistant district attorney, was named in 1923 by Governor Pat Neff to office of district attorney, 30th district, where he earned a strong reputation in fight against Ku Klux Klan.

Married Joe Betsy Miller, of Wichita Falls, and had three sons: James V. Jr., William David, and Sam Houston Allred.

As Texas Attorney General 1931–1935, won many victories over monopolies; put "teeth" into gasoline tax law, to halt evasions; corrected a number of unfair trade practices; defended oil proration laws, winning the very first test case; successfully fought attempts of Federal officials to tax the income of Texas schools; established school fund's title to West Texas oil royalties worth over twenty million dollars. In 1934 race for Governor, James V. Allred was victorious over five opponents. In 1935 he was named "outstanding young man in America" by the National Junior Chamber of Commerce. Won second term by landslide, in 1936. As governor, 1935–1939, he implemented strong executive, legislative and judicial programs to correct social and economic ills; led fight that outlawed pari-mutuel gambling in Texas.

During his administration, Social Security amendments were added to Texas Constitution, and on Nov. 19, 1935, he signed the state's first old-age assistance bill; soon instituted aid to dependent children, aid to needy blind, and a teachers' retirement fund. Secured for schools the greatest per capita apportionment that they had known; obtained for the instructors fairer salaries; advanced building programs for colleges and other state institutions.

Set up a board of pardons and paroles to correct old system whereby it was alleged a governor might "sell" pardons; initiated prison reforms; revised Industrial Labor Commission; instituted unemployment insurance system.

Combined Texas Rangers and highway patrol to form State Department of Public Safety.

In 1937 gave encouragement to an aspiring statesman, Lyndon B. Johnson, then running for Congress and later to be 36th President of the United States. Befriended many others seeking high public office, including later U.S. Senator Ralph Yarborough, Secretary of Treasury Robert B. Anderson, and Chief Justice of Texas Supreme Court Robert Calvert.

Named to Texas Judiciary its first woman member—Judge Sarah T. Hughes, of Dallas.

After his two terms as Governor, Allred was twice appointed United States District Judge, and was on bench at time of his death. He is buried in Riverside Cemetery, Wichita Falls.

Outstanding Texas statesmen series, 1968.

BOYS RANCH (Oldham Co.)

US 385, 2 mi. N in roadside park

The Historic LS
(Headquarters 3 mi. SE)

Great early ranch well known to badman Billy the Kid and other famed western characters. The LS was founded in 1870s by former Indian territory trader W. M. D. Lee and New York financier Lucien Scott. Through Lee's efforts, the LS had water and grass for over 100,000 cattle and sometimes drove 6 or 7 herds a year up the trail. When thefts followed Billy the Kid's visits, LS men rode west and brought back their cattle: and when Tascosa gunfights put men into Boot Hill graves, the LS escaped disaster. But drouth brought heavy losses in 1886; and grant of

3,000,000 acres of Panhandle lands to the XIT (State of Texas' payment for constructing capitol in Austin) cut old LS range in half. Lee left in 1890 to promote a ship canal in Houston. Scott died 1893. W. H. Gray and E. F. Swift of Chicago bought LS in 1905.

Memorable LS men included for foreman J. E. McAlister, later a Channing merchant. One of the $25-a-month cowboys was E. L Doheny, later a multi-millionaire oil man involved in 1920's Teapot Dome scandal.

Ownership of brand and 96,000 acres of LS range passed to Col. C. T. Herring, rancher and civic leader of Amarillo; his estate still operates it.   (1968)

BOYS RANCH (Oldham Co.)   *US 385 on Boys Ranch*
Tascosa Courthouse, 1884
Served 12 counties in Panhandle. Site of trials for killings that had filled Boothill cemetery. Until 1915 Oldham County seat. Many years headquarters, Julian Bivins ranch. Birthplace of Cal Farley's Boys Ranch, 1939.   (1965)

BOYS RANCH (Oldham Co.)   *US 385 between Vega and*
the Hartley Co. Line

Old Tascosa
Old Tascosa, cowboy capital of the plains, lay one-half mile northeast. In its brief span it became the center of the open-range world, stamping ground for some of the West's most notorious bad men and focal point for cattle thieves and ranchmen.

Because of the easy crossing of the Canadian River at the site, it early became a meeting place where Indians and Mexican traders (comancheros) exchanged contraband goods, including women and children. With the passing of the buffalo came the first permanent settlement, made by Mexican sheepherders in 1876. Charles Goodnight and Thomas S. Bugbee brought the first cattle to the free-grass empire the same year. Smaller ranchmen and nesters followed and the boom was on.

Hundreds of miles from the general line of settlement, Tascosa lured the lawless and the lawmen: Billy the Kids and Pat Garretts. To accommodate those who "died with their boots on" in growing gunfights, a cemetery was set aside in 1879. It was named for the famed "Boot Hill" in Dodge City, Kansas, to which Tascosa was tied by cattle and freight trail. Heaviest toll in a single shoot out occurred March 21, 1886, when three cowboys and a restaurant owner died in a five-minute duel. All went to Boot Hill.

The cattle trails, Tascosa's lifeblood, began to be pinched off with the coming of barbed wire, first commercial use of which was on the nearby Frying Pan Ranch in 1882. The noose was drawn still tighter when the vast XIT spread fenced its 3 million acres. By 1887 Tascosa was completely closed in. When the railroad bypassed it the same year, its fate was sealed.

By the time the Oldham County seat was moved to Vega in 1915, only 15 residents remained. Sole remnants of the old town today are Boot Hill and courthouse.

BRACKEN (Comal Co.)   *FM 3009, .7 mi. NW of Gardenridge*
Schoenthal School
Incorporated into the present structure is the Schoenthal School, built in 1872. A late example of the German Fachwerk style of architecture.

The school provided educational facilities for grades 1 through 7 until 1937. The Germanic name means "beautiful valley."   (1972)

BRACKEN (Comal Co.)   *FM 1337, at the church in Bracken*
Zion's Kirche
Organized 1871, with 52 German members, by the Rev. William Felsing, itinerant minister of the Methodist Episcopal Church. Building was erected 1872 of native limestone; enlarged 1893; had brick facade and bell tower added, 1913. Still in congregation are heirs of founders of this church.   (1972)

BRACKETTVILLE (Kinney Co.)   *US 90, 5 mi. E, Fritter Park*
Kinney County
Formed from Bexar County; created January 28, 1850; recreated February 2, 1856; organized December 3, 1869. Named in honor of Henry L. Kinney (1813–1861), founder of Corpus Christi.

Member of the first state constitutional convention. Brackettville, county seat a leading wool and mohair producing county.

BRACKETTVILLE (Kinney Co.) *FM 674, Courthouse Grounds*
Fort Clark, C.S.A.

Located southwest edge of town. Upon secession and surrender of U.S. posts, Texas troops occupied the fort to give protection against Indians. They seized the four 24-pounders and two 8-inch Howisters located there and sent the cannon for use in defense of the Texas coast. On supply line for Arizona, New Mexico campaign to make the South an ocean to ocean nation. Although the frontier defense line was pulled east more than 50 miles in 1862 and posts set a day's horseback ride apart from the Red River to Rio Grande, Fort Clark remained occupied by Confederate and State troops to keep Indian uprisings in check to protect against bandits from Mexico and to constantly watch for U.S. invasion along the Rio Grande.

BRACKETTVILLE (Kinney Co.) *US 90W right-of-way, about 8 mi. SW*
Dolores Townsite
(About 8 mi. S)

Only settlement founded in John Charles Beales' ill-fated Rio Grande colony of 1834–1836.

Beales (1804–1878)—empresario of 70,000,000 acres in present southern and western Texas and New Mexico—was Texas' largest known land king. In 1833 he and a partner brought 59 settlers here to colonize a town to be named for Beales' Mexican wife.

Indian raids and drouth soon took their toll, but the death blow came in 1836. As the group fled the Mexican Army during the Texas Revolution, Comanches killed all but 7 of one party. This ended the town's existence. (1970)

BRACKETTVILLE (Kinney Co.) *FM 3348, 5 mi. SW*
Seminole Indian Scouts Cemetery
(Founded on Fort Clark Reservation, Sept. 1, 1872)

Burial site of heroic U.S. Army men, families, and heirs. These Seminoles came mainly from Florida about 1850; lived in northern Mexico or Texas; joined Lt. (later a General) John L. Bullis and Col. Ranald S. Mackenzie in ridding Texas of hostile Indians, 1870s. (1971)

Incise on plate on back of marker:

The following are among the many scouts buried here:

John Bowlegs	George Kibbit
Elijah Daniels	Issac Payne
Pompey Factor	Pompey Perryman
Renty Grayson	Joseph Phillips
John Jefferson	Billie Wilson
Billy July	Issac Wilson
Sampson July	Kelina Wilson

BRACKETTVILLE (Kinney Co.) *US 90, Entrance Fort Clark*
Military Roads in Texas

The routes that moved troops in early Texas often followed old Indian trails and were usually little more than deep wagon ruts. This one, the Chihuahua Road, joining Fort Clark with other Southwest posts, was widely used, 1850–1880.

The Comanche War Trail, part of the Chihuahua Road, carried women, children, and horses stolen by Indians, from Mexico to the north.

The Spanish era opened El Camino Real (the Old San Antonio Road) in 1691 to join Louisiana to Mexico. After 1836, Republic of Mexico settlers demanded forts for safety from Indians; a main 1840 supply road followed present Austin-Dallas highway. Central National Road, 1844, linked Trinity and Red Rivers.

(Its rules required all trees to be cut 12 inches or less from the ground).

From 1848–1860, surveys by U.S. led to a network of military roads in West Texas. In 1849, Captain Randolph B. Marcy blazed a West Texas trail used by California gold hunters. Famed U.S. 2nd Cavalry made Fort Belknap—San Antonio Road a military artery in 1850s.

During Civil War supplies moved from Mexico to Texas over the Cotton Road. The Indian campaigns of Captain R. S. Mackenzie in 1870's opened trails across the Staked Plains; but by 1881, the railroad had begun to replace Texas's once famous military routes.

BRACKETTVILLE (Kinney Co.)   *2 mi. S. of US 90 in Fort Clark Springs*
Seminole Scout Camp on Fort Clark
Under Spanish rule, Florida was a haven for freed or escaped slaves in the 1700s. Once there, many integrated into the Seminole tribe, intermarrying and adapting to the culture. Florida became a U.S. territory in 1821, and after approximately 30 years of warfare, the majority of the Seminoles were forced to relocate to the Indian Territory (Oklahoma). Tribal leaders Coacoochee (Wild Cat) and John Horse gathered a group of Seminoles in 1850 and left the Indian Territory for Mexico. There, under an agreement with the Mexican government, they settled and fought against raiding tribes along the Rio Grande. In 1870, the U.S. Army offered the group pay and rations to move to Fort Clark, established in 1852 to protect settlers along the border. The Black Seminoles became scouts for the Army, serving under Lt. John L. Bullis and other noted officers during Texas' Indian wars. The Seminole-Negro Indian scouts, as they were known, lived on the fort in a settlement referred to as "The Camp." They built homes in the Mexican jacal style, using wattle and daub construction and thatched roofs. The scouts and their families also built dams and irrigation systems along Las Moras Creek for farming. The Seminoles lived on the fort until 1914, when the scouts were disbanded. Some returned to Mexico, many stayed in the Brackettville area and some moved to Oklahoma, where the Seminole nation was granted sovereignty. Still others remained, buried in the scouts' cemetery (1.5 mi. SW), which was established in 1872. Among those buried there are four scouts who earned Congressional Medals of Honor: Adam Payne (Paine), Isaac Payne, John Ward and Pompey Factor.   (2002)

BRADY (McCulloch Co.)   *FM 1311, 16 mi. SW*
Site of Indian Battle
On November 21, 1831, James Bowie, Rezin Bowie, Daniel Buchanan, Cephas D. Hamm; Matthew Doyle, Jesse Wallace, Thomas McCaslin, Robert Armstrong, James Coryell with two servants, Charles and Gonzales, held at bay for a day and night, 164 Caddos and Lipans. After 80 warriors had been killed, the Indians withdrew.

BRADY (McCulloch Co.)   *US 87 at US 190*
General Ben McCulloch, C.S.A.
(1811–1862)
Distinguished ranger, frontier surveyor, Indian fighter, lawman, statesman and military commander.

Born in Tennessee. Followed David Crockett to Texas to fight in war for independence. Commanded one of the "Twin Sisters" cannons in the Battle of San Jacinto, April 21, 1836. Served in the Congress of the Republic of Texas. In 1846, during war with Mexico, led Ranger company in successful scouting mission 100 miles behind enemy lines.

During 1849 California Gold Rush was sheriff of Sacramento County. Home again in 1852, became U.S. Marshal, Eastern District of Texas.

Led Texas volunteers in San Antonio Feb. 16, 1861, when U.S. arsenal was surrounded and its surrender demanded—an encounter in a charged atmosphere that could have become the first armed conflict of the Civil War, although it ended without the firing of a shot, and with U.S. troops leaving the state.

President Jefferson Davis offered him first general staff commission in the Civil War. Made a brigadier general on May 14, 1861, he had charge of troops, in Arkansas and Indian territory. Was the Confederate commander in victory at Wilson Creek, Mo., 1861. Was killed in Battle of Pea Ridge, Ark.

BRADY (McCulloch Co.)   *US 377, 2 mi. N*
Curtis Airfield
Named for Harry Lamar Curtis, mayor of Brady who instigated offer of this field to the United States government during World War II. Born 1903 in Dallas, H. L. Curtis was educated at the

University of Dallas, Southern Methodist University, and Texas A. & M. He married (1929) Marjorie McCall of Brady and moved here after business successes in Dallas. Served on city council 1936 to 1940 and as mayor 1940 to 1944.

In 1940 Mayor Curtis obtained designation of Brady Airfield as a national defense airport, with funding for enlargement and hard-surfacing. Small old field was relinquished and this larger tract provided. City paid about $40,000; Federal grant was $141,631. Brady's clear skies, dry climate, and freedom from commercial air traffic made it a favored site. A contract school moved here from Love Field, Dallas, on March 16, 1941, and became Brady Aviation School, Ltd. Mayor Curtis led the city to grant free use of the field for ten years, with one dollar a year charged for utilities.

Over 10,000 cadets trained here before the school closed in Aug. 1944. This was final duty for a few: 21 cadets, six instructors, a personnel officer lost their lives in accidents. This was one of 17 Texas civilian fields training military pilots during World War II. (1972)

BRADY (McCulloch Co.) *US 190, 6 mi. NE*
Onion Creek Indian Fight
(Battleground 1 mi. NE of Marker)
One night in 1866, five men from Richland Springs (about 25 mi. NE) recovered stolen horses from Indians camped near here. A metal arrow hit a Mr. Lafferty, slid halfway around his skull, was cut out with a pocket knife, and Lafferty survived. The grave of an Indian casualty is about 300 yards north. (1973)

BRADY (McCulloch Co.) *SH 71, N side of bridge over San Saba River*
Voca Waterwheel Mill
(¼ mi. E)
Built 1876, by H. A. Chadwick and Sons, William and Milam, who constructed other mills in the region. Water was diverted from river by a still-visible, 1300-yard millrace. Originally used to grind wheat and corn; a saw was soon added to provide "rawhide" lumber. First cotton gin in the county, powered by this wheel and producing 3 bales per day, was constructed in early 1880s. A store operated near the mill for a short time, but moved to Voca after landlord refused to allow the sale of bitters. Mill operated until washed away by flood, June 1899. (1972)

BRADY (McCulloch Co.) *US 283, 10 mi. N near Cow Gap*
Western Trail
Through this gap in hills called "Brady Mountains" passed the Western Cattle Trail, also known as "Dodge City Trail," "Fort Griffin Trail," or "The Beef Trail." Said to have originated in 1876, this was the last of the old-time Texas cattle trails, those east of here having been closed by farmers. Large numbers of cattle were driven up this trail 1876 to 1886 — over 200,000 head in 1881 alone. This trail started near Brownsville and came up to San Antonio, then northwest through or near Uvalde and Kerrville. Skirting the Nueces River, it came over the divide, crossing headwaters of the South Llano River, fording San Saba River at Pegleg Crossing, going downriver about six miles, then turning north. Near Brady, feeder trails came from Fort McKavett and points west, and from San Saba, to the east.

After leaving Cow Gap (likely so named from Cow Creek, about 500 yds. W. of this marker), it went northwest and over the Colorado at "Beef Crossing" in Waldrip's Bend, then to Coleman, Baird, Fort Griffin and Vernon, spanning Red River at Doan's Crossing. Northward through Indian country it went to Dodge City, Kans., and later into Wyoming and Montana. This trail was of great worth to the territories it traversed. (1970)

BRADY (McCulloch Co.) *US 377, 2 mi. S of FM 502*
Geographic Center of Texas
Five miles northwest is the geographic center of Texas, an imaginary point whose coordinates divide the state into four equal areas. In straight-line distance it is 437 miles from the state's most westerly point on the Rio Grande River above El Paso, 412 miles from the most northerly point in the northwest corner of the Panhandle near Texline, 401 miles from the most southerly point on the Rio Grande below Brownsville and 341 miles from the most easterly point on the Sabine River near Burkeville. Maximum border-to-border distance is 801 miles from north to south and 773 miles from east to west.

Enclosed within the 4,137-mile perimeter of the state are 267,339 square miles or 7.4 per cent of the nation's total area. Fifteen of the 50 states could be readily accommodated within Texas' borders—with more than 1,000 square miles left over. Brewster, in southwest Texas, is the largest of the state's 254 counties with 6,208 square miles, an area larger than the state of Connecticut. Smallest county is Rockwall in northeast Texas with 147 square miles.

Texas elevations rise from sea level along the 624-mile coast of the Gulf of Mexico to 8,751 feet atop Guadalupe Peak in the Guadalupe Mountains. Altitude at this point is 1,545 feet. Terrain varies from the subtropic Rio Grande Valley to the trackless Great Plains, from the lush forests of East Texas to the rugged Trans-Pecos region where mountain ranges thrust 90 peaks a mile or more into the sky. But perhaps nowhere are Texas contrasts more pronounced than in average annual rainfall: from more than 56 inches along the Sabine River, nearly as much as Miami's, to less than 8 inches in the extreme west, as little as Phoenix's.

BRADY (McCulloch Co.)   *US 190/377, North Bridge St.*
Union Passenger Depot
The Fort Worth and Rio Grande Railway built the first rail line into Brady in 1903. Eight years later the Gulf, Colorado & Santa Fe Railroad constructed a second line into town. This depot, built in 1911, was designed for passenger use for freight service. Prominent features of the depot include the corbeled brickwork, segmented arches, the red tile roof, and a parapet over the observation bay.   (1984)

BRANDON (Hill Co.)   *SH 22 at FM 1243, in front of old schoolhouse*
Old Brandon Mill
(1.5 mi. SW)
One of earliest grist mills in Hill County. Built (1868) by Dr. Jas. T. Harrington, who also founded town of Brandon. Corn meal, basic to settlers' diet, was ground here.

Dr. Harrington built a dam on White Rock Creek near here as a water source for power in the millhouse. His grist mill served a wide area for nearly 50 years.

A grist mill was primary need in every early community. Where bread could be made, settlements thrived. A good water supply and a grist mill were essential to a successful town.

Today only store foundations of old Brandon mill remain.   (1967)

BRAZORIA (Brazoria Co.)   *FM 521, 4 mi. SW*
Site of Home of James Walker Fannin
Site of plantation home established 1834 by James Walker Fannin 1805–1836 who with his troops was massacred at Goliad March 1836.

BRAZORIA (Brazoria Co.)   *SH 332, 0.9 mi. E of SH 36*
Brazoria Bridge
The town of Brazoria began in 1828 as a port and trading center in Stephen F. Austin's colony. Partially burned in 1836 during the Texas Revolution, it rebuilt and served as county seat until 1897. To escape floods and to enjoy a better life, the townspeople moved to "new town" near the St. Louis, Brownsville, and Mexico Railway in 1912. This town became "old town." The first traffic bridge, built across the Brazos River in this historic region in 1912, provided a vital link between eastern and western Brazoria County. Falling victim to the elements and lack of maintenance, the wood-decked bridge fell into the river in the 1930s.

Built in 1939, during the great depression, using local labor, county bond money, and funds from the public works administration, this Brazoria Bridge sustains the historic transportation route. Nicknamed "The Bridge That Goes to Nowhere" before the soil embankments were built, this 1124-ft. concrete and steel bridge has three Parker through truss spans. It is supported by concrete-filled caisson and concrete piling, and approaches composed of 14 concrete-supported I-beams with steel guard rails. An important example of its style, this Brazoria Bridge is a significant part of Brazoria County history.   (1991)

BRECKENRIDGE (Stephens Co.)   *US 180, 5 mi. E*
Stephens County
Created as Buchanan County January 22, 1858. Organized September 20, 1860. Named changed to Stephens December 17, 1861.

Named in honor of Alexander H. Stephens, 1812–1883, Vice-President of the Confederate States.

Breckenridge, the county seat. (1936)

BRECKENRIDGE (Stephens Co.)   US 183, 20 mi. NW in roadside park
Stephens County
C.S.A.

Created as Buchanan County, 1858; organized 1860; renamed 1861 to honor Alexander H. Stephens, Vice-President Confederate States of America.

Crossed in 1850s by Fort Belknap-Austin Military Road, gained a few settlers of the boldest type; John R. Baylor, Indian agent, Civil War general, Confederate congressman; and Peter Gunsolus, a doctor whose 7 marriages gave him 51 children. During the Civil War, the few residents "forted up." County men were on Confederate frontier defense line from Red River to Rio Grande, patrolling this area. Until they were subdued in 1875, hostile Indians harassed the settlers and hindered county development.

Reorganized 1876, with Breckenridge as county seat. Growth was aided by sawmill for rawhide lumber (cut from local wood and used green, before it had time to warp and get too tough to be nailed). An 1878 visit by train robber Sam Bass and gang excited the area. But so few prisoners ever occupied the early jail that it was used for storage of cotton.

The 1919 oil boom brought a railroad. Region became center of petroleum production, processing, well servicing and supply. Also has farming, ranching, industrial and recreation facilities. (1965)

BRECKENRIDGE (Stephens Co.)   Eastland Highway at S edge of town
B. T. Brown House

One of the oldest structures in Breckenridge, this ranch house was erected by Benjamin Tarver Brown (1831–1905), a Confederate Army captain who came to Stephens County in 1866. He built this house in 1876, the year Breckenridge was founded as county seat. Limestone blocks were cut nearby for the 18-inch thick walls, and other building materials were hauled by wagon from Fort Worth. The structure was restored by Mr. and Mrs. H. C. Kelley, who purchased it in 1941. (1975)

BRECKENRIDGE (Stephens Co.)   US 183, 1 mi. N
Picketville
(0.5 mi. E)

One of Stephens County's first white settlements, Picketville was founded before the Civil War (1861–1865) on Gunsolus Creek. Without military defense during the war, families "forted up" here for protection against hostile Indian attacks. The name probably came from picket construction in which tree limbs were placed on end and chinked with mud. Picketville served as the county seat until Breckenridge was settled in 1876. Then the town began to decline, leaving only a cemetery. After many graves were accidentally destroyed, Boy Scout troops restored and fenced the site. (1975)

BRECKENRIDGE (Stephens Co.)   SH 67, 15 mi. N
South Prairie Cemetery

Founded in 1880, this cemetery was the community burial ground for South Prairie, a settlement which once included homes, a post office, blacksmith shop, mercantile, and school. The community gradually declined in favor of the nearby towns of Ivan and Eliasville. The oldest burial in the cemetery is that of six-month-old Birddie G. Norton. Among the graves here are those of area pioneers and veterans of the Civil War, World War I, and World War II. Maintained by a cemetery association, the graveyard is the last visible reminder of South Prairie. (1990)

BREMOND (Robertson Co.)   117 S. Main St.
Bremond

Part of the 1841 Mary Peterson Grant, the land on this site was sold to William Baker and a group of investors in 1869. The investors immediately granted right-of-way to the Houston and Texas Central Railway. The first train pulled into Bremond, named for railroad executive Paul Bremond, in 1870. It was met by a crowd of more than 1,000. The town was incorporated and a post office opened that year with Sam Morehead as postmaster. By 1871 Bremond had several merchants, churches, three doctors, a law firm, a school and a newspaper called The Central

Texan. Joseph Bartula and his family were among the first of many Polish immigrants to arrive in the 1870s. The town continued to grow throughout the 19th and 20th centuries. In 1999, Bremond had an estimated population of 1,300. (2000)

BREMOND (Robertson Co.) *FM 1373, 3.5 mi. W*
Wootan Wells
Famous early health spa and resort. First well was dug 1878 by landowner Francis Wootan. Water tasted good, but turned dishes yellow and clothes red. Even so, it seemed to possess amazing curative properties.

Wootan soon built a hotel and in 1879 a resort town made its debut. He formed promotion company with T. W. Wade and more hotels, a bottling works, dance pavilion, and school sprang up. Leading socialites came for miles to "take the waters."

Disaster struck in 1915 when fire swept the town. In 1921 the last buildings also burned. (1969)

BRENHAM (Washington Co.) *US 290, 4.3 mi. W*
City of Brenham
Established in 1844, named in honor of Dr. Richard Fox Brenham, 1810–1843, surgeon in the army of the Republic of Texas. Member of the Mier Expedition, killed at Salado, Mexico February 11, 1843.

BRENHAM (Washington Co.) *Loop 318 at US 290 E*
Brenham
Founded 1843. Named for Richard Fox Brenham (1810–1843), Republic of Texas patriot. Railhead and supply center in Civil War. Blinn Memorial College founded here, 1883. Center for farming, trade and manufacturing. Home of famous annual Maifest, colorful folk tradition. Historical sites marked.

BRENHAM (Washington Co.) *US 290, 11 mi. SE in roadside park*
Early Texas River Steamers
River-shipping efforts in pioneer Texas by steamboat were centered primarily on the Brazos (about 2 mi. E.); and Washington-on-the Brazos (about 15 mi. N.) was an important distribution point for commercial interests. The Brazos flowed through most productive cotton and sugar region in Texas; steamers greatly aided shipment of these items to markets in New Orleans. The first steamer reached Washington in 1840; by 1849 its docks were busy with steamboats making regular river trips.

Between 1820–1840 settlers made journey to Texas on the Red River in steamers if the river was high enough and there were no obstructions. Buffalo Bayou, extending from Houston to Galveston Bay, was waterway traveled most often by steamers, and took over trade from Brazos River because it had a better outlet to the sea. Navigation of the Trinity, Colorado, and Sabine Rivers also increased inland growth and development.

While rivers in Texas seemed to offer possibilities for steamboat travel, the story of river navigation is largely one of disappointment. Most meandering rivers were too shallow, often flooded, needed clearing; many were choked with driftwood. These hazards greatly retarded economic and social development of the state. By 1865 the importance of river steamers was gone. (1967)

BRENHAM (Washington Co.) *SH 36 at FM 390, 7 mi. N*
La Bahia Road
One of the first overland routes used by European explorers of Texas, La Bahia road was originally an east-west Indian trail in southeastern Texas and Louisiana. Earlier it may have been animal trail.

Although not as famous, or long, as El Camino Real (The San Antonio Road), La Bahia is probably older and it figured quite importantly in the movement of explorers, soldiers, traders, and settlers across Texas.

Possibly the first European to set foot on the road was La Salle, who explored for France in this area during 1685–1687. Almost certainly it was traveled by the Spaniard Alonso de Leon, who searched for the French intruders in 1689.

From 1812 on, the trail and its westernmost town, La Bahia (now Goliad), served agents of both war and peace. The Gutierrez-Magee Expedition, part of Mexico's revolt against Spain, used the road in 1812–1813.

In 1821 the first Anglo-American colonists in Texas, the vanguard of the "Old 300," came down La Bahia into this area. During the 1836 Texas Revolution, the road found use by troops of the Texan Army; Col. James Fannin and his 400 men were massacred near the road—in Goliad. In the 20th century, La Bahia's route helped surveyors map modern Texas highways. (1971)

BRENHAM (Washington Co.) *SH 36, 6.1 mi. N*
Robert Starke Armistead
(November 5, 1800–June 14, 1866)
A native of North Carolina, Robert Starke Armistead moved with his family to Alabama in 1818. He married Ann Sylvesta Carney in 1826 and they came to Texas in 1835. Armistead served in the Republic of Texas Army in 1836 and with forces defending San Antonio during the Vasquez Invasion in 1842. He was a charter trustee of Baylor University in 1845. Settling in Washington County, the Armisteads operated a large agricultural enterprise and in 1863 adopted a daughter, Sallie. Robert and Ann are buried nearby in a family cemetery on land once a part of their farm. (1990)

BRENHAM (Washington Co.) *SH 36, 9 mi. N, then 2.6 mi. E on FM 390, then 0.9 mi. N on CR 58 (Mayfair Lane)*
Oak Rest Cemetery and Site of Prospect Presbyterian Church
The Rev. Hugh Wilson (1794–1868) organized Prospect Presbyterian Church at this site in February 1839. On land included in a Mexican land grant to James F. and Emily Perry, it was the second Presbyterian Church founded in Texas. Worship services were conducted in a log school-house where in 1840 the First Presbytery (Brazos) of Texas was organized.

The congregation's second pastor, the Rev. James Weston Miller (1815–1888), founded Live Oak Female Seminary in 1853, and the church building housed some school classes. Under Miller's direction a foundation was laid here for a new sanctuary prior to the Civil War. The foundation stones, though never used, still exist. A new building was erected south of here near the seminary in 1872. The church disbanded in 1928 and its members transferred to Brenham Presbyterian Church. The 1872 building was dismantled in 1956.

Among those interred in Oak Rest Cemetery are many pioneer members of Prospect Presbyterian Church, including the Miller family, and veterans of the Texas Revolution and the Civil War. Along with the nearby site of the Live Oak Female Seminary, the cemetery and church foundation stones serve as reminders of the area's pioneer heritage. (1994)

BRENHAM (Washington Co.) *CR 51, 7 mi. N, intersects with SH 36*
Thomas Affleck
Born and educated in Scotland, Thomas Affleck (1812–1868) emigrated in 1832 to the United States, where he became one of the most well-known agriculturalists of his time. A prolific writer, Affleck was associated with several agricultural and horticultural publications. An early advocate of scientific farming, he wrote and theorized on topics such as forage, erosion control, hedging, livestock improvements, and plantation management. His publication, "Affleck's Southern Rural Almanac and Plantation and Garden Calendar," was published yearly from 1845 to 1861.

During the late 1850s, Thomas Affleck and his wife, Anna (Dunbar) Smith, came to Texas and established their Washington County plantation, which included what is now the Gay Hill Community. The Affleck Plantation, known as "Glenblythe," was extensive and highly organized. It included a wagon factory, where wagons and ambulances were made for the Confederacy.

After the end of the Civil War, Thomas Affleck was active in developing plans for Texas' economic recovery. He traveled to England and Scotland, encouraging investment and emigration. Upon his death at the age of 56, Affleck was buried near this site in the graveyard he established on the grounds of "Glenblythe." (1985)

BRIDGE CITY (Orange Co.)   *SH 87, 3 mi. S at Neches River*
Rainbow Bridge
The rapid growth of the petrochemical industry in Orange and Jefferson Counties in the early 20th century led to increased population in this area. In order to serve the transportation needs of workers and others in this vicinity, the Dryden Ferry was established in 1926. It soon proved inadequate for the volume of traffic, however, and plans began for the construction of a bridge to span the Neches River.

Jefferson County, the State of Texas, and the federal government (through the public works administration) all provided funding for the bridge's construction. While the citizens of Orange County also supported the project, the county's economic situation did not permit monetary assistance.

Construction of the bridge began in 1936, and was not completed until over two years later. Measuring 176 feet in height and 7,760 feet in length, it was the largest bridge ever built by the state of Texas up to that time. Dedication ceremonies were held on Sept. 8, 1938, attracting a crowd of approximately 20,000. Among the activities were a boat regatta on the river and a stunt diver's plunge from the top of the bridge into the water below. The structure was officially named "Rainbow Bridge" in a 1957 contest.   (1990)

BRIDGEPORT (Wise Co.)   *SH 114 in City Park*
Bridgeport Coal Mines
Once a staple of Bridgeport's economy, coal was discovered here in latter part of 19th century. Diggers hit vein 60 feet deep while seeking water. Mine No. 1 lies under northeast Bridgeport, and entire area is honeycombed with tunnels and shafts.

Wise County Coal Company was chartered Aug. 23, 1882, by C. D. Cates, J. C. Carpenter, J. G. Halsell, J. J. Lang, H. Greathouse, and D. Waggoner. The firm was bought in 1900 by Col. Wm. H. Ashton of Virginia. Renamed Bridgeport Coal Company, it had 500 employees at zenith.

Mines closed in 1929 due to increased use of oil and gas.   (1971)

BRIDGEPORT (Wise Co.)   *FM 920, near the river*
Toll Bridge
and
Old Bridgeport
When Butterfield Overland Mail traversed this area (1858–1861) on St. Louis to San Francisco route, a crossing over west fork of the Trinity was a necessity. Col. W. H. Hunt on Feb. 11, 1860, obtained a charter and built a toll bridge here (50 yd. W). The Overland Mail ceased operating as Civil War began. The bridge soon collapsed. However, a settlement had begun here, and in 1873 Charles Cates, a Decatur merchant, spanned the river with an iron bridge.

When the Rock Island Railroad built to this point in 1893, town moved but retained historic name.   (1972)

BRIGGS (Burnet Co.)   *US 183*
The Community of Briggs
Pioneers mainly from the old south settled here on the Aaron Boyce land grant in the 1860s and 70s. They had a school, and held church services, at Gum Springs in the 1880s. In 1888 a post office opened at Taylor's Gin Store; this was renamed in 1898 for Mrs. Henry D. Briggs, an early settler. On April 12, 1906, a tornado destroyed much of the village. Afterward Briggs was rebuilt on a platted townsite: it thrived from 1906 to 1920, but began declining after a 1928 fire. Many of the townspeople have worked since 1950 at Fort Hood, in neighboring Bell County.   (1977)

BRIGGS (Burnet Co.)   *US 183, 3.2 mi. S*
Prairie View Cemetery
Pioneer settlers in this vicinity met together for worship services in the Gum Springs Schoolhouse until 1892, when Stephen Taylor deeded land at this site for church and cemetery purposes. This historic cemetery began in the churchyard of the First Methodist Episcopal Church, south, (also known as Prairie View Church) in the early 1890s.

The earliest documented grave in the cemetery is that of Scottish native James Smith (1836–1892), who immigrated to Texas in 1884. Those interred here include pioneer settlers; a number of infants and small children; and veterans of the Civil War, World War I, World War II, and Korea.

The Prairie View Church moved to Briggs in 1906 and became the Briggs Methodist Church. The congregation later was dissolved, and the members attended worship services in neighboring communities, and the church building was moved to Lampasas in 1951 and converted into a parsonage.

The Prairie View Cemetery serves as a physical reminder of the area's pioneer heritage. The Prairie View Cemetery Association, organized in 1977, provides maintenance for the historic graveyards. (1991)

BRONTE (Coke Co.) US 277, 12 mi. NE
Fort Chadbourne
Established by the United States Army, October 28, 1852, as a protection to frontier settlers against Indians. Named in honor of Lieutenant T. L. Chadbourne, killed at Resaca de La Palma, May 9, 1846. Occupied by Federal troops, 1852–1861, 1865–1867. An important station on the Butterfield Overland stage route, 1858–1861.

(Fort Chadbourne, Coke County)

BRONTE (Coke Co.) US 227, 11 mi. NE in roadside park
Southern Overland Mail, 1858–1861
(Butterfield Stage)
Passed near this site, providing for the first time combined passenger and mail service between Pacific and Atlantic coasts. Operating west from St. Louis and Memphis, John Butterfield's company used 1350 horses and mules and 90 Concord coaches and wagons.

Stage traveled at a run, despite lack of good roads. A signal given approaching a station would have fresh horses ready and food on the table for crew and passengers. Route had stations 12 to 13 miles apart, and was sometimes changed to get water. Crew and passengers wore guns; to reduce danger of Indian attacks, mules (less coveted than horses) were used west of Ft. Belknap. The trip one way took 25 days—seven spent crossing Texas, from Preston (now under Lake Texoma) to Jacksboro, Ft. Belknap, Ft. Chadbourne and El Paso. One way fare for the 2700 miles was $200. Passengers rarely stopped off, because they might not find seats on a later stage. Merchants in Jacksboro and other towns used Butterfield's light freight service to make mail-order sales.

Greatest contribution of the Overland stage was its carrying news; coaches also brought mail from the west one to 10 days faster than it came by ship.

Service was ended in 1861 by the Civil War. (1966)

BRONTE (Coke Co.) US 277 at SH 158
Bronte
Eastern gateway to Permian Basin, in Coke County. Called Oso and Broncho in early 1800s. Formally named for English novelist Charlotte Bronte, in 1890. Incorporated 1907.

Basic agricultural economy, predominantly ranching. Site of major oil and gas development since 1948. (1964)

BRONTE (Coke Co.) SH 158 West (West Main St.)
Bronte Depot
Built by local stonemason James C. Lammers (1874–1942), this depot was completed in 1911, two years after the first train arrived in Bronte. Built of locally quarried materials, the depot features stone lintels and window sills and a red tile roof. Originally owned by the Kansas City, Mexico, & Orient Railway, the Bronte depot was sold in 1928 to the Atchison, Topeka, & Santa Fe Railway Company, which discontinued operations here in 1967.

(Recorded Texas Historic Landmark—1989)

BRONTE (Coke Co.) SH 70 at US 277, about 8 mi. N
Indian Rock Shelters
Throughout this area during the last several centuries, rock ledges gave protection to Lipan, Kickapoo, Comanche, and Kiowa Indians. In one typical shelter archeologists found evidence of 3 periods of occupation, plus numerous intricate petroglyphs (rock carvings). River shells, turkey and

deer bones, flint knives, scrapers, and points lay about the area. One of several hearths (2' × 3' in size) consisted of small pieces of sandstone lining a natural rock trough. On the highest level was found green bottle glass from nearby Fort Chadbourne (1852–1867). (1970)

BROOKSHIRE (Waller Co.) FM 1489 at Old US 90
Kellner Townsite
(In NE Part, Stephen F. Austin Grant to Wm. Cooper)
First town in area. Platted 1893 by John G. Kellner (1846–1933), donor, Missouri, Kansas & Texas Railroad right of way and station site. Kellner's rich Brazos River watershed farm and ranch lands produced rice, cattle, peanuts, pecans, and (later) natural gas. His old home is nearby. Town was renamed Brookshire.

BROWNFIELD (Terry Co.) US 380, 10 mi. E in roadside park
Terry County
Formed from Young and Bexar Territories
Created August 21, 1876, organized June 28, 1904. Named in honor of Colonel Benjamin Franklin Terry (1821–1861). Leader of the famous Terry's Texas Rangers. Brownfield, county seat. Primarily a farming area.

BROWNFIELD (Terry Co.) US 380, 4.4 mi. W
½ mi. S of this Marker Stood Town of Gomez
In 1903, owners of land here in center of then-unorganized Terry County platted this town, secured a post office named for Spanish-American patriot Maximo Gomez, drilled a public water well, and induced merchants and citizens to move here. This was the first inhabited townsite in the county. Its promoters hoped it would be the county seat, but that honor went to Brownfield (4.4 mi. E) in 1904 when the county was organized. Gomez had a post office until 1926, school until 1941. A church, some businesses (.75 mi. NW), and the old cemetery retain the name. (1974)

BROWNFIELD (Terry Co.) US 380, 6 mi. W
Gomez Baptist Church
On August 3, 1903, nine worshipers gathered together under a wagon sheet tent to organize a Baptist church. Led by the Rev. J. R. Miller, the congregation met once a month in the Gomez schoolhouse. A one-room sanctuary, erected in 1909, was moved three-quarters of a mile northwest when Gomez was relocated due to highway construction. A larger church building was erected in 1936, and by 1942 the church had its first full-time pastor. The Gomez School, converted for church use in 1953, was destroyed by fire in 1960 and was replaced by a new structure. (1988)

BROWNFIELD (Terry Co.) US 380 right of way, 18 mi. W
Tokio School
Early classes in the Tokio area were held in the ranch house of the J Cross Ranch near the turn of the century. In 1911, a school building was constructed near the center town (about 300 feet N), and classes were relocated. Larger school buildings later were erected, once due to fire and twice due to changing space needs. The school facilities continued to serve the community's educational as well as religious and civic needs until 1941, when Tokio School was consolidated with the Brownfield Independent School District. (1991)

BROWNFIELD (Terry Co.) SH 137, 13.7 mi. SE
Mail Relay Station
(500 yds. W)
W. J. French (1859–1930) settled here in 1903, and built two-story house. Site became regular water stop for freighters and drovers.

In 1905, French obtained the mail contract between Lamesa and Gomez, via Brownfield. Five-passenger "hacks" started each day from Lamesa and Gomez, and met at this half-way point at noon to exchange mail and passengers and change horses. After riders were served a hot meal, cooked by Mrs. French, "hacks" returned to starting points, completing a 40-mile round trip.

Service was discontinued in 1910, when mail was rerouted. (1973)

BROWNFIELD (Terry Co.)   *US 62/82, 2.5 mi. SW of Meadow*
Route of Nolan Expedition
Army and civilian effort in 1877 to halt raiding of chief "Old Black Horse's" Comanches.

In group were 60 Negro troops of Co. A, 10th U.S. Cavalry, and 22 buffalo hunters known as "The Forlorn Hope." Troops departed Fort Concho in early July, led by Capt. Nicholas Nolan.

Eluded by Indians and finding water holes dry, on July 27 men were thirst-crazed. By drinking horse blood and urine, soldiers lived 86 parched hours; finally reached old supply base. Hunters left group; found water alone.

All but 4 soldiers survived this heroic test of endurance.   (1972)

BROWNFIELD (Terry Co.)   *US 62 at US 82, N edge of city*
The Oak Grove
Landmark for pioneers, freighters, these "shin oakes" are unusual for growing spontaneously on treeless high plains.

BROWNSBORO (Henderson Co.)   *SH 31 at FM 314*
Site of Old Normandy
(0.5 mi. SE)
First Norwegian colony in Texas. Founded in 1845 by Johan Reinert Reierson (1810–1864) and Ole Reierson, of Holt, Norway.

In "Christianssandsposten," J. R. Reierson urged Norwegians to find "A Rich Life" by migrating to Texas. His associate editor, Elise Tvede (1815-1895), also came to Texas and continued writing for publications in Norway. She married Wilhelm Warenskjold, lived in this area, and opened home to Norwegian newcomers.

By 1853 a Norwegian-Lutheran church and cemetery had been established here. Normandy was later renamed Brownsboro.   (1970)

BROWNSBORO (Henderson Co.)   *SH 31 E at the edge of town, S side*
Brownsboro Norwegian Lutheran Cemetery
After migrating from Norway in 1845, Ole Reierson bought the land that included this cemetery site (1.1 mi. ESE). He chose the spot for his burial and carved several of the plain brown gravestones before he died in 1852. The cemetery's 24 marked and 81 unmarked graves are mostly those of Norwegian immigrants. A Lutheran church, built nearby in 1889, served as a cemetery chapel until the 1920s. Will Tergerson tended the site for many years. An association formed in 1974 by descendants of early settlers now maintains it.   (1976)

BROWNSVILLE (Cameron Co.)   *US 77, N city limits*
Cameron County
Created February 12, 1848 from Nueces County; organized August 7, 1848.

Named in honor of Ewen Cameron, 1811–1843. Captain in the Mier Expedition, shot at Queretaro. County seat, Santa Rita, 1848–1849. Brownsville, since. The earliest battles of the Mexican War and the last battle of the Civil War were fought in this county.

BROWNSVILLE (Cameron Co.)   *The corner of E. Elizabeth St.*
                    and International Blvd.

The Chisholm Trail
Iberian range cattle, progenitors of the Texas Longhorn, were brought into Texas by Spain in the 1600s and 1700s. The cattle thrived on the area's rich grasslands and roamed throughout Texas. At the time of the Texas Revolution (1835–1836) vast Mexican ranchos with their illustrious vaqueros (Spanish for cowboys) were an established tradition in the Rio Grande Valley. By 1860, cattle ranching dominated land use in the region.

Demand for beef rose dramatically after the Civil War. Longhorn cattle worth $2 and $3 in Texas sold for $30 and $40 in midwestern railroad centers such as Kansas City and Chicago. Area ranchers, aware of the longhorn's stamina, united to drive their cattle to frontier railroad terminals in Abilene and Dodge City.

The Rio Grande was the southernmost point at which cattle were gathered for the drive north through Austin, Fort Worth, Red River Station, and into Oklahoma. There the trail joined the original 220-mile Chisholm Trail into Kansas established by Indian trader/guide Jesse Chisholm in 1865. The entire route and its feeder trails soon became widely known as the Chisholm Trail.

An estimated 10 million cattle were driven north along the Chisholm Trail by the late 1870s when use of the trail was drastically curtailed by quarantines. (1994)

BROWNSVILLE (Cameron Co.) *US 281, 20 mi. NW*
Las Rucias
Here Colonel John S. Ford of the Confederate Army defeated the Union Forces June 25, 1864.

BROWNSVILLE (Cameron Co.) *SH 4, 16 mi. NE*
Site of Camp Belknap
In May 1846, when war was declared against Mexico, the U.S. Congress authorized the raising of 50,000 volunteer troops to supplement the regular U.S. Army. General Zachary Taylor was quickly inundated with volunteer soldiers arriving at Brazos Santiago, and was forced to place them in temporary encampments.

Camp Belknap, located on this site, was established in the summer of 1846. The camp was located on a long narrow rise of land, measuring about 2 miles in length and one-half mile at its widest point. It was the first high ground encountered after leaving the Gulf Coast. Thought to be the largest encampment for volunteer soldiers, troop estimates total 7,000–8,000 men including several regiments from eight states. Soldiers suffered exposure to the elements, unsanitary living conditions, overcrowding, biting insects, thorny plants, and disease. Many died a premature death, often resulting in one to two funerals daily.

No enemy attacks took place despite one false alarm. During August and September most of the volunteers were moved upriver either to camps nearer Matamoros, or farther to Camargo. The camp was completely empty by December 1846. (1996)

BROWNSVILLE (Cameron Co.) *SH 4, 12 mi. E*
Battle of Palmito Ranch
The last land engagement of the Civil War was fought near this site on May 12–13, 1865, thirty-four days after Robert E. Lee surrendered at Appomattox.

Col. Theodore H. Barrett commanded Federal troops on Brazos Island 12 miles to the east. The Confederates occupied Fort Brown 12 miles to the west, commanded by Gen. James E. Slaughter and Col. John S. (Rip) Ford, whose troops had captured Fort Brown from the Federals in 1864.

Ordered to recapture the fort, Lt. Col. David Branson and 300 men advanced from Brazos Island. They won a skirmish with Confederate pickets on May 12. Barrett reinforced Branson's troops with 200 men on May 13 and renewed the march to Fort Brown. Confederate cavalry held the Federals in check until Ford arrived with reinforcements that afternoon. Ford's artillery advanced and fired on the northern end of the Federal line while the cavalry charged. The Confederate right charged the southern end of the Federal line and captured part of the Union infantry. Barrett ordered a retreat toward the U.S. position on Brazos Island.

While the Confederates reported no fatalities in the Battle of Palmito Ranch, the Union forces reported 4 officers and 111 men killed, wounded, or missing. (1963, 1990)

BROWNSVILLE (Cameron Co.) *SH 4, 20.3 mi. E at Boca Chica*
Palmetto Pilings
These palmetto piling are the remains of the Boca Chica crossing of the railroad from Boca Chica inlet to White's ranch on the Rio Grande. Begun by General Francis H. Herron, U.S.A., in 1864 and completed in 1865 by General Philip H. Sheridan for the transportation of military supplies.

The cypress piling, 1,000 feet north are what remain of a floating bridge constructed across Boca Chica inlet by General Zachary Taylor in 1846 as a part of the road from Brazos Santiago to the White ranch landing and Clarksville on the Rio Grande, for transportation of military supplies.

BROWNSVILLE (Cameron Co.) *FM 511 at SH 48, at Navigation District Admin. Building*
Port of Brownsville
The first serious attempt to study the possibility of construction of a deep-water seaport in this part of South Texas was undertaken in 1854 when a survey was conducted by United States Army engineers. At that time, the only natural harbor in the area was located at Brazos de Santiago Pass

near Point Isabel (16 mi. NE). Shipping through that pass dated to the 16th century, but the presence of shifting sandbars prevented large vessels from anchoring at that point.

In 1906, Louis Cobolini, a commercial fisherman in Point Isabel, took on the cause for a deep-water port. He compiled data that convinced U.S. Army engineers that such an undertaking was practical and deserved federal economic support. During the next 20 years, various attempts at dredging channels and eliminating the sandbars were made without much success.

Recognizing the need for deep-water transportation to assure sound economic growth, the citizens of Brownsville created a navigation district in 1929 to provide local support for the federal government to build a deep-water port. Between 1934 and 1936, this ship channel, linking Brownsville and the Gulf of Mexico, was dredged. The port facilities were formally dedicated in May 1936. (Texas Sesquicentennial 1836–1986)

BROWNSVILLE (Cameron Co.) *SH 774, 8 mi. N*
"Rancho Viejo"
Here Jose Salvador de la Garza built his ranch El Espiritu Santo in 1771, first European settlement in Cameron County.

BROWNSVILLE (Cameron Co.) *US 281, 4 mi. NW*
Sabas Cavazos Cemetery
Established in 1878 with the burial of rancher and businessman Sabas Cavazos, this small cemetery has served the Cavazos and related families for more than a century. It is located within the Potrero de Don Sabas Cavazos, a portion of the Espíritu Santo Land Grant conveyed to José Salvador de la Garza by the King of Spain in 1781.

Born December 4, 1809, in Camargo, Nuevo Santander, Mexico, Sabas Cavazos was the son of José María Francisco Cavazos and Estefana Goseascochea, and a great-grandson of José Salvador de la Garza. Encompassing more than one-quarter million acres of land, the Espíritu Santo Grant included the future sites of Fort Brown and the city of Brownsville. The De la Garza family established Rancho Viejo, the first settlement in the Brownsville area. The communities of San Pedro, El Carmen, La Gloria, and La Puerta were established by Doña Estefana.

Although in use since 1878, the cemetery was not officially recorded in deed records until 1947. Among those buried here are members of the extended Cavazos family, their relatives, and members of the San Pedro community. The site is maintained by descendants of persons buried here. (1995)

BROWNSVILLE (Cameron Co.) *US 281, 22 mi. NW in roadside park*
Thornton Skirmish
The spot where "American blood was shed on American soil" April 25, 1846. Here Captain Seth B. Thornton and 62 dragoons were attacked by Mexican troops.

BROWNSVILLE (Cameron Co.) *1300 Mexico Blvd.*
Brownsville-Matamoros Bridge
The St. Louis, Brownsville and Mexico Railroad arrived in Brownsville in 1904. The Rio Grande separated the U. S. railway from the Mexican National Railway line. Congressman John Nance Garner (1868–1967), later vice president of the United States, introduced a bill into Congress in 1908 providing for the construction of a bridge spanning the river and connecting the two railways. The Brownsville-Matamoros Bridge Company, owned equally by the St. Louis, Brownsville and Mexico Railway and the Mexican National Railway, was incorporated in 1909 to handle bridge operations. In 1909 St. Louis, Brownsville and Mexico Railway magnate Benjamin F. Yoakum (1859–1929) met with representatives of the Mexican National Railway. An agreement was reached, and Yoakum hired the Foundation Company of New York to build the concrete foundations and the Wisconsin Bridge Company of Milwaukee to erect the steel spans. Work on the structure began in April 1909. The entire structure, a swing bridge of riveted construction, was completed in summer 1910. It was swung open in July of that year for inspection and was photographed by Robert Runyon. By that time, river traffic in the area had ceased, and the swing function was unnecessary. The approximate cost of the bridge, which totaled 227 feet in length, was $225,000. The bridge was renovated for heavier automobile traffic in 1953 and 1992. Although the Brownsville-Matamoros Bridge Company erected an adjacent bridge in 1997 for automobile traffic, the original bridge continues to be used for rail and truck traffic.
(1999)

BROWNWOOD (Brown Co.) *US 67/84/377, E city limits in roadside park*
Brown County
Created August 27, 1856; organized March 21, 1857.
Named for Capt. Henry S. Brown. Came to Texas in 1824. Indian trader and fighter.
Commanded a company at the Battle of Velasco, member of the convention of 1832.
County seat, Brownwood, 1856. Moved to new site of same name, 1867.

BROWNWOOD (Brown Co.) *US 67/84, at city limits in established roadside park*
City of Brownwood
(First Site 1 mi. E; Second, 5 mi. SE, Present Location)
Settled 1857. Acquired a post office 1858. An oil vein ruined 1860s water well of townsite donor Greenleaf Fisk. Wagon-yard keeper Martin Meinsinger sold medicinal oil from 1878 well. Commercial drilling began 1889.
Farming, cotton sales, business town since 1880s; was reached by Santa Fe Railroad, 1880; Frisco, 1890. Two colleges—Daniel Baker and Howard Payne—were situated here in 1889. Camp Bowie, World War II military post, operated in Brownwood from 1940 to 1946.
Center for agriculture-retail sales-industry. Has a coliseum, parks, 110 miles of lake shore. (1968)

BROWNWOOD (Brown Co.) *US 67/84, 2½ mi. W in roadside park*
Greenleaf Fisk (1807–1888)
"Father of Brownwood"
Donor of present townsite of Brownwood, Fisk was noted as a soldier, public servant, surveyor, and businessman. The son of English parents, he was born in New York. As a boy he was so studious that he voluntarily gave up recess periods to read. In 1834 he abandoned his preparation for the Presbyterian ministry and, with a friend, embarked down the Ohio River on a skiff to brave the Texas frontier.
Settling at Mina (present Bastrop), he fought in the Battle of San Jacinto in 1836. He later served in various county offices in Bastrop and Williamson Counties and was a senator in the Republic of Texas. As a government surveyor in this period, he mapped this region and liked it so well he determined to settle here. Having received in 1846, for his service in the Texas Revolution, a large land grant in this vicinity, he moved here in 1860. Besides teaching, he also served as county judge and in other offices.
When difficulties arose over the location of the county seat, he donated 60 acres for the town and 100 acres for county purposes. He then persuaded many citizens to move here from the old townsite.
At his death in 1888, Fisk was buried in Greenleaf cemetery. He married twice and had 15 children. (1968)

BROWNWOOD (Brown Co.) *SH 377, Greenleaf Cemetery*
Robert E. Howard
(January 24, 1906–June 11, 1936)
Born in Parker County, Robert Ervin Howard grew up in the Brown and Callahan County communities of Cross Cut, Cross Plains, and Brownwood. He attended Brownwood High School and Howard Payne College, and published his first works of fiction in school newspapers. He later wrote poetry and short stories for popular magazines. His main interest was in science fiction and fantasy. In 1932, he created the character Conan the Barbarian. Howard committed suicide at age 30. His Conan character has become known worldwide through books, magazines, and movies. (1991)

BROWNWOOD (Brown Co.) *SH 377, 6 mi. W at sign*
pointing to Indian Creek Cemetery
Katherine Anne Porter
(May 15, 1890–September 18, 1980)
Born Callie Russell Porter in Indian Creek, Katherine Anne Porter moved to Hays County with her family following her mother's death in 1892. She left Texas in 1915 and worked as an actress, teacher, reporter and publicist in such places as Chicago, Denver, Mexico, and New York. Her first book of short stories was published in 1930. Her acclaimed 1962 novel, *Ship of Fools,* was followed by the Pulitzer prizewinning *The Collected Stories of Katherine Anne Porter* in 1965. Upon her death in 1980, her ashes were buried next to her mother's grave in Indian Creek Cemetery. (1990)

BRUCEVILLE (McLennan Co.) *IH 35N, rest stop*
Martin Irons
A native of Scotland, Martin Irons (1833–1990) came to the United States at the age of fourteen as a machinist's apprentice. After learning the trade, he lived and worked in numerous places throughout the country. By 1884, he was employed as a machinist in the Missouri Pacific Railway shop in Sedalia, Missouri.

A firm believer in organization as a means by which individuals could improve their lives, Irons became an active participant in groups such as the Knights of Pythias and the Grange. While working in Sedalia, he became interested in an early union society known as the Knights of Labor and was instrumental in organizing workers employed by Jay Gould's Network of Southwestern Railroad Lines.

The railroad union, known as District Assembly 101, went on strike in 1886. Irons, then chairman of the executive committee, came into prominence as its leader. The strike was marked by violence, and when it ended, Irons was blacklisted. He retired in nearby Bruceville but remained active in social reform movements until his death. Irons' grave in the Bruceville Cemetery is marked by a monument, placed in 1911 by the Missouri Federation of Labor. (1984)

BRYAN (Brazos Co.) *SH 6, 1.7 mi. S*
Brazos County
Created from Robertson and Washington Counties in 1841. First called Navasota, changed 1842 to Brazos after two rivers on county's boundaries. Organized in 1843, with Booneville as county seat; Bryan, county seat since 1866.

Area originally included in Stephen F. Austin's second colony, 1828. Became a part of the Washington municipality, 1837, under the Mexican government.

First railroad reached Millican in 1860. A. & M. University opened, 1876.

Economy based on agricultural, industrial and educational activities. (1966)

BRYAN (Brazos Co.) *SH 21, 8 mi. SW*
Route of El Camino Real
(Also known as Old San Antonio Road and Old Spanish Road)
Great thoroughfare of pioneer Texas, stretching 1,000 miles from Saltillo, Mexico, to present Louisiana. The general route followed ancient Indian and buffalo trails, but the oldest marked portion, known as "Trail of the Padres," was blazed in 1691 under Domingo Teran de Los Rios, first governor of Texas. This part joined Monclova, then capital of the province, to the Spanish missions of East Texas. San Antonio, military nerve center of the region, was a major stop.

Over the centuries, explorers, traders, smugglers, armed men, and civilians traversed this road. In 1820 Moses Austin traveled it to San Antonio to request a land grant from Spanish officials. The colonizing venture he started later brought thousands of Anglo-Americans over the road to help settle Texas.

In 1915 the Texas legislature appropriated $5,000 to survey and mark the route. The Daughters of the American Revolution and other patriotic groups sponsored and endorsed the project, and V. N. Zivley was commissioned to make the survey. In 1918, the State and D. A. R. placed granite markers approximately every five miles along the Texas section of the road.

Today many modern highways, particularly State 21, follow the original route of El Camino Real. (1973)

BRYAN (Brazos Co.) *FM 2154 at FM 159, 16 mi. S*
Millican, C.S.A.
Millican was Texas' northernmost railroad terminus when the War Between the States began in 1861. It became a vital Confederate shipping point for the area extending to the Red River on the north and to be frontier settlements in the west. The products of that region moved over the rails of the Houston and Texas Central Railroads from Millican to Houston, Beaumont, Galveston and Alleyton.

Confederate troops came by rail to nearby Camp Speight, a training and rendezvous point. Many marched overland from here for duty in Arkansas and Louisiana. Others entrained here for Houston and Beaumont where they boarded ships for Neblett's Landing on the Sabine and other debarkation points.

During the war cotton from North Texas and the Brazos Valley went to market through Millican to Alleyton, the state's southernmost railroad terminus, where it was transported over the Cotton Road by wagons and carts to Brownsville and Matamoros, Mexico. Returning wagons and carts brought military supplies and merchandise which eventually reached Millican by rail for wide distribution.

Millican, which had been born with the coming of the railroad in 1859, flourished with the railroad, and declined with the northward extension of the railroad that began in 1866.

BUCKHOLTS (Milam Co.)   *US 190/SH 36, 6 mi. W at "Bryant's Station"*
Major Bryant's Home
Major Bryant's home and trading post stood six miles southeast of this marker.

BUFFALO (Leon Co.)   *US 79, 4 mi. S*
Colonel Robert Simonton Gould (1826–1904)
Born in North Carolina. Educated at University of Alabama. Came to Texas in 1850. Practiced law in Centerville. Served as the first district attorney, then as judge in the old 13th Judicial District.

Represented Leon County as member of secession convention, 1861. Afterward, as this county voted 534 to 82 in favor of secession, raised locally troops which as Co. B. became nucleus for 6th Texas Cavalry or (Gould's Battalion), in the Confederate Army. First as major, then as colonel, Gould led battalion for 4 years in Louisiana and Texas. Saw duty in Red River campaign to prevent invasions of Texas, fighting in the 1864 repulses of Federals at Mansfield and Pleasant Hill. At Jenkins Ferry, Ark., Col. Gould had his horse killed under him.

After the war he was reelected judge of the old 13th District, but was removed in 1867 by military authorities in charge of reconstruction in Texas.

Appointed Assistant Justice of Texas Supreme Court in 1874, he was afterward elected, and served until Dec. 31, 1882 (being Chief Justice in 1880–1882).

Was named, along with Governor O. M. Roberts, as one of two first professors of law at the University of Texas, holding tenure 1883–1889. Died in Austin.   (1965)

BUFFALO SPRINGS (Clay Co.)   *FM 174, 18 mi. SE*
Buffalo Springs
A landmark as early as 1849. Watering place for buffalo hunters. Site of a proposed permanent United States Army post, July, 1867. Abandoned due to lack of water and timber, November 19, 1867, and Fort Richardson on Lost Creek was established instead, November 26, 1867. Served as a stage stand and camp ground between that post and Fort Sill. Scene of battle, July 12, 1874, between Indians and George W. Stevens, captain of Texas Rangers.

BUFFALO SPRINGS (Clay Co.)   *SH 148 at FM 174*
Buffalo Springs, C.S.A.
On line of sentry forts along Red River and far frontiers of North Texas, 1861–1865. Used at intervals by cavalry, especially at such times as 1863 massing of 3,000 Federals to the north, in Indian territory. Soldiers here saw little of war's glory, had large share of fighting and shortages of guns, ammunition, food, clothing and horses.

Site of "forting up" of families wishing to stay, with goods and stock, near frontier homes. Lived in picket houses in fortified square, placing guards on water or wood gathering parties; in 1862 left during water famine.   (1965)

BURKBURNETT (Wichita Co.)   *US 277/281 near Red River Bridge*
Burkburnett
("Boomtown, U.S.A."; 1 mi. SW)
One of the most famous Texas boom towns. Name was given to post office at request of President T. R. Roosevelt after his 1905 wolf hunt with rancher Burk Burnett in this area. Townsite was laid out in 1907 by Joseph A. Kemp and Frank Kell, surveyors and promoters of Wichita Falls & Northwestern Railroad. First oil discovery was Chris Schmoker No. 1, in 1912.

A 2200-barrel gusher was brought in on S. L. Fowler farm about a mile from this site, July 29, 1918, by a company formed by Fowler, his brother, W. D. Cline, and J. I. Staley. In 3 months 200 wells had been completed in Burkburnett townsite—a forest of derricks. Money and oil flowed freely. A bank capitalized at $25,000 got monthly revenue of $10,000 from a well drilled at its back door. The town's population jumped from 1500 to 15,000 in a year. Boom area was extended by finds on properties of Burk-Waggoner Company and by Kelly-Allen operations to the southwest.

Town was made world famous in 1941 by the movie "Boomtown," filmed from a popular story entitled "Lady Comes to Burkburnett."

Economy is dependent on agriculture and oil. An important neighbor is Sheppard Air Force Base.   (1966)

BURKBURNETT (Wichita Co.)   *At point of entry into Texas,*
at Red River Bridge inside city limits
The Red River
Named for the red soil across which it flows; the main stream is 1,360 miles long, and for 440 miles the river forms the Texas-Oklahoma boundary.

For years this was an international boundary. The 1819 treaty with Spain established the course of the Red River to the 100th meridian as part of the boundary between the United States and New Spain. Until after the 1845 annexation of Texas, this river did not lie entirely within the United States.

During the colonial period, the waterway and the crossing here became a main gateway into Texas. In the mid-19th century, brisk steamer traffic went on at eastern end of the river. A military expedition under Capt. Randolph B. Marcy in 1852 explored the Red to its upper reaches in land held by wild Indians.

In 1921, the Burkburnett oil boom here led to a dispute between Texas and Oklahoma over ownership of the valuable river bed. The Supreme Court in 1921 and 1923 upheld the south bank as the Texas border.

This site is 25 miles west of important old Fort Sill crossing on the major military road that once linked the Oklahoma fort to outposts on the Texas frontier. The bridge here, opened to traffic in 1927, is the second free bridge to span the Red River.   (1968)

BURKBURNETT (Wichita Co.)   *SH 240, 14 mi. W*
Tenth Cavalry Creek
First called Getty's Creek, this stream was renamed by cowboys and settlers who found near its mouth, on Red River, remains of a military outpost garrisoned by the U.S. Tenth Cavalry from 1873 to 1875.

Most of the Negro soldiers and white officers stationed there had previously served in the Federal Army during the Civil War (1861–1865) and at Fort Sill, in Indian territory.

This staked timber outpost was attacked by Indians; legend says that all the officers, men and horses killed in the battle were buried in a common grave somewhere along this creek.

BURKBURNETT (Wichita Co.)   *SH 240, 7.1 mi. W*
Ghost Town of Clara
Herman Specht migrated in 1870 to Galveston from Germany. In 1884, he married Clara M. Vogel Lange (1853–1912), a wealthy widow. Adding to earlier property holdings in Galveston, he began buying extensive tracts of land in northern Wichita County, which eventually totaled 21,000 acres. In 1886, he platted the town of Clara which he named for his wife. The streets were named for Texas heroes. He donated this site for the Trinity Lutheran Church. Specht advertised for German colonists from other states to settle here.

Specht built his home in Iowa Park in 1890 and ran a ranch at Clara where he grew wheat. North of the church site, he had a large experimental nursery for unusual plants. The 1891 drought wiped out the nursery and Specht's crops. The 1900 Galveston storm destroyed the remainder of their vast holdings.

Clara included a church, schools, store, garage and post office. Hampered by an inadequate water supply, the town began to decline with the consolidation of the school with the Burkburnett schools. During the oil boom of the 1920s, many residents moved to Wichita Falls. Good roads and cars made it possible to shop elsewhere. The town finally vanished except for the church, rectory, and cemetery.   (1978)

BURKBURNETT (Wichita Co.)   *FM 240, 6 mi. W*
The Receiver Bridge
A natural border of the Louisiana Territory when it was acquired by the United States in 1803, the Red River later served as a boundary between the states of Texas and Oklahoma. The exact location for the line of separation was challenged in 1920 soon after an extension of the Burkburnett oil field led to increased drilling activity in the area, including the banks and the bed of the stream. Since the Red River meandered, causing wide flood plains, the state of Oklahoma initiated a suit to determine ownership of the land. By authority of the United States Supreme Court, the disputed land was temporarily placed under the jurisdiction of the federal government.

Frederick A. Delano, whose nephew Franklin Delano Roosevelt later became President of the United States, was named as the receiver in charge of the property. As part of his plan of supervision, he had a one-lane wooden bridge (2.5 mi. N) built to the center of the river, providing access to the drilling sites.

The boundary between the two states was set as the south bank of the Red River in 1923. It was not until four years later that a special commission completed the actual survey work. The bridge was partially destroyed later during a 1935 flood.   (1981)

BURKEVILLE (Newton Co.)   *SH 63 W of SH 87*
Blum Male and Female College
(200 ft. NW)
Chartered February 26, 1880, by 36 incorporators; named for Leon Blum, Galveston merchant, largest holder in $20,000 capitol stock—$5 per share. First directors were: R. J. Brailsford, H. J. Casey, W. W. Downs, W. A. Droddy, T. W. Ford, M. D. Hines; first president was Joseph Syler.

Pupils ranged in age from 5 to 50 years; those under 12 met in downstairs of 2-story building; older pupils and adults met upstairs. Average enrollment per term was 100 resident and boarding pupils.

School "took up" at 8 am.; closed at 4:30 p.m. Students entered and left school by lining up— boys on one side and girls on the other—a division which continued inside the school room. Lessons were recited on a recitation bench; all tests were oral, often an occasion for community gathering. Subjects offered besides the 3 r's were: philosophy, Latin, grammar, algebra, history, geometry, rhetoric, and geography. Friday afternoons were devoted to spelling matches, recitations.

A well in school yard furnished water; most students brought lunch from home in a tin bucket which was covered with a lid ventilated by nail holes.

Soon was called Burkeville School, and after expiration of college charter on February 20, 1905, the building served that purpose until torn down in 1912.

BURKEVILLE (Newton Co.)   *SH 63, 11 mi. NE near Sabine River Bridge*
Site of Old Burr's Ferry
(At Highway Bridge)
An important communications point between Texas and the United States, especially during settlement era of early 1800s. Named for Dr. Timothy Burr (1790–1852), second cousin of U.S. Vice President Aaron Burr.

Dr. Burr is said to have come to the Sabine area in 1809, but moved his family down from Ohio in 1820s. He practiced medicine from home plantation on the Sabine. Family operated the ferry in the 1840s. Town of Burr's Ferry grew up on east side of the river.

This crossing (earlier called Hickman's Ferry) gave pioneers the means to enter Texas with their stock, household goods, and other property. It was one of four main points of entry on Texas-Louisiana border. Besides the famous El Camino Real (King's Highway) from Natchitoches, other entry roads were the "upper" route, from present-day Shreveport; "lower" route, from Opelousas; and this one, called "The Old Beef Trail" because it was used to drive thousands of cattle from Texas to Alexandria for shipment to such cities as New Orleans, as early as the 1820s and '30s.

This crossing was considered strategic in 1860s, during the Civil War. Breastworks were built on east bank, and timber cleared here on west bank in effort to guard against Federal invasions. (1968)

BURKEVILLE (Newton Co.)
SH 63 at Shankleville Rd., 2 mi. SW
Shankleville Community
Named for Jim and Winnie Shankle, known as first Newton County blacks to buy land and become local leaders after gaining freedom by emancipation.

Both were born in slavery: Jim in 1811, Winnie in 1814. After Winnie and her three children were sold to a Texan, Jim ran away from his Mississippi owner. He traveled by night, foraged for food, swam streams (including the Mississippi River), walking out of sight the 400 miles to East Texas. At dusk one day he found Winnie beside her master's spring (800 ft. W). After slipping out food for several days, Winnie told her master, who arranged to buy Jim. The couple worked side by side, bringing up Winnie's children and six of their own: Wash Rollins, Tobe Perkins, Mary McBride, George, Henry, Houston, John Harriet (Odom), B. M. (Lewis).

In 1867, they began buying land, and with associate, Steve McBride, eventually owned over 4,000 acres. In their neighborhood were prosperous farms, churches, a cotton gin, grist mills, sawmills, schools—including McBride College (1883–1909), built by Steve McBride.

Jim and Winnie Shankle are buried in Jim Shankle Cemetery (600 ft. SW). A great-grandson, A. T. Odom, has been guardian of this heritage. Annual homecomings have been held since 1941.
(1973)

BURKEVILLE (Newton Co.)
SH 87, 8.25 mi. NW
The Old Beef Road
Early 19th century trade routes across the Sabine River were few, and served all travelers and traders. The Beef Road, which replaced earlier "Zavala Road," was an important route by 1840, crossing this area. Named for cattle trade, it began in Huntsville and Liberty regions, and ran through Zavala, Jasper, and into present Newton County, where it forked near this site, forming three routes. The northern fork, to Natchitoches, crossed the Sabine at Bevil's Ferry (later Haddon's); the middle route, to Alexandria, led to Hickman's Ferry (later Burr's). The southern branch, to Opelousas, crossed at New Columbia. The cattle were corraled at night in "Beef Pens," located at points along the trails, including Weeks' Chapel and Toledo.

During Civil War, the Beef Road was an important supply artery to the Confederate states, until the Federal Army gained control of the Mississippi River in July 1863. This halted the eastern cattle drives. Sabine River crossings were fortified against attack, as the roads would be a necessity for an invading force, but the expected invasion never came.

Railroad expansion into Kansas, in the later 1860s, diverted the cattle drives to the north, and led to decline of Beef Road as a major cattle trade route.
(1973)

BURKEVILLE (Newton Co.)
SH 87, 2 blocks S of SH 63 on W side
Colonel John R. Burke Home Site
A few feet west of this marker was built, 1845, first home in Burkeville, by founder of the town, donor of land for Newton County courthouse; friend of Andrew Jackson and Sam Houston; an 1853–1855 member of Texas legislature.

Burke died in 1855. Heart pine-house, razed in 1947 was rebuilt elsewhere.
(1965)

BURKEVILLE (Newton County)
SH 87, 7 mi. N in front of Survey Church
The Survey Community
William Williams, an early 1800s Sabine Valley pioneer, obtained a large land grant in 1834 from the Republic of Mexico. His surveyed land attracted settlers, who called the location "The Survey." In 1847, Wade H. Mattox (1800–1863) built the first frame house in the settlement, using lumber hauled from Alexandria, La., by a neighbor, Ezekiel Cobb (1825–1864). By the 1850s, The Survey had settlers named Booker, Bush, Dade, Clark, Collins, Conner, Droddy, Garlington, Hardy, Joiner, Jones, McGee, Mitchell, Smith, Trotti, and Weeks. The economy was based on farming and (later) lumbering. At least 16 Survey community residents fought for the Confederacy in the Civil War (1861–1865).

In 1889, the Methodists built a church on land given by Mr. and Mrs. J. W. Mattox. The building was also used for school purposes. Surveyville post office, opened in 1903, was soon renamed "Mayflower."

Population shifts starting in the 1940s caused the school to consolidate with Burkeville (1949), the post office to close (1951), and the church to disband (1961). Public facilities, including the church building, Mattox cemetery, and several other burial grounds, are now maintained by the Survey Cemetery Association. (1975)

BURKEVILLE (Newton Co.) *SH 63, 11 mi. W*
Farrsville
In the 1830s, this area was part of the Lorenzo de Zavala land grant. One of the early settlers was American Revolutionary War veteran Thomas C. Holmes. Once called Farr's Mill, the community was named for Alfred Farr, who established nearby Farr's Chapel Methodist Church. Before the Civil War large plantations stood along the military and stagecoach road. A water mill, grist mill, cotton gin, sawmill, and tannery made this a major trade center. Farrsville post office operated until 1948. After consolidation with the Burkeville district, the schoolhouse became a union church. (1966)

BURKEVILLE (Newton Co.) *FM 692 and River Road, 15 mi. N*
Toledo Bend
The Sabine River's Toledo Bend has played a major role in the history of East Texas. An area initially inhabited by Indians and buffalo, it was a landmark for Spanish explorers and missionaries. The latter possibly named it for a similar bend in the River Tagus at Toledo, Spain. It might also have been named for Gen. Jose Alvarez de Toledo, who camped here after his defeat in the 1813 Battle of the Medina.

Toledo Bend was located on the western edge of the neutral territory, the border area disputed by the United States and Spain during the early 1800s. Situated a few miles south of El Camino Real, the King's Highway, it became a major route of trade and migration. It was also the site of steamboat landings and a crossing of the old beef trail.

Anglo-Americans arrived before 1820 and the bend became known as Bevil's Crossing and later Hadden's Ferry. It developed under such leaders as W. C. Lenehan, farmer, merchant, ferry operator, and postmaster. The area became a center of the southeast Texas pecan industry through the work of Mrs. W. A. Steele, who planted the first trees, and R. L. Odom, who patented several varieties of pecans. A region rich in history, Toledo Bend is now a major resort area of Texas. (1982)

BURLESON (Johnson Co.) *IH 35W, 5 mi. S*
Bethesda Community
The Bethesda Community traces its history to 1853, when pioneer farmer David R. Jackson donated land for a community cemetery. Unmarked graves date to 1844, and the earliest marked burials are from 1856.

Bethesda Baptist Church was organized on August 13, 1855. It was the first Baptist church in the county and was called Cross Timbers Bethesda Baptist Church. Services were held in a log cabin. Initially served by circuit riding ministers, the church's first pastor was William Robinson. A Sunday school was organized in 1887. Services were held monthly until 1944, when weekly meetings were begun.

After the original log cabin church burned in 1878, a new wooden structure was built. A brick sanctuary was constructed in 1959, and became a fellowship hall in 1980 when a new facility was completed.

A community school was organized in 1855. Located at the head of Crill Miller Creek, it was called Crill Miller School. In 1918, it was consolidated with the Post Oak and Village Creek schools to form Bethesda School. A four-room schoolhouse was built and served as a center for many community activities. Bethesda School was incorporated into the Burleson Independent School District in 1950. (1987)

BURNET (Burnet Co.) *SH 29, .2 mi. W*
Site of Fort Croghan
Established by Lieut. C. H. Tyler, United States Second Dragoons, by order of the War Department, March 18, 1849, as protection to frontier settlers against hostile Indians. Abandoned in December, 1853 as the settlements had extended farther west. (1964)

BURNET (Burnet Co.)   *US 281, 6 mi. N in Dobyville Cemetery*
Mr. and Mrs. Jacob Wolf
Jacob Wolf (1812–1874) and wife, Adeline Faulkner Wolf (1814–1870), came from Tennessee to Texas about 1850. Obtaining land grant in Burnet County, they settled at Dobyville, and were pioneers, supplying their own provisions, buildings, medicines, and school.

Menaced by Indian raids, and aware of need for government, Wolf in 1854 helped organize Burnet County. Of the 8 children, 2 sons became sheriffs—one in Burnet, one in Lampasas County.   (1967)

BURNET (Burnet Co.)   *SH 29, 2 mi. W at Fort Croghan*
Peter Kerr, 1795–1861
One of "Old 300" of Stephen F. Austin's first colony; from Pennsylvania. Took part in 1836 War for Texas Independence. He made and lost several stakes.

In 1851 bought a league and labor of Burnet County land, including site of Fort Croghan.

Amassed wealth as army beef contractor. Gave 100 acres and town square for Burnet county seat. To build a college here, he willed $23,500 and 6,359 acres of land to Burnet. The will was broken; city got a 2-acre site for a public school. It is said "He never refused to help when he observed its need."   (1970)

BURNET (Burnet Co.)   *SH 29, approx. 1 mi. E on south side*
Airy Mount Barn
Kentucky native Adam Rankin Johnson (1834–1922) came to Texas in 1854. After attaining the rank of brigadier general in the Confederate Army, Johnson later settled in Burnet County where he was active in business and civic affairs. In 1882, he donated land for the railroad that carried Burnet County granite for the Texas State Capitol. This stone barn, on the homestead he called "Airy Mount," was built in the early 1880s and remained in the Johnson family until 1915.   (1986)

BURNET (Burnet Co.)   *Park Road 4, between US 281 and SH 29*
Longhorn Caverns
Rich in history and folklore, a young geologic formation only a few million years old. Bones of elephant, bison, bear, are found here. When white men came to area in 1840s, Indians knew the caverns: Rangers once found and rescued a kidnapped girl from Indians in the "Council Room."

During the Civil War (1861–1865), gunpowder was manufactured and stored here. In 1870s outlaws, including the Sam Bass Gang, sometimes lived in the cavern. It was the site of a night club in the 1920s and has many unique features. It was opened to the public in 1932.   (1967)

BURNET (Burnet Co.)   *US 281 at SH 29, 1 mi. S*
Magill Family Cemetery
Surrounded by a rock wall, the small pioneer family cemetery just west of this site is located on land that was once part of the William H. Magill homestead. Magill, a veteran of the Battle of San Jacinto, moved his family to Burnet County in 1850. He established this graveyard with the burial of his 15-year-old son, John, In 1863. The remaining four marked graves include William H. Magill (1813–1878); his second wife, Elizabeth (1831–1914); and his parents, Nancy (1792–1865) and Samuel (1783–1865) Magill. At least one unmarked grave is known to exist.   (1985)

BURTON (Washington Co.)   *SH 390 at FM 1948, 3 mi. NE*
Leander H. McNelly
(March 12, 1844–Sept. 4, 1877)
Born in Virginia; was valiant Confederate soldier.

In 1870, appointed one of four state police captains by Gov. E. J. Davis. Then with Texas Rangers, McNelly was assigned a special force, "The Washington County Volunteer Militia," to mediate the Sutton-Taylor feud. Company then assigned to Rio Grande border to control international cattle thieves in "Las Cuevas War."

His men always proudly called themselves, "Little McNellys."

BURTON (Washington Co.)   *FM 2780, 2 mi. N*
Site of Union Hill
The Hugh and Lucy Kerr family from Tennessee started the Kerr settlement in this area in 1831. W. B. McClellan (1804–1880) from North Carolina bought land from W. P. Kerr in 1844 and

began a second settlement. Union academy was operating by 1850. Mrs. Lucy Kerr gave acreage at this point for a Methodist church; Masonic lodge and school soon shared the site. Stores, a hotel, and other buildings stood to the west. Unincorporated, the town of 800 dwindled after 1870, as railroad facilities in Burton (2 mi. south) drew away the local businesses. (1976)

BURTON (Washington Co.) *FM 2780, 1.5 mi. NW*
The Gantt-Jones House
One of the homes in the early Union Hill settlement, this Greek revival residence was built about 1860 for Dr. William Henry Gantt (d. 1867), a physician and scientist who later taught at Galveston Medical College. The second owner, 1865–1890, was Henry B. ("Jo-He") Jones, the inventor of a multi-purpose medicinal ointment. The family of Louis Prenzler lived here from 1908 to 1973. The structure was then purchased and restored by Mr. and Mrs. George L. Temple. (1976)

BUSHLAND (Potter Co.) *IH 40, 1 mi. E in roadside park*
Tecovas Springs
Located 6 miles northwest of this marker. Favorite campsite of prehistoric Indians, and of later traders, military parties and hunters, from time of 18th century Spanish explorations.

Meeting place of 19th century Plains Indians with traders, smugglers and the renegade peddlers called comancheros.

Summer range home ground of Mexican shepherds before the cowmen came in the 1870s.

Since 1881, location of the headquarters of the Frying Pan, ranch started by J. F. Glidden and Henry S. Sanborn, inventors and promoters of barbed wire. (1964)

BYNUM (Hill Co.) *SH 171 at school grounds*
Bynum School
The first school in Old Bynum Community began in 1880 before the settlement had a name. After a store and a post office were built, the area adopted its name from a nearby creek. The school was moved to the new townsite on the railroad in 1905, and an independent school district was organized. Over the years, the following schools consolidated with Bynum: Davis, GroveCreek, part of Honest Ridge, Pecan, Pierce (1905–1914); Watson (1931); Massey, McMurry (1938); Brandon (1953); and Irene (1958). The school now is a historic reminder of the region's heritage. (1984)

CADDO (Stephens Co.) *US 180 at FM 717*
Caddo
The 1860 census reported fewer than 200 residents in Stephens County. That year, Joe Schoolcraft settled on Caddo Creek, 15 miles south of a Caddo Indian village. He built his home on the north bank of Caddo Creek at Elm Creek. The town grew during the next decade, and in 1876, local ranchers began recording their brands at the courthouse. Early settlers included Jere Hart, C.J. Johnson, A.W. Corbett, Tom Thompson, W.B. Richardson, William Copeland, John Robinson and Josephus Knott, as well as the Graceys, Swensons, McMeens, Lees and Winstons. Perry K. Taylor opened a store in 1875. Shortly thereafter, R.Q. Lee and the Butlers opened "the Big Red Store," which became Sandidge, Lee & Co. in 1906. The Caddo post office opened in 1877. In 1883, the town hired Dora Mandy as the first schoolteacher. A two-story structure was built in 1890 and was used for school, church and Masonic lodge meetings; it burned in 1910, and residents then built a red brick and rock schoolhouse on Caddo Creek. The first physician came in 1886, and the town's early doctors included a woman named Dr. Evans. Local churches organized in the 1890s; the Baptist congregation built its sanctuary in 1894. Early settler Tom Lay hauled water to local residents, who also had access to telephone service in 1898. Cattle, horses, sheep and cotton were the mainstay of the town until 1916, when the first oil well came in. In 1919, Caddo led the state in oil production. The boom, which attracted thousands of new residents and numerous businesses, lasted until the early 1920s. By World War II, the population had declined. The last class of maroon and white Caddo Cougars graduated in 1945; the town consolidated its school with Breckenridge. Highway construction bypassed the town in the 1950s, and Caddo's population continued to decrease. Fewer than 50 people lived in the town in 2000, most relying on agriculture and oil. (2002)

CALDWELL (Burleson Co.)   *SH 21 at 36*
Burleson County
Farmed early as 1744 by Indians under guidance of Spanish missionaries. In 1830, Ft. Tenoxtitlan, guarding Brazos crossing, San Antonio Road, attracted Anglo-Texans, who lived off wild game in early years.

County created and organized in 1846. Named for Gen. Edward Burleson (1798–1851), veteran of Battle of San Jacinto; Indian fighter; Republic of Texas vice-president and senator; later a state senator. County seat, Caldwell (named for Mathew Caldwell, signer of Declaration of Independence).

During the Civil War, furnished troops, cotton and food to Confederate Texas.   (1965)

CALDWELL (Burleson Co.)   *SH 21 E just outside city limits*
City of Caldwell
Founded 1840 by Lewis L. Chiles, a veteran of Battle of San Jacinto. Named for Mathew "Old Paint" Caldwell, Indian fighter and signer of the Texas Declaration of Independence. This was county seat, Milam County, in 1845; since 1846 county seat of Burleson County.

Home Burleson County Fair.   (1967)

CALDWELL (Burleson Co.)   *SH 21 in roadside park, 8 mi. SW*
John Mitchell
Born in Tennessee c. 1836–37, John Mitchell came to Texas in 1846. He began purchasing land in this area in 1870, the same year he married Viney Cox. As a member of both the 12th and 14th Legislatures, Mitchell championed increased educational opportunities for African Americans. Elected as a delegate to the 1875 Constitutional Convention, he defended the policies of Gov. Davis and was one of 11 members to vote against adoption of the new constitution, which ultimately marked the end of reconstruction in Texas. John Mitchell returned to Burleson County as a farmer and rancher, and donated land for a church and school that bore his name. Upon his death in 1921, he was buried in a family graveyard.   (2002)

CALDWELL (Burleson Co.)   *SH 21, 9.4 mi. SW at edge of rest area*
Site of El Camino Real
(The Old San Antonio Road)
Great thoroughfare of early Texas. Following ancient Indian and buffalo paths, sometimes on same course as 1691 "Trail of the Padres," stretches 1,000 miles from Saltillo, Mexico, to present Louisiana. Highway for explorers, traders, smugglers, adventurers, settlers, armies. Was surveyed about 1800 and given name of "King's Highway." Here, as in some other areas, the modern highway follows historic El Camino Real.

Also, in this particular area, El Camino Real marked boundary between the major early 19th century colonies of Stephen F. Austin and Sterling C. Robertson.   (1968)

CALDWELL (Burleson Co.)   *SH 21, 4 mi. E*
Duewall House
Rudolph and Anna Duewall established a family farm here in the 1880s upon moving to Burleson County. Their son Edward (1885–1944) and his wife, Lizzie (Herrmann) (1890–1947), continued the farm operations. In 1928, they built this house on the site of the original Duewall House to accommodate their family of six children. Carpenter Otto Berndt used materials from the first farmhouse and from the second Burleson County courthouse in the home's construction. The vernacular farmhouse features exposed rafters and a cross-gabled roof.   (2001)

CALDWELL (Burleson Co.)   *SH 21, 5 mi. E in roadside park*
"Dream Capital of Texas"
Fort Tenoxtitlan
(Site about 8 mi. NE)
Founded by Mexico as a bulwark against Anglo-American immigration, this fort and its nearby city were twice proposed for the capital of Texas.

Alarmed by the influx of Anglo settlers into Texas, Mexico in 1830 sought to erect a line of forts to keep out the intruders. The ancient Aztec name for Mexico City (originally pronounced "Ten-Ox-Teet-Lan") was given this site; it means "Prickly Pear Place." So hopeful of the fort's success was the military commandant of the region that he envisioned it as the capital of Texas. But Anglo immigration did not cease. Instead it thrived on the friendship of the local soldiers and incoming pioneers. The colonizer Sterling C. Robertson introduced scores of settlers.

In 1832, the soldiers were withdrawn and the fort finally defaulted to the Anglos. Subsequently it was a supply center and mustering point for expeditions against the Indians. During its brief life many Texas patriots lived here, including 5 signers of the Texas Declaration of Independence, a martyr of the Alamo siege, and 7 soldiers of the Battle of San Jacinto.

Tenoxtitlan was again suggested for the capital of Texas during the Republic, but Austin won out. In 1841, after many Indian raids, the site was abandoned. (1970)

CALDWELL (Burleson Co.) — SH 21, in Cooks Point

Near Homesite of Judge Andrew S. Broaddus
(1810–1891)

Noted pioneer leader. Member Virginia House of Delegates (1844–1845). Piloted to Texas (1854) a mile-long wagon train of 200 people, who built Salem Baptist Church—reminder of their Virginia home.

Broaddus debated the Hon. Sam Houston at Waugh Campground (8 mi. W), 1857. He served in 1861 in Texas Secession Convention; 9th (1861–1863) Texas Legislature; 13th Texas Legislature (1873); also on commission to locate and build Texas Agricultural & Mechanical College (now University); Judge, 32nd District (1874–1875; 1879–1880).

Married twice, had 13 children. (1971)

CALDWELL (Burleson Co.) — SH 21, 10 mi. NE between FM 50 and Brazos River Bridge

Moseley's Ferry

Situated where the Old San Antonio Road crossed the Brazos River, this public ferry was begun by Michael Boren (1806–1875) about 1846. The ferry and a settlement nearby were named for Daniel Moseley (1787–1856), who took over the service in 1849 and whose family ran it until 1868. Other ferrymen continued to transport travelers, livestock, and freight across the river until 1912, when the Houston & Texas Central (now the Southern Pacific) constructed a railroad bridge at this location. Today a highway bridge spans the Brazos where Moseley's Ferry once operated. (1975)

CALDWELL (Burleson Co.) — SH 21, 5 mi. E in roadside park

One Mile North to Site of Elizabeth Chapel
Methodist Church

First Methodist church in the county. Began as Sunday school in home of Isaac Addison, early settler. Later moved to home of Mrs. Elizabeth Scott. Organized about 1839 by Robt. Alexander, famous pioneer minister. Soon a small, hand-hewn frame building was erected and named for Mrs. Scott. Land containing both the church and cemetery was given to Methodist Episcopal Church, south, by Mrs. Scott's son, Philip, in 1878. Membership reached peak of 165 in 1885.

Church merged with the Cooks Point Church about 1907. (1970)

CALDWELL (Burleson Co.) — SH 21, 5 mi. E

Cooks Point United Methodist Church

This congregation began in 1881 to serve the German speaking population in the area. Organized largely through the efforts of Anna Duewall, who had come to Burleson County with her family in 1880, the fellowship originally was known as the German Methodist Church, Caldwell. The Rev. Jacob Ott served as first pastor. Worship services were held in the members' homes until a sanctuary was built in 1883. The congregation adopted the name Cooks Point in the 1940s and continues to play an important role in the surrounding rural area. (1984)

CALDWELL (Burleson Co.) — SH 21, 8 mi. W

An Arm of the
Chisholm Cattle Trail

The Chisholm Trail, which was developed following the Civil War, allowed Texas cattle to be driven to railheads in Kansas for shipment to eastern markets. An arm of the celebrated route, reaching from Matagorda County to the main trail near present McGregor, passed through this area. With the establishment of James L. Dean's store, later the site of Deanville, and the White Inn, the trail became a significant commercial road. Vital to the development of Burleson County's cattle industry, it declined in use after rail lines reached the area in the late 1870s.   (1981)

CALLIHAM (McMullen Co.)   *FM 99, 8.2 mi. N at site of Jambers Ranch Road*
Site of Old Crowther Ranch
Townsite of 1600 acres established by 1902. Named in honor of Samuel Crowther on whose land it was located. Purchased by S. A. Hopkins in 1903. Extensive promotion failed to develop community into oil and farming center despite early oil discoveries. Became a ghost town by 1921. Bought by George T. Jambers, 1933.   (1968)

CALLIHAM (McMullen Co.)   *SH 72 by gymnasium*
Calliham
In 1918 had a post office, Guffeyola, in store of H. H. McGuffey. After oil and gas discoveries, 1917–1922, was tent city, then town of shotgun houses. Piped first natural gas to San Antonio.

Name was changed 1923 to honor J. T. Calliham, rancher and townsite owner. Still produces oil and exports fine rocks and petrified wood.   (1966)

CALLIHAM (McMullen Co.)   *SH 72, City Square*
First Producing Gas Well in McMullen County
and First Gas Pipeline to San Antonio
(South of Frio River, 1 mi. NE)
Thirty years before the first producing gas well was drilled in this county, traces of salt water, sulphur, gas, and oil in water wells gave hints of the presence of petroleum here. For years wild-cat drilling went on, but with only moderate success.

Then in 1908, a well on Charles Byrne's land began to blow warm sulphur water and gas 120 feet into the air every 8 days, arousing much interest. After this discovery, Byrne, a promoter, set out to locate capitalists to develop his petroleum deposits.

Armed with a picture of the gusher and a bottle of area oil, he attracted the attention of W. M. "Bee" Stephenson, his sons Light and Donald, and others.

The well they drilled here in 1917–1918, on the Tom Brown tract, blew in at 816 feet with 62,000,000 cubic feet of natural gas a day, but for 3 months it spewed out of control because of the intense subsurface pressure and inadequate equipment.

After other producers were drilled, W. M. Stephenson arranged to pipe gas to San Antonio, 68 miles north, in 1922. Among those joining this enterprise was H. A. Pagenkopf, a Wichita Falls oil man. Thus, petroleum took a leading role in the economy of McMullen County.   (1970)

CALLISBURG (Cooke Co.)   *FM 2896 right of way in Callisburg*
First Oil Well in Cooke County
Located on the Bud W. Davis farm (1 mile E), Cooke County's first producing oil well came in on Nov. 9, 1924, heralding the beginning of a multi-million dollar industry and a new life style for the surrounding farm community. Carnival atmosphere prevailed while sightseers and reporters flocked to the lease. One enterprising man charged admission until questioned by a worker. The discovery well, drilled by C. A. Doudrick's Big Indian Oil Company, continued to produce until 1970 when it was plugged.   (1976)

CALVERT (Robertson Co.)   *SH 6, 3 mi. N*
Site of Extinct Town of Hammond
Dr. Ben F. Hammond moved here from Alabama in 1853 and built a plantation home about a mile to the west. Neighbors included James Love and Robert S. McCall. Hammond depot and post office were opened at this point on the Houston & Texas Central Railroad after the doctor granted right-of-way through his land in 1869. Near the depot, used by planters for their shipping, were a few stores. As the railroad declined, the town had vanished by 1950. Area residents are mostly the descendants of persons given land at emancipation (1865) by Dr. Hammond and other planters.   (1976)

CALVERT (Robertson Co.)   *SH 6, 5 mi. N*
Site of Harvey Massacre
(1 mi. W)
At this site on Sunday night in November 1836, the family of John Harvey was attacked by an Indian raiding party. Harvey, his wife, and son were all killed, Mrs. Harvey's blood staining the open pages of the family Bible. Their daughter Ann, aged 5, and a servant girl were taken captive, later to be sold as slaves. The price of Ann was a few blankets.

After four years in Mexico, Ann was recovered by her uncle, James Talbot of Alabama. In 1848 she wed Sanders Briggs and in 1853 they moved to Texas, where they built a home—ironically —near the site of the massacre. (1972)

CALVERT (Robertson Co.)   *SH 6, access rd.*
Home Area of Chinese Farmers
Imported from Asia about 1874 to help in cotton fields, these exotic workers wore queues and attracted much notice. At least 24 families were brought here; many became permanent residents, respected for their good work.

Over 25 ethnic groups settled in Texas—many having preceded the Chinese. Other than American Indians, first permanent Texas settlers were cattle raisers from the Canary Islands. Other migrant groups included Cuban cigar makers and European lace makers. Given new opportunities, their descendants now are in industry, business, professions. (1968)

CAMDEN (Polk Co.)   *US 59 on FM 62*
Moscow Camden & San Augustine Railroad
Texas' shortest (and one of its oldest) "mixed"-train railroads. Has passenger and freight cars pulled by a single engine on a 7-mile system, 5 days a week.

Chartered 1898 by Lumberman W. T. Carter to connect sawmill town of Camden with Texas & New Orleans Railway at Moscow.

"Panama No. 201," now retired to Camden with other steam engines, was used in building the Panama Canal in 1914. It was the last locomotive in service here, 1965.

Passenger coach with original rattan seats began its career 1898 on Long Island Railroad. (1968)

CAMERON (Milam Co.)   *US 77, 8 mi. N*
Milam County
A part of Robertson's Colony in 1834, a part of the Municipality of Viesca, 1835. Name changed to Milam December 21, 1835 in honor of Benjamin Rush Milam, 1788–1835, who fell at San Antonio. After Burleson and Robertson Counties were cut off, Nashville became the county seat in 1837. The later creation of Williamson, Bell, McLennan and Falls, reduced Milam County to its present size.

Cameron, the county seat since 1846.

CAMERON (Milam Co.)   *US 77, 1.6 mi. E*
Site Where Steamboat *Washington* Landed
In the winter of 1850–1851 with Captain Basil M. Hatfield, Commander, the Steamboat *Washington* landed here with a shipment of merchandise from Washington-on-the-Brazos to J.W. McCown and Co., merchants at Cameron. The first, last and only steamboat to navigate Little River.

CAMERON (Milam Co.)   *US 190, at site, City Park*
Site of First Home in Cameron
Boyhood home of L. S. "Sul" Ross (1838–1898), Texas governor from 1887 to 1891. His father Shapley P. Ross, Indian agent and Ranger, built the house after moving here about 1841; he chose this site because it had a good spring. L. S. Ross, who was a Confederate general, served as president of Texas A&M College after holding office as governor.

In 1890, this pavilion was erected to accommodate band concerts, meetings, and rallies. It was the scene in 1892 of a landmark debate between two gubernatorial candidates: Gov. James S. Hogg and George Clark. (1969)

CAMP VERDE (Kerr Co.)

FM 480 at FM 689 (SH 173)

Camp Verde
General Store and Post Office

Mercantile Business opened 1857 as Williams Community Store, serving trade around Camp Verde Army Post (site of U.S. War Department's 1857–1869 camel experiment). Post office opened in 1887.
(1971)

CAMP VERDE (Kerr Co.)

SH 173 (FM 689)

Camp Verde, C.S.A.

Texas Frontier Regiment Outpost was established 1862, southeast and near old U.S. Post Camp Verde. Part of Red River-Rio Grande line of posts a day's horseback ride apart. The troops furnished own guns, mounts, but often lacked food, clothing, supplies. Still, scouting parties, patrols effectively curbed Indian raids until war's end. Kerr County population was 585. County voted 76–57 for secession 1861. 75 men served in Confederate and state forces. Some sent to protect Texas coast from Union invasion, some helped to defend frontier in this region, others fought on distant battlefields. 19 men from county served in Texas Union Forces. Old U.S. Post Camp Verde was taken by C.S.A. troops Feb. 1861. The Confederates captured 80 camels and two Egyptian drivers with other U.S. property. These camels were used to haul cotton—life's blood of South—to Mexico to swap for vital supplies, including salt from lakes north of Brownsville. During post dances ladies rode a camel "Old Major" around the parade grounds. 600 Union soldiers captured leaving Texas early in Civil War were confined in prison canyon southwest of the camp. 3 cliffs, described as "very difficult to ascend" surrounded the prison area. Prisoners, held from Aug. 1861 until sometime in 1862, were allowed to build shacks and get adequate exercise with little risk of escape. One Union prisoner performed as ventriloquist at post dance, scaring ladies with unseen pig sounds.
(1963)

CAMP WOOD (Real Co.)

SH 55, .3 mi. N

Site of the Mission San Lorenzo de la Santa Cruz

Founded by Franciscan missionaries among Lipan Apache Indians in 1762. Abandoned in 1769.
(1936)

CAMP WOOD (Real Co.)

SH 55, .5 mi. N

Site of Camp Wood

Established May 20, 1857, as a means of preventing Indian raids on the San Antonio-El Paso route and the Rio Grande Valley. Abandoned March 15, 1861, when Federal troops were withdrawn from Texas.

CAMP WOOD (Real Co.)

SH 55, 4 mi. N

Private Frank Marshall, C.S.A.

Buried here, ³/₁₀ mi. from Camp Wood. A 29-year-old Harrison Countian, symbolizes Texans who died for the Confederacy in the Arizona-New Mexico campaign. Served from April 19, 1861, till death June 16, in W. P. Lane Rangers in second front stretched from San Antonio to Santa Fe. Frontier posts at Camp Wood, Ft. Inge, Ft. Clark, Camp Hudson, Howard Spring and Ft. Lancaster supported the 1861–1862 campaign to make the Confederacy an ocean-to-ocean nation. Combat forces included such Texans as Tom Green, Wm. R. Scurry, W. P. Hardeman and Wm. Steele, all later to be generals in the Confederate Army.

Green and Scurry commanded troops that won battle of Valverde in Feb. 1862. This victory and others enabled the Confederacy to occupy Arizona and New Mexico and hope to gain California. However, Texas troops found their lines too long and supplies an impossible problem. With scanty food, no blankets, no means of transportation, the army limped back to Texas. On reaching San Antonio, troops hid near the Menger Hotel, pooled their rags to dress one man, then sent out for clothes to cover them so they could go home. Yet these same men re-grouped and won many victories later in the Civil War.
(1965)

CAMP WOOD (Real Co.) 　　　　　　　　　　　　　　*SH 55, Lindbergh Park*
Charles A. Lindbergh in Texas
Texas was important in the career of Charles A. Lindbergh (1902–1974). When he bought his first W. W. I surplus Jenny in Georgia, he flew it to Texarkana in 1923 so he could say he had flown in Texas, the ambition of every barnstormer.

With Leon Klink, in March 1924 he landed Klink's Canuck in Camp Wood while trying to fly to California. Next day in attempting to take off, he accidentally crashed into Warren Pruett's store. No one was hurt and his offer to pay for the damage was rejected. Then called "Slim," Lindbergh made many friends here.

Two weeks after visiting Camp Wood, he became a U.S. Air Service Cadet at Brooks Field, San Antonio.

He completed advanced flight training at Kelly Field in 1925. On May 20–2l, 1927, he made the first solo flight from New York to Paris, to world acclaim.

Later in 1927, he returned to Texas. Surveying the first commercial transcontinental air-route through Amarillo; in 1929 he inaugurated U.S.-Mexico air mail in Brownsville. A great aviation pioneer, he drew up and proved many major air routes. He flew combat W.W. II, collaborated in medical research, helped organize Berlin Airlift, and remained a hero to the people of Camp Wood, Texas.

CAMPBELL (Hunt Co.) 　　　　　　　　　　*FM 513 ¼ mi. from downtown*
Henry and Emerson Colleges
Prominent early institutions, Henry College founded 1892 by educators Henry Bridges and Henry Eastman, was re-established and renamed in 1903 for writer Ralph Waldo Emerson, closed 1907 other early colleges in Hunt County were Calhoun 1887-1899, Texas Holiness 1899–1906, The Elmwood Institute 1898–1906, Burleson 1895–1931, Wesley 1914–1937. Only East Texas State University, opened in 1894, still operates in Commerce. Although short lived, these colleges, like more than 200 chartered in Texas, 1836–1875, helped shape early culture.　　(1968)

CANADIAN (Hemphill Co.) 　　　　　　　　　　　　*US 60, .3 mi. N*
Hemphill County
Formed from Young and Bexar Territories. Created August 21, 1876; organized July 5, 1886. Named in honor of John Hemphill, 1809–1862, First Chief Justice of the Supreme Court of the State of Texas, Adjutant General of the Somervell Expedition, Member of the first State Constitutional Convention, Member of the United States Congress. Canadian, the county seat.　　(1936)

CANADIAN (Hemphill Co.) 　　　　　　　　　　　*US 60-83, 1 mi. N*
Canadian River Trail
Trade, exploration and hunting trails along the Canadian are older than recorded history—old when used 1541 by Spaniard Coronado hunting Golden Cities of Cibola. Route in 1840 for Josiah Gregg and 34 Missouri men with goods worth $25,000 headed for trade in Santa Fe. Used by 1849 parties escorted by U.S. Army Captain R. B. Marcy on way to California Gold Rush.

Hunters, cattlemen, settlers used Canadian River trails in 1870s and '80s, as Panhandle was opened to civilization.

River's name, "Canadian," came from Spanish for "boxed-in."　　(1966)

CANADIAN (Hemphill Co.) 　　　　　　　　　　　*SH 83, 13.2 mi. S*
Gen. Nelson Miles' Expedition
(Headquarters Dugout, 2.3 Mi. W, on Washita River)
Indian raids brought Miles' men to Texas from north in 1874 as part of U.S. Army pincers' tactic operating from a dugout post. The 12 infantry and cavalry units had supply camps on the Canadian, Red and Washita Rivers.

On Nov. 8, 1874, Miles' troops recovered three captive German sisters; fought 8 Indian battles during winter. At this post Gen. Miles nominated for medal of honor several of his men—among them renowned Panhandle settler, Billy Dixon.

In 1875, Ft. Elliott was opened at Old Mobeetie to continue frontier protection.　　(1967)

CANADIAN (Hemphill Co.)   *US 60 at FM 2266, 1 mi. N*

Gene Howe Wildlife Management Area

The Gene Howe Wildlife Management Area contains approximately 6,000 acres of upland sand-hills, pastures, natural meadows and woodlands fronting the north bank of the Canadian River.

Named for Eugene A. Howe, Amarillo newspaper publisher, dedicated conservationist and member of the Texas Game and Fish Commission for more than 19 years, the area was acquired by the state in 1951. The objectives: to develop through research and demonstration, better meth-ods of game management which can be applied to major vegetative types found in the High Plains and Panhandle regions of Texas.

Chief projects on the area involve the white-tailed deer, wild turkey, bobwhite quail and migra-tory waterfowl. Lesser prairie chickens and ring-necked pheasants may be found throughout the year and winter brings a wide variety of visiting shorebirds.

To improve wildlife habitat and increase the yield of natural foods for wildlife, dikes have been constructed to create marshes which are planted with waterflow food plants; brush clearings have been made in the cottonwood thickets and bottomlands to provide suitable feeding areas and game openings; small grain is sowed for winter feeding of deer and turkey.

Scientific information acquired through work done on this federal-state cooperative project is available to surrounding landowners and others who are interested. Game surpluses produced on the area are harvested periodically by hunters under a controlled public hunt program.

CANADIAN (Hemphill Co.)   *US 60, 17 mi. SW*

Fossil Beds
(3 mi. SE)

Cited as one of most prolific fossil fields of Lower Pliocene Age at time of discovery, these beds are about 13,000,000 years old. Geologists of Rio Bravo Oil Company found them in 1928 on C. C. Coffee ranch, and their reports brought specialists from several major institutions to the area.

The fossil bones buried here included (among others) those of a prehistoric camel, a kind of antelope, horse, bone-crushing dog, mastodon, and wild pig.

Further studies led scientists in 1941 to adopt "Hemphillian" as the name for the geologic age represented by these fossils.   (1970)

CANADIAN (Hemphill Co.)   *US 60/83, 6.5 mi. S near Highway Station 525*

58 yds. W to Routes of Historic Trails

During the mass slaughter of buffaloes in the Panhandle, 2 trails arose to meet the needs of the hunters and their ever-hungry markets. Started about 1876, both moved vast convoys of wagons across the plains.

Charles Rath—transporting gun powder, lead, tobacco, whiskey and food staples—blazed a road from Dodge City to the Double Mountains. In 2 years, however, the best hunting was over and the route fell into disuse. Ed Jones and Joe Plummer forged a trail from Kansas to Ft. Elliot. Their route became a freight road and finally a cattle trail.   (1969)

CANADIAN (Hemphill Co.)   *SH 33, 21 mi. SE*

Site of Lyman's Wagon Train Battle
(2.5 mi. S, 1.7 mi. E)

During the U.S. Army campaigns in 1874 against marauding Indians, Capt. Wyllys Lyman led a wagon train to Camp Supply, Okla., for rations for Gen. Nelson A. Miles' troops on duty in Texas. On the way, Indians attacked, and the longest Indian battle in Panhandle history ensued.

Fighting from a wagon corral Sept. 9 to 14 Lyman and 95 soldiers held off about 400 Comanche and Kiowa Indians. A scout escaped and reached Camp Supply for help.

Company K, 6th Cavalry, traveled 80 miles without rest in a raging rainstorm to aid the wagon train. On its arrival, the Indians fled.   (1967)

CANADIAN (Hemphill Co.)   *US 60/83, 7.9 mi. S*

Route of Marcy Trail

This overland route, blazed in 1849 by energetic and efficient army Captain R. B. Marcy, was best known as part of the California Gold Trail. Starting in Oklahoma, Marcy led an expedition across the Texas Panhandle and back through Central West Texas. Both of the wagon roads he laid out served the emigrant traffic.

In 1853 this section was planned as part of the route for the first transcontinental railroad in America, but the Civil War shifted sentiment to northern routes. Its importance declined after the railroad came through this county, 1887. (1969)

CANADIAN (Hemphill Co.)   *US 60, 3 mi. N*
Robert R. Young
(February 14, 1897–January 25, 1958)
A leader in America's finance and transportation. Born here, in house built by lawyer Temple Houston, son of Republic of Texas President Sam Houston.

His grandfather was traildriver, pioneer rancher; his father, president of the first bank in Canadian.

Educated at old Canadian Academy, Culver Military Academy (where he won highest honors), University of Virginia. Married, 1916, Anita O'Keeffe, sister of the famous painter Georgia O'Keeffe. Had a daughter. One of close friends was King Edward VIII of England.

Assistant to treasurer of General Motors, 1920s. Made fortune in stock market in 1929. After years on Wall Street, won acclaim of financial world in a proxy battle to gain control of and modernize New York Central Railroad. In this fight, enlisted aid of Texas friends Clint Murchison and Sid Richardson.

Until 1939, retained banking interests in Canadian. Was a lifelong member of Presbyterian Church here. Remembered native state with gifts of rare papers to University of Texas. Restored an historic local burial ground, naming it "Edith Ford Cemetery," to honor an aunt who reared him after early death of his mother. Maintained close ties (in visits, hunting trips, correspondence) with people known in boyhood.

CANADIAN (Hemphill Co.)   *US 60/83, 1.7 mi. NE*
Site of Old Springer's Road Ranch
(12.2 mi. E)
First post office in Hemphill County. Unique for tunnel from dugout home-store to corral.

On 1870s trail from Ft. Elliott (35 mi. SW) to Ft. Supply, Ind. Terr., to Ft. Dodge, Kans. Established by A. G. Springer; besides running 300 head of cattle, Springer's was a stagecoach stand, tavern; store (mainly for teamster, hunters) had liquor, canned goods, hunting equipment. Poker-expert Springer was frequent host to soldiers seeking entertainment in tavern.

In 1877, he and Tom Ledbetter, his partner, were killed in gun battle with angered soldiers, and were buried at the ranch. (1967)

CANTON (Van Zandt Co.)   *SH 64 at county courthouse*
Cadwell Walton Raines (September 18, 1839–August 2, 1906)
Born in Georgia, Raines came to Texas in 1858, after serving in Gen. R. M. Gano's Texas Cavalry Regiment in the Civil War, he was a teacher in New Braunfels and a lawyer in Canton. Van Zandt County judge from 1876 to 1878, he played a major role in the infamous County Seat War of 1877. He published newspapers at Wills Point, Mineola, and Quitman, where he became Wood County judge and was appointed state librarian in 1891 by his friend Governor James Stephen Hogg. Raines rebuilt the neglected State Library and began its invaluable collection of Texana in 1895. (1998)

CANTON (Van Zandt Co.)   *SH 64 at county courthouse*
Oran Milo Roberts (July 9, 1815–May 19, 1898)
A South Carolina-born Alabama legislator, Oran M. Roberts came to San Augustine, Texas in 1841. He served in district and state judicial positions, including the First District Court in Canton in 1850, and was president of the Secession Convention in 1861. After service as a colonel in the 11th Regiment, Texas Infantry, his postwar career included a second turn as a state supreme court judge; he made the 1877 ruling that ended the Van Zandt County Seat War. Roberts was elected governor of Texas in 1878. He was a law professor at the new University of Texas until 1893. Roberts helped form the Texas State Historical Association in 1895. (1998)

CANTON (Van Zandt Co.) — SH 243, 8 mi E
Shelby Expedition Through Van Zandt County
Gen. Joseph O. Shelby's command refused to surrender at the close of the Civil War. Shelby's men, the First Missouri Cavalry of the Confederate States of America, marched via Clarksville to Van Zandt County, proceeding through Grand Saline to Canton and on to Stone Point soon after learning of Gen. Robert E. Lee's surrender. From about April 22 to May 29, 1865, Shelby's troops camped at Stone Point while their leader attended a Confederate conference at Marshall, Texas. Determined to continue the war, Shelby's men journeyed to Mexico, stopping where they were needed to enforce the peace in a ravaged postwar Texas. (1998)

CANTON (Van Zandt Co.) — SH 64, 1 mi. SE
Van Zandt County
A portion of the original Mercer Grant, created from Henderson County 1848.

Named in honor of the illustrious statesman Isaac Van Zandt. Born in Tennessee, July 10, 1813. Delegate to the Annexation Convention in 1845.

Died in Texas, October 10, 1847. Canton the county seat; Van, the oil field center; Grand Saline, famed for its salt industry.

CANTON (Van Zandt Co.) — City Lake Dr., 1 mi. E in City Park
Dipping Vat
Before discovery of a dip (1894) and vaccine (1898), the American cattle industry faced ruin, as it lost $40 million annually from cattle tick fever. In 1918, tick eradication began in East Texas, with colorful, exciting "dipping days" enforced every two weeks from spring to fall. Sometimes citizens resented the compulsory dipping, and dynamited vats or held shootouts with authorities.

This dipping vat is typical of 50 built in Van Zandt County. It was on property of G. M. Hilliard (1856–1931), pioneer rancher and merchant. His estate in 1968 sold this park site to city of Canton. (1973)

CANTON (Van Zandt Co.) — SH 19 at SH 64, 2 blks. N
Hillcrest Cemetery
Located within the original 1850 town plat of Canton, this cemetery has served citizens of this area for well over a century. The oldest documented burial is that of Ann Calhoon (1807–1860). Among those buried here in marked and unmarked graves are Van Zandt County pioneers; veterans of the Civil War, World War I, and World War II; and business and community leaders. Serving as a reminder of Canton's pioneer heritage, the Hillcrest Cemetery is a reflection of the history of the town and its citizens. (1990)

CANTON (Van Zandt Co.) — SH 64, 22 mi. SE
Roseland Plantation Home
Built 1854 by B. H. Hambrick, from Virginia. Headquarters for 3,000-acre property. Colonial architecture. Pegged mortise and tenon construction. Joists are 48-ft. timbers. Bricks were hand-made on the plantation.

Site, halfway between Dallas and Shreveport, at times served as overnight stagecoach stop and change station for horses.

An early-day social center.

Restored in 1954 by Mrs. W. C. Windsor. (1966)

CANYON (Randall Co.) — 4 locations: US 87/60 N; US 60, 15 mi. W; US 87 S; SH 217 E
Randall County
Created 1876; named for Confederate General Horace Randall. Settled 1877 by Rancher Leigh Dyer, brother-in-law of Chas. Goodnight, man who brought first cattle to Panhandle. Organized in 1889. County seat: Canyon, home of West Texas State University, Panhandle-Plains Historical Museum, Palo Duro State Park, Buffalo Lake. (1965)

CANYON (Randall Co.) *SH 217, 12 mi. E at Palo Duro Canyon State Park*

The Battle of Palo Duro Canyon
September 28, 1874

One of the most significant battles of 1874–1875 Indian campaign; columns of troops converging from five directions harassed Indians on the Panhandle Plains for over six months.

The 4th Cavalry under Col. Ranald S. Mackenzie, moving north from Fort Concho, tracked a large band of Indians to their secret canyon camp.

Moving silently at dawn down a perilous path on the south rim, the first troops reached the floor of the canyon before the aroused camp fled.

Some of the warriors took up positions on the canyon walls from which they fired on the troops, seeking to give their families time to escape.

Realizing his tactical disadvantage, Mackenzie ordered the Indian camp and supplies burned and withdrew, taking along 1,400 captured horses (1,000 of which he later destroyed).

The cavalry suffered no casualties in the fight and only four Indian dead were counted.

Having lost half their horses as well as all their supplies and shelter, the Indians drifted back to their reservations at Fort Sill and Fort Reno.   (1967)

CANYON (Randall Co.) *FM 217, ¾ mi. E of Courthouse*

Site of an
Early Barbed Wire Fence
in the Panhandle

In the latter 1800s, when fencing was needed in the treeless Texas Panhandle, the solution proved to be barbed wire. Joseph F. Glidden of Illinois devised and by 1876 was manufacturing (with I. L. Ellwood) the first really practical barbed wire on the market. H. B. Sanborn was sent to Texas as their agent, and remained to become a builder of the Panhandle.

Wanting free access to water and grass, ranchers at first resisted fencing. Cowboys disliked it, as fewer range riders were needed on fenced lands. The old-timers grew bitter, because of blocked trails—herds had to be hauled rather than driven to market.

Yet newcomers wanted fencing, in order to have use of land purchased for ranching. Merchants and city-builders wanted fences, to assure settlement.

The T-Anchor, owned by Jot Gunter and Wm. B. Munson, real estate investors of Grayson County, built a line fence on this site in 1881, enclosing a 240,000-acre horse pasture. Also built in this area, by popular subscription, was a "drift" fence to hold cattle back from wandering south in blue northers and blizzards.

Barbed wire gradually came into general use. It saved the cattle industry, because improvements in breeding and feeding were possible on fenced ranges.

CANYON (Randall Co.) *SH 217, 4 mi. E*

Francisco Vasquez De Coronado
on the Texas Plains

On April 22, 1540, Francisco Vasquez de Coronado (1510–1554) set out from Culiacan (in present Sinaloa, Mexico) with an expedition of 1500 men to search for seven golden cities reported far to the north. Coronado entered the present United States in Arizona and proceeded northeast to the Rio Grande pueblos in New Mexico, where he spent the winter of 1540–1541. On April 23, 1541, Coronado left the Rio Grande, traveling eastward to seek the golden city of Quivira.

A native guide called "El Turco" led the conquistadores aimlessly across the arid plains in an attempt to get them lost. On May 29, 1541, with supplies depleted, Coronado entered Palo Duro Canyon, where wild fruit and water abounded. While in the canyon, Coronado discovered the guide's betrayal. On June 2, Coronado selected 30 men and started northward in quest of Quivira. The rest of the expedition, under command of Tristan de Arellano, remained in the canyon for 2 weeks before returning to the Rio Grande. According to legend, Fray Juan de Padilla conducted a feast of thanksgiving for the group while in Palo Duro Canyon.

In 1542, after failing to find the Seven Cities of Gold, Coronado returned to Mexico a broken man.   (1973)

CANYON (Randall Co.)
14 mi. E, grounds of Panhandle-Plains Museum
situated on the commemorative
Charles Goodnight Trail

The Charles Goodnight Memorial Trail

The highway from this museum to the Palo Duro State Park (12 mi. E) approximates course used by Charles Goodnight, outstanding Texas cowman and trail blazer, when he trailed 1600 cattle from Colorado to found first ranch on the staked plains of Texas in 1876.

He entered precipitous Palo Duro Canyon by way of Old Comanche Indian Trail; drove thousands of buffalo from what is now park area; established his home ranch a few miles farther down canyon.

Goodnight was born in Illinois, March 5, 1836. At age of 9 he rode bareback to Texas behind covered wagon driven by his parents; he hunted with Caddo Indians beyond the frontier at 14; guided Texas Rangers fighting Comanche and Kiowas at 25; blazed cattle trails about 2,000 mi. long with Oliver Loving at 30.

In partnership with John G. Adair, he expanded his original Palo Duro ranch into the giant JA and other holdings of more than a million acres and 100,000 cattle. He preserved the buffalo, founded a college, encouraged the settlement of the plains and led in a long fight for law and order.

This foremost plainsman died March 12, 1929, and is buried at Goodnight, Texas.   (1968)

CANYON (Randall Co.)
SH 217, about 14 mi. at entrance
to Palo Duro State Park

The Old JA Ranch

In 1876, veteran Texas cattleman Charles Goodnight entered Palo Duro Canyon by way of an old Comanche Indian Trail near here, to establish the first ranch in this area.

In 1877, Goodnight in partnership with Englishman John Adair moved farther down the canyon to lay out headquarters of the JA Ranch. This pioneer venture became one of the greatest cattle operations in the world, taking in more than a million acres of land and grazing 101,023 head of cattle.

Goodnight had become acquainted with the Palo Duro as a scout and guide for Texas Rangers during the Civil War. He knew that the canyon, fenced in by the overhanging caprock, was an ideal spot for a ranch: it furnished water and shelter in the winter and the adjacent plains provided ideal grazing in the summer.

Upper division of this ranch (the park area) was reserved for the purebred, or JJ herd. The vast lower end of the JA was ranged by longhorns—gradually being improved by better blood.

In 1887 the Goodnight-Adair partnership was ended. Adair retained the JA which, in the hands of his heirs, is still one of the great ranches of Texas.   (1968)

CANYON (Randall Co.)
SH 217, 4 mi. E

Los Ciboleros
(New Mexican Buffalo Hunters)

For centuries Pueblo Indians of present New Mexico trekked to the plains to hunt buffalo to supplement their diet of beans and corn. After acquiring horses from the Spanish in the 17th century, the annual trips were made more easily and with greater success. By the 19th century, the ciboleros (from "Cibolo"—Spanish for buffalo) became very important, providing food for the growing New Mexican population and hides for the rich Santa Fe-Chihuahua trade.

Cibolero expeditions often included as many an 150 people. The daring cazadores (hunters), picturesque in leather jackets and flat straw hats, rode into the herds armed only with lances, killing 8 to 25 bison each in one foray, and depending on the speed, ability, and skill of their horses for safety. Others, including occasional women and children, cut meat into strip for drying and cured the hides for tanning. With their carts laden with fruits of the hunt, the ciboleros returned to New Mexico and a hero's welcome.

The Plains Indians, protecting their hunting grounds, maintained constant warfare against the ciboleros throughout the 19th century, but the colorful lancers survived until Anglo-American hunters decimated the great buffalo herd in the late 1870s.   (1973)

89

CANYON (Randall Co.) *US 60/87 at SH 217, 1.9 mi. N*
T-Anchor Ranch Headquarters
Built by Leigh R. Dyer, 1877, of logs cut from Palo Duro Canyon. Oldest surviving house in Texas Panhandle.

Dyer did first Panhandle farming. Sold 1878, to Gunter, Summerfield and Munson. Became center of area ranching and development. (1967)

CANYON (Randall Co.) *US 87, 1.5 mi. SW*
Homesite of
W. F. Heller, Pioneer Farmer
Native Texan, Civil War Veteran (1861–1865); settled here in 1887. Was first to farm area successfully.

Was elected first clerk when county organized 1889. Also helped organize first Sunday School, 1890. Married Susan Roberts, Sept. 1897.

Helped start West Texas State Normal College. A Friend to Strangers in Our County (1968)

CANYON (Randall Co.) *SH 217, 4 mi. E*
First Thanksgiving in America, 1541
Feast of first Thanksgiving by Pedro Fray Juan de Padillo for Coronado and his troops in Palo Duro Canyon 79 years before the Pilgrims.

Marker placed by Texas Society Daughters of the American Colonies. (1959)

CANYON (Randall Co.) *US 87, 14 mi. S*
Site of
Old Happy
The Hugh Currie family home, "Happy Hollow" (built 1891, near this site), was for many years only house of Amarillo-Tulia freights and stage lines. Settlers got mail and freight here. The U.S. Postal Department cut name to "Happy" for the post office. The town moved (2 mi. W) to Santa Fe Line, 1906. (1973)

CARRIZO SPRINGS (Dimmit Co.) *US 83, 3.7 mi. N*
Dimmit County
Created February 1, 1858. Organized November 2, 1880. Named in honor of Philip Dimmitt, a pioneer trader and captain in the Texas Army who died in 1841. Carrizo Springs, the County Seat.

CARRIZO SPRINGS (Dimmit Co.) *103 N. 5th St. (US 277)*
Dimmit County Courthouse
Named for one of the framers of the Texas Declaration of Independence, Dimmit County was created from four other counties in 1858. The county was formally organized in 1880, and Carrizo Springs was chosen as the county seat. On November 12, 1883, the County Commissioners Court chose noted architect Alfred Giles to design a permanent courthouse for Dimmit County. Later that month, on November 26, the court reversed its decision and selected J.C. Breeding & Sons of San Antonio to act as both architects and builders. Probably working from Giles' initial plans, they erected a structure which featured a double gallery porch. The building's cubical form and Italianate detailing resemble Giles' designs for other Texas courthouses erected about the same time. By the 1920s, the thriving Dimmit County needed a larger government facility. The Commissioners Court called in Henry T. Phelps to design an expansion. At Phelps' instruction, the San Antonio Construction Company demolished the north second story wall, removing exterior rock from the lower north and south walls and adding new, longer wings on each end. As was his custom, Phelps worked along a Classical Revival plan, requiring a symmetrical façade. He relocated the main entrance to the west side of the building, highlighting it with four massive columns and a recessed porch. The 19th century windows were widened, and Phelps changed the Second Empire roofline to an elaborate cornice. The architectural character of the Dimmit County courthouse was transformed from a simplified Italianate style of the late 1880s to the restrained Classicism popular in the 1920s. (2000)

CARRIZO SPRINGS (Dimmit Co.)
US 277, .4 mi. NW
Burleson Cemetery
Among the earliest settlers in the area later named Dimmit County, the Burleson family settled near Carrizo Springs between 1865 and 1870. James A. (1869–1895), Joseph E. (1870–1895), and Samuel (1877–1895) Burleson died suddenly, probably of food poisoning. The following July, Marion M. Burleson (1853–1895) succumbed to heat stroke and was buried on family land with his brothers and a Burleson child. As time passed, the graves on this site became a mystery. Investigations at the end of the twentieth century by the Texas Department of Transportation found it to be the final resting place of the Burleson family. (1998)

CARTHAGE (Panola Co.)
US 79, 24 mi. NE
Site of Bethany
A thriving town of the fifties. Through it passed the Shreveport Road, over which many emigrants entered Texas.

CARTHAGE (Panola Co.)
US 59, 12 mi. S just off hwy.
Woods Methodist Church
Organized as Methodist Church Concord; had a house of worship before 1858. Present site was deeded to church Nov. 28, 1876, by E. S. Hull. This building was erected by men of community in winter of 1876–1877. About 1900 name was changed, to conform to local post office (named for first postmaster, Theodorick B. Wood, appointed Jan. 16, 1854).
This church is one of oldest buildings in Panola County still in use. (1970)

CARTHAGE (Panola Co.)
US 79 at 59, Anderson Park on the square
Margie Neal
(1875–1971)
A native of Panola County, Margie Elizabeth Neal began her career as a teacher in 1893. She became editor and owner of the *East Texas Register* newspaper in 1904. A respected educator and leader in the woman suffrage movement, she was the first woman appointed to the State Normal School Board of Regents in 1921. Five years later she made history as the first woman elected to the Texas Senate. After serving in several federal positions in Washington, she returned to Carthage in 1945 and was active in civic affairs for many years. (1988)

CARTHAGE (Panola Co.)
US 79 (109 W. Panola St.)
The Panola Watchman
Tom M. Bowers (1837–1916) printed the first issue of *The Watchman* on July 2, 1873. He had published the *Carthage Banner* here from 1859 until he left about 1861 to serve in the Confederate Army. Type was handset, and news items came from other publications and letters to the editor. Following Bowers' ownership, the paper was headed by three state representatives—T. E. Boren, Jasper Collins, and O. P. Carswell—between 1884 and 1906. R. M. Park added a Linotype machine in 1915. In 1971, the publishers converted to offset, sending printing to Marshall. In 1984, the first offset press was installed. (Texas Sesquicentennial 1836–1986)

CARTHAGE (Panola Co.)
US 79, 4.5 mi. E
The Respess Family and Respess Creek
In the 1870s Richard Ormand Respess (1839–1906) and his wife Nannie Lois Williams moved here from Harrison County. Respess gave the land and taught at the first school built in the Frog Pond community, known later as Liberty Chapel. His oldest son Charlie O. (1859–1917) lived near this site and operated a general store. During the years that the family allowed free access for perch and cat fishing, the stream became known as "Respess Creek." It is the only reminder of the pioneer family who lived here. (1979)

CARTHAGE (Panola Co.)
FM 1971, 16 mi. SW
Walter Prescott Webb
(April 3, 1888–March 8, 1963)
The world-renowned American historian Walter Prescott Webb was born near this site. His parents were Casner P. and Mary Elizabeth (Kyle) Webb. C. P. Webb farmed and taught school. The

family moved in 1893 to the edge of central West Texas. There a startling new terrain spurred young Walter to study the influence of the frontier on American history.

Alternately studying and teaching, Walter Webb earned his B.A. degree in 1915, his M.A. in 1920, and his Ph.D. in 1932, all at the University of Texas. In 1918, he joined the history faculty of the University in Austin, where he taught for 45 years. Visiting lectureships in the U.S. and abroad included a term as Harmsworth Professor at Oxford University in England. An inspiring teacher, he molded a generation of historians and scholarly writers. *The Great Plains, The Texas Rangers, Divided We Stand, The Great Frontier,* and his other books are works of splendid vision. Recipient of many honors and offices, he was the first Southwesterner to serve as President of the American Historical Association.

He married (1) Jane Oliphant, by whom he had one daughter, Mildred (Mrs. W. B. Bugg), and (2) Mrs. Terrell Maverick. He is buried in the Texas State Cemetery.   (1977)

CASTELL (Llano Co.)   *FM 2768, on north side of Llano River*
German Settlements
In 1847 on Fisher-Miller Land Grant, three settlements were begun by German Emigration Company under Commissioner General John O. Meusebach.

Castell; settled by Fredericksburg pioneers of the German Emigration Company, was first only permanent Llano County settlement.

Leiningen; site three miles to the East. Non-existent today.

Bettina: First communal settlement in Texas. Located where Elm Creek enters Llano River. Abandoned in less than a year, when supplies ran out.   (1964)

CASTROVILLE (Medina Co.)   *US 90, 1 block N, Isabelle and Paris St.*
Cordier-Tschirhart-Seal House
Jean Baptiste Cordier (1804–1881) built this Alsatian pioneer dwelling after migrating to Texas in 1844. The native limestone structure had three downstairs rooms and an attic. Cordier sold the cottage in 1847 to blacksmith Stephan Ahr (1821–1903) and shoemaker Jacob Biry (1810–1867), whose families occupied it together. In 1906 the house was purchased by Eugenia Beck (Mrs. Sebastian) Tschirhart (1861–1938). It was restored by her descendants, Mr. and Mrs. Adrian L. Seal.   (1976)

CASTROVILLE (Medina Co.)   *Houston Square*
Alsatians of Texas
In 1842, empresario Henry Castro brought his first colonists to Texas to settle land west of the Medina River. Most of the immigrants were from the Rhine River area of Europe. Many claimed the province of Alsace, on the border of France and Germany, as their homeland. The Alsatian colonists brought with them their combined French and German heritage, which has left a distinctive mark on this area of the state.

In 1844, Castro laid out a townsite, which the settlers chose to name Castroville. It became the center of Alsatian culture in Texas. The houses, European in style, are primarily single-story dwellings of cut limestone, mortared with adobe, and white-washed. Over the years, farming has been the major occupation of people in the area, as it was in Alsace.

The Alsatian immigrants and their descendants have made a distinct impression on area politics, holiday customs, cuisine, and religion. Winemaking, using grapes grown along the Medina River, is another early tradition that has continued over the years.

The history of Alsatians in Texas is a reflection of ethnic and cultural diversity in the state's rich heritage.   (1985)

CASTROVILLE (Medina Co.)   *US 90 W, Moye Formation Center*
Moye
Named for the Rev. John Martin Moye, founder (1762) of the Sisters of Divine Providence, religious order that opened school in Castroville in 1868, and built first part of this structure in 1873: first mother house of the order in the United States.

Occupants since 1900 have been Providence Industrial School, St. Philip's Seminary, refuge for persecution victims, and several other endeavors.

Repurchased 1939 by Sisters of Divine Providence and used as military academy for boys. Now used as training center for religious life. (1972)

CASTROVILLE (Medina Co.) *E US 90 approach to Medina Bridge*
Landmark Inn
Built as a one story home and store, about 1844 by French settler Caesar Monad. Later became Vance Inn, after top floor and bath house were added to accommodate travelers.

Civil War bullets were made of the lead lining peeled off a room of the bath house in 1860s.

After 1927, Jordan T. Lawler and his sister Ruth Lawler, natives of New Orleans, La., owned and restored Inn.

CASTROVILLE (Medina Co.) *US 90, 1 block N*
St. Louis Church
Built by Alsatian settlers of Castro Colony, in Republic of Texas. Dedicated by Rt. Rev. John Odin, C. M. First Catholic Bishop of Texas, on November 9, 1846.

Claude Dubuis, 1847 pastor, was later Bishop of Texas. Here in 1868 Sisters of Divine Providence opened their first permanent school in Texas. First Mother House of Order in Texas. Marked 100th anniversary of founding of the Sister of Divine Providence in Texas.

CATARINA (Dimmit Co.) *19290 S US 83*
Catarina Hotel
Catarina grew around headquarters of the Sinton-Taft Ranch, later called Taft-Catarina Ranch. Kansas businessmen C.H. Kearny, J.E. Jarrett and H.V. Wheeler bought the ranch in the 1920s for development, attracting many buyers. By 1928, the town had approximately 2,500 residents and many businesses, including this hotel. In 1925–26, C.H. Kearny and Lee Peters designed and built the hotel in the Spanish eclectic style, with features including tile roofs and mission elements, cast stone detailing, and a U-shaped plan with courtyard and fish pond. The building, which once also housed a bank, café, shops and offices, is a reminder of the town's boom era. (2002)

CEDAR HILL (Dallas Co.) *102 S US 67 at Belt Line Rd.*
City of Cedar Hill
Prospective settlers who traveled to this area during the 19th century were attracted to its high prairie hill and established a community here known as Cedar Hill in the late 1840s. Its early economy was based on providing support services for the surrounding farm communities. Cedar Hill was struck by a disastrous tornado in 1856, which slowed growth until the railroad came through in 1882. The town experienced a transition from rural to urban development during the late 20th century. It remains one of Dallas County's oldest settlements. (1985)

CELESTE (Hunt Co.) *US 69, at east edge of Celeste*
Audie Murphy
Most decorated soldier in World War II. Born 4.5 miles south, June 20, 1924, sixth of nine children of tenant farmers Emmett and Josie Killian Murphy. Living on various farms, Audie Murphy went to school through the 8th grade in Celeste—considered the family's home town. He had to quit school to help support the family, acquiring marksmanship skills by hunting to provide food. On his 18th birthday, after being rejected by the Marines because of his size (5 feet, 7 inches; 130 pounds), He enlisted in the Army while working in Greenville.

For unusual courage and bravery, he received 24 decorations, including the U.S. Congressional Medal of Honor; the French Legion of Honor, Chevalier; the Distinguished Service Cross; and a Silver Star.

After the war he became a successful actor, his most prominent role portraying himself in the film "To Hell and Back," his war career autobiography.

Following his untimely death in a plane crash in Virginia, May 28, 1971, and burial in Arlington National Cemetery, the U.S. Congress paid him a final tribute, dedicating a new veterans' hospital in San Antonio to the memory of this American hero.

Survived by widow Pamela, sons Terry and James. (1973)

CENTER (Shelby Co.)

US 84, 1.5 mi. E of Paxton Switch

Site of 1870s–1900 Town of Spivey

Founded by Civil War veteran James Jackson Spivey; brothers Elisha P. and George W. Spivey lived nearby. In early days mail arrived by wagon. Houston East & West Texas Railroad crossed the founder's land, building Spivey Station, 1886. During late 1880s Hicks Lumber Mill and workers' houses were erected. U.S. post office was established in 1891, with Isaac W. Spivey, postmaster. Friendship Baptist Church was organized in 1890s with James M. Spivey, pastor. After 1900, town gradually moved over to Paxton Switch. Friendship Cemetery, with 33 graves, marks the old site. (1971)

CENTER POINT (Kerr Co.)

SH 27, .5 mi. E of FM 480

Site of Zanzenberg

Home of Dr. Charles de Ganahl (1824–1883), a signer of the Texas Articles of Secession in 1861 and army surgeon for the Confederate States of America.

The home was erected in 1856 and named after Dr. Ganahl's ancestral home in the Austrian Tyrol of Europe.

Here the first post office in Kerr County was established in 1857 with his wife Virginia (1834–1895) as the first postmaster. (1968)

CENTERVILLE (Henderson Co.)

SH 85, 1.25 mi. S of; 6 mi. NW of Eustace

Site of Centerville

Replaced Buffalo as county seat, 1848, due to central location in county; on land donated by James Harper Starr (1809–1890), Texas statesman. Clerk's records were kept in a log cabin court-house. When county was reduced in area, 1850, county seat was moved to Athens, and Centerville died. (1973)

CHANDLER (Henderson Co.)

.2 mi. E of post office

C. R. Yarborough Home

Occupied since 1903 by Charles Richard and Nannie Jane Spear Yarborough and 3 generations of descendants. Birthplace in 1903 of United States Senator Ralph Webster Yarborough.

In this house Charles R. Yarborough, as Justice of the Peace, performed many marriage ceremonies. In this house, he and Mrs. Yarborough, on June 13, 1939, celebrated their 50th wedding anniversary. Here on Jan. 1, 1959, he administered to his son the oath of office as senator of the United States.

C. R. Yarborough died here Oct. 24, 1964, aged 100 years, 11 days. (1966)

CHANNING (Hartley Co.)

Main Street

XIT Headquarters 1890

Business office for 3,000,000-acre ranch of syndicate that built the Texas State Capitol. (1964)

CHANNING (Hartley Co.)

Courthouse Square

Hartley County Courthouse

Hartley County was created in January 1891, and an election held that year designated the town of Hartley as county seat. A frame courthouse was built on the town square.

In October 1896, largely due to XIT Ranch interests, a second election was held which resulted in the removal of the county seat to Channing. The frame courthouse was dismantled and moved to the new county seat, where it was reconstructed.

In May 1905, the commissioners court approved the construction of a new courthouse. Contracts were awarded to Solan & Wickens, Contractors, and O. G. Roquemore, architect. The two-story structure was completed in October 1906 at a cost of $10,525. The Beaux Arts style building features a triumphal arch on the front facade, native sandstone base, and Roman Ionic paired columns. When completed, the top story provided a courtroom and two offices, and there were five offices and a lobby on the first floor. At the time of construction, the building was served by its own water well and lighting system. A vault was added to the county clerk's office in 1927. A second vault and jury dormitories were built in 1935.

(Recorded Texas Historic Landmark—1987)

CHAPPELL HILL (Washington Co.)   *US 290 at FM 1155*
Chappell Hill
Founded 1847. Named for Robert Chappell, an 1841 settler. Early education center, with Chappell Hill Male and Female Institute, 1852, and Soule University, 1850.

Male students marched away to Civil War in 1861. C.S.A. Quartermaster Depot located here. Many early Texas landmarks in vicinity.

CHAPPELL HILL (Washington Co.)   *Old US 290, 1 mi. E*
Lockhart Plantation
Home built 1850 by Dr. John W. Lockhart, Chappell Hill physician and frequent host of Sam Houston. House is of cedar and black walnut handcut on rich 1,000-acre place that had its own blacksmith shop, cotton gin, store, other facilities.   (1964)

CHEROKEE (San Saba Co.)   *SH 16, at site of college (now high school)*
Site of Old Behrns West Texas
Normal and Business College
Opened 1895 by noted educator Francis Marion Behrns. A 3-story native blue marble main hall and frame dormitory were built by interested local citizens.

Courses included mathematics, natural sciences, Latin, oratory, commercial subjects, literature, psychology, music and painting. Character building was stressed. Its graduates led in teaching and other professions.

After the Behrns school closed in 1903, buildings were used by Cherokee Junior College; after 1921, by public schools. In 1945, fire destroyed old main hall.   (1966)

CHERRY SPRINGS (Gillespie Co.)   *US 87, 2.5 mi. S in roadside park*
John O. Meusebach
(1812–1897)
To be a Texan, Meusebach gave up title of baron in 1845. As commissioner-general, German Emigration Company, he founded Fredericksburg in 1846 as gateway to Fisher-Miller Land Grant, hunting ground of the Comanche. By emptying his fire-arms, he won trust of Indians and made treaty to provide for unmolested settlement. Indians called him "El Sol Colorado" (The Red Sun).

State senator, 1851. In 1854 issued colonists' headrights.

To his family motto, he added "Texas Forever." Lived in Loyal Valley. Grave near Cherry Spring.   (1964)

CHESTER (Tyler Co.)   *FM 1745, 11 mi. NE at Fort Teran Park*
Fort Teran Park
Named an historical site by the Texas Centennial Committee, 1936—101 years after closing of fort.

Park was donated in 1966 to Tyler County Historical Survey Committee by Mrs. Winnie Wilson in memory of her husband, S. Earl Wilson, who preserved fort site.   (1968)

CHICO (Wise Co.)   *FM 1810, 2 mi. E*
Indian Captives Dot and Bianca Babb
(Captured 2 mi. S; This Town on Getaway Route)
Two of Texas history's best-known Indian captives, 13-year-old T. A. "Dot" Babb (1852–1936) and his 9-year-old sister Bianca (1855?–1950) were stolen by Comanches from their home near here in September of 1865.

While at play one day, the children were surprised by a raiding party of 35 to 40 Indians. Mrs. Babb was killed and Dot, Bianca, and a Mrs. Luster (a visitor) were taken to Indian Territory (present Oklahoma). After helping Mrs. Luster escape on the way, Dot was very nearly executed, but so stoic was he in facing death that the Indians admiringly spared his life.

For the next two years Dot and Bianca lived, in different tribes, as adopted Comanches. Bianca later recalled that the Indians held a feast—with coffee, a luxury—upon her arrival and that they colored her blonde hair with charcoal and buffalo tallow.

Dot, after a winter as the squaws' flunky, asserted his male rights and thereafter spent his time taming horses. He was taken on raids against other tribes and showed signs of becoming a fine warrior.

After two years, the children's father ransomed them and a joyful reunion occurred. Both Dot and Bianca spoke with sympathy, however, of many Indian customs and of kind treatment during captivity. (1971)

CHILDRESS (Childress Co.)   *17 mi. N*
Site of Buck Creek Stage Stand
Established in 1882 by Frank Chriss. A stop on the mail route from Wichita Falls to Tascosa. Abandoned in 1886 after the Ft. Worth and Denver Railroad reached this region. (1964)

CHILDRESS (Childress Co.)   *US 287, 3 mi. SE in roadside park*
(moved to Courthouse Square)
Colonel Wm. Edgar Hughes
of the Mill Iron
Born 1840. Came from Illinois to Texas, 1859. During Civil War rose from private, 1st Texas Artillery, to colonel in 16th Cavalry. Was in bloody battles of Shiloh, Chickamauga, Nashville, Richmond. After war, when "didn't have 2 pairs of pants," taught school and read law in Weatherford. As lawyer, took many land cases. In 7 years became organizer and president, City Bank of Dallas (now 1st National, Dallas). Later an officer in Exchange Bank, Dallas; Union Trust Co., St. Louis; Continental Trust Co., Denver.

In 1880 bought half interest in Mill Iron Ranch. Purchased small holdings from Pease to Red River—Bridle Bits, DV'S, Diamond D's and others. Range lay in Childress, Cottle, Hall, Motley Counties. In 1885 added windmills, wells, to run larger herds—up to 50,000. In early years used dugouts, chuckwagons for headquarters. First small ranchhouse was built at windmill 62, near Estelline.

Bought out Rocking Chair Ranch, Collingsworth County, 1896. Until 1898 ran only longhorns. Was said to have had the largest men, most practical jokers, longest cattle drives, biggest horses in Texas. He sold off the last Mill Iron herd in 1918—year of his death. (1965)

CHILDRESS (Childress Co.)   *US 83 at FM 1034, 20 mi. N of Childress*
On Old Shoenail Ranch Land, Community of Loco
(2 mi. E)
Named for weed found here in 1880s by early settlers—the families of Dick Brown, Walter Campbell, and Bobby Payne. The Browns survived the last Indian battle of Buck Creek in 1887.

Soil-based local economy moved from mule-power to tractors with lugs, to rubber-tire tractors, to irrigation farming. The Loco Post Office was established in 1892. Town at its height had 4 churches, a high school, a garage, 2 cotton gins, 3 stores, barber shop, blacksmith shop, cafe, and a golf course. Little now remains except the school's storm cellar. The post office closed in 1964. (1970)

CHILLICOTHE (Hardeman Co.)   *301 Avenue J South (US 287)*
Chillicothe First Methodist Church
Originally organized in 1886 in the Jackson Springs community, this church was first served by circuit riders C. T. Neese and J. T. Hosmer. Shortly after the Fort Worth and Denver City Railway came through Chillicothe in 1887, the Jackson Springs Church moved into town. This edifice was erected at the church's second Chillicothe location. Designed by prominent area architect Rockwell Henry Stuckey (1855–1936) in 1916, the structure features classical columns, cornice and eaves. Notable elements include the ornate stained glass windows and octagonal dome, a feature often associated with Stuckey's work. The original stained glass windows were crafted in Germany during World War I and crossed the Atlantic three times before being accepted at New York and shipped to Chillicothe by train. (1998)

CHILLICOTHE (Hardeman Co.)

FM 392, 6 mi. SW on grounds of Research Station

Texas Agricultural Experiment Station, Substation No. 12
Home of Hybrid Sorghums

Forage crop field station at which in 1909 (when situated 6 mi. NE) was planted the United States' first Sudan grass, a sorghum especially adaptable to semi-arid regions. The United States Department of Agriculture had brought the seed from Khartum, Africa. Here ensued more than a half-century of sorghum breeding under supervision of A. B. Conner, J. R. Quinby, J. C. Stephens and other scientists, culminating in hybrid seed for more productive crops that revolutionized the agriculture of the Great Plains. (1971)

CHILTON (Falls Co.)

US 77, 6 mi. N

Site of North Prairie School

On June 8, 1896, the citizens of North Prairie petitioned the Falls County Commissioners Court for a community school district, and North Prairie School District No. 65 was created. In 1910 a 2-room school housed two teachers and about 20 students. By 1926 the North Prairie School had grown to include about 30 students with three teachers providing instruction in nine grades. World War II called away many of North Prairie's young people. The community declined in population as did many community schools of the era, and in 1946 the North Prairie School District was consolidated with nearby Chilton schools. The North Prairie schoolhouse was razed within a few years, but remains a significant part of local history. (1999)

CHIRENO (Nacogdoches Co.)

SH 21, 3 mi. NW

Half Way House—Old Stage Coach Inn
Built 1850

Pre-Texas Revolution stage stop on King's Highway from San Antonio Nacogdoches-San Augustine-Natchitoches; also a post office under the Republic; overnight accommodations to progenitors of Texas Revolution.

CHRIESMAN (Burleson Co.)

SH 36, 7.5 mi. NW of Caldwell

Alexander Thomson
(August 29, 1785–June 1, 1863)

A leader in colonizing Texas. Born in St. Matthews Parish, S. C.; lived also in Georgia, then in Tennessee where in 1830 he became partner of the Empresario in development of the Sterling C. Robertson Colony. Conducting a number of families who had signed agreements to settle in the Robertson Colony, he crossed into Texas and came to Nacogdoches three days after Mexican officials there received notice of 1830 law requiring passports of immigrants. After Thomson tried unsuccessfully to have rule waived for hardship reasons, the party bypassed Nacogdoches, making a new trail often used afterward and known as the Tennesseans' Road. Thomson lived for a time in Austin's Colony, representing District of Hidalgo (now Washington County) at Texas Convention of 1832. By 1835, when he was consultation delegate from Viesca (later Milam Municipality), he was living and serving as official surveyor in Robertson's Colony. Still a leader, he was Robertson's executor in 1842. Married twice, father of 13, he was ancestor of many noted Texans, including Thaddeus A. Thomson, United States envoy to Colombia and sign-er of the Thomson-Urrutia Treaty in 1914. Alexander Thomson is buried in Thomson Family Cemetery one mile to the northeast.

CHRIESMAN (Burleson Co.)

SH 36 at FM 1363

Chriesman

Chriesman (originally "Yellow Prairie," 0.5 miles east). Settled by Alexander Thomson, Jr., early Texas patriot and partner of the colonizer Sterling C. Robertson. When railroad came through in 1880, the settlers moved to tracks. Renamed, 1884, after Capt. H. C. Chriesman, surveyor for Stephen F. Austin. Now serves surrounding ranches.

CHRISTOVAL (Tom Green Co.)   *US 277, at Anson Clubhouse*
Christoval
Frontiersmen began to immigrate into the south Concho Valley in 1870s, locating along the "Toe Nail" Trail from Fort McKavett to Fort Concho. By mid-1880s the settlement began to develop and a union church was organized. The South Concho Irrigation Co. was established in 1885, and built a dam and 3 miles of canals to furnish water to dry farmland.

Christopher C. Doty (1857–1944), who had arrived in Texas in 1879, opened a store and applied for a post office in 1888. After rejection of application for "Alice," due to another office of that name, Doty suggested "Christobal" (Spanish for Christopher). Confirmation of establishment of the office and Doty's appointment as postmaster arrived in Jan. 1889, but the spelling of the name had been changed to Christoval.

After flood in Aug. 1906, a tract of bottomland was purchased for a city park, which became popular Baptist campground and site of Confederate reunions, both attended by thousands of regional residents. A bath house, built in 1915 at nearby Mineral Wells, was first of several local health facilities.

Arrival of the Panhandle & Santa Fe Railroad, in 1930, made Christoval a shipping point for area sheep, wool, and cattle industries.   (1973)

CIBOLO (Guadalupe Co.)   *SH 78, City Park*
Cibolo
A town began to grow here after the Galveston, Harrisburg and San Antonio Railroad built a line through western Guadalupe County in 1875. A general store, operated by George Schlather and Ernst Jenull, was opened the following year to serve the predominantly German population. A post office was established in 1876, and the town was named Cibolo from an Indian word for buffalo. The community was also known as Fromme's Store after Charles Fromme purchased the general store in 1882. Cibolo was officially incorporated in 1965.   (Texas Sesquicentennial 1836–1986)

CLAIRETTE (Erath Co.)   *SH 6*
Clairette Cemetery
Joseph and Elizabeth Salmon and their children moved to the Republic of Texas in 1839. They settled in this area in 1854. When their 15-year-old son, Albert, died in 1858, he was buried at his favorite campsite in a grove of oak trees on the family land. Albert's brother, Joseph Salmon, Jr., deeded the acre of land surrounding the grave site for use as a community cemetery in 1876. Additional land acquisitions over the years have increased the size of the cemetery. The diverse styles of gravestones found here serve as reflections of the area's pioneer heritage.   (1991)

CLAIREMONT (Kent Co.)   *US 380 at SH 208*
Old Kent County Jail
Built 1894, of red sandstone quarried nearby. Horse and cattle thieves, murderers, moonshiners most common prisoners. One of most difficult West Texas jails from which to escape. No attempted break successful.   (1965)

CLARENDON (Donley Co.)   *US 287 at SH 70 in roadside park*
Donley County
Formed from Young and Bexar Territories. Created August 21, 1876; organized March 22, 1882. Named in honor of Stockton P. Donley 1821–1871, a Confederate officer elected to the Texas Supreme Bench in 1866. Clarendon, the county seat.   (1964)

CLARENDON (Donley Co.)   *SH 70, 5 mi. N*
Clarendon Cemetery
In this first cemetery of Donley County, sixteen rods west lie the first dead of Old Clarendon. Here white civilization sank its roots in sadness, and from the graves in this sacred acre strong pioneer spirits turned to face the future with greater love for the land and a firmer determination to build for a tomorrow which we know today. To those of the Old Clarendon Colony who first found rest on this bold promontory and to their survivors, this stone of imperishable Texas granite is loyally and lovingly dedicated. Erected by the State of Texas, July 4, 1938.

CLARENDON (Donley Co.) *SH 70, 5 mi. N*
Replica of First Donley County Courthouse
(Originally about 6 mi. NW)
Soon after founding in 1878 of Clarendon Colony by the Rev. Lewis H. Carhart, workers were brought from Vermont to quarry local stone and erect 2-story structure for hotel, stagecoach stand, and public meeting hall.

With organization of Donley County, April 11, 1882, Clarendon was named county seat. The hotel became (and remained for years) the first courthouse—and third courthouse in entire Panhandle of Texas. It served settlers in an 8,000-square mile area, since eight unorganized counties were for years attached for judicial purposes to Donley County.   (1967)

CLARENDON (Donley Co.) *SH 70, 20 mi. NNW*
Boydstun Cemetery
(3.7 mi. SW)
Pioneer area settler Henry S. Boydstun (1858–1942), a native of Illinois, moved his family to this area in 1890. That year, his infant son, Eddie, died and was buried in the southwest corner of the family farm. In 1898, Boydstun deeded two acres at the site for use as a public burial ground. A small farming community that developed near there included a school and, from 1891 to 1940, a post office (listed as Boydston). Although Boydstun deeded land for the cemetery, he and his wife, Mary (d. 1950), were interred in the nearby town of Groom.   (1988)

CLARENDON (Donley Co.) *SH 70, 4 mi. N of Salt Fork*
Old Mobeetie Trail
(To Early Town, About 40 mi. NE)
A road older than recorded history, carved out in centuries of wintertime travel to the south, spring migration to the north, by millions of bison and by Indians who lived by hunting these large animals.

Important in era of Texas Panhandle settlement.

Used in 1873–1874, when first lifelong residents put dugout dwellings in the Panhandle and began to hunt buffalo to fill demand for hides and meat.

Fort Elliott, established 1875 to regulate Indians resisting white settlement, soon had as a neighbor the town of Mobeetie, which for some years was the county seat for 28 counties and a place to go for medical aid, supplies and access to stage travel.

In 1876 Kansans came this way south for better hunting, calling this "Rath Trail," for their leader. Also in 1876 cattlemen began to bring herds here. By 1880 this ancient path was a southern arm of Jones and Plummer Trail, over which cowboys moved longhorns to railroads and northern cattle markets.

Beginning about 1887 the Mobeetie Trail was used by "nesters" taking up farm lands alongside the old great ranches. Those it served founded and expanded agricultural-commercial economy of the Panhandle.   (1966)

CLARKSVILLE (Red River Co.) *US 82, 1 mi. W*
A House of the
William Becknell Family
William Becknell (1788–1856) of Missouri is renowned for opening the Santa Fe Trail from the United States into Spain's new world empire in 1821. He and his wife Mary settled in 1835 near here, on Becknell's prairie, with a daughter and two sons. On the way to the Alamo, David Crockett visited them. Becknell himself fought in 1836 in the Texas War for Independence. After milled lumber became available, he or his family built the earliest portion of this house. It was later enlarged and relocated.   (1978)

CLARKSVILLE (Red River Co.) *US 82, 1 mi. W*
City of Clarksville
Incorporated December 29, 1837. Named in honor of James Clark who settled here in 1834.

CLARKSVILLE (Red River Co.)
Shiloh Cumberland Presbyterian Church
US 82, 6 mi. E, Shiloh Cemetery

In this vicinity Shiloh Cumberland Presbyterian Church was organized in June 1833 by Rev. Milton Estill.

CLARKSVILLE (Red River Co.)
J.D. Tippit
SH 37 at CR 1280, 6 mi. SW

Slain in the line of duty while on alert for President John F. Kennedy's assassin, J.D. Tippit (1924–1963) grew up on his family's farm near this site. He served as a paratrooper in the 17th Airborne Division during World War II and received the Bronze Star. J.D. married his high school sweetheart in 1946 and started a family in Red River County. He joined the Dallas Police Department in 1952 and later was honored for his quick thinking and outstanding judgment. On November 22, 1963, Tippit was working a beat in central Oak Cliff when he stopped Lee Harvey Oswald for questioning. Oswald shot and killed him. J.D. Tippit, who left a wife and three children, is buried at Laurel Land Memorial Park in Dallas. (2001)

CLARKSVILLE (Red River Co.)
Site of McKenzie College
SH 37, 3.5 mi. SW

An outstanding school in the Southwest before the Civil War. Established in 1841 by the Reverend John W. P. McKenzie (1806–1877), pioneer missionary of the Choctaws, circuit rider in Texas in 1838. Opened in a log cabin, it expanded to four large buildings on 900 acres. Chartered January 10, 1854. Enrolled 300 boarding pupils annually. Closed in 1869.

CLARKSVILLE (Red River Co.)
The Rev. William Stevenson
(October 4, 1768–March 5, 1857)
Courthouse Sq.

Frontier minister; friend of Stephen F. Austin, Father of Texas.

A circuit rider in Missouri Conference, Methodist Church, Mr. Stevenson in 1815 made a pastoral trip to Pecan Point, home of Claiborne Wright, member of newly-arrived Anglo-American colony on Texas side of the Red River. Records indicate that his preaching to Wright and friends in 1815 constituted the first Protestant sermons ever given in Texas, then part of Catholic "New Spain." He thus established a beachhead for religious freedom in Texas at this point of entry. (1972)

CLARKSVILLE (Red River Co.)
Red River County Jail
SH 37 at West Madison St.

This building was completed in 1889 as the second jail for Red River County. Architects Maj. S. B. Haggart and Marshall Sanguinet designed the structure as a companion building to the county courthouse, which had been completed five years earlier. The elaborate high Victorian Italianate styling of the Red River County jail features finely crafted stonework and intricate metal cornices. (1982)

CLAUDE (Armstrong Co.)
The Great Panhandle Indian Scare of 1891
Courthouse lawn

Although most Indians had left the Panhandle plains by the 1880s, fear of Indian attacks was still prevalent among settlers who arrived in the next decade. On Jan. 29, 1891, rumors of approaching Indians spread throughout the entire region. For three days settlers hastily prepared to defend themselves by fleeing or barricading their homes and replenishing their weapon and ammunition supplies. Later it was discovered that the rumored Indian war cries and smoke signals were actually ranchers in pursuit of a steer they finally caught and cooked over an open fire. (1983)

CLAUDE (Armstrong Co.)
Armstrong County
Courthouse lawn

Created 1876. Name honors several Texas pioneers named Armstrong. Ranching became the chief industry when huge JA Ranch was established here in 1876.

Farming was introduced after the railroad came through, 1887. County was organized in 1890. Present courthouse was built 1912. (1969)

CLAUDE (Armstrong Co.)   *US 287, one block W of town square, at site*
Armstrong County Jail
Erected in 1953, this building is constructed of stone used to build the first masonry jail in Armstrong County, 1894. Stone for the structure (which replaced a primitive, frame "calaboose") was quarried 14 miles south at Dripping Springs in Palo Duro Canyon and then hauled here in wagons driven by local citizens. The rock was cut at this site.

The 1894 building had two stories, topped by a dome, and 20-inch walls. So sturdy was it that dangerous convicts from other counties were kept here. Old-timers remember that only three prisoners ever escaped.   (1969)

CLAUDE (Armstrong Co.)   *US 287, 1.5 mi. W and 1 mi. N*
Claude Cemetery
(Established 1890)
Dan Cavanagh settled here in 1885 and bought this land in 1888. In 1890, he gave a grave site for railroad worker Neal DeBerry. Settler C. C. Bates was buried in 1890, and early burials from the Fort Worth & Denver Railroad right-of-way were later moved here. James and Harriet Grimes deeded the cemetery land to the public in 1905. A cemetery association was organized in 1912, and perpetual care began in 1936 with a $10,000 gift from Jim Hill. Also interred here are veterans of the Civil War, the Spanish American War, World Wars I and II, Korea, and Vietnam.   (1973, 1990)

CLAUDE (Armstrong Co.)   *FM 1258—23 mi. SW, at*
      Harrell Ranch Headquarters
Old Home Ranch
First ranch in the Panhandle, established in 1876 by Charles Goodnight (1836–1929). The original ranch headquarters, located on the south side of the Prairie Dog Town fork of the Red River (7 miles SE), was built by Goodnight in the fall of 1876. In June 1877, Goodnight entered a partnership with Irishman John G. Adair and founded the "JA" Ranch. Adair died in 1855, and his wife, Cornelia Ritchie Adair, assumed the partnership with Goodnight until its dissolution in 1887. The old home ranch headquarters burned in 1904. Edward Harrell purchased 35,000 acres of the "JA" in 1917, including the old ranch.   (1970)

CLAUDE (Armstrong Co.)   *SH 207, about 16 mi. S*
The S. P. Hamblen Family
Pioneered at this site, in dugout to the west. S. P. Hamblen (1846–1930) and wife Virginia Ann (1861–1950) settled in Lakeview area (9 mi. S. of Claude) in 1889. Hamblen helped establish Lakeview School, 1890. He engaged in farming and stockraising, and also dealt in cedar posts cut in Palo Duro Canyon and sold in Amarillo at 3¢ each. Hauls over the Old Indian Trail were made with such great effort that W. H. Hamblen (oldest son, who helped his father) longed for good roads and later was designer of Hamblen Drive.

Mrs. Hamblen, at home with her children, tended the ranch, courageously protecting family from the prevalent rattlesnakes, and repulsing vicious lobo wolves that attacked the young cattle.

The Hamblens lived at this site, known as Mesquite Flat, in 1901–1902. The father and older sons, W. H., David and Claude, put up corrals and a barn, and then built the rockwalled 24 × 36-foot dugout. The tenth child of the family, Luther Ray Hamblen, was born in the Mesquite Flat dugout on March 3, 1902.

Moving from this place, the Hamblens sought the best location for educating their children, who in the tradition of their parents became respected citizens of the West.   (1970)

CLAUDE (Armstrong Co.)   *US 287 at FM 2250, 15 mi. W,*
      frontal road in town of Washburn
Town of Washburn
Planned by R. E. Montgomery, son-in-law of Fort Worth & Denver City Railway Builder-President Gen. G. M. Dodge. Named for family friend. Promoted 1887, Washburn for a time was F. W. & D. C. Line's terminus. It had first newspaper of plains—"Armstrong County Record." Also had general store, lumber yard, 2 hotels, 2 saloons. Became junction point, branch line connecting F. W. & D. C. with Santa Fe Railway at Panhandle.

Remaining as town dwindled: Judge Jas. Logue, donor cemetery site and founder Washburn State Bank, 1908; H. E. White, owner of store, lumber yard and elevators.   (1970)

CLAUDE (Armstrong Co.)   *SH 207, 26 mi. S in roadside park*
First Battle of the Palo Duro
(Aug. 30, 1874)
Opening fight in 1874–75 U.S. action against tribes supposedly on Indian Territory Reservations (present Oklahoma), but actually occupying the Texas Panhandle.

South from Fort Dodge, Kans., marched 750 soldiers under Gen. Nelson A. Miles, who on Aug. 28 had to leave guards with his stalled supply train. Attacked on Aug. 30 in rugged terrain by superior numbers of Cheyennes, Comanches, and Kiowas, Miles won victory in 5-hour fight at Battle Creek (10 mi. E. of here)—first of 14 fights in Red River War that broke the Indians' power in Texas Panhandle.   (1971)

CLAUDE (Armstrong Co.)   *SH 207, 13 mi. S, then 3.5 mi. E*
                                               on FM 2227 right-of-way
Dugout of W. M. Dye
William Miles Dye was born in Kentucky in 1864 and moved to Texas with his parents in 1870. He settled in this area in 1891, one year after the organization of Armstrong County. By hauling rock from Palo Duro Canyon, Dye helped in the construction of the first county jail in Claude (13 mi. N). Still visible (10 yds. N) is the lower portion of the dugout he built for his family. Dugouts often were constructed in areas, such as the Texas Panhandle, where building materials were in short supply.   (1983)

CLAYTON (Panola Co.)   *SH 315, Old Bethel Churchyard*
Church Bethel
Organized on Saturday before the 4th Lord's Day in September 1843 by Rev. Isaac Reed, a pioneer Baptist minister, in his home two miles northwest, moved to this spot in 1874. The original minutes of organization are in the possession of this church. Erected by State of Texas.   (1936)

CLEBURNE (Johnson Co.)   *SH 171, 5 mi. N*
Site of Buchanan
(¼ mi. SW)
Johnson County's second seat of government. (Wardville, just west of Nolan River, at US 67, was first.) Buchanan, named for President-elect of the United States, was founded in Dec. 1856 on 60-acre townsite donated by John P. Bailey. A jail (first for the county) and office for the district clerk were built 1858. But lack of a reliable water supply hindered town's growth.

Later resurvey of county lines showed necessity for a new site. In 1867, Camp Henderson (renamed Cleburne, July 4, 1867) was chosen. Cemetery is only remaining trace of old Buchanan townsite.   (1972)

CLEBURNE (Johnson Co.)   *US 67, 4 mi. SW off hwy.*
Lake Pat Cleburne
Named to honor famous Confederate general and leader of Texas troops.

Built to supply city water needs after $3,200,000 bond issue approved Aug. 14, 1962. Lake covers 2,000 acres of land. Treatment plant has normal daily capacity of 3,000,000 gallons of water. Lake completed in Oct. 1964.   (1967)

CLEBURNE (Johnson Co.)   *US 67, 50 yds. W of city limits*
Site of Wardville
(¼ mi. S of marker)
First county seat of Johnson County, chosen in Aug. 1855, and located on an 80-acre donation from William O'Neal. Named for Thomas William Ward (1807–1872), a Republic of Texas soldier and second commissioner of General Land Office of Texas. The first courthouse, 16 feet square, was built by O'Neal of logs overlaid with clapboards, at cost of $49.

When Wardville was found to violate Texas Constitution's requirement that a county seat be within 5 miles of center of county, it was abandoned (1856). Ironically, later county line changes made it near the center.   (1972)

CLEVELAND (Liberty Co.)   *SH 321, 9 mi. SE, on building*
Old Wells' Store
Center section built about 1875 by D. D. Proctor & Company; later operated by L. L. Wells.

This structure and earlier one on same site each served as general mercantile store. This building was center for visits and exchange of local news at "Tarkington's Prairie" community. Building has been used as post office, wagon stop, credit house, and voting place. Was located on old Nacogdoches-Lynchburg Trail, a 19th century thoroughfare.   (1968)

CLEVELAND (Liberty Co.)   *SH 321, 5.5 mi. SE*
Burton B. Tarkington
Burton B. Tarkington (1790–1861) and his wife Sarah Berry Tarkington migrated with their family from Indiana in the mid-1820s to the Mexican state of Coahuila. They settled west of the Trinity River in present northwest Liberty County, and began ranching and raising crops. The area around their farm became known as Tarkington's Prairie, and a creek in the area is called Tarkington Bayou. According to family legend, the Tarkingtons and other early settlers had to vacate their property in 1836 when Santa Anna's forces advanced prior to the Battle of San Jacinto.

Apparently, Tarkington did not have a land grant from the Mexican government for the land he claimed, but when Texas gained independence from Mexico in 1836, he received a headright land grant of one league and one labor (4,605 acres). The grant was patented in 1847 by the new state of Texas and became known as the Tarkington Survey.

Tarkington became a leader in the community. He served in the Texas Militia in 1842, and was elected Liberty County commissioner for three terms beginning in 1854. He received recognition for his service from Governor H. R. Runnel. Tarkington died Feb. 2, 1861, and is buried in the McGinnis Cemetery (.25 mi.W).   (1996)

CLIFTON (Bosque Co.)   *SH 6, 4 mi. S at reunion grounds*
Election Oak
One of three polling places in first election held after Bosque County was organized in 1854. Of 21 votes cast on that occasion (Aug. 7, 1854) in county, 17 were polled under this tree. J. K. Helton was election judge.

Officials elected were L. H. Scrutchfield, judge; P. Bryant, sheriff; Jasper N. Mabray, clerk; Isaac Gary, assessor-collector; Archibald Kell, treasurer.

In later years, Bosque County Old Settlers Association used this site for reunions, by the courtesy of Tom M. Pool, owner of the land. Site was known locally as Pool Park.   (1970)

CLIFTON (Bosque Co.)   *FM 182 at FM 219, 7 mi. W*
Norwegian Settlements in Bosque County
Though never as numerous as some national groups emigrating from Europe, Norwegians left an imprint on rural life in Texas.

Hundreds sailed to the United States beginning in the 1830s. For those who settled in Texas, Bosque County had great appeal, because with its woods, hills and steep, sloping streams, it resembled parts of Norway.

In 1854 Ole Canuteson started here what became Texas' largest Norse settlement. Until past the turn of the century, the Gary Creek Valley settlers spoke mainly Norwegian and retained many customs of their homeland.   (1969)

CLIFTON (Bosque Co.)   *SH 219, 8.5 mi. W*
Cleng Peerson
(May 17, 1782–Dec. 16, 1865)
Called the "Father of Norwegian immigration to America," Cleng Peerson migrated to the United States from his native Norway in 1821. He traveled extensively and encouraged his countrymen to settle on land he selected in the East and Midwest. Coming to Texas in 1849, Peerson discovered Norwegian families living near Dallas and located sites where others might move. In 1853, he led a group to Bosque County, beginning the large Norwegian settlement in this area. Peerson lived on the O. Colwick farm (.5 mi. S) until his death. He is buried in the church cemetery at Norse.   (1975)

CLINE (Uvalde Co.)   *US 90, 19 mi. W, south side of hwy.*
Cline Community
(½ mi. S of this site)
First settler, Celeste Pingenot came to this area in 1870. He built first house on south bank of Turkey Creek, 1871. Established stagecoach stand, store and inn; named it Wallace. He was first postmaster, commissioned, 1878.

Community protected from Indians by small detachment of soldiers billeted at "The Spring," nearby.

August Cline was employed by Pingenot to operate store and stagecoach stand. When railroad came in 1883, built rock house and post office on north bank. Became postmaster. Renamed community, Cline.   (1967)

COLDSPRING (San Jacinto Co.)   *SH 150, .5 mi. E*
San Jacinto County
Eighteenth century Spanish explorers gave to the hyacinth-choked stream the name of Saint Hyacinth. Anglo-Americans settled here after 1820. Formed from portions of Polk, Montgomery, Liberty and Walker Counties.

Created January 5, 1869; recreated August 13, 1870; organized December 1, 1870. County seat, Cold Springs, 1870; later, Coldspring.

COLDSPRING (San Jacinto Co.)   *Byrd Ave. at SH 150*
San Jacinto County Courthouse
A fire in 1915 destroyed the San Jacinto County courthouse. Landowners donated land at this site and relocated the center of county government to "new town" Coldspring. The county hired builders Price and Williamson to construct the new courthouse based on plans by the Houston firm of Lane and Dabney. It was constructed in 1916–17 of brick fired locally from local clay. Merchants and citizens followed the courthouse to the new location, and by 1925, "old town" Coldspring was deserted. Repairs in 1936 modified its appearance somewhat, but the courthouse retains elements of its original Italian Renaissance design in its arched doors and windows on the east and west elevations.   (2000)

COLDSPRING (San Jacinto Co.)   *SH 150, 2 mi. in rest area*
The Big Thicket, C.S.A.
In early Texas, a paradise for settlers liking solitude. During the Civil War, became notorious as haunt of army deserters or men avoiding conscript officers and living off the country.

The thicket was so hard to penetrate that it was the despair of commanding officers. Soldiers who remained loyal were somewhat demoralized by seeing that men camping in the big thicket were safe from punishment for desertion. On at least two occasions, however, the men were discovered. Once a fire was set in a circle around them, and smoked them out. A later camp was located by a veteran hunter whose pack of bear dogs brought out the deserters.

Before they were hunted out, the deserters found thicket life good. They feasted on game and wild honey. Their wives, living nearby, would visit the men occasionally. Except when conscript officers were in the locality, the wives would visit caches established by the men and remove meat, hides or honey to be marketed for the support of the family. These people felt justified in deserting. Many were foreign-born and had sworn allegiance to the U.S. only 5 to 10 years earlier. Confused by the onset of war, they had fled from their homes.   (1965)

COLDSPRING (San Jacinto Co.)   *SH 150 right-of-way, 13.8 mi. W*
Old Waverly
Early center of culture for this part of Texas. Settled 1835–1850's, mainly by people from Alabama. Community was named for the Waverly novels of Sir Walter Scott, then very popular.

To provide education equal to any, Waverly Institute was founded in 1854, with separate departments for boys and girls.

Plantation system prevailed until 1860s. During Civil War, Federal troops camped in heart of Waverly, on Soldier's Hill.

Of three early churches, only the Presbyterian (organized in 1860) still exists; its present building was erected in 1904.   (1969)

COLEMAN (Coleman Co.)   *US 84, 0.6 mi. N*
Coleman County
In early Texas this area had Apache, Comanche, Kiowa camps and mountain lookouts. A white settlement began at Camp Colorado, U.S. 2nd Cavalry Post on Jim Ned Creek, 1857. The county was created Feb. 1, 1858 and named for Robert M. Coleman (1799–1837), a signer of Texas Declaration of Independence and a hero of the Battle of San Jacinto.

To south part of county, 1862, came John Chisum, to raise cattle to be furnished to Confederate troops fighting Civil War. The county was organized Oct. 6, 1864, and courts first met at Camp Colorado. Coleman was approved as county seat April 28, 1876.   (1965)

COLEMAN (Coleman Co.)   *SH 206 S*
County Named in 1857 for Robert M. Coleman (1799–1837)
Born in Kentucky. Came to Texas in 1832. Commanded company of volunteers at siege of Bexar (San Antonio), Dec. 5–10, 1835. Delegate to Constitutional Convention where he signed Texas Declaration of Independence, 1836. Aide-de-camp to Gen. Sam Houston at Battle of San Jacinto, 1836. Later fought Indians as a Texas Ranger.   (1966)

COLFAX (Van Zandt Co.)   *IH 20, 5 mi. E in roadside park*
Battle of the Neches
(Site 15 mi. SE)
Main engagement of Cherokee war fought July 15 and 16, 1839, between 800 Indians (including Delawares and Shawnees) and 500 troops of the Republic of Texas.

An extraordinary fact is that David G. Burnet, Vice President of the Republic; Albert Sidney Johnston, Secretary of War; and two other high officials took active parts in the fighting.

When killed, Chief Bowles, aged Cherokee leader, carried a sword given him by Gen. Sam Houston. After the defeat of the tribes, they scattered, thus virtually ending Indian troubles in the settled eastern part of Texas.   (1968)

COLLEGE STATION (Brazos Co.)   *FM 60, 6 mi. W*
The Brazos River
Largest river between the Red and the Rio Grande, the 840-mile Brazos rises in 3 forks: The Salt, Clear and Double Mountain Forks.

According to legend, this river saved Coronado's expedition of 1540–1542 from dying of thirst, so the men thankfully named it "Los Brazos de Dios" (Arms of God).

On its banks were founded historic San Felipe, capital of Stephen F. Austin's colony, and Washington where in 1836 Texas' Declaration of Independence was signed. Vast plantations thrived in the fertile Brazos Valley, making cotton "king" in Texas until the Civil War.   (1969)

COLLEGE STATION (Brazos Co.)   *SH 6 Bus. off Texas Ave*
                                                      at Main entrance, A&M Campus
Texas A&M University
The State Legislature authorized the Agricultural and Mechanical College of Texas April 17, 1871, under terms of the Federal Morrill Act. Constitutionally a part of a chartered, yet-unorganized state university, A&M gained its own directorate in 1875 with Governor Richard Coke as board president. Brazos Countians provided its 2,416-acre site. Committed to "teach . . . branches of learning . . . related to agriculture and mechanic arts . . . to promote liberal and practical education," A&M opened Oct. 4, 1876, as the first state institution of higher learning actually operating in Texas. Thomas S. Gathright was president. Its original six students in seven academic departments grew to 28,038 students in eleven academic colleges by 1976. Initially an all-male, all-white school, it was desegregated as to color in 1963 and made fully coeducational in 1971. The Legislature recognized its diversified programs and international leadership in education and research by awarding the new name, Texas A&M University, on Aug. 23, 1963. On Sept. 17, 1971, the U.S. Congress made this one of America's first four Sea Grant colleges. National defense has drawn from Texas A&M thousands of ROTC men, including 29 general officers for World War II.   (1978)

COLMESNEIL (Tyler Co.)   *FM 1745, 4 mi. W*
Site of one of Earliest Tyler County Landmarks
Enloe Mill
(1 mi. S.)

A major contributor to county and state history. Built about 1840 on Billums Creek, where the swift current made by inflow of Belts Creek would turn a water-wheel, to generate power.

Mill took name from owner Benjamin Enloe, an 1837 settler who bought this property in 1849. Enloe, his son David and grandson George were known to several generations as mill operators. From this mill came lumber for the first frame courthouse in Woodville, built in 1852 while David Enloe was county sheriff.

Since people came from wide area to this mill, there grew up one of area's main roads (later known as Boone's Ferry Road), connecting Fort Teran with the Old Spanish Trail from Liberty to Nacogdoches and crossing present road at this point.

Enloe's Mill, one of 27 in Tyler County by 1857, produced essentials of life for settlers: cornmeal for their bread and lumber for erecting homes and other buildings. This mill also ginned cotton, their "money" product.

Although long known for its raw materials rather than manufactured goods, Texas gained self-reliance from early landmarks such as Enloe's Mill.   (1968)

COLMESNEIL (Tyler Co.)   *US 69 North*
Zion Hill Missionary Baptist Church

Zion Hill Missionary Baptist Church is one of the earliest churches to serve this area's African American community. In the early 1880s, a freedmen's colony grew here in response to the availability of jobs at a newly opened sawmill. The Rev. George Durden and his congregation, with the assistance of the Rev. A. Venerable, moderator of the Trinity Valley Baptist Association, officially organized Zion Hill Missionary Baptist Church in 1881. It was the first Black church congregation in Colmesneil. Worship services were held in a log cabin built by the congregation until the early 1900s.

The church has occupied several locations and has served not only as a place of worship, but also as a school for Black children. In the early 1900s Zion Hill Missionary Baptist Church was moved to a site east of the Southern Pacific Railroad tracks adjacent to the Odd Fellows Hall. In 1933, the church was rebuilt at this site six blocks southwest of its original location.

For over one hundred years Zion Hill Missionary Baptist Church has served the community with a variety of worship and educational programs and maintained a leadership role in civic activities.   (1991)

COLMESNEIL (Tyler Co.)   *US 69 South*
Colmesneil-Mount Zion Cemetery

According to local oral tradition, African American residents of Colmesneil began using this land for burial purposes as early as the 1850s. The property remained in the hands of absentee landlords until the 1930s, when the new owner allowed burials to continue at the site.

The oldest legible tombstone in the graveyard is that of Henry Mitchell, who died September 11, 1859. There are a number of unmarked graves, however, and some possibly predate Mitchell's burial. Among the more than two hundred interments here are those of prominent members of Colmesneil's Black community, including ministers, doctors, teachers, railroad employees, and veterans of World War I and World War II.

Known as the Colmesneil Cemetery until 1972, the graveyard was renamed Mount Zion Cemetery to avoid confusion with another Colmesneil cemetery in the city. The new name was taken from a combination of the names of two local churches with which the cemetery historically has been associated—Mount Hope Baptist Church and Zion Hill Missionary Baptist Church. The cemetery serves as a visible reminder of the area's African American heritage.   (1992)

COLORADO CITY (Mitchell Co.)   *E on SH 208 S*
Colorado City Standpipe

In response to the need for a water supply system for Colorado, as this town was then known, the city's governing body issued waterwork bonds in 1884. The bond money was used to build this standpipe and to lay mains through which the city's water supply could run. The 90-foot steel standpipe was erected in 1884 by Riter and Conley of Pittsburgh, Pennsylvania, and continues in use as a storage facility for emergency water needs. The development of the city's water services was a major factor in the town's survival in the dry West Texas area. (1985)

COLORADO CITY (Mitchell Co.) *SH 208, 6 mi. S*
Seven Wells
(Site Located 1 mi. S)
This area, now covered by Lake Champion, was once the site of springs that originated from underground water which also supplied Champion Creek. They were called "wells" because the seven spring basins closely resembled man-made wells.

Buffalo tracks cut deep into the creek banks of soft sandstone indicated this was a watering place for great herds of bison. At least four trails crisscrossed the area where North and South Champion Creeks converged.

For hundreds of years Indians also camped here, and in the 1880s a small, early Mitchell County settlement grew up near the wells. The place remains today one of scenic beauty. (1968)

COLORADO CITY (Mitchell Co.) *SH 208, 6 mi. S*
Union Methodist Church
Organized March, 1891, by Rev. J. W. Montgomery. First church built by J. M. Dorn and neighbors. All faiths worshipped here. Was also used as schoolhouse and community meeting place.

Present church built 1905, and renamed Dorn Chapel. Planks over nail kegs were early pews. (1967)

COLORADO CITY (Mitchell Co.) *SH 163, 25 mi. SW*
Spade Renderbrook Ranch
Founded in buffalo and Indian days of 1870s by Taylor Barr. Owned 1882–1889 by D. H. and J. W. Snyder. They built "White House" headquarters; sold ranch, 1889, to Isaac L. Ellwood, an inventor of barbed wire, in DeKalb, Illinois.

Ellwood paid in wire for Spade Cattle from Donley County, to stock ranch. Added Sterling and Coke lands to original 130,000 acres; to distinguish this from range bought 1902 near Lubbock, called this Renderbrook (from name of spring where Indians shot a U.S. Cavalry officer in the 1870's). Ellwood heirs still run Spade brand on 2 ranches. (1965)

COLORADO CITY (Mitchell Co.) *SH 208, 12 mi. S on Country Road*
The 96 Ranch
Cattlemen began settling Mitchell County in the later 1870s, before the arrival of businessmen and farmers. This marker stands on one of the area's important early ranches, the 96 Ranch, founded by James Durham Wulfjen (1845–1933).

Wulfjen was a merchant in Round Rock before he visited Mitchell County in 1884. Inspired by the booming ranch economy, he filed on three sections of land, brought in a herd of cattle, and built a cabin near the Colorado River at the site of an old buffalo hunter's camp. He then persuaded his wife Mary Jane (Cocreham) (1854–1950) to give up the comforts of town life and settle on an isolated ranch.

On March 11, 1885, at the Mitchell County courthouse Wulfjen registered the "96" brand, still used by his descendants. He and his sons increased the size of the ranch to 19 sections (12,160 acres), on which they raised fine Durham cattle and saddle horses. The land is still owned by various members of the family.

The Wulfjens helped build a school an church at nearby Seven Wells and contributed to the stability of the ranching frontier. To provide education for their six children and others in the area, they donated funds for schools in Mitchell and Scurry counties. (1976)

COLUMBUS (Colorado Co.) *US 90, .3 mi. E*
Benjamin Beason's Crossing of the Colorado River
Site of the camp, March 19–26, 1836, of the Texas Army under General Sam Houston, who directed the retreat from Gonzales to the San Jacinto. (1964)

COLUMBUS (Colorado Co.)

SH 71, 1.5 mi. NW

Colorado County

A part of Stephen F. Austin's first colony; created March 17, 1836; organized in 1837.

The river traversing the region was called "Colorado" (Red) by Spanish explorers who mistook it for the reddish Brazos. From the river, the county took its name, Columbus, the county seat. (1964)

COLUMBUS (Colorado Co.)

US 90, 2 mi. W

Site of the Camp

March 20–26, of one division of General Santa Anna's army under the command of General Joaquin Ramirez y Sesma. It crossed the Colorado at Atascosita Ford, eight miles below Columbus. (1964)

COLUMBUS (Colorado Co.)

US 90 at FM 102, 2.5 mi. E

Alleyton, C.S.A.

Born as war clouds gathered. Alleyton was a key point on the supply line of the Confederate States of America during the Civil War. It was both beginning and end of the cotton road leading to the Confederacy's back door on the Rio Grande River.

By 1860 the Buffalo Bayou, Brazos and Colorado Railroad extended from Harrisburg, near Houston, to Alleyton. As a railhead Alleyton became the site of an important cotton station and quartermaster depot during the war.

Cotton came here from north and east Texas. From Louisiana, and from Arkansas on the rails of the B.B.B. & C. and via wagon roads. From Alleyton the south's most precious trading commodity was carried to a point on the Colorado River across from Columbus. It was then ferried across the start of a long, tortuous journey to the Rio Grande. The bales of cotton were hauled on big-bedded wagons and high-wheeled Mexican carts, pulled by mules, horses or oxen.

The cotton road led to Goliad, San Patricio, the King Ranch and finally to Brownsville. Shreds of white fluff on bush and cactus marked the trail of the wagon trains. From Brownsville the cotton was taken across the river to Matamoros, Mexico and subsequently placed on board ships bound for Europe. As the only major gap in the Federal naval blockade of the Confederacy, neutral Matamoros was the place of exchange for outgoing cotton and imported munitions, clothing and medicine.

When Federal forces took Vicksburg in 1863 the Mississippi River was sealed off and the Confederacy divided. The Texas-Mexico trade routes then became the South's major military supply lines in the Trans-Mississippi West.

Alleyton was a main destination of the wagon trains returning from the Rio Grande. Rifles, swords, shirts, pants, alum, arrowroot and other items needed by soldier and civilian in the harried Confederacy were unloaded here for new destinations.

COLUMBUS (Colorado Co.)

SH 71 at S end of Colorado River Bridge

Site of Robson's Castle
and
Columbus, Texas, Meat & Ice Company

Robert Robson (1804–1878), one of many Scotsmen seeking fortune in North America, came to the Texas Republic in 1839. On land he owned at this site, he built a concrete "castle," using native lime and gravel. It had running water, pumped from the Colorado into a tank on the roof, then through wooden pipes to its many rooms. It also had a roof garden and an encircling moat, with drawbridge. From Bastrop to Matagorda, it drew guests to champagne suppers, card parties, and balls. Undermined by an 1869 flood, it became a ruin and was razed when site was put to new use in 1880s.

Columbus, Texas, Meat & Ice Company built its 3-story plant on this site in 1884. It was then one of three packing houses in Texas. Established to process at place of origin, the plant could handle 125 cattle a day. Some of its beef went to Queen Victoria's London. Robert E. Stafford (1834–1890), a wealthy trail driver and rancher, veteran of Civil War service with famous Hood's Texas Brigade, owner of a private bank and extensive Colorado County properties, was president and major stockholder in the packing house. In the early 1890s, after Stafford died, the plant closed. (1973)

COLUMBUS (Colorado Co.) *Courthouse Square*
The Rangers of Austin's Colony
By March 1822, Stephen F. Austin had attracted 150 colonists to Texas. The pioneers faced many hardships, including concern for their protection from Indians along the Colorado and Brazos Rivers. In December of that year, Trespalacios, the Mexican governor, divided the colony into two districts, each having an alcalde to preside over matters of local administration and a captain to handle protection of the colonists.

In 1823, after several Indian attacks on members of Austin's Colony, Captain Robert Kuykendall and Alcalde John Tumlinson of the Colorado district requested permission from Trespalacios to raise a company to protect the colonists. Ten men were recruited to serve under the command of Moses Morrison.

When Stephen F. Austin returned from Mexico City in August 1823, he found the colony still plagued by Indian disturbances and announced that he would employ ten additional men, at his own expense, to serve as "rangers" for the common defense.

Although the law enforcement group known as the Texas Rangers was not formally organized until 1835, the "rangers" of Austin's Colony are the earliest recorded force of this type raised in Texas and served as a model for the later formation of the Texas Rangers.

(Texas Sesquicentennial 1836–1986)

COMANCHE (Comanche Co.) *US 377/67, .25 mi. W*
Comanche County
First settled in 1854 by five families, the county, created and organized 1856, was named for Comanche Indians, Lords of Texas frontier, who were losing hunting grounds to settlers. First county seat was Cora. Comanche has been county seat since July 18, 1859. Indians harassed settlers, stealing cattle and horses, and keeping farmers out of fields. Food from neighboring Bell County kept people here from starvation in 1862. By 1879 a stage line crossed county; the Texas Central Railroad came through in 1880; Fort Worth & Rio Grande Railroad in 1890. An oil boom occurred in 1918–1920. Agriculture has long been major industry. (1967) 1936 Text: Created January 25, 1856; Organized May 17, 1856; Named for the Comanche Indians, nomads of the Plains; successful hunters, superb horsemen, and courageous warriors; the terror of Texas frontier settlers, who dispossessed them of their hunting grounds. County Seat Troy (changed to Cora), 1856; Comanche, since July 18, 1859 (1936)

COMANCHE (Comanche Co.) *SH 16, 12 mi. S*
Captain James Cunningham, 1855
Capt. Jas. Cunningham home, 1855. Lumber hauled from Waco by ox wagon. Local stone, place of county's first wedding. (1965)

COMANCHE (Comanche Co.) *US 67/337, 5 mi. E*
Hasse Community
Began as "Cordwood Junction," a siding on the Fort Worth & Rio Grande Railroad. Flatcars loaded wood here to be shipped over a wide area. As demand for the fuel increased, the railroad built a station house at site.

It was named in 1892 for O. H. Hasse, thought to have been the local railway agent, 1890s.

Cotton and cattle brought more business to town. A cotton gin, stock pens, and lumber yard were built. With the advent of automobiles, migration to urban centers, and highways, however, Hasse began to dwindle. Today only a few buildings remain. (1970)

COMANCHE (Comanche Co.) *US 67/377, ¼ mi. W*
Old Corn Trail
Surveyed in 1850 by army engineers. This was the first wagon road to penetrate this area. Point of origin was San Antonio, site of U.S. Army District Headquarters after annexation of Texas in 1846.

This segment of road extended from Fort Gates (in Coryell County) to Fort Griffin (Shackelford County) and Fort Belknap (Young County). Although used for communications and troop movements, most common traffic was in supplies—especially feed for army horses and mules. Hence the name "Corn Trail."

Presence of the road and its traffic from fort to fort encouraged settlement. In 1851 John A. and J. M. McGuire moved to a site near here on Indian Creek. James H. Neel settled on Resley's Creek in 1852; in 1854 James Mercer and Capt. Frank Collier pitched tents on Mercer Creek, soon to be joined by their families and the Holmsleys and Tuggles. Collier put up first log house; Holmsley plowed first furrow.

By Christmas of 1855 there were enough citizens here to petition for a county, and Comanche County was created by the Texas Legislature Jan. 25, 1856.

The Corn Trail was a main civilian thoroughfare, and continued to serve its original purpose as a route for frontier troops and supplies. (1967)

COMANCHE (Comanche Co.) *SH 16, 9 mi. S*
Cunningham Family Reunion
James (1816–1894) and Susannah (1817–1899) Cunningham came to the Republic of Texas in 1839–1840 and settled in this area in 1855. An influential family in the county, the Cunninghams were active in military defense against hostile Indians. In 1889, James, Susannah, and their 12 children gathered for their first family reunion. Additional reunions were held sporadically until 1901, when they became an annual event. Acreage adjoining the family property was purchased to insure continuation of the historical gatherings, which take place for two days each summer. (1989)

COMANCHE (Comanche Co.) *SH 16, 10 mi. S at site*
South Leon Baptist Church
First Baptist church formed in Comanche County. Organized by the Rev. Richard Howard and 8 charter members, under a brush arbor built here, 1857. Early services were held in a log schoolhouse (300 ft. W). Later combination church-school was built near cemetery. In 1906 the present building was erected.

Church was dissolved, 1859, due to Indian troubles; reorganized in 1872 with James Cunningham and F. H. Neely as deacons.

Has official Texas Historical Medallion Plate. (1968)

COMFORT (Kendall Co.) *FM 473, 1.5 mi. E*
Hygieostatic Bat Roost
This shingle style structure was built in 1918 to attract and house bats in an effort to eradicate mosquitoes and thereby reduce the spread of malaria. It was designed for Albert Steves, Sr., a former mayor of San Antonio, by Dr. Charles A. R. Campbell, an authority on bats who had served as the health officer in the same city. Named "Hygieostatic" by Steves, the bat roost is one of 16 constructed in the United States and Italy between 1907 and 1929. (1981)

COMFORT (Kendall Co.) *SH 27 at Cypress Creek*
First Pharmacy in Comfort
Using trees growing on nearby Cypress Creek, log portion of this house was built 1857 by Emil Serger and Paul Hanisch. Housed first pharmacy in Comfort. West wing and "Sunday House" were built in 1870, 1885. Restoration by Mr. and Mrs. J. C. Rice, 1947.

Medallion Plate. (1965)

COMFORT (Kendall Co.) *US 87, 6 mi. N*
Stieler Ranch House
Designed and built 1890–1892 by Hermann Stieler, German rock mason and local sheep rancher. He came from Germany; hauled freight for Charles Schreiner Company and to Camp Verde.

Made this place a shearing station for fellow ranchers. Coaches from nearby stage line often stopped for food, repairs.

Style is typical of era. Each floor has two rooms on either side of central "dog trot" hall.

Interior was remodeled in 1937. Has Medallion Plate. (1970)

COMFORT (Kendall Co.) *Treue Der Union High St.*
"Treue Der Union"
(Loyalty to the Union)
This German language monument, erected 1866, houses the memory of 68 men (mostly Germans) from this region who were loyal to the Union during the Civil War.

Trying desperately to reach U.S. Federal troops by way of Mexico, about 40 of the men were killed by vengeful Confederates bent on annihilating them, in the Battle of the Nueces (on Aug. 10, 1862) and a later fight (Oct. 18).

The bodies of the slain and those who drowned swimming the Rio Grande were left unburied. A group of Germans gathered the bones of their friends and buried them at this site in 1865.

COMFORT (Kendall Co.)   *301 SH 27*

Freidenker (Nineteenth Century Freethinkers)

From 1845 to 1861, a number of German Freidenker ("Freethinkers") immigrated to the Texas hill country. Freethinkers were German intellectuals who advocated reason and democracy over religious and political authoritarianism. Many had participated in the 1848 German revolution and sought freedom in America. The Freidenker helped establish Bettina, Castell, Cypress Mill, Luckenbach, Sisterdale, Tusculum (Boerne) and Comfort. Laid out in 1854, Comfort soon was home to about half the population of hill country Freethinkers. Freethinkers valued their new-found freedoms of speech, assembly and religion. Their settlements, where a knowledge of Latin was considered essential for a cultured intellectual society, became known as "Latin Colonies." They strongly supported secular education and generally did not adhere to any formal religious doctrines. They applied themselves to the crafts of physical labor and divided their time between farming and intellectual pursuits. Freethinkers advocated universal equal rights, and their moral values were dominated by their respect for life. They actively supported such social issues as the abolition of slavery and the rejection of secession. Their loyalty to the Union during the Civil War cost many their freedoms and their lives. Following the war, many Freethinkers relocated to nearby urban areas, while others returned to Germany.   (2000)

COMMERCE (Hunt Co.)   *1501 Monroe Street*

Site of Birthplace of
Maj. Gen. Claire L. Chennault (1890–1958)

Organizer-Commander of the famous "Flying Tigers" of the China-Burma-India Theater in World War II. An outstanding air strategist, Chennault had retired from a pioneer flying career when, in 1937, he was asked by Gen. Chiang Kai-Shek to help China develop an air force to combat threatening raids by Japan.

Four years later, with World War II spreading, he received permission from the U.S. to seek a corps of American airmen to help train the Chinese. A total of 252 men—87 pilots and 165 ground personnel—joined the "American Volunteer Group." Its popular name resulted from a misunderstanding of the sharks' teeth painted on the noses of the aircraft.

The Tigers formed three squadrons—"Adam and Eve," "Panda Bears," and "Hell's Angels"—supported by the expert pilots of the China National Aviation Corps, a daring supply transport group. So effectively had Chennault studied Japanese air tactics that his tiny band officially destroyed 539 enemy aircraft while losing only 90 itself. During 1941–1942, they checked Japan's invasion of China, then joined regular units.

Jack Cornelius, also a native of Commerce and a close friend of Chennault's, was a member of the first pursuit squadron of the Tigers.   (1968)

COMSTOCK (Val Verde Co.)   *US 90 W, approx. 8 mi.,*
in roadside park

Pecos River High Bridge

High canyon walls dominate the last 60 miles of the Pecos River before it enters the Rio Grande. The Southern Pacific Railroad built the first high bridge across the Pecos River in 1891. The first highway bridge to span the river was built one mile downriver from here in 1923. Just 50 feet above water, the 1923 bridge was destroyed by floodwaters in 1954. Two temporary low-water bridges built nearby in 1954 and 1955 also were destroyed by floodwaters. A new 1,310-feet long bridge was completed here in 1957. At 273 feet above the river it is the highest highway bridge in Texas.   (Sesquicentennial of Texas Statehood 1845–1995)

COMSTOCK (Val Verde Co.)
US 90 W, approx. 8 mi., in roadside park
Near Site, Southern Pacific Ceremony of
Silver Spike
Marked completion of Southern Pacific Railway. Eastern part originated in Texas in 1850s; then was rechartered 1870 by Texas Legislature as Galveston, Harrisburg & San Antonio Rwy., designed to join Houston and San Antonio to the Rio Grande.

T. W. Peirce of Boston gained control in 1874. Meantime, C. P. Huntington of California was building the Southern Pacific eastward; he wanted a Texas line to join his tracks, and reached agreement with Peirce. On Jan. 12, 1883, the two railroads met near the Pecos High Bridge, and were joined by a silver spike. (1967)

CONCAN (Uvalde Co.)
US 83 & SH 127, S city limits
C.S.A. Saltpetre Mine
(6 mi. SW)
Worked in the 1860s. Had vast deposits of bat guano, which by natural decay became saltpetre, chief ingredient of gunpowder used in the Civil War. As mixed with small parts of charcoal and sulphur, saltpetre from here powered Confederate cannon and smaller ammunition. Some was shipped east of Mississippi.

Cave inhabited by bats, source of the guano, extends about 23 miles. One room in the great bat den is 585' × 325', and has a 45' ceiling. Narrow gauge railway with mule drawn cars was used in the digging. Cave had corrals for the mules. (1965)

CONCAN (Uvalde Co.)
US 83 at SH 127 in roadside park
Silver Mine Pass
(2 mi. W)
Named for silver mine opened near pass by Spaniards in 1700s or earlier. Ore was inferior, and mine was abandoned; but 14 shafts (some interconnecting) remain.

Near the mine are remnants of a fortification made by 30 men under leadership of James Bowie, later (1836) a hero of the siege to the Alamo. In 1831, while at work at this mine, Bowie's men repulsed a Comanche attack in a fierce, all-day battle.

Hero of the fight was Bowie's slave, "Black Jim Bowie," who risked his life by leaving the fortification to bring water to the besieged. (1968)

CONE (Crosby Co.)
US 62, at site
Village of Cone
Named in 1903 for S. E. Cone, who helped carry mail here from the nearby town of Emma. Post office was established same year in general store of R. E. Chapman, who became the first postmaster. Town once had a school, stores, and churches. Now center of irrigated section, which produces cotton, sorghum grains, and wheat. (1969)

CONROE (Montgomery Co.)
US 75, 4 mi. N
Montgomery County, C.S.A.
A wealthy farm area in 1861. In Civil War, supported Texas with goods, funds and men. 2 companies from here were in famed Hood's Texas Brigade—with only 9 men in one living to return. Young boys, old men and the partially disabled formed 5 Home Guard and State Companies. The county clothed its own soldiers. The courthouse, then on this site, had a sewing room for that work; home looms, cotton cards and needles also cooperated.

Homefolk ate sparingly, had few new clothes. By 1864, so much was given to war effort that not a store was open in Montgomery. (1965)

CONROE (Montgomery Co.)
SH 105, 15.5 mi. W
Site of the Home of
Charles B. Stewart
(1806–1885)
Member of the Consultation, 1835. First Secretary of State. Signer of the Texas Declaration of Independence. Delegate from Montgomery County to the Constitutional Convention of 1845. Member of the Texas Legislature.

CONROE (Montgomery Co.) *FM 1485, 8 mi. SE in field*
Conroe Oil Field
One of the great petroleum areas of the Texas Coastal Region. Opened Dec. 13, 1931, by the discovery well of George Strake (No. 1 South Texas Development Co.), about 1.4 miles west of here. Initial daily flow: 15,000,000 cubic feet of gas, along with white gasoline. Strake's Second Well, a 900-barrel-a-day producer, and the Heep Oil Corp.-No. 1 Freeman (both coming in during June 1932) proved existence of a large field. Fast-paced drilling ensued. In Jan. 1933 Madeley No. 1, of Kansas Standard, came in as a wild well and on fire. TNT charges and tons of earth did not smother the fire; it burned about three months.

Cratering spread to Harrison and Abercrombie well nearby, and that gushed out of control. In Jan. 1934 a driller for Humble "killed the blowout," by using directional drilling for first time in coastal Texas. This saved the field. (The crater is 600 feet deep.)

The Conroe Field was the first in Texas to adopt 20-acre spacing, before this was mandatory under conservation rules. It has yielded over 400,000,000 barrels of oil; now produces at the yearly rate of 5,300,000 barrels. After the dramatic discovery here, Montgomery County developed 11 other oil fields, and has vast reserves for continuing production. (1967)

CONROE (Montgomery Co.) *FM 1485, 7 mi. SE, .5 mi. from crater and 300 yds. from Crater Hill*
Crater Hill
Placid Crater Lake—600 feet deep—is only evidence today of the disastrous blowout of a gas-oil well drilled here in 1933.

Madeley No. 1 of the Kansas Standard Oil Co. came in on fire; cratering began and spread to 2 other wells. The future of one of the richest petroleum areas in Texas was threatened.

The blaze raged 3 months as firefighters poured in tons of water and mud and exploded TNT to smother the flames.

Humble Oil Co. at last halted fire by drilling directional well and pumping in mud. First use of this method on the Texas coast. (1967)

CONROE (Montgomery Co.) *SH 105, 7.5 mi. W near Lake Conroe dam site*
West Fork of the San Jacinto River
Patiri and other Indians lived here in Archaic and Neo-American Periods. When Spanish incursions began in the 1700s, the river was named either for hyacinths or for the saint on whose day it was discovered. Pioneers from the United States settled on the San Jacinto before Stephen F. Austin founded his colony to the west in 1821. Upon their wish to join him, he took this area into his colony in 1824.

The San Jacinto won world fame when beside its lower channel Mexican Dictator Santa Anna with 1700 troops was defeated on April 21, 1836, by General Sam Houston and Texas volunteers fighting for freedom.

Riverside farms became plantations, often shipping cotton by keelboat down the San Jacinto, in 1845–1861. Until woodlands vanished during the years 1880–1930, sandhill cranes and bear abounded. Reforestation, begun in 1936, brought back timber industries and small game. The lake now makes this a residential and recreational paradise, but covers such landmarks as Grandma Ed'ards Fishing Hole, Indian Camp Creek, and the White Sugar Sand Crossing. Downriver, after this fork and the East Fork unite, the San Jacinto forms part of the Houston Ship Channel, the link between Port of Houston, the Gulf, and the High Seas. (1975)

COOKS POINT (Burleson Co.) *SH 21 near FM 1362 intersection*
Cooks Point
Founded about 1840 where colonial road from southeast crossed San Antonio Road. Settler Gabriel Jackson had two story log cabin-trading post here. Community was named for Silas L. Cooke, who surveyed much land in this vicinity. It is now a thriving rural village. (1969)

COOKS POINT (Burleson Co.) *FM 50, 2 mi. E of SH 21*
Brazos River Levee
Destructive Brazos River floods have often plagued residents of Burleson County. In 1899, a 30-inch rain killed 35 and caused about $9 million in property damage. Again in 1900, 1902, and 1908 Brazos River bottom inhabitants endured serious flooding. In 1909, W. S. Mial and 49 other

citizens asked the commissioners of Burleson County to build levees along the Brazos to protect the valuable farm land. In July 1909, voters unanimously approved the issuance of bonds and the higher taxes to pay off the debt.

Contractors Roach and Stansell built the 8-foot levee which extended south for 30 miles. Its test came in December 1913, with a storm far worse than the 1899 flood. Residents of this area, depending on the levee for safety, did not flee until the water had risen dangerously. Too late, they discovered the levee trapped water and then broke, unleashing a wall of destruction from which there was no escape. Victims rode out the flood on roofs and in treetops. There were 180 deaths and $8 million property loss. Still convinced of the value of the levees, voters in 1914 approved reconstruction bonds. The indebtedness was not retired until 1963, long after modern flood control methods made the area safe. (1978)

COOKVILLE (Titus Co.) *US 67*
W. A. Keith House
Oldest house in Cookville. Erected in 1880 by W. A. "Doc" Keith (1850–1930), farmer, county attorney (1895), postmaster.

Built of rough-milled, hand-planed pine with hand-hewn oak sills. Originally had three rooms and hall. Has been remodeled slightly. Has Medallion Plate. (1970)

COOPER (Delta Co.) *SH 24, 4.5 mi. NE*
Erected in the Centennial Year, to Commemorate Founding of
Delta County
Named for shape, resembling Greek letter, and for evident origin of its land—sedimentation at fork of North and South Sulphur Rivers. The first (1820–1830) political activity here was oversight by the Sulphur Forks Indian Commission (of the United States) of the Caddo, Delaware, Quapaw, and Seminole inhabitants.

After Texas Independence in 1836, the Delta came under jurisdictions of Red River, Lamar, and Hopkins Counties. Families and wagon trains from Kentucky, Tennessee, and other states—and from other parts of Texas—settled here as early as the 1830s.

The people of the Delta in 1868 petitioned for creation of the county; in 1870 the Legislature of Texas complied. The county seat, a new town to be in the geographic center, was named for Leroy Cooper, chairman of the House Committee on Counties and Boundaries. Gov. E. J. Davis named as commissioners to organize the county: Joel Blackwell, John P. Boyd, James Hamilton, J. W. Iglehart, and Thomas J. Lane. To supervise sales of lots in Cooper, Erastus Blackwell was appointed sheriff. The organizing election was held on Oct. 6, 1870, naming Charles S. Nidever as chief justice. Commissioners elected were John P. Boyd, J. F. Alexander, Alfred Allen, and J. M. Bledsoe. (1970)

COOPER (Delta Co.) *SH 19/154, 6 mi. SE*
DeSpain Bridge
(Site 4.2 mi. SW)
Located where the Bonham-Jefferson Road crossed the South Sulphur River, this pioneer bridge served the area's rich cotton trade for some 20 years.

It was constructed before 1850 by landowner Brig DeSpain and his neighbors to provide access to the county seat—Tarrant—in Hopkins County. The land was originally awarded to the family of Randolph DeSpain a Texas Revolutionary soldier who was killed in the massacre at Goliad in 1836.

Strongly built of native oak and bois d'arc wood, the bridge withstood heavy traffic of ox-wagons and horse-drawn vehicles. The narrow ridge of land where it was situated was known as "Granny's Neck," for Mrs. Mary Sinclair, who lived in the vicinity.

Until cotton and corn became important crops, the South Sulphur River ran clear. Afterward, eroded dirt from plowed fields muddied its waters.

Shortly after 1870—the year Delta County was organized—heavy rains washed out the bridge. The state of Texas built a new one, which took the name of G. W. Harper, toll keeper. Later Hopkins and Delta Counties assumed maintenance of this new bridge, which continued to channel cotton and corn wagons between the two regions for several decades. (1970)

COOPER (Delta Co.)
SH 64, 3½ mi. W, N side of road
The Pioneer Smith Brothers
Tall, strong men who helped to carve Delta County out of Texas frontier. Benjamin, Charles, Gilford and Mira J. Smith came to Texas from Arkansas before or during the 1840s. They obtained from heirs title to the Moses Williams Land Grant, patented 1849, and surveyed by Major George W. Stell. After 1853 several generations of the Smith family lived here.

The brothers were each 6 feet, 4 inches or taller and weighed over 250 pounds. They cut logs and built their cabins with puncheon (split-log) floors, riven-board roofs, and homemade furniture. Instead of nails wooden pegs were used: instead of glass windows, board shutters. Chimneys were of black clay mud plastered over sticks. Bear meat was the main food, obtained by hunting with flintlock rifles in such dangerous places as Jernigan Thicket, 2 miles west. Charles H. Smith kept bees, and was known as "Honey."

Mira J. Smith was a key man in settling of Delta County, because he was an early blacksmith. His first son, Moses, became a tanner; the second son, Henry a blacksmith. The women of the four families carded cotton and wool, and spun, wove, and sewed clothing. Young Moses Smith also made men's buckskin suits.

Grant has produced over $1,000,000 worth of cotton. (1968)

COOPER (Delta Co.)
SH 64, 2 mi. E
Hiram Rattan
(Homesite .3 mi., Grave .4 mi. N)
Delta County pioneer, born 1805. Settled in Texas, 1835, on brother Larkin Rattan's 1,000-acre land grant; later became site for city of Paris. Both Rattan families moved to Delta County in 1839. Hiram obtained two third-class land grants for producing grain and livestock. Larkin later joined the California Gold Rush, then returned to his native Illinois.

Four Rattan relatives were massacred by Texas Indians.

Civil War and politics divided family but never their devotion to Texas. Descendants include educators, military and political leaders. (1967)

COOPER (Delta Co.)
SH 24, 2 mi. W
Pioneer Citizen
Leroy Nelson DeWitt
(Mar. 20, 1840–May 23, 1918)
Prosperous merchant and farmer. Native of Virginia; moved here with parents, 1854. Married Miss Mary Collier, 1861; they had 9 children.

In 1862, joined Confederacy to serve on frontier until end of war. Became recognized leader in civic and church affairs, area development. (1967)

COPPERAS COVE (Coryell Co.)
US 190, 1 mi. S
Ogletree Stagestop and Post Office
(.5 mi. W)
After Marsden Ogletree (1819–1896) and his family migrated from Georgia, he received a land grant in 1878. Inscriptions on two stones in this house indicate the structure was erected the same year. It served as the family home, grain store, and stopping place for the Lampasas to Belton stagecoach. Since the mail arrived by stage, a post office was opened here in 1879 with Ogletree as postmaster. Legend says that the settlement received the name "Coperas Cove" from a copperas-tasting spring in the cove of a nearby mountain.

Samuel Gilmore served as the second postmaster. In 1881, Gilmore's father-in-law Jesse M. Clements (1822–1900) and his wife Charley deeded land for the right-of-way to the Gulf, Colorado & Santa Fe Railroad. The following year the railroad laid out the new townsite of Coperas Cove. Soon the center of the community, including the post office, moved over to the railroad. Later the town corrected the spelling of its name to "Copperas Cove."

In 1891, Clements bought this house and used it as the headquarters for his large ranching operations. The old stone stagestop remains a visible link with the community's pioneer heritage. (1979)

CORPUS CHRISTI (Nueces Co.)   *FM 286 at FM 70, 12 mi. S at Chapman Ranch*
Chapman Ranch

In Jan. 1919, Philip Alexander Chapman (1847–1924) purchased 34,631 acres of the Laureles Division of the King Ranch for development as farm lands similar to others he owned in East Texas and Oklahoma. He sent his son, J. O. Chapman (1883-1953), to supervise operations. Arriving in Sept. 1919, J. O. Chapman began dividing "Nueces Farms" into 160-acre tracts and leasing them to tenants. In 1924, the name was changed to Chapman Ranch.

The town, founded in 1925, had a hospital, cotton gin, 2 schools, its own power plant, and "The Commissary," which housed grocery, hardware, and merchantile stores, a barber shop, soda fountain, automobile agency, service station, post office, and ranch headquarters offices.

In 1926, over 20,000 acres were in cultivation. The ranch contracted with manufacturers to test modern farm equipment. Several implements were invented here. In the later 1920s, Chapman Ranch was advertised as the world's largest mechanized farm. During the 1930s, the ranch conducted extensive crop experiments, and developed a superior strain of long-staple cotton, the seed of which was marketed worldwide.

By 1941, the town had dwindled away, and the land was partitioned among P. A. Chapman's children, whose heirs continue to operate the ranch.   (1973)

CORPUS CHRISTI (Nueces Co.)   *SH 358 at Laguna Shores Rd.,*
near intersection

Flour Bluff

In the spring of 1838 France blockaded the coast of Mexico during the Pastry War, so-called because of the mistreatment of French citizens, including pastry chefs, living in Mexico. The strategic location of Corpus Christi Bay led to the revival of smuggling in this area. Supplies were carried overland across the Rio Grande, and the illicit trade flourished as Mexico bought sorely needed goods in Texas. Although President Sam Houston did not wish to antagonize Mexico, Mexican patrols at Corpus Christi offended many Texans. In July, 1838, authorities at Texana heard reports of Mexican activity near the bay. A captured Mexican sea captain said that his government had declared Corpus Christi a port of entry and had dispatched about 400 men to protect it. A summons was issued, calling Texans to rally at Texana, Aug. 7, to drive the invaders from the Republic's boundaries. By the time the volunteers reached the area, some of the Mexicans had landed their supplies near the tip of Corpus Christi Bay and returned to Matamoros. The rest scattered, leaving about 100 barrels of flour and parts of a steam engine. The Texans confiscated the usable flour, and other contraband, and the site became known as Flour Bluff.   (1976)

CORPUS CHRISTI (Nueces Co.)   *IH 37, Violet Rd. exit, on frontage rd.*
Nuecestown
(4 mi. N)

Henry L. Kinney (b. 1814), who founded Corpus Christi, established Nuecestown in 1852 at the location of the first ferry crossing on the Nueces River west of Corpus Christi. He sent agents to Europe, primarily England and Germany, to promote his new settlement. Each immigrant purchased 100 acres of land, a town lot, and 10 head of cattle.

Nuecestown, known locally as "The Motts" because of several clusters of trees, grew to have, in addition to the ferry, a hotel, packery, and one of the county's first cotton gins. A post office opened in 1859.

After the Civil War it was a gathering place for cattle drovers in the area herding longhorns to be driven to northern railheads. On Good Friday, March 26, 1875, Mexican bandits entered the region on a raid, causing many Corpus Christi residents to flee. After plundering the Frank store (3 mi. E), the raiders turned on Nuecestown, looting and burning T. J. Noakes' store and post office, killing one man, and capturing several hostages. A party of citizens pursued the attackers unsuccessfully, and another man was killed.

When bypassed by the St. Louis, Brownsville, & Mexico Railway about 1905, Nuecestown began to decline. The post office closed in 1927.   (1973)

CORPUS CHRISTI (Nueces Co.)   *FM 666, 9 mi. N at bridge over Nueces River*
Santa Margarita Crossing
Ranchers occupying the 1804 Spanish Land Grant of Jose Herrera established this crossing of the Nueces and named the scattered settlement Santa Margarita. In 1828, John McMullen and James McGloin received a land grant from the Mexican government for an Irish colony north of the river and founded the town of San Patricio. This site soon became a major crossing on the Matamoros Road into Texas. To protect the crossing, the Mexican Army, in 1831, established nearby Fort Lipentitlan, which was captured Nov. 4, 1835, by insurgent Texians. On Feb. 27, 1836, Gen. Jose Urrea's army defeated the Texian forces of James Grant and F. W. Johnson here before marching to Goliad. After Texas won independence, Gen. Vicente Filisola led the defeated Mexican troops back to Mexico along this road.

After crossing the river here in summer of 1845, Gen. Zachary Taylor held his army in this region until March 1846, when he moved to the Rio Grande, the action which precipitiated the U.S. War with Mexico (1846–1848).

During the Civil War the Old Matamoros Road, then called the "Cotton Road," served as a trade outlet for the Confederacy. Texas products were transported via the Santa Margarita Crossing to Mexico, circumventing the Federal blockade of Confederate ports.   (1973)

CORPUS CHRISTI (Nueces Co.)   *Park Road 22, 20 mi. SE, on Padre Island*
The Pat Dunn Ranch
Patrick Francis Dunn, the son of Irish immigrants Thomas and Catherine H. Dunn, was born Oct. 10, 1858, in Corpus Christi. He married Clara J. Jones Aug. 30, 1883.

In Dec. 1883, Pat Dunn entered a partnership with his mother and brother, Thomas, to graze cattle on Padre Island, and as manager moved to the island in Jan. 1884, settling 20 miles down the coast. Laguna Madre and the Gulf of Mexico served as natural fences; during roundup, ranch hands drove stock into several corrals scattered along the 110-mile island.

When his children reached school age, Dunn moved back to Corpus Christi and established headquarters at the north end of the island. In 1907, after buying his brother's interest, he built a 2-story house on Corpus Christi Pass (0.5 mi. E.), using lumber washed ashore from shipwrecks. Much of the house and corrals were constructed of fine mahogany. The house was destroyed in the hurricane of 1916, the year of his mother's death, which left Dunn as sole owner of the ranch.

Pat Dunn sold his Padre Island interests in 1926, retaining grazing rights, which he used until his death March 25, 1937. His son, Burton Dunn, continued ranching operations until his death Sept. 8, 1970, after which the last cattle were removed from Padre Island.   (1973)

CORPUS CHRISTI (Nueces Co.)   *Water Street, under the High Bridge*
Early History of
The Port of Corpus Christi
Protected by offshore islands, the shallow waters of Corpus Christi Bay were a haven for smugglers before the Texas Revolution (1836). Commercial activity began when Henry L. Kinney (1814–1860s) opened a trading post here about 1838. After the Mexican War (1846–1848), Corpus Christi became a departure point for the California Gold Rush (1849) and a main stop on the route between San Antonio and the Rio Grande Valley.

In 1854 the city authorized dredging operations to make the harbor accessible to deep water vessels. In 1857 a circuitous 32-mile long channel was opened from Corpus Christi Bay to Aransas Pass. Blockaded by Federal ships during the Civil War (1861–1865), Corpus Christi remained a major port for Confederate trade with Mexico until the harbor was captured in 1864. The ship channel was widened and deepened in 1874.

Elihu Harrison Ropes of New Jersey came to Corpus Christi in 1890 with ambitious plans for development of the city and port. Using a steam dredge, he began digging a 14-mile long, 15-foot deep pass across Mustang Island. The "Ropes Boom" collapsed in the Panic of 1893, but Ropes' efforts laid a foundation for the opening of the Port of Corpus Christi of Sept. 15, 1926, and its success as one of the nation's largest seaports.   (1977)

CORPUS CHRISTI (Nueces Co.)   *IH-37, Courthouse Grounds*
Nueces County
Named for Rio Nueces (River of Nuts), its northern border.

In 1519, Pineda, one of the first Spanish explorers, paused briefly in this area. Spain founded Fort Lipantitlan nearby in 1531. Post, named for an Indian village, fell into Anglo-American hands in 1835 during Texas Revolution.

Strategic value of this area (with its outlet to the sea) was recognized in 1845 when U.S. Army forces camped here en route to battlefronts in Mexican War.

County was created in 1846 and organized in 1847 with Corpus Christi as the county seat.
                                                                                        (1970)

CORPUS CHRISTI (Nueces Co.)   *City Park on Ocean Drive*
Alonzo Álvarez de Pineda
In 1519, the Spanish government commissioned Alonzo Álvarez de Pineda (1494–1519) to explore the coast of the Gulf of Mexico in the hope of finding a water passage from the Gulf to the Orient. Ships, men, and money for the expedition were provided by the Governor of Jamaica, Francisco de Garay, who had been on Christopher Columbus' second voyage to the New World.

Pineda followed the coast from what is now western Florida to present-day Vera Cruz, Mexico. During his 9-month expedition he mapped nearly 800 miles of shoreline, including the rivers and bays that emptied into the Gulf. He arrived in Vera Cruz in August 1519 to find that another explorer, Hernán Cortés, already had claimed the land. After escaping from Cortés, who had attempted to capture him, Pineda sailed north, stopping briefly near a river that was probably the Rio Grande. He may have died of wounds received in an Indian fight there, since his return to Jamaica never was confirmed.

Pineda's report and detailed map were forwarded to Governor Garay and then to King Charles I of Spain. Although Pineda's expedition was a failure in that he found no passage to the Orient, it did encourage further exploration along the Gulf Coast that led to colonization by Spaniards and other Europeans.   (1983)

CORPUS CHRISTI (Nueces Co.)   *Ocean Dr. at South Alameda*
Karankawa Indians
Among the first Indians encountered in Texas by 16th and 17th century European explorers were the nomadic Karankawas, who lived along the coast from Galveston Bay to the Corpus Christi area. A primitive tribe, the Karankawas fished and gathered roots and cactus fruit for food. The men were usually tall and wore their hair long or braided with colorful bits of flannel and rattlesnake rattles. The women were shorter and stouter. The Indians often smeared their bodies with alligator grease and dirt to repel mosquitoes. At first friendly to Europeans, they later gained a reputation for savagery. Persistent reports that the Karankawas were cannibals may be traced to occasional ritualistic practices.

Attempts by Spanish Franciscans to found missions for this coastal tribe were not successful. Never large in numbers, the Karankawa population dwindled as a result of diseases contracted from Europeans. During the 19th century, many of the Indians were killed in warfare with Jean Lafitte's pirates and with Anglo-American colonists. Remaining members of the tribe fled to Mexico about 1843. Annihilation of that remnant about 1858 marked the disappearance of the Karankawa Indians.
                                                                                        (1976)

CORPUS CHRISTI (Nueces Co.)   *IH-37, Frontage Rd. at Mountain Trail*
Calallen
The rural Nueces County settlement of Calallen was established by the Calvin Townsite Company on August 18, 1910. The president of the firm was the prominent local cattleman Calvin J. Allen (1859–1922), for whom the town was named. The area's abundant water supply and the settlement's location on the St. Louis, Brownsville and Mexico Rail Line resulted in Calallen's development as an important agricultural center of the region.

Calallen's greatest period of growth occurred from the 1920s to the 1940s. During that time it was the site of a hotel, funeral home, lumberyard, post office, doctor's office, bank, churches, a variety of stores and a school district, formed in 1914. Major employers here included a Corpus

Christi water plant and the vegetable packing firm of C. E. Coleman. Residents of the community included some of the prominent cattlemen and business leaders of South Texas.

Calallen's decline began as new roads resulted in dramatic growth for Corpus Christi. Although the Calallen school remained in operation, the rural town was annexed by Corpus Christi in 1970. Today the area serves as a reminder of the early residents who were vital to the growth of Nueces County. (1982)

CORRIGAN (Polk Co.) US 287, 1 mi. N
P. B. Maxey Home
Built early 1860s on a 160-acre tract by P. B. Maxey, farmer and rancher.

Constructed of pine logs, using pegs, square nails, and hand-riven shingles, house had two rooms and a kitchen.

Remodeled 1947, the home is still in Maxey family. Has Medallion Plate. (1968)

CORSICANA (Navarro Co.) US 75 cut off, 1 mi. N
Navarro County
Formed from Robertson County. Created April 25, 1846; organized July 13, 1846. Named in honor of Jose Antonio Navarro 1795–1871. Soldier, patriot and statesman, signer of the Texas Declaration of Independence, member of the Texas Congress 1838, Commissioner on the Santa Fe Expedition, delegate in 1845 to the Constitutional Convention. County seat Corsicana.

CORSICANA (Navarro Co.) SH 22 (1465 W 2nd)
James Clinton Neill
Born in 1790 in North Carolina, James Clinton Neill came to Texas in 1831 with Stephen F. Austin's third colony. He settled in Milam County and represented his neighbors at the Convention of 1833.

On September 28, 1835, Neill entered the Texas Army as captain of artillery, and was promoted to Lt. Colonel in December. He was in charge of artillery at the Siege of Bexar, and soon thereafter was appointed by Sam Houston to the Commandancy of San Antonio and the Bexar District, including the fortifications at the Alamo. When he received word in February of illness in his family, Neill left the Alamo in the command of William B. Travis, and so was not among the defenders who lost their lives on March 6.

In charge of an artillery unit with Sam Houston's army in April, Neill was wounded in a skirmish on April 20, one day before the Battle of San Jacinto. He was appointed Indian commissioner in 1844. Neill was living in present Navarro County when it was created from Robertson County in 1846. He and two partners donated land for the county seat.

James Clinton Neill and his wife, Margaret Harriet were the parents of three children. Neill died in March 1848, and is buried in Grimes County. (Texas Sesquicentennial 1836–1986)

CORSICANA (Navarro Co.) SH 22 W, Collins Catholic School
James L. Collins
Born in Weston, West Virginia, James Lawrence Collins (1883-1953) began his career in the petroleum industry at age fourteen. New oil discoveries in Texas brought him to the Corsicana area about 1923. He soon formed a partnership with two brothers, John and Robert Wheelock, and founded the Wheelock & Collins Oil Co.

Collins' business was instrumental in the development of the Corsicana field, the East Texas field, and other oil fields around the country. His success and expertise were widely recognized throughout the industry and led him into positions of leadership in several national petroleum associations.

Never married, Collins provided upon his death that his $13 million estate be divided among four organizations. These included Dallas' Scottish Rite Hospital for Crippled Children and St. Joseph's Orphanage. Part of the estate went to his local Roman Catholic parish, which used the money to build and operate the school at this site. The remainder of his estate went to create scholarships for graduates of Corsicana High School.

Collins' contributions as a businessman and civic leader played an important role in the development and history of the Corsicana area. (1983)

COTTONWOOD (Callahan Co.)   *SH 21, eastern edge of city*
Site of Cottonwood Springs
After Indians on High Plains were subdued (1874) by Gen. R. S. Mackenzie, settlers started to pour into this area, where they found abundant game, water, and good soil for ranching, farming.

Cottonwood Springs, at head of Green Briar Creek, was one of first villages founded (in 1875). The town soon became a trading center for southeastern part of county. It had several stores, two churches, and a school; and although usually peaceful, it experienced many gun battles.

The town name was shortened to "Cottonwood" after first post office was established in 1883.
(1967)

COTULLA (La Salle Co.)   *IH 35, .5 mi. S beyond Nueces River Bridge*
                                                      about 1 mi. off IH 35 on S side
The Nueces River
Until 1836 this river formed the undisputed western boundary of Texas. By the Treaty of Guadalupe Hidalgo, signed in February 1848, the boundary line between Mexico and the United States was fixed at the Rio Grande.

COTULLA (La Salle Co.)   *Cotulla courthouse lawn*
La Salle County
The Presidio Rio Grande brought travel to this area for centuries. In 1852, the U.S. Army built Fort Ewell, to protect the region. William A. Waugh, the first settler, established a ranch in 1856 near Cibolo Crossing on the Spanish road. On Feb. 1, 1858, the county was created but not organized. It was named for Robert Cavalier, Sieur De La Salle (1643–1687), first French explorer of Texas. The county's first post office opened in 1871 at the Guajuco Crossing. County government was organized at Crarey's Rancho on Nov. 2, 1880. Offices were at temporary sites until 1884, when Cotulla was made the County Seat.

COTULLA (La Salle Co.)   *SH 468, Cotulla Cemetery*
Cotulla Cemetery
Land for this cemetery was first given by Joseph Cotulla, the town's founding father. The earliest marked grave is dated 1882. Numerous graves bear the date 1886, when smallpox struck La Salle County. Many community leaders, including Joseph Cotulla, and the Rev. V. E. Covey, early Texas educator, are buried here. The cemetery was originally divided into Mexican and Anglo-American sections. In 1941, six acres of land were added to the first site. Under the care of the Cotulla Cemetery Association since 1915, this is the chief burial ground in La Salle County.
(1981)

COVE (Chambers Co.)   *FM 2354 S—Cedar Point Rd.*
Site of Home of General Sam Houston
Constructed about 1860. Occupied by him as a residence during part of 1861 and a part of 1862.

CRANDALL (Kaufman Co.)   *Gleason and South Main (Bus. 175)*
Crandall
Named for The Rev. C. F. Crandall (1827–1906), Methodist minister who came here from Indiana, 1877, and bought 1800 acres of land. When Texas Trunk Line Railroad built east from Dallas in 1880, he gave bonus for rail service and was first postmaster when post office was created in 1881. Baptists, Disciples of Christ, and Methodists built churches. Townsite plat was recorded in 1889. The city school system was established in 1901. By the early 1900s, town had a lumber yard, several stores, 3 physicians, 3 banks. It remains a center for agriculture and recreation.
(1971)

CRANE (Crane Co.)   *Two locations: US 385, 7 mi. S in roadside park;*
                                                    also, US 67/385, 15 mi. S
Horsehead Crossing of the Pecos
Well known to frontiersmen and used by emigrants for several years preceding. This crossing was an important point on the Southern Overland Mail (Butterfield Route) which linked St. Louis and San Francisco with semi-weekly mail and stage service (1858–1861).

CRANE (Crane Co.)   *US 385, 7 mi. S in roadside park*
Castle Mountain
(2 mi. E)
About 3000 ft. elevation. Since 17th century, a landmark in travel from Texas points to Mexico and California. According to tradition, named by Spaniards for resemblance to ancient castles. Has association with stories of lost trains of gold and other treasures.

CRANE (Crane Co.)   *US 385, 10 mi. N*
Crane County
Formed from Tom Green County. Created February 26, 1887; organized September 3, 1927. Named in honor of William Carey Crane (1816–1885), a Baptist minister, president of Baylor University (1863–1885). Crane, County Seat.

CRANE (Crane Co.)   *Crane on FM 1601, 8 mi. NW*
One Hundred Million Barrels of Oil
From Block 31 Unit
A discovery well completed in Nov. 1945 about a mile to the northeast has led to vast production of oil—one hundred million barrels by July 27, 1969.

The discovery well, University A No. 1, was drilled by the Atlantic Richfield Company. This development is on land belonging to the University of Texas, designated as Block 31 Unit, and leased to Atlantic Richfield (the operator), Phillips Petroleum Company, Continental Oil Company and Champlin Petroleum Company. The unit—7,200 acres in area—has 72 wells approximately 8,500 feet deep, into the earth stratum known as the Devonian Formation.

Through the years, unusual processes were used to increase unit oil recovery. High pressure natural gas was injected, to wash oil from subterranean rock. Later, exhaust gas was injected instead of the costlier natural gas.

Research and farsighted policies made possible unusually high recovery in this reservoir. Credit for the conservation and good management of this unit goes to the Texas Railroad Commission (as the regulatory body with oversight of oil production), the University of Texas and owners of the unit.   (1969)

CRANE (Crane Co.)   *US 385 (S Gaston)*
Charles Booth Curry
(1890–1962)
Born in the Smith County town of Troup, C. B. Curry became a law enforcement official at an early age. In Jan. 1933, he joined the Texas Rangers and served for two years in Falfurrias and San Angelo. He came to Crane in 1935 as special investigator and helped preserve order during the town's oil boom days. He later served as deputy sheriff and chief of police before going into private business.

Curry was married twice and had seven children.   (1977)

CRANE (Crane Co.)   *US 385, 5 mi. N*
Church & Fields Oil Discovery Well
(Drilling site 2.25 mi. SE)
Since 1839, Texas has set aside her public lands to finance education. The University of Texas at Austin acquired the land at this site in 1883, after the first owner, a railroad company, returned it to the state as worthless. For years McElroy Ranch grazed cattle here. On similar terrain 70 miles to the southeast the Santa Rita gusher blew in during 1923, and soon other university lands were being explored for oil.

Church & Fields Exploration Company, composed of George M. Church and Robert Fields of San Angelo, obtained a permit late in 1925 to drill in Section 34, Block 30, in university land on McElroy Ranch. On Dec. 28, 1925, contractor Burton F. Weekley and driller John Garlin started the Church & Fields well, 2.25 miles southeast of this spot. In March 1926 this became Crane County's first oil producer, opening a new major field for West Texas. Soon other wells were drilled and local population rose from 27 to about 4,500. In Sept. 1927, county government was organized as a result of the oil field activity.

Until 1955, the discovery well continued to produce. Since the day it proved successful and an asset to education and energy production, over a billion barrels of oil have come from University of Texas lands. (1978)

CRAWFORD (McLennan Co.)   *9162 Cedar Rock Parkway (FM 185)*
Crawford
Located in an area of McLennan County once inhabited by Tonkawa Indians, the community of Crawford grew slowly from an 1850s settlement centered around Tonk Crossing (two miles northeast). The first townsite was at the crossroads of the Waco to Gatesville and Belton to Fort Graham trade routes. The exact source for the town's name is unknown, but possibilities include Coryell city resident William Nelson Crawford, who graded the Tonk Creek Crossing, A.C. Crawford of Galveston, a director of the Gulf, Colorado & Santa Fe Railroad, or Texas Ranger George Crawford, who was stationed here.

Development increased following the Civil War, and the post office opened in 1871. By the latter part of that decade, the town included several stores, a tavern, a blacksmith shop and a school with an enrollment of about 100.

In 1881, the Gulf, Colorado & Santa Fe Railroad, building north from Temple to Fort Worth, bypassed the original townsite, and residents began moving here along the new line. Crawford experienced economic growth as a result, and there were soon four churches, a cotton gin and a grain mill. Incorporated in 1897, the town remained an important agricultural center throughout the twentieth century, at times boasting more than 700 residents, two banks and dozens of local businesses.

In July 1999, Texas Governor George W. Bush and his family bought the former Englebrecht Ranch (Prairie Chapel Ranch) west of town. His election as President of the United States in 2000 turned the ranch into the "Western White House," the site of gatherings for U.S. officials and foreign Heads of State. Crawford gained international media attention and served as the official voting place for President Bush and First Lady Laura Bush. (2004)

CRESSON (Parker Co.)   *US 377, Texas Refinery Recreation Ranch*
Goforth Graves
Burial place of 4 people, on land settled in 1857 by J. L. and Elizabeth Goforth.

A 2-year-old son, John L. Goforth, Jr., was buried here 1863, while Goforth was in 18th Tex. Cav., in Civil War.

Chadwick family, neighbors, also used this cemetery. (1966)

CRESSON (Parker Co.)   *US 377, Texas Refinery Recreation Ranch*
Sunshine Special
Ellsmere
One of the most elegant private cars in the world when it was built in 1914 for the personal use of Dr. W. S. Webb, president of Wagner Palace Car Company.

When New York Central's "20th Century Limited" express broke New York Chicago rail passenger speed record 1932, this was the rear car.

Owned 1920–1961 by T & P Railway presented in 1962 to Fort Worth Childrens Museum.

CRESSON (Parker Co.)   *US 377, 6 mi. W Cresson*
Elizabeth Crockett
Three miles south to the grave of Elizabeth Crockett, wife of hero of the Alamo. Died March 2, 1860, age 74.

CROCKETT (Houston Co.)   *SH 21, near FM 227 intersection, 19.5 mi. NE*
Site of the
Daniel McLean Claim
Daniel McLean (1784–1837) first came to Texas in 1813 with the Gutierrez-Magee expedition, and was one of 93 survivors of the fateful Battle of the Medina.

Returning with his wife Hannah (Sheridan) in the original Austin Colony, he settled this league in 1821 and became first permanent resident of area now in Houston County. McLean and his brother-in-law John Sheridan were killed by Indians May 10, 1837, near site of present town of Elkhart, Texas.

Daniel and Hannah McLean are buried near this marker. Because of their pioneering spirit, this has been McLean land since 1821. (1972)

CROCKETT (Houston Co.) *SH 21, 17.7 mi. NE*
Glover School
Established in 1881, the Glover School served residents of the rural Glover community. Under the direction of teacher James Breeze, a one-room schoolhouse was built on A. E. Sloan's land, now the site of the old Glover cemetery. A consolidated school district was formed in 1936 and the third schoolhouse was built at this site soon after. Destroyed by fire in 1938, it was rebuilt the next year. The school merged with the Kennard district in 1967, but community identity and pride provided by the early school are reflected in biennial reunions of ex-students and teachers.
(1981)

CROCKETT (Houston Co.) *SH 19, .8 mi. N*
Houston County
Houston County, created from Nacogdoches County, June 12, 1837; organized the same year; named in honor of Sam Houston 1793–1863, Commander-in-Chief of the Texan Army at San Jacinto, President of the Republic and Governor of the State of Texas, Senator in the United States Congress, 1846–1859.
Crockett, the County Seat.

CROCKETT (Houston Co.) *SH 21 at FM 1280, 14 mi. SW at Austonio*
Site of Old Block House
Established before 1836; used by Elisha Clapp and neighboring settlers as a place of defense against Indians. Abandoned about 1844. (1936)

CROCKETT (Houston Co.) *SH 21, 4 mi. E*
Stage Coach Inn
Built as a home by Joseph D. Rice, Sr., who came to Texas in 1828. In 1838 it was designated as a stopping place for the stage coach from Nacogdoches to Crockett.

CROCKETT (Houston Co.) *SH 21, 1.5 mi. E*
A. E. Gossett Home
House on typical southern plan, with separate kitchen in back yard. Built 1835 by A. E. Gossett, owner of large land grant from Mexico. An early 1836 visitor was former Tennessee neighbor, Col. David Crockett, on his way to the Alamo, and camping with his company for a night at the spring nearby. Has Medallion Plate. (1964)

CROCKETT (Houston Co.) *Old SH 21 at Loop 304, .5 mi. W*
Smith Brothers
Houston County natives Francis Albert (1875–1949) and James Henry (Jim) (1878–1930) Smith formed a business partnership in 1904 called Smith Brothers. Among their early business enterprises were a livery stable, family farms, and real estate. Following the advent of the automobile industry, they also sold cars and became interested in road construction.

Using their own funds, the Smith Brothers constructed a 6.9-mile section of Old State Highway 21 west of Crockett in 1923. It was the first paved highway in the area. The company also paved roads in the city, including brick paving on the courthouse square.

The brothers' business grew to include projects in California, Kansas, Florida, Illinois, North Carolina, Oklahoma, Louisiana, Tennessee, and New Mexico. Other Smith Brothers companies, formed in Dallas and San Antonio, included contracting and cement operations, as well as real estate development and investments in hotels in San Antonio, Corpus Christi, and Crockett. They also owned ranches in Houston and Concho Counties.

Following Jim Smith's death in 1930, many of the company's assets were liquidated. The partnership was finally dissolved in 1937. (1989)

CROCKETT (Houston Co.) *SH 7 right-of-way, 6.6 mi. W*
Oakland
Named for the oak trees in the vicinity, Oakland was a rural settlement in the late 19th and early 20th centuries. A townsite was never platted, and the community was composed of

scattered homes between the Trinity River and Crockett. A church, cotton gin, and school were in operation for a brief time. Among the early settlers of the area were Wilson E. Hail, who later served as Houston County sheriff, and Z. S. Thompson. The settlement began to decline by the 1930s. Some descendants of early settlers remain in the area. (1988)

CROCKETT (Houston Co.) — SH 7, 1 mi. W of Ratcliff
Four C Mill
R. M. Keith, agent for Central Coal & Coke Co., Kansas City, Mo., in Oct. 1899, began purchasing the virgin pine timberlands of this region. Lumber for construction of a new mill was cut by a small sawmill bought by Keith, Jan. 10, 1901, from local landowner, J. H. Ratcliff. Although known as "Four C" Mill, it was operated by the Louisiana & Texas Lumber Co., organized by Keith in July 1901. The mill began sawing lumber in June 1902, producing 300,000 board feet per 11-hour day.

The Texas Southeastern Railroad laid tracks from Lufkin; tram roads and tap lines were built into the forest to haul fresh-cut timber to the mill.

The company built houses and a "company store" at the mill, and several logging camps in the forest to house and feed lumberjacks. Hostility erupted when town of Ratcliff was begun nearby, competing for the workers' trade. Between the mill and Ratcliff the company erected a 16-foot fence, which was dynamited several times, thwarting the attempts to establish a company-controlled town.

By 1917, the company had exhausted the 120,000 acres it had purchased. The mill was shut down and dismantled in 1920, due to shortage of good timber.

Nearby Ratcliff Lake was the Four C Millpond. (1973)

CROCKETT (Houston Co.) — SH 7, 12 mi. E
Randolph Community
(1 mi. N)
Settled 1838, by Cyrus Halbert Randolph (1817–1889) on the San Felipe de Austin-Nacogdoches mail route. Randolph was member of Snively Expedition, county justice of peace, coroner, chief justice, and sheriff; state legislator and treasurer.

School was opened about 1850, and post office established June 30, 1858. Had 2 stores, blacksmith shop, saloon, and barber shop in 1860, when it tried to wrest the county seat from Crockett, after which Randolph slowly began to decline in population. Demise of the settlement was marked by the closing of the post office September 29, 1881. (1973)

CROCKETT (Houston Co.) — US 287 at SH 19 and FM 2160, 3 mi. N
John Wortham
A pioneer area landowner and farmer, John Wortham (1804–1867) was a petitioner for the creation of Houston County in 1837. He later served as captain of an independent Ranger company, as Major in the Republic of Texas Army, and as Quartermaster of the Texas Militia. In addition to his military service, he was a trustee of Trinity College and was appointed to the first Board of Land Commissioners for the Texas Republic. He also owned a local sawmill and gristmill. Twice married, Wortham was the father of 12 children. He was buried on his land (2.3 mi. SW). (1982)

CROCKETT (Houston Co.) — SH 19, 3 mi. S
Givens Homesite
Solomon George Givens and his wife Lula (Burleson), both born in Houston County in 1871, were the children of former slaves. They were married in Crockett in 1891, and in 1892 they bought 34 acres of land here. Their farm proved a success and in 1893 they built a large 8-room house at this site.

The Givenses were noted for their charity and as leaders in the development of a nearby school and Baptist church; baptism services took place in a tank on their land. For many years their home was the center of an African American farming community known as "Givens Hill." (1994)

CROCKETT (Houston Co.) — US 287 right-of-way, 7 mi. SE
Hopewell Community and Gudeblye School
The Hopewell Community began as a freedmen's town in the 1870s. At its height it included homes, farms, small businesses, a church, and a school. Established on land once owned by an Anglo teacher named Good Blye (Bly), the school's name evolved into Gudeblye over the years.

In 1925, it became a part of Houston County's Agricultural Training School program, and by 1949 it was annexed to the Crockett School System. Descendants of the early settlers and alumni of the school still reside in the area. (1990)

CROCKETT (Houston Co.) — *US 287 S, 15 mi. SE*
Albert Holley House
In 1857, Albert Holley (b. 1828), his mother and two brothers, migrated to Houston County from Alabama. While the others journeyed to Texas by boat, he brought the family's supplies overland by wagon with 137 slaves. By 1860, he and his wife Julia (Russell) (1840–1897) had begun homesteading this land. After serving in the Civil War, where he was a prisoner of war, Albert continued to farm here. In 1867, he constructed a new home for his family at this site. He died in 1907, but his land remained in the ownership of Holley family members until 1976. (1983)

CROCKETT (Houston Co.) — *SH 21 (near), 4 mi. NE*
Original Site of
The Joseph R. Rice Log Cabin
Joseph Redmond Rice (1805–1866) and his wife, Willie Masters Rice (1809–1881), natives of Tennessee and Kentucky, built a one-room log cabin on this site in 1828. Rice's brothers and his father-in-law, Jacob Masters, probably helped with the building. The men cut the logs in the woods, and Willie Rice drove a team that snaked them to the clearing for the house-raising. Menaced by hostile Indians, the Rices fled to Louisiana, but returned in the 1830s. Over ensuing years, they enlarged the cabin and increased their family to eleven children. Their dwelling became known in the Republic of Texas as a place to lodge or take meals on the San Antonio Road, between the towns of Nacogdoches and Crockett. After Joseph and Willie Rice died, descendants lived in the log house until 1919, when a grandson shifted it some 300 feet and built a new frame house on the original site. The historic house was then used to store grain and shelter farm implements and the family automobile.

The Rice homesite was commemorated in 1936 by the Texas Centennial Commission, and in 1973 the old log house was given to the state. Relocated in Tejas Mission Park (16 mi. NE), it has been restored and is on exhibition as a relic of frontier days. (1976)

CROCKETT (Houston Co.) — *SH 21, 14 mi. NE*
Pine Springs Campground
A favorite campsite of Tejas Indians in the years before European settlers arrived, this location was used in turn by explorers, Spanish missionaries, traders, and armies. Travelers were attracted by abundant game, including deer and wild turkey, and fresh water which flowed from springs 300 feet from El Camino Real (The King's Highway). Nineteenth-century pioneers ringed their wagons in the grove and rested en route to settlements. Hunting parties later camped at Pine Springs for weeks at a time. (1972)

CROSBY (Harris Co.) — *US 90 at San Jacinto River, about 1 mi. SW*
Humphrey Jackson
(November 24, 1784–January 18, 1833)
Educated in law, Humphrey Jackson left his native Ireland in 1808, during a period of political conflict. He migrated to the United States and settled on a sugar plantation in Louisiana. While there, he served in the 1815 Battle of New Orleans.

Unable to manage his plantation without the use of slavery, which he opposed, Jackson sold his land and came to Texas in 1823 to join Stephen F. Austin's colony. Not realizing he was locating outside the colony's boundaries, he settled on land at this site. When the error was discovered, he joined other area settlers in successfully petitioning the Mexican government to form the San Jacinto District under control of the Austin Colony. Jackson was elected to serve as alcalde of the new district.

One of the pioneer settlers in present Harris County, Jackson was active in the early local government. His efforts on behalf of the surrounding settlement and his ability to mediate disputes impartially led to further development of the area.

In 1833, Jackson was killed by a falling tree while clearing his land. Twice married, he was the father of four children. His descendants include prominent business, professional, and political leaders. (1982)

CROSBYTON (Crosby Co.)　　　　　　　*US 82, 4 mi. E of 1½ mi. N of Old Dewey Lake*

Old Dewey Lake

Once an important landmark for early surveys of this area, Dewey Lake got its name after surveyors returned from here to headquarters and found, to their embarrassment, they had not yet named this site. Gallantly, they decided to call it after land office employee Miss Dewey.

Lake shore was site of Texas Ranger Camp "Roberts" (1879–1882) and the "Stag House," barracks for the cowboys of the Two-Buckle Ranch. Surveyors often camped here too.

The lake disappeared in the 1880s after two creeks eroded its banks, forming a new channel which drained the lake basin.　　　　　　　　　　　　　　　　　　　　　(1967)

CROSBYTON (Crosby Co.)　　　　　　　　　*US 82, 3 mi. E in roadside park*

High Plains Pioneer
Henry Clay Smith (1836–1912)

First to set up a post office and farm in Crosby County; first to break land and build a water well on High Plains.

At the start of the Civil War, he was a miner at Pinos Altos, New Mexico, and joined in moves to take over gold and silver mines for the South. But Indian raids closed mines.

When the Confederate Army withdrew from Arizona and Mexico in 1861, Smith along with others joined the South's cause. He served four years in Texas and spent rest of his life here.

A replica of the old rock house he built near here in 1877 is now shown in the museum at Crosbyton.　　　　　　　　　　　　　　　　　　　　　　　　　(1965)

CROSBYTON (Crosby Co.)　　　　　　　　　*US 82 and FM 2591, 3 mi. E*

Two-Buckle Ranch Headquarters
Kentucky Cattle Raising Company

Headquarters for the Two-Buckle Ranch was built near this site, at Silver Falls, in 1884 by the Kentucky Cattle Raising Company, which had been founded two years earlier by a group of Louisville, Kentucky, distillers. Claude Tilford was hired by the company to manage the 145,240-acre ranch. A variety of grain and hay crops were grown. The ranch's cattle operation featured cross breeding and separation of breeding stock.

In 1901, the C. B. Livestock Company bought 90,000 acres of the land and used the established headquarters for its -N- ranching and plains land development operations. A dipping vat was built in 1912 and was used by all area cattlemen to combat Texas cattle fever. Since the 1915 breakup of the C. B. Livestock Company, succeeding owners have continued to add to and preserve the original headquarters site. A barn, garage, concrete storage tank, as well as a dam across White River were added during the 1920s.

Over the years, this land has been home for a number of families who have contributed to Crosby County's ranching heritage. The Two-Buckle Ranch headquarters is a historic reminder of this early West Texas industry.　　　　　　　　　　　　　　　　　(1984)

CROSBYTON (Crosby Co.)　　　　　　　　　*US 82, 3 mi. E in roadside park*

Main Supply Camp on Historic
Mackenzie Trail
(3 mi. SE)

Trail followed by Gen. Ranald Mackenzie, U.S. 4th Cavalry in 1871 frontier campaign. He camped at Dewey Lake after brush with Indians.

In 1872, he was again ordered to ferret out the Comanches.

From his main supply camp on Brazos River Freshwater Fork (now White River) he launched a drive against Quanah Parker.

Ended with fights in Palo Duro and Tule Canyons, last battles between Indians and Cavalry in this area: opened the plains to white settlement.　　　　　　　　　　　　(1966)

CROSBYTON (Crosby Co.)　　　　　　　　　*SH 82 at FM 2591, 4 mi. E*

Texas Ranger Campsite
(1 mi. N)

Law and order for plains area began here in 1879 with creation of Camp Roberts, first ranger station in Panhandle. Company C of the newly formed Frontier Battalion of Texas Rangers was located here and commanded by Capt. G. W. Arrington, Civil War veteran, hard-fighting ranger, later a Panhandle sheriff and rancher. Battalion commander was Maj. John B. Jones.

Frontier Battalion was created to protect settlers from marauding Indians and outlaws; rowdy cowboys also needed disciplining. Capt. Arrington's C Company was to have 75 men to meet these duties—he never had more than 28. A large territory and few men to cover it meant scouting parties always on the move.

Living conditions on the vast, arid plains, scouting trips, encounters with violence, long watches over dangerous captives made a Ranger's life hard. Each man was self supporting, furnishing his own saddle, ropes, guns, clothing, horse, bedding; he received small salary, ammunition and food from the state. Shooting matches provided much of his off-duty entertainment.

By 1881 local Indian menace was removed; rangers went to new frontier, 1882. Remnants of Camp Roberts today are foundations of three sod buildings around an old well used by the Rangers. (1967)

CROSBYTON (Crosby Co.) — *US 82 at FM 836, 10.3 mi. E*
Near Site of Pansy Baptist Church
The Pansy Baptist Church was organized in 1905 by J. V. Leatherwood, John Holt, P. H. Leatherwood, Snow Loyd, and J. M. Leatherwood to serve the residents of the Pansy community, and church services were conducted in the school building until 1916 when the congregation constructed its first sanctuary. An arbor was built on the church grounds for revival services.

Church building was moved two miles south in 1946 for the convenience of the membership. A parsonage was erected in 1947 for the congregation's first full-time pastor and a new sanctuary was built and was dedicated on July 16, 1950. The church building burned in August 1965, and services were held in a church member's barn until December, when a new structure was completed. The church supported a strong mission outreach program.

Through the years population dwindled in the rural community of Pansy. In 1995, the remaining members of the Pansy Baptist Church voted to disband. The church building was donated to the Mt. Zion Baptist Church, an African American congregation in Floydada.

The building was moved 32 miles by 140 volunteers from Crosbyton, Pansy, Floydada, and Wiley. (1996)

CROSS PLAINS (Callahan Co.) — *SH 36 W, in Treadway Park*
1 mi. E to
Fort Mason—Camp Cooper
Military Road
Route for U.S. 2nd Cavalry and supplies from San Antonio to Fort Mason (about 100 mi. S of here) to Camp Cooper (about 65 mi. N.) in campaigns of 1851–1861 against Plains Indians. Great military men of American history traveled this road. Including Robt. E. Lee (later a commanding general, C.S.A.) and Geo. T. Thomas, "Rock of Chickamauga."

CROSS ROADS (Henderson Co.) — *RR 3273 E right-of-way, 3.5 mi. SE*
Science Hill
A group of pioneers from Tennessee, Mississippi, Arkansas, and Louisiana founded the Science Hill community when they arrived in this area in 1846. Their hope for the settlement was that it would become a cultural and educational center for the county. Soon after their arrival, the residents started mills, cotton gins, mercantile businesses, churches, and schools.

The decade of the 1850s was one of growth and progress for Science Hill. A Methodist church was organized by the Rev. William D. Sansom, and the Science Hill Masonic Lodge began meeting in 1857. Members of the lodge and other citizens helped found Science Hill Academy, which opened in 1858. The first school of higher education in Henderson County, the academy offered classes in arithmetic, geography, history, elocution, Latin, Greek, natural science, and logic. Educator A. J. Fowler (1815–1886) was instrumental in its founding and served as first principal.

During the harsh years of the Civil War and reconstruction, families began moving away from Science Hill. The academy closed in 1872. By 1878, the Masonic Lodge had only 12 members, and its charter was surrendered. Science Hill became a ghost town, leaving only its history as a reminder of the community. (1984)

CROWELL (Foard Co.) *SH 6, 2 mi. N*
Foard County
Formed from Hardeman, King, Cottle and Knox counties. Created March 3, 1891; organized April 27, 1891.

Named in honor of Robert L. Foard 1831–1898. A Confederate officer. Prominent lawyer of Columbus, Texas.

Crowell, the county seat. Traversed by a railroad in 1908.

CROWELL (Foard co.) *SH 6, courthouse lawn*
Robert L. Foard
Star and Wreath
County named honor Texas Confederate officer (1836–1898) Came to Texas from Maryland, 1853. Prominent pioneer lawyer and citizen. Lt. Columbus Grays Texas Militia Co. 1861. Confederate major 13th Texas Infantry Regiment, which successfully guarded portion Texas coast against raiding parties from Union blockading vessels. 13th stationed 7 weeks, 1863, Brashear City, LA., as part campaign to prevent split of South by loss of Mississippi River. Returned to coast duty until war's end. A memorial to Texans who served the Confederacy. (1963)

CROWELL (Foard Co.) *SH 6, 4½ mi. N at site*
Site of Old Pease City
Founded in 1880 by Benjamin E. Lower, John Wesley and wife, first settlers. Lower became the first postmaster, 1880; Mrs. Wesley was second, 1882. Place was named for Pease River and E. M. Pease, Texas governor (1853–1857 and 1867–1869).

Second group of settlers was family of W. T. Dunn.

Stone post office-trading post served 3,500 square miles of sparsely settled country. Mail delivery was by stage or horse.

The post office was abolished 1885 when Margaret became seat of Hardeman County. In 1891 site of Old Pease City and Margaret became part of Foard County. (1967)

CRYSTAL CITY (Zavala Co.) *US 83, 1.9 mi. N*
Zavala County
Explored as early as 1691 by the expedition of Domingo Teran de Los Rios, Spanish governor of Texas. The historic San Antonio Road crossed this region from southwest to northeast and was used by most of the Spanish explorers and travelers of the 18th century. French-American explorer St. Denis used it in 1714, as did the Canary Islanders, who made one of the first civil settlements in San Antonio, in 1718.

The county was created in 1858 from Uvalde and Maverick Counties and named for Texas patriot and statesman Lorenzo de Zavala. Not until 1884, however, did enough people reside here to permit it to be organized. The first county seat was Bates City, later renamed Batesville. First judge was J. M. Downs and commissioners were W. C. Mangum, E. P. Waller, V. M. West and G. B. Kenney. Before 1884 was out, a school election had been held in Palo Blanco, and a $7,500 contract had been let for a courthouse and jail.

When the county seat moved to Crystal City (1928) courthouse and jail were built here. New courthouse erected 1969 at cost of $475,000 was commissioned by 1968–1969 county courts: Irl Taylor, judge; Cecil Davis, Jr..; F. D. Keller, Jr.; H. R. Reynolds; E. B. Ross; Jesus Rodriguez; and Henry Volz, Jr., commissioners. (1969)

CUERO (DeWitt Co.) *US 183 & 77A right-of-way, 2.6 mi. S*
Near Clinton Cemetery, Burial Place
James Norman Smith
(1789–1875)
"Uncle Jimmy the Peacemaker." Son of Sgt. James Turner Smith, veteran of American Revolution.

Born and educated in North Carolina. Lived for 32 years in Tennessee, where he taught James K. Polk, later a U.S. President.

Taught first school in area now DeWitt County, 1840 (year he came to Texas). Surveyed DeWitt County; was first county clerk. Organized Presbyterian Churches at Victoria, Hochheim,

Clinton, Peebles Ranch, Mill Creek, Live Oak and Cuero. Organized first Masonic Lodge in county. At 1857 political rally, introduced old Tennessee friend, Sam Houston.   (1970)

CUERO (DeWitt Co.)   *US 183 at US 77A, 4 mi. N*
Site of Friar-Cardwell Stage Stand
In 1839 or 1840 at the junction of the La Grange-La Bahia and Victoria-Gonzales Roads (.5 mi. E), Daniel Boone Friar (1800–1858) built a home and store that served as a social, political, transportation, and trade center for early DeWitt County. In 1841 the two-story frame structure became an overnight stop on stagecoach lines between San Antonio and coastal towns. It was designed as a temporary courthouse for the short-lived judicial county of DeWitt in 1842. When the county was actually organized in 1846, the court met at Friar's place for several months. It was also the county's first post office, established on May 22, 1846, and named Cuero, with Friar as postmaster.

In 1849 Friar sold the building to Crockett Cardwell (1812–1891), who continued to operate it as a stage stand, store, post office, and community meeting place. The county's first Masonic Lodge, Cameron Lodge No. 76, A. F. & A. M., was organized in an upstairs room in Nov. 1850 and met there until Jan. 1853. When the Gulf, Western Texas, and Pacific Railroad located the town of Cuero four miles south of the Cardwell Stand in 1873, the post office was moved to that site. As the town along the railroad grew, other activities at the old stage stand ended. It was torn down in 1916.   (1974)

CUERO (DeWitt Co.)   *US 183, 7 mi. N*
Dr. William Watt White
(1829–1914)
Surgeon of Waul's Legion, Confederate Army.

Came to Texas about 1850. In 1856 got M. D. Degree in Philadelphia. During Civil War, saved many lives, but took typhoid, which contributed to loss of his eyesight. After blindness, practiced rest of his life. Was local educational and civic leader, this county.

Confederate doctors had many problems with drug supply, surgical tools, horse-drawn ambulances and hospitals. Instruments had to be bought in Europe (shipped through naval blockade) or captured from the foe. Drugs came in by blockade-runner or were brought from north by ladies who hid them in their pompadours, bustles, petticoats. Scarcities led to use of dogwood, willow and poplar bark tea as substitute for quinine. Mullein and other wild herbs were also medical substitutes. Garden poppies were milked for opium. Sutures were made of horse-hair softened by boiling, or by raveling silk cloth.

Female nurses were used for first time in army hospitals. This was first war to use anesthetics. Amputations left severed limbs stacked like wood around the field hospitals. Ambulances seemed never at hand for casualities; many died awaiting aid. Till the atom bomb, the Civil War was history's bloodiest.   (1965)

CUERO (DeWitt Co.)   *US 183 right-of-way, 7 mi. N*
George Washington Davis
Pennsylvania native George Washington Davis (1797–1853) brought his family to Texas in 1831. He selected a league of land near present-day Cuero in the Green DeWitt Colony and became an active participant in the movement toward Texas Independence, serving as a delegate to the second Convention of Texas in 1833 and as a delegate to the Consultation at San Felipe in 1835. After the revolution, Davis held a number of local public offices. He and his wife, Rebecca (d. 1846), are buried 1.8 miles west of this site.   (Texas Sesquicentennial 1836–1986)

CUERO (DeWitt Co.)   *US 87, 6 mi. SE*
Burns Station Cemetery
Reminder of DeWitt County's earliest settlement, Irish Creek, begun in 1826 when Arthur Burns (1780–1856) migrated from Missouri and Iowa to Texas. He joined colony of Green DeWitt and built a 2-story log home near here. Used as a refuge during Indian raids, the house was also visited by General Sam Houston, 1836. On Dec. 19, 1837, President Houston appointed Burns to Board of Land Commissioners, Victoria County (which then encompassed this portion of DeWitt County).

Area's first grist mill (operated 1856–1869 by Moses Rankin) was established by Burns. Near it clustered the Sherman & Thomas General Store, Charlie White's Blacksmith Shop, and Warn Hardware. The Irish Creek settlement became known as Burns Station, as it was a stage stop on the Victoria-Gonzales Road.

Cemetery site, donated 1853 by Ardelia Burns Cook, daughter of Arthur Burns, adjoined the Irish Creek Methodist Church. In oldest marked grave lies Joseph Allen (1812–1853), born in Ireland. Here also is buried Sarah, Arthur Burns' widow. (Burns is buried in Iowa.)

In 1870s, Burns Station lost business to Thomaston and Cuero, but was a stop on the Gulf, West Texas & Pacific Railroad until the name was changed in 1902 to "Verhelle," honoring a railroad official. (1970)

CUERO (DeWitt Co.) US 183, 4 mi. N
Chisholm Trail

From site near here, 1800 longhorns were moved out April 1, 1866, on first trail drive from this area to northern markets. Crockett Cardwell, owner of cattle bed ground, had gathered the herd. The trail boss was Thornton Chisholm, a native of DeWitt County. Indian Scout Jesse Chisholm in 1865 had marked the upper trail from the North Canadian to the Arkansas River.

Road here became a prong of the famous Chisholm Trail, going past Gonzales, San Marcos, Austin, Round Rock, Georgetown, Gatesville, Glen Rose and Red River Station, into Indian Territory. The 30 men of this 1866 drive to St. Joseph, Mo., were gone 7 months, 10 days. The cook and many of the men made numerous later drives; but Thornton Chisholm died in 1868.

260,000 cattle—accumulated in Texas in 4 years of Civil War—went in 1866 up the Chisholm Trail, a flood channel from a vast reservoir of beef. Sold in northern markets or to the U. S. Government to feed Indians on reservations or soldiers in forts, the trailed cattle helped Texas recover from the war.

From 1866–1895 at least 10,000,000 cattle were driven up the Chisholm Trail by courageous Texas cowboys—the greatest movement of animals under the control of men in all history. (1966)

CUERO (DeWitt Co.) US 183, 10 mi. N
¼ mi. E to Site of
Concrete College (1865–1881)

One of most respected schools in Texas in its day. Founded by the Rev. John Van Epps Covey (1821–1898), noted educator and minister. Embraced primary through Collegiate levels, accepting only students over 12 years old for college work. Broad course offerings included classical and modern languages, penmanship, music (piano, guitar, violin, flute), plus homemaking and etiquette for girls. A well-attended business school taught bookkeeping, banking, commercial law, and letter-writing. Enrollment, including boarding and day students, averaged 100; peaked at 250 in 1873.

On weekdays pupils rose at 5 a.m., took a brisk walk before breakfast, heard devotional services, and went to classes. Nights were reserved for study and discussion, with "lights out" at 9 p.m. Gambling, liquor, smoking, and profanity were strictly forbidden.

Students wrote their lessons on slates, as paper was expensive, then recited them to the instructor. June graduation was the ceremonious occasion of public speeches and oral examinations.

In 1881 the college closed after epidemics broke out and the railroad bypassed town of Concrete. Years later rock walls of main building were crushed and used to surface roads. Only rubble marks site today.

CUERO (DeWitt Co.) US 183 at US 77A, N
Cuero

Founded 1873 with arrival of Gulf, Western, Texas & Pacific Railroad. County seat moved here from Clinton, 1876. Population grew after coastal storms of 1875 and 1886 destroyed Indianola and refugees from there made a new start here.

Home of Turkey Trot, begun in 1912.

Farming, ranching, oil and gas center. (1968)

CUERO (DeWitt Co.) US 183, 7 mi. S
Hopkinsville Community—A Colony of Freedmen

Members of the Hopkins family came to DeWitt County in 1854 as slaves of Judge Henry Clay Pleasants (d. 1899). They worked for a time on a Gonzales County plantation and returned to this area after the Civil War as freedmen. In 1872, Henry Hopkins bought 42 acres of land and established the Hopkinsville Community (1 mi. W). Residents of the settlement organized the Antioch

Baptist Church in 1873 and began a school about ten years later. Although the school closed in 1956, members of the Antioch Baptist Church continue to worship near Hopkinsville.   (1983)

CUERO (DeWitt Co.)   US 183, 3 mi. S
Clinton
(0.6 mi. E)
Created in 1846, DeWitt County was named for empresario Green DeWitt. The county seat, originally at Cameron, was moved in 1848 to the pioneer town of Clinton, named for DeWitt's son. County government returned briefly to Cameron, but Clinton again served as the county seat from 1850 until 1876, when Cuero was named the seat of government. Courthouses here included a log cabin and two frame buildings. A cemetery and well remain at the site of Clinton, evidence of the once-thriving community that was the home of many prominent area pioneers.   (1967)

CUMBY (Hopkins Co.)   SH 11, 6 mi. N
Mt. Zion Churches and Cemetery
Mt. Zion Methodist Episcopal Church organized here before creation of Hopkins County, 1846.

Also at Mt. Zion, 1849, Harmony Cumberland Presbyterian Church was organized, with 13 members, by the Rev. Anthony Travelstead.

After years of worship in oak groves, brush arbors and homes, church edifice was built jointly 1861. Site given by David Findley, Nicholas Harlow. More land given 1904 by J. A. Rains, Chas. E. Brown.

In 1901 Harmony Cumberland Presbyterian Church became Mt. Zion Cumberland Presbyterian Church; continued to function.

Methodists moved away in 1914.   (1967)

DAINGERFlELD (Morris Co.)   SH 11/49 north right-of-way, at entrance to
                                    Daingerfield State Park, 2 mi. E of city
Caddo Trace
(1 mi. N)
Hunting and trade route for area between Arkansas and Red Rivers; used by Caddo Indians, who occupied the northeast corner of Texas and adjacent states.

Like many Indian trails, it was later usurped by whites; after 1840, it became part of stage and mail routes. Teamsters used it transporting goods to market; soldiers marched along it to and from several wars.

The Trace follows or crosses in places 3 other early trails: Cherokee, Choctaw, and Trammel's.

Today State Highways 11 and 49 (Hughes Springs to Daingerfield) follow the same general route.   (1967)

DAINGERFIELD (Morris Co.)   SH 338 at US 259, 7 mi. N
Spring Hill
Primitive Baptist Church of Christ 1852–1935. Meeting house erected 1859. Awarded Medallion.   (1964)

DAINGERFIELD (Morris Co.)   US 259 and FM 1400
Daingerfield, C.S.A.
Civil War center for manufacturing, supply and travel. Place of enrollment of several Confederate Army units. Local industries supporting the war effort included 3 tanyards—sidelines of the beef slaughtering trade that helped feed troops and civilians. The tanyards made leather for soldiers' boots and shoes and for cavalry saddles, bridles, and harnesses. On nearby rivers or ponds were 3 sawmills, one grist (corn meal) mill, and a distillery. Foundries in the area were predecessors of the 20th century Lone Star Steel Company.

An "old" town before the Civil War. Founded about 1830 at a spring where Capt. London Daingerfield was killed by Indians. The square was laid off in 1841 when this was designated seat of justice for judicial county of Paschal. Courts continued to he held here, though Paschal was abolished in 1842.

One noted 1842 trial was for a group that included Stephen Peters (one of the men who had platted the town square), accused of murdering Robert Potter. Potter, formerly Secretary of the

Navy and one of the authors of the Constitution of the Republic of Texas, had been killed in the Regulator-Moderator Feud, a political power struggle in East Texas. (1964)

DAINGERFIELD (Morris Co.) US 259 N, 6 mi. N
Rocky Branch
The abundance of creeks attracted travelers to this area, settled as early as the 1820s, and local tradition holds the community was named for the rocky beds of the creeks. The Rocky Branch Community grew throughout the 19th century; the earliest church, Spring Hill Primitive Baptist, was built in the 1850s. Over the years, the settlement boasted businesses, including lumber, grist and syrup mills, cotton gin, broom factory and general store. It also had a rodeo arena and base-ball team, as well as a precinct courthouse, post office (1890–1904), community center and a Woodmen of the World band. Families made mattresses and canned foods at the community's school (1879–1943), which consolidated with the Paul H. Pewitt and Daingerfield districts in 1951. (2002)

DALHART (Dallam Co.) Off FM 1879, 27 mi. N
Buffalo Springs
Its permanent water made it known at opening of 17th century as a great hunting ground alive with buffalo and mustangs. A cow camp before 1878. Since 1882, headquarters of XIT Ranch, once largest fenced ranch in the world consisting of three million acres. Exchanged for the con-struction of the state capitol.

DALHART (Dallam Co.) US 87, 1 mi. NW
Dallam County
Formed from Young and Bexar Territories. Created August 21, 1876; organized July 28, 1891. Named in honor of James W. Dallam 1818–1847. Compiler of digest of decisions of Supreme Court of the Republic of Texas, 1845. County seat, Texline, 1891–1903 Dalhart, since. This area was once part of XIT Ranch. (1964)

DALHART (Dallam Co.) US 87 at US 385, at "Empty Saddle" monument
Mrs. Cordia Sloan Duke
(Jan. 10, 1887–July 23, 1966)
Chronicler of a unique era in the history of the Southwest.
Born in Belton, Mo. At 17, taught school in Indian Territory (Okla.).
In 1907 she married Robert L. Duke, a ranch hand who had risen to division manager of the XIT Ranch (then world's largest). In addition to her own family, she "looked after" the 150 cow-boys who worked the 3,000,000-acre spread. Kept a diary of everyday events in ranch life around here and successfully encouraged 81 others to do likewise. Thus was preserved an authentic account of a passing phase of American life—the cowboy and his work. (1969)

DALHART (Dallam Co.) US 87 at US 385, at top of V-shaped underpasses
Heartland of Old
XIT Ranch
Great Texas ranch of international fame. Payment made in an 1882 contract for the construc-tion of granite capitol building in Austin. As contractors, some out-of-state investors (headed by the wealthy Chicago merchants, John V. and Senator C. B. Farwell) built the largest state capitol in North America and received in payment 3,000,000 acres of land.

The grant, 200 miles long and of varying widths (enclosed later by a 6,000-mile barbed wire fence), extended from near site of present Lubbock to the Oklahoma line 40 miles north of here. It included land in counties of Bailey, Castro, Cochran, Dallam, Deaf Smith, Hartley, Hockley, Lamb, Oldham and Parmer.

Trail Boss Abner Blocker delivered first herd to Buffalo Springs in 1885 and scratched the "XIT" in corral dust with boot heel to design famous brand.

Although its land was parcelled and sold, the XIT lives in Texas memories—especially here, 32 miles south of its Buffalo Springs headquarters. Dalhart holds an annual XIT reunion with rodeo and parade featuring a horse with an empty saddle, in honor of range riders of the past. Permanent tribute of XIT cowboys is this "empty saddle" monument, designed by western artist Bobby Dycke, dedicated in 1940. (1968)

DALLAS (Dallas Co.)   *Dallas County Historical Plaza*
Dallas County
After Texas became a republic in 1836, the Trinity River separated Robertson County to the west and Nacogdoches County to the east. This area, called "Three Forks" for the confluence of three branches of the Trinity, was settled mainly by Peters colonists after 1841. A town named Dallas was on this site by 1842.

Its founder, John Neely Bryan, led efforts to create Dallas County in 1846, which included the settlements of Dallas, Cedar Springs, Farmers Branch, and Hord's Ridge. The legislature possibly named the county for George Mifflin Dallas (1792–1864), then Vice-President of the United States. The town of Dallas was confirmed as county seat by election in 1850.

The 1850 census showed 2,743 settlers in the county, most of whom were farmers. Railroads came in the 1870s and the population leaped in 1880 to 33,488, one-third living in the city of Dallas. In 1885, farmland sold for $15 per acre; by 1920, with cotton prices briefly soaring, farmland was worth $300 per acre.

Railroads, interurban lines, and highways aided the urbanization of the county, which accelerated during the 1930s depression. After World War II the county became primarily urban. In 1980, the county population was 1,556,549, less than two percent rural.

(Texas Sesquicentennial 1836–1986)

DALLAS (Dallas Co.)   *City Hall Plaza*
City of Dallas
Pioneer John Neely Bryan (1810–1877) settled on the banks of the Trinity River just west of this site in 1841. A town he called Dallas grew up around his cabin. Chosen as county seat four years after the creation of Dallas County in 1846, the city of Dallas was incorporated in 1856, with Dr. Sam B. Pryor serving as first mayor.

Although John Neely Bryan had anticipated that river navigation would lead to growth for the city, it was the arrival of the Houston and Texas Central Railroad in 1872 and the Texas and Pacific Rail Line the following year that helped to establish Dallas as a major commercial center.

By 1890, Dallas was the state's most populous city. Wheat and cotton production provided impetus for continued growth. Insurance and banking also contributed to the city's prosperity, and its selection as the site for a regional Federal Reserve Bank in 1914 was an economic milestone. Following the discovery of oil in East Texas in 1930, Dallas banks concentrated on providing financial services for that industry.

Noted throughout its history for aggressive civic leaders, Dallas won the right to host the Texas Centennial Exposition in 1936.   (Texas Sesquicentennial 1836–1986)

DALLAS (Dallas Co.)   *SH 289, University Park at Park Cities YMCA*
Preston Road
Named for Ft. Preston, built 1841 at best ford on upper Red River (N of here). Followed pre-Columbian Indian trail.

Republic of Texas staked out road to fort from Austin. "Preston Road" later served as cattle trail from ford of Trinity River at Dallas to Oklahoma border.   (1968)

DALLAS (Dallas Co.)   *7405 W NW Hwy., Hillcrest Memorial Park*
Governor W. Lee O'Daniel
(March 11, 1890–May 11, 1969)
Born in Ohio, Wilbert Lee O'Daniel moved to Texas in 1925. A flour mill executive, he pioneered in radio advertising and country music. His "Hillbilly Boys" theme song resulted in his nickname "Pappy." In his first try for public office he won a primary over 12 opponents and became Governor of Texas (1938). During his second term in 1941 he won a special election to the U.S. Senate, defeating Lyndon B. Johnson and others. He was elected to a full term in 1942.

(1981)

DALLAS (Dallas Co.)   *3630 Harry Hines Blvd.*
Turtle Creek Pump Station
Constructed in 1909 as a 15-million-gallon per day primary pumping station for the city water supply, this brick industrial building was designed by Dallas architect C. A. Gill. Its location on high ground afforded protection from floods that had damaged earlier stations. The building

features ornate masonry detailing in the Italianate style. Last used as a pump station in 1930, the structure is a symbol of Dallas' growth at the turn of the century. (1983)

DALLAS (Dallas Co.) *2807 Harry Hines Blvd.*
Pike Park
The city of Dallas purchased this site in 1912–1913 for a neighborhood park. Developed as Summit Play Park, it served a predominantly Mexican-American community by the 1920s. The park name was changed in 1927 to honor a former park member, Edgar L. Pike. During World War II, Pike Park was an important gathering place for Mexican-American servicemen, both residents of "Little Mexico" and those visiting the city. It has become the focal point of the community's cultural, recreational, and political interests. Annual festivities, including Cinco de Mayo and Diez y Seis de Septiembre, reflect a proud heritage. (1981)
(Inscription also appears in Spanish.)

DALLAS (Dallas Co.) *Dallas Love Field*
Oath of Office of President Johnson
Near this point on November 22, 1963, Vice-President Lyndon Baines Johnson took the oath of office as 36th President of the United States. He is the first Texan to hold the office of President.

The ceremony was held in the central compartment of "Air Force One," the military aircraft assigned to the President. The plane was parked on the concrete ramp at Gate 28, east concourse of this terminal.

United States District Judge Sarah T. Hughes, of Dallas, a friend of long standing, was summoned to administer the oath. (Judge Hughes thus became the first woman in history to give the oath of office to a President of the United States.)

The new Chief Executive, with Mrs. Johnson on his right and Mrs. John F. Kennedy on the left, was sworn into office at 2:38 p.m. In the stresses of the day President Johnson had executive duties thrust upon him immediately, during the flight to the Capitol.

For over 30 years he had been in public service. Like some of his ancestors (including a university president) he had taught school as a young man.

He had served with distinction in Congress, 1937 to 1949; and in the U.S. Senate, 1949 to 1960, with an unsurpassed record as Senate Majority Leader. (1966)

DALLAS (Dallas Co.) *10600 Preston Rd.*
St. Mark's School of Texas
St. Mark's School has its foundation in three 20th-century preparatory schools, each of which contributed to its high standards and national reputation for academic excellence. Founded in 1906 by educators Menter and Ada Terrill, the Terrill School opened in a Swiss Avenue home with 42 students. The Terrills were strict disciplinarians and demanded high levels of scholastic competence. The school attracted the sons of many of Dallas' prominent families. By the late 1920s, athletics had begun to replace academics as the primary focus, and in response, several Dallas families began the Texas Country Day School for Boys to provide a strong academic preparatory education for their sons. When it opened with ten students and four faculty members in September 1933, Texas Country Day School was located two miles north of the Dallas city limits. With the post-World War II economic boom, this area became an affluent suburban neighborhood, and many of its youth attended Texas Country Day School. Meanwhile, the Cathedral School for Boys opened under the auspices of the Episcopal diocese of Dallas after the Terrill School closed in 1946. In 1949, negotiations to merge the Cathedral School and Texas Country Day School resulted in the formation of St. Mark's School of Texas, which held its first classes in September 1950 on the former Texas Country Day School campus. In the last half of the 20th century, St. Mark's School solidified its place in Texas' educational history as a significant college preparatory institution through expanded facilities and exemplary faculty, which led to increased enrollment and solid financial support. (2002)

DALLAS (Dallas Co.) *5200 Buckner Blvd.*
Buckner Baptist Children's Home
Founded out of concern for dependent, orphaned children, this institution opened in 1879 under the guidance of the Rev. Robert Cooke Buckner (d. 1919). Originally known as Buckner Orphan's

Home, the first structure on this site was built in 1880 and housed six children. By 1910, the orphanage was caring for 600 children. Supported by the Baptist General Convention of Texas since 1914 and later renamed Buckner Baptist Children's Home, the facility now primarily cares for children from broken homes. For more than 100 years, the Buckner Home has been a leader in Texas child care. (1983)

DALLAS (Dallas Co.)   *Atlanta and South Blvd., SW of Texas State Fairgrounds*
South Boulevard-Park Row Historic District
This neighborhood is one of the few remaining intact residential districts that reflects the early 20th century suburban development of Dallas. Construction of homes in this vicinity began soon after the Jewish Temple Emanuel El was moved here in 1913 from its downtown location. Many early residents of the neighborhood were prominent leaders of the Dallas Jewish community.

Included in the district are homes designed by the leading area architects of the time. The structures feature a variety of popular architectural influences, representing details of the Midwestern Prairie, Mission Revival, Classical Revival, and Georgian styles.

A gradual migration of area residents to newer suburban developments began following the end of World War II. During the 1950s, the South Boulevard-Park Row neighborhood became the home of many prominent black leaders of the Dallas area. Residents here have included educators, lawyers, merchants, clergymen, doctors, and business executives. Since the early 20th century the neighborhood has been a symbol of the growth, prosperity, and vitality of Dallas. (1981)

DALLAS (Dallas Co.)   *SH 352, State Fair Grounds*
State Fair of Texas
Founded in 1886, the State Fair of Texas now ranks as the most largely attended state fair in the U.S. It was begun as a private, nonprofit corporation for civic purposes by Capt. W. H. Gaston and other pioneer business and civic leaders of Dallas.

Since 1904, the fair grounds have been owned by the city, which maintains them as a public park except during the annual two-week fair.

The fair suspended operations for two years in order to permit the central exposition of the Texas Centennial Celebration to be held here in 1936. In 1937, the Pan American Exposition used the grounds.

Over the years great names have appeared here, including wild west showman Buffalo Bill, Harry Houdini the magician, silver-tongued orator William Jennings Bryan, and Comanche War Chief Quanah Parker.

Federal, state, and city governments have erected a series of permanent buildings on the fair grounds, including the Hall of State, five other museums, music hall, livestock coliseum, and "Cotton Bowl."

Originally 80 acres in size, the grounds have been successively enlarged to include the present 250 acres. Over 100,000,000 persons have entered its gates during annual expositions. (1969)

DALLAS (Dallas Co.)   *N end of Esplanade facing Hall of State; Fair Park*
Texas Centennial Exposition
As plans began to take shape for the centennial celebration of Texas Independence, a group of Dallas businessmen led by R. L. Thornton, Sr., Fred Florence, and Nathan Adams, joined together to promote the city as the host of the major centennial event.

The Centennial Exposition Corporation, formed in 1935, took temporary control of the State Fair grounds, and a team of over 100 architects, artists, and craftsmen soon began designing the exposition complex. Employing thousands of people in the midst of the great depression, the project resulted in the creation of impressive structures, works of art, and landscaping.

Officially opened by Gov. James Allred on June 6, 1936, activities of the exposition included a spectacular parade through downtown Dallas, guest speakers, and nationwide news coverage. In his speech to the crowd, U.S. Secretary of Commerce Daniel Roper declared, "America, here is Texas!" President and Mrs. Franklin D. Roosevelt visited the exposition on June 12.

The exposition ran for 178 days, entertaining over six million people. It was a turning point in the development of the city of Dallas and left a legacy of art, history, architecture, and culture to generations of Texans. (1988)

DALLAS (Dallas Co.)   *Bryan Colonnade, Dealey Plaza, Elm & Houston Streets*
John Neely Bryan, 1810–1877
Margaret Beeman Bryan, 1825–1919
In 1839, Tennessee lawyer John Neely Bryan chose this high bluff and shallow ford on the Trinity River as site for a trading post. Finding Indians scarce when he returned in 1841, he platted a town, installed a ferry, and called the place Dallas. In the 1840s, the Republic of Texas opened its Central National Road from here to the U.S. border, and drew settlers to this area with liberal land grants.

Margaret Beeman was a daughter of John Beeman, a prosperous man from Illinois, of North Carolina heritage. At 15, she met Bryan at the Cross Roads Camp Ground, Bowie County. Her father staked his claim about eight miles from Bryan's town. She and Bryan married in 1843, and became parents of six children. Margaret, her father, and other relatives strongly supported Bryan's work as "Father of Dallas."

Bryan went to the California Gold Rush in 1849, but gained no fortune. After his return, he donated 98 city lots for a courthouse and county seat, then sold his ferry and remaining interest in the townsite. In poor health for many years, he died in Austin at 67. Margaret Beeman Bryan lived to age 94, and saw Dallas attain a population of over 150,000.   (1978)

DALLAS (Dallas Co.)   *US 80 Bus., nearby at Dealey Plaza*
Site of First Ferry and Bridge
(About 300 ft. W)
First ferry on the Trinity River at Dallas was started here, 1842, by John Neely Bryan (1810–1877), the founder of Dallas. Alexander Crockrell (1820–1858), early builder and developer, replaced ferry with wooden toll bridge, 1854.

This crossing played an important part in the development of the city.   (1968)

DALLAS (Dallas Co.)   *411 Elm Street*
Formerly the
Texas School Book Depository Building
This site was originally owned by John Neely Bryan, the founder of Dallas. During the 1880s, French native Maxime Guillot operated a wagon shop here. In 1894, the land was purchased by Phil L. Mitchell, president and director of the Rock Island Plow Company of Illinois. An office building for the firm's Texas division, known as the Southern Rock Island Plow Company, was completed here four years later. In 1901, the five-story structure was destroyed by fire. That same year, under supervision of the company vice-president and general manager F. B. Jones, work was completed on this structure. Built to resemble the earlier edifice, it features characteristics of the commercial Romanesque Revival style.

In 1937, the Carraway Byrd Corporation purchased the property. Later, under the direction of D. H. Byrd, the building was leased to a variety of businesses, including the Texas School Book Depository.

On November 22, 1963, the building gained national notoriety when Lee Harvey Oswald allegedly shot and killed President John F. Kennedy from a sixth floor window as the Presidential motorcade passed the site.   (1980)

DALLAS (Dallas Co.)   *Dealey Plaza, Elm, Main, and Commerce Sts.*
Kennedy Memorial Area
John Fitzgerald Kennedy 35th President of the United States was mortally wounded on November 22, 1963, feet to the right of this marker as the Presidential car was headed toward the underpass to the west on Dallas' Elm Street. Firing from the window on the extreme right of the sixth floor of the building immediately northeast of this spot, the assassin also wounded critically, but not fatally, Governor John Connally of Texas, riding with the President. From this spot, the President was rushed to Parkland Hospital where he died. This marker commemorates the tragic loss of a great American, mourned by the nation he served.

DALLAS (Dallas Co.)   *SH 183, California Crossing Park*
California Crossing
(Some 500 ft. N)
Here thousands of 49'ers crossed Trinity River in heroic trek west—following California gold discovery.

Crossing was in shallow part of stream on southern transcontinental route to Pacific. Later used by stage lines, railroad; route passed through Dallas and Cedar Springs on to El Paso.   (1967)

DALLAS (Dallas Co.) *Belle Starr Lane & Scyene Road, Loop 635*
Site of the Scyene Meeting Place
In the 1840s, settlers held public meetings under a tree at this site. Beginning in the 1850s, several successive 2-story frame buildings stood here and housed Masonic Lodge, church, elections, and social activities. Scyene Meeting Place housed one of the first public school sessions in Dallas County. In her girlhood, outlaw Belle Starr was a pupil in that school. In 1872, Texas & Pacific Railroad bypassed Scyene and the town dwindled. Yet the Woodmen of the World and other groups continued to meet in the community building, and school was held here until 1927.
(1976)

DALLAS (Dallas Co.) *McCommas Bluff*
Navigation of the Upper Trinity River
Since the founding of Dallas, many of the city's leaders have dreamed of navigation on the upper Trinity River, but none of their attempts achieved lasting success. Fluctuating water levels and massive snags in the river below Dallas hindered early navigation. In 1866, the Trinity River Slack Water Navigation Co. proposed dams and locks for the waterway. Capt. James H. McGarvey and Confederate hero Dick Dowling piloted *Job Boat No. 1* from Galveston to Dallas, but the trip took over a year. In 1868, the Dallas-built *Sallie Haynes* began to carry cargo southward.

Rising railroad freight charges spurred new interest in river shipping in the 1890s. The Trinity River Navigation Co., formed in 1892, operated *Snag Puller Dallas* and the *H. A. Harvey, Jr.,* which carried 150 passengers. The Harvey made daily runs to McCommas Bluff, 13 miles downstream from Dallas, where a dam, dance pavilion, and picnic grounds created a popular recreation spot.

In 1900–1915, the U.S. government spent $2 million on river improvements, including a series of dams and locks, before World War I halted work. A critical 1921 corps of engineers report ended further federal investment. Despite sporadic interest in later years, the dream of Dallas as an inland port remains unrealized.   (1985)

DANEVANG (Wharton Co.) *SH 71 at FM 441*
Danevang
("Danish Meadow")
The first successful Danish community in Texas. Established in 1894 on a portion of 25,000 acres secured through option by Danish Folk Society from Texas Land and Cattle Company.

Most immigrants came first to the northern United States, where other Danes had settled, and then to Texas, desiring to preserve their national culture, language, and religion. A Lutheran church was erected in 1895.

Hardships included disease, insects, poorly drained land, and primitive transportation: but hard work, farming ability, and cooperation brought success.   (1970)

DAWN (Deaf Smith Co.) *US 60 E access road, north side*
at Dawn Community Park

Town of Dawn
Had second post office in county, in 1889. Named by pioneers who saw here the "dawning of a new country." Santa Fe Railroad station house (a box car) was first building on site, 1905. Town was developed by W. E. Neal and Sons in 1914, with lumber yard, hotel, bank, and store, Now center of farming industry.   (1970)

DAWSON (Navarro Co.) *SH 31, 1 mi. W*
Battle Creek Burial Ground
A surveying party of 25 Texans ran into about 300 Kickapoo Indians on a buffalo hunt; failing to heed warning to leave, the Texans were ambushed on Oct. 8, 1838. Only seven survived, and four of these were wounded. After the escape, they came back to bury their comrades in a common grave.   (1966)

DAWSON (Navarro Co.)   *FM 709, 3.5 mi. NE*
Spring Hill
Oldest Community in Navarro County
The springs at this site supplied water to Indians for centuries before white settlers arrived. In 1838 Dr. George Washington Hill (1814–1860) built a trading post near the springs, and in October of that year a skirmish between a surveying party and Kickapoo Indians occurred in this vicinity.

After serving as Republic of Texas Secretary of War under President Sam Houston, Dr. Hill returned here about 1843, reopened the trading post, built a home, and began practicing medicine. In Jan. 1847, his brother-in-law, Robert Harve Matthews (1814–1894), settled here. A post office was established on Nov. 5, 1849, with Dr. Hill as postmaster. A building erected in 1850 served as both church and schoolhouse; by 1855, Matthews had opened a store. During the Civil War, a Confederate training camp was located here.

At the height of its growth, in the 1870s, Spring Hill boasted general mercantile stores, blacksmith shops, saloons, a drugstore, hotel, Masonic Lodge, flour mill, cotton gin, and rock quarry. Decline began in 1881, when the community was bypassed by the Cotton Belt Railroad. The post office closed on June 15, 1906. The cemetery and a few foundations bordering deserted streets remain to mark site of Spring Hill.   (1974)

DAWSON (Navarro Co.)   *FM 709, 2 mi. N in roadside park*
Near Site of Trading Post of
Dr. George Washington Hill (1814–1860)
Dedicated frontier physician and public servant of the Republic and State of Texas. Born in Tennessee, Hill received his medical degree from Transylvania University. He came to Texas in 1836, where he was a surgeon for Fort Houston at the opening of his lifelong practice. In 1837 Hill became the medical censor for Milam County. Later that year, he moved to newly created Robertson County, where he married Miss Matilda Slaughter. He entered public office as Robertson County Representative in the Congress of the Republic, 1838–1841 and 1842–1843.

In 1838 Hill was reported operating a trading post near here. His home, called Spring Hill, became the first settlement in Navarro County. Later that year, however, it was connected with a tragedy. A few days after spending the night at Hill's Place twenty-one surveyors (including Hill's brother) were virtually annihilated by several hundred Kickapoos.

Hill was named Indian agent for the Republic in 1841, and in 1843 he became Secretary of War. After Texas joined the Union he served in the legislature.

Throughout these years he continued to practice medicine, facing many dangers in order to render aid. In 1853 Hill County was named in his honor.   (1970)

DAWSON (Navarro Co.)   *FM 677, 4 mi. NE via SH 31*
The Navarro Mills Community
A flour mill built here in the 1860s drew pioneer commerce to this site. Flour was a luxury, used mostly for yeast bread, cakes, and biscuits served on Sundays or special occasions. People traveled for considerable distances with their wheat, and waited sometimes for days to have it ground. The original mill property was bought from R. A. Younger in 1867 by John Summers and sons. Several local residents owned shares in ensuring years. The waters of Rock Creek furnished power. Besides this mill and a cotton gin, there may have been other mills here.

The Navarro Mills Post Office opened in 1874. A store, school, blacksmith shop, and other facilities were developed. Local leaders included Confederate veterans W. C. French (1821–1897) and R. J. Wright (1837–1926).

The flour mill ceased operating in 1881. The post office closed in 1882, to be revived only briefly in later years. The community continued to thrive, however. An 1880s newcomer was a former county judge, James C. Key (1817–1910), whose surname survives in the landmark Tandy Key Road.

The cemetery, the Baptist Church that was formed in 1901, and the tabernacle built in 1915 mark the site of the historic village.   (1976)

DAYTON (Liberty Co.)   *US 90, in Dayton*
The Runaway Scrape
Famous flight of Texians to escape Santa Anna's invading Mexican Army. Tales of the Alamo butchery on March 6, 1836, and the continuing retreat of Gen. Sam Houston's army prompted colonists to abandon homes and property and seek refuge in East Texas.

Families left beds unmade, breakfast uneaten, and ran for their lives, traveling in wagons, carts, sleds, on foot, or by horseback, dropping gear as they went.

Many Liberty Countians remained at home until mid-April, helping refugees struggle toward the Sabine in order to cross to safety in the United States. Terrible hardships plagued the runaways trying to ferry the swollen Trinity River. In rain-soaked camps many children died of measles and other ills. Wading through flooded bottomlands, the wayfarers came with relief to the prairie and the Samaritans in Liberty.

After resting a few days, tending the sick, and burying the dead, most of the wanderers moved on toward Louisiana. East of Liberty stragglers heard the cannonading at the Battle of San Jacinto on April 21, 1836. Fearing that Santa Anna's legions had whipped the ragged Texian forces, they hurried on, but shortly heard joyful news: "Turn back, turn back." Freedom had been won for them by Sam Houston's Army.   (1972)

DAYTON (Liberty Co.)   *US 90 right-of-way, 2.5 mi. W*
Stilson
The community of Stilson traces its origins to the arrival in the 1890s of the Texas and New Orleans Railroad. Out-of-state developers O. H. Stilson and Rodney Hill bought land in 1896 and immediately began planning a town. They advertised the new community to farmers in Iowa, and a number of families came here to begin new lives. Among those who came to build homes and establish farms were many Swedish immigrants, including C. F. Seaberg and C. D. Nelson.

By the late 1890s the town boasted a fourteen-room hotel, a general store, a gin, a blacksmith shop, a rice mill, a warehouse, a barber shop, a post office, a railroad depot, and a school.

The one-room Stilson School served students in all grades, taught by one teacher. The school was closed in 1918 when area children began attending classes in Dayton.

The Stilson post office was established in 1898 and was located in the general store operated by C. S. Brown. The post office was discontinued in 1925, and rural mail delivery from Dayton began in 1926.

Stilson began to decline when the population gradually shifted to nearby Dayton. Descendants of many early settlers still reside in the area.   (Texas Sesquicentennial 1836–1986)

DE BERRY (Panola Co.)   *FM 31*
DeBerry
Site of 1850 sawmill and grist mill. Settled mostly by cotton planters. Center for markets and gins. Oil development after 1900.

Named for Col. Alfred W. DeBerry (1829–1903), 28th Texas Cavalry, Dismounted, Confederate Army. In 1863-65 legislature, helped pass laws to give Confederacy men, revenue and supplies, support soldiers' families and defend Texas frontiers.

In 1874–1876 was Secretary of State under Gov. Richard Coke, who put Texas government into hands of the people after nine years of Federal rule.   (1965)

DE KALB (Bowie Co.)   *US 82, DeKalb City Limits*
De Kalb
Named for Maj. Gen. Johann de Kalb—a hero of the American Revolution—upon suggestion (1836) of David Crockett, a visitor on his way to fight in Texas War for Independence. Other Texas heroes traveling through here were James B. Fannin and Wm. B. Travis.

Settled by 1831, when land was given for a public school by Dr. W. H. Boyce, Wm. L. Browning, D. M. Chisholm, Clement R. John and Judge (and Dr.) James W. Smith.

Site of first college in Bowie County, founded in 1839 and of ninth Masonic Lodge in Texas, organized 1840. Served as county seat, 1840–1841. On two early stagelines. A stopover for U.S. immigrants to Texas Republic, and 49'ers on way to California Gold Rush.

In 1870s hideouts of train robbers Sam Bass, Jesse James, other notorious characters were nearby. Texas & Pacific Railroad reached here 1876. Site in 1889 of P. S. Ramseur's sawmill which shipped high quality lumber all over United States; to get logs to mill, he built a railroad, traces of which still exist. Although in 1896 and 1923 most of businesses were destroyed by fires, city prospers today. Center of ranching, truck farming, and pulpwood production.

Known as "The Pride of East Texas."   (1966)

DE LEON (Comanche Co.)   *303 N. Texas Street (SH 16)*
De Leon Peanut Company

Cotton was the major cash crop for farmers in Comanche County until the early 20th century. The combined effects of disastrous weather conditions in 1908–1809, a national economic downturn, and a major infestation of the Mexican boll weevil in 1914 caused many Comanche County farmers to abandon their decades-long reliance on cotton and turn to the more lucrative prospect of peanut farming.

Because shipping peanuts to Fort Worth for processing reduced local farmers' profits, N. T. Haskins organized the De Leon Peanut Company in 1912. Its first board of directors included R. W. Higginbotham, W. H. Williams, B. T. Higginbotham, Jr., J. B. Wilson, A. E. Hampton, and W. E. Lowe. By 1914, peanuts were the leading cash crop in the county, and the company enlarged its operations to meet growing demand. A six-story main building was completed in 1917; soon the plant was processing up to ten railroad carloads of peanuts per day.

The business survived an economic crisis in the 1920s and remained a strong force in the local community, which has been called "the peanut capital of the world." Acquired by a national company in 1967, the De Leon Peanut Company has played a vital role in Comanche County history.

(1994)

DE LEON (Comanche Co.)   *302 N. Texas Street (SH 16)*
Texas Central Railroad

Railroad construction in Texas, interrupted by the Civil War and by the national economic depression of the early 1870s, began a period of recovery in the late 1870s and early 1880s. Chartered on May 31, 1879, the Texas Central Railway was owned by the Houston & Texas Central Railway and was in competition with the Texas Pacific to build a line westward through North Central Texas.

Extending from Ross Station near Waco in 1879, the Texas Central reached the Erath-Comanche County line in 1880. The Texas Central laid out the town of De Leon on April 10, 1881, and railroad official Robert M. Elgin conducted the sale of town lots from the back of a flatcar on July 7. Although the initial sale of lots was slow, the town soon developed and attracted new settlers from the southeastern United States. Railroad offices, shops, and a roundhouse were built here, and De Leon became the area's primary shipping point for cotton and, later, peanuts and other products.

Acquired by the Missouri-Kansas-Texas (Katy) Railroad in 1910, the line continued to operate until 1967, when local backers purchased part of the line and continued to provide shipping service to customers along "the peanut line" connecting Dublin, De Leon, and Gorman. (1994)

DE LEON (Comanche Co.)   *SH 6*
Frances Marie Sparks Brown
(October 17, 1849–January 1, 1934)

Frances Marie Sparks, a native of North Carolina and daughter of Daniel and Kezziah Sparks, married Thomas Brown in 1865. They lived in Grayson County, Texas, before moving to a 410-acre farm near here about 1876. During the 1880s and 1890s, Frances served as a midwife and lay doctor for families in the area. Known as "Aunt Fanny," she often rode 6–8 miles by horseback at night to deliver a baby. Despite her husband's death in 1912 Frances skillfully managed her farm and reared 12 children while continuing to nurse many of her neighbors back to health.   (1993)

DE LEON (Comanche Co.)   *SH 16, 8 mi. N at Victor Cem.*
William H. Pate
A San Jacinto veteran. Born in Georgia. Died August 29, 1879. His wife Jane Pate born March 10, 1827. Died March 18, 1906.

DECATUR (Wise Co.)   *US 81/287, N city limits*
Butterfield Overland Stage Line
Through Decatur passed the Butterfield Overland Mail Line connecting St. Louis and San Francisco with semi-weekly stage and mail service, 1858–1861. The length of the route, 2795 miles and the superior service maintained made this a pioneer enterprise of the first magnitude.

DECATUR (Wise Co.)   *Courthouse grounds*
Randolph Vesey
(1832–1908)
Respected Negro citizen and homeowner. Champion pioneer fiddler, popular at Forts Belknap, Griffin and Richardson and Over County. Once when he was an Indian captive, held in Kansas, Texans sent ponies to ransom him. He is buried in Oaklawn, Decatur.

Born in Georgia. He served during the Civil War as body servant and voluntary battle aide to Gen. W. L. Cabell of the Confederate Army. Vesey's courage and loyalty were typical. Hundreds of slaves went to war with masters. Many operated farms and ranches of soldiers away at war, producing cotton and food for the Confederacy. Others did work for hire, with wages supporting the master's family. On patrol duty they protected homes from Indians, bandits, outlaws.

During war years, 1861–1865, some 30,000 to 50,000 Negroes—free and slaves—aided Confederate armies. They served with the nitre and mining bureau and departments of medicine, engineers, quartermaster general, ordnance and commissary general. They built fortifications on coasts from Brownsville, Texas, to Norfolk, Virginia, and its inland points. Many were army teamsters, wheelwrights, blacksmiths, butchers, shoemakers, cooks and nurses. Texas and other states later provided land grants and pensions for many.   (1965)

DECATUR (Wise Co.)   *900–904 US 81/287 S*
Texas Tourist Camp Complex
Local businessman E. F. Boydston (1888–1945) purchased this site, a former feed lot, in 1927 for $400. Recognizing a potential business opportunity in offering services to the traveling public, he built a wooden shed and gas station in 1927. Travelers were allowed to build camp fires during overnight stays, and by 1931 Boydston added three wooden cabins with garages to the camp complex. The buildings later were faced with rock, and more cabins and garages were added in 1935. The original wooden gas station was covered with petrified wood in 1935 when the highway was widened and remained in operation by the Boydston family until 1988.

The Texas Lunchroom, a one-room frame building, was built in 1929. Renamed the Texas Cafe in 1935 and faced with stone to match other buildings in the complex, it was enlarged to provide second-floor living quarters. Popular with local high school and college students, as well as families and the traveling public, it was closed in the 1960s after a highway bypass built west of town diverted traffic from this area. The cafe reopened in 1993. One of the few intact examples of tourist camps built throughout Texas in the mid-20th century, this property is significant for its association with the early development of automobile tourism.   (1995)

DECATUR (Wise Co.)   *US 287, 2 mi. NW*
First Record of White Men in This Area
Battle of the Knobs
(SE)
Fought Oct. 10, 1837, between 18 men of Republic of Texas Army and 150 Indians. Hunting stolen horses, the Texans were led by Lt. A. B. Benthuysen. Three were veterans of the Battle of San Jacinto; one of the three, Lt. A. H. Miles, had been in the group that captured Gen. Santa Anna.

Ten Texans and fifty Indians died. The slain Texans (left, of necessity, without burial) were: Alexander Bastwick, Jesse Blair, James Christian, Joseph Cooper, J. Josslin, Lt. Miles, Wesley and William Nicholson, Dr. William Sanders, and Lewis F. Sheuster.

Their memorial is "The Knobs."

DECATUR (Wise Co.) — *Courthouse Square*
Charles Vernon Terrell
(May 2, 1861–November 17, 1959)

A leading public man in Texas, 1896–1939. Born in Wise County to early (1854) settlers. After two years at Texas A. & M., read law and began practice in 1886. Served 1888–1892 as Decatur city attorney; 1892–1896 as county attorney; 1896–1901 and 1909–1913 from Denton-Montague-Wise Counties, in Texas Senate. There he sponsored act creating North Texas State University. He was State Treasurer of Texas from 1921 to 1924.

Appointed in 1924 to the Texas Railroad Commission (chairman 2 terms), he served during landmark years when Texas was catapulted into role of a major world energy supplier. Through regulation of oil and gas shipping, the Railroad Commission became the agency for making production rules. When East Texas in the 1930s began to produce oil in volumes such as the world had never known, and the state invoked martial law to quell strife there, Commissioner Terrell and associates pioneered in conservation without the sacrifice of industrial leadership.

After his retirement in 1939, his native county had an oil discovery at Park Springs, in 1942. The Chico Field came in with larger yields in 1947.

C. V. and Etta (May) Terrell were parents of Tully Vernon, John Preston, and Margaret (Mrs. F. T. Ward). (1972)

DECATUR (Wise Co.) — *SH 24, 10 mi. E, ¼ mi. N of the crossing*
Cattle Trail Crossing
(Located ¼ mile S, on Denton Creek)

Near this site ran one of the many "feeder" branches of the famous Chisholm Trail, best-known of all the cattle trails that once linked the vast grasslands of Texas with the meat-hungry markets of the North.

The original trail, which stretched from the North Canadian to the Arkansas River, was blazed in 1865 by Jesse Chisholm, a half-Scottish and half-Cherokee trader. The 220-mile route, soon taken up by drovers, was extended north and south. Branches all the way from the Rio Grande gradually snaked up to join the main trail at the Red River.

Although unpredicatable Texas weather and hostile Indians sometimes prevented the drovers from keeping to the main route, certain points were fixed. One of these was the Trinity River Ford at Fort Worth, just south of here, where cattle might have to wait for weeks to cross if the river had recently flooded.

In 1895, the fenced range, railroad, and quarantines against the fever tick had reduced to a trickle the flood of cattle leaving Texas on the hoof; but by this time, the trail had helped restore the economy of Texas (wrecked by the Civil War) and it had left a legacy in folksong and legend of cowboy days on the untamed Texas frontier. (1968)

DECATUR (Wise Co.) — *SH 24, 5 mi. E*
Old Campsite of Jesse and Frank James
(Approximately 1 mi. S)

Famous western frontier outlaws, who had many Texas hide-outs along a line from the Rio Grande to the Red River. The camps—extending into Missouri, their home state—were used for hiding stolen horses until posses could be thrown off the trail. The campsites were sometimes known to scattered settlers, who feared or befriended the bandits.

Also friendly with the James Brothers (and also operating sometimes in Texas) were fellow Missouri outlaws Cole Younger and "bandit queen" Belle Starr.

This was an era of widespread lawlessness in Texas. Billy the Kid roamed into West Texas. The Daltons, John Wesley Hardin, Cullen Baker, Bill Longley, Sam Bass and many others found it easy to kill and rob and then hide in wild areas where they were beyond the reach of local officers, and food was plentiful.

After reconstruction ended in 1874, Texas Rangers were reorganized, to restore respect for the law. Given special powers, in 1889–1890 they arrested 579 wanted men (including 76 alleged murderers). Jesse James and some other notorious badmen by then were dead. Frank, reformed, worked as a salesman in Dallas, Paris, and other Texas towns.   (1967)

DECATUR (Wise Co.)   *US 380 right-of-way, 5.5 mi. E*
Dr. William Renshaw
(1822–1887)
Born in Illinois, William Renshaw studied medicine and set up practice in Sparta, Tennessee. His wife Sarah received from the Mexican Government a grant of land in Texas, where her father Samuel Worthington lost his life in a colonization attempt in 1828. Dr. Renshaw traveled to Texas in 1853 to locate this headright, which encompassed many acres of Wise County north of this marker site. Dr. Renshaw returned to Sparta and served two terms in the Tennessee Legislature before moving his family to Texas in 1859.

The first doctor to settle permanently in Wise County, Dr. Renshaw was often away from home for long periods, with a practice extending from Denton to Jacksboro. The Renshaws organized one of the county's earliest schools, taught by J. D. White, for their own and neighbor children. After the Civil War, the family moved to Decatur, where Dr. Renshaw and his son Lute opened a drugstore. They were devout Baptists and supported Decatur Baptist College.

Dr. Renshaw died in 1887 and was buried at Oak Lawn Cemetery in Decatur. As his 10 children married, each received a portion of the Worthington Survey. Two family members still own part of the property. A number of descendants became doctors.   (1976)

DECATUR (Wise Co.)   *SH 51, at entrance to Reunion Grounds, edge of Decatur*
The Wise County Reunion
The Confederate veterans of Wise County are said to have held occasional reunions in the 1860s–1870s. Old settlers invited both the Confederate veterans and Wise County Pioneers to an 1881 reunion at Cold Springs. This was on July 12, the anniversary of Capt. George Stevens' victory over hostile Indians in 1874.

About 5,000 people attended the 1881 reunion. The "Wise County Messenger" reported a successful day—"only the music being a failure." Events included speeches and picnicking. The reunion began to occupy the present site in 1896. By 1900 it extended to three days—honoring old settlers on the first, the veterans on the second, and daughters and sons of Confederates on the third. Sometimes 12,000 would attend, parading from courthouse to camp ground. Programs included candidates' speeches, rodeos, and sham battles. Evenings were devoted to visiting.

In 1901, the grounds were leased for 25 years. Later, campsites were leased and improved by participants.

The Wise County Old Settlers Association, formed in 1904, sponsored a 1907 Pioneer History by C. D. Cates.

Extended to a week, with visiting in daytime and stated events in the evenings, this reunion is now the oldest recurring public event in the county.   (1976)

DEL RIO (Val Verde Co.)   *US 90 E, 2.5 mi., on grounds of*
Women's Club on San Felipe Creek
Val Verde County
Formed from Crockett, Kinney and Pecos Counties. Created March 24, 1885; organized March 31, 1885. Named in honor of the battle fought at Val Verde near Fort Craig, New Mexico, February 19, 1862. Del Rio, the County Seat.

DEL RIO (Val Verde Co.)   *Museum Grounds*
Roy Bean, C.S.A.
(1824–1903)
Born in Kentucky. A trader in Mexico, 1848. Mining in New Mexico when Civil War broke out. As spy and scout, joined Texans in the command of Gen. John R. Baylor during the 1861–1862 Arizona-New Mexico campaign. Organized irregular company called "Free Rovers." In a narrow canyon, took part in capture of 800 Federals by 250 Confederates. After 1862 was a Confederate freighter, hauling cotton to Matamoros from San Antonio and bringing into Texas wartime goods guns, ammunition, medicine, cloth, shoes, food.

In 1882, began following with a tent saloon crews building railroad along the Rio Grande. Cooperating with Texas Rangers, was appointed Justice of Peace "Law West of the Pecos." Tamed rough frontier town of Langtry, where he spent his life. Won fame in unique court decisions, as in trial and fining of dead man for carrying a concealed weapon. Most widely celebrated show he staged was Fitzsimmons-Maher World Championship boxing match, on a Rio Grande sand bar near his saloon in 1896.

Court was held in the saloon, where he displayed pictures of "The Jersey Lily"—British actress Lily Langtry, whom he never met. She visited town at his invitation, but only after Judge Bean's death.

DEL RIO (Val Verde Co.)   *US 90, 8 mi. E at E end of bridge*
Site of Chihuahua Road
(Crossing at West End of Bridge)
In the 19th century, a life line that connected Chihuahua, Mexico, with the Texas port of Indianola.

Opened to exploit rich trade in Mexican silver and gold, the road eventually carried every type of goods (including, in 1860, 27 camels), adventurers, settlers, soldiers, and "Forty-Niners" bound for the California Gold Rush.

All sorts of vehicles used the Chihuahua Road: stagecoaches, wagons, ox-carts, and traveling ambulances, which were light carriages with 4-foot wheels.

Not until the railroad came to San Antonio, 1877, did this road lose its commercial importance. (1967)

DEL RIO (Val Verde Co.)   *US 277, San Felipe Creek, City Park*
San Felipe Springs
Named by 17th Century Spanish Explorers in honor of San Felipe de Jesus 1560–1597. First Mexican martyr. A watering place on road blazed in 1849 between San Antonio and the Pacific. A stage stand on the San Diego Route 1857 to 1883.

DEL RIO (Val Verde Co.)   *US 90 W, .5 mi. W of San Felipe Springs Rd.*
Canal System of Del Rio
Crude irrigation systems, drawing water from San Felipe Springs and Creek, were first devised by Indian and Spanish inhabitants of this area. Anglo-American settlers also saw the need for irrigation in this arid region, and about 1869 a group of landowners formed the San Felipe Agricultural, Manufacturing & Irrigation Company. Among early stockholders were W. D. Adams, Donald Jackson, Joseph Ney, Randolph Pafford, James H. Taylor, and A. O. Strickland. They dammed San Felipe Creek just below the Springs, and by 1871 had built canals diverting water to 1,500 acres of land.

Under the 1875 irrigation law, the company received a 99-year state charter authorizing the digging of two canals: five-mile long "Madre Ditch" and mile-long "San Felipe Ditch"—plus lateral canals. In 1876 the state inspector reported that the San Felipe Company had irrigated about 3,000 acres. Land grant provisions of an 1876 law awarded the company 5,000 acres of state land for the total mileage of its canals.

In addition to promoting agricultural development the work of the San Felipe Company stimulated the growth of Del Rio, since the irrigation canals provided water to the city as well. Today this vital water supply system is still in operation.

DEL RIO (Val Verde Co.)

US 90, 6 mi. E near main gate
to Laughlin Air Force Base

Military Aviation in Val Verde County

In 1911, eight years after the Wright Brothers' historic flight at Kitty Hawk, North Carolina, Galbraith Perry Rodgers landed his plane at Del Rio while on the first transcontinental flight across the United States. The arrival of a plane in Del Rio was a major event then, but it became a common sight in later years. During World War I, the town was the center of aerial patrols along the United States-Mexico border. In 1919, planes were dispatched to the area in reaction to Pancho Villa's border raids. One pilot stationed here to fly border patrols was Lt. James H. Doolittle, who later gained international attention in World War II.

In the 1940s, Del Rio was chosen as the site of an air base because of the flat terrain and the mild climate. Opened as the first B-26 bombardier school, Laughlin Air Force Base was named in honor of Lt. Jack T. Laughlin, the first pilot from Del Rio killed in action in World War II. Later a pilot training school, it closed after the war. In 1952, through the efforts of local residents, it was reopened. Laughlin has been utilized for astronaut training, Strategic Air Command U-2 reconnaissance missions, the development of Air Training Command's undergraduate pilot training mission, and other important innovations. (1981)

DENISON (Grayson Co.)

US 75, 5 mi. N

Colbert's Ferry

Established about 1853 by Benjamin F. Colbert. Across it came thousands of immigrants into Texas in the fifties. The stages of the Southern Overland Mail Line, which provided mail and passenger service between St. Louis and San Francisco, crossed there, 1858 to 1861. Abandoned in 1931 when a highway bridge spanned the Red River.

DENISON (Grayson Co.)

US 75A, 4 mi. NW, overlook area

Lake Texoma

Completed 1944. Texoma is today the second largest lake in Texas and the eleventh largest reservoir in capacity in the United States. Its main purposes are flood control, power generation and recreation. Lake Texoma was promoted largely through the efforts of Sam Rayburn (1882–1961), noted speaker of the House who represented District 4 in Congress for 49 years.

In normal operation, lake shoreline covers 550 miles, with the Red River arm (45 miles) in Texas and the Washita arm (30 miles) in Oklahoma covering 93,080 acres. The waters are impounded by Denison Dam.

When Texoma was created, it caused the relocation of railroads, highways, utilities and cemeteries. The site of Preston, historically the Red River crossing for the Butterfield Stage, was submerged, as were the sites of Hagerman and part of Cedar Mills, Texas.

In 1966 numerous areas on Texoma drew 8,500,000 tourists who could also visit Eisenhower State Park at the southeast end of the lake. The park was named in honor of Dwight D. Eisenhower, the thirty-fourth president of the United States.

Texoma is one of more than 200 major inland lakes and reservoirs in Texas which contribute greatly to the economic and industrial growth of the state.

DENISON (Grayson Co.)   *US 69/75, 1 mi. S of the Red River*
at Texas Travel Information Center

1931 Free Bridge Controversy

As a result of late 1920s legislation in Texas and Oklahoma, the two states cooperated on a project to build free highway bridges spanning the Red River to accommodate rapidly increasing highway traffic. One of these bridges was near Colbert Bridge, a toll bridge descended from the mid-19th century Colbert's Ferry.

When the free bridge was ready to open in early July 1931, the Red River Bridge Company, operators of Colbert Bridge, obtained a federal restraining order against the opening of the free bridge until contractual payments had been made to compensate the company for their anticipated loss. Texas Governor Ross Sterling complied, but Oklahoma Governor William Murray, who was not a party to the contract between the Texas Highway Commission and the Red River Bridge Company, asked Governor Sterling to join him in protesting the injunction. Sterling refused. Murray ordered the removal of barricades erected by the Texas Highway Commission.

For twelve hours, traffic flowed freely across the bridge. By July 17, Texas Rangers guarded the southern side. Oklahoma highway crews rerouted traffic from Colbert Bridge to Preston Bridge several miles away and dismantled the approach to the Colbert Bridge from Oklahoma.

As tensions came close to breaking in the summer heat, the injunction was suspended; the Texas Rangers opened the bridge on July 25. The new bridge was officially opened on Labor Day, 1931. It served until 1995, when it was replaced by a new structure. A portion of the free bridge was placed in a park in Colbert, Oklahoma, about two miles north.   (1998)

DENISON (Grayson Co.)   *US 75, 1.5 mi. S of FM 120*

The Civilian Conservation Corps at Loy Park

Grayson County officials became aware of a growing need for a public recreation facility for the area's approximately 65,500 residents in 1930. Three years later the federal government agreed to create a small lake on land provided by the county. The county commissioners court purchased a site 2.5 miles southwest of Denison in October 1933 and secured the services of the Civilian Conservation Corps (CCC), a federal public works program, to construct the dam and build a recreational park.

In early November, 200 men from Wisconsin who comprised CCC Company 857 arrived in Grayson County to begin construction. Many men returned home in April 1934 at the end of the six-month CCC contract. Though it was unusual to employ CCC workers in their own areas, 48 Grayson County men were enlisted to replenish the supply of workers in Company 857. By 1934 the CCC men had created a recreation center with a lake, a roadway, 13 culvert bridges, 6 "battleship" picnic units, a baseball diamond, and a partially completed central tower of native stone.

Initially called Grayson County Park, the facility was renamed Judge Jake L. Loy State Park in 1934 in an effort to secure state assistance in completing the park. The commissioners court retrieved custody of the park in 1937 after no state maintenance had occurred. Under the supervision of the county commissioners court, the facility created by the depression-era Civilian Conservation Corps program continues to be enjoyed by area citizens.   (1998)

DENISON (Grayson Co.)   *US 75, at site of home, Old Settlers' Village*
in Loy Lake Park, Loy Lake Road

Old Bass Home
(Originally at 215 W Houston, Sherman)

Oldest extant house in city. Erected in 1850s by Dr. R. L. Bullock. Built around typical "dog run," or entry hall. Had first window glass in county.

Family home of Confederate Col. T. C. Bass since 1867. His daughter Nettie, born here 1868, lived in home 97 years.   (1968)

DENISON (Grayson Co.)   *US 75, corner of Loy Lake Rd. & Park Lane*
Sand Springs
(About 100 yds. N)
A noted watering place on pioneer trails, known as early as 1840 to settlers and prospectors who camped near the strong currents of water boiling up at the foot of a rocky bluff. The sandstone of the bluff's face became an inscription rock, in which travelers carved names or initials and dates of their visits, sometimes to assure friends or relatives who were to follow later over the same trail.

The campsite for prospectors, including California-bound gold seekers passing this way, 1849–1850s, the spot was mapped in 1857 as a watering spot for the Southern Overland Mail coaches of John Butterfield, racing from Saint Louis to San Francisco. After the Civil War (1861–1865), many cattle herds passed this way for water while being driven north to market.

When Missouri, Kansas & Texas Railroad was built to Denison townsite in 1872, Sand Springs gained new importance, feeding Waterloo lake, built in late 1800s and used for many years (prior to 1908) as city's main water supply. But the old campsites were inundated. Other steps in man's progress reduced flow of the water. The area remained a popular picnic ground for years. Its history is revealed by the weathered carvings still visible on the inscription rocks.   (1972)

DENISON (Grayson Co.)   *Lamar Avenue and Day Street, at site*
Birthplace of Dwight D. Eisenhower
Thirty-fourth President of the United States; born here Oct. 14, 1890, third son of David J. and Ida Elizabeth Stover Eisenhower.

Dwight Eisenhower graduated from the U.S. Military Academy, 1915; in 1943, during World War II, was appointed Commanding General of Allied Forces in Europe; served as president of Columbia University, 1948–1952; was President of U.S., 1952–1960; active elder statesman later.   (1968)

DENTON (Denton Co.)   *US 377 at FM 407, 7 mi. SW*
Denton County
Created April 11, 1846 from Fannin County; Organized July 13, 1846 with Denton as county seat. Both town and county are named in honor of John B. Denton 1806–1841. Pioneer preacher, lawyer and Indian fighter.

First county seat designated as Pinckneyville. 1846. Site selected in 1848 called Alton. Permanently located at Denton in 1857.   (1964)

DENVER CITY (Yoakum Co.)   *SH 214, 6 mi. N, Yoakum County Park*
Discovery Well in the Wasson Field
L. P. and Ruth Bennett moved to Yoakum County in 1916 to take over the ranching operation they had inherited from Ruth's father Dr. J. R. Smith of Munday. In 1927, they leased part of the ranch to the Texas Pacific Coal and Oil Company for the drilling of exploratory oil wells.

By the mid-1930s the Bennett's cattle business was declining as a result of the economic depression and a severe area drought. They were in danger of losing their property through foreclosure when oil was discovered on the ranch. The find was made on October 10, 1935 at the Ruth Bennett No. 1-678 (6 mi. NE), a well supervised by Fort Worth wildcatter Red Davidson and crews of the Honolulu Oil Company. With the discovery, the Bennetts were able to pay all claims against their land.

Increased drilling activity in the area created a "boom town" atmosphere and led to the founding of Denver City (6 mi. S) in 1939. Petroleum remains the major industry in Yoakum County, a national leader in the production of crude oil.

In 1964, Gene H. Bennett, the youngest son of L. P. and Ruth Bennett, donated this portion of the Bennett ranch to the county for use as a park.   (1981)

DESDEMONA (Eastland Co.)
SH 16, city limits
Fort Blair, C.S.A.
A few miles to the southwest. Largest far western "family fort" used throughout Civil War. Started by C. C. Blair, 1857 settler. 1861–1865 occupants were Wm. Arthur, Blair, J. M. Ellison: Jasper, Jim and Tom Gilbert; W. C. McGough, W. H. Mansker and sometimes others. The fort had 12 log cabins, 14 ft. square, 14 ft. apart in two parallel rows. Pickets walled spaces between cabins. Ammunition and supplies could be bought only by making long, dangerous trips to the Brazos settlements or to the south. Men were hard to spare for a trip, from the fort's defenders against Indians.

Candles, soap, soda, food, clothing were made in the fort, by use of rat renderings, beeswax, wood ashes, wild herbs, bark, roots, berries, animal skins. Families had to promote education for their children.

Other area forts included Allen's Ranch, also in Eastland County; Lynch and Green ranches, Shackelford County; Buffalo Springs, Clay County; Bragg's and Murray's Forts, Young County; Picketville, Fort Davis, Owls Head and Mugginsville, Stephens County.

After the war, Desdemona was established as a stop on the Old Waco-Ft. Griffin Road. It boomed to fame when oil was discovered in 1918. Its call for help to end lawlessness added new glory to Texas Rangers. (1965)

DESDEMONA (Eastland Co.)
SH 16, 1 mi. S
Desdemona Cemetery
The town of Desdemona was a well established frontier community by the 1870s. A post office opened there in 1877. J. S. and Rosa Jones deeded one acre from the D. W. Funderburgh land survey for a "public graveyard" in 1880. The earliest marked grave is that of William E. Wright (1815–1878). It is likely that older unmarked burials exist among the oak trees here.

Native rocks incised with initials or dates mark some early graves. Those buried here include pioneer settlers and their descendants; frontier matriarch Mrs. Kate (Kizzie) Shuler; veterans of the Civil War, World War I and World War II; Capt. A. J. O'Rear, a county commissioner and postmaster; S. E. Snodgrass, a physician who served the area for 50 years; local citizens who profited from the 1918 oil boom: Joe and Almeda Duke, owners of the site of the first oil gusher; and many young children. In 1918–1819, oil discoveries surrounded the cemetery with flowing wells and oil derricks.

H. H. Williams' estate donated two acres of land in 1965. The Desdemona Cemetery Association manages and maintains the site. The cemetery continues to serve the area as it has for more than a century. (1996)

DETROIT (Red River Co.)
FM 410, 6 mi. SW
Birthplace of John Nance Garner
In this house John Nance Garner, Vice President of the United States since 1933, was born November 22, 1869. A member of Texas Legislature, 1896–1902. Member of United States Congress since 1903. Speaker of the House 1931.

DETROIT (Red River Co.)
200 S. Main, Detroit
John Nance Garner (1868–1967)
As a young lawyer lived, 1889–1892, in this house owned by his parents. He rose from Uvalde county judge (1893–1896), to Texas Legislature (1898–1902), to U.S. Congress (1904–1932, with a term as Speaker, House of Representatives), to Vice President of the United States, 1933–1941. Awarded Medallion. (1971)

DEVERS (Liberty Co.)
SH 61, 4 mi. S
Homestead of John S. and
Jane Susanna Lee Brown, 1856
On Spanish Land Grant. Building materials came by sea from Mobile, Ala., to Anahuac, thence by ox-cart to present site. Lumber was hand-planed; pegs and square nails were used. Awarded Medallion. (1965)

148

DEVINE (Medina Co.)   *US 81 at SH 173*
Judge Thomas J. Devine
(1820–1890)
Born in Nova Scotia. Came to Texas in 1843. Became district judge, 1851. On the powerful Public Safety Committee of the Texas Secession Convention, 1861. Named with Samuel A. Maverick and Philip N. Luckett to take possession of the Federal property in Texas. Backed by Col. Ben McCulloch and 1,200 Minute Men, forced surrender of 3,000 troops with arms, ammunition, supplies and $30,000 cash.

Served throughout the Civil War as one of two Confederate judges in Texas. Tried cases of persons accused of Union sympathies; dispositions of goods owned by northern enemy; and maritime disputes arising from the coastal blockade and shipwrecks.

In 1864 was made special commissioner to settle disputes among foreign merchants handling cotton (South's only medium of trade for vital supplies) across the Mexican boundary.

At war's end, left with other Texas leaders hoping to continue fight from Mexico. On his return became only southerner besides President Jefferson Davis to be twice indicted for treason. Was pardoned in June 1867 by President Andrew Johnson.

On Texas Supreme Court and University of Texas Board of Regents. This town named for him in 1882.

DEVINE (Medina Co.)   *SH 173 right-of-way, 3 mi. N*
Spanish Exploration in Medina County
In 1531, Spain ruled present Mexico, Central America, the Caribbean, half of South America, and much of the United States. The desire to claim new lands north of the Rio Grande led to continuous Spanish expeditions through present Texas during the 16th, 17th, and 18th centuries.

The expedition of Alvar Nuñez Cabeza de Vaca traveled through Texas between 1526 and 1537, exploring and mapping the unknown territory. Later Spanish expeditions, which established missions, presidios (forts), and townships, included those led by Alonso de Leon; Father Manuel de la Cruz; Father Juan LaRios and Fernando del Bosque; Domingo Teran de los Rios; and Father Isidro de Espinosa.

At least twenty Spanish expeditions led by soldiers, missionaries, and settlers crossed present Medina County before 1844. Detailed descriptions of the area appear in the official accounts of many of the expeditions. Many of the county's geographical features retain the names given them by Spanish explorers of the 16th, 17th, and 18th centuries. Spanish names associated with early settlements, sites, rivers, and streams serve as reminders of the rich Spanish heritage of the area now known as Medina County.   (1989)

DEWEYVILLE (Newton Co.)   *SH 12, on Texas side of Sabine River Bridge*
Deweyville
Original site, called "Possum Bluff," was purchased with a team of oxen by Pierre Lavine from Bill Morrison, 1886.

Town was renamed for Admiral George Dewey during Spanish-American War.

Leading industry, sawmill, was built by Sabine Tram Co., 1897; and was owned 1919–1943 by Peavy-Moore Lumber Co.   (1967)

D'HANIS (Medina Co.)   *US 90, 1.5 mi. E in Old D'Hanis*
Now Known as Old D'Hanis
Established in 1847 by 29 families under the leadership of Theodore Gentilz, representing Henri Castro (1781–1861), distinguished pioneer and colonizer of Texas who introduced the early settlers of Medina County.

Named in honor of Guillaum (William) D'Hanis manager of the Colonization Society. When the Southern Pacific Railroad missed the town its citizens moved to present D'Hanis.   (1936)

D'HANIS (Medina Co.)   *US 90, 1½ mi. E in Old D'Hanis*
Site of
Saint Dominic Catholic Church
and Cemetery
Congregation formed in 1847 with founding of D'Hanis Colony by settlers from Alsace, France.

In 1853, when town became a mission parish, limestone church was built, using timber hauled by ox-wagon from Medina River.

Sandstone extension was built in 1868 upon arrival of first resident pastor but abandoned after 1914 when new church was built in "New" D'Hanis (1½ miles west).

Cemetery, dating from burial of child of colonists in 1847, was used until 1893, when new cemetery was started following diphtheria epidemic. (1972)

D'HANIS (Medina Co.) *FM 1796 (Main St.), 1 block N of US 90*
J. M. Koch's Hotel
J. M. and Mary Ann Koch owned and operated a hotel in D'Hanis beginning in 1898. They purchased the land on this site in July 1902, and built this hotel in 1906. Reportedly constructed by Chinese railroad laborers, it is built of early bricks from the D'Hanis brick plant. In December, 1914, the Koch family sold the building, which continued as a hotel until 1920. The Farmers Exchange of D'Hanis purchased it that year for use as a feed store, adding a cotton scale to the east side of the structure. A later owner operated it as a boarding house. A simple but elegant early 20th century hotel with late Victorian details, the edifice's notable architectural features include its symmetrical plan, three-bay façade with central door, paired round-arch windows, 2-story porch and corbelled brickwork on the parapet. (2000)

DIANA (Upshur Co.) *US 259, 1 mi. S 400 yds. E of Railroad Crossing*
Two Early Railroads
(Crossing, 400 yds. E)
The Marshall & East Texas Railroad, chartered 1908 was part of a line built 1882. Operated a passenger train nicknamed the "Misery & Eternal Torment," and ran a logging train until 1917.

The Port Bolivar & Iron Ore Line was founded 1911 to haul ore from Upshur County to the Texas coast, but never built farther than Longview, 30 miles south. It ceased operations in 1929.

The history of these lines is that of many "special interest" railroads. They thrived during the early days of Texas industry, but today have been abandoned or incorporated into larger lines. (1967)

DIBOLL (Angelina Co.) *US 59, 3 mi. S*
Site of Clark's Ferry and Clark's Ferry Cemetery
Established by I. D. Clark in 1856, this ferry provided an important crossing on the Neches River between Angelina and Polk counties. When Clark died in 1859, his widow, Ann, operated the ferry with the help of two slaves until her own death in 1863. Ownership of the land remained in the Clark family.

In 1881, W. B. Clark was issued a license to operate the ferry. A town was platted at the ferry crossing and named Clark's Station, also known as Miami. In 1860, a community cemetery was established north of the town.

The ferry was phased out after modern highways were built. (1996)

DIBOLL (Angelina Co.) *400 Kenley at Temple St. (US 59)*
Diboll
A sawmill established here in 1894 by T. L. L. Temple gave rise to a town that by 1900 contained a commissary, post office, churches, homes, and schools run by the Southern Pine Lumber Company. The town was named for the Diboll family of New Orleans from whom Temple initially purchased timber rights.

Diboll remained a company town until Southern Pine Lumber Company began promoting private ownership of homes and businesses in the 1950s. Diboll was incorporated in 1962 and today boasts a multi-ethnic citizenry which supports numerous community activities. (1994)

DIBOLL (Angelina Co.) *US 59, 1 mi. N on, then 1.1 mi. NW on FM 2497*
Ryan Chapel
Founded 1866, after new settler, Rev. Isaac Ryan, had Methodist revival in home before occupying it. His brother John was one of 19 charter members. L. H. D. and Sallie Guinn gave 7½ acres for church and cemetery. First 16 by 20-ft. church had puncheon seats and floor. First pastor, Rev. Henry Wright, was paid in bacon, corn syrup. (1964)

DICKENS (Dickens Co.)   *Dickens Springs Park on US 82*
Dickens Springs
At one time, water covered this area. Sandstone, the prominent rock around this site, is porous, causing exposed strata at canyon rims to form a natural drainage outlet for upland aquifers, making possible the existence of these springs. Situated at the head of a canyon ravine immediately below the upper prairie region of the rolling plains, the ancient springs have been a favored human habitat since the earliest human occupation in this region. Many nomadic tribes have used the site, leaving behind a wealth of archeological evidence. John A. Askins and his family settled near these springs in late 1883, and it became known to pioneers as Askins Springs. A traveling real estate developer called Dr. M. S. Crow arrived here in 1891 and was a driving force in the organization of the town of Dickens about a half-mile west of the Askins land. In 1891 he gave a speech proclaiming his intent to give ten acres around "Crow Springs," as he called them, to the town of Dickens. The new city park became known as Dickens Springs. Generations of Dickens citizens and tourists, attracted by the rugged and colorful scenery and the unique collection of plants, have visited this site for picnics and social gatherings. In 1978 the Departments of Anthropology and of Park Management at Texas Tech University made an intensive survey of the land surrounding Dickens Springs. Though many artifacts were lost to souvenir hunters, the university workers uncovered a variety of ancient tools, rarely of local origin. In the 21st century, Dickens Springs continues to provide water and beauty to the area for modern visitors as it did for the nomadic peoples of the past.   (2000)

DICKENS (Dickens Co.)   *SH 114, 0.5 mi. E*
Dickens Cemetery
The only cemetery to serve the town of Dickens, this graveyard began in 1891, the same year the town was founded. Mrs. C. F. Jones, wife of pioneer settler and town barber C. F. Jones, died in 1891 and was buried by her husband at the foot of a hill overlooking the Croton Breaks. The owner of the property, M. S. Crow, at the suggestion of his attorney W. C. Ballard, donated five acres of land surrounding the grave site for a community cemetery. W. C. Ballard, considered by many to be the "Father of Dickens," died in 1913 and was buried here, as well.

Many early settlers and city and county officials are interred in this graveyard. Also buried here are veterans of the Civil War, the Spanish-American War, World War I, World War II, the Korean War, and the Vietnam War.

Through the years, the size of the Dickens Cemetery has increased through additional land donations. Fence was erected in 1919, and in 1948 local citizens formed a cemetery association to care for the grounds and monument. Now encompassing more than eighteen acres, the cemetery serves as a reflection of area history.   (1994)

DICKENS (Dickens Co.)   *US 82, 17 mi. E*
Pitchfork Ranch
Irish-born Jerry Savage established an open range ranch at this site about 1879. In 1881, St. Louis businessman Eugene F. Williams and Texas cattleman Dan B. Gardner purchased the ranch and in 1883 joined forces with landholder Sam Lazarus to form the Pitchfork Land and Cattle Co., Inc. Williams' heirs later acquired controlling interest of the cattle empire. The first structures here were dugouts in the river bank, while the present buildings date from 1902. Pitchfork Ranch has doubled its original size to 165,000 acres and now operates ranches in Kansas and Wyoming.
                                                                   (1983)

DICKINSON (Galveston Co.)   *SH 3, School Admin. Bldg.*
Townsite of Dickinson
Oldest mainland settlement in Galveston County, named for John Dickinson, one of "Old 300" settlers in original colony (opened in 1821) of Stephen F. Austin. Townsite is on Dickinson Bayou land grant of James F. and Emily Austin Perry (brother-in-law and sister of Austin), surveyed in April 1830 by Austin and his friend Seth Ingram. Early settlers here included Alexander Farmer, who in 1831 obtained a land grant where he built home after Texas War for Independence ended in 1836; and Herman Benson, whose mid-1840s dog trot cabin still stands. Gen. E. B. Nichols, merchant, statesman, and leader in Houston-Galveston area in 1857 built summer home still standing in Dickinson.

Colonial era economy was based on agriculture and cattle raising. Toward end of 19th century produce was shipped by eight trains a day; for a time area was known as "Strawberry Capital of the World." The Coast County Fair was held here 1895–1896. Picnic and fairgrounds with exhibit building stood alongside Galveston, Houston & Henderson Railway tracks.

Community's first church (Methodist) was organized in 1876, and served by circuit riders. Dickinson post office was opened in March 1890; first tax-funded school, in 1892. Town remains a coastal beauty spot. (1972)

DIME BOX (Lee Co.) — *FM 141 at Stayton Avenue on NW side*
Dime Box

Founded 1913. Name derived from the practice of leaving dimes in community mailbox on old San Antonio Road in return for items from Giddings.

Nation's first town to contribute one hundred per cent to "March of Dimes" program, 1945. Official national program opening held here in 1946. (1968)

DIME BOX (Lee Co.) — *SH 21, 5 mi. NW*
County's Second Oldest Community
Old Dime Box

Located in Texas, founder Stephen F. Austin's "Old Three Hundred" colony. First known as Browne's Mills.

Present name derived from practice of leaving dimes in box at Joseph S. Browne's Mill so that postman John W. Ratliff would bring items from Giddings to community members. (1968)

DIMMITT (Castro Co.) — *SH 94 at US 385, in roadside park at city limits*
Castro County

Formed from Young and Bexar Territories. Created August 21, 1876; organized December 8, 1891. Named in honor of Henri Castro, 1786–1861, a distinguished pioneer and colonizer of Texas. Founder of the towns of Castroville, Quihi, Vandenburg, and D'Hanis, in Medina County. Dimmitt, the county seat. (1964)

DIMMITT (Castro Co.) — *Jones Street on Courthouse Square*
Shoot-out on Jones Street

At an 1891 meeting to discuss the selection of a Castro County seat, words were exchanged between Ira Aten, a retired Texas Ranger speaking on behalf of Castro City, and Andrew McClelland, a spokesman for Dimmitt. The inflammatory remarks led to a gunfight between the two men on Dec. 23, five days after Dimmitt was chosen county seat. In an exchange of shots in the middle of Jones Street, Aten wounded Andrew McClelland and his brother Hugh. Aten was acquitted of the assault charges and a short time later was appointed Castro County sheriff. (1983)

DIMMITT (Castro Co.) — *FM 145 and FM 1055, 10¾ mi. SW*
The J. W. Carter Family
and the 7-UP Ranch

The first permanent settlers in Castro County, the James W. Carter family moved to this area in 1884. A tent and dugout served as home until a house was constructed (100 yds. W). Their cattle, which they brought with them, were marked with the 7-UP brand. Their daughter Lizzie (b. 1886) was the first white child born to a permanent settler in the area. James Carter (1845–1916) was instrumental in the organization of the Castro County government in 1891 and served on the first commissioners court. Carter and his wife Ellen (1855–1942) later opened a hotel in Dimmitt. (1981)

DIMMITT (Castro Co.) — *SH 86, 5.8 mi. E of FM 2567*
Summerfield-Dameron Corner

In 1876, English native John Summerfield (1853–1918) began his work locating and surveying millions of acres of land in present-day Randall, Deaf Smith, Castro, and Swisher Counties. One of the earth monuments he erected that year was located near this site and became a starting point for surveys in many Panhandle counties. In 1925, a group of Castro County citizens placed a concrete monument at the site, which has become known as Dameron's Corner after a local landowner. The monument was buried in 1958 when a road was cut through the area. (1985)

DINERO (Live Oak Co.)   US 281, 3.5 mi. NW
Site of Fort Merrill
Established by Captain S. M. Plummer, First U.S. Infantry February 26, 1850. As a protection to settlers against Indians.

Named in honor of Captain Hamilton W. Merrill, Brevet Major Second Dragoon. Gallant officer in the Mexican War.

Permanently abandoned Dec. 1, 1885.   (1936)

DINERO (Live Oak Co.)   *On oil derrick near post office*
Town of Dinero
Settled about 1838 by farmers and ranchers. First named "Barlow" after the local ferry operator. Townspeople were instrumental in organizing Live Oak County, 1856; started a school by 1858.

About 1872, rumors of money ("Dinero" in Spanish) buried here led town to change of name. A post office was established in 1885.

Town buildings were moved a mile west, 1913, to be on new rail line. In 1925 Dinero piped first natural gas to Houston. Oil, gas continue to bolster economy.

Local landmark is hanging tree. Famous resident was J. Frank Dobie (1888–1964), Texas author.   (1970)

DODGE (Walker Co.)   *Farris St. and FM 405*
Town of Dodge
In area of pioneers: W. H. Palmer (Parmer), 1825; W. H. Barker, 1830; John Roark, 1832; Ed Farris, 1836.

When Houston & Great Northern Railroad (later International & Great Northern, and now Missouri Pacific) was built in 1872, right of way was given by Thomas Akin, W. J. Johnson, and others. Johnson stipulated depot be placed here.

12-block town soon had Masonic Lodge, churches, school, blacksmith shop, cotton gin, stores. From 1901 to 1936, this was junction for Trinity Valley Southern and I. G. N. Railroads. With timber phased out, town declined. Community well and a few businesses remain.   (1972)

DONNA (Hidalgo Co.)   *Bus. US 83 at S 8th St.*
Donna
Two East Texas men, T. J. Hooks and A. F. Hester, began developing this area for settlement in the late 1890s. Through formation of the La Blanca Agricultural Company, they set up farms and irrigation systems and advertised the area's favorable climate and resources. In 1904, when a rail line was built here, they founded the town of Donna, named for T. J. Hooks' daughter. Ed Ruthven opened the first store and, in 1908, the town incorporated with R. P. Boeye as mayor. Since the earliest days of the 20th century, Donna has developed as one of the leading cities of the Rio Grande Valley.   Texas Sesquicentennial 1836–1986

DONNA (Hidalgo Co.)   *FM 493, .7 mi. S; 2.7 mi. E on US 281*
Balli Cemetery
Juan Jose Hinojosa (1700–1789) was granted land including this site posthumously in 1790. His great-grandson Antonio Balli Cavazos (1813–1887), was the first to live on the land, which he named the Balli San Antonio del Esterito Ranch in 1839. He established the family cemetery. The earliest marked grave is that of Atilano Pina (d. 1874), the husband of Francisca Natividad Balli Rubalcaba. Antonio Balli Cavazos was laid to rest with his wife Manuela Rubalcaba in 1887. The last burial was that of Apolonio Balli Salazar in 1956. There are 17 marked and at least 16 unmarked graves in the Balli Cemetery. The graveyard is all that remains of a 7,000-acre cattle ranch that dominated this part of the Valley for 120 years.   (1998)

DOUGLASS (Nacogdoches Co.)   *FM 225, 6 mi. S*
Site of the Mission Nuestra
Señora de La Purisima Concepcion
Established by Franciscan missionaries in 1716 with the hope of civilizing and Christianizing the Indians of the region. Abandoned temporarily due to the French incursions from Louisiana in

1719. Restored by the Marquis of Aguayo in 1721. Removed to the Colorado River in 1730 and finally situated on the San Antonio River in 1731.

DOUGLASS (Nacogdoches Co.)   *FM 225, 7 mi. S*
Site of Town of Mount Sterling
Established by John Durst in 1837. Near the ruins of the Mission La Purisima Concepcion de Maria. He built a saw and grist mill, in the town, a large warehouse. From his house he could see the boats moored to the wharves on the Angelina. The Cordova Rebellion in 1838 sealed the doom of the town. Durst moved to Leon County.

DOUGLASSVILLE (Cass Co.)   *SH 8*
Douglassville Cemetery
Williamson Petty (1820–1861), Sulphur River ferryman, donated land for this cemetery from a claim which he settled in 1850. Col. John C. Douglass (1818–1863), from Georgia, bought in 1855 all of the Petty claim not previously reserved for school and church. The cemetery took its name from his town of Douglassville. The earliest legible stone (1859) marks the grave site of Mrs. Henrietta Cook and her infant twins. Additional land was acquired in 1928 and 1939. The cemetery has about 400 graves and a governing association.   (1976)

DRIPPING SPRINGS (Hays Co.)   *US 290*
The Marshall-Chapman Home
Burrell J. Marshall (1826–1872) built this residence in 1871 by adding rooms of native lime-stone to an existing frame structure. He used his home briefly as a post office while he was post-master. When Marshall died in 1872, his widow, Martha, (1835–1924) married Wm. Thomas Chapman (1835–1917), who also became postmaster and a trustee of the Dripping Springs Academy. Marshall and Chapman family members owned the house until 1942, when John and Clara Wilson bought it.   (1976)

DRISCOLL (Nueces Co.)   *US 77 at FM 665*
Site of Santa Petronila Ranch
Appointed in 1764 by the Governor of the Spanish colony of Nuevo Santander, Captain Blas Maria de la Garza Falcon (1717–1767) established an outpost and way station (8 mi. E), the first in present-day Nueces County. He was commissioned to explore the coast and establish a mission for Christianizing the Indians. By 1766, he had moved his family, friends and herds of live-stock to what was called Rancho de Don Blas or Santa Petronila Ranch. Until 1836, many colonists came from the Rio Grande area.

The ranch served as headquarters for expeditions including those led by Falcon and his son Alferez Don Joseph Antonio de la Garza who explored the islands along the Gulf Coast. Falcon probably named Santa Gertrudis Creek after his only daughter, Gertrudis de la Garza. He played an important role in settling towns along the Rio Grande and Nueces River and Padre, Mustang and St. Joseph's Islands. Soldiers at the garrison patrolled the region against the fierce Karankawa Indians and foreign invasion. Many colonists returned to the Rio Grande settlements because of Indian raids and the Texas War for Independence (1836). After the war they reestab-lished homes here. Many of their descendants still live in the area.   (1978)

DUBLIN (Erath Co.)   *SH 6, 8 mi. W*
Round Grove Baptist Church
First church in western Erath County. Organized by the Rev. R. D. Ross in 1871 with 16 char-ter members. Had first Sunday school reported in county, 1872.

Original church of logs and rough native lumber was built on site given by Ross family; rebuilt 1938.   (1972)

DUMAS (Moore Co.)   *US 87/287, 6 mi. S*
Moore County
Created 1876 from Bexar Land District. Named in honor of Edwin W. Moore (1810–1865), Commodore of the Navy, Republic of Texas.

County was organized July 5, 1892, with Dumas (named for promoter of the townsite) as coun-ty seat. Stagecoach and freighters furnished transportation in early days.

The county was thinly settled; ranching was the main industry prior to discoveries of oil and gas in 1926. A zinc smelter was built in 1936. Economy is now based on petrochemicals, helium, oil, gas, cattle feeding, ranching, grains, soybeans, sugar beets and castor beans.   (1969)

DUMAS (Moore Co.)   *US 287/87, S city limits*
Geological Riches of Moore County
Have proved beneficial from earliest times when prehistoric man developed first industry in Texas by mining flint deposits along the Canadian River. Items made from these quarries have been found over a large portion of the western United States.

Slabs of dolomite from area were used to build sturdy, warm homes; interiors were coated with mixture of sand, clay and caliche—an advance uncommon in prehistoric North America.

Modern man has established 31 industries based on oil and gas, to take advantage of geological riches untapped by ancient man.   (1970)

DUMAS (Moore Co.)   *US 87/287, S edge of Dumas*
Site of Historic Drift Fence
Until the mid-1880s, no range fences existed in the Texas Panhandle. Thus when winter blizzards came, cattle drifted from Oklahoma, Colorado and Kansas to the Texas ranches of ("T Box T"—Dominion Cattle Co. Ltd.), K ("Seven K"—York, Parker & Draper), CC ("Bar C's"—Creswell Land & Cattle Co.), ("Turkey Tract"—Hansford Land & Cattle Co.), LX (Bates & Beal), LIT (Littlefield) and LE (Lee & Reynolds). The influx caused these ranches in the Canadian River breaks to be overgrazed, for by spring roundup there were as many northern as local cattle in the herds.

To prevent the costly and time-consuming job of separating the cattle, each Texas rancher agreed to construct a fence along his north boundary line. The resulting fence was 200 miles long and ran from the northeast corner of the Panhandle southwest to near the site where Dumas was later founded, then west about 35 miles into New Mexico. It was a 4-strand, 4-bar fence with posts 30 feet apart and a gate every 3 miles. The materials amounted to about 65 carloads of wire and posts hauled from Dodge City.

In 1890, however, to comply with an 1889 state law prohibiting any fence from crossing or enclosing public property, most of the fence was removed.   (1969)

DUMAS (Moore Co.)   *US 87/287, 6½ mi. S*
Route of Tascosa-Dodge Trail
Founded 1877 for cattle drives and freight hauls from Tascosa (38 mi. SW) to market in Dodge City, Kans.

A mail route. The first stagecoach stop out of Tascosa was 3 mi. SW of here. Tascosa had a post office, 1878; was county seat, Oldham County, 1880; declined after 1887.   (1966)

DUMAS (Moore Co.)   *FM 1913 at Plum Creek Rd., 24.8 mi. SE*
Exploration Route of Lt. James W. Abert
(Campsites: 5 mi. SW and 3 mi. NE of Marker)
The United States government had the Canadian River explored in 1845, just before Texas joined the Union. Topographical engineer James W. Abert (1820–1897), a West Point graduate, had charge of a 33-man party, and spent two or more days in the vicinity of this marker. Near here he was visited by Kiowa Indians, who said that they were at war with Texans. Abert was made welcome after he proved to be an American. His map of the river and notes on geography and the Indians proved valuable to Texas and the nation.   (1976)

DUMAS (Moore Co.)   *SH 152, 12 mi. E*
Route of Tascosa-Dodge City Trail
As ranchers and merchants settled in this part of Texas during the 1870s, the need for a direct supply line became evident. This trail was established in 1877 for cattle drives and freight hauls from Tascosa (38 mi. SW) to markets in Dodge City, Kansas. It also served as a stagecoach and mail route. The town of Tascosa received a post office in 1878 and was the Oldham County seat from 1880 until 1915. The coming of the railroad in 1887 led to the decline of the town and to the abandonment of the Tascosa-Dodge City Trail.   (1966)

DUMAS (Moore Co.)   *US 287/87, Courthouse Square*
Moore County Courthouse
Land for this courthouse square was donated by Louis Dumas, who laid out the townsite in 1891. One year later, Moore County was formally organized as a government, and in 1893 the county's first courthouse was built. The original courthouse was replaced by the current structure, built by C. S. Lambie and Company at a cost of $155,000. The brick building was occupied by county officials during the first week of August 1931. Both courthouses have held all county records and have served as focal points for the community and for the entire county.   (1984)

DUNDEE (Archer Co.)   *US 82, 1.5 mi. E*
Alex Albright
(September 22, 1861–April 8, 1937)
A pioneer American Karakul breeder. Born in Nebraska; grew up in cattle business. In 1890, came to Dundee; opened a general store. Built Elm Lodge Ranch (1,400 acres on Holliday Creek, 4 mi. SE). At first raised purebred Lincoln sheep. In 1910, with help of U.S. ex-President Theodore Roosevelt and the Czar of Russia, he imported valuable Karakul sheep from Asia. Later his upbred flock of 1,200 took prizes all over the world.

Albright's first wife, Dorothy Jane Duncan, died in 1900. Second wife, Marie Sahores, assisted him in ranching business. Daughters were Zella, Ester, and Marie.   (1971)

DUNN (Scurry Co.)   *SH 208 at Post Office*
Dunn
Started as change station for teams hauling goods north after T.&P. Railway reached Colorado City in 1881. Freighters camped here beside creek. A blacksmith shop and store were started to supply them. In time a town developed. Mail was dropped at home of Mr. and Mrs. A. T. Dunn. Post office, granted 1890, was given their name; Mr. Dunn was first postmaster. In 1890, the first school was built.

A well, windmill and trough were added for travelers and town. Because it was in middle of the road, well was covered when highway was paved in 1938.   (1966)

EAGLE LAKE (Colorado Co.)   *US 90A 2 mi. W*
Navigation of the Colorado River
Because overland travel in early Texas was an enterprise often fraught with hardship, frustration, and danger, many individuals looked to rivers for a solution to the problem. From 1829 to the Civil War, optimistic Texans attempted to ply the area's long meandering rivers, but met repeated disappointment.

The most serious drawback to navigation of the Colorado was "The Raft." This was a series of timber masses—some floating, some sunken—choking off the river about 10–15 miles above its mouth. The length was variously given as 3–8 miles. In spite of this, the keelboat *David Crockett* became the first boat to navigate the river, in 1838. After that, flatboats brought cotton, hides, lumber, and pecans down as far as the raft, but there goods had to be taken off and hauled laboriously by wagon to Matagorda.

The Republic of Texas incorporated 2 companies to clear the river and the state authorized the construction of a new channel around the raft, but the obstruction remained an impediment and hazard.

Although shallow-draft boats managed occasional trips, the more efficient railroads eventually took away much business. After the Civil War, Texas rivers ceased to be an important factor in transportation.   (1969)

EAGLE LAKE (Colorado Co.)   *FM 102, 1.8 mi. S*
The Lakeside Sugar Refinery
The sugar industry, which began in Texas before the Civil War (1861–1865), was revived in the later 1800s by cheaper refining methods. One of the leading sugar producers in Colorado County was William Dunovant. In 1898 he and several men from Eagle Lake built the Cane Belt Railroad to take care of the mill. Later extended, the profitable rail line was purchased by the Santa Fe Railroad in 1902.

The success of the railroad encouraged Dunovant to build a refining plant for the area. Lakeside Sugar Refinery, erected at this site about 1902, processed up to 1000 tons of cane each day and produced 5,000,000 pounds of refined sugar each year. A train called the "Whangdoodle" carried cane from the nearby fields to the refinery. By 1910 Lakeside Mill was one of the largest in Texas, with about 100 employees. It stimulated the local economy and attracted able business men, such as Rudolph Wintermann and son Oscar J. Wintermann.

After its best season in 1908–1809, the sugar industry declined. A state law forbidding use of convict labor raised production cost. A tropical storm damaged the refinery, and an early freeze destroyed much of the sugar crop. Sold in 1913, the Lakeside Refinery was dismantled in 1918 and rebuilt in Jamaica. (1976)

EAGLE PASS (Maverick Co.) 3.3 mi. E (relocated at Courthouse grounds)
Maverick County
Created Feb. 2, 1856, from Kinney County. Organized July 13, 1871. Named for Texas Revolution veteran, signer of Declaration of Independence, Texas Legislator Samuel A. Maverick (1803–1870). The county centers in an area of dairies, farming, ranching.

Hard-traveled El Camino Real (path into Texas history for Louis St. Denis, Spanish missionaries, Moses Austin and countless troops and settlers) crossed the Rio Grande near Eagle Pass, the county seat.

Site of Spanish mission ruins, military posts. Fort Duncan, now a military park, housed both U.S. and Confederate troops. (1965)

EAGLE PASS (Maverick Co.) US 57, 8 mi. NE
Dead Man's Hill
(¾ mi. E)
A knoll by which the old Uvalde road passed.

Hill acquired name in 1877 when three traders from Guerrero, bound for San Antonio, were killed here by a party of Lipan-Apaches. The victims' mutilated bodies were found hanging from the wheels of their carts. (1968)

EAGLE PASS (Maverick Co.) US 277, 2 mi. N
Eagle Pass Coal Mines
Although the Indian, Spanish, and early Anglo-American inhabitants knew of this area's large bituminous coal deposits, commercial mining did not begin until 1885, when F. H. Hartz opened a hillside mine near the Rio Grande. For a time, it was the largest producing mine in Texas, but damage from an 1892 fire caused it to close several years later. Hartz then started another mine for the Maverick County Coal Co., which evolved into the Olmos Coal, Coke, and Oil Co. Under the direction of Pasquale and Rocco DeBona, this company reached a production peak of 1,200 tons a day.

Another mining operation was the Eagle Pass Coal and Coke Co., formed in 1893 by Louis Dolch, J. B. Dibrell, and Emil Moshiem. Their mines (.25 mi. S) supplied fuel for Southern Pacific Railroad locomotives until 1902. The town of Dolchburg, now called Seco Mines, was built in 1905, with housing for 90 workers. After Dolch's death in 1907, the International Coal Mine Co. took over the operation. By 1910, this firm employed 350 men and produced about 1,000 tons of coal a day.

Competition from oil, natural gas, and other fuels caused the mines to decline. The main Olmos Co. shafts closed in 1912, but Olmos' Lamar Mine (3.5 mi. NE) and the International Co. Mines were operating as late as 1925. (1975)

EAGLE PASS (Maverick Co.) In front of old post headquarters, Fort Duncan
Fort Duncan
Established March 27, 1849, by Capt. Sidney Burbank with companies A, B, and F, First U.S. Infantry. Name honors Col. James Duncan, a hero of the Mexican War.

Fort served as frontier outpost near trail of California emigrants; base of operations against hostile Lipan Apache Indians. In 1851, it became the headquarters of the First Infantry. By 1856, Garrison included units of Mounted Rifles and First Artillery. Abandoned May 1859, post was regarrisoned in March 1860 because of border assaults by Juan N. Cortina, desperado of the area. At outbreak of the Civil War, 1861, fort was again abandoned, only to be occupied later as "Rio Grande Station," by Confederate forces.

In 1868, Fort Duncan was regarrisoned by the 9th Infantry and Headquarters Company of 41st Infantry, under Col. William R. Shafter. Seminole-Negro scouts, organized here Aug. 16, 1870, played a large part in ridding Western Texas of Indians. After 1883, post declined in importance; known as Camp Eagle Pass, it was abandoned about 1900. Mexican border troubles in 1916 again brought reoccupation; its use as a training camp continued during World War I.

In 1938, the fort property was purchased by city of Eagle Pass, for use as park and recreation area. (1970)

EARTH (Lamb Co.) US 70, 4.7 mi. W
First Irrigation Well in Lamb County
Dug by hand in 1902 for crops, cattle, and household use of Ewing Halsell (1877–1965), son of land promoter and settler W. E. Halsell. An irrigation ditch carried water half a mile to headquarters of Halsell's "Mashed O" Ranch. Six feet in diameter but only 30 feet deep, well is no longer in operation. (1972)

EARTH (Lamb Co.) US 70, 5.2 mi. W
Spring Lake
Indian camp and watering place extensively used in hunting buffalo. Became cattle territory in 1882 when Tom Lynch drove his herds from New Mexico. After acquisition by the Capitol Syndicate, this became headquarters of largest division of the XIT Ranch.

EAST COLUMBIA (Brazoria Co.) SH 35, 2 mi. E in roadside park
James Britton "Brit" Bailey
(1779–1833)
Pioneer Texan noted for his courage, integrity, and eccentric behavior. Came to Texas in 1818 with wife and six children.

He settled on what came to be "Bailey's Prairie." Joined Stephen F. Austin's colony, 1824.

Bailey became a captain in the local militia. Fought in battles preceding 1836 Texas Revolution.

At his request he was buried standing up, facing west, gun at side so no one could look down on him, even in death. (1970)

EASTLAND (Eastland Co.) US 80, .6 mi. E
Eastland County
Formed from Young and Bexar Territories. Created February 1, 1858. Organized December 2, 1873. Named in honor of Captain William Mosby Eastland, 1806–1843. Hero of San Jacinto. Member of the Mier Expedition he drew the first black bean at Salado, Mexico, and was executed, on March 25, 1843. Eastland, county seat.

EASTLAND (Eastland Co.) IH 20 access road, 2 mi. E
Hargus Farm
North Carolina native Larry Hargus (1810–1887) and his wife Mary (Corder) (1824–1910) came to Eastland County in 1879. In 1881, they bought the original tract of their farm at this site from C. U. Connellee, a founder of Eastland. Members of the Hargus family were active in the development of a local Methodist Church and a son, James, was a Texas Ranger and a Civil War veteran. The family farm was later inherited by Larry Hargus' son Barry, who lived here with his wife Mackie (Gilbert) and eight children. This land has remained in the family for over 100 years. (1982)

EDEN (Concho Co.) US 83 & Town Square
Eden
Founded 1882. Incorporated 1910. Named for Frederic Eden, native of England and pioneer ranchman on whose land the town was located, and who donated land for this public square.

Farming and ranching area. Wool and mohair marketing center. Elevation 2,052 feet. Location of Concho County Hospital.

EDEN (Concho Co.) *Town Square (Paint Rock (US 83) at Blanchard)*
General Ira C. Eaker
Ira Clarence Eaker was born April 13, 1896, in Field Creek, Llano County, Texas. In 1906, his parents, Young Yancy and Ladonia (Graham) Eaker, moved the family to the Eden area, where he and his brothers attended school. Eaker enlisted in the army on April 7, 1917, one day after the U.S. declared war on Germany. He was recruited into the army's early aviation program and continued his pilot training through the war, after which he commanded a squadron in the Philippines. There he helped devise an aircraft level instrument, which was further developed by the Air Corps Material Division. In 1926–27, Eaker served as a pilot in the Pan American Goodwill tour. He also conceived and tested innovative flight procedures. During the 1930s, he earned a journalism degree and graduated from the Army Command and General Staff School in Kansas. At the outbreak of World War II, Eaker was sent to England to organize and oversee the U.S. 8th Army Air Force Bomber Command, coordinating efforts with the Royal Air Force in round-the-clock bombing of Germany's war works. He sometimes accompanied his men, believing a commander should know what his troops face in combat. He commanded the 8th Army Air Force and later the Mediterranean Allied Air Forces. Near war's end, he served at the Pentagon as Deputy Commanding General of the Army Air Forces. Eaker retired in 1947 and worked for Howard Hughes and then for Douglas Aircraft Company, from which he retired in 1961. He launched a newspaper column a few years later and involved himself in military commentary for the rest of his life. Remembering his foundation in Eden and his Eden classmates, he returned here often for family and community events. The recipient of more than 50 awards and decorations, including knighthood in England and a U.S. Congressional Gold Medal as "aviation pioneer and air power leader," he died August 6, 1987. (2003)

EDINBURG (Hidalgo Co.) *US 281, 16 mi. N, 1 mi. E*
La Coma Ranch Headquarters
William Frederick Sprague, who left wealth and position in Rhode Island to come to Hidalgo County in 1883, stayed to convert a run-down ranch into a productive farm and cattle ranch which he named La Coma from a native tree that thrives and yields abundant berries. Sprague's enterprise and vision yielded one of the best success stories of the late 19th and early 20th century decades. After experimenting with sheep raising, he changed to cattle raising for both volume and quality. He was the first in the county to raise cotton and his example spread to other land owners to whom he brought cotton seed. He built a cotton gin in 1898, the first between here and Brownsville, to process the crop of 1,000 to 1,500 bales.

Headquarters for the growing ranch holdings were established near the center of Sprague's activities, 80 miles from the railroad at Hebbronville. The home was an oasis of luxury and elegance in the midst of a vast brushland. Running water was available in the brick residence which was illuminated by acetylene gas since electricity was not available. Nearby was a general store and also a public school established for the children of the ranch workers.

Mr. Sprague's influence was felt throughout the county. He served as a county commissioner from 1890 to 1912, helping to pioneer in forming water districts and building farm roads. He gave the largest land bonus of any rancher to help bring the railroad west from Harlingen to Sam Fordyce. Earlier, he had used ox carts, then a stage coach line of his own to bring visitors and friends to settle in the Valley, using the route from Hebbronville to La Coma. His ranch was a refuge to soldiers and Rangers sent to the area during the 1914–1916 bandit troubles. Awarded Medallion Plate. Was large ranch on route from Mexico to El Sol Del Rey.

EDINBURG (Hidalgo Co.) *100 N Closner St., Hidalgo Plaza*
Padre Miguel Hidalgo y Costilla
Miguel Hidalgo y Costilla (1753–1811), for whom the county of Hidalgo is named, was born near Guanajuato, Mexico, while the country was still under Spanish rule. After being ordained a priest in 1779, he served churches in Colima, San Felipe, and Dolores, where he emerged as a champion of human rights who feared the colonial system would never allow independence and justice for all citizens. A firm believer in economic independence from the mother country, Hidalgo worked toward that goal by teaching farming methods and industrial techniques to Indians and others in his parish.

In 1810, Padre Hidalgo, along with military leader Ignacio de Allende, conspired to overthrow the royalist government. Warned that officials suspected their plot, Hidalgo gathered sympathizers in Dolores. Following early mass on the morning of Sept. 16, 1810, Hidalgo made his famous "Grito de Dolores," a call to arms which in effect began the revolt that led to Mexican Independence from Spain in 1821. During a battle on the bridge of Calderon, Padre Hidalgo was captured and later was unfrocked and shot.

Considered "the father of Mexican Independence," Padre Hidalgo continues to be honored for his leadership throughout Mexico and the Southwest. (1983)

EDMONDSON (Hale Co.) SH 194
Running Water Community
(2 mi. S)

Attracted by abundant water from Running Water Draw, J. W. and T. W. Morrison established a ranch in 1881 with headquarters about ten miles west of here. Most of the early settlers in this region worked for the ranch. Later, several partners joined the operation, including wealthy cattleman C. C. Slaughter.

In 1884, Dennis and Martha S. Rice purchased several sections of land along the draw south of this site. Rice hoped to start a town and lure the railroad across his land. He began Wadsworth post office in his dugout in 1890. It was renamed Running Water in 1891. Rice organized the Running Water Townsite and Investment Company and staged a picnic and barbecue, July 4, 1892, for the purpose of selling town lots.

Soon the community had a blacksmith shop, grist mill, a two-story store building, several residences and churches. The early one-room schoolhouse was later replaced by a brick structure.

Although the Fort Worth & Denver Railroad bypassed Running Water in 1928, it remained a thriving village for several years. In 1935, the post office moved to Edmondson switch on the railroad and many residents relocated here. In 1937, the name of this settlement was changed to Edmondson. (1978)

EDNA (Jackson Co.) US 59, SW, then left on FM 1822 for 2.8 mi., left 2 mi.
Site of Camp Independence

A part of the first army of the Texas Republic, under the command of General Felix Huston, and later of General Albert Sidney Johnston. Was stationed here from December, 1836, until furloughed by order of President Sam Houston on May 18, 1837.

Captain Henry Teal was assassinated here as he slept in his tent on the night of May 5.

EDNA (Jackson Co.) US 96, 5 mi. NE, St. Agnes Catholic Church grounds
Mission Nuestra Señora del
Espiritu Santo de Zuniga

Situated in the present county of Jackson. Was the Mission Nuestra Señora del Espiritu Santo de Zuniga.

Established by Joseph de Azlor, Marquis of Aguayo, and Father Fray Agustin Patron, O.F.M. in 1722 for civilizing and Christianizing of the Karankawa, Cujane, Coco, Copane, and other Indian tribes. Under the protection of the Presidio de Nuestra Señnora de Loreto. Both moved to Mission Valley on the Guadalupe River in 1726. Moved finally to Santa Dorotea, now Goliad near the San Antonio River in 1749.

EDNA (Jackson Co.) SH 111, 8 mi. SE, right on FM Loop 1822
Site of Old Town of Texana

Founded in 1834 by Dr. F. F. Wells, personal friend of Stephen F. Austin. County seat of Jackson County from 1835–1883.

Old home of Capt. Clark L. Owen of Civil War fame.

Here the following were first organized in Jackson County: Methodist church in 1838, Masonic lodge in 1852, Presbyterian church in 1855.

EDNA (Jackson Co.) 401 N Wells St.
Site of
William Millican's Gin House

First cotton gin in Jackson County. Here was held the memorable "Lavaca-Navidad Meeting" on July 17, 1835.

At this meeting resolutions were adopted protesting against the treatment of the Texas colonists by the Mexican government. James Kerr was chairman of the meeting and S.C.A. Rogers, secretary. The first formal public protest was a forerunner of the Declaration of Independence, March 2, 1836.

EDNA (Jackson Co.) *401 Wells St. at Texana Museum*
The Famous Lavaca-Navidad Meeting of 1835
At the cotton gin of William Millican, near here, on July 17, 1835, occurred the significant Lavaca-Navidad meeting, held by pioneers living near the two rivers. James Kerr, the founder of Gonzales, was chairman and the Rev. S.C.A. Rogers, secretary. The meeting adopted resolutions protesting mistreatment of Texas colonists by the government of Mexico. This early formal public protest was a forerunner of the Declaration of Independence on March 2, 1836, and the constituting of the Republic of Texas. (1974)

EDNA (Jackson Co.) *SH 111, 7 mi. E*
Enon Cemetery
In 1856 the Rev. Joseph I. Loudermilk (1816–1880) came to Jackson County and organized Enon Baptist Church—the first church of that faith in the county. He was pastor from that time until his death, and was buried here. A five-acre site was given by John and Clarissa Andrews on Oct. 23, 1858, for the church and cemetery. The first interment (1862) was Isaac J. Sheppard. There are now 65 graves and cemetery is still open for burials. Site of the church is partially enclosed by cemetery fence. (1972)

EDNA (Jackson Co.) *FM 822, 7 mi. N*
Major James Kerr
(September 24, 1790–December 23, 1851)
Born in Danville, Ky.; served in War of 1812 and as sheriff, state representative, state senator in Missouri. Came to Texas as DeWitt Colony's surveyor-general; laid out town of Gonzales, July 1825. In 1827 moved to Jackson County, which he represented in 1832, 1833 conventions, serving in 1833 on committee to draft constitution for proposed State of Texas. On July 17, 1835, was chairman of the Lavaca-Navidad meeting, an early public protest against Mexican authorities' mistreatment of settlers. Served in Republic of Texas Congress in 1838–1839. He was also a practicing physician. (1972)

EDNA (Jackson Co.) *SH 111, 12 mi. NW in Morales*
Old Morales Store
Originally built in early 1860s of rough pine. Local gathering place then—as now. Exterior appearance is same. Awarded Medallion Plate. (1967)

EDNA (Jackson Co.) *US 59, Courthouse*
Jackson County, C.S.A.
In 1861, voted for secession 147 to 77. With its beef and cotton, helped supply South. Furnished salt from beds near Cox's creek; hides and tallow from a plant between Port Lavaca and Texana; lead from Navidad mine (now a "lost mine"). Homefolk molded bullets and sent them to fighting men, along with clothes woven, sewed or knitted by the family.

Couriers operated along a line that skirted blockaded coast from mouth of Caney Creek to Brownsville. Home guard kept enemy ships off the shores. A Confederate gunboat, chased from Lavaca Bay, sank in the Navidad. (1965)

EGYPT (Wharton Co.) *FM 102, Near Post Office*
Community of Egypt
One of the most historic towns in county. Named following the drought of 1827, when pioneers of Stephen F. Austin's colony came to this fertile region to obtain corn. They called it "going down into Egypt for corn," after a Biblical passage.

Noted patriots were among earliest settlers. Eli Mercer, one of first sugar producers in Texas; and W. J. E. Heard, leader of citizen soldiers. Others were dairy king Gail Borden; William Menefee, a signer of the Texas Declaration of Independence; and Maj. Andrew Northington, stagecoach operator and surveyor. (1970)

EL PASO (El Paso Co.)   *US 80*
El Paso
On May 4, 1598, Don Juan de Onate, Adelantado and Captain-General, Governor of New Mexico, first named El Paso Del Rio Del Norte.

Through this old pass, the lowest snow-free feasible route from the Atlantic to the Pacific through the Rocky Mountains, extend today the great trunk lines of telegraph and railroad. The city of El Paso marks the place and perpetuates the name.   (1964)

EL PASO (El Paso Co.)   *US 62/80, 30 mi. E*
Hueco Tanks
One of the most historic spots in the Southwest. Famous watering place for Indians, emigrants, and travelers. Near here on many occasions the Apache challenged the right of the white man to pass through and disturb his country. Here was a station of the Southern Overland mail line which linked St. Louis with San Francisco, 1858–1861.   (1964)

EL PASO (El Paso Co.)   *IH 10 W, on grounds of Anthony Tourist Bureau*
El Paso
Largest U.S. city on the Mexican border. Named for the mountain pass: Historic gateway for Indians, priests, gold-seekers, traders, stages.

Federal troops occupied this area longer than any other in Texas during the Civil War.

Agricultural, industrial and military center. Texas Western College (now University of Texas at El Paso), Spanish missions.

EL PASO (El Paso Co.)   *US 80, right-of-way, Alameda Avenue in Ysleta*
Oldest Mission in Texas
Originally founded in 1613 at Isleta Pueblo, in New Mexico, and dedicated in 1621 as San Antonio de Isleta. Removed to El Paso area, 1680 (during Pueblo revolt), by Tigua Indians who brought along the patron saint as they accompanied fleeing Spaniards.

Re-established here in 1682, it has been named successively: Sacramento de Los Tiguas de Ysleta; Corpus Christi de Los Tiguas de Ysleta (1691); San Antonio de Los Tiguas de Ysleta (1744); and Nuestra Señora del Carmen (1874). Present chapel has walls and bells of 1744 building.

Still ministers to the Tiguas.   (1970)

EL PASO (El Paso Co.)   *US 62 (Paisano Dr.) and East Wald Kip Way*
The Pass of the North
Historically a major trade and travel artery for North America because it is the northernmost Rocky Mountain pass that stays snow-free throughout the year.

Indians used pass long before Spaniard Cabeza de Vaca, thought to be first white man in area, crossed it about 1536. Juan de Onate brought first cattle into U.S. through the pass in 1598.

Route was heavily traveled during California gold rush, 1849, and in later years important stage lines and railroads crossed Rockies here. Today the pass lies on one of three major travel routes across the continent.   (1968)

EL PASO (El Paso Co.)   *1720 W. Paisano Dr. (US 85)*
Franklin Canal
For centuries, the Rio Grande has been molded and shaped by the humans living along its banks. Informal irrigation systems have existed along the life-sustaining river from the Spanish Colonial period. As early as the 1840s, area farmers began more modern improvements on these systems. By 1889 El Paso developers needed a means to efficiently provide water to farmers in the El Paso Valley. The El Paso Irrigation Company began construction on the Franklin Canal the following year. A dispute between the U. S. and Mexico over water rights led to the International Treaty of 1906, in which it was agreed that the U. S. would deliver 60,000 acre feet of water to Mexico via the Franklin Canal. Completed in 1912, the canal began at the international dam and extended five miles, paralleling the Rio Grande on its north bank and continuing through downtown El Paso. It was intended to deliver water thirty miles into the El Paso Valley. Demands on the canal increased as the area's population grew. Upgrades began in 1914 and continued into the 1930s. The American Dam was created in 1938 to hinder the efforts of Mexican citizens to

siphon water from the Rio Grande. Modifications have been made to Franklin Canal throughout the 20th century. It is an important element in the history of water control along the U.S.-Mexico border. Essential to irrigation on both sides of the Rio Grande, the canal continues to affect development in both countries. (1998)

EL PASO (El Paso Co.) *Loop 375, eastbound, at mile marker 17.4*
Fusselman Canyon

Below is Fusselman Canyon, which follows the Fusselman Canyon Fault, a major natural cut into the Franklin Mountains. For centuries it has served as a natural corridor for the movement of people, goods and livestock between the river valley to the west and the desert basin to the east. The canyon also served as a source of seasonal water, plants and animals for the many Native Americans who inhabited this region. It is named in honor of Charles H. Fusselman (1866-1890), Texas Ranger and U.S. Deputy Marshal. In the late 19th century, El Paso was a booming town, but outlying areas were still plagued by frontier conditions. On April 17, 1890, local rancher John Barnes reported that his horses and cattle had been stolen. Later that day, Charles Fusselman was deputized and led Barnes and city policeman George Herold into the Franklin Mountains to chase the rustlers. The thieves intended to drive the horses and cattle through the canyon (along the path of today's Woodrow Bean Trans Mountain Road), through Smuggler's Gap at the top of the canyon, and then into the Rio Grande Bosque near Canutillo, Texas. Fusselman's party captured one of the rustlers before encountering the outlaws' camp. There they were met with a barrage of gunfire, and Fusselman was shot and killed. The outlaws escaped after the outnumbered Barnes and Herold left their prisoner and fled the scene. Fusselman's body was later recovered and taken to Lagarto, Texas, where he was buried. For the next ten years, lawmen pursued the rustlers. Geronimo Parra, the outlaw leader, was finally arrested, tried and found guilty of Fusselman's murder. He was legally hanged in January 1900 in El Paso. The canyon became known as Fusselman Canyon in honor of the slain deputy and ranger. (2002)

EL PASO (El Paso Co.) *FM 258, entrance to Socorro Mission*
The Camino Real

For more than 200 years the Camino Real, or Royal Road, was the major route for transporting commercial goods from Mexico City and Chihuahua to Santa Fe and Taos. First traveled by Juan de Oñate during his 1598 expedition to New Mexico, the Camino Real followed the San Elizario, Socorro, and Ysleta road, crossed the Rio Grande west of present downtown El Paso, and continued north into New Mexico. When the Rio Grande was established as the U.S.-Mexico boundary in 1848, this section of the old Camino Real became part of the United States. (1983)

EL ZACATAL (Hidalgo Co.) *US 281 right-of-way, approx. 25 mi. E*
Battle of La Bolsa

In 1859 and early 1860, a series of raids on Texas settlements led by Juan N. Cortina (1824–1894) led to skirmishes with companies of Texas Rangers and U.S. soldiers. These conflicts became known as the Cortina Wars. On February 4, 1860, a battle occurred at La Bolsa Bend (ca. 1 mi. S) between Cortina's raiders and Capt. John S. "Rip" Ford's Texas Rangers. The Rangers successfully defended the riverboat *Ranchero*, traveling downstream from Rio Grande City, from an attack by Cortina's band. Cortina escaped into Mexico and later became a general in the Mexican Army. (1991)

ELDORADO (Schleicher Co.) *US 277, 11 mi. N*
Christopher Columbus Doty
(April 16, 1857–October 26, 1944)

First permanent citizen of Schleicher County. Came to Texas from Missouri, 1879. Soon bought headquarters at Ten-Mile Water Hole (½ mi. East). Drilled first water well in county 1882 and erected first windmill south of Concho River, thus establishing area's agricultural industry.

The organization of this county in 1901 included his property, and he was elected first tax assessor-collector. Later was justice of the peace, a rancher, active Methodist and a Mason. He married Alice Pancoast on June 3, 1887, and they had one daughter, Annie Marie. (1968)

ELDORADO (Schleicher Co.)   *US 277, 5 mi. N*
Site of Verand
First town in present Schleicher County. Named for the Vermont Cattle Company, on whose land it was situated. Post office established 1892; closed 1895. 49er's crossed this area on way to gold fields of California. Site of Comanche and Apache Indian raids in 1870s, 1880s.   (1968)

ELDORADO (Schleicher Co.)   *US 277, 10 mi. S*
Site of J. D. Earnest Ranch
Stage Stand
During the ownership of rancher J. D. Earnest, this site was used as a rest stop on the stage line between San Angelo and Sonora. Owned and managed by Theodore Jackson Savell (1872–1954), the operation began providing mail and passenger service to the area in 1894. Each weekday two stages pulled by four horses made the 75-mile run. On rare rainy occasions the passengers helped push the stagecoach up muddy hills. The Savell Line remained in operation until 1909, when mail was first delivered to the county by automobile.   (1980)

ELDORADO (Schleicher Co.)   *US 277, 15.4 mi. N*
Site of Mark Fury Ranch
Stage Stand
Originally part of the Mark Fury Ranch, this site was used as a stagecoach stop from 1894 to 1909. Theodore Jackson Savell (1872–1954) owned and operated the line between San Angelo and Sonora. Six mornings each week a horn was blown to announce the arrival of the stage. In emergencies on the road, help was prompt because the line served as a thread of life for this remote area. The Savell stages were instrumental in the early development of the region, providing passenger, mail, and express service.   (1980)

ELECTRA (Wichita Co.)   *SH 25, 12 mi. S*
The Old Buffalo Road
(About 100 yds. W)
Named for its traffic in buffalo hides and bones, this North Texas road gave subsistence to pioneers while aiding in mass "harvest" of the American bison. As long as buffalo survived (providing food, shelter and clothing) the Indians were lords of the plains. Recognizing this, the authorities encouraged hunting. Harvested hides were taken to market over this road.

The buffalo and Indians gone, permanent settlers arrived. In adverse years (while a man tried to get a start at farming, ranching or storekeeping), bones were salvaged and sold for grocery or seed money.

This old road was route of hundreds of wagons taking buffalo hides to market before 1878 and hundreds of wagons taking bones to Wichita Falls and Henrietta before 1890. The road came east from the Plains, near south line of Foard and Wilbarger Counties to Guide Mound; then three miles east (near this marker) and south to Wichita River bridge; then to the county line three miles west of Holliday. Next it passed the north edge of Holliday, and south of Lake Wichita, then crossed at the old Van Dorn Crossing five miles south of Jolly. Pioneers also called it "Great North" Road or "Good Creek" Road. It proved invaluable to economy and mapping of area.   (1970)

ELECTRA (Wichita Co.)   *SH 25, 1 mi. N*
Clayco No. 1 Oil Well
Clayco No. 1 Woodruff Putnam, 1628 feet. Here flowed oil April 1, 1911, opening one of the world's greatest oil fields.
(Crew also listed)

ELECTRA (Wichita Co.)   *SH 25, 14 mi. S*
The Kadane Discovery Well
(About 700 ft. SW)
Oil development in this part of Wichita County began in 1919 from shallow depths in the KMA field. As the original wells went dry, and a severe national depression blighted the country in the 1930s, the oil industry sought new production. The Mangold family, owners of land at this site, offered liberal terms for deeper exploration, but at first found no driller willing to take the risk on the scant capital then available. Finally, veteran operator George K. Kadane (1881–1945) and sons

Edward, Jack, and Mike had the courage to drill in this area of negative geologic readings. On Nov. 11, 1937, they struck oil at a depth of 3,800 feet, bringing in Mangold No. 1 as a gusher. The discovery effected an extension of the KMA Field. This spot was labeled "Kadane Corner" on local maps.

Other operators rushed in, starting a new Wichita County boom. Along with a rapid rise in population came new housing construction, new industries, new jobs, and an era of financial growth. In 1942, a test well on the Griffin ranch came in at 4,300 feet. Final development of the field resulted in more than 2,000 producing wells in an area of 75,000 acres. Over a 40-year period, the field has yielded 250 million barrels of oil. (1978)

ELGIN (Bastrop Co.) SH 95, 8 mi. S
Camp Swift
Named for Major General Eben Swift (1854–1935) Camp Swift, established primarily for infantry division training, was a major military training facility for 300,000 men and women during World War II. The camp was active from May 1942 until July 1946, and covered nearly 56,000 acres. Shaped like a triangle, the reservation was like a self-contained city and included 2,750 buildings. The camp had the capacity to house and train 45,000 people.

The 95th, the 97th, and the 102nd Infantry Divisions and the 10th Mountain Division trained here during the war. The 2nd Infantry Division was processed through the camp after the war. More than 32,000 casualties were suffered by these 5 divisions. The camp also provided training for more than 100 separate non-divisional combat and other support units, and the only nurses combat training program in Texas. About 4,800 German prisoners of war were also held at Swift.

At the end of World War II the camp shifted from war time training to processing more than 12,400 officers and enlisted personnel from the service to civilian life. On June 30, 1946, the camp became inactive, and utilization was transferred from the U.S. Army to the State of Texas in December 1948. (1996)

ELKHART (Anderson Co.) SH 294, .5 mi. W of Elkhart
Pilgrim Predestinarian Regular Baptist Church
Organized in Crawford County, Illinois by Elder Daniel Parker in 1833 with the following charter members: Daniel Parker, Pheby Parker, Patsey Parker, Julious Christy, John Parker, Rachel Christy, Salley Brown.

The first Baptist church in Texas. First meeting held in Stephen F. Austin's Colony January 20, 1834. First log church built in 1839. Pilgrim Baptist Church grounds. (1964)

ELKHART (Anderson Co.) US 287, 3 mi. N at site
Starr Cemetery
Family graveyard of the descendants of John Starr (1797–1872), Texas pioneer. First person buried here, Starr lies beside wife Susannah. Interred nearby are 6 of their 8 children; 2 of the sons here served in the Confederate Army, Civil War. Ancestral home is on nearby Starr Hill. (1969)

EMORY (Rains Co.) US 69, .2 mi. NW
Rains County
One of the earliest areas of Texas to be settled. J. H. Hooker, first known settler, built a grist mill on the Sabine River here in the 1840s.

Emigrants from the Old South came in after 1840 although the county was not created until 1870. The name honors pioneer Emory Rains (1800–1878). He served as senator in 8th Legislature from district out of which this county was later carved and had a long public service career.

Rains County is known as the birthplace of the Farmers Cooperative and Educational Union of America, founded in 1904. (1970)

EMORY (Rains Co.) US 69, 3 mi. E at site
Site of Fraser Brick Company
Here in 1905 Walter B. Fraser (1877–1968) built a pioneer Texas factory which produced bricks and hollow clay building tile. This was the first industrial plant in Rains County and it employed about 40 men.

When, in 1909, a post office was established near here, its name "Ginger" was taken from the distinctive color of the burnt clay bricks made at the plant.

Operations ceased when this clay supply neared exhaustion in the 1940s. Walter B. Fraser retired in 1944. The business prospered at its other Texas locations until sold in 1961.   (1968)

EMORY (Rains Co.)   SH 275, 4 mi. N
Dougherty Community Homeplace
Robert Newberry Dougherty, son of Dougherty community founder James W. Dougherty, assumed management of his father's farm in the 1860s and by 1870 was sole owner of the family land. At this site in 1880–1881 he erected a one-room house to which later additions were made. The Dougherty family has maintained the home since its construction and has often opened it for community gatherings. Over the years, the homeplace has been the site of weddings, music festivals, and family reunions, and at one time served as headquarters for the Dougherty Rural Telephone Co.   (1983)

ENCINO (Brooks Co.)   US 281, 6.5 mi. N
Falfurrias to Encino Road
Visible from this site is a small section of roadway that dates from the earliest efforts of the State Highway Program to oversee road construction. In 1918, one year after the establishment of the Texas Highway Department, plans were drawn for the Brooks County segment of what would become U.S. 281. That portion of the road constructed in 1918 was a soft sand thoroughfare terminating at Encino (6.5 mi. S). A caliche surface was applied in 1920, and the concrete paving now in evidence was laid in 1928. The remaining portion of the Falfurrias to Encino Road is a reminder of early road construction methods and transportation networks into the Rio Grande Valley.   (2002)

ENCINO (Brooks Co.)   US 281, 1 mi. S
El Encino del Poso
(The Oak in the Hole)
In this vicinity once stood a magnificent live oak tree that was an early landmark on the South Texas Plains for many years. Noted for its size and its wide canopy, it was located in a large hollow created by livestock that gathered beneath its branches and by winds that eroded the exposed soil. El Encino del Poso was a landmark for early trails and land grants. It also served as the location of a stagecoach station and as the basis for naming Encino (1 mi. N). The tree died in the 1890s, before the formation of Brooks County, the victim of an extended drought.

(Texas Sesquicentennial 1836–1986)

ENNIS (Ellis Co.)   US 287 & NW Main St.
Town of Ennis
Founded 1872 as market town on Houston & Texas Central Railway; named for an H.&T.C. official, Cornelius Ennis (1813–1899).

Cumberland Presbyterians built first church, 1872; first school session opened 1873. Czechs settled here 1874, adding a new segment to Anglo-French-Mexican-Texans employed in cattle and cotton economy. In 1892, banker Joseph Baldridge and associates secured H.&T.C. division shops for the town. In 1911, St. John's School was established here.

In 20th century, local industry, recreation areas, and municipal services spur continuing growth.   (1972)

Ennis (Ellis Co.)   501 W. Ennis Ave. (US 287) at Ennis Public Library
Jack Lummus
(October 22, 1915–March 8, 1945)
Born on an Ellis County farm, Jack Lummus attended school at Alma and Ennis, and Baylor University on an athletics scholarship. He played minor league baseball in Texas and football for the New York Giants. He joined the U. S. Marines in 1942 and on February 19, 1945, landed with the Fifth Marine Division in the first wave of assault troops on Iwo Jima. On March 8, after fighting without respite for two days and nights, Lummus and his rifle platoon slowly advanced toward a complex of pillboxes before being halted by Japanese forces. Despite injuries from two grenade explosions, Lummus single-handedly destroyed three enemy emplacements before step-

ping on a land mine, sustaining fatal wounds. His Congressional Medal of Honor celebrates his "conspicuous gallantry and tenacious perseverance in the face of overwhelming odds." (1999)

ENNIS (Ellis Co.) *US 287, 5 mi. W*

Thomas C. Neel
(1825–1863)

Georgia native Thomas C. Neel married Willia E. Latimer in 1848. The couple moved their family to Texas in 1854 and to Ellis County in 1855. They established a cotton and wheat plantation near what would become Ennis. Neel called his wife "Will" and the plantation became known as Will's Town, which later was shortened to "Wilton." A post office opened on the plantation in 1857; it served under both the United States and Confederate governments. In 1861 Neel was appointed a delegate to the Secession Convention. Later that year, he was elected to represent the 42nd District in the House of Representatives in the 9th Legislature. Shortly after that term ended, he was elected state senator from the 19th District, but he became ill and died before he was able to serve in the 10th Legislature. (2000)

EUREKA (Navarro Co.) *US 287, ½ mi. W*

Home of
Whitney Montgomery, Poet
(1877–1966)

Born in Navarro County in white-columned house across pasture south of this site. Began to write poetry when he was 15 years old. Author of more than 500 published poems which appeared in many major magazines; won numerous poetry prizes.

Moved to Dallas, 1927. Was editor and publisher of "Kaleidograph" magazine and press. Helped to organize and was vice president of the poetry society of Texas.

His home was honored in this poem:

I Own a Home
I can not boast of a broad estate,
But I own a home with a rose at the gate.

I hold the title, and I keep the keys,
And in and out I can go as I please.

My home is not grand, but I live content,
For no man sends me a bill for rent.

And no man comes with a brush and a pail
To paint a sign on my door, "FOR SALE."

I can not boast of a broad estate,
But I own a home with a rose at the gate. (1967)

EUSTACE (Henderson Co.) *US 90 and FM 316 intersection, 4.5 mi. SSW*

Payne Springs Methodist Church and Cemetery

For over a century, this church and cemetery have served the community of Payne Springs, originally known as Mallard Prairie. By 1880, the church already had a large membership and met in a log structure. The church building served as a gathering place for elections and political rallies. Summer revivals were held under a brush arbor on the church grounds. The revivals often lasted two weeks and were social as well as religious events.

Local tradition indicates the cemetery was started when a child from a family traveling west was buried by a small cedar tree in the churchyard. The first marked grave was that of a mother and daughter who were buried on the other side of the cedar. Elenor Reynolds (1812–1880) and her daughter, Mary Ann Davis (1829–1880), died within a day of each other.

The Mallard Prairie school once stood near the church and cemetery. It later moved across the road, and the growth of the cemetery took in land where the school and early church buildings stood. The burial ground now contains over 1,000 graves. An annual July 4th workday evolved into a fund raising event for the cemetery's upkeep. (1984)

167

EVADALE (Jasper Co.)

SH 105, .2 mi. W between G.C. & S.F. tracks & Evadale School

Site of Former Settlement of
Richardson's Bluff

Homesite of Benjamin Richardson (1775?–1848?), an 1830 De Zavala Colony settler. With his sons, Richardson operated a ferry that was of great service, especially in 1836 Runaway Scrape, aiding civilians as they fled toward the U.S. in fear of Santa Anna.

Place later was renamed Ford's Bluff, for family with mill site here in 1852. In 1894 Mannie Cox opened a local shingle mill that was sold in 1902 to Kirby Lumber Company. When Kirby built sawmill in 1904, the site was renamed in honor of Miss Eva Dale, a teacher at the Southeast Texas Male and Female College in Jasper. (1972)

EVANT (Coryell Co.)

US 281 in town square

Evant

The town of Evant traces its history to an earlier settlement in this area. Langford Cove, founded in 1855 by Asa Langford (1820-1970), was located adjacent to and partly within the south boundary of the present town of Evant. A United States Post Office was authorized in 1876 under the name Cove. Evan T. Brooks and his family arrived in the area in 1876. In 1881 Brooks platted a townsite which was filed in Hamilton County records as Brooksville. The same plat appeared in Coryell County records in 1884 as Evant, so named from a combination of Brooks' first name and middle initial. Streets and blocks were carefully planned, including a town square. The Cove post office was transferred to Evant and renamed in 1885. In 1878 a one-room plank schoolhouse was erected on land donated by Asa Langford in 1875. It was replaced in 1888 by a stone structure which, with additions and modifications, served Evant Independent School District until 1976. Over the years, businesses were established and churches and community groups were organized. The citizens of Evant voted to incorporate in an election held in December 1976. (1986)

FAIRFIELD (Freestone Co.)

US 84, Wm. L. Moody Reunion Grounds

Colonel Wm. L. Moody
(1828–1920)

Came to Texas from Virginia, 1852. Organized and was captain of Co. G, 7th Texas Infantry, the first Freestone County unit to go into battle in the Civil War.

Captured at Fort Donelson, Tenn., Feb. 1862. Exchanged, soon won promotion to colonel for bravery on battlefield. Commended for personally leading and rallying men in hand-to hand combat in thick woods.

Wounded and returned to Texas, where he served till war ended.

In 1866 moved to Galveston. Became leader in financial, business, philanthropic and civic affairs.

FALCON (Zapata Co.)

US 83

Old Falcón

In 1745, Col. José de Escandón was commissioned by the Viceroy of New Spain to lead the colonization of this area. The first settlers arrived 3 years later and were assigned land on which to build their homes. A survey conducted in 1767 resulted in the allocation of individual land grants to the settlers, which marked the start of private property ownership in the area.

About 1800, José Eugenio Ramírez established a ranch on the north bank of the Rio Grande and named his headquarters Ramireño. The settlement that grew up around his home was plagued throughout the 19th century with Indian raids, particularly when military protection was withdrawn during the years of the Mexican Revolution (1810–1832). In the early 1900s, Ildefonso Ramírez opened a general store, and, when a post office was established in 1915, the name of the village was changed to Falcón in honor of José Eugenio's wife, María Rita de la Garza Falcón.

After Falcón Dam was completed in 1952, the town was flooded, and residents were forced to relocate to this site. The history of Old Falcón, however, with its ties to 18th-century Spanish colonialism, remains an important part of their heritage. (1983)

FALFURRIAS (Brooks Co.)   *US 281, 10 mi. S in state roadside park*
Brooks County
Formed from Hidalgo, Starr and Zapata Counties, created March 11, 1911; organized September 2, 1911. Named in honor of James Abijah Brooks, Captain of Texas Rangers, 1882–1906, Member of Texas Legislature, County Judge, Brooks County since 1911. Falfurrias, county seat.   (1964)

FALFURRIAS (Brooks Co.)   *SH 285 & FM 1418, 3 mi. NE*
Don Pedro Jaramillo
(1829–1907)
Called "The Healer of Los Olmos." Born in Jalisco, Mexico. Said to have been cured through faith, then given the gift of healing in a vision. He came to Los Olmos Ranch in 1881. Many came to him because, unlike other faith healers, he claimed no power of his own, but said that God's healing was released through faith. He made no charges. Patients gave or withheld as they chose. But whatever was given voluntarily he often gave to the poor—food as well as remedies. He traveled widely to visit the sick. Hundreds gave testimonials of their healings.

Llamado "El Curandero de Los Olmos." Nació en Jalisco, México. Se dice que fue curado por la fé, después recibió el don de curar en una visión. Vino al Rancho De Los Olmos en 1881. Muchos venían a él porque, no como otros curanderos, él no reclamaba su propio poder sino decía que el curamiento de Dios era obtenido por la fé. No cobraba. Los pacientes pagaban si querían. Pero lo que se le daba voluntariamente, acostumbraba dárselo a los pobres—comida tanto como remedios. Viajó extensivamente visitando a los enfermos. Cientos han dado testimonios de sus curamientos.
(1971)

FALFURRIAS (Brooks Co.)   *SH 285, 4.2 mi. E*
.5 mi. S is Site of Town of
Flowella
On 1831 "Loma Blanca" grant and 1873 land of Perez family, who in 1898 sold "Parrita" (Little Grape Vine) to Mrs. King of King Ranch.

Flowella was founded 1909 by E. O. Burton and A. H. Danforth as trade town for a projected farm colony, and named for a flowing well in middle of townsite. The Calahan family opened hotel in 1909, store and post office, 1910. School building, also erected in 1910, provided a social-cultural center for some 100 residents. In adverse seasons, closings began: the store, 1911; hotel, 1915; post office, 1923; school, 1928. None of the original buildings remain.   (1973)

FALFURRIAS (Brooks Co.)   *US 281 at FM 1418, .5 mi. N*
Site of Los Olmos
The first permanent settlement in Brooks County, Los Olmos was located at the southwest corner of El Paisano Land Grant, given to Ramon de la Garza about 1830 by the Mexican State of Tamaulipas. Situated near the main route to the Rio Grande, the village served a region settled originally by ranchers from Northern Mexico. By 1880, it had a post office, stores and a school, which operated until 1945. The schoolhouse was the site of services conducted by traveling priests. As the town of Falfurrias grew, Los Olmos began to decline. Descendants of its founders still reside in this area.   (1976)

FALFURRIAS (Brooks Co.)   *US 281 at SH 285, at Pioneer Park in city*
Falfurrias
Founded as a cattle shipping point by Edward C. Lasater in 1904, the town bears the name of a village on land he purchased in 1893. When the San Antonio & Aransas Pass Railroad extended its lines, Lasater (1860–1930) platted present townsite, built a hotel, general store, water and power plants, and cotton gin. He opened the area to truck, citrus, and dairy farms. He founded South Texas' first creamery—now widely recognized. A post office, newspaper, churches, and schools were opened. A citrus packing plant was built in 1914. Still later the city became an oil and gas production center.   (1971)

FANNIN (Goliad Co.)   *FM 2987, 1 mi. N*
Site of Battle of El Perdido
During 1810–1819 efforts to expel Spain from Texas, a bloody clash occurred here on June 19, 1817, between the forces of Col. Antonio Martinez, last Spanish Governor of Texas, and a Mexican Republican Army of Invasion that was on its way to attack and capture La Bahía.

Republicans had 42 men under Col. Henry Perry and Maj. James H. Gordon, former U.S. officers, veterans of the 1815 Battle of New Orleans. Outnumbered 3-to-1, Perry and Gordon refused offer of safe surrender, saying they would die first. Along with 24 of their men, both were killed.
    (1967)

FARMERSVILLE (Collin Co.)   *SH 78 & McKinney St.*
Farmersville
Originated 1849 as a settlement on the Jefferson-McKinney Road, and near Republic of Texas National Road. Named by pioneers for their chief occupation. After 1854, the Yearys and their neighbors of Sugar Hill (2 mi. NE) began relocating here. Dr. H. M. Markham, practicing here by 1855, is said to have been Collin County's earliest physician. The First Methodist Church was organized in 1856. William Gotcher on March 4, 1859, donated land for the public square. A school was operating as early as the 1860s. The First Baptist Church was organized on May 14, 1865.

The town was incorporated on June 2, 1973. First mayor: John S. Rike. Aldermen: James Church, Ben King, John Murchison, Tom Tatum, John P. Utt. Marshall: Jeff Hines.

Institutions of the 1880s still in operation include Farmersville *Times* and the First National Bank.

As town became a trade center, agriculture kept pace. Farmersville in 1930s was known as the "Onion Capital of North Texas," annually shipping over 1,000 carloads of onions. Along with some small industry, cattle, cotton, and maize crops remain important.

Audie Murphy, the most decorated American hero of World War II, had been a resident of Farmersville before he entered the United States Army.   (1973)

FARMERSVILLE (Collin Co.)   *223 McKinney St. (SH 78)*
First National Bank of Farmersville
Named for the occupation of many of its citizens, the town of Farmersville was founded in the mid-1850s. A private bank, an exchange bank, was established in 1885, and housed in the rear of the Aston Brothers Store. A national bank charter was obtained on January 17, 1887, and the exchange bank merged with the First National Bank of Farmersville. Pioneer doctor A. H. Neathery served as the first president. The bank building, then located at 119 S. Main Street, was destroyed by fire in 1905 but it was rebuilt.

The First National Bank absorbed the Farmersville National Bank in 1929. In 1933 the First National Bank of Nevada, from the small town of Nevada south of here, was also absorbed. Despite experiencing heavy losses am undergoing two reorganizations during the depression of the 1930s, the bank never failed and its customers suffered no interruption of services.

The bank moved to its present location in 1970, and expanded the building in 1979. The bank converted to a state bank charter in 1986, and changed the name to the First Bank at Farmersville. The bank, one of the 20 oldest independent banks in Texas, has served Farmersville and the surrounding communities continuously for more than 110 years.   (1996)

FARWELL (Parmer Co.)   *US 70, .5 mi. E*
Martin Parmer
Formed from Young and Bexar Territories. Created August 21, 1876; organized May 7, 1907. Named in honor of Martin Parmer. Came to Texas in 1825 and located at Mound Prairie. A leader in the Fredonian War in 1826. Signer of the Texas Declaration of Independence. Died in 1850. County seat Parmerton, 1907 Farwell, since 1909.

FARWELL (Parmer Co.)   *US 84, 0.5 mi. SE in roadside park*
Near Route of Coronado Expedition
One of first explorations of North America by Spain. Began in Mexico, crossing into Texas at or near present Parmer County.

The party, led by Francisco Vazquez de Coronado, was sent to investigate reports of great wealth among the Indians. In one city, Quivira, the ruler reputedly ate from gold plates.

After entering Texas, Coronado and 36 men separated from the main group and continued north.

In August, 1541, on the present Kansas-Nebraska line, he found Quivira—an ordinary Indian village.

After the winter of 1541–1542, he returned to Mexico. (1969)

FARWELL (Parmer Co.) US 70, .5 mi. E
Parmer County

Created Aug. 21, 1876, from Bexar County. Named for Martin Parmer ("The Ringtailed Panther"), signer of Texas Declaration of Independence. Organized May 7, 1907.

The XIT Ranch, extending across nine counties, initially owned most of Parmer. The Capitol Syndicate, which built Texas' capitol, received in payment 3,050,000 acres of land and established the XIT in 1885. By 1890, population of the county was only 70. But with syndicate land sales, buyers came on the new railroad in 1904. Brisk settlement began, with many small farms. Farwell is the county seat. (1965)

FASHING (Atascosa Co.) FM 99 at FM 2924
Town of Fashing

Near the Old San Patricio Trail, leading to San Antonio from McMullen and McGloin Colony, in area of Gulf of Mexico. In this vicinity were stage stops at Belle Branch, Rock Spring, Rountree's, and Tordilla. Land was part of the Butler, Hickok, Tom and Rountree ranches. Town was platted in 1915 as "Hickok." However, after the U.S. Post Office Department disapproved that name, the tag on a popular tobacco—"Fashion"—inspired adoption of the name "Fashing" for the town.

First schoolhouse was built in 1917; a second, 1921. The Methodist Church, organized 1922, erected first house of worship (building moved in from Bastrop) in 1925. In 1934, St. Elizabeth Catholic Church was built. The Martin Luther Lutheran Church was erected 1948. Present school building was completed in 1952.

A center for mineral development. First local oil production was from Weigang Field, 1946. Tordilla Hill (5 mi. N) was site of first major uranium discovery in Texas in 1954. After further petroleum strikes in Fashing Edwards Limestone Field, 1958, gas and sulfur processing plants were built by the Elcor Chemical Co., Lone Star Producing Co., Sinclair Oil and Gas Co., and Warren Petroleum Corp. Currently, the only commercial uranium operation in Texas is near here. (1968)

FAYETTEVILLE (Fayette Co.) SH 159 at FM 955
The Sladek-Hillman House

F. J. Sladek, a Bohemian immigrant, built this home about 1896. In 1899, ownership was transferred to Anna Hillman, the widow of Ludwig Hillman, one of the early settlers of the Fayetteville area. She lived in the house until her death in 1923. The interior of the Victorian cottage features 12-foot ceilings and millwork carvings of intricate detail. The front porch columns are bracketed and the bay window is decorated with fish scale siding. (1979)

FERRIS (Ellis Co.) FM 983, at Main
City of Ferris

Site was occupied in 1851 by the Ephraim Andrews family and their in-laws, the McKnights, settling a purchased land grant. The Duffs, Greens, McDaniels, and Orrs also pioneered here. The Cumberland Presbyterian Church was founded in 1858. The Andrews family (1874) deeded 100-acre townsite, named for Judge J. W. Ferris (1823–1899), to the Houston & Texas Central Railway. Post office opened June 22, 1874, in store of the first postmaster, Jackson J. Straw. First cotton gin opened in 1880; first newspaper in 1889. The Ferris Institute was operated 1892–1907. City has been a brick-making center since 1895. (1974)

FIELDTON (Lamb Co.) FM 1072, ¾ mi. S
One of the Trails of Ranald Mackenzie

Col. Ranald S. Mackenzie (1840–1889) of the United States Army was ordered in the 1870s to conquer Indians on Texas frontiers. He led 240 enlisted men and eight officers in an expedition along the draw here. Heading toward New Mexico, he hoped to break up a ring of traders paying Indians to steal cattle and horses. He marched past this point about August 1, 1872; in a swift, secret move against the traders. The path beaten out by his men was serviceable later to scouts and settlers. Its traces are still known as Mackenzie's Trail. (1877)

FLATONIA (Fayette Co.)
SH 95, 8.25 mi. N
Colony Cemetery
The Colony Community, settled in the 1870s by former residents of Mississippi, at one time included three churches, several stores, and a post office. John A. and Margaret Young donated land at this site in 1876 for a Methodist Church and cemetery. The graveyard became the primary burial ground for the community. The oldest documented grave is that of Methodist minister Samuel J. Brown (1813–1879). Also interred here are numerous other pioneer settlers, infants and children, and military veterans. The cemetery serves as a reflection of the area's pioneer heritage. (1994)

FLORESVILLE (Wilson Co.)
US 181, 3 mi. NW
Casa Blanca
Home of Don Erasmo Seguin who died here in 1857. By appointment of the Spanish Governor he inducted Stephen F. Austin into Texas, 1821. Texas Deputy to the Mexican Congress, 1824.

On October 13, 1834 in a convention in Bexar he made the first effort to organize a provisional government in Texas.

FLORESVILLE (Wilson Co.)
US 181, ¼ mi. NW
Cemetery of Canary Islanders
Cemetery of Canary Islanders predates church built 1732 by colonists who arrived 1731, led by Juan Leal Goras. They farmed and raised stock. Their villa, San Fernando, was first municipality in Texas.

Among unmarked graves is that of flamboyant Doña Maria Cavillo.

Site now county-owned. (1967)

FLORESVILLE (Wilson Co.)
FM 536 & Goliad Road
on W edge of Floresville
Site of Old Town: Lodi
Community in an area known by 1720 as land of the Cayopines, a Coahuiltecan Indian tribe. The site was important to Spanish Missions of San Antonio, since here along the river their herds were pastured. For the herdsmen, adobe huts were built. After the Apache Indians began to raid the area in 1731, the herdsmen took refuge across the river within the stronger walls of the Mission Cabras, The Pena brothers had Rancho San Eldifonso del Chayopin here from 1756 to 1787, and a nephew applied for title when mission lands were secularized in 1794. However, award was made to Simon and Juan Arocha. Their neighbors (descended from Canary Island colonists of 1731) included Jose Maria Flores and Erasmus Seguin.

Stephen T. Cook settled here in 1858, putting in a store and securing office of postmaster. He may have named Lodi for a town in Mississippi, his old home state. Wilson County was organized in an election held Feb. 13, 1860. Samuel W. Barker (husband of local aristocrat Josefa Flores) became the first sheriff of the new county. Improved roads were built here.

After the Civil War, Wilson County voters on Dec. 8, 1867, designated Lodi county seat—an honor lost to Floresville in 1872. Area then reverted to ranching. (1971)

FLOWER MOUND (Denton Co.)
FM 3040 at FM 2499, NE corner
Flower Mound
Settlers of the Peters Colony named this smooth, dome-shaped hill for the abundant wild flowers that grow on it. Rising fifty feet above the surrounding prairie, Flower Mound long has been a point of interest in the area. According to local legends, no structure was ever constructed on top of the mound, nor has any tree grown here.

Before W. S. Peters began bringing settlers to the land issued him by the Republic of Texas Congress, Wichita Indians inhabited the area. During the 1840s, Peters colonists began moving to the prairie in search of good farmland. In 1844, John R. Wizwell was granted 640 acres of land that included the mound. His widow, Edy, later remarried and sold this land to George L. Beavers. Flower Mound remained in the Beavers family well into the 20th century.

Although the hill has remained in private ownership, it historically has been identified with the community that grew up around it. Flower Mound Presbyterian Church was the first to officially use the name in 1854. Once a sprawling agricultural community, Flower Mound has begun to expand with the urban growth of nearby Dallas and Fort Worth, leaving this formation as a historic reminder of its pioneer days.   (1984)

FLOYDADA (Floyd Co.)   *US 62, 5 mi. S*
Floyd County
Formed from Young and Bexar Territories. Created August 21, 1876; organized May 28, 1890. Named in honor of Dolphin Ward Floyd, a captain who died at the Alamo. County seat, Floyd City, 1890. Floydada, since 1892.   (1965)

FLOYDADA (Floyd Co.)   *SH 207 & FM 786 intersection, 5 mi. N*
Della Plain
A severe drought in the mid-1880s brought Baylor County rancher T. H. Braidfoot to this area in search of better conditions for his cattle. In 1887, with the support of J. R. McLain of Seymour, he founded the settlement of Della Plain at this site. Other early contributors to the town's development included Seymour residents I. R. Darnell and Dr. L. T. Wilson. Named for J. S. McLain's daughter Della and for the surrounding terrain, it was hoped the town would become the county seat when Floyd County was formally organized.

Della Plain became an early agricultural center for the region and was soon the site of a school, church, post office, stores and a newspaper, the Della Plain Review. Growth, however, was limited by an inadequate water supply and by the establishment of the nearby towns of Lockney (1889) and Floydada (1890). Rapid decline began after Floydada was named the seat of Floyd County in 1890. Four years later the community cemetery was all that remained of Della Plain. Despite its brief history, the pioneer town had a dramatic impact on the region. Its residents led in the later development of the county and nearby cities. Their descendants still live in the area.   (1982)

FLOYDADA (Floyd Co.)   *US 62, 8 mi. S, in roadside park*
Coronado in Blanco Canyon
From 1540 to 1542, Francisco Vazquez de Coronado led the first organized European exploration of the southwest in search of the fabled "cities of gold." With a company of more than a thousand men and women and thousands of horses and mules, cattle and sheep, Coronado trekked north from Culiacan, Mexico, through land that became Arizona, New Mexico, Texas, Oklahoma and Kansas. The exact route along which their Indian guides led the Spaniards between Pecos Pueblo in New Mexico and the Arkansas River in Kansas has long been a subject of debate among historians. Surviving documents are brief, vague and occasionally contradictory. Twice in the spring of 1541, the company camped long enough to have created detectable archeological evidence; the first time, they chose the site of a Teya Indian camp. A hailstorm struck, destroying most, if not all, of their pottery. They occupied a second camp for two weeks in a canyon that was described as being "a league wide." In the 1950s and 1960s, two pieces of chain mail were discovered by local ranchers in and near Blanco Canyon. Since 1993, a series of other objects, both European and from other parts of the southwest, have been found in the same area. They include projectile points similar to those used on crossbow arrows. Crossbows were obsolete after this expedition and are unlikely to have been used by any other group of significant size. In the late 1990s, archeologists began the task of confirming this area as the location of one of Coronado's camps. Evidence and artifacts recovered supported the theory that Coronado passed through Blanco Canyon.   (2000)

FLUVANNA (Scurry Co.)   *11th St., ¾ mi. E*
Former Townsite of Light
Established in 1899, with the granting of a post office on land owned by D. C. McGregor. The school on "Jumbo" Ranch (in area settled in 1890s) was relocated here and Light began to grow. In 1905 a new two room school building was constructed.

A decline set in however when the town of Fluvanna was surveyed in 1907 at the terminus of Roscoe, Snyder and Pacific Railroad. Soon citizens moved their buildings and belongings a mile west to be on the rails.

Although the town of Light has vanished, area still supplies water to Fluvanna.   (1972)

FLUVANNA (Scurry Co.)

US 84, 6 mi. SE

McDermott

Named for S. P. McDermott, who had crossroads store and was an early postmaster. Began as a community called Dark, 1½ miles northeast. (School in area was named Bookout.) Town moved 1909 to the Roscoe, Snyder & Pacific Railroad. It had a hotel and a number of businesses. The Santa Fe was built in 1911, and the competing railroads made this a busy cattle shipping center, with full loading pens. Town moved 1915 to Santa Fe Railroad.

The R. S. & P. tracks were taken up in 1942. The town had new population in the later 1940s, during county oil boom.

(1966)

FOLLETT (Lipscomb Co.)

SH 15, ½ mi. from W city limits

Follett

A gateway to Texas Panhandle's "Golden Spread." Founded as "Ivanhoe," on a site across state line, in Oklahoma. Town moved twice to locate on a railroad. Situated here in 1917, and renamed for Horace Follett, railroad surveyor.

Economy based on wheat, cattle, grain sorghums and (since 1950s) oil and gas production.

(1967)

FOLLETT (Lipscomb Co.)

SH 15, 8 mi. E

Northeast Corner of Texas
(3.56 mi. N)

Established by law in 1850 as intersection of 100° longitude and 36° 30' latitude, this point remained in dispute 70 years.

Of some nine surveys made to locate corner of ground, almost none coincided. Even so, three blocks were annexed to Texas from Oklahoma (1903–1929)—to confusion of landowners. One man claimed he went to bed in Oklahoma and awoke in Texas.

In 1929 U.S. Supreme Court had a final survey run. Some people with land formerly in Oklahoma could not afford to repurchase it in Texas, but exact site of corner was at last determined.

(1970)

FORESTBURG (Montague Co.)

FM 455, 5 mi. S

Butterfield Overland Stage Line Crossing

This is the crossing used by the Southern Overland Mail Line connecting St. Louis and San Francisco with semi-weekly stage and mail service, 1858–1861.

The length of the route, 2795 miles, and the superior service maintained made this a pioneer enterprise of the first magnitude.

FORNEY (Kaufman Co.)

113½ Old US 80

The Forney Messenger

The Forney Messenger is the oldest newspaper in continuous operation in Forney. Founded in 1896 by M. J. Cox, the first issue was printed on April 16 and contained a personal column, school news, a local church directory, and news from surrounding communities. In 1919, *The Messenger* was merged with *The Forney News* and was known as *The Forney News and Messenger* until 1921, when it again became *The Forney Messenger.* For many years *The Messenger* has provided residents of Forney and the surrounding area with news of local interest.

(Texas Sesquicentennial 1836–1986)

FORNEY (Kaufman Co.)

IH 20 access road (south) near FM 740 intersection

Brooklyn Lodge No. 386, A.F. & A.M.

Following the arrival of the Texas and Pacific Railroad in the village of Brooklyn in 1873, the town name was changed to Forney in honor of John Wein Forney, a director of the railroad. The local Masonic Lodge was organized the same year, using the original town name. The lodge first met in a building shared with the local school and union church. Over the years, lodge members have contributed to the community with projects such as laying the cornerstone of Lewis High School in 1922. A new lodge was completed in 1966.

(1988)

FORRESTON (Ellis Co.)   *US 77, 1 mi. S*
Chambers' Creek
Named in honor of Thomas Jefferson Chambers, (1802–1865), to whom the first land grant within present Ellis County was made in 1834 by the Mexican Government. Also known as Howe's Settlement in honor of William R. Howe, first settler in the region in 1843. An early post office in Robertson County. First county seat of Navarro County, 1846–1848.   (1964)

FORT DAVIS (Jeff Davis Co.)   *SH 17, 1 mi. NE*
Fort Davis
Established by Lieut. Colonel Washington Seawell with six companies of the U.S. Infantry on October 7, 1854 for the purpose of protecting Presidio del Norte from Indian raids.

Named in honor of Jefferson Davis, then Secretary of War.

Evacuated by Federal Troops April 13, 1861. Permanent buildings were erected when reoccupied in 1867. Abandoned as a military post in 1891 after the country had been cleared of Indians and bandits.

FORT DAVIS (Jeff Davis Co.)   *SH 17, 1 block S of courthouse*
Jeff Davis County
Formed from Presidio County. Created March 15, 1887. Organized May 16, 1887.

Named in honor of Jefferson Davis, 1860–1868, president of the Confederate States. Fort Davis, County Seat. Presidio County, 1875. County Seat, Jeff Davis County, since 1887.

FORT DAVIS (Jeff Davis Co.)   *Intersection of SH 17 and SH 118*
Jeff Davis County Courthouse
Designed by the architectural firm of L. L. Thurman and Co. of Dallas, this building was erected in 1910-1911 and replaced the original 1880 adobe courthouse. This concrete and stone Classical Revival edifice, erected by the Falls City Construction Company of Louisville, Kentucky, is dominated by a massive portico supported by Doric columns. Other distinctive design elements include the alternating horizontal bands of pink rusticated stone made of locally quarried materials and the Beaux Arts style clock tower, which features a Seth Thomas timepiece. The courthouse continues as the seat of local government.   (2000)

FORT DAVIS (Jeff Davis Co.)   *SH 17/118*
St. Joseph Catholic Church
Catholic clergy began serving residents of the Fort Davis area about 1872. Father Joseph Hoban was appointed pastor in 1876 and the First St. Joseph Catholic Church building was erected in 1879. Father Hoban was followed by circuit-riding priest who regarded St. Joseph's as the central church of the region. Father Brocardus Eeken came to Fort Davis in 1892. He and fellow Carmelite friars traveled thousands of miles each year, ministering to the 18 churches and mission stations in the Trans-Pecos and Big Bend. A new church was consecrated in 1899. Many parishes, including those in Alpine and Marfa, were created from this parish. Father Brocardus retired in 1935. St. Joseph Catholic Church continues to serve a large and diverse congregation.
                                                                       (1999)

FORT DAVIS (Jeff Davis Co.)   *SH 118, 6 mi. SE*
Musquiz Ranch
Ruins of the ranch home of Manuel Musquiz, a pioneer who settled here in 1854. Abandoned due to Indian raids. The deserted buildings served as a Ranger station intermittently, 1880–1882, while the country was being cleared of Indians and bandits.

FORT DAVIS (Jeff Davis Co.)   *SH 17, 12 mi. NE*
Wild Rose Pass
In early days the Indian trail through these mountains followed the gorge below, known as Limpia Canyon. To avoid the floods, travelers over the San Antonio-El Paso road, emigrants, U.S. Troops, supply trains and the mail chose this higher pass famed for its wealth of wild roses.

FORT DAVIS (Jeff Davis Co.)   *SH 17, 2 mi. NE*
Barry Scobee Mountain
(1 mi. N 6,300 ft. elev.)
Camp grounds and lookout post (1850s–1880s) for military, mail coaches, freighters, travelers, emigrants. Site of area's last Indian raid, 1881. Part of John G. Prude Ranch.

Named by Gov. John Connally Dec. 21, 1964, to honor Barry Scobee, whose efforts were largely responsible for the preservation of Old Fort Davis.

He was born 1885, in Missouri. Served in U.S. Army in Philippines and later on merchant ship in World War II. Was editor, reporter, printer, publisher. Came to Fort Davis in 1917 and became an authority and writer on Trans-Pecos history.   (1965)

FORT DAVIS (Jeff Davis Co.)   *SH 166, 17 mi. SW*
Bloys Camp Meeting
Held each year since 1890. Founded by Rev. W. B. Bloys, a Presbyterian. His camp pulpit was an arbuckle coffee crate. First campers, 48 people from remote ranches and towns, slept in tents, wagons. Family groups had chuck-box meals, sharing with guests. Some 1,500 attend mid-August meetings today. Still nothing is ever sold in camp.

Baptists, disciples of Christ, Methodists and Presbyterians incorporated the Cowboys' Camp Meeting in 1902. Site, Skillman Grove, has been a camp ground since the 1850s. Elevation is about 6,000 feet.   (1965)

FORT DAVIS (Jeff Davis Co.)   *SH 118, 12 mi. SE on roadside*
First Rural School
West of Pecos River
(240 ft. S)
Built 1881 of adobe brick by settlers P. H. Pruett, Cal Nations, James Dawson, Joe Dorsey. At the same time Pruett built home a half-mile west. A Texas Rangers' camp in area gave protection from Indians. Mrs. Pruett once made a midnight ride to alert Rangers to approach of Apaches.

Pruett sold home, 1883, to Fort Davis Commandant B. H. Grierson, and founded "Lone Cottonwood" ranch 4 miles north. School was closed after he moved. In 1912 Pruett sold "Cottonwood" to H. L. Kokernot; now several Kokernot ranches use it as headquarters.   (1967)

FORT DAVIS (Jeff Davis Co.)   *SH 166 access rd., 14 mi. NW*
McDonald Observatory
of the University of Texas
Original unit in complex forming one of the great observatory centers of the world. Built in the 1930's under terms of legacy from William Johnson McDonald (1844–1926), a Paris (Texas) banker interested in the stars. A well-educated man, McDonald lived frugally. As a hobby, he read science books and viewed planets through a small telescope. His will granted to the University of Texas $800,000: "To build an observatory and promote the study of astronomy."

This site was selected because of its high ratio of clear nights, its 6,800-foot altitude, its distance from artificially-lighted cities, and its quite low latitude that permits observation of southern skies.

The observatory was operated for its first 25 years mainly by astronomers from the University of Chicago, more recently primarily from the University of Texas. Until 1948, its 82-inch telescope was second largest in the world. Its fine work and site have resulted in the addition of other telescopes, including a 107-inch instrument sponsored jointly by the National Aeronautics and Space Administration, the National Science Foundation, and the University of Texas.

Discoveries made here have included interstellar polarization and the satellites of several planets.   (1968)

FORT DAVIS (Jeff Davis Co.)   *Fort St., just outside south gate of*
Ft. Davis Nat'l Historic Site
San Antonio-El Paso Road
Westward expeditions opened trails from San Antonio to El Paso in the late 1840s. Two routes, called the Upper and Lower Roads, converged at the Pecos River to traverse the Davis Mountains.

Henry Skillman (1814–1864) began a courier service along the road in 1850 and was awarded a U.S. government contract to carry the mail. He formed a partnership with George H. Giddings

(1823–1902) in 1854, and they established relay stations along the route, including one at the new U.S. Army post at Fort Davis.

During the Civil War, control of the area passed to the Confederates, and Giddings continued mail service for the new government.

By 1867, Fort Davis was occupied by four companies of the 9th U.S. Cavalry. After Federal reoccupation, stage and courier routes were more frequently utilized, with travelers often accompanied by army escorts from Fort Davis and other posts.

After the arrival of railroads in West Texas in the 1880s, use of overland roads declined sharply, though the trails did provide access to new settlers and were still used by the army as links between forts. Vestiges of the Old San Antonio-El Paso Overland Road can still be seen in Fort Davis and surrounding areas. (Texas Sesquicentennial 1836–1986)

FORT HANCOCK (Hudspeth Co.) *SH 148 Spur at railroad tracks*
Fort Hancock Mercantile
Established when the town of Fort Hancock was founded in 1883, this general store is the oldest in Hudspeth County. Started by a Mr. Ross, later the first area postmaster, it was sold in 1916 to Q. A. Hare and his wife. In 1960, they transferred the business to their daughter Mrs. Bob Sims and her husband. It has remained in continuous operation, serving the Mexican border area with modern supplies as well as items like horse collars and coffee mills. (1967)

FORT HOOD (Bell Co.) *US 190, at 2nd Armored Division Museum*
Gen. Patton's "Hell on Wheels"
The 2d Armored Division
United States Army
Formed to meet 20th Century challenges, this force includes Battery A, 1st Battalion, 3rd Field Artillery, which has been in service since 1778. That battery and other veteran units have found new capabilities in this age of mechanized combat involving lightning mobility and massive firepower. In 1940, as German Panzers overran France, the United States Congress created the 1st and 2nd American Armored Divisions. The 2nd was organized July 15, 1940, at Fort Benning, GA., by Gen. Charles L. Scott, and received its "Hell On Wheels" name in 1941 from Gen. George S. Patton, Jr.

First U.S. Armored Force in combat in World War II, "Hell On Wheels" landed in North Africa on Nov. 8, 1942. It won great victories at Safi and Casablanca, in the assault on Sicily, the 1944 Normandy Invasion, the Battle of the Bulge, and other campaigns. Along 11,702 miles of combat advance, the 2nd won 7 French Croix de Guerres, 19 distinguished unit citations, and was first foreign division ever given the Fourragere of Belgium, the 2nd provided honor guard for President Harry S. Truman at the Potsdam Peace Conference. Since 1945, Fort Hood has been 2nd's permanent base. (1975)

FORT HOOD (Bell Co.) *Headquarters Ave., Bldg. 2218*
The 1st Cavalry Division
First in Manila—first in Tokyo—first in Pyongyang.

The Fifth Cavalry Regiment, raised and posted in 1855 to Fort Belknap, Texas, is the oldest unit in the 1st Cavalry Division, United States Army. Next (1866) were the Seventh and Eighth Regiments. The Eighth initially saw duty at Fort Concho, Texas. On Sept. 13, 1921, the Division was constituted of these and one other Regiment (later dropped) at Fort Bliss, Texas, to defend the United States-Mexico border. In 1933, the Twelfth Regiment, formed in 1901 at Fort Sam Houston, San Antonio, Texas, came into the Division.

Dismounted in 1943 and sent to the Pacific, the Division captured the Admiralty Islands, joined the invasion of Leyte, and captured Manila on order of General Douglas MacArthur to act as his "First Team." During United Nations action in Korea, the Division swept over 100 miles in 11 hours to reach Osan and win victory. It was the first force to enter the North Korean Capital, Pyongyang. On July 1, 1965, at Fort Bening, Ga., it was converted to an Airmobile Division—the first in U.S. Military History. It had a distinguished record in Vietnam. Since 1971 it has been based at Fort Hood, in the state of its creation and earliest service. (1976)

FORT McKAVETT (Menard Co.)

US 190, 17 mi. W Menard, then 6 mi. SW on 864

Site of Fort McKavett

Established March 14, 1852 by the United States War Department as a protection to frontier settlers against hostile Indians. Named in honor of Captain Henry McKavett, who fell at the Battle of Monterrey, September 21, 1846. Evacuated by Federal Troops, March 22, 1859. Reoccupied April 1, 1868. Abandoned June 30, 1883.

FORT STOCKTON (Pecos Co.)

US 67, 1.5 mi. E

Pecos County

Formed from Presidio County. Created May 3, 1871. Organized March 9, 1875.

On March 9, 1875, the following county officers were elected: George M. Frazer, Chief Justice; Cesario Torres, Commissioner; Francis Rooney, Commissioner; Hipolito Carrasco, Commissioner; Martin Hufmann, Commissioner.

Fort Stockton, County Seat. Oil was discovered in the Yates Field in 1926.

FORT STOCKTON (Pecos Co.)

US 67, 15 mi. NE

Pecos County Camptosaur Tracks

In the arroyo southwest of this site are dinosaur tracks made 120 million years ago when area was part of sea that extended north from the Gulf of Mexico.

These tracks, embedded in rocks of the Comanchean Cretaceous Period, were left by a Camptosaurus Dinosaur, ancestor to the better known duck-billed Trachodon.

According to research, this plant-eating animal was about 20 feet long and ten feet tall. His hind legs were strong and longer than his arms which were used to grasp and tear food. His neck was short; head small; the tail long, perhaps equal in length to the body.

Measurement of the exposed tracks (17½ in. wide and 21 in. long) determine that this Camptosaur's stride was 5 ft. 10 in. from toe to heel; his pace, 11 ft. 8 in.

The shallow sea in which this dinosaur (and other forms of animal and plant life) lived and died was gradually covered by deposits of mineral-laden earth. As this area rose and settled through hundreds of centuries, the buried organic matter was gradually converted through chemical changes to vast resources of petroleum, natural gas and sulphur.

This Camptosaur's tracks remain to remind mankind of the Prehistoric Age in which the oil industry had its infant beginnings. (1968)

FORT STOCKTON (Pecos Co.)

IH 10 in roadside park

Pioneer Stagecoach Stand Operators
Mr. and Mrs. Isaac J. Rude

On their way to California from Tennessee in the 1850s, Isaac J. and Sarah Isabella Rude settled in West Texas. In the Davis Mountains, Rude built and operated a station for the Butterfield Overland Stage; here passengers had meals while mules were unharnessed and exchanged for a fresh team. Soon Butterfield—the pioneer passenger and mail service (1858–1861) from St. Louis to California—had Rude move here to Ft. Stockton and build another stand. In 1859, when a stop was added at Leon Water Hole, 5 mi. west of Ft. Stockton, Rude built and ran the stand there. The food there was the best on the route, said a journalist.

Sarah Rude (1834–1916) carried a pistol under her apron to protect her children. When Indians attacked the Davis Mountains stand, the men loaded guns and handed them to Mrs. Rude, a calm, sure marksman. Just over 5 ft. tall, she butchered and skinned beeves to feed her family when her husband was away.

After stages stopped operating in 1861, Isaac Rude, like others associated with the Overland Mail, joined the Confederate Army. Later he became a prosperous businessman in McKinney. Born in 1829, he died in 1902. (1967)

FORT WORTH (Tarrant Co.)

800 Main, General Worth Square

General William Jenkins Worth
(1794–1849)

William Jenkins Worth, a native of Hudson, New York, was severely wounded at Lundy's Lane during the War of 1812. In 1820, he became instructor of infantry tactics and soldierly discipline at the United States Military Academy at West Point. He was appointed the first commandant of cadets in 1825. When Worth was reassigned in 1828, Robert E. Lee was serving as cadet adjutant.

Worth was involved in defenses along the Canadian border in the 1830s, and in 1841–1842 led an expedition against the Florida Seminole Indians. He was awarded a commendation from the Florida Territorial Legislature and was promoted to brigadier general.

During the Mexican War, Worth fought at the Battle of Monterrey. He received a Sword of Honor from the U.S. Congress and a promotion to major general.

While serving as commander of the Texas and New Mexico military districts, Worth died of cholera in San Antonio in 1849. Fort Worth, a frontier post established after his death, was named in his honor. Worth was buried in New York City. His grave, at Broadway and Fifth Avenue, is marked by a fifty-foot monument and is surrounded by a fence of cast iron swords, copies of his New York State Sword of Honor.   (1987)

FORT WORTH (Tarrant Co.)   *108 W Bluff St., Heritage Park*
Fort Worth-Yuma Mail
(Star Post Route No. 31454)

By the 1870s remote areas of the frontier not served by the railroads needed mail delivery routes. In response the U.S. Post Office Department, in 1873, began establishing Star Post Routes.

On Aug. 15, 1878, Star Route No. 31454 was opened between Fort Worth and Yuma, Arizona Terr., under contract to J. T. Chidester. Stagecoaches carried the mail along much the same route used by the Butterfield Overland Mail in the late 1850s.

Fort Worth to Yuma mail was discontinued after completion of the Southern Transcontinental Railroad in 1881.   (1976)

FORT WORTH (Tarrant Co.)   *300 W Belknap (US 377), on yard of courthouse*
Fort Worth
"Where the West Begins"

Founded June 6, 1849, as frontier post of Co. F, 2nd Dragoons, 8th Dept., U.S. Army. The Commander, Maj. Ripley Arnold, named the camp for his former superior officer, Maj. Gen. William Jenkins Worth. In 4 years of operations, the post had but one serious Indian encounter. A town grew up alongside the fort, as center for supply stores and stagecoach routes.

In 1856, Fort Worth became county seat of Tarrant County. A boom started after 1867 when millions of Longhorns were driven through town en route to Red River Crossing and Chisholm Trail. Herds forded the Trinity below Courthouse Bluff, one block north of this site. Cowboys got supplies for the long uptrail drive and caroused in taverns and dance halls.

After railroad arrived in 1876, increased cattle traffic won city the nickname of "Cowtown."

By 1900, Fort Worth was one of the world's largest cattle markets. Population tripled between 1900 and 1910. Growth continued, based on varied multimillion-dollar industries of meat packing, flour milling, grain storage, oil, aircraft plants and military bases. Fort Worth also has developed as a center of culture, with universities, museums, art galleries, theatres and a botanic garden.   (1969)

FORT WORTH (Tarrant Co.)   *100 blk. of E Exchange Ave.*
Fort Worth Stock Yards Entrance

Spanning Exchange Avenue, this gateway to the Fort Worth Stock Yards was completed in 1910. Constructed by the Topeka Bridge & Land Co. for the Fort Worth Stock Yards Co., it was a significant feat of concrete work for that era. The columns are 22 feet high and 13 feet in circumference. The sign is 36 feet long and 4 feet high. The entrance is a significant landmark in this historic area of Fort Worth.   (1985)

FORT WORTH (Tarrant Co.)   *131 E Exchange Ave.*
The Fort Worth Stock Yards Company

The Fort Worth Stock Yards Company was created in 1893, when Boston capitalist Greenlief W. Simpson led a group of investors in purchasing the Fort Worth Union Stock Yards. Under Simpson's leadership, the company earned the support of the Texas Cattle Raisers Association and lured the prominent meatpacking companies of Armour and Swift to open plants here. Publicity through the company's market newspaper and annual fat stock show, both begun in 1896, resulted in a significant increase in the number of animals brought to market. The Stock

Yards Co. built the area's livestock-related facilities and had controlling interest in many north Fort Worth businesses and properties.

The first five decades of the 20th century were the most successful for the Fort Worth Stock Yards Co. During World War I, foreign governments purchased draft animals, making Fort Worth the largest horse and mule market in the world. In 1917, overall livestock market receipts reached 3,500,000 and in 1944, sales exceeded 5,000,000 head of livestock. However, by the 1950s, local auctions were drawing sellers away from this central market. Today the Fort Worth Stock Yards Co. continues as a significant part of the city's unique heritage. (Texas Sesquicentennial 1836–1986)

FORT WORTH (Tarrant Co.)   *US 80/377, Veterans' Park, 4100 Camp Bowie Blvd.*
Camp Bowie Boulevard
In 1917–1918, this roadway was the main artery through Camp Bowie, a World War I training center. Narrow strips of asphalt paving flanked streetcar tracks that ran the length of the avenue, then called Arlington Heights Boulevard. After the war, business and residential development spread into this area. In 1919, the street was renamed Camp Bowie Boulevard. In 1927–1928, like many of the major thoroughfares in Fort Worth, it was paved with durable Thurber bricks. Today, this street is a reminder of Fort Worth's heritage and a source of pride to area residents. (1979)

FORT WORTH (Tarrant Co.)   *4600 Camp Bowie Blvd.*
Arlington Heights Lodge No. 1184,
A.F. & A.M.
Chartered on December 9, 1921, Arlington Heights Lodge no. 1184 is located on land donated by lodge members W. C. Stonestreet and F. H. Sparrow. This building, designed by lodge member John C. Davies (1885–1963), was dedicated January 3, 1923. The classical revival structure with strong Greek temple influence features pedimented gables, brick pilasters with stone capitals, round-arch upper windows and entry, stone motif details, and art glass transoms. (1987)

FORT WORTH (Tarrant Co.)   *US 80 southside, .25 mi. E of Marys Creek Bridge*
Chapin School
The Chapin School was begun for Mary's Creek Community in the late 1870s in a log cabin on land deeded by Ivory H. Chapin (2 mi. SE). In 1884, the school was moved one mile west to a 2-room frame house on Mary's Creek on land donated by J. Fielding Dunlap (0.5 mi. S). It was moved again in 1936, to a rock structure on Chapin Road. In 1961, the Fort Worth Independent School District annexed the Chapin Common School District. The name Chapin School continued to be used for an elementary school, however, until 1968, when it closed. (1985)

FORT WORTH (Tarrant Co.)   *Loop 820 & John T. White Rd., NW corner*
Site of
Ray-Manship Cemetery
Razed in 1984, the cemetery that once was located at this site contained twelve known burials and numerous unmarked graves of early Tarrant County settlers. The graveyard was located on the William Ray survey. Ray, a Peters colonist, and his wife, Lucinda, were buried here in the mid-1880s. The earliest known burial, that of Sarah Clark (b. 1880), took place in 1883. Three members of the Manship family, early area farmers, were known to have been buried here. Several graves were reinterred in Rose Hill Cemetery as area land development began.
(Texas Sesquicentennial 1836–1986)

FORT WORTH (Tarrant Co.)   *3419 E. Belknap (US 377)*
Riverside Methodist Church
According to local oral tradition, Riverside Methodist Episcopal Church, South, began in March 1888, when the Rev. C. F. Vance and ten people held Sunday school in an abandoned saloon at East First and Sylvania Streets.

After organizing a congregation, the members bought land at the corner of East First and Ross Avenue (now Retta) in 1893 and built a frame sanctuary.

In its early years, the congregation was served by visiting ministers and by students at Polytechnic College (Now Texas Wesleyan University). The church building was moved to the southeast corner of Noble Street and Frey Avenue (now Riverside Drive) in 1907. It continued in use until 1925, when it was replaced by a basement for a new structure and the name of the church was changed in 1924 to Sylvania Heights Methodist Episcopal Church, South, but in 1935 it reverted to its original name when Frey Avenue was renamed Riverside Drive. A sanctuary was completed over the 1925 basement in 1937, and a new facility was built on adjacent lots in 1951.

Highway construction and changing neighborhood dynamics led to the church's relocation to this site in 1982. After a denominational name change in 1968, it became known as Riverside United Methodist Church. (1991)

FORT WORTH (Tarrant Co.) *SH 360, E side near SH 183*
Founder of World-Famous Cattle Trail
Jesse Chisholm (1806–1868)

Represented the Republic of Texas and President Sam Houston in many negotiations with Indians. Half Scotsman, half Cherokee; a scout, hunter, trader, and trailblazer. Spoke 40 Indian languages and dialects, and was a respected influence among Southwestern tribes, including the wild Kiowas and Comanches.

In 1843, near here at Bird's Fort on the Trinity, was interpreter for a peace conference; in 1849, was in negotiations at Grapevine Springs, to the north.

He is best known for marking the Chisholm Trail across Oklahoma and Kansas. Cowboys driving cattle north to seek favorable markets used his direct route which avoided deep rivers and lay in grassy, watered land. He thus helped rebuild Texas economy that had been wrecked in 1861–1865 by the Civil War. Cattle had increased greatly in wartime. Texas had no market; drives were necessary, so $5 Longhorns could go to northern markets to bring $30 or more per head. In 1867, the Chisholm Trail was extended to Abilene, Kansas, where cattle loading pens and railroad shipping cars were provided.

This was the best known of several cattle trails from Texas over which some 10,000,000 beeves were driven from the state during the years 1866–1884. (1967)

FRANKLIN (Robertson Co.) *US 79, 1.3 mi. E*
Robertson County

Settled by people from Tennessee under an 1822 contract held by Sterling Clack Robertson (1785–1842), who later signed the Texas Declaration of Independence. Colony and county were named for him. County was created Dec. 14, 1837; organized March 1838.

County Seats: "Old Franklin," 1838–1850; Wheelock, 1850–1855; Owensville, 1855–1869; Calvert, 1870–1879; Franklin since 1879.

Sent 5 troop companies into Confederate service in Civil War. Established mill to make flour, cotton and wool cloth. Furnished cotton cards, medicines, flour, bacon and salt to soldiers' families. (1965)

FRANKLIN (Robertson Co.) *FM 2446, 4 mi. E*
General Walter Washington Williams
(Nov. 14, 1842–Dec. 19, 1959)

Reputed to have been last surviving soldier of the Civil War (1861–1865). Born in Ittawamba County, Miss., Williams during the war was a forage master for the celebrated Hood's Texas Brigade. Soon after the war he moved to Texas and farmed near here. He was twice married and had a large family, with the descendants numbering over 200 when he died.

He had lived very quietly until in extreme old age he gained fame as one of a very few remaining veterans. After the nation lost all other men who had fought in the Civil War, he was given honorary rank of general by President Dwight D. Eisenhower. When Gen. Williams died in Houston at home of a daughter, President Eisenhower proclaimed a period of national mourning.

Williams rests here in Mount Pleasant Cemetery among families who migrated to Texas and braved the dangers of the frontier for years before he came. This is one of the oldest public burial grounds in Robertson County, situated within boundaries of colony planted north of El Camino Real by the pioneer Sterling C. Robertson, from Tennessee. The Robertson Colony was founded in the 1820s and was a major civilizing influence in East Texas. (1970)

FRANKLIN (Robertson Co.) *FM 979, 4 mi. N*
Site of Owensville

Robertson County's third county seat was located here, 1855–1869, on land given by D. H. Love (1816–1866). The town was Owensville, named for Harrison Owen (1803–1896), who was the first county clerk, 1838–1847. Public officials, doctors, lawyers, businesses moved here and town thrived. It was on Houston-Waco mail, stage, and freighting road.

As Civil War (1861–1865) county seat, this place armed and dispatched soldiers, and cared for civilians.

After Houston & Texas Central Railway bypassed Owensville in 1868, county records were moved to Calvert. Owensville Cemetery, oldest in county, marks townsite. (1974)

FRANKSTON (Anderson Co.) SH 155
Frankston Railroad Depot
In 1900 the Texas & New Orleans Railroad, now part of the Southern Pacific Line, platted the town of Frankston. The station was first called Frankfort and the post office Ayres. Both were renamed Frankston in 1902 for Miss Frankie Miller, who gave land for a city park. In 1906 this frame depot was built. The railroad connected local farmers with distant markets and provided passenger service from 1903 to 1964. The depot was restored in 1976 as a museum. (1977)

FRANKSTON (Anderson Co.) FM 837, 9.5 mi. SW
Anderson Campground
Located on a spring near Brushy Creek Community, this area was first settled in the 1850s. In 1873, it was set aside for use as a religious campground by members of the local Methodist congregation. The land was purchased from E. S. Jamison of Galveston County for sixty dollars in gold. The tabernacle was built the following year of pine beams, sweet gum piers, and wooden pegs.

Religious camp meetings were conducted here each summer. During the week-long services, residents of the surrounding area, representing several faiths, lived in tents on the grounds. The spring provided water for the campers and for baptisms. Although the meetings were primarily times of religious revival, they also allowed distant neighbors a chance to visit and exchange ideas.

A sanctuary for the Brushy Creek Methodist Church, built here in the 1870s, was replaced by the present building in 1894. A parsonage for use by the circuit preachers burned in 1916. As rural life became more modernized, camp meetings declined in popularity. The last ones here were held in the 1930s. Still used for religious meetings, Anderson Campground is the site of an annual September homecoming. (1981)

FREDERICKSBURG (Gillespie Co.) FM 965, 18 mi. N
Enchanted Rock
From its summit, in the fall of 1841, Captain John C. Hays, while surrounded by Comanche Indians who cut him off from his Ranging Company, repulsed the whole band and inflicted upon them such heavy losses that they fled. (1965)

FREDERICKSBURG (Gillespie Co.) SH 16, 7 mi. SW in roadside park
Gillespie County
The trails of roving Indians crossed these hills, settled by German pioneers, in 1846. A group of Mormons settled at Zodiac in 1847. Created February 23, 1848. Organized June 5, 1848. Named for Richard Addison Gillespie, a Texan from 1837, a defender of the Texas Frontier, Captain in the Mexican War, who fell at Monterrey, September 22, 1846. Fredericksburg, the County Seat. (1965)

FREDERICKSBURG (Gillespie Co.) US 290, 3 mi. SE
Site of Fort Martin Scott
Established by the United States Army December 5, 1848 as a protection to travelers and settlers against Indian attack. Named in honor of Major Martin Scott, Brevet Lieutenant Colonel, 5th United States Infantry, killed at Molino del Ray, September 8, 1847. Its garrison participated in many Indian skirmishes. Occupied intermittently after 1852. Held by the Confederates, 1861–1865. Permanently abandoned in December, 1866.

FREDERICKSBURG (Gillespie Co.) US 290 on E right-of-way, 2 mi. E
The Pinta Trail
Origin of the Pinta Trail is attributed to nomadic plains Indian tribes. Early Spanish and Mexican expeditions followed the general route of the trail, which extended from San Antonio de Bexar to the San Saba River near present Menard. A survey by German immigrants in 1845 provided a wagon road over part of the trail, and, after the discovery of gold in California in

1849, the trail was utilized by U.S. military companies seeking to open new routes to the western States. Use of the trail declined with the advent of railroads in the late 1800s and early 1900s.

(Texas Sesquicentennial 1836–1986)

FREDERICKSBURG (Gillespie Co.)
US 290, 8 mi. E in roadside park
Texas Rancher
General E. Kirby Smith, C.S.A.
(1824–1893)

Born in Florida. Graduated from West Point. Fought in Mexican War. On the Texas frontier in the 1850s, commanded Camps Belknap, Cooper and Colorado.

In 1860 and many years afterwards was a partner of J. M. Hunter of Fredericksburg in a Texas ranch.

Resigned from U.S. Army, 1861, to serve Confederacy. Was appointed 1863, to command all the area west of the Mississippi. At that time Federals held the river, all of Missouri, much of Arkansas, Louisiana and Indian Territory, and were trying to take Texas and her supplies of food, cotton and horses.

The Trans-Mississippi Dept. had many problems. The French under Maximilian were approaching from Mexico. Indians and bandits constantly raided frontiers. Freighters and blockade runners had to be employed for exporting cotton—the only product the south had for trading to get guns, ammunition and goods.

Texas was chief source of the cotton Gen. Smith used for financing his army. It was place of safety to which he sent his wife and children. It gave him ovations as he went to Mexico after the war ended.

Young Texans studied, 1875–1893, in his mathematics classes at the University of the South, Sewanee, Tenn.

(1965)

FREDERICKSBURG (Gillespie Co.)
FM 965 2 mi. N
Cross Mountain

This marl and limestone hill elevation 915 feet, was an Indian signal point, advancing news of the intrusions of white settlers. The hill was first recorded and described by the German geologist, Dr. Ferdinand Roemer in 1847. A timber cross found on the hilltop the same year suggests that Spanish missionaries recognized it as a landmark on the path from San Antonio to Mission San Saba. John Christian Durst (1825–1898), arriving with his family in 1847 from Germany, received a town lot and 10 acres of land, including this hill. On finding the cross, he named it "Kreuzberg," or Cross Mountain. The Easter fires on Cross Mountain and the surrounding hills recall a German tradition of burning the old growth to make way for the new, and also commemorate the 1847 Treaty made by John O. Meusebach and the settlers to establish peace with the Comanche Nation.

In 1849, a Bohemian priest, Father George Menzel, erected a more substantial cross as a symbol of redemption and civilization. Easter sunrise services were held on the mountain for many years prior to 1941. In 1946 the Very Rev. F. X. Wolf threw the switch to illuminate the permanent cross of metal and concrete built by St. Mary's Catholic Church.

(1976)

FREDERICKSBURG (Gillespie Co.)
US 290, 315 W Main Fredericksburg
Sunday Houses

Small townhouses built by German settlers who lived in distant rural areas. Used over weekends by families while they traded or attended church.

A typical early Sunday House had one room with a lean-to kitchen and a half-story above, which was reached by outside stairway or ladder. Built during 1890s–1920s. Most Sunday Houses were frame but some were rock.

Homes found use during school sessions, periods of religious instruction or serious illness.

Some of the large ones made comfortable retirement homes for elderly German farmers.   (1970)

FREDERICKSBURG (Gillespie Co.)
511 E Main St.
Ressmann-Boos House

An evolution of pioneer building methods is evident in this home. The earliest part, built about 1845, is of Fachwerk construction typical in early German houses. Later additions were of log and clapboard frame construction. Early area settlers Christian and Katharina Ressmann purchased the home in 1866 and in 1946 members of their family sold it to Hilmar and Christine Boos. The house remained in the Boos family until the 1970s. (1983)

FREDERICKSBURG (Gillespie Co.) *714 W Main St.*
Schneider-Klingelhoefer House
Built about 1870 for watchmaker and stonemason Ludwig Schneider, this home features German Fachwerk construction. Owned by builder Louis Preiss from 1883 to 1890, it was acquired in 1924 by banker Arthur Klingelhoefer, who lived here from 1925 until his death. Prominent features of the home, which remained in the Klingelhoefer family until 1976, include an unusual porch roof parapet, gable-end chimneys, and a decorative wood balustrade. (1988)

FREDERICKSBURG (Gillespie Co.) *US 290, Pioneer Plaza, Main Street*
Vereins Kirche
Church for all denominations, school and community hall.

Built, summer 1847, after the Comanche Peace Treaty made by John O. Meusebach, commissioner, German Emigration Company.

Located in Main Street between courthouse and Market Square of early Fredericksburg.

Razed after the celebration of fiftieth anniversary of the arrival of first settlers, 1896.

Replica, first used as museum, and library, constructed 1934–1935. (1967)

FREDERICKSBURG (Gillespie Co.) *Corner of Main & Washington*
Nimitz Hotel
This property was purchased by Charles Henry Nimitz, Sr., in 1855. By 1860, the Nimitz Hotel was established, hosting frontier travelers and providing a home for the large Nimitz family. Expanded in the 1870s to feature a steamboat shaped facade, the hotel was a center for community activities. It was sold by the family in 1926 and underwent major alterations. In 1964, it became a museum honoring fleet Admiral Chester W. Nimitz and those who served with him in World War II. The steamboat facade was later rebuilt and remains a local landmark. (1989)

FREDERICKSBURG (Gillespie Co.) *US 290, at site, East Main Street*
Birthplace of
Fleet Admiral Chester W. Nimitz, USN
Typical early Fredericksburg home built 1866 by Carl Basse. Property of the Henke family since 1873. Heinrich Henke, early settler, Confederate freighter had butcher counter on front porch; meat processing was done in back yard; there the horses that pulled meat vending cart were stabled. Shop later built on foundation of stone walls surrounding lot.

He and his wife Dorothea (nee Weirich) added the long dining room and kitchen with sloped roof to accommodate their twelve children. Many of their furnishings are preserved by Udo Henke, a descendant.

In small room to rear of front bedroom, on Feb. 24, 1885, their daughter, Anna Henke Nimitz, gave birth to Chester William Nimitz, destined to command the greatest naval armada in history.

A 1905 honor graduate of the U.S. Naval Academy, Nimitz was Chief of Staff to Commander, Atlantic Submarine Fleet, W.W. I. Installed first naval ROTC unit in U.S. Navy, 1926; selected Commander in Chief Pacific Fleet after attack on Pearl Harbor; appointed Fleet Admiral, U.S. Navy, 1944. As representative of the U.S. he signed Japanese surrender documents on his flagship, *USS Missouri,* Sept. 2, 1945 in Tokyo Bay. Admiral Nimitz died in San Francisco on Feb. 20, 1966.

FREDERICKSBURG (Gillespie Co.) *S. Adams (SH 16) & Hale St.*
Fredericksburg Lodge No. 794, A.F. & A.M.
Fredericksburg Masonic Lodge No. 794 traces its history to 1896 when a warrant of dispensation was granted by the Grand Lodge of Texas, Ancient Free and Accepted Masons. The First Worshipful Master, D.C. Darroch, was installed by Neal Caldwell, Deputy District Grand Master of the 47th Masonic District. Members joined from Willow Creek, Kerrville, and Johnson City, and first met in the Schandua Building.

In 1910, the Otto Kolmeier Building located on East Main Street was acquired as the second home for the lodge, and was shared with the Eastern Star Organization. The lodge moved to the Beckmann Building on West Main Street in 1925. Lodge meetings were held on the first floor, and the second floor housed Eastern Star meetings. The cornerstone for a new lodge building was laid in 1963 at South Adams and Hale Streets.

Lodge members maintain a strong tradition of supporting education. An award named for Republic of Texas President Mirabeau B. Lamar has been given annually, in addition to a scholarship. Many charitable causes have received assistance from the Masons, who continue to serve the community as they have for more than a century. (1997)

FREDERICKSBURG (Gillespie Co.) *SH 16 right of way, 2 miles S*
Guenther's Live Oak Mill

By 1848, Carl Hilmar Guenther (1826–1902), master millwright, had completed his apprenticeship in Germany and immigrated to the U.S. In search of opportunities and a good gristmill site, he journeyed south from Wisconsin to New Orleans, and then west to Texas. In 1851 he bought land and water rights on Live Oak Creek near Fredericksburg. After six months of construction, his mill was operational, but a flood destroyed the first dam. One month after the flood the mill was working again.

Ox drawn wagons loaded with harvested crops converged on the mill in the mornings, and after the farmers' business was completed the men remained to visit with each other. The mill became a center of social life in the hill country community. Guenther was granted U.S. citizenship in Gillespie County in 1854. He married Dorothea Pape in 1855. They lived in a home near the mill and were eventually the parents of seven children.

In 1859, Guenther chose a site about one mile from the center of San Antonio as a new site for his mill operation. Guenther Mills soon became the Pioneer Flour Mills, an enterprise which became a flourishing business in Texas and the Southwest. (1991)

FREEPORT (Brazoria Co.) *SH 36, 8 mi. NW*
⅛ mi. S to Peach Point

Home of Mrs. Emily M. Perry, 1795–1851, only sister of Stephen F. Austin, who regarded the place as his home after the burning of San Felipe on March 29, 1836. (1964)

FREEPORT (Brazoria Co.) *Ave. B and Skinner St. in Velasco*
4 mi. SE to the Original Town of Velasco

Landing place of the "Lively," first vessel bringing immigrants to Austin's Colony in 1821. There the Battle of Velasco, between Texas Colonists and Mexican Troops, was fought June 26, 1832. A treaty of peace between Texas and Mexico was signed there May 14, 1836, by Presidents David G. Burnet and Antonio Lopez de Santa Anna but was never ratified by Mexico. (1964)

FREEPORT (Brazoria Co.) *SH 332, 1 block S of Intracoastal Waterway*
Velasco

Four miles southeast to the original town of Velasco, landing place of the "Lively," first vessel bringing immigrants to Austin's Colony in 1821. There the Battle of Velasco, between Texas Colonists and Mexican Troops, was fought June 26, 1832. A treaty of peace between Texas and Mexico was signed there May 14, 1836, by Presidents David G. Burnet and Antonio Lopez de Santa Anna but was never ratified by Mexico. (1964)

FREEPORT (Brazoria Co.) *SH 36, 9 mi. W*
Major Guy M. Bryan, C.S.A.
(1821–1901)

Born in Missouri. Rode a mule to Texas in 1831 to join his uncle, Stephen F. Austin, Father of Texas. A private of Texas War for Independence. Legislator, Congressman, Member of Texas Secession Convention.

Enlisted as a private in the Civil War. But his administrative ability, diplomacy and political understanding soon cast him in the role of trouble-shooter and liaison man between State and Confederate Governments and the military. Convinced C.S.A. leaders of need to leave enough troops in Texas to guard coastline and prevent Indian attacks.

Arranged 1862 Conference of Governors of Missouri, Arkansas, Louisiana and Texas, and delivered their request to President Jefferson Davis for creation of a strong military department west of the Mississippi River. Helped reorganize armed forces in east Texas. Served as confidential adjutant to both Pres. Davis and Trans-Mississippi Commanding General. Settled dispute among military, state of Texas and Confederacy on acquisition and sale of cotton—lifeblood of the South. Took part in battles in April 1864 to prevent Federal invasion of Texas. Arranged Governors' Conferences in 1863 and 1865.

Buried in State Cemetery in Austin.

FREEPORT (Brazoria Co.) *SH 332, 1 block S of Intracoastal Waterway, 5 mi. E*
Old Velasco, C.S.A.

Historic and key Texas port of entry located near here. During the Civil War was fortified by troops and 8 gun batteries at the mouth of the Brazos River to provide shelter and landing facilities for blockade runners, to protect rich farmlands, and to prevent Federal invasion.

The South exchanged cotton for European guns, ammunition, milled goods and medicines for army and home use. Velasco was one of the busiest ports. Federal vessels attempted to stop vital trade, and constantly fired upon runners as well as the shore defenses and patrols. The runners would approach the port on dark nights when the waters were smooth, and by the use of sounding lines could determine nearness to shore and avoid blockaders. Boilers would be kept well fired with hard coal that burned with a minimum of smoke, in case it became necessary to outrun Federal patrol ships.

Union ships had to go to New Orleans for drinking water, food and fuel, because Texas Marines on rafts or dredgeboats or Texas Cavalry and Infantry units kept them off the shores. The raw courage of the Texas coastal defenders made this a most dramatic story in the history of the Confederacy.

FREEPORT (Brazoria Co.) *15 mi. NE, on San Luis Island*
at Balboa Blvd. & Beach

Titlum-Tatlum

Nearby island. Resort for fishermen, hunters, small boats. During the Civil War, 1861–1865, used by such Captains as H. C. Wedemeyer, a peacetime shipbuilder, as base for operations defying Federal blockade.

Ships loaded with cotton entered waterways around Titlum-Tatlum and hid among willows, out of range of observers with spyglasses on the tall masts of Federal blockading ships. On dark nights or in bad weather, blockade-runners would slip out of here to the open seas, hugging shores, sometimes being towed by men on land until deep water was reached.

Cotton taken overseas by such ships would buy for the Confederacy (hampered by lack of manufacturing facilities) guns, gunpowder, medicines, coffee, cloth, hardware and shoes. Purchases came into Texas by the same route that cotton was freighted out.

Aside from such havens as Titlum-Tatlum, blockade runners needed every advantage over the foe, for they supplied life-blood to the Confederacy. Texas gave them unstinted support: From her coast guard and from infantry and cavalry that would not let Federals land even to get drinking water or wood; so that blockade ships often had to drop duty and take off for New Orleans for supplies and repairs. (1965)

FREEPORT (Brazoria Co.) *SH 36, 9 mi. W at the Bryan marker*
Battle of Jones Creek

Fought by Texan Army of 23 men under Capt. Randal Jones (1786–1873), sent out 1824 by Stephen F. Austin to the lower Brazos to fight cannibal Karankawa Indians. Scouts found the camp here. Attack at dawn found Indians ready with spears. Jones' guns got 15 Indians, dispersed the rest. (1965)

FREEPORT (Brazoria Co.) *SH 332, 4 mi. E, at turnout near high bridge*
Gulf Intracoastal Waterway

This complex of barge canals and natural channels—most valuable waterway in America—stretches 1,116 mi. from Brownsville, Texas, to St. Mark's, Florida. Is longer and carries more tonnage than Suez, and Panama Canals. Is a vital link in economy of Texas and has been one of main causes of rapid development of Gulf Coast area.

The Canal system was begun in 1854 when a short canal was built from Galveston Bay to mouth of Brazos River as aid to Texas trade; it was 50 ft. wide 3½ ft. deep and dug by hand-labor and mule teams. Later projects widened, lengthened canal along the coast.

Most important period in growth of the waterway system was result of determined efforts by two Texas businessmen, Clarence S. E. Holland and Roy Miller. In 1905–1907 these men organized the initial financial support, arranged construction and won congressional backing for canal improvements. By 1966 annual total tonnage on the waterway exceeded 78,500,000 tons.

Hundreds of companies now have plants or warehouses along the canal; its impact on growth of Gulf Coast has been immense. Several inland cities have become seaports; canal helped to make Houston nation's third largest port. Low shipping costs created by waterway have brought prosperity to entire Texas Gulf Coast. (1967)

FREEPORT (Brazoria Co.) *SH 36, 9 mi. SW*
Gulf Prairie
Pioneer cemetery. Originally of Peach Point Plantation.

Used by descendants of James Franklin Perry and wife, Emily Austin Bryan Perry, Stephen F. Austin's sister, and by the community since 1829.

In 1836, Austin, the "Father of Texas," was buried here.

His remains were reinterred in the State Cemetery in the city of Austin in 1910. (1967)

FREEPORT (Brazoria Co.) *SH 36, 7 mi. W*
Little Peach Point House:
Awarded
The Texas Historical Building Medallion
Site of the Texas home of Austin's sister, Mrs. James F. Perry, was selected by Austin himself. It is near the Brazos River but not subject to overflow.

FREEPORT (Brazoria Co.) *SH 36, 9 mi. SW, Gulf Prairie Cemetery*
Major Reuben R. Brown
(February 3, 1808–March 2, 1894)
In Texas War for Independence, joined Matamoros expedition of January 1836. In detachment that captured horses of Gen. Urrea of Mexican Army, Brown was made captive in a counterattack, and spent 11 months in prison in Mexico, but finally escaped.

In his old age, he lived at "Sur Mer," home of his daughter, Mrs. James Perry Bryan, a great-granddaughter by marriage of Moses Austin, whose courage had led to colonization of Texas.
(1970)

FREEPORT (Brazoria Co.) *SH 36 at rd. leading to plantation*
Old Oakland Plantation
Founded 1828 by Henry Wm. Munson, who bought site from Stephen F. Austin, Father of Texas. This land joined Peach Point Plantation, Austin's home.

Munson, one of Texans in uprising over injustices at Anahuac and Velasco in 1832, died in yellow fever epidemic in 1833. (1965)

FREEPORT (Brazoria Co.) *SH 36, 9 mi. SW, Gulf Prairie Cemetery*
William Joel Bryan
(December 14, 1815–March 3, 1903)
Grandson of Moses Austin, whose dream of Anglo-American colony changed course of Texas history.

Came to Texas with his mother and stepfather in 1831; served in Texas army from 1835 to 1838. A highly successful planter, he was instrumental in building of deepwater port at mouth of the Brazos. Town of Bryan, Texas, is named for him. He married Lavinia Perry. Lived at "Durazno" plantation—a gift of his uncle, Stephen F. Austin. Had 7 children. (1970)

FREEPORT (Brazoria Co.) *SH 36, 9 mi. SW, Gulf Prairie Cemetery*
Henry William Munson
(January 15, 1793–October 6, 1833)
Heroic early Texas soldier. Fought in Battle of the Medina, near San Antonio, 1813. Returned east afterward, but moved to Texas as a colonist in 1824. Fought on behalf of Mexico to quell Fredonian Rebellion, 1827; but against Santa Anna's agents in 1832 Battle of Velasco.

187

Munson married Ann Pearce. In their family of 8 children was a son, Mordello, named for the Mexican officer who saved life of H. W. Munson at the Medina. (1970)

FREEPORT (Brazoria Co.)   *SH 36, 9 mi. SW, Gulf Prairie Cemetery*
Major James Peckham Caldwell
(January 6, 1793–November 16, 1856)
Adjutant of the Texas Army in Battle of Velasco, June 26, 1832. Wounded there, he was guarding civilians at time Texas won independence in Battle of San Jacinto, April 21, 1836.

A bosom friend of Stephen F. Austin, Caldwell received land grant from Mexico in 1824. In 1830s he had a sugar mill, said to be the first on the Brazos.

He married Ann Munson, widow of his friend H. W. Munson. They had a son and a daughter. (1970)

FREEPORT (Brazoria Co.)   *SH 36 1 mi. W, Stringfellow Ranch gate*
Stringfellow Ranch
Born at Old Brazoria, Robert Edward Lee Stringfellow (1866–1941) began his career on a cattle ranch at the age of 14. Soon he acquired his own herd. He opened a Velasco meat market in 1890 and provided beef for workers building jetties at the mouth of the Brazos River. Stringfellow's ranch holdings here in southern Brazoria County increased to 20,000 acres. A philanthropist and civic leader, Stringfellow was an early builder and investor in Freeport townsite. After he was injured in the 1932 hurricane, his wife Nannie (Maddox) (d. 1971) operated the ranch and Freeport interests. (1980)

FREER (Duval Co.)   *US 59 SW in roadside park*
John C. Duval
Escaped the massacre March 27, 1836, and was the last survivor of Fannin's Army to die. Born in Kentucky in 1816. Died in Fort Worth, Texas, January 15, 1897.

FREER (Duval Co.)   *SH 16, 27 mi. S*
Barroneña Ranch
The Barroneña Ranch is an important reminder of early South Texas ranching. Named for a creek (now called Los Machos) which traverses the property, the ranch was part of a larger tract owned by Diego Hinojosa, who received a grant of five leagues from the Republic of Mexico. In 1856, Hinojosa received a state of Texas patent for 2,237 acres of this land.

James O. Luby (1846–1932) later owned a part of the ranch. A native of England and a confederate veteran of the Civil War, Luby became the first county judge of Duval County in 1876.

Barroneña Ranch was purchased by J. M. Bennett (1831–1920) in 1905 and has remained in the Bennett family since that time. The nucleus of the ranch is a 19th century adobe house, reportedly a stage stop between Goliad and Laredo. Other structures include a native rock water trough and storage tank; a native rock wall more than one mile long; remains of a dipping vat and smokehouse; and rock foundations of other buildings, including a blacksmith shop.

Richard King, grandson of the founder of the King Ranch, leased the Barroneña Ranch in the 1920s. Santa Gertrudis cattle, developed by the King Ranch, were introduced here following World War II. (1989)

FRELSBURG (Colorado Co.)   *FM 109 at city limits*
Frelsburg
First German settlement in Colorado County. Founded in 1837 by William Frels who immigrated to Texas in 1834 and fought for independence, 1835–1836. Proposed site of Hermann University, first institution of higher learning sponsored by Germans. Chartered by the Republic of Texas in 1844, but never established.

FRIENDSWOOD (Galveston Co.)   *502 S Friendswood*
Friendswood
This community was founded in 1895 by a group of Friends (Quakers) led by F. J. Brown and T. H. Lewis. They acquired the land from J. C. League and named the settlement Friendswood.

From the very beginning, church and school were central to the life of this community. In 1900 an academy building was built on this site, with lumber from huge pine trees felled by the 1900 hurricane. The Friends Church, which until 1958 was the only church in the community, used the academy building for both worship and education. In the early years it provided the only secondary educational facilities for the surrounding area. The last school term was held in 1938, but the building continued to be used for worship until 1949 when it was replaced by a more modern structure.

The heritage of this community, received from its founders, is based on Christ's words: "Ye are my friends, if ye do whatsoever I command you." John 15:14

FRIONA (Parmer Co.) *US 60, .5 mi. E*
Friona
Originally called Frio, after Frio (cold) Draw, when established by XIT Ranch, in 1898, as a shipping point on recently built Pecos & Northern Texas Railroad.

In 1906, the George G. Wright Land Co. took options on area lands and initiated a colonization project, promising fertile land and a healthful climate to attract prospective settlers from Ohio to Kansas, and erecting a hotel, livery stable, and bank.

Name was changed to Friona when the post office opened, March 16, 1907, with Sarah D. Olson, postmaster. The first organized church was Union Congregational Church, June 1907. School opened in 1908, and was one of first districts in Texas to use buses, in 1917.

A controversy between Friona and Farwell over location of the county seat led to an election in 1913, won by Farwell, contested by Friona, and settled in 1916, by a court ruling favoring Farwell. By this time, S. A. Harris was publishing a newspaper, the "Friona Sentinel." The city was incorporated in 1928, and John W. White elected mayor.

Now a regional marketing center for agricultural and beef products, Friona claims the distinction of "Grain Sorghum Capital of the World." (1973)

FRISCO (Collin Co.) *SH 289, 4 mi. S in Lebanon*
The Shawnee Trail
In 1838, the Republic of Texas Congress appropriated money for construction of a north-south road opening the Northern Texas area to trade. The project leader, Colonel William G. Cooke, followed an existing Indian trail which reached from the Red River to Austin. A supply fort established on the river near the trading post of Holland Coffee was named for Captain William G. Preston, a veteran of the Texas Revolution, who was in charge of troops stationed there in 1840. The part of the road running south from the Red River to the Trinity River crossing was known as the Preston Road. At the Trinity crossing in 1841 John Neely Bryan began the settlement of Dallas.

By the 1850s, the road was known as the Shawnee Trail and was used by immigrants coming to Texas. It also served as a cattle trail, leading to northern markets. The number of cattle drives decreased as new trails were opened to serve the growing Texas Cattle Industry. Further decline occurred when rail lines were completed to the area in the 1870s.

Lebanon served as an assembly point for cattle drives on the Shawnee Trail. Bypassed by the Frisco Railroad in 1902, the town declined. The post office, opened in 1860, closed in 1905. (1980)

FRISCO (Collin Co.) *SH 289, NW corner of Gaylord and Preston Rd.*
Site of Lebanon
Settlers traveling to this area of Texas after it opened for settlement as part of the Peters Colony found free land, clear spring water and plenty of timber. Those who decided to stay named it Lebanon and began to establish homes and farms. On March 1, 1860, the U.S. Postal Service granted a post office to Lebanon, with Phillip Huffman serving as first postmaster. Although a general store begun by Z. T. Rainey in 1858 closed during the Civil War, other businesses soon were established. Located on the route of the historic Preston Road/Shawnee Trail, Lebanon was a popular stopping place for cattle drivers who used that road as their north-south route. Primarily a farming community, the town grew in the 1880s and 1890s to include a blacksmith shop, dry goods store, a saddlery, churches, doctors' offices, a hotel, tavern and other businesses. A two-story union school was built in 1885 to serve the schoolchildren in the community. In 1902, the St. Louis and San Francisco Railroad bypassed Lebanon, which resulted in an exodus of residents and businesses to the new railroad town of Frisco. The school closed in 1947, and by 1959 there were fewer than a dozen homes remaining in Lebanon. As the 21st century dawned, only three

buildings stood from the original townsite, but the history of Lebanon remains as a part of the urban and suburban development in this part of Collin County. (2002)

GAIL (Borden Co.)
FM 669 at US 180, Courthouse
Borden County
Originally a part of Bexar District. Created August 21, 1876. Organized March 11, 1891.

Named in honor of Gail Borden 1801–1874. Pioneer surveyor, newspaper editor, and inventor of the process of condensing milk. Gail, county seat.

GAIL (Borden Co.)
FM 669 at US 180 at Museum
1902–1904 Land Rushes
Cowboys and settlers fought here in early days for right to claim lands placed in public domain in 1902 by Texas courts. To keep land they were using, ranchers sent their men, wearing blue ribbon arm bands, to file claims at office of county clerk. Nesters, with red ribbons, rushed for same land. To avoid bloodshed, sheriff W. K. Clark disarmed them. For three days prior to deadlines, the cowboys and nesters had knockdown dragout fights at the filing window.

Later nesters starved out, because of droughts: land they took up reverted to grazing. (1970)

GAINESVILLE (Cooke Co.)
US 77/82, 1 mi. N
Butterfield Overland Stage Line
Gainesville was a station on the Southern Overland Mail Line (Butterfield Route), which provided semi-weekly mail and stage service between St. Louis and San Francisco, 1858–1861.

The line was 2,795 miles long—one of the longest stage transportation routes ever established. (1964)

GAINESVILLE (Cooke Co.)
SH 51, 1 mi. W at Elm Creek Bridge
Cooke County
Created March 20, 1848. Organized March 10, 1849. Named in honor of William G. Cooke, 1808–1847, captain of the "New Orleans Greys," 1835; assistant inspector general at San Jacinto, 1836; member of the Santa Fe Expedition, 1841; Secretary of War and Marine, 1845; adjutant general, 1846–1847. County seat, Gainesville. (1964)

GAINESVILLE (Cooke Co.)
US 82, 5 mi. E in roadside park
The Cross Timbers
Two long, narrow strips of timber extending parallel to each other from Oklahoma to Central Texas form a marked contrast to adjacent prairie.

The more fertile East Cross timbers begin here in Cooke County. Area was famous pioneer landmark as well as obstacle to travel because of its dense growth. It divided the hunting grounds of the Plains and East Texas Indians. Until 1870s it marked boundary of settlement, for Plains Indians avoided the timber. Forests' most important function was (and is) causing soil to retain water. (1970)

GAINESVILLE (Cooke Co.)
IH 35 at FM 1202, 5 mi. NW
Site of Camp Howze
(1 mi. W)
In operation from 1942 to 1946, Camp Howze served as an infantry training facility during World War II. It was named for General Robert Lee Howze (1864–1926), a native Texan whose distinguished career in the United States Army began with his graduation from West Point and included service in France, Puerto Rico, Germany, a South Dakota Indian war and the Philippine Insurrection, 1899–1902.

Clifford McMahon of the Gainesville Chamber of Commerce first contacted federal authorities with the idea of establishing a military installation here. Attracted by the community's active endorsement of the plan, the government activated Camp Howze on August 17, 1942, under the command of Colonel John P. Wheeler. In addition to infantry training, the base was also the site of a German prisoner of war camp and an air support command base, now part of the Gainesville Municipal Airport. Services provided for the soldiers included camp exchanges, libraries, chapels, theaters, service clubs and a base newspaper, the *Camp Howze Howitzer*.

The economic and social impact of Camp Howze on Gainesville was significant and was instrumental in the town's rapid growth and development. (1982)

GAINESVILLE (Cooke Co.)   *IH 35, Leonard Park at California St.*
The Great Hanging at Gainesville, 1862

Facing the threat of invasion from the North and fearing a Unionist uprising in their midst, the people of North Texas lived in constant dread during the Civil War. Word of a "Peace Party" of Union sympathizers, sworn to destroy their government, kill their leaders, and bring in Federal troops caused great alarm in Cooke and neighboring counties. Spies joined the "Peace Party," discovered its members and details of their plans. Under the leadership of Colonels James Bourland, Daniel Montague, and others, citizens loyal to the Confederacy determined to destroy the order; and on the morning of October 1, 1862, there were widespread arrests "by authority of the people of Cooke County." Fear of rescue by "Peace Party" members brought troops and militia to Gainesville, where the prisoners were assembled, and hastened action by the citizens committee. At a meeting of Cooke County citizens, with Colonel W. C. Young presiding, it was unanimously resolved to establish a citizens court and to have the chairman choose a committee to select a jury. Sixty-eight men were brought speedily before the court. Thirty-nine of them were found guilty of conspiracy and insurrection, sentenced, and immediately hanged. Three other prisoners who were members of military units were allowed trial by court martial at their request and were subsequently hanged by its order. Two others broke from their guard and were shot and killed. The Texas Legislature appropriated $4,500 for rations, forage used by state troops here during the unrest.   (1963)

GAINESVILLE (Cooke Co.)   *SH 51, Elm Creek Bridge*
Cooke County, C.S.A.

Military, defense center in Civil War. Cooke voted 221 to 137 anti-secession, yet nine military units served Confederacy from here. In constant danger of Federal or Indian attack, Col. Wm. C. Young of Cooke, with 1,000 men took Indian territory forts from Federals April–May 1861. Commissioners set up regular patrols, forted a home as refuge for dependents, and gave $4,000 for munitions and wool cards to make cloth. Cotton gin, grist mill, gunsmiths, blacksmiths made war goods. C.S.A. was furnished epsom salts from Indian Creek. Corn, beef, pork, wheat, other produce fed the military, home front. County swapped 25 steers for salt for dependent families. People worked hard, sacrificed much, protected homes of fighting men of Confederacy.

2nd Frontier Regiment

Organized Oct. 1863 with Gainesville as headquarters, the Second Frontier Regiment, Texas Cavalry C.S.A. guarded counties along Red River to keep down outlaws, Indians, deserters. Col. James Bourland (1803–1868) was appointed commander and it became known as "Bourland's Border Regiment." Union invasion from north of Red River was constantly threatened. These mounted troops patrolled, maintained posts along river and in Indian territory. Confederate Seminole troops served with the unit. Famous Confederate Indian Gen. Stand Watie and his Cherokee Brigade shared duty along perilous border. Bourland also worked with frontier regiment, state troops, that maintained line posts 100 mi. west, a day's horseback ride apart, from Red to Rio Grande Rivers, and with a state militia line 30 mi. to the west.   (1963)

GALVESTON (Galveston Co.)   *SH 87, NE at site of Pass Bolivar Peninsula*
Roll Over Fish Pass

This favorite spot of fishermen is so named because, on this narrow neck of land, freebooters rolled their barrels and supplies from the Gulf to Galveston Bay.

GALVESTON (Galveston Co.)   *1417 Ave. A*
Jean Lafitte

Notorious pirate. Settled here in 1817 with his buccaneers and ships; under Mexican flag, continued his forays against Spanish shipping in the Gulf.

On this site, he built his home, Maison Rouge (Red House), which was part of his fort; and upper story was pierced for cannon. It was luxuriously furnished with booty from captured ships.

Leaving Galveston in 1821, upon demand of the United States, he burned his home, fort and whole village; then sailed to Yucatan.

In 1870, present structure was built over old cellars and foundations of Maison Rouge.   (1965)

GALVESTON (Galveston Co.)   *2219 Market St.*
William Lewis Moody, Jr.
(January 25, 1865–July 21, 1954)
Famed for a long career of dynamic leadership in Galveston business, civic affairs, and philanthropy.

Born in Freestone County; son of William Lewis and Pherabe Elizabeth Bradley Moody. Educated at Virginia Military Institute, he later traveled and studied abroad before joining his father's cotton firm in Galveston in 1886. He organized in 1889 W. L. Moody and Co., a private bank (still operating). He founded American National Insurance Co. (1905); City National Bank, later called the Moody National Bank; National Hotel Co. (1930); and other firms. He owned *Galveston News* (Texas' oldest newspaper), *Galveston Tribune, Texas City Sun,* 11 ranches, and many other interests.

He took active part in relief and reconstruction after the disastrous Galveston hurricane of 1900.

He married Libbie Rice Shearn in 1890. Their children were Mary Elizabeth (Mrs. E. C. Northen), W. L., III, Shearn, and Libbie (Mrs. Clark W. Thompson).

Known as one of the ten richest men in America, W. L. Moody, Jr., in his lifetime gave the state a school for cerebral palsied children. With his wife he set up (1942) the Moody Foundation, which has since given millions of dollars for charitable, scientific, educational and religious purposes throughout Texas.   (1971)

GALVESTON (Galveston Co.)   *2618 Broadway*
The Moody Home
Family residence, W. L. Moody, Jr. Built about 1894, and for many years home of Mr. Moody, prominent financier and philanthropist who established the Moody Foundation.

Late Victorian architecture. Said to have been first Texas residence built on steel frame. Has magnificent stained glass windows, ornate ceilings, rare handcarved woodwork. A large handsome home, famed for its hospitality.   (1967)

GALVESTON (Galveston Co.)   *2217 Broadway*
J. F. Smith House
Designed by Nathaniel Tobey, Jr., and built in 1884 for the family of John Francis Smith. This house is an excellent example of Italianate architecture. Prominent features of the house include paired brackets, a bay window, balcony, and hood moldings over large windows. Smith, who founded the J. F. Smith & Bro. Hardware Company on the Strand, probably ordered much of the woodwork, including doors and windows, from supply catalogs.   (1990)

GALVESTON (Galveston Co.)   *1703 Broadway*
Adriance-Springer House
This house was built in 1914 for the family of businessman John Adriance, who was instrumental in Galveston's early development. It was sold in 1929 to business and civic leader Oscar Springer, whose family continued to live here until 1960. Designed by L. S. Green, the house reflects a mixture of styles and features an entry portico with colossal Doric order columns, a craftsman style gable, wraparound porch, porte cochere, and arched basement.   (1989)

GALVESTON (Galveston Co.)   *1427 Broadway*
St. Paul United Methodist Church
Founded in the late 1860s, St. Paul Methodist Church can trace its history through two earlier Methodist congregations in Galveston. Charter members of St. Paul Church included Methodists from the Reedy Chapel Methodist Church (originally part of the Ryland Chapel congregation), who broke away when that membership elected to join the African Methodist Episcopal denomination.

The Rev. Samuel Osborn served as first pastor of the new church. A sanctuary was built on the eastern end of the island on Avenue H between 8th and 9th Streets. A larger building was later erected to serve the growing congregation, but was destroyed in the 1900 storm.

Under the leadership of the Rev. Frank Gary, the congregation acquired property at this site and built a new sanctuary in 1902. The church has continued to thrive here, serving many generations of Galveston families. It is known locally as the "mother church" of Galveston's Wesley

Tabernacle United Methodist Church. St. Paul Methodist Church counts among its members descendants of some of its founding families. (1990)

GALVESTON (Galveston Co.) *1402 Broadway*
The Bishop's Palace
Built, 1886–1893, by Col. Walter Gresham, civic leader and U.S. congressman. Nicholas J. Clayton was architect. One of the most lavish and massive homes in U.S. House is a Victorian adaptation of Renaissance style.

Silver and onyx mantle in music room won first prize, 1886, at New Orleans Exposition. Mrs. Gresham painted murals, ceilings.

Catholic Diocese bought home, 1923, made one room into chapel with stained glass windows. (1967)

GALVESTON (Galveston Co.) *1114 Broadway (SH 87)*
Boddeker House
The son of German immigrants, Joseph Boddeker came to Galveston with his parents about 1850. After service in the Civil War, he worked as a riverboat pilot and purchased this lot for his family home in the 1870s. When the original Boddeker House was destroyed in the 1900 storm, Capt. Boddeker purchased and relocated this 1893 house from 12th and Sealy. His son James (1875–1940), who lived here with his wife, Elizabeth, was a successful businessman and civic leader, serving as county commissioner from 1912 until 1940. Upon his death, Elizabeth completed his term as commissioner, becoming the first woman in Galveston County to hold that post. (2001)

GALVESTON (Galveston Co.) *2106 Seawall Blvd., Moody Civic Center*
Galveston: Gateway to Texas
From the days of European conquest, the Gulf of Mexico was the main road to Texas. Some settlers of the 1820s even came by keelboat, going ashore along the way to kill game, in the same way an overland party would live off the country while traveling. Planters from the old South and some farmers from the mid-continent came by land. But roads, wet and rough, had too many rivers crossed only by costly, ill-tended ferries; and cutthroats haunted many of them.

Galveston in the 19th century was chief port of entry. It was sister city to New Orleans, so well organized was passage from one to the other. Texas ports of entry included Velasco, Quintana, Lavaca, Indianola, Matagorda, Point Isabel, Houston, and Corpus Christi. Yet Galveston—with the best natural harbor between Pensacola and Vera Cruz—dominated travel into Texas. This port welcomed statesmen, speculators, teachers, soldiers, clergymen, doctors, merchants, craftsmen, tourists, European immigration.

Col. Wm. Lewis Moody (1828–1920), a Virginian, landed here in 1852, entered business world, courageously led unit in the Civil War, founded a fortune. Gifts of his family to Texas for educational and humane purposes have included facilities at this site. (1965)

GALVESTON (Galveston Co.) *57th St., between Avenue S and Seawall Blvd.,*
entrance to Lake View Cemetery, at gravesite
Burial Site of David G. Burnet (1788–1870)
Provisional President of Texas (March 16, 1836–Oct. 22, 1836)
A man of strong principle who carried a gun in one pocket and a Bible in the other, Burnet acted as a cohesive force in the chaotic days of early Texas independence, though his dour, quick-tempered disposition kept him from ever winning wide popularity.

As an idealistic youth, he took part in the Miranda expeditions (1806 and 1808) to free Venezuela from Spain, almost losing his life to yellow fever.

He bought a trading post, 1817, in Louisiana, but had to sell it after developing tuberculosis. Though weak from the disease, he rode to West Texas, where he fell into the hands of unusually friendly Comanches. He lived with them for 18 months, thus becoming an expert on the pre-settlement days of these Indians.

Burnet began his statesman's career in 1833 when Texas was beginning her fight for independence from Mexico. In 1836, he ran as a compromise candidate for the presidency of the Republic of Texas and won by 6 votes. His interim government was mainly concerned with winning military victory and escaping, sometimes only by minutes, Mexican troops.

In later years he held various offices under the Republic and State of Texas. He married Hannah Este in 1830 and they had four children.

GALVESTON (Galveston Co.)   *2100 block of Seawall Blvd.*
Hotel Galvez
Built at a cost of $1,000,000, this hotel was financed by local businessmen and public subscribers to help the economy of Galveston following the 1900 hurricane. Completed in 1911, it was designed by the St. Louis firm of Mauran and Russell. The Spanish colonial revival styling includes a red tile roof and white stuccoed brick walls. The hotel and city are named in honor of Count Bernardo de Galvez (1746–1786), Spanish Governor of Louisiana and Viceroy of Mexico.

(1980)

GALVESTON (Galveston Co.)   *2100 block, Seawall Blvd.*
The Original Galveston Seawall
On Sept. 8, 1900 a devastating hurricane and tidal wave destroyed much of Galveston and left 6,000 persons dead. After the tragedy, the city appointed a board of three engineers, Brig. Gen. (Ret.) Henry M. Robert (1837–1923), author of *Robert's Rules of Order*, Alfred Noble, and H. C. Ripley, to devise protection from future storms. Work on their proposal, to be financed jointly by city, county, and state governments, was started in 1902. To prevent flood damage, buildings were jacked up and the surface of the entire city upgraded, increasing the elevation to a maximum of 12 feet above sea level. As a shield against high waves, a solid concrete wall was built along the gulf shore of the island.

The original section of the seawall, begun in Oct. 1902, stretched 3.3 miles. Founded on wooden pilings, the 17-foot high barrier was backed by a sand embankment and protected in front by stone riprap. The Gulf side of the wall curved outward to prevent water from washing over the top. Finished in July 1904, the seawall proved its value in 1915, when a hurricane more severe than the storm 15 years earlier did far less damage. Since then, the wall has been periodically lengthened. Freed from the threat of further destruction, Galveston has grown into a modern and prosperous city. (1975)

GALVESTON (Galveston Co.)   *Park at intersection of 13-mile Road*
and Termini Road
West Galveston Island
First known to world history in 16th century, from report of Spanish soldier Cabeza de Vaca, who was shipwrecked on this island in 1528. Area was also visited by French explorer La Salle in 1685. Second known Caucasian to live here was the buccaneer Jean Lafitte, who had to fight Karankawa Indians for site he chose as operating base for his pirate fleet in 1815 or 1816. In the 1820s, a debarkation point for illegal slave ships developed on West Island.

Humane and civilized traffic afterward found its way here. Stagecoach service was established in the 1850s from Galveston to Old Velasco (now Freeport) on a west beach road, with a ferry at San Luis Pass. An important lace manufacturing concern was located here, and by 1885 the Galveston & Western Railway carried visitors by the hundreds to a race track near the center of the island.

Since 1957, West Island has rapidly become a major recreational and resort area, with leisure homes fronting the Gulf, the canals, and the bay. There is still enough wilderness to attract migratory shore birds; more than 95 percent of the known species in America annually spend some time on this island. (1967)

GARDEN CITY (Glasscock Co.)   *SH 158 at FM 33*
Glasscock County
Created in 1887. Organized in 1893 with Garden City county seat. Named for George W. Glasscock (1810–1868), flatboating partner of Abraham Lincoln in Illinois. Came to Texas 1834 and fought 1835–1836 in the War of Independence from Mexico. Built first Central Texas flour mill, Williamson County. Georgetown was named for him. Was in Texas legislature 1864–1868.

Of the 254 counties, 42 bear Indian, French, Spanish names. Ten honor such colonizers as Stephen F. Austin, "Father of Texas." Twelve were named for Washington, Clay and other American patriots. Ninety-six were named for men like Glasscock who fought in the Texas War

194

of Independence at the Alamo, 15 dying at the Alamo, signed the Declaration of Independence or served as statesmen in the Republic of Texas. Twenty-three have the names of frontiers men and pioneers. Eleven honor American statesmen who worked for the annexation of Texas. Ten leaders in Texas since statehood, including jurists, ministers, educators, historians, statesmen, and 36 men prominent in the Confederacy during Civil War. Midland and eight others have geographical names. San Jacinto and Val Verde were named for battles, Live Oak and Orange, for trees, and Mason for a fort.

GARFIELD (Travis Co.)   *SH 71 E*
Haynie Chapel Methodist Church
Founded 1839 in the Republic of Texas by Rev. John Haynie (1786–1860). First church was of logs, and located a mile north on land of Andrew Deavers Houston. This building, the third, was put up in 1907.

Plaque erected by Houston descendants, Mr. and Mrs. E. W. (Nellie Houston) Schuhmann. History given by Rev. Olin W. Nail, present pastor. Awarded Medallion Plate.   (1964)

GARLAND (Dallas Co.)   *6th & Main Sts.*
Garland
Settlement of this area began in the 1840s. A small community named Duck Creek was established and by 1846 a log cabin was serving as a community center, school, and union church. Early businesses included a general store, grist mill, and cotton gin.

In 1886, the Gulf, Colorado, & Santa Fe Railroad built a line through Dallas County, passing about one mile east of Duck Creek. A new town, named Embree in honor of one of Duck Creek's early doctors, was laid out along the rail line. The Missouri, Kansas, & Texas Railroad built a second rail line north of the Santa Fe tracks. The original Duck Creek settlement declined in favor of New Duck Creek on the MKT Rail Line.

A U.S. post office was authorized for the area in 1887 and was positioned between the two towns. Named for U.S. Attorney General A. H. Garland, the site became a new town into which the earlier communities merged. The citizens voted to incorporate in 1891, and M. Davis Williams was elected first mayor.

Garland flourished in the early 20th century and survived the Great Depression. Rapid transportation and industrial growth following World War II changed the city's economic base. Garland continues to be an important part of Dallas County history.   (1991)

GARLAND (Dallas Co.)   *SH 78 & DeWitt Rd., 1 mi. NE*
William Sachse Cemetery
William Sachse, a native of Prussia, arrived in nearby Collin County in 1845 as a Peters colonist. He became a successful businessman, rancher, and trader, and participated in several cattle drives to Kansas. His business successes over time allowed him to acquire more than 5000 acres of land in Collin and Dallas Counties. In 1886, Sachse gave some of this land to the Gulf, Colorado & Santa Fe Railroad for a railway line and townsite. The community that grew up around the railroad was named Sachse in his honor. Sachse moved his family to the new town and soon set aside two acres of land for a church and this cemetery.

The graveyard has been used throughout its history as a public burial ground. The oldest marked grave, that of William Sachse, is dated 1899. Sachse's second wife, Martha (Frost), a number of their descendants, as well as many early settlers and their descendants also are buried here. Some of the family names recorded here are Salmon, Herring, Ingram, House, Harper, and Brand.

The William Sachse cemetery, with its ties to early settlement in this part of the state, is an important reminder of the area's heritage.   (1985)

GARWOOD (Colorado Co.)   *SH 71 at FM 333, 2 mi. N*
First Producing Gas
Well in Colorado County
(12 mi. W)
Completed on July 17, 1932, as Nelson No. 1 Well, at a depth of 4,052 ft.; was drilled by Coyle-Concord Oil Company, owner of 30,000 acres of block leases in area. Many other wells were soon drilled as a result of success here. Site called Garwood Field.

In 1932 no market was found for this gas. Two extensions of the field were later located and commercial outlets obtained. Gas production has contributed to prosperity of the county.

Texas reserves of natural gas are nearly 119 trillion cu. ft., or 42.3% of United States reserves.

(1967)

GATESVILLE (Coryell Co.) US 84, 2 mi. E
Coryell County
Formed from Bell County. Created February 4, 1854. Organized March 4, 1854. Named in honor of James Coryell, born in Tennessee in 1796. A member of the Bowie Expedition to the old San Saba silver mines in 1831. A Texas Ranger. Killed by Indians near Fort Milam, May 27, 1837. County seat, Fort Gates, 1854. Gatesville since.

GATESVILLE (Coryell Co.) US 84, 4.5 mi. SE
Site of Fort Gates
First settlement in Coryell County. Established by Brevet Colonel W. R. Montgomery, 8th U.S. Infantry, October 26, 1849, on the Military Post Road between Austin and Fort Graham as a protection of the frontier against hostile Indians. Named in honor of Collinson R. Gates, gallant officer in the Mexican War. Abandoned in March, 1852, as the frontier line had advanced further westward. Used as a place of defense by settlers during Indian raids. First seat of Coryell county February 4–May 27, 1854, when Gatesville was established.

GATESVILLE (Coryell Co.) SH 107, 9 mi. E
Pecan Grove Baptist Church
On August 7, 1882, this church was organized as Coryell Creek Baptist Church of Christ by Monroe M. Smith, James M. Davidson, Joe F. and Martha J. Alsup, and Cordelia C. Beaty, with the help of D. J. Hardin and the Rev. J. M. Wright. An additional seven members joined that day.

Early services were held at Blackfoot and Davidson Schools and at annual brush arbor meetings at Pecan Grove on the west side of Coryell Creek. In 1903, the congregation, then known as Coryell Creek Missionary Baptist Church, built a tabernacle on the east side of Coryell Creek on land donated by Frank M. Martin.

In 1929, the congregation changed its name to Pecan Grove Baptist Church and began building a sanctuary at this site. In 1930, the tabernacle was enlarged to accommodate the large number of people attending annual camp meetings. Church facilities have been enlarged and modernized over the years.

Pecan Grove, recognized by Baylor University for its support of ministerial students, has held memberships in the Leon River, Coryell, and Tri-Rivers Baptist Associations, and the Southern Baptist Convention. As many as six generations of some local families have been members of this congregation. Pecan Grove continues to serve the area with various outreach programs. (1994)

GAUSE (Milam Co.) US 79
The Town of Gause
William J. Gause (1829–1914), born in Alabama, moved to Texas in 1849, to the Brazos region in 1856, and to this locality in 1872. Buying lumber in Montgomery, he gave his friend Dan Fowler half in return for hauling it here. The two built the first homes in this settlement. In 1873, Gause gave right of way and 100 acres of land to the International & Great Northern Railroad, and the town was platted. Gause post office opened in 1874, with James S. Reynolds as postmaster. The I.G.N. freighted out great quantities of cotton, and the town thrived. Cotton gins, stores, blacksmith shops, a lumber yard, a bank, hotels, livery stables, a newspaper and other businesses were established. Besides W. J. Gause, civic leaders included Dr. J. E. Brown, Richard Cox, Dr. James Dollar, Lafayette Ely, Bill Faubian, Dan Fowler, J. C. Lister, C. C. Moore, Dr. John Porter, Frank Thomas, and T. L. Watts. Churches were organized and a Masonic Lodge chartered. The county's first independent school was established in Gause.

Good highways, mechanized farming, and decline of railroading halted commerce in the town of Gause. It survives, however, as a residential site chosen by descendants of the pioneers and by commuters to industrial plants and businesses in this vicinity. (1974)

GAUSE (Milam Co.)
US 79, 4.5 mi. SE
Site of Town of Nashville
Surveyed in the fall of 1835 as the capital of Robertson's colony. Named for Nashville Tennessee, where Sterling C. Robertson and many of his colonists had formerly lived.

Seat of Justice Milam Municipality 1836; Milam County, 1837. First home in Texas of George C. Childress, chairman of the committee who drafted the Texas Declaration of Independence.

GAY HILL (Washington Co.)
FM 390 in Gay Hill
Glenblythe Plantation, Home of
Thomas Affleck
In the 19th century, one of the world's foremost researcher-writers on agriculture and horticulture. Lived 1858–1868 on his 3,500-acre plantation 2 mi. S of here, developing famous "Central Texas Nurseries" and experimental fields for new plant varieties. On this property gained recognition as one of earliest promoters and developers of conservation farming.

Born 1812 in Scotland; came to the United States in 1832, soon starting in Mississippi one of the South's finest nurseries; gained wide fame as scientist and writer on agriculture. Before moving here, landscaped state capitol grounds for both Louisiana and Texas.

Surrounded Glenblythe Mansion and guest houses (2 mi. S) with ornamental gardens and greenhouses, vegetable garden, orchard, a church, hospital, day nursery, store, homes, workshop, stock pens, flour and lumber mills.

During Civil War (1861–1865) built ambulances, wagons; fed Waul's Legion in training camp near here. After the war, was key figure in rehabilitation of farming of Texas; made a trip to Europe to recruit settlers.

Died 1868, and was buried near his home. Writings, especially "Affleck's Southern Rural Almanac," were influential for years. His "Report on Agricultural Grasses" was a senate executive document of 1879.
(1967)

GENEVA (Sabine Co.)
SH 21 near bridge
Gaines Memorial Bridge
Named by the Highway Departments of Louisiana and Texas in honor of two brothers: James Gaines, who owned and operated a ferry here, 1819 to 1844, and was a signer of the Texas Declaration of Independence, and General Pendleton Gaines, an officer in the U.S. Army, prominent in Louisiana history, and who was stationed near here in 1836 to observe the Campaign in Texas.

GENEVA (Sabine Co.)
SH 21, 2 mi. W
County Line Baptist Church and Cemetery
This congregation began soon after the end of the Civil War in the freedmen's community known as Weeks Quarters (about 2 mi. S). Early prayer meetings and worship services were conducted in homes.

Led by the Rev. M. McBerry, the congregation built its first sanctuary in 1868. Worshipers came from a large surrounding area to attend services in the small frame building, which also served as a community schoolhouse. The church's name originated from its location near the Sabine-San Augustine county line.

In 1885, the members voted to relocate the church to the nearby Hankla Community, next to the County Line Cemetery (about ³⁄₁₀ mi. N). The oldest documented grave in the cemetery dates to 1902, although local oral tradition suggests burials occurred much earlier. Many early graves are unmarked.

In 1944, the congregation voted to move once again to this location. Since that time additional facilities have been built to serve the growing congregation. County Line Baptist Church continues to serve members from a large area in both San Augustine and Sabine Counties.   (1990)

GENEVA (Sabine Co.)
SH 21, 5.5 mi. W
McMahan's Chapel
The oldest Methodist church having a continuous existence in Texas. Organized as a "Religious Society," September, 1833, at the home of Colonel Samuel McMahan by the Rev.

James P. Stephenson (1808–1885), as a Methodist church July, 1834, by the Rev. Henry Stephenson. First building was completed in 1839 by the Rev. Littleton Fowler and given the name of McMahan's Chapel. Displaced by a new building in 1872 and again in 1900.

GENEVA (Sabine Co.) *SH 21, near post office*
In This Vicinity Was Historic Spanish Rancho Called El Lobanillo
Pueblo of Gil Ybarbo (1729–1809), where his ill mother and other refugees remained when Spain evacuated colonists from western Louisiana and East Texas in 1773. Granted 1794 to Juan Ignacio Pifermo, and inherited in early 1800s by John Maximillian (1778?–1866), this is now known as oldest continuously occupied site in East Texas. (1972)

GEORGE WEST (Live Oak Co.) *US 281, 23 mi. S*
Fort Ramirez
As late as 1920 dilapidated rock walls stood on this site known as Fort Ramirez. Treasure hunters pulled them down and workmen on the pipe-line passing near hauled them to the hollow below. Erected at an unknown date by two brothers named Ramirez, from whom Ramirena Creek derived its name. The structure is believed to be the first in what is now Live Oak County. It was combined ranch dwelling and fort. The owners were run off or killed by Indians in 1813. A full account of the fort and its traditions is given in "Coronado's Children" by J. Frank Dobie.

GEORGE WEST (Live Oak Co.) *US 281, 1.4 mi. S*
Live Oak County
Formed from Nueces and San Patricio Counties. Created February 2, 1856. Organized August 4, 1856. So named from its live oak trees. County seat, Oakville, 1856. George West, since 1919.

GEORGE WEST (Live Oak Co.) *Two locations: US 281, 16 mi.*
S in roadside park; and FM 3162, 6.9 mi. E
Old Dobie Ranch, Birthplace of
J. Frank Dobie (Sept. 26, 1888–Sept. 18, 1961)
A strong individualist and noted folklorist who added a new dimension to literature of Southwest. Collected and published more than 30 volumes of folk tales and legends. His works best preserve the heritage of people of the brush country—the rancher, the miner and the cowboy. (1970)

GEORGE WEST (Live Oak Co.) *US 281, 4.2 mi. N*
Near Crossing Of
Old Ox-Cart Road
From the early days of Spanish Colonial Texas well into statehood, the only "Highways" in the area were private dirt roads. Although many had names, others were simply called "Oxcart roads" for the sturdy Mexican carts so frequently seen on them.

In the 19th century this site was a junction for two of these roads, one extending from Brownsville to San Antonio, the other from Laredo to Goliad, then over to Indianola on to the Gulf. This strategic location helped Oakville grow in to a thriving town and become county seat of Live Oak County in 1856.

Ox-carts were unique in being constructed entirely of wood, fastened by wooden pins and rawhide thongs. The two wheels stood taller than a man and the bed was usually fifteen feet long, covered by a thatched roof. To stop the deafening squeak of the wheels, drivers greased the hubs with prickly pear leaves.

Pulled by several yoke of oxen, the carts usually traveled in groups. Their arrival meant fresh coffee beans, salt, and sugar for isolated settlers.

Although gradually replaced by wagons, carts were for two centuries almost the only freight vehicles in Texas. Reminders of their former importance long remained in the names of these two old roads. (1968)

GEORGETOWN (Williamson Co.)　　　　　　　*SH 29 4 mi. E of Liberty Hill*
and 11 mi. W of Georgetown
In This Vicinity
Manuel Flores
An emissary of the Mexican government, with a small group of men conveying ammunition to the Indians on the Lampasas River, was surprised by Rangers under Lieutenant J. O. Rice in May, 1839, and killed.　　　　　　　　　　　　　　　　　　　　　　　　　　(1936)

GEORGETOWN (Williamson Co.)　　　　　　　　　　*US 81 at IH 35 S*
Williamson County
Formed from Milam County. Created March 13, 1848. Organized August 7, 1848. Named in honor of Robert McAlpin Williamson, 1806–1859. Pioneer, editor, lawyer, patriot and statesman, veteran of San Jacinto. Georgetown, county seat.

GEORGETOWN (Williamson Co.)　　　　　*IH 35, West side near FM 2243*
(Leander Rd.) exit
Page-Decrow-Weir House
Built in 1903, this house was owned by a succession of area ranchers. J. M. Page had the home built for his family, but sold it to his brother-in-law Thomas Decrow in 1903. The home was purchased in 1920 by Horace M. Weir, and in the 1930s a polo training center was operated on the property. A Georgetown landmark, the Queen Anne style home features an octagonal tower, two-tiered wraparound porch, and a two-story bay window.　　　　　　　　　　(1988)

GEORGETOWN (Williamson Co.)　　　　　*IH 35, 1 mi. S at cave entrance*
Inner Space Cavern
(Laubach Cave)
Discovered in May 1963 on land of W. W. Laubach by core-drilling team, Texas Highway Department. Exploration began in November 1963 and continues to present.

Carved by water from Edwards limestone, cave lies along the Balcones Fault and is estimated to be 100 million years old. 95 percent of formations are still growing. Cave was apparently open during late Pleistocene (20,000–45,000 years ago), for bones of many extinct mammals have been found in debris cones filling former natural entrances. Remains of sabre-toothed cats and mammoths are represented.　　　　　　　　　　　　　　　　　　　　　　(1973)

GEORGETOWN (Williamson Co.)　　　　*SH 195, 5 mi. N in Berry's Creek*
James B. Williams 1821–1891
James B. Williams and his wife, Sarah Coffey, were born in Kentucky. Soon after their marriage, he led a wagon train headed for Texas. They reached Berry's Creek, Dec. 24, 1848, the same year that Williamson County was organized. In a few years, they moved to San Saba County where he served as sergeant in the 2nd Co. of Texas Rangers under his uncle, Capt. John Williams, the famous Indian Scout. After Capt. John was scalped by the Indians in 1862, James B. moved his family back to Glasscock Valley in Williamson County. They raised 10 children, most of whom raised large families and they in turn played an influential part in shaping the destiny of the fledgling Williamson County.　　　　　　　　　　　　　　　(1973)

GEORGETOWN (Williamson Co.)　　　　　　　　　　*SH 29 E, 7 mi.*
Jonah
On 1820s land grant to Nashville Colony, settled 1851 by wagon train from Arkansas, and called Water Valley. In 1884, repeated ill-luck in selecting an acceptable name for post office led to renaming the town Jonah. This was site of famous grist mill, 1865–1912.　　　　(1970)

GEORGETOWN (Williamson Co.)　　　　　　　　　　*SH 29, 9.5 mi. E*
Jonah Cemetery
Jonah Cemetery was established in 1902 when community leaders J. M. Barrington, W. S. McMakins, C. Brady, A. J. McDonald, and R. H. Northcutt purchased two acres near the San

Gabriel River to be used as a cemetery. Burials were free to area residents. The earliest marked grave is that of George N. Northcutt. Other graves of interest are those of Confederate veterans Isiah S. Hicks and M. G. Walton. Twin sisters Sarah E. (Yoes) Robbins and Margaret (Yoes) Barrington are interred here near many of their 22 children. One of the last physical remnants of a once-thriving rural community, the Jonah Cemetery continues to serve the area.   (1998)

GEORGETOWN (Williamson Co.)   *SH 29, at edge of town*
Old Dimmitt Home
Built in 1866 by John Jones Dimmitt; of native limestone hauled in by ox drawn wagons. Home of prominent citizens in Georgetown over 100 years.

Dimmitt—a surveyor, lawyer, mathematician, linguist, one time county attorney, and partner in building of Georgetown Railroad—was civic leader; instrumental in getting Southwestern University moved to Georgetown. Awarded Medallion Plate.   (1967)

GEORGETOWN (Williamson Co.)   *SH 29, 5 mi. E in roadside park*
Texan Santa Fe Expedition
A dramatic chapter in administration (1838–1841) of Republic of Texas President Mirabeau B. Lamar. Aware of United States-Mexico commerce crossing Texas by the Santa Fe Trail near the Canadian River, President Lamar sought similar trade advantages for Texas.

He initiated the Texan Santa Fe Expedition early in 1841, with Dr. Richard F. Brenham, Col. Wm. G. Cooke and Jose Antonio Navarro as commissioners. Cooke began recruiting in April, forming an artillery and five infantry companies. Remainder of 321 members included merchants (with $200,000 worth of goods), teamsters, guides and others. George W. Kendall, of the New Orleans "Picayune," joined to write classic book on the venture. Travel was by 21 slow ox-wagons.

First day's March, June 19, 1841, ended on the San Gabriel, and expedition's campsite is near here.

Before reaching the Santa Fe Trail some 600 miles north, the men were to have torturing experiences with drouth and unknown terrain. Ill from hardships, the group was betrayed into the hands of Mexican authorities and sent as prisoners to Mexico City. However, this penetration of upper Texas gave the republic stronger claims to her northern lands.   (1970)

GEORGETOWN (Williamson Co.)   *SH 29, 3.2 mi. E*
Mankins Crossing
(100 yards W)
This historic crossing on the San Gabriel River was named for pioneer settler Samuel Mankins, who purchased land along the river in 1849. The limestone bed in the river provided a convenient crossing for area farmers. A nearby community included a school, church, and cotton gin. A 1914 concrete and gravel causeway was replaced by a state highway department concrete bridge in 1931. After the highway department built a new bridge on higher ground at Highway 29 in 1958, the Mankins Crossing Bridge became a popular recreational site for area residents.   (1990)

GEORGETOWN (Williamson Co.)   *SH 29, 3.2 mi. E*
The Double File Trail
Laid out about 1828 by Delaware Indians, "The Double File Trail" got its name because two horsemen could ride it side by side. The Delawares carved this trace migrating ahead of expanding white settlements. They moved from what they called "The Redlands" in East Texas to Mexico near present Nuevo Laredo. Of the 200 to 250 families reported in East Texas in the 1820s, only about 150 remained after the move. Early sites in Williamson County were settled where this trail crossed waterways. Texas Rangers and the Sante Fe Expedition also traveled the track.   (1978)

GERONIMO (Guadalupe Co.)   *SH 123, .25 mi. S*
Navarro School
The original Navarro School, named for early Texas leader Jose Antonio Navarro, was a one-room building located about one-half mile northeast of this site in 1889. A second structure was added in the early 1900s. In 1912, the Navarro Agricultural High School was built on land purchased from L. H. Heinemeyer. It was replaced in 1953 by new elementary and high school facilities on this site. Sports and other extra-curricular activities were established as the school grew. For over a century Navarro School has served students in the Geronimo area.   (1989)

GIDDINGS (Lee Co.)

US 290, 2.3 mi. W

Lee County

Located on Old San Antonio Road, on land surveyed in 1821 as part of the original colony of Moses and Stephen F. Austin.

In 1854 became site of major settlement by Wends, from Northern Europe, under the leadership of Pastor Johann Kilian. Had only school in the U.S. that taught in the Latin-like Wendish language.

County created from parts of Washington, Fayette, Bastrop and Burleson. Organized in 1874. Named for Robert E. Lee (1807–1870), General of the Army of Northern Virginia in the Southern Confederacy, 1862–1865.

Giddings is the county seat.   (1965)

GIDDINGS (Lee Co.)

FM 2239, 6 mi. S;
1.8 mi. from junction with FM 488

Serbin

Trilingual (Wendish-German-English) community founded 1854 by 588 Wends under leadership of the Rev. John Kilian. The Rev. Kilian (Evangelical Lutheran) named place Serbin because the Wends were descendants of Serbs.

A thriving town 1865–1890; had grocery, dry goods, jewelry, drug and music stores; shops of wagon maker, blacksmith, saddler; post office, 3 doctors, 2 dentists.

On Smithville-Houston Oxcart Road—sending out cotton, other produce, and hauling in staples. Decline began about 1890 as railroads bypassed settlement by several miles.   (1969)

GIDDINGS (Lee Co.)

US 77 at E. Hempstead

City of Giddings

County seat of Lee County. Named for Jabez D. Giddings (1814–1878), of Washington County, one of four brothers from Pennsylvania who were Texas transportation pioneers and business leaders.

The town was established as a shipping point when Houston & Texas Central Railroad (in which J. D. Giddings was a stockholder) reached here in 1871. A second and third railroad (San Antonio & Aransas Pass, 1889, and Hearne & Brazos Valley, 1913) increased city's prestige. Commission form government was adopted in 1913. A diversified economy developed.   (1971)

GIDDINGS (Lee Co.)

In roadside picnic area on SH 21,
4 mi. from Bastrop at Lee County border

King's Highway—El Camino Real—Old San Antonio Road

First opened by Louis de St. Denis, 1715, route from Mexico to Louisiana.   (1918)

GILMER (Upshur Co.)

5.5 mi. SE

Indian Rock Village

An ancient Indian people, their name unknown, located this rock suited to their need and caused it to serve them in preparing food. Without tools but with great patience and skill, they fashioned these Stone Age mortars in which to grind their corn. Their successors in the land the Texans of 1936, salute the industry and skill of these original inhabitants.

GILMER (Upshur Co.)

SH 155, 12 mi. SW

Upshur County

Named in honor of Abel Pucker Upshur, 1790–1844.

Distinguished debater and orator as Secretary of State under President John Tyler.

He began negotiations in 1843 for the annexation of Texas. Gilmer, the county seat.

GILMER (Upshur Co.)

SH 155, 8 mi. NE Gilmer

Old Coffeeville, C.S.A.

Ferry Point near this site, on Big Cypress. Important town of 1850s, with an academy, 2 dry goods stores, 2 groceries, drug store, 3 doctors, Methodist and Presbyterian churches, a hotel and Masonic lodge.

During Civil War, lived up to its name, selling coffee when other towns had none.

Had a Confederate camp of instruction, one of three in Upshur County, established in response to June 8, 1861, call of Governor Edward Clark for such camps to be set up at expense of local citizens. Trained infantry and cavalry.   (1965)

GILMER (Upshur Co.)   *US 271, S city limits*
Gilmer
Founded 1846. Named for Thomas W. Gilmer, U.S. Secretary of the Navy and ardent champion of annexation for Texas.

Supply, training, production and educational center during the Civil War.

Farming, lumbering and oil hub. Home of famous annual yamboree, Sweet Potato Festival.

GILMER (Upshur Co.)   *SH 154, E Gilmer city limits*
Meshack Roberts
A faithful slave. Came to Gilmer with his master, O. E. Roberts before 1850. While Mr. Roberts was away in the Civil War, ran the farm and looked after the family. To get money to finance farm costs, shod horses for soldiers and others, baked and sold ginger cakes. Was example of the sincere loyalty found over the South.

At war's end, master gave him freedom, land and material to build a home. Later, moved to Marshall, where served in the Texas Legislature. In 1882, helped establish Wiley College for Negroes.

GILMER (Upshur Co.)   *SH 155, south edge of town*
Gilgal Baptist Church
In 1865, the Rev. John Baptist led the founding of this congregation. The members built a brush arbor here and chose the name "Gilgal" after the site of the Israelites' first encampment in the Promised Land.

Tom Littlepage gave two acres for the church grounds and for a black school. Later, three acres were purchased from Judge J. R. Warren. The first frame church building was erected here in 1872 during the ministry of the Rev. J. H. Hill.

In 1900, after serving this fellowship, the Rev. W. L. Dickson founded an orphanage, fulfilling his lifelong dream. The Dickson Colored Orphans Home, near Gilmer, operated for years before the State Government took charge and moved the facility to Austin.

The Rev. S. H. Howard served longer and baptized more members than any other pastor of this congregation. About 1905, during Rev. Howard's ministry, this structure was completed. The building was veneered with brick during the pastorate of an evangelist, the Rev. H. W. Gray. The first fulltime minister, the Rev. Floyd D. Harris, led in the building of the educational annex. A parsonage was constructed during the pastorate of the Rev. U. L. Sanders.   (1979)

GILMER (Upshur Co.)   *US 271, 5 mi. N*
Ben Phillips Place
Built 1872 with square nails, broadax hewn boards. Center for talk of politics and news. "A stranger never passed this home." Many marriages performed here by Ben F. Phillips (1845–1927), Church of Christ minister, student of politics, philosopher, Confederate veteran. He represented Upshur-Camp Counties, 1890-94, in Texas legislature. Married Mattie Fambrough (1856–1937) and had nine daughters. Awarded Medallion Plate.   (1964)

GILMER (Upshur Co.)   *US 271 right-of-way, 8 mi. S*
West Mountain Cemetery
Part of a Republic of Texas land grant formerly occupied by Caddo and Cherokee Indians, this cemetery was established in the mid-1850s by plantation owner Alpha Phillips. The first grave, that of his father, William, is marked with a stone cairn. The family cemetery came to be used by neighbors, West Mountain Community residents, and transients. A volunteer association was begun in the 1920s to maintain the grounds, and its members have added acreage to the graveyard over the years. Originally known as Old Phillips Cemetery, it has been called West Mountain Cemetery since 1933.   (1985)

GILMER (Upshur Co.)   *US 271 in S section of Gilmer at site*
Site of the Pioneer
Dickson Orphanage
Only home in Texas for Negro orphans for thirty years, 1900–1929. Founded by W. L. Dickson, Negro Baptist minister, only superintendent home ever had.

Orphans remained here until they reached 21, unless adopted or indentured by good families. A choir of children made good-will trips to raise funds.

In Aug., 1929, home was deeded to the State, together with 700 acres of land and 27 buildings. Name was then changed to the Gilmer State Orphanage for Negroes, which ran until 1943, when the children (about 180) moved to State Home in Austin.   (1968)

GILMER (Upshur Co.)   *US 271, 11.6 mi S*
The John O'Byrne Home
Social, cultural, political center. Built 1888 in the O'Byrne's Mill settlement that included sawmill, planer, grist mill, cotton gin.

O'Byrne, Irish emigrant, father of 13, built first Catholic church in Upshur and also started first school in community. Awarded Medallion Plate.   (1964)

GILMER (Upshur Co.)   *SH 155, 9.5 mi. SW*
New Hope
Missionary Baptist Church
Organized September 22, 1855, with 15 charter members, in New Hope community (4 mi. NW). Monthly meetings were held in a one-room log school. The building, with 2 acres of land, was given to the church in 1872.

A new sanctuary erected in 1883 was torn down and rebuilt at Crossroads community (2 mi. NW), 1914.

In 1950 the church purchased an acre of land at the present site. A new building was erected, again using lumber from the old structure. Many present members are descendants of people who composed original congregation.   (1970)

GILMER (Upshur Co.)   *SH 154 at FM 1002, 16 mi. W at site*
Town of Rhonesboro
Founded 1902; named for W. M. Rhone, only sawmill operator in area until 1901, when arrival of Marshall & East Texas Railroad created a town which grew to have 15 sawmills, 10 stores, 2 churches, a school, hotel, bank, gin, and cotton yard. Mill operators were Connally; Barton and Smith; McWhorter; Cone and Watkins; Whitter; Dacus; Waterman; Nolan; James; Swann; Beavers and Meek; P. K. Williams; M. C. and F. C. Florence; Roger and J. O. Schrum.

After pine forest here was depleted (1917), the mills moved and the railroad was abandoned.   (1967)

GILMER (Upshur Co.)   *SH 155 N at Coffeeville Cut-Off*
C.S.A. Camp Talley
Camp of instruction. Set up near Old Coffeeville soon after governor's June 8, 1861, proclamation requesting voluntary popular support for troop training. Merchants were to give goods; farmers, food; laborers, their work; camp officers, leadership. Trainees received no pay until mustered into the Confederate Army.   (1964)

GILMER (Upshur Co.)   *SH 155, 14 mi. NE*
Tarver's Ferry
(Site ⁹⁄₁₀ mi. E)
Once located at a strategic crossing of Big Cypress Creek, this pioneer ferry transported settlers moving west into Texas through populous Jefferson, on Big Cypress Bayou. Those going to the interior of Texas often came by horse or oxen, stopping for provisions at nearby town of Coffeeville. The ferry operator probably was James L. Tarver, who lived on Coffeeville Road, 1860s.

Many years before, the Caddo Indians forded stream at this same point in their travels.

By 1867 a bridge was built at the crossing and the ferry was no longer needed.   (1968)

GILMER (Upshur Co.)
FM 1844, SE via Lease Road

Upshur County Discovery Well
J. D. Richardson No. 1

Completed May 6, 1931; first of 4,000 county wells that produced over 225,000,000 barrels of oil. Drilled by Mudge Oil Co.; bought by General American Oil Co. (1952).

Total depth of well: 3754 ft., initial daily production: 35,000 barrels of oil and 10,000,000 cu. ft. of gas. Contractor was Clark and Cowden Drilling Co.

Drilling supervisor: T. P. Kirk; Dave McCullough and R. D. Kirk, drillers. Crew: Jess Wright, John Bloomfield, W. B. Stroheim, Grady Williams, R. E. Powers, C. O. Kirk, W. D. Emerson, Tommie Thompson.

Is an extension of East Texas Oil Field, one of world's richest. (1967)

GIRVIN (Pecos Co.)
FM 11, 20 mi. NW, 3 mi. N

Horse Head Crossing on the Pecos River

Here crossed the undated Comanche Trail from Llano Estacado to Mexico. In 1850 John R. Bartlett, while surveying the Mexican boundary, found the crossing marked by skulls of horses; hence the name "Horse Head." The Southern Overland Mail (Butterfield) Route, St. Louis to San Francisco, 1858–1861, and the road west from Fort Concho crossed here. The Goodnight-Loving Trail, established in 1866 and trod by tens of thousands of Texas longhorns, came here and turned up east bank of the Pecos for Fort Sumner and into Colorado. (1936)

GIRVIN (Pecos Co.)
FM 11, 10 mi. N

Horse Head Crossing
(2 Miles NE)

Famed ford of the Pecos River, named for abundance of horse and mule skulls lining the banks in the 19th century. Many water-starved animals, stolen in Mexico by Indians and driven along the Comanche War Trail, died after drinking too deeply from the river.

After the California gold strike in 1848, Horse Head Crossing became a major landmark on the trail west, as it provided the first water for about 75 miles on the route from the East. Emigrants arriving here either turned northwest along the river or crossed and continued southwest to Comanche Springs at Fort Stockton. In 1858, the crossing became an important stop on the Butterfield Overland Mail Route from St. Louis to San Francisco. An adobe stage stand was built and a ferry put into operation, but both were abandoned in 1861, when mail service was terminated.

In late 1862, during the Civil War, Federal forces kept a close watch at the crossing in reaction to a threatened Confederate invasion. Cattle began to be trailed across the Pecos in 1864, and in 1866, Charles Goodnight and Oliver Loving blazed their famous trail, which came to this point and turned upriver.

Completion of two railroads across West Texas in the early 1880s caused abandonment of the crossing. (1974)

GLADEWATER (Gregg Co.)
US 80 near Glade Creek

Gladewater

Founded as St. Clair, about 3 miles east. Moved to present site on Glade Creek and T & P Railway, 1872. Population grew from 500 to 7000 after oil was discovered in 1931. It became hub of production and refining operations.

Manufacturing, clothing, medical, farming and dairy center.

Home of annual East Texas Quarter Horse Show. Has world's richest self-supporting cemetery.

Round-Up Association sponsors June rodeo, nationally known, in unique arena—an abandoned crude oil storage pit. (1965)

GLADEWATER (Gregg Co.)
2.5 mi. S, Country Club Rd. &
SH 135, Shepperd Family Cemetery

John Ben Shepperd (October 19, 1915–March 8, 1990)

Gladewater native John Ben Shepperd was appointed Texas secretary of state in 1950. Elected attorney general in 1952 and 1954, he retired from public office in 1957 and moved to Odessa.

He became a prominent insurance, banking, and petroleum executive. At the request of governors and presidents, he served on 7 state and national boards, including those concerned with the arts and historic preservation. He was Texas and U.S. Jaycees president. (1992)

GLEN ROSE (Somervell Co.) *SH 144, 4 mi. N*
Squaw Creek Indian Fight, 1864
Civil War frontier victory, near this site. About 25 raiding Indians jumped a fox hunter, Rigman Bryant, killed him, shot his dog, stole his horse. That afternoon the Indians and stolen horses were seen by a minister, Silas Scarborough, W. C. Walters and a Negro bringing home a turn of meal from the gristmill. Scarborough and Walters headed into a cedar brake. The Indians urged the Negro to join them, shot him full of arrows when he refused. In a few hours the Cavalry attacked the Indians, recovered the horses, killed one Indian, chased the others away. One settler was shot. In a week the wounded Negro died.

Many of the 1848–1861 settlers on the Paluxy and Squaw Creek were away in the Confederate Army. Very young boys and elderly men joined defense forces. Some drew military duty for 10 days, were off 10 days to look after mills, cattle, horses and farms.

For safety, women dressed as men while their sons, husbands and fathers were away. At times 50 to 100 tents were used in hasty "forting up" of families.

During the war, Alex McCammant established county's first tannery, using cedar leaves in processing hides. For cloth making, county's first cotton was grown. (1965)

GLEN ROSE (Somervell Co.) *US 67, 8 mi. E*
Barnard's Trading Post No. 2
The Torrey brothers of Connecticut and their childhood friend George Barnard, with President Sam Houston as a partner, contracted to build a series of trading posts along the Brazos River in 1843. Barnard's friendly manner made the Indians his friends, paving the way for more peaceful frontier settlement. In 1846, George ransomed a young girl, Juana Cavasos, from a group of Comanches at the post on Tehuacana Creek near Waco for $300. By 1847, she had married his brother Charles.

In 1849, Charles and George established a post within this valley where Charles and Juana would live. In view of Comanche Peak in modern-day Hood County, the second post was four miles north of this site and near a Shawnee-Delaware village, trading goods from a bulletproof "dog-run" log house, the brothers did an excellent business, and Juana's influence on the region equaled theirs. Two Anglo communities sprang up in the area: George's Creek and Fort Spunky.

The government relocated the area's Indian population to Oklahoma in 1859; the need for a trading post dwindled. 1860 found Charles and Juana beginning a community on the Paluxy River, where he built a large stone gristmill. The town that grew around the mill was called Barnard's Mill, later renamed Glen Rose. (1998)

GLEN ROSE (Somervell Co.) *US 67, 2 mi. W*
Booker Home
This home was built in the early 1870s by William G. McCamant, who came to Texas about 1856. McCamant, who had worked for the creation of Somervell County, was appointed one of the county's first commissioners. The house was sold to Civil War veteran George L. Booker in 1896, during his 36-year tenure as county surveyor. The house features 18-inch thick walls made of limestone that was quarried nearby. The chimneys on either end are typical of 1870s frontier homes. (1963)

GLIDDEN (Colorado Co.) *US 90 at 8th St.*
Glidden
Before the railroad came to Colorado County, this area was the origin of several cattle drives to northern markets. Early settlers in the region were area gravel industry pioneer J. N. Mahon; John Turnbough, a contractor who came in 1877; rancher J. L. Townsend, who purchased land in 1879 and later served as Colorado County sheriff; T. J. Oakes, A. A. Oakes, and A. J. Folts, founders of a mercantile business that remained in operation for more than 100 years; and the L. H. Schulenburg family, who developed the first addition to Glidden.

In 1882, T. J. Oakes sold land to the Galveston, Harrisburg & San Antonio Railway Company. A switchyard, depot, roundhouse, turntable, water well, and section house were built. H. T.

Youens was station agent in 1885. The townsite of Glidden, named for railroad engineer F. G. Glidden, was platted that year and quickly developed as a rail center for the surrounding area.

Many Scotch-Irish and English railroad workers were attracted to Glidden during its early years. In 1888, the post office was established, and by 1897 a school had opened. Although Glidden has continued as a railroad town, many changes have taken place in the rail industry and in the community. The history of Glidden is an important part of Colorado County's heritage.   (1985)

GOLDSMITH (Ector Co.)   *SH 158, 6 mi. E*
North Cowden
Site of Ector County's second big oil strike. Named for ranching family of John M. Cowden, an 1885 Permian Basin settler. One of 4 brothers, ranching community leaders on Texas frontier.

Oil and gas development began here with the L. No. 1 discovery. Post office granted 1947. Town continues as a Permian Basin petroleum source. (Only the site now remains.)

GOLDTHWAITE (Mills Co.)   *US 84, .4 mi. N*
Mills County
Formed from Brown, Comanche, Hamilton and Lampasas Counties. Created March 15, 1887. Organized August 30, 1887. Named in honor of John T. Mills, 1817–1871.

Judge of the Third and Seventh Judicial Districts in the Republic of Texas.

Goldthwaite, county seat.

GOLDTHWAITE (Mills Co.)   *Loop 15, US 183*
Mills County Jail, 1888
First structure built by newly organized county, before county seat was chosen. Awarded Medallion Plate.   (1965)

GOLDTHWAITE (Mills Co.)   *US 183 right-of-way, 7 mi.*
S in Lady Bird Johnson Roadside Park
The San Saba Peak
Rising to an altitude of 1,712 feet, San Saba Peak is an oblong promontory with rimrock edges on the north and west sides. The Spanish governor of Texas, Don Juan Antonio Bustillo y Cevallos, named the ancient landmark in 1732. Tales of lost silver mines have centered on the surrounding area for centuries. Inhabited by early Indians, San Saba Peak has been a landmark for pioneers, surveyors, and cowboys; the site of battles between Indians and early settlers; a signpost on the Fort Phantom Hill supply road; a register for Western travelers; and a setting for Easter services.   (Texas Sesquicentennial 1836-1986)

GOLDTHWAITE (Mills Co.)   *FM 574 at US 183*
The Regency Suspension Bridge
(Near Extinct Town of Regency, 22 mi. SW)
This area's first Colorado River bridge was at Regency, on Mills-San Saba County line. Built 1903, it served ranchers and farmers for going to market, but fell in 1924, killing a boy, a horse, and some cattle. Its successor was demolished by a 1936 flood. With 90 percent of the work done by hand labor, the Regency suspension bridge was erected in 1939. It became the pride of the locality, and youths gathered there in the 1940s to picnic, dance, and sing. Bypassed by paved farm roads, it now (1976) survives as one of the last suspension bridges in Texas.   (1976)

GOLDTHWAITE (Mills Co.)   *US 84, 7 mi. E*
Center City Community
Settled in 1854 by the families of William Jenkins and David Morris (1811–1889), this community was called "Hughes Store" after W. C. Hughes and his wife opened a store here in the 1870s. They platted a townsite in 1876, hoping to attract the railroad and to become county seat. An ancient live oak (l00 yds. S), by tradition once considered the center of Texas, was site of temporary court and school sessions and religious services. Renamed "Center City," this thriving town boasted several stores and businesses until the railroad bypassed it in 1885. The post office remained until 1920.   (1977)

GOLIAD (Goliad Co.)   *US 59, 4.5 mi. W*
Goliad County
First known to Spanish settlers as Nuestra Señora de Loreto, later called La Bahía del Espiritu Santo.

Established as a mission in 1749. Became a strategic fort under Spanish, Mexican, Texas occupancy, 1810–1821, 1835–1836. Name changed to Goliad and created a Mexican municipality in 1829. Scene of massacre of Fannin and his command in 1836.

Organized as a county, 1836, with town of Goliad as the county seat.

Home of Confederate General Hamilton P. Bee. From population of 3,384, county sent several army companies to the Civil War.   (1965)

GOLIAD (Goliad Co.)   *US 77A, 1 mi. S, Goliad State Park*
Site of the
Mission Nuestra Señora del
Espíritu Santo de Zuñiga
First established at the site of La Salle's fort on Garcitas Creek, Victoria County, among the Coco, Cujanes, Karankawa and other Indian tribes in 1722. Moved to Mission Valley, Victoria County, on the Guadalupe River among the Jaranames and Tamiques in 1726. Located on the present site in 1749 for the same Indian neophytes. Secularized in 1794. Here Franciscan friars attempted to civilize and Christianize even the cannibalistic Indians of the region.   (1965)

GOLIAD (Goliad Co.)   *US 77A, 1 mi. S, Goliad State Park*
Mission Nuestra Señora del Espíritu Santo de Zuñiga
Mission of Our Lady of the Holy Spirit of Zuñiga
Founded in 1722 by the Aguayo Expedition on "La Bahía del Espiritu Santo" (the Bay of the Holy Spirit), present Lavaca Bay. This mission reflects its former site in the popular name, "La Bahía." Its formal name (in part) honored Baltasar de Zuniga, Viceroy of New Spain.

Because of threats from the French and the Indians, Spain founded this mission and its auxiliary fort, Presidio Nuestra Señora de Loreto de La Bahía (now ¼ mi. SE) to defend its territory and convert the natives.

Difficulties, however, caused both to be moved, in only four years, to the Guadalupe River, and again in 1749 to this site on the San Antonio River.

At its peak of success the mission possessed huge herds of cattle and supplied settlements in Mexico, as well as missions in present Texas.

In 1758 about 180 persons resided at the mission and fort. All about were Indian "Jacales," crude clayplastered brush huts thatched with grass. Spacious grazing lands and fertile fields surrounded the area, where colonists had formed a small community.

After a general decline caused the mission to be secularized in 1830, it fell into ruin. In 1932, this land was deeded to the state by Goliad County. The mission complex was partially restored, 1936–1939.   (1969)

GOLIAD (Goliad Co.)   *US 59, 4 mi. W at site*
Site of Mission
Nuestra Señora del Rosario
(Mission Our Lady of The Rosary)
Founded in 1754 for the Cujane Indians. Capt. Manuel Ramirez de la Piseina, commander of nearby Presidio la Bahía, named this mission for his parish church in Spain, and Fray Juan Dios Camberos ministered to the first converts here. The Indians were taught crop-raising. In the years following, much livestock, including 30,000 head of cattle, belonged to Rosario. But these, along with Indian land at the mission, had to be surrendered later to the Spanish crown. In 1807 Rosario was permanently abandoned and its lands were distributed to Spanish settlers.   (1969)

GOLIAD (Goliad Co.)   *US 183/77A, ¼ mi. S in Goliad State Historical Park*
Cattle Drive from La Bahia
After Spain joined the American colonists in declaring war on England in 1779, Spanish soldier Bernardo de Galvez traveled to New Orleans to raise an army. Aware of the great number of

207

wild cattle in Texas from his time spent stationed in the region, Galvez asked the Spanish governor of Texas to send cattle to feed his troops. As a result, about 10,000 head of cattle from Texas missions and ranches were assembled at Presidio La Bahia. Between 1779 and 1782, in what is believed to be the first major Texas cattle drive, cattle were herded from La Bahia to Spanish soldiers preparing to fight in the American Revolution along the Gulf Coast.   (1999)

GOLIAD (Goliad Co.)   *US 183, Goliad State Park*
Judge James Arthur White and the Civilian Conservation Corps at Goliad State Park
Mississippi native and Goliad County Judge James Arthur White (1878-1953) possessed a fervent interest in Texas history, notably that of his adopted city of Goliad. He began in 1928 to organize support for a state park to protect Goliad's many significant historic sites. Judge White drafted a bill in 1931 to create the park and a state-funded bridge and highway (later U.S. 183). Despite the bleak financial prospects of the Depression era, Judge White secured funding and labor from the Federal Civil Works Administration in 1933. When funds were expended by 1934, White applied to the Civilian Conservation Corps (CCC) program. Preliminary study of the site began in March 1935. Forty cottages, each to house six men, were constructed in May. The first CCC enrollees to arrive were veterans of the Spanish American War, the Boxer Rebellion in China and World War I. They had their own newspaper, "The Goliad Veteran," and their evening schedules included an extensive educational program. Historians and architects traveled the U.S. and Mexico researching Spanish Colonial Mission architecture. Supervised by National Park Service architects and local craftsmen, the CCC workers ultimately reconstructed a school-workshop, church and granary at Mission Espiritu Santo and also erected maintenance and shop buildings, a latrine, custodian's lodge, museum and administration building and developed a state park road and picnic facilities. Judge White served on the Texas Centennial Commission, and through his influence Goliad received $100,000 in state and federal funds for Memorial Auditorium (1937) and a burial monument for Col. J. W. Fannin and his men (1939). The CCC camp was closed by June 1941 due to the threat of World War II.   (2000)

GOLIAD (Goliad Co.)   *1 mi. S, US 77A, Goliad State Park*
Aranama College
Named for 18th century Indian converts of mission Espiritu Santo de Zuniga.
A men's college. Founded 1852 by Western Presbytery of Texas. Used buildings of old mission plus funds given by Goliad. Taught Latin, Greek, geography, surveying, bookkeeping, writing, reading, elementary and higher mathematics, English grammar and orthography.
Closed like most of Texas 25 colleges after the Civil War began (1861) and most students joined the Confederate Army. Had its buildings wrecked by the great storm of 1886.   (1965)

GOLIAD (Goliad Co.)   *US 183, W side, 1 mi. S at Goliad State Park*
Battle of Coleto and Goliad Massacre
After the fall of the Alamo, March 6, 1836, Colonel James Walker Fannin, with about 400 soldiers, mostly volunteers from the United States in the Texas War for Independence, was ordered by Texas General Sam Houston to retreat from Goliad to Victoria.
March 19, the heavy Mexican force of General Urrea surrounded the withdrawing Texas contingent near Coleto Creek, and bitter fighting ensued. Fannin's volunteers hurled back the assaults of the Mexican force. On the following day, faced with several times their number, the Texans surrendered in the belief they would be treated as prisoners of war of a civilized nation. After removal to Goliad, the Fannin men were marched out and massacred on Palm Sunday under orders of Santa Anna, the General of the Mexican Armies. Thus Dictator Santa Anna added another infamy to that of the Alamo and gave to the men who saved Texas at San Jacinto their battle cry, "Remember the Alamo, Remember Goliad."
The memorial to Fannin and his men is near Goliad.   (1974)

GOLIAD (Goliad Co.)   *US 183 S at Goliad State Park*
General Ignacio Zaragoza
(January 14, 1829–September 8, 1862)
Nacio en este lugar cuando se llamaba "Bahía del Espiritu Santo." En 1855, al mando de un ejercito de voluntarios Mexicanos, contribuyo a la derrota del Dictador Santa Anna.

Siempre fue caudillo en la defensa de su patria, el 5 de Mayo de 1862, durante la invasion de las fuerzas Francesas de Napoleon III y Maximiliano, en la Batalla de Puebla y al mando de 4,000 soldados mal armados, derroto a 8,000 Zuavos veteranos Franceses. Esta heroica victoria dio a Mexico su gran fiesta patriotica nacional "El Cinco de Mayo."

Born on this site when it was called "Bahía del Espiritu Santo." In 1855, at the head of an army of Mexican volunteers, contributed to the defeat of Dictator Santa Anna.

Always a leader in the defense of his country, on May 5, 1862, during the invasion of the French forces of Napoleon III and Maximilian, in the Battle of Puebla, he led 4,000 poorly armed soldiers to defeat 8,000 veteran French Zouaves. This heroic victory gave Mexico its great national patriotic anniversary, "El Cinco de Mayo." (1967)

GOLIAD (Goliad Co.) US 183/77A, 14 mi. N
Weser

Many German and Polish immigrants came to Texas in the 19th century on a ship named "Weser." Arriving at the Port of Galveston, a number of the pioneer settlers made their way overland to this area, establishing a community in the 1850s and 1860s. By 1881, when a post office was granted, it was officially named Weser for the ship that had brought the immigrants to America. By 1900 the settlement included, in addition to the post office, a general merchandise store, a steam grist mill, a cotton gin, a school, a blacksmith shop, a Western Union Telegraph office, a saloon, a Sons of Hermann Lodge hall and a dance hall. A community brass band entertained residents and played for local celebrations. The population of Weser consisted primarily of farmers and ranchers and their families. The school they established for their children served as a focal point and gathering place for area residents. Early facilities were replaced with a new building erected by volunteers in 1903. It continued to serve students in the Weser area until 1943, when it closed its doors. The building was later sold and moved out of the community. The highest population figure recorded for the town was 153 in 1904. It remained steady until the 1920s, when new generations began moving away to larger cities for greater economic opportunities. By the 1930s only two businesses remained in Weser, and the population had dropped to 50, a figure that remained steady for the remainder of the 20th century. Although smaller in number now, the Weser community represents a typical rural settlement in Goliad County. (1999)

GOLIAD (Goliad Co.) US 77A/183, 3 mi. NE
Geraldus B. Smart Home
Awarded The Texas Historical Building Medallion

North of this old homestead is the camp site of the freight line that ran from Indianola on the coast to San Antonio. Mr. Smart was one of the drivers in the freight line. This trail crossed his land.

GOLIAD (Goliad Co.) US 77A & 183, S near the grave, in an enclosure off Spur 71
Grave of Col. J. W. Fannin and His Men

After Battle of Coleto (March 19–20, 1836), where a Texas army under Col. James Walker Fannin met defeat by Mexicans in superior numbers, the Texas soldiers were held in Presidio la Bahía, supposedly as war prisoners. However, by order of Mexican Gen. Antonio Lopez de Santa Anna, approximately 400 of Fannin's men were marched out and massacred on Palm Sunday, March 27, 1836. The wounded were shot one by one in the fort compound. Col. Fannin was the last to die.

Because of their profession, Drs. J. H. Barnard, J. E. Field and Jack Shackelford were spared; about 25 men were saved by a Mexican woman, "The Angel of Goliad." Approximately 30 escaped by feigning death or by swimming the San Antonio River. The Texans' corpses were stripped and partly burned, but left unburied.

This atrocity three weeks after the fall of the Alamo gave Texans part of the battle cry- "Remember the Alamo! Remember la Bahía!"-under which decisive victory was won at San Jacinto on April 21, 1836.

Gen. Thomas J. Rusk and the Texan army afterwards marched here and gathered the bones of Fannin's men from the terrain. From Presidio la Bahía, the remains were carried in procession to the grave, and there given a military funeral and burial on June 3, 1836.

GOLIAD (Goliad Co.)   *US 77A/183, 1 mi. S*
La Bahía Mission
The Mission of Espíritu Santo de Zuñiga or La Bahía was established as an Indian school in 1749 and that of Rosario de los Cujanes 1754. A non-mission school for the families of soldiers and settlers was begun by Juan Manuel Zambrano with Jose Galan as teacher in 1818. The buildings of the old mission were leased by Rev. John Hillyer for a girls' school in 1848 and were used by the Presbytery of Western Texas for more than 20 years as Aranama College. Beginning in 1852 Payne Female Institute was conducted in Goliad, 1852–1885.

GOLIAD (Goliad Co.)   *Courthouse grounds*
Santa Anna's Surrender Ratified
Gen. Vicente Filasola, second in command of Mexican armies in Texas War for Independence, fled from area of his nation's defeat at San Jacinto, April 21, 1836. Filasola's aim was to go back to Mexico with his army.

After he had passed through Goliad, he was overtaken at Mujerero Creek (12 mi. SW) by Texan army couriers, Col. Ben Fort Smith and Capt. Henry Teal.

Signing the ratification of peace at Mujerero, May 26, 1836, were Gen. Filasola, Gen. Eugene Tolsa, Col. Augustine Amat, Col. Smith, and Capt. Teal.   (1970)

GOLIAD (Goliad Co.)   *1 mi. S of city limits, compound of Presidio La Bahía*
Replica of
Texas Independence Flagpole
Displays a replica of banner unfurled Dec. 20, 1835, at signing of Declaration of Independence of Texas from tyranny of Santa Anna's regime in Mexico. That declaration, drafted by staunch early patriots Philip Dimitt and Ira Ingram, and signed by 92 citizens and soldiers, was later suppressed as premature, but it forecast coming events.

A battle flag used 11 weeks earlier (and sometimes called "First Flag of Texas") lacked the support of a formal declaration of independence. The Goliad flag also waved over an army-one in possession of fort at La Bahía.   (1968)

GOLIAD (Goliad Co.)   *US 183 at Presidio La Bahia, 1.5 mi. S*
Manuel Becerra
Born at Presidio La Bahía del Espíritu Santo in 1762, Manuel Becerra played a significant role in the settlement and politics of the region. Becerra and his wife, Juana María Cadena, and their two daughters, María Josefa and Gertrudis, were leading citizens of La Bahía. In 1820, Antonio María Martínez, the last Spanish governor of Texas, called for the formation of the ayuntamiento of La Bahía as required in the Spanish Constitution of 1812. The ayuntamiento, or town council, included Manuel Becerra, who was elected its first secretary. Becerra's involvement with colonization efforts came the following year, as he was selected to accompany Stephen F. Austin to the Colorado River to find a suitable site for Austin's first colony. His friendship with empresario Martín de León led to his eventual responsibility within de León's Guadalupe Colony in 1827, when de León placed Becerra in charge of the colony's political and business affairs. The same year, Becerra helped negotiate a treaty with the Coco and Karankawa tribes to enhance peace and stability in the region. In 1832, Becerra received a land grant of 8,856 acres in what is now Refugio County and later assisted colonizer James Power in the colonization of the Power Colony at Villa de Refugio. As a citizen under the flags of Spain, Mexico, the Republic of Texas and the United States, Manuel Becerra bore witness to many of the formative events in Texas history and played a significant role in colonization efforts. He died in what is now Refugio County about 1849.   (2001)

GOLIAD (Goliad Co.)   *US 59, 4 mi. E of Goliad*
Site of September 1824 Indian Treaty
After finding bones of 2 men eaten by Karankawa Indians, Stephen F. Austin and 100 Texans met near here with a priest and men of La Bahía, where the Indians had taken refuge. The Indians were pledged to keep away from Texas colony. Breaking of the treaty caused tribe later to be driven from Texas.   (1967)

GOLIAD (Goliad Co.)   *SH 239 and Pettus Lane, 13 mi. W*
Pettus Cemetery
Virginia native John Freeman Pettus (b. 1808) came to Texas in the early 1820s as a member
of Stephen F. Austin's first colony. During the Texas Revolution he served with Ben Milam in
the siege of Bexar and participated in the Battle of San Jacinto. Soon after moving his family to
Goliad County about 1876, he chose this site near his home as the family burial ground. Pettus
died in 1878 and was the first buried here. Graves include those of 3 other Austin colonists:
Elizabeth Pettus, Sarah Pettus, and Phoebe Scott; and a San Jacinto veteran, James Austin
Clements.   (1981)

GOLIAD (Goliad Co.)   *US 77A/183, 1 mi. S*
Presidio de Nuestra Señora de Loreto de la Bahía
(Fort of Our Lady of Loreto of the Bay)
One of the most historic Spanish forts in Texas. Popularly called Presidio la Bahía, it was
founded on Espiritu Santo (present Lavaca) Bay in 1722. Twice moved, it was re-established here
in 1749 to protect Espiritu Santo Mission (¼ mi. NW). In the chapel is the statue of Our Lady of
Loreto placed here in 1749.
    The turbulent history of this fort has often rung with the sound of revolution. Between 1812
and 1820 several irregular "filibustering" forces, including the Gutierrez-Magee Expedition and
others led by James Long and Henry Perry, occupied or assailed the fort for various idealistic and
profiteering motives.
    Here, too, 92 Texas citizens and soldiers drew up and signed Texas' first formal Declaration of
Independence on December 20, 1835. In the ensuing War for Texas Independence, Col. James
Fannin and 341 prisoners of war were held here and, on Palm Sunday, 1836, were massacred in
and around the fort by their Mexican captors.
    When the fort was authentically restored, 1936–1967, by the Kathryn O'Connor Foundation,
nine "levels of occupancy" were uncovered. Church services are now held in the chapel. The presidio has been named a registered national historic landmark.   (1969)

GONZALES (Gonzales Co.)   *US 183, S city limits at turnout*
Battle of Gonzales
The first battle of the Texas Revolution, fought on the west side of the Guadalupe River about
four miles above Gonzales on October 2, 1835, came to be known as the Lexington of Texas. The
incident grew out of Col. Domingo de Ugartechea's demand late in September for a cannon given
to the settlement for defense against Indians. When the colonists refused to deliver the cannon,
Ugartechea sent 150 dragoons to demand the weapon. Alcalde Andrew Ponton, in the meantime,
sent word to other colonists that he had refused to surrender the cannon, which on September 29
was buried in George W. Davis' peach orchard. From September 30 to October 2 the number of
defenders at Gonzales had grown from 18 to about 160. Under command of John H. Moore and
J. W. E. Wallace they dug up the cannon, mounted it on ox-cart wheels, filled it with chains and
scrap iron, crossed the river and marched toward the enemy. When the Texan scouts discovered
the Mexican force early October 2, they fired their pieces and retired with the Mexicans in pursuit. A discharge from the six-pounder caused the latter to retreat. When the Texans opened with
their artillery and charged the enemy his force was driven back in the direction of San Antonio.

GONZALES (Gonzales Co.)   *SH 97, 7 mi. SW*
The First Shot of the Texas Revolution
One and one-half miles from here the first shot of the Texas Revolution was fired from a small
cannon by Texans under the command of Col. John H. Moore, October 2, 1835.   (1965)

GONZALES (Gonzales Co.)   *US 183, 1 mi. S at Guadalupe River Bridge*
18 Texians
On this site, September 29, 1835, began the strategy of the 18 Texians who by advising with
Alcalde Andrew Ponton, held for two days 150 Mexican dragoons sent to demand the Gonzales
cannon, allowing colonists time to mass recruits for the Battle of Gonzales.

"THE OLD EIGHTEEN"

Captain Albert Martin, Almond Cottle, Jacob C. Darst, Ezekiel Williams, Winslow Turner, Simeon Bateman, Wm. W. Arrington, Joseph D. Clements, Gravis Fulcher, Almaron Dickerson, George W. Davis, Benjamin Fuqua, John Sowell, Valentine Bennet, James B. Hinds, Charles Mason, Thomas R. Miller, Thomas Jackson.   (1965)

GONZALES (Gonzales Co.)   *US 90A, 10 mi. E*

⅛ mi. N is
Sam Houston Oak

⅛ mile north is where General Sam Houston established his headquarters camp, March 13, 1836, after burning the town of Gonzales. Under this oak his small army was joined by many volunteers from the eastern settlements, who went with him to San Jacinto.   (1965)

GONZALES (Gonzales Co.)   *US 183, 1.7 mi. S*

Santa Anna Mound

Extending from this point one-quarter mile west is Santa Anna Mound, formerly De Witt Mound, now site De Witt family cemetery. Here Mexican troops camped between September 29 and October 1, 1835, awaiting delivery of the Gonzales cannon. Colonists refusing to surrender cannon, the Mexicans retreated toward Bexar, where on October 2, five miles west, the Texians overtook them. The Battle of Gonzales ensued with Texians as victors.   (1965)

GONZALES (Gonzales Co.)   *SH 97, 3 mi. SW on Spur 95*

Site of the First Shot of the Texas Revolution
Near Gonzales

Near here on October 2, 1835 was fired the first shot of the Texas Revolution of 1835–1836, the shot heard round the world. At Gonzales the Texians defied the Mexican government and refused their demand for the Gonzales cannon with the "Come and Take It" challenge until reinforcements arrived from other parts of De Witt's colony and from the colonies on the Colorado and Brazos. They then pursued the Mexicans from Gonzales to near this point and fired upon them with this cannon, driving them back to Bexar.

This shot started the revolution and was directly responsible for adding more territory to the United States than was acquired by the freeing of the original thirteen colonies from England.

GONZALES (Gonzales Co.)   *US 183, 1 mi. S*

Site of Gonzales Cannon Dispute

On this site September 29, 1835, the Mexican government troops demanded the return of the Gonzales cannon. After two days delay, awaiting recruits, the colonists answered, "Come and Take It."   (1965)

GONZALES (Gonzales Co.)   *200 block of St. Louis St.*

First Shot of the Texas Revolution

On this site September 29, 1835 the Gonzales cannon was buried from the 150 Mexican dragoons sent to demand it.

Three days later it was mounted on ox-cart wheels, loaded with chains and scrap iron, and fired at the Mexican army, the first shot of the revolution. This location was known as George W. Davis peach orchard.   (1965)

GONZALES (Gonzales Co.)   *US 90A, 12 mi. SE, 1st Rd.*
on left part of Peach Creek Bridge

Braches Home

Braches house marker has only a Texas historical marker on the front. There is no inscription plate. Following is the "Statement of Significance" for the Braches house in the national register application: "The Braches home, twelve miles southeast of Gonzales, Texas, is a handsome Greek Revival plantation house and stage stop, built while Texas was an independent republic. The building is large and its full two-story Greek Revival gallery was quite advanced in comparison to most of the structures of inland Texas at this time. In front of the house there is a large old live oak that is marked by the State of Texas as the site of at least one significant incident in

Texas history. It is said to have been Sam Houston's location on March 11, 1863, nine days after the signing of the Texas Declaration of Independence, when as Commander-in-Chief of the Texas Army he heard of the fall of the Alamo. It was there that he sent orders to Fannin to retreat from Goliad, and made plans for his men to fall back in order to induce Santa Anna to divide his forces in pursuit. Panic took the settlers and most abandoned their homes to flee east. This event is known as 'The Runaway Scrape,' the tree as the 'Runaway Speech Oak' and the Sam Houston Oak. Santa Anna is supposed to have followed and stayed in this same location for three weeks."

GONZALES (Gonzales Co.)   *US 90A, 2 mi. E near Ken Creek*
David Burkett
(1798–1845)
Progressive patriot and citizen soldier in Texas War for Independence. A member of Green DeWitt's colony. Came to Texas with his family, 1830. Served as a guard for women and children fleeing Gonzales before the approach of Santa Anna, 1836. Is buried on his 4,428-acre land grant extending south from this site.   (1966)

GONZALES (Gonzales Co.)   *SH 80, 1.6 mi. N of Nixon*
Ghost Town of Dewville
(Site 7 mi. NW)
Small farming community. Started in 1850s. Named for Frank Dew (1862–1940), early settler. The main buildings were a store, Masonic lodge hall, gin, Sandies Chapel (Methodist, founded 1897), a school (1898). Post office was established in 1901.
After populace dwindled, post office closed, 1955.   (1971)

GONZALES (Gonzales Co.)   *US 90A, 2 mi. NW*
Duncan Ferry
(Site 1 mi. S)
Started about 1834 by Benj. Duncan (1793–1866), a Scotchman.
According to tradition, Mrs. Almaron Dickinson stopped first at Duncan's home on her way to tell people of Gonzales of fall of the Alamo. She was one of few survivors of this bloody Battle of Texas Revolution in which many Gonzales men died.
Upon hearing news, General Sam Houston ordered retreat of the Texas Army (camped in Gonzales) and on night of March 13, 1836, he had town and ferry burned to keep them from enemy hands. Duncan later rebuilt ferry, which was operated until 1866.   (1971)

GONZALES (Gonzales Co.)   *US 90A, 2 mi. E*
Kerr's Creek
Commissioned to found a capital for colony of Green DeWitt, ex-Missouri state Senator James Kerr settled here. He and six other men built homes on this stream-known ever since as Kerr's Creek.
After a destructive Indian raid in 1826, the settlement was abandoned.   (1966)

GONZALES (Gonzales Co.)   *US 90A, 6 mi. E*
2 mi. N to Site of
Maurin Quarry
In operation 1883–1908, this quarry supplied sandstone for buildings in Gonzales, Shiner, Moulton, Flatonia, Hallettsville. Stone was first dynamited, then cut by hand. It was shipped by wagon until railroad was built. The founder was Firmin Maurin, from Marseilles, France.   (1969)

GONZALES (Gonzales Co.)   *US 90A, about 2 mi. E on Spur 146*
Route of Old Chisholm Trail
Blazed by trail boss Thornton Chisholm on an 1866 drive from Cardwell's Flat, near Cuero, to Austin (Texas) and Missouri, this section of the famous trail was used until 1869.
Over it thundered thousands of cattle headed for northern markets, where sale of beef meant cash to Texas cattlemen and economic growth during the post-Civil War period.
Until the railroad was built from Texas to Dodge City, trails such as this were also the only supply line for U.S. forts, Indian reservations and large Kansas-centered markets.   (1967)

GONZALES (Gonzales Co.)   *SH 97, 6.5 mi. SW at Spur 95*
The First Shot of the Texas Revolution
(Erected by the School Children of Gonzales)
This is the site of the first battle of the Texas Revolution and the monument marks the exact spot where the first shot of the Texas fight for freedom was fired. Here, over the Texas forces commanded by Col. J. H. Moore and Lt. Col. J. W. E. Wallace, waved the famous battle flag inscribed "Come and Take It." When the cannon was fired, the Mexican forces broke rank and fled in terror, leaving one dead on the battlefield.

GONZALES (Gonzales Co.)   *US 90A, 2 mi. E*
Kerr Settlement
In this general area the first settlement of Gonzales was built in August, 1825. Major James Kerr commissioned by Green DeWitt to select the site on which to build a capitol for his colony. Kerr and six men chose this area where the San Marcos and Guadalupe Rivers join together. The beauty of the country, rich lands, and abundant water supply made this the ideal spot for their purpose.

GONZALES (Gonzales Co.)   *US 90A at FM 794*
Site of Confederate Fort
Fort Waul—A confederate fort built in 1863–1864 at Gonzales, is thought to be the only similar structure commissioned west of the Mississippi River by the Confederate States of America. The fort was built in Gonzales to protect against inland invasion by Yankee troops following an attack by Federal gunboats at the old port of Indianola.

GONZALES (Gonzales Co.)   *US 97, 6 mi.*
Memorial Monument—First Shot Texas Revolution
The monument in this roadside park was erected by the State of Texas in recognition of the fact that the first shot of the Texas Revolution was fired near here on October 2, 1835.

Bronze and granite, designed and cast by Waldine Tauch, world famous sculptress.

GONZALES (Gonzales Co.)   *US 90A 1.2 mi. W*
                                                       past San Marcos River bridge
James Hodges, Sr.
James Hodges, Sr., came to Gonzales in April 1835. Soon after his arrival, he purchased four leagues (17,721 acres) of land at the forks of the San Marcos and Guadalupe Rivers for $3,000 in silver.

On September, 26, 1835, in an election held under the auspices of the Gonzales Committee of Public Safety, Hodges was elected one of six delegates to the consultation of 1835. Convened in San Felipe de Austin on November 3, delegates to the consultation created a provisional government and organized an army under the command of Sam Houston.

Returning to Gonzales after the consultation, Hodges provided supplies for the Texas Army in 1836. He and his family left the area during the Runaway Scrape, but later returned to Gonzales County. In 1838, Hodges served on the county's Board of Land Commissioners.

Twice married, James Hodges was the father of eight children. He and his family continued to live on their land on the San Marcos and Guadalupe Rivers. After his death on December 24, 1846, Hodges was buried on the family farm in a plot which became known as the Hodges Family Cemetery (about one mile southeast).   (1990)

GONZALES (Gonzales Co.)   *US 183 right-of-way at US 90A, .25 mi. N*
Fort Waul
Named for Confederate General Thomas N. Waul, Fort Waul was built to defend inland Texas from possible Federal advances up the Guadalupe River from the Gulf of Mexico, as well as to provide protection for military supply trains. Construction of the earthen fortification was overseen by Col. Albert Miller Lea, Confederate Army engineer. Begun in late 1863, the fort was partly built by slave labor and measured approximately 250 by 750 feet. Surviving records do not indicate whether the fort was ever actually completed.   (1988)

GOODNIGHT (Armstrong Co.)   *US 287 and FM 294, 1 mi. E near intersection*
Site of Old Goodnight Ranch
First ranch in the Texas Panhandle. Established in 1876 by Charles Goodnight, 1836–1929.
Noted scout, Indian fighter, trail blazer and rancher, the Burbank of the range.   (1964)

GOODNIGHT (Armstrong Co.)   *US 287, E city limits in roadside park*
Town of Goodnight
Named in honor of Charles Goodnight, 1836–1929.
Noted scout, Indian fighter and trailblazer, who established the first ranch in the Texas
Panhandle in 1876 and is also known as the "Burbank of the Range."

GOODNIGHT (Armstrong Co.)   *US 287 near old Goodnight Home*
Charles Goodnight
1836–1929
Texas Ranger, Indian fighter. At age 19, on way to California gold fields, saw ranching possi-
bilities, settled and started ranch in Palo Pinto County, 230 miles southeast of here.
In Civil War, scout, guide and hunter for frontier regiment Texas Cavalry, protecting settlers
from Indian raids and federal invasion.
With Oliver Loving, moved cattle herds across arid West Texas and New Mexico lands domi-
nated by Comanche Indians, establishing Goodnight-Loving Trail northeast to U.S. forts.
Founded Old Goodnight College.

GORMAN (Eastland Co.)   *FM 8, 3 mi. NE*
Ellison Springs
(¾ mi. N)
Used for centuries by Indians inhabiting the region. Named for James Madison Ellison
(1840–1923), a native of Alabama, who was the first settler in this section of Eastland County,
erecting a cabin near the springs in Oct. 1858. He soon married Eliza McGough, a member of
another pioneer family, and had 3 children.
During the Civil War, frontiersmen organized militia companies for mutual protection against
the Indians. Ellison joined the company mustered from Eastland, Shackelford, and Callahan
Counties. On Aug. 9, 1864, a group of 12 scouts from the company was attacked near the springs,
and took refuge in Ellison's cabin. The commander, Capt. Singleton Gilbert, and Leroy "Button"
Keith were killed, and Ellison, Tom Gilbert, and Tom Caddenhead wounded. Ellison was disabled for life.
After cessation of Indian activity, Ellison Springs became the center of social and cultural
functions for the scattered settlers in the area. Picnics, community gatherings, and brush arbor
camp meetings were held at the site. In the early 1870s, a Baptist Church was constructed, with
the Rev. C. Brashears as minister. A cemetery was begun in the mid-1870s. The present frame
house at the springs was built by Ellison in 1886.   (1974)

GRAFORD (Palo Pinto Co.)   *SH 254, 2 mi. E*
The George Rice Bevers Homesite
On the Fort Worth-Fort Belknap Road, near Flat Rock Crossing of Keechi Creek. Occupied
1854 when such travelers as Indian agent Robert S. Neighbors were fed or housed overnight by
Bevers. First Palo Pinto County school opened in vicinity in 1856, on a path smoothed by oxen
pulling a log. In Bevers cemetery lies a victim of 1860s Indian raids that sent settlers to refuges
as remote as the courthouse in Fort Worth.
Bevers (1825–1904), his wife, Lucinda Jane Tacker (1825–1873), and children lived near
Curetons, Goodnights, Slaughters, other noted pioneers.   (1971)

GRAFORD (Palo Pinto Co.)   *SH 254, 3 mi. E in roadside park*
Simpson Crawford
A native of Kentucky, Simpson Crawford (1824–1908) served in the Mexican War
(1846–1848) at Vera Cruz and Mexico City. Following the war he returned to Kentucky and married Elizabeth Evans. In 1852, they moved to Texas, settling first in Titus County. In 1854, they
came to Palo Pinto County and built a home (¾ mi. NW) in the Keechi Valley area of Peters

Colony. A successful rancher owning 3,100 acres, Crawford also served in the Texas Rangers. His first wife died in 1858 and he married Mary Brown four years later. He is buried in Crawford Cemetery (1.5 mi. N). (1980)

GRAFORD (Palo Pinto Co.) *FM 2353, .5 mi. S of , 15 mi. SW, Observation Point*
Morris Sheppard Dam and Possum Kingdom Lake—
A Project of the Brazos River Authority

Built in response to disastrous Brazos River flooding, Morris Sheppard Dam and Possum Kingdom Reservoir were early attempts at water conservation and flood control in Texas. The U.S. Government funded $4,500,000 of the three-year, $8,500,000 project through the Works Progress Administration, a Depression era recovery agency. Named for U.S. Senator Morris Sheppard and completed in 1941, the dam is 2,740 feet long and 190 feet high. Nine spillway gates allow for the passage of flood waters and drift material. Power generating facilities consist of two 11,250-kilowatt units which serve much of the surrounding area.

The creation of Possum Kingdom Lake from the impounded waters of Morris Sheppard Dam sent bridges, roads, and an entire town underwater. Recovery was initially slow, but quickly picked up after World War II with the establishment of major fishing lodges, camping areas, and other recreational facilities. The growth and success of the area is a tribute to the spirit of the surrounding communities which continue to benefit from the project's original purposes of water conservation and supply, and hydroelectric power generation. (1983)

GRAHAM (Young Co.) *SH 16, in Graham*
Brazos River Indian Reservation

In February 1854 the Texas legislature designated 12 Spanish leagues (or 53,136 acres) of land to be maintained as Indian reservations by the federal government. In August 1854, Major Robert S. Neighbors, United States supervising Indian agent, and Captain Randolph B. Marcy, of the United States Army, made surveys in both Spanish and American measurements; American dimensions were platted, totaling 69,120 acres. In the 8-league tract here in Young County—on either side of the Brazos River—were placed tribes of Anadarko, Caddo, Tehuacana, Tonkawa, Waco and others, together with splinter groups of the Cherokees, Choctaws, Delawares, Shawnees and some other remnants. The southern Comanches had their 4-league reservation about 45 miles to the west.

Under the guidance of United States agents, the Indians of the Brazos River Reservation made much progress in agriculture, stock raising and other arts of civilization. Drouth and other adversities, however, led to closing of the reservations.

Emptied in 1859 when the Indians were removed to vicinity of present Anadarko, Oklahoma, lands of the reservation reverted to the state, and were opened to the pre-emption of Texas citizens in 1873. (1970)

GRAHAM (Young Co.) *SH 16, 8 mi. NE*
Warren Wagon Train Massacre

On Salt Creek Prairie (1.5 mi. W), on May 18, 1871, Kiowas and Comanches from the Fort Sill Reservation, in present Oklahoma, attacked a train of 12 wagons owned by Capt. Henry Warren, a contractor of supplies of U.S. forts in this frontier region. Seven teamsters were killed. The chiefs who led the raid were soon arrested. In a nationally spotlighted trial at Jacksboro, Satana spoke with great eloquence on behalf of his people. Texas' governor, E. J. Davis, later commuted the death sentences given by the court. Satana committed suicide. (1977)

GRAHAM (Young Co.) *SH 199, 6 mi. SE of Olney*
Little Salt Creek Indian Fight
(Battleground about a Mile to the North)

Duel between a cattle roundup crew and Indians, on May 16, 1869.

Cowboys attacked at their work were Shapley Carter, Bill Crow, and Henry Harrison, all of Palo Pinto County; crew captain Ira E. Graves, J. W. Gray, W. C. Kutch, and Jason McClain, of Jack County; Joe Woody, Parker County; George and John Lemley and Rube Seachrist, Young County; Dick, the cook, from Tarrant County. All day the crew held at bay 57 Comanches, who left that night. Nine cowboys were wounded—Carter, Crow, and John Lemley died. Texans never forgot the unprovoked attack. (1971)

GRAHAM (Young Co.)

SH 67, off hwy. between 5th & 6th Sts.
on the east bank of Salt Creek

Graham Salt Works

Saline residue found along the banks of Salt Creek attracted settlers to this area in the 1850s. The first person to undertake commercial production of salt here was Martin V. Bowers, who arrived in the area prior to the Civil War. A farmer and local politician, he later sold his business to A. B. Gant and moved to Parker County.

Gant, a Confederate veteran, operated the salt works until 1871, when he was elected to the Texas Legislature. He sold the operation to Gustavus A. (1836–1906) and Edwin S. (1831–1899) Graham, brothers who had come to Texas with the Texas Emigration and Land Company.

The Grahams improved the salt works by adding new equipment in 1872. With a capacity of producing 2,500 pounds of salt per day, the Graham Salt Works was in operation for only two years. The salt, sold to merchants in nearby towns, cost more to transport than to produce, and the operation was discontinued.

Although short in duration, the Graham Salt Works played a vital role in local development. The Graham brothers donated land for a town, named for their family, as well as for Oak Grove Cemetery, where both brothers were later buried. (1987)

GRAHAM (Young Co.)

SH 67, 5 mi. SW

The Tonk Valley Community

Earliest known attempt at permanent settlement in this valley was made in 1851 by Elijah Skidmore, who was killed after a few months on the frontier.

Locality takes its historic name from the Tonkawa nation, known in its own language as "the most human of people." In 1855 the Tonkawa were placed in this valley on a reservation provided by an act of the Texas legislature; but in 1859 the tribe was removed to Indian Territory (now Oklahoma).

After the Civil War ended in 1865, and especially after the Indian reserve was opened to settlers in 1873, pioneers established livestock farms here.

Their children went to school in a log cabin with dirt floor and homemade split log benches. Schoolmistress Addie McNabb accepted as salary a gray plow pony and a small amount of cash. In 1877 Baptists organized a church with the Rev. G. W. Black as pastor; also in 1877 Methodists founded Monk's Chapel, with the Rev. B. H. Johnson as pastor. The first building strictly for church use was erected 1909.

School consolidations (1922) enlarged community and (1948) saw local children transported into Graham. Community life is centered in the churches. (1972)

GRANBURY (Hood Co.)

US 377, 5 mi. E on FM 167

Site of the
Home of Elizabeth Crockett

Wife of David Crockett, hero of the Alamo. She died here March 2, 1860, age 74.

GRANBURY (Hood Co.)

FM 4 and FM 167, Acton

Acton Public Square

The oldest community in what is now Hood County, Acton was settled during the 1850s. First called "Comanche Peak" when a post office was established here on March 10, 1856, the town was renamed "Acton" before the post office was reopened, March 16, 1868. Clarence P. Hollis, pioneer merchant and early postmaster, donated 1.43 acres of land for this public square in the 1860s. Once the hub of commercial activity, the square declined after many of the buildings around it burned. The site was resurveyed in 1974 and restored as center of this rural community. (1976)

GRANBURY (Hood Co.)

SH 144 near FM 51

Wright-Henderson-Duncan House

The three principal owners of this home each served terms as sheriff of Hood County. A. J. Wright (1819–1889) began the limestone structure about 1873 as a one-story dogtrot dwelling. James F. Henderson, who acquired the house in 1881, added the second floor and Victorian galleries. Charles M. Duncan (1878–1957) and his wife Emma (Wade), owners for a long period in the 20th century, helped preserve the residence. (1977)

GRANBURY (Hood Co.)

SH 144, 3.5 mi. S

Comanche Peak

Prominent Indian and pioneer landmark. Actually a mesa, the peak rises 1,229 feet (above sea level). May have had ceremonial value for local tribes or have been a lookout point for game and enemies. A Comanche trail crossed county in this vicinity.

In 1846, whites and Indians en route to the so-called "peak" for a meeting also failed to find it because of its flat top.

Later settlers held dances here and students from Add-Ran College (about 10 miles N) had picnics at the peak. Boys also hunted wolves and rattlesnakes among caves and rocks on the top.   (1969)

GRANBURY (Hood Co.)

Courthouse square, Bridge St./Crockett St.

Site of Schultz Blacksmith Shop

Carl Severin Schultz was born in Copenhagen, Denmark, in 1876. After marrying Nelsina Vestermann (b. 1871), he came to the United States and settled in Granbury. Schultz had several professions, including ownership of a soft drink factory. He later became the village blacksmith and operated his shop on this site, which he had purchased in 1900. Known throughout the county for his fine craftsmanship, Schultz represents the type of settler and business leader who lived in Granbury at the turn of the century.   (1984)

GRAND PRAIRIE (Dallas Co.)

800 Skyline Road at S. Belt Line Rd.

Avion Village

As early as the mid-1940s, housing was scarce in Dallas as well as in other centers of defense production and military activity throughout the nation. The private housing industry was unable to keep up with the demand for shelter in these areas. Some federal officials saw the situation as an opportunity for experimentation in architecture and planning, as well as establishment of a pilot program aimed at lowering the cost of quality housing through the use of prefabrication and mass production building techniques. Defense housing officials also wanted to introduce industrial workers to mutual home ownership as an alternative to traditional suburban home ownership. Avion Village was one of several early developments intended to be permanent additions to community housing stock. The facility's layout promoted both privacy and resident interaction. Built under the auspices of the Federal Works Agency and its assistant administrator, Texas native Lawrence Westbrook, the facilities were designed by Roscoe DeWitt and David R. Williams in cooperation with Richard J. Neutra. Avion Village was launched amid high media attention in May 1941 as two teams of workers raced to complete the first house in the planned 300-unit development. The first unit was built in less than one hour. The entire development was finished in 100 days with the help of an on-site makeshift prefabrication plant. Civilian employees of the North American Aviation Company were the first to live in the complex. The Avion Village Mutual Housing Corporation purchased the development from the federal government in 1948. Avion Village continues to be mutually owned by residents.   (1999)

GRAND SALINE (Van Zandt Co.)

US 80 at FM 857, .5 mi. E

Grand Saline, C.S.A.

This large saline deposit was a major source of salt in Texas during the Civil War. Salt was first obtained by the Indians. In 1854, works were built. Sam Richardson, the owner in 1861, went to war and left his wife to run the works until the Confederate government took over production. Because salt was considered a strategic industry, salt workers were exempt from army service for a time. Many wells were sunk to obtain the more than 10,000 pounds of salt made daily for the civilians and army west of the Mississippi River. Mule-powered pumps drew the brine from the wells. Gum logs, hollowed out and pinned together, formed a pipeline to huge iron evaporating kettles. Salt was then sacked, purchased and hauled away on horseback, in wagons and oxcarts. During the Civil War, the demand for salt, the only known way to preserve meat, increased to supply the Southern Army. Meat was salted, smoked and then packed in salt for the long, hot trips to army camps. Horses and mules used by cavalry, artillery, and quartermaster units required the vital mineral, too. Salt too preserved hides for making shoes, harness and saddles. When the Confederate government levied a meat tithe on farmers, the demand for salt increased. Often cattle and cotton were exchanged for salt, which itself became a medium of exchange. When salt became scarce, women dug up smokehouse floors to extract salt from the soil. Other Civil War salt works were operated along the coast and in other East, Central and West Texas counties.   (1963)

GRAND SALINE (Van Zandt Co.)
SH 110, 1 mi. S
Morton Salt Company
Awarded Medallion. Around 1835, the Cherokee Indians made first salt at Grand Saline. Salt has been mined continually since that time.

GRAND SALINE (Van Zandt Co.)
US 80 (Garland St.) and SH 17 (Main St.)
Wiley Hardeman Post (1898–1935)
Pioneer aviator Wiley Hardeman Post was born on November 22, 1898, in the community of Corinth in Van Zandt County, to William Francis and Mae Laine Post, who moved to Oklahoma when Wiley was a boy. Wiley was inspired as a youth to learn to fly.

In the late 1920s, he obtained flight training, made his first solo flight, and acquired an air transport license. Despite the loss of one eye in an oil-field accident, Post worked as a barnstormer, commercial pilot, and flight instructor.

Post set many flight records and won the national air races in 1930. He and Harold Gatty circled the world, flying 15,474 miles in less than 9 days in 1931. Post soloed around the world in less than 8 days in 1933.

Post invented and developed the first pressurized flight suit, explored stratospheric flight, and used an early Sperry autopilot mechanism. He worked with the U.S. Army Air Corps on an experimental automatic direction finding (ADF) radio compass, and was a pioneer in the use of liquid oxygen for high-altitude flight. Post and humorist Will Rogers died in a plane crash on a trip to Alaska in 1935. His plane the "Winnie Mae" is in the Smithsonian Institution's Air and Space Museum in Washington, D.C. (1996)

GRANDFALLS (Ward Co.)
SH 18, 1.5 mi. S
Butterfield Overland Stage Line
One of the longest stage routes ever established, the Southern Overland mail line (Butterfield Route), which provided semi-weekly service, St. Louis to San Francisco, 1858–1861. Followed substantially the route of this highway through Ward County.

GRAPEVINE (Tarrant Co.)
SH 121, 2.5 mi. NE at Tarrant-Dallas Co. Line
The Missouri Colony
In 1844, related families from Platte County, Missouri, settled in this area. James Gibson, one of the earliest settlers in Tarrant County, owned this site. In 1845, more relatives and friends arrived. They became known as the "Missouri Colony." The pioneers raised cattle and grain. John A. Freeman taught school and preached to the settlers at Lonesome Dove. Some original colonists moved to pioneer other frontier regions. Others remained to help build the northeastern section of Tarrant County, the first permanently settled area in the county. (1979)

GRAPEVINE (Tarrant Co.)
SH 26, ¼ mi. SW of Bethel Road
Morgan Hood Survey
Pioneer Cemetery
Originally part of the Morgan Hood Survey, this small cemetery (75 ft. SE) has been abandoned for over a century. Its one visible grave is marked with portions of a sandstone burial cairn, a common method of marking graves in this area in the 1850s–1870s. The subject of speculation since no written records remain, the graves may be those of members of the Peters Colony, early pioneers who entered the Grapevine area in 1844. Although nearly all traces of the cemetery are gone, it serves as a reminder of Tarrant County's early days of settlement. (1983)

GRAPEVINE (Tarrant Co.)
SH 26, .1 mi. E of Bear Creek Bridge
The Peters Colony
in Tarrant County
In 1841, W. S. Peters of Kentucky and associates contracted with the Republic of Texas to bring immigrants to this area. By 1848, Peters Colony land covered nearly 2 million acres in North Central Texas, including all of Tarrant County. Speculation in unlocated land certificates was rampant. About 150 colonists and their families, most of whom were American-born farmers of meager means, settled in Tarrant County. As the most extensive empresario enterprise undertaken by the Republic, the Peters Colony helped open this area of Texas to settlement.
(1985, 1990)

GREENVILLE (Hunt Co.)　　　*American Cotton Museum, Paul Matthew Blvd.,*
just off 600 IH-30
Ende-Gaillard House
German native Charles Frederick von Ende (b. 1832) came to Greenville in 1857 and established a mercantile business on the town square. He became one of the community's most active civic leaders, serving on the school board and city council, and helping to establish the local Odd Fellows lodge. In 1857–1859, Ende built this home for his bride, Amelia Reinecker. Their daughter, Louise, and her husband, Dr. David I. Gaillard, bought the home in 1883. After Louise's death in 1945, the house became part of a lumberyard and was threatened with demolition. Originally located just north of the courthouse square, the Ende-Gaillard House was moved to a city park in 1957 and then to the American Cotton Museum in 1996.　　　(2002)

GREENVILLE (Hunt Co.)　　　*2821 Washington St., at Municipal Building*
Greenville
In 1846, the Texas legislature created Hunt County and specified that Greenville would be the name of the county seat, honoring Texas War for Independence veteran Thomas J. Green. Voters ultimately selected this location, on land donated by Tennessee surveyor McQuinney Howell Wright, for the new community of Greenville. The townsite was platted in May 1846 and the first lots were sold at auction the following January, although Wright did not file the deed officially conveying his land until March 22, 1850. Albert G. Hamilton served as first mayor after the town incorporated in 1852. Unlike most north central Texas counties, Hunt County voted in favor of secession during the national crisis in the 1860s. Economic hardship, occasions of violence, and occupation by federal troops characterized the Civil War and Reconstruction period in Greenville. The arrival of the Missouri, Kansas and Texas railroad in October 1880 was a watershed in Greenville's history. The railroad provided cotton farmers with easier shipping access, and cotton production and processing became major economic activities. New businesses and service industries, including banks, hotels, street cars, and the state's first municipally owned electric utility, developed to serve the growing community. Greenville was home to Majors Army Air Field and three colleges in the 20th century. Its location at the crossroads of major state and national highways helped Greenville develop over the years to become an industrial and trade center in northeast Texas.　　　(2001)

GREENVILLE (Hunt Co.)　　　*SH 24, 11 mi. NE on granite shaft*
containing marker for Scatter Branch Church
Fourth-Sunday Singing
(Held on Fourth Sunday of Each Month)
A monthly music "convention" founded in 1885 or 1890 by this church at old location (½ mile east). Began when G. J. Oslin of Arkansas held a 20-day music school here.

Singers came from wide area; a tuning fork was used to give pitch until instruments were obtained. The present officers are J. G. Murphy, president, and Mrs. Ola Speight, secretary.

Also in 1885, the village of "Hoover's Gin" was founded near here by John T. Hoover, merchant. Awarded Medallion Plate.　　　(1968)

GREENVILLE (Hunt Co.)　　　*US 69, 1.3 mi. NW of Celeste*
Headwaters of the Sabine River
A half mile to the west rises the Sabine River, lower channel of which separated new world empires of France and Spain and in 1836 became Republic of Texas-United States border. Fork here is called Cow Leach, for Indian chief who lived in the area. This marker is on a 3-way watershed. Flow to the north goes into the Sulphur and to the Mississippi; the west drains to the Trinity; south goes into the Sabine, which forms Texas-Louisiana boundary and pours more water into Gulf of Mexico than any other Texas river (6,400,000 acre feet annually).　　　(1971)

GREENVILLE (Hunt Co.)　　　*FM 35, in West Tawakoni*
Lake Tawakoni
One of the largest lakes wholly within Texas. Completed 1960, it covers 36,700 acres. Impounded by 5.5-mile-long iron bridge/dam on Sabine River, it has a shoreline of 200 miles. Constructed and owned by the Sabine River Authority of Texas. Financed by city of Dallas under terms of a water supply contract. Other towns also by lake's water.

Prehistoric animal bones and remains of a Tawakoni Indian village were discovered here. Lake is operated under Iron Bridge Division, S.R.A. of Texas. It embraces Wind Point Park, a public recreational resort. (1970)

GREENVILLE (Hunt Co.) — *SH 34, 13 mi. N*
Old National Road Crossing
One mile northeast below junction of Short Creek and Sulphur River.

The Central National Road of Texas (Republic) was created by act of Texas Congress, 1844, with intent to give the new nation a unified transportation route.

From present Dallas to the head of navigation on the Red River, northwest of Clarksville, road linked to Northeast Texas the military routes of West and Central Texas; connected with routes east at Jonesborough and Paris. It failed to gain international status congress hoped for, due to population shifts, coming of railroads and development of other routes. (1967)

GREENVILLE (Hunt Co.) — *SH 24, 11 mi. NE, front lawn of church*
Scatter Branch Church
Jointly owned Methodist and Baptist edifice. The two congregations hold united communion, Sunday school services; share upkeep. Pastors alternate Sundays.

Partnership began 1893. Moved here 1927 and built present building. Named for branch that spreads over area in flood time. (1967)

GREENVILLE (Hunt Co.) — *SH 24, 1 mi. W on old road*
Route of
Old Colony Line Road
Early travel artery. Followed the north boundary line of the Chas. F. Mercer colony, a 6,500 square-mile tract granted to Mercer in 1844 by Sam Houston (President of the Republic of Texas) for purpose of bringing colonists into Texas. Southern half of Hunt County once lay in this pioneer colony.

Over the road came ox-wagons from Jefferson to supply stores in Greenville, McKinney, Dallas, Fort Worth and the frontier.

Settlers from the old south traveled it in a steady stream of covered wagons. Highway 24 today traces part of the road. (1968)

GREENVILLE (Hunt Co.) — *US 69, 6 mi. N at Kellogg*
Central National Road
of
The Republic of Texas
Surveyed and established by virtue of an act of the Congress of the Republic of Texas in 1844, running from the Trinity River to the Red River. It crossed the highway near this point.

"An Old Road is the Soul of the Past." (1926)

GREENVINE (Washington Co.) — *FM 2502, and CR 2*
Greenvine Gas Discovery
(2 mi. NW)
Apparently the first use in Texas of natural gas for fuel occurred in 1879 near here.

William Seidel, a farmer, grist mill and cotton gin owner, and merchant, trying to dig a water well, struck gas at approximate depth of 106 feet. The gas was piped to a farmhouse nearby.

Production of gas and oil has spread to 210 Texas counties; 27 pipeline companies export gas. Annual rate of production is about 8 trillion cubic feet. Texas has 42.3 percent of the proven gas reserves in America, and it has a 19,895-foot well, believed to be world's deepest. (1967)

GRIT (Mason Co.) — *US 83, Grit Cemetery*
John Bate Berry (1813–1891)
Forefathers resisting America's foes on many frontiers inspired John Bate Berry, who came to Texas from Kentucky in 1826. He fought (1835–1836) in the Texas War for Independence and in the 1842 Mier Expedition to stop Mexican raids on the Republic of Texas. Captured, imprisoned, then freed in 1844, he scouted for the American Army in 1846, during the Mexican War. Later he married, lived in this locality, and fought to make frontiers safe for settlement. (1977)

GROESBECK (Limestone Co.)

SH 164, 10 mi. NW

Fort Parker

Built 1834 for protection from Indians. Named for leaders who brought first Predestinarian Baptist church body to Texas: elder Daniel Parker; his father, elder John; brothers Jas. W., Benjamin, Silas, John. Also here were Kellogg, Frost, Nixon, Duty and Plummer families. On May 18, 1836, raiding Comanches killed Benjamin, John and Silas Parker; Samuel and Robert Frost and others; captured Elizabeth Kellogg, Rachel Plummer and son James, and Silas' children, John and Cynthia Ann. In captivity, Cynthia Ann married Chief Peta Nacona; her son, Quanah, was last Comanche chief. With her baby, Prairie Flower, in 1860 she was captured by Texas Rangers. She, the baby and Quanah are buried at Fort Sill.   (1965)

GROESBECK (Limestone Co.)

SH 14, 1.5 mi. N, Fort Parker
Memorial Park Cemetary

Fort Parker Memorial Park

Site of the grave of victims of the massacre at Fort Parker by Comanche and Kiowa Indians on May 19, 1836, in which Cynthia Ann Parker and others were captured. The trunk of the oak tree under which they were buried still stands, and the grave is marked by a granite slab. Also site of state monument to the Pioneers, erected in 1922, and the graves of other old settlers and veterans of the Texas War of Independence.

GROESBECK (Limestone Co.)

SH 164, 10 mi. NW

Lost Prairie Cemetery and Church

Established by volunteers in 1846; sponsoring group formed about 1900. According to legend, a man lost in the surrounding woods named the site when he stumbled onto the prairie. The graves of many early settlers include Azariah G. Moore, a soldier in the Texas War for Independence. First officials of the cemetery association were Jeff Rambo, chairman, and Beulah Holloway, secretary. Successors include Dan Dove, Jake Hudson, W. C. Jackson, Bill Kennedy, I. M. Kennedy, Joe Lansford, Cliff Sims and J. B. Sims. Others helping in preservation of site were R. L. Dossey, J. A. Easterling, W. K. Hardison, W. L. Henderson, A. B. Sims, E. E. Sims, J. J. Sims, J. L. Sims and R. A. Sims. Others have served as caretakers since the grounds were opened; among them George Henry, J. N. Henry and Bill Sims.

Baptist church was situated here about 1850. Present building is fourth structure to serve as a church.

First pastor was Rev. William Clark. Founding members included the Beavers, Browns, Easterlings, Gregorys, Henrys, Kennedys, Lansfords, Mortons, Rambos, Sandifers, Shugarts, Sims, Summers, Thompsons and Waylands. One early church member, A. J. Rogers, was named a deacon after returning from the Civil War.   (1967)

GROESBECK (Limestone Co.)

SH 14, 5 mi. NE

Old Springfield

Named for the large spring on townsite donated Jan. 6, 1838, by Moses Herrin, who gave 4 lots to any person agreeing to settle in the town. Twelve families later in 1838 were forced out by Indian hostility. Post office was established in 1846. When Limestone County was created April 11, 1846, Springfield—its only town of any size—became county seat. First courthouse was built 1848 near Navasota River; new 2-story brick courthouse in 1856 on the hill.

Home of Springfield District of Methodist Church—from which stemmed the Northwest Texas Conference.

Also had active Baptist and Disciples of Christ churches. Springfield College was established, but closed during the Civil War. The Navasota Stock Raisers Association was organized here.

When Houston & Texas Central Railroad was built some miles to the east in 1870, population dwindled.

In 1873 there were 2 great fires in the town-one burning the courthouse. Surviving buildings were moved away. Groesbeck became the county seat. The old cemetery and Springfield Lake, both in Fort Parker State Park, retain the historic name of the once important town. Lake Springfield provides recreation, irrigation and municipal water.

GROVETON (Trinity Co.)   *US 287 in front of courthouse*
Groveton
Named for a grove of black jack oak trees, Groveton resulted from the establishment of the Trinity County Lumber Company sawmill in 1882. After the Trinity and Sabine Railroad Company built a sixty-five mile branch line through area forests, the Trinity County Lumber Company bought about 29,000 acres of land from the Trinity and Sabine Timber Company, leaving acreage on either side of the railroad tracks for a town. The county seat was moved from Pennington to Groveton in 1882. By 1884 the first permanent court house was completed and the town included a barber shop, grocery store, drug store, hotel, boarding house, several saloons, homes, and a school. The city was incorporated on September 29, 1919 and officials were elected. By 1930 all the timber for miles around had been cut; consequently, the sawmill closed December 31, 1930. The once prosperous town of Groveton went into decline. The Civilian Conservation Corps was responsible for road construction and a reforestation program in the 1930s. Through the years Groveton has seen economic booms and hard times, but as the county seat, it has survived to leave a rich heritage. (1991)

GROVETON (Trinity Co.)   *US 287, 5.5 mi. SE*
Site of Town of Sumpter
First county seat, Trinity County. Land granted in 1850. County seat located here in 1854. Town was laid out November 20, 1855, incorporated in 1862. Courthouse and records were destroyed by fire in 1872. In 1873 the county seat was removed to Trinity.

GRUVER (Hansford Co.)   *SH 136, 9 mi. S*
Site of Cator Buffalo Camp
Established by James H. and Bob Cator in the spring of 1872 while hunting buffalo in the fall of 1875. The camp became a trading post known as Zulu. (1965)

GRUVER (Hansford Co.)   *SH 15, 2 mi. SE*
Old Farwell
Established 1886 about ½ mile northeast of this site. Intended to be county seat of Hansford County, created 1876, organized in 1889. Lost election to town of Hansford, which served till 1928 but is also now non-existent.
Named for early surveyor John V. Farwell and members of his family, Chicago department store executives who operated XIT Ranch in this and 9 other counties—their fee in payment for the building of the Texas state capitol, 1882–1886.
Stones here are from the casing of a 200 foot well dug by hand to supply water to the town.
(1964)

GUNTER (Grayson Co.)   *FM 121, 1.5 mi. W*
Town of Gunter, on Old Gunter Ranch
Established 1880s by Jot Gunter, developer of Texas real estate, prominent Grayson County businessman. In mid-1890s his ranch exceeded 20,000 acres. Gunter, born in North Carolina in 1845, came to Texas to practice law after he served in Confederate Army. The town of Gunter, incorporated in 1914, was named for him. (1968)

GUSTINE (Comanche Co.)   *SH 36 County Seat, Cora*
First Comanche County Courthouse
A dwelling before county organization, 1856. Served as courthouse in town of Cora until 1859, when Comanche became the county seat; then reverted to use as a residence. Moved here and restored by Mr. and Mrs. A. P. Burks. Awarded Medallion Plate. (1965)

GUSTINE (Comanche Co.)   *FM 591 W of FM 1702, 8 mi. NE*
The Choctaw Robinson Tree
The Rev. William Robinson (1809–1898), pioneer Baptist missionary, was born in North Carolina and came to Texas in 1848. He organized and served as pastor to churches in Rusk, Johnson, Erath, and Comanche Counties. At the same time, he supported his large family by

farming. He was called "Choctaw Bill" because a band of Choctaw Indians once complained about his long sermons. The Rev. Mr. Robinson often preached for hours beneath this tree, near a rough frontier town. While he spoke, he rested his gun in the fork of the tree. His grave is located in nearby Baggett cemetery. (1975)

GUTHRIE (King Co.) US 82, 1.5 mi. S
King County
Created Aug. 21, 1876, from Bexar County, whose diamond-shaped boundaries extended from the Rio Grande to the Panhandle to El Paso. Named for William King, who died at the Alamo. Chief industry, ranching, is reflected in its famous brands: "6666," "Pitchfork," "JY," "SMS," and "MATADOR."

A population of only 173 in 1890 was aided in formal organization by petitions signed by itinerants. Names of favorite horses were also added. Organization came on June 25, 1891. In establishing county seat, cowboys voted for Guthrie, which won over Ashville, choice of the ranchers.

(1965)

HALE CENTER (Hale Co.) US 87, 7.5 mi. S
The Stant Rhea Stage Stand
(6 mi. E, on Private Property)
Early settlers in this area kept in touch with the world by picking up their mail at railheads. Federal mail delivery to post offices began when W. L. Tharp took a route from the new railroad town of Amarillo to Plainview and Estacado in July and August, 1888. There were no roads; the round trip took six days. About 1889, W. H. Fuqua of Amarillo, who had a new U.S. mail contract, used a compass and laid off a route with several stations—one of Plainview. He soon added passenger service, but then disposed of the line, which about 1890 fell into the hands of Stant Rhea and Robert Montgomery. Buying out Montgomery, Rhea carried the mail for 19 years.

Sidney Stanton "Stant" Rhea (1862–1922) was a small, red-haired man who drove wild Spanish mules hitched to a buckboard (or carriage). He made the 240-mile round trip from Amarillo to this area three times a week. With later route changes and better roads, he came this way daily. Six miles east of this spot he had a mule corral and a dugout. Stage passengers and mail patrons used the dugout as a waiting room. Until railroads outmoded his service, Stant Rhea's route and stage stand were important in the development of the South Plains. (1976)

HALE CENTER (Hale Co.) IH 27, ½ mi. S
Ranching and Farming in Hale County
Pioneer ranchers began to settle Hale County in the early 1880s. Land was plentiful and cheap, but life was hard. Many settlers lived in dugouts. Supplies were freighted from Colorado City until the railroad reached Amarillo. Cattle roamed the free grazing land until roundup time, when they were separated according to brands. Ranchers earned extra income by selling buffalo bones for fertilizer, working on the railroad, or hiring out to larger ranches. Many worked at the Circle Ranch of Col. C. C. Slaughter, which covered land in four counties. Other significant ranches included the Callahan, Barton, and Norfleet ranches.

When the public land was gone and free grazing ended, the larger ranches were divided into smaller tracts. The transition from ranching to farming was difficult. By the early 20th century, wheat farming and dairy production began to replace ranching operations.

The dust bowl and depression of the 1930s brought new hardships. Soon after World War II, however, a high percentage of the cultivated acreage in Hale County was under irrigation. This allowed for crop diversification with high yields of grain sorghum, corn, soybeans, wheat, vegetables, and livestock production. Cotton has become the leading cash crop. (1985)

HALLETTSVILLE (Lavaca Co.) US 77, at fire station
Hallettsville
Founded 1833 when John Hallet erected a log cabin near Lavaca River. Town was named for his widow, Margaret, who gave the land when town became county seat in 1852. Farming, livestock, poultry processing, and cotton marketing center. State championship high school rodeo held annually in June. (1968)

HALLETSVILLE (Lavaca Co.)

US 77, 5.5 mi. S

John Himes Livergood
(September 10, 1815–October 3, 1893)

A native of Pennsylvania, John Himes Livergood came to Texas in 1837 and received 640 acres of land on Peach Creek near Gonzales. From that time until Texas' annexation to the United States nearly ten years later, Livergood played an integral role in the defense of frontier settlements and in several major events during the Republic period. In 1840, Livergood joined Capt. Adam Zumwalt to pursue an Indian party that had attacked his neighbors. The chase ended with a decisive victory at the Battle of Plum Creek. Later he served in several scouting expeditions, including the Spy Company of the Texas Rangers under John (Jack) Coffee Hays. He took part in the Battle of Salado Creek and the Somervell Expedition in 1842. As a member of the doomed Mier Expedition to invade Mexico, he was a survivor of the Black Bean Episode and was finally released from Perote prison in 1844. While visiting family in Missouri in 1847, John H. Livergood met Sarah Ann Elizabeth Perkins (1828–1909). They married in 1847 and established a home (eventually with 13 children) on the Lavaca River. The Livergoods helped found Mossy Grove Methodist Church and were active leaders there. A farmer and rancher, Livergood also entered the political life of Lavaca County, serving as Chief Justice (County Judge) from 1850 to 1852 and later as Justice of the Peace. In his final military service, Livergood served in the Lone Star Guard, the Texas State Troops and the Confederate Army during the Civil War. Both he and Sarah Ann Livergood are buried at Mossy Grove Cemetery. (2001)

HALLETTSVILLE (Lavaca Co.)

US 77, 9 mi. N in roadside park; SH 95 at American Legion Hall in Moulton

Route of the Texas Army

In Texas Revolution, Gen. Sam Houston and his Texas Army crossed Rocky Creek near this spot, March 15, 1836, retreating eastward from town of Gonzales.

Their victory 5 weeks later over Santa Anna's Mexican army, in Battle of San Jacinto, brought freedom to Texas, April 21. (1969)

HALLETTSVILLE (Lavaca Co.)

US 90A, in Sublime

The Wild Man of the Navidad

A mysterious runaway Negro slave who alternately terrified and aroused pity of settlers in this region for about 15 years.

The mysterious exile, at first with a companion, appeared along the Navidad bottoms about 1836.

Hiding in trees during day, he stole into kitchens at night for food, but always left half. He also took tools, returning them later, brightly polished. Slaves called him "The Thing That Comes," fearing a ghost.

Captured in 1851, the wild man proved to be an African chief's son. Resold into slavery, he died peacefully as "Old Jimbo" in 1884. (1970)

HALLETSVILLE (Lavaca Co.)

US 77, 1 mi. S

William Smothers
(1760–1837)

A veteran of the American Revolution, a native of Virginia, William Smothers was orphaned at 12 when Indians killed his father, and his mother died of shock. In the American Revolution, he fought at King's Mountain, Guilford courthouse, Camden, and Eutaw Springs. He moved to Kentucky in 1781, built two forts near present Hartford, originally called "Smothers Station," and in 1798 founded an Ohio River port that later became Owensboro. He was a leader in civil affairs in early Kentucky, was a militia captain, and commanded troops in the War of 1812. Smothers Park in Owensboro is named in his honor.

Smothers scouted in Texas before 1820, returned in 1821 with the exploring party of Stephen F. Austin, and helped build Fort Bend for the safety of the "old 300" settlers. In 1824 Mexico gave him a land grant; in 1826 he and two sons helped settle DeWitt's colony, receiving land grants in the vicinity of this marker. Fearless and a skillful guide, he often hunted with his friend Jim Bowie. Reputedly he tomahawked bears in hand combat. Married twice, he was ancestor of many leading Texans. He died in 1837, after seeing a son and three grandsons help to win the Texas War for Independence. (1977)

HAMILTON (Hamilton Co.) — US 281, 1 mi. N
Hamilton County
Created February 2, 1842, from Montgomery and Houston Counties. Recreated January 22, 1858. Organized August 2, 1858. Named in honor of General James Hamilton, 1786–1857, lawyer and Governor of South Carolina. Appointed diplomatic agent to Europe by President Lamar. Hamilton, the county seat. (1965)

HAMILTON (Hamilton Co.) — US 281, 10 mi. N in roadside park
Hamilton County, C.S.A.
Created and organized in 1858. By 1860 had 489 people in 78 families from 15 states. Vote in 1861 was 86-1 in favor of secession. 60 farmers were organized as Hamilton County Minute Men, a unit of part-time soldiers. Others joined Confederate regiments and fought at Vicksburg, Shiloh and other memorable battles.

During the Civil War travel was on horseback and hauling by ox wagon. Homes were of logs split from timber along creeks and rivers. About half an acre a day was farmed, with homemade wooden tools. Corn and wheat were raised. On burned-over ground each family grew its own tobacco, hanging the leaves inside the living room to dry. Diet was mostly beef, cornbread and coffee substitutes. Homes were lighted by wicks stuck into tallow-filled eggshells.

With few men on hand to brand and herd, feuds rose over thefts and straying cattle. In differences over war issues, 2 men fled to Mexico to join Federals. Later they returned, trying to recruit neighbors into a unit disloyal to Texas to welcome planned Federal invasion. Further trouble came from many Confederate deserters who took refuge along the streams and lived by theft and violence. (1965)

HAMILTON (Hamilton Co.) — 121 S. Rice Avenue (US 281)
Manning-Gordon-Henderson House
Local contractor Louis V. Manning built this house between 1880 and 1885 on land inherited from his father, pioneer Exekiel Manning, and lived here until 1904. The John H. and Abbie Gordon family owned the house from 1907 to 1936 and the Oliver Dow and Minta Henderson family took up residence here in 1936. A simple example of a cross-gabled roof Queen Anne house, its distinguishing details include fish-scale textured gables, cutaway bay windows, and a front entry porch with ornamental posts and brackets and a jigsawn frieze. Also of interest is the unusual siding flanking the entry door. (1999)

HAMILTON (Hamilton Co.) — 222 Baker St. (Alt. US 281)
Twin Oaks
Named for historic trees. Built 1904 by Dr. Chas. C. Baker (1872–1942), city's first resident dentist, descendant of the Beemans, one of Dallas' founding families; graduate, Baltimore College of Dental Surgery, Republican state executive committeeman for 26 years. Dr. Baker built "Twin Oaks" with ball and billiard rooms unique in Hamilton. At death of widow, Alma Nicholson Baker, 1958, the home was sold to Andrew Campbell. (1968)

HAMLIN (Jones Co.) — South Central Ave. (US 83) between 2nd and 3rd Sts.
Hamlin
Early settler R. D. Moore conveyed 320 acres of land to the International Construction Co. (also called the Orient Land Co.) of Kansas City, Missouri, for a town site along the Panhandle Gulf Railway in September 1902. Probably named for Orient executive W. H. Hamlin, the Hamlin community was organized in 1905, the same year it received its first post office. The Kansas City, Mexico and Orient Railway reached Hamlin in 1906 and a newspaper, the Hamlin Herald, was first printed that same year. Hamlin was incorporated as a town and a school system was established in 1907. By autumn 1908, Hamlin had grown to more than one thousand citizens as more railroads reached the area. Hamlin quickly became a major shipping point, with its economy based on agriculture and the railroad. Among the town's business operations were cotton compresses, a cotton oil mill, an ice plant, a cement and plaster plant, a grain elevator, several cotton gins, an electric generating plant, an ice cream factory and bottling works, and a telephone company. Churches formed in Hamlin's early days included Church of Christ, Baptist, Methodist

and Church of the Nazarene. A movie theatre opened in 1907. Central Nazarene College was established in 1909. The Oscar Depriest School System for African American students began operation in 1925. Oil was discovered near Hamlin in 1928, broadening the area's economic growth with oil and gas exploration. In 1950, the town's population was 3,564. The school system was integrated in 1965. The population of Hamlin in 1990 was 2,791. At the dawn of the 21st century, Hamlin remains a center for farming and varied manufacturing. (2000)

HAMSHIRE (Jefferson Co.)   *3 mi. E*
Arceneaux House
Typical "daubed" house in which lower walls are plastered with moss, mud and sassafras strips. Built by Moise Broussard about 1856 when he brought to it his bride, Mary Gadrac Arceneaux, great-great-granddaughter of Louis Arceneaux, the "Gabriel" of Longfellow's poem "Evangeline." 1880-house passed to brother, Athenas Arceneaux, area pioneer in rice planting, and his heirs.

Trees here came from acorns of oak shading "Evangeline" grave. Awarded Medallion Plate. (1966)

HANDLEY (Tarrant Co.)   *SH 303, Near Lake Arlington Golf Course*
General Edward H. Tarrant
In this vicinity May 24, 1841, General Edward H. Tarrant with 79 men attacked several Indian villages situated along a creek (now called Village Creek) and recovered many horses and much stolen plunder. 12 Indians were killed and many wounded.

Of the Texans, Captain John B. Denton was killed. Captains Henry Stout and Griffin were wounded. (1936)

HAPPY (Swisher Co.)   *IH 27, N city limits on a windmill*
Harman-Toles Elevator
(¼ mi W)
Holland E. Toles (1894–1941) opened a grain elevator in this area in 1926, and was joined by Vernon Harman in 1938. After Toles' death, Harman formed a new partnership with John F. and Holl Ed Toles. World War II, increased irrigation, and a Federal grain program created a need for larger storage facilities. On March 1, 1945, construction was begun on this six-unit concrete elevator. Labor was provided by the U.S. government, utilizing 50 Italian prisoners of war from a camp near Hereford, under Geneva Convention provisions. The project was completed on July 10, 1945. (1974)

HARLETON (Harrison Co.)   *SH 154, Centennial Park*
Harleton
Although settlement in this area between the forks of Big and Little Cypress Creeks began in the 1830s, notable growth did not occur until the arrival of a railroad here in 1891. The railroad was a vital part of a venture financed by John H. Inman, organized by Edwin J. Fry, and executed by brothers Robert H. and James W. Harle, to exploit the area's virgin forests. Organized as the Hope Lumber Company, they constructed a depot and large commissary, installed a band sawmill, and extended a tram road into the Eagle Creek area.

The nearby village of Grady was unable to compete against the Harles' well-stocked store and dance hall and soon faded. Its post office, renamed Harleton after the Harle brothers, was relocated to the Harle Store.

Harleton's economy boomed as timber production led to increased farm activity, and local merchants such as D.C. Webb and Son, Dreyfus-Little Mercantile Co., J.P. Craver and Son, and R.W. Taylor General Merchandise increased stocks to meet a growing demand for wares.

By the late 1890s, however, Hope Lumber Company had processed the area's available timber and closed its mill. The railroad later joined with the Marshall & East Texas Railroad. Harleton continued, supported by agriculture and other timber operations in the area. (1993)

HARLETON (Harrison Co.)   *SH 154, 7 mi. NW on S side, on open land*
Site of Davidson Homestead
On this land, purchased by Isaiah Davidson (1814–1900), one of the first frame houses in this section of the state was built in 1867. Davidson, of Scottish descent, moved to Texas from Georgia with his wife, Mary Little, and children Elias, Frank, Lizzie, and Houston. His oldest

son, John, who was a Confederate soldier, acquired land adjoining. Two other sons, Whitfield and Henry, died in the Civil War.

This site soon became a mecca for members of the Davidson clan as they moved to Texas. The land was also on an old wagon road over which crops were hauled from "Blackland country" (around Dallas) to port of Jefferson.

Family property, which totals 3,200 acres (five sections), is today owned by descendant T. Whitfield Davidson.

Early History
of Davidson Property

This land was sold on December 15, 1859, by Richard Key to E. J. Glover, who soon built a hewn-log house here. The first Masonic lodge in this area was named for Glover, who sold the property on August 31, 1867, to Isaiah Davidson.

HARPER (Gillespie Co.)   *US 290*
Harper Presbyterian Church

Organized in 1881 as the Barnett Spring Presbyterian Church, this congregation originally met in a schoolhouse. The fellowship moved to Harper in 1901 and erected this frame church on land donated by Arch Austin. Sale of property given by R. W. Crosley helped finance the construction. In 1903 a bell was purchased for the belfry. This structure housed the Harper school in 1906 and again in the 1940s. It also served as a worship site for other denominations.   (1976)

HARPER (Gillespie Co.)   *US 290 at FM 783, 300 ft. S*
Site of the McDonald Massacre

Pioneer preacher Matthew Taylor and the families of his daughter and two sons moved here in 1863 from their homestead on the Llano River. They built a cabin on this site near the source of the Pedernales River. In August 1864, Matthew and his son Jim returned to the Llano for a load of hay, leaving in charge Eli McDonald, husband of Matthew's daughter Caroline.

On August 8, 1864, at a nearby spring, Jim Taylor's wife, Gill, was surprised by a band of Kiowas and wounded by an arrow. Before she died, she warned the others, who took refuge in the cabin. After a brief fight, the Indians killed Eli McDonald. They captured his wife, Caroline, and daughters, Mahala and Becky Jane; and Alice, James, and Dorcas, children of Matthew's son Zed. Matthew's wife, "Aunt Hannah," escaped and hid in a cave in what is now Harper Community Park.

Matthew and Jim Taylor discovered the tragedy the next day and sought help from Eli McDonald's nephew Monroe. The two victims of the massacre were buried near Spring Creek, twelve miles east of Harper. "Aunt Hannah" was found and reunited with her husband. The captives wandered as far north as Oklahoma with the Kiowa tribe before they were located and ransomed by the U.S. government.   (1976)

HARPER (Gillespie Co.)   *FM 783 at US 290*
First Baptist Church
of Harper

Organized in 1887 with nine members, the First Baptist Church congregation initially met in the local school building and a brush arbor. A wooden sanctuary and parsonage were built in 1897. The congregation has been involved in community activities and mission work for many years. Harper High School held classes in the church building in 1921 and 1941–1942. A native stone structure was erected in 1944, consisting of a sanctuary and Sunday School rooms. A fellowship hall annex was added in 1971. This church has been part of Harper history for over one hundred years.   (1987)

HARTLEY (Hartley Co.)   *US 87, 1.8 mi. SE*
Hartley County

Formed Young and Bexar Territories. Created August 21, 1876. Organized February 5, 1891.

Named in honor of two brothers Oliver Cromwell and Rufus Hartley, distinguished members of the Texas bar. Hartley, county seat.

HASKELL (Haskell Co.)   *US 277, 1 mi. N*

Haskell County

Created February 1, 1858. Recreated August 21, 1876. Organized January 13, 1885.

Named in honor of Charles Ready Haskell, 1817–1836, a Tennessean who was shot with Fannin in the massacre at Goliad.

Haskell, the county seat. Crossed by Capt. R. B. Marcy in surveying a route to California in 1849. First settlement at Haskell, 1882.

HASKELL (Haskell Co.)   *US 277, 6.5 mi. S*

Capt. R. B. Marcy Trail
1849–1858

Erected by American Legion Haskell, Texas.

HASKELL (Haskell Co.)   *US 277 at US 380, .5 mi. N*

The Mackenzie Trail Historical Marker
Located 1 mi. N Stamford

This is the largest such marker between Vicksburg, Miss. and the Pacific. Erected by descendants of Open Range Ranchers.

The MacKenzie Trail was the only way west between T. P. and F. W. & D. Rwys for decades. MacKenzie Trail Memorial Assoc.

HAWKINS (Wood Co.)   *FM 778, 11 mi. NW at site*

Macedonia School
(Site 600 ft. SW)

One of first one-teacher schools in Wood County. Served the county's earliest community— Macedonia, which was renamed Redland in 1900. Land for school was donated by W. M. McCarroll in 1885. W. M. Harris was one of first teachers. The school consolidated with the Hawkins Independent District in 1944.   (1969)

HEARNE (Robertson Co.)   *FM 391, E City Limits*

Brazos Manufacturing Company, C.S.A.
(About 6 mi. E)

Established in 1863 on a Brazos River tributary. Intended to make flour and cloth of cotton and wool. Chartered by 9th Texas Legislature in all-out effort to supply the goods necessary to Confederate victory in the Civil War. Up to now Texas had not had factories because she could more economically trade agricultural products for manufactured goods. Wartime imports, however, were limited to small shipments run in through Federal coastal blockades.

To finance its purchases of machinery, materials and labor, Brazos Manufacturing Company received cotton from Texas planters, especially in this area.

Subscription of a bale of cotton gave a planter the right to export one bale for his own benefit. Since neither factory nor farm had any other way to pay running expenses than by cotton sales, much cotton was donated to the corporation.

This corporation met the fate of many chartered by Texas during the Civil War: paper mills, bridge and ferry companies, iron works, railroads, foundries, cotton cards plants and others. Although Brazos Manufacturing Company did help to clothe army and civilians, its production was small and was achieved too late in the war.   (1965)

HEBBRONVILLE (Jim Hogg Co.)   *SH 16, 205 N Smith St.*

Hotel Viggo

The original part of this hotel was built by C. F. Luque in 1915 for the owner, Viggo Kohler, to accommodate businessmen and area travelers. Soon after it opened, Hotel Viggo served as a fortress when area ranchers feared an attack by Pancho Villa's men. As a result of the town's oil boom, a south wing was added in 1924. The Mission Revival hotel has been a landmark on the Jim Hogg County courthouse square since Hebbronville's early days.   (1983)

HELENA (Karnes Co.)   *FM 81 at SH 80*
Helena
Founded in 1852 on San Antonio River by Thomas Ruckman, a graduate of Princeton, and Lewis Owings, later first governor of Arizona Territory. Town was named in honor of Owings' wife, Helen.

Situated on branch of famed Chihuahua Trail (running from Indianola to San Antonio to Northern Mexico), Helena was to experience quick growth. Much traffic of wagon freight and gold bullion travelled trail. Four-horse stages daily passed through town.

Helena was designated county seat when Karnes County was created and organized in 1854. First election of county officials was held on gallery of Ruckman-Owings store.

During Civil War, Karnes County mustered six companies, including Helena guards, for service. Helena was a confederate post office and issued its own stamps. Much Confederate cotton destined for Mexican ports passed through Helena.

During its heyday, Helena had a courthouse, jail, newspaper, academy, drugstore, blacksmith shop, two hotels, and several saloons and general stores.

Bypassed by the S.A. & A.P. Railroad in 1886, town died. County seat was moved to Karnes City in 1894 after hotly contested election.

HELENA (Karnes Co.)   *FM 81, Old Helena Courthouse*
Ox-Cart Road (Section of Chihuahua Road)
After centuries of use by buffalo and Indians, this trail from San Antonio to the Texas coast gained importance when opened to colonial travel by the Alarcon Expedition in 1718.

Spanish conquistadores and priests, the Gutierrez-Magee Expedition (which invaded Spanish Texas in 1812), Stephen F. Austin, Alamo heroes, Santa Anna's messenger ordering the death of prisoners at Goliad, Polish, and German settlers of Texas—all traveled the road.

Rich trade in gold, silver, and leather with Mexico and the West was conducted along the road from San Antonio to Powderhorn. The U.S. 2nd Cavalry forts, established to protect the Texas frontier, moved men and supplies over it. Materials were transported in two-wheeled ox-carts, prairie schooners, Wells-Fargo wagons drawn by sixteen mules, and by pack animals.

In 1852, Helena was founded on the road as a midway point between San Antonio and Goliad; Lewis S. Owings operated a daily stage line here, 1854. Major incidents of the bizarre Cart War of 1857 between Texan and Mexican teamsters occurred near Helena.

Herds of longhorns from South Texas crossed the road here enroute to market. After the railroad came through county in 1886 the Ox-Cart Road was abandoned.

HELOTES (Bexar Co.)   *SH 16 N, 9 mi.*
Gallagher Ranch
Fort and ranch house built by Peter Gallagher (1812–1878), Irish-Texan engineer, merchant, ranger, and diarist of the Texan-Santa Fe Expedition. The hacienda of native stone, with rifle slits to protect from Indian attack, was bought 1927 by H. V. McNutt as headquarters of early Texas guest ranch. The rambling Mexican-style home has known distinguished guests and the routine of a working ranch. Awarded Medallion Plate.   (1967)

HEMPHILL (Sabine Co.)   *SH 87 right-of-way, 4.5 mi. N*
Matthew Arnold Parker
(May 17, 1801–March 19, 1862)
First chief justice of Sabine County, Republic of Texas. Parker was born in Georgia. He came here from Louisiana in 1822, settling at this site which was on land later included in his headright grant from the Republic. In 1836 he served in the defensive Sabine Volunteers. President Sam Houston appointed him chief justice (or county judge) in Dec. 1836, and he was on a commission to detect fraudulent land claims in 1840. After his wife, Mary (Isaacs), died (1845), he married Elizabeth Lowe. He was father of 16 children. He died in DeWitt county, and was buried near Nordheim.   (1974)

HEMPSTEAD (Waller Co.)   *FM 359, 4 mi. SE*
Plantation of Charles Donoho
In this vicinity on the Plantation of Charles Donoho the Texas Army under General Sam Houston encamped April 14–15, 1836, before beginning its march to Harrisburg.

HEMPSTEAD (Waller Co.)   *SH 159, 2 mi. SW*
The Camp Site of the Texas Army
Five miles southeast to the camp site of the Texas Army March 31 to April 13, 1836, when it crossed the Brazos on the steamboat Yellowstone and began its march toward Harrisburg.

HEMPSTEAD (Waller Co.)   *US 290, 1 mi. N*
Waller County
Created from Austin and Grimes Counties, April 28, and organized Aug. 16, 1873. Named for Edwin Waller (1800–1861), a signer of the Texas Declaration of Independence, 1836; Postmaster General, Texas Republic; first mayor of Austin.

Site of rich 1831–1874 Groce plantations, later home of sculptress Elisabet Ney.

Hempstead, founded 1857 during building of Houston & Texas Central Railroad, an important transportation center, is the county seat.

Since 1878, county has been site of Prairie View Agricultural & Mechanical College.

Economy is based on industry, diversified agriculture, and oil production.   (1967)

HEMPSTEAD (Waller Co.)   *US 290 2.9 mi. E in roadside park*
Clear Creek Confederate
War Camps
Although no physical evidence has been found of the Confederate camp sites in this area, historical accounts have established that this part of Waller County was the location of several Civil War encampments. The close proximity of Clear Creek, the railroad, and the city of Hempstead made this area a logical site for training soldiers and for holding Federal prisoners. Although Camp Groce and Camp Herbert were the most widely known, other camps were known to have been established as the need existed and were abandoned when no longer necessary.   (1985)

HEMPSTEAD (Waller Co.)   *US 290, 3.3 mi. E, rest area,*
                                                    near entrance to Liendo Plantation
Groce Family Plantations
Pioneers in this Texas area. Had early cotton gin and ferry. Founder of family was Jared E. Groce (1782–1836), who came to Texas in 1822. His large wagon train brought elaborate plantation equipment. Groce built "Bernardo" and "Groce's Retreat." Heirs built "Pleasant Hill," "Eagle Island" and "Liendo" (the only surviving Groce mansion, 2 mi. NW of here).

A contribution of the family to the cause of Texas freedom was providing rations and ferry service to army of Gen. Houston on eve of San Jacinto victory. Descendants have contributed leadership to the state.   (1970)

HEMPSTEAD (Waller Co.)   *FM 529, 14.8 mi. S*
Norris Wright Cuney
(May 12, 1846–March 3, 1898)
Born in the slave quarters of Sunnyside plantation (3.2 miles SE), Cuney displayed such intelligence as a boy that in 1859 he was sent to Wiley Street School for Negroes in Pittsburgh, Pa. On returning to Texas after the Civil War, he studied law and began operating a wharf contracting company in Galveston.

Cuney soon became an active member of the Texas Union League, which urged black political activity and Republican Party loyalty. In 1870 he organized the Negro Longshoremen's Association. In later years he served Galveston as a city alderman, school board member, and U.S. customs collector, and ran twice without success for the state legislature. On July 5, 1871, he married Adelina Dowdie; they had two children.

After 1872 he emerged as leader of the Republican Party in Texas, attending national party conventions as chairman of the Texas delegation. He served on the Republican National Executive Committee in 1891–1892. The party broke his power in Texas in 1896 by refusing to seat his delegation, an action which deprived blacks of a voice in Texas politics until the 1960s.

Cuney, one of the most prominent blacks in Texas history, died in San Antonio, where he had moved for his health. He was buried in Galveston.   (1973)

HENDERSON (Rusk Co.)

US 79 at US 259, (Jackson at W Main St.), on traffic island

Henderson

Founded as the county seat for the newly created county of Rusk in 1843, Henderson was named for Republic of Texas pioneer and statesman James Pinckney Henderson, who would later become the first governor of the state of Texas. Land for the town was donated by W. B. Ochiltree, who stipulated that it be named for his friend Henderson, and by Republic of Texas General James Smith, who is known as the "Father of Henderson."

Town lots were sold soon after the city was established, with land set aside for both churches and schools. A wooden courthouse was built in the center of town in 1849, and the town grew steadily as homes and businesses were constructed.

A disastrous fire destroyed much of the central business district in 1860. Following the Civil War and the arrival of the railroads in this area in the 1870s, a large number of brick structures were built in the downtown area.

The discovery of the vast East Texas oil field in 1930 caused an economic boom in Henderson. The population increased from 2,000 to 10,000 within a matter of months. The town continues to serve as a center of commerce and civic activities. (1989)

HENDERSON (Rusk Co.)

SH 64, 6 mi. W in roadside pk.

East Texas Oil Field Discovery Well
The Joiner No. 3 Daisy Bradford

Discovery genius was C. M. (Dad) Joiner, 70 year old Oklahoman, who for years had believed there was oil in Rusk county. Driller was E. C. Laster. Final crew: Dennis May, Dave Cherry, Glenn Pool, Jim Lambert and Dave Hughes.

Two previous attempts had been made by Joiner on the Miller farm, both ending in mechanical failure. A bit jammed in the first hole, and the second was abandoned on the advice of Laster because the drill pipe was stuck. Rig was skidded 300 feet down slope (derrick had a broken sill). "This is as good a place as any," said Laster, and the Joiner no. 3 Daisy Bradford was spudded in on May 8, 1929.

Equipment consisted of an old rotary rig powered by one single cylinder engine, one 45 hp boiler and one old cotton gin boiler fired with soggy oak and pine chunks by Dan Tanner, roustabout. The depression was on and money hard to raise. The crew often went without pay and Dad Joiner sacrificed much of his 10,000 acre block of leases to keep the venture going.

Finally on Sept. 5, 1930, a drill stem test logged at 3536 feet into the Woodbine formation showed oil. A better rig had to be brought in to complete the well. Casing was set at 3400 feet and on October 3, 1930, the well blew in and oil went over the crown block. The news spread like wildfire. Cars were bumper to bumper on all roads leading to the well, and the boom was on. Derricks rose in all directions. In its first 30 years, this great field produced in excess of 3½ billion barrels of oil. It now covers some 200 square miles, largest in the world.

HENDERSON (Rusk Co.)

SH 64, 6 mi. W

Gaston Public School Complex

An oil boom here in the early 1930s prompted the formal organization of the Gaston Independent School District in 1931 to cope with the community's rapidly expanding student population. The district chose Dallas architects Emory White and Howard DeFee to design both an elementary and a 2-story high school building. These brick structures were completed at this site, along with a football field, in 1932.

The district added a wooden gymnasium and brick auditorium in 1936, home economics cottage in 1938, brick cafeteria in 1939 and shop building in 1940. Linked by arcades, the structures exhibit classically articulated features and sophisticated cast-stone and window details. The rustic style landscaping, which includes walls made of native stone from the nearby Hardy farm, was completed by the Works Progress Administration in 1936–1940.

Students at this institution earned county, district and regional championships in football, basketball, and track, as well as awards in journalism, band, debate and other literary areas, including a Rhodes Scholarship, during the 1940s and 1950s. Gaston schools merged with the London School System in 1965 to form the West Rusk County Independent School District.

Recorded Texas Historic Landmark—1993

HENDERSON (Rusk Co.)

US 79, approx. 11 mi. SW

Pleasant Grove Methodist Episcopal
Church South Cemetery

The East Texas farming community of Pleasant Grove, also known as "Shake Rag," was established during the 1850s by southern planters. Among the first settlers were Judge Stephen Decatur Morris (1819–1898) and his wife, Mary (Bradford) (1823–1906), on whose plantation early Methodist worship services in the area were held. About 1853, a sanctuary for the Pleasant Grove Methodist Episcopal Church, South, was built.

The Methodist Cemetery was established here in 1873, with the burial of James Bradford Morris (b. 1856). He was the son of Stephen and Mary Morris. Others buried here include Dr. Richard H. C. Shelton, an eminent southwestern surgeon; other friends and relatives of Stephen and Mary Morris; and pioneer settlers.

Church trustees Seaton Moore, Simpson Moore, and G. D. Boatwright purchased this land for the church and cemetery in 1877. The Pleasant Grove Church eventually disbanded, with the remaining members joining St. Paul's Methodist Church in Henderson (11 mi. NE). By 1929, the year of the last burial in this graveyard, most Methodist families were using the city cemetery in Henderson, The Pleasant Grove Cemetery remains an important part of the record of early settlement in this part of Rusk County. (Texas Sesquicentennial 1836–1986)

HENDERSON (Rusk Co.)

Two locations: US 79, 13.5 mi. E;
also, Tatum (Rusk Co.) SH 149

Trammel's Trace

An early Indian trail later named for Nicholas Trammel who surveyed it in 1813 for the U.S. Used in describing most of the boundary between Rusk and Panola Counties. Portions of the trace are incorporated into the county line road 7/10 of a mile south of this marker.

It passes through Tatum, placing the town site in both counties.

The trace extended from Red River to Nacogdoches and brought in great numbers of pioneers, including many who became Texas heroes.

HENDERSON (Rusk Co.)

S. Main and Henderson St.

General James Smith
1792–1855

On this hill, as he wished for burial in sight of courthouse, is grave of General James Smith, one of the founding fathers of Henderson. A South Carolina native, he fought for the United States in War of 1812. Moved to Texas in 1835, returned to United States to raise troops for Texas War for Independence. Later he fought in Republic's Indian Wars; Regulator-moderator uprising in 1840s in East Texas; and in Mexican War.

He was first judge, East Texas District; a legislator; honored in naming of nearby Smith County. His wife, Hannah Parker, is buried beside him in this park. Also buried here is Burt M. Smith, a son who died in 1863, and it is believed that a daughter also, Frances Smith Timmons is buried here. She and her husband also donated land to Henderson. Both of these latter graves are unmarked and lost.

HENDERSON (Rusk Co.)

South Main Street (SH 154)

Howard-Dickenson House

First brick home in county. Built 1855 by brothers, David P. and Jas. Logan Howard, settlers from Richmond, Va. The Howards made bricks with mud mill and later with a patented machine and kiln on the premises.

(Howard bricks and carpentry went into the old courthouse on square—and most of city's major construction in later 1800s.)

Structure is iron-reinforced; has hand-wrought woodwork and oldest plastered walls in city.

A frequent visitor in early years to this house was Texas statesman Sam Houston, a cousin of Martha Ann (Mrs. Dave) Howard.

The home was bought in 1905 by Mrs. M. C. Dickenson, the daughter of Dr. Alfred Graham, a pioneer physician of Rusk County. To the original house, the Dickensons added a frame wing at the rear.

Purchased in 1950 by Mr. and Mrs. Homer L. Bryce, and given by the Bryces in 1964 to the Rusk County Heritage Association, the house was restored in 1967 by work of Friends of Texas History. (1968)

HENRIETTA (Clay Co.) *US 82 at US 287, East city limits*
Clay County
Formed from Cooke County. Created December 24, 1857. Organized August 6, 1860. Disorganized in 1862 because of Indian raids. Reorganized August 4, 1873. Henrietta, headquarters for buffalo hunters until 1878. The first Hereford cattle in Texas were brought to Clay County 1875 from Beecher, Illinois by William S. Ikard. Original county seat Cambridge moved to Henrietta 1874. (1964)

HEREFORD (Deaf Smith Co.) *US 60, 4 mi. SW*
(moved to courthouse grounds)
Deaf Smith County
Formed from Young and Bexar Territories. Created August 21, 1876. Organized October 3, 1890. Named in honor of Erastus "Deaf" Smith 1787–1837. Came to Texas in 1821. Rendered valuable service as a scout and spy during the Texas Revolution and was conspicuous for his bravery in the Battle of San Jacinto.

County seat, La Plata, frequently called Grenada, 1890–1898. Hereford, since 1899. (1964)

HEREFORD (Deaf Smith Co.) *US 385 and W 4th Street*
Town Without a Toothache
Hereford's "miracle water" was brought to national fame in 1941 when Dr. Edward Taylor, state dental officer, told the American Dental Association that tooth decay was almost unknown here.

This ideal situation had been discovered by a local dentist, Dr. George Heard, originally from Alabama. In a cross-section survey, dentists found that few local people had dental cavities. Hereford's mineral-rich water and soil are thought to prevent tooth decay.

Demand arose for Hereford water to be shipped all over the U.S. and to foreign nations.

. (1967)

HEREFORD (Deaf Smith Co.) *US 60 at US 385*
Site of Great Cowboy Strike
(3 mi. E)
Began in spring of 1883 when range hands from LS, LX, LIT and other large ranches organized a strike for better wages; was a reaction to loss of privileges given earlier and to attitude of big land owners toward cowboys.

Several hired hands gathered at Alamocitos, headquarters of LS, to protest. Men on every ranch soon asked for higher pay, but strike failed due to surplus of cowboys and no means to enforce demands.

Strike gave force to little men opposing cattle barons and three years later erupted in Tascosa into one of the bloodiest gun fights the West had ever seen. (1967)

HEREFORD (Deaf Smith Co.) *US 60, 4 mi. SW in roadside park*
Ghost Towns of Deaf Smith County
Here as in many Texas counties, ghost towns and ghost post offices outnumber living ones.

La Plata (formerly Grenada) thrived as county seat and was a major stop of New Mexico-Amarillo Road, 1880s and '90s. Its 28 houses and businesses were removed to Hereford with the county government in 1898.

Ayr, which lost county seat to La Plata, 1890, had a early post office and a few frame buildings. Other nonexistent post offices include Escarbada (on XIT ranch), 1889; Dean, 1892–1899; Mirage (probably on LS ranch), 1891–1894; Kelso, 1907–1908. (1969)

HEREFORD (Deaf Smith Co.) *US 60 at 385, 4.2 mi. SE*
Mackenzie Trail
Along this lonely, arid trail Gen. Ranald S. Mackenzie led his troops on scouting forays in the 1870s. Known for bravery and skill as a Civil War officer, he was sent to Texas and quickly adjusted to dangers and problems of frontier fighting. He fought against Comanches at Blanco and Tule Canyons. On Sept. 28, 1874, in Palo Duro Canyon, he led his men in one of the last

major Indian battles in Texas where he slew more than 1,000 horses to cripple Indian action; thus he helped bring peace to the Texas Panhandle, making it safe for settlers.   (1965)

HEREFORD (Deaf Smith Co.) *US 60, 2 mi. SW*
Prisoner of War Camp Chapel
(3.5 mi. S)
A prisoner of war camp, used primarily for Italian soldiers, was in operation near this site during World War II. Known as the Hereford Military Reservation and Reception Center, it was first used in 1943 for prisoners captured in an invasion of North Africa. Many of the approximately 7,000 Italian soldiers imprisoned here became friends with local residents and with American troops. Since the war, some have returned for visits and others have settled in the region. The camp chapel, constructed by the prisoners, is the only building remaining at the site.   (1982)

HEREFORD (Deaf Smith Co.) *US 385, 4.5 mi. S in Castro County*
Prisoner of War Camp Chapel
(3 mi. W)
Near this site during World War II the Hereford Military Reservation and Reception Center, a prisoner of war camp, was established. During nearly three years of operation, approximately 7,000 Italian soldiers were imprisoned. Through their work on area farms and such projects as the painting of religious murals in St. Mary's Catholic Church at Umbarger (25 mi. NE), many of the soldiers made lasting friendships with local residents and with American troops at the camp. The center's chapel, constructed by the prisoners, is the only building remaining at the site.
(1982)

HERMLEIGH (Scurry Co.) *US 84 at S Harlan*
St. John's Catholic Church
This area was settled in the early 1900s by a number of farm families from South Texas. Catholic services were first conducted by priests from Abilene in the homes of Albert J. Kuss, Sr. (1863–1945) and other settlers. The Church of Francis Xavier was built in 1908 on land donated by Robert Herm (1874–1927) in the new town of Hermleigh. In 1936, the name of the church was changed when funds were given to the congregation with the stipulation that its name be St. John's. Included in the new diocese of Lubbock in 1983, St. John's is the oldest parish in the diocese.   (1988)

HICO (Hamilton Co.) *US 281 at First St.*
First United Methodist Church of Hico
In 1881, the Rev. John W. Hearn and Elder L.B. Hickman led 29 members in a newly organized Methodist church in Hico. The congregation held its early services in the Hico schoolhouse, and charter members included the L.T. Dillashaw, J.B. Hillyer, George D. Autrey and D.G. Barrow families. During a 10-day revival in winter 1884-85, evangelist R.R. Raymond helped raise money for a church sanctuary. Texas Central Railway donated land in 1886 for the use of the Methodist Episcopal Church, South, congregation of Hico. A sanctuary was completed in spring 1887 at this site. The structure served the congregation, which had grown to more than 300 members, until 1902-03, when the current sanctuary was built of wood with handcrafted benches and pulpit. The church held an open house and homecoming in 1954, showing to former members and pastors a new education building and remodeled sanctuary, with an enclosed bell tower and new tan brick façade over the original wood cladding. The congregation's numbers grew during the 20th century as other area churches merged their memberships into Hico's. These churches represented the communities of Carlton, Clairette, Duffau, Fairy and Pleasant Hill. During its years as a congregation, the church has contributed to area communities through its many services, including Boy and Girl Scout programs, community dinners, and clothes and food pantry, as well as its youth, music and education programs, missionary funding, study and worship.   (2002)

HICO (Erath Co.) *SH 6, 7 mi. NW*
Clairette Schoolhouse
The first Clairette schoolhouse was a one-room log structure built as early as 1871. This two-story building was constructed in 1912, one year after the creation of the Clairette Independent School District. It served until 1949, when the rural school was closed. The native stone building

was then used for various community functions. The old Clairette schoolhouse features a one-story porch with Tuscan columns at the entryway. (1985)

HIDALGO (Hidalgo Co.) *US 281 Spur, terminus at the Rio Grande River*
Hidalgo-Reynosa Bridges
At the time of the formation of Hidalgo County in 1852, the village located here, originally named Edinburgh, became the new county seat. A ferry service was operating between the village and Reynosa, Mexico.

By 1861, the town's name was changed to Hidalgo, and regular ferry service was inaugurated in 1910 by Crisoforo Vela (1856–1932). First using rowboats and, later, raft-like conveyances, the ferry continued in operation until Joe Pate erected a bridge here in 1926.

The 1926 suspension bridge was damaged by floods in 1933. Although rebuilt and strengthened, it fell into the river and was destroyed in 1939 after cable anchors on the U.S. side failed to hold. A second suspension bridge was erected the following year and was purchased by the city of McAllen in 1960. A four-lane prestressed concrete bridge was opened to traffic on June 1, 1967. The suspension bridge was removed for salvage in 1971. Construction of an additional four-lane bridge was completed in 1988.

For over six decades, the Hidalgo-Reynosa bridges, operated jointly by McAllen, Hidalgo, and Mexican interests since 1960, have facilitated transportation and fostered international cooperation and friendship between Texas and Mexico. (1989)

HIGGINS (Lipscomb Co.) *US 60, 1 mi. E*
Lipscomb County
Formed from Young and Bexar Territories. Created August 21, 1876. Organized June 6, 1887.

Named in honor of Abner S. Lipscomb, 1789–1856. Secretary of State in President Lamar's Cabinet. Member of the Constitutional Convention, 1845. Associate Justice of the first Supreme Court of Texas.

Lipscomb, the county seat.

HIGGINS (Lipscomb Co.) *US 60, E edge of city limits*
Higgins
Town platted, post office opened and first train arrived, 1887. Named for G. H. Higgins, wealthy railroad stockholder. Early cattle shipping point. Devastating tornado struck April 9, 1947. An estimated 45 were killed, 140 injured. Ranching, farming and oil are chief area industries. Oil drilling was begun in 1957. (1967)

HIGGINS (Lipscomb Co.) *US 60, W edge, city park*
Will Rogers
(Nov. 4, 1879–Aug. 15, 1935)
One of America's best loved humorists, whose stage act, gently mocking man's foibles, was highlighted by rope tricks learned here in his youth.

Born in Oklahoma. In 1898, threatened with discipline for pranks, he left school and came to Texas. He became a cowboy on the Little Robe ranch near Higgins and made a lifelong friend of young Frank Ewing, son of his employer.

In 1902 he joined a Wild West show; was famous by 1918.

Rogers died in a crash during a globe-circling pioneer flight with aviator Wiley Post, 1935. (1967)

HIGH ISLAND (Galveston Co.) *SH 87, 10 mi. SE on Bolivar Peninsula in the Caplen Community*
The Breakers
Terrence Meche, a ship's carpenter, built this beach house in 1884, using materials shipped in from Pensacola, Florida. Although the house withstood the devastating 1900 storm, Meche and his family abandoned it. William D. and Ruth McLean Gordon purchased the house in 1905 and named it "The Breakers." Used as a vacation home by the Gordon family for many years, The Breakers underwent a number of alterations, including relocation to higher ground. It survived the 1915 hurricane and subsequent gulf storms, and has become a noted local landmark. (1990)

HILLSBORO (Hill Co.)   *SH 309, 7 mi. NW*

Woodbury Missionary Baptist Church

Organized Sept. 28, 1871, by Elder Samuel Lacy, assisted by Elder S. E. Brooks. Early members came from the Bigham, Brooks, Ezell, Posey, Reed, Rozell, Skinner, Stearnes, and Witty families. Sunday school was organized in 1902. Present building was erected 1933.   (1972)

HILLSBORO (Hill Co.)   *SH 22, 4 mi. W*

Site of Old
Lexington Village
(1 mi. S)

Founded about 1851 on Jack's Branch. Was Hill County's first settlement and only polling place when county organized on May 14, 1853. For 4 months two log homes functioned as a courthouse until a special election put the county seat at Hillsboro.   (1965)

HILLSBORO (Hill Co.)   *SH 171, 6 mi. NW on ranch*

The Lackawanna Ranch

Dr. John S. Scofield (1826–1901) chose the Indian name "Lackawanna" for the 2500 acre tract of land he bought here in 1858. After moving with his family from Kentucky, he served Hill County as a doctor and county judge. Later he was a director and vice-president of Sturgis National Bank. Dr. Scofield introduced shorthorn cattle to this area. His son, Frank (1887–1974), who inherited this part of the ranch in 1901, raised prize-winning shorthorns. After the first house on this site burned, the present structure was built in 1917. The Lackawanna ranch was purchased in 1945 by E. G. Murphree.   (1975)

HILLSBORO (Hill Co.)   *SH 22 & County Rd., opposite Hill Junior College*

Confederate Veterans and
Old Settlers Reunion Grounds
(1 mi. S)

Formed in 1901, the Confederate Veterans and Old Settlers Association of Hill County acquired 73 acres of wooded land as a site for its summer reunion. The 3–5 day encampment, held annually from 1902 to 1924, was an important social and recreational event in this locality. Many families traveled by wagon and camped at the site. Special trains from Hillsboro brought other visitors, and a gravel auto road was completed in 1909. The reunion usually attracted a crowd of several thousand persons. Activities included speeches, musical programs, baseball games, and, on one occasion, a carnival midway show.

Located on the grounds were a spring-fed lake, large pavilion, and baseball park. Some families leased their camp lots and built summer cottages. The Fraternal Picnic Associations's July 4th picnic, 1908–1914, and other meetings and social events were also held here.

With the reopening (1916) of the Hill County Fair and a decrease in numbers of veterans and old settlers, reunion attendance dropped sharply at the end of World War I (1918). The association deeded its property to the state in 1924 to be developed as Jefferson Davis State Park, but those plans were never realized.   (1977)

HITCHCOCK (Galveston Co.)   *SH 6 at FM 2004*

Hitchcock

In region held before 1820s, by Karankawa Indians, and afterwards by cattle raisers. The Gulf, Colorado & Santa Fe Railway built through the area in 1870s, naming station for Galveston civic leader and late landowner, Lent Munson Hitchcock (1810–1869). On the railway, George Henckel in 1880s opened a produce commission house. Leaders among fruit and vegetable growers included Emil and Hypolite Perthius, H. M. Stringfellow, and Jacques Tacquard. Stores, a butcher shop, bakery, hotel, and saloons were established. The townsite was platted and public school opened 1894.

Churches were active. St. Mary's (later Our Lady of Lourdes) Catholic Parish had first house of worship. A building for Protestants, soon a Methodist church, was erected 1894. Other faiths arrived later.

After 1920, truck farming declined; packing houses closed. In 1930s, local men found work in Texas City.

237

A coast auxiliary army replacement center opened here in 1940; it later became Camp Wallace, an anti-aircraft training center. A blimp base was operated 1941–1945, for surveillance against enemy submarines.

Hitchcock remains a center of small business and industry, with modern homes on garden acreage owned and occupied by urban and industrial workers.   (1973)

HITCHCOCK (Galveston Co.)   *SH 6, at entrance to Jack Brooks Park*
U.S. Naval Air Station (Blimp Base)
(⁷⁄₁₀ mi. S)

In an effort to defend U.S. coasts and shipping lanes against German submarine activity during World War II, the U.S. Navy established bases to house huge lighter-than-air (LTA) craft, also known as blimps. With the ability to hover above a target, the blimps were uniquely qualified for coastal defense and observation.

Because of its site on the flat Texas Coastal Plain, Hitchcock was chosen as the location for one of the nine new blimp bases. Construction began in 1942, and the facility was commissioned on May 22, 1943. The resulting military personnel build-up caused an economic boom in the community.

The Hitchcock base consisted of forty-seven buildings, including a massive hangar to house six blimps, administration buildings, warehouses, living quarters, and recreational facilities. Aircraft from the base, in addition to their regular patrolling duties, were also used to assist with hurricane relief efforts and war bond drives.

In 1944, after the blimps were no longer needed, the Hitchcock base was redesignated for other purposes. Following the war some of the buildings were used by private interests, and after hurricane damage in 1961 the blimp hangar was razed.   (1989)

HITCHCOCK (Galveston Co.)   *SH 6, 0.5 mi. W of entrance*
to Jack Brooks Park
Camp Wallace

Named for World War I Army Colonel Elmer J. Wallace, Camp Wallace was established as a training facility for military personnel during World War II. The U.S. government acquired more than 3,300 acres of land between the towns of Hitchcock and Alta Loma on State Highway 6 for placement of the facility.

Construction began in November 1940. Before the erection of structures, 17 miles of access roads were built, 29 miles of electrical lines were installed, and a 3.9-mile spur rail track from the main rail line were laid. The site contained a total of 399 structures. Some buildings were constructed at Galveston's Fort Crockett and transported to the site, including a cold storage depot, bakery, laundry, and morgue. The camp contained a medical facility, 161 barracks, and a service club.

By May 1941, the camp accommodated 10,250 people, including officers, enlisted personnel, and civilian staff and training continued through World War II. The site also housed German prisoners of war. In April 1945, Camp Wallace was transferred to naval supervision, and later served as a distribution center releasing veterans back into civilian life. The site was used by the Red Cross in 1947 following the explosions at Texas City. The camp was declared surplus by the U.S. government in 1947.   (1996)

HITCHCOCK (Galveston Co.)   *7902 SH 6*
Stringfellow Orchards

Nationally and internationally recognized horticulturist Henry Martyn Stringfellow (1839–1922) started an experimental garden and orchard at this location in 1883. In 1890, he published a treatise containing innovative organic gardening methods that were adopted by Japanese, German, and many American fruit and vegetable growers. Silver medals garnered at two world fairs and world-wide acclaim for additional publications solidified his stature as a premier experimental horticulturist of his time, vestiges of his handiwork were evident here over 100 years later.   (1992)

HOCHHEIM (DeWitt Co.)   *US 183, 4 mi. S Hoch House Stage Stand*
Stagecoach Inn
(.15 mi. W)
Built of hand-quarried native stone in 1856 by V. Hoch, a settler. Served as an inn on the Austin-Indianola Stage Road.

While drivers changed four-horse teams, the passengers welcomed the chance to enjoy the inn's food and hospitality.   (1965)

HOCHHEIM (DeWitt Co.)   *US 183*
Hochheim (Hoch's Home)
Founded near home and stage stand of Valentine Hoch on old Austin-Indianola road, 1856. In 1864 German Methodist Church was built; post office opened 1969. County's first protestant church (organized 1841 on Cuero Creek by J. M. Baker and James N. Smith) moved here in 1882 as Hochheim Presbyterian Church. The Baptist church was founded later (1923). Concrete Lodge No 182, AF & AM (chartered 1856 with F. J. Lynch first Worshipful Master), became Hochheim Lodge, 1884, buying 1885 upper story of school house for lodge hall. In 1921 bought lower story, housing school until 1938.

HOCHHEIM (Dewitt Co.)   *US 183, 4 mi. N*
Valentinook II
or
Stagecoach Inn
Built of hand-quarried native stone in 1856 by V. Hoch, a settler. Served as an inn on the Austin-Indianola Stage Road.

While drivers changed four-horse teams, the passengers welcomed the chance to enjoy the inn's food and hospitality.   (1965)

HOCHHEIM (DeWitt Co.)   *US 183, on bluff near Guadalupe River*
Cuero I
Archeological District
Extending 45 miles along the Guadalupe River Basin, Cuero I Archeological District was created to define and preserve cultural resources threatened by a proposed reservoir. Archeological investigation in 1972–73 revealed 352 significant prehistoric and historic sites spanning 9,000 years of human occupancy. The remains include the camps of prehistoric nomads and of historic Indians such as Tonkawas and Comanches. Other sites mark early Anglo-American settlement, which began with the colonizing efforts of Green DeWitt in the 1820s and '30s.   (1979)

HOLLIDAY (Archer Co.)   *US 82, 1 mi. N*
Captain John Holliday
(Dec. 8, 1811–Aug. 19, 1842)
Born Hollidaysburg, Pennsylvania; came to Texas about 1835. Joined Texian Army, and was one of 24 survivors of the Goliad Massacre, March 27, 1836. Joined Texian-Santa Fe Expedition, and en route to New Mexico, Aug. 4, 1841, carved his name on a tree in this vicinity. After reaching Santa Fe, the party was arrested and marched to Perote Prison near Mexico City. In Aug. 1842, Holliday was released, but he died of yellow fever aboard ship two days from Galveston, and was buried at sea.

Nearby Holliday Creek and the town of Holliday were named for the carving on the tree.
     (1973)

HOLLIDAY (Archer Co.)   *SH 25, 2 mi. SE*
Stonewall Jackson Camp
106 acres of land bought 1898 by United Confederate Veterans of Archer County for reunion grounds. Meetings lasting 3 days were held annually until 1935. Approximately 500 people attended each year. Activities included ball games, dancing, visiting, contests, shows, and rodeos.

HONDO (Medina Co.)

US 90, 3.5 mi. E

Medina County

Formed from Bexar County. Created February 12, 1848. Organized August 7, 1848. Named for river which traverses the county. County seat, Castroville, 1848–1892. Hondo, since.

Primarily a farming and ranching area.

HONDO (Medina Co.)

1600 Ave. M

Hondo

Spanish explorers passed this way several times in the centuries preceding Anglo settlement of the area. The original village that would become Hondo was situated on "El Arroyo Hondo" named by the Spanish. Permanent settlers to the area began arriving with Henri Castro in the 1840s. The Galveston, Harrisburg and San Antonio (GH & SA) Railroad began to consider the busy village on Hondo Creek for the location of a depot in the late 19th century. They ultimately chose 188 acres 5 miles west of the town. The first deeds were executed in 1881.

A post office for Hondo City was approved in 1882. Knowing that the county seat might be moved from Castroville to a more central location, the GH & SA donated land for a courthouse in 1883. The county seat was relocated to Hondo City in 1892. In the early 20th century, the town, by then known simply as Hondo, developed as a trade center and cotton shipping point. Oil was discovered in the area in the 1920s. The population grew steadily with commerce; by 1940 it reached 2,500.

The town's population exploded in 1942 when an army air corps base was built to the northwest. Hondo was incorporated that year and the federal government provided educational funds and installed a sewage system to accommodate the boom. At its peak Hondo had an estimated population of 12,000. The base was closed in 1946, but continued to operate as a civilian pilot training center through the 1950s.

Hondo grew steadily in the late 20th century. Its population in 1998 was more than 8,000. The community continues to thrive.   (1999)

HONDO (Medina Co.)

US 90, SH 173 & FM 2676, 6.8 mi. NE

The Wiemers Oak

The land on which this live oak stands was purchased by German migrant Johann Wiemers, who came here in 1854. The Rev. John Schaper held services under the tree and converted Johann and his wife, Aalke, to Methodism. They became charter members of the New Fountain Methodist Church. The first church building was erected near this site. This tree also shaded the Wiemers and their neighbors as they met for reunions or used a mule-drawn press in molasses making. The land was inherited by Wiemers' descendants, who built a home near the ancient oak.

(1977)

HONEY GROVE (Fannin Co.)

FM 904, 4 mi. E of Ladonia,
near intersection with FM 64

Central National Road

Created 1844 to connect Texas Republic with the United States. Route began in Dallas, to go to Kiomatia Crossing on Red River.

Surveyed by Maj. George W. Stell, road was to be 30' wide and clear of tree stumps more than a foot high. Route ran north of land of John H. Loring (1 mi. E of present Ladonia), coming eastward to make abrupt north turn here and push over Sulphur River at crossing named for Isaac Lyday, who came here in 1836. A small segment of the road may still be seen (1972) skirting Lyday cemetery in the W. D. Wehrmann, Jr., pasture, just east of FM 904, southwest of Dial.   (1972)

HONEY GROVE (Fannin Co.)

US 82, 3 mi. W

Wheeler House

First Classic Revival house in area. Has unusual stairway. Built 1852–1854, with slave labor. Fifth house on Bonham-Paris Stagecoach Road. Chimney stones and lumber hand-hewn. Joists were pegged rather than nailed.

Sold in 1884 by Wiley Halsey, builder, to Confederate veteran Peyton Wheeler and wife, Martha Jane Hamil. Their descendants have erected this marker. Awarded Medallion Plate.   (1965)

HOOKS (Bowie Co.)
IH 30 near a Stuckeys park

Pecan Point Signers
of the Texas Declaration of Independence

Five of the most prominent delegates to the Constitutional Convention of Texas, held March, 1836, hailed from Pecan Point, in this vicinity. Richard Ellis (an attorney and judge) was chosen president of the meeting and later served four terms in the Senate of the Republic.

Collin McKinney (a magistrate) helped draft the Declaration and served three terms in the House. A. H. Latimer (an attorney) served two terms. Samuel Price Carson (attorney) became Texas' Secretary of State and with Robert Hamilton (financier) was an agent to the United States.

(1969)

HOUSTON (Harris Co.)
6 locations, all near San Jacinto Park Cemetery

Battle of San Jacinto

At mid-afternoon April 21, 1836, two miles to the north, General Sam Houston with about 1,000 Texans in 18 minutes annihilated the 1,400-man army of Antonio Lopez de Santa Anna, President of Mexico.

Screened by trees and rising ground, Houston's men formed with Edward Burleson's regiment at center, Sidney Sherman's on the left wing, artillery under George W. Hockley on Burleson's right, the infantry under Henry Millard on the right of the artillery. Under M. B. Lamar, a future President of Texas, the cavalry took the extreme right, to cut off possible flight of Mexican troops.

Their 4-piece band playing a popular love song, "Will You Come to the Bower," the Texans attacked at a run, crying, "Remember the Alamo! Remember Goliad!" Such was their fury that 630 of the enemy were killed, 730 captured. Enemy lead shattered Gen. Houston's ankle, but he lost only 9 men killed or mortally wounded and 30 wounded less seriously.

San Jacinto stands as one of the world's greatest victories. It gave Texas independence, and with her annexation 9 years later brought into the Union all or parts of Arizona, California, Colorado, Kansas, New Mexico, Nevada, Oklahoma, Utah, and Wyoming.

HOUSTON (Harris Co.)
SH 134, San Jacinto Park

Battle of San Jacinto

Near here on the afternoon of April 21, 1836, the Army of the Republic of Texas commanded by General Sam Houston was drawn up to attack an invading Mexican Army commanded by General Antonio Lopez de Santa Anna (3.5 mi. S San Jacinto State Park, State Hwy. 134).

The Texas Army attacked in four divisions: the cavalry on the right, commanded by Mirabeau B. Lamar, next, the infantry under Lieutenant Colonel Henry Millard; the "Twin Sisters" cannon under Colonel George W. Hockley; the 1st regiment in the center under Colonel Edward Burleson; the 2nd regiment, the left wing, under Colonel Sidney Sherman. (3 mi. S San Jacinto State Park, State Hwy. 134).

Within a few minutes the Battle of San Jacinto was over. According to General Houston's report 630 Mexicans lay dead on the field. 208 were wounded and 730 were taken prisoners. Money, arms and equipment were captured. The Texans had 9 killed and 30 wounded (1.4 mi. S San Jacinto State Park, State Hwy. 134).

The Mexican cavalry was on the left wing; infantry and artillery in the center behind a fortification of boxes and baggage; while the extreme right was far extended. (2.5 mi. S San Jacinto State Park, State Hwy. 134).

To the tune of "Will You Come to the Bower" the Texans advanced; "Remember the Alamo! Remember Goliad" was their cry. With cannons and gunshot, clubs and Bowie knives they fought; no quarter was given; the route was complete—the slaughter terrific.

HOUSTON (Harris Co.)
US 90 at Crosby-Baytown Rd., 22 mi. NE

Lynch's Ferry

Established before 1824 by Nathaniel Lynch, one of Austin's first colonists, on land granted August 19, 1824. Granted exclusive privilege to operate ferry at this point January 1, 1830, by Ayuntamiento of San Felipe. Now known as Lynchburg Ferry.

HOUSTON (Harris Co.)   *SH 134, 22 mi. E, San Jacinto*
                                                           Battlefield Park near Battleship Texas,
1 mi. NE to Site of
Lynch's Ferry

A pioneer ferry of Texas under Mexico and the Republic. Established at the confluence of Buffalo Bayou and the San Jacinto River, 1822, by Nathaniel Lynch, one of Stephen F. Austin's "Old Three Hundred" colonists. Usual charges at ferries like this were man and horse, 25 cents; cattle, 4 cents a head. But rates could be raised for risky high-water service.

Lynch, from Missouri, was an active Texas merchant and judge. After a small settlement grew up near his ferry, he platted the town of "Lynchburg" about 1835, but few shared his enthusiasm for the spot.

In March and April, 1836, as Texan settlers fled the Mexican Army during the War for Independence, hundreds crossed the San Jacinto at Lynch's Ferry. By April 2 the prairie was covered with wagons, horses, mules, tents, and baggage; but 19 days later at the Battle of San Jacinto, the Mexican General Santa Anna, hoping to cut off a Texan retreat at the ferry, was himself defeated near the site.

In later years Lynchburg became a steamboat stop for the picturesque stern-wheelers plying Buffalo Bayou, as eastbound freight was transferred there.

Today the modern, motor-driven "Lynchburg Ferry."   (1969)

HOUSTON (Harris Co.)   *Zavala Point across Buffalo Bayou*
                                                              from Battleship Texas
Site of the Home of Lorenzo de Zavala (1788–1836)

Signer of the Texas Declaration of Independence, Vice-President of the Republic of Texas. His plank-covered log house, the first in the municipality of Harrisburg, built in 1829, served as a hospital for the wounded after the Battle of San Jacinto. Here de Zavala died November 15, 1836.

HOUSTON (Harris Co.)   *Channel View at Market St. and*
                                                             De Zavala Rd., 3 mi. E
Lorenzo de Zavala
(1788–1836)

Three miles east is homesite and grave of a signer of the Texas Declaration of Independence and first Vice-President of the Republic of Texas—an illustrious statesman of two nations. He was born in Mexico.

De Zavala, an ardent liberal and earnest advocate of democratic reforms, served his native country as representative in the Spanish Cortes, Madrid; Minister of the Treasury; President of Chamber of Deputies; Governor of State of Mexico and Ambassador to France. De Zavala tired of Santa Anna's tyranny, resigned his ambassadorship and moved here in 1835.

When Mexican officials learned of his taking refuge in Texas and ordered his arrest, he became a strong leader in cause of Texas Independence. Voters in Harrisburg sent him in 1835 to the Consultation at San Felipe de Austin and later to the Independence Convention at Washington-on-the-Brazos.

The De Zavala home, a plank-covered log house across from San Jacinto Battleground, served as a hospital for both sides after the battle.

An observer on the scene described de Zavala as "the most interesting man in Texas"—He was a leading author, learned publicist, philosopher, historian, economist and constant lover of liberty.
                                                                             (1968)

HOUSTON (Harris Co.)   *US 59, City Hall Plaza*
Houston City, Republic of Texas

By vote of Congress, Nov. 30, 1836, chosen temporary capital for new Republic of Texas. At the time a small townsite at the head of Buffalo Bayou navigation. Into a "Houston City" of mud, tents, cabins on April 1, 1837, came President Sam Houston and his government. Finding its quarters unfinished, Congress postponed its opening session until May 1. The capitol building was a 2-story plantation style house, with columned porches. It was scene of many important Indian treaties, diplomatic negotiations, legislative functions. As no church yet graced the city, it also was used for religious services.

That muddy April saw the city hold its first big social event—the anniversary celebration of the San Jacinto victory, with parade, reception, and ball.

On Dec. 5, 1837, some war heroes and other leaders founded in the capital the Texas Philosophical Society, the Republic's first learning organization.

In a powdered wig, and dressed to resemble George Washington, President Houston made a 3-hour farewell address, after which Mirabeau Buonaparte Lamar was inaugurated his successor on Dec. 10, 1838.

In 1839, removed to Austin, the capital returned here, but only briefly, 1842, during the Mexican invasion. (1965)

HOUSTON (Harris Co.)

San Jacinto St., East lawn,
old Harris County Courthouse

Harris County

Inhabited during the 17th century by Karankawa and Orcoquiza Indians, and considered in 1756 by Spain for site of Presidio de San Agustin de Ahumada, this region was settled permanently in 1822 by the colonists of Stephen F. Austin. In 1824, John R. Harris (1790–1829) received title to 4,428 acres of land in Buffalo Bayou-Braes Bayou junction area, and started village named for his family and for Harrisburg, Pa., founded by his grandfather. Colonial settlements in the vicinity were Cedar Bayou, Lynchburg, Midway, Morgan's Point, New Kentucky, and Stafford's Point.

First step toward local government was taken when Stephen F. Austin and the Baron de Bastrop met (1824) with colonists at the house of William Scott, Midway, to explain colonization laws. Harrisburg, a town by 1826, was one of the original and most influential colonial municipalities, with a major role in Texas War for Independence, which won freedom in 1836.

The county of Harrisburg (later Harris) was created Dec. 30, 1836. The capital of the Texas Republic was within its boundaries for several years. In the Civil War, it was a command and ordnance center (1863–1865), of Trans-Mississippi Department, Confederate Army. It has since grown into a center for world commerce. (1972)

HOUSTON (Harris Co.)

Park under Viaduct, Main St.

The Original Port of Houston
Allen's Landing
1837

This Houston city park, created in 1967, is on the site of Houston's first port. Ocean-going ships, both steamers and sailing vessels, loaded and unloaded freight here, beginning with the visit of the steamer *Laura*, which docked on January 26, 1837.

The farsighted Allen brothers, Augustus C. and John K., located their city here primarily because they considered Houston "the head of navigation" on Buffalo Bayou. Although shallow and winding, Buffalo Bayou contributed immeasurably to growth of Houston from its earliest days. The confluence of Buffalo and White Oak Bayous provided a natural turning basin for the small ships of the day.

The port of Houston was officially established by the city on June 8, 1841. Over the years Houston has labored for deeper water. In 1910, the United States Congress adopted the "Houston Plan," whereby the navigation district and federal government shared costs of dredging a ship channel from the Gulf to the present turning basin, 4.25 miles east of this point. This deep water channel brings the world's commerce to one of the largest ports in the nation. However, to this day barges move much freight on up the bayou to downtown Houston. (1967)

HOUSTON (Harris Co.)

515 Rusk

Edward Mandell House
(July 26, 1858–March 28, 1938)

Edward Mandell House, son of Houston businessman and mayor Thomas W. House, was born in a two-story frame house at this site. He attended the Houston Academy and later continued his education in Virginia and at Cornell University.

E. M. House married Loulie Hunter in 1881, and they were the parents of two daughters. In 1885, the family moved to Austin, and House became involved in Democratic party politics. He was instrumental in the election of four Texas governors—James S. Hogg, Charles A. Culberson, S. W. T. Lanham, and Joseph D. Sayers.

House gained national political prominence in 1912 when he was instrumental in the nomination of Woodrow Wilson for President. House became a trusted advisor to President Wilson, participating in foreign policy negotiations during and after World War I. He played a major part in drafting the Fourteen Points, Wilson's plan for ending the war, and was a delegate to the Paris Peace Conference in 1919.

House died in New York in 1938 and was buried in Houston's Glenwood Cemetery. Known as Colonel House for many years, he is remembered as one of the most politically influential people of Texas and the United States, although he never held elective office.   (1989)

HOUSTON (Harris Co.)   *1302 Heights Blvd*
Houston Heights
Representatives of the American Loan and Trust Company of Omaha, Nebraska, came to Houston in 1890 to scout locations for land development. Under the leadership of O. M. Carter, D. D. Cooley, and others, company directors purchased 1,756 acres of land northwest of Houston. They led efforts to electrify Houston's streetcar system in 1891 and extended the lines to their new community, named Houston Heights due to its elevation 23 feet above that of downtown Houston.

Directors of the Omaha and South Texas Land Company, formed by American Loan and Trust in 1892, developed streets, sidewalks, and utility systems; built and marketed homes; and encouraged the establishment of business and industry in Houston Heights. The city of Houston Heights was incorporated in 1896, and W. G. Love served as first mayor. He was followed in that office by John A. Milroy, David Barker, Robert F. Isbell, and J. B. Marmion.

Seeking a broader tax base with which to support their public schools, voters of Houston Heights agreed to annexation by the city of Houston in 1918. Houston Heights grew rapidly in the 20th century, but continued to maintain its unique identity. It remains a distinctive neighborhood with many historic structures.   (1991)

HOUSTON (Harris Co.)   *US 90A, at Houston ship-turning basin*
Constitution Bend
Now Houston's famous ship-turning basin, this bend in Buffalo Bayou was named for the *Constitution*, first steamboat to turn around here, in June 1837.

At the time, Houston was less than a year old. It was serving as temporary capital of the Republic of Texas, which was itself barely more than a year old. According to one story, the town's founders, John and Augustus Allen (brothers), paid the captain of the boat $1,000 to make the trip as a publicity measure. The trading vessel was approximately 150 × 24 × 8 feet in size, with one deck, no mast, a round stern, male figurehead, and a cabin on the deck.

The *Constitution's* trip up Buffalo Bayou was not easy. Lines were run from it to trees and the boat was laboriously hauled forward by windlass. It ran aground twice. At one grounding, famous passenger Thomas Jefferson Chambers (patriot of the Republic) had enough time to visit a friend on shore. Upon their arrival at Houston, 35 of the 150 passengers memorialized the captain for his landmark voyage.

The exit of the *Constitution* was no more graceful than her entrance: she had to back down the narrow bayou until she reached a spot wide enough to turn around. The name of this bend records that event.   (1970)

HOUSTON (Harris Co.)   *On Buffalo Bayou, near Milam Street Bridge*
Site of Sunken Confederate Ship
In late 1862 and early 1863, during the Civil War, the Federal blockade of Galveston reached its peak. Confederate ships bearing vital goods could get to the main supply depots and arsenals at Houston only by slipping around wary Federal patrols.

One ship, believed to have been the *Augusta,* had arrived safely in Houston when it sprang a severe leak. Although it was quickly towed to the Milam Street landing, it sank before it could be unloaded. Then, inexplicably, the Confederates abandoned it.

For years afterward, when the bayou water level was low, the ship would reappear, and divers were able to recover many relics. About 1910, however, due to unknown causes, the ship was blown up and its remains sank slowly into the bayou silt.

In 1968, the Southwestern Historical Exploration Society determined to retrieve artifacts from the ship. At 8 a.m., July 20, an 80-ton dragline atop the Milam Street Bridge began dredging several feet of mud, and at 2:30 p.m. an aged cannon ball dropped out of the dragline "clamshell." Subsequently, musket balls, bayonets, coins, square nails, chest locks, and numerous pistol balls were raised—slightly over a century from the date that they sank. (1970)

HOUSTON (Harris Co.)

Site of Dick Dowling Statue, Hermann Park,
1700 block of MacGregor Dr.

Major Richard William (Dick) Dowling, C. S. A.
(January 14, 1837–September 23, 1867)

Born in 1837 near Tuam, County Galway, Ireland, Richard Dowling emigrated to New Orleans in 1846 during the Irish potato famine. In 1857, Dick married Elizabeth Anne Odlum in Houston. By 1860 he had owned 3 bars, installed Houston's first gas lighting in his home and business, and was a charter member of Houston Hook and Ladder Company No. 1. During the Civil War, Dick was First Lieutenant, Company F, Cook's Regiment, First Texas Heavy Artillery. He was in command at Fort Griffin in 1863. On September 8 he held fast with only 6 cannons and 47 men inside the fort despite rumors of a Federal invasion and orders to retreat. Twenty-seven ships carrying Maj. Gen. William B. Franklin and 5,000 Union troops sailed into Sabine Pass; Dowling and "The Irish Davis Guards" shot so accurately that Franklin's forces surrendered in 45 minutes. The Confederate Congress called the Battle of Sabine Pass "one of the most brilliant . . . achievements . . . of this war." Discharged as a major in 1865, Dick reopened his most famous bar, "The Bank of Bacchus." In 1866 he formed the first oil company in Houston. By 1867, he owned more than 22 square blocks of downtown Houston and vast lands across Texas. Dick Dowling died of yellow fever at age 30 and is buried in Houston's St. Vincent's Cemetery. (1998)

HOUSTON (Harris Co.)

7401 Katy Freeway (IH 10)

First Baptist Church of Houston

In February 1841, the Rev. James Huckins visited the fledgling city of Houston, where a small group of Baptists had been meeting informally since 1838. Under Huckins' leadership, a congregation was organized on April 10, 1841, with 16 charter members. Noted Texas minister William E. Tryon became the Houston church's first resident pastor in 1845. His first concerns were the erection of a church building and increasing the membership. The new structure, located at the corner of Travis Street and Texas Avenue, was dedicated in May 1847, and membership increased dramatically. Pastor Tryon succumbed to yellow fever in 1847. Under the leadership of his successor, Dr. Rufus C. Burleson, membership grew to 140 by 1852. Membership declined during the Civil War and Reconstruction, reaching 100 again in 1871. The church began a mission in nearby Richmond in the 1870s, followed by two mission chapels north of Buffalo Bayou and Tuam Mission in South Houston in the 1890s. These and other missions sponsored by the First Baptist Church became self-supporting Baptist churches. In 1907 the church joined with others in establishing the Star of Hope Mission and the Baptist Sanitarium (later Baptist Memorial Hospital). The congregation persevered during the Depression and World War II. The congregation experienced unprecedented growth in the early 1970s, and on April 3, 1977, relocated to this site from 1010 Lamar in downtown Houston. Membership increased to 21,000 by the year 2000. In addition to evangelism, discipleship and missions, the church became known for other specialized ministries, including music and pageantry, programs for the deaf, community service and support to smaller churches. (2001)

HOUSTON (Harris Co.)

7934 SH 6

Heritage Presbyterian Church

Originally constructed near the banks of Little Cypress Creek (11 mi. NW) in 1916, this chapel served the congregation of St. John Lutheran Church. Designed with Gothic detailing, it was built by German craftsmen. When the fellowship grew too large for the sanctuary, it was purchased by the members of Windwood Presbyterian Church and moved to Grant Road (8 mi. NE). Heritage Presbyterian Church relocated it here in 1980. (1980)

HOUSTON (Harris Co.) *SH 6, on the E side, approximately 235 ft.*
N of Patterson Road

Bear Creek Methodist Church
and Cemetery

German immigrants settled in the area surrounding the junction of Langham and Bear Creeks in the 1840s. Settlers traveled to nearby churches for Sunday services until about 1879, when 7 charter members established the Bear Creek German Methodist Church. The congregation initially met in members' homes. The church was subsequently made a mission of the Rose Hill Methodist Church near Tomball.

In 1890, a small church building was erected near the Hillendahl family cemetery. The site proved to be poorly drained and often inaccessible, and in 1902 the congregation moved the sanctuary here on 3 acres donated by Fred and Katherine Brandt. A part of the acreage was laid out as a cemetery. Christine Backen's burial in 1904 was the first recorded here. The cemetery is still active and is maintained by the Addicks Bear Creek Cemetery Association.

A summer storm destroyed the sanctuary in 1915, but by the end of that year a new church building had been erected. Area flooding in 1935 resulted in the construction of the nearby Addicks Reservoir in 1940 and the subsequent removal of the church to another site about 1.7 miles south of here. The congregation changed its name to Addicks United Methodist Church in 1968.   (1994)

HOUSTON (Harris Co.) *Corner of Broadhurst and Almeda Rd.*
(SH 288/FM 521)

Almeda

In 1892, Illinois investors bought land here, near a pre-Civil War railroad line, and platted the town of Almeda. With its mild climate, the town was marketed as a citrus farming community, but unusually severe freezes caused many farmers to turn to dairy production by the 1920s. Almeda became a prosperous dairy farming town. In 1893, residents founded a school district that served children from parts of three counties. Although Almeda became part of the city of Houston in 1959, it remains a part of local history.   (1992)

HOWE (Grayson Co.) *East side of Denny Street, (SH 5)*
between O'Connel and Haning

Mame Roberts
(Aug. 19, 1883–Dec. 24, 1976)

The daughter of James M. and Martha Sue (Baxter) Roberts, Mame Roberts lived her entire life in or near the community of Howe. Largely self-taught, she worked as a substitute teacher in the lower grades at the Howe Public Schools in the early 1900s before turning to her life's work—promoting civic improvements and beautification. As the writer of a weekly column in the Howe Messenger, Mame Roberts promoted her hometown and encouraged its beautification. Her campaign to make Howe the "prettiest little town in Texas" motivated other small Texas towns to take similar action. A series of articles in the Dallas Morning News provided step-by-step instructions for carrying out beautification efforts, and she was in great demand as a speaker at garden club gatherings throughout this part of the state. Mame's work attracted the attention of Life magazine and Reader's Digest, and she was named "Woman of the Day" on May 14, 1949, on Eleanor and Anna Roosevelt's national radio program. Her leadership positions included: president of the Grayson County Federation of Women's Clubs; president of the Texoma Redbud Association, which urged the planting of redbuds along highways in Texas and Oklahoma; and founder and president of the Howe Sesame Club. Her work, which spanned the decades before and after World War II, is a significant part of the civic history of Howe and of all the towns that put her lessons into action.   (2002)

HUBBARD (Hill Co.) *SH 31 at SH 171, 1 block E*

Hubbard

Founded 1881, as a shopping and supply point on the St. Louis and Southwestern Railroad. Named for Richard B. Hubbard (1832–1901), colonel in 22nd Texas Infantry during the Civil War, Texas governor (1876–1878), United States minister to Japan (1885–1889). Banking & market town. Has mineral waters.   (1964)

HUCKABAY (Erath Co.)
FM 219, near Huckabay Cemetery
The Community of Huckabay
In 1875 a small group of pioneers from Arkansas and Tennessee acquired land here on the headwaters of the Bosque, starting the "Flat Woods" settlement. Confederate veteran John Copeland (1841–1886) taught the first local school sessions (1876, 1877) in his home, and gave land (1879) for a cemetery and (1883) for a school. A Church of Christ congregation was formed in 1876. G. W. Glenn opened the first store in 1878. Baptist and Methodist churches were founded in 1881.

John Huckabay, a farmer-storekeeper who brought the settlers' mail from Stephenville, led in securing a post office (1888), which was named for him. He was postmaster in 1888–1891 and 1893–1895. By 1890, town had general stores, groceries, drugstores, 2 blacksmiths, barber shops, and undertaker; and later (briefly) a bank. John Huckabay and W. C. Rigsby opened a cotton gin, 1891.

C. H. Hale, an outstanding teacher, founded (1902) the Huckabay Academy, a high school that later offered college courses. It is said the academy won every debate, oratory event, and athletic contest it ever entered. It closed in 1914. The village dwindled in changing economic and travel conditions. The school, churches, cemetery, and tabernacle became focus for the community. The post office closed in 1965. (1975)

HUGHES SPRINGS (Cass Co.)
SH 11, E side of Hughes Springs
Trammel's Trace
Entered Cass County at Epperson's Ferry. Continued south and west in an arc, passing through Chalybeate Springs (Hughes Springs).

This 1813 pioneer trail originated in St. Louis and linked the "Southwest Trail" with the King's Highway to Mexico. It was laid out by Nicholas Trammel (1780–1852). (1967)

HUMBLE (Harris Co.)
110 W Main St.
City of Humble
A pioneer oil boom town. Originated as crossroads community named for settler Pleasant Smith Humble (1835?–1912), who lived here before 1889, hewing his timber into railroad ties, mining gravel from his land, keeping store, and serving as justice of the peace. Neighbors included the Bender, Durdin, Isaacks, Lee, Slaughter, and Williams families. Economic bases were farms and saw-mills. The post office opened 1902.

In 1904, C. E. Barrett (1866–1926) drilled for oil in this area, securing small production on Moonshine Hill. On Jan. 7, 1905, he brought in the No. 2 Beaty well which yielded 8,500 barrels a day, opening the great boom. From a village of 700, Humble grew at once into a town of 20,000. Field production—the largest in Texas for the year 1905—was 15,594,923 barrels of oil. The field was named for the town. A group of its operators, including Ross S. Sterling, later (1931–1933) Governor of Texas, in 1911 incorporated a new oil company named for the field, thus spreading into the annals of world commerce the town's name.

Production from several strata here exceeded the total for fabulous Spindletop by 1946. Known as the greatest salt dome field, Humble still produces and the town for which it was named continues to thrive. (1972)

HUNGERFORD (Wharton Co.)
SH 60 and Old US 59
Site of Post West Bernard Station
(3.5 mi. NW)
In the summer of 1837, Post West Bernard Station was established as an ordnance depot of the army of the Republic of Texas. Its location on the West Bernard River was strategic in protecting Houston, then capital of Texas, from possible invasion by Mexico. Cannons, rifles, muskets, powder, and shot were stored at the station. Troops under Lt. H. L. Grush and later Capt. Martin K. Snell maintained the post despite harsh living conditions. In 1838–1839, this station transferred its inventory of ordnance to the newly completed Houston arsenal. (1985)

HUNGERFORD (Wharton Co.)
SH 60 and US 59
Site of Quinan Community
(¼ mi. W)
The village of Quinan was established about 1872 on the Wharton-Richmond road. It was named for Judge George E. Quinan (1819–1893), who lived south of here on Peach Creek. A

native of Ireland, Quinan served in the Texas Senate and on the State Court of Civil Appeals. He was one of the founders of the State Bar of Texas. The community named for him had a school, Methodist church, and a post office located in John C. Habermacher's store. The Quinan community declined after the founding of Hungerford in 1882. The post office and businesses were relocated here later. (1985)

HUNGERFORD (Wharton Co.) SH 60 at US 59
New York, Texas & Mexican Railroad
and the Community of Hungerford

Attracted by the State of Texas' offer of free land to railroad developers, a charter for the New York, Texas & Mexican Railroad was secured in 1880. Its major investor, John W. MacKay, made his fortune in the Nevada silver mines. His brother-in-law, Count Joseph Telfener of Lombardy, Italy, arranged for the construction. Work began in 1880 on the 91-mile stretch of railroad track between Rosenberg and Victoria. The pasta diet of many of the Italian laborers lent itself to the railroad's nickname, the "Macaroni Line."

Telfener and MacKay established six stations along the line—Inez, Louise, Edna, Hungerford, Telfener, and MacKay—and named them for themselves and family members. The community of Hungerford was named for their father-in-law Daniel E. Hungerford, who served as vice-president of the New York, Texas & Mexican Railroad. Not the successful business venture they had envisioned, the company was sold to Southern Pacific Railway in 1885.

With an economy based on farming and ranching, the community of Hungerford has continued to flourish over the years. Its origin is a reflection of the varied history of the railroad in Texas. (Texas Sesquicentennial 1836–1986)

HUNGERFORD (Wharton Co.) SH 60 at US 59
J. D. Hudgins Ranch

Joel Hudgins (1800–1873) of North Carolina came to the Republic of Texas in 1839 and settled in the Hungerford area. He married Rachel Ann Northington McKenzie (d. 1903) in 1847. He was elected county commissioner in 1854.

After Joel's death, Rachel and their four sons began to buy more land and expand the ranching operation. Josiah Dawson (J. D.) Hudgins (d. 1928) headed the family's interests. He also owned a store, cotton gin, sawmill, and grew rice. In 1897, the four brothers divided the family property and operated independently.

In 1915, J. D. and his children purchased their first purebred Brahman cows, descendants of the herd brought from India by A. P. Borden in 1906. J. D.'s son Walter Hudgins (d. 1943) helped organize the American Brahman Breeders Association in 1924.

The Hudgins Ranch acquired the bull "Manso" in 1933. Manso's descendants are the cornerstone stock from which the ranch's American Gray Brahman herd was developed, now one of the largest registered American Gray Brahman herds in the world. Cattle from this ranch have been exported to over 42 countries and 34 states in the U.S. In 1962, the ranching partnership was reorganized into five separate entities, with each division operated by descendants of J. D. Hudgins. (1985)

HUNT (Kerr Co.) SH 39, 1 mi. E, East of river bridge
Schumacher Crossing on the Guadalupe River

Christian Schumacher emigrated with his family from Germany to Texas in 1845, the year he was born. He came to Kerr County in 1860, later marrying Sarah Brazeal Sublett and moving to land along the Guadalupe River, near the site of an antebellum sawmill operation built by Gustav and Fredrich Tegener. In the 1920s, son John Randolph Schumacher built a series of dams across the river, providing security from raging floodwaters for a stream crossing and new road to Hunt. Today the dams remain and an improved highway bridge crosses the stream. Schumacher Crossing is still enjoyed for its scenery and access to the river. (2003)

HUNTSVILLE (Walker Co.) SH 19, 8.2 mi. NE
Akin Hill
(3 mi. SE)

A landmark on the "Old Colony Road" between Huntsville and Ryan's Ferry on the Trinity River. Named for Thomas Akin (1828–1878), a native of Mississippi, who came to Texas in 1853 with his wife, Ruth Leakey Akin, whom he met and married in Bienville Parish, La., along the way. Akin, a horse trader, farmer, and singing teacher, came to this area in 1854, settled in the rural community of McGuire, and built a cabin at the base of the hill. While Akin served in the Civil War as a courier for Confederate Gen. John B. Hood, Mrs. Akin moved the family a few miles to the east. The couple had 7 children. (1974)

HUNTSVILLE (Walker Co.) *IH 45 frontage road at FM 1696, 7 mi. N*
Near Gravesite of
Veteran of American Revolution
Mark Manning
(1750–1850)
Served in American Revolution from Halifax district of North Carolina, his native state. Later lived in South Carolina and in Conecuh County, Ala., coming to Texas at 97 to live with sons who had large land grants and helped to settle Walker County.

Some 20 or 30 veterans of the American Revolution followed the nation's westward movement to Texas, perpetuating here their devotion to freedom and liberty.

Manning's sons fought in the Texas Revolution before he came to the new Republic. Manning is buried in family cemetery (2 mi. NE). (1972)

HUNTSVILLE (Walker Co.) *US 75, 6 mi. S*
Walker County
Created from Montgomery County in 1846, shortly after Texas became a state, Walker County was named for U.S. Senator Robert J. Walker (1801–1869) of Mississippi, a major advocate of Texas annexation. Because of Walker's Union sympaties in the Civil War, the honor was withdrawn in 1863 and the county was renamed for Captain Samuel H. Walker (1817–1847), a noted Texas Ranger who was killed in action during the Mexican War. Huntsville has always served as Walker County seat. Parts of Madison and San Jacinto Counties were carved from Walker County. (1982)

HUNTSVILLE (Walker Co.) *US 75, 4 mi. N*
Hillary Mercer Crabb (1804–1876)
Georgia native Hillary Mercer Crabb, a veteran of the militia in his home state, moved his family to the Mexican state of Texas in 1830. While awaiting a land grant they settled in the Sabine District. From there Crabb joined the Texas Militia and served in such action as the 1832 Battle of Nacogdoches. In 1835, he was granted property at this site. The rural community that developed around his homesite (400 yds. W) became known as Crabb's Prairie.

Crabb was instrumental in the early development of Huntsville and Walker County. A leader in civic and social activities, he became the first probate judge when the county was created in 1846. He also served as a justice of the peace and chief justice (county judge). In 1852, he was elected to serve the unexpired term of State Representative F. L. Hatch. Among Crabb's accomplishments as a legislator was the introduction of a bill to create Madison County.

Opposed to secession, Crabb moved to Lavaca County at the outbreak of the Civil War. He later moved to Madison County, where he served as sheriff. His influence as a prominent landowner, church leader, Mason and public servant had a dramatic impact on the early growth of this area. (1982)

HUNTSVILLE (Walker Co.) *US 75, approx. 7 mi. N*
Cook Springs Baptist Church
Baptists organized here in 1901 and held services at the Guinea Glade school (about 2 mi. NW). Brother Elisha E. Day (1848–1936), pastor of the Woodville Church (about 10 mi. SW), helped establish the congregation and conducted its first services. Charter members included Mr. and Mrs. Jim Cauthen, Mr. and Mrs. W. H. Hill, Mr. and Mrs. Jesse Petree, Mr. and Mrs. John L. Petree, Mrs. Mary Petree, Mr. and Mrs. Peter Petree, Mr. and Mrs. E. H. Tharp, and Miss Ruth Tharp. Mrs. Sarah Brown Gaines, wife of Toliver L. Gaines, organized the Sunday school.

In 1903, Mrs. Scisely Wells Cook Rose (1830–1912), also a charter member, gave this spring-fed site for a church building. She asked that the church be named for her late husband, John William Cook, who died in 1864 in the Civil War.

Records date from 1907, when deacon Edwin Harris Tharp (1849–1922) was church clerk and C. W. Matthews was the first called pastor listed. By 1912, a wooden sanctuary was completed. Services were held one weekend per month, Saturday night and Sunday morning.

A new building was dedicated in 1945, assembled and furnished largely by the labors of the congregation. Many additions indicate the growth of the church, yet the original spring survives, occupying a revered site. (Texas Sesquicentennial 1836–1986)

HURST (Tarrant Co.) *SH 183 W, NE of Loop 820*
Parker Cemetery
Land for cemetery donated by Isaac Duke Parker, Jan. 14, 1901. He was son of Isaac Parker, pioneer politician for whom Parker County was named and who was the uncle of Cynthia Ann Parker, white girl captured by Comanche Indians in 1836 and reared as an Indian. She was the wife of Comanche Peta Nocona and mother of Quanah Parker, the last great Comanche war chief.

Both Isaac Parker and Isaac Duke Parker served as members of the Texas legislature.

Isaac Duke Parker is buried here. Cemetery also contains a public burial section. (1968)

HUTCHINS (Dallas Co.) *New Dowdy Ferry Rd., .5 mi. E of IH 35*
Dawdy's Ferry
Illinois Native Alanson Dawdy (1826–1901) came to Dallas County in 1847. In 1854, he was granted a license to operate a ferry at this site on the Trinity River, the southernmost crossing at the time. An important route for citizens living on both sides of the river, the ferry continued in operation until about 1876. Ferry charges included one dollar for a wagon with four or more animals, ten cents for a man and horse, and five cents for a person on foot. The first permanent bridge was installed at this site in 1888. Dawdy was a veteran of the Mexican and Civil Wars.

(Texas Sesquicentennial 1836-1986)

HUTTO (Williamson Co.)

US 79 at FM 1660, ½ block E
Hutto
Located near Shiloh, one of the earliest villages in Williamson County, this area was settled in 1855 by J. E. Hutto (1824–1914) and Adam Orgain, a former slave. Hutto sold land for this townsite to the International & Great Northern Railroad in 1876. A post office was established in 1877 with Hutto as postmaster. By 1882, the town had a school and a Baptist church. By 1898, there were six churches, a Masonic lodge, newspaper, hotel, bank, two gins, and several stores. Hutto grew rapidly after Swedish immigrants turned nearby farms to cotton production. The town was incorporated in 1911. (1976)

HUTTO (Williamson Co.) *FM 1660, 5 mi. SE*
Norman's Crossing
The settlement of Avery was established in the mid-1800s by Daniel Kimbro, veteran of the Mexican War and Williamson County pioneer. The small farming community later was known as Norman's Crossing after pioneer M. B. Norman (1856–1921) who came to the area from Alabama in 1872. Besides farming a large tract of land along Brushy Creek, Norman, along with M. R. Kennedy, built and operated the local cotton gin. By 1914, the village boasted a general store, school, church, and a garage and machine shop. Descendants of some of the settlers still live in the area. (1982)

HYE (Blanco Co.) *US 290*
Hye Post Office
Named for Hiram ("Hye") Brown, founder of store, in 1880. Post office established 1886. Present store with Bavarian metalwork built in 1904. Owned by Deike family since 1923.

At age four, Lyndon B. Johnson, future U.S. President, mailed a letter here—a postal customer for first time in his life.

Postmaster General Lawrence F. O'Brien was sworn into cabinet of President Johnson at this post office in 1965. Awarded Medallion Plate.

INDEPENDENCE (Washington Co.)   *FM 390 E of intersection with FM 50*
Independence
Local legend tells of Dr. Asa Hoxey who, celebrating the Texas Declaration of Independence in 1836, moved to change the name of Coles settlement to Independence. Actual county records show an 1835 origin for the town of Independence, with C. Baker, J. G. W. Pierson, A. F. Burchard, and R. Stevenson, proprietors. The still-strong Independence Baptist Church was established in 1839 with Pastor T. W. Cox. Local resident Sam Houston was baptized in Little Rocky Creek in 1854. The wealthiest town in Texas by 1845, Independence won the bid for Baylor University, newly chartered by the Republic of Texas. J. B. Root became its first U. S. Postmaster in 1846. By the 1850s Independence had a hotel, jail, stagecoach depot, Masonic lodge, cemetery, and small commercial district. Both the city leaders and Baylor administrators refused to grant right-of-way to the Santa Fe Railroad. By the 1880s, trade was going to competing towns and Independence began to decline. Baylor University moved its schools to Waco and Belton in 1886. By the 1990s, Independence was a rural community with a population of 140. Remaining attractions include the Baptist church and numerous historical sites in the area.
(1997)

INDEPENDENCE (Washington Co.)   *FM 390, 3 blocks W of FM 50/*
FM 390 intersection
Old Baylor Park
Under a charter issued in 1845 by the Republic of Texas, Baylor University was established on this site and operated here until its removal to Waco and Belton in 1886. Afterward the site was bought by John Thomas Hairston (1835-1918), a church leader in Independence for over 40 years. Passed to his son, the land was returned in 1933 to Baylor by Dr. Thomas Coke Hairston (1875–1954), a grandson of Albert Gallitan Haynes, an original trustee of Baylor University who served on the board for 25 years. In 1965 the park became part of Texas Baptist Historical Center.

INDEPENDENCE (Washington Co.)   *FM 390 at FM 50*
Old Baptist Church
Organized in 1839. Here Sam Houston was converted and baptized in Rock Creek in 1854. The present building was erected in 1872.

INDEPENDENCE (Washington Co.)   *FM 50, 5 mi. S*
General Sam Houston
General Sam Houston was baptized by Rufus C. Burleson, Baptist minister and president of Baylor University, November 19, 1854, in Rocky Creek.

INDEPENDENCE (Washington Co.)   *FM 50 at FM 390, .3 mi. W*
General Sam Houston Home
Site of the home of General Sam Houston and family. Original house built in 1837 by Thomas Barron. First occupied by the Houstons in 1854. Torn down and rebuilt in 1897 by James Dallas.

INDEPENDENCE (Washington Co.)   *FM 50 at FM 390, 1 block S*
Site of Home of General Jerome B. Robertson
Home built in 1845 by General Jerome B. Robertson (1815–1891), a captain in the Army of the Republic of Texas 1836. A captain in the Somervell Expedition 1842. Representative and senator in the Texas Legislature. Brigadier General of Hoods Brigade, C.S.A.

INDEPENDENCE (Washington Co,)   *FM 390 at FM 50, .3 mi. E*
Margaret Lea Houston House
Margaret Lea Houston, Gen. Sam Houston's widow, lived here with their 8 children, 1863–1867. House built in 1830s.   (1965)

INDEPENDENCE (Washington Co.)   *FM 390 at FM 50*
Houston-Lea Family Cemetery
When the widow of Sam Houston died of yellow fever during the epidemic of 1867, the danger of contagion made it impossible to carry her to Huntsville for burial beside her husband. She lies here, with her mother, Mrs. Nancy Lea, near the sites of their last homes and the old church they both loved.   (1965)

INDEPENDENCE (Washington Co.) *FM 390 at FM 50*

Margaret Moffette Lea Houston
Wife of Gen. Sam Houston
April 11, 1819–Dec. 3, 1867
and her mother
Nancy Moffette Lea
May 1, 1780–Feb. 7, 1864

Women of character, culture and staunch devotion to their families and church, each in her own way greatly influenced the career of Sam Houston and the course of Texas history.

A daughter, Madora Cole McCrocklin, gave the site.

Many statesmen, educators, physicians, lawyers, war veterans and other "old Texians" are buried here. (1970)

INDIANOLA (Calhoun Co.) *SH 316, 15 mi. SE from Port Lavaca*

Site of the Town of Indianola (1844–1886)

First called by German immigrants Karlshaven, an important port of Texas. Cargoes of ships were hauled to and from points in Texas and Mexico by carts until 1860 when the San Antonio and Mexican Gulf Railroad and the Indianola Railroad were completed to Victoria.

The town was partly destroyed with great loss of life by a hurricane, September 17, 1875. It was rebuilt but completely destroyed by another hurricane, August 20, 1886. (1964)

INDIANOLA (Calhoun Co.) *SH 316 Terminus*

Indianola

Many currents of the mainsteam of Texas history flow in this onetime port. Pineda explored the coast in 1519 and LaSalle planted a settlement near here in 1685. Once an Indian trading point, it was a major seaport from 1844 to 1875. Texas colonists, including Germans led by Prince Carl of Solms-Braunfels, entered through Indianola. "Forty-niners," supplies for frontier forts, and experimental army camels were landed here.

During the Civil War Indianola and Fort Esperanza, which controlled the gateway to Indianola through Pass Cavallo, were objectives of Federal blockading vessels. Pass Cavalo, ten miles south, was one of several entrances to the inside waterway created by Matagorda Peninsula and the offshore islands extending to the Rio Grade. To deny Confederate use of this waterway for commerce through Mexico, the Federals had to seize control of these entrances.

Before Confederate defenses at Fort Esperanza were completed, two Federal steamers slipped through Pass Cavallo to Indianola and on October 31, 1862, demanded the surrender of Lavaca (now Port Lavaca) to the northwest. The Confederate command refused, stood off the naval guns with land batteries, and forced the withdrawal of the Federal ships.

Federal forces attacked Fort Esperanza November 22, 1863. The Confederates withstood the assault of naval and land forces for six days then spiked their guns, destroyed their magazines, and withdrew to the mainland. Indianola then fell December 23. On Christmas Eve, Federal and Confederate forces clashed at Norris Bridge, eight miles north. Two days later Lavaca was occupied and the entire Matagorda-Lavaca Bay area remained in Federal control until wars end.

Indianola was partially destroyed by a hurricane in 1875 and completely destroyed by another in 1886.

INDUSTRY (Austin Co.) *SH 109 S (7453 Ernst Pkwy)*

Education in Industry

German settlers established the town of Industry in 1831. Shortly after they arrived in December 1840, the Rev. Louis C. Ervendberg and Dr. Joseph Anton Fischer founded the town's first school. Fischer is recognized as the first teacher in Industry, and Ervendberg is credited as being tutor to the children of town founder Frederick Ernst. Tutors were common, with families hiring teachers to give lessons in their homes. By 1842, 37 area residents had petitioned the Texas Congress for the creation of a German institute of higher learning, Hermann's University. The school received its charter in 1844, and although the charter was amended in 1846 when Texas became a state, the project never materialized. Accustomed to the free education offered in their native Germany, Industry settlers were part of the free public school movement in Texas. In 1864, Civil War veteran Christian William Hander opened a school in the residence of the Niebuhr family. His school grew out of the private home and became the Industry Day School in 1865. Other schools at that time were operated by Rudolph Franke and John Simmons. These schools required tuition, though, from their students. Austin County established several public schools by 1880, including five in Industry, which created its own school district in 1912. Nearby Star Hill consolidated with it in 1928. Legislation in 1948 consolidated Industry, Shelby, Henkhaus, Rockhouse and New Bremen into West End Rural High School District, with grades 1–9 in Industry and 10–12 in Bellville. The district erected a new brick building in 1952, as well as a new structure for the African American campus, the Mary Bethune School. Following integration, the school consolidated into the Bellville Independent School District. The 1952 West End School building continued to serve as an elementary campus for the children of the area. (2002)

INDUSTRY (Austin Co.) *FM 1457 at FM 389, 8 mi. NW*
Town of Shelby
Named for 1822 settler David Shelby, this town grew up at the mill of German pioneer Otto Von Roeder. The Ohlendorfs, Vogelsangs, Rothermels, and Vanderwerths arrived in 1845; other Germans came in ensuing years. The post office opened 1846 with Shelby as postmaster. A school (1854), an agricultural society, a singing society and a band were started. Mission work, begun in 1876, led to founding of Peace Lutheran and St. Paul Lutheran Churches. By 1900 there were at least a dozen businesses here. Decline of farming led residents to live on ancestral land and work in cities. (1974)

INDUSTRY (Austin Co.) *SH 159, 2 mi. W in roadside park*
Charles Fordtran
(May 7, 1801–Nov. 1, 1900)
In Jan. 1831 Charles Fordtran, a German of Huguenot descent, joined the colony of Stephen F. Austin. His first work was to survey land for Austin's partner, Samuel May Williams. He was given a league (4,428.4 acres) as his fee. Soon he brought in two families of settlers who worked for him for a time, then obtained their own land in present Fayette County.

On July 4, 1834, he married Almeida Brookfield (1817–1887), daughter of a noted Indian-fighting family. Fordtran also fought Indians who stole livestock and kidnapped the wives and children of colonists. In the Texas War for Independence, he joined the "Spy Rangers" under Capt. John Bird, defending civilians who were fleeing to escape the Mexican invaders.

Charles Fordtran was one of the first Teutonic settlers in Texas—arriving some years before the main tide of German immigration. Music and good living abounded in his home. He and his wife had 14 children, with nine living to adulthood. Of four sons in the Confederate Army during the Civil War (1861–1865) two survived. His descendants have made contributions to Texas history as industrialists, engineers, lawyers, physicians, and teachers. This marker stands on land he received in 1831. (1976)

INEZ (Victoria Co.) *US 59 at FM 444*
Fort St. Louis
Thirteen miles southeast of Inez is located the site of Fort St. Louis, first French settlement in Texas, attempted by Rene Robert Cavelier Sieur de La Salle in 1685. Devastated by the Karankawa Indians. Burned by members of the Alonso de Leon Expedition in 1689. On its remains the Spaniards constructed Presidio de Nuestra Señora de la Bahía del Espiritu Santo. Established by Joseph de Azlor Marquis of Aguayo and Father Fray Augustin Patron, F. M., in 1722 as a protection for the Mission of Nuestra Señora del Espiritu Santo de Zuniga for civilizing and Christianizing of the Indian tribes of the vicinity. Moved to Mission Valley on the Guadalupe River near present Victoria in 1726. Moved finally to Santa Dorotea, now Goliad, near the San Antonio River.

INGRAM (Kerr Co.) *SH 39, 2 mi. W*
Site of Sherman's Mill
A pioneer Kerr County water-powered mill located near Kelly Creek-Guadalupe River confluence. It ground corn, sawed lumber, ginned cotton. Built in 1870s by John Sherman, it was in use until destroyed by flood in 1932. Sherman, his wife, and 8 children lived in house still standing nearby. (1972)

INGRAM (Kerr Co.) *SH 27*
Nichols Cemetery
Born about 1805, Rowland Nichols settled in Kerr County where he served as county commissioner. Upon his death at the hands of Indians, Nichols was buried, as he wished, under a live oak tree on his farm on April 11, 1859. This site became a community burial ground and the burial place of many area pioneers, including J. C. W. Ingram (1829–1902), for whom the town of Ingram was named. Additional property was later purchased from Lafayette Nichols to enlarge the cemetery. For over a century Nichols Cemetery has served the residents of this part of Kerr County. (1982)

INGRAM (Kerr Co.) *SH 27, approx. 2 mi. NW at Henderson Branch Rd.*
Henderson Cemetery
(2 Mi. N)
Howard Henderson (1842–1908) came to Texas in 1857. He was a survivor of the Civil War Battle of the Nueces in 1862, in which he and other Unionists were ambushed by a Confederate force near the Nueces River. He later served as a Texas Ranger. Henderson married Narcissa Turknett in 1866 and they settled near this site. In 1870, upon the deaths of their infant twin sons Thomas and Philip, they began a family burial ground which became known as Henderson Cemetery. Other family members and neighbors were also buried in the graveyard. (1990)

IOWA PARK (Wichita Co.) *Valley View School grounds,*
FM 1206 & FM 2226, 8 mi. SW
Van Dorn Trail
(1 mi. N)
First important wagon road in Wichita County. Blazed by Brevet Major (later General) Earl Van Dorn in September 1858 with 200 men of the crack 2nd U.S. Cavalry. Just ahead of him went young L. S. "Sul" Ross (Governor of Texas 1887–1891, and president of Texas A & M College 1891–1898) with 100 Indian scouts from the Brazos Reservation. Loyal Tonkawa Chief Placido guided Ross and his party.

After opening the trail, Van Dorn camped on Otter Creek, in present Oklahoma, for over a year. He routed the Comanches in a battle near Rush Springs (70 mi. E), although he and Ross were wounded in the fighting.

In 1859 Van Dorn won another decisive victory over the Comanches in Ford County, Kansas. Famous persons in this battle were Kirby Smith (later a noted Confederate general) and Fitzhugh Lee (later Governor of Virginia). They had recently ridden up the west branch of the trail. The 15 army wagons which brought supplies to the men leveled a trail much used by pioneer settlers who came afterward.

The trail ran from Fort Belknap, near Newcastle, Texas, to Camp Radziminski on Otter Creek, north of Frederick, Oklahoma. At Van Dorn crossing the road branched off to Montague County for supplies. (1969)

IRA (Scurry Co.) *SH 350, 4 mi. SW*
Campsite of the Marcy Expedition
At a grove of mesquite and wild china trees by a creek near here, Capt. R. B. Marcy's expedition camped Oct. 7, 1849. While blazing the famous Marcy Trail, they saw nothing deadlier than quail and wild turkeys in the area, but the next day tragedy struck.

Lt. Montgomery Pike Harrison (1826–1849)—grandson of President Wm. Henry Harrison and older brother of later President Benjamin Harrison—left camp alone to scout a ravine. When he did not return by dark, the company fired a Howitzer to signal him, but received no answer. Searchers the next day found signs that Harrison, always friendly to the Indians, had stopped and smoked with two Indians, believed to be Kiowas.

He was disarmed, however, taken one mile south and then shot with his own rifle. The Indians scalped and stripped the body and threw it into a ravine on Canyon Creek, They were pursued, but never captured.

Marcy later reported that when his men heard of Harrison's death, many hid their faces "to conceal their tears." The body was packed in charcoal and taken in a coffin made from a wagon bed to Ft. Smith for burial.

Despite this tragedy, Marcy's trail became a major wagon road, taking gold seekers to California and troops and supplies across the West Texas frontier. (1967)

IRA (Scurry Co.) *SH 350 at FM 1606*
J. J. Moore No. 1 Oil Well
(1.4 mi. S)

First producing oil well in Scurry county; opened a major West Texas petroleum area. Drilled February to October 1923 by E. I. (Tommy) Thompson, W. W. Lechner and E. E. (Buddy) Fogelson of Loutex Corp. W. A. Reiter located the well. Leon English was field geologist. Drillers were Jesse Thomas, Begossa Murphy, Tom Mann, Charlie Dodson, Sim Taylor. The tool dresser, James O. Jarmon, was the only man working the well from top to bottom. Pat and Mike Moore, the young sons of the landowner, helped to fire the steam boiler.

The drill struck a pressurized reservoir of "cold air" (nitrogen and helium), unique in Texas at that time. It blew mud and water 60 feet above the well head. Soon harnessed, it replaced steam to operate the drilling. It also refrigerated food and water.

Completed to 3575 feet and plugged back to 1800 feet in the San Andres formation, the J. J. Moore No. 1 has yielded over 500,000 barrels of oil; is still producing. Several "dusters" were drilled nearby in 1924. Exploration was further discouraged in the 20s by low prices. Eventually, however, here in the Sharon Ridge Field over 2200 wells have been brought in.

In 1948 deep wells began to tap the canyon reef in Scurry. The county now has over 4,000 oil wells. (1966)

IRA (Scurry Co.) *SH 350 at FM 1606*
Ira

Named for Ira Green, who had a crossroads store near this site. First homes and school were half-dugouts (cellars with windows set above ground level). Post office established 1896. On opening of block 97 to settlers, 1899, area became active farm and ranch community. Oil production since 1923. (1966)

IRAAN (Pecos Co.) *US 190 W at Marathon Oil Co. office*
Marathon Oil Company Discovery Well

Opening one of the greatest fields in the world, Marathon Oil Company (then Ohio Oil Company) brought in the I. G. Yates "A" No. 1 Well on October 29, 1926. It was a gusher from a shallow depth of 1,004 feet.

Previously oil men had said, "You won't find any oil west of the Pecos." This did not stop the work of Marathon Oil Company's predecessor firm and its partners in many ventures, the veteran wildcatters Michael L. Benedum and Joseph C. Trees, of Pittsburgh, Pennsylvania. Their strike was sensational.

Within a year, the Yates field had more than 100 wells—two with even higher yields than Yates No. 1.

Under the 20,000-acre Ira G. Yates ranch lay one of the largest oil reserves in the world. The many developers voluntarily adopted proration. Their plans for allocating and restricting Yates Field production were approved in 1928 by the Railroad Commission of Texas. This was the first complete proration of an oil field in the state—and an important milestone in petroleum conservation.

The discovery well has since been deepened to 1,283 feet. It still has a potential daily flow of 77,760 barrels. The Yates Field now has 607 wells. (1966)

IRVING (Dallas Co.) *200 block S Main*
City of Irving

Permanent settlement in this part of Dallas County began before the Civil War with the establishment of small farming communities and supply centers. In the early years of the 20th century, while working on the construction of the Rock Island railroad extension from Fort Worth to Dallas, two members of the survey party—its chief, J. O. Schulze, and a surveyor, Otis Brown—purchased just over 80 acres of land from pioneer farmer H. W. Britain. Soon they had platted a townsite, which they named Irving.

On December 19, 1903, Schulze and Brown held a barbecue and auction for the sale of town lots. The first issue of the Irving "Index" was distributed to those in attendance. Approximately

40 lots were sold, and construction of buildings soon began. The post office, which had been located at Kit, moved to Irving in 1904.

Co-founder Otis Brown served as Irving's first mayor after the town was incorporated in 1914. Over the years Irving grew to be a modest suburb of Dallas. With the construction of the Dallas-Fort Worth airport, Texas Stadium, and the Las Colinas Business Park, Irving experienced major economic growth during the last quarter of the 20th century.

(Texas Sesquicentennial 1836–1986)

ITASCA (Hill Co.)   *FM 934, 8 mi. E*
Site of Fort Smith
One of the chain of fortifications extending from the Colorado to Red River. Established in about 1846 as a protection against Indians. Named for Major Thomas I. Smith.

ITASCA (Hill Co.)   *FM 66, 5 mi. E*
Pioneer Home of David S.
and Sarah Ann Files
Built 1846 in Files Valley. Hewn log frame; salt-box style, with many later additions.

Four young Files sons—Adam, Francis, George and Thomas—were sworn into Confederate Army under an elm tree in front of the house, in 1861 ceremony. Awarded Medallion Plate.

(1966)

ITASCA (Hill Co.)   *FM 66, 6 mi. E*
Home of Francis Marion
and Jane Simpson Files
Built 1868. Dog-run style. Lumber hauled by ox-wagons from Waxahachie. Has square nails and pegs in framing; a fireplace in each room.

Builder was a Confederate veteran, large landowner, business executive, and a devout Presbyterian leader. Awarded Medallion Plate.   (1966)

ITASCA (Hill Co.)   *FM 66, 5 mi. E in vicinity of subject*
Southwestern Presbyterian
Home and School for Orphans
Orphanage originated in Dallas when First Presbyterian Church women arranged care for four children of a deceased member. Church then decided to found a statewide orphanage, for which D. S. Files family gave this land. Home opened in 1906 with Rev. J. D. McLean as first president. From beginning, home has used modern "cottage plan" and has maintained reputation for its outstanding staff, facilities, and program. Home's school was closed in 1957. Orphanage now part of Presbyterian Children's Home and Service Agency.   (1969)

ITASCA (Hill Co.)   *FM 67 at FM 934*
Site of Switzer College
Founded 1902 by David and Rebecca Switzer as woman's college and conservatory of music. Offered liberal arts, sciences, music. Had average of 125 students.

Social activities included literary societies, lyceum courses, receptions. Moved to Dallas, 1912. Plant was sold, dismantled in 1917.   (1966)

JACKSBORO (Jack Co.)   *US 281, city limits*
Butterfield Stage Line
Here ran the Southern Overland Mail Line connecting St. Louis and San Francisco with semi-weekly stage and mail service, 1858–1861. The length of the route, 2795 miles, and the superior service maintained made this a pioneer enterprise of first magnitude.

JACKSBORO (Jack Co.)   *US 281, .5 mi. S*
Fort Richardson
Established November 26, 1867 by the United States Army to defend the frontier against the Indians. A mail station on the Butterfield Overland Stage Line 1858–1861. Abandoned as a military post May 23, 1878.

JACKSBORO (Jack Co.)   *SH 199-US 281, at city limits*
Fort Richardson
Cavalry Post Hospital, 1867
In fort built to halt Indian depredations in North Texas. One of buildings and units on inspection in May 1871 by Gen. Wm. Tecumseh Sherman when news came of massacre of Warren Wagon Train, 24 miles northwest. Killers, later found at Ft. Sill, were brought to trial in Jacksboro—first time Indians were ever tried in the white man's court in North Texas. Awarded Medallion Plate. (1965)

JACKSBORO (Jack Co.)   *US 281, Ft. Richardson Grounds*
Officers' Quarters
Built in 1867 of lumber cut from cottonwoods growing in nearby river bottoms. One of 5 original officers' quarters. Outlasted fort's barracks and stables, which were built of small vertical timbers (pickets).

Style typical of 19th century army posts in the West. Only one left standing in the U.S.

Among men quartered here was Gen. Ranald S. Mackenzie, who sent Indians back to reservations, 1871–1874.

Restored by city of Jacksboro. Maintained by Girl Scouts.   (1964)

JACKSBORO (Jack Co.)   *FM 1156, 10 mi. E*
Wizard Wells
The Kiowa Indians first visited this location and used the mineral waters for medicinal purposes. George Washington Vineyard settled here in the 1870s, taking up a claim originally established by David Rowland. Vineyard dug this well for his home but the mineral-tasting water was not used. He suffered from sore eyes and from ulcers on his legs but was cured by bathing in and drinking the water. The news spread and visitors suffering from arthritis, rheumatism, stomach disorders, and skin diseases began coming to the well.

Those seeking treatments often camped along Bean's Creek in their wagons. Soon three hotels and several bath houses opened to serve the increased visitor population. The town of Vineyard was laid out in 1882 and J. H. Grisham opened the first general store. The town later included several churches, a newspaper, school, sawmill, blacksmith shop, and post office.

In 1898, the Rock Island Railroad bypassed Vineyard and Sebree Community was started (2 mi. S). Visitors arriving by train took a hack to the resort. H. F. Stamper and his sons, Clint and H. F., Jr., petitioned the Legislature in 1915 and the name of Vineyard became "Wizard Wells." Sebree was changed to Vineyard.   (1980)

JACKSBORO (Jack Co.)   *US 281, Sewell Park, on Lost Creek, near bridge*
Sewell Park
This site became Jacksboro's first park after tract here on Lost Creek was donated to city on June 25, 1921, by pioneer teacher-lumberman-rancher-public benefactor Dan Roland Sewell (1872–1957). City's first waterworks were installed during Sewell's service as mayor, Feb. 17, 1913 to April 11, 1921.   (1972)

JACKSONVILLE (Cherokee Co.)   *301 W Larissa (1 blk. off US 69)*
Larissa House
Oldest home in Jacksonville. Begun in Texas colonial style, 1857. W. A. Brown (1841–1933), veteran of Gen. N. B. Forrest's confederate cavalry, built main structure, 1874. Victorian additions in 1890s.

Lumber, hand-sawn heart pine, cut nearby. Square nails. Brick of local iron ore clay. While making fine walnut staircase, craftsman lived with family. Reared here was J. L. "Lem" Brown, merchant, author of Larissa, a history of this area.

(Recorded Texas Historic Landmark 1965)

JACKSONVILLE (Cherokee Co.)   *US 175, 1 mi. NW at site*
Old Neches Saline Road
(Crosses Highway 175 Here)
Originally an Indian trail. Used in 1765 by the Spanish priest Calahorra on an Indian peace mission. Gained importance, 1820s, for use in hauling salt from Neches Saline to Nacogdoches.

Survivors of the Killough family massacre of 1838 fled via the road to Fort Lacy. The Texas Army used it en route to fight Mexican rebel Cordova in 1838 and in Cherokee War, 1839.

Some of Kentucky volunteers went this way to the Mexican War, 1846. After Indian wars, road brought in many settlers.

Jacksonville, Dialville, and Larissa grew up along its path. (1970)

JACKSONVILLE (Cherokee Co.) *FM 347, 4 mi. S*
Old Rusk Tramway
(Roadbed Visible Behind Marker)

Equipped with pine rails that warped out of shape and a speed often exceeded by mule wagons, the Rusk tram began operations in 1875. Bypassed 2 years earlier by another railroad, local citizens rejoiced over the $47,500 tram. Rolling stock consisted of an aged street car, 3 flat cars, and a steam engine—the "Cherokee." Passengers usually had to help replace train on tracks before it reached end of the 16-mile line: Jacksonville. In 1879 the tram was sold for $90. However, it had fostered growth by helping attract Cotton Belt Railroad, iron works, and state prison. (1970)

JACKSONVILLE (Cherokee Co.) *FM 347, 5 mi. S*
Dialville

In 1866, Confederate John J. Dial (d. 1928) joined a group of 60 wagons headed for Texas. He arrived in this area the same year and soon began farming the land. With the 1882 arrival of the Kansas & Gulf Short Line Railroad, Dial opened a general store near the rail line. The following year, Dial and his wife, Ida Mae (Jones), deeded eight acres of land to the railroad for a flag stop station. The townsite he platted at the site of the station was named Dialville when the post office was established in 1885.

There was little growth in Dialville until 1897, when the flourishing tomato and peach production and shipping business revitalized the area. In that year, John T. Bailey opened a store and reactivated the post office. Dialville's first school was established in 1899. C. D. Jarratt, a leading East Texas fruit and vegetable sales agent, arrived about 1900 and helped develop the town into a leading shipping point for tomatoes and peaches.

Dialville was the scene of much commercial activity during the early years of the 20th century, but by the mid-1920s had begun to decline. It remains an important part of the regional and agricultural history of Cherokee County. (1985)

JACKSONVILLE (Cherokee Co.) *US 69, 4 mi. N in park*
Love's Lookout

On this nine-mile-long ridge there are two historic lookout points which command a view of 30 to 35 miles. Between this site, with an elevation of 713 ft., and Point Lookout (¼ mi. NW), lies a narrow valley. An Indian trail and later a pioneer road crossed this valley. The pass became known as McKee's Gap in 1846, after Thomas McKee led a group of Presbyterians here from Tennessee and began the town of Larissa (3.5 mi. NW). Named by McKee's son the Rev. T. N. McKee, the village flourished as the location of Larissa College from the 1850s until the 1870s. Point Lookout was a popular recreational area for citizens of Larissa until the railroad bypassed the town and it declined.

Around the turn of the century, John Wesley Love (1858–1925) bought this land and developed a 600-acre peach orchard. Known as Love's Lookout, the scenic point was used for outings by area residents. After Love's death, his family gave 22.22 acres, including the lookout site, to the state for a park. The city of Jacksonville bought 25 adjoining acres and developed both tracts as a WPA project.

J. L. Brown (1866–1944) and Jewel Newton Brown (1873–1966), former Larissa residents, gave the city 122 acres next to the park in 1940 in tribute to pioneers of Larissa. (1978)

JACKSONVILLE (Cherokee Co.) *US 69, 2 mi. S; W of hwy.*
Town of Craft

Known first as Independence, the town of Craft grew up in the 1890s on the railroad. When a post office was established in 1891, the name Craft was chosen to honor Thomas J. Craft, first postmaster and community leader. In 1896, C. D. and S. H. Jarratt and W. R. Stout began commercial tomato growing and production here. By 1917, 90 percent of Texas' tomatoes were shipped from this area. The town declined in the 1930s but is important for its early role in the East Texas tomato growing and shipping industry. (1985)

JASPER (Jasper Co.) *SH 63, 13 mi. NW*
Site of Town of Zavala
The town, called De Zavala, was named after Lorenzo de Zavala, a Mexican Impresario who became a Texas patriot in the Republic's fight for independence. De Zavala was incorporated on Christmas Eve, 1838, and was a postal office until the Civil War.

JASPER (Jasper Co.) *SH 63, 4 mi. W*
Bevilport
Important river shipping and trading point; was made seat of Bevil municipality, 1834. Named for John Bevil, Texas Ranger, a delegate (1835) to Consultation on Texas Independence, chief justice of Jasper County (1839), farmer.

On Angelina River, Bevilport shipped cotton, hides and other East Texas products to markets in New Orleans. Its docks were busy with flatboats, keelboats—its stores packed with travelers.

Texas rivers flowing to Gulf of Mexico were favorite areas for settlement; Bevil and others prospered on rich "bottom" lands, using river as road to market. (1967)

JASPER (Jasper Co.) *US 96, 6 mi. S*
Zion Hill Missionary Baptist Church and Cemetery
Local tradition and Baptist church records indicate that the Zion Hill Missionary Baptist Church was organized in 1852 with the Rev. John Bean as first pastor. The first church building on this site is thought to have been a small log house. On August 16, 1853, Aurin Goodgame Horn donated 3 acres including the graveyard to the Zion Hill Baptist Church.

The oldest marked grave is that of Joseph Wood, who was born in 1792 in North Carolina and died in Jasper County on September 16, 1854.

The original church building was quickly replaced by a board-and-batten structure and, in the 1880s, a large frame building. This stood until 1967, when it was demolished and replaced by a modern brick edifice outside the cemetery's north fence.

Of over 1,186 graves in Zion Hill Cemetery, 36 are unmarked or unknown. Several were citizens of the Republic of Texas; 75 war veterans are interred on this site. The graves of 102 young children bear witness to the high infant mortality rate among pioneers. Another notable grave is that of the Rev. A. C. Sims (1845–1920), who was born in the Republic of Texas, served in the Confederate Army, and was a pastor of Zion Hill Baptist Church. (1998)

JASPER (Jasper Co.) *FM 1131, 6.4 mi. S of Evadale*
Wiess Bluff
(300 yds. E)
End of tidewater navigation of Neches River; called Grant's Bluff in 1840, when Niles F. Smith laid out town and Simon Wiess (1800–1868) built wharf and warehouses to ship area products downriver. Post office, established 1847 at Pattillo's, in Jefferson County, was moved here July 21, 1853.

Area flourished after 1885, when J. G. Smyth & Co. built tram roads into forest and began to cut timber. Beaumont Lumber Co. bought out Smyth in 1888. As good timberland dwindled after 1900, local population declined. The Wiess Bluff post office closed Sept. 15, 1908. (1973)

JAYTON (Kent Co.) *SH 70, 3 mi. N in roadside park*
Putoff Canyon
(East of Here)
Named for a Mr. Putoff, early settler. In region of salt water, canyon was noted for its freshwater spring "strong enough to swim a horse". Area was a resort, 1900–1914, for many artists. Western writer Zane Grey used region as setting for his novel *The Thundering Herd.* (1969)

JEFFERSON (Marion Co.) *US 59, 2 mi S*
Jefferson
Home to the Caddo Indians for centuries, this area of Texas attracted Anglo-American colonists to settle here in the early 1800s. Founded in 1839, Jefferson developed along a double-grid pattern.

Daniel Nelson Alley platted the townsite in a true North-South and East-West pattern, while Allen Urquhart drew a plan with streets leading diagonally to and from Big Cypress Bayou.

Jefferson was a center of commerce and an important shipping point on the Red River system. Riverboats arrived at the wharves daily, making it a major inland port of entry for Texas pioneers. It was the seat of Cass County from 1846 to 1852, and was named seat of the new county of Marion in 1860.

During the Civil War, Jefferson served as a major supply center for the Confederacy. The late 1860s saw the imposition of martial law by Federal reconstruction troops, and a devastating fire in 1868 destroyed much of the central business district.

Destruction of a massive logjam on the Red River in November 1873 diverted the river's flow and lowered the water in Big Cypress Bayou. The decline of Jefferson's economy due to the loss of its port continued until 20th-century tourism began to revive the town. (1990)

JEFFERSON (Marion Co.) SH 49, 4.5 mi. W
Site of Early Bell Foundry
From a log blacksmith shop in 1854 grew a bell foundry owned by G. A. Kelly which manufactured cowbells widely used by pioneer ox-team freighter. Later the Kelly plow, one of the first modern plows made in Texas, was manufactured here.

JEFFERSON (Marion Co.) SH 49, 5 mi. W
Kellyville
Named for George Addison Kelly. Died in 1909. Proprietor of an early foundry which cast cowbells widely used by ox-team freighters. After 1860 his factory turned out the first modern plows used in Texas.

JEFFERSON (Marion Co.) SH 49, Blackburn Syrup Works
Site of First Ice Factory in Texas
Established by Boyle and Scott about 1875. Sold ice at ten cents per pound. B. T. Benefield delivered it. The plant was later moved to Harrisburg.

JEFFERSON (Marion Co.) SH 44 at US 59
Civil War Meat Packing Plant
About 2 miles to the southwest, the meat plant of J. B. Dunn dressed, packed and shipped beef, pork and mutton to the Confederate Army. In 1861 began by packing 150 beeves a day. Well located, on the cypress bayou shipping route, with cattle in trailing distance, in East and North Texas. Herds were bought at $20 to $40 a head.

Used 42-gallon wooden barrels. Filled these with meat and brine. Obtained salt from New Iberia, La., and elsewhere through the Confederate government. Yet even with use of preservative salt, bloody water was sometimes found in the packed meat. The army complained it was made to accept this, though regular customers would have rejected it.

The greater portion of cattle went out of Texas on the hoof, to be served as fresh meat after being slaughtered in the army camp. So much beef, pork, mutton, grain, sugar, salt, peas, beans, flour and corn meal was shipped away that Texas became known as the breadbasket of the Confederacy.

Supplying of food was only one part of the Texas war effort, which included yielding her cotton crops as currency to buy guns and ammunition and other goods, and sending her men and horses into the fight. (1964)

JEFFERSON (Marion Co.) SH 49, E city limits
Jefferson, C.S.A.
Metropolis of commerce and culture for East Texas, Jefferson became important center for Confederate activity. Major quartermaster depot for northern Texas established 1862 supplied clothing and camp equipment. Cotton bureau station set up to buy cotton, "life blood of the confederacy." Two iron works in county made plows, kettles, skillets and cannon balls. Thousands of cattle and sheep were driven to slaughter house for processing and shipment. Boot and shoe factory helped outfit army. Debarkation center for troops leaving Texas. A memorial to Texans who served the Confederacy. (1963)

JEFFERSON (Marion Co.)   *FM 729, 20¾ mi. W*
Nash Iron Works
(500 yds. N on Alley Creek)
First iron furnace in Texas. Built by Jefferson S. Nash, who came here in 1846. He found much iron ore, wood for charcoal, and clay to make molds. From ridge back of the furnace, charcoal and ore were poured down the smokestack. Under the furnace grate, melted iron collected in a puddle, to be put into molds for shaping farm tools, cooking pots, smoothing irons, and—in the Civil War—cannon balls and possibly guns. Nash had trouble with securing capital, labor, transportation and machinery.

In the 1800s, at least 16 iron works operated in East Texas.   (1965)

JEFFERSON (Marion Co.)   *SH 59, 1 mi. S on east side, north of the bridge*
Trammel's Trace
Traces began as foot paths used by the Indians to mark their trails through wilderness areas. They later were used by surveyors in mapping early land grants. In 1824, Nicholas Trammel (1780–1852), a government scout, began opening up the trace that now bears his name. Trammel's Trace was, for many years, an important route of immigration into Texas. Approximately 180 miles long, it began at Fulton, Arkansas, and continued to Nacogdoches, Texas. Trammel's Trace entered Marion County on its northern boundary and left the county about 3.5 miles south of Jefferson.

(1984)

JEFFERSON (Marion Co.)   *US 59, 1.6 mi. S*
Bluebonnet Farm
Raised cottage; begun in 1847. Main wing, built 1869, is of heart pine cut on the home place. Awarded Medallion Plate.   (1966)

JEFFERSON (Marion Co.)   *US 59, Big Cypress Bridge approach*
Jefferson Turn Basin
Wide, deep lagoon in Cypress Bayou, used for turning around ships in Gulf-Red River trade.

First steamer to reach here was the *Lama* in 1844, by way of Red River, which for 200 miles above Shreveport was clogged by a "raft" of debris that had begun forming about 1529. Cypress Bayou thus was best travel route into Oklahoma, Western Arkansas, and North Texas. Until federal government in 1873 removed the raft, Jefferson was Southwest's greatest inland port, with this basin its business center. Last steamer operated here in 1903.   (1964)

JEFFERSON (Marion Co.)   *SH 49, 4 mi. NE*
T. J. Taylor, Jr. Home
On an original land grant of the Republic of Texas. Built about 1852 by Berry Hodge, prominent surveyor, using slave labor.

Among later owners was a civic leader who published the "Jefferson Jimplecute."

Restored in 1950 by the now deceased T. J. Taylor, Jr., brother of U.S. First Lady, Mrs. Lyndon B. Johnson. Awarded Medallion Plate.   (1964)

JERMYN (Jack Co.)   *SH 114, about 3 mi. W, 300 yds. S of site*
Site of
Loving Ranch House
Built 1872 by J. C. Loving, the son of pioneer trail driver Oliver Loving. J. C. Loving was an organizer and first secretary of Texas and Southwestern Cattle Raisers Association.

Organization's first office was at the ranch, which was later operated by Loving's son, Oliver II.
(1968)

JOAQUIN (Shelby Co.)   *FM 2787, 2 mi.*
Fellowship Baptist Church
One of the oldest Baptist churches in Texas. Founded by settlers who came by ferry across Sabine River as early as 1818. After a number of homes were built on hills near good springs of water, a church was considered essential. It is recorded that this one ministered to spiritual needs

in Republic of Texas era. Congregation assembled by riding many miles, usually in farm wagons, and with baskets of food.

Original log building, heated by 8-foot fireplace, with mud chimney, had split log benches.The windows, without glass, had shutters on wooden hinges.

In season, school was held in this early building.

The name "Fellowship" honored loyalties among the pioneer families. First pastor was the Rev. Wyatt S. Childress, a kinsman of Geo. C. Childress, one of the authors of the Texas Declaration of Independence. First church clerk was Dr. John Moses Taylor.

Erected after sawmills were in use in the 1870s was second church building, of plank construction. This was several times relocated and remodeled. The present structure was built in 1939; enlarged 1967.

The old "Busbee Place" spring, initially responsible for choice of this site, still supplies water for the church and baptistry. (1969)

JOHNSON CITY (Blanco Co.)

US 281, 3 mi. N of Round Mountain then 1.6 mi. W on Round Mountain Llano Lane

Blanco County

Formed from Burnet, Hays, Gillespie and Comal Counties. Created February 12, 1858. Organized April 12, 1858. Named for the stream which traverses the region. County seat, Blanco City, 1858–1890. Johnson City, since. (1.6 mi. E Johnson City, U.S. Hwy. 281–290.) (1964)

JOHNSON CITY (Blanco Co.)

US 281, 11 mi. NE in roadside pk.

Home County of Pioneer Leader
Joseph Wilson Baines
(1846–1906)

Born in Louisiana; in 1850 came to Texas, where his father, Rev. Geo. W. Baines, founded a church newspaper and was president of Baylor University. Served in the Williamson cadets, in Civil War.

Lived in Collin County, 1867–1883. Married Ruth A. Huffman. Was a teacher, lawyer; founder and publisher of McKinney "Advocate."

Served 1883–1887 as Secretary of State for Texas. Practiced law in Blanco, 1888–1903. Died in Fredericksburg.

His daughter Rebecca (Mrs. Sam Ealy Johnson) became the mother of Lyndon Baines Johnson, 36th President of the United States. (1965)

JOHNSON CITY (Blanco Co.)

US 290 at entrance of Johnson Ranch Headquarters

Blanco County Trail Drivers

From this headquarters site in the 1870s, the brothers J. T. and Sam Ealy Johnson started thousands of cattle up trails to Kansas and other shipping or market points. To the west, at Williamson's Creek, and at Deer Creek (southeast) the Johnsons had gathering and processing pens. They had largest individual trail driving outfit in Blanco and six nearby counties, sending north several herds of 2,500 to 3,000 each season. Sam Ealy, the younger Johnson brother, is known to history as grandfather of 36th President of the United States, Lyndon Baines Johnson. (1969)

JOHNSON CITY (Blanco Co.)

US 290 W, 1 blk. off

Boyhood Home, 36th U.S. President,
Lyndon Baines Johnson

Built 1886. Bought 1914 by Sam Ealy Johnson, Jr., Texas legislator, and his wife Rebekah Baines, daughter of later Secretary of State in Texas. On 2 ell porches Mrs. Johnson grew roses. On east porch, 1937, Young Lyndon, protege of President Franklin Roosevelt and a former Congressional aide, made first speech in first campaign for national office, for Congress, 10th district of Texas. Awarded Medallion Plate. (1965)

JOHNSON CITY (Blanco Co.)

US 290/281 at Ave. H

Dr. James Odiorne
1816–1887

Prominent pioneer physician, civic leader. Practiced medicine in Illinois and Kentucky before settling in Texas in 1857, moved to Blanco County in 1860. He was Civil War surgeon at Fort Mason, Texas. Served as commissioner and chief justice of Blanco County, 1860. Owned a newspaper, 1885-1887.

As doctor, he went by horseback or gig, regardless of weather. Scarcity of drugs led him to use native herbs for medication; for a sedative (opium), grew and milked garden poppies. He died of burns when alcohol exploded during the compounding of medicine in his drugstore near this site.

(1972)

JOHNSON CITY (Blanco Co.)

US 290, 9 mi. SE at Miller Creek Cemetery

Thomas C. and Eliza V. Felps

Born in Tennessee in 1836, Thomas C. Felps came to Texas in 1850 and to this area in 1856. He earned a living by freighting joined the Blanco County rangers during the Civil War. In 1863 he married Eliza V. White (b. 1846), a native of Ohio. In the summer of 1869, the couple lived with Eliza's parents while Thomas recovered from a fever. Her father, newly-appointed county judge S. T. White, had gone to Blanco on July 21, 1869, when Thomas and Eliza were killed by a band of Indians on Cypress Creek. Only Eliza was scalped. The couple's orphaned children, Thomas and Caroline, were cared for by Eliza's parents. (1975)

JONES CREEK (Brazoria Co.)

SH 36 right-of-way at Gulf Prairie Presbyterian Church, just N of cemetery

Emily Margaret Brown Austin Bryan Perry
(1795–1851)

Born near Austinville, Virginia, as was her brother Stephen Fuller Austin (1793–1836), Emily moved with her father Moses Austin (1761–1821) and mother Maria Brown Austin (1768–1824) to Missouri in 1798. The family operated lead mines there and founded the town of Potosi, south of St. Louis.

Emily was sent to schools in Kentucky and New York and returned to Missouri in 1812. She married James Bryan (1788–1822) in 1813 and gave birth to five children at Hazel Run, Missouri. After James died, Emily subsisted by taking boarders and teaching school. She married James Franklin Perry (1795–1853) in 1824 in Missouri; their union produced six children.

By the end of 1831, the Perry family—including Emily, James, four Bryan children, two Perry children, James' niece, and nine slaves—had joined Emily's brother Stephen in Texas. They settled at San Felipe and built a house at Stephen's Peach Point Plantation, providing a home and counsel for her bachelor brother.

The Bryan and Perry offspring contributed greatly to the development of Texas. Emily's sons served as soldiers and statesmen, and preserved the Austin bloodline. Emily died at Peach Point shortly after a trip to Philadelphia, and was buried here at Gulf Prairie Cemetery.

(Texas Sesquicentennial 1836–1986)

JONES CREEK (Brazoria Co.)

SH 36 and Gulf Prairie Cemetery Rd, Gulf Prairie Presbyterian Church

James Franklin Perry
(September 19, 1790–September 13, 1853)

A native of Allegheny County, Pennsylvania, James Franklin Perry moved to Potosi, Missouri, in 1808. He joined the mercantile business of his relatives Samuel and John Perry, and became a partner in 1818.

While living in Potosi, Perry met and married Emily Margaret Austin Bryan, a widow with four children. They were eventually the parents of six additional children.

Emily's father, Moses Austin, and her brother, Stephen F. Austin, were pioneer leaders in the movement to colonize Texas. Upon the urging of Stephen F. Austin, James and Emily Perry and their family moved to Texas in 1831. James Perry established a mercantile business in San Felipe and a farm on Chocolate Bayou. By 1832, the family moved to Peach Point Plantation on the Brazos River.

James Franklin Perry was an active supporter of the Republic of Texas, serving at conventions and on the committee of safety. As executor of Stephen F. Austin's estate, his reports to the government concerning colonial affairs, maps, and land papers became important to the archives of Texas. Perry died of yellow fever while visiting Biloxi, Mississippi, in 1853 and is buried there.

(1989)

JOSHUA (Johnson Co.) *SH 174, 4 mi. N*
Sam Bass Holdup
Along with two partners, Sam Bass, daring Texas outlaw, stopped a Fort Worth-Cleburne stage near here Dec. 20, 1877. Without firing a shot, they disarmed the driver, robbed passengers of $11.25. One outlaw, shot by a witness, was left by Bass to die. Less than a year later, Bass too was slain. (1966)

JOURDANTON (Atascosa Co.) *SH 97, 1 mi. NE in roadside park*
Atascosa County
As early as 1722 El Camino Real (the King's Highway) from the Rio Grande to San Antonio was well established in this area. The Spanish word "Atascosa," denoting boggy ground that hindered travel, gave region its name. The county was created in 1856 from land formerly in Bexar County. Jose Antonio Navarro, whose 1831 claim was the first grant recorded in area, gave land in 1857 for first county seat, Navatasco. County seat moved to Pleasanton in 1858, to Jourdanton in 1911.

Livestock, oil, gas and strawberries are well-known products of the county. (1969)

JOURDANTON (Atascosa Co.) *FM 2504, 24 mi. NW via SH 173*
Rossville
First Scottish community in Southwest Texas. Founded 1873 by brothers William F. Ross and John C. Ross. Born in North Scotland, they came to Texas in 1867. Here they were awarded a contract to carry U.S. mail. On the route, they noticed fertile soil and plentiful game of this region. They soon settled here and persuaded other Scottish families to join them.

Rossville came to have a one room school, cotton gin, post office (established 1877), two grocery stores, a bakery and a saloon; but it declined after being passed by the railroad.

JUNCTION (Kimble Co.) *US 83 at US 290/IH 10*
Kimble County
Jumano and Apache Indians inhabited region when Spanish explorers traveled across it in the 17th and 18th centuries, and were displaced by the Comanche tribe by the mid-19th century. Area was under military jurisdiction of Forts Terrett (1852–1854) and McKavett (1852–1859, 1868–1883), which were aided in defense by the Texas Rangers.

County was created from Bexar County, 1858, named for George C. Kimble (1801–1836), who died defending the Alamo. Organized in 1876, with the county seat first at Kimbleville, then Junction in 1877. Haven for lawless element until the Rangers restored peace in 1880s. Ranching is primary industry, producing wool and mohair. (1973)

JUNCTION (Kimble Co.) *US 290/IH 10, 4.3 mi. NW*
Old Bear Creek
Texas Ranger Camp
(300 yds. S)
Established October 1877 as patrol base for Co. E, Frontier Battalion, Texas Rangers, on the lookout for Indians and outlaws along the Llano River. Area was popular refuge for cattle and horse thieves, murderers, mail robbers—and within a few weeks many were captured by the unit of 30 men commanded by Lt. N. O. Reynolds. The Rangers in 1878 helped fight off one of the last Indian raids in the area.

Ranger protection given from this camp (used until mid-1880s) opened the way for peaceful settlement in Kimble and nearby counties. (1966)

JUNCTION (Kimble Co.)   *US 377, 1.7 mi. SW*
Bradbury Settlement
One of earliest communities opened by James Bradbury, great grandfather of O. C. Fisher. He was killed by Indians in 1872. His land was sold in 1875.

JUNCTION (Kimble Co.)   *US 290/IH 10, 4.5 mi. NW*
Campsite of
Marques de Rubi, 1767
In 1764 King Charles III of Spain ordered the Marques de Rubi, a Spanish army field marshal, to tour and inspect all presidios in New Spain.

Rubi arrived in Mexico in February 1766, and was joined by Nicholas de LaFora, engineer and mapmaker. They made a tour of the Northwest and California Territory and entered Texas on July 17, 1767. Rubi chose this location for his campsite July 23, 1767.

His report suggested small Texas missions be closed. This was done in 1772. Only Goliad and San Antonio remained.

JUNCTION (Kimble Co.)   *RR 1674, 17.8 mi. NW*
Coalson-Pullen Colony
(Cabin Chimney at site, about 3 mi. NW)
Opened 1866 by Nick and Jennie (Blackwell) Coalson, who moved from Menard area. Stockraising and hunting provided livelihood. Their "bacon" was cured bear meat.

Indians often stole horses, and in Dec. 1870 attacked cabin when Coalson and Charlie Mann had gone hunting. Ranch hand Joe Harris was killed. Mrs. Coalson in man's attire held off Indians until her husband returned.

Later Coalson sold the ranch to surveyor-Civil War veteran Dr. Asa Pullen and wife, Juliet (Gilliland), who had 6 daughters. Many descendants of this family still live in Kimble County.

(1970)

JUNCTION (Kimble Co.)   *US 290 N, 13 mi. W in front yard of church*
First Church in Community
Copperas Methodist Church
Organized in 1881 by circuit rider, Andrew Jackson Potter, who helped firmly establish the Methodist church in West Texas. Before construction of church on this site in 1917, services were held in schoolhouse or under brush arbor ¾ mi. SW, on west bank, Copperas Creek.

Building site was donated by J. A. Cowsert. Lumber was hauled here by wagon from Menard. Labor was donated by members and other local residents. Awarded Medallion Plate.   (1967)

JUNCTION (Kimble Co.)   *US 83, .3 mi. N*
First Court in Kimble County
(Site: ½ mi. NW, on Main Llano River)
Held in spring of 1876, under a live oak tree that had a hive of wild bees in its trunk. The site, "Old Kimbleville," had been suggested as the county seat.

District Judge W. A. Blackburn, of Burnet, arrived by horseback.

District attorney was Frank Wilks. The jury was seated on two logs. Another log was the judges bench, and a piece of gnarled live oak limb the gavel. Prisoners awaiting trail were chained to nearby trees. Major trials were for horse thefts. Texas Rangers were on hand to testify and to guard court, as this was during lawless era.   (1967)

JUNCTION (Kimble Co.)   *US 290/IH 10, 18 mi. W*
Ft. McKavett-Ft. Clark
Military Road
From nearby Ft. Terrett, this road in 1852 led south to Ft. Clark and north to Ft. McKavett.

Selected mainly because it had water available, it served as route for freight and mail, 1868, when forts were reactivated. Over it went troops, supplies, a few immigrants and pioneer ranchers. It was noted also for passage of forays of Col. Ranald Mackenzie against the hostile Indians to the northwest.

After forts were abandoned in 1883, ranchers drove cattle to market over parts of the road.

(1966)

JUNCTION (Kimble Co.) *US 377, 4 mi. SW of courthouse*
Site of Four Mile Dam (100 yds. S)
Built under an 1896 charter, obtained for the Junction City Irrigation and Power Ditches, to furnish power for mills and mining, supply city mains, water extensive lands and livestock.

At first under engineering supervision of G. W. Ragsdill, a local man, then of R. J. Hand, San Antonio, project was sold 1903 to Jay E. Adams, San Antonio, and A. C. Green, of Palestine, Texas.

Dam was of native stone and cypress wood; ditches were 4 ft. deep, 20 ft. at top, 12 at bottom. Big ditch carried water late as 1925; but was unprofitable. Charter was forfeited in 1950.

(1967)

JUNCTION (Kimble Co.) *US 290/IH 10, 7.8 mi. E*
Near Route of Old Military Road
Supply line from U.S. Army headquarters in San Antonio to Fort Terrett, 1852–1854.

In the 1850s two-thirds of Texas was held by Comanches or threatened by raids. Posts such as Fort Terrett stood from Red River to the Rio Grande, for protection. The Fort Terrett road paralleled Johnson (Elm) Fork of the Llano, and crossed the main Llano near Junction.

The army closed Fort Terrett in 1854, but settlers used the route as their main road to San Antonio. It appeared on Kimble County maps until 1930. Parts of the road are still visible. (1966)

JUNCTION (Kimble Co.) *FM 2291, 12.1 mi. NW at site*
Morales Ranch
350 yards southwest stands a small rock house built in 1881 by settler Meliton Morales (1837–1924).

Born in Mexico, Morales was kidnapped by Indians as a youth and spent 9 years in captivity. Moved to Texas in 1855. Came here from Duval County in 1874, bringing 200 Spanish goats and 2,000 sheep to start ranching.

He and wife, Ramona (Pena), had 9 children. He served on jury of first court convened after organization of county. He and wife are buried on the Manuel Morales ranch in Schleicher County, near Kimble County line.

Descendants own this land. (1970)

JUNCTION (Kimble Co.) *US 377, 10.8 mi. SW*
Doom of the
Outlaws of Pegleg Station
Here the climax of a western track-down occurred on Jan. 18, 1878, when Texas Rangers killed suspected murderer Dick Dublin, member of a gang of outlaws.

Although a friend yelled for him to run, Dublin was shot (150 yds. S) as the intrepid James B. Gillett and 3 other Rangers rushed his hide-out (60 yds. E).

Dick's brothers (Role and Dell), Mack Potter, and Rube Boyce were captured after a partner of the gang turned informer.

Three of them (plus two others) were convicted Aug. 23–24, 1880, of the 1877 robbery of the U.S. mail at Pegleg Station. (1968)

JUNCTION (Kimble Co.) *US 377, 10 mi. SW*
R. M. Turner Family
On April 28, 1879, R. M. Turner (1858–1928) entered Kimble County with bride, Emma (Scarborough), (1863–1945), from DeWitt County. They settled near this site, on the north bank of the South Llano River, where Turner soon became a prominent cattle and sheep rancher. Of ten children born to the Turners, eight reached adulthood. Most of them remained in the county to become leading citizens. Most noted was Jack Turner, conductor of the first Angora doe sale in Texas, and one of the organizers of National Angora Goat Breeders Association, in 1925, serving as the first secretary, then president. (1973)

JUNCTION (Kimble Co.)   *US 377 NE, 1½ mi. from*
courthouse, in roadside park

The Killing of Sam Speer
(⁹⁄₁₀ mi. W, Hwy. 290; and 200 yds. S)

On Dec. 24, 1876, a band of Indians killed Sam Speer, only 17 years of age, who was driving in horses near here. A 50-caliber gun his brother was using failed to fire.

This was the last Indian murder in Kimble County.

Speer is buried in the North Llano cemetery.   (1967)

JUNCTION (Kimble Co.)   *FM 385, 32 mi. E in roadside turnout*

Spanish Road to Santa Fe, 1808

Most direct road from San Antonio to Santa Fe, during Spanish era in Texas, 1519–1821. Charted for closer ties between Mexico City and New Mexico, after American explorer Zebulon Pike blazed trail from U.S. to New Mexico. Spanish road of 1808 was mapped by Capt. Francisco Amangual and 200 soldiers.

Amangual, veteran of 46 years of service to Spain, left San Antonio on March 30, 1808. On April 8, coming into this valley 5 miles to the south, he followed the East James (then called El Chimal Creek, for its bordering bluffs that resemble Indian headdresses), and camped that night by this red bluff. The party saw much game, including buffalo, and killed a bear.

Stampedes and losses of horses and mules (some loaded with crude sugar and other food) made the trip difficult. The route pointed north-northwest.

The party reached Santa Fe on June 19, and six months later returned to San Antonio.

Although Zebulon Pike (discoverer of Pike's Peak) had traveled with only eight men, Amangual had to field a large party. One goal of his expedition was to impress the wild and fierce Plains Indians with the might and glory of Spain. The road measured in 1808 has traces visible today, parallel to auto roads.   (1967)

JUNCTION (Kimble Co.)   *US 377, 8 mi. E*

Teacup Mountain

Named for its peculiar formation. Probably used as a lookout post by both whites and Indians in pioneer days. Near here occurred the Indian killing of pioneer James Bradberry, Sr., 1872; and the capture of a wanted man by Lt. N. O. Reynolds and four fellow Texas Rangers in 1878.

(1967)

JUNCTION (Kimble Co.)   *FM 1871, 20 mi. E*

John L. Jones Ranch

Established about 1875 by Jim Ike and John L. Jones (1852–1912). John Jones drove thousands of cattle to Kansas railheads, and by 1885 had bought his brother's interest in the ranch, which he increased to 25,000 acres. Originally he ran large herds of cattle, but later added sheep and goats to his range. He built a stone drift fence, possibly first in county; portions of this still stand.

He was persuaded by friends to run for sheriff in 1896, to help rid the county of rustlers; he completed the job in one term.

Descendants own much of this original ranch property today.   (1973)

JUNCTION (Kimble Co.)   *US 377, 1 mi. SW of courthouse*

Isaac Kountz

Killed on this spot by Indians on Christmas Eve, 1876. He was 16 years old, and herding sheep for his father, Dr. E. K. Kountz.

A brother, Sebastian, aged 11, escaped. A posse and Texas Rangers chased the Indians to the Guadalupe River.

Young Kountz was buried in Junction cemetery.   (1967)

JUNCTION (Kimble Co.)   *US 377, 5 mi. S*

Hoggett Home

First two-story house in county. Built 1877–1879 on the caliche soil, with no foundation, by Civil War veteran B. F. Pepper, who led a wagon train of settlers to Texas from Missouri.

Since 1905 in family of Dr. R. H. P. Wright. The girlhood home of Fay Wright, 1941–47, First Lady of Texas, as wife of Governor Coke Stevenson. (1965)

JUNCTION (Kimble Co.) US 377 3 mi. S

John James Smith
(March 4, 1822–April 22, 1924)

Illinois native John James Smith came to Texas shortly before enlisting for service in the Mexican War, 1846–1848. He later served as a Texas Ranger, helping protect frontier areas from attacks by hostile Indians. During the Civil War, Smith joined the Confederate Army and served for four years. Following his discharge from the military, he served as city marshall of Greenville, Texas, for two years. Smith moved to Kimble County in 1881, where he was a farmer and a respected citizen. He lived at his nearby farm home (300 yds. SE) until his death at the age of 102. (1981)

JUNO (Val Verde Co.) FM 189 at SH 163, 2 mi. N

Hood's Devil's River Fight

The men of Company G, a small unit of the U.S. 2ND Cavalry, left Fort Mason on July 5, 1857, under the command of Lt. John Bell Hood (1831–1879), in pursuit of Comanche Indians in the vicinity.

Traveling northwest, they discovered a fresh Indian trail leading southward toward Mexico. Crossing bluffs near the Devil's River on July 20, the men encountered an Indian camp on a ridge about two miles from the stream, marked by a white flag. Suspecting an ambush, Hood proceeded cautiously toward the ridge.

A small band of Indians advanced to meet Hood's party. Then, throwing down the flag to signal their concealed allies, the Indians attacked. Outnumbered, and hampered by brush fires set by Indian women, the soldiers were forced into fierce hand-to-hand combat. The Company fell back to reload their weapons, only to hear the loud cries of Comanche women through the smoke and dust, indicating an Indian retreat.

Two cavalrymen, William Barry and Thomas Ryan, were killed, and five others, including Hood, were wounded. Later reports revealed that nineteen Indians were killed, and many more wounded. Hood and his men were later cited for valor in army reports. (1987)

JUSTICEBURG (Garza Co.) US 84, NW of Justiceburg post office

Garza County's First Oil Well
(3½ mi. E)

After several unsuccessful ventures from 1911 to 1919, the first oil producer in the county was completed on J. M. Boren property at Justiceburg in 1926.

The well was begun in 1924 by Phelps, Caldwell and Blackwell Oil Company. It produced a total of 1,641 barrels before it was abandoned in 1932.

In 1932 four producing wells were completed south of Post. A refinery was built near city.

Garza County has a number of fields, and its 1,500 wells have produced more than 85,000,000 barrels of oil.

KARNACK (Harrison Co.) FM 134 at Taylor Avenue

Home Town of
Mrs. Lyndon B. Johnson
(Wife of 36th President of the United States)

On December 22, 1912, in the family home 2.7 miles south, was born Claudia Alta Taylor. She was third child (only daughter) of Thomas Jefferson and Minnie Pattillo Taylor. Her father had a general store in Karnack for many years. Young "Lady Bird" (a pet name originated by her nurse, Alice Tittle) attended public schools in Fern community, near here, and in Jefferson and Marshall, and earned Bachelor of Arts and Journalism Degrees at the University of Texas.

On November 17, 1934, she married Lyndon Baines Johnson, congressional staff member who became head of National Youth Administration in Texas in 1935.

The Johnsons are parents of two daughters, Lynda Bird and Luci Baines.

During her husband's rise to world leadership—as United States Congressman, Senator, Senate Majority Leader, Vice President, and President—Mrs. Johnson added to role of wife and mother that of hostess to many of the greatest statesmen of the world.

As First Lady of the United States, she is true to her East Texas heritage of love for gardens, trees, unspoiled natural scenery, and historic sites. She sponsors vital natural programs of conservation, beautification, and historical preservation. (1967)

KARNACK (Harrison Co.) *FM 1915, 2 mi. N in Caddo State Park*
Old Town of Port Caddo
(Site located in and around Caddo State Park)
Ancestral home of Texas Caddo Indians, this region gained a distinctive character in the 19th century. From 1806 to 1845 it lay in an area disputed by various countries and designated, from 1819, as the "neutral ground." Settlers living here were far from neutral, however. They became independent and resisted paying taxes levied by any "outside" authority.

Port Caddo, founded 1838 on Caddo Lake, soon grew to importance, and its rowdy reputation grew, too, as ship's crews, gamblers, and Indians filled its streets. Meanwhile, new towns and roads sprung up nearby.

Continuing upheaval led to the assassination of the tax collector in 1840 and townsmen joined in the factional "Regulator-Moderator War" from 1840 to 1844. When Texas proposed to join the Union in 1845, Port Caddoans saw a chance to end their problems and voted strongly in favor of statehood.

From 1845 to the 1850s Port Caddo thrived, growing to 500, but then declined as the port of Jefferson and the county seat of Marshall drew away business.

With the end of the great plantations after the Civil War, falling of the water level in Caddo Lake, and coming of the railroad to nearby Karnack (1900), Port Caddo gradually faded out of existence. (1968)

KAUFMAN (Kaufman Co.) *SH 34, 1.5 mi. S*
Kaufman County Poor Farm
As did many Texas counties of the era, Kaufman County created a poor farm in 1883 in order to provide the indigent residents and families of the area with food, shelter, and medicine. This work program replaced earlier relief efforts. All able-bodied persons were required to work, including resident guards and county inmates convicted of minor crimes who were originally brought from the jail daily for labor; by 1893 they were housed on the farm. In the 1930s the farm was used to demonstrate new agricultural techniques. Usually filled to capacity, the farm operated until the 1970s. By 1997, a cemetery and a few buildings remained. (1997)

KELLER (Tarrant Co.) *US 377*
Keller
After Texas and Pacific Railroad came through this area, H. W. Wood, a druggist, set aside 40 acres on July 19, 1881, for this townsite. He named the new village "Athol." Within a year, the name became "Keller," honoring John C. Keller, railroad construction crew foreman. Many businesses grew up to meet the needs of the surrounding farms. In 1886, the post office was established. There were two hotels, three doctors, a newspaper, and a school. The Baptist, Methodist, and Presbyterian congregations erected a union church building in 1886. Keller was incorporated in 1958. (1980)

KEMPNER (Lampasas Co.) *US 190, W city limits*
Kempner
Founded 1882. Named for Texas philanthropist, banker, railroad magnate Harris Kempner (1837–1894). An immigrant from Poland, Kempner joined Parsons' Brigade, Confederate Army. Wounded in Red River campaign, he was left on the battlefield for dead, but recovered and served to the war's end. Then he helped to rebuild Texas.

KENDALIA (Kendall Co.) *FM 473, city limits*
George Wilkins Kendall
1809–1867
A molder of world opinion. His theme: Greatness of Texas. Born in New Hampshire, learned printing and worked in New York, Boston and Washington, D. C.

With Francis A. Lumsden, in 1837 founded New Orleans "Picayune." Joined the Texan-Santa Fe Expedition, 1841, as a reporter. Was imprisoned along with other ill fated members. Wrote a book on the expedition. During Mexican War, 1846–1848, often rode with the Texas Rangers, in world's first war coverage by a foreign correspondent. Filed his news by Pony Express.

In 1847 settled on Texas sheep range, at Post Oak Springs. Continuing news columns brought him in a single mail 300 letters from far away as Sandwich Islands, inquiring about Texas.

During the Civil War, produced wool for Confederate uniforms, blankets. Proposed a weaving mill on Comal River, for making cloth near the flocks. Received no government response. To keep producing wool, had to fight Comanches, range fires, freezing disasters. When roaming vandals threatened to kill sheepherders, he and his teenage son tended flocks themselves.

To end of his life, his regular dispatches to the "Picayune" continued to praise good life in Texas.   (1965)

KENDLETON (Fort Bend Co.)   *US 59, 30 yds. E*
Kendleton
The site on which Kendleton now stands was originally a Mexican land grant to settler Elizabeth Powell, whose house was an early-day stage stop.

During the Texas Revolution, in 1836, Santa Anna's Mexican Army camped near here. Later the settlements of Oak Hill and Humbolt existed briefly.

Kendleton began during Civil War reconstruction when Wm. E. Kendall sold land, for as little as 50 cents an acre, to assist freed Negroes in starting their own farms. The rural village was named in his honor when the railroad came through, 1884.   (1969)

KENNARD (Houston Co.)   *SH 7 & Main Street (FM 357)*
Kennard
The town of Kennard was founded in 1903 by the Louisiana and Texas Lumber Company and platted on 160 acres. Land agent Alexander McTavish also acted as Kennard's first postmaster. The town served as a terminus for the Eastern Texas Railroad, a line established to transport timber to Angelina County.

Many businesses and citizens from earlier settlements nearby moved to Kennard when the rail line located here. Schools were built nearby as early as 1864 and served the area until Kennard school opened in 1903. Religious observances began with tent meetings conducted by traveling ministers. Permanent churches were soon organized, early establishments included a bank, hotel, drug store, general merchandise stores, cafe, meat shop and Woodmen of the World Lodge. In the 1920s and 1930s the timber industry and farming grew while other businesses came to town including a cottonseed mill, cotton gins, syrup mills, a blacksmith shop, gas stations, and a boardinghouse. In 1933, State Highway 7 was built through main street, shifting the town's business center there.

Incorporated as a city in 1969, Kennard continues as an active and involved community located in the heart of the Davy Crockett National Forest.   (1996)

KENNARD (Houston Co.)   *SH 7, near school campus*
A Former Rosenwald School
(Now "The Little Red Schoolhouse")
A symbol of Black America's pride in education, plus crusade of Julius Rosenwald (1862–1932), a Chicagoan who in 1913 began to fund school buildings for Negroes. By 1920, when this one-teacher structure was built at Ratcliff (4 miles East), Rosenwald's grants had to be matched—in this case, by Houston County funds.

Alfred Foy (1865–1944), a veteran of brush arbor and log cabin classrooms, taught in this building at Ratcliff 1920–1923 and 1924–1927; Miss Detroit Denman, 1923–1924; Mrs. Evola Colbert Dorn, 1927–1955. Their pupils' playground equipment consisted of a baseball diamond, basketball goal, mulberry tree and swing. Yet patrons—true to zeal that helped obtain the building—brought in food and saw that the children had hot lunches.

Sessions ceased in 1955 when the Ratcliff school was consolidated with Kennard Common School District No. 75. The Ratcliff building was used 1955–1968 as the community center for socials and public meetings. In 1968 the "Old Rosenwald School" was moved to Kennard for use by Headstart and related programs.

Texas had a total of 518 school buildings funded in part by the Rosenwald Foundation—22 of them in Houston County—providing classrooms for thousands.   (1973)

270

KENNARD (Houston Co.)
SH 7, 1.2 mi. E at Hagerville turnoff
Hagerville Community
(5 mi. SE)
Kentuckian James Murphy Hager (1822–1879) and his wife Naoma (Clark) came to Texas in the 1840s. Hager, a farmer and cabinet maker, opened a blacksmith shop and mill in Houston County. The Nacogdoches-to-Navasota stage and mail road ran beside his log home. Hager's son James Polk began a post office in 1891 and named the area "Hagerville." Another son W. J. (Bill) donated land for a schoolhouse that was used for worship. Many residents moved closer to the sawmills and the post office closed in 1905. Business declined but the community retains its identity. (1979)

KENNARD (Houston Co.)
SH 7, 1.4 mi. E
Community of Coltharp
(1.2 mi. SE)
By the 1850s, Eli Coltharp lived beside Cochina Bayou. He opened a store and post office at his home on the stage route west of Nacogdoches. The farm area called Coltharp Hill boasted a gin, gristmill, blacksmith, and millinery shops. A school building housed Coltharp Masonic Lodge No. 419, now in Kennard. When the railroad bypassed Coltharp and a sawmill opened nearby in 1901, residents worked at the mill and farming declined. The post office closed in 1909 and Coltharp school consolidated with Kennard in 1925. Many descendants of early settlers remain in the area. (1979)

KENNEY (Austin Co.)
Old SH 36 right-of-way, 2.5 mi. S
James Bradford Pier
(Nov. 23, 1813–Feb. 5, 1888)
A native of Circleville, Ohio, J. B. Pier came to Texas in 1835 with his wife, Lucy (Merry). The Piers settled in this area near the site of the early Texas town of Travis. Pier served as a member of the Texas Army during the War for Independence. He was detailed as a rear guard at the camp opposite Harrisburg during the Battle of San Jacinto. In later years, he was a farmer, stock raiser, teacher, and merchant. He served as justice of the peace of Austin County and was the first postmaster of the Travis community. Pier is buried in the nearby Travis Cemetery. (1985)

KERMIT (Winkler Co.)
SH 115 10 mi. NE in roadside park
Winkler County
Formed from Tom Green County. Created February 26, 1887. Organized April 5, 1910. Named in honor of C. M. Winkler, 1821–1882, statesman, soldier and jurist.

Kermit, the county seat. A petroleum producing and cattle raising area.

KERMIT (Winkler Co.)
SH 302, 12 mi. E
Blue Mountain
(Elevation 3,500 ft.)
Projection of Staked Plains. Winkler County's highest point. Lookout and landmark for red men and whites. Indians found here fuel, sheltering caves and water. Left artifacts and 138 mortar holes for grinding food. On cave walls bragged of their prowess as horse wranglers, hunters, fishermen, by using crushed stone paints to make pictographs 4 inches high. Also gave story of a fight between two lizards. A directional sign told of a waterhole 9 days by trail to the northeast.

Pass is called Avary Gap for John Avary, first settler, 1880.

KERMIT (Winkler Co.)
SH 302, 1.5 mi. W city limits
Old Duval Townsite
First post office in Winkler (then part of Tom Green) County opened near here (1908) on John Howe ranch. Mail came in twice weekly to serve 300 persons.

Duval townsite, promoted all over the United States by the Pueblo Investment Co., opened on March 19, 1910, with free lots, a picnic, and cowboy tournament.

In April, Kermit became seat of Winkler County; post office moved there in October. Duval failed to develop and townsite rights were canceled after 1928 oil discovery here. Ownership of many valuable lots sold in 1910 is still unclear today. (1968)

KERMIT (Winkler Co.)   US 302, E. city limits
Kermit
County seat of Winkler County. Organized in 1910. Incorporated in 1938. Named for Kermit Roosevelt, son of President Theodore Roosevelt, who had visited a local ranch. One of the top oil and gas producing counties in state. Ranch center. Gateway to New Mexico.

KERMIT (Winkler Co.)   SH 115 at FM 784, 1.1 mi. NE
The Sand Hills
Mapped by U.S. government, 1849, for gold seekers and settlers. Known earlier to Indians and many Spanish explorers, a 100-mi. belt of sand in Winkler and 4 other Texas Counties and in New Mexico. Width varies from 3 to 20 mi. Outer dunes are held by dwarf oaks. Water at 2' depth supports willows, cottonwoods, and a plum thicket. (The plums gave food to early settlers.)

Many dunes more than 70' high. Heavy, shifting sands a natural barrier to travel. Campsite and game reservation for Indians. Now part of expansive cattle ranges and rich oil fields.   (1967)

KERMIT (Winkler Co.)   SH 18, 10 mi. N adjacent to state line
Texas Territorial
Compromise of 1850
Four miles east of this site is an official corner post marking agreement of Texas to give up some of the land won in her 1836 War for Independence. It also marks New Mexico's southeast corner.

When Texas was annexed to the United States, 1846, her territory included 98,300 square miles now in the states of Colorado, Kansas, New Mexico, Oklahoma and Wyoming. After the Mexican War (fought 1846–1848, over the annexation), anti-slavery forces in the U.S. sought to trim the size of Texas, a slave state.

To raise money and establish a definite boundary, Texas accepted the compromise of 1850 and agreed to give up a third of her area in return for payment of $10,000,000. The money paid debts of the former Republic of Texas, set up a $2,000,000 public school fund, and erected state buildings, including a new capitol (which subsequently burned in 1881).

By the 1850 compromise, the western boundary of Texas follows the 103rd Meridian south from 36°30'; near here intersects the 32nd Parallel, then goes west along the parallel to the Rio Grande. The corner marks not only a peaceable boundary pact, but also shows an unbroken stretch of Permian Basin lands, unified in geography and common goals.   (1966)

KERMIT (Winkler Co.)   SH 18, 12 mi. S
Willow Springs
6.6 miles east in Sand Hills. Water hole vital to Comanche, explorer. "Judge" A. Hayes found charred remains of 40-wagon train massacre in 1901. Ox bows, human bones, flintlocks, other relics of the ill-fated and unidentified group in Sul Ross State College museum at Alpine.   (1964)

KERRVILLE (Kerr Co.)   SH 27, 3.6 mi. SW
Kerr County
Formed from Bexar County. Created January 26, 1856. Organized March 22, 1856. Named in honor of James Kerr, 1790–1850. The first American settler on the Guadalupe River. General manager of Dewitt's colony. Signer of the Declaration of Independence. Member of the Third Texas Congress. County seat, Kerrville, afterwards Kerrville (1856 to 1860). Comfort 1860–1862. Kerrville, since.

KERRVILLE (Kerr Co.)   SH 16, ½ mi. N
Site of
Animal Health Discovery
In this building (at Menard) during late 1930s, Dr. Edward F. Knipling (b. 1909) advanced the theory screwworms might be eradicated by releasing sterile male flies to break chain of reproduction and save livestock from role of host to parasitic larvae that destroy livestock and wildlife.

During 1950–1951, this laboratory (removed to Kerrville area) was site of sterilization of male screwworms with irradiation, in procedures by Dr. R. C. Bushland and D. E. Hopkins. The outcome: eradication of the screwworm and saving of domestic and wild animals of the United States.   (1972)

KERRVILLE (Kerr Co.)   SH 27, 17 mi. NW
The Dowdy Tragedy of 1878
The pioneer family of Susan (1830–1913) and James Dowdy (1818–1900) moved from Goliad to Kerr County in 1878 and settled on Johnson Creek. Shortly after the family arrived, four of the Dowdy children, Alice, Martha, Susan, and James, were killed by Indians while tending sheep near their home. The attack occurred on Oct. 5, 1878, at a site about 3.5 miles northwest of present Ingram. The victims were buried the following day at Sunset Cemetery, northwest of Ingram. This incident was one of the last Indian raids in Kerr County.   (1979)

KERRVILLE (Kerr Co.)   700 Main St. (SH 27)
James Kerr
(1790–1850)
Kentucky native James Kerr, the son of a Baptist minister, was reared in Missouri. Kerr fought in the War of 1812 and was later sheriff of St. Charles County, Missouri. He married Angeline Caldwell in 1818 and served in the Missouri Senate and House of Representatives. Kerr was appointed Surveyor General of the Texas colony of Green DeWitt in 1825. With his wife, three children and several slaves, he joined Stephen F. Austin's "Old Three Hundred" colony in Brazoria. In August 1825 he set out to select a site for the DeWitt Colony. Kerr named the community Gonzales in honor of the Governor of Coahuila, Mexico. By this time, Angeline Kerr and two of the children had passed away. Kerr was active in area politics and law enforcement during the formative years of the Republic of Texas. He acted as attorney and surveyor for Benjamin Rush Milam in 1827. He negotiated for peace before the Fredonian Rebellion, signed a treaty with the Karankawa Indians and fought other tribes. He was the Lavaca delegate at the Convention at San Felipe de Austin in 1832 and served as a member of the Second and Third Conventions. Two years later, he married Sarah Fulton. He became a major in the Texas Rangers in 1835 and in the Republic of Texas army in 1836. He was elected to the Third Texas Congress in 1838. Kerr's later years were spent practicing medicine in Jackson County. In 1856, pioneer Joshua Brown gave the land around this site in order that Kerr County be named for his longtime friend, Texas frontiersman and patriot James Kerr.   (2000)

KERRVILLE (Kerr Co.)   2100 Memorial Blvd (SH 27)
Schreiner College (Schreiner Institute)
Kerrville leaders began to envision a college in the early days of the 20th century. Negotiations with the Presbyterian Synod of Texas were pursued from 1904, when plans were made for an annual camp meeting that might one day evolve into a boys' school. In 1914, local businessman Charles Schreiner (1838–1927) announced his plan to donate 140 acres of land and at least $100,000 to the Synod of Texas to fund the Charles Schreiner Institute for Boys. The plan was delayed by World War I. Finally, on September 18, 1923, the school's opening ceremonies were held, with James J. Delaney (1879-1959) as president. Ninety-five students were enrolled in the first year. The school stressed military discipline and religious instruction as a backdrop for general education. In 1932, girls were admitted as day students. Many students and younger faculty left Schreiner for military service and defense work during World War II, and a naval flight school was established at the institute for the war's duration. Sixty-six alumni lost their lives in World War II. Military training became optional in 1957. In 1971, the board of trustees voted to discontinue military training. Female boarding students were enrolled, and the recruitment of minority and disadvantaged students was instituted. The last high school class graduated in 1976. In 1984 the school became a four-year baccalaureate college. Schreiner College continues to evolve as one of Texas' leading private institutions.   (1998)

KERRVILLE (Kerr Co.)   FM 1341, 10 mi. E
Indian Sites On Cypress Creek
Named "Sturdy Oak Farm" for an ancient live oak, this property has belonged to the Lich family since 1879. Mr. and Mrs. Ernst Perry Lich became the owners in 1945. Three significant prehistoric sites on this property indicate its importance for human habitation for at least 10,000 years. Tools from the sites represent several archeological periods from Paleo-Indian through archaic times. The sites are near spring-fed pools in Cypress Creek. Artifacts discovered at the three locations include arrowheads, knives, beads, and stone tools left by nomadic tribes that once wandered this area.   (1978)

KILGORE (Gregg Co.)   *US 259, N city limits*
"Oil City of the World"
Kilgore
Founded 1872 with coming of the I. G. N. Railroad. Named for site donor, a Confederate colonel, Constantine B. Kilgore, state senator and U.S. congressman.

Geographical center of huge East Texas oil field. World's greatest concentration of steel derricks. Petroleum production, service, supply, processing hub.

Commercial, industrial, farm, education and medical center.

Home of Kilgore College and its famous "Rangerettes," women's precision drill team; and of Van Cliburn, international concert pianist.   (1965)

KILGORE (Gregg Co.)   *Main and Commerce Sts.*
World's Richest Acre
Part of fabulous East Texas oil field discovered in 1930. This 1.195-acre tract had first production on June 17, 1937, when the Mrs. Bess Johnson-Adams & Hale No. 1 Well was brought in.

Developed before well-spacing rules, this block is the most densely drilled tract in the world, with 24 wells on 10 lots owned by six different operators. This acre has produced over two and a half million barrels of crude oil. Selling at $1.10 to $3.25 a barrel, it has brought more than five and a half million dollars.

A forest of steel derricks for many years stood over the more than 1,000 wells in downtown Kilgore, marking the greatest concentration of oil wells in the history of the world. Dozens of these derricks still dot city's internationally famous skyline.

Since 1930, the East Texas oil field has produced nearly four billion barrels of oil. It now has more than 17,000 producing wells, and geologists predict a future of at least 45 years for this "granddaddy of oil fields." Its development has attracted to the area many diversified industries and a progressive citizenship with a high degree of civic pride.

KILGORE (Gregg Co.)   *1 mi. N of I-20 on old 135-Gladewater Hwy., 4 mi. N*
Liberty City
Historic rural community in oil-rich Gregg County. Settled before Civil War. Has also been known as Sabine, Mount Moriah, McCrary's Chapel, Goforth and Hog Eye (for an early settler with an "eye" for hogs). Present name adopted in early days of famous East Texas oil boom. Area served by Sabine School District, established 1893; an example of excellent schools in county. Also crossed by great system of improved, all weather county roads—finest in state. Center of farming, livestock raising. Has fine churches, park and community meeting places.   (1965)

KILLEEN (Bell Co.)   *US 190 Bus. at Conder in Conder Park*
City of Killeen
When the tracks of the Gulf, Colorado and Santa Fe Railroad were extended from Temple to Lampasas in the early 1880s, a switching station was installed near the midway point. The settlement that grew up around the site became the town of Killeen, named for Frank P. Killeen, a native of Ireland and a senior official of the rail company. The first train arrived on May 15, 1882, marking the beginning of the town.

Many early residents of Killeen came from the nearby pioneer communities of Sugar Loaf (6 mi. N) and Palo Alto (3.5 mi. NE). Town lots were sold by the GC&SF Railroad and one of the earliest structures built was a wooden community school, which opened in the fall of 1882. By the following year, Killeen was the site of two gristmills and a cotton gin. The town was incorporated in 1893, and W. E. Hudson was elected to serve as the first mayor.

In the early years of Killeen's development, the town was primarily an agricultural center for the production of cotton, grain, wool, and cattle. In 1942, it became the home of Camp Hood, now Fort Hood. The federal installation's growth as a major military base has had a dramatic impact on the city, making it one of the fastest growing towns in Texas.   (1982)

KILLEEN (Bell Co.)   *2201 E. US 190 Bus.*
John Blackburn Log House
John Churchill Gaines Blackburn (1832–1912) was born in Tennessee and came to Texas in 1853. He and his wife Mary Ann Chambers Blackburn (1831–1908) first stopped with other family members in Williamson County, then moved to Bell County in 1854. Blackburn's father, John

Porter Blackburn (1786–1855) had previously established claims in Texas, including land in this county near the Palo Alto community (then about 4 mi. NE).

There John C. G. Blackburn established a 30-acre farm. He enlisted in the Confederate State Militia in 1861 when the Civil War began. Blackburn built this oak-log structure in 1863, according to family tradition, just before enlisting in the Confederate cavalry. He was then assigned to frontier duty along the Rio Grande for the duration of the war.

The Blackburns built a larger house at Palo Alto in 1883. This structure survived at its original site until 1954, when a Fort Hood expansion prompted its removal to Westcliff Road in Killeen (2 mi. NE). It remained there until 1976, when the cabin was moved here and rebuilt as an artifact of frontier life in Bell County.

John C. G. and Mary Ann Blackburn are buried at the Blackburn cemetery near their homestead on old Schwald Road (about 4 mi. NE on Fort Hood property).

(Texas Sesquicentennial 1836–1986)

KINGSLAND (Llano Co.)   *1001 King St.*
Antlers Hotel
The juncture of the Llano and Colorado Rivers has attracted visitors for millennia. European settlers, including Martin D. King, began moving to the area in the 19th century. King purchased land here in 1877, and it is for him that Kingsland is named. In 1892, the Austin and Northwestern Railroad built a railroad bridge at the Llano-Colorado River confluence and a depot between the tracks in Kingsland. At the same time, the railroad company purchased this land from Mrs. N.J. King. The company started construction of the Antlers Hotel in 1900. The two-story wooden hotel, which opened in 1901, was designed to welcome railroad passengers, who could easily walk here from their train. Hotel porches afforded views of both rivers, and guests could also stay in small cabins later built on the grounds. Visitors walked across the street to enjoy a park full of Cottonwood trees that featured a pavilion with stage and dressing rooms. Behind the hotel, guests and residents fished in the adjoining lake, then called Crescent Lake. Pleasant and convenient, the railroad resort was frequented by tourists as well as business travelers. As the automobile's influence slowed rail travel, the hotel business quieted; C.E. Schults purchased the hotel in 1913 and later sold it to the Van der Stucken family. In 1923, former hotel guest Thomas H. Barrow of Austin bought the Antlers, and he and his family spent summers and vacations here. He also purchased surrounding land and, after his death in 1936, his family continued to enjoy the property until they sold it in 1993. The hotel and cabins were refurbished and reopened as a hotel complex in 1996, once again offering Texas hill country scenery and recreation to its many guests. (2002)

KINGSLAND (Llano Co.)   *FM 1431, overlooking the lake*
Lake Lyndon B. Johnson
This lake, originally Granite Shoals, was renamed for the President of the United States on April 22, 1965, by the board of directors, Lower Colorado River Authority (LCRA); in gratitude for his work as U.S. Congressman and Senator toward the development of the project. Mr. Johnson devoted much time and skill to the completion of LCRA programs creating flood control, water conservation and low cost electric power for the people of the Highland Lakes country.

A native of this hill country, Mr. Johnson maintained a home on the lake and used it often as a place for relaxation and the entertainment of guests. It is near his ranch and boyhood home.

The body of water impounded by the Alvin J. Wirtz Dam has 6,200 surface acres and 138,000 acre-feet. Construction was begun on the dam in 1949 and since its completion the lake has primarily been a source of hydroelectric energy from the overflow of Lake Buchanan to the north. It is also one of Texas' most outstanding boating and fishing areas.

This lake, some 20 miles long, is one of seven in the LCRA which extend 100 miles up the Colorado from Austin. Together they form the largest hydroelectric system in the state. (1967)

KINGSTON (Hunt Co.)   *US 69, 1.5 mi. S*
Audie Murphy
Most decorated soldier in World War II. Born 4.5 miles south, June 20, 1924, sixth of nine children of tenant farmers Emmett and Josie Killian Murphy. Living on various farms, Audie Murphy went to school through the 8th grade in Celeste—considered the family's home town. He had to quit school to help support the family, acquiring marksmanship skills by hunting to

provide food. On his 18th birthday, after being rejected by the marines because of his size (5 feet, 7 inches; 130 pounds), he enlisted in the army while working in Greenville.

For unusual courage and bravery, he received 24 decorations, including the U.S. Congressional Medal of Honor, the French Legion of Honor, Chevalier, the Distinguished Service Cross, and a silver star.

After the war he became a successful actor, his most prominent role portraying himself in the film *To Hell and Back,* his war career autobiography.

Following his untimely death in a plane crash in Virginia, May 28, 1971, and burial in Arlington National Cemetery, the U.S. Congress paid him a final tribute, dedicating a new veterans' hospital in San Antonio to the memory of this American hero.

Survived by widow Pamela, sons Terry and James. (1973)

KINGSTON (Hunt Co.) *US 69, .9 mi. S*
Harrell Camp Ground
(¹⁄₁₀ mi. W)

One of first religious sites in Hunt County. Influential for 50 years. Cabins and brush arbor built in 1850's by early settler Richard Harrell (1813–1895).

Methodist gospel services drew people here from many counties in summers while crops grew and work was slack. With milch cows, cook stoves, bedding, wash tubs, water barrels, families forded Sabine River to camp for weeks. Children and adults sang hymns, studied scriptures, listened to sermons—diversions in hard and lonely lives. In months between camp meetings, passing travelers often were sheltered in camp. (1965)

KINGSVILLE (Kleberg Co.) *SH 141, 1.2 mi. W*
Kleberg County

Formed from Nueces County. Created February 27, 1913. Organized June 27, 1913. Named in honor of Robert Justus Kleberg, 1803–1888, a pioneer German settler in Texas. A veteran of San Jacinto. Kingsville, county seat.

KINGSVILLE (Kleberg Co.) *SH 141 W, entrance to King Ranch*
King Ranch, C.S.A.

A major South Texas way-station on Cotton Road, lifeline of southern states in the Civil War. Had water, food, mules, oxen and bunks for drivers of wagons hauling cotton to trade for war goods. Also bivouacked Confederate troops in war marches.

Founded 1853 by Capt. Richard King, who by 1861 had—in partnership with Mifflin Kenedy and James Walworth—20,000 cattle and 3,000 horses. Walworth was a delegate to Texas Secession Convention. In wartime, King managed ranch and salt works on coast to benefit Texas and the Confederacy. Kenedy ran the partnership's 22 boats from gulf to Rio Grande City; ferried cotton from Texas to Matamoros, Mex., where it was exchanged for guns, factory goods, ammunition, medicines and coffee, scarce in the Confederacy; and took cotton from Bagdad, Mex., out to ocean vessels riding high seas to dodge the Federal blockade.

King and partners were supply agents for the Rio Grande military sub-district. With concentration of goods here, ranch tempted bandits and was target of Federals seeking to break up Cotton Road activity and get beef, cotton and horses for their planned Texas conquest. After Federal raids, was patrolled by the Confederate cavalry of Col. John S. (Rip) Ford. (1965)

KINGSVILLE (Kleberg Co.) *SH 141 W, at entrance to King Ranch*
The King Ranch

Richard King (1824–1885), a Rio Grande steamboat captain, bought two Spanish land grants on Santa Gertrudis Creek and founded the legendary King Ranch in 1853. He brought longhorn cattle from Mexico and battled droughts and cattle thieves to build a profitable ranch. Operating first in partnership with G. K. ("Legs") Lewis and later with Mifflin Kenedy and James Walworth, King became sole owner in the late 1860s. During the Civil War (1861–1865), The King ranch was a way-station for Confederate cotton going to Mexico. Herds carrying King's famous "Running W" brand followed the cattle trails to northern markets in the 1870s.

After King died, his widow, Henrietta (Chamberlain) (1832–1925), named as ranch manager Robert Justus Kleberg (1853–1932), who later married her daughter Alice Gertrudis King (1862–1944). The ranch became less isolated in the early 1900s, when the railroad arrived and the town of Kingsville was settled. Constant improvement of herds by King-Kleberg descendants produced a new breed of cattle, the Santa Gertrudis, and fine quarter horses and thoroughbreds. Petroleum was discovered on ranch property in the 1930s. Today the King ranch has grown to almost one million acres in South Texas, plus holdings in other states and nations.   (1977)

KINGSVILLE (Kleberg Co.)   *SH 141 W, across from entrance to King Ranch*
Santa Gertrudis
Headquarters of the King Ranch
On this site, part of the De la Garza Santa Gertrudis Land Grant purchased by Captain Richard King in 1853, has stood each of the King Ranch headquarters. The first, an adobe jacal, was replaced by a frame cottage which later burned. Under the direction of Robert J. Kleberg, Sr., this house was designed by Carlton W. Adams for Mrs. Henrietta King. Completed in 1915, it is the family home of Captain King's descendants who are owners of the King Ranch.   (1980)

KINGSVILLE (Kleberg Co.)   *SH 141 at FM 1898*
Plaque dedicated to memory General Joseph Dorst Patch
Camp Kingsville, U.S.A.
(1915–1917)
Established in September 1915 by Lt. Joseph Dorst Patch, acting under orders of the United States Army during the troubles on the Mexican border. This camp served as the operational base for companies K, L, and M of the 26th Infantry, U.S. Army. These units were detailed to defend the Armstrong, Kenedy and King ranches and the rail line from San Antonio to Norias against raids by Mexican insurgents striking north of the Rio Grande. Early in 1917, this camp was visited by the U.S. border commander, Gen. John J. Pershing, who later that year chose men of the 26th Infantry to become a vanguard regiment of the now famous First Division, American Expeditionary Forces in World War I. With departure of the chosen troops, bound for France, Camp Kingsville was closed.

Joseph Dorst Patch, born December 8, 1885, at Fort Huachuca, Ariz., enlisted in 1909 and was commissioned in 1911. He married Minerva King of Agua Dulce. He served in two world wars, and was awarded the Purple Heart, the Distinguished Service Cross, the Croix de Guerre with bronze star, and the Order of the Bath (British). Retired in 1945 as a major general, he turned to writing as a vocation. His home was in Corpus Christi, where he died November 21, 1966.   (1971)

KINGSVILLE (Kleberg Co.)   *US 77, 3 mi. N at San Fernando Creek*
Camp San Fernando
(1862–1864)
Military post on San Fernando Creek, near this site. Guarded the lifeline of the Confederacy, the Cotton Road, export-import route that ran from the Sabine River in East Texas to the Rio Grande. Manned 1862 by 32nd Texas Cavalry flying Bonnie Blue flag; in 1863, a banner lettered: "We Fight for Our Rights."

Temporarily occupied, Nov. 1863, by Gen. H. P. Bee. In Feb. 1864 a strong complement arrived under Col. J. S. (Rip) Ford. Col. Matt Nolan reported to Ford a victory over Federals under Capt. C. Balerio 50 mi. southwest of Banquete. Winning troops were under Capt. Thomas Cater, Wm. Tate, Taylor, and A. J. Ware, plus home guard under Capt. Santiago Richardson. (Capt. Richard King, of King Ranch, also served in the home guard.)

Col. Ford's "Cavalry of the West" included Maj. Felix A. Von Blucher, chief of staff; Capts. H. C. Merritt and J. Littleton, commissaries; Col. Albert Walthersdorff, technician; Capt. W. G. M. Samuels, ordnance.

On March 30, 1864, the Arizona companies of Lt. Col. Daniel Showalter reached camp San Fernando. In April Col. Ford and Col. Santos Benavides attacked the Federals in the Rio Grande Valley. Cols. Nolan and B. F. Fry continued to watch over the Cotton Road and "keep an eye" on Corpus Christi.   (1966)

KINGSVILLE (Kleberg Co.)   *US 77, near Missouri-Pacific RR and Caesar Pens*
Historic Cattle Dipping Vat
In 1894 this vat—believed to be the first in the world—was built to stop the spread of tick fever, which was destroying thousands of U.S. beef cattle.

By the 1880s, the disease had become widespread, and official and "shotgun" quarantines prevented cattle from moving across the affected area, bounded by a line from the Rio Grande to the Atlantic.

Although the mortality rate from tick fever (also called "Texas" and "splenetic" fever) sometimes reached 90 percent, longhorns and other native southwestern cattle were immune. They did, however, carry the insect, which could infect other animals.

Efforts to eradicate the tick (*Margaropus annulatus*) centered here, headed by officials from Texas A. & M. College and the U.S. Bureau of Animal Industry. Manager of the King Ranch, R. J. Kleberg, allowed the vat to be built, and 25,000 tick-infested cattle from the ranch were dipped. An effective formula of oil and sulphur was found here. In October 1898, the U.S. quarantine was lifted for cattle treated in the dip.

This eradication program not only introduced a new weapon for controlling cattle diseases, but also freed the industry from restrictive quarantines, thus increasing the value of cattle throughout the U.S. (1967)

KINGSVILLE (Kleberg Co.) US 77, 3 mi. S
First Producing Gas Well in Kleberg County
(3.3 mi. E)
Natural gas was first encountered in 1912 by Frank House while drilling for water on the Oscar Rosse farm. Other efforts to obtain fresh water resulted in more gas pockets or water contaminated with salt or oil. An unsuccessful attempt was made in 1915 to develop gas production. In Oct. 1919, the Kleberg County Oil & Gas Company was formed in Kingsville by lumber and hardware merchants Charles H. Flato and his son, Charles, Jr.; oil sales manager H. C. Dennett; grocer J. J. Ivey; postmaster Marcus Phillips; Kingsville mayor J. C. Nolan; and retail merchants Sam Sellers, Ben F. Wilson, and C. M. Allen. The company leased the Rosse farm on Oct. 30, 1919, and contracted Hammill & Bess Drilling Company of Bay City to drill a well. The Rosse No. 1 was completed on Jan. 16, 1920, at a depth of 3,000 feet. Pipelines were soon laid into Kingsville to supply businesses and residences with gas. Another well, the Rosse No. 2 completed in March 1920, was the first producing oil well in the county.

The discovery of gas and oil in the county provided a foundation for economic growth through development of petrochemical and refining industries. (1974)

KINGSVILLE (Kleberg Co.) SH 141, 5.5. mi. W
Near Site of Hide and Tallow Plant
(King Ranch, 1866–1869)
Business founded by Capt. Richard King to advance economic recovery after the Civil War had ended in 1865. The King ranch beef herds were "money on the hoof," but cull animals also had value if by-products (hides for leather, tallow as a soap ingredient, etc.) could be salvaged from them. A slaughtering plant was built on Santa Gertrudis Creek, about two miles west of ranch headquarters and north of this marker.

Baled, cured hides and barreled tallow were hauled by oxcarts to ships on the bay, then sent to market.

The tallow was rendered in round iron vats about 18 feet long and six feet in diameter. In service only a short time (plant closed within four years), two of these remained at the old site for 50 years. One of the two was later moved to the Kingsville oil field for use as a storage tank. When it proved unsatisfactory, it was returned and placed at Sillo Barro pens for water storage. Second vat was cut up for scrap iron during World War II. Site of the old plant is still called "matanza" (slaughter) pasture. Descendants of the hide and tallow plant employees are working a century later as King Ranch cowboys. (1971)

KINGSVILLE (Kleberg Co.) SH 141, 1.4 mi. W at park area
Mexican Activities at
Santa Gertrudis in the 1830s
As a favored camp, important in Mexico's relations with early Texas. Visited June 1832 by Matamoros citizens on their way to compliment Irish settlers with a feast at Banquete Lake, 25 miles to the north.

Gen. Juan Urrea camped here Feb. 25, 1836, with his unit of Santa Anna's invading army. With him were several persons who became agents of mercy to the Texans—a famous Mexican woman

278

known as "The Angel of Goliad," Col. Francisco Garay, and Lt. Col. Juan Holsinger. But also with Urrea was Lt. Col. Jose de la Portilla, who under orders from Gen. Santa Anna carried out the 1836 Palm Sunday massacre at Goliad.

The Mexicans left Santa Gertrudis to fight Texans at San Patricio, Agua Dulce, Refugio, and Coleto.

Santa Gertrudis soon afterward saw Mexican armies in retreat. Gen. Urrea returned here in May, heading south. Gen. Vicente Filisola and other officers also returned here June 11, as aftermath of defeat of the Mexican Army at San Jacinto. With them were 4,500 soldiers, throngs of camp followers, numerous fleeing Negro Slaves, thousands of draft and cavalry horses, and even herds of captured range cattle.

The camp at Santa Gertrudis was used often after 1830s by soldiers of Texas and the United States. (1967)

KINGSVILLE (Kleberg Co.)   *Kleberg Ave. at Missouri-Pacific RR depot*
Uriah Lott
(January 30, 1842–March 29, 1915)

Merchant, banker, builder of railroads to the Rio Grande. Born in Albany, N.Y. Came to South Texas in 1868. Chartered the Corpus Christi, San Diego & Rio Grande narrow gauge railroad in 1875. Later, reorganized it as the Texas-Mexican Railroad, to be built from Corpus Christi to Laredo. In 1884 he chartered and became president of the San Antonio & Aransas Pass Railway, which in time had 688 miles of track, and gave South Texas a new outlet to the Gulf of Mexico and international trade.

Setting out (1900) to run a railroad to southmost tip of Texas, he obtained right of way for segment of the St. Louis, Brownsville & Mexico Railway from Robstown to Brownsville. The "Lott railroad" tracks reached this point in Feb. 1903. When, for the first time, a passenger train ran all the way from Corpus Christi to Brownsville, July 4, 1904, the new town of Kingsville held a special Fourth of July celebration.

For some years prior to his death, Lott lived in Casa Ricardo Hotel in Kingsville. He and his wife, the former Mary Cicele Reynolds, are buried in the Chamberlain cemetery, Kingsville.

Lott's work, vital to South Texas development, also enhanced national prosperity at turn of the century. (1972)

KINGSVILLE (Kleberg Co)   *US 77 S*
Taylor Camp Site, 1846

In 1846 Zachary Taylor's army marched from Corpus Christi to the Rio Grande. On March 10, 11, 12, 13, the four regiments in succession camped at this spot on Santa Gertrudis Creek.

War with Mexico over the boundary of Texas began soon. The first battles—Palo Alto and Resaca de la Palma—occurred near present Brownsville. General Mariano Arista led the Mexican army.

The results of the war: the boundary of Texas was fixed at the Rio Grande; the Treaty of Guadalupe Hidalgo gave the United States New Mexico, Arizona, Nevada, and California; a notable group of men got training for later public service. Of the 251 officers camped here, many rose to national fame.

THE HONOR ROLL

Twelve leaders in the Texas battles gave name to United States forts in Texas: Wm. G. Belknap, Jacob Brown, J. E. Blake, W. W. S. Bliss, Theodore L. Chadbourne, James Duncan, Clinton R. Gates, Zebulon P. M. Inge, George T. Mason, J. B. McIntosh, Samuel Ringgold, William Jenkins Worth.

Many who camped here became commanders of great armies in the Civil War. Among them: Augur, Bee, Bragg, Kirby Smith, Longstreet, Meade, Pemberton, Reynolds, Twiggs, Whistler.

Two of them—Zachary Taylor and Ulysses Simpson Grant—became President of the United States.

KNICKERBOCKER (Tom Green Co.)   *FM 2335, in front of Community Church*
Knickerbocker

Attracted by irrigable land and the available water supply in Dove Creek, farmers, sheepmen, and cattlemen came to this area in the 1870s. First to arrive were the Baze brothers, who dug an irrigation ditch in 1875 to grow melons and hay for nearby Fort Concho. Others soon followed, including cattleman Joseph Schmidt, cotton farmer S. D. Arthur, and the Ryan, Martinez, Jaques, Villareal, Soto, Byler, Atkins, Beck, Duncan, Foster, and Etheridge families. In 1877, New Yorkers Morgan and Lawrence Grinnell, Joseph Tweedy, and J. B. Reynolds drove their sheep into the valley. They named their ranch headquarters after Washington Irving's character Diedrich Knickerbocker.

The Knickerbocker post office was established in 1881. In 1889, the town was moved to a location just south of the original site in order to tap a new water supply. By 1890, the settlement had stores, hotels, saloons, blacksmith shops, two churches, and two schools.

As was typical of many West Texas rural areas, Knickerbocker declined with the advent of the automobile and improved road systems. Farmers left to find work in San Angelo (18 mi. NE). The settlers of Knickerbocker, however, left a rich heritage. Many of their descendants still live in the area. (1983)

KNIPPA (Uvalde Co.)

US 90, in beautification area off to north side

Town of Knippa

Served by the Texas & New Orleans Railroad since 1882, this area was settled in 1887 by George Knippa. A freighter who worked between East Texas and Mexico, Knippa also encouraged many friends to move to the fertile land of this county.

In 1899 gold-mining was tried here by an aged, white-bearded stranger known as Wilson. In 1900 the community acquired a post office and in 1909 a town was laid out. Previously called Chatfield, it was renamed Knippa. The Trap rock mine, a stone and gravel business which started in 1913, is still in operation. (1969)

KNIPPA (Uvalde Co.)

SH 90W right of way, near entrance to
Vulcan Materials Co.

Knippa Trap Rock Plant

Volcanic lava deposited here more than 60 million years ago cooled and hardened over time to form basalt, a dark igneous rock also known as trap rock. M. B. (Pete) Walcott purchased acreage here about 1904 and in 1907 formed the Genevieve Mining Co. to search for gold. Although little gold was found, substantial quantities of high quality trap rock were discovered.

The Texas Trap Rock Company established a quarry about 1911 and shipments of rock began in 1912. A large highly-visible screening house was completed in 1914. By 1919, Knippa's trap rock plant, the largest in Texas at that time, was capable of producing about 100,000 tons of trap rock per year. The company transported the trap rock by spur line to the Southern Pacific Railroad in nearby Knippa.

The company and its employees became an integral part of the community. Knippa High School named its football team the "Rockcrushers" in 1946. The trap rock operation, purchased by White's Mine Company in 1968, was acquired by Vulcan Materials Company in 1987.

Trap rock has been applied to various uses such as railroad ballast, decorative stone, and as insulation material. Its historic and primary use, however, has been as a road paving material. (1994)

KOSSE (Limestone Co.)

SH 7, 1 mi. E

Eutaw

(Site of Extinct Town is .3 mi. N)

Settled in 1840s. On Franklin-Springfield, Waco-Marlin stage routes. Post office opened 1856 with Nathan Gilbert postmaster. Eutaw Lodge No. 233, A. F. & A. M., was chartered 1859. Among early settlers were Henry Fox, Allen McDaniel, Charles C., Frank and Wesley McKinley, and T. A. Polk. Town had churches, school, stores, blacksmith shop, wagon yard. The "Eutaw Blues" (Co. K, 12th Tex. Cav., C.S.A.) fought in Civil War, 1860s. Officers: Capt. A. F. Moss, 1st Lt. A. H. McDaniel, 2nd Lt. J. P. Brown.

Bypassed in 1870 by Houston & Texas Central Railroad, town died. Salem Baptist Church marks site. (1973)

KOSSE (Limestone Co.)   *SH 7, 3 mi. E*
Old Moss Home
On Capt. A. F. Moss land grant from Mexico. Put up 1860 with square nails, pegs. Lumber hauled by oxen from Houston County. Awarded Medallion Plate.   (1965)

KOUNTZE (Hardin Co.)   *SH 326 at courthouse lawn*
General Braxton Bragg, C.S.A.
(1817–1876)
Born in North Carolina. Graduated in 1833 from West Point. In 1845 came to Texas with army of General Zachary Taylor, to fight in Mexican War. In 1850s retired from army to be a planter. Also served as Commissioner of Public Works, state of Louisiana.

Appointed a brigadier general of the Confederacy, 1861. Made great captures of guns and prisoners at Battle of Shiloh, 1862. Victor at Chickamauga, 1863. Strong disciplinarian. Devoted patriot. Had stern sense of duty. Became military advisor, 1863–1865, to President Jefferson Davis. After surrender of General Lee, traveled with President Davis toward Florida and a suggested escape route. Was captured by Federals and paroled in Georgia in May 1865.

Alabama Commissioner of Public Works, 1866–1870. Then served in Texas as chief engineer of Gulf, Colorado & Santa Fe Railway. Later, state inspector of railroads built under Texas land grants. Lived several years in Galveston, where he died.

Old town at this site on G. C. & S. F. (1901–1934) was named in General Bragg's honor. It is one of many towns and counties in Texas named for military leaders, statesmen, public officials and soldiers.   (1965)

KOUNTZE (Hardin Co.)   *US 69, 15 mi. SE*
Former Townsite of Concord
First town in Hardin County. Established in 1858 at a strategic crossing from Beaumont to points north. Original name was Benton. Rapidly became a thriving steamboat port and reached a population of about 300, but declined in the 1880s with coming of the railroad.   (1970)

KOUNTZE (Hardin Co.)   *SH 326, 3 mi. SW*
"Old" Hardin
Founded 1859 as first county seat of Hardin County, created in 1858. Prospered until bypassed by Sabine & East Texas Railroad in 1881. A fire of suspicious origin razed the courthouse here on Aug. 8, 1886. In an 1887 election, Kountze, on the railroad, was named the county seat.   (1970)

KOUNTZE (Hardin Co.)   *US 69, 7 mi. S*
Hardin-Concord Road
(In use 1859–1900)
One of oldest landmarks in area. Formed by wagon and horseback travel from early settlements on Pine Island Bayou (to the SE) to Hardin, first county seat of this county (to the NW). Much of old road can be traced today. The highway crosses its course here.   (1971)

KOUNTZE (Hardin Co.)   *7 mi. N on US 69 at FM 420,*
                                     Big Thicket National Preserve Visitors' Center
Richard E. Jackson
Conservationist Richard E. Jackson was born August 12, 1880, in Leary, Georgia. In 1886, he came with his parents to Jasper, Texas, where they opened a general mercantile store. As a teenager, he worked for the family store and carried mail from Jasper to Woodville. In 1896, he was the first ticket agent for the GB & CK Railroad at Silsbee "Junction." Working as a conductor for the Santa Fe by 1904, he carried freight to sawmills and oilfields. In 1907, he married Velma Ophelia (Byrum), of Gainesville, and settled in Silsbee. Because of his admiration for the Big Thicket, Jackson began leasing land in the region, which was threatened by development,

timber activity and oil explorations. His leases exceeded 18,000 acres, and he formed the Hardin County Co-operative Pasture and Game Preserve Group. Envisioning a park and hunting club, in 1929, he began an effort for the area's preservation and attracted wide support. In 1936, Jackson called a meeting in the offices of the Beaumont Chamber of Commerce and organized the East Texas Big Thicket Association with 52 members. He hosted field studies for scientists, offered tours for public leaders, used his leases to show off the Big Thicket and delivered speeches publicizing it throughout the state and the region. Among other factors, the Great Depression and World War II contributed to the collapse of this early organization, but Jackson continued his conservation efforts until his death in 1957. Many of his followers later joined to establish the Big Thicket Association. Due to Jackson's early initiative and vision in preserving the unique landscape he loved, a national preserve was finally created here in 1974. Because of his unselfish dedication, R.E. Jackson is widely recognized as the "Father of the Big Thicket." (2003)

KOUNTZE (Hardin Co.) *US 69 North*
Kountze Church of Christ
This congregation was established in 1886, one year before Kountze was named Hardin county seat. First services were held in the Masonic hall and in the courthouse. In 1891, a permanent building was constructed on Brown Road on land given by Judge and Mrs. W. W. Cruse. It served the congregation until 1952 and was equipped with an 1819 church bell that provided the traditional call to worship. First elders of the church were John R. Bevil and J. W. Daniels, with D. A. Leake serving as first minister. For over a century, the Church of Christ has been an important part of the history of Kountze. (Texas Sesquicentennial 1836–1896)

KOUNTZE (Hardin Co.) *SH 326 at Pine St.*
First United Methodist Church
of Kountze
The town of Kountze developed in the 1880s, after the Texas and New Orleans Railroad was built through this area. The county seat, which had previously been located at the town of Hardin, was moved to Kountze in 1886.

Soon after the town's creation, a group of worshipers led by the Rev. James S. Murphy joined together to organize a Methodist congregation. Land was acquired in 1887 from P. S. Watts, and plans were made to erect a sanctuary to be used by all denominations. The cornerstone was laid on May 11, 1888, and the first church building in Kountze soon was completed. Worship services were held on alternate Sundays by Methodists and other denominations. Murphy continued to serve as circuit-riding minister to the Methodists until December 1888, when he was succeeded by the Rev. V. A. Godbey.

The Methodist Church in Kountze continued to grow over the years. Sunday school and missionary programs were organized, and in 1940 the congregation became a full charge in the denomination, with its own full-time pastor. A new sanctuary was built in 1951 to serve the growing congregation. The church has been a part of Kountze history for over a century. (1989)

KOUNTZE (Hardin Co.) *100 Munro (US 69 at SH 326)*
First Baptist Church of Kountze
The Baptist Church of Hardin was organized in 1860 with Pastor D. W. Jordan. When the railroad bypassed Hardin (then the county seat) in 1881, area residents began moving to nearby Kountze. Hardin Baptists are believed to have followed, probably meeting in a multi-denominational building known as the first house of worship in Kountze erected in 1887. Southern Baptist Convention records list the origin of the Baptist Church of Kountze in 1890; the congregation declared itself in 1893 under Pastor J. W. Rhodes.

In 1908, a loan from the Southern Baptist Convention to the First Baptist Church of Kountze facilitated the erection of a frame structure on Redwood Street. It was located two blocks from the original building, which had become the Methodist Church.

In 1951, fund raising and planning began for a new brick building, dedicated in 1955. By 1979, a two-story wing was added; in the 1980s the church library and sanctuary were expanded and new youth programs established. The First Baptist Church of Kountze marked its 100th anniversary with a celebration lasting from the spring of 1990 to January of 1993. With such developments as a new fellowship hall added in 1997, the church continues to serve the community. (1998)

KRESS (Swisher Co.) *FM 145, 10 mi. E*
First Baptist Church of Claytonville
Organized as New Hope Baptist Church of Christ in 1891, this congregation changed its name in 1912 to Whitfield Baptist Church. It acquired a good church plant, a parsonage, and a cabin site at Plains Baptist Assembly grounds. Steps began in 1960 to relocate on the paved highway in this new business community growing up around the cotton gin built in the 1950s by M. C. Clayton (1899–1963). The new church building—first in the town—was erected in 1962–1963. The present name was adopted in 1964. Peak membership for the congregation has been 206.   (1975)

KYLE (Hays Co.) *Old Stagecoach Rd., 4 mi. SW*
Claiborne Kyle Log House
Col. John Claiborne Kyle (d. 1867) and his wife Lucy (Bugg) (d. 1863), natives of Tennessee, came to the Republic of Texas from Mississippi in 1844. They built this four-pen dog trot log home soon after they purchased land here in 1850. Constructed of hand-hewn cedar logs, it was located on the Austin-San Antonio stage route. An active political leader, Kyle had five sons who served in the Confederate Army during the Civil War, including Capt. Ferg Kyle, for who the town of Kyle (4 mi. NE) was named. The Kyle house now serves as a reminder of this prominent pioneer family.   (1982)

LA GRANGE (Fayette Co.) *SH 159 at SH 71*
Fayette County, C.S.A.
Although voted 600 against to 580 for secession, began Confederate recruiting in June 1861. La Grange was headquarters for 22nd Brigade, Texas state troops, Brig. Gen. Wm. G. Webb commanding, of which 18 companies (1,238 men) and 72 officers were from Fayette.

Special county war taxes provided relief for soldiers' families. Funds were also raised by the famous "Cow Order" for seizure of strays. Censors here banned exchanges of mail with the U.S. Confederate cotton gathered in and stored at La Grange and Round Top was freighted to Mexico by local men hauling 5 or more bales on each 3-months-long trip. In 1863 a dozen teamsters lost outfits and barely saved themselves when bandits struck near Roma, on the Mexican border.

Gen. Webb and Cols. John C. and Wm. F. Upton were Fayette County men. Local C.S.A. units were commanded by Capts. Ira G. Killough and Ben Shropshire, who fought in the Arizona-New Mexico campaign. Gen. Tom Green, first county surveyor, an Indian fighter and hero of San Ja-cinto and the Mexican War, had a part in such Confederate victories as the recapture of Galveston and the Battle of Mansfield, La.

LA GRANGE (Fayette Co.) *US 77, 4.5 mi. N*
Rabb's Prairie
This portion of Fayette County is named for William Rabb (1770–1831), a prosperous miller from Pennsylvania who came to Texas in 1821 with members of his family. Rabb claimed a site on the east side of the Colorado River he had selected during an exploratory trip in 1819. He was a member of Stephen F. Austin's first colony in Texas, and recipient of one of the earliest and largest land grants of more than 22,000 acres, of which 13,285 acres comprised Rabb's Prairie. Part of Rabb's agreement with Austin was to build a gristmill for future settlers of the colony.

Two grinding stones for the mill weighing about one ton each were imported from Scotland and unloaded at the mouth of the Colorado River on the Gulf of Mexico. In order to transport the heavy stones to the site of the gristmill, Rabb constructed a wooden axle and attached a round stone on both ends to serve as wheels. He then hitched oxen to the vehicle and pulled it about 100 miles overland to his mill. Rabb and his sons completed the mill in 1831; Rabb died shortly afterward. Through the years his descendants played significant roles in the development of Texas. The community of Rabb's Prairie was named for this pioneer family.   (1996)

LA GRANGE (Fayette Co.) *US 77, 4 mi. S*
The Oldest
Czech Settlement in Texas
Was established at Hostyn when in November, 1856, the families of Josef Janda, Valintin Kolibal, Frantisek Koza arrived here from Czechoslovakia.   (1964)

LA GRANGE (Fayette Co.)

SH 71 at FM 955, 10 mi. SE

James J. Ross

Born in South Carolina in about 1787, James Jeffres Ross was a member of the "Old Three Hundred." He arrived in Stephen F. Austin's colony in late 1822 or early 1823, moving onto the league granted him near Eagle Lake in Colorado County. In 1828, he moved to the S. A. Anderson league and built a home about one mile southwest of this site.

Col. Ross, as he was known, soon assumed a position of leadership as captain of the militia of the Colorado district. He was a delegate to the second convention at San Felipe in 1833 and was one of those appointed in 1834 to help obtain Austin's release from imprisonment in Mexico. He helped establish a stage line and a stop that became the town of Fayetteville.

An important figure during the early years of settlement in this part of the state, Ross was a successful farmer, rancher, trader, and merchant. Ross Prairie and Ross Creek, both in this vicinity, bear his name. He was killed by angry neighbors in January 1835 for sheltering Indians at his home and was buried in nearby Ross Cemetery. His home, which came to be known as the Ross/Martinek House, was owned by Czech immigrant Joseph Martinek and his descendants for nearly seventy years.

LA GRANGE (Fayette Co.)

SH 237, 3 mi. NE

Rutersville College

First institution of higher education in Texas, recommended in 1837 by Martin Ruter, D. D. Chartered as a Methodist school in 1840. Granted four leagues of land by the Republic of Texas. After educating more than 800 students, it merged in 1856 into the Texas Monument and Military Institute.

(1964)

LA GRANGE (Fayette Co.)

SH 159, 4.8 mi. N in Rutersville

Asa Hill of Rutersville
(1788–1844)

Born in Martin County, N. C. Married Elizabeth Barksdale in Georgia, Oct. 6, 1808. Came to Texas 1835. In army in 1836, was sent by Gen. Houston to warn people in enemy's path. Settled here 1839. In 1840, enrolled eight children in Rutersville College. With sons Jeffrey and John C. C., joined the 1842 expedition to Mier, Mex. Captured, he drew a white bean—thus escaped death, but was in prison until Aug. 1843. Jeffrey was wounded, captured, likewise imprisoned. John C. C., then 14, was adopted by Gen. Santa Anna.

Asa Hill died here; was buried on Cedar Creek, off SH 159. (1973)

LA GRANGE (Fayette Co.)

SH 159, 5.3 mi. NE of Fayetteville

Breeding Family Cemetery
(300 yds. NW, across the highway)

David and Sarah Davis Breeding came to Texas from Kentucky and settled here in 1833 with sons John, Richard, L., Napoleon B., Fidelio S., and Benjamin W.; John, Napoleon, and Fidelio Breeding fought in Texas army during the War for Independence, participating in the victory at San Jacinto on April 21, 1836.

In 1838 David Breeding was a member of the board of land commissioners of Fayette County. John was the first county sheriff, also taking office in 1838.

Family cemetery was opened with burial of David Breeding, 1843. Sarah and John Breeding also lie here.

First School in Fayette County

In a log house on Breeding's land, the first known school session in Fayette County was taught in 1834 by a Mr. Rutland. Attending were Edward, George, Gus, and James Breeding, orphan nephews of David Breeding; Lyman Alexander, Patsie Dougherty, Marian and Sally York, and Emily Alexander (later Mrs. Joel Robison, wife of one of the captors of Santa Anna), whose father Sam Alexander kept four students as boarders. Capt. Jesse Burnham (or Burnam) brought his children 15 miles and built a shed tent with a long bedstead for the girls; the boys slept under the trees.

LA GRANGE (Fayette Co.)   *SH 71, 12 mi. W at roadside park*
First Roadside Park in Texas
Established fall 1933, when a local state highway official built tables and benches (since then replaced) here to encourage motorists to stop and rest.

Texas was one of the first states to sponsor building of roadside parks, which provided work for many of the unemployed during the 1930's depression.

Early highway beautification efforts also started here. Today areas along Texas highways are noted for their landscaping and abundance of native wildflowers.

Texas roadside parks, many of which have restrooms and cookout areas, totaled 1,008 in 1967.
(1968)

LA GRANGE (Fayette Co.)   *SH 159, 4.8 mi. NE*
Rutersville
Founded in 1838 upon the recommendation of Dr. Martin Ruter (1785–1838), as a site for an institution of higher learning. Named in honor of Dr. Ruter, a pioneer Methodist missionary who entered Texas on Nov. 21, 1837, and weakened by his travels, died on May 16, 1838. Later in the year of his death, a company of ten Methodists bought a tract of land, platted the townsite, and began to build Rutersville.

In 1840, Rutersville College was chartered by the fourth congress of the Republic of Texas as the republic's first Protestant college. The legislation specified the school should not be exclusively for the benefit of Methodists, and it was patronized by families of various faiths. Rutersville students were noted for their loyalty to neighbors, sometimes spending days away from class, pursuing Indians.

The Rev. Chauncey Richardson, A. M. (1802–1852), whose grave is nearby, was first president of the college. The campus was half a mile southeast of this marker.

After the Civil War ended in 1865, the original inhabitants of Rutersville sold their property. It was later purchased by German immigrants, whose descendants now live here in large numbers. (1972)

LA JOYA (Hidalgo Co.)   *US 83, 2.7 mi. W*
Hidalgo County's First Oil Well
John M. Lawrence No. 1 oil well was brought in Sept. 18, 1934, near this site by veteran driller Otto C. Woods. Well flowed 1,000 or more barrels a day. At first the oil formed a lake beside the well. County has produced 20 million barrels of oil. (1967)

LA JOYA (Hidalgo Co.)   *US 83, 1.8 mi. W, Havana Cemetery*
Havana
Located on land known as Porcion 46, ceded by the crown of Spain to Don Jose Matias Tijerina in 1767, the community of Havana was named for Havana, Cuba, where Tijerina had stopped on his journey from Europe. Among the early settlers here were the families of Josefa de la Garza Salinas and Civil War Union soldier Patricio Perez. A frame church was built in 1891 and named for St. Joseph. Descendants of early settlers still live in the area. Many Havana pioneers are buried here in the Havana Cemetery. (1988)

LA PRYOR (Zavala Co.)   *US 83, roadside park at Nueces River*
The Bosque-Larios Expedition
(April 30–June 12, 1675)
In the 16th century, Northern Mexico was torn by strife as the Indian inhabitants resisted Spanish efforts to enslave them. A century later, wealthy humanitarian Antonio Balcarcel set out to invoke justice and help missionaries Christianize the land.

In the spring of 1675, Balcarcel sent out an armed expedition under Fernando del Bosque to accompany Fray Juan de Larios on a mission north of the Rio Grande. Also in the party was Fray Dionisio de San Buenventura, an army chaplain. Entering Texas at a site near present Eagle Pass, the expedition marched almost to the present site of San Antonio.

Three days after entering Texas, when they were in camp on the Nueces, about nine miles southwest of present Uvalde, they set up a portable altar. The expeditionaries gathered with some 1,172 Indians to hear Fray Larios chant the mass. Later Fray Larios baptized 55 infants and instructed the adult Indians so that they might be baptized at a future time.

The celebration at the Nueces on May 16, 1675, is known as the earliest recorded occasion of a high (sung) Mass in Texas. Missionary activity that began on that day eventually brought about the founding of the Texas mission system. (1975)

LA PRYOR (Zavala Co.) US 83, 8 mi. N in roadside park
Camp Nueces, C.S.A.

Founded April 1862 near this site, to guard vital traffic as it crossed the Nueces on the San Antonio-Eagle Pass road. A post of the Confederacy's frontier regiment, under Col. James M. Norris. Its duty was to see that cotton got through to Mexico and munitions, medicines and factory goods came north to supply the Confederacy. One of the chain of posts a day's horseback ride apart, on line from Red River to Rio Grande. Never able to relax, in constant danger of Indian raids; short of food, horses and guns, Nueces (like other frontier camps) had none of war's glory and more than its share of hardships.

Located in Zavala County, created in 1858 and named for Lorenzo de Zavala. This is one of 10 counties to commemorate colonizers. Of the 254 counties, 42 have Indian, French or Spanish names. 12 honor Washington and other American patriots. 96 were named for 1836–1846 heroes of the Republic of Texas (including 15 who died in the Alamo). 23 have names of other early statesmen. 11 honor U.S. leaders in the campaign to annex Texas. 10 honor state jurists, ministers, educators, statesmen, historians. 36 are named for leading men of the southern Confederacy. 14 have names from local geography. (1965)

LA VERNIA (Wilson Co.) US 87
Old Chihuahua Road

Mexican cart road from central Mexico to Texas coast at Indianola. Route of marauding Indians as well as Alsatian, German, Polish, Irish immigrants seeking freedom in new world. After 1835 was important in gold and silver exporting; in 1850s for army travel. (1967)

LA VERNIA (Wilson County) 624 W. US 87
Applewhite Homestead

The family of Henry Applewhite (1630–1704), who sailed from England to Jamestown, Virginia, in 1656, remained in Virginia for several generations. Applewhite's descendant, Thomas Applewhite, was born in North Carolina in 1791 and served as a sergeant in the War of 1812.

In 1842 Thomas married his second wife, Elizabeth Oglesby (1820–1898). The Applewhites, accompanied by 8 slaves, moved to this area of Texas in 1853. They purchased 214 acres of farmland here in 1854 and by 1860 the Applewhites owned 9 slaves, some of whom had taken the Applewhite name.

According to local oral tradition, at one time the Applewhites' homestead may also have served as a brief stop for stagecoaches traversing the area along an alternate route of that part of the Chihuahua Road extending from Indianola to San Antonio.

Thomas (d.1864) and Elizabeth Applewhite are buried in LaVernia in concrete cemetery. A number of Applewhite families, the descendants of African Americans who established homes here during the 1860s, remained in the area for many generations. Thomas and Elizabeth Applewhite's original stone house was mostly destroyed during highway construction in the 1950s. (Sesquicentennial of Texas Statehood 1845–1995)

LADONIA (Fannin Co.) FM 904, 8 mi. NE
Site of Fort Lyday
(1 mi. E)

Early Texas pioneer Isaac Lyday built a fort in this area soon after settling here in 1836. The compound consisted of living quarters, storerooms, and a large community well. As many as eighty families gathered inside the fort during Indian attacks. Due to an increase in Indian raids, the settlement was almost abandoned until Texas Ranger Captain William B. Stout came in 1838 to organize a Ranger force. Lyday was elected captain of the company and served until 1839. Fort Lyday continued to shelter settlers until Indian trouble subsided after the Civil War. (1983)

LADONIA (Fannin Co.) Off FM 6, 4.5 mi. E
Site of Hockaday Homestead

After a noted career as an educator and founder of Giles Academy (4 mi. E), Virginia-born Thomas Hart Benton Hockaday (1835–1918) bought over 280 acres in this area in 1870. He farmed the land and built and operated a cotton gin. He later sold much of the property but maintained an eighty-acre homestead on this site for his wife Maria and their seven children. Following Maria's death in 1881, he married Misouri Bird in 1892.

Hockaday sold his property to Laurence Pickard in 1916 and moved to Ladonia (4.5 mi. W) where he spent the remaining two years of his life. Pickard moved the Hockaday house in 1921 and divided it into rent houses for the farm's employees. Although the house itself is gone, the existing barn was constructed from Hockaday's cotton gin.

T. H. B. Hockaday's youngest child, Ela (1875–1956), followed her father's footsteps into education. In 1913, at the peak of a teaching career that began at age eighteen, she established the Hockaday School in Dallas. In the thirty-three years she was with the school, Hockaday earned national recognition as an excellent college preparatory school for girls. Ela was instrumental in the founding of the Hockaday Alumnae Association which continues to carry on the Hockaday tradition. (1981)

LAKE JACKSON (Brazoria Co.)

SH 332, 1 mi. W,
Lake Jackson Wilderness Park

Joseph H. Hawkins

Native Virginian Joseph H. Hawkins practiced law in Kentucky, where he served as State legislator and U.S. congressman before moving to New Orleans. There he befriended Stephen F. Austin, who was broke and reluctant to complete his father's colonization plans on his own. Hawkins encouraged him to continue, offering him a job and, later, capital for the project. In 1821, the two men formalized an agreement in which Austin acknowledged receipt of $4,000 and agreed to divide equally the lands he would receive as colonizer, or empresario. Hawkins sent boats of supplies and colonists to meet Austin in Texas but died in 1823, leaving his wife, George Ann (Nicholas), and five children deeply in debt. She returned with the children to her native Kentucky to be near her family and Hawkins' brother, Littleberry. She appointed Nathaniel Cox to help settle her husband's estate. In 1824, the Mexican government gave Austin, as empresario, almost 100,000 acres, but law required a person to reach majority age and live in Texas to own land, so the Hawkins children could not immediately claim their share. Austin worked with Cox to find a suitable agreement and, in 1833, conveyed to the Hawkins heirs some 42,000 acres of land in and around Brazoria County. Each of Hawkins' children lived briefly in Texas. Edmund St. John (d. 1836) was the first, followed by Norbourne, who died at Goliad in 1836, George (d. 1837), and then Joseph Thomas (d. 1850). Mary Jane came in 1839 but, after her husband died, returned to Kentucky, where she stayed. Although none of his heirs persevered in Texas, Hawkins' legacy in Texas is apparent in the success of Austin's first colony and all that sprang from the early Texas settlement. (2002)

LAKE MEREDITH (Potter Co.)

SH 136 & Alibates Road, 40 mi.
NE of Amarillo on park road

McBride Ranch House
(Built 1903)

A pioneer settler quarried Alibates dolomite from the canyon rim to build this house, mortared with lime burned on the site. Wood in ridge beams, door and window lintels, ice house, and corral came from old railroad bridge timbers salvaged from Canadian River. The floors are of masonry mortar.

The builder, David Nichols McBride, was born Oct. 22, 1849, in Henry County, Ill.; married Abigail Catherine Stringer at Fort Sill, Indian Territory, July 2, 1876; and settled near village of Amarillo Sept. 17, 1887—just 18 days after Potter County was organized. The McBrides had seven children. This site (in "watered homestead") and three alternate "dry grazing" school lands sections were situated in center of the famous LX ranch, owned by the American Pastoral Company of London. Patent for his land was issued to McBride in 1901, upon proof of three years' occupancy. The homestead section cost $1.50 an acre, with payments extending over 40 years at 3% interest. The grazing land cost $1.00 an acre. McBride died June 26, 1928, in Needles, Calif. Heirs sold this property in 1963 to the Canadian River Municipal Water Authority. It is now administered by the National Park Service, Sanford Recreation Area, Lake Meredith. (1971)

LAMESA (Dawson Co.)   SH 137, 12 mi. S
The Hardy Morgan Homestead
One of first ranch homes in Dawson County. Property of Morgan, (1870–19?), a native of
Arkansas who came to Texas in 1883 and worked for Bar Oto and Long S ranches. After acquiring cattle and land in Gaines County, he removed here in 1895. In 1904 he married a pioneer
schoolteacher, Bessie Pearl Andrus of Howard County. In 1905 they built this ranch home where
they brought up a family of five and lived as useful citizens and leaders in development of
Dawson County.

LAMESA (Dawson Co.)   FM 2592, ½ block E of N 22nd St. Park
Site of Chicago
W. C. Bishop of Chicago, Ill., and wealthy lumberman George N. Fletcher established the OTO
(later Bar TO) ranch about 1887 on Fletcher's extensive landholdings in Dawson County. A post
office was opened at the ranch headquarters on May 15, 1889, and named Chicago, both in honor
of Bishop's home town and in humorous reference to the sparse population of the area. The postal
facility served other large ranches in this vicinity, such as C. C. Slaughter's Long S.

In the 1890s, Fletcher left the ranching venture, and A. F. Crowley and W. H. Godair became
Bishop's partners. By that time, a village had begun to grow up around the post office. A. B.
Oden served as OTO ranch foreman and postmaster of Chicago from 1894 to 1903. When Walter
Stemmons replaced him in both positions in 1904, the settlement was renamed Stemmons. The
same year, a post office was established in the new town of Lamesa, two miles south of Chicago.

Dawson County was organized in 1905, and both towns entered the contest for county seat.
When Lamesa won, residents of Chicago quickly relocated their homes and businesses there. The
school and Baptist and Methodist churches also moved to Lamesa. Within days, the community
of Chicago had disappeared.   (1977)

LAMKIN (Comanche Co.)   SH 36
Lamkin
Originally established in 1870, one-half mile north on banks of the Leon River. Named for
George Lamkin, donor of land for the townsite. Business firms included general store, blacksmith
shop, gin, post office, and drugstore. Despite several floods and fires, pioneer merchants gamely
rebuilt. Only after the flood of 1908 destroyed old Lamkin was town moved to present site.

Two years later with the coming of the Cotton Belt Railroad, Lamkin developed into a shipping center for farmers and ranchers. By 1920, the town had 2 gins, a hotel, bank, produce house,
lumberyard, blacksmith shop, 3 general stores, post office, 4 churches, telephone exchange and
drugstore. Consolidated public school had an average attendance of over 200. Basketball team
was county champion for 4 consecutive years. Annual attraction was horse and mule show. In
1922, fire destroyed a major portion of business firms. Lamkin rebuilt but failed after railroad
discontinued, 1936.

An often-related pioneer story was of 1869 Indian raid 2 miles east of here on Resley's creek.
The home of Mrs. Elizabeth Ewell was ransacked by 19 renegade Indians. The widow and her 2
sons were not at home but on their return were greeted by clouds of feathers from ripped mattresses. A posse drove the Indians away.   (1967)

LAMPASAS (Lampasas Co.)   US 190, 1 mi. E
Hughes Springs
One of the Lampasas sulphur springs named in honor of first settler in the vicinity in 1833,
Moses Hughes, whose wife regained health through its waters.

LAMPASAS (Lampasas Co.)   US 190, 3.8 mi. E
Battle Branch
This branch of Sulphur Creek was named for an event in the Horrell-Higgins feud. On the
morning of March 26, 1877, Tom and Mart Horrell were going to Lampasas to attend district
court. En route they were ambushed by gunmen hiding in the brush near this location. The
Horrells returned fire and the attackers rode away. Mart took his wounded brother to a nearby
residence and continued to town for help. He led a squad of Texas Rangers to the site, but officers never caught the attackers. Many believed a Higgins faction had set up the ambush. The feud
would continue with additional gunfighting for several more months.   (2003)

LAMPASAS (Lampasas Co.)

US 281, 3 mi. N in roadside park

Lampasas County

Organized 1856; had 1028 people in 1860; favored secession by 85 to 75 vote in 1861. Sent 2 units to serve in Texas state troops, 2nd frontier District; one unit to 17th Texas infantry; 2 units to 27th Brigade, Texas militia.

Also had 48 minute men in 6 patrols to guard home front land property of men away at war. After a week of duty, each unit returned home to aid women and children tending cattle, crops. Helped supply frontier troops and miners in Longhorn Caverns.

Indians still roamed here during Civil War, stealing horses, killing hunters and others. (1965)

LAMPASAS (Lampasas Co.)

US 190E & Snell Dr.

First United Methodist Church
of Lampasas

Methodists in Lampasas were holding church services as early as 1866. The Rev. William F. Cummins is the first known pastor to have served the Methodist circuit in this area.

Although the exact details of the organization of the First United Methodist Church of Lampasas are unclear, it is known that a sanctuary was built on Fourth Street in 1880, during the pastorate of the Rev. E. F. Kahle. Four years later, the congregation sponsored the opening of Centenary College. The Christian boarding and preparatory school was located in Lampasas and was in operation for about ten years. In 1900, under the leadership of the Rev. J. S. Braswell, the fellowship moved to a new church home on Key Avenue. The congregation relocated to Highway 190 East and Alexander Drive (1 mi. N) in 1966.

Mergers with the Black Methodist congregation known as Alice Chapel and a rural Methodist church at Ogles have strengthened the membership. With ties to the reconstruction era in Texas history, the First United Methodist Church of Lampasas has played a long and distinguished role in the leadership of this community. Descendants of some of the earliest known members still worship with the congregation. (Texas Sesquicentennial 1836–1986)

LAMPASAS (Lampasas Co.)

US 183 at US 190

C.S.A. Salt Works

Located between Tow Valley and Old Bluffton, 15 miles NE. Since 1935 under Lake Buchanan.

During Civil War made salt for table, curing meat and hides, feeding cavalry horses.

A day's boiling in 100 iron, 250-gallon kettles produced 20 to 30 bushels of salt. Cooled, sacked and hauled out, this met Texas' wartime shortages.

First Llano County district court was held at salt works. Stagecoach stop was nearby.

Brine here was from Cambrian sea waters trapped 500 million years ago in sand and strata. Indians led first settler here. (1964)

LAMPASAS (Lampasas Co.)

US 190, 9 mi. NW

Pleasant Valley
Farmers' Alliance No. 1

First chapter of the farmers' alliance in Texas. Founded 1877, it became one of the strongest arms of the national agrarian reform movement of the era.

The group was begun by John R. Allen on Donaldson Creek (1 mi. S) in a "rawhide" (rough) lumber school. Its main purpose was to improve ruinous farm living and economic conditions. Missing livestock were traced by 2 secret officers known as "Grand Smokies."

In 1887 the 3,000 sub-alliances merged with the "farmers' union," then helped spark the Populist Party Drive of the 1890s; but by 1900 they had died out. (1969)

LAMPASAS (Lampasas Co.)

US 281, 3 mi. N in roadside park

Indian Culture Sites

Scattered throughout this area, campsites, flint quarries, and rock paintings testify that primitive tribes lived here for centuries. Tonkawas, Comanches, and Lipan Apaches were the main inhabitants in the early 1800s.

Typical of the sites was a burial found near a river. The shallow grave contained the tightly flexed skeleton of a man aged about 60 at his death. Pitted bones (indicating disease), a broken arm, and worn teeth suggested the difficulty of his life. A pebble painted with black lines, probably an offering, was also found near the burial. (1969)

LAMPASAS (Lampasas Co.) US 281 & FM 1690
2.5 mi. E is Birthplace of
Stanley Walker
(1898–1962)
Noted Texas journalist and editor. Began his career in Austin and Dallas. From 1920 to 1935 was with New York *Herald-Tribune*, where as city editor, he trained many writers. Also was on staff of Philadelphia *Ledger*. He wrote *The Night Club Era, Mr. Astor's Horse*, 5 other books, many articles. Spent last years here. (1966)

LAMPASAS (Lampasas Co.) US 281, Hancock Park
Hancock Springs
First white settlers in 1850s found Indians using curative waters here. Town was quickly developed around the springs. Stage and freight routes and many cattle drives came this way. The springs took the name of landowner, John Hancock.

On a hill to the north about 1882, promoters of the Santa Fe Railway built the 200-room Park Hotel, with boardwalk to the springs, bathhouses, many other luxuries. It gained wide fame as south's finest health resort.

Closed in a few years as a hotel, it later housed Centenary College, until it burned in 1895. Area is now a city park. (1966)

LANCASTER (Dallas Co.) SH 342, 1 mi. S
The Rawlins Homestead
In 1845, Roderick Rawlins the elder settled this area. His son Roderick A. Rawlins (1833–1910) married his teacher, Virginia Bledsoe, daughter of the founder of Lancaster. They started this house in 1855. After serving as a Confederate officer during the Civil War (1861–1865), Capt. Rawlins rebuilt his home in the popular Greek Revival style. It stood halfway between Waxahachie and Dallas. Travelers obtained water and sometimes camped at its well.
(1964)

LANGTRY (Val Verde Co.) Torres St., across from TxDot Visitors Center
Langtry
Langtry was created in 1882, when the Galveston, Harrisburg & San Antonio Railroad, later known as Southern Pacific, signed a deed with the Torres family, who owned the land. The town, which provided water for locomotives, developed from a tent town to a bustling settlement after the rail line was completed. The town was most likely named for George Langtry, who led an area rail building crew. Lore, though, links the town's most famous inhabitant to its naming; Roy Bean, who owned a local saloon and served as Justice of the Peace, became known as "The Law West of the Pecos." He was enamored of Lillie Langtry, a popular British actress, and although she was probably not the town's namesake, she did visit here in the early 20th century. In addition to the infamous Bean, other local men and women contributed to the town's western ambience. J.P. Torres, part of the town's founding family, also served as Justice of the Peace and operated a store and saloon. He, like many of the area residents, also raised livestock, most often sheep or goats. Accessibility to the trains attracted many ranchers, who supported local businesses. Langtry supported other industries, including a rock crushing plant created for the railroad. The town also attracted tuberculosis patients who came in hopes of regaining their health. During the Mexican Revolution, soldiers came to Langtry for goods, guns and munitions. The rail line was rerouted in the 1920s, and Langtry's population declined, today existing primarily as a tourist site. The landscape and the remaining buildings still speak to what once was a bustling West Texas town. (2003)

LANGTRY (Val Verde Co.) Law West Museum
Jersey Lilly Saloon
1882–1903 "Law West of the Pecos" courtroom. Named for Judge Bean's idol, actress Lillie Langtry. Awarded Medallion Plate. (1965)

290

LANGTRY (Val Verde Co.)
Law West Museum
Law West of the Pecos

Judge Roy Bean lived a life in which fiction became so intermingled with fact that he became a legend within his lifetime. Basis for his renown were the decisions which he reached in this building as the Law West of the Pecos. Court was held as frequently on the porch, spectators grouped about on horseback, as within the building. Nor was Bean above breaking off proceedings long enough to serve customers seeking services dispensed by the other businesses carried on in his courtroom-home.

The judge's "law library" consisted of a single volume, an 1879 copy of the Revised Statutes of Texas. He seldom consulted it, however, calling instead on his own ideas about the brand of justice which should apply. This he effectively dispensed together with liberal quantities of bluff and bluster. Since Langtry had no jail, all offenses were deemed finable with Bean pocketing the fines. Drunken prisoners often were chained to mesquite trees in front of the building until they sobered up enough to stand trial.

Bean reached a peak of notoriety when, on February 21, 1896, he staged the banned Fitzsimmons-Maher heavyweight title fight on a sand bar in the Rio Grande River, a stone's throw from his front porch. By holding it on Mexican territory he outwitted Texas Rangers sent to stop the match—and turned a handsome profit for his shrewdness.

This building was named the "Jersey Lilly" for the famous English actress Lillie Langtry whom Bean admired and for whom he claimed to have named the town. His lamp frequently burned into the night as he composed letters to her. But he never saw her since her only visit to Langtry occurred in 1904, less than a year after Bean died.

LAREDO (Webb Co.)
US 83, 2.5 mi. S
Mission Dolores A Visita

Established in 1750 as a part of Jose de Escandon's project to settle the region and civilize and Christianize the Indians.

LAREDO (Webb Co.)
US 83, NW Laredo
Poblacion de Delores

Oldest Spanish settlement on north bank of the Rio Grande. Founded August 22, 1750 by Jose Vasquez Borrego, Lieutenant of Jose de Escandon.

LAREDO (Webb Co.)
US 81/83, 1 mi. N
Webb County

Formed from Nueces County. Created January 29, 1848. Organized March 16, 1848. Named in honor of James Webb 1792–1856, Attorney General and Secretary of State of the Republic of Texas, 1838–1841. Laredo, the county seat, founded in 1755 by Tomas Sanchez.

LAREDO (Webb Co.)
US 59, Laredo Catholic Cemetery
Bishop Peter Verdaguer (1835–1911)

Born in the Cataluna region of Spain, the Most Rev. Peter Verdaguer de Prat studied in the United States. He was ordained (1862) in San Francisco and ministered at Catholic Indian missions in California. While serving at Our Lady of the Angels Church in Los Angeles, he was nominated for the vicariate of Brownsville. Consecrated a bishop in Barcelona in 1890, he sailed to Corpus Christi and in 1891 took up residence in Laredo.

Entrusted with the care of 42,500 Catholics. Bishop Verdaguer faced two severe problems: the extreme poverty of the vicariate and the mobility of the many Mexican-Americans among his flock. The great drought of the early 1890s aggravated the situation. Bishop Verdaguer spent much of his time traveling on horseback from Laredo to Victoria and Brownsville, baptizing, marrying, and confirming the faithful on South Texas ranches.

Despite hardship, three new churches were built in Laredo from 1896 to 1909. During the tenure of the Most Rev. Verdaguer, the number of Catholics in the vicariate rose to 82,000 and the number of churches, schools, and clergy increased significantly. After his death, the vicariate continued to exist until 1913, when the diocese of Corpus Christi was established.   (1978)

LATEXO (Houston Co.)   FM 2663, .3 mi. E
Town of Latexo
Early community called Oldham, near Bethel Church and school, was renamed Starks' Switch when International & Great Northern Railroad in 1872 laid sidetrack to serve Starks' sawmill (2 mi. W).

Latexo post office opened in 1907, after the Louisiana Texas Orchard Company platted 3,000 acres of fruit land and a town here. Lumbering later stripped timber from area, but permanent settlers grew fruit and cotton. About 1915 Latexo became first Houston County school to teach agriculture. Ranches sprang up, 1960s. Unincorporated, town has fire squad, other civic services.

(1972)

LATEXO (Houston Co.)   SH 19/US 287 at FM 2663
Latexo Baptist Church
The community of Stark Switch, originally known as Oldham, was the home of Protestant worship for early settlers from the mid-19th century. Stark Switch Baptist Church of Christ was organized on July 19, 1900, with 27 charter members. The Louisiana Texas Orchard Company became the community's major employer in the early 1900s. The community name changed to Latexo in the company's honor, and the Baptist church name changed to Latexo Baptist Church in 1905. The congregation moved into the local schoolhouse in 1905 and purchased the building from the county in 1912. After 1930 the community gradually moved east with the new main highway, and Latexo Baptist Church followed in 1945. The church thrived in its new location, building new facilities to meet the needs of its members and programs. Celebrating a century of service in the year 2000, the church continues in the traditions of its founders.   (2000)

LEAKEY (Real Co.)   US 83, 1 mi. NE
Real County
Located on the Edwards Plateau, Real County is in an area of rolling terrain broken by the canyons of the Frio River. Because of raids by Comanche, Apache, and Lipan-Apache Indians, white settlement was hindered until after 1881. Mission San Lorenzo de la Santa Cruz was founded by the Spanish in 1762 near present Camp Wood.

The county was created on April 3, 1913, from Edwards, Kerr, and Bandera Counties. Organized on July 26, 1913, it was named in honor of Julius Real (1860–1944), a prominent businessman and state senator, 1909–1914 and 1924–1928. Leakey, the county seat, was established by John Leakey (1824–1900), a pioneer settler in the region.   (1968)

LEAKEY (Real Co.)   US 83, Courthouse Square
John Leakey
Tennessee native John Leakey (1824–1900) came to Texas in 1847, settling for a time in Henderson County where he was a brickmason and rancher. He and his wife Nancy (Patterson) moved to Uvalde County in 1852 near present day Sabinal. A desire to pursue other endeavors took him to the Frio Canyon where there was an abundance of cypress timber. Despite constant threats of Indian attacks, Leakey settled his family and started a cypress shingle business. He served the Confederacy as a freighter during the Civil War, hauling provisions for the troops. Leakey returned to his home after the war to establish a steam sawmill and to attend to his ranching interests. He also began a school for the children of the community, and his home often served as a resting place for itinerant preachers.

The town, situated on the Bandera-Edwards county line, was laid out in 1833 and named in honor of the resourceful pioneer who donated land for this plaza, a church, school, and cemetery. Leakey served as county seat of Edwards County until 1891, and became county seat of Real County when it was organized in 1913.

A successful businessman, Indian fighter and pioneer, John Leakey's contributions and leadership were vital to the early growth of the area.   (1983)

LEAKEY (Real Co.)   4th Street, courthouse square
Real County Courthouse
Leakey was the county seat of Edwards County from 1883 to 1891 when a vote moved the seat to Rocksprings. Real County, named for businessman and State Senator Julius Real, was organized from parts of Edwards, Kerr and Bandera counties in April 1913. Leakey was named the

county seat and a temporary building was erected on the square. Controversy over the site of the county seat continued for several years, so Judge D. D. Thompson began planning for a permanent courthouse upon his election in 1917. Voters approved bonds to finance a permanent structure. The bonds were financed through Hanover National Bank of New York. Architect H. A. Reuter designed the 1918 courthouse, and the firm of McCreary and Schott served as contractors. According to oral history, a local builder known as "Scotty" Archibald made a significant contribution, as well. E. F. Vanderbilt was construction superintendent. Using native limestone quarried from Tucker Hollow near the site, workers erected Reuter's vision of a Classical Revival edifice with a fortress-like façade. The rusticated limestone bands were laid in regular courses with quicklime bonding to create the building's texture and solid feel. A stone pediment with simple cornice topped by a standing seam metal roof contributes to the building's character. Renovations and additions made in 1978 transformed the original doors into large central windows with flat arch and transoms. The fine structure retains its original flavor and distinctive features and remains the center of Real County government. (2000)

LEAKEY (Real Co.) *US 83, 5.2 mi. S at site*
Near Route of
Famous Cattle Trail
One of many "feeder trails" in Texas that converged with the legendary Chisholm Trail above the Red River, this route directed thousands of longhorns to northern markets during the first years after the Civil War.

Many local settlers took part in the drives, which lasted for months, and their tales are full of stampedes and Indian raids.

At times, the trail was used by herds of 200–300 hogs being driven 40 miles to local markets.

The cattle industry and trails such as this helped save Texas' economy—torn by the Civil War— and enriched pioneer folklore. (1968)

LEANDER (Williamson Co.) *US 183 at FM 2243*
Webster Massacre
1½ miles east to the grave of the victims of the Webster massacre, which occurred August 27, 1839, when John Webster and a party of about thirty, enroute to a land grant in Burnet County, were attacked by a band of Comanche Indians. After attempting to flee under cover of darkness, they were trapped on an open prairie. Mrs. Webster and her two children were made prisoners. All others were killed. In death they rest together in one grave. (1936)

LEANDER (Williamson Co.) *US 183, 1.5 mi. NE*
Old J. C. Bryson Home
Pioneers' house. Antedating town of Leander, this place was a 3-day wagon distance from Austin. First two rooms were built (1872) by J. C. and Nancy Bryson, of rock from San Gabriel River and Jenks Branch; hewn cedar logs and shingles from Bastrop area. Had several additions, for family of eight children. Awarded Medallion Plate. (1970)

LEANDER (Williamson Co.) *US 183*
Leanderthal Lady
On Dec. 29, 1982, Texas Highway Department archeologists uncovered the skeleton of a prehistoric human female at the Wilson-Leonard Brushy Creek site (approx. 6 mi. SE). Because of the proximity of the grave site to the town of Leander, the skeleton became known as the Leanderthal Lady. Carbon testing indicates the woman lived 10–13,000 years ago. She was about 30 years old at the time of death and measured 5'3" in height. As one of the earliest intact burials uncovered in the United States, the site is a valuable source of information on the nation's pre-historic past. (1985)

LEESVILLE (Gonzales Co.) *SH 80 at FM 1682, ¾ mi. E*
Leesville Baptist Church
The first meeting place of this congregation, organized in 1875, was destroyed by a storm in 1886. The membership then moved across O'Neal Creek to this site, purchased from pioneer settler N. H. Guinn, and erected this simple frame church in 1887–1888. The steeple which once topped the building was removed in 1924. After a disastrous flood in 1936, Leesville was

relocated along the state highway (¾ mi. W). This church is one of the structures that mark the old townsite. (1976)

LEFORS (Gray Co.) *SH 273, 1 mi. SE*
Captives Rescued
Ten miles southwest of here Lieutenant Frank D. Baldwin, commanding two companies of United States troops, attacked a large band of Cheyenne Indians and rescued two white girl captives, November 8, 1874. (1965)

LEFORS (Gray Co.) *SH 273, 10 mi. SE*
Battle of North Fork of Red River
On Sept. 29, 1872, Col. Ranald S. Mackenzie (1840–1889) found on this site a 262-tepee village of Comanches defying treaties that sought to confine them on Indian Territory reservations. Mackenzie's 231 U.S. Cavalry and Infantrymen captured the village in half an hour and routed Chief Mow-Way's warriors, who made a desperate resistance from sheltering creek banks. That night the Indians succeeded in recapturing their horses from an army guard detail. This taught Mackenzie a lesson that led to his eventual victory in the 1874 campaign to subdue the Indians. (1972)

LEONA (Leon Co.) *US 75, 1 mi. N*
Leon County
Formed from Robertson County, created March 17, 1846. Organized July 13, 1846.

Named in honor of Martin de Leon, 1765–1833, a Texas empresario, founder of Victoria. County seat, Leona 1846. Centerville, since 1850. (1936)

LEONA (Leon Co.) *IH 45 Rest Area*
Fort Boggy
Pioneers who settled in this area about 1840 included members of the Middleton, Byrns, Staley, Erwin, Jones, Capp, Bloodworth, Philpott, Easton, Howell, and Hinton families. Nearby Kichai and Kickapoo Indian camps afforded these early settlers little sense of security. On February 5, 1840, Christopher C. Staley was ambushed and killed by a group of Indians while out hunting near his home. This incident led to the building of Fort Boggy for the protection and safety of the settlers.

Named for its proximity to Boggy Creek, the fort consisted of two blockhouses with eleven dwellings inside an area of about 5,000 square feet. A military company, authorized by Texas President Mirabeau B. Lamar, was formed under the leadership of Capt. Thomas Greer to protect the fort. According to one account, 77 people moved into the fort upon its completion. Illness proved to be a major problem for them.

In 1841, while leading a scouting party beyond the fort, Captain Greer was killed in an Indian attack. Soon after, the threat of raids lessened, and the need for Fort Boggy no longer was vital. For many years, however, a community church and school retained the name "Boggy."

As an early aid in the settlement of this area, Fort Boggy remains significant to the history of Leon County. (1985)

LEONARD (Fannin Co.) *SH 78, 6 mi. W*
Indian Creek Baptist Church and Cemetery
The oldest readable gravestone in this burial ground bears the date 1870, four years before the founding of the Indian Creek Baptist Church. Worship services were first held in a schoolhouse ¼ mile south of this site. Dock Holcomb donated this property adjacent to the cemetery, and a church building was completed in 1882 using lumber hauled by wagon from Jefferson. For over a century the burial ground was under the direct care of the congregation. An annual cemetery decoration day was begun in 1900. (1982)

LEONARD (Fannin Co.) *SH 78, 3 mi. E*
Savage
William Hamilton "Uncle Billy" Savage (1822–1909) and his wife Elizabeth (Henson) moved to this area in 1869. Due to bad road conditions, they often stocked extra supplies and sold them to their neighbors. Their store became the center of Savage community (2.5 mi. E). The village had a doctor, blacksmith, cotton gin, stores, school, church, and a post office established in 1891.

Savage began to decline after World War I (1917–1918) when it was bypassed by construction of new roads in the area. Annual reunion activities are held in Leonard (3 mi. SW). (1980)

LEONARD (Fannin Co.) *SH 78, 4 mi. W*
East Shady Grove Baptist Church
Organized Oct. 26, 1884, by 18 members who met at nearby school to found a missionary Baptist church. T. P. Reece was the first of 25 pastors here.
The Sunday school was founded Feb. 22, 1885.
Dedication of present church was July 16, 1911. (1968)

LEVELLAND (Hockley Co.) *FM 597, 21 mi. NW at White Ranch Hdqts.*
Casas Amarillas (Yellow Houses)
Most famous landmark on the South Plains. Ancient Indian camp ground visited in the 17th century by Spanish missionaries. Here the whites recovered, through trade, property stolen by Indians. Camp site for buffalo hunters, freighters and cattlemen. Acquired by XIT syndicate, 1882; by George W. Littlefield, 1901. (1936)

LEVELLAND (Hockley Co.) *US 385, 4.2 mi. N in roadside park*
Hockley County
Formed from Young and Bexar Territories. Created August 21, 1876. Organized February 21, 1921. Name in honor of George W. Hockley, commander of the artillery San Jacinto. Secretary of War of the Republic of Texas. Died in 1851. Levelland—called Hockley City until 1912—county seat. (1936)

LEVELLAND (Hockley Co.) *SH 114, 2.4 mi. W of Smyer*
The Spade Ranch
Founded by Isaac L. Ellwood (1833–1910), inventor who made a fortune in barbed wire, and bought (1889) from veteran cattlemen D. H. and J. W. Snyder an 8 × 25-mile range (128,000 acres in Hale, Hockley, Lamb and Lubbock Counties. This range was used for Spade-branded calves from Renderbrook Spring, his southmost ranch, in Mitchell County. He continued buying South Plains land until Spade range was 54 miles long. Headquarters (originally in Lamb County) was moved to South Camp (³⁄₁₀ mi. N of here) after farm-land sales in 1920's.
Ellwood's descendants still own and operate the Spade. (1972)

LEWISVILLE (Denton Co.) *FM 1171 W, City Park*
Within Area Encompassed by
The Peters Colony
A reservation of land made under an empresario contract by the Republic of Texas, 1841. Its purpose was to introduce colonists into this area. Under the first of four contracts, W. S. Peters and 19 partners agreed to introduce 600 families in three years, to furnish each with seed, shot, and a cabin, and also to survey the land. Each family was to receive 640 acres of land free and each single man, 320 acres; of this, the company could take half for its services.
Three later contracts altered terms somewhat, and although the land company underwent several internal upheavals, by 1848 there were approximately 1,800 colonists and their families in the area. Resentment over the company's share of land climaxed in 1852 when settlers drove out the unpopular agent, Henry O. Hedgcoxe, in the so-called "Hedgcoxe War."
Because of its success in opening a large area of the frontier and its later effect on Texas land and immigration policy, the law establishing this colony was one of the most important in the republic.
In spite of unusual tumult and hardship, the final Peters Colony Area today extends over five counties and encompasses one-fourth of the state's population, including its largest combined metropolitan area. (1969)

LEWISVILLE (Denton Co.) *Lewisville Lake Park, off Lake Park Rd.*
Lewisville Prehistoric Site
(1.5 mi. SE)
During the construction of Lewisville Dam in 1950, a number of aboriginal artifacts were unearthed. Archeologists conducted several excavations (1952–1957) before the waters of Garza-Little Elm Reservoir covered the site. The excavations revealed 21 hearths, vegetable matter,

animal bone fragments and lignite (coal) which was used for fuel. Scientific radiocarbon dating techniques indicate the organic material is approximately 12,000 years old. The Lewisville discoveries are similar in age and content to findings at the Clovis site in New Mexico.   (1980)

LEXINGTON (Lee Co.)   *US 77, near S city limits at roadside park*
Indian Camp Branch
Located along an old buffalo trail, this creek was once fed by a spring and was a favorite camping place for Indian hunting parties. It was named Indian Camp Branch by James Shaw (1808–1879), a veteran of the Battle of San Jacinto (April 21, 1836), to honor the hospitality of a band of friendly Tonkawa Indians he encountered near this site in 1837. Shaw built a cabin in this area and was soon joined by other Anglo-American settlers. A teacher, surveyor, and postmaster, Shaw also served as a senator and representative in congresses of the Republic and State of Texas.   (1976)

LIBERTY (Liberty Co.)   *SH 146, 3 mi. NE*
Atascosito Marker
1756—Liberty Bicentennial, observance 1956 Atascosito, established Indian village prior to 1690. Established as district on Atascosito Road by Spanish government in 1857 to prevent French trade with Indians.
Bill Daniel, director general; W. D. Partlow, chairman, historical marker committee.

LIBERTY (Liberty Co.)   *SH 146, 23 mi. N*
Site of the Town of Grand Cane
Here General Sam Houston built a home in 1843 and in it resided until 1845. A post office was established May 22, 1846, with Vernon B. Lea as postmaster. It was discontinued October 25, 1868, and reestablished April 26, 1869. The name of the town was changed to Ironwood August 26, 1869. The post office was discontinued March 15, 1900.

LIBERTY (Liberty Co.)   *US 90, on Trinity River*
The Trinity River
Longest river lying entirely within Texas. The watershed of the Trinity covers 17,969 square miles, an area larger than any one of the nine smallest states of the union. More than 20 percent of the people in Texas reside in this area—more people than in any one of the 24 least populous states.

The first recorded exclusive navigation rights to the Trinity were given by Mexico in 1833 to district commissioner J. Francisco Madero, but before he could exercise his rights, the Texas Revolution intervened.

As early as 1838, during the Republic of Texas, steamboat navigation had begun on the Trinity. The famous steamer *Ellen Frankland* plied it regularly. In 1852 a survey authorized by the U.S. Congress reported that "the Trinity River is the deepest and least obstructed river in Texas." The river played a vital role in the Civil War, when a company of Alabama-Coushatta Indians transported key military supplies and boats from Anderson County to waiting Confederate officials in Liberty. Until 1874 steamers chugged from Galveston to as far north as Porter's Bluff in Ellis County. Under the River and Harbor Act of 1965, Congress authorized the comprehensive development of the Trinity basin's water resources.   (1970)

LIBERTY (Liberty Co.)   *SH 146 & FM 1011*
Atascosito
A Spanish settlement on the Atascosito Road was established here in 1757 to prevent French trade with the Indians. Four and one-half miles east of here the road crosses the Trinity. There Alonso de Leon, Spanish explorer crossed in 1690. The road from Goliad to Opelousas, Louisiana, known as the Lower Road, extensively traveled from 1750–1850, also crossed here.

1936
1756–1956 Liberty Bicentennial Observance. Atascosito established Indian village prior to 1690. Established as district on Atascosito Road by Spanish government in 1857 to prevent French trade with Indians.

LIBERTY (Liberty Co.)   *US 90 East*
Mexican Hill
Following the decisive battle of San Jacinto in the Texas War for Independence, most of the Mexicans captured in the battle were taken to Galveston. Problems concerning a lack of provisions and the threat of attack persuaded Texas President David G. Burnet to transfer some of the prisoners to Liberty. In August 1836, some 60 Mexicans were transported by schooner to Anahuac, where they were met by William Hardin, who took them on to Liberty.

Georgia native William Hardin (1801–1839) had come to Liberty from Tennessee in 1825. During the years before the Texas Revolution, he served as commissioner of police and alcalde of Liberty. Hardin was elected a delegate to the convention of 1833 at San Felipe and later served as an election judge in Nacogdoches and as a primary judge in Liberty.

The Mexican prisoners stayed on Hardin's property near this site, which has come to be called Mexican Hill. Among the men were General Martin Perfecto de Cós and Ten. Colonel Pedro Delgado, who wrote an account of his time in Liberty. According to Delgado, the Mexicans were treated well and given the best care available during their stay, which lasted until the government of Texas released them on April 25, 1837.   (1985)

LIBERTY (Liberty Co.)   *US 90 at Trinity River*
Early Meat-Packing Plant
Probably first commercial meat-packing plant in Texas. In the early 1840s, English firm of Jones & Co. established a beef-preserving plant at Liberty Landing. British gold bought beef on hoof at four cents a pound. In processing, barrels of meat were put in iron cylinders and air was expelled, causing a vacuum. Brine was then added. When beef was removed, it was packed in salt and shipped to Galveston by steamer and on to West Indies in English sailing vessels. Firm also made candles, tallow, neat's-foot oil and glue. A flood destroyed the factory in 1844.   (1969)

LIBERTY (Liberty Co.)   *400 block Travis Street*
Casa Consistatorial
(Courthouse Square)
Originally one of five squares platted for public use in 1831 by J. Francisco Madero, General Land Commissioner of Texas (under Mexican government), in accordance with the provisions of 1825 Law of Colonization-Article 34.

Madero changed name of site from Atascosito, meaning boggy, to Liberty to reflect his hopes for the future of Texas.

The first courthouse was built on this square, 1831; a second in 1857; a third in 1877; a fourth in 1895–1896; and the present one in 1930–1931.

Many Texas statesmen including Sam Houston and David G. Burnet practiced law here.
(1968)

LIBERTY HILL (Williamson Co.)   *SH 29, 2 mi. NW*
Liberty Hill Cemetery
Weathered gravestones show use of this spot for burials since 1852, when the earliest settlers were establishing homes in area. The first formal grant of land here as a community burial ground was made by John T. and Amelia Edwards Bryson in 1875, when three and one-half acres were deeded to the Liberty Hill cemetery trustees: T. N. Bryson, C. C. Chance, W. H. Poole, J. B. Roddy, and T. S. Snyder. This acreage was protected by a stone fence built with their own hands by the Brysons and their neighbors. Additions to original plot include land formerly owned by John T. Bryson and donated by Dr. and Mrs. H. L. Fowler. Royal Arch Masons in 1932 established an adjacent three-acre Masonic cemetery, later transferring title to the Liberty Hill Lodge No. 432, A. F. & A. M., which gave it in 1959 to the Liberty Hill Cemetery Association.

By later land purchases, the cemetery now contains more than twenty acres. Funds have come by bequests from Walter Gardner, Arthur Gray, and T. L. McDaniel. Many other persons have also contributed to funds for the cemetery. In 1953 the Liberty Hill Cemetery Association was incorporated, with Dr. J. Gordon Bryson as president; C. L. Chance, vice president; C. F. Hickman, treasurer; and Mrs. Letitia Russell, secretary.   (1971)

LIBERTY HILL (Williamson Co.) *SH 29, 1 mi. NW*
Bryson Stagecoach Stop
John T. Bryson (d. 1894) and his wife Amelia (d. 1897), prominent early settlers of the Liberty Hill community, constructed this home in the 1850s. Built on a frame of notched and fitted hewn cedar logs and featuring chimneys of native stone, the original open dog-trot construction is typical of pioneer Texas houses. The Bryson residence also served as a stop on the stagecoach route between Austin and Fort Croghan, near present Burnet. (1981)

LINCOLN (Lee Co.) *SH 21/FM 1624, 1½ miles SW*
Old Evergreen Tree
Said to have sheltered in 1714 explorer Louis de St. Denis—probably first white man ever here. Site of pioneer court trials in 1870s. (1967)

LINCOLN (Lee Co.) *FM 1624/SH 21, 1.5 mi. E.*
King's Highway—El Camino Real—Old San Antonio Road
First opened by Louis de St. Denis, 1715; route from Mexico to Louisiana. This location within sight of famous "Old Evergreen Tree." (1918)

LINDALE (Smith Co.) *US 69, 3 mi. E*
Vial-Fragoso Trail
In this vicinity extended the Vial-Fragoso Trail.
Blazed in 1788 by Pierre Vial and Francisco Xavier Fragoso on their way from Santa Fe, New Mexico, to Natchitoches, Louisiana.

LINDEN (Cass Co.) *US 59, 7 mi. NE in roadside park*
Cass County
Formed from Bowie County land. Created April 25, 1846; organized July 13, 1846.
Named in honor of Gen. Lewis Cass (1782–1866), United States soldier and statesman, a strong advocate of annexation of Texas.
Important river port city of Jefferson was county seat until Marion County was carved out of Cass in 1860; Linden, near center of county, then became county seat.
During wave of sectional patriotism in 1861, the name "Cass" was changed to "Davis," in honor of Jefferson Davis, President of the Confederate states. The original name was restored in 1871. (1971)

LINDEN (Cass Co.) *US 59, 9 mi. S in roadside park*
Texas Confederate Legislator
Dr. M. D. K. Taylor
(1818–1897)
Alabama physician. Came to Texas, 1847. Served Cass County in Texas House and Senate for 24 years. Was called the ablest parliamentarian of his time.
Served as one of the speakers of Texas House of Representatives in critical Civil War years, 1861–1865. Legislators passed laws to raise, equip and supply 90,000 Texas soldiers who fought on all fronts and provided for defense of state's 2000 mile frontier and coast against Indians, enemy troops and ships.
As naval blockade reduced imports, the legislature established plants to make guns, powder, cloth, salt. Contracts, subsidies and land grants were provided to encourage private industry to help meet heavy wartime demands for arms, supplies, clothing, food.
Taylor and the other lawmakers taxed property and business and required farmers to turn in tithes of produce to meet the crisis. Funds were voted to buy cotton for state exchange for goods in Mexico to aid soldiers' dependents and to provide hospitals and medical care for troops—in and out of state.
The legislature was in almost continuous session. Poor pay and inflated Confederate money caused many members to live in tents and covered wagons on the capital grounds and cook over campfires. (1965)

LINDSAY (Cooke Co.)

US 82, 2.3 mi. W in roadside park

First Cooke County Surveyor
Daniel Montague
(1798–1876)

Born in Massachusetts. Moved to Texas 1836. Accepted post of surveyor, Fannin Land District, helping settlers locate claims and fight Indians. Joined Snively expedition to capture Mexican traders trespassing in Republic of Texas, 1843. Captain of company in Mexican War, 1846. When Cooke County was created, 1848, Montague was named county surveyor.

Like most surveyors, took land as pay for duty that called for constant risk of life. Rifles to stand off Indians were in field kits. Like surveyor-Senator John H. Reagan, Montague was honored in having a county named for him. (1968)

LINGLEVILLE (Erath Co.)

FM 219, 0.2 mi. S of FM 8

Lingleville Tabernacle

Built in 1913, this tabernacle served as a permanent structure for summer religious revivals, and eliminated the need to rebuild or repair the brush-covered arbors that had been used in earlier years. Local Baptist, Methodist, and Presbyterian church congregations helped erect the structure, which included the hand-made benches. Like many tabernacles, it also served as a community meeting place. It is still used for the annual Lingleville homecoming. (1983)

LINN (Hidalgo Co.)

SH 186, 4 mi. E

El Sal Del Rey, C.S.A.

Large salt lake located 26 miles NE was principal source of salt in South Texas during the Civil War. Put under state guard and agent 1862. Salt sold to families, Texas military board, army of Confederacy and wagons returning north on Cotton Road—vital trade route for South thru Mexico. Due to military and domestic importance, Union Forces periodically wrecked the salt works from November 1863 until war's end. It was also a Texas Confederate base for the 1864 recapture of Brownsville. (1936)

Salting or smoking were only ways to preserve meat at time of Civil War. When South levied a meat tithe, salt was necessary to cure bacon and beef for military. Salt was a must for horses and mules used by cavalry, artillery and supply wagons. Hides were preserved with it to make leather for shoes and harness. Other wartime salt works were operated along coast and in 7 counties in Central, East and West Texas. El Sal del Rey, Spanish for "salt for the king" also played a significant role in the history of Texas mineral law. A legal controversy raged for years over its ownership. Under Spain, mineral rights belonged to crown. Mexico retained the principle of the state ownership of minerals. Texas, as republic and state, kept minerals in the public domain. Private possession of the lake began with the 1866 Texas Constitutional Convention which relinquished all minerals to landowners. The principle of private ownership was readopted in the constitutions of 1869 and 1876.

LINN (Hidalgo Co.)

US 281 right-of-way, .5 mi. S

La Noria Cardeneña

Parts of present Hidalgo, Cameron, Willacy, and Kenedy Counties were once included in two Spanish land grants, San Juan de Carricitos and San Salvador del Tule. The original grantee of the Carricitos grant was Jośe Narciso Cavazos. After his death, ownership of the land passed to his heirs.

The Tule lands were granted to Juan Jośe Ballí in 1798. Ballí obtained a business loan from Antonio Cárdenas of Reynosa, Mexico. Following Ballí's death and subsequent litigation over the loan, the lands reverted to Cárdenas heirs in 1828.

The Cárdenas family established La Noria Cardeneña Ranch in 1829, so named because of the fresh water wells (norias) found in the region. Gradually, the Cárdenas and Cavazos families were joined by a number of marriages, which also combined property interests. Although the families endured many hardships, including years of Indian and bandit attacks, they continued to run a strong ranching operation.

Still in existence on part of the ranch is a small cemetery, begun in 1835 and named Niño Jesús de Praga in 1863. Also surviving are the mid-19th century main ranch house and a church built next to the cemetery in 1944. (1988)

LIPSCOMB (Lipscomb Co.) *SH 305 at Spur 188*
Lipscomb, Texas
Established 1886, by settlers hoping to benefit from proposed Santa Fe Railroad in Panhandle. Post office was opened in 1886; Lipscomb Town Company sold land for $3 an acre in 1887. In first month, seven businesses started.

When county was organized in 1887, Lipscomb became seat, named for A. S. Lipscomb, Secretary of State in Republic of Texas and Justice of State Supreme Court. Hotel from undeveloped town of Dominion moved here, 1887.

First courthouse was built in 1887. The first school—in a church—had 25 pupils, 1888. A new courthouse was erected in 1916. (1967)

LIPSCOMB (Lipscomb Co.) *Main St. (SH 188)*
Lipscomb County Courthouse
Established in 1886 and organized the following year with Lipscomb as county seat, Lipscomb County was named for Abner S. Lipscomb, an associate justice of the Texas Supreme Court in the 1840s–1850s. A one-story wood frame building served as the first county courthouse. During the first decade of the 20th century, the number of farms and ranches in the county more than doubled, and the population more than tripled that of the 1900 census. In 1915, county voters approved the issuance of bonds for a new, larger courthouse to serve the governmental functions of a growing county. The Commissioners Court selected William M. Rice of Amarillo as both architect and general contractor for the project. Edward S. Altmiller, who had been the contractor for the 1910 Lipscomb County jail, served as construction superintendent. Rice designed the courthouse in the Classical Revival style, with style-defining features such as the arched doorway and the triangular pediment supported by Doric order columns over the entrance. Design and construction took place primarily during 1916, with final details completed in early 1917. Despite its status as the smallest town in the county, largely the result of being bypassed by the railroad, Lipscomb retains its designation as county seat. The Lipscomb County courthouse, which dominates the town site, continues to function as the center of government and politics for county residents. (2000)

LITTLEFIELD (Lamb Co.) *US 84 at Delano Street*
Replica of XIT's Giant Windmill
Yellowhouse division of the 3,050,000-acre XIT Ranch built (1887) a 132-foot windmill southwest of here. Set in a canyon, it had to be tall to catch breezes and pump water. It was known as the world's tallest windmill until it was toppled by winds in 1926. This replica was erected May 27, 1969. (1970)

LITTLEFIELD (Lamb Co.) *US 84, NW city limits*
Major George W. Littlefield
(1842–1920)
Came to Texas 1850. In Civil War, with Terry's Texas Rangers, fought at Shiloh, Chickamauga, Lookout Mountain and other bloody battles.

Helped open South Plains, the Panhandle and New Mexico to ranching. His "LIT" and "LFD" herds were famed all over the West and in Canada.

Became Austin banker, devoted friend and benefactor to the University of Texas. Financed studies, donated property and established the Littlefield Grant for Southern History.

Founded town of Littlefield.

LITTLEFIELD (Lamb Co.) *FM 54, 8 mi. W*
Comanchero Trail
One of several routes used by traders dealing with Indians, primarily Comanches (hence name). Weapons, whiskey and trade goods were swapped for stolen Texas cattle, horses and captives.

Pursuit apparently began in the 1760s when Mexican hunters ventured out on "Staked Plains" (Indian domain) to hunt buffalo for New Mexico meat markets.

Early explorers Zebulon Pike (1807), Josiah Gregg (1830), and Capt. R. B. Marcy (1848) told of finding Comanchero campsites and wagon trails on the plains. The Comancheros ceased to operate in the mid-1870s. (1970)

LITTLEFIELD (Lamb Co.) — *US 385 right-of-way, 12 mi. N*
Rocky Ford Crossing and Community
(The Ford was .5 mi. W)
The 840-mile Brazos River was both friend and foe to settlers. Here near the source of Double Mountain Fork, after XIT ranch was sold to smaller operators about 1912, the river that had attracted settlers was found to obstruct wet-weather travel. In 1926, the settlers built a gyprock road across the valley and lined the river bed with rock to make a passable road. They also built a tabernacle for church, elections, and other gatherings. New roads bypass Rocky Ford, yet the community still thrives. (1976)

LIVINGSTON (Polk Co.) — *US 190, 16 mi. E at entrance to reservation*
Village of Alabama-Coushatta Indians
Who came into Texas early in the 19th century and have always been friendly with the whites.

LIVINGSTON (Polk Co.) — *Reservation, US 190, 16 mi. E*
Confederate Service of Alabama and Coushatta Indians
Alabama and Coushatta Indians of Polk County were trained as cavalrymen in 1861 by Indian agent Robert R. Neyland as the War Between the States advanced. In April 1862, nineteen Alabama and Coushatta, including Chief John Scott, enlisted in the Confederate Army as members of Company G, 24th Texas Cavalry. They trained in Hempstead, Texas, and in Arkansas, where their commander, General Thomas C. Hindman, converted them to infantrymen. After voicing displeasure with the change from cavalry to infantry duties, they were permitted to return to their Polk County homes to await further orders. Following brief service in the Confederate Navy under Galveston Bay Commander W. W. Hunter, they were reorganized as a cavalry company in the 6th Brigade, 2nd Texas Infantry Division. In 1864 the company roster listed 132 men. Their primary job was to build and operate flat-bottomed boats (scows) to transport farm produce and other supplies needed by the confederacy down the Trinity River to the port at Liberty, Texas. Official correspondence of wartime Texas Governors Francis R. Lubbock and Pendleton Murrah refer to the Alabama and Coushatta Indians' loyalty in their role as Confederate infantry, cavalry, and navy servicemen. (1994)

LIVINGSTON (Polk Co.) — *US 59, N city limits*
Polk County
Created from Liberty County March 30, 1846. Organized July 13, 1846 with Livingston as county seat. Named for James Knox Polk, 1795–1849, President of the United States who favored the annexation of Texas. Early settlements were Drew's Landing, Mariana, Swartwout. On 1,280 acres granted by the State in 1854, the descendants of the Alabama Indians still live.

(1936)

LIVINGSTON (Polk Co.) — *101 W. Church Street (US 190 at US 59 Bus.)*
Polk County Courthouse
Completed in 1924, this is the fifth courthouse to serve Polk County. Citing "lack of space and modern conveniences," the Commissioners Court hired the Houston architectural firm of McLelland & Fink to design their new building. Contractor Isaac Young completed demolition of the 1884 courthouse by July 1923, and the first court meetings were held in this building by the fall of 1924. Designed to include an auditorium, library, American Legion hall and post office, which were replaced in later years by administrative and judicial offices, the Polk County Courthouse features Classical Revival styling with Beaux Arts influences. It stands as a significant part of Livingston's architectural heritage. (2001)

LIVINGSTON (Polk Co.)   *US 190, 16 mi. E*

Alabama-Coushatta Reservation
Awarded
The Texas Historical Building Medallion

Although there are no old buildings on the reservation, the site itself is of much historic interest. The Alabama-Coushatta tribe has been a friendly tribe since the beginning of their recorded history.

LIVINGSTON (Polk Co.)   *FM 1988, 7 mi. SW*

Paddlewheels on the Trinity
(Nearest Point on River, 7 mi. SW)

Once the most navigable of Texas' winding, debris-choked rivers, the Trinity links Dallas to Galveston across the rich farm lands of East Texas.

Of 17 landings in Polk County, Smithfield, Drew's Landing, and Swartwout were 3 of the most important. At times, 8 or more steamboats, stern- and side-wheelers could be seen at a busy landing, where stevedores loaded goods as curious citizens hailed the passengers.

Although the Trinity played a leading role in Texas commerce, 1850–1900, railroads eventually ended the steamboat era.   (1965)

LIVINGSTON (Polk Co.)   *6 mi. SW, Lake Livingston Viewing Area*

Early Roads in Polk County

Travel was of great importance in Polk County's early days. Civilized Indians—particularly Creeks, Alabamas, Coushattas, and Kickapoos—were numerous and had many trails for intercommunication. Long King's Trace (named for a chief) led from Alabama villages through site of present Livingston, past site of this marker. The Coushatta Trace began in Louisiana, wound through what is now Polk County, joining (more than 100 miles west) an ancient road into Mexico. The Alabama Trace branched off El Camino Real (The King's Highway) east of Nacogdoches and came to the site of present Alabama-Coushatta reservation. Indians started many other local roads.

A Mexican-Indian trail became the Nacogdoches-Liberty Stagecoach Road, after white settlement began in 1820s. Settlers brought in goods by Trinity River boats, establishing 20 landings (or wharves) on the 72 miles of Polk County riverfront. Roads led to the interior from the landings; boat handled shipping of county produce for many years.

Northeast of Livingston is the "Old Israel Road"—named for a religious colony whose buildings have disappeared. As with many of the Indians, memory of these people is preserved only in the road's name.   (1970)

LLANO (Llano Co.)   *SH 16 at FM 965, 15 mi. S*

Enchanted Rock

Nine miles west is Enchanted Rock.

From its summit, in the fall of 1841, Captain John C. Hays, while surrounded by Comanche Indians who cut him off from his ranging company, repulsed the whole band and inflicted upon them such heavy loss that they fled.   (1936)

LLANO (Llano Co.)   *SH 16, 10 mi. S*

Oxford Cemetery
(¼ mi. E)

The Oxford Community was founded in 1880 when Confederate veteran A. J. Johnson came to Llano County and laid out the townsite. In 1881, a burial ground was established near this site for the use of the families of Oxford. Burials date from 1883, although some of the graves that were moved from a neighboring cemetery bear earlier death dates. Among those interred there are the town's founder, A. J. Johnson (1832–1912); and James R. Moss (1843–1924), who captained the Packsaddle Mountain fight, an 1873 battle that drove raiding Indians out of Llano County.   (1985)

LLANO (Llano Co.)   *601 Bessemer (SH 16)*

Badu House

Built in 1891 during the city's iron production boom days, this structure originally housed the First National Bank of Llano. In 1898 it was purchased by French native N. J. "Professor" Badu, a noted local mineralogist, for use as a residence. Designed by the Austin firm of Larramour and

Watson, it features Renaissance Revival detailing and a distinctive band of native granite in a checkerboard pattern. Badu's descendants lived here for many years.   (1981)

LLANO (Llano Co.)   *SH 16, 3.3 mi. N*
Llano County
(Plaque missing—probably vandalized)
(Inscription read)
The name "Llano" first given by Spanish explorers in the 18th century to the river traversing the region, is a corruption of the French name given the Lipan Indians.

First settlements were made by Germans about 1850.

The county, created from Gillespie, Bexar, February 1, 1856, with Llano as the county seat.

LLANO (Llano Co.)   *SH 71, 12 mi. NW*
Community of Valley Spring
O. C. J. Phillips, first settler, arrived in 1853. Whistleville combined with Bugscuffle to form Valley Spring, with post office established 1878.

This was birthplace of James Field Smathers (1888–1967), inventor of electric typewriter.
                                                                              (1970)

LLANO (Llano Co.)   *SH 71, 14 mi. SE*
2.5 mi. E of
Packsaddle Mountain
In a battle fought August 4, 1873, Captain J. R. Moss, Stephen Moss, William B. Moss, Eli Lloyd, Arch Martin, Pink Ayers, E. D. Harrington, and Robert Brown routed a band of Indians thrice their number.

The last Indian battle in this region.   (1936)

LLANO (Llano Co.)   *SH 29 at SH 261, 16 mi. E*
C.S.A. Salt Works
Located between Tow Valley and old Bluffton, 15 miles NE. Since 1935 under Lake Buchanan. During Civil War made salt for table, curing meat, and hides, feeding cavalry horses.

A day's boiling in 100 iron, 250-gallon kettles produced 20 to 30 bushels of salt. Cooled, sacked and hauled out, this met Texas wartime shortages.

First Llano County district court was held at Salt Works. Stage coach stop was nearby.

Brine here was Cambrian Sea waters trapped 500 million years ago in sand and strata. Indians led first settler here.

LLANO (Llano Co.)   *SH 71, 15 mi. E near Honey Creek*
Early Explorers In Llano County
By commission of the governor of Spanish Texas, Bernardo de Miranda in 1756 examined Cerro del Almagre, a red ochre hill supposedly rich in silver. His party of 23 from San Antonio struck Honey Creek near here. Then went to the junction of the Llano and Colorado Rivers. Three pounds of ore from Cerro del Almagre assayed only ten ounces of silver to 100 pounds of ore. Plans for further explorations were therefore abandoned as such low yield, coupled with transport problems and Indian threats, made mining seem unattractive.   (1971)

LLANO (Llano Co.)   *SH 71 & SH 16 S*
Llano County Granite Industry
(Original Quarry 6 mi. W)
A major source of American building granite. First stone polished 1888 by J. K. Finlay, using water wheel. First quarry opened 1890 on David Stewart land. Frank Teich (1856–1939), famous Texas sculptor, worked here in Llano granite. Largest stone quarried (40 tons) is base for statue of a Terry's Texas Ranger, at State Capitol.   (1967)

LOCKHART (Caldwell Co.)   *US 183, 3 mi. N in roadside park*
Dr. D. Port Smythe
(1824–1889)
Pioneer Lockhart physician, from Alabama. Studied medicine, University of Pennsylvania.

Was Civil War surgeon, Texas Mounted Rifles and Cavalry, on Texas frontier and in Louisiana, Arkansas and Indian Territory.

Typical of Texas Confederates, his letters home show concern for wife and children: contain instructions on teaching child to read, crops, plowing, animal care, fences, debt collection.

Professor of Chemistry, 1871, Galveston Medical College. A & M College physician, 1879–1882. First to serve full time in any Texas college or university.   (1965)

LOCKHART (Caldwell Co.)   *US 183, Lions Club City Park*
Battle of Plum Creek

The harsh anti-Indian policies of President Mirabeau B. Lamar and Mexican efforts to weaken the Republic of Texas stirred Indian hostilities. Hatred increased after the Council House fight in San Antonio, March 19, 1840, where 12 Comanche chiefs were killed.

After regrouping and making plans for revenge, 600 Comanches and Kiowas, including women and children, moved across Central Texas in early August. They raided Victoria and Linnville (120 mi. SE), a prosperous seaport. About 200 Texans met at Good's Crossing on Plum Creek under Major-General Felix Huston (1800–1857) to stop the Indians. Adorned with their plunder from Linnville, the war party stretched for miles across the prairie.

The Battle of Plum Creek, August 12, 1840, began on Comanche Flats (5.5 mi. SE) and proceeded to Kelley Springs (2.5 mi. SW), with skirmishes as far as present San Marcos and Kyle. Mathew Caldwell (1798–1842), for whom Caldwell County was named, was injured in the Council House Fight but took part in this battle. Volunteers under Edward Burleson (1793–1851) included 13 Tonkawa Indians, marked as Texan allies by white armbands. Texas casualties were light while the Indians lost over 80 chiefs and warriors. This battle ended the Comanche penetration of settled portions of Texas.   (1978)

LOCKHART (Caldwell Co.)   *SH 20 right-of-way, 5.4 mi. E of US 183*
Lincecum Cemetery

Garland R. Lincecum, cousin of Alamo hero James Bowie, and his wife Emmaline left Mississippi and settled on land he had purchased here in 1847. Lincecum, who signed a petition with others to create Caldwell County in 1847, died in 1853 and was the first person buried here. Three of his daughters were married to the sons of fellow Mississippian Alexander Roberts, who settled in this area in 1843. The last person buried here was Jacob G. Roberts, Lincecum's grandson, in 1938. Members of the pioneer Roberts and Lincecum families and their descendants are interred here.   (1993)

LOEB (Hardin Co.)   *US 69*
Former Townsite of Concord

First town in Hardin County. Established in 1858 at a strategic crossing from Beaumont to points north. Original name was Benton. Rapidly became a thriving steamboat port and reached a population of about 300, but declined in the 1880s with coming of the railroad.   (1970)

LOMETA (Lampasas Co.)   *US 190, 9 mi. W*
Chadwick's Mill
(Site 3 mi. N)

Famous pioneer sawmill, flour mill, and cotton gin. Built 1874 by Henry A. Chadwick and son, Milam. A sturdy oak dam across river supplied power. A millrace chiseled in sandstone channeled water to millstones. Mill and gin house were also sandstone. A fish trap in millrace offered food and sport to customers, who often had to wait several days for a turn at the mill.

This scenic spot grew to be a popular resort around 1900, with hotel and dance platform. Attracted hundreds of campers.

Change in course of river, 1915, forced mill to be abandoned.   (1970)

LOMETA (Lampasas Co.)   *US 190, 1.25 mi. W*
Phantom Hill Road

In 1851–1852, in a major reorganization of the frontier defense system, the U.S. Army built a line of 7 forts between the Red River and the Rio Grande to protect the scattered remote settlements and travel routes to California. On Nov. 14, 1851, Fort Phantom Hill was established near present Abilene (120 miles NW) by Col. J. J. Abercrombie and the 5th Infantry.

The Phantom Hill Road, the vital transportation and communication link between the fort and military headquarters at Austin (80 miles SE), was the first road in Lampasas County, and crossed at this site. Supply trains of up to 24 wagons drawn by mules, horses, and oxen passed along this route to the frontier fort. The road was used primarily by the military until the abandonment of Fort Phantom Hill on April 6, 1854, but also served as a thoroughfare for early settlers entering the region and continued in that capacity until after the Civil War.

About 1870, traffic passing through the area was diverted to the Senterfitt Stage Station (1.5 miles SW), and this section of the road abandoned. Several isolated segments of the Phantom Hill Road remain in use in the county, and physical evidence of the Emy's Creek Crossing (200 yards S) still exists. (1974)

LOMETA (Lampasas Co.) *US 183, at edge*
Scholten Railroad
(Owned by the "Scholten Brothers Cedar Company")
A 25-mile narrow gauge railroad that operated about 1912–1920 from Lometa to San Saba County.

Constructed by Edward and Alfred Scholten (from Holland). Line hauled cedar posts and piling to Santa Fe line at Lometa to be distributed to fast-growing West Texas. Employees totaled 500.

Headquarters were located 100 yards west. (1968)

LONDON (Kimble Co.) *US 377, 1.5 mi. SW*
Reichenau Gap
Travelers between Mason and Junction passed through this gap, named for a German emigrant who settled nearby in 1866.

LONE STAR (Morris Co.) *US 259 S near Big Cypress Bridge*
Site of Old Spearman's Ferry
(1 mi. W)
Operated along with a mill by E. B. Smith during the Republic of Texas. Bought by John Spearman in 1850. At this site in 1870 the state authorized a toll bridge. Fees ranged from 2¢ for a sheep to $1 for an 8-horse team and loaded wagon. This was at Big Cypress Bayou on Pittsburg-Jefferson Stage Road. (1966)

LONGVIEW (Gregg Co.) *US 80 at North High*
Gregg County
Formed from Rusk and Upshur Counties. Created April 12, 1873. Organized June 28, 1873. Named in honor of General John Gregg (1828–1864), delegate to Secession Convention and to the Provisional Congress of the Southern Confederacy. A Confederate officer. Longview, the county seat. (1965)

LONGVIEW (Gregg Co.) *US 80, 7.7 mi. W*
Cherokee Trace
In 1821 near this site, Cherokee Indians blazed a trail from near Nacogdoches, Texas, to their home reservation at White River, Ark. They slashed trees, cleared path, planted "Cherokee" roses, and established camps at springs.

Used by Sam Houston, friend of the Cherokees, on his move to Texas; by David Crockett, other soldiers of the Texas Revolution, and thousands of immigrants.

After June 1839, when Texas settlers drove the Cherokees out of the state, the Indians departed over this trail; others traveled it for years thereafter. (1967)

LONGVIEW (Gregg Co.) *US 80 near W city limits*
Longview
Named for "long view" from rock hill when in 1870 surveyors laid off townsite. Incorporated June 24, 1871. Became county seat of Gregg County, and railroad, agricultural and lumber center.

Early home of Governors Thos. M. Campbell and James S. Hogg.

Since nearby 1931 Lathrop Well discovery extended East Texas oil field—world's largest—has become oil, financial, industrial, medical, cultural, religious hub.

Home of Letourneau College, combination technical school and industrial plant, producing some of the world's largest equipment. (1965)

LONGVIEW (Gregg Co.)

IH 20 at FM 2087, 3½ mi. W

Old Fredonia Townsite

Founded by Haden Edwards, a land grantee who contracted in 1825 with Mexican Government to establish 800 families of settlers in East Texas. A later misunderstanding with Mexico caused him to organize famous Fredonian Rebellion, and flee to the U.S. in 1827 in failure.

Town of Fredonia prospered, however. It was important ferry crossing and river port. Had 40 or 50 buildings, including homes, 3 warehouses (mainly for cotton), and a brick kiln. After the Civil War, post office was given up. Bypassing by railroad caused abandonment of town about 1870.   (1967)

LONGVIEW (Gregg Co.)

US 80 at FM 1403, W city limits

Rockwall Farm

Colonial mansion built in 1854, 50 yards north. Overnight stop on W. T. Brooks' stageline from Monroe, La., to Tyler via Pine Tree and Earpville post offices, both now in city of Longview.

Slaves hewed lumber and made chimney bricks on site. First floor partitions folded away, making big ballroom for square dancing, fiddlers' contests. Favorite game table upstairs was black walnut coffin made for first owner, Thomas Harris.

Last owners, J. Roy Sparkman and J. Jack Castleberry families, restored, opened to visitors. House burned in 1952.   (1964)

LOPEÑO (Zapata Co.)

US 83

Old Lopeño

Development of this area began about 1749 when Col. José de Escandón began bringing colonists to establish permanent settlements along Mexico's northern frontier. When parcels of land were granted to the colonists by the Spanish government in 1767, Ysabel María Sanchez, widow of early settler and rancher Joseph López, was allotted more than 6,000 acres. The village of Lopeño that later developed on part of the land was named in honor of the López family.

During the early 1800s, part of the López land passed to the ownership of the Ramírez family, founders of the nearby village of Falcón. In 1821, Benito Ramírez built a combination home, fort, and chapel that later came to be called Fort Lopeño. Federal troops briefly occupied the fort during 1856 while in the area helping to ease border disturbances.

The general store established in Lopeño in the early 1900s by Seraffín Benavides served as the area's only supply point at the time. A post office as established in 1920, and in 1934 oil and gas wells were successfully drilled just outside the village.

When Falcon Reservoir was created in 1952, residents relocated their village to this site.

     (1984)

LORAINE (Mitchell Co.)

IH 20, 2.5 mi. SE, 1.3 mi. S off hwy.

D. W. "80 John" Wallace
(1860–1939)

Born of slave parents, Victoria County. At 15 became a cowboy. Rode from Old Mexico to Kansas.

In 1877, came to this county, riding for Clay Mann, whose "80" brand gave him name for rest of life. On Mann's advice, bought land; past 25, and 6'3" tall, went back to school. Left Mann's for own ranch, 1891. Eventually had fine cattle and crops on 12½ sections of land. Also oil was found on his property. Up to 74, still rode bucking horses.

Married Laura Owen; 3 of their 4 children became teachers. His interest in education caused a school to be named for him.   (1965)

LOS EBANOS (Hidalgo Co.)

FM 886 S at ferry crossing

Los Ebanos Ferry Crossing

Apparently this is an ancient ford. First recorded usage was by Spanish explorers and colonists under Jose de Escandon in 1740s on the Rio Grande. A salt trail led from here to El Sal del Rey (40 mi. NE). The ford was used by Mexican War troops, 1846; by Texas Rangers chasing cattle rustlers, 1874; by smugglers in many eras, especially during the American prohibition years, 1920s and 30s. The ferry and inspection station were established in 1950. Named for the ebony trees here, this is known as the only government-licensed, hand-pulled ferry on any boundary of the United States.   (1974)

LOTT (Falls Co.)   *SH 320 & Judge R. W. Bailey Dr., NW corner*
Lott
Located on a straight line from Cameron to Waco, this site was the natural choice for development of a new town along the San Antonio and Aransas Pass Railroad in 1889. The Texas Townsite Company bought land from area pioneers Captain and Mrs. George H. Gassaway, who had purchased 7,000 acres in 1871. The railroad was given a right-of-way, and development began on a town, named in honor of railroad president Uriah Lott (1842–1915).

As the construction crew worked to complete the rail line, businesses sprang to life in the new town. A post office was established, and the city was incorporated in a November 1890 election. City officers were elected in December, and Albert B. Hemphill became the first mayor.

The Texas Townsite Company donated land to the town for a school and churches. the first school opened in 1890, followed by churches of several denominations. Fraternal organizations were established, and the Lott volunteer fire department was organized in 1895.

Following the completion of the railroad, Lott experienced a time of rapid growth. Although the railroad route closed in 1949, the town flourished.   (Texas Sesquicentennial 1836-1986)

LOTT (Falls Co.)   *SH 320, 8 mi. SW*
Church of the Visitation
German natives who settled originally in Colorado County came here in 1879 looking for better land. Pleased with the soil and location, they brought their families and immediately purchased 100 acres for a church and school. The earliest mass was said in 1882 in the home of the first settler, Theodore Rabroker. The original church building, completed in February 1884, was destroyed the following May by a terrible storm. The congregation rebuilt the structure by July.

Large numbers of German-American Catholic families moved into the area. Westphalia was named after the province from which the early settlers came. Visiting priests served until 1893 when the Rev. Michael Heintzelmann was assigned as the permanent pastor. He led the congregation for the next 36 years. In 1895, with A. Fuchs of Waco as the designer and contractor, the present church house was completed. The stones were shipped by railroad from Muldoon, Texas, to Lott (8 mi. NE) and then hauled here by wagon. The central church area forms a Latin cross. For safety in storms, six inches of sway was built into the bell towers. The original-design stained glass windows are very rare and priceless. This is one of the largest wooden church buildings in the state.   (1978)

LOTT (Falls Co.)   *SH 320, 9 mi. S*
Homesite of Theodore Rabroker
Founder of Westphalia Community
In 1866, Theodore Rabroker (1835–1905) and his wife Mary Ann (Brucktrops) (1836–1886) immigrated from Westphalia Province, Germany. They lived for a time in Pennsylvania and Iowa. In 1877, while moving to Frelsburg, Colorado County, Rabroker saw the fertile land in this area and visualized a German-Catholic community here. In 1879, he and his wife and three children became the first settlers. In 1881, Rabroker purchased 271 acres from William Neyland and became Neyland's land agent, encouraging Frelsburg families to come here. Rabroker provided a place for prospective residents to live until they bought property. Only German-Catholics were invited to settle within a five-mile radius; this resulted in strong community traditions.

The Rev. John Lauth celebrated the first mass in 1882 in the Rabroker home (400 yds. W). The residence served as the center for village religious and civic activities until a church building was completed in February 1884. After a storm destroyed the structure in May, Rabroker led efforts to erect a new church edifice, completed in July 1884.

After his first wife died, Rabroker married Theresa Halfman (1854-1932) and they had six children. The Rabroker home was destroyed by fire in 1975.   (1979)

LOVELADY (Houston Co.)   *SH 19, at park*
Town of Lovelady
Founded by Houston & Great Northern Railroad investors as line was built through grant of Cyrus Lovelady, near communities of Nevil's Prairie, Pennington, and Weldon. Post office opened on Nov. 8, 1872. Town soon had livery stables, stores, blacksmith shop, and hotels, prospering as market and shipping point. By 1876 day school and Sunday School were held in a log house. A two-story structure was shared 1881–1888 by Baptists and Lovelady Lodge No. 539, A. F. & A. M.

Churches of other faiths were built later. The town, incorporated 1927, is now center for ranching, pulpwood production. (1972)

LUBBOCK (Lubbock Co.) — *US 82, entrance to Mackenzie State Park*
General Ranald Slidell Mackenzie
Born in New York City on July 24, 1840, Mackenzie attained the rank of major general during the Civil War. On February 25, 1871, at Fort Concho, Texas, he assumed command as colonel of the 4th Cavalry, which soon became the finest regiment in the army.

He commanded three expeditions into this region against the Indians. The first, in 1871 against the Comanches, was unsuccessful; but in 1872 he found two feasible routes across the vast, hitherto unexplored Llano Estacado; and on September 29, he defeated the Comanches on the north fork of the Red River.

After a successful raid into Mexico in 1873, he commanded three of five columns of army troops in a final campaign against the Comanches, Kiowas, and southern Cheyennes; and on September 28, 1874, he surprised and destroyed three of their villages in the depths of Palo Duro Canyon, also capturing 1,424 horses and mules in the engagement. Left without food, shelter, supplies and horses, the Southern Plains tribes then submitted to life on the reservation, thereby opening Western Texas to white settlement.

Later promoted to brigadier general, Mackenzie died in New York, January 19, 1889, and was buried in West Point Cemetery. This park is named in his honor. (1968)

LUBBOCK (Lubbock Co.) — *US 84, NW city limits*
Lubbock
Founded 1891. Named for Col. Thomas S. Lubbock, Texas Republic soldier and Civil War hero.

Incorporated 1909. Commercial-marketing-processing heart of a mechanized-irrigated cotton, grain and cattle area.

Home of Texas Tech, Lubbock Christian College, West Texas Museum, Mackenzie State Park.

LUBBOCK (Lubbock Co.) — *US 84, approx. ½ mi. NW of Loop 289 overpass*
Lubbock Lake Site
This bend in the Yellowhouse Canyon has seen the passing of many from the time of the prehistoric mammoth-hunting Llano culture of 12,000 years ago. An archeological site of great importance lies in the bottom of this valley; here is recorded the evidence of periodic visits by nomadic hunting groups and Plains Indians. Springs and water holes made this spot a favored hunting and camping site in prehistoric and early historic times, but it is noted mainly for providing the first radio-carbon date on the Folsom Culture of 10,000 years ago and the association of man-made artifacts with bones of extinct mammoths, horses, bison, and camels.

Some historians think Coronado passed here in 1541 and Spanish expeditions coming from Santa Fe to the Concho River looking for fresh-water pearls passed this way in the middle 1600s. Later visitors were buffalo hunters and Indian fighters in the 1870s.

A general store—first commercial building in the area—was built here about 1880 by George W. Singer. Patronized by ranchers, cowboys, and dwindling numbers of buffalo hunters and friendly Indians, Singer's became a post office in 1884 and a widely known landmark by 1885. The first building burned, 1886. (1970)

LUBBOCK (Lubbock Co.) — *US 87 directly across from entrance to Lubbock Country Club*
Site of Old Lubbock
A predecessor of present Lubbock, this area was, in 1890, a subject of heated dispute by three factions (led by W. D. Crump, W. E. Rayner, and Frank Wheelock) that vied in the founding of the county seat.

Unlike most county seat debaters in Texas, though, these men had no long-established town to support. Their main interest was in organizing the county.

In the course of the rivalry, the groups founded two settlements. The Crump faction, later joined by the Wheelock group and several financial backers, started "Old Lubbock" at this site. Called "North Town" because it was located north of Yellow House Canyon, the site took in section 7, Block A, bounded by the present streets of Quirt, Ash, Erskine, and Kent.

The site soon attained a population of about 50 and boasted a reported 37 buildings, including the most historic one in the county: the Nicolett Hotel.

Rayner's rival settlement south of the canyon was named "Monterey" and was popularly called "South Town."

Surprisingly, though, the factions did not reach the permanent hostility common to such disputes. On December 19, 1890, they united in a compromise unique in West Texas history; and as a result, the city of Lubbock was founded on the site where it now stands. (1968)

LUBBOCK (Lubbock Co.) — Loop 290 at US 84
Site of G. W. Singer's Store
(1877–1886)
"Old Man Singer" catered first to the buffalo hunter and then to the cattleman. He became the first postmaster in Lubbock Co. in 1884. Two military trails crossed here, one from Ft. Griffin to Ft. Sumner and one from Ft. Stockton to Ft. Elliott. Aside from Estacado this was the only store on the South Plains for several years. R. C. Burns

LUBBOCK (Lubbock Co.) — Loop 289 & US 84
The Free Range Era of Ranching
Northwest Texas, 1878–1885
After Indians and buffalo were removed in 1870s, several hundred cattlemen with small herds came to rolling plains near site of later Lubbock, to graze free range. Vital natural water sources were found east of the caprock, where springs and streams were fed from the Ogallala formation of the High Plains.

Here, with good years and rising prices, the free rangers prospered until 1884, when syndicates began purchasing land and enclosing large blocks with barbed wire. Free range men had to sell their herds to the syndicates or move farther west.

The Spur Ranch alone acquired over 500,000 acres of land and bought cattle and brands from 37 of the free rangers. Similar ranches were developed by the Curry Comb, Ioa, Jumbo, Long S, Magnolia, Matador, Pitchfork, Square and Compass, T Bar and Two Buckle interests. By 1885, all free range operations were transformed into large, enclosed ranches.

Some free rangers exchanged cattle for stock in syndicates, others were employed by syndicates, and a few moved to Arizona, New Mexico or Wyoming. A few—including the Edwards, Long, and Slaughter families—acquired land and became sizable operators. (1970)

LUBBOCK (Lubbock Co.) — SH 114, W of Loop 289
Carlisle Cemetery
The pioneer Carlisle community was named for W. Augustus "Uncle Gus" Carlisle (1849–1920), who settled here with his wife Lizzie (Spikes) (d. 1914) in 1890. A cattleman and a prominent landowner, Carlisle made significant contributions to the development of the area, including a donation of land for a school. In 1918, he set aside this part of his property for use as a public cemetery. It was first used for the burial of George W. Wood (b. 1879), a victim of the 1920 influenza epidemic. Other graves include those of pioneers, area settlers and early leaders of Carlisle. (1983)

LUCKENBACH (Gillespie Co.)
FM 1376, 10 mi. SE of Fredericksburg
Luckenbach School
In 1855, pioneer area settler Peter Pehl deeded a two-acre tract of land at this site for the construction of a schoolhouse to serve the Luckenbach School District. A log building, it was used until 1905, when the present native limestone schoolhouse was completed. Herman Toepperwein was the first teacher in the log building. The Luckenbach school remained in operation until 1964, when it was consolidated with the Fredericksburg District. (1982)

LUFKIN (Angelina Co.) — US 69, .5 mi. S
Angelina County
Created and organized in 1846. Originally a part of Nacogdoches county. Bears the name of the river traversing the region. The following towns have served as the county seat: Marion, 1846–1854; Jonesville, 1854–1858; Homer, Feb. 3–May 17, 1858; when its name was changed to Angelina, 1858–1890; Lufkin, 1890. (1963)

LUFKIN (Angelina Co.)   *US 69, 6 mi. SE*
Site of the Town of Homer
Also known as Angelina. Third county seat of Angelina County, 1858-1890.   (1964)

LUFKIN (Angelina Co.)   *US 69, 12 mi. SE*
Site of the Town of Jonesville
Second county seat of Angelina County, August 22, 1854–May 19, 1858.   (1964)

LUFKIN (Angelina Co.)   *SH 103 (1903 Atkinson Dr.),*
                                                   Texas Forestry Assn. grounds
Equipment Typical of Early
Texas Logging
One of last ox-drawn or mule-drawn carts skidding logs to railroad from the forests. Built 1950 for W. T. Carter & Brother, a lumber firm, and replaced 1951 by tractor-powered equipment, this slip-tongue, high wheel cart is a relic of early logging methods.   (1972)

LUFKIN (Angelina Co.)   *SH 103 (1903 Atkinson Dr.),*
                                                   Texas Forestry Assn. grounds
Machinery from Early East Texas
Logging Railroads
Steam Locomotive and Tender No. 3 were bought 1908 by Carter-Kelley Lumber Co., for use in building a sawmill at Manning (about 18 mi. S); then in railroad building, logging, and passenger and freight hauling schedules.

The 1906 wood-burning steam loader was also used by Carter-Kelley in building Manning Mill, and later served on "portable" logging railroads. Its cables could skid logs to tracks from distances of 300 to 500 feet.

Carter-Kelley merged (1930s) with W. T. Carter & Brother. This equipment was retired in 1950s.   (1972)

LUFKIN (Angelina Co.)   *US 69, 1 mi. N*
Kurth Home Awarded
The Texas Historical Building Medallion
Built by Joseph Kurth, who founded the oldest lumber company in Texas still in continuous operation.

LUFKIN (Angelina Co.)   *US 59, City Service Club Park*
City of Lufkin
Founded 1882. Soon became a thriving sawmill community. Named for E. P. Lufkin, chief of crew that surveyed railroad through town. Has been county seat of Angelina County since 1892. Now a regional manufacturing and commerce center. Products include paper and wood products, oilfield pumps, trailers, and foundry castings.   (1970)

LUFKIN (Angelina Co.)   *US 59, 4 mi. N at inter. with CR 110*
Redland Baptist Church
Liberty Baptist Church, established in the Redland community in 1859, became Redland Baptist Church after reorganizing in 1895. Worship services were held in a local schoolhouse until 1924 when the congregation built its first sanctuary. A new church building was erected in 1939, and in 1942 the first full-time pastor was called. Growth in church membership resulted in the construction of new facilities in 1960 and a larger sanctuary at this site in 1976. Redland Baptist serves the community with a variety of programs and supports a wide range of missionary work.   (1994)

LUFKIN (Angelina Co.)   *SH 103, 3 mi. E*
Southland Paper Mills, Inc.
First plant to turn southern pines into newsprint, mill here revolutionized paper industry in the Southern United States. Seeking local paper rather than foreign supplies, Southland was incorporated in 1938 and began operations, 1940. Its mills made possible use of southern pine (earlier rejected for newsprint because of its high resin content).

In 1942, additional facilities were built to supply bleached pulp.

Success of this pioneer complex gave Texas an avenue for aiding world in supply of vital paper. (1968)

Oldest church in Caldwell County. Organized in 1848, with J. Isaac, pastor. Building erected in 1850; hand-hewn oak frame was morticed with pegs; lumber hauled from Port Lavaca. Land for church and adjoining cemetery was donated in 1857 by John H. Hargis and Thomas L. Burkhead. (1973)

LUFKIN (Angelina Co.) SH 103, 17 mi. E
Ewing

The boom town of Ewing stood for two decades on the west bank of the Angelina River. Named for plantation owner James A. Ewing, the town was located near a rail line and virgin hardwood forests. In 1919, H.G. Bohlssen purchased a 100-acre tract of land and built a saw mill. A company town, Ewing grew rapidly and at its peak contained a post office, commissary, church/school, boarding house, and a population of 850.

After many men left to serve in World War II, or in war related industries, the mill closed in December 1944. (1997)

LUFKIN (Angelina Co.) US 59, 9 mi. N near Angelina River Bridge
Don Joaquín Crossing on Bedias Trail

Used by Indians, explorers, traders, and missionaries, this trail ran from Bedias Indian camps on the lower Trinity River to Spanish missions near Nacogdoches. Don Joaquín de Orobio y Basterra, captain of the presidio at La Bahia (present Goliad), led reconnaissance troops along trail in 1746 and gave his name to the Angelina River Crossing. Italian born trader Vincente Michiuli owned a large ranch near the crossing before 1800. Bedias Trail was important in Angelina County's development. Railroads and major highways later followed the trail's route. (1979)

LUFKIN (Angelina Co.) SH 94 and Ellis Street
Lufkin CCC Camp

Created by President Franklin Roosevelt and approved by an Act of Congress in 1933, the Civilian Conservation Corps (CCC) provided youth employment programs during the Great Depression. The Lufkin CCC Camp, located near this site from 1933 until 1942, was administered by the Texas Forest Service. Young men helped to build roads and bridges, string telephone lines, and plant trees. The Lufkin CCC Camp proved to be instrumental in relieving unemployment but also helped revive the East Texas forest industry through its use of progressive forestry techniques. (1984)

LUFKIN (Angelina Co.) 805 E. Denman Ave., SH 278
First United Methodist Church of Lufkin

Margaret (Fullerton) Abney, born in Alabama in 1829, joined the Methodist Church with her family at a camp meeting held at nearby McKendree Campground in 1863. Because the nearest Methodist church was ten miles away, Mrs. Abney held Bible study meetings in her home on Sunday afternoons. This group of Abney family and friends formed the nucleus of the membership of the Methodist Episcopal Church, South, when it organized a Lufkin congregation in 1882. One of eight churches in the Homer circuit, the congregation met once a month in a local school building to hear the sermons of the Reverend H. H. Vaughan. In 1884 a 200-seat frame church building was erected in downtown Lufkin on land donated by the railroad. The building was shared with local Presbyterians and Baptists. By 1891, membership had grown to 100 and the pastor held services twice a month. Ten years later, the membership numbered 286 and the pastor was serving full-time. Completed in 1905 at a cost of $14,750, a new sanctuary seated more than 800 people. The church prospered, requiring an educational building by 1928. Despite the difficult times of the Depression era and World War II, the congregation continued to grow, and the church was relocated to Denman Avenue in 1959. By 1978, when the congregation celebrated the 100 years since Mrs. Abney began her Sunday School, the church complex included six buildings. The First United Methodist Church of Lufkin continues an active tradition of community and missionary service. (1998)

LUFKIN (Angelina Co.)
First St. and Frank Ave. (SH 94)
Lufkin Telephone Exchange
Telephone service in Lufkin began in 1898 when Dr. Alexander Madison Denman and his friend Judge Edwin James Mantooth strung telephone wires between their offices. The system was so popular that the pair soon formed the Lufkin Telephone Exchange with partner Eli Wiener, operating from offices on this site. In 1908 they contracted with the Southwestern Telegraph and Telephone Company to provide long distance service. The company grew as rapidly as telephone technology itself, eventually acquiring the telephone exchanges of a large portion of East Texas. In 1985 the corporation was reorganized as the Lufkin-Conroe Telephone Exchange.
(1998)

LULING (Caldwell Co.)
US 183 N, Blanche Sq.
William Johnson Cabin
The Rev. William Johnson (1822–1889), farmer and Baptist minister who came to Texas in 1833, built this shotgun-style cabin near Tenney Creek (11 mi. NE of Luling) in 1870s. Family included five children. His son, W. E. (Billie) became a physician in Tilmon.

Since 1893 the Jeff Connolly family has owned Johnson's land. T. B. Coopwood, M.D., used cabin as office in late 1890s. Mr. and Mrs. Jeff Connolly donated structure in 1972 to be relocated here.
(1973)

LULING (Guadalupe Co.)
US 90 right-of-way, 3 mi. W
San Marcos Primitive Baptist Church
The San Marcos Primitive Baptist Church, so named because of its proximity to the San Marcos River, was organized in 1853 at the home of George Daniels, who also served as the congregation's first pastor. The five charter members of the church were William Baker, Vashti Baker, Hannah Daniels, I. D. Owen, and Sylvanna Daniels.

George Daniels served as pastor until 1862, when James Milton Baker (1831–1910) began his 48-year service as minister of the San Marcos Church. A native of Alabama, Baker was the son of charter members William and Vashti Baker. The family had come from Alabama to Texas in 1852 and had settled in this area during the following year.

The first church building and early records of the church were destroyed in a flash flood that probably occurred in 1869 or 1870, but the congregation continued to meet. In 1886, J. M. Baker deeded land at this site for the church and cemetery.

In 1930, the San Marcos Primitive Baptist Church moved to Luling (3 mi. E) but continued to meet here occasionally until 1970. This historic site serves as a reminder of the heritage of the Luling congregation.
(1985)

LUTIE (Collingsworth Co.)
US 83, 3 mi. N
Nicholson School
Once the center of a thriving agricultural community, Nicholson school was named for county judge Arthur Clyde Nicholson, during whose term the school was opened in 1915. As Nicholson school increased in enrollment, reaching a peak of 150 students in 1929, additional teachers and classrooms were added. Consolidation with other rural schools began in 1934 and was completed in 1937, when the last classes at Nicholson school were held. A concrete cellar near this site is all that remains of the original school property.
(1984)

LUTIE (Collingsworth Co.)
US 83 at FM 1439, just S of intersection
Site of Lutie School
The community of Lutie, named for early settler Lutie Gresham Templeton, traces its history to 1909. Two years previously, local citizens had formed the Pleasant Valley School about one mile northeast of the town site. Community leaders moved the school to Lutie in 1912, renamed it and added a room. A third room was added in 1929, and the school continued to serve area children until 1937, when it consolidated with the school in Samnorwood (4 mi. NW). Land where the school was located reverted back to the family of the original donor, John Henry Young, Sr. (1874–1950).
(1992)

LYONS (Burleson Co.)   *SH 36, on N approach to town, near Community Center*
Lyons
An 1878 railway work camp; in 1880 became town of Lyon's Station, named for site donor, W. A. Lyon. Soon had 3 cotton gins, an oil mill, many businesses. In 1894 hosted first auto ever seen in this county, with rides for the daring.
Now gateway to Lake Somerville Recreation Area.   (1968)

MADISONVILLE (Madison Co.)   *US 75 & US 190, 3.5 mi. N*
Madison County
Formed from Grimes, Walker and Leon counties. Created January 27, 1853. Organized April 4, 1853. Named in honor of James Madison (1751–1836), "Father of the Constitution," fourth President of the United States. County seat, Madisonville.

MADISONVILLE (Madison Co.)   *SH 21, 15.5 mi. NE*
Robbins Ferry
First known as Paso Tomas (Thomas Ford) at the crossing of the San Antonio and La Bahia roads over the Trinity. Ferry established about 1821 by Joel Leakey. Named in honor of Nathaniel Robbins, who operated it many years. Acquired about 1852 by Elisha Clapp, whose descendants operated it until 1930 when Clapps Ferry Bridge was constructed.

MADISONVILLE (Madison Co.)   *SH 21, 15 mi. NE*
Site of Trinidad
Later known as Spanish Bluff. A fort and town as early as 1805. Captured by the McGee-Guitierrez Expedition in October, 1812. Near here the survivors of the Battle of the Medina were executed in 1813. Inhabitants of the town were butchered by order of the Spanish Commander and the town desolated.

MADISONVILLE (Madison Co.)   *SH 21, 1 mi. SW of courthouse on south side*
CCC Camp site
A part of the National Civilian Conservation Corps program of the New Deal era, Camp Sam Houston in Madisonville was a soil conservation camp. Begun in July 1935 and occupied by workers one month later, the camp provided jobs for 196 men. Members of the camp worked with area farmers and ranchers, demonstrating techniques of soil erosion control and pasture management. Covering a radius of 21 miles, CCC improvement projects included all of Madison County, as well as portions of Grimes, Leon, and Walker Counties. The camp was closed in 1941.
                                                                                   (1988)

MADISONVILLE (Madison Co.)   *SH 21, 4.5 mi. NE of Midway*
Nuestra Señora del Pilarde Bucareli
In this vicinity, at Paso Tomas on the Trinity, was the Spanish Town Nuestra Señora del Pilar de Bucareli (1774–1779).
Indian troubles had caused Spain to move Louisiana colonists to Bexar (San Antonio). These people, however, pled to return to East Texas, and secured the consent of Viceroy Antonio Maria Bucareli. Led by Gil Ybarbo (1729–1809), they built at the Trinity crossing a church, plaza, and wooden houses, and grew to a town of 345 people. But ill luck with crops, a few Comanche raids, and river floods sent the settlers farther east. Again led by Ybarbo, they rebuilt the old town of Nacogdoches, 1779.   (1972)

MADISONVILLE (Madison Co.)   *SH 90 right-of-way, 3 mi. S at Ranch Lane*
Site of Bullard Community
(3 miles east)
Alabama native Calvin Cullee Bullard (1824–1882) brought his family to this area from Hunt County, Texas, in 1867 and settled on 160 acres of land between Bedias Creek and Caney Creek. In their new home, he and his second wife, Zillah (Woodbury), reared three of Bullard's children from his first marriage and six of their own. Calvin Bullard had a blacksmith shop in the community that bears his name, and several of his descendants followed in his footsteps. The Bullards were also farmers, as were other families in the area, raising cotton as their primary cash

crop. Active beyond their community, Calvin E. Bullard served a term as county tax assessor-collector and Rube Bullard was a justice of the peace and five-term Madison County commissioner. A one-room schoolhouse was built in the Bullard community to address the educational needs of the neighboring children. It operated from 1890 until 1923. Worship services were held in the schoolhouse, as well as in an outdoor brush arbor when the weather permitted. Calvin and Zillah Bullard and many of their descendants are buried in the Bethel Cemetery in nearby Grimes County. Their contributions to Madison County history as early settlers and the founders of a community reflect the settlement patterns in this part of Texas and remain an important part of the area's history. (2001)

MALONE (Hill Co.) *SH 171 at FM 308*
German Settlers in Hill County
Germans first came to Texas in 1821, immigrated by the hundreds in the 1840s, and in the 1880s began to move into Hill County. Here land was made available by such earlier settlers as G. W. McNeese, the Savage family, A. D. Walling, the Whites, the Worleys. First to arrive (1882) were Fritz Lentz and Alex Radke. Later came families named Degner, Dietz, Gehrels, Gehring, Geltmeier, Hodde, Huse, Kaddatz, Kelm, Klein, Klinert, Krueger, Kunkel, Maas, Manske, Manthei, Meyer, Neumann, Piel, Reinke, Schronk, Schulz, Sonnenberg, Schmidt, Steffer, Strauch, and Zettler.

Pastor J. C. Rieger came from West (16 mi. SW) and held church services in settlers' homes. Salem Lutheran congregation was organized with 15 charter members on June 6, 1886, and erected a church building three months later. St. Peters Lutheran Church was founded July 1, 1906, at Walling with nine charter members. Religious leaders (some of whom also taught in the parochial school) have included Pastors Bartel, Finke, Gaertner, Heinmeier, Hodde, Hopmann, Kramer, Liefer, Manchina, Oertel, Seils, Walters, and Wunderlich.

By diligence and thrift, these people made garden spots of their farms; and with love of God, of family, and of music, they created a goodly heritage. (1974)

MANKINS (Archer Co.) *US 82*
The D. S. Dudley Show
Founded in late 19th or early 20th century as a wild west circus, the D. S. Dudley Show has been chief industry in Mankins for over half a century. Dick "Cheyenne" Dudley (born in 1896), a prize-winning bronco rider, bought the show in 1914, interrupted his career to serve overseas in the U.S. Army in World War I, came back and married Ruth Wolf of Mankins. Together they toured the Southwest with the show 8 months of the year, employing as many as 250 people, wintering here with their exotic animals. Younger generations of their family continue with the show. (1974)

MANOR (Travis Co.) *Loop 212*
City of Manor
In area first settled by James Manor (1804–1881), who came from Tennessee with Sam Houston in 1832, later returning for his family and a sister and brother. Until 1852, area was subject to Indian raids. Other pioneers included A. F., W. M., and James Boyce, Sterling Chamberlain, Dave Eppright, J. I. Haynes, Ed Harrington, A. C. and W. H. Hill, W. B. Howse, N. A. Rector, W. L. Shipp, E. D. Townes, and Joe, Bill, Sam, and Walter Vaughan. In 1854, a boys' school was opened and a Methodist church organized. Isaac Wilbahn (1857) gave site, and Parsons Female Academy (named for a leading contributor) was established, to become one of the celebrated schools of 19th century Texas. Its teachers included the Rev. and Mrs. D. H. Bittle, and T. C. Bittle; its students, T. B. Wheeler (1840–1913), Mayor of Austin (1872–1877), Judge of 12th District (1880–1886), Lieutenant Governor of Texas (1887–1891); and John C. Townes (1852–1923), Judge of 33rd District (1882–1885), 26th District (1888), and Dean of the University of Texas Law School (1901–1902, 1907–1923).

In 1871, James Manor donated right of way for the Houston & Texas Central Railroad. The town founded and named for him in 1872 was incorporated in 1913.

Cotton, king here for years, has been supplanted by cattle raising as base for the local economy. (1972)

MANSFIELD (Tarrant Co.)   *100 blk. US 287 at Alice Ponder Elementary School*

Earle C. Driskell

Born in Indiana in 1883, Earle Claud Driskell came to Texas with his parents in 1888. Educated as a lawyer, he started his journalism career in 1907 when he joined the staff of the Fort Worth *Star*. He soon gained recognition for his work as an advocate of a county bond program to improve the quality of local roads and highways. Largely through his editorial efforts, a major road bond package was passed in 1911 that set an example for other state and local highway programs. Driskell died of smallpox at his Fort Worth home the following year.

(Texas Sesquicentennial 1836–1986)

MARATHON (Brewster Co.)   *US 385, 42 mi. S near entrance of Big Bend Nat'l Pk.*

Comanche Trail

You are now traveling the Comanche Trail, blazed by Comanche Indians, en route from the Western Plains to Mexico, and traveled later by emigrants and soldiers. It extended south from the Horse Head Crossing of the Pecos by Comanche Springs (Fort Stockton) to the Rio Grande.

MARATHON (Brewster Co.)   *US 385 at US 90 E, nearby*

Colonel Lewis Given Harman
(1818–1902)

Typical of those who served the South and then moved into new counties of western Texas. Surveyor, Indian agent, soldier, legislator, justice of the peace.

Born in Tennessee. Moved to Texas 1838. Fought in Mexican War. Though 43 when Civil War began, immediately joined 11th Texas Cavalry, in swift 1861 campaign to place Confederate Forts in Indian Territory. Was post commander, Fort Arbuckle, I. T., June to August 1861.

Civic leader in Marathon after its founding in 1882. Had town's first Masonic funeral.

(1964)

MARATHON (Brewster Co.)   *US 90 at US 385, 1 mi. E at roadside park*

Denuded Ouachita Rock Belt

In highway cuts toward the east are excellent exposures of almost vertical rock layers—part of the Ouachita Fold Belt, a northeasterly trending, folded and faulted mountainous range which was uplifted about 275 to 290 million years ago. The deformation is comparable in age to the uplift that formed the Appalachian Range of the Eastern United States. The term "Ouachita" for this earth formation comes from the Ouachita Mountains of Arkansas and Oklahoma. (These were named by the Indians, whose words were rendered into written language by 16th century French explorers.)

In the hillside toward the northeast, the highly deformed strata are overlaid by almost horizontal layers of "younger" rock—formed about 135 million years ago. Erosion wore down the old mountains; and when the area was again covered by the sea, the horizontal layers were deposited on the sea floor.

Later uplifting earth movement comparable in age to the forming of the Rocky Mountain Range gently elevated this area, exposing it to erosional forces which have shaped the topography seen today.

This region abounds in vivid lessons in geology, and is under constant study by scientists. (1970)

MARATHON (Brewster Co.)   *US 385, 35 mi. S on Maravillas Creek*

Double Mills

A natural watering place in prehistoric times, as evidenced by artifacts found here. Used later by Indians and Spaniards on road from Northern Mexico.

As Maravillas Creek developed from a draw into water channel, old water hole vanished. About 1900 an early rancher, George Miller, dug two wells and put up twin windmills. After that, site was called Double Mills.

Became campsite for ranchers driving cattle and horses from Mexico or the Chisos Mountains to railroad at Marathon. Also for wagon trains of ore; and for U.S. troops on border duty. (1967)

MARATHON (Brewster Co.) *US 385, 1 mi. E*
Marathon
Fort Pena Colorado, the last active fort in this area, on the Old Comanche Trail, about 4 miles to the southwest was established in 1879.

Marathon was founded in 1881. Named by an old sea captain, A. E. Shepard, for the Plain of Marathon, in Greece, of which the hills here reminded him.

Cradle of West Texas cattle industry. Among the first noted ranchers here were Mayer M. Halff and brother, owners of the famous Circle Dot brand.

Original gateway to the Big Bend National Park. (1965)

MARATHON (Brewster Co.) *US 385, 12 mi. S*
Los Caballos
(In Core of the Ouachita Structural Belt)
Highly deformed rocks in the Ouachita Fold Belt, a northeasterly trending range, uplifted about 275 to 290 million years ago. The intricate folding is shown by whitish rock bands—called caballos (the Spanish word for horses)—exposed on both sides of this highway. The Ouachita Fold is comparable in age to the uplift that formed the Appalachians in the eastern part of the United States.

The northwesterly trending Del Norte-Santiago Range (southmost extension of the Rocky Mountains) forms the southwestern skyline. The rocks of this range were deposited in a sea that covered the Ouachita Fold Belt after erosion had reduced the highlands and a later submergence lowered the area. Santiago Peak (named for a local man who was killed by Indians and buried beneath the peak) is the high, flat-topped mountain to the southwest. It was once a mass of molten magma that cooled and hardened underneath the earth's surface and was uncovered by later erosion. The Del Norte-Santiago Range, uplifted and folded 40 to 60 million years ago, is not half the age of the Ouachita Fold. This is a remarkable fusion of "old" and "young" mountains—and is unmatched at any other site in North America. (1976)

MARATHON (Brewster Co.) *US 385, 38 mi. S at Stillwell-Heath turnoff*
Black Gap Wildlife Management Area
Black Gap, a natural cleft in the basalt ridge northeast of the Sierra del Carmen, frames the headquarters site of the Black Gap Wildlife Management Area.

Established in 1948, the "Gap" contains approximately 100,000 acres representative of the rugged Big Bend country—the typical arid, mountainous Southwest.

Owned by the people of Texas and operated by the Game and Fish Commission, the area is the scene of research and developmental work dedicated to the conservation and restoration of wildlife species indigenous to the region.

Mule deer, javelina, prong-horned antelope and scaled quail are among the principal game species managed. Work is in process to restore the bighorn sheep which, by the 1960s, were all but eliminated from Texas.

Scientific land use practices, designed to increase the yield of natural foods for wildlife, have been instituted by the commission. Water retention and utilization is accomplished by the construction of water impoundments, diversion dams and "push ups" seeded with native vegetation.

Research findings, through demonstrations and educational extension programs conducted on this Federal-State cooperative project, are available to surrounding landowners and others who are interested. Game surpluses produced on the Black Gap are harvested periodically by hunters under a controlled public hunt program.

MARATHON (Brewster Co.) *Ave. C North at US 90*
The Gage Hotel
This brick hotel building, designed by the El Paso firm of Trost and Trost, was constructed in 1926–1927 for Vermont native Alfred S. Gage. A cattleman, Gage founded the largest ranching operation in the Trans-Pecos, consisting of over 600 sections of land. After moving to San Antonio, where he became a successful businessman and banker, the hotel served as his Marathon residence and as the headquarters for his local cattle and banking interests. (1981)

MARBLE FALLS (Burnet Co.)
FM 1431, 1 mi. W
Granite Mountain
This 866-foot dome of solid pink granite, covering 180 acres, contains the largest quarry of its kind in the United States. This mountain, like all granite formations, was once melted rock similar to lava. As the molten rock cooled thousands of feet below the earth's surface, it hardened into large crystals of quartz, feldspar, and several dark-colored minerals.

Wherever strength, durability and beauty of finish are required, granite is a favored building stone.

The mountain was part of a grant made to Texas colonist William Slaughter. The site became famous commercially when a dispute arose in the 1880s over the type of stone to be used in the Capitol in Austin. The issue was settled in 1885 when Governor John Ireland resisted demands to use non-native limestone.

Following this decision, a special track was built to haul the granite to the rail line in Burnet. The stone was generously donated to the state by quarry owners G. W. Lacy, N. L. Norton, and W. H. Westfall.

Today, granite from the quarry here is shipped to all parts of Texas, the U.S. and foreign countries for use in monuments, shafts, jetties, and buildings. It has been used in the Galveston Sea Wall and in new state office buildings near the Capitol in Austin. (1979)

MARBLE FALLS (Burnet Co.)
US 281, N of Colorado River Bridge
Marble Falls Factory Site
The potential of water power on the Colorado River led town developer Gen. Adam R. Johnson and Farmers Alliance members to build a cotton mill on this site in the 1890s. The two-story stone factory, 300 ft. long and 100 ft. wide, was erected for the Marble Falls Cotton and Woolen Co., formed in 1892. New machinery run by hydroelectric power was installed by the Marble Falls Textile Mills Co. in the 1920s. Woolen goods, surgical gauze, and air conditioners were made here before the factory was gutted by fire in 1964 and razed in 1971. (1977)

MARBLE FALLS (Burnet Co.)
US 281 at Third St.
The Roper Hotel
George C. and Elizabeth Roper constructed this double-galleried hotel building about 1888. In the growing town of Marble Falls, the Roper Hotel became a popular stop for visiting businessmen and dignitaries. It was purchased by W. F. Smith in 1926 and later operated as the Central Hotel and the Francis House. His son R. O. Smith, who became manager in the 1930s, later served as mayor of Marble Falls. The hotel remained in the Smith family until 1963. (1981)

MARBLE FALLS (Burnet Co.)
US 281 at Ave. H
Marble Falls Depot
The town of Marble Falls was laid out in 1887. Texas Mining & Improvement Co. deeded land for a depot to Austin & Northwestern Railroad. This building was erected in 1893 and then Southern Pacific Railroad bought the line and property. Area residents gathered at the depot to visit and watch for the train. Excursions were offered and passenger service provided. Hogs, horses, cattle, cedar posts, cotton, pecans, and hides were shipped to market from here. In 1937, passenger service was discontinued and the depot was closed in 1968. It was moved to this site in 1976. (1979)

MARBLE FALLS (Burnet Co.)
US 281 at 819 7th St.
Governor O. M. Roberts' House
President of the 1861 Secession Convention and a Confederate officer, Oran M. Roberts (1815–1898) served as Governor of Texas from 1879 to 1883. After leaving office, he became a law professor at the University of Texas. He built this cottage at Third and Main Street and settled there after his retirement in 1893. Mr. and Mrs. H. E. Faubian bought the house in 1901 and moved it to this site. They altered the front porch and roofline, adding Victorian touches. (1978)

MARBLE FALLS (Burnet Co.)
US 281, 6 mi. N, then 2 mi. W on FM 1855
Crownover Chapel
Backbone valley's first public building, started 1859 on 7-acre tract donated that year by heirs of settler Jefferson Barton. Finished 1870, chapel was named for the Rev. Arter Crownover

(1810–1876), whose preaching of Methodist faith opened its use. Building soon also housed a school. The nearby cemetery was in use by 1872.

A school room was added but later removed. Chapel now bears original appearance, and is used as church and community center. Awarded Medallion Plate. (1972)

MARFA (Presidio Co.) US 67/90, 13 mi. E
Paisano Pass
Legend recounts that two Spaniards meeting here greeted each other as "Mi Paisano" (My Countryman). First known to history when Juan Dominguez de Mendoza camped here on January 3, 1684. Well known after 1850 as a point on the Chihuahua Trail, an emigrant road to California.

MARFA (Presidio Co.) US 67/90, .7 mi. E
Presidio County
Formed from Bexar County. Created January 3, 1850. Organized March 13, 1875.

So named for the early "Fortress Garrisoned by Soldiers." Erected for the protection of the Big Bend Missions. County seat: Fort Davis, 1875; Marfa since 1885.

MARFA (Presidio Co.) US 67, .7 mi. E
Presidio
Oldest town in Americas. At confluence of Concho and Rio Grande rivers.

A settlement for over 10,000 years. Site of first recorded wagon train crossing into Texas December 10, 1862. (?-date not legible). Headed by Antonio de Espejo. Marker placed jointly by Texas Society Children of the American Revolution, Texas Society Daughters of the American Colonists. (1961)

MARFA (Presidio Co.) US 67/90, 5 mi. E
Marfa Lights
The Marfa Lights, mysterious and unexplained lights that have been reported in the area for over one hundred years, have been the subject of many theories. The first recorded sighting of the lights was by rancher Robert Ellison in 1883. Variously explained as campfires, phosphorescent minerals, swamp gas, static electricity, St. Elmo's Fire, and "ghost lights," the lights reportedly change colors, move about, and change in intensity. Scholars have reported over seventy-five local folk tales dealing with the unexplained phenomenon. (1988)

MARIETTA (Cass Co.) 8 mi. NW, US 67 near county line
Stephenson's Ferry
Established about 1838 by Joseph A. Stephenson on whose grant it was located and whose name it bore. Remained in operation until about 1910.

MARION (Guadalupe Co.) SH 78, Cactus Garden
Founding of Town of Marion, 1877
The Galveston, Harrisburg & San Antonio Railway was chartered in 1870 to give interior Texas ready access to Gulf of Mexico ports. As the tracks proceeded west of the Guadalupe, Col. Thomas W. Pierce (1818–1885), major investor in the G. H. & S. A., bought land here near a country store and hotel. Platting a town named for his daughter, he obtained a U.S. Post Office on May 31, 1877. A public sale of lots was held on June 20, 1877. Within a year, Marion's 3-acre railyard was known for vast quantities of shipping. By 1900, public school, churches and other facilities were thriving. (1977)

MARLIN (Falls Co.) SH 6, 4.5 mi. S
Falls County
Created Jan. 28, 1850, from Limestone and Milam Counties. Organized Aug. 5, 1850. Named for Falls on the Brazos River which flows through the center of the county.

White colonization in the area pre-dates the Texas Revolution, but colonists fled on news of Santa Anna's assault, 1836. John Marlin, for whom county seat was named, returned and settled near present city. Growth was steady and the first railroad reached the county in 1870.

A center for farming, manufacturing and dairying. Curative artesian water gives Marlin recognition as a health spa. (1965)

MARLIN (Falls Co.)
125 Bridge St. (SH 7)
Falls County Courthouse
The Texas legislature created Falls County in 1850. The first courthouse was a log cabin, possibly located on this site. In 1855 the county seat (then Adams) was renamed Marlin, and construction was completed on what became the courthouse square. The second courthouse, built of native white cedar, burned about 1870. The third courthouse was completed by 1876 but was damaged in an 1886 storm. Houston architect Eugene Heiner drew the plans for a fourth courthouse, which was completed in 1888. It deteriorated quickly, and county officials began to seek funding for a new edifice. Work began on a fifth Falls County courthouse in 1938. A county bond issue for $130,000 was matched with a 45% Public Works Administration grant in 1938. The cornerstone was leveled by the Grand Lodge of Texas, A. F. & A. M., on July 4, 1939, and the building was completed by December. Much of the façade is Austin shellstone; Texas pink granite makes up the entry steps. The courthouse was designed in the Art Moderne style by architect Arthur E. Thomas of Dallas, and was constructed by San Antonio contractors Hill and Combs. Its symmetrical façade is dominated by a three-story central entry tower with key pattern stonework across the tower parapet. Among its unusual features are the massive shellstone entry surrounds and decorative corner pilasters. Arthur E. Thomas designed various other notable structures in Texas from the late 1930s to 1970, including other courthouses and projects for the Marlin Independent School District. The 1939 Falls County courthouse continues to serve as the center of county government. (2000)

MARLIN (Falls Co.)
SH 6, 4.5 mi. S
Indian Battlefield
At this site, near the pioneer home of George Morgan, a battle took place, January 16, 1839, between settlers in this region and Indians under Chief Jose Maria in which the colonists were defeated.

A treaty with these Indians made soon after brought comparative peace to this region. (1964)

MARLIN (Falls Co.)
SH 6, 5 mi. SE in roadside park
C.S.A.
General Thomas Harrison
(1823–1891)
Youngest of only trio of Texas brothers who all gained rank of General in Confederate Army. Lived in Falls County in 1850s.

Veteran of Mexican War and of Texas Frontier Defense. Rose in Civil War to command of Terry's Texas Rangers. Rode with cavalry of Gen. N. B. Forrest, who got "Thar fustest with the mostest." Fought at Shiloh, Murfreesboro, Ft. Donelson, Knoxville, Atlanta. Was wounded 3 times and had 5 horses shot from under him.

Elected district judge in 1866, was removed by reconstruction regime. Served as trustee of Waco University. (1965)

MARLIN (Falls Co.)
FM 712, 5 mi. SW, E bank of Brazos at site of falls
Falls of the Brazos River
When Anglo-Americans began to settle in Texas, the falls of the Brazos were located 2 miles southwest of here. At that time, the water fell about 10 feet over a rocky ledge. The falls served the Indians and early settlers as a trail landmark, meeting point, and campsite. In 1834 colonizer Sterling C. Robertson (1785–1842) established the town of Sarahville de Viesca at the fall line on the west bank of the Brazos, but it was abandoned in 1836 because of Indian hostilities. Later renamed Ft. Milam, the settlement lasted only a few more years. It was followed by the town of Bucksnort, begun in the 1840s on the east side of the river. The falls also formed a natural fording place for frontier travel; the rocky stream bed was the only hard-bottom crossing of the Brazos within 200 miles of the coast. The rapids marked the limit of the river's 19th century steamboat traffic as well.

Organized in 1850, Falls County was named for this distinctive landmark. Marlin became the county seat in 1851, and Bucksnort soon disappeared. The Brazos River changed course in 1866, moving the fall line to the present site and lowering the rapids to about 2 feet. Today a county park is located along both sides of the river at the falls. (1975)

MARLIN (Falls Co.)

SH 6, 5 mi. E at roadside park

**Site of Colonial Capital
Sarahville de Viesca
(1 mi. SW)**

Founded 1834 by Sterling C. Robertson, colonizer of a 100 by 200-mile area embracing all or part of 30 later Texas counties.

Situated near falls of Brazos River, where over a stony ford passed much traffic between east and southwest Texas, this was Robertson colony capital. An important Sarahville site was land office, where settlers applied for their titles.

Town was named for Robertson's mother, and for Agustin Viesca, governor of the province of Coahuila and Texas.

Target of Indian hostilities, Sarahville was abandoned, 1836. (1970)

MARSHALL (Harrison Co.)

US 80, 6 mi. E in roadside park

Harrison County

Formed from Shelby County. Created January 28, 1839. Organized June 12, 1842. Named in honor of Jonas Harrison, a pioneer statesman of New Jersey who came to Texas in 1820. A member of the first convention of Texas held at San Felipe in 1832. Died in 1836. Marshall, the county seat. Named in honor of John Marshall, Chief Justice of the United States Supreme Court.

MARSHALL (Harrison Co.)

SH 154, 5 mi. NW

Nesbitt Cemetery

Robert Jameison (1810–1886) and Nathan L. Nesbitt, twin brothers from Tennessee, settled this area in 1847. First grave here was that of Nathan's wife, Psyche ("Sackey") Walker Nesbitt (1815–1851). Robert's wife, Susan Adeline Nesbitt (1827–1901), who often nursed sick neighbors in the absence of a community doctor, donated this site for the family cemetery. After her husband died, she used her pension from his service in the Mexican War (1846–1848) to fence the plot. Nesbitt descendants, led by Julian Womack Nesbitt, established a trust fund for perpetual care of the cemetery in 1969. (1976)

MARSHALL (Harrison Co.)

US 59, N city limits

Marshall

Founded 1839. Named for John Marshall, Chief Justice of U.S. Supreme Court.

Supply, ordnance, medical, telegraph and military headquarters during Civil War. The Confederate capital of Missouri was located here.

Trade, industry, rail and historical center.

MARSHALL (Harrison Co.)

US 80, in roadside park

Marshall, C.S.A.

As a center of activity for the Confederacy west of the Mississippi, this East Texas town played a major role in the Civil War.

Headquarters of the Trans-Mississippi Department Medical Bureau and Postal Service were here plus two military hospitals and a commissary bureau. An ordnance bureau, depot, arsenal, and laboratory produced and distributed powder, pistols, saddles, harness and clothing.

Following the occupation of Missouri by Union forces, the governor and other officials of that state made this the wartime Confederate capital of Missouri from November, 1863 to June, 1865.

Three wartime conferences of governors and Confederate military officials of Texas, Arkansas, Louisiana and Missouri met here. One, in 1862, resulted in the establishment of a separate department for these states. In 1863 military and civil authority was consolidated under Gen. E. Kirby Smith, commander of the department. On May 15, one month after Appomattox, discussion of continued resistance or surrender resulted in a stalemate.

Prominent Confederates from Marshall were Edward Clark and Pendleton Murrah, wartime governors of Texas; Louis T. Wigfall, a "state's rights" leader in the U.S. Senate prior to secession and member of Confederate senate; Dr. James Harper Starr, Trans-Mississippi postal agent; and Brigadier-Generals Matthew D. Ector, Elkanah Greer, Walter P. Lane and Horace Randal.

This was the home of Lucy Holcomb Pickens, "Sweetheart of the Confederacy," the only woman whose portrait graced Confederate currency.

Rather than surrender at War's end, a number of high-ranking Confederate military and civil officials began an exodus from Marshall to Mexico.

A memorial to Texans who served the Confederacy.

MARSHALL (Harrison Co.)   *US 59, 8 mi. N*
John Barry Henderson Home
Rear wing built before 1861. Way station on route of Shreveport-to-Daingerfield stage. Main part built 1868–1871 by Henderson, who during Civil War had furnished beef to the Confederate Army.

Thick ground floor walls are of hand-cut local iron-ore rock (only 19th century native stone home in county). Frame second story has narrow cantilevered porch with ornamental railing.

Still in family of Henderson. Awarded Medallion Plate.   (1965)

MARSHALL (Harrison Co.)   *SH 43 at Pine Bluff Rd., 5.5 mi. NE*
Marshall-Shreveport Stagecoach Road
Before the Civil War (1861–1865), the stage road was the main transportation artery between Marshall and Shreveport, providing a link with New Orleans and distant markets. Extending northeast from Marshall, the stage road paralleled the later route of State Highway 43 and passed about 2.5 miles north of this site. Merging with the route from Jefferson, it turned southeast toward Waskom. In some areas, iron-rimmed wheels and horses' hooves trampled the narrow roadbed as much as 12 feet below the surrounding terrain. Travel over the dirt road was uncomfortable in dry weather and often impossible in rainy seasons.

Regular stage service was established by 1850, with three arrivals and three departures weekly from Marshall. Arrival of the stage was a major event. At the sound of the driver's bugle, townspeople rushed to meet the incoming coach. By 1860, Marshall had several stagecoach lines and a network of roads.

The Marshall to Shreveport line was operated by plantation owner William Bradfield and his son John. The stage continued to run during the Civil War, despite the shortage of drivers and horses. Use of the stage road declined after the war, when the Southern Pacific completed a rail line to Shreveport.   (1979)

MASON (Mason Co.)   *US 87, 18 mi. SE*
Homesite of John O. Meusebach, 1812-1897
(14 mi. SE, in Loyal Valley)
By 1848, German colonization reached area under direction of John O. Meusebach, who succeeded Prince Carl of Solms-Braunfels as colony leader and who signed treaty with Comanches allowing peaceful settlement of the land between the Llano and San Saba Rivers. He later retired here to a 640-acre farm where he died.

His colonists have influenced Texas through their ingenuity, thrift, and enterprise. They came seeking political and personal freedom and remained to create a unique culture through their blending of German custom with American necessity.   (1969)

MASON (Mason Co.)   *0.5 mi. N of courthouse on US 87 right-of-way*
Two Sheriffs of Mason County
A native of Kentucky, Thomas S. Milligan (1810–1860) moved to this area in 1855 and operated a change station for the stage line. He was also a rancher and supplied beef to the soldiers at Fort Mason. Shortly after Mason County was organized in 1858 he became the first elected sheriff. Two years later he was killed by hostile Indians near his home (1.6 mi. NW.). His grandson Allen Thomas Murray (1880–1929) became county sheriff in 1924 and like his grandfather died in the line of duty. He was killed by a bootlegger near this site in 1929.   (1980)

MASON (Mason Co.)   *US 377 at US 87, 1 mi. N in roadside park*
Old Fort Mason
Situated near a spring long used by Indians; built of stone quarried from Post Hill, fort helped protect Texas frontier from Indians. Colonel Robert E. Lee, stationed in Texas 2 years, commanded Fort Mason from Feb. 1860 to Feb. 1861. Here he made his decision as to his part in the Civil War, saying: "If the union is dissolved, . . . I shall return to my native state and . . . save in

defense . . . draw my sword on none." He left Fort Mason Feb. 13, 1861. In wartime he remembered "the enemy never sees the backs of Texans." (1965)

MASON (Mason Co.)
US 87, 1 mi. N
Crosby Cemetery
The first burial ground for the citizens of Mason and Koocksville, this cemetery traces its history to the 1850s. The oldest documented burial is that of Kate Lemburg, who died in 1856. Also interred here is Mason County's first sheriff, Thomas Milligan (1810–1860). The Crosby family purchased the property surrounding the cemetery in 1866, and it has been known as Crosby Cemetery since that time. Those buried in the cemetery include members of the Crosby and other pioneer families. It stands as a reflection of the area's heritage. (1988)

MASON (Mason Co.)
US 87/SH 29, 2 mi. N
Mason County
Created January 22, 1858, and organized August 2, 1858, this county was named for its most important settlement, Fort Mason.

Garrisoned intermittently from July 6, 1851, to March 23, 1869, Fort Mason was named for Lt. G. T. Mason of the United States 2nd Dragoons, killed in Mexican War action on April 25, 1846, near Brownsville. Fort Mason was one of a chain of posts situated a day's horseback ride apart, from Red River to the Rio Grande, for protecting frontier against Apaches, Comanches, other Indians. (1971)

MASON (Mason Co.)
Broad St. at Comanche Creek
Broad Street Bridge
In 1914, citizens of Mason petitioned the County Commissioners Court for a reliable means of crossing Comanche Creek, which separated north and south Mason. Initial construction bids were deemed too high and a second petition was presented in 1917. Because Mason had no railroad to transport large pre-fabricated building materials, the Alamo Construction Company crafted the bridge of reinforced concrete on site in 1918. Perhaps the last concrete truss bridge to remain in Texas, the Broad Street Bridge continued to support vehicular and pedestrian traffic in Mason in 1998. (1998)

MASON (Mason Co.)
Live Oak and SH 29
Mason House Hotel & Stage Station
Built in 1869–70 by S. F. (Lace) Bridges, the Mason House was a hotel and stagecoach stop on the San Antonio to El Paso Road. It was a popular stopping place, providing respite for many weary travelers and hearty meals for local residents. A tragic fire in 1900 resulted in the death of 23-year-old Annie Medlock. Eventually the building was converted into apartments, and some alterations occurred in the 1930s, including the addition of an exterior stairway. A number of historic features still remain on the property, including the original kitchen cistern and stone fences. (1999)

MATADOR (Motley Co.)
US 70, 1 mi. S in Virginia Walton Pk.
Motley County
Formed from Young and Bexar Territories. Created August 21,1876. Organized February 5, 1891. Named in honor of Dr. Junius William Mottley, 1812–1836. Signer of the Texas Declaration of Independence. Aide to General Rusk at the Battle of San Jacinto where he was mortally wounded.

Matador, the county seat.

MATADOR (Motley Co.)
SH 70 right-of-way, .5 mi. S near ranch headquarters
Matador Ranch
The Matador Cattle Company began as an open range ranch in 1879 when Henry H. Campbell, A. M. Britton, and three others bought range rights in this area.

In 1882 the ranch was purchased by Scottish investors, who formed the Matador Land and Cattle Co., Ltd. The ranch utilized one and one half million acres of owned and leased range in Motley, Floyd, Dickens, and Cottle Counties. In 1902, the ranch acquired the 210,000-acre Alamocitas Ranch in Oldham County. Additional pastures were leased in the Dakotas, Montana, and Canada. At its height the ranch owned 90,000 cattle and title to 879,000 acres of Texas land.

In 1913, the Quanah, Acme, and Pacific Railroad was built through the ranch in Motley County and the town of Roaring Springs was established.

General managers of the ranch were Britton (1879–1890), Murdo Mackenzie (1890–1911, 1923–1937), John MacBain (1912–1922), and John Mackenzie (1937–1951). The general manager's office was located first in Fort Worth and later in Trinidad and Denver, Colorado. Corporate offices were maintained in Scotland from 1882 until the ranch's liquidation in 1951. The ranch headquarters was purchased by Koch Industries, Inc. and became the Matador Cattle Co.

(Texas Sesquicentennial 1836–1986)

MATADOR (Motley Co.) US 70, 12 mi. W
Henry H. Campbell
(1840–1911)

A native of North Carolina, Henry Harrison Campbell arrived in Texas with his family in 1854. Following his service in the Confederate Army, he worked as a cattle drover. In 1879, with four other investors, he founded the Matador Ranch at Ballard Springs (ten miles southeast).

Campbell's wife, Elizabeth Bundy, joined him at the ranch in 1880. Refusing to live underground in a dugout, she insisted on camping in a tent until lumber could be hauled in for a two-room house. She served as hostess and nurse at the ranch, and later was post-mistress at Matador.

In its first three years, the Matador Ranch holdings grew to include 40,000 head of cattle on 100,000 acres of land, with an additional 1.5 million acres of free range rights. In 1882, the ranch was bought by a Scottish syndicate, the Matador Land and Cattle Company, Ltd. Campbell continued his association with the ranch, serving as ranch superintendent until 1890.

Henry H. Campbell led efforts to create Motley County in 1891. After serving two terms as county judge, he retired to concentrate on his ranch interests on Dutchman Creek. He died in Matador on May 23, 1911. (1964, 1988)

MATADOR (Motley Co.) US 70, E city limits
The Motley County Railroad

Pioneer carrier for cattle and farm goods. Chartered June 20, 1913, by 92 people of Motley and nearby counties. One man is said to have invested $50,000. Matador Land & Cattle Company also provided bonus funds.

Original directors were J. C. Burleson, A. B. Echols, J. N. Gaines, T. E. Leckie, I. E. Martin, R. P. Moore, J. D. Morriss, J. E. Russell, and A. C. Traweek.

Trains used cattle sweepers, as 8-mile track ran through unfenced ranches. Line joined Quanah, Acme & Pacific tracks near Roaring Springs. The M. C. R. R. ceased to operate in 1936.

(1970)

MATADOR (Motley Co.) US 62/70, 10 mi. E, in roadside park
Tee Pee City

At the junction of the Middle Pease River and Tee Pee Creek (8 mi. NNE), is the site of Tee Pee City. In the 1870s, traders established an outpost there to take advantage of the area's buffalo hide trade. The small community of picket houses and tents derived its name from abandoned tipi (tee pee) poles found along the creek. Charles Rath, an important figure in West Texas history, was among the partners in the original operation that resulted in the formation of the settlement, bringing in wagons, cattle, mules and dance hall equipment. Rath then continued south to establish his headquarters on the Double Mountain Fork of the Brazos, leaving management of the Tee Pee City camp to others. An 1877 account of the settlement identified one or two saloons, a dance hall, gambling hall and two-room hotel, as well as other businesses. The 1880 census listed 12 residents. The R.V. Fields and A.B. Cooper families arrived in 1879, the same year Tee Pee City's post office opened. By then, few buffalo remained in the area. Hunters had killed thousands, nearly depleting the southern herd. Cooper freighted supplies and ran a general store out of a dugout. The community supported a post office (1879–1900), as well as a school (1895–1902), but Tee Pee City was best known for its rowdiness, brawls and shootings, which warranted the attention of G.W. Arrington's Texas Rangers. In 1904, the Matador Land and Cattle Company bought the land and closed down the saloon, which had been off limits to Matador employees due to its wild reputation. A 1936 state monument placed at the townsite was moved here in 2002. Little remains at the original site, now on private land. (2002)

MATAGORDA (Matagorda Co.)   *SH 60, E city limits*
Dale-Rugeley-Sisk Home
CA. 1830. Has withstood many hurricanes. A cultural, social, political center. Home of A.C. Horton, 1st Lieutenant-Governor of Texas and governor 7 months; Rev. Caleb Ives, 1st rector of 1st Episcopal Church in Texas; W. L. Sartwell, partner in Ives-Sartwell-Academy; a leading churchwoman, Mrs. S. M. Dale; F. L. Rugeley, son of a Confederate leader; Robt. J. Sisk, pioneer in rice, oil and land development. Awarded Medallion Plate.   (1964)

MATAGORDA (Matagorda Co.)   *SH 60, Matagorda City Park*
Early Texas Freighting
Industry that moved goods to build, sustain distant settlements in 18th–19th century Texas. Teamsters defied Indians, bandits, and Texas weather to supply outlying forts and inland towns, which suffered if imports from the Gulf Coast, U.S or Mexico slackened.

One of few regular runs was Austin-Matagorda. Wagons left each city on 1st and 15th of every month, crossing Matagorda, Wharton, Colorado, Fayette, Bastrop, and Travis Counties. Houston was major Texas freight center because of access to Galveston Bay. George T. Howard and Charles Ogden were early freight men.

First carts, later wagons with 3000–7000 lbs. of cargo were drawn by 3 to 6 yoke of oxen or mule teams. "Grass rates" for oxen, grazed on way, were less than "corn rates" for faster mules. Early wooden carts were 15 ft. long with two 7-ft. wheels and a thatched roof. Their hubs were greased with prickly-pear leaves. For heavy loads, rough roads, the 2-ton "prairie schooner" was best. Caravans varied from 5 to 150 wagons.

When resting or attacked, wagons formed a round, protective corral and trained mules took their places instantly. Teamsters often banded together for mutual assistance. With coming of the "iron horse" in 1853, the freighter began slowly to disappear from the state. Early travel, transportation and communication series.   (1967)

MAUD (Bowie Co.)   *US 67, 1 mi. NE*
Site of Epperson's Ferry
At this crossing, constructed by nature and used by Caddo Indians, early French and Spanish explorers, and travelers over Trammel's trace, Mark Epperson before 1837 established a ferry used until the construction of a wooden bridge antedating the modern structure erected in 1924.

MAVERICK (Runnels Co.)   *SH 158, E city limits*
Maverick
Founded in the 1870s. Named for Samuel A. Maverick (1803–1870), who came to Texas 1835. Fought in the Texas War for Independence. In secession convention, 1861, he was made one of the commissioners to negotiate surrender of United States troops in San Antonio. In 1853 he had land in this important ranching area.

MAY (Brown Co.)   *US 183 right-of-way*
The May Community
Originally part of a Mexican land grant given to Empresario John Cameron in 1827, May developed in the 1870s when several pioneer families settled here. Baptists and Methodists quickly organized churches. A one-room school known as Old Swayback provided the first formal education for the children. Nathan L. May built a trading post in 1879 and became the town's first postmaster in 1881. By 1907, the village had a blacksmith shop, general store, newspaper, and bank. The early history of May climaxed in 1911 with the coming of the railroad.   (1981)

MAY (Brown Co.)   *18001 US 183 N*
May United Methodist Church
Methodists in this area were initially served by circuit-riding preachers. First to come to the region in the 1860s was the Rev. Hugh M. Childress, and worship services were held in private homes. In 1882, the Rev. Peter Gravis organized Mt. Zion Methodist Church, which later merged with the congregation at Byrds. Both of these communities, along with Bethel, Brooks, Clio, Gap Creek, Green's Chapel, Holder, Pleasant Valley, Rocky, Shrum, Verbena, Williams, Windham and Wolf Valley became part of the May charge. Brush arbor revivals were held each summer. The May Methodist Church was formally organized in 1886. Members gathered for services in nearby Verbena until 1890, when they began meeting in the newly constructed May schoolhouse.

Four years later, members built their own one-room church, which served until they constructed a new brick building with memorial stained glass windows in 1929–30. After 70 years of service, the church building was destroyed by fire in January 2000. Throughout its history, the May United Methodist Church has upheld the ideals and traditions of its pioneer founders. Despite the Depression, droughts, floods, wars and fire, the church has served its members and the May community for more than 100 years. (2001)

MAYDELLE (Cherokee Co.)
US 84, in front of the Texas State Railroad depot
Maydelle
In 1906, the Texas State Railroad built to this area for timber to fuel iron manufacturing at the penitentiary in Rusk. The branch prison established at the railhead was called Camp Wright. When Rusk native Thomas Campbell became governor, he persuaded the Legislature to extend the line to Palestine, where it met the I&GN Railway. The line brought new settlement to the Camp Wright area, and in 1910, residents platted the new town of Maydelle, named for the governor's daughter, who sang at the townsite's dedication. The town was an early center for cotton, timber and tomato production, but its population, like in other rural Texas towns, declined by the latter part of the 20th century. (2003)

MAYDELLE (Cherokee Co.)
US 84, 1 mi. N
Pleasant Grove Missionary Baptist Church
This congregation was organized in 1854 and represents one of Cherokee County's oldest Baptist churches. The Rev. G. W. Slover served as first pastor. The first church building, erected here on land donated by Green B. Hill, was replaced with a frame sanctuary after the Civil War. Sunday School and other church facilities have been added over the years. Several early church members and their descendants are buried in the nearby Pleasant Grove Cemetery. The church, whose past membership has included several area civic leaders, continues to provide spiritual guidance for the area. (1994)

MAYDELLE (Cherokee Co.)
US 84 right-of-way at FM 747, 4 mi. W
Mewshaw State Sawmill and Maydelle CCC Camp
In operation from 1908 to 1912, the Mewshaw State Sawmill at this site produced 35,000 board feet of lumber daily and was staffed by convict laborers from the nearby Rusk Penitentiary. The village of Maydelle later developed on the rail line which ran between Rusk and Palestine, and in 1933 a forest conservation camp under the auspices of the Federal Civilian Conservation Corps (CCC) was established here. The camp was closed in 1937, but the benefits of its programs are still evident in the I. D. Fairchild State Forest, now a wildlife sanctuary. (1991)

MAYDELLE (Cherokee Co.)
US 84 right-of-way, 6 mi. W at the Neches River
Ben Cannon Ferry
Native Americans and early Anglo settlers in this region forded the Neches River at this site called Duty Crossing for early settler Richard Duty. A significant link in the history of transportation across the river, the Ben Cannon Ferry is first documented in Cherokee County commissioners court records in 1848. Pioneer settler Ben Cannon operated the ferry until 1851. A toll bridge operated north of the ferry site from 1854 to 1924. The route of the Texas State Railroad crosses the Neches just north of the ferry site. (1991)

MAYSFIELD (Milam Co.)
US 190 and county road, 11 mi. E
Fort Sullivan
Early important trade and educational center. Established by Augustine W. Sullivan in 1835. River navigation extended to this point for many years. The Austin-East Texas and Houston-Waco roads crossed here. On this spot was located Port Sullivan College. Established in the early fifties, incorporated December 16, 1863. Destroyed by fire in 1878.

McADOO (Dickens Co.)
FM 264 at US 82, 3 mi. S
Marshall Clinton Formby, Jr.
Marshall Clinton Formby, Jr. (April 12, 1911–December 27, 1984) born in Hopkins County in East Texas. Marshall Clinton Formby, Jr., moved with his family to McAdoo (3 mi. N) when he was five years old and spent his adult life working for the betterment of this part of the state. Educated at Texas Technological College (now Texas Tech University), the University of Texas

and Baylor University school of law, Formby used his talents in a variety of business and public service opportunities. Marshall Formby maintained extensive farming interests in West Texas in addition to oil ventures and radio, newspaper and cable television enterprises. He served as Dickens County Judge from 1936 to 1940 and was elected to the Texas Senate, although his participation as a U.S. Army captain in the European theatre of World War II kept him away from the state capitol for much of his term. Formby continued his statewide public service as a governor-appointed member of the Texas Highway Commission in 1953–59, including two years as chair. During his tenure, he worked for the paving of Farm-To-Market roads and for the implementation of the Interstate Highway System in Texas. A member of the Texas Tech Board of Regents, he also served 12 years on the state's College Coordinating Board. Active in the Baptist church and in numerous civic organizations, Marshall Formby received many awards and honors for his service to his community, region and state. He died at his home in Plainview in 1984 and is buried in the McAdoo cemetery. (2002)

McALLEN (Hidalgo Co.) *351 S. Main St.*
Campsite of "The Fighting 69th"
Famed New York Infantry Regiment. Encamped in McAllen during 1916–1917 bandit troubles, guarding the border and preventing the smuggling of arms across Rio Grande to Pancho Villa. Tour of duty here seasoned the men for rigors of World War I, wherein regiment won undying glory in France. (1970)

McCAMEY (Upton Co.) *US 67, Santa Fe Park*
Adrian Building
Western bungalow. Built 1915, in Girvin, by R. F. Mayse, first merchant. Moved to McCamey, 1946. Mr. and Mrs. Hal Holmes gift. Awarded Medallion Plate. (1965)

McCAMEY (Upton Co.) *US 385, 12 mi. NW*
Castle Mountain
About 3,000 ft. elevation.
Since 17th century, a landmark in travel from Texas points to Mexico and California. According to tradition, named by Spaniards for resemblance to ancient castles. Has associations with stories of lost trains of gold and other treasures. (1966)

McCAMEY (Upton Co.) *SH 67, Campsite*
Early Humble Camp in Permian Basin
The world's largest complex of oil wells in the 1920s was developed in this area. Key to success of this vast petroleum field lay in finding ways to convey oil to growing fuel markets. First efficient transportation came in 1925 with the laying of the Humble pipeline from Kemper station, near Big Lake, to Comyn station (a distance of about 500 miles), to connect with existing Comyn-Baytown system.

Early camp for pipeline construction crews was built here 1926 when Humble extended its line west from Big Lake field. Camp's site led to growth of McCamey and building of a refinery. McCamey became important center of oil production and operation.

A constant flow of oil went through Humble's pipeline on its long journey to the Gulf Coast. Even with use of pipeline and railroad tank cars, more oil was produced than could be marketed. New practices had to be used to prevent overproduction and waste. Thus Humble pipeline became involved in the first voluntary proration in Texas, when in 1928 producing capacity of local wells was reduced to a level consistent with transportation facilities.

Today in Texas, Humble has 15,000 oil and gas wells; 9,545 miles of pipeline; and one refinery. (1967)

McCAMEY (Upton Co.) *US 385, 3 mi. NW at site*
King Mountain
Probably named for Guy King, rancher who drilled first water well on top of mountain about 1900. Elevation is 3,000 feet.

Part of an uplift in southern Permian Basin; associated with county oil fields. Many Indian relics have been found along the rim rock. (1968)

McCAMEY (Upton Co.)   *US 385 at Discovery Well Rd.*
McCamey
Founded 1926. Had 10,000 people in 1927. Named for Geo. B. McCamey, driller of discovery well that by 1964 had led way to opening of 31 oil and gas fields in Upton County. (Discovery well is 2.3 miles north of town.)

Center for horse, sheep, goat ranching. Has 5 parks. Home of Mendoza Trail Museum. (1964)

McCAMEY (Upton Co.)   *US 67, 5 mi. E*
Castle Gap
Castle Gap, famous early pass for southwestern trails, lies 14 miles northwest along the Upton-Crane County line. Through this mile-long gap between Castle and King mountains flowed the full panorama of Texas history—Indian, Spaniard, Stage and Trail Herd Driver, Settler, '49er. In prehistoric time Castle Gap was a landmark for nomadic Indian tribes and later guided the Comanches on their war trail into Mexico. The first white man to discover the pass was probably the Spanish explorer Felipe Rabago y Teran in 1761. Then came the '49ers in their frenzied rush to the California gold fields, to be followed by other, more permanent settlers. From 1858 to 1861 the famed Butterfield Overland Mail coaches rumbled through the pass on their 24-day journey from St. Louis to San Francisco, pausing briefly at the adobe-walled Castle Gap station for fresh teams. Then they were off again, fording into the sunset. By 1866 the Goodnight-Loving cattle trail was firmly established at the gap, funneling tens of thousands of brawling longhorn cattle to the northern markets. During this same period, legend holds that a treasure-laden aide of Emperor Maximilian of Mexico, fleeing the country when the regime collapsed, buried gold and jewels in the area. Dust of the pioneers settled long ago. Today Castle Gap slumbers peacefully, disturbed only by visitors, occasional treasure hunters and those who probe for ruins of the Butterfield station and the rapidly fading ruts of coach and wagon.   (1962)

McCAMEY (Upton Co.)   *US 67, 5.5 mi. E*
Rodman-Noel Oil Field
Discovered 1953. Initial well, about 2½ miles south of this spot, was drilled by E. G. Rodman and W. D. Noel as No. 1 Radford Grocery. It was completed January 13,1953, for a natural flowing potential of 960 barrels in 24 hours, from Grayburg formation and at total depth of 1744 feet. It is located 1980 feet from the south and west lines of section 1 of the Gulf, Colorado and Santa Fe survey in Railroad Commission District 7C.

The field has a number of wells completed for natural potentials in excess of 3,000 barrels a day.

The drillers Rodman and Noel were oil business veterans at the time they brought in this Upton County field. Already experienced in various phases of petroleum development, E. G. Rodman became an independent producer in Texas in 1938. W. D. Noel became an independent producer in Texas in 1940. Their interests extend into international exploration and other phases of oil development, including manufacture of petrochemicals.

Their opening of this field—which contributed substantially to the 1925–1960 Upton County total of 272,628,476 barrels of production—was made 28 years later than the great boom in McCamey.   (1964)

McCAMEY (Upton Co.)   *US 67, 7.5 mi. E at site*
Square Top Mountain
Named 1919 by students and professors making a geological survey for the University of Texas. The peak rises 450 feet above its base and may be part of King Mountain, 1.5 mi. W.

This pioneer landmark contains fossil shells 450 million years old from a prehistoric sea. (1967)

McCAMEY (Upton Co.)   *US 67, 8 mi. E at site, S*
Table Top Mountain
Round, flat-topped mesa rising 475 feet above its base; part of an uplift in Permian Basin, which was once a prehistoric sea.

The limestone-topped buttes and mesas in this area are remnants of rock that covered county 115 million years ago, but has now been mostly eroded.   (1967)

McCAMEY (Upton Co.)
SH 329, 7 mi. NW of Rankin
"Weir No. 1" Oil Well
Except for the original Yates Ranch gusher of 1926, most dramatic oil discovery in Upton County. Brought in December 6, 1961. West of this site 3.5 miles.

First quadruple completion in West Texas, called by American Association of Petroleum Engineers the most important development of the year 1961—and the most prolific discovery in many years. Drilled to depth of 12,432 feet. Plugged back at 9,925 feet. Produced from upper, middle and lower Strawn zones, and from the bend, with perforations in lower detrital gas zone. Contractor was Brahaney Drilling Co.

Discovery made by E. G. Rodman, W. D. Noel and Odessa Natural Gasoline Co., founded by Rodman and Noel, and affiliated with El Paso Natural Gas Products Co.

Rodman and Noel, who began their Upton County operations in 1940, have been responsible for numerous significant discoveries in the Permian Basin of Texas and New Mexico, and have led in the establishment of a vast petrochemical complex in Odessa. This utilizes in the making of such things as plastics, many petroleum by-products once scrapped as waste.

Such leadership and such wells as Weir No. 1 have enabled Upton County to remain for many years one of the outstanding production areas in Texas. (1964)

McCAMEY (Upton Co.)
US 67 at FM 305, 1.9 mi. SW
Bobcat Hills
(West of Highway)
Named for dens of lynx (bobcats) found here 1919 by a University of Texas geology team mapping the resources of the county.

These hills, cretaceous formations, are part of an uplift in the southern Permian Basin. Associated with this uplift are the oil fields of the county. (1967)

McDADE (Bastrop Co.)
US 290 & Loop 223
McDade
Laid out 1871; named for James McDade, Brenham lawyer. Became a thriving town, important freight center and early day stage stop. School-church built 1872.

Vigilantes (organized 1883) lynched 3 men on Christmas Eve, causing a shoot-out next day at the Rock Saloon (now a museum). (1968)

McKINNEY (Collin Co.)
SH 380, 3 mi. W
Site of Buckner
John (Jack) and Polly McGarrah and family came to this site from Tennessee in 1842. The third settler in present Collin County, McGarrah opened a trading post to barter for hides and furs. While in the act of building a family fort, he and his men had to defend themselves from roaming hostile Indians.

The Texas Legislature created Collin County on April 3, 1846, directing that its county seat, to be named "Buckner," would be no more than three miles from the geographic center. Buckner townsite was soon laid out here in McGarrah's settlement. On the Fourth of July, citizens met here and elected their first county officials. They also raised a military company for the Mexican War. On Sept. 21 there was an auction of Buckner town lots; on Nov. 25, 1846, the post office opened, with McGarrah as postmaster.

By 1848, it was noticed that Buckner townsite was outside the legal limits for the county seat. The legislature ordered another election and named the new county seat "McKinney," honoring early settler Collin McKinney, a signer of the Texas Declaration of Independence. Residents moved their homes and other buildings to McKinney (3 mi. E), and Buckner townsite reverted to agricultural land uses. (1978)

McKINNEY (Collin Co.)
US 380, 3 mi. W
Buckner Cemetery
The land surrounding this historic cemetery was part of a grant obtained by John McGarrah, a member of the Peters Colony who arrived in this area in 1843. McGarrah founded a trading post near this site, and soon the Fort Buckner settlement was established. It would later become the first county seat of Collin County.

David William O'Brien (1808–1885) came to Collin County with his family in 1857. He eventually acquired the part of the McGarrah Land which included this site. The Buckner Cemetery, which was established on the O'Brien Land, has also been referred to as O'Brien Cemetery over the years.

Although there may be earlier unmarked graves, the oldest documented burial is that of Franklin O'Brien (1851–1870). Many early pioneers of Collin County are interred here, including victims of a smallpox epidemic in the 1870s. According to local tradition, a Kiowa Indian named Spotted Tail also lies here in an unmarked grave.

The only physical remnant of the Buckner community, this cemetery serves as a reminder of the early history of Collin County. (1988)

McKINNEY (Collin Co.) *US 75 access road, 7.7 mi. N via Throckmorton Rd. Exit*
Governor James Webb Throckmorton
(February 1, 1825–April 21, 1894)
A doctor's son, James W. Throckmorton was born in Tennessee. He migrated with his parents to the Texas frontier in 1841 and settled near this site. At age 17, he became hunter and scout for his pioneer neighbors. He served in the Mexican War (1846–1848). In 1848, he married Annie Rattan (1828–1895) and built a home near McKinney.

Trained as a physician, Throckmorton disliked medicine and in 1851 entered law and politics. He served 1851–1857 in the Texas Legislature, where he promoted railroad building. Later he became attorney for Texas & Pacific Railroad. He was state senator, 1857–1861 and 1863–1865.

Although he upheld the right of secession, he was one of seven men who voted against Texas leaving the union at the Feb. 1861 Secession Convention. During the Civil War (1861–1865), he fought in the Confederate Army. Elected governor in the summer of 1866, he grappled with postwar problems of frontier defense and Federal military occupation. In July 1867, Gen. Philip H. Sheridan, commander of the 5th Military District to which Texas was assigned, removed Throckmorton from office as "an impediment to reconstruction" and named E. M. Pease provisional governor. Throckmorton continued his political career in the U.S. Congress, serving his North Texas district in 1875–1879 and 1883–1887. (1977)

McKINNEY (Collin Co.) *US 75, 2.5 mi. S*
Collin County
Formed from Fannin County. Created April 3, 1846. Organized July 13, 1846. Named in honor of Collin McKinney, 1766–1861 land surveyor, signer of the Texas Declaration of Independence, member of Congress, Republic of Texas, member of the Texas Legislature. County seat, Buckner, 1846–1848. McKinney, since.

McKINNEY (Collin Co.) *US 75, N city limits*
McKinney
Founded 1845 by Collin McKinney, a signer of the Texas Declaration of Independence.

In Civil War, Gen. J. W. Throckmorton (later a governor of Texas) organized McKinney's Co. K, 6th Texas Cavalry, an outstanding Confederate fighting unit.

Manufacturing, trade and hospital center.

McKINNEY (Collin Co.) *SE corner of Chestnut & Virginia (SH 359)*
1911 McKinney Post Office
Designed by architect J. H. Suttle, the 1911 McKinney Post Office is a characteristic and well-preserved example of an Italianate post office. The tile roof, ornamental columns, eaves and window configuration are common to the American post office after 1910. These elements and the three-bay arched recessed entry define the façade. The fourth post office to serve the area, the structure was deeded to Collin County by the federal government in 1959 and in 1982 became a Collin County museum. (1997)

McKINNEY (Collin Co.) *Courthouse Square, Virginia (SH 359)*
& Louisiana Streets
1927 Collin County Courthouse
Collin County was formed in 1846 and its only town, Buckner, was automatically selected as the county seat. To comply with state law, an election was held to relocate the county seat to the

center of the county. Only eleven people participated due to inclement weather, and when the vote was tallied McKinney was established as the county seat in 1848. The first courthouses in McKinney were modest wooden structures. A third courthouse was erected on this site during 1874–1875, and was opened for use in 1876. The 2-story Victorian structure was made of native limestone blocks with a steep mansard roof and a main entrance that faced east. The building's architect, often mistakenly identified as Charles Wheeler, was Charles Wheelock of Sherman. The much-celebrated courthouse on the square became a backdrop for parades and other events. The structure was overcrowded and in poor condition by the mid-1920s. Extensive exterior and interior renovations included the removal of the mansard roof and tower caps, as well as the addition of a third story and basement. Overseen by W. A. Peters of the Paris, Texas, architectural firm of Sparger and Peters, the work resulted in a Classical Revival edifice completed in 1927. Original features included tripartite windows with flanking double classical columns on the north and south façades. The new structure was commonly known as the "Temple of Justice," and continued to be the center of activity for city and county functions. It remained in service as a courthouse until 1979. The structure remains a fine example of 20th century Classical Revival design and a monument to Collin County history. (1998)

McKINNEY (Collin Co.)

Courthouse Square, between Virginia (SH 359) & Louisiana Sts.

Old Collin County Courthouse

Collin County was created from Fannin County in 1846. It was named for pioneer area settler Collin McKinney (1766–1861), a signer of the Texas Declaration of Independence. The first county seat was established at Buckner (2 mi. NW). In 1848 William and Margaret Davis conveyed 120 acres of land at this site for a more central seat of government, which became the community of McKinney. The first two courthouses in the new town were built of wood. In 1874 county commissioners approved plans for a more substantial courthouse on this site. Sherman architect Charles Wheeler designed the building and O.J. King served as general contractor. Constructed of stone from a local quarry (3.5 mi. NE), it was completed in 1876. A grand ball was held in the courthouse to celebrate the event. By the 1920s the courthouse was inadequate to meet the needs of a growing county. Extensive changes, including the addition of a basement and a third floor, were made in 1926–27 under the direction of architect W.A. Peters of Paris, Texas. The site of many political speeches and events, the building was used as a courthouse until 1979. It now serves as a historic reminder of the county's early development. (1982)

McKINNEY (Collin Co.)

SH 121 at FM 274 (Wilmeth Road) N of the NE corner

Site of Wilmeth-McKinney Homestead

Joseph Brice (J.B.) Wilmeth (b.1807) and Nancy Ferguson (b.1807) were married in Tennessee in 1826. They settled here on 320 acres of virgin prairie in 1846. They began to farm their land and soon built a grand two-story family home at this site.

Elder J.B. Wilmeth, along with pioneer settler Collin McKinney, established Collin County's First Christian Church at Liberty in 1846. J.B. organized McKinney's First Christian Church in 1848, and early worship services were held in his home. Between 1848 and 1887, the Wilmeth home also was the site of a free school taught by J.B. and his children. J.B. served on the commission that selected the Collin County seat and later served as district clerk and county judge, and in 1850 the Wilmeths' daughter, Martha, married Daniel L. McKinney, grandson of Collin McKinney. Following the deaths of J.B. and Nancy in 1892, Martha and Daniel lived in the Wilmeth home until Daniel's death in 1906. The homestead was next occupied by Martha and Daniel's son, John Brice, and his wife, Annie (Magers), until their deaths in 1968. Materials from the original Wilmeth home were used to build a new house here in 1941. The property continues to be recognized as an important site in early Collin County history. (1994)

McKINNEY (Collin Co.)

SH 5 & SH 121

Pecan Grove Memorial Park

This park is situated on property granted by the Republic of Texas to Samuel McFarland in 1845, only four years after the first permanent settlement in this area was begun by a pioneer from Tennessee, Dr. William E. Throckmorton (1795–1843), and his family. By the 1850s, when the first known burials occurred, R. A. Davis owned the land. The name of the spot was derived from a handsome stand of trees. Ownership by the public began in 1870 with the purchase of a

21.3-acre tract by Isaac F. Graves, I. D. Newsome, G. A. Foote, E. R. Stiff, and Thomas J. Brown. The original charter was issued in 1889 to Pecan Grove Cemetery Association, Inc., a private corporation. Additional land was purchased in 1892 and 1960.

The name "Pecan Grove Memorial Park," granted in a new charter in 1964, commemorates the courageous and compassionate pioneer men and women of this vicinity. One of these, Dr. James Webb Throckmorton (1825–1894), was a Texas legislator in the 1850s; became a Confederate brigadier general during the Civil War; was governor of Texas in 1866–1867; and was in the United States Congress intermittently from 1875 to 1888.

Pecan Grove Decoration Day is held every spring.   (1976)

McMAHAN (Caldwell Co.)   FM 713, 8 mi. W, then 0.25 S on
                                                       SH 304, at Delhi Community Center
Delhi

The earliest known permanent settlers in this area were Orrin L. and Susannah Winters and their extended family. By 1873, enough of a settlement existed to make application for a U.S. Post Office. Postal officials rejected the first name selected for the community, but accepted the second name, Delhi. According to local tradition, Delhi was the name of a traveling salesman who stayed in the area for a time dispensing patent medicines and providing entertainment for the settlers. John P. Reid served as first postmaster.

The first store in Delhi was in operation by the early 1870s in the home of Daniel T. Winters. The Delhi community experienced some growth in the 1880s with the founding of two churches, a school, and two cotton gins. Over the years, additional businesses, including a blacksmith shop, casket shop, and a syrup mill have served the community, and although the post office closed in 1929 and the public school consolidated with the McMahan District in 1947, Delhi remains a strong rural community in eastern Caldwell County. Many of its residents are descendants of the town's pioneer families.   (1992)

McNARY (Hudspeth Co.)   IH 10, 10 mi. E at site of replica, at "Tommy's Town"
Replica of
Fort Quitman
(Site of Real Fort, 5½ mi. SE)

In 1858 travel here was made so hazardous by Apache Indians and Mexican bandits that Fort Quitman was founded to protect stages and wagon trains.

The fort was given over to Confederates during the Civil War, but afterward became the center of efforts against the "Apache Napoleon" Victorio.

In 1877, disputes over rights to use salt deposits north of here led to the bloody El Paso Salt War. This caused cavalry patrols to be continued in the area even though the Indian menace was over and fort was abandoned earlier that year.   (1967)

MELVIN (McCulloch Co.)   US 87 and FM 503, 1.5 mi. NW
"1870's Cowboy-Indian Fight"
(Battleground 1 mi. N of Marker)

Near here in 1874 or 1875, 18 Indians attacked W. B. Brown and two comrades, spooking one horse and capturing bedrolls and grub, but sparing the men, who thankfully escaped. In the 1870s, when they were being driven off the range, capture of supplies meant victory to the Indians.

MEMPHIS (Hall Co.)   Heritage Hall Main and 6th St.
Hall County

Formed from Young and Bexar Territories. Created August 21, 1876. Organized June 23, 1890. Named in honor of Warren D. C. Hall 1788–1867.

Member of the San Felipe Convention in 1832. Second in command of the Texans at Anahuac, 1832. Memphis the County Seat.

MEMPHIS (Hall Co.)   SH 256, 12 mi. W
Shoe Bar Ranch Headquarters

On first ranch in Hall County, started in 1880s by pioneer cattlemen T. S. Bugbee and O. H. Nelson. This residence was built about 1884. A nearsighted owner, J. K. Zimmerman of Kansas City, was wary of surprise visitors, and put in only one outer door.

Adobe building bricks were made nearby. The tamped clay walls are 24 inches thick.

At this headquarters, citizens met on May 4, 1890, and organized Hall County's local government. Awarded Medallion Plate. (1962)

MENARD (Menard Co.) *US 83, 3.4 mi. N in roadside park*
Menard County
Formed from Bexar County. Created Jan. 22, 1856. Organized June 25, 1866. Named in honor of Michael Branaman Menard, 1805–1856.

Signer of the Texas Declaration of Independence, member of the Texas Congress, founder of Galveston. Menard, county seat.

MENARD (Menard Co.) *US 190, 1 mi. W*
Real Presidio de San Saba
Originally established on the San Gabriel River as the Presidio of San Francisco Xavier in 1751. Moved to the present site in 1757 as a protection to the Mission Santa Cruz de San Saba, known as the Presidio de San Lois de Las Amarillas, 1757–1761. After March, 1761, the name was Real Presidio de San Saba.

The stone building was completed in 1761. (1936)

MENARD (Menard Co.) *US 190, 1 mi. W, Celery Creek*
Arroyo de Juan Lorenzo
Name used by Spaniards of Presidio de San Saba (in existence from 1757 to 1770) for this stream now called Celery Creek.

Stone to build Presidio was quarried from bluffs along the creek and deep banks let hostile Indians approach undiscovered to attack the Presidio, half a mile to the southwest.

MENARD (Menard Co.) *US 83 at Canal Street*
"The Ditch"
The Vaughn Agricultural and Mechanical Canal Company was chartered in 1874 by William J. Vaughn, president; William Tipton, director; and James H. Comstock, director and secretary. Major H. M. Holmes was appointed attorney.

Irrigation for 2,000 acres of valley land and power for grist mills are furnished by gravity flow from San Saba River. Use of "the ditch," running from 5 miles above town to 5 below, began in 1876. Vaughn sold his controlling interest to Gus Noyes in 1886.

Since 1905 "the ditch" has been operated by Menard Irrigation Company, using the original dam.

MENARD (Menard Co.) *US 190, 1 mi. W*
Mission San Saba
Medallion
This building was originally built as a presidio or fort and mission was apart from it. After the mission was attacked and burned by Indians, all personnel moved into the presidio.

MENARD (Menard Co.) *US 190 at US 83*
Paso de La Santa Cruz
(Holy Cross Ford)
Spot where in 1753 Juan Galvan, Spanish explorer, put up a huge cross, to show his choice of site for Mission San Saba. Indians gathered at the cross, remaining to participate in the first known Christian worship service in this area.

The mission, 2 miles east, and the river ford were both named for the cross. (1964)

MENARD (Menard Co.) *SH 29, about 10 mi. SE at roadside park*
Pegleg Crossing
on the San Saba; about 1 mi. NE
An hourglass-shaped pass through the hills where McDougal Creek joins San Saba River. For years a favored Indian campground, it entered written history, 1732, as site of Spanish-Apache battle.

Saw passage of adventurers, mustang hunters, Indian fighters, German settlers, gold-seekers.

Probably named by landowner Wilhelm Harlen for one-legged land commissioner T. W. Ward. Crossing became station on stage line. Gained notoriety for many hold-ups that occurred at "robbers' roost" (1 mi. W). Pegleg served in later era as crossing on Great Western cattle trail.

(1970)

MENARD (Menard Co.) US 83 S in roadside park
Puerto de Baluartes
(Haven of the Strong Points)

In this pass between the hills—location of present day Menard—a site for an important spanish mission to the Apaches was chosen in 1754 by Don Pedro de Rabago y Teran, second explorer sent on the assignment by the viceroy of New Spain.

Suitable to be fortified and farmed, this pass had its mission built in 1757.   (1964)

MENARD (Menard Co.) US 83
Frisco Depot

Seeking a rail line to speed marketing of their livestock, residents of this area in 1909 asked the Fort Worth-Rio Grande Railroad, a branch of the Frisco System, to extend track from Brady (40 mi. NE) to Menardville. Ranchers donated right of way, while townspeople erected this depot and shortened the town's name to "Menard." Celebrations marked the arrival of the first train, Feb. 10, 1911 and completion of this Mission Revival station, July 4, 1911. The Santa Fe System later acquired the line. After rail service ended in 1972, this building became a historical building.   (1978)

MENDOZA (Caldwell Co.) SH 21 at FM 1854, 2 mi. N
Harris Cemetery

Sidon H. Harris and his family arrived in Texas in 1851, and moved to this vicinity in 1856. Harris and his wife, Amanda, bought two parcels of land, and this family cemetery was begun when Sidon died in 1861. Two Harris children were buried here in 1862, followed by Amanda in 1866. Descendants later sold the land, with the understanding that the cemetery would be maintained. Destruction of the cemetery in 1984 led to the replacement of the original grave markers. The cemetery reflects the history of an early Caldwell County family.

(Texas Sesquicentennial 1836–1986)

MENTONE (Loving Co.) SH 302, ½ mi. W at rest area
Goodnight-Loving Trail

Blazed from the Fort Griffin-Dodge City trail through New Mexico, to Colorado about 1860 by Oliver Loving, 1812–1867, first cattle trail driver from Texas.

MENTONE (Loving Co.) Courthouse grounds
Loving County

Formed from Tom Green County. Created February 26, 1887. Organized July 8, 1893. Named in honor of Oliver Loving, 1812–1867, farmer, rancher and an early trail-driver. Mentone, county seat.

MENTONE (Loving Co.) SH 302, NE city limits
Oliver Loving C.S.A.
(1812–1867)

Only Texan instrumental in mapping 3 major cattle trails: Shawnee, Western and Goodnight-Loving Trails.

Born in Kentucky. Came to Texas 1845, to farm, haul freight, deal in cattle. Started large Palo Pinto County ranch. In 1858, drove herd to Chicago—first time in history Texas cattle trailed to northern market. In 1859 drove to Denver.

When Civil War broke out, 1861, was Confederate beef contractor, furnishing meat to army commissaries. Served on 24-hour patrol squad against Indians in frontier town of Weatherford.

Mapped an 1862 expedition by 300 or more Texans to wipe out depredating Indians on the home grounds in Colorado, but failed to get necessary men to put this plan into action.

After the war, with Charles Goodnight, drove cattle from Palo Pinto to Horse Head Crossing on the Pecos, then up the river to Indian reservations and forts in New Mexico. In 1867 on this trail, was shot by Comanches: crawled 5 miles, chewing an old kid glove for food. Hauled at price of $250 to Fort Sumner by Mexican traders, he had wounds treated, but died of gangrene. Partner packed corpse in charcoal, hauled him to Weatherford for burial, fulfilling last wish.

Loving County was named for him in 1887. (1965)

MENTONE (Loving Co.) *SH 302, 3 blks. N of courthouse*
Mentone Community Church
Built 1910 in Porterville, a town abandoned after Pecos River flood of 1930. Moved here for school and social center. Also used by various church groups and for non-denominational worship.

Oldest building in Loving County. Awarded Medallion Plate. (1964)

MENTONE (Loving Co.) *US 285 at SH 302, 6 mi. SW*
Smallest County Seat in Texas
Mentone
Only town in Loving County—last organized, most sparsely populated (both in total and per square mile) county in Texas.

Established 1931 and named for an earlier town (10 miles north) which legend says was named by a French surveyor-prospector after his home on the Riviera.

With population of 42, Mentone has no water system. (Water is hauled in.) Nor does it have a bank, doctor, hospital, newspaper, lawyer, civic club, or cemetery.

There are only two recorded graves in county; some Indian skeletons, artifacts are found. Oil, farming, cattle country. (1967)

MENTONE (Loving Co.) *SH 302, .5 mi. SW in roadside park*
Route of
Old Butterfield Stagecoach Road
Over these tracks passed the Butterfield Stage, 1858–1861, providing for first time in history a combined passenger and mail service from Atlantic to Pacific Coast. Operating westward from St. Louis and Memphis, John Butterfield's company used 1,350 mules and horses and 90 concord coaches and wagons.

Stages traveled rapidly, despite lack of real roads. A signal given approaching a station would assure food on table for travelers, and fresh horses ready.

Stations were 12 to 113 miles apart. Route changes were often made to obtain water. The passsengers and crew wore guns. Indians liked horses, so to reduce the danger of Indian attacks, mules were used West of Ft. Belknap. Trip one way took 25 days—7 consumed in crossing Texas, from near Preston (now under Lake Texoma) to Jacksboro, Ft. Belknap, Ft. Chadbourne, and El Paso. One-way fare for the 2,700 miles was $200.

This marks a 113-mile span, from Emigrants' Crossing (82 mi. S) to Pope's Crossing (31 mi. N), that on inaugural trip, Sept. 16–Oct. 12, 1858, had no team-change. Route ran parallel to Pecos River. By November there were 3 change stations in this area, one being Skillman's Stop (6 mi. N). Route was shortened in 1860, going by Forts Stockton, Davis and Quitman, west of the Pecos. (1968)

MERCEDES (Hidalgo Co.) *US 281, 4 mi. S*
Relampago Ranch
Originally part of a Spanish land grant, Relampago (Lightning) Ranch community lay along the stage and military route from Rio Grande City to Brownsville. In 1852, Thaddeus Rhodes (1828–1904) acquired acreage here when he came as Hidalgo County clerk. Later he served as commissioner and judge. He and Jose Maria Mora (1824–1884), who bought adjoining land about 1856, helped bring economic and social stability. Mora and later his son Melchor, a deputy sheriff and Texas Ranger, farmed, ranched, and had the only general store in the area. Descendants still live on the property. (1980)

MERCEDES (Hidalgo Co.)   *US 83 right-of-way at FM 1015,*
3 mi. W in roadside park

The Rev. Pierre Yves Keralum
"The Lost Missionary"
(1817–1872)

Architect Pierre Yves Keralum was ordained an oblate priest at Marseilles, France, in 1852. That same year he came to South Texas as a member of the Missionary Oblates of Mary Immaculate (O.M.I.). Evidence of his architectural skill can be seen at Our Lady of Refuge Church in Roma and the cathedral in Brownsville. As a missionary, Keralum covered a large area of South Texas, ministering to thousands of people. He disappeared while traveling in this area in 1872. His remains were not discovered until ten years later.   (1989)

MERIDIAN (Bosque Co.)   *SH 22, .7 mi. W*

Bosque County

Named for the Bosque (Spanish for "woods") River. The territory now part of this county was traversed in 1841 by the Texan-Santa Fe Expedition. Maj. George B. Erath, noted surveyor and soldier, explored the region prior to its settlement. The first colonists established homes in 1850–1851. Among the national groups who immigrated here were the English (at Kent), Norwegians (at Norse and elsewhere), and the Germans (in eastern part of county).

Formally created and organized in 1854, Bosque County had traditionally had farming-ranching economy. The Chisholm Cattle Trail crossed the area in the 1870s.   (1973)

MERIDIAN (Bosque Co.)   *SH 144, 1 mi. NW in roadside park*

¼ Mile West to Boyhood Home of
John A. Lomax (1867–1948)

Only a log kitchen now marks the homesite of John Lomax, one of the foremost collectors of American folksongs. Here, on part of the Chisholm Trail, young Lomax heard cowboys croon-ing and yodeling to restless herds; Negro servants taught him jig tunes, chants, work songs, and calls; and on winter nights his family sang songs and swapped stories around a blazing fire.

Lomax began to write down this music while still a boy; and when he left Bosque County at age 20, he carried with him a roll of cowboy ballads—the nucleus of his lifelong work. (1970)

MERKEL (Taylor Co.)   *FM 1235, 7 mi. S, in vicinity of fight*

Vicinity of Indian Fight

On New Year's Day, 1871, Indian raiders who had stolen horses in Coleman County were pur-sued and overtaken here by 18 Texas Rangers and cowboys. Leaders of the group were Captain James M. Swisher and rancher Sam Gholson.

The Indians took refuge in the heights west of Mountain Pass. The ensuing battle lasted all day, and at nightfall the raiders left the horses and fled.

Of the fewer than one dozen Indians, one was killed, several wounded. One cowboy was wounded and another, J. M. Elkins, recorded the battle in his book "Indian Fighting on the Texas Frontier."   (1968)

MERKEL (Taylor Co.)   *FM 1235, 7 mi. S*

Castle Peak
(2.6 mi. WSW)

The Butterfield Overland Mail, the first public transportation facility spanning the area from the Mississippi to the Pacific with passenger and mail service, 1858–1861, used the 2,400-ft. peak to the northeast as a beacon. The drivers and passengers viewed it for 30 to 40 miles. In that era it was called Abercrombie Peak, for Col. J. J. Abercrombie of the U.S. Army, active in defense of this frontier. Waterman Ormsby, a newspaper reporter riding the first Butterfield stage to pass this way, noted that the peak resembled a fortress. Later the height was renamed Castle Peak.   (1968)

MERTENS (Hill Co.)

Mertens Baptist Church

On June 14, 1884, a small group of Baptists, led by W. J. Priddy, D. P. Sanders, and J. C. Osborne, met to organize a Baptist church. Originally known as Richland Baptist Church, the congregation worshiped in the Richland school until 1892, when they moved a few miles northwest to the town of Mertens. Now known as Mertens Baptist Church, the membership has grown and expanded its facilities over the years. Throughout its history the congregation has provided significant service and leadership to the residents of this part of Hill County. (1984)

MERTZON (Irion Co.) *8.5 mi. SW near county line, off US 67, courthouse grounds*

Dove Creek Battle

On January 8, 1865 eight miles east of here Confederate troops and Texas militiamen engaged a large party of Kickapoo Indians. The Indians, formerly hostile to the South, had entered Texas without authority and were making their way to Mexico. The troops attacked them and following five hours of desperate fighting, withdrew, having suffering the loss of 22 killed and 19 wounded. Indian losses from the encounter were probably less. Later raids by the Kickapoos were traced to the Dove Creek fight.

Texas Civil War Indian Trouble

War brought turmoil to Indians living in Kansas and the Indian Territory, with unfortunate results for Texans on the frontier. Most Cherokees, Choctaws, Creeks and Seminoles aided the South, while others adhered to the North. Few Comanches made a treaty with the South; but a great majority with their allies, the Kiowas, held aloof from either side and plundered the frontier at will. Apaches and Kickapoos did the same from Mexico. Texas and Confederate troops, despite poor arms and mounts, held defense lines until war's end.

MERTZON (Irion Co.)

US 67, 2 mi. E

Irion County

Created March 7, 1889. Organized April 16, 1889.

Named in honor of Robert Anderson Irion, 1806–1860. Came to Texas, 1833, and located at Nacogdoches. Member of the First Texas Congress, secretary of state in the cabinet of President Houston, 1837–1838.

Sherwood the county seat, later moved to Mertzon.

MESQUITE (Dallas Co.)

18680 IH 635

Site of Galloway Farmstead

Confederate veteran Benjamin Franklin Galloway (1833–1912) and his wife Eliza (Fletcher) (1852–1883) came to Texas from Tennessee in 1872. Their son Bedford Forest is said to have been born in a covered wagon at Duck Creek (Garland) in 1873. They purchased 101 acres in 1874 and Benjamin Galloway erected a cabin where they lived while a two-room house was built. A farmer, he also raised horses, mules and cattle. A second son, Nathan Lemmon, was born in 1876. Twin sons were born in 1883, but they lived only a day, and Eliza Galloway died soon after. Her niece, Clara Gentry, came to live with the family that year. At that time Benjamin had a Blackland Prairie hay company. Dallas clients included Tennessee Dairy, Caruth Farm and Ringling Brothers Circus. Benjamin Galloway married Amanda Jane Miller (1848–1938) of Tennessee in 1887 and built a 1½ story addition onto the home place. The structure eventually featured an entrance hall, bedroom, parlor, and a kitchen on the first level, with children's rooms upstairs. A son was born in 1888, but died at birth. Bedford returned home after attending college in Waco and New Orleans and made his living farming, baling hay and ginning cotton. He and his first wife, Nannie Lawrence, had four children. After her death in 1915, he married Bertha Dakan in 1917 and they had two daughters. Bedford was a city alderman, a member of the school board, and served as mayor of Mesquite from 1927 to 1940. A Galloway descendant restored the house between 1949 and 1950 and built another addition in 1955. Designated a Recorded Texas Historic Landmark in 1973, the Galloway Home Place was moved from this site to a more rural location in Sunnyvale in an effort to protect it from encroaching urban development. (2000)

MEXIA (Limestone Co.)

US 84 (Comanche Crossing Road), 9 mi.
W at entry of Booker T. Washington Park,

Booker T. Washington Park
(Near the Historic Comanche Crossing of the Navasota River)

Set aside by deed in 1898 as a permanent site for celebrating June 19th—the anniversary of the 1865 Emancipation of Slaves in Texas. It was 2.5 miles south of this site that slaves of this area first heard their freedom announced.

Limestone County in the 1860s—era of initial celebrations here—had many able Negro leaders. It sent to the Texas Constitutional Convention of 1866 one of its Negro citizens, Ralph Long. From among people who lived in this locality at the time of emancipation came Negro legislators Giles Cotton, Dave Medlock and Sheppard Mullins.

Even before land was dedicated for the park here, this was site of annual celebrations of June 19th. For many years the Honorable Ralph Long was the featured orator, speaking at times from bed of a wagon parked in the shade. As many as 20,000 often gathered for the occasion. On July 7, 1912, the 19th of June organization was chartered, to administer the park and perpetuate regional history.

The Negro people of Texas have shown outstanding initiative in fields of civic leadership, education, culture and business. In 1860 they numbered 187,921; in 1960 there were 1,187,125 Negroes in the state.

MEXIA (Limestone Co.)   *SH 14 SW*

Joseph F. Johnston Reunion Grounds
(Camp No. 94, United Confederate Veterans)

Established 1889, in era when Texas looked to Civil War veterans for state leadership. One of numerous parks on river banks or other favored sites that drew large, popular annual encampments. Statesmen came to make speeches. There were orations by old soldiers; memorial programs, reviews, concerts.

In 1892 the camp purchased this 70-acre tract; sold lots to shareholders; named streets for Lee, Jackson, other heroes. During week of full moon each August, members came to encampments; set up housekeeping in tents, shacks or brush arbors; entertained, feasting on fried chicken, barbecue, brunswick stew, sweet potato pie, watermelons. Special trains were run for year from Fort Worth, Dallas, Houston. In peak years 5,000 people assembled here. Until 1940, the dawn and dusk salutes shot by Old Valverde, Civil War cannon, were heard far into neighboring counties.

Besides giving honors to Confederate veterans, the encampments were occasions for family reunions.

After the Mexia oil boom began in 1920, Col. A. E. Humphreys, a leader in petroleum development, built club facilities and promoted use of the park.

The reunion grounds still are dedicated to the memory of the late Confederate veterans.

(1965)

MEXIA (Limestone Co.)   *SH 171, 2.5 mi. NW*

Horticulturist-Educator-Farmer
Joseph W. Stubenrauch
(February 7, 1852–September 21, 1938)

Argricultural genius, born in Ruelzheim, Rhenish Bavaria, of a family of horticulturists. Educated in Germany. Migrated to New York in 1871 and to Texas 1876. In Limestone County (surrounding this marker site) lay 100 acres of open prairie land which he purchased.

He discovered that fruit varieties then being grown here were unsuited to the climate. By cross-pollination, budding and grafting, he developed some 100 new varieties of peaches. More than 20 which were propagated for commercial purposes included "Anna," "Barbara," "Carman," "Frank," "Fredericka," "Katie," "Liberty," "Lizzie," "Miss Lola," and "Tena."

In 1882, his younger brother, Jacob, also came and settled nearby. Both men were outstanding citizens.

Joseph W. Stubenrauch shared his findings through his writings for *Farm and Ranch, Rural New Yorker* and *Holland's Magazine.* He practiced and advocated terracing, crop rotation and diversification, soil testing, fertilization and irrigation.

Many of his ideas of conservation farming and agricultural education were incorporated into U.S. Government programs. He was nationally recognized for his contributions to American agriculture. (1970)

MEXIA (Limestone Co.)
SH 14, on S edge
Mexia Oil Boom
One of great free-wheeling oil booms of America—before proration was enforced. Population in Mexia increased from 4,000 to 50,000 within days after oil discovery in 1920 at Rogers No. 1 Well, located 1.6 miles west of this marker, just off FM road 1633.

Earlier (in 1912), Blake Smith and other Mexia men had brought in a gas field. Believing oil also could be found here, they interested a veteran operator—flamboyant wildcatter A. E. Humphreys—who struck oil at 3,105 feet. By May, 1921 gushers were flowing. Humphreys had 2,000 men; did a $4,000,000 business. His fortune later was estimated at $37,000,000.

The boom was on. Other companies were formed. A second renowned wildcatter, J. K. Hughes, shared the leadership in developing the field to capacity.

Millionaires, merchants, celebrities, operators and workers swarmed to Mexia for a share in the "black gold." Many undesirables came, also, and one day were ousted by the thousands by Texas Rangers. In 1920–1921, first boom year, $5,000,000 went into construction: tanks for over 30 million barrels of oil were built; but even so storage area was inadequate for output.

A park and clubhouse developed near this site by Col. Humphreys—mementos of boom—are still in use. (1967)

MIAMI (Roberts Co.)
US 60 at S Mobeetie St.
Miami Railroad Depot
When the Southern Kansas Railway Company of Texas built a line through Roberts County in 1887, Miami developed at the end of the track as a campsite for workers. The crew set up a kitchen and a tent hotel. Soon the railroad built a public water well and telegraph lines to nearby Fort Elliott. Passengers and supplies for the post and nearby town of Mobeetie began arriving by rail. This depot was erected in 1888 between North Main and Birge Street. The Santa Fe Railroad bought the line in 1899 and this structure remained in service until 1978. (1979)

MIAMI (Roberts Co.)
US 60, 5 mi. NE
Roberts County
Formed from Young and Bexar Territories. Created August 21, 1876. Organized January 10, 1889.

Named in honor of John S. Roberts, a signer of the Texas Declaration of Independence, and Oran Milo Roberts, governor of Texas, 1878–1882.

County seat, Miami, to October, 1889. Parnell, to August 1, 1898. Miami, since.

MIAMI (Roberts Co.)
301 Commercial (US 60)
Roberts County Courthouse
Prominently sited atop a grassy slope overlooking the town of Miami, the Roberts County Courthouse was built in 1913, during a time of regional economic development spurred by the oil and ranching industries. One of six Texas courthouses designed by architect Elmer George Withers of Stamford, the Roberts County Courthouse features Beaux Arts styling with simple Classical features. As the center of social and governmental activity for this rural county, the building has played an important role in the county's history. (2000)

MIAMI (Roberts Co.)
FM 283, 20.5 mi. N
Parnell
Roberts County was created on Aug. 21, 1876, by the Texas Legislature, but remained unorganized, as in that year it had only one settler. Its 1880 population was 32. After the Santa Fe Railroad was built across this area in 1887, settlement increased. A Jan. 1889 election to organize the county was invalidated by fraudulent voting. However, the disqualified officers opened a courthouse in a vacant store in Miami (the county seat according to the contested election), placing the records in a heavy safe with a secret combination. The legally-elected authorities later obtained records by hiring a gunman to impersonate a landowner and capture the safe when it was opened.

Hauled to the legal county seat (20.5 mi. NW), safe was set on blocks and a 2-story frame courthouse was built around it. First called Oran (supposedly for Texas Governor Oran M. Roberts) the town was renamed Parnell when the United States Post Office opened in March, 1890. Parnell had a few businesses, about 12 residences, a school, a saloon called "The Bat's Cave." Guests rode 25 to 30 miles to dances in the courthouse; but men attending court in Parnell had to camp out as hotel was small. Miami became county seat in 1898, and Parnell was abandoned. (1974)

MICO (Medina Co.)   *FM 1283, near post office*
Medina Dam
Henri Castro, who colonized this area in the 1840s, envisioned irrigated farms along the Medina River. The project was delayed, however, until after the turn of the century, when Dr. Fred Stark Pearson, an internationally known engineer, persuaded British investors to finance construction of a dam at this site. Completed in 1912, Medina Dam was hailed as the largest in Texas and the fourth largest in the United States. Limestone boulders from a nearby quarry added bulk to the massive concrete structure. Four miles downstream, a small diversion dam conducted water into a system of irrigation canals. Gravitational force delivered the water to fields.

The outbreak of World War 1 (1914) disrupted ties with British investors. Seeking new capital, Dr. Pearson and his wife left for England in 1915 on the *Lusitania* and were killed when a German submarine torpedoed the ship.

The irrigation network created by Medina Dam brought new prosperity to this region. Vegetables raised in irrigated fields became a valuable crop. Water and electricity were made available to rural residents. In 1925, voters established the Bexar-Medina-Atascosa Counties Water Improvement District No. 1 to manage the project.   (1978)

MIDLAND (Midland Co.)   *Two locations: US 80, .5 mi. E in roadside park;*
IH 20, 4.8 mi. E in roadside park
Midland County
Created and organized, March 1885. First known as the junction of many trails and site of the last Comanche raid into Texas.

In 1881 the Texas and Pacific Railroad was built; equidistant between El Paso and Fort Worth, this became known as Midland. First settler was sheepman in 1882. Cattlemen came with herefords in 1888. Water wells and windmills lured small farmers.

Became headquarters for 1928 Permian Basin Oil Discovery. In 1945 its first well came in.

The "Midland Man," oldest skeletal remains in North America (18,500 B.C.), was found in 1954.   (1967)

MIDLAND (Midland Co.)   *SH 158, 12 mi. SE*
Greenwood Baptist Church
Organized 1907 in unused saloon in Slaughter. Named for two missionaries, the Revs. Green and Wood.

Services were later held in various schools. Present structure built in 1926 on land donated by John M. King, an organizer, charter member and deacon.

MIDLAND (Midland Co.)   *IH 20, 4.8 mi. E in roadside park*
Marcy Trail
Platted in 1849 by a U.S. Army surveying expedition under Capt. Randolph B. Marcy. Guided by Manuel. a Comanche Indian, Marcy crossed the dreaded staked plains of West Texas, proving their feasibility for travel, and opening a new and shorter road west.

Marcy's trail from Dona Ana, N.M., to Fort Smith, Ark., became a major road to the California gold fields. Later the Overland Stage followed it for about 125 miles and in 1881, Texas and Pacific Railroad built along part of the route.

MIDLAND (Midland Co.)   *SH 158, 6 mi. W*
(1 mi. E of junction of SH 158 and FM 1788)
Site of Old Roadbed
Midland & Northwestern Railroad
Standard gauge 66 mile line built by David Fasken, Sr., to carry cattle, ranch supplies, passengers.

Operated 1916 to 1920—critical era of World War I and world starvation aftermath. Linked towns of Fasken, Florey, and Seminole with Texas & Pacific Railway at Midland. At first, operated with locomotive borrowed from T. & P.

Train had to stop for pasture gates to be opened. Crew shot coyotes and rattlesnakes.

In a breakdown, the passengers were fed, sheltered at Fasken. Work crew slept on the prairie.

Flooded out in 1920, M. & N. R. was abandoned. Roadbed still is visible.   (1967)

MIDLAND (Midland Co.)   *US 80 1 mi. W air terminal*
Midland County
(Created and Organized, March, 1885)
First known as the junction of many trails and site of the last Comanche raid into Texas.

In 1881 the Texas an Pacific Railroad was built; equidistant between El Paso and Fort Worth, this became known as Midland. First settler was a sheepman in 1882. Cattlemen came with Herefords in 1888. Water wells and windmills lured small farmers.

Became headquarters for 1928 Permian Basin Oil Discovery. In 1945 its first well came in.

The "Midland Man," oldest skeletal remains in North America (18,500 B.C.), was found in 1954.   (1965)

MIDLAND (Midland Co.)   *SH 158 10 mi. SE*
Midland County's First
Producing Oil Well
Humble Oil and Refining Company's No. 1 Mrs. O. P. Buchanan staked by Rowan Drilling Company Aug. 17, 1944. Spudded Sept. 14, 1944.

Completed Nov. 6, 1945, at total depth of 12,574 feet. Well flowed 332 barrels in 29 hours. Geologist: H. L. Beckman.   (1966)

MIDLAND (Midland Co.)   *US 80, 10 mi. SW at Terminal*
Site of Old
Midland Army Flying School
Old Sloan Field, built 1931, in 1942 became Midland Army Flying School, for bombardier cadets. At one time it was called largest bombardier training center in the world. One of over 25 World War II airfields in Texas, its cadets flew 861,510 hours in Beech "AT-11" aircraft, dropping 1,245,107 bombs. Last class of cadets graduated in Jan. 1945.

The field was used as an army air force instructor school (bombardier) until World War II ended later that year.

After military phase-out, 1947, commercial field opened, 1950.

MIDLOTHIAN (Ellis Co.)   *FM 1387, .5 mi. E*
Site of Old Hawkins Spring
(About 100 ft. E)
William Alden Hawkins (1800–1867) and wife, Anna Eddy (1800–1895), from La Porte, Ind., arrived with family at this site in May, 1848, becoming first settlers in area. The family included Marcellus Tolbert (1824–1896); Mary Melissa (1824–1884), with her husband, Harrison F. Hinkley and child, Annie Lucretia; Benjamin Franklin (1828–1891) and wife, Mary; James Emerson (1829–1912); William Alden (1831–1889); Elizabeth Ann (1838–1903); David Peter (1838–1863); John Wesley (1841–1876); and George Washington (1842–1931). As members of Peters Colony, Wm. A. Hawkins and adult children claimed about 2,500 acres of land. In a critical period of 28 days prior to July 1, 1848, logs were cut and hauled from Dallas County cedar brakes to build five houses, to sustain the claims. Hawkins Spring, about 100 feet from the Wm. A. Hawkins home, supplied water for all households and often for passers-by. Upon the organization of Ellis County in 1850, William A. Hawkins (1800–1867) was appointed first chief justice (county judge).

Currently situated on Hawkins family lands are part of Midlothian business district east of Santa Fe Railroad, on the Wm. A. Hawkins survey; Northeridge Shopping Center, on Harrison Hinkley survey; First United Methodist Church, on B. F. Hawkins survey.   (1971)

MIDWAY (Madison Co.)

SH 21, 2 mi. W

James and Calpernia Mitchell

James (1795–1870) and Calpernia (Franklin) (1805–1865) Mitchell came to Texas from Virginia in 1833 and received a Mexican land grant. In 1837, James served as a member of the commission to locate the seat of the newly formed Montgomery County; in 1846, when Walker County was formed, he became one of the first county commissioners. The Mitchell house and inn on the old San Antonio road provided rest for weary travelers and served as an area post office from about 1840 to 1850. The parents of Edwin, Thomas, James, Nathan, Anthony Wayne, Calpernia, and James are interred in the family cemetery near this site. (1998)

MIDWAY (Madison Co.)

SH 21, 3.7 mi. E at Antioch Rd. (CR 248)

Antioch Church of Christ

Believed to be among the oldest independent African American churches in Texas, this congregation was established on the Hayes Plantation and named Antioch after a biblical passage. The church moved from the plantation in 1865 and relocated in Midway, where trustees acquired property. The church building also served as a school until a bungalow schoolhouse was erected in 1915. In 1917 a second Church of Christ was formed in the area. The two congregations merged in 1924 and the school was replaced as a Rosenwald School the next year. New church structures were erected in 1937 and again in 1990. The active congregation continues to serve the community with a variety of outreach and worship programs. (1999)

MILAM (Sabine Co.)

SH 21 at SH 87

Milam

Founded in 1828 as Red Mound. Named in 1835 for Benjamin Rush Milam. Seat of Justice of Sabine Municipality, 1835; of Sabine County, 1837–58. Incorporated December 29, 1837. Internal Revenue Post during the Republic Headquarters of the Quartermaster's Department C.S.A. for Sabine County, 1861–1865. First home in Texas of John S. Roberts, a signer of the Texas Declaration of Independence. Home of John C. Hale, martyr of San Jacinto.

MILAM (Sabine Co.)

SH 21 at SH 87, W side

In This Vicinity Was the Well-Known
Las Borregas Camp Site

Las Borregas Creek formed east line of Spain's 1794 grant to J. I. Pifermo, first landowner in present Sabine County. Upstream, about 1800 at Jack Cedar Crossing of Crow Ferry Road, Spain had an army post to protect settlers and travel. The "Father of Texas," Stephen F. Austin, spent his first night (July 16, 1821) in Texas on this creek. (1973)

MILAM (Sabine Co.)

SH 21, .25 mi. E

The Milam Masonic Institute

Many pioneers belonged to the Ancient, Free and Accepted Masons, an order active in education. Among Masons settling in this area by 1845 were Republic of Texas leaders William Clark, James Gaines, D. S. Kaufman, Willis H. Landrum, and F. M. Weatherred.

The Rev. Littleton Fowler (1803), a Mason, opened in 1845 in this county the Midway Institute, which was soon absorbed by Red Mound Seminary. Set to work at Red Mound (Milam), 1847, was Jackson Lodge No. 35, A. F. & A. M., with John Boyd, G. A. Norford, A. D. Oliphint, O. J. Polley, and J. T. Scruggs as officers. The Lodge soon operated the Milam Masonic Institute, successor to the earlier schools. On the charter application (1853) M. M. I. was listed as already "a flourishing school."

Later, Sexton Lodge No. 251, A. F. & A. M., operated M. M. I., a great contributor to East Texas culture until tax-funded education became universal in the 1870s.

Among supporters of M. M. I. were Masons with the family names Anderson, Causey, Davis, Deweese, Dorsey, Elliott, Gellately, Halbert, Harper, Harris, Jacks, Low, McCloskey, McGown, McMahan, Mason, Nethery, Noble, Pratt, Reeves, Renfro, Sanders, Slaughter, Smith, Speights, Sweet, Tucker, Vickers, Watson, White, Whittlesey, Williams, and Yeiser. (1974)

MILLERSVIEW (Concho Co.)

FM 2134, 12 mi. N

Site of Mission San Clemente

At the juncture of the Concho and Colorado Rivers.

Established March 16, 1684, by the Mendoza Expedition for the purpose of civilizing and Christianizing the Indians of the region. (1964)

MINEOLA (Wood Co.)   *101 E. Broad St. (US 80) at Johnson St.*
Site of Public Mineral Water Well

Mineola settlers chose this area, nicknamed "the Forks of the River," for its abundance of water. The town's first water service was administered by A. W. Front, who made daily deliveries to his 50 clients. A water well was located on this site as early as 1885; workmen drilling for salt between 1889 and 1890 discovered mineral water. In 1896 a 60-foot windmill tower with a 3,000-gallon cypress wood tank was constructed and a mineral well dug to 150 feet by Henry L. Beaird. This became the town's main water source. A 1913 analysis of the water revealed more than 12 minerals associated with healing properties. In 1906, an electric motor replaced the windmill. The well was capped in 1924 when the street was bricked over. The exact site of the public mineral water well was the center of the intersection of Highway 80 and Johnson Street. (1998)

MINERAL WELLS (Palo Pinto Co.)   *US 281, 9 mi. N*
Site of the Home in 1885 of
Oliver Loving
1812–1867

First trail driver of Texas cattle. Loving Valley and a county in Texas bear his name.

MIRANDO CITY (Webb Co.)   *FM 649, near S city limits*
Oliver Winfield Killam
(April 27, 1874, January 1, 1959)

Discoverer of first commercial oil field in South Texas; founder of Mirando City, as base of operations.

Born in Lincoln County, Mo.; graduated in law at University of Missouri, 1898. Operated stores and lumber yards and served 8 years in legislature of Oklahoma. Came to Texas to explore for oil in 1920.

After drilling twice unsuccessfully, he brought in as a pumper the first commercial well south of San Antonio, Mirando Oil Co. No. 3 Hinnant, April 17, 1921.

With Colon Schott of Cincinnati, Ohio, drilled Schott No. 2 (1 mi. S of here), which came in as a gusher Dec. 10, 1921—opening the South Texas oil boom. The U.S. Post Office in Mirando City opened May 18, 1922, to serve town that jumped suddenly in population to a reputed 13,000. All sorts of businesses boomed; and churches, school, and medical facilities expanded.

O. W. Killam was crowned "King Petrol" at Oil Men's Jubilee, Laredo, July 4, 1937. He was also esteemed by ranchers aware of oil lease benefits to the area.

Killam and his wife Hattie (Smith) had 3 children: Winfield (Hank now deceased), Louise (Mrs. John Hurd, also deceased), and Radcliffe. The O. W. Killam shops and Radcliffe Killam's oil operations continue as Mirando City celebrates its 50th anniversary. (1972)

MISSION (Hidalgo Co.)   *US 83 Business at Conway Ave., NW corner*
The Border Theater

A fine example of a mid-20th century motion picture theater with regional stylistic influences, the Border Theater was completed in 1942. Dallas architect William J. Moore designed the structure, which was built by contractor George Holliday. The theater was large enough for 740 patrons and housed the office of owners Mr. and Mrs. R. N. Smith. Changes to the edifice's exterior include a raised marquee and the addition of a tile canopy. The Border Theater remains a monument to Mission's architectural and cinematic history. (Recorded Texas Historic Landmark 1997)

MISSION (Hidalgo Co.)   *FM 495, 1 mi. N on Bryan Rd.*
Home of William Jennings Bryan
(1860–1925)

Once the lands of the Mission of the Oblate Fathers, this property (160 acres) was owned by Bryan from 1910 to 1916. While residing here, he wrote many articles and engaged in a magazine debate with Senator Albert J. Beveridge.

MISSION (Hidalgo Co.)
FM 1016, 2 mi. S
Chimney Park
Site of Mission Canal Co. Pumping Plant
In 1907, John J. Conway and James W. Hoit began the Mission Canal Co. Irrigation System, which was instrumental in the early agricultural growth of the area. Here they built the first pump station out of hand made brick from Madero. The 106-ft. chimney carried smoke from wood-fired boilers which produced steam to drive the pump. The plant was later operated by John H. Shary and by Hidalgo County Water Control and Improvement Districts No. 7 and No. 14. The property was developed for recreational use after a new pumping plant was built upstream in the late 1950s.
(1985)

MISSION (Hidalgo Co.)
FM 1016, 3.2 mi. S
Spiderweb Railroad
Begun in 1912, when dirt roads hampered area transportation, the San Benito & Rio Grande Valley Railroad was instrumental in the early development of the region's towns and commerce. It grew from the Brownsville Street & Interurban Railroad Company, established by Sam A. Robertson (1867–1938), a local civil engineer and land promoter. As the line grew and spurs were constructed to remote farm communities, it became known as the Spiderweb Railroad. With just over 100 miles of track, the company became part of the Missouri-Pacific system in 1924.
(1982)

MOBEETIE (Wheeler Co.)
SH 152, 1 mi. W
Site of Fort Elliott
Established June 5, 1875. One of the last forts established in Texas for the purpose of clearing the region of Indians. Around it Mobeetie, rendezvous of buffalo hunters and traders, grew up. The post was abandoned in 1889.

MOBEETIE (Wheeler Co.)
SH 152, at old jail
Fort Elliott Flagpole
First stood about a mile to the northwest, at Fort Elliott, established 1875 to protect the Texas Panhandle from Indians.

J. J. Long, teamster-merchant, who arrived with the soldiers, was hired to provide a flagpole for the fort. In cedar breaks near antelope Hills, 30 miles away, he cut two huge trees and hauled them here by wagon to build this 50-foot pole.

After Fort Elliott closed in 1890, Long bought the pole and placed it in front of his store. Later at Mobeetie School for 20 years; it was erected here 1949.
(1966)

MOBEETIE (Wheeler Co.)
SH 152
Old Wheeler County Jail, 1886
First jail in Panhandle of Texas. Central holding place for badmen. Built at cost of $18,500, including $1200 for a hangman's device put in to meet state requirement. Stone quarried on farm of Emanuel Dubbs, first county judge. Awarded Medallion Plate.
(1965)

MOBEETIE (Wheeler Co.)
SH 152
Mobeetie
Oldest town in Texas Panhandle. Originally a trading post, 2 mi. south, 1874; moved nearer Fort Elliott, 1875. Earlier called Sweetwater, was renamed in 1879.

Courthouse was completed by Mark Huselby, first county tax assessor, and other citizens.

Popular with hunters, cowboys, gamblers—town in 1881 became judicial center of 35th District.

Temple Houston, son of the hero, Sam Houston, was district attorney and the first state senator for this district.

After bypass by the Santa Fe Railroad (1888) and a destructive 1898 tornado, Mobeetie declined.
(1967)

MONAHANS (Ward Co.)
IH 20 in roadside park
Ward County
Formed from Tom Green County. Created February 26, 1887. Organized March 29, 1892.

Named in honor of Thomas William Ward, 1807–1872, at the storming of Bexar, December, 1835; commissioner of the General Land Office, 1841–1848; United States Consul at Panama, 1853–1856.

MONAHANS (Ward Co.)   *US 80, 6 mi. E*
Monahans Sandhills State Park and Museum
In these shifting seas of sand, rich in stone evidences of primitive men, today's visitors find flint points, sandstone metates and manos of peoples who were here as early as 10,000 years ago and late as the 1870s. Bones of great mammoths and gigantic bison prove that this desert was in post-glacial times a land of lakes and tall grasses.

Cabeza de Vaca in 1535 and Antonio de Espejo in 1583 encountered Jumanos, historic tribe which hunted here. In 1590 Castano de Sosa found a tribe he called Vaqueros because they lived by hunting cows (buffalo)—the tribe later called Apaches.

For more than 100 years at this stop on Great Comanche War Trail extending into Mexico, Apache fought Comanche for pools of water and acorns of dwarf shinnery oak. The California or Emigrant Trail through the Sand Hills started with the gold rush, was first mapped in September 1849 by Capt. Randolph B. Marcy. U.S. Topographical Engineers, and in 1854 by Capt. John Pope, who explored a railroad route toward the Pacific Ocean.

3,840 acres of sand hills were designated in 1957 as a state park, after acquisition and construction of museum by Ward County. Has picnic facilities.

MONROE CITY (Chambers Co.)   *SH 65 at entrance to old Humble Oil Camp*
Anahuac Oil and Gas Field
Although oil production of major value began in Chambers County in 1916, this prolific Anahuac Field was discovered on March 3, 1935, with completion of Humble Oil & Refining Company's A. D. Middleton No. 1(1.8 mi. SE). The camp which housed Humble crews who developed the field was adjacent to this site.

The field encompasses some 14,000 acres of prime rice and grazing land and produces from 21 zones in a highly faulted domal structure. Producing depths range from 6,600 feet to 8,600 feet. Peak production was reached in World War II, when in 1944 annual total was 11,916,137 barrels. Discovery well had an original potential of 144 barrels a day from depth of 7,050 feet. It was deepened to 7,088 feet and recompleted March 14, 1935, with a new potential of 518 barrels. Through 1966, A. D. Middleton No. 1 has produced in excess of 390,000 barrels of oil.

Over 177 million barrels of oil and 268 billion cubic feet of gas have been produced from the field. (In Chambers County, a pioneer oil producing area, over 475 million barrels of oil have been produced since 1916). At present, there are 408 wells in the Anahuac Field, and it is expected that production will continue into the 21st century.   (1967)

MONT BELVIEU (Chambers Co.)   *SH 146, at roadside park*
Barbers Hill Oil Field
While digging a 65-ft. water well near his home in 1889, Elmer W. Barber (1854–1935), whose father, Amos Barber, first settled this area, encountered inflammable gas near the top of the salt dome known as Barbers Hill. After the Spindletop discovery in 1901, prospectors sought leases here. In 1902, Fattillo Higgins (1863–1955), an early Spindletop promoter, drilled on the Northwest slope of the hill. His shallow well, like those of other early operators, yielded little, and the low price of crude oil discouraged large investment.

The United Petroleum Co. No. 1 Fisher, drilled in 1918, produced 70 barrels a day, the field's first oil in commercial quantities. Drilling resumed in 1926, when the Mills Bennett Production Co. and the Humphreys Corp. brought in the A. E. Barber No. 1, yielding 500 barrels a day. The success later that year of their B-2 Kirby, reaching a depth of 4,174 ft., triggered a leasing campaign and launched a period of rapid expansion which lasted until the late 1930s.

Rows of oil derricks and tent dwellings were a common sight during the boom. As the population of the community grew, oil money helped upgrade and enlarge school facilities. By 1977, the local economy had shifted from production to storage of petroleum.   (1977)

MONT BELVIEU (Chambers Co.)   *IH 10 at FM 565, 6 mi. E*
Cove
In 1824, Joseph Lawrence of New York, a reputed member of Jean Lafitte's privateering band, settled on a nearby marshland ridge. Known as Lawrence's Island, it became the nucleus of later

settlement, which included James Haney and members of the Dugat, Mackey, Stubbs, and Wilburn families. In 1827, A. B. J. Winfree came here from Louisiana and settled on a land grant. The wide-spread community around his property soon became known as Winfree's Cove and later simply as Cove.

The economy of the Cove community was originally based on cattle, but later included farming, fishing, and fur trapping. Several businesses were located here, including ferries, a shipyard, and general stores. The settlement also included a post office from 1885 to the 1940s, a school which was established in the 1870s and consolidated with the Barbers Hill District in 1937, and churches.

In order to avoid annexation, Cove was incorporated as a municipality in 1973. An important agricultural center for Chambers County and the upper Texas coastal region, the town of Cove has maintained a form of local government that reflects the residents' values, independence and rich heritage. (1982)

MONT BELVIEU (Chambers Co.) *FM 1409, .5 mi. N of FM 565, 2.5 mi. NE*
Old River
Formed as a channel of the meandering Trinity River, Old River rises in southwestern Liberty County and flows to the southeast, joining the Trinity in northwestern Chambers County. During the 1820s and 1830s the tributary was the center of early area settlement. Among the first pioneers to migrate here were Robert and Eleanor (Dorsett) Wiseman, who settled on nearby land grants in 1827.

Fertile soil for farming and abundant grassland for raising cattle made the Old River area an important early agricultural center of Southeast Texas. Goods from the community, including animal skins, timber and charcoal, were shipped to market in Galveston.

Commercial activity in the Old River settlement grew as the population increased. Dr. James P. Alford pioneered in the area's shipping and business trade with Galveston, which led to the development of shipbuilding firms such as that of Capt. William Icet. Other significant businesses here included the brick kiln of P. Almeras and river ferry operations.

The early residents of Old River set patterns of residential and industrial growth which are evident today. Descendants of the pioneer Southeast Texas settlers still live in the area. (1982)

MONTALBA (Anderson Co.) *SH 19, 3.5 mi. N*
Old Montalba
In area known as Beaver Valley, settled about 1853—the year that pioneer P. G. Oldham built his home a half-mile northwest of this marker. This was on the Palestine-Athens Road, the route taken by mail hacks in early days. To the east was a campground where travelers often spent the night, and where later inhabitants of the area used to gather for seasonal religious camp meetings. Near the Oldham home was the Beaver Valley Primitive Baptist Church. Mr. Oldham donated land for a cemetery adjoining the church. Nearby stood a noted early school, Beaver Academy. The church was later known by name "Holly Springs."

The first local physician, Dr. T. J. Adams, built his homestead in the woods of Beaver Valley in 1859, and conducted a wide practice until he was past 80.

During the Civil War, while the young men of the area were away in the army, an iron foundry in this valley made arms and bullets for the Confederacy.

In 1880 a post office was granted under the name Montalba—suggested by early settler Tobe Hamlett, inspired by snowclad mountain on the horizon. Mrs. Mollie Hamlett was the first postmaster. In later years Montalba settlement was moved southward, and now thrives as a market and supply point for valley. (1970)

MONTELL (Uvalde Co.) *US 55, 20 miles NW of Uvalde*
Church of the Ascension
Bishop W. P. Elliott held first Episcopal rites in Montell, 1890. Church was built with donations from friends throughout the world, under the leadership of the Rev. Richard Galbraith, who came from Ireland in 1883. The first service was held in this edifice Christmas Day, 1890. Services of Consecration by the Right Rev. J. S. Johnston, Bishop of West Texas, 1891. (1965)

MONTELL (Uvalde Co.)

General John R. Baylor

SH 55 just inside Montell

Born in Kentucky. Came to Texas Republic 1839. Colorful Indian fighter. In war against Cherokees 1840. Member Texas Legislature 1853. Comanche agent 1855–57. Delegate from Weatherford, Secession Convention. Commanding detachment of Second Regiment Texas Mounted Rifles occupied, took over supplies, Ft. Bliss, June 1861—during campaign to extend Confederacy westward to the Pacific. Repulsed Federals, Mesilla, N. Mex., July 25. With 200 men took 700 Federals, their transports, arms, ammunition, 200 horses, 270 beeves, four cannon at San Augustin Springs, July 27. With Capitol at Mesilla, organized government, proclaimed Confederate control of Arizona, Aug. 1. Baylor became military, civil governor. Sent C.S.A. Treasury $9,500 captured at Ft. Fillmore. Supervised gold, silver mining for C.S.A. Order to kill instead of capture troublesome Apaches incensed authorities against him, had Baylor recalled to Texas, stripped of rank. As private "served guns in hottest of the fight" to recapture Galveston, Jan. 1, 1863. Salvaged U.S. warship parts to make cannon light enough to go into battle on back of mule. 1863–65 in Confederate Congress. Given new command. Made Brigadier-General 1865. Raised, led troops in frontier defense. Fear of his moves pinned down thousands of Federals in California, Arizona. Climaxed war service on Northwest Texas border. Post-war lived in San Antonio. Farmed, ranched Uvalde County. Buried in Montell. (1963)

MONTELL (Uvalde Co.)

Montell Methodist Church

SH 55, behind Church of the Ascension

A Methodist Church mission was established in the community of Montell in 1889. Served by missionary N. W. Keith, the congregation met in a number of locations, including a brush arbor in the summer months. A Union Sunday School was organized by 1895. A permanent church building was dedicated on June 1, 1908. Services were held once a month except for a period during World War II when they were temporarily suspended. Since 1948 the congregation has met for worship on alternating Sundays. Descendants of pioneer members remain active in the church. Texas Sesquicentennial 1836–1986

MONTELL (Uvalde Co.)

Near Site of Nuestra Señora de la Candelaria Mission

SH 55 just inside city limits

Third mission under this name founded in Texas. Established near here on the Nueces River in 1762 by Franciscan missionaries for the conversion of the Indians and protection of Spanish lands. Typical of many Spanish missions in Texas, Candelaria had twice moved closer to centers of civilization since its first founding in 1749 on the San Gabriel River. Beset with friction between friars and soldiers, the first Candelaria was abandoned in 1755 and then moved to the San Marcos River. Soon, however, the friars found that the Indians were more concerned with protection than with Christianity. In 1757 the mission was again discontinued. In 1762 Candelaria was re-established here, and about 100 Lipan-Apaches quickly volunteered to live within its walls. A chapel, large thatched building, a house, and possibly other structures were erected. But once more, difficulties arose—scarcity of meat, unrest and insincerity among the mission Indians, inadequate defense, devastating raids by Comanches and Apaches. About 1767 the mission was abandoned for the last time. Little remains of it today, for the smooth building stones were taken by Anglo settlers in the 1800s to build their houses. (1968)

MONTGOMERY (Montgomery Co.)

Bennett's Early Homesite

SH 105, 1 1/2 mi. E in rest area

Place of residence of an early great legislator and civic and military leader.

Joseph L. Bennett settled here in 1834. Served as colonel in Texas Army during War for Independence. Attempted to reach the Alamo in March, 1836, to aid in that battle. Later joined Gen. Sam Houston's army and commanded 2nd Regt., Texas Volunteers, at Battle of San Jacinto. He received bounty certificates in 1838 for 960 acres of land for Republic of Texas military service. Was appointed in May 1837, by President Sam Houston to command a regiment of mounted gunmen for defense of Texas Frontier. He also carried mail from Houston to Montgomery.

Represented Montgomery County in Republic of Texas Congress, Nov. 5, 1838–Feb. 3, 1840. Participated in 1842 in Somervell Expedition, a Republic of Texas campaign to punish Mexico for three destructive raids made in Texas. Founded near here in Jan., 1842, one of county's earliest schools.

346

Lived here until 1848 when he moved to Navarro County to settle on his headright survey with his wife, Elizabeth, son, Seaborne, and daughters, Julia Ann, Frances, Lillian and Adaline. He died later that year. Buried in family cemetery near Streetman. (1968)

MONTGOMERY (Montgomery Co.)

SH 105, 1 blk. S, between FM 149 and Pond St.

The Railroad in Montgomery

Problems with transporting farm crops to market, along with the growing importance of rail transportation were major factors that prompted area businessmen to organize the Central and Montgomery (C&M) Railroad in 1877. Completed by 1880, the C&M consisted of a 25-mile track connecting Montgomery with the Houston & Texas Central Railroad at Navasota.

A combined passenger and freight station constructed near this site was often the center of social activity. After the county seat was moved from Montgomery in 1889, a small jail, moved to the railroad yard, held prisoners awaiting transportation.

In 1882, the Gulf, Colorado & Santa Fe Railroad purchased the C&M, thus acquiring access to the prized timber trade of East Texas. By extending the rails east and west, this line became the Beaumont-Somerville branch of the Sante Fe. The eastern extension joined the original C&M line a mile west of town at a point that became known as "The Junction." Travel delays resulted from trains backing to or from the depot to the main line.

Passenger service was discontinued in 1951. Later, the mile of railroad track from "The Junction" to the depot in Montgomery was removed. (1984)

MORAN (Shackelford Co.)

SH 6 at FM 576

Cottle No. 1
First Natural Gas Well in Shackelford County
(2 mi. NE)

The appearance in 1908 of oil and gas in water wells in this vicinity prompted the Texas Company (later Texaco, Inc.) in June, 1909, to begin leasing large tracts of land. After a surface geological survey, a wooden derrick complete with cable tools and steam engine was erected by contractor F. J. Winston on a prospective location on the Jim Cottle Ranch and on Sept. 23, 1909, drilling operations began. Equipment breakdowns were frequent and sometimes lengthy, but finally, on Nov. 9, 1910, after 13 months of drilling, the Cottle No. 1 struck natural gas at a depth of 2660 feet. This discovery opened the Moran Field, and was the first commercial gas well completed in this vast West Texas area.

In the spring of 1911, gas was piped to Moran for residential and business use. Within two years (in 1913) the cities of Albany, Cisco, and Abilene were supplied for the first time with natural gas. By Oct. 1913, with five producing gas wells, the Moran field won recognition as one of the most important sources of fossil fuels in Texas. Although the Cottle No. 1 was plugged years ago, Moran Field continues to be an economic mainstay in this area. (1974)

MORAN (Shackelford Co.)

SH 6 at FM 576

Moran

Pioneers came to this area as early as the 1860s. During the Civil War (1861–1865), they built the temporary fortress settlement of Mugginsville on Deep Creek. At one time, a branch of the Western Cattle Trail passed nearby. Population increased after the arrival of the Texas Central Railroad in 1881. The town of Moran was established by Swope Hull, who opened a grocery store at the rail crossing on Deep Creek in 1883. He was postmaster of the community's first post office, called "Hulltown," which opened August 29, 1883. Hull bought 160 acres between Post Oak and Deep Creek and platted a townsite in March 1884. Most of the property was bought by I. B. (Ben) Scott, who sold his interests in 1890 to M. D. Bray (1845–1926), a prominent local merchant and landowner.

The town's name was changed in 1890 to "Hicks" and in 1892 to "Moran" for Texas Central Railroad president John J. Moran. By the 1890s, the community had a school and Baptist, Church of Christ, Cumberland Presbyterian, and Methodist congregations. A newspaper was begun in 1895 and bank in 1902. Incorporated in 1919, Moran was a shipping point for drilling supplies during the oil and gas boom of 1910–1930. Today the area's economy is based on farming, ranching, and oil and gas production. (1976)

MORGAN (Bosque Co.)

SH 174, 10 mi. E in Kimball Bend Park

Chisholm Trail
Kimball Crossing

Kimball, one of the first towns in Bosque County, was established at this site in the early 1850s. One of the westward wagon routes forded the river at this crossing until a ferry was built in 1865.

The famous Chisholm Trail made its major crossing of the Brazos here. During the 1870s tens of thousands of Texas Longhorn cattle forded the river and were driven to Northern markets.

Building of barbed wire fences and railroads in the 1880s caused abandonment of the Chisholm Trail. Kimball, with no railroad and loss of the cattle trail, became a ghost town by the middle 1900s.

MORGAN (Bosque Co.)

SH 174, 4.5 mi. N

Union Hill School

Started before 1879, the Union Hill School was one of several rural schools that served the early settlers of Bosque County. A two-room 1888 schoolhouse, located across the road, was used until 1914, when a two-story building was constructed at this site. A nearby stable housed the students' horses during the school day. Enlarged by the 1926 merger with the Auburn Hill District, Union Hill became part of the Kopperl District in 1939. Former students, which include many area business, professional, and agricultural leaders, still meet for a biennial school reunion. (1981)

MORTON (Cochran Co.)

SH 24, 5 mi. E

Cochran County

Created August 21, 1876, from Bexar County. Named for a native of New Jersey, Robert Cochran, a private who died for Texas Independence in the siege of the Alamo.

Indian hostilities and the distance to market and supplies made settlement slow. The 1900 census listed 25 cowboys. In 1910 there were 75 persons; then 67 in 1920.

Organized May 6, 1924, with Morton as county seat. Oil discovery and development of irrigation caused rapid growth, and made it a farm and petroleum center.

Site of Silver Lake, a saline known to early Spanish explorers as Laguna Quemado. (1965)

MORTON (Cochran Co.)

SH 214, 2.5 mi. S, then .8 mi. W

C. C. Slaughter Ranch

Headquarters for pioneering C. C. Slaughter Ranch, made up of 246,669 acres of Cochran and Hockley County lands. Col. C. C. Slaughter—a leader in banking, ranching and religious life in Texas—purchased land 1898–1901.

First headquarters was a half-dugout. In 1915, C. C. Slaughter Cattle Company, Inc., brought men from Mexico to build this adobe and concrete quadrangle, on order of a Spanish hacienda. This was one of the finest Texas ranch buildings of its era. Awarded Medallion Plate. (1962)

MOSCOW (Polk Co.)

US 59, near Loop 177 intersection at park

Modern Texas Statesman
William Pettus Hobby
(1878–1964)

Born in Moscow, son of a state senator, Judge Edwin E. Hobby. At age 17 joined staff of *Houston Post* and rose to managing editor at 23. Was named publisher of *Beaumont Enterprise* in 1907.

Elected lieutenant governor 1914 and 1916, became governor at Ferguson's impeachment in 1917. Won reelection to serve his own full term, 1919–1921.

Appointed to first board of regents, Texas Technological College, 1924. President of *Houston Post* 1924–1964.

Married in 1931 Oveta Culp, parliamentarian of the Texas House of Representatives. For the next quarter-century shared with his wife editorial administration of the *Post,* sparing her during World War II to serve as commander of Women's Army Corps of the United States Forces, and during 1953–1955 to serve in the cabinet of President Dwight D. Eisenhower. Their children were Willlam Pettus, Jr., and Jessica.

As governor, term was marked by initiation of free schoolbooks, compulsory school attendance law, budget system in state government, state drouth relief, Texas participation in World War I, and the effecting of woman's suffrage in the State and Nation. (1964)

MOSS HILL (Liberty Co.)   *SH 146, 13 mi. N*
Concord Baptist Church
Organized May 24, 1845, with the following members: Nancy Lea, Margaret Houston, Antoinette L. Bledsoe, Joseph L. Ellis, Benjamin F. Ellis, Archer B. Worsham, and B. G. Brown, pastor. It sent delegates to the Baptist State Convention, organized September 8, 1848, at Anderson, Texas. General Sam Houston attended services here.   (1936)

MOSS HILL (Liberty Co.)   *SH 146, N of intersection with SH 105*
Kalita
Chief of the Coushatta Indians. Friend of the Pioneers. D.A.R., Liberty, Texas.

MOULTON (Lavaca Co.)   *SH 95 at Nelson St.*
Moulton
Founded (about 2 mi. NW) in early 1850s. Moved to this site after 1887 when the San Antonio & Aransas Pass Railroad extended its line from Yoakum to Waco, placing a station at this point. Sam and Will Moore, brothers, took lead in building an outstanding school here in 1901. Town remains an agricultural and shipping center.   (1970)

MOUNT CALM (Limestone Co.)   *SH 31, 1 mi. SW*
Col. Leonard Williams
Served in the Army of Texas. Participated in the storming of Bexar. A trader and interpreter among Indian tribes.

MOUNT ENTERPRISE (Rusk Co.)   *US 84, 12 mi. E then 1 mi. N*
Monte Verdi
Frontier version, southern Greek architecture. So placed that most of Rusk and much of Cherokee and Nacogdoches Counties are visible from upstairs porch. Built on his 10,000 acre plantation by Julien Sidney Devereux (1805–1856), justice of the peace, county commissioner, legislator. Awarded Medallion Plate.   (1964)

MOUNT ENTERPRISE (Rusk Co.)   *US 84, 12 mi. E then 1 mi. N*
Medallion House
Birdwell House
Built in early 1840s for Allen Birdwell, 1851 county commissioner; member Texas Legislature 1853–1854 and 1863–1864.

House is excellent example of "Saddle bag" architecture–story-and-half double house.

Built of hand-hewn logs with squared morticed corners. Later "boarded over." Has four main rooms, two on each floor. First floor rooms have exposed beam ceilings. Moved to Monte Verdi plantation. Restored by Mr. and Mrs. E. F. Lowry, 1965.   (1967)

MOUNT ENTERPRISE (Rusk Co.)   *US 84, 5 mi. E at Concord Community*
Dennard Home
A native of Missouri, Augustus "Gus" Dennard (d. 1933) came to Texas with his parents in 1883. A leader in the Concord community, Dennard was a merchant, farmer, and blacksmith. He operated a forge on part of the land he purchased in 1901. A year later, he completed this home for his family. A good example of East Texas vernacular style architecture, the house features paired gables over the porch, which is supported by turned posts with decorative brackets.   (1984)

MT. PLEASANT (Titus Co.)   *US 67, 1 mi. E in roadside park*
Titus County
Formed from Red River and Bowie Counties. Created May 11, 1846. Organized July 13, 1846. Named in honor of Andrew J. Titus, 1814–1855; pioneer of Northwest Texas; soldier in the Mexican War; member of the Texas Legislature. County Seat, Mt. Pleasant.

MT. PLEASANT (Titus Co.)   *SH 49 in Dellwood Park*
Dellwood Park
Before 1830, Caddo Indians had campgrounds here around mineral springs flowing red, white, and blue waters. First home at future Mount Pleasant was built here in 1830s by Benjamin Gooch.

A health-recreational resort by 1895, springs area was site (1909–1916), of the lavish Dellwood Hotel, built by the Red Mineral Springs Development Co., headed by Dr. T. M. Fleming. These steps are from Dellwood Hotel, which burned.

Favorite spot for Confederate conventions, political rallies, and other meetings, the site was acquired 1951 by City of Mount Pleasant, as Dellwood Park. (1973)

MT. PLEASANT (Titus Co.)   *N. Madison and W 4th St.*
First Presbyterian Church of Mt. Pleasant

This church was organized by the Rev. William Waldo Brimm (b. 1837), an early area evangelist, on Aug. 14, 1881. Two years later the congregation bought the land at this site and soon after began constructing a white frame church building. Despite hardships in its developing years, the church grew rapidly in the 1900s. The frame structure was moved to another location and replaced by a brick building in 1923. Continued expansion led to the need for an educational facility, built in 1955. For over one hundred years this church has continued to be a vital part of community life. (1981)

MOUNT SELMAN (Cherokee Co.)   *US 69, ¼ mi. S of Bullard*
The Burning Bush Colony

From 1913 until 1919 a religious community operated in this vicinity, on the former Joseph Pickens Douglas Plantation. The colony was established by the Metropolitan Church Association, commonly called the Burning Bush Society, an evangelical organization founded in Chicago about 1900. This 400-member Burning Bush Colony was set up to be a self-sustaining agricultural community. It operated its own school, sawmill, power plant, water system, and sewage disposal facility. Unable to pay its debts, the colony disbanded after the close of World War I. (1984)

MT. VERNON (Franklin Co.)   *US 67 at SH 37*
Franklin County

Formed from Titus County. Created March 8, 1875. Organized April 30, 1875. Named in honor of Benjamin C. Franklin, 1805–1873, hero of San Jacinto, district judge of the Republic of Texas. Member of the legislature. Mt. Vernon, county seat.

MT. VERNON (Franklin Co.)   *US 67, 4 mi. E at Ripley Creek Crossing*
Ripley Massacre

Ambrose Ripley and his wife Rachel (Wood) brought their family to Texas in 1837, settling near here in what was then Red River County. They established their home near the Nacogdoches Road (Cherokee Trace) and a stream now known as Ripley Creek.

On April 10, 1841, while Ripley was away, a band of Indians attacked his farmstead, killing first his eldest son who was plowing in the field. Mrs. Ripley and five children were killed trying to reach a canebreak and one infant died when the house was burned. Two of Ripley's daughters eluded the Indians and made it to a neighboring farm. Charles Black and Charles S. Stewart led a group of settlers north in pursuit of the band. Near the Sulphur River they encountered Indians, who may or may not have been involved in the massacre, and attacked them, killing several.

The Ripley family massacre was an isolated incident in this area, but it proved to be a rallying point for increased frontier defenses and for support of the anti-Indian policies of Texas president Mirabeau B. Lamar. The attack also influenced the formation of a militia unit under the leadership of Gen. Edward H. Tarrant and Cols. James Bourland and William C. Young to rid the area of Indians. (Texas Sesquicentennial 1836–1986)

MOUNTAIN HOME (Kerr Co.)   *SH 41, 16 mi. W at entrance to ranch*
Y. O. Ranch

Charles Armand Schreiner (1836–1927), a native of Alsace-Lorraine, immigrated to Texas with his family in 1852. He joined the Texas Rangers at age fifteen, and in 1857 entered the cattle business at Turtle Creek in Kerr County. He left to serve in the Third Texas Infantry during the Civil War, and returned to Kerr County in 1865. Moving to Kerrville in 1869, he opened a successful mercantile business. The threat of Indian raids in the area soon prompted the formation of the Kerrville Mounted Rifles, and Schreiner was appointed captain by Governor Richard Coke in 1875.

In 1880, he bought the Taylor-Clements ranch and its Y. O. Brand. Texas longhorn cattle became Captain Schreiner's primary concern, and over 300,000 head were driven from this area to Kansas railheads. Because of Schreiner's venture in raising sheep and goats, Kerrville was known as the "mohair center of the world."

The last cattle drive from the ranch was held in 1941, the stock being moved to Kerrville for shipment to Fort Worth. The Y. O. Ranch has also become known throughout the world for its Texas longhorn cattle and its native and exotic wildlife conservation programs.

(Texas Sesquicentennial 1836–1986)

MUENSTER (Cooke Co.)   *US 82 near City Park*
Muenster
In 1889, brothers Anton, August, and Emil Flusche contracted to sell 22,000 acres of this land along the Missouri, Kansas & Texas Railroad. Jot Gunter gave 25 acres for a school, church, cemetery, and park. The first mass, celebrated Dec. 8, 1889, marked the official beginning of this German Catholic town. Despite drought, typhoid fever, and tornadoes destroying the first two church buildings, the area grew and farming and dairy business increased. Farmers established an insurance company and a marketing group for buying products in bulk. An oil boom in 1926 added to the prosperity.   (1979)

MULESHOE (Bailey Co.)   *US 84, .5 mi NW in roadside park*
Bailey County
A part of Bexar Territory, 1836–1876. Created August 21, 1876. Organized November 5, 1918. Named in honor of Peter James Bailey, 1812–1836, a Kentucky lawyer killed in defending the Alamo. Muleshoe, the county seat.   (1964)

MULESHOE (Bailey Co.)   *FM 746, 15 mi. SW*
Coyote Lake
One of numerous natural, salt lakes in the Texas Panhandle; its waters, although brackish, have been welcome enough at various times to Indians, buffalo hunters, and thirsty cattle on hot, dry days.

The lake, having a shoreline of over six and a half miles and a bed area of 829 acres, is one of the largest of the many saline lakes in the region.

In early days, the Comanches were masters of this area, but after the 1874 Battle of Adobe Walls, they no longer hindered settlement of the staked plains. Today, artifacts found near the lake shore show that this was once a favorite Comanche camp site.

Even while the Indians were still a menace, buffalo hunters swarmed into the Panhandle, and they, too, often camped on Coyote Lake. Until 1877, they killed so many of the huge, shaggy beasts that the southern herd, once numbering millions, nearly became extinct.

From 1885 to about 1910, Coyote Lake served as a watering spot for cattle on the huge (3,050,000 acres) XIT Ranch, which blanketed the western Panhandle. In 1898, when the Pecos & Northern Texas Railroad built through Bovina (30 miles north), the lake watered thousands of cattle en route from southern ranches to the railhead, and from there to Northern markets.   (1968)

MULESHOE (Bailey Co.)   *SH 214, 2.5 mi. N*
.5 mi. W to Townsite of Old Hurley
First town in Bailey County. Promoted in 1907 by land company of Stevens A. Coldren (d. 1924). He had a townsite surveyed and named it for Patrick J. Hurley (1883–1963) New Mexico political leader. Company built a general store, hotel, and livery stable. Wide plowed furrows indicated future streets. In August 1907 a post office was established.

Settlers came in and a church and school were begun.

In 1913 however, the railroad bypassed town. Efforts to start "New Hurley"—on the rail line— failed. After Muleshoe became county seat, 1918, Hurley expired.   (1970)

MULESHOE (Bailey Co.)   *SH 214, 20 mi. S on refuge entrance road*
Muleshoe National
Wildlife Refuge
Founded in 1935 as a wintering area for migratory waterfowl, Muleshoe Wildlife Refuge is on the "central flyway" in a chain of refuges from Mexico to Canada. Migrating birds begin arriving in August and remain until April. The largest wintering concentration of sandhill cranes in North America is most noticeable here from October through March. The site, covering over

5,000 acres, provides habitat for many other species of birds and wildlife. Muleshoe is one of several National Wildlife Refuges in Texas that protect migratory water-fowl, endangered wildlife species, or unique natural habitats. (1967, 1985)

MULESHOE (Bailey Co.) *FM 214, 2 mi. S*

The
XIT Ranch South Line
(About 100 ft. S of This Marker)

One of most famous boundaries in Texas. Marked edge of XIT—Ranch empire bartered away by Texas for its capitol building.

The 16th Legislature in 1879 designated a 3,000,000-acre tract to be used in payment for the capitol. The grant extended 200 miles north from line here. Besides portion in this county, it included land in counties of Castro, Cochran, Dallam, Deaf Smith, Hartley, Hockley, Lamb, Oldham, and Parmer. Heading the investors who built the capitol were wealthy Chicago merchants John V. and C. B. Farwell. Their surveying was begun in 1886. (1970)

MULLIN (Mills Co.) *US 84*

Site of
the Settlement of Williams Ranch
(4 mi. S)

Once a prominent frontier town, Williams Ranch grew up around the homestead of cattleman John Williams (1804–1871), who came to this area in 1855. The community flourished during the Civil War (1861–1865) because of trade with Mexico and by 1874 had stores, saloons, a hotel, mill, and blacksmith shop. In 1875 Henry Ford and J. M. Parks bought most of the land in the village and platted a townsite. They proposed the name "Parksford" but "Williams Ranch" prevailed when the post office opened in 1877. The community was a stagestop and a roundup point on the Western Cattle Trail. It claimed the first hotel, newspaper, telegraph, and public school in Brown and Mills Counties. In 1881 it was one of the towns considered as a site for the University of Texas. Williams Ranch reached its peak of activity in the early 1880s, with a population of over 250.

The settlement began to decline when the railroad bypassed it in 1885. An outbreak of mob violence was quelled by the Texas Rangers in 1887. By 1892 the post office and all businesses had closed. Today the site is marked by the natural springs that attracted the original settlers and by Williams Ranch Cemetery, burial place of many pioneers and their descendants. (1976)

MUMFORD (Robertson Co.) *FM 50, 2 mi. W*

Big Brazos Bridge

An 1895 engineering victory—longest Brazos bridge in that era—spanning heavy flow below ford of "Little River" (San Andres) with "Big Brazos." This bridge stood where immemorial Indian trails crossed the river. Later these paths became part of El Camino Real (The King's Highway). About a mile downstream in 1830 Fort Tenoxtitlan was established. In 1855 Jesse Mumford (founder of Mumford) operated a ferry at the trail crossing.

Authorized by commissioners court of Robertson County, this landmark iron bridge served until removed by a flood, 1899. (1968)

MYRTLE SPRINGS (Van Zandt Co.) *SH 64, 3 mi. SW*

Hayden Baptist Church

The organizational meeting for this congregation was held in October 1878. Led by Dr. George D. Staton, who also served as first pastor, the fourteen charter members adopted the name Myrtle Springs Baptist Church and agreed to meet monthly. A church building, constructed in 1889, served the congregation until 1900, when the meeting place was moved to the Cow Prairie Schoolhouse, which was located near this site. Four years later, the fellowship built a new sanctuary and adopted the name Hayden Baptist Church. The pioneer church continues to serve the surrounding rural area. (1985)

NACOGDOCHES (Nacogdoches Co.) *US 59, 3 mi. N*

Nacogdoches County

Home of the Nacogdoches Indians in the 17th century.

Spanish settlements, 1716, alternately settled and abandoned in 18th century due to French encroachments. Scene of the Fredonian Rebellion in 1827.

Organized a municipality, 1832, under the Mexican government. Created a county March 24, 1837. Nacogdoches, established 1779, became the county seat in 1836.

NACOGDOCHES (Nacogdoches Co.)   *FM 225, 14 mi. W and 6 mi. S of Douglass*
Presidio Nuestra Señora de los Dolores
Built by Capt. Domingo Ramon 1716. Repaired and enlarged by Marquis of San Miguel de Aguayo, 1721.

Abandoned about 1730. Built by the Spanish government as a fort and headquarters for soldiers to guard the East Texas missions and the borders of the New Phillipines.

NACOGDOCHES (Nacogdoches Co.)   *SH 21, 8 mi. E*
Site of El Atascoso
In the 1778 return to East Texas of settlers removed in 1772–1773, this Atascoso Bayou-to-Puentesuellos segment of El Camino Real was site of many camps, and here Jose Mora established Rancho "El Atascoso." Others settled nearby, joining him for protection against the original Indian inhabitants. (1973)

NACOGDOCHES (Nacogdoches Co.)   *SH 21, 3.5 mi. E*
Sam P. Smith Place
A good example of an East Texas farm home, this house originally had five rooms, four porches, and an enclosed dog trot. It was built in 1880 for Samuel Pharr and Mary Spencer Smith by Smith's brother-in-law Andrew B. Ireson. A local cabinetmaker and carpenter, Ireson also designed the woodwork and some of the furniture. Sam Smith, who grew up in Nacogdoches County, was a farmer. He and Mary had 12 children and lived here until their deaths in 1941. (1985)

NACOGDOCHES (Nacogdoches Co.)   *US 59, 5 mi. N at Millard's Crossing*
The Millard-Lee House
Built about 1837 by Nacogdoches merchant-deputy postmaster-road overseer Robert F. Millard (1803–1847) a family home that sometimes was also a boardinghouse. In 1859 David Lee, a blacksmith-merchant-county official, bought the house, then situated near public square in Nacogdoches (5 mi. S), it remained until 1960 the Lee family home. In 1970, Mrs. Albert (Lera Millard) Thomas bought, moved, and restored it here at Millard's Crossing, named for the builder's family. (1974)

NACOGDOCHES (Nacogdoches Co.)   *US 59, 5 mi. N at Millard's Crossing*
Burrows-Millard House
Confederate veteran Elijah M. Burrows (1844–1893) built the rear portion of this pioneer farmhouse before he married Mary Josephine (Molly) Millard (1848–1901) in 1867. Between 1869 and 1874, he added the rooms and porch across the front. Members of the Burrows family occupied the structure until 1972, when George Van Burrows gave it to Lera Millard (Mrs. Albert) Thomas, descendant of the builder. She moved it ½ mile north to this site and restored it. (1976)

NACOGDOCHES (Nacogdoches Co.)   *Fredonia at El Camino Real (Main)*
The Battle of Nacogdoches
(August 2, 1832)
One of the opening actions of the Texas War for Independence, this battle occurred soon after settlers drove out the Mexican garrisons at Anahuac and Velasco. In 1832, Col. Jose de las Piedras, in command of over 300 soldiers, ordered the residents to surrender all firearms. Citizens of Nacogdoches and other East Texas towns resisted by forming the "National Militia," commanded by James W. Bullock.

When Piedras refused to support the constitution of 1824, the militia marched toward the Mexicans on the square and the Mexicans opened fire. In hand-to-hand combat, the militia took the stone fort and several nearby structures, but the Mexicans continued to hold Piedras' headquarters in the Red House. Adolphus Sterne showed San Augustine "Redlanders" how to outflank the Mexicans. Piedras' men fled during the night and were captured August 3 by militiamen near Loco Creek. Fighting ended after the Mexicans arrested their leader at John Durst's home. A peace treaty was signed on August 6. Piedras lost 47 men. Four Texans died, including the Alcalde of Nacogdoches, Encarnacion Chireno. Because of this incident, Mexican troops were never again stationed in East Texas, leaving settlers free to meet and air their grievances.   (1979)

NACOGDOCHES (Nacogdoches Co.)

1936 North St., in front of Rusk Bldg., SFASU campus

Alton W. Birdwell
(1870–1954)

Born near Elkhart in Anderson County, Alton W. Birdwell was reared in the Piney Woods of East Texas. His early education was provided through home schooling; he earned money for later study by hand-molding clay bricks and hewing railroad ties. Birdwell attended classes at the University of Texas, the University of Missouri, and the University of Chicago. His first teaching position was at Pleasant Retreat in Smith County in 1892. Birdwell served as principal in Tyler, superintendent of schools in Troup, and superintendent of Smith County schools. He became a professor of history at Southwest Texas State University (SWT) in 1910, and married fellow teacher Maude Margaret Shipe in 1914. He took courses in normal school administration at Peabody College in Nashville, Tennessee, where he was acclaimed for his work in education theory. He earned a master's degree from Peabody in 1916 and returned to SWT as dean of the faculty. Birdwell was appointed president of the newly-created Stephen F. Austin State Normal School in 1917. Because World War I delayed the opening of the school, he remained at SWT, serving the war effort in various defense groups. In August 1922, Birdwell and his family arrived in Nacogdoches. Delays in construction of the Austin building forced him to postpone the opening of the college in 1923; he nevertheless opened the institution in borrowed facilities. Birdwell selected the faculty, taught history, and worked with area schools to support the college. He was equally resourceful in expanding the school in the 1920s and in protecting the college from collapsing enrollment and legislative cuts during the Great Depression. After his retirement in 1942, Birdwell remained on the faculty and served as president emeritus until his death.   (1999)

NACOGDOCHES (Nacogdoches Co.)

Corner of North (US 59) & Rusk St.

Homesite of Thomas J. Rusk
(1803–1857)

Soldier-statesman of the Republic of Texas. A hero of San Jacinto. Commander in chief of the army 1836. Chief justice of the Supreme Court 1839. President of the Constitutional Convention, 1845. United States Senator, 1846. He called Nacogdoches his home from 1835 to 1857. (1936)

NACOGDOCHES (Nacogdoches Co.)

1936 North St. (US 59) at SFASU campus between Austin & Rusk buildings

Pioneering Higher Education in East Texas

The absence of an institution of higher learning to train teachers in East Texas became obvious in the early 20th century. "Normal institutes" or ad hoc college courses were important statewide attempts to supplement the educational level of the teachers in rural school systems. The Legislature's decision in 1909 to abolish the community school system in favor of public school systems further increased demand for trained teachers. To address the needs of the East Texas region, the Legislature in 1915 authorized the placement of a normal college east of the 96th meridian. Legislative, sectional, and political difficulties delayed the charters until 1917. By the time the schools were funded in 1921, the state had passed the compulsory education law for children and the certification law for teachers, creating a huge demand for educated instructors in Texas. In the rural districts of Texas, 24% of public school teachers had not completed high school, 22% had normal college training, and 13% were graduates of other college and university programs. Stephen F. Austin State Teachers College opened in 1923. The faculty consisted of 24 instructors selected by President Alton W. Birdwell. The majority of the educators' degrees came from Texas universities, but other major national institutions were represented. The vast majority of students came from East Texas, particularly the counties surrounding Nacogdoches. The early faculty, staff, and students of Stephen F. Austin State Teachers College transformed teaching into a profession in East Texas while making education an attainable goal in the region. These men and women laid the foundation for public education in East Texas.   (1999)

NACOGDOCHES (Nacogdoches Co.)   *1936 North St. (US 59),*
                                                      SFASU campus
Rusk Building
Built on the homestead lands of warrior statesman Thomas Jefferson Rusk, Stephen F. Austin State Teachers College (SFA) was swollen with success shortly after taking over its new facilities, the Austin Building and Aikman Gymnasium, in 1924. The board of regents had approved the erection of the Rusk Building in their original plan, but cost-cutting measures in the State Legislature led to a delay in its construction until 1926. Designed by architect W. E. Ketchum, it was built by F. A. Mote, the same contractor who had completed the Austin Building in 1924. An excellent example of a Classical Revival public building, the Rusk Building features a fifteen-bay primary façade, a grand staircase, pedimented three-bay entry, Doric columns and cast stone details. An important academic facility for a variety of SFA programs, it initially housed the college library, departments of education and business, and the demonstration school for teacher training. In later years it was home to the departments of applied arts and sciences, communications, continuing education, social work and criminal justice, as well as administrative offices of the registrar, admissions staff and student services. The Texas Folklore Society and university printing services have occupied the basement. An extensive renovation project in 1987 returned the Rusk Building to its original grandeur. The structure retains a high degree of architectural integrity and remains a central facility on the Stephen F. Austin State University Campus.   (1998)

NACOGDOCHES (Nacogdoches Co.)   *1936 North St. (US 59) in front*
                                             of Rusk Building, SFASU campus
Thomas Jefferson Rusk
(1803–1857)
Born in South Carolina, Thomas Jefferson Rusk showed an early aptitude for the law, passing the bar at age twenty-one. He began to practice law in Georgia, where he married Mary F. Cleveland in 1827. Rusk was so taken with Nacogdoches that he sent for his family and became a citizen of Mexico in 1835. Quickly becoming involved in the independence movement, he organized a group of Nacogdoches volunteers and joined Stephen F. Austin's army. The provisional government named him inspector general of the army. He signed the Texas Declaration of Independence as a delegate from Nacogdoches and was appointed secretary of war. Rusk fought with Sam Houston at the Battle of San Jacinto and was briefly commander in chief of the Army of the Republic of Texas. After the war, Rusk was again appointed secretary of war and major general of the Texas Militia. Elected to the Republic of Texas Congress, he chaired the House Military Committee. In 1840, he retired from his position as Chief Justice of the State Supreme Court to return to a successful law practice in Nacogdoches, but he was called again to the militia in 1843 and was soon elected major general by the Congress. Returning home in June, Rusk focused his energies on the establishment of Nacogdoches University. Following his term as president of the convention of 1845 to annex Texas to the United States, Rusk was elected to a U. S. Senate seat in 1846. He and Senator Sam Houston established the southwestern boundary of Texas, and he promoted construction of a transcontinental railroad route through Texas. Mary Rusk died of tuberculosis in 1856, and an ill and despondent T. J. Rusk took his own life in 1857.
                                                      (1999)

NACOGDOCHES (Nacogdoches Co.)   *1936 North St. (US 59), SFASU*
                                       campus between Austin & Rusk buildings
The University Tradition in Nacogdoches
The Spanish friars who built the Mission of Our Lady of Nacogdoches passed to the townspeople a sense of scholarship and educational responsibility. Prominent citizens such as Sam Houston and Thomas J. Rusk were well known for their attention to education. Town citizens pursued the establishment of a university in the 1840s. The Republic of Texas granted a charter for a school in February 1845. Nacogdoches University was a preparatory school with some college subjects included in the curriculum. Townspeople gave money, materials, land and labor to support the school and secure for their children the best education possible. The school moved into its permanent home on Washington Square in 1858. Hard times began with the Civil War; later, several entities operated the institution, including the Catholic Church, local Masons, and

Keachi College of Louisiana. In 1904, the trustees deeded the campus to the newly created public school district of Nacogdoches. Citizens began a movement in 1906 to lobby for the formation of a new college. This culminated in the first, although ultimately unsuccessful, attempt to establish an East Texas normal school in 1915. When legislation in 1917 called for a college "east of the 96th meridian," Nacogdoches organized a citizens' committee. A pamphlet entitled "Twenty-three reasons why Stephen F. Austin State Normal College ought to be located at Nacogdoches . . ." stated their case. As they had 70 years earlier, the people of Nacogdoches lobbied heavily for the new college, pledging 208 acres of land, 250 students, paved streets, and free electricity to the institution. When the opening was postponed from the summer of 1923 to the fall, the town recruited students from all of East Texas and even supplied a temporary home for a year—Washington Square. (1999)

NADA (Colorado Co.) *SH 71*
Nada Post Office
The post office in Nada was established in 1894 when William J. Engbrock, Jr., was appointed the first postmaster. The post office was located in the general store owned by his father, William Engbrock, Sr., until 1898.

Subsequent locations of the post office changed several times over the years, depending on the profession of the succeeding postmasters. Twice it was housed in the medical office and pharmacy of Dr. Francis Daehne, appointed in 1898, and Dr. John A. Halamicek, appointed in 1915. The post office returned to the general store during the terms of Joseph H. Labay, named in 1900, and Joseph J. Patter (Potter), appointed in 1903. Adolph Hruzek became postmaster in 1911 and moved the post office to his general store across the street. Appointed in 1921, Antone Lichnovsky moved the office in 1935 to his general store built near the newly constructed State Highway 71. His daughter, appointed in 1946, also served from his store. In 1953, the post office moved to the site of the postmaster's new service station and garage, where it remained for thirty years.

In 1987, a new post office facility was built here on land purchased from the Braden family. (1996)

NAPLES (Morris Co.) *US 67 E in roadside park*
Morris County
Created and organized in 1875, with Daingerfield as county seat. Named for William W. Morris (1805–1883), who came to Texas in 1849. When the Civil War began in 1861, was in 8th Legislature that armed the state, enacted soldiers' families' relief laws and set up 2,000 mile frontier and coastline defenses. Also in 13th Legislature, 1873–1875.

Of the 254 Texas counties, 42 bear Indian, French or Spanish names. 10 honor such colonizers as Stephen F. Austin, "Father of Texas." 12 were named for Washington, Clay and other American patriots.

96 were named for men who fought in the Texas War for Independence (15 dying at the Alamo), signed the Declaration of Independence from Mexico, or served as statesmen in the Republic of Texas.

23 have the name of frontiersmen and pioneers. 11 honor American statesmen who worked for the annexation of Texas; 10, leaders in Texas since statehood, including jurists, ministers, educators, historians, statesmen; and 36, men like Morris prominent in the Confederacy during the Civil War.

Delta and 8 others have geographical names. San Jacinto and Val Verde were named for battles; Live Oak and Orange, for trees; and Mason for a fort. (1964)

NAPLES (Morris Co.) *US 67*
Naples
When railroad by-passed prosperous town of Wheatville (3 mi. N), this rival town emerged at railroad. Post office moved here Jan. 1882, and was called Station Belden. Name was changed to Naples by U.S. Post Office Department, Feb. 1895.

With depletion of hardwood forests, economy returned to cattle and agriculture. (1967)

NAPLES (Morris Co.)

US 67 right-of-way, near "Motor Inn"

Home Town of
United States Senator Morris Sheppard
(1875–1941)

One of great lawmakers of the United States. Born near Naples, son of John L. and Alice Eddins Sheppard. Attended local schools. Received degrees of B. A. and LL. B., University of Texas; LL.M., Yale; LL.D., Southern Methodist University. Entered law practice in 1898.

Served in United States Congress 1902–1913; United States Senate, 1913–1941. Active in legislation for agriculture, waterways, topographical and geological surveys, development of helium and potash deposits, construction and improvement of federal buildings (including national archives), federal insurance for bank deposits, and air mail service. Author in senate of Federal Credit Union Act, the Federal Maternity and Infancy Act, and the 18th (Prohibition) Amendment. He supported the 19th (Women's Suffrage) Amendment.

One of creators of World War I aircraft board, he continued to champion military aviation, even when air power was discredited during 1920s and '30s. His leadership prevented disastrous curtailment of air power and helped prepare nation's air defenses in World War II. He was chairman Senate Military Affairs Committee, 1933–1941. Sheppard Air Force Base, Wichita Falls, was named in his honor in 1942. He married Lucile Sanderson; they had 3 daughters.   (1968)

NASH (Bowie Co.)

US 82

Town of Nash

Begun about 1873; first named "T. C. Junction" for its location on transcontinental division of Texas & Pacific Railroad. In 1884 post office was established and named "Park," after Dr. J. N. Parker, the first postmaster.

First school started 1885 in single room. New buildings have been erected in 1904, 1924, 1967.

In 1906 the town was named in honor of Martin Manny Nash, division superintendent of Texas & Pacific. Noted resident was Dr. Joseph Abner Dodd (1871–1944), who served 6 terms in Texas House of Representatives. Present town population stands at 2,000.   (1970)

NATALIA (Medina Co.)

IH 35, 1.9 mi. NE, rest areas

Robert Lee Bobbitt
(Jan. 24, 1888–Sept. 14,1972)

Robert Lee Bobbitt was born near Hillsboro, Texas, the son of Joseph A. and Laura Duff Bobbitt. He graduated from North Texas Normal College in 1911, and from the University of Texas Law School in 1915. After opening a law practice in Laredo, Bobbitt married Mary B. Westbrook on April 20, 1918, while an officer in the 90th Infantry Division during World War I.

Bobbitt was elected to the Texas Legislature in 1923, served three two-year terms, the last as speaker of the House of Representatives, and was appointed attorney general in 1929. He returned to private practice in San Antonio in 1931, and served on the board of directors of the Texas College of Arts and Industries. In 1935, he was selected as an associate justice of the San Antonio Court of Civil Appeals, a post from which he resigned in 1937 to receive an appointment as the chairman of the Texas Highway Commission. During Bobbitt's six-year term, the Texas Highway Department made great strides toward a goal of a connected system of paved roads in the state.

In 1944, Bobbitt was a presidential elector, and, in 1958, was appointed to last public service post, as member of the board of regents of North Texas State College, his alma mater.   (1974)

NAVASOTA (Grimes Co.)

SH 105, 11 mi. SE

Home of
Rosanna Ward Britton Grimes
(1803–1871)
and
Jesse Grimes
(1788–1866)

Signer of the Texas Declaration of Independence and the Constitution of the Republic of Texas member of the Congress of the Republic; state senator. In his honor Grimes County was named.
(1965)

357

NAVASOTA (Grimes Co.)

Primus Kelly

A faithful Negro slave. Came to nearby Courtney, Grimes County in 1851 with his master, John W. S. West from North Carolina. West was a prominent and wealthy pioneer planter and landowner.

At the outbreak of the Civil War, West sent Kelly "to take care" of his three sons—Robert M., Richard and John Haywood—who joined the famous Terry's Texas Rangers, where they served with distinction.

Kelly was not content "to wait on" his charges but joined them in battle, firing his own musket and cap and ball pistol. Twice Kelly brought to Texas the wounded Richard, twice took him to the front again.

After war, bought a small farm near "Marse Robert," raised a large family and prospered. Died in 1890s.

The courage and loyalty of Kelly was typical of most Texas Negro slaves. Hundreds "went to war" with their masters. Many operated the farms and ranches of soldiers away at war, producing food, livestock, cotton and clothing for the Confederacy. Others, did outside work to support their master's families. They protected homes from Indians, bandits and deserters and did community guard and patrol duty.

At war's end, most slaves, like Primus Kelly, became useful and productive citizens of Texas.
(1965)

NAVASOTA (Grimes Co.)

SH 90, 2 mi. E

R. B. S. Foster Home

Early Texas plantation home in architectural style of the Atlantic States, Malcolm Camp, wealthy cotton planter, built this structure in 1859, with lumber hauled from East Texas sawmills. High-ceiling rooms are very large. Formal dining room in sandstone-lined cellar was unique. Had detached kitchen.

Purchased 1883 by a leading local citizen, R. B. S. Foster (1848–1889), this was birthplace of his three children—Georgia, Robert F. and Nettie Rose. So stable is this locality that home was continuously occupied until 1966 by Fosters or their agents. (1968)

NAVASOTA (Grimes Co.)

SH 90, 400 blk. E Washington, W end Esplanade

Rene Robert Cavalier Sieur de la Salle

Treacherously slain by his own men near this spot in March, 1687. Born Rouey, France, November 22, 1643. Explorer of the Mississippi River. Frontier statesman, empire builder, nobleman in rank and character.

NECHANITZ (Fayette Co.)

FM 2145, 10 mi. N of La Grange

Earthman Farm

Established 1835 with one-room log cabin as settlers' dwelling.

In 1841, a party of Indians was alleged to have killed, scalped, and mutilated the body of young Henry Earthman, who was hunting horses (with his brother Fields) near their home. Fields Earthman took the news of the murder to Rutersville College (8 mi. E), and nearly all boys at school spent the ensuing three weeks hunting fruitlessly for Indians.

Present house was built 1877. Awarded Medallion Plate. (1972)

NEEDVILLE (Fort Bend Co.)

SH 36, 250 ft. N of junction with FM 1236

Town of
Needville

Had beginning in 1892 when settler August Schendel opened general store here, on his land. Blacksmith shop, cotton gin, and room for post office had been added by 1894, when Schendel was appointed first postmaster.

He suggested naming place "Needmore" because it needed more of everything, but another town already had that name.

Slowly village became trade center. First church service was held 1891; school opened by 1897.

Early economy, based on stock-raising and farming, was altered radically with discovery of oil, natural gas, and sulphur, 1920–1930s. (1971)

NELSONVILLE (Austin Co.)   SH 159
First Czech Immigrants in Texas
People from Czechoslovakia began to come to America for liberty as early as 1633. First known Czech in Texas was Jiri Rybar (George Fisher), customs officer in Galveston in 1829. Others arrived individually for years before letters sent home by the Rev. Josef Arnost Bergman, an 1849 Czech settler at Cat Spring (9 mi. S), inspired immigrations in large numbers.

Josef Lidumil Lesikar (1806–1887) was instrumental in forming the first two large migrations, 1851 and 1853, with names of family parties listed on ship logs as Silar (Shiller), 69; Lesikar (Leshikar), 16; Mares (Maresh), 10; Pecacek (Pechacek), 9; Rypl (Ripple), 7; Coufal, 6; Rosler (Roesler), 6; Motl, 5; Jezek, 4; Cermak, 3; Janecek, 3; Jirasek, 3; Kroulik, 2; Tauber, 2; Marek, 1; Pavlicek, 1.

With pastor Bergman's counsel, many of the Czechs began to farm in Austin County. Other immigrations occurred in the 1850s, and became even heavier in the 1870s. Czechs eventually spread throughout the state, gaining recognition for industry, thrift, and cultural attainments. To preserve their heritage they succeeded in having a chair of Slavic languages established (1915) at the University of Texas, and later at other schools. Their ethnic festivals have been held in various cities for many years.   (1974)

NELSONVILLE (Austin Co.)   SH 159, 2 mi. W
The Old Roesler Place
August Roesler (1836–1933), who migrated to Texas from Germany during the 1850s, built a simple frame dwelling at this site in 1873. Near a busy public road, it was a frequent stopping place for travelers. In 1892, after the Roesler family had moved to a larger residence on the property, their first home burned. With help from his neighbors, Roesler then constructed this board and batten farmhouse, a replica of the earlier structure.   (1977)

NEW BOSTON (Bowie Co.)   US 82 N, city parking lot
New Boston
Established as shipping point when Texas & Pacific Railroad was built across Bowie County in 1870s. Drawing business from original town of Boston (4 mi. S). New Boston townsite was platted in 1876; its post office opened Jan. 26, 1877, with L. C. Demorse as postmaster. Baptists organized church here in 1880; Methodists, 1883; Church of Christ, 1943. The first building designated as a school was erected in 1886.

New Boston men who have served in the Texas Legislature: Blair McGee (1889); Norman L. Dalby (1909–1910); R. M. Hubbard (1929, 1931), and Joseph White, Jr. (1939).   (1971)

NEW BOSTON (Bowie Co.)   1 mi. W on US 82 in roadside park
Bowie County
In 1836 a part of Red River County. Created December 17, 1840. Organized February 1, 1841. Named in honor of James Bowie, 1785–1836; member of Long's expedition; defender of Texas liberty; a martyr of the Alamo.

Old Boston, 1841, Texarkana and New Boston have served as county seat.

NEW BOSTON (Bowie Co.)   US 82, 6 mi. E on U.S. Government Reservation
Site of the Home of
Hardin R. Runnels
1820–1873
Governor of Texas, 1857–1859. The house was built in 1853. Destroyed by fire in 1914. Here Governor Runnels died. He was buried nearby. His remains were later removed to the state cemetery at Austin.   (1964)

NEW BOSTON (Bowie Co.)   SH 8, 7 mi. N in roadside park
Site of the Texas Home of
Richard Ellis
A Virginian by birth and education jurist and statesman of Alabama, 1813–1825. Came to Texas, 1825. President of the Constitutional Convention, March 1836, and member of the Congress of the Republic of Texas. Born February 14, 1781. Died here December 20, 1846.   (1964)

NEW BOSTON (Bowie Co.)   *SH 8, 7 mi. N in roadside park*
Harvey C. Sanders, C.S.A.
(1837–1925)

Native of Kentucky. In Civil War, fought at Shiloh, Chickamauga and other battles. After being wounded twice, became a guard at Confederate White House.

When Richmond fell on April 3, 1865, was placed in escort for the departing president. Rode 5 weeks toward Florida, where President Jefferson Davis was planning to sail for Mexico to join many other Confederate leaders. (These southerners intended to regroup an army, march north to Texas and continue their fight for states' rights.)

President Davis and his guards were followed by thieves trying to steal the Confederate treasury, the horses and the wagons. The assassination of Abraham Lincoln on April 14 and the offer of a reward of $100,000 caused many adventurers to hunt for President Davis. Just before dawn of May 10, near Irwinsville, Ga., federals captured him and his party, including 2 Texans, Postmaster-General John H. Reagan and Presidential Aide F. R. Lubbock, a former governor of Texas. Mrs. Davis and children were soon freed, but all the men were imprisoned.

Sanders was released in a year. Later he came to Texas and lived near this site after 1887—honored for years as the last man of the Davis bodyguard.   (1965)

NEW BOSTON (Bowie Co.)   *US 82, 6 mi. E on U.S. Government Reservation*
Black Cherry Tree

In early days, source of lumber and shingles. Bark had medicinal use.

This was judged the largest black cherry tree in Texas in 1965.   (1969)

NEW BOSTON (Bowie Co.)   *IH 30, 20 mi. SW in rest area*
SE of Sulphur River Bridge,
Early Protestant Preaching

The Rev. William Stevenson (Oct. 4, 1768–March 5, 1857), a Missourian, friend of Stephen F. Austin, preached in 1815 at Pecan Point on the Red River, north of here. Records indicate that his were the first Protestant sermons ever given in Texas, then part of Catholic "New Spain." Many settlers also entered Texas through Red River County.   (1970)

NEW BRAUNFELS (Comal Co.)   *Bus. IH 35, N of intersection with SH 46*
Comal County

Formed from Travis and Bexar land districts. Created March 24, 1846. Organized July 13, 1846.

Named for the river so called from the pancake shape of the islands formed by its springs.

New Braunfels, county seat established March 21, 1845. Named in honor of the founder, Prince Carl of Solms-Braunfels.   (1964)

NEW BRAUNFELS (Comal Co.)   *SH 46, 2.5 mi. NW*
Approximate Site of Mission
Nuestra Señora
de Guadalupe

Established by Franciscan missionaries in 1757 for the purpose of civilizing and Christianizing the Tonkawas, Mayeyes, and their associates. Formerly at mission San Francisco Xavier on the San Gabriel River. Abandoned in 1758.   (1964)

NEW BRAUNFELS (Comal Co.)   *150 N. Seguin St.*
New Braunfels

Founded on Good Friday, March 21, 1845, by German immigrants led by Prince Carl of Solms-Braunfels. Named for Braunfels, on the Lahn River, Germany.

Earlier inhabitants were Karankawa, Lipan, Tonkawa and Waco Indians. Land (1,265 acres) was acquired for the German colonists by sales contract from Rafael L. Garza and wife, Maria Antonia Veramendi Garza. A drawing for plots was held among colonists in 1845.

City was incorporated by the Texas Legislature on May 11, 1846, but charter was not ratified until 1847. By 1850, New Braunfels was one of largest cities in Texas. Because of ideal climate and abundant natural resources, agriculture and industry thrived. Early craftsmen included bakers, blacksmiths, butchers, button-and-fringe makers, cabinetmakers, carpenters, coppersmiths, locksmiths, machinists, saddlers, tailors, shoemakers, tanners, tinsmiths, turners, wagonmakers. Industries included brick kilns, cotton gins, door and blind factory, flour and grist mills, breweries, sawmill, soap and candle house, and woolen mill.

This city was undaunted by early hardships. It had courageous citizens under superior leadership. Many old-world customs survive among descendants of the original colonists.   (1970)

NEW BRAUNFELS (Comal Co.)
FM 306, about 12 mi. NE at
N lookout on Canyon Dam
German Pioneers in Texas
In this area, now covered by Canyon Lake, German emigrants were the first settlers.

A society of nobles (Mainzer Adelsverein) sponsored the emigration of 7,380 Germans to Texas from 1844 to 1847. They founded New Braunfels in 1845. Moving west, they established Fredericksburg in 1846.

Their Comanche Indian treaty opened 3,800,000 acres between the Llano and Colorado Rivers to peaceful settlement.

Farmers and artisans, scholars and scientists, they triumphed over epidemic and privation to help build Texas and the West.   (1968)

NEW BRAUNFELS (Comal Co.)
FM 1863, 15 mi. NW via SH 46
Natural Bridge Caverns
Discovered March 27,1960, by four students of St. Mary's University, San Antonio. Named for the rock bridge that marks entrance. Dedicated on August 5, 1964 by Governor John Connally. Of early cretaceous age; still forming. Site of artifacts from 5,000 B.C., and human remains at least 8,000 years old; also Indian campsites.   (1967)

NEW BRAUNFELS (Comal Co.)
On Gazebo Circle in city
Site of
Nuestra Señora de Guadalupe Mission
Our Lady of Guadalupe Mission
Established in 1756 on the Guadalupe River at or near present New Braunfels as an extension of the ill-fated Mission San Francisco Xavier de Horcasitas (1746–1755). Earlier located 100 miles northeast, San Francisco Xavier had been shaken by attacks, disease and strife between friars and soldiers, which had climaxed in the murder of a friar in 1752.

Although most of the personnel and Indian converts (Neophytes) fled, the mission continued until 1755. After that time it moved to the Guadalupe River to gather its scattered Mayeye Indians, who refused to enter Valero Mission (the Alamo) in San Antonio. Like the other three San Xavier Missions, San Francisco Xavier was short-lived.

Good features at this site included five springs, fertile fields, timber, meadows and the nearby river. Two friars ran the small mission, with a citizen guard, so as to avoid friction. Four Spanish families and 41 Indians (27 of them Baptized) comprised the inhabitants of the mission as of January, 1757.

Never a strong mission, Guadalupe continued only until March, 1758. At this time the church withdrew its staff because of increasingly dangerous raids by Comanches and other northern tribes.(1968)

NEW BRAUNFELS (Comal Co.)
SH 46 N, ¹⁄₁₀ mile N of Loop 337
Mission Nuestra Señora de Guadalupe
Established by Franciscan missionaries in 1757 for the purpose of civilizing and Christianizing the Tonkawas, Mayeyes, and their associates. Formerly at Mission San Francisco Xavier on the San Gabriel River. Abandoned in 1758.   (1936)

NEW BRAUNFELS (Comal Co.)
SH 46, entrance to Wurstfest Assn. Grounds
First Patented Wire Fence
Virginia native William H. Meriwether (b. 1800), an early Comal County plantation owner, ran a sawmill, cotton gin, and gristmill at this site. As an agriculturalist, he was aware of the need for an economical and practical source of fencing material. His interest led to the development of a smooth wire and board fence that effectively resisted the temperature changes that had been so damaging to earlier wire fences. His invention, known as snake wire fencing, was awarded patent No. 10211 on November 8, 1853. It was the first patent for a wire fence issued in the United States.

Although not widely accepted, Meriwether's fence was an important step in the development of an economical fencing material. It also played a role in later wire fence patent disputes. Meriwether sold his mill site to German native Joseph Landa in 1859 and moved to Tennessee, where he died in 1861. (1982)

NEW CANEY (Montgomery Co.)
US 59 South, between frontage road and Courthouse annex

New Caney

Permanent settlement in what is now New Caney began in the 1860s. The area was first called Presswood for the pioneer family of Austin and Sarah (Waters) Presswood. The Presswoods came to Texas in 1862, purchased land in the area, and raised cattle on the open ranges. The family of John Wesley Robinson (1819–1903) also settled here in the 1860s and began farming, cattle raising, and cotton ginning operations.

When the Houston, East and West Texas Railway Line was laid through Montgomery County in the 1870s, the community became a shipping point for livestock. It was then known for many years as Caney Station, named for the dense cane brakes growing along nearby creeks. In 1882, when a post office was established, the name New Caney was adopted.

Early industries in New Caney were confined chiefly to those that were necessary to carry on farming and cattle raising. As the timber industry began to flourish, however, mining props, used to support the earth along the side and roof of mining tunnels, were shipped out of New Caney.

The settlement and early history of New Caney are important reminders of the rich heritage of this part of East Texas and Montgomery County. (1984)

NEW LONDON (Rusk Co.)
SH 42, south steps of cenotaph

New London School Explosion

On March 18, 1937, a massive explosion destroyed the New London Junior-Senior High School, instantly killing an estimated 296 students and teachers. The subsequent deaths of victims from injuries sustained that day brought the final death count to 311. The explosion was blamed on a natural gas leak beneath the school building. Within weeks of the disaster the Texas Legislature passed a law requiring an odor to be added to natural gas, which previously was odorless and therefore undetectable. This memorial to victims of the explosion was erected in 1939. (1989)

NEW LONDON (Rusk Co.)
SH 42 at Phillips St.

London Baptist Church

London Baptist Church traces its history to 1856. By 1857, church members shared meeting facilities with the Odd Fellows Lodge in a jointly owned building located on the stagecoach route from Henderson to Waco. The structure was destroyed by fire in 1877. In 1897, a new building was constructed near the same location. When oil was discovered in the area in 1930, London became a boomtown and the church prospered, as well. Throughout its history, London Baptist Church has served the community with a variety of worship, educational and outreach programs. (1991)

NEW SUMMERFIELD (Cherokee Co.)
SH 110, 1 mi. S

McDonald Cemetery

Located on the original homestead of William and Clarissa Johnson and their family, this community cemetery began in the 1850s. Although there may have been earlier interments (possibly including William Johnson) the earliest documented burials, those of two young daughters of Dr. and Mrs. J. C. Privett, took place in 1856. Dr. Privett died in 1857 and was buried next to his daughters.

After Clarissa Johnson married Thomas McDonald in 1858, her homestead became known as the McDonald Farm. By 1870 the small graveyard on Clarissa's farm had become a community burial ground known as McDonald Cemetery, although it was not formally designated as such in deed records until 1930.

Among those buried in the McDonald Cemetery are members of the Johnson and McDonald families. There are over 550 documented burials, as well as a number of unmarked graves. The original one-acre plot of land set aside for the graveyard was enlarged in later years by additional land acquisitions.

For well over a century, the McDonald Cemetery has served as a reminder of Cherokee County's pioneer heritage. It remains one of the area's important cultural resources. (1990)

NEW SUMMERFIELD (Cherokee Co.) *SH 110*
New Summerfield Methodist Church
Founded about 1878 in the Union Chapel community (approximately ¼ mi. SE of this site), this congregation has been in continuous existence since that time. Built on land donated by Dr. and Mrs. G. F. Fullerton, the Methodist Episcopal Church, South, was used as a union church, providing a place of worship for all denominations in the community. Public school classes were held in the building during the week.

A new community built up about the turn of the century at this location. Named Summerfield after the pioneer Summers family, it gradually replaced the Union Chapel community. The Methodist church relocated to the new town and became known as Summerfield Methodist Episcopal Church, South. The congregation moved into a new building in 1919. It continued to occupy that facility until 1931, when a new brick structure was completed.

When the town was renamed New Summerfield in 1938, the church's name changed once again. After the merger of the Methodist and Evangelical United Brethren denominations in 1968, it became known as New Summerfield United Methodist Church. A part of Cherokee County history for over a century, the church continues to serve its community. . (1989)

NEW SUMMERFIELD (Cherokee Co.) *SH 110, 4 mi. N, Blackjack Community*
Samuel Smith Homesite
Samuel Smith (1800–1873), a native of Switzerland, came to Knox County, Tennessee, at the age of 19. In 1823, he married Oney Karnes and received his United States citizenship four years later. In 1849, the Smiths joined a group of immigrants from North Carolina and Tennessee who journeyed to Texas and founded the town of Knoxville in northeast Cherokee County.

Samuel and Oney Smith brought six of their seven children with them to Texas. They purchased land three miles southwest of Knoxville in the Blackjack community. Smith built a farmhouse at this site in 1859, and the homestead remained in the family until 1874.

As the patriarch of a family that made significant contributions to the rural Blackjack community, Samuel Smith is an important figure in the context of northeastern Cherokee County history. Members of the Smith family deeded land for the church and cemetery, operated the first blacksmith shop in the settlement, and were associated with the International & Great Northern Railroad when it came through the area in 1872. (Texas Sesquicentennial 1836–1986)

NEW SUMMERFIELD (Cherokee Co.) *SH 110, 4 mi., 2 mi. E*
Site of Griffin
Founded by settlers who came here from Griffin, Georgia. In the early 1850s became a flourishing town.

Birthplace of John Benjamin Kendrick (1857–1933), Texas cowboy who settled in Wyoming in 1879 after going up the trail for years with herds of cattle. He served in Wyoming State Senate, 1910–1914; as governor, 1914–1916; then as U.S. senator, 1916–1933.

Town of Griffin gradually lost people and businesses to railroad towns after 1872. Last store here was closed, 1930. (1965)

NEW WAVERLY (Walker Co.) *FM 2693, 10 mi. NE*
Winters Memorial Park, Set Aside to Honor Family of
James and Rhoda Creel Beall Winters
Pioneers who led their large family here in 1834 from Tennessee. Two older sons, Wm. Carvin and John Frelan Winters, came to Texas in 1832. On receiving their good report, the parents moved to this land between east and west forks of San Jacinto River. With them came 10 of their children, some in-laws, and grandchildren. A daughter, Mrs. Caroline W. Fannin, died and was buried en route, on the Trinity River.

James Winters, veteran of several American wars, was 62 when he left his new home to fight for Texas in 1835 conflict with Mexico. In the 1836 Texas War for Independence, he and a 15-year-old son, Benjamin, hauled supplies to the Texas Army. In that war were three sons, Wm. C., J. F., and James W. Winters; and two sons-in-law, Jackson Crouch and Charles D. Edwards.

Members of the Winters family helped to settle Caldwell, Frio, Hays, Lavaca, Live Oak and McMullen Counties. The mill of Wm. Winters made much of the furniture for the 1859 Texas capitol. In 1901 James W. Winters served Texas by helping mark battlefield at San Jacinto, where we fought 65 years earlier.

The senior James Winters (born 1773) died in 1848; he is buried two miles south, at Waverly. Rhoda (1784–1859) is buried at Oakville, Live Oak County.   (1968)

NEWCASTLE (Young Co.)   SH 51, 3 mi. S on grounds of Fort Belknap
The Butterfield Overland Stages
Connecting St. Louis and San Francisco with semi-weekly service, 1858–1861, traversed this county, with a station at Fort Belknap.

NEWCASTLE (Young Co.)   SH 251, 2 mi. S
Fort Belknap
Established in 1851. The largest military post in northern Texas until the Civil War. The first county seat of Young County. A station on the Southern Overland Mail Line connecting St. Louis and San Francisco. (1858–1861)

NEWCASTLE (Young Co.)   SH 251, 3 mi. S
Military Road Fort Belknap—Fort Worth
Past this point extended, in 1851, a military road connecting Fort Belknap and Fort Worth. Surveyed in 1849 by Colonel J. E. Johnson, who was detailed by the U.S. War Department to locate the most feasible route from Red River to El Paso. Blazed in 1851 by Lieutenant Francis T. Bryan of the U.S. Army. Traveled by troops, supply trains and frontier settlers. From 1851 to 1854 it connected two frontier forts, Belknap and Phantom Hill, 73 miles apart. Traveled 1858 to 1861 by stages of the Butterfield Line which connected St. Louis and San Francisco.

NEWCASTLE (Young Co.)   SH 251, S city limits
Site of Camp Van Camp
Established April 30, 1859, by the United States Army. Named in honor of Cornelius Van Camp, 2nd lieutenant, Second U.S. Cavalry, killed in action at the Wichita Village, October 1, 1858. Abandoned August 28, 1859.

NEWCASTLE (Young Co.)   SH 251, 3 mi. S on grounds of Ft. Belknap
Camp Belknap, C.S.A.
Confederate frontier post Camp Belknap located this vicinity. Local soldiers, determined to guard edge of settlement against Indian raids, Union invasion from Indian territory, joined frontier regiment of Texas Cavalry and Rangers. Chain of posts from Red River to Rio Grande patrolled. Regiment concentrated vicinity this camp, spring 1863. Fought Comanche attack near Elm Creek 1864. Constantly looking for marauders, short on food supplies and ammunition, these Confederates effectively protected settlers and supply trains.   (1963)

NEWCASTLE (Young Co.)   SH 24, 9 mi. W near Proffitt
Indian Raid on
Elm Creek, C.S.A.
Indian troubles continually plagued the Texas frontier in the Civil War, with great loss in lives and property.

One of the most serious raids occurred near here on Oct. 13, 1864, at Fitzpatrick Ranch. Comanches killed seven ranch people and five Confederate soldiers. Six women and children were kidnapped. 10,000 cattle were stolen.

Brit Johnson, Negro slave who that day lost his whole family, later "joined" the Comanches, got their confidence, and freed his people. Later Indians punished him with mutilation and death.

NEWCASTLE (Young Co.)   SH 251, 3 mi. S on grounds of Ft. Belknap
Tonkawa Scout, C.S.A.
By the time of the Civil War, 1861–1865, Texans knew the horrors of Indian warfare. Hostile tribes made a business of stealing horses, cattle, women and children. The paths they followed in the "bright Comanche moons" were marked by fires and ruin.

The Tonkawa tribe, by contrast, sought friendship with Texans. They became valued allies in the Civil War, scouting against hostile Indians and watching for signs of Federal invasion. Old Texas Indian fighters, who once had fought Tonkawas along with others, in wartime asked for Tonkawa scouts. Along the frontier defense line from Red River to the Rio Grande, commanders valued them so much they fed them at personal expense when necessary to obtain their help. A few Tonkawa scouts were more useful than two or three companies of regular soldiers. They could stalk enemies better than bloodhounds.

They paid for their Confederate loyalty. On Oct. 25, 1862, near present Anadarko, Okla. Hostile Indians attacked the Tonkawa camp, killing 137 men, women and children out of 300. When later their Chief Castile requested a tribal home in Texas, they were located at Fort Griffin, where they remained until 1884, and then were removed to Oklahoma.

NEWCASTLE (Young Co.)

SH 251, 3 mi. S on grounds of
Ft. Belknap on Powder Magazine

Old Fort Belknap Powder Magazine

Best preserved of the original structures at Fort Belknap. The fort, named for its builder, Brig. Gen. W. G. Belknap (1794–1851), was one of the frontier posts placed by the Federal Government along a line from the Red River to the Rio Grande to guard settlers from Indians, soon after Texas joined the union. This was one of nine stone and seven picket houses on the site by 1853. Restored by the State of Texas in 1936. Awarded Medallion Plate.   (1962)

NEWCASTLE (Young Co.)

SH 251, 3 mi. S

Major Robert S. Neighbors

As Indian agent, forceful peacemaker and humanist, Maj. Neighbors had more influence over Texas' Indians than any other man of his era; came to Texas in 1836.

He served as quartermaster in Texas Army, 1839–1841. While on Texas Ranger duty in San Antonio, 1842, he was taken as a prisoner of war to Mexico by Gen. Adrian Woll and spent 18 months in Perote Prison.

Began his service to the Indians in 1845. As agent for Lipan-Apache and Tonkawa tribes, he used field system of control, visiting Indian homes, learning a red man's way of life, improving living conditions, helping them to trade. He ably defended their rights, was counselor and friend, and sought new homes for them, never faltering in commitment to their safety.

As a Texas commissioner in 1850 he organized El Paso County; he was also a state representative, 1851–1852, and a presidential elector in 1852.

Major Neighbors later became the supervising agent for all of the Indians in Texas. Frontier civilians and soldiers failed to support his Indian policies. Many became hostile. On Sept. 14, 1859, he was murdered near here by a white man as he was returning after safely removing all reservation Indians from Texas. He was buried in Belknap Cemetery (½ mi. E of town).   (1967)

NEWCASTLE (Young Co.)

US 380, 2.5 mi. SW

Joseph Alfred Woolfolk

A native of Kentucky, Joseph Alfred Woolfolk (1836–1918) earned a law degree from the University of Louisville in 1856. He moved to Belknap, Texas, in 1858 and was hired by the Texas Emigration and Land Company to survey land grants in the Peters Colony. Licensed to practice law by the First District Court in Young County, he served as county attorney and county clerk.

At the outbreak of the Civil War, Woolfolk joined a home guard Texas Rangers unit, and in late 1862 transferred into the regular Confederate Army. Captured by Union Troops in West Virginia in July 1863, he spent the remainder of the war in a prison camp in Ohio. Upon his release in 1865 he returned to his native Kentucky, where he married Elizabeth J. Lewis (1846–1922). They became the parents of 9 children.

The Woolfolks returned to Texas in 1867 and settled in Weatherford. In 1871, Woolfolk gained notoriety when he was appointed by the court to defend Satanta and Big Tree, Kiowa Indians on trial for murder in the infamous Salt Creek Massacre near Jacksboro. Woolfolk moved his family to a ranch in Young County in the late 1870s. He again served as county attorney in 1881. He and Elizabeth are buried in a private family cemetery near this site.   (1994)

NEWCASTLE (Young Co.)

US 380, 0.5 mi. E

Harmonson Rancho

Kentucky native Peter Harmonson (1797–1865) came to Texas in 1845 as a settler in the Peters Colony. The following year he helped form Denton County, where he served as the first sheriff. In 1854, he brought his family here and established a ranch near this site known as Harmonson Rancho. An organizer of Young County, he served as its first chief justice. He died from a wound received in an Indian raid on the Elm Creek community. In 1869, after it was sold, his ranchsite and his son Z. J. "Jack" Harmonson figured in a skirmish between Indians and local cattlemen. (1982)

NEWCASTLE (Young Co.)

US 380, 8 mi. SW

Proffitt Cemetery

Members of the Robert Smith Proffitt family came to this area about 1862 and established homes. A son, John Proffitt (1846–1925), amassed large land-holdings and built a gin and other businesses. The developing community was named Proffitt. At its height it boasted homes, a post office, school, retail businesses, a Methodist church, and Baptist church.

On July 17, 1867, three young men were killed in an Indian raid near this site. They were buried in a common grave on John Proffitt's land about one mile south of town. Theirs was the first burial in the community graveyard which became known as the Proffitt Cemetery.

The cemetery contains both marked and unmarked graves of area pioneers. The numerous interments of infants and children illustrate the often harsh conditions of frontier life. The largest number of burials occurred in the years between 1910 and 1920, and include many victims of the World War I-era influenza epidemic. Also buried here are veterans of the Civil War, World War I, and World War II.

Maintained by a cemetery association, this historic graveyard stands as a memorial to Young County Pioneers. (1990)

NEWTON (Newton Co.)

US 190, 3 mi. SE in roadside park

Newton County

Formed from Jasper County. Created April 22, 1846. Organized July 13, 1846. Named in honor of Sergeant John Newton, 1752–1807, hero of the American Revolution.

County seat, Newton, 1846; Burkeville, 1848; Newton since 1853.

NEWTON (Newton Co.)

US 190, 3 mi. SE

Newton County, C.S.A.

Supply and military center in the Civil War. Target area for Federals trying to move up the Sabine or across Louisiana and take Texas. Confederates built breastworks and maintained arsenal at Burkeville.

Major supply route, "The Old Beef Trail," begun 1823 through area later Newton County, was road taken by thousands of cattle being sent from Texas to feed armies and civilians as far eastward as Mobile, Ala. Sabine ferries were equipped with cattle pens; also ferrymen kept oxen trained to lead herds swimming across the river. Some local beef went eastward, too.

Farrsville, a town founded about 1850 on Cow Creek, had a military campground and corrals furnishing fresh stagecoach teams. Its tanning vats and shops made boots and shoes for the Confederacy. Its water mills ground corn for bread, sawed lumber, ginned cotton-products used in supplying the South.

The commissioners court made appropriations to outfit military units (buying horses for men unable to furnish their own), aid dependent families, and supply the people with cotton cards to turn the lint into batts for spinning, weaving and knitting.

The county, which had voted 178 to 3 for secession, sent about 400 soldiers into the Confederate Army. (1965)

NIXON (Wilson Co.)

FM 1681, 6 mi. NW on grounds of
Union Valley Homecoming Association

Site of Old Town of Union Valley
(Settled in 1860s)

Original schoolhouse of logs on site given by Harriet Smith Beaty in 1872 to trustees John Coleman, King Holstein, and Samuel McCracken, was replaced 1877 by a frame one on William

Cope land, serving as Masonic hall, church, court room. Union post office opened 1883. Stores, gins, saloons, blacksmith and butcher shops were owned by men named Burnside, Cone, Creech, Dunn, Hightower, Hoy, Hudson, Irvin, Johnson Murray, Magee, Patterson, Spear, Treadwell, Watkins, Wiley and Wright. Town dwindled when bypassed in 1906 by Galveston, Harrisburg & San Antonio Railroad. (1972)

NIXON (Wilson Co.)
FM 1681, 6 mi. NW on grounds of
Union Valley Homecoming Association
Albuquerque
(2.5 mi. to the NE)
Near 1857 ranch of Samuel and Martha (Hastings) McCracken. Post office, opened 1869, was named by veterans of Sibley's Civil War campaign in New Mexico. Town had businesses, school, blacksmith, shop where DeWitt County sheriff Jack Helm died (1873) of blast from gun of John Wesley Hardin. Post office closed 1883. (1972)

NOCONA (Montague Co.)
US 82, 6 mi. W
Red River Station, C.S.A.
Established nine miles northwest 1861 as Civil War outpost near major buffalo and Indian crossing. Local soldiers, determined to guard edge of settlement against Indian raids, Union invasion from Indian territory, joined by Texas frontier regiment cavalry company. Families of settlers, cattlemen built log cabins within post stockade. Poorly fed, clothed and short on horses and ammunition Confederates patrolled area effectively. Comanche, Kiowa raid at Illinois Bend 15 miles east Jan. 1863. Major cattle crossing after war.

Texas Civil War Frontier Defense
1861–1865
Texas made an all-out effort for the Confederacy after voting over 3 to 1 for secession. 90,000 troops, noted for mobility and heroic daring, fought on every battlefront. An important source of supply and gateway to foreign trade thru Mexico, Texas was the storehouse of the South. Red River station and other posts on this line were backed by patrols of State Rangers, organized militia, and citizens' posses scouting from nearby "family forts." This was part of a 2000 mile frontier and coastline successfully defended by Texans.

NOCONA (Montague Co.)
FM 103, 10 mi. N
North Nocona Oil Field
Montague County
Oil Discovery, 1922
Pennsylvania oil man George Williams, backed by Cad McCall, drilled for oil intermittently, 1918–22, beginning at Eagle Point (4.5 mi. SE). Leasing by individuals and major companies—including, Phil Lesh, A. E. Humphrey, and the Texas Co.—kept rigs working. Gas blew in at 800-foot depth on J. W. Maddox-J. E. Lemons land, one well yielding over 100,000,000 cubic feet daily. The gas was piped to Nocona and rural homes.

Oil was discovered in 1922 on Maddox site, at about 1,000 feet. Production continued at 1,000–2,000 feet, there and elsewhere. The gas caused trouble: a capped well blew mud from prairie dog holes and gas from water well a quarter-mile away. In 1925, a gas well on W. W. Jones land (2 mi. W) blew out a gigantic crater. Another well (.75 mi. W) caught fire, burned its rig, and was finally doused by nationally-famed oil well fire fighter Tex Thornton.

With an estimated 100,000,000 barrel total on record, this 12,295-acre field still produces.
(1972)

NOCONA (Montague Co.)
US 82, ½ mi. E at rest area
Red River Station
A frontier post for state militia most northwestern outpost of Confederacy. Became thriving settlement and main crossing on Red River for vast herds of Texas cattle "going up" the Chisholm Trail to northern markets. Town abandoned, 1887. This trail driving through this area marked the advance of American settlement westward.

NOME (Jefferson Co.)   US 90 W
Opelousas Trail
Named for one of several Atakapan-speaking Native American tribes originally connected by this trail, the Opelousas Trail ran from La Bahia (later Goliad) to the Mississippi River in Louisiana. Evidence of cultural interchange between tribes indicates the presence of such a trail for hundreds of years.

Spanish explorers, soldiers, and vaqueros employed this route. By the 1750s, French traders had been traveling the trail for about twenty years. After 1820 settlers began to arrive from Louisiana and other southern states. Don Martin de Leon and anglo cattlemen such as James Taylor White and William B. Duncan herded large droves of cattle, mules, and horses to market in New Orleans. A post route was established along the Opelousas in early 1836. That spring, Texas pioneers fled along this path during the "Runaway Scrape." Later, Santa Anna was led down the trail toward New Orleans and ultimately to Washington, D.C., as a prisoner of war. A stage and mail route followed the trail after 1850; the Confederate Army used the road to move troops during the Civil War.

Use of the route continued throughout the 20th century. Many segments of the trail were incorporated into U.S. Highway 90 from Liberty to Orange.   (1998)

NORDHEIM (DeWitt Co.)   FM 239, .5 mi. SE
Pilot Knob
(Elevation: 447 ft. Above Sea Level)
A beacon for early Texas pioneers. Because the hill could be seen for miles, it guided travelers from old Indianola (on the coast) inland to Helena and San Antonio during the 19th century. On the hill, they discovered charred rocks and artifacts from a previous Indian camp ground.

The area was first surveyed in 1838 by the Goliad Land District and in 1886 the San Antonio & Arkansas Pass Railroad was built through this region. For years a sign at the Weldon Switch (present Nordheim) depot proclaimed its 400-foot elevation was highest on the line between Houston, San Antonio, and Waco.

In 1895 Nordheim was platted. Afterward numerous German immigrants were attracted to the area. Under the sturdy oaks on Pilot Knob, young and old enjoyed typical German and pioneer activities, including band concerts, shooting matches, harvest and May festivals, and Easter egg hunts. A refreshment stand and dance platform were built on the hill, which became the center of social life for Nordheim citizens.

Here the townspeople also buried their dead, and since most activities had been moved into town by about 1910, Pilot Knob gradually settled into its present use as the community cemetery.
                                                                           (1968)

NORMANGEE (Leon Co.)   W of junction of FM 39 and Old Spanish Road
El Camino Real
The Old San Antonio Road
First blazed in 1691 by Captain Don Domingo Teran de los Rios, first provisional governor of Texas, in an expedition officially directed by Father Fray Damian Massanet, O.F.M. Apostolic missionary and explorer in Texas. The general route was northeast from the Rio Grande to the San Antonio River, thence across the Guadalupe, San Marcos, Colorado, Brazos and Trinity Rivers to the missions in East Texas. Other expeditions taking the same route: Espinosa, Olivares Aguirre in 1709; St. Denis in 1714; Ramon in 1716; Alarcon in 1718; Marquis of Aguayo in 1720; Moses Austin in 1820. The Republic of Texas officially made this road a boundary between a number of Emperarial Land Grants.

Normangee home of the old San Antonio Road Association.

NORMANNA (Bee Co.)
US 181, on south edge of town,
near the Medio Creek crossing
Community of Normanna
Settlement dates from about 1850. First town, two miles west, was called San Domingo for its location near junction of San Domingo and dry Medio Creeks. After railroad was built, 1886, citizens moved to Walton (new flag station) to be on line. Name honored Sheriff D. A. T. Walton.

When Norwegians settled area, 1890s, Walton became Normanna. Word originally suggested the qualities of old Norse heroes, but through local usage came to mean "Home of the Norseman."

Town thrived for years; then declined after series of fires and advent of the automobile. (1969)

NORTH COWDEN (Ector Co.)
SH 158, N city limits
North Cowden
Site of Ector County's second big oil strike. Named for ranching family of John M. Cowden, an 1885 Permian Basin settler; one of four brothers, ranching community leaders on Texas frontiers.

Oil and gas development began here with the 1930 discovery. Post office granted 1947. Town continues as a Permian Basin petroleum source. (1965)

NORTON (Runnels Co.)
FM 383, town square
Town of Norton
Named for George W. Norton of Kentucky, who about 1882 bought and later developed the divide between Oak and Valley Creeks. Post office, established in 1894, was a first in home (1.5 mi. NE) of Postmaster Marion A. Wilkerson. This facility and a few country businesses—including stores, cotton gins, blacksmith shops—were drawn into town, which was platted by O. C. Bivins in 1903.

First homes are said to have been built by Dr. W. W. Mitchell and Less Trimmier. High school was established in 1906. Early institutions included several churches and a Masonic lodge.

(1970)

NOTREES (Ector Co.)
SH 302, Shell Office Bldg.
Town of Notrees
Post Office established 1944 in drug store of C. J. Brown, Jr., who named it in response to title suitable to locality. Residents have since made history by planting shade trees. Now production hub of Permian Basin; center of gas processing industry, and home of Otto's Boys Ranch. (1965)

NURSERY (Victoria Co.)
US 87
Murphy Home
Built 1897 combining Southern plantation and New England saltbox styles of architecture.

Home of prominent Nursery citizens R. S. Fowler, John M. Horton, E. S. Jennings, Louie Carpenter, and for many years, W. M. Murphy, Sr. Has Medallion Plate. (1966)

O'DONNELL (Lynn Co.)
Off US 87, City plaza
O'Donnell
Named for Tom J. O'Donnell, promoter of South Plains railroads, including 60 miles of Santa Fe line from Slaton to Lamesa. On this new railroad (important as freight hauler) town of O'Donnell was founded in 1909 by H. E. Baldridge and Charles H. Doak—two of the organizers and first officials of Lynn County. Doak built a hotel in projected town of O'Donnell in 1909. L. G. Phillips established the first store.

On July 4, 1910, a big picnic was held to celebrate arrival of first Santa Fe train. Old "Central" post office (previously on Dee W. Harris Ranch, 5.5 mi. NW) was moved to new town in 1910 and was officially renamed O'Donnell on Feb. 7, 1911. W. R. Standefer was employed to survey townsite in 1911. H. E. Baldridge offered free building lots to churches. A Methodist church was organized in 1911; Church of Christ and Presbyterian churches in 1912; First Baptist in 1914.

Town was incorporated in 1923, with W. R. Sanderson as first mayor. School, improved dramatically since its early wooden building, serves a large area. A graduate was actor Dan Blocker ("Hoss" Cartwright).

Now a dryland farming center, O'Donnell in 1961 had what was then largest cotton gin in the world, ginning 21,000 bales of cotton during that year. (1969)

OAK HILL (Travis Co.)   *Roadside park on US 290, 500 ft. W of Williamson Creek*
Oak Hill
First settlers arrived in area in 1840s. The community founded here in 1856 was called Live Oak Springs; in 1865 it was renamed Shiloh. Later schools known as Live Oak and Oatmanville gave names temporarily to the settlement. It has been known as Oak Hill since 1900.

Limestone quarries were opened, 1882, to supply stone for capitol building in Austin. By 1886, ten carloads of stone were shipped daily over railroad which joined quarries with capitol grounds. It is estimated that one-third of capitol's walls are lined with limestone from Oak Hill quarries. (1969)

OAKHURST (San Jacinto Co.)   *3 mi. SE on FM 946, 2 mi. off rd.*
Site of Raven Hill
Plantation home of General Sam Houston, who was called "The Raven" by the Cherokee Indians. Built in 1844. Sold before 1860.

OAKVILLE (Live Oak Co.)   *In front of post office on FM 1358 at Main St.*
Oakville Post Office
Irish immigrants settled this area as part of the John McMullen and James McGloin Mexican Land Grant. Located on the Sulphur tributary of the Nueces River, this site was known as "On the Sulphur." Live Oak County was organized in 1856 and Oakville was named county seat. Thomas Wilson gave 640 acres for the townsite stipulating that separate squares be marked as public, graveyard, church, and school squares. Oakville grew as stores, two hotels, a livery stable, a school, and two churches were established.

The Oakville post office was established May 11, 1857, with Joshua Hinton as the first postmaster. The mail came four times a week on stagecoaches traveling from San Antonio to Corpus Christi and on to Brownsville. By 1879, the San Antonio-Corpus Christi stage left both ends of the line six days a week. Stage travel became less popular with the arrival of the railroad. When the San Antonio, Uvalde & Gulf Railroad bypassed Oakville in 1913, the town began to decline. The county seat was relocated in 1919 at George West.

In 1966, the Oakville post office was designated as a rural branch of the Three Rivers post office and continues to serve the community. (1979)

ODEM (San Patricio Co.)   *US 77, 4 mi. S*
Angelita
("Littlest Angel")
Angelita was one of several rural communities which grew up in San Patricio County after the Civil War. A schoolhouse was erected in the 1880s and was the center of community life. After the arrival of the St. Louis, Brownsville, and Mexico Railroad in 1904, a town was platted and businesses were established. The railroad station at Angelita provided a shipping point for agricultural products and cattle from nearby farms and ranches. The relocation of the post office and school to Odem in 1916 caused the town of Angelita to decline and eventually vanish. (1988)

ODESSA (Ector Co.)   *IH 20, 14 mi. W at roadside park*
Odessa
Founded 1881. Legend says name came from an Indian princess who wandered into camp of Texas & Pacific Railroad construction gang. Others say it was for Odessa on Russian plains— area West Texas resembles. County seat ever since Ector was organized, 1891. Has had great growth since 1926 oil strike. Center for one of the two largest oil fields in the world. Has largest inland petrochemical complex in United States, alone with many other diversified industries. It is also the oilfield supply capital of the world. Odessa College has served area since 1946. City has 143 churches; a symphony orchestra; clubs for sports, service, culture. Recreational attractions include nation's second largest meteor crater; exact replica of Shakespeare's 16th century Globe Theatre; 4 museums; a planetarium; industrial tours; "Permian Playhouse"; "Prairie Dog Pete" park; world's largest jackrabbit statue; and 21 playground-parks. Unique "Presidential Room" depicts lives of U.S. Presidents in art, documents, and memorabilia. Sandhill Hereford

and Quarterhorse Show opens annual rodeo season for entire Southwest. World famous Permian Basin Oil Show is held biennially. (1967)

ODESSA (Ector Co.) *Bus. IH 20, E of Loop 338*
Ector County
Created February 26, 1887 from Tom Green County. Organized January 15, 1891. Named in honor of Matthew Duncan Ector, 1822–1879, member of the Texas Legislature, a Confederate officer, and outstanding jurist. Odessa, the county seat. (1964)

ODESSA (Ector Co.) *US 385, 10 mi. N*
Near Site of
Baker Ranch School
Since there were no public schools in rural Ector County, R. W. Smith and Teague Baker in 1906 erected an 8' × 10' school building in Baker's pasture. They hired a teacher at $15 a month, plus room and board, which each furnished on alternate months.

Ranch schools like this one taught not only children of ranchers, but also those of cowboys and nesters—small farmers coming west to homestead or to buy land at nominal prices.

Baker Community later had a public school. Till the Permian Basin had good roads and buses, ranch schools served it well. (1965)

ODESSA (Ector Co.) *US 385, 4 mi. SW on Bessye Cowden Ward Ranch House*
(Home has since burned and been rebuilt.)
Cowden F. Bar Ranch
Built 1922 on ranch of J. Hal Pegues. Here since 1932, it has been home to five generations, Walter and Eva Cowden family. Stopping place for horsedrawn and early auto traffic of remote ranches for water—from area's first windmill and unique tankhouse—and change to town clothes. Hospitality maintained under ownership of Odessa's former "First Lady," Bessye Cowden Ward and Walter Fay Cowden Averitt. Awarded Medallion Plate. (1964)

ODESSA (Ector Co.) *US 385 and 42nd St.*
The Cable Tool Rig
Equipment that replaced the spring pole drilling method used in America's earlier oil fields. The cable tool rig used a bit suspended on a steel drilling cable. The bit is dropped in the hole and the impact breaks up the formation. The broken pieces are removed by a bail. This method made possible the deeper penetration so necessary in the Southwest.

The cable tool rig was introduced in Texas in 1866. (Some use of cable tools had been made around 1840 in the North.) Texas gave the Southwestern oil industry the first lease, the first oil pipe line, the first wooden and iron storage tanks, the first iron drums for transporting crude oil, and first use of the auger principle later employed in rotary rigs.

The cable tool rig brought in the first important wells of the Permian Basin. This rig was reconstructed from parts of several rigs actually used as Big Lake, Reagan County, where the No. 1 Santa Rita blew in during May 1923 as the first well in the first major oil field in the Permian Basin.

To the cable tool rig and the men who used it goes credit for the great development in the Permian Basin. (1964)

ODESSA (Ector Co.) *IH 20, 13 mi. W in rest area*
The Caprock
A range of flat-topped ridges and cliffs stretching from Texas Panhandle to 20 miles south of this point and extending into New Mexico. The name also refers to tough limestone that caps ridges, rising sharply 200 to 1,000 ft. above plains. This section, Concho Bluffs, marks western edge of caprock escarpment, called the "break of the plains" because it divides the Staked Plains from the North Central Plains of Texas.

Observed by Coronado's Expedition, 1540–1541. Provided shelter in storms, but delayed entrance of settlers to Staked Plains. Herds of stampeding cattle at times plunged over its edge. In this area, the caprock blocked eastbound wagons, including some from California gold fields in 1850s. Because of scarce surface water, Staked Plains were too dry for farming or ranching until wells were drilled and windmills installed.

Ridges and canyons here hindered railroad building. In 1881 workmen earned $2.50 a day—highest wages ever paid until then on a Texas railroad job—at "Colt's big rock cut" (the mile-wide, 17-ft. chasm visible here). A tragic accident with dynamite injured several of Colt's men and killed three. Their graves, known to the pioneers around Odessa, were on a hill northeast of the tracks, but cannot now be found. (1967)

ODESSA (Ector Co.) Bus. IH 20, E of Loop 338
Comanche War Trail
A barbed, bristling flying wedge—the Comanches—rode into 18th century Texas, driving the Wichitas and Caddoes east, the Apaches west, becoming lords of the South Plains. Harassed the Spanish and Anglo-Americans along frontier from Corpus Christi on the Gulf up to the Red River. Wrote their name in blood clear down to Zacatecas, Mexico. Captured women, children and horses along their road of blood, tears and agony.

Many roads converged into the Great Comanche War Trail, which passed about 20 miles southeast of this marker.

ODESSA (Ector Co.) US 385 at 4400 Andrews Hwy. at
Permian Basin Oil Show Grounds
El Paso Natural Gas Company's
First Compressor Transmission Engine
A landmark tool in man's conquest of energy. This compressor went into use in Culberson County, Tex., on Oct. 1, 1931, and served until 1969, aiding in the rise of the Southwest as an industrial empire.

This was the first compressor transmission engine at the number one transmission station of El Paso Natural Gas Company, founded in 1928 by Paul Kayser, a Houston attorney.

The pioneer transmission station of the El Paso Natural Gas Company was one of the earliest in the Permian Basin. A Cooper-Bessemer Type 19, this machine is an 800-horsepower horizontal tandem reciprocating compressor engine. Equipped with two 10¼-inch by 24-inch gas compressor cylinders, it weighs about 173,000 pounds. It served under load for 152,064 hours, compressing more than 144 billion cubic feet of natural gas in its working lifetime. It conveyed production from fields at Jal, N. M., and in Winkler County, Tex., to city of El Paso and southern New Mexico and Arizona. It was the first machine of its kind in a system that expanded into 22,000 miles of forwarding lines furnishing low-cost energy for industries and households in eleven western states. (1970)

ODESSA (Ector Co.) US 385, 4.6 mi. N
Emigrant Trail
Gateway to the West
Road of stubborn seekers of 1849 California gold fields and better life. Bringing the old, infant, the yet unborn and all worldly goods, family wagons entered Texas at Preston, on Red River, to go southwest via springs (including some now in Monahans Sandhills Park) to Emigrants' Crossing on the Pecos, then upriver and west through Guadalupe Pass to El Paso. Old wagon parts by the trail tell of some disasters.

Capt. R. B. Marcy in 1849 and Capt. John Pope in 1854 made army surveys of the trail. It passed near this spot. (1964)

ODESSA (Ector Co.) US 80, 4 mi. E at Mausoleum, Sunset Memorial Gardens
Homer Robert Henderson
(February 24, 1881–April 8, 1963)
Texas Ranger, deputy sheriff, county commissioner in Ector and (later) in Crane County.

Born in Wilson County; one of 12 children of Robert and Mary Elizabeth (O'Neal) Henderson.

Came to Odessa as member of Company A, Texas Rangers, under command of Capt. J. A. Brooks, in 1906. This was in period when Rangers kept the peace during citizens' filing of land claims.

Married Annie Henderson here, October 8, 1908. Ranched in area. (1967)

ODESSA (Ector Co.) US 385 at SH 158, 11 mi. N
LeGrande Survey of 1833
(SE Corner 18 mi. E of This Site)
Made in era of Mexican rule in Texas for John Beales, who through partnership, acquired 70,000,000 acres of land and gained the title of "Texas' Largest Land King."

Alexander LeGrande's survey covered about 2,000 miles in West Texas, Oklahoma Panhandle and Eastern New Mexico—then south to the 32nd parallel. Hardship and tragedy plagued LeGrande's party. Attacked by Indians, he abandoned survey.

First exploration here is usually credited to Capt. R. B. Marcy, U. S. Army. LeGrande's work was years earlier.

(1967)

ODESSA (Ector Co.)   *US 385, Odessa College, Globe of the Great Southwest*
Mrs. John L. Morris
(Marjorie)

Originator, promoter of the Globe of the Great Southwest, world's most nearly authentic replica of the Globe Theater in England made famous by the plays of William Shakespeare.

Mrs. Morris was educated at North Texas State University and joined the English faculty at Odessa College. In 1961 the college named her "Teacher of the Year." She was honored 1961 as an outstanding teacher in Texas colleges.

She also founded the Permian Basin Museum and area "Writers Roundup" contest, both of which are sponsored by Odessa College. (Outstanding Women of Texas Series, 1967).

ODESSA (Ector Co.)   *US 385*
Site of
Odessa College, 1889–1891

Established through efforts of Odessa Townsite Co., which gave $12,000; a Northern Methodist group matched this fund in 1888.

Rev. M. A. Daugherty, Pittsburgh, Pa., was placed in charge, and a 20-acre plot was allotted to the college. Erection of a two-story building began in 1890. In 1891 classes for 14 students were taught by Miss Alice Wright, of Maine. A "mystery" fire destroyed the college after one session.

This church-sponsored college was never rebuilt. In 1946, the new Odessa College was founded to fulfill aims of leadership in education.

(1967)

ODESSA (Ector Co.)   *IH 20, 14 mi. W in rest area*
Pivot Point of the Permian Basin
Odessa

Founded 1881. Legend says name came from an Indian princess who wandered into camp of Texas & Pacific Railroad construction gang. Others say it was for Odessa on Russian plains—area West Texas resembles.

County seat ever since Ector was organized, 1891. Has had great growth since 1926 oil strike. Center for one of the two largest oil fields in the world. Has largest inland petrochemical complex in United States, along with many other diversified industries. It is also the oilfield supply capital of the world.

Odessa College has served area since 1946. City has 143 churches, a symphony orchestra, clubs for sports, service, culture. Recreational attractions include nation's second largest meteor crater, exact replica of Shakespeare's 16th century Globe Theatre, four museums, a planetarium, industrial tours, "Permian Playhouse," "Prairie Dog Pete" Park, world's largest jackrabbit statue, and 21 playground-parks.

Unique "Presidential Room" depicts lives of U.S. presidents in art, documents, and memorabilia.

Sandhills Hereford and Quarterhorse Show opens annual rodeo season for entire Southwest. World-famous Permian Basin Oil Show is held biennially.

(1967)

ODESSA (Ector Co.)   *US 385 N & 42nd St., Coliseum Grounds*
The Permian Basin

One of the two richest oil fields in the world. Discovery began in 1920 at a Mitchell County well. Next came the 1923 Big Lake strike, then the wild 1925 boom in Upton County, followed by production in Andrews, Crane, Ector, Martin, Midland, Pecos, Ward, Winkler and 24 other counties. In some years new wells averaged 38 a week. Fortunes were made, lost, then regained—all within months. So great were yields that oil brought 50 cents a barrel, while drillers paid $5.00 barrel for drinking water.

Area is 88,610 square miles, with center here at Odessa. Extends across a deeply buried prehistoric sea that more than 250 million years ago contained much fish and reptile life, including dinosaurs. Shores and islands later grew giant vegetation, until earth changes buried animals and plants in pockets that turned hydrocarbons into petroleum.

In 40 years from its discovery, the Permian Basin was producing 53% of total oil in Texas and 20% of U.S. crude oil. It is one of the world's largest producers of channel carbon black. Other by-products are sulphur, asphalt, synthetic rubber ingredients and petrochemicals.   (1964)

ODESSA (Ector Co.)   *IH 20, 10 mi. W*
Odessa Meteor Crater
The Odessa Meteor Crater, second largest in the United States and sixth in the world, was formed some 20,000 years ago when an iron meteorite believed to weigh 1,000 tons crashed into the earth near this site. Impact was so great that 4.3 million cubic feet of rock was expelled or shifted, forming a cone-shaped crater 500 feet wide and nearly 100 feet deep.

Action of wind and water during subsequent centuries filled the cavity with silt so that today its concave surface is only five to six feet below the level of the surrounding plain. It retains its original broad diameter, surrounded by a low, rock-buttressed rim created when limestone formations were shattered and forced to the surface by the burrowing mass.

Fragments of the meteorite collected around the crater indicate that it was 90 percent iron, with small amounts of cobalt, copper, carbon, phosphorus, sulphur and chromium. Although the main mass has never been found, it is believed to lie embedded 179 feet below the surface.

In addition to the principal crater, scientific investigation has revealed the presence of two smaller adjoining depressions, formed by less massive bodies that fell in the same meteor shower which sent the large mass to earth. Although not now discernible, they were from 15 to 50 feet wide, and from seven to 17 feet deep. Neither penetrated deeply enough to encounter solid rock but was formed primarily in clay-like deposits.

Meteors are believed to have been formed by the breaking-up of a planet similar in size and composition to the earth. The body is thought to have been part of the solar system . . . perhaps the mythical planet between Mars and Jupiter whose disruption must have created the asteroids.

OLDENBURG (Fayette Co.)   *SH 237*
Oldenburg
The land in this area was included in a Mexican land grant awarded to Nathaniel Townsend in 1838. Portions of the grant were sold to a succession of different people over the years, and in 1885 August Heintze and Gus Steenken purchased about eighteen acres. Heintze and Steenken, both natives of Oldenburg, Germany, founded a community and named it after their hometown.

The majority of the settlers in this area were immigrants from Germany and Bohemia. At its height Oldenburg boasted homes, farms, and a number of businesses and institutions, including stores, saloons, a cotton gin, tin shop, doctors' office, blacksmith shop, post office, church, dance halls (festplatz), and schools.

The first school in the community was known as the German and Bohemian Oldenburg School. Founded in 1898, it was succeeded in 1922 by Oldenburg Common School District No. 5. A separate school for black students opened about 1930. By 1944, both schools were consolidated with the Fayetteville school district.

Descendants of early German and Bohemian settlers continue to reside in this vicinity. (1990)

OLIVIA (Calhoun Co.)   *SH 172 at city limits*
Olivia
Established in 1892, the community of Olivia was named for Olivia Haterius, wife of the Rev. Carl J. E. Haterius, a Swedish Lutheran minister who bought land in the area and advertised a new settlement to other Swedish immigrants in the midwest. Twelve Swedish families responded to the initial advertisement and moved to Olivia with others following in a few years.

By 1900, a number of non-Swedish families had settled here, as well. The first public building in Olivia was a one-room schoolhouse where children were taught during the day and parents attended classes at night to learn English. The Eden Lutheran Church held services in the schoolhouse until 1910, when a sanctuary was built.

John Lind built the first store in the community on Carancahua Bay in 1894. The post office was housed in Lind's store and mail was delivered once a week. Lind moved his store to the center of the townsite in 1900. In 1906, Edward Wilson, another Swedish immigrant, bought the Olivia store and was appointed postmaster.

Other businesses included a hotel doctor's office, grocery store, blacksmith shop, and cotton gin. Since 1900, the thriving community has changed and grown, but retains its proud Swedish heritage. (1992)

OLIVIA (Calhoun Co.) SH 172 at CR 317
Olivia Cemetery
In 1892, the Rev. Carl J. E. Haterius of Galesburg, Illinois, acquired land at this site with the intention of establishing a community for Swedish settlers. He named the settlement for his wife, Olivia. When the townsite was laid out in 1893, land was set aside for this burial ground in association with the Swedish Lutheran Eden Church. The earliest marked grave is that of Anna Berardino Wilson, who died in 1902. Swedes and non-Swedes together contributed to the early development of Olivia, and the community cemetery serves as a reminder of their contributions.
(Texas Sesquicentennial 1836–1986)

OLNEY (Young Co.) SH 199, 9 mi. SE
Site of Cottonwood Spring
19th century oasis around a lone cottonwood tree and a good spring. Wagon ruts from heavy traffic attracted here are still visible on hill to the southwest. In 1849, Capt. Randolph B. Marcy, U.S. Army, camped with his soldiers at this spring as they mapped a gold-seekers' road to California. Capt. Marcy was to return as escort (1851) for Col. W. F. Belknap, en route to establish Fort Belknap (15 mi. SW), and with Maj. Robert S. Neighbors (1854), exploring for Indian reservation sites. Maj. Enoch Steen of the 2nd U.S. Dragoons was here in 1855, platting a route to Fort Riley, Kan. The Leach Wagon Train camped here in 1857 while opening the Butterfield Overland Mail Route, along the Preston Road to Red River. Riding to the north of Red River to fight wild Comanche raiders, two expeditions camped here in 1858: Capt. John S. ("Rip") Ford with Rangers, in April; Maj. Earl Van Dorn with U.S. Cavalry in the fall. Maj. Neighbors in Aug. 1859, escorting Texas Indians to reservations in present Oklahoma, found the spring dry.

Water returned, however. Cattlemen used the spring for generations, until in mid-20th century, the water table dropped permanently and the cottonwood died. (1974)

OLNEY (Young Co.) SH 79, 3 mi. N in Archer Co.
The Confluence of the
Brazos, Trinity, and Red
River Watersheds
The Trinity, a major Texas river, rises 250 yards west of this 1250-foot mound. South of this site water drains to the Brazos, and north and west to the Red. This high point has been important in Texas history. It guided Capt. Diego Parilla to battle Indians on the Red in 1759 and aided Capt. R. B. Marcy in mapping a California trail in 1849. Marcy and Maj. R. S. Neighbors used it as a beacon point in finding a site for an Indian reservation in 1854. It also was on U.S. Cavalry maps for 1870s Indian campaigns. (1976)

OLTON (Lamb Co.) US 70, 1.5 mi. E in roadside park
Lamb County
Formed from Young and Bexar territories. Created August 21, 1876. Organized June 20, 1908. Named in honor of George A. Lamb, 1814–1836, a second lieutenant who fell in the first charge at the Battle of San Jacinto. Olton, county seat.

OMAHA (Morris Co.) US 67 W
Concord Meeting House & Baptist Church
Built about 1860 to replace log church; used for school, voting. Now a Baptist church. Awarded Medallion Plate. (1966)

OMAHA (Morris Co.) US 259, 6 mi. N city limits
Omaha
On Seidicum Line, the old Bowie-Red River Counties boundary surveyed in 1840. Thompson Morris laid out "Morristown" in 1880, but post office was "Gravett." To arbitrate, a drawing from a hat suggested "Omaha," for old home of a settler from Alabama. Town is now a shipping center for plants and farm products. (1966)

ORAN (Palo Pinto Co.)

FM 52, 2 mi. from SH 254, W of Graford

Charles Goodnight

Here at Black Springs in the Keechi Valley in 1857, the celebrated pioneer open range cowman and trail driver Charles Goodnight (1836–1929) located his first ranch on the extreme Indian frontier of Texas. From here he took part in the 1860 Pease River fight when Cynthia Ann Parker was recaptured from Comanches. He served as scout and guide for the Texas Rangers during the Civil War and in 1866 he laid out the Goodnight-Loving Cattle Trail, over which thousands of longhorns were driven to market in New Mexico. In 1867, at Fort Sumner, New Mexico, his partner Oliver Loving died from wounds suffered in an Indian attack. Without the aid of an undertaker, Goodnight carried the body by wagon through hostile Indian territory for burial at Weatherford (24 mi. SE).

Goodnight extended his cattle trails to Wyoming and to Colorado, where he started a ranch near Pueblo. In 1876, he established the first cattle ranch in the vast Texas Panhandle, which became the internationally known JA Ranch. Involved in the preservation of the area's native buffalo, he also bred the first herd of cattalo by crossing buffalo with range cattle.

Goodnight's pioneer efforts led to the development of the frontier and the Texas cattle industry.

(1982)

ORANGE (Orange Co.)

US 90, 3 mi. W

Orange County

Formed from Jefferson County. Created February 5, 1852. Organized March 20, 1852.

Named for the fruit grown in this district since the earliest settlements near the mouth of the Sabine River.

County seat, Madison, 1852. Name changed to Orange, February 6, 1858.

ORANGE (Orange Co.)

Front and 4th St., Riverwalk Park

Atakapan Indians of Orange County

The Atakapans Indians, a tribe associated with Southeastern U.S. Bands, lived in this area for centuries. Studies have suggested their presence covered a large region of Southeast Texas. Their name comes from the Choctaw Indians, and means "man-eaters."

It is believed that Indians encountered by Spanish explorer Cabeza de Vaca in 1528 along the Gulf Coast may have been Atakapans. The first documented contact with the tribe was by French sailor Simars de Bellisle in 1719. Put ashore with four others to collect fresh water, the men were abandoned, and de Bellisle, after the deaths of his companions, was made a captive of the Indian tribe for a time.

Later contact with the Atakapans included trade with French and Spanish explorers. The tribe was evidently a fairly loose confederacy of small, scattered bands. Archaeological evidence suggests they subsisted mainly on small game, fish, and wild plants, and evidently were not farmers. Shell middens found indicate the existence of Atakapan campsites in this vicinity.

The tribe disappeared from Texas in the early 19th century, either becoming extinct or integrating into other tribes. (Texas Sesquicentennial 1836–1986)

ORANGE (Orange Co.)

Front and Third Streets

Old Niblett's Bluff, C.S.A.

On high point SE, across the Sabine, in Louisiana. Busiest East Texas port of entry in the Civil War. Target for enemy movements west across Louisiana repeatedly in 1862–64. Confederate defense post. Supply depot to support constant troop movements, both for fighting and for patrols and recruiting. Crossroads for land and river traffic. Ferry point on old road through swamps. Cotton concentration point. A boom town with saloons, gambling, night life.

Patrolled on both sides of the Sabine by Texans, to protect troop movements, commercial shipping, stagecoach travel routes, freighters' trains, and herds of cattle and hogs going east on the hoof.

Passed Texas troops through by thousands, to go eastward through marshlands and sloughs toward Brashear City and New Orleans or upper Mississippi River crossings, to eastern battlefields. Many units went by trail from Houston to Beaumont, then to Sabine Pass and up the river by steamer.

Niblett's Bluff welcomed steamers unloading guns, ammunition, clothing, medicines and other goods vital to the Confederacy—swapping these for Texas and Louisiana cotton, called "money of the Confederacy" because of its purchasing value in world trade.

ORANGE (Orange Co.)

William Henry Stark

A native of San Augustine County, William Henry Stark (1851–1936) lived in Burkeville and Newton before moving to Orange in 1870. Here he worked in the early area sawmills and became acquainted with every phase of the lumber industry.

In 1881, Stark married Miriam Melissa Lutcher (1859–1936), the daughter of Henry Jacob Lutcher, a partner in the Lutcher and Moore Lumber Company. Stark joined his father-in-law's firm and, because of his knowledge of milling operations, was soon placed in charge of two mills in Louisiana.

Stark's success in the lumber industry led him to invest in other businesses, including iron and coal production, real estate, and ranching. His progressive ideas, including deep water ports on the Sabine River and an irrigation system that provided stimulus for the region's rice industry, led to increased growth for the city of Orange. Stark also served as a regent for the University of Texas, 1911–1915, an office later held by his son Lutcher Stark, who became Chairman of the University Board.

The many contributions W. H. Stark made to Orange are reflected in the city's steady growth, industrial strength, and community pride. (1982)

ORANGE (Orange Co.)

IH 10, 10 mi. W, Claiborne West Park

Claiborne West (1800–1866)

Born in Franklin County, Tennessee, Claiborne West moved as a young man to Louisiana. He married Anna Garner in 1824 and they had nine children. His family immigrated to this area in 1825 and received a land grant in the Cow Bayou settlement.

Soon West joined in the struggle for independence from Mexico. As one of the representatives from Liberty Municipality, he attended the 1832 convention and the 1835 consultation at San Felipe de Austin. West was responsible for the designation of Cow Bayou as Jefferson Municipality, the forerunner of Jefferson and later Orange County. He served as a representative from the municipality to the general council and acted as local postmaster.

At the general convention at Washington-on-the-Brazos on March 2, 1836, West was one of 58 signers of the Texas Declaration of Independence. He helped draft the Republic of Texas Constitution. From July to October, 1836, West served in Franklin Hardin's company of volunteers. He then served in the first Congress of the Republic of Texas.

West moved from here to Montgomery County and later settled in Seguin. He was buried in the Riverside Cemetery at Seguin. (1979)

ORLA (Reeves Co.)

US 285, 10 mi. NW

Red Bluff Dam
(3 mi. NE)

Constructed for irrigation and electrical power purposes during 1934–1936, dam is located on Pecos River 8 miles south of Texas-New Mexico state line. It impounds an 11,700-acre lake occupying parts of Reeves and Loving Counties, Tex., and Eddy County, N.M. Floods first filled the reservoir in June, 1937.

Capacity is 310,000 acre feet of water. Main embankment—9,230 feet long—rises 105 feet above steams bed at highest point. Dam has top width of 25 feet.

These waters irrigate about 140,000 acres, which extend for 100 miles along the Pecos River. (1972)

ORLA (Reeves Co.)

US 285 at FM 652

Orla

Gateway to Red Bluff Lake, Guadalupe Mountains, Carlsbad Caverns recreational areas.

Established 1890 on Pecos Valley Railroad. Developed during land promotions. Had school, general stores, hotel, livery stable. In 1931 remaining merchant and postmaster Hal Olds moved ¼ mi. west to new highway. (1965)

OVERTON (Rusk Co.)

SH 42, 4 mi. NE on county road near Leverett's Chapel

Leverett House

Original house was built near a spring on land patented to a Georgian killed at Goliad. Present house has been built around and incorporates into its walls the original log house begun in 1840.

The two front rooms and central hall of the original house are virtually unchanged as to plan and comprise the library, central hall and living room of the present house. In the library, the original walls, ceiling, mantel and door, put together with pegs and rubbed smooth without paint or varnish, are still in use. House has Historical Building Medallion, and although not open to the public, is a beautiful and majestic site from the highway. Mr. M. B. Leverett was early planter in the area, operating on an extensive scale. Served Confederacy during Civil War.

OZONA (Crockett Co.) *IH 10 in roadside park*
Crockett County
Formed from Bexar Territory. Created January 22, 1875. Organized July 7, 1891.
Named in honor of David Crockett, 1786–1836, member of the United States Congress from Tennessee. Killed at the Alamo. Ozona, county seat. (1964)

OZONA (Crockett Co.) *US 290, 33 mi. W (moved to Courthouse Grounds)*
Fort Lancaster, C.S.A.
Site 33 miles west on U.S. 290. Upon U.S. surrender Texas forts start Civil War, made part Confederate far western frontier line. Occupied by 2nd Texas Cavalry. On supply line to and from Arizona-New Mexico campaign 1861–1862. Intended to make Confederacy an ocean to ocean nation. When regular patrols to guard supply trains and check Indian activities grew dull, life spiced by camp newspaper and nightly sport of shooting pesky coyotes. (1963)

OZONA (Crockett Co.) *US 290, 33 mi. W*
Ruins of Fort Lancaster
Established in 1855 by the United States government as a protection to travelers and mail on the Overland route from San Antonio to San Diego. Abandoned in 1861. Reoccupied in 1868 for a short time. (1964)

OZONA (Crockett Co.) *SH 137 at US 190, 22 mi. NW*
Crockett County's First
Producing Oil Well
In 1923 World Oil Co., owned by Chester R. Bunker, Ft. Worth publisher and printer, began drilling on the L. P. Powell ranch. Work progressed slowly, depending on the availability of money, under the direction of superintendent Mickey Green and the tool pusher known only as "Dangerous Dan." The wildcat operation proved successful in the spring of 1925, when the first well (10 mi. NW) came in at a depth of 2647 feet and began producing 25 barrels of oil a day. The strike opened up the World pool, more commonly known as the Powell Field, which is still yielding oil. Eventually 180 wells were drilled by a number of companies on Powell's 9260-acre ranch. Bunker, a New York-born World War I veteran, sold his rights to Humble and Marland Oil Co. after the strike, but Powell's heirs still own the land. Powell No. 1 has produced continuously since 1925 and now, under the operation of Petro-Lewis, yields 10 barrels a day.
Powell No. 1 was the beginning of a vital new industry for Crockett County, before 1925 primarily a ranching area. The next important strike occurred in the Crockett Field in 1938. There are currently over 2000 producing oil and gas wells in the county. (1975)

OZONA (Crockett Co.) *IH 10 and Taylor Box Rd. E*
Emerald Townsite
(¾ mi. N)
First townsite in Crockett County. Established 1889 by T. A. Wilkinson, agent for Fort Worth and Rio Grande R. R. as colonization project with the prospect of railroad extending into this area. Advertising from Maine to Minnesota, with mild climate and fertile land as major attractions. Post office opened April 8, 1890, with mail service via Knickerbocker was discontinued Dec. 7, 1891. Charles Hatch and E. E. Moore, postmasters. Site of first school in county, taught in a tent by Mrs. John Noyes in 1890. After wood structure was built teachers included Mrs. John Ketchpaw and Miss Ada Williams, who taught the last term in 1893.
In August 1890, prairie fire threatened Emerald, but valiant efforts of residents turned the fire which could be seen for two days before and two days after it reached the settlement.
Although the only town in the county, Emerald was doomed to extinction when it lost its bid for the county seat to the E. M. Powell Well (Ozona) in July 1891. Wilkinson challenged the elec-

tion but lost, and his community disintegrated as residents began to migrate to the Powell Well only one of many failures of colonization projects in West Texas. (1972)

OZONA (Crockett Co.) — *SH 163, about 9 mi. N at roadside park*
High Lonesome Stage Stand
(Site 11 mi. NE)

First station after leaving Ozona on the San Angelo-Ozona mail line. Here, at the 20-mile point of an 86-mile run, fresh horses awaited. The stand, built in 1902, served one of Texas' last commercial stage lines.

Ten horses were kept here, as at the three other stations: Shoeingstand (where the horses were re-shod each six weeks), Sherwood and Knickerbocker.

Frequent riders were whiskey drummers (peddlers), lightning rod salesmen and preachers.

Automobiles (1908) and finally the railroad (1910) put the "hacks" on this line out of business. (1969)

OZONA (Crockett Co.) — *SH 163, 20 mi. S*
Site of Comstock-Ozona Stage Stand
(Flagstone ruins nearby mark)

Site of early 1900s stage stand. First stop on passenger and mail line connecting Ozona with Southern Pacific railhead at Comstock—80 miles distant.

When stage pulled in about 8:30 a.m. (having left Ozona at 5:00) agent had fresh horses in harness for next 20-mile run.

Agent's family lived in tent with a flagstone floor. Other structures here were rock pens for a pig and cow and probably a corral for horses. Automobile replaced stage about 1914, but wagon ruts are still visible. (1972)

OZONA (Crockett Co.) — *US 290, 36 mi. W, Visitors' Center Parking Area, Fort Lancaster*
Howard's Well
(19 mi. to the SE)

First known to civilized men in the 18th century, when, according to legend, Franciscan Padre Alvarez prayed for water to ease his thirst, put down his staff, and saw a spring gush forth from the ground, this landmark of western travel was named for its rediscoverer, Richard A. Howard of San Antonio, an ex-Texas Ranger. Howard and other men, along with 15 Delaware Indian guides, made up an expedition sent out in 1848 under Col. John Coffee Hays to map a wagon road from San Antonio to El Paso. Although aided by the discovery of the well, the expedition failed, turning back in a state of near-starvation.

In 1849 the U.S. Army made its maps of the route, with Howard along as a guide. Many forty-niners went this way to the California gold rush. In 1853 the first regular San Antonio-to-El Paso mail line was routed by way of the well. So were many later ventures. Although white travelers seldom caught sight of them, Indians frequented the well. There, on April 20, 1872, Comanches and Kiowas surprised a large wagon train led by a man named Gonzales, and killed 16 persons. This was one of the events that led to the U.S. Government's cancellation of hunting permits for reservation Indians. (1976)

OZONA (Crockett Co.) — *US 290, 30.5 mi. W, Lancaster Hill roadside park*
Old Government Road

Route of march and troop supply on Texas frontier. Followed in part pre-Columbian Indian trails and "Old Chihuahua Trail" that ran from San Antonio to El Paso and Mexico. In 1840s this was extended to Gulf Coast Port of Indianola, where imported goods arrived from the United States and Europe, and were freighted out to be exchanged in Chihuahua for ore of silver and gold, leather goods, and other products.

In 1848 water holes and camp sites were marked as this road was re-charted for use of U.S. troops sent to protect Texas frontiers from Indian invasions. Army posts were built along this road: Fort Clark, between San Antonio and Del Rio, 1852; Fort Davis, in the Davis Mountains, 1854; Camp Lancaster, at this site, became Fort Lancaster in 1856. Camp Hudson and Fort Stockton were founded in 1857 and 1859. With all the army traffic, trail won new name of "Government Road."

Pioneer settlers, adventurers, California-bound gold seekers—even camel trains in government service—traveled this road in spite of frequent encounters with Comanches, Apaches, Kiowas, and other Indians. The army finally stationed troops in continuous picket line from San Antonio to El Paso. However, it was not until 1870 that relatively safe passage was assured.   (1968)

OZONA (Crockett Co.)   *SH 163 right-of-way, 7 mi. N*
Ozona-Barnhart Trap Company
By the 1920s, many ranchers in Crockett County had fenced their land, preventing their neighbors from driving sheep and cattle to the railroad shipping point in Barnhart (23 mi. N of here). A solution to the problem was offered by the Ozona-Barnhart Trap Co., which was organized in Ozona in 1924. By buying or leasing land for trails, traps (small pastures), pens, and water wells, the company established a corridor through which ranchers could drive their livestock to the railroad without crossing their neighbors' fences or destroying his grass supply. The main trail extended about 34 miles, from south of Ozona to Barnhart, with branch lines throughout the county. The McNutt traps (2 mi. NW), with 1340 acres of pasture, were the hub of the trail. Sale of stock to area ranchmen financed the enterprise, and operating expenses were handled by a charge per head of livestock for services used. The O. B. Trap Co. saved the ranching industry at a time when it was the only important business in Crockett County.

The need for the trail dwindled with the rise of truck transportation in the 1930s, but drives were still held until the 1950s. The O. B. Trap Co. now leases its land for grazing or gas production.   (1974)

OZONA (Crockett Co.)   *US 290, 36 mi. W, Visitors' Center*
Parking Area, Fort Lancaster
The Chihuahua Trail
and
Escondido Water Hole
The Chihuahua Trail was opened by segments, but was not called by this name until the 19th century. A small part of the route, along the nearby Pecos River, was followed by the Spaniard Gaspar Castano de Sosa in 1590, during an expedition to New Mexico. By 1850, the trail was finally extended to connect the city of Chihuahua and the Texas gulf coast, by way of San Antonio. Gold seekers going to California found it practical because it touched at all known water holes in this rugged terrain. Heaviest use of the trail came during the mid-1870s, when freighters transported tons of silver and copper from the state of Chihuahua for shipment to the eastern U.S.

One of the landmarks along the Chihuahua Trail in this part of western Texas was Escondido ("Hidden") Water Hole, seven miles southeast of Fort Lancaster. A small, deep well in the side of a rugged canyon, this water source was very hard to find, but saved the lives of many travelers. However, it is flanked by rock cairns marking the graves of some who died near the water hole of accidents or disease.   (1976)

OZONA (Crockett Co.)   *Between IH 10 and US 290, Fairground Park*
The Emerald House
Although the early history of this structure is unrecorded, it is known that the house originally was built in the townsite of Emerald (9 mi. E). Established in 1889 as Crockett County's first settlement, Emerald was the colonization project of railroad agent T. A. Wilkinson. When Crockett County was organized formally in 1891, an election was held to determine the site of the county seat. Emerald lost its bid for the seat of government to a newly developing area that became the town of Ozona. Within a few years, many of Emerald's buildings, including this house, were moved to the new county seat. As a result, Emerald eventually disappeared.

Until 1981, when it was moved to this site, the Emerald house was located on one of Ozona's main streets. It had been owned by many of the town's prominent citizens, including E. M. Powell, an early area surveyor who gave the land for many of the town's public buildings and parks; pioneer merchant Phil Perner; newspaper publisher W. A. Cochran; ranchers George L. Harrell and J. W. Friends; and E. B. Deland.

As one of Crockett County's earliest structures and a survivor of its first settlement, the Emerald house is a significant reminder of the county's heritage.   (1984)

PADUCAH (Cottle Co.)

US 70 at US 62, E

Cottle County

Created in 1876, organized in 1892, in area where the Pease and Little Wichita Rivers break level terrain. Named for George Washington Cottle (1798–1836), an 1832 settler in Dewitt's colony, who after fighting in 1835 Battle of Gonzales entered the Alamo March 1, 1836, and died there defending Texas.

Of the 254 counties, 42 bear Indian, French or Spanish names. 10 honor such colonizers as Stephen F. Austin, "Father of Texas." 12 were named for Washington, Clay and other American patriots.

96 were named for men who fought in the Texas War for Independence (15, including Cottle, dying at the Alamo), signed the Declaration of Independence or served as statesmen in the Republic of Texas.

23 have names of frontiersmen and pioneers.

11 honor American statesmen who worked for the annexation of Texas; 10, leaders in Texas since statehood, including jurists, ministers, educators, historians, statesmen; and 36, men prominent in the Confederacy during the Civil War. 8 have geographical names. 2 were named for battles, 2 for trees, one for a fort.

Cottle is noted for fine farms and ranches, with Paducah the principal market and shipping point. (1964)

PAINT ROCK (Concho Co.)

US 83, 4 mi. N

Confederate Beef Contractor
John S. Chisum
(1824–1884)

On this site during the Civil War and later, grazed by tens of thousands the longhorns of cattle baron John S. Chisum. Ranch headquarters were 10 miles east. Here in 1863–1865, Chisum not only ranched but also was buyer of cattle to feed Confederate armies stationed west of the Mississippi River.

Born in Tennessee, he came to the Republic of Texas in 1837. After a term as Lamar County Clerk, started ranching in 1853. For room to expand, moved his well known "Jingle-Bob" herds to the Concho in 1863.

Though he was not the man who gave the name to the famed northbound trail (this was Jesse Chisolm) John S. Chisum's drives were heroic. Herds bound in wartime for Louisiana army camps had to by-pass or to fight Indians, rustlers and occasionally a federal patrol. Concho cattle had to swim across the deep, cold Brazos River. Here cowboys would prod a heavy, wild bull till he was angry; then he would turn on men and horses. Or the Brazos itself killed men and horses. Still, beef went through to the Confederates.

After the war, Chisum developed ranches in New Mexico and was a bystander in the Lincoln County Wars of Billy the Kid and other desperados. (1965)

PAINT ROCK SPRINGS (Edwards Co.)

SH 377, 21 mi. NE

Stopping Place on the
Fort Clark–Fort McKavett
Military Road

One of many roads built to connect frontier cavalry posts in Texas, this route led south to Fort Clark and north to Fort McKavett (both established in 1852). Paint Rock Springs, located here at the head of the South Llano River, was a natural midway rest stop. In 1877, Major John B. Jones' Texas Rangers assembled here to begin a major offensive to capture frontier outlaws. In addition to its military uses, the Fort Clark–Fort McKavett Road provided an accessible route for immigrants, cattle drovers, pioneer ranchers, mail carriers, and freighters. (1968, 1990)

PALACIOS (Matagorda Co.)

FM 521, 7 mi. NE

Home of Horace Yeamans

A member of the 1829 colony of Stephen F. Austin, and one of organizers of Tres Palacios Baptist Church. Homesite is land given him for service in Army of the Republic of Texas. House was built, 1850s, by shipwright. Awarded Medallion Plate. (1965)

PALACIOS (Matagorda Co.)   *SH 35 Bus., 1.5 mi. W*
Site of Camp Hulen
Camp Palacios was established on this site in 1925 as the summer training camp for the 36th Infantry of the Texas National Guard. Located on the Turtle and Tres Palacios bays, the land was donated by Palacios area citizens. Over 6,000 guardsmen arrived in July of 1926 for the first training session. Renamed for Major General John A. Hulen (1871–1957) in 1930, the new camp supported the largest concentration of troops for field training in the United States military.

In 1940, the War Department leased Camp Hulen; first to undergo anti-aircraft training were National Guard units from several states. By 1941, the city of Palacios suffered a housing shortage that was alleviated by government housing near Camp Hulen. After extensive development the camp had facilities for 12,000 military personnel. Basic training continued until early 1944 when U.S. soldiers were removed. German prisoners of war, guarded by a small contingent of U.S. personnel, were housed here from 1943 to 1945.

In 1946, the War Department returned Camp Hulen to the National Guard, for whom it had become too small. Buildings were slowly dismantled and sold. In 1965, the property was sold jointly to a group of Palacios citizens and a development company.   (1997)

Correction:

36th Infantry should read 36th Division. Formed during World War I, it was redesignated 36th Infantry Division during World War II. The division trained here each summer, 1926–1937 and 1939.   (1998)

PALACIOS (Matagorda Co.)   *Loop 141 W (Main Street), off SH 35 Business*
General John Augustus Hulen
Missourian John Augustus Hulen (1871–1957), citizen soldier and railroad executive, came to Texas with his family in the 1870s. He later attended Virginia's Staunton Military Academy and returned to Texas. He joined a militia unit and later served in the Spanish-American War and then in the Philippines. There he earned a Silver Star and a Congressional Citation. In World War I, he earned a French Croix de Guerre and a U.S. Distinguished Service Medal. After the war, he was instrumental in establishing Camp Palacios in 1925, renamed Camp Hulen in 1930 in his honor. In 1935, he retired from service a Lieutenant General, the highest rank in the militia.

(2002)

PALESTINE (Anderson Co.)   *US 79, 4.7 mi. NE*
Anderson County
Created March 24, 1846, from Houston County. Organized July 13, 1846 with Palestine as the county seat. Named in honor of Kenneth Lewis Anderson, vice-president of the Republic of Texas 1844–1845.   (1964)

PALESTINE (Anderson Co.)   *US 79, 2.7 mi. W*
Home of John H. Reagan
Fort Houston
A fort and stockade built about 1836 on the public square of the Town of Houston (then in Houston County), as a protection against the Indians, by order of General Sam Houston, commander-in-chief of the Texan Armies. The town was abandoned in 1846 for Palestine, the new seat of Anderson County, the fort about 1841. The site is now a part of the historic home of John H. Reagan, which is called Fort Houston.   (1964)

PALESTINE (Anderson Co.)   *SH 155 right-of-way at Old Kickapoo Road*
                                                       (Brushy Creek Road)
Site of
Northeast Texas Christian Theological
and Industrial College
(about 1 mi. N)
Led by the Rev. A. J. Hurdle, the Northeast Texas Christian Missionary Convention of the Christian Church (Disciples of Christ) was formed in Daingerfield in 1900. Established to serve Black members of the denomination, its primary purpose was the creation of a college.

The Christian College Building Association was formed by a group of women within the organization, and by 1904 enough funds had been raised to purchase forty-nine acres of land near

Palestine, Texas. Contractor J. L. Randolph was hired in 1910, and on May 26, 1911, the cornerstone was laid for the main college structure.

Opening with seven students in January 1912, the Northeast Texas Christian Theological and Industrial College consisted of several large frame buildings and had a faculty of four. D. T. Cleaver served as the first president and was succeeded by I. Q. Hurdle. In addition to their classroom studies, the students farmed the college lands and raised livestock.

After the main college building was destroyed by fire about 1920, the school closed. The remaining buildings were later razed, leaving no visible reminders of the institution that once provided an education to students from several states. (1989)

PALESTINE (Anderson Co.) SH 155 at FM 321, 7 mi. N
C.S.A. Iron Works

Near old towns of Plenitude and Mound Prairie, John Billups, native of Georgia, as early as 1847 used Anderson County ore for iron to manufacture grist mills and cotton gins.

In the Civil War, with partner D. D. Hassell, made Confederate rifles—some with bayonets.

As part of program to increase wartime production of arms, the state exempted men and gave subsidies to the plant. Texas also made pistols, percussion caps, gunpowder. Plants were at Lancaster, Austin, Bastrop, Fredericksburg, Rusk, Tyler.

PALESTINE (Anderson Co.) US 79 at FM 1990, 2 mi. S, ¼ mi. N of Ft. Houston
Fort Houston
(Site ¼ mi. S)

A stockade and blockhouse of The Republic of Texas. Built in 1835–1836 to protect settlers who founded Houston, a pioneer town, now in Anderson County.

Friendly Indians would come to trade at the site, but wary settlers often slept inside the 25-foot-square blockhouse, built of heavy logs. Trappers bought supplies there and men from Houston formed one of the first Ranger units in Texas. The fort defended a large area of the frontier, 1836-1839, but it was abandoned about 1841. The site later became part of home of John H. Reagan, Texas statesman. (1969)

PALESTINE (Anderson Co.) US 287 at CR 499, 20 mi. NW
Early Settlement of Northwestern Anderson County

Early Texas settlements were often centered around institutions such as churches and schools. Even those that were short-lived played significant roles in the historical development of the state. When Anderson County organized in 1846, the area west of Catfish Creek was only sparsely populated. Community development began in the 1840s on land owned by Georgia-native Charles Gilmore (1796–1880). His house served as first polling place, first school and location for early meetings of the Gilmore's Chapel Methodist Church, the first area church. He then donated land for its cemetery and sanctuary. In 1854, local Baptists met there and organized Judson Baptist Church, moving later to a nearby site (1 mi. N) and then to Cayuga (3 mi. NW). Wild Cat Bluff (7.5 mi. NW), near the confluence of Wildcat Creek and the Trinity River, was also settled in the 1840s. It was an important ferry crossing and flourished until after the Civil War, when the river became unnavigable. Just over in Henderson County, settlers came as early as 1846 and founded a Masonic lodge. In 1852, Bethel Post Office, the first in the area, opened with Gilmore as postmaster. Soon the center of activity moved near the present-day community of Bethel (2.5 mi. SE), and Gilmore's Chapel Community disappeared. Although some of these communities and institutions did not survive, their stories demonstrate early settlement patterns and reflect the goals and needs of area pioneers, who established schools, churches and businesses, relying on mutual support and effort to develop Anderson County. (2002)

PALESTINE (Anderson Co.) US 287, 6 mi. S
Campbell Cemetery

Typical of a number of small family cemeteries located throughout the state of Texas, this graveyard was established by the Campbell family, who moved to the Mound Prairie community in this area in 1844.

Albert Gallatin Campbell (1808–1876), his wife Jenny Elvira, and their children John Bartlett, Isadore, and James, established a farm. Soon the family grew with the addition of another daughter, Jettie, and another son, Alexander.

John Bartlett Campbell (1834–1915) returned home after service in the Civil War and worked in a hardware store to earn money to purchase his own farm. He eventually purchased 270 acres and built a large home, where he and his wife Mary Elizabeth (1853–1927) reared their twelve children.

John Bartlett Campbell set aside one acre of land on his farm for a family burial ground, and in 1876 his father, Albert Gallatin Campbell, became the first person buried here. Albert's was the only burial in the graveyard for twenty-four years, until his grandson, 23-year-old John Bartlett Campbell, Jr., died in 1900 of scarlet fever. The cemetery is still in use by Campbell family descendants. (1994)

PALESTINE (Anderson Co.) *US 287, 6.5 mi. S*
John Starr House
Home of 1848 settler Starr and wife Susannah (sister of religious leader Daniel Parker, aunt of famed Indian captive, Cynthia Ann Parker).

Late Greek revival style. Built in 1856, fireplaces are of handcut native sandstones. Awarded Medallion Plate. (1968)

PALESTINE (Anderson Co.) *US 287 W, .5 mi. W from US 287 at SH 19*
Lone Pine Baptist Church
This congregation traces its history to a small group of worshipers who gathered together in the early 1890s to hold services in a small schoolhouse near this site known as Rocky Point. A plot of land was purchased by the church in 1903, and a one-room frame structure was built for school and church purposes. The one pine tree on the property gave the church its name: Lone Pine Baptist Church.

Although the congregation met regularly before then, the church was formally organized on July 8, 1908, with thirty-four charter members. The Rev. A. M. Thompson was called as first pastor, a position he held until his death in 1911.

In 1916, a larger building was erected for the combination church and school. About one year later the two institutions were divided and a church structure was built in June 1920. Called The Tabernacle, it had permanent walls and a roof, but the interior floor was of dirt.

Continued growth over the years enabled the congregation to improve The Tabernacle and build additional facilities. A new church auditorium was dedicated in 1957. The church continues to serve the community as it has for over eight decades. (1989)

PALESTINE (Anderson Co.) *US 84, 2 mi. E*
Texas State Railroad
The Texas Prison System built a short rail line from the Rusk State Penitentiary to hardwood timber stands where charcoal was made for firing the prison's iron ore furnaces. The rail line became the foundation of the Texas State Railway, organized in 1896 to make the prison self-supporting and to develop the region's economy.

Built by prisoners and supervised by the state penitentiary system, the line was completed in 1909 to Palestine (30 mi. W) where it connected with existing route. Financial woes and the closing of the furnaces led to the line being leased to the Texas & New Orleans Railroad and later the Texas & Southeastern Railroad, which operated the line until 1969.

Control of the line was transferred to the Texas Parks and Wildlife Department in 1972 for development as a state park. Restoration of the tracks between Rusk and Palestine was accomplished by Texas Department of Corrections inmates. New depots and parks were built at each terminus. Vintage steam locomotives and rail cars were purchased to provide tourist passenger service from Palestine to Rusk. The park has become one of the most popular tourist attractions in the state. (1997)

PALESTINE (Anderson Co.) *US 84, 11 mi. E*
Fields Chapel Methodist Church and Cemetery
Pioneer settlement began in this vicinity in the late 1830s and early 1840s, this area was the location of several camp revival meetings. The Rev. John W. Fields organized the Methodist Episcopal Church in 1852 and the church was named for him. Trustees elected were W. R. Anglin, J. J. O'Quinn, E. W. Hassell, Joseph Shaver, A. J. Killion, L. D. Fulton, and A. K. W. Jones. Adrian Anglin donated land to this congregation and property deeds were signed on June

23, 1853. The church members built a church that also served as a school. That structure was in use until the late 1940s, when a white brick sanctuary was erected.

The cemetery may have been in use prior to the date of the church organization, as there is evidence of more than 100 unmarked graves identified only by iron ore rock, native to the area. The oldest marked grave, dating to November 8, 1858, is that of Arminda Florence Langston, infant daughter of Willis B. and Amarillo Anglin Langston. The burials include many pioneer settlers and their descendants and veterans of the Civil War. The community has gathered for homecoming, a social event held annually on these grounds. The church and cemetery continue to serve this area of Anderson County. (1996)

PALESTINE (Anderson Co.) 5300 N. Loop 256
Alonzo Marion Story
Alonzo Marion Story (1882–1966) was born in New Orleans to parents John and Mary Story. He attended public schools and graduated from Louisiana's Leland College before doing postgraduate work in Texas and Colorado. Story came to Texas at the age of 21 and taught mathematics in Midway. He also served as a mail clerk before moving in 1912 to Palestine, where he taught math at Lincoln High School, the school for African American students. He taught there until 1917, when he moved to Austin to be principal of the state's Deaf, Dumb and Blind Institute for African Americans. In 1924, Story was offered a job as principal in Dallas. Instead, he returned to Palestine's Lincoln High School, where he taught math and served as principal. Beloved and respected, Story stayed until retiring in 1949, teaching his last years with no eyesight. After retirement, he tutored from his home. In 1953, the school district opened a new facility and named it Alonzo Marion Story High School in honor of the revered educator. After desegregation, the school became a junior high and then an elementary school before being destroyed by a tornado in 1987. In 1990, the district built a new school named for him. Story dedicated his life to education. In addition to his roles as teacher and principal, he was director of religious education at West Union Baptist Church and served on the executive committee of the Texas State Teachers Association and as vice president of the East Texas Teachers Association. His immeasurable contributions to Palestine are reflected in the communit's commemoration of his life. (2002)

PALO PINTO (Palo Pinto Co.) US 180, 2 mi. W at rest area
Palo Pinto County
Created Aug. 27, 1856, from Navarro and Bosque Counties; organized in 1857. Spanish name Palo Pinto refers to spotted oak, a common regional tree having bark with a mottled appearance.

Good hunting and abundant water made area a favored Indian locality. The first Anglo-American settlers arrived in 1850s, including Texas cattlemen and trail-blazers Charles Goodnight and Oliver Loving. The discovery, in 1880, of mineral water and arrival of Texas & Pacific Railroad brought an influx of settlers and helped establish a strong economy.

The county seat, first named Golconda in 1856, was renamed Palo Pinto in 1858. (1973)

PALO PINTO (Palo Pinto Co.) US 180, 12 mi. W
Brad Cemetery
According to local tradition, a young girl died as her family traveled past Thomas Lindsey's land in the 1870s. A short time later, Lindsey buried his sister near the girl's grave. The earliest marked grave is that of Tump Mapes (June–October 1877). The Lindsey Cemetery was deeded to William and Ada Graves in 1911, shortly after the site became known as Ioni Cemetery. In 1929, the land was conveyed to trustees Cozby, Fitzgerald, and Slemmons; it became known as Brad Cemetery in the 1940s. The cemetery association was incorporated in 1973. With more than 400 graves, the cemetery continues to serve the people of the area. (1998)

PALO PINTO (Palo Pinto Co.) SH 4, 5 mi. N
George Webb Slaughter
(May 10, 1811–March 11, 1895)
Born in Lawrence County, Miss. Came to Texas with his parents in 1830, settled in Sabine County, and began a freighting business. He participated in the Texas War for Independence,

serving as a courier for Gen. Sam Houston, and on one occasion took a dispatch to Col. William B. Travis at the Alamo in San Antonio.

Slaughter married Sarah Mason on Oct. 12, 1836, the first marriage sanctioned under laws of the Republic of Texas. The couple had 11 children, including the prominent cattlemen Christopher C. (1837–1919) and John B. Slaughter (1848–1928). George W. Slaughter in 1844 was ordained a Baptist minister. He began raising cattle in Freestone County in 1852, and moved in 1857 to his Palo Pinto County homestead (¼ mi. E). He organized (1861) a Baptist church near his home, and rode a circuit in the area, preaching and practicing "saddlebag" medicine. He and his family survived several Indian attacks.

From 1868 to 1875, thousands of his cattle went up the trail to Kansas railheads. Slaughter moved (1870) to Emporia, Kan., but returned here in 1875. In 1882, he founded the First Baptist Church in Mineral Wells. He ceased ranching in 1884. He was moderator (1886) when Slaughter Valley Baptist Church merged with the church in Palo Pinto, where he was later buried.   (1974)

PALO PINTO (Palo Pinto Co.) *US 180, off NE corner of Courthouse Square*
Jonathan Hamilton Baker
(July 13, 1832–October 18, 1918)
Virginia native Jonathan Hamilton "Ham" Baker came to Texas in 1858 with his brother G. W. Baker and his uncle Eli Young. Stricken by malaria while a teacher in Fort Worth, he later moved to Palo Pinto County where his uncle Frank Baker was homesteading. Here he opened a school, believed to be the first regularly organized school in Palo Pinto, and soon after helped establish the town's first Methodist church.

In 1859, Baker was chosen to lead a company of local men organized to defend the area against Indian attacks. He first served under Capt. J. R. Baylor and later participated with Capt. Lawrence Sullivan Ross in the recovery of Cynthia Ann Parker, the white woman seized by Comanches in 1836. During the Civil War he served as the leader of the home guard.

Baker was also an open range cattleman, and in 1869 he began driving his herds to Kansas railheads. Active in local government, he served as deputy sheriff, justice of the peace, deputy postmaster, and clerk of the county and district. In 1890, he moved to Granbury, where he became a successful nurseryman.

For over 60 years Baker kept a detailed diary, which now provides a thorough account of his distinguished life and the frontier of Texas.   (1983)

PAMPA (Gray Co.) *US 60, 2 mi. E*
Gray County
Formed from Young and Bexar territories. Created August 21, 1876. Organized May 27, 1902. Named in honor of Peter W. Gray 1819-1874, member of the First Legislature of Texas. Member of the Confederate Congress. Appointed to the Texas Supreme Bench in 1874. County seat, Lefors, 1902. Pampa, since 1928.   (1965)

PAMPA (Gray Co.) *SH 70, 17 mi. S*
Indian Battlefield
In this vicinity Lieutenant Frank D. Baldwin, commanding two companies of United States troops, attacked a large band of Indians and rescued two white girl captives, November 8, 1874.   (1965)

PAMPA (Gray Co.) *SH 70, 6 mi. S*
The Red River Expedition of 1852
In 1852, U.S. Army captain and explorer of the Southwest Randolph B. Marcy and George B. McClellan, later Democratic candidate for President against Abraham Lincoln, led Company D, 5th Infantry into the Texas Panhandle to locate the headwaters of the Red River. Their findings had great impact on the determination of Texas' border with the state of Oklahoma.

Until the 1852 journey, it was not known that there are two large branches of the Red River that intersect the 100th meridian, which forms the eastern boundary of the Texas Panhandle. On June 16th, the company discovered the headwaters of the north fork (approx. 1 mi. SE). On July 1st, they found the source of the southern, or Prairie Dog Town, fork in Palo Duro Canyon. Marcy's report to Congress is one of the earliest known written records of Gray County.

Since several early treaties had used the Red River as a boundary and since there was an extensive area of land between the two branches, the question arose as to which fork was in the minds of the contracting parties when the boundary was first defined. Marcy testified before a Congressional committee that the south fork should be the boundary, and an 1896 Supreme Court decision confirmed his findings. (1984)

PAMPA (Gray Co.) *SH 152 at FM 3302, 11 mi. E*
Site of Pampa Army Air Force Base
In the early 1940s, Pampa Mayor Fred Thompson and a delegation from the city's chamber of commerce traveled to Washington, D.C. to promote this area as a possible site for a military base. Attracted by the terrain, climatic history, available land, and community response, army officials chose this site for the establishment of an installation to train pilots and support personnel for World War II.

Construction of the Pampa Army Air Force Base began in June 1942, under the direction of the Tulsa, Oklahoma office of the Corps of Engineers. Overseeing the initial stages of the operation was Col. Norman B. Olsen. Temporary offices were set up in the Rose Motor Company and Culberson-Smalling buildings in town. Col. Daniel S. Campbell became the commanding officer in September 1942, and within two months the first planes and aviation cadets had arrived.

The Pampa Army Air Force Base closed September 30, 1945, after just three years of operation. During that time 6,292 aviation cadets and 3,500 mechanics were trained. The base's safety record was one of the best in the U.S. training command during World War II. Despite a brief history, the base had a dramatic impact on the development of the Pampa area. (1982)

PANHANDLE (Carson Co.) *US 60, 2.5 mi. NE*
Carson County
Formed from Young and Bexar territories. Created August 21, 1876. Organized June 29, 1888. Named in honor of Samuel P. Carson, 1798–1840, statesman of the United States and the Republic of Texas. Wheat, oil and gas contribute to its wealth. Panhandle, county seat. (1964)

PANHANDLE (Carson Co.) *405 Elsie (SH 207)*
Conway Community Church
Residents of Conway, established 9 miles south of here in 1905, attended non-denominational services in a relocated school house until this Union Church building was completed in 1912. It became an important gathering place for the Conway community and housed regular worship services until 1968. Membership in the congregation dwindled and the building fell into disrepair. Former church members and area volunteers devoted thousands of hours to restore this structure to its historic condition and relocate it here to the Square House Museum complex in 1991. (1993)

PANHANDLE (Carson Co.) *SH 207, N*
6666
Dixon Creek Ranch
Takes name from creek where noted buffalo hunter and scout Billy Dixon established first dugout home of High Plains, 1874.

Ranch founded, 1882, by Francklyn Land and Cattle Co., English firm backed by Cunard Steamship Co.

Fenced, 1884, with barbed wire hauled here from railroad at Dodge City; posts were of Palo Duro Canyon cedars.

Purchased in 1903 by S. Burk Burnett (1849–1922), trail driver, rancher; an organizer and for 45 years on executive board, Texas Cattle Raisers Association. Host during 1905 wolf hunt to U.S. President Theodore Roosevelt.

(Ranch not open to public.) (1965)

PANHANDLE (Carson Co.) *SH 207, Pioneer Park of Carson County*
Pioneer Dugout
In the 1874–1888 era, the High Plains (a sea of grass) had no native timber, stone, or adobe building materials. Homes were dugout or, if settlers, wagons went some 300 miles for lumber, half-dugouts. Dugouts were warm in winter, cool in summer. Some were carpeted and cloth-lined. Some

had an extra room for the schoolteacher or other guests. The cooking and heating stoves burned buffalo chips, cow chips.

This exact replica of a Carson County half-dugout was donated by Opal Purvines to honor her parents, the John F. Weatherlys, and other pioneer families. (1967)

PANHANDLE (Carson Co.) *SH 207, 18.8 mi. N*
First Rotary Drilling Rig Used in Texas Panhandle
(2.5 mi. SE)
In October 1923, W. T. Willis, J. E. Trigg, and H. D. Lewis, partners in one of Texas' largest drilling firms, broke ground at the S. B. Burnett 6666 Ranch with the first rotary drilling rig used in the Texas Panhandle. Success of this drilling method was a major event in this region. Drilling equipment included a $25,000 rotary rig; a 6-inch diameter drill pipe; a derrick; 3 steam boilers; 2 mud pumps; and other tools. Rotary rigs began to replace cable tool rigs on the Texas Gulf Coast about 1900, but the lack of a rotary drill bit capable of piercing rock delayed its use here. (1993)

PANHANDLE (Carson Co.) *SH 207, 18.8 mi. N*
Gulf Burnett No. 2 (1 mi. SE)
(Carson County Oil Discovery Well)
The Panhandle's first oil well, Gulf Burnett No. 2, was struck by the Gulf Production Company on May 2, 1921, on the 6666 Ranch of S. B. Burnett. The prediction of oil in this area by U.S. geologists in 1904 and the discovery of natural gas nearby in 1918 induced Amarillo business-men to finance Burnett No. 2. Though the first oil was of poor quality, major oil discoveries in the nearby Borger and South Pampa fields in 1926 spurred a regional oil boom and established the Panhandle as one of Texas' richest petroleum areas. Carson County has produced 150 million barrels of oil since 1921. (1993)

PANHANDLE (Carson Co.) *US 60, 4.5 mi. SW*
First Tree
Texas High Plains
Set in front of dugout home by Thomas Cree, 1888. Good luck symbol of settlers through drought, blizzard and heat.

Note: This tree, which had survived nature's worst, was killed a few years back by a crop-duster's poison, which was being sprayed on a nearby field.

Cree's Bois D'Arc tree died in the 1970s. County residents planted a new tree here in 1990 as a memorial to the area's early pioneers.

PANHANDLE (Carson Co.) *US 60, 4.5 mi. SW*
Thomas Cree Homesite
After serving as a teamster in the Civil War (1861–1865), Thadium (Thomas) B. Cree worked for the Union Pacific Railroad. In 1888, he and his wife came to the High Plains. They acquired this land and, with no trees for lumber, they build a dugout home. Cree traveled 35 miles at his wife's request to find a sapling and planted it here. He watered it from a nearby lake that he dug from a buffalo wallow. The tree never grew but lived many years despite blizzard, heat, and drought. Gov. John Connally dedicated a historical marker in 1963 to the first tree in the Panhandle. (1980)

PANHANDLE (Carson Co.) *SH 207, 18.8 mi. N*
3.5 mi. SE to site of
No. 2 Burnett
Carson County Oil Discovery Well
First oil well in the entire Panhandle. Brought in May 2, 1921, by Gulf Production Company on the 6666 Ranch of Captain S. B. Burnett. The first oil was of poor grade and transportation facilities were inadequate but interest grew, for the area was to become one of the world's largest producing gas fields.

The discovery of the prolific Borger and South Pampa Fields (1926) caused great excitement and established the Panhandle as one of Texas' richest petroleum areas. Since 1921, Carson County has produced over 140,000,000 barrels of oil. (1970)

PANHANDLE (Carson Co.) *SH 207, within city limits*
Square House
Built 1887–1888 for official of Southern Kansas Railway when terminal track was laid from Kiowa, Kansas to Panhandle, Texas.

This pioneer cottage was home of famous Panhandle pioneers: banker-judge James Christopher Paul; rancher-judge J. L. Harrison; innkeeper James B. Wilks; and Sheriff Oscar L. Thorp.

Was oldest house in Panhandle when purchased in 1965 for restoration as Carson County Museum. Awarded Medallion Plate. (1966)

PANHANDLE (Carson Co.) *US 60, at city limits*
Terminus of the Santa Fe Railroad
Panhandle, Texas
Originally "Carson City," town name was changed 1887 when this site appeared to be the future metropolis of the Panhandle: it was to be at the junction of Santa Fe (under name "Southern Kansas") and Fort Worth: Denver City Railroads.

Plans changed, however, and the F. W. & D. C. took a route 16 mi. south, bypassing Panhandle. (Amarillo was soon founded on the F. W. & D. C.)

Even so, Panhandle became a major shipping center. During great ranching era and again in 1926 oil boom, it moved more freight than any other town on Santa Fe Line except Chicago. (1968)

PANNA MARIA (Karnes Co.) *Main St., FM 81*
Town of Panna Maria
Oldest Polish settlement in Texas. Established December 24, 1854 by The Reverend Leopold Moczyge, MBA, O.F.M., who was instrumental in bringing from Poland about 100 Polish peasant families. Within a few months, the majority sought homes in other localities in Texas.

PANNA MARIA (Karnes Co.) *FM 81, .75 mi. E of SH 123*
Immaculate Conception
Church
Oldest Polish parish in America. Offered its first mass on Dec. 24, 1854 (altar under an oak tree). First building erected 1855. This church with 100-foot tower built 1877; remodeled 1937. Awarded Medallion Plate. (1966)

PANNA MARIA (Karnes Co.) *Main St., FM 81*
Oldest Permanent Polish Colony in America
Settled by 100 Polish families who came to Texas to gain economic, political and religious freedom.

Led by Father Leopold Moczygemba, O. F. M. Conv., they made a contract in 1854 with John Twohig, a San Antonio banker and merchant, for land at this site.

The colonists, natives of upper Silesia and Krakow, landed at Galveston after a hard voyage of nine weeks on a sailing ship. They hired Mexican carts to haul their farm implements, featherbeds, and the cross from their parish church in Poland. The 800 men, women and children walked—some in boots, others barefoot—the 200 miles inland to their new home. Babies were born on the way, and some of the people died. All suffered from hunger and exposure.

On Dec. 24, 1854, they reached this site. They named it Panna Maria (Virgin Mary) placing it under the patronage of the immaculate conception. Beneath a large oak they offered their first midnight mass of Thanksgiving and petition for strength and courage.

They camped out until they could put up huts of mud, straw or wood, later building in stone. In spite of hardships, they founded a stable community, aided in settling other frontiers, pioneered in education and gave Texas many patriotic, dedicated citizens.

PARADISE (Wise Co.) *SH 114 & FM 2123, 8 mi. S*
Cottondale
Area's oldest settlement. Platted by landowner B. F. Banks, who also gave lots for public use. Named, 1875, for lush growth of cotton planted by John Bridges, blacksmith, to finance a trip to Alabama to bring back his bride. Paradise took over town's post office, 1912; school 1933.

(1968)

PARADISE (Wise Co.) *Paradise Cemetery*
Dr. M. W. Matthews
(December 29, 1806–April 13, 1891)
Pioneer physician and preacher. Born in Kentucky. As army surgeon in Texas Revolution (1836), treated Gen. Sam Houston at Battle of San Jacinto. Served in the 1st and 7th Congresses of the Republic. Took part in Mexican War (1846). A firm Unionist during Civil War (1861–1865), he once barely escaped hanging at hands of Southern vigilantes.

Founded many churches across state. Was married twice; first to Sarah Gehagan and later to Margaret Spencer. (1971)

PARIS (Lamar Co.) *US 82, W city limits in roadside park*
Lamar County
Created December 17, 1840, from Red River County. Organized in 1841. Named in honor of Mirabeau B. Lamar, 1798–1859. Father of Texas education. President of the Republic of Texas, 1838–1841.

Lafayette 1841, Mount Vernon 1843. Paris, originally called Pinhook 1844. Has served as county seat.

PARIS (Lamar Co.) *US 82, 5.5 mi. W*
Smiley-Woodfin
Native Prairie Grassland
This meadow, approximately 2,100 acres, is the largest section of native grassland existing in Texas. It was originally part of a prairie system that stretched throughout the midwestern United States and into Canada. Since the earliest settlers arrived in this area in the 1830s, when Texas was part of Mexico, this grassland has remained uncultivated, providing an annual harvest of native grasses.

A lack of fuel and surface water made this area unsuitable for pioneer farmers. Although similar land nearby was tilled and planted, often resulting in erosion of overworked soil, this site was saved by the owner M. L. Smiley (1872–1953). A native of Lamar County, he used the meadow for cattle grazing and for hay production.

Early harvests consisted of cutting and stacking the grasses for drying, or transporting the hay to nearby steam-powered presses. The process was later simplified by the use of gasoline-powered machines that harvested and baled the hay on the site.

After Smiley's death, the meadow was inherited by brothers George S. and Gene M. Woodfin. Today the Smiley-Woodfin prairie grassland is the largest supplier of native hay in the state.

(1981)

PARIS (Lamar Co.) *US 82 at FM 38, 8 mi. W*
Tridens Prairie
In 1841, when Zacharia Westfall was granted 1280 acres of land in this area, much of the northeastern region of Texas was covered with natural prairies. Over the years most of them have been plowed or destroyed. Tridens Prairie, which covers 97 acres of Westfall's original grant, is an undisturbed remnant of the blackland prairie that now is under preservation management.

Tridens Prairie is part of a natural grassland that extends from Texas through the midwestern United States and into southern Canada. Its name is derived from the native, perennial bunch grass known as long-spiked tridens. Over 150 species of grasses and wildflowers have been identified in Tridens Prairie. Dominant grasses of the prairie include *Sporobolus silveanus* (silveanus dropseed), *Tridens strictus* (long-spiked tridens), *Paspalum floridanum* (Florida paspalum), and *Tripsacum dactyloides* (eastern gama).

One of the few remaining native grasslands in the state and once part of a large hay-producing region, Tridens Prairie is an important part of Texas' natural history. It is being preserved by the Texas Nature Conservancy and Texas Garden Clubs, Inc. (1985)

PARIS (Lamar Co.) US 82, 1 mi. W
Central National Road
of the Republic of Texas
Designed as a military highway, intended to make linkage with United States military road built to the north of the Red River in the 1820s.

This was part of the national effort of Republic of Texas to open a good road system. Congress in 1839 passed a bill for a road east from Washington-on-the-Brazos to the Sabine River; 1841 legislation called for a road from the Nueces to the Red River and another from Austin to Santa Fe, New Mexico.

The Central National Road was created in 1844, to reach from mouth of Elm Fork on the Trinity to Kiomatia Crossing on the Red. It went down a main street in Paris, which was founded in 1844; near its south end was the 1841 John Neely Bryan home, around which the City of Dallas originated.

Major George W. Stell surveyed the 130-mile route. Plans called for a road 30 feet wide and clear of tree stumps over 12 inches high. For each mile of road built (including bridges), grants of 160 acres of public lands were offered. Commissioners were Roland W. Box, Harrison County; James Bradshaw, Nacogdoches County; William M. Williams and Jason Wilson, Lamar County; John Yeary, Fannin County.

The route is roughly followed by later roads. (1968)

PARIS (Lamar Co.) Entrance #5, off US 271 about 9 mi. N
Camp Maxey
Recognizing in 1940 that hosting peacetime draftees might revive the county's economy, the city of Paris sent a request for the army to build a training camp here. The local American Legion acquired land options. Delegations from the Chamber of Commerce of Lamar County received initial support, but Congressman Lyndon Johnson moved the planned camp to his district at Bastrop. In response U. S. Senator Tom Connally and army officials ensured a camp for Paris, confirmed in July 1941. The 70,000 acre site was being surveyed when the U. S. entered World War II in December. Camp Maxey, named for C. S. A. General and U. S. Senator Sam Bell Maxey from Paris, was activated on July 15, 1942. Its main entrance was "Gate 5" marked by stone portals at this site. Two infantry divisions, the 102nd "Ozark" and 99th "Checkerboard," trained here with the 250th Field Artillery and other army units. A regional hospital and a prisoner of war camp hosting 7,000 Germans were part of the reservation. Local women formed the "Maxey Command" to host dances for the total of 194,800 soldiers stationed here. Area residents housed thousands of dependents and filled 10,300 civilian jobs on base. The camp was closed when the P. O. W. stockade was vacated in early 1946. (1992)

PARIS (Lamar Co.) West side of city plaza, downtown, on US 82
John James Culbertson
(March 16, 1853–September 27, 1932)
Born in Cincinnati, Ohio, John James Culbertson grew up in large northeastern cities. He married Emily Lou Lee of New Jersey in 1882 and soon became a salesman for a cotton product company based in Alabama. During his southern travels, Culbertson saw the potential for profit from cottonseed oil. He moved to Paris and was instrumental in building the first Paris cotton mill about 1884. The company, Paris Oil Works, was sold to American Cotton Oil Trust in 1887, and Culbertson moved to Arkansas to manage a southern oil company plant. Four years later the Culbertsons returned to Paris, where he built a small cottonseed oil empire through the Paris Oil and Cotton Company, later known as Southland Cotton Oil Company. Culbertson was asked to participate in a master plan for the growth of Paris in 1913. As an influential Texas financier, he was appointed to the Board of Directors of the Federal Reserve Bank in Dallas when it was formed in 1914. His nationwide reputation as a cotton producer led President Woodrow Wilson to appoint him to the board that organized a bureau to oversee cotton and cottonseed products for the U. S. Food Administration in 1917. After Paris was ravaged by fire in 1916, John and Emily Culbertson were among leading citizens who rebuilt the city. Held in high esteem by the people of Paris, the Culbertsons gave many public spaces, monuments and works of art to the city and

several local institutions, including the Paris Public Library and the fountain of imported Carrara marble on the city's central plaza. (1999)

PASADENA (Harris Co.)
SH 225, W city limits
City of Pasadena
This area has progressed from Indian territory to pioneer ranch land to space-age Pasadena.

Known at one time for its strawberry patches, it is now acclaimed for its oil and chemical industries.

The Vince Brothers, members of Stephen F. Austin's original 300 settlers, developed area as ranch land.

The armies of both Sam Houston and Santa Anna traveled through what is now Pasadena in 1836 to San Jacinto to decide the future of Texas. "Deaf" Smith destroyed a bridge on the Vince Ranch to block possible escape by the Mexican Army. After the brief battle, Santa Anna eluded the victorious Texas Army on a horse stolen from Allen Vince. He was captured approximately one mile from this marker. Site of the bridge and capture may be seen by following signs to the north.

In 1850, surveyors of the Galveston, Harrisburg and San Antonio Railroad called the area "Land of Flowers."

Col. J. H. Burnet, a land developer from Galveston, founded Pasadena in 1895. He said, "Pasadena will be the hub of a vast, rich agricultural area." The area fully justified his vision for, by 1908, "delicious strawberries, figs, oranges and vegetables" were the boast of Pasadena.

(1967)

PASADENA (Harris Co.)
SH 225, near Allen–Genoa Rd. intersection
Allen Ranch
This busy commercial area was once part of the Allen Ranch, one of the oldest and largest ranches in Southeast Texas. A portion of the land was granted to Morris Callahan in 1824 by Mexico and inherited by his niece, Rebecca Jane Thomas (d. 1919), who married Samuel William Allen (1826–1888) in 1844. Allen bought additional land, including a 1300-acre tract belonging to his friend, Governor Francis R. Lubbock, and began operation of a prosperous cattle ranch. He helped organize the firm of Allen & Poole to ship cattle to eastern and foreign markets.

Samuel Ezekiel Allen (1848–1913) took over operation of the ranch from his father in 1881. He and his wife Rosa Lum (d. 1931) built a large home near the junction of Buffalo Bayou and Sims Bayou (1 mi. N). Allen was a leading Houston businessman as well as a cattleman.

At the time he died, Allen's property included 13,000 acres in Harris County and 10,000 acres in Brazoria County. In 1917, Rosa Allen sold 700 acres to the Sinclair Oil Company (now Atlantic Richfield Corporation) as a refinery site. The remaining land was later divided for industrial, commercial, and residential use. The ranch house was moved to Galveston Bay, where it became Camp Allen of the Episcopal Diocese of Texas. (1976)

PATTISON (Waller Co.)
US 90 and FM 362
James Tarrant Pattison
Homesite
Located at important junction of Atascosito Road and the San Felipe Trail, this homesite was established by James Tarrant and Sarah Smith Pattison on their Republic of Texas land grant and became a stage coach stop. Their plantation of 5,000 acres had its own grist mill and cotton gin. The first church and school in the community were founded through the efforts of Pattison. Town developed here before 1854 was named by a son, George Madison, for the original settler, James Tarrant Pattison (1810–1872). Heirs still live here.

PATTISON (Waller Co.)
FM 1458, 2 mi. W
Judge Edwin Waller
(March 16, 1800–January 3, 1881)
Virginia native Edwin Waller migrated to Texas from Missouri in 1831 as part of Stephen F. Austin's third colony. An active participant in the earliest stages of Texas' struggle for independence, Waller participated in the 1832 Battle of Velasco, served as Alcalde of Brazoria, and represented the town of Columbia in the Consultation of 1835 at San Felipe.

A framer of Texas' Declaration of Independence and Constitution, Waller also served in the army during the 1836 Texas Revolution. After the war he became postmaster general and later a land commissioner for the new republic. In 1839, as a government agent, he platted the townsite of Austin, the new capital of Texas. The next year he became the first mayor of the city. Resigning during his first term, he moved to his plantation home, just north of this site.

The Waller plantation was the center of a large rural area. Here Waller opened a post office and store and provided for a school and church. For many years he also served as Austin County Judge. In 1873, a new county, which included this area was formed from Austin and Grimes Counties and named in his honor. Buried on his plantation, his body was later reinterred in the State Cemetery at Austin. (1982)

PATTISON (Waller Co.) FM 1458, 1.2 mi. W
Isaac Best
(1774–1837)
One of "Old 300" settlers of the Austin Colony. Spent early life in Pennsylvania and Kentucky. Moved (1808) to Missouri. There he built a mill and Best's Fort, which was a pioneer refuge from Indians, particularly during War of 1812. About 1824, with his wife, May Margaret Wilkins Best (1776–1852) and several of their nine sons and daughters, he came to Texas by wagon train. On Aug. 19, 1824, he was granted land east of the Brazos and about 30 miles north of Austin's capital, San Felipe. He sold that, bought other tracts, later owning about 8,000 acres. Best Creek (.5 mi. W) bears his name.

PEARLAND (Brazoria Co.) SH 35 & Halik Rd.
Old Settler's Cemetery
(0.2 mi. W)
Settlement of this area began as a result of railroad development through north Brazoria County in 1882. First known as Mark Belt, the townsite was platted in 1894 and named Pearland because of the abundance of pear orchards in the vicinity. An advertising campaign featuring favorable farm conditions brought many settlers to the area in the 1890s. Although some were discouraged by storm and freeze damage to their homes and crops in the early years, many remained and established permanent homes.

A community graveyard was begun with the burial of pioneer Echolean C. Ackerly, who died August 11, 1894. Four years later her burial plot and the surrounding land was officially dedicated as a cemetery. Six Civil War veterans are interred in the graveyard.

The cemetery contains many types of burials. The early practice of scraping the earth over graves was followed by cement paving, gravel cover, and bricking. Styles of gravestones range from simple stone markers to tombstones featuring elaborately carved decorations.

Old Settler's Cemetery remained the primary community burial ground until 1936. It continues to serve as a reminder of Pearland's early history. (1988)

PEARSALL (Frio Co.) US 81, 1.5 mi. N
Frio County
(Created 1858, Organized 1871)
Home of Pachal Indians before Spaniards arrived in Mexico (1519). First area explorer was Alonso De Leon, 1690, searching for Fort St. Louis founded by La Salle.

Upper Presidio Road—artery of travel from Saltillo, Mexico, to East Texas—crossed Frio River and became a King's Highway, 1720. Frio Town, first county seat, was located on the road, over which Santa Anna marched to destroy defenders of the Alamo in 1836.

County took name from Frio (a Spanish word which means "cold") River. The county seat moved to Pearsall, 1883. Jail, built 1884, is the oldest building in town. (1968)

PECOS (Reeves Co.) US 285 at First St.
The Pecos Cantaloupe
Nationally famed melon, originated in this city. Residents from 1880s grew melons in gardens, noting sun and soil imparted a distinctive flavor. Madison L. Todd (March 22, 1875–Sept. 10, 1967) and wife Julia (Jan. 30, 1880–Feb. 5, 1969) came here from East Texas and New Mexico. In 1917, Todd and partner, D. T. McKee, grew eight acres of melons, selling part of crop to dining cars of Texas & Pacific Railway, where Pecos cantaloupes first became popular and in wide demand. McKee soon quit business, but Todd remained a leader for 41 years.

Famed lecturer Helen Keller, Presidents Eisenhower and Johnson, and many other distinguished persons have ordered and appreciated Pecos cantaloupes. Exclusive clubs in New York, Chicago, St. Louis, and other cities are regular clients of Pecos growers.

Genuine Pecos cantaloupes begin ripening in July and continue on the market until late October. The varieties are the same as those grown in other areas. Climate, soil, and special cultivation methods account for the distinctiveness of Pecos melons. 2,000 acres are now planted annually.

M. L. Todd was known in his later years as father of the industry. He and his wife and family were leaders in civic and religious enterprises. (1970)

PECOS (Reeves Co.) — *US 285 at First St.*
Reeves County–Pecos, Texas

Flat, arid, grassy land with a moderate water supply from the Pecos River and springs in Toyah Valley. Yuma Indians are thought to have done irrigated farming here in 16th century. Mexicans later raised vegetables, grain.

Cattlemen moved in during the 1870s. Texas & Pacific Railway opened route to El Paso in 1882. Farmers, merchants, mechanics settled in Pecos City and Toyah. County was organized in 1884.

Modern irrigated agriculture began about 1900. Only dam on Pecos River in Texas was built in this county 1935. Privately owned deep wells are also used. (1967)

PECOS (Reeves Co.) — *US 285 at First St.*
Emigrants' Crossing
(20 mi. SE)

One of the few spots where pioneer travelers could cross the Pecos River by fording. At Emigrants' Crossing, the deep, treacherous river flows over exposed rock. It is one of only three fords in a 60-mile segment of the stream, and was the one favored by parties migrating in 1849 from the eastern United States to West Coast Gold Fields.

Often called the California Emigrants' Crossing, or the Red River Trail Crossing, it was also the one used in 1858 by coaches of Butterfield Overland Mail, which had an adobe station and a high-walled adobe corral there. (1972)

PECOS (Reeves Co.) — *US 285 at First St.*
Spanish Explorers

Antonio de Espejo in 1583, after exploring among Pueblos in New Mexico, reached the Pecos River southeast of Santa Fe. He named it Rio de Las Vacas (River of Cows), for the abundance of buffalo. On his return route to Mexico, he went down the river to near the present town of Pecos. Jumano Indians led his party to their camp on Toyah Lake. He then went down Toyah Creek and through the Big Bend.

While Espejo was first to explore the Pecos, Castano de Sosa, on his way into New Mexico in 1590, was the first European to travel its full length. (1966)

PECOS (Reeves Co.) — *Walthall St. & US 285, Rodeo Grounds*
World's First Rodeo

Held a block south of Pecos courthouse, July 4, 1883. Started with claims of cattle outfits—NA, Lazy Y, and W Ranches—that each had fastest steer ropers.

Settlers in town for Fourth of July picnic were spectators. The prizes were blue ribbons cut by pocket knife from new dress of a 4-year-old girl in the crowd.

Best roper was Morg Livingston of the NA; second, Trav Windham, Lazy Y. Others entered: Howard Collier, Fate Beard, Jim Mannin, George Brookshire, John Chalk, Jeff Chism, Jim Livingston, Jim and Henry Slack, Brawley Oates, Henry Miller, E. P. Stuckler. (1965)

PENWELL (Ector Co.) — *US 80, 2½ mi. W; 2 mi. N of site*
Ector County
Discovery Well
(2 mi. S)

The discovery of oil in Ector County December 28, 1926, marked the beginning of a new economic era for this region.

The first well, "J. S. Cosden No. 1–A W. E. Connell," was named for the driller and owner of land. Its meager initial output of 38 barrels per day did not cause much excitement, but experts insisted that vast oil deposits lay under area (Permian Basin).

In 1929, Robert Penn's gusher catapulted Odessa to boom-town fame. Oil has sustained the area economy since then, although the discovery well was plugged and abandoned in 1940. (1967)

PENWELL (Ector Co.) *US 80, W city limits*
Penwell

Birthplace of Ector County's oil boom. First civic development here was wide-open town, "Derrick City," platted March, 1927, after Dec. 28, 1926, oil discovery by driller Josh Cosden on land of W. E. Connell, near the old farming and cattle station, Judkins.

However, when Connell well began pumping only 20 barrels a day, the boom crowd moved away. The city was abandoned.

As nearby counties off the railroad struck oil that had to be shipped by the Texas & Pacific to refineries, Ector County in 1927 had a "truck drivers boom"—a foretaste of the leadership in supply and servicing that was to develop progressively.

Then on Oct. 14, 1929, on Robert Penn's land here, a 375-barrel per day well came in. With that showing, exploration continued, soon followed by the Penn Well, the 600 to 700-barrel a day gusher.

In a busy, bustling and prosperous tent city, the Penwell post office was established June 30, 1930. This has remained a central distributing and shipping point for numerous fields in several Permian Basin counties, thereby establishing an earned reputation as "the crossroads of the oil patch." (1965)

PERRY (Falls Co.) *SH 6 right-of-way*
Judge Albert G. and
Harriet Elizabeth Grimes Perry

Tennessee native Albert G. Perry (1807–1874) began the study of law at age sixteen in his brother's Alabama law office. He became a successful attorney, but in 1831 left for Texas, settling in Washington, where he opened a law office. The following year, on January 8, he married Harriet Elizabeth Grimes (1816–1888), the daughter of pioneer Jesse Grimes (1788–1866), signer of the Texas Declaration of Independence. In 1826, Harriet had arrived in Texas with her father and eight siblings, one of whom, Albert Calvin Grimes, later died at the Alamo.

In late 1833 or early 1834, Perry became secretary to the alcalde at Sarahville de Viesca in Robertson's Colony (in present Falls County), and in 1835 was First Lt. of a frontier defense ranger company. He was a member of the Viesca Committee of Safety, and was a delegate to the Consultation of 1835.

The Perrys lived in Washington from 1836 to 1843, when they moved to Anderson in present Grimes County. In 1852, they moved to Falls County, where they farmed, and he was county and district judge.

In 1883, when the railroad bypassed the community of Peyton, a new settlement developed along the rail line and was named Perry in honor of Albert G. Perry.

(Texas Sesquicentennial 1836–1986)

PERRYTON (Ochiltree Co.) *US 83, 13 mi. S, 4 mi. E on Lake Fryer Rd.*
Buried City

In 1907 Dr. T. L. Everly, Floyd V. Studer and other archaeologists discovered here the Buried City.

These Pueblo ruins were built by the Panhandle Pueblo Indians who were agriculturists, stone house builders, pottery, and basket makers.

Dr. Warren K. Moorehead partially excavated this ruin in 1919–1920.

Some archaeologists and historians agree that the well-built stone houses were in ruins when Coronado explored this region in 1541.

PERRYTON (Ochiltree Co.)   *US 83, 13 mi. S, 1 mi. E on Lake Fryer Rd.*
Site of the
Trading Post
Established by C. E. Jones in 1874 on the Jones and Plummer Trail, which extended from Dodge City, Kansas, to Mobeetie. Here, food and clothes were traded to Indians for hides and later ranchmen purchased general supplies hauled from Dodge City.

PERRYTON (Ochiltree Co.)   *SH 70, 8 mi. S*
Ochiltree Townsite
(Bordering This Highway)
This county was created in 1876 and named for noted Texas Jurist William Beck Ochiltree (1811–1867). In 1876 it was attached for judicial purposes to Clay and later to Wheeler County. In 1886, pioneers began to settle in dugouts here on the prairies near Wolf Creek, saying they lived "in Ochiltree." For convenience in making land and tax transactions, and establishing law and order, they organized the county in 1889, making their village the county seat. First elected officials were William J. Todd, county judge; Dave C. Kettell, sheriff and tax collector; George M. Perry, county clerk; Myrtle L. Daily, treasurer. In 1891 a 2-story courthouse was built (100 yds. E) of lumber freighted from Dodge City, Kans. This also served as church, schoolhouse, and social hall for the town. By 1903, Ochiltree had 600 people, churches, a high school, a newspaper, bank, flour mill, and other facilities.

In 1919, the Santa Fe Railway founded a new town between Ochiltree and Gray, Okla., and induced people from both places to relocate by offering free lots. In 1919 steam engines and heavy equipment hauled the improvements from Ochiltree to the new site (8 mi. N), called Perryton, in honor of veteran county official George M. Perry.   (1976)

PERRYTON (Ochiltree Co.)   *SH 70, 9 mi. S*
Ochiltree Cemetery
In 1902, Jim McLarty and J. V. Stump fenced off 90 acres for a cemetery in the town of Ochiltree. Soon afterwards, Jim was thrown from his horse and killed, and at age 21 became the first person buried in the cemetery. In 1927, the county acquired the deed from Mr. J. M. Blasingame; in 1930, a cemetery association was formed. During the depression of the 1930s, an entry gate was built with help from the Works Progress Administration, veterans of the Civil and Spanish American Wars, World Wars I and II, and the conflicts in Korea and Vietnam are among the citizens buried here.   (1997)

PETTUS (Bee Co.)   *US 181, 2 mi. N*
Bee County
Named for Col. Barnard E. Bee (1787–1853), who served Republic of Texas as Secretary of War, Secretary of State, and Minister to the United States. County was created by legislative act on Dec. 8, 1857; organized Jan. 25, 1858, from land earlier in Goliad, Karnes, Live Oak, Refugio, and San Patricio Counties. County seat in 1858 was on Medio Creek; since 1860 at present Beeville.

A cattle region since Spanish times, Bee County became important beef producer in 1865. San Antonio & Aransas Pass Railroad provided first modern transportation in 1886. Oil was discovered here in 1929.   (1971)

PETTUS (Bee Co.)   *US 181, 3 mi. N in a roadside park*
Town of Pettus
(Located 3 mi. S)
Oil capital of Bee County, Pettus was settled in the 1850's when John Freeman Pettus (1808-1878) set up his sprawling ranch about 4 miles south of here.

The son of one of Stephen F. Austin's first 300 colonists, Pettus was an extensive cattle and horse breeder. The town, previously called "Dry Medio" for a nearby creek, was named for him during the Civil War.

The community was in the vicinity of two important Indian skirmishes in Bee County in 1859 and the 1870s; but the town slept until 1886, when the tracks of the San Antonio & Aransas Pass Railroad reached this site. It then awoke to become the cattle shipping center for the area. In the same year, John S. Hodges, a pioneer citizen, laid out the townsite and donated land to be used for streets and S. A. & A. P. right-of-way.

For years the railroad stockyards and depot were places of bustling activity as freight trains came for loading and wood-burning steam engines took on water. In 1909 the presidential train of Wm. H. Taft stopped at the Pettus water tank. The tank—a final monument to steam railroading here—was razed, 1965.

In 1929 the Houston Oil Co. brought in its well "No. 1–Maggie Ray McKinney" and from that time Pettus has played a continuing useful role in Texas economy.   (1968)

PETTY (Lamar Co.)   *US 82 and on FM 38, 6 mi. NW*
The Historic Persimmon Grove
and Capt. Hill's Military Camp

Up to 1860, pioneers found here a grand 100-square-mile prairie overgrown with high grass. The grove of persimmons 100 yards west of this spot formed an island on the north-central edge of the prairie. The locality's only trees, the persimmon grove, was a gathering place where settlers swapped news or livestock and followed other casual pursuits.

When Texas and other states seceded from the Union and prepared for war, Lamar Cavalry Company No. 2 was organized here on June 10, 1861, by Methodist Lay Minister and Mexican War Veteran James Hill (1827–90). Capt. Hill drilled his men for several months on the prairie beside the grove. Then it became known that militia laws would forbid such cavalry units to leave the State of Texas. Disbanding, Hill's men formed Company E, 9th Regiment, Texas Infantry, and were mustered into Confederate service on Nov. 26, 1861. In Ector's brigade, French's Division, army of Lieutenant General Polk, they fought at Shiloh, Murfreesboro, Chickamauga, and other actions.

Farmers later plowed up the prairie and planted trees that obscured the persimmon grove. Yet it has become a landmark of pioneer days.   (1977)

PFLUGERVILLE (Travis Co.)   *FM 1825, Pecan & 3rd St.*
Pflugerville

Henry Pfluger (1803–67), who migrated from Germany to Texas in 1849–1850, moved his large family here in 1853. Other settlers joined them, and in 1872 a school was begun on Henry Lisso's farm. Immanuel Lutheran Church was founded in 1874. Primarily a farming settlement, Pflugerville had no commercial businesses until 1890, when Louis Bohls built a general store. A post office was opened there in 1893 with Bohls as postmaster. In 1891, two community organizations were formed: the German-American Mutual Assurance Association, to insure townspeople against natural disasters; and "Pflugerville Schuetzen and Kegel Verein," a shooting and bowling club.

The village began to grow when the Missouri, Kansas & Texas Railroad arrived in 1904. George Pfluger (1834–1910) and his son Albert (1878–1969) platted the townsite, and George donated land for a train depot and a school. Early businesses included drugstores, groceries, a hotel, grist mill, cotton gin, ice factory, and a blacksmith. In 1907, La Rue Noton and Archie Ward started a telephone system. Farmers State Bank, chartered in 1906, became First State Bank in 1933. A newspaper, *The Pflugerville Press,* was published from 1907 until 1942.

In 1958–1962, the Pflugerville High School football team gained national fame by winning 55 consecutive games.   (1976)

PHARR (Hidalgo Co.)   *US 281 at I Road, 7.25 mi. S*
Jackson Ranch Church

This fellowship was founded in 1874 by the Rev. Alexander H. Sutherland (1848–1911), an early Methodist missionary, on Juan Manuel de la Vina's El Capote Ranch. In 1883, the congregation began meeting near this site on the Jackson Ranch when owner Martin Jackson donated the land. He later built a small chapel for their use. In 1910, most of the church members moved to the new city of McAllen, and only a few families continued to worship here. As one of the first Protestant congregations in Hidalgo County, this church has continued to serve area residents.   (1983)

PHARR (Hidalgo Co.)   *Old US 83 at Fir St.*
First Pharr–San Juan–Alamo School

The common school district of Pharr and San Juan began construction of this school in 1915. First used for the 1916–1917 school year, its enrollment was 143, with twelve teachers and a graduating class of nine. The name was changed in 1919 to Pharr–San Juan Independent School District. Although the town of Alamo was also founded that year and contributed students to the school, the Alamo name was not officially added until 1959. In 1961, this became Jefferson Junior High. It was named Memorial Junior High in 1979 in honor of all Pharr–San Juan–Alamo veterans.

(Texas Sesquicentennial 1836–1986)

PIERCE (Wharton Co.)
Corner of Kruttschnitt St. and US 59 bypass
Site of Pierce Hotel

Here, in the 1890s, the celebrated Texas cattleman A. H. "Shanghai" Pierce (1834–1900) platted the townsite of Pierce, which he hoped would become the Wharton County seat. Its proximity to his ranch headquarters in the central part of the county was a major factor in his choice of location for the town. He laid out a public square, courthouse square, academy square, and a cemetery. He built several structures in the town, including a three-story hotel located at this site.

The Pierce Hotel was designed to accommodate cattle buyers, traveling salesmen, and others attracted to the area by the railroad and Pierce's ranching interests. Located near the Southern Pacific Railroad depot and across from the present Pierce ranch entrance, the hotel was designed as the center of the town's planned growth, which did not develop. Although never opened to the public as a hotel, the building was used for various purposes by several long-term tenants. A landmark on the Texas coastal prairie for more than eighty years, the Pierce Hotel was razed in 1980.

Still at this site of the hotel is its Widow's Walk, which was preserved as a symbol of the structure's historical significance.

(1984)

PIERCE (Wharton Co.)
US 59, 1.1 mi. SE
Shanghai Pierce Ranch House

Built 1886, in lavish style. On first floor was office of highly successful ranch.

Legend says Pierce (cattle king famed for introducing Brahmas in Texas) used to stand on porch and call orders to Southern Pacific station, a mile away. Awarded Medallion Plate.

(1967)

PILOT POINT (Denton Co.)
US 377 at Strittmatter Rd., southeast corner
Skinner Cemetery

In the early days of Pilot Point, Lucinda (Glasscock) and Richard Skinner set aside a 2.44-acre piece of land to be used as a cemetery. The first recorded burial was that of 5-year-old Josiah Taylor in March of 1858; his father, Josiah Sr., died the following July.

Predominantly of Anglo-Saxon protestant descent, most of those buried here came from Kentucky, Virginia, Missouri, Arkansas, and Tennessee. Many were farmers or ranchers. Significant graves include that of J. D. Merchant, Sr., a local businessman who built the first brick building in the area. Also here are several victims of yellow fever, including Prissie and Sarah Wilson, sisters who died within 2 months of one another during the epidemic of 1872 and 1873. Two people named James Graham, born on the same date two years apart, died on the same September day in 1867.

Lucinda Skinner, the last charter member of the Pilot Point First Baptist Church, died in 1890. By 1900, there were probably 200 graves in the cemetery. The land was sold by John Skinner to the Skinner Cemetery Association in 1905; the last recorded burial was that of Joe Mylo Phipps, an infant who died in 1928. The Skinner Cemetery remains a vital link to the early settlers of the Pilot Point community.

(1998)

PINE SPRINGS (Culberson Co.)
Guadalupe Mountain National Park, US 62
Ruins of "The Pinery" or
"Pine Spring" Stage Stand

Built in 1858 as a station on the Butterfield Overland Mail Route. St. Louis to San Francisco. Abandoned in 1859, when the line was shifted to the Davis Mountain Route.

(1964)

PINE SPRINGS (Culberson Co.)
US 180/62, 3 mi. SW in roadside park
Guadalupe Peak

Guadalupe Peak, Texas' highest mountain at 8,751 feet, dominates one of the most scenic and least-known hinterlands of the old frontier. It lies behind and to the right of 8,078-foot El Capitan, the sheer cliff that rises more than 3,000 feet above this spot to mark the south end of the Guadalupe Range.

Starkness of the mountainside belies the lushness which the Guadalupes conceal. Tucked away in their inner folds are watered canyons shaded by towering ponderosa pine, douglas fir, juniper and quaking aspen. McKittrick Canyon, scene of a four-mile trout stream, is also the habitat of the state's only known herd of wild elk. Deer and wild turkeys abound.

Stories of hidden gold go back to Spanish days. The Conquistadores who rode north from Mexico wrote about fabulous deposits. Geronimo, the Apache chief, said the richest gold mines in the western world lay hidden in the Guadalupes. Legend holds that Ben Sublett, a colorful prospector of the 1880's, slipped off at night to a cave and returned with bags of nuggets.

Probably less is known about the archeology of the Guadalupes than of any other area in the Southwest. Excavators have found spearheads, pictographs and human remains together with bones of long-extinct bison, dire wolf and musk ox in cliff caves. At Hermit Cave in Last Chance Canyon, carbon-14 dating indicates occupancy 12,000 years ago.

Geologically, the Guadalupes present a spectacular exposure of the famous Capitan prehistoric barrier reef, said to be the most extensive fossil organic reef known.

PITTSBURG (Camp Co.)   *US 271, 1.7 mi. N*
Camp County
Formed from Upshur County. Created April 6, 1874. Organized June 20, 1874. Named in honor of John La Fayette Camp, 1828–1891, soldier-lawyer-statesman, member of the Constitutional Convention, 1866, state senator in 1874. Pittsburg, the county seat.   (1964)

PITTSBURG (Camp Co.)   *US 271, 1.7 N*
Colonel John L. Camp
(1828–1891)
Came to Texas from Alabama in 1849. Practiced law and taught school in Gilmer.

In Civil War, organized and was elected captain of Co. E, 14th Texas Cavalry (dismounted), unit in famed Gen. M. D. Ector's Brigade. In thick of fight, in Tennessee and Georgia, was wounded twice, captured twice. Was in prison camp at the war's end.

Elected to Congress in 1866, was denied his seat because of Confederate service. Served as district judge and state senator. Campaigned for adoption of constitution of 1876, to end reconstruction in Texas.   (1964)

PITTSBURG (Camp Co.)   *FM 21, 6 mi. NW*
Cherokee Trace
This Indian trading route to Arkansas and Oklahoma was laid out by Cherokees. A tribesman with a keen sense of direction pulled buffalo hides behind his horse to press down the tall grass. Groups of Indians followed blazing the trail, removing logs and underbrush, and marking fords. Others located springs and good camping places. After the road was established the Cherokees planted roses and honeysuckle which still mark the old trace. After the Indians were driven out, settlers came into Texas by this route. The first residents in Camp County lived on the trail.   (1979)

PITTSBURG (Camp Co.)   *SH 11 at FM 1519, 7 mi. W*
Leesburg Cemetery
Dwight Hays Townsend (1834–1906) donated land for this cemetery about 1870. The graves of two children which were relocated here from the Leesburg school yard are thought to be the earliest burials on the site. The oldest marked grave is that of Tapley Wylie (1836–1870). This cemetery is the primary burial ground for the rural community of Leesburg. Those interred here include pioneer settlers, community leaders, a large number of infants and children and veterans of the Civil War, World Wars I and II, Korea, and Vietnam.   (1992)

PLAINS (Yoakum Co.)   *US 380, 1 mi. E on courthouse grounds*
Yoakum County
Created August 21, 1876. Organized September 21, 1907. Named in honor of Henderson Yoakum, 1810–1855. Author of a "History of Early Texas." A soldier in the Mexican War. Plains, the county seat.

PLAINVIEW (Hale Co.) *US 87 Bus., 1 mi. S at city limits in roadside park*
Hale County
Formed from Young and Bexar territories. Created August 21, 1876. Organized August 13, 1888. Named in honor of John C. Hale, a lieutenant who fell at San Jacinto. Plainview, county seat. (1965)

PLAINVIEW (Hale Co.) *US 70, 5 mi. W*
The Slaton Well
(.5 mi. N)
The Plainview Commercial Club, led by President J. O. Wyckoff, saw the potential of irrigation during a 1910 visit to wells in New Mexico. Local banker and farmer J. H. Slaton agreed to bear cost of a test well sunk on his land if it succeeded. G. E. Green and J. N. McNaughton completed the well in Jan., 1911. At 130 feet, using a nine-inch centrifugal pump, it yielded 1,700 gallons of water a minute. The success of the Slaton Well led to extensive irrigation. It transformed this semi-arid area of West Texas into one of the most productive food crop regions in the world. (1976)

PLAINVIEW (Hale Co.) *US 70 at W 5th Ave.*
Plainview Points
The first of this distinctive type of early man dart point was found by 15 year old Val Keene Whitacre in 1941, in a caliche quarry on Running Water Draw. In 1944, quarry workers uncovered a fossil bone deposit, which was noted by scientists surveying the geology of the Plains. The next year a team of archeologists from the University of Texas, including Dr. E. H. Sellards and Dr. Alex D. Krieger, excavated the site and found 26 man-made artifacts, including several of the points, in association with the remains of about 100 extinct bison (Bison Talori), about twice the size of modern species.
The bone bed probably resulted from the primitive hunting method of stampeding bison over a cliff, and butchering of the dead and crippled animals for food. The cliff eroded away, and covered the bones with 12 to 14 feet of silt. When exposed, the bone bed was 62 feet long, up to 10 feet wide, and 1.5 feet thick. Radiocarbon dating indicates that this site is 8,000 to 9,000 years old. The Plainview Point is found most commonly in the Great Plains Region of North America, but has been located also in Alaska and Mexico. (1973)

PLAINVIEW (Hale Co.) *US 70 at FM 179, 14 mi. W*
Halfway
Settlers came to this area seeking abundant grass, fertile soil, and water. This site, acquired by R. L. Hooper (1872–1952) and his wife Ada Mae (Huguley) (1880–1955) in the 1890s, received its name because it stood "halfway" between Olton and Plainview. It made a good rest stop for ranchers, with a windmill for water and overnight camping. Early pioneers raised enough grain for their stock. Arrival of the railroad in Plainview in 1906 and use of irrigation systems developed a vast agricultural region.
In 1908, Hooper provided six acres and helped build a schoolhouse for his seven and the neighbors' children. Hooper donated land in 1910 for Edgar Howard to build the first store where he ran a post office and wagon yard. Methodist and Baptist congregations met in the school building until they erected sanctuaries. The post office closed in 1914 but the settlement boasted a blacksmith shop and a cotton gin. In 1917, Hooper gave one acre for a burial ground.
Although population decline caused the Halfway school to consolidate with Plainview in 1952, the community is still prospering. Located here is the High Plains Research Foundation to aid farmers in the surrounding 19-county area. (1979)

PLAINVIEW (Hale Co.) *US 87, 4 mi. N*
Liberty Community and Finney Switch
In 1887, Joseph B. Leach and his brothers, John and Dee, immigrated to this area from Liberty, Kentucky. Joseph filed on a 160-acre homestead and built a half dugout and sod house and a windmill. The Leach brothers often hauled freight for Plainview merchants.
More families arrived in this five-mile square area. By 1892, there were enough children for a schoolhouse to be erected. Methodist and Baptist services and community activities were held in the building. The settlement was called "Liberty" for Joseph Leach's Kentucky home.

William R. Finney and his family settled nearby in the early 1900s. When the Santa Fe Railroad from Amarillo to Plainview located a switch in 1906 on Finney's land, the site became "Finney Switch."

Soon irrigation wells improved agriculture and dairy farming began. Liberty schoolhouse was moved in 1912 and in 1920 a four-room brick building was erected south of Finney. About 1925 the first business, a store, opened. The Baptist and Methodist congregations built sanctuaries by 1940. With the consolidation of the Liberty and Plainview schools in 1948 and changes in farming, the population decreased. (1979)

PLEASANTON (Atascosa Co.)
Main Street and Goodwin

Pleasanton
(Founded 1858)

Named for early Texas settler John Pleasants, by John Bowen (d. 1867), San Antonio's first Anglo-American postmaster. Bowen, assisted financially by associate Henry L. Radaz, in Sept. 1858 founded this town at the juncture of Atascosa River and Bonita Creek as the county seat of Atascosa County. The first courthouse in Pleasanton (second in county) stood on this site. Men from this and surrounding counties met here in Civil War (1862) to form Co. E, 32nd Texas Volunteer Cavalry, Confederate Army, under Captain Lewis Maverick. In an area thick with longhorns since Spanish and Indian days, Pleasanton became a cattlemen's capital. Beginning in 1860s, the Stock Raisers' Association of Western Texas often convened here. This was place of publication of "Western Stock Journal," founded 1873. Here gathered the hardiest and most skillful cowboys, including those driving herds from Mexican border to shipping points in Kansas. In spring of 1873 they drove 43,000 Atascosa County cattle up the trail. Pleasanton was county seat until 1911, and still grows. In 1961 it absorbed North Pleasanton (founded 1912 as site for San Antonio, Uvalde and Gulf Railroad shops). County's largest town, it is famous for live oak trees, and commerce in beef, peanuts, and petroleum. (1973)

PLEASANTON (Atascosa Co.)
SH 97, 4 mi. E, then 2.3 mi. N on IH 37 right-of-way

Site of
San Augustine Church

Between 1850 and 1860, Manuel, Enrique, and Francisco Esparza brought their families to settle in what is now Atascosa County. The brothers, along with their sister and mother, were within the walls of the Alamo when it fell to the Mexicans in March 1836. Their father, Gregorio, died in that battle.

The Esparza brothers farmed and ranched the open land near this site. Almost immediately after arriving, Enrique and Manuel constructed a small chapel for family worship. In 1869, Enrique and his wife, Gertrudes, donated five acres of their land to the Roman Catholic Church. About the same time, the Esparzas constructed a larger church building of native stone. The small mission church was named San Augustine.

A storm damaged the church building in 1940 and services were discontinued, although San Augustine was not formally closed until 1942. By the late 1960s, only three exterior rock walls remained, and these were later razed.

Many settlements in Texas sprang from the activities of mission churches such as San Augustine that were located at river crossings or ranch headquarters. Although many have disappeared or have been forgotten, they are an important part of the state's heritage.

(Texas Sesquicentennial 1836–1986)

POINT BLANK (San Jacinto Co.)
SH 156 at US 90

Governor George Tyler Wood
(1795–1858)

Born in Georgia and married there in 1837 to Martha Evans Gindrat (1809–1863), a widow with 3 children, George T. Wood came to Texas with his family in 1839 and settled along the Trinity River near Point Blank. Wood studied law and was elected to the 6th Republic of Texas Congress, 1841–1842, and the Annexation Convention of 1845. As a state senator in 1846, he sponsored a bill creating Tyler County. Woodville, the county seat, was named for him, as was Wood County, created in 1850.

Wood left the senate in 1846 to fight in the Mexican War (1846–1848). His military heroics helped make him the popular choice for governor in 1847. Under Gov. Wood, the recently-organized state government faced the problems of recurring Indian hostilities and a boundary dispute in Santa Fe County (now part of New Mexico). Gov. Wood urged sale of public lands to pay the large public debt. His administration saw the establishment of a state library and a penitentiary.

Mrs. Wood, who raised silkworms and made her own silk cloth, did not accompany her husband to the state capital at Austin, then a rough frontier town without an official governor's residence. After failing to win a second term in 1849, Gov. Wood returned to his home at Point Blank. He died at age 63 and was buried nearby. (1976)

POINT BLANK (San Jacinto Co.) *US 190, 4 mi. E*
Isaac Jones (October 4, 1793–May 27, 1878)
Individualistic pioneer of Texas. Born in Mississippi; moved here 1834, receiving Mexican land grant on west bank of Trinity River. Served 3 years in Army of Texas Republic 1836–1838. Operated ferry at Jones Bluff 1858–1861. Wife: Elizabeth (Martin). (1970)

POINT BLANK (San Jacinto Co.) *SH 156, .75 mi. S*
The Robert Tod Robinson House
Adjacent to property of Governor George T. Wood, and on high ground near juncture of waterways and land trails important in early Texas, this was originally a log house with wide front verandas on the two floors. It was built in 1857 by Point Blank planter Robert Tod Robinson (1826-1878), copying style from his native state of Alabama. He brought up a large family; his descendants include soldiers, statemen, and civic leaders. The log house was covered with siding in 1919, and facade was modified in 1970s. A descendant owns and preserves it. (1975)

POINT BLANK (San Jacinto Co.) *SH 156, S, then 3 mi. SE*
Mount Zion Cemetery
John R. Johnson, whose 1849 land grant included this property, gave 4.25 acres in 1850 to Mount Zion Methodist Church. Churchyard burials may have begun earlier, but oldest gravestone is dated 1870. The church building was dismantled in 1928 after it fell into ruin. In 1958, descendants of Harrells' Settlement, Mount Zion, and Stephens Creek pioneers began a yearly homecoming here at the sole public landmark of their ancestors, the cemetery. As of 1976, there are about 250 graves—most of them identified and a number marked through efforts of a special committee. (1976)

POINT COMFORT (Calhoun Co.) *SH 35, 6 mi. NE of Port Lavaca*
Site of Cox's Point
An early landing place of supplies for the interior. Captain Jack Shackelford's "Red Rovers" of Alabama disembarked at this point.

A town established here in 1836 was burned by Indians in 1840. (1964)

POLLOK (Angelina Co.) *Paul Townsend Rd. (CR 4A) at SH 7*
Pollok Baptist Church
Founded as Warren Chapel Baptist Church in 1891, this congregation became known as Pollok Baptist Church in 1896. The first meeting place was shared by the Methodist and Presbyterian churches. Land acquired in 1906 by the Baptists was the site of the first church building. Early baptisms were performed in the Angelina River. Services were held once or twice monthly until 1945 when the first full time pastor was called. Fire destroyed three church buildings in 1932, 1955, and 1960; the congregation rebuilt each time, and continues to serve the area. (1996)

POLLOK (Angelina Co.) *7622 US 69N, 3.8 mi. SW on US 69*
Central Consolidated School
This school traces its origin to five small schools in the Pollok-Central area: Union, Durant, Pollok, Clawson and Allentown. An effort to solve the problem of inadequate funding for each of these rural schools led to their consolidation in 1929 as the Central Consolidated Common School District. A new brick building at this site greeted approximately 200 students in grades

one through eleven when it opened in September 1929. With J. W. Dunn presiding as superintendent, Central Consolidated boasted nine teachers and had eight students in its first graduating class. Over the years, Central Consolidated became the focal point of the community. Its growth led to the construction of separate buildings for primary, elementary, junior high and high school classes, three gymnasiums, a cafetorium, and technology and agricultural buildings. Additional schools, including Cordaway Springs and Simpson, merged with Central Consolidated in 1939–40. In 1955, Central converted from a common school district to an independent school district. Providing a strong educational foundation and extracurricular activities for students in the northwestern part of Angelina County, Central Consolidated has played a significant role in the county's educational history. (2002)

PONTA (Cherokee Co.) *CR 4401, 1 block NE of SH 204*
Ponta
In 1901, a new townsite was laid out on the Texas & New Orleans Railroad. Promoted by brothers Lee D. and William T. Guinn, it was named Hubb for county surveyor Hubbard S. Guinn. It was renamed Ponta (an adaptation of the Latin "Ponte" which means bridge) when the post office was established in 1903. Ponta was a shipping center for such local products as lumber, cotton, tomatoes and peaches. In time, the town boasted such businesses as general stores, restaurants, banks, blacksmiths, cotton gins and sawmills, as well as a hotel, a Masonic lodge, churches and schools. Large scale greenhouse cultivation began in the area in the 1950s. The railroad ceased operation after World War II and the post office closed in 1972. Ponta plant nurseries remain a major factor in the Cherokee County economy. (1999)

PONTOTOC (Mason Co.) *SH 71*
Pontotoc and San Fernando Academy
(Site of academy is 100 yd. N)
Pontotoc, settled about 1859, was named by first merchant, M. R. Kidd, for his former home town in Mississippi. Post office was opened 1878 in B. J. Willis home, with Mrs. Willis post master.
Founded by interested citizens, San Fernando Academy (probably named for nearby creek) opened 1883. Pupils (200 during academy's career) took regular subjects or courses leading toward teacher certificates. Principals were K. T. Hamilton and W. C. Roaten. After academy failed site was sold by W. J. and B. J. Willis and used by the public school until 1927. (1972)

PORT ARANSAS (Nueces Co.) *SH 361, 4.2 mi. NW*
Aransas Pass, C.S.A.
Aransas Pass, 5 miles to the southeast, a gap between Texas coastal islands, was strategic in the Civil War because it let in friends, kept out foes.
Admitted goods to be hauled on the overland road from the coast to San Antonio. A haven to blockade runners, who came to Corpus Christi, Copano or Aransas Bays with ammunition, guns, medicines, steel, rope, crockery, cloth, trenching tools, shoes, bar iron or other goods. They took out 50 to 250 bales of cotton a trip. Holds and decks were so full that men had to walk on cotton to work the sails.
Behind the island chain which Aransas Pass helped to guard, mail and goods traveled along a 300-mile inlet from Bagdad and Matamoros in neutral Mexico up to Matagorda. The islands, inlet and passes were fortified by Confederate infantry, cavalry and marines manning dredge-boats, rafts or prize ships.
Confederates won victories at Aransas Pass on Feb. 22 and April 22, 1862. With 1,900 Federal troops, Gen. N. P. Banks took the 100-man Aransas garrison on Nov. 17, 1863, but failed to hold the mainland behind the pass. In June 1864, the Federals withdrew.
To the war's end, blockade runners fed vital goods into the Confederacy by way to Aransas Pass.

PORT ARTHUR (Jefferson Co.) *SH 73, 15 mi. SW*
Sabine Pass
Richard Dowling
In memory of Lt. Richard W. Dowling and his men.
Texas remembers the faithfulness and valor of her sons and commends their heroic example to future generations.

Thus it will be seen that we captured with forty-seven men two gunboats mounting thirteen guns of the heaviest caliber and about three hundred and fifty prisoners. All my men behaved like heroes, not a man flinched from his post. Our motto was victory or death. Official report of Lt. Richard W. Dowling.

At this site on Sept. 8th, 1863 Dick Dowling and forty-seven men comprising Company F Texas Heavy Artillery, Jefferson Davis Guards C.S.A., from a mud fort repulsed an attack made by four warships and twelve hundred men of the Federal Army, thus saving Texas from invasion by the enemy.

There is no parallel in ancient or modern warfare to the victory of Dowling and his men at Sabine Pass, considering the great odds against which they had to contend. Jefferson Davis.

PORT ARTHUR (Jefferson Co.)
SH 87 at Neches River
Rainbow Bridge
The rapid growth of the petrochemical industry in Jefferson and Orange Counties in the early 20th century led to increased population in this area. In order to serve escalating transportation needs, plans began in the 1920s for the construction of a bridge to span the Neches River.

Due to the depressed economy and differences of opinion among business leaders, the campaign to build the bridge (led by the Port Arthur *News* and American Legion Post No. 7) lasted for seven years. In 1934, Gov. Miriam A. Ferguson signed a special law to enable county bond and federal public works administration funds to pay for state highway and bridge construction.

The project engineer, G. G. Wickline, used innovative techniques to design a bridge that would cross 7,742 feet of marshy terrain and river bottom. The bridge's 680-foot central span, designed to clear a navy ship carrying a moored dirigible, was, at 176 feet, the world's highest elevated roadbed over tidal waters.

The final cost of the bridge was $2,750,000. Its dedication on September 8, 1938, drew huge crowds and was a major local event. In a 1957 contest sponsored by the North Port Arthur Lions Club, it was named "Rainbow Bridge." (1990)

PORT ARTHUR (Jefferson Co.)
SH 87 about ¼ mile south of Taylor's Bayou Bridge
Early Oil Tanker Service
Part of the huge transportation complex that moves petroleum to world markets. Traffic in oil tankers and barges in Texas mushroomed two months after the state's first oil gusher, "Spindletop," roared in. On March 11, 1901, the first boat to transport the Spindletop product, the *Atlas*, left Sabine Pass with about 3,000 barrels of crude oil.

Port Arthur exported one of the earliest large shipments of oil about April or May, 1901, on the *Atlas* and two other vessels. The cargo was bound for the refineries of Standard Oil Company of Philadelphia to be tested for "illuminating" purposes. Many persons then scoffed at the idea of using oil as a fuel.

One year after Spindletop, Texas commerce, formerly based on cattle and cotton, had been vastly changed by petroleum. More than half of all ships entering Sabine Pass and Port Arthur were connected with the oil industry. By April of 1902, shipments had already exceeded the 1,750,000 barrels exported in 1901.

By 1902, steamers were burning Texas oil as fuel and the Guffey Petroleum Company had begun to build Texas' first tanker fleet—five ships.

Today the value to Texas' economy of crude oil alone totals more than three billion dollars yearly. (1968)

PORT ARTHUR (Jefferson Co.)
SH 87, 0.2 mi. SW of Avenue I
The Port Arthur Refinery
The eruption of the Lucas Gusher at the Spindletop Oil Field in January 1901 established Texas as a major oil source and signaled the beginning of a significant economic boom to the state. The new town of Port Arthur benefited tremendously from its proximity to the oil field. In early 1901, a consortium of men from Pittsburgh, Pennsylvania, formed the J. M. Guffey Petroleum Company to finance and develop an industry for the oil from its Spindletop leases. In need of refining facilities and a sales organization, the consortium chartered the Gulf Refining Company on November 10, 1901, and built a refinery at Port Arthur for the purpose of making the crude

oil into a usable commodity. Early products of the refining company included gasoline, kerosene and engine oil. In 1907, assets of the J. M. Guffey Petroleum and Gulf Refining companies were merged into the Gulf Oil Corporation. At the end of 1910, Port Arthur was the company's lone refinery until a second was built in Fort Worth the following year. Innovative production, refining and retailing techniques after World War I kept the company on solid economic footing. Expansion continued after World War II, and by 1955, Gulf Oil was the nation's largest producer of ethylene. By 1960, the Port Arthur facility was refining 270,000 barrels of crude oil per day into 600 different products. Gulf Oil became part of Chevron in 1984. In 1995, Clark Refining took ownership of the Port Arthur plant, and in 2000, Clark's name was changed to Premcor. Upholding an excellent safety record, the Port Arthur refinery has been a significant factor in the city's development as a major petrochemical center. (2001)

PORT ARTHUR (Jefferson Co.)

Between bank, Sabine River at the Sabine Pass and 1st Avenue

Spanish-American War Fortifications

As tension mounted between the United States and Spain during the late 1890s, U.S. Representative Samuel Bronson Cooper of Texas recommended the War Department begin plans for the defense of the strategic Sabine Pass area. Maj. James B. Quinn of the Army Corps of Engineers in New Orleans was authorized to direct construction of two forts on land granted by Augustus F. Kountze. Work on the batteries was underway by May 1898, one month after the formal war declaration. Military efforts were coordinated with area residents by government engineer J. L. Brownlee.

Although the emplacements were soon completed, the shore guns were never part of military action here. The Spanish-American War ended December 10, 1898, with the signing of the Treaty of Paris.

Later efforts were made to locate permanently a military installation at the site following the war. The plans were dropped, however, by 1901. In 1913, fifteen years after the war, the fortifications were the site of a tragic accident, in which a Sabine boy was killed when an abandoned ammunition cache exploded. Evidence of the fortifications has been severely damaged by hurricanes, but the site remains a symbol of an important era in U.S. history. (1983)

PORT ARTHUR (Jefferson Co.)

2232 Seventh St.

Birthplace of
Babe Didrikson Zaharias
(June 26, 1911–September 27, 1956)

One of seven children, Mildred Ella "Babe" Didrikson was the daughter of Norwegian immigrants Hannah Marie (d. 1945) and Ole Didrikson (d. 1943). For the first several years of her life, the family occupied a frame house at this location. Later they moved to Beaumont. The Didriksons encouraged their children to develop their natural athletic abilities. Called "Baby" by her family, Mildred was later nicknamed "Babe" for baseball star Babe Ruth.

Babe first demonstrated her athletic skill as a high school basketball star. After training in track and field events, she won two gold medals at the 1932 Olympic Games in Los Angeles. An exceptionally versatile athlete, Babe excelled in baseball, bowling, tennis, and other sports. Eventually, she concentrated her efforts on golf and won many tournaments as both an amateur and a professional. The Associated Press named her the "woman athlete of the first half of the 20th century."

In 1938, Babe married George Zaharias. Popular with sports fans for her skill and personality, she won further admiration during a long and courageous battle against cancer. She died in Galveston and was buried in Beaumont. (1979)

PORT BOLIVAR (Galveston Co.)

At Old Lighthouse

Point Bolivar

Headquarters for Long's Expedition which attempted to free Texas from Spanish rule in 1819. Named in honor of Simon Bolivar (1783–1830), leader in the Spanish-American War for Independence. Here Mrs. Long and a small group remained until news of her husband's death came in 1822. A lighthouse was erected by the Republic of Texas.

PORT BOLIVAR (Galveston Co.)

US 87

Old Fort Travis

A strategic location in the military history of Texas, this site has been fortified by Mexican rebels, the Confederacy, and the United States Government.

In 1816–1817, while Mexico was attempting to win freedom from Spain, this location was a bivouac for rebel irregulars. Here they drilled while planning a campaign into Mexico and awaiting reinforcements.

Victory was closer four years later when the adventurous Dr. James Long built a mud fort here as headquarters for his efforts to liberate Texas. His young wife Jane fought her own battle at the fort—against the elements and hostile Indians—as she vainly awaited her husband's return. She was later to gain renown as "The Mother of Texas."

During the Civil War (1861–1865) the Confederate Army here built an outpost called Fort Green. With the beginning of Federal coastal defense in 1898, Fort Travis was established at this site. Named for Texas revolutionary hero, William B. Travis, it is supported by a specially built, 17-foot seawall. Fortifications include raised gun mounds and earthworks. For years the Galveston ferry made connections with Highway 87 here. Occupied by U.S. troops in both World Wars, the fort was named a civil defense shelter in 1960. (1970)

PORT ISABEL (Cameron Co.)

N. Tarnava St. and P 100

Old Point Isabel Lighthouse

The beacon for the commerce of the Rio Grande.
Erected by the United States government in 1852.
Extinguished during Civil War. Discontinued, 1888–1895. Permanently discontinued, 1905.

PORT ISABEL (Cameron Co.)

Maxan St. and Yturria St.

Point Isabel, C.S.A.

After Texas seceded and joined the Confederacy, the Federal navy in later 1861 blockaded this port with the U.S. *Santiago de Cuba*. Commerce stoppage caused removal of customs offices to Brownsville and some civilians to neutral Bagdad, Mexico. The Confederates ceased to use the lighthouse, and it became a watchtower for blockade runners, and thus Laguna Madre their haven. Boats from the U.S.S. *Brooklyn*, in May 1863, attacked vessels in port and a Confederate unit near the lighthouse. The Confederates tried to blow up the tower—a defense measure—but only succeeded in damaging fixtures.

The French, supporting Maximilian in Mexico, prohibited the landing of war material at Bagdad. Defying both the French and U.S. naval patrols, Mexican lighters from the Rio Grande landed here in Sept., 1863 with a large cargo of C.S.A. arms.

In Nov. 1863, U.S. forces from the expedition of Gen. N. P. Banks occupied Point Isabel. The blockade was lifted and the port reactivated. In Aug., 1864, the Confederates drove the Federals across the bay to Brazos Island. The next March, Federal Gen. Lew Wallace (later author of *Ben Hur*) met Confederate officers here to talk peace. (1964)

PORT ISABEL (Cameron Co.)

S. García St. and P 100

Port Isabel
(Old "Point" Isabel)

An historic haven for gulf shipping. Visited 1520 and named for Queen Isabella (1451–1504) of Spain by map-maker Alonso Alvarez de Pineda. In early eras, when cargo was loaded and unloaded by small boats, ocean vessels would anchor beyond Brazos Santiago Pass and have goods ferried across shallow Laguna Madre to this place, a site of civilized habitation ever since a village was established here in 1786. From here, freight went to the Rio Grande and from there to places far inland in northern Mexico.

Point Isabel, however, had a grave access problem: adjacent lowlands hampered the oxcarts that moved freight to and from the port. Charters were issued for railways in 1850 and 1853, but the roads were never built, although by 1859 some $4,000,000 worth of imports and exports passed this way annually.

In 1866, Mifflin Kenedy, Capt. Richard King of the King Ranch, and other powerful businessmen got a charter but built no road. Finally in 1871 the Rio Grande Railroad Company built and put into use 22 miles of track, from Brownsville to a terminus here (200 ft. N of this site). Although often damaged by storms, this railroad served until 1933, when shipping was diverted to the new deepwater port in Brownsville. (1970)

PORT ISABEL (Cameron Co.) *Park Rd. 100, 3 mi. E at approach to causeway*
Padre J. Nicolas Balli
Padre Island, off the South Texas Coast, is named for Padre Jose Nicolas Balli (177?–1829), whose family migrated from Spain in 1569 and became large landowners in the Lower Rio Grande Valley. In 1800, Balli applied to King Charles IV of Spain for 11½ leagues of land on the island, and in 1804 started its first settlement, Rancho Santa Cruz. Padre Balli served as collector of finances for all the churches in the Rio Grande Valley and founded the first mission in present Cameron County. Padre Balli's ministry was a great influence on the lives of early South Texas settlers. (1983)

PORT LAVACA (Calhoun Co.) *SH 35 between SH 238 & Half Moon Dr., at Bauer Community Center*
Port Lavaca
Founded in the aftermath of a Comanche raid on the nearby settlement of Linnville, the town of Lavaca ("the cow") was established in 1840. The busiest port in the Matagorda Bay area and a major center for overland export of cattle and other goods, Lavaca was an able successor to Linnville.

Lavaca was the first Calhoun County seat from 1846 to 1852, when Indianola assumed the role. The county seat was returned to Lavaca briefly during the Civil War, when the town withstood fire from federal gunboats, then returned to Indianola. In 1886, Indianola was ravaged by a hurricane and Lavaca was again county seat.

With railroad expansion in Texas, Lavaca moved away from cattle and turned to seafood. Called Port Lavaca from the late 1880s, the village boomed. Tourism and the population increased; several factories were opened; the town became a general law city in 1909. The Gulf Intracoastal Waterway was connected to Port Lavaca in 1913 and a seawall was completed in 1920. Shrimp and frozen seafood became major items for export. Natural gas and oil were discovered in 1934 and 1935. From the late 1940s major manufacturing began to contribute to Port Lavaca's growth. Port Lavaca became a home rule chartered city in 1956, and a deep water port was located here in 1965. Port Lavaca celebrated 150 years of rich history in 1990. (1998)

PORT LAVACA (Calhoun Co.) *SH 316, 14 mi. SE*
Rene Robert Cavelier
Sieur de la Salle
Born in Rouen, France, November 22, 1643. Came to Canada in 1666. Founded a first settlement near Montreal, led several expeditions on the Great Lakes and the Ohio and Illinois Rivers. Completed the exploration of the Mississippi 1682. On July 24, 1684 La Salle sailed from France to establish a colony at the mouth of the Mississippi. Landed at Matagorda Bay February 15, 1685. There established Fort St. Louis. While on his way to Canada he was murdered near the Trinity River, March 19, 1687.

A gentleman but not a courtier. A proud independent yet timid nature. An explorer of bold vision and untiring energy.

La Salle's colony on Matagorda Bay gave the United States its first claim to Texas as a part of the Louisiana Purchase.

"America owes him an enduring memory, for, in this masculine figure, she sees the pioneer who guided her to the possession of her richest heritage." Francis Parkman. (1964)

PORT LAVACA (Calhoun Co.) *SH 316, 14 mi. SE via SH 328*
Mrs. Angelina Bell Peyton Eberly
(About 1800–March 15, 1860)
A Tennessean, Angelina Peyton came to Texas in 1822. With her husband, J. C. Peyton, she operated an inn in San Felipe, capital of the Austin Colony. Peyton died in 1834; in 1836 the widow married Jacob Eberly. She and Eberly had a hotel in Austin by 1842, when Angelina

Eberly discovered men secretly removing records from the capital. Firing a cannon, she started the "Archives War," and rescued the original records of the Republic of Texas. Later she lived at Indianola. Her burial place and marker (¾ mi. NW) were destroyed in a flood in 1875. (1978)

PORT LAVACA (Calhoun Co.) — *SH 35, Bay Front Park*
Half Moon Reef Lighthouse
Constructed in 1858, this three-story hexagonal lighthouse was originally located in Matagorda Bay, at the southern tip of Half Moon Reef. The beacon served as an aid to ships trading in Port Lavaca and the nearby town of Indianola (14 mi. SE). During the Civil War the light was disabled by Confederate troops in an attempt to disrupt Federal efforts to capture Southern blockade runners. The lighthouse was restored to full operation in 1868 and remained in service until 1943 when it was moved to Point Comfort (7 mi. NE). It was relocated here in 1979. (1980)

PORT LAVACA (Calhoun Co.) — *200 block of Commerce St. (SH 238)*
Civil War Bombardment of Port Lavaca
As part of the U.S. Naval initiative to control Texas Confederate ports, the gunboats *Clifton* and *Westfield* turned to the town then known as Lavaca after easily taking Galveston and Indianola. On October 31, 1862, under a flag of truce, Commander Willliam B. Renshaw demanded the surrender of Lavaca. Maj. Gen. Daniel D. Shea refused. After an evacuation period of merely 90 minutes, Renshaw's ships attacked the town. The city garrison returned the fire. Partially disabled, the Union boats fell back, but rained a steady barrage upon the town until night came. They resumed shelling the following morning, then retreated. The city streets were ravaged by gunfire, but Port Lavaca remained in Confederate hands until December 1863. (1998)

PORT LAVACA (Calhoun Co.) — *300 block Commerce St. (SH 238)*
Alsatian Immigration through Lavaca Bay
Texas land empresario Henri Castro contracted to bring colonists of various European nationalities to Texas beginning in 1842. The first of these were Alsatians, most of whom spoke German and held German sympathies. They arrived at Galveston, their official port of entry, with 114 passengers from France in early 1843; most then sailed for Lavaca (later Port Lavaca). They waited here before beginning their overland journey to what became Medina County, to establish the town of Castroville. Another, largely Alsatian, group of 129 arrived at Galveston January 1, 1844. About 40 continued to Lavaca, landing on the 10th. Conditions were difficult, and many immigrants succumbed to various coastal fevers. Other ships followed in 1845 and 1846. Castro's contract expired in 1847, after he had transported more than 2,000 colonists to Texas, most through Lavaca Bay. (1999)

PORT LAVACA (Calhoun Co.) — *200 S. Ann St. on courthouse grounds*
Calhoun County Hurricanes
Severe storms with high winds, heavy rains and tidal surges, hurricanes have played a significant role in events that shaped Calhoun County's history. Entire towns, including Indianola (a key Gulf seaport and Calhoun County seat) and Saluria (Republic-era port on Matagorda Island) were destroyed by 19th-century storms. Over the centuries, residents have dealt with wind and water damage to property, and lives have been lost during hurricanes. Stories of survival and rebuilding in the aftermath of these torrential storms also figure prominently in Calhoun County history. (2001)

PORT LAVACA (Calhoun Co.) — *US 87, 6 mi. NW*
Moses Johnson, M.D.
(1808–1853)
Born in Virginia, Dr. Moses Johnson settled in Port Lavaca about 1837. After moving to Austin in 1840 to practice medicine, he was elected city alderman and then mayor. An active Mason, he served as Grand Marshal of the Grand Lodge of Texas, A. F. & A. M. in 1844. When Anson Jones was elected president of the Republic in 1844, he named his friend Johnson treasurer. In 1845 Johnson's Austin home and the treasury records were destroyed by fire. He moved his family back to Port Lavaca the next year. He died in a yellow fever epidemic there on Oct. 2, 1853 and is buried ¼ mile west of this site. (1975)

PORT LAVACA (Calhoun Co.) *SH 35 right-of-way, 12 mi. SW*
Green Lake
Named for the nearby tidal lake of the same name, the community of Green Lake began to develop in the late 1840s, although records indicate there were some settlers in the area before that time. A group of wealthy planters from Kentucky migrated to the area about 1849, along with their families and many slaves. They established extensive cotton plantations and built large and impressive homes.

Early in its history, in 1851, a tornado struck the settlement, but miraculously caused little property damage and no injuries. A private school was established in 1852 and served children of the Green Lake and surrounding communities.

The outbreak of the Civil War caused many changes in Green Lake. Following the U.S. surrender by General David Twiggs in 1861, Federal troops camped near here awaiting transport ships. With its agricultural economy based largely upon slave labor, Green Lake declined following the war when landowners, facing a labor shortage, began to leave the area. By 1875 most of the original settlers were gone.

Although in existence a relatively short period of time, Green Lake contributed to the history of Calhoun County. (1988)

PORT MANSFIELD (Willacy Co.) *On the waterfront*
Port Mansfield
Dedicated April 23, 1949 by Hon. Beauford H. Jester, Governor of Texas. Named in honor Hon. Joseph J. Mansfield of Columbus, Texas, "Father of Inland Waterways." Willacy County Navigation District. F. E. Macmanus, R. F. Allen, Gustin Garrett.

PORT NECHES (Jefferson Co.) *Grigsby Dr., across from City Park*
Grigsby's Bluff
(1834–1902)
Joseph Grigsby (1771–1841) and family migrated from Kentucky to the Sabine area in 1827. He is said to have been the first grower of cotton in East Texas. In 1834 he received a grant of 17 labors (3,009 acres) of land on the Neches. Here he built a wharf for sidewheel steamers and founded town of Grigsby's Bluff. He served in 2nd, 3rd and 5th Congresses of the Republic of Texas. His settlement became Port Neches, and his family has given many leaders to Texas.

A huge pecan tree (at Texaco Refinery, 6 blocks SE) marks site of Grigsby's Bluff. (1969)

PORTLAND (San Patricio Co.) *US 181 access road (Old Hwy. 35),*
at N end of bridge (E side of hwy.)
Site of Indian Point Mass Grave of 1919 Hurricane Victims
In the early morning hours of Sunday, September 14, 1919, a hurricane made landfall in Corpus Christi after gathering strength in the Gulf of Mexico for two weeks. Crowds packed the North Beach area for their last weekend of the summer season, most continuing to ignore the last-minute evacuation warnings of police officers, firefighters and soldiers from Fort Brown. The rapidly rising water blocked vacationers from escaping to higher ground. As the water rose, people climbed to their rooftops and tied ropes to themselves and their children so that they might not be lost. A giant wave of water carrying oil from ruptured tanks on Harbor Island, timber from Port Aransas and cotton bales from a dock in Corpus Christi crashed down on North Beach, sweeping its victims into the black waters of Nueces Bay. On Monday morning the sun rose on a scene of terrible destruction. Though the official death toll was 284, estimates place the actual number, including those lost at sea, at one thousand. In the ensuing days, the survivors worked together to rebuild their homes, rescue the injured and bury the dead in mass graves, some containing more than fifty bodies, using farm implements as undertaking tools. A month later the bodies were removed to Rose Hill Cemetery in Corpus Christi and other sites as requested by friends and family members. Property damage and crop losses were estimated at twenty million dollars. The great storm of 1919 was the worst disaster to hit Corpus Christi in the twentieth century. The mass graves at Indian Point were about one hundred yards east of this site. (2000)

POST (Garza Co.)

US 84, 3 mi. NW

C. W. Post Rain Battles

Site of 1911–1914 dynamiting to produce rain, carried on by C. W. Post, Texas farm colonizer and cereal foods millionaire.

After reading that rain often accompanies cannonading in war, Post planned "battles" to relieve
drouths. He thought vertical air currents would condense vapor in atmosphere and cause rain. He
first used dynamite airborne by kites, but soon replaced this dangerous method by setting off
explosions on edge of caprock.

Post's experiments were said to have been 40% effective, and cost $5,000. He battled drouth
of farms until his death, 1914.

(1967)

POST (Garza Co.)

US 380 W

Dry-Land Farming

This low rainfall area, limited usually to grazing, was colonized in 1907 by C. W. Post, creator
of Post Foods, and a philanthropist. By introducing new agricultural techniques, he was able to
make farming profitable for colonists.

Cotton, milo maize, Indian corn, and oats were grown here. Post also experimented with several types of fruits and vegetables.

Men of small means could buy farms on easy terms from Post. He provided good houses,
fences, windmills, and electricity.

Also built Post textile mill to provide supplemental work and income for the colonists.

(1967)

POST (Garza Co.)

SH 207, 11 mi. N

Duffy's Peak
(3 mi. E)

Height so prominent it was Garza County's earliest bench mark, designated by peg-legged surveyor Jasper Hays, who in 1877–1878 was marking bounds of Llano Ranch, first property to be
occupied by settlers in county. Hays began at a corner established for the Houston & Great
Northern Railroad Company near the White River in Crosby County, and shot west toward this
peak. Tradition has it that a member of Hays' crew died and was buried near this peak which was
afterward named for him. Local heights named for natural wonders include "The Ice Cream
Cones," "Cow Head Mesa," "Indian Head Point" and "The Chimneys." Other interesting uplands
are "Two Bush Hill," "The Devil's Breakfast Table," "Needlepoint Peak" and "Buffalo Point."
Two balanced rocks known to early settlers have now disappeared because of wind and weather
erosion.

Duffy's Peak, like most of the scenic formations, is of sandstone, clay and sand. It still figures
in local land transactions, as Hays' original notes (unearthed from mason jars he buried on the
peak) formed basis for later surveys—including those of A. L. Marhoff in 1906, establishing
boundaries for the farm colony of "Cereal King" C. W. Post.

(1969)

POST (Garza Co.)

*US 84 in roadside park at Highway Department
and at courthouse grounds*

Garza County

Created in 1876. Attached to Borden County 1891–1907. Organization came July 8, 1907 at
the OS Ranch. According to legend, even the horses "voted" to gain the required 75 ballots. First
court was held under a tent; first courthouse built in 1908.

It is to the memory of these pioneer men who became the first county officials that this marker is dedicated in sincere appreciation for the part they played in the organization and development of Garza County: J. M. Boren, county judge; O. B. Kelly, sheriff; H. B. Murray, clerk; B.
F. Wilks, treasurer; D. W. Stiles, tax assessor; M. L. Harkey, county attorney; A. L. Duren, justice of the peace; Marion McGinty, constable; H. C. Callis, hide and animal inspector;
Commissioners: Sam C. Wilks, Jobe Davies, J. L. Barrow, W. V. Roy.

(1965)

POST (Garza Co.)   *US 84, 8 mi. SE*
O S Ranch
Founded on open range, 1878, brand was owned in 1881 by R. H. Overall.
Acquired 1901 by W. E. Connell, who had about 200 sections of land.
Ranch house a community center—for barbecues, roundups, parties. In 1907 it was site of election organizing Garza County.   (1966)

POST (Garza Co.)   *US 380 at FM 669*
Old Post High School
Built 1928, incorporating in lower walls native Garza County stones from the town's first (1909) school, erected soon after the founding of City of Post.

This historic preservation occurred under leadership of Supt. John E. Watson, outstanding educator, veteran of World War I service in the heroic Rainbow Division. The Parent-Teachers' Association backed Watson's stand, and bond issue passed in spite of adverse circumstances.

When later growth called for a larger educational complex to meet community needs, this became Post Junior High School.   (1968)

POST (Garza Co.)   *US 84, entrance to city-county park*
Post
Founded 1907 by industrialist C. W. Post.

Early abundant water supply by windmills above Caprock. Later from White River Lake. Extensive ranching and farming. Postex Cotton Mills, making sheets and pillowcases, furnish year-round employment. Service center for over 1,750 oil wells in county.   (1967)

POST (Garza Co.)   *US 380, .5 mi. E*
Terrace Cemetery Gateway
From Double "U," "Lazy S," Connell and Curry Comb Ranch canyons, round rocks were collected and made into gate piers in 1908 when cereal king C. W. Post founded Post City.

George Samson designed and with fellow Scotsman James Napier built the gateway. Samson was a community leader 50 years.   (1963)

POST (Garza Co.)   *US 84, 6.5 mi. SE, then a county road*
5.5 mi. from Post City; in grove
near OS Ranch headquarters
The Famous Post Picnic of 1906
After this area was freed of Indians, Garza County was created and named in 1876 for a patriotic family of early Texas. With its ranching population rising from 36 in 1880 to only 180 by 1900, Garza remained attached for judicial purposes to Borden County.

In 1906 Charles William Post (1854–1914), "The Cereal King" from Battle Creek, Mich., sought Texas land for development. In the month of March, he and his wife and daughter visited here at the OS Ranch, where a barbecue picnic was given in their honor. In the gathering, Post made a speech suggesting the county be organized for self-government, as he proposed to establish a model farm colony and a modern town.

Cowboys from a wide areas were at the OS that day working in spring roundup. Immediately they called an informal election in the bunkhouse. A boy who had won all the money gaming the previous evening now gave a dollar to each voter, to be placed in a fund to defray expenses of a future, legal election. It is said that even the horses voted in favor of the Post proposal. After a petition was filed on May 13, 1907, the election was held and the county organized on June 15, 1907. By that time Post City was being built as county seat. County and city still prosper.   (1972)

POST (Garza Co.)   *US 84, 3 mi. NW at roadside park*
Twin Chimneys
(100 yds. N)

Used as a landmark in the 19th century by surveyors sighting from Duffy's Peak, located ten miles northeast. Jasper Hays, earliest recorded surveyor of this area, used the peaks during 1877–1878 for charting the Llano Ranch, later bought by C. W. Post, the cereal king. Hays established, in addition, lines from which section surveys were made.

Civil Engineer A. L. Marhoff, using the original field notes and book of Hays, surveyed the land bought by Post, 1906. This included the section on which the town of Post was founded, 1907, as well as other property.   (1970)

POST (Garza Co.)   *US 84, 6 mi. SE in rest area*
Llano Estacado

Stretching across the horizon as a range of flat-topped mountains is the caprock escarpment, eastern boundary of the vast Llano Estacado or "Staked Plains." The Llano, one of the world's most perfect plains regions, is an elongated oval extending from north to south. Some three quarters of it, 20 million acres, are in Texas. The remainder is in eastern New Mexico. Its naturally treeless surface, unbroken except for several canyons, slopes gradually from an altitude of 2,700 feet at its eastern edge to more than 4,000 feet along the New Mexico border.

The caprock escarpment is the result of surface erosion that began in the early Pleistocene Period some 750,000 years ago. Composed of tough caliche, the caprock has protected the softer materials underlying it, thus resisting the erosive factors with varying success. The escarpment begins in Borden County 25 miles south of this point and extends northward, in a sweeping arc 170 miles into the Texas Panhandle. It rises from 300 feet to 1,000 feet above the lower plains at its base, giving the impression of having been thrust upward out of the surrounding land.

First white man to visit the Great Plains was the Spanish Conquistador Francisco de Coronado who crossed them in 1541 on his search for the fabled Seven Cities of Cibola. He was especially impressed by the sea of grass which covered the soil so completely that the tracks of his expedition left no permanent mark. The Spaniards, it is said, staked their route so they would be guided on the return trip—hence the term "Staked" Plains.

Because of the scarcity of surface water, the Llano was generally shunned by buffalo and Indians until the encroachment of settlers in the lower areas drove them onto it. The native grasses supported an immense ranching empire following the extinction of the buffalo. More recently the Llano has become one of the nation's leading cotton, wheat and grain sorghum producing areas.

POTEET (Atascosa Co.)   *4th St. & Ave. I*
Poteet

The town of Poteet traces its history to the 1880s, when Francis Marion Poteet (1833–1907) established a mercantile store northeast of this area. A blacksmith and farmer as well as a merchant, Poteet began providing mail service to his customers.

Poteet sold his business to Henry T. Mumme (1870–1947) before 1900. Mumme continued to offer postal service at the store, and in 1910 he and his wife Ida (1869–1942) donated 400 acres of land for a new townsite. Since the area had been referred to as Poteet as a result of the early mail service, the new town was named in honor of Francis Marion Poteet. Mumme moved his store to the new townsite in 1911.

Mumme drilled the town's first artesian water well and is credited with introducing the cultivation of strawberries here. The artesian water, together with the sandy soil of the region, proved ideal for growing the berries. Known statewide for its superior quality strawberries, Poteet has been nicknamed the "Strawberry Capital of Texas."

The town grew steadily after 1910, with the establishment of schools, churches, homes, and businesses. It was incorporated in 1926.   (1989)

POTH (Wilson Co.)   *US 181, 4 mi. S*
Beauregard Ranch

Founded 1852, by Augustin Toutant-Beauregard, of landed Creole gentry who traced lineage to 16th century Spanish nobility.

Brother was Confederate General Pierre Gustave Toutant-Beauregard.

Stone-mounted iron rings were part of scaffolding used to butcher hogs.   (1967)

POTTSBORO (Grayson Co.)
FM 120, 4 mi. N
Site of Fort Johnson
Established by William G. Cooke in 1840 as a part of the defense of the military road from Red River to Austin. Named in honor of Colonel Francis W. Johnson (1799–1888), commander of the Texas Army at the capture of San Antonio, December 10, 1835. Place of rendezvous for the Snively Expedition which set out April 2, 1843. The settlement in the vicinity was known as Georgetown. (1965)

POTTSBORO (Grayson Co.)
FM 120, 8 mi. N
Site of the
Trading Post
of Holland Coffee
Established about 1837 for trade with the Indians of the Red River region and the western plains. Here many white captives of red men were redeemed. From its vicinity the Snively Expedition set out for New Mexico on April 25, 1843. Abandoned after Coffee's death in 1846. (1965)

POTTSBORO (Grayson Co.)
FM 120, 8 mi. N
Confederate Lady Paul Revere
Sophia Porter (1813–1899) settled 1839 at Glen Eden, site now under Lake Texoma. North of here, husband Holland Coffee, early trader, built a fine home, welcomed (1845–1869) U.S. army officers, including Robert E. Lee and Ulysses S. Grant. During the Civil War, wined and dined passing Federal scouts, found they were seeking Col. Jas. Bourland, Confederate defender of the Texas frontier. While guests were busy, she slipped out, swam her horse across icy Red River, warned Col. Bourland, helped prevent invasion of North Texas.

POTTSBORO (Grayson Co.)
FM 120, 5 mi. NW
Ninth Texas Cavalry, C.S.A.
A distinguished regiment in Ross' Texas Brigade. Organized and mustered into service Oct. 2, 1861, at Brogdon's Springs, near this site. Officers: Col. William B. Sims, Lt. Col. Nathan W. Townes, and Maj. William Quayle.

Cos. A and D were from Tarrant County; Co. B from Fannin County; Co. C, Grayson County; Co. E., Red River County; Cos. F and I, Titus County; Cos. G and K, Hopkins. The Ninth was part of Gen. Van Dorn's Army that almost captured Gen. Grant in Dec. 1863. It was also a unit in the cavalry assault that captured and burned the Federal gunboat *Petrel* in 1864. (1971)

POWELL (Navarro Co.)
SH 31, across street from Powell State Bank
The Powell Oil Field
One of the world's most noted petroleum fields. Discovered 1905; developed in three periods. A number of early shallow wells (800'–1,000' in Nacatoch sand) drilled by Claude Witherspoon, are still producing.

Field's second and greatest era came as a result of three heartbreaking years of drilling. On Sunday, Jan. 7, 1923, the W. H. Warren–R. K. Blackshear "J. H. Burke No. 1" (2,933' in Woodbine sand) blew in a gusher, triggering a feverish drilling boom. As this was prior to spacing and proration regulations, derricks sprouted by the dozens. The site of "J. H. Burke No. 1" is one mile southwest of this marker.

On May 8, 1923, another great gusher, the "J. K. Hughes–W. J. McKie No. 1" (2.25 mi. SW), blackened the area with oil which soon ignited, causing 15 deaths. This 8,000-barrel-a-day gusher defined the main pool.

By fall, the six-square-mile field was outproducing Pennsylvania plus nine other oil states. On Nov. 23, 1923, came the peak day of 354,893 barrels. The population skyrocketed. Corn and cotton patches became townsites for Oil City, Tuckertown, Wildcat. In 1923, Powell ran over 30 million barrels; in 1924, over 40 million. It then declined, with its last million-barrel year in 1931.

Waterflooding ushered in the third yield period in 1964. (1973)

POYNOR (Henderson Co.)   *FM 315, 4 mi. N at Fincastle Cemetery*
Fincastle
One of the earliest settlements in Henderson County, Fincastle developed during the early 1850s. At that time, this part of the state was a center of economic activity with a growing number of plantations and farms.

In 1851, John Tindel (1796–1864) purchased 1,091 acres in the Jan Jose Martinez Survey and later platted the community townsite. He laid out fourteen lots, measuring 60 feet by 70 yards. The community attracted farmers, tradesmen, professional people, and other settlers who came to Texas. Fincastle was the scene of much activity during the Civil War, as Capt. William H. ("Howdy") Martin came in 1861 to raise troops. In addition, a quartermaster and commissary department was established here.

By 1880, Fincastle had several stores, a blacksmith shop, cotton gins, saloons, a combination drugstore and doctor's office, several churches, and a school. Farmers from surrounding areas came here to sell their cotton and produce and to buy supplies for their homes and farms.

About 1900, most of the members of the settlement moved to the county seat of Athens, and Fincastle declined. A church, the pioneer cemetery, and the nearby home of John Tindel are all that remain of this early trade center.   (1984)

PRAIRIE VIEW (Waller Co.)   *FM 1098, off US 290, University campus*
Prairie View A&M University
Authorized by the Texas Legislature in 1876, the "Agricultural and Mechanical College for Colored Youth" was Texas' second state-supported institution of higher learning. As a land grant college, it occupied a 1,434-acre former slave plantation. Organized by the Texas A&M board of Directors, Prairie View has remained a part of the Texas A&M system.

The first eight students enrolled on March 11, 1878, but low enrollment caused the school to close. The following year the "Prairie View Normal Institute" was organized with emphasis on preparing teachers in trade and agricultural subjects. A coeducational college, Prairie View's enrollment of 16 soon reached 60. In ten years, industrial training was added to the curriculum. Inter-collegiate athletics began in 1904. By 1931, the campus boasted 31 main buildings and 50 cottages.

In 1934, the Southern Association of Colleges and Secondary Schools granted a Class "A" rating. In 1947, the institution became "Prairie View Agricultural and Mechanical College." Integrated during the 1960s, the name changed to "Prairie View A&M University" in 1973. The university's motto is "Prairie View produces productive people."   (1982)

PRESIDIO (Presidio Co.)   *FM 170, 4.5 mi. E, Fort Leaton State Historic Site*
El Fortín de San José
(The Little Fort of Saint Joseph)
About 1773, the Spanish garrison at Presidio del Norte, present Ojinaga, Mexico, established El Fortín de San José in this vicinity to protect local farmers. The settlement retained the name after the post was abandoned about 1810. After Ben Leaton had acquired extensive property in the area in 1848, the community came to be called Fort Leaton. Ben Leaton's fortress is all that remains of the old settlement. Fort Leaton is neither the site of the original Presidio del Norte nor the Spanish Mission Apostal Santiago, as stated erroneously by earlier markers at this location.   (1978)

Approximate Site of
Mission San Francisco
de los Julimes
One of nine missions established in the Big Bend country by Father Fray Nicolas Lopez, O. F. M., and Don Juan Dominguez de Mendoza in 1683–1684. Maintained by Franciscan missionaries for the civilizing and Christianizing of the Jumano, Julimes and other Indians of this area.

Presidio del Norte

Approximate site of Presidio del Norte de la Junta, established by Captain Alonzo Rubin de Celis in 1759–1760. Name of the post retained in part by the present town and county. In this vicinity the missions of San Antonio de los Publiques, San Francisco de los Julimes, Santa Maria la Redonda, San Pedro Alcantara, El Apostol Santiago, San Cristobal, were first established in 1683 by Don Juan Dominguez de Mendoza and Padre Fray Nicolas Lopez O. F. M. Maintained by Franciscan missionaries for the Christianizing and civilizing of the Apache Natages, Faraones, Publiques, Julimes, Jumanos, Zumas, and other Indian tribes. Administered and controlled in 1746 by the custodia of New Mexico.

PRESIDIO (Presidio Co.)   *O'Reily St. (US 67) in St. Francis Plaza*
Captain Henry Skillman, C.S.A.

Renowned southwestern mail and stagecoach man. Born in Kentucky. Came to Texas before 1846. Served as a U.S. Army scout in Mexican War.

About 1851 established the first mail service from San Antonio to El Paso. When the first Butterfield Overland Stagecoach in 1858 made bid to establish fast service to the West Coast, was selected to drive perilous Comanche Indian area from Horsehead Crossing on the Pecos to El Paso. Made it in 4 days without rest or relief, his 6-foot frame draped with revolvers and Bowie knives.

A Confederate scout in the Civil War. From July 1862, when Federals seized El Paso and the Davis Mountains (to make the longest enemy occupation in Texas), served as liaison between regular Confederate troops and the C.S.A. patriots who plotted in their refugee colony in Juarez to recapture West Texas. Knowing country well, came and went at will. Spread false rumors of Confederates massing in deserts, to divert Federal troops from combat. Came to be most dreaded scout known to the occupation. Was hunted by special force commissioned to take him alive. In showdown at Spencer's Ranch near here on April 3, 1864, fought to his death.   (1964)

PRIDDY (Mills Co.)   *SH 16*
Zion Evangelical Lutheran Church

In the 1870s and 1880s many settlers of German ancestry began arriving in this area. In 1889, under the leadership of the Rev. R. Seils, Zion Evangelical Lutheran Church was organized. Early worship services were held in the Bismark schoolhouse (approx. 2 mi. S). Beginning with twenty-three charter members, the congregation grew steadily. By 1892, a small sanctuary was constructed and a cemetery was established on the church property (2 mi. SW).

Another group of families began meeting together for worship services in the Priddy community, and in December 1903 organized St. John's Lutheran Church. Services were held in the Becker Mountain schoolhouse (approx. 2 mi. E). Soon both German Lutheran congregations were being served by the same minister.

In 1929, the Zion congregation moved to Priddy and built a new sanctuary. In 1941, by mutual consent, the Zion and St. John's congregations joined together to become one church under the Zion Evangelical Lutheran Church name.

A part of Mills County history for generations, this church continues to serve the community with many forms of outreach.   (1989)

PROCTER (Comanche Co.)   *US 67/377 at Procter Grocery Store*
Confederate Texas Poet
Mollie E. Moore
(1844–1909)

During the Civil War, wrote poems Texans memorized, cut out of newspapers, sent their boys on the battlefront: About the deaths of heroes, Texans' units, Confederate victories and such topics. She also did social work and nursing at Camp Ford, Tyler.

She was a lively, spirited girl who went horseback riding with a pistol strapped to her side.

After war, became nationally known poet, novelist, columnist. Married a newspaper editor. Led New Orleans society 20 years.

Near this marker site, at old Mooresville (now Proctor) often visited her brother's family.

(1965)

PROGRESO (Hidalgo Co.)
Former Station Site of Spiderweb Railroad
The agricultural boom that marked the early development of this area was due in large part to the San Benito & Rio Grande Valley Railroad. Begun in 1912 by Missouri native Sam A. Robertson (1867–1938), it was called the Spiderweb Railroad because of its intricate network of lines and spurs. The railroad built a station here in 1926 as the hub of a community and citrus production center planned by the Progreso Development Co. Through early valley shipping centers such as Progreso, local produce was first transported to markets nationwide. (1982)

PROSPER (Collin Co.)
Preston Road (SH 289) at Rock Hill Rd., 2 mi. S
Site of Rock Hill
Probably named for the white rock escarpment on which it was built, Rock Hill was established by December 1854 when John Moore became its first postmaster. By the early 20th century the town boasted two schools, four churches, three doctors, a grist mill, general store, cotton gin, blacksmith, drugstore, dry goods and grocery and a population of 115. In 1902 the St. Louis and San Francisco Railroad bypassed the town, and within months most of the businesses, townspeople and churches had relocated to Prosper. The little community survived for several more years. In the mid-1930s an African American Baptist church was the only one remaining. The Anglo school closed in 1948; the Black school closed in the 1960s. A general store, the last remnant of Rock Hill, was razed in 1973. (2000)

PUTNAM (Callahan Co.)
US 80, 2 mi. E
The Original Burkett
Pecan tree, bred from a native tree, 1900, by J. H. Burkett (1861–1945), Texas pecan industry leader. (1966)

PUTNAM (Callahan Co.)
FM 2945, 4 mi. E
Hittson Ranch Headquarters
On Battle Creek
Nearby Battle Creek was given its name in 1840 by a small band of men who had traveled to this area in search of hostile Indians. A fight took place near the creek when a raiding party attacked the group. Approximately twenty years later, cattleman John Hittson (1831–1880) established his ranch headquarters at the site of the battleground. The headquarters, used only when cattle were rounded up from surrounding lands, consisted of corrals, branding pens, and a small shelter. It is believed to be the first ranching headquarters established in Callahan County. (1984)

PYOTE (Ward Co.)
IH 20, across from West Texas Children's Home
Rattlesnake Bomber Base
(Pyote Army Air Base)
Nicknamed for the numerous rattlesnake dens that were uncovered during its construction, Pyote Army Air Base was established in 1942 to train replacement crews for bombers during World War II. Located on 2,700 acres of University of Texas land, the base consisted of two 8,400-ft. runways, five large hangars, and hundreds of buildings used to house 3,000 to 4,000 soldiers and 2,000 civilians.

On Jan. 1, 1943, the 19th Bombardment Group (later known as the 19th Combat Crew Training School), a heavily-decorated fighting unit from the Pacific Theater, arrived to begin training B-17 bomber crews. Pyote came to be highly regarded as a top training field, and its crews set many new records for flying hours. This reputation continued after the transition to B-29s was made in July 1944.

During the post-war years, the base served as a storage facility, at one time housing as many as 2,000 aircraft, including the *Enola Gay*, the plane that dropped the first atomic bomb. Pyote also was used for a short time as a radar station, but by 1966 it was no longer economical to maintain such a large base for so small an operation, and the facility was closed. (1984)

QUANAH (Hardeman Co.)   US 287 W, Quanah Garden Club Park
Hardeman County
Created February 1, 1858; recreated August 21, 1876; organized December 30, 1884. Named in honor of Bailey Hardeman, 1785–1836, signer of the Texas Declaration of Independence, and Thomas Jones Hardeman, 1788–1854, member of the Texas Congress and Legislature.

County seat, Margarette, 1884–1890, Quanah, since, in honor of Quanah Parker, a Comanche chief.   (1965)

QUANAH (Hardeman Co.)   US 287, E
Old Railroad Depot
Medicine Mound Depot, 1910. Built by Kansas City, Mexico & Orient Railway as passenger and freight station, in area where Chief Quanah Parker's Comanches prayed and rolled in gypsum, believing it was healing dust.

Later Santa Fe Station. Site of holdups and shootings. Has bullet holes, but escaped a 1935 fire that burned entire town. Retired from use, 1959; was moved via Highway 287 to its present site. Awarded Medallion Plate.   (1964)

QUANAH (Hardeman Co.)   222 S. Main St. (SH 6)
Simpson Building
After serving as manager of the Cameron lumberyard in Quanah and then as a general manager in Waco, L. Simpson began his own lumber company and returned to Quanah in 1906. In 1910, Simpson had this three-story commercial building constructed to house his offices; other local businesses, including the corner drug store from 1920 until 1998; and the Elks Lodge, which occupied the top floor. Featuring decorative brick detailing and a corner entry, the Simpson Building is a significant part of Quanah's architectural heritage.   (2001)

QUANAH (Hardeman Co.)   409 S. Main St. (SH 6)
First Presbyterian Church of Quanah
This congregation was organized in 1892 at the home of Mrs. A. E. DeGraffenried by the Rev. Jacobs and eight charter members. This beaux arts classical style church building, erected by Chillicothe contractor R. Henry Stuckey in 1909, features stucco over frame construction, an inset entry under large columns, arched stained glass windows, and an elaborate stained glass dome. This structure is a symbol of the church's continuing service to the community.
(Recorded Texas Historic Landmark 1995)

QUINLAN (Hunt Co.)   SH 34 right-of-way at SH 34 Bus., 1 mi. S
Roberts
In 1882, the Houston and Texas Central Railroad bought 100 acres of land from Texas Governor Oran Roberts. As the terminus of the company's Northeastern Line, Roberts quickly attracted business people. The town boasted a school for white students and another for Black students, a post office with daily mail service, a doctor, a blacksmith, a carpenter, dry goods and grocers, general stores, and saloons.

Roberts gained a reputation as a boomtown, full of opportunity and vice. In 1892 the bankrupt Houston and Texas Central sold its Northeastern Line to New Yorker Hetty Green who reorganized the railroad as the Texas Midland under the leadership of her son Edward "Ned" Green. A land dispute between the two railroad companies led Ned Green to purchase land just north of Roberts, establishing a depot there and platting the new town of Quinlan.

Merchants and business people soon moved their facilities to Quinlan, followed by the First Missionary Baptist Church of Roberts and others wishing to escape Roberts' lawlessness. The Quinlan depot and post office were dedicated on October 17,1894; the Roberts depot and telegraph office were promptly dismantled by railroad agents. A fire of unknown origin destroyed Roberts in 1895.   (1998)

QUITAQUE (Briscoe Co.)   FM 1065, 5.5 mi. NW, Caprock Canyon State Park
Lake Theo Folsom Bison Kill Site
Stone tool fragments were discovered in 1965 and 1972 on the shores of Lake Theo, named for former landowner Theodore Geisler. Archeological testing in 1974 revealed a campsite and bison butchering and processing area dating back to the age of Folsom Man, between 10,000 and

12,000 years ago. Projectile points and scraping tools were found at a depth of four feet, along with over 500 bones from an extinct type of bison. Ponds in Holmes Canyon, now covered by Lake Theo, probably attracted prehistoric men to this area. (1978)

QUITAQUE (Briscoe Co.)
Roadside park 7 mi NW on SH 86

Trading Area of Jose Tafoya and Other
Comancheros
In Quitaque area, Comancheros (peddlers in Comanche domain) from New Mexico traded flour and other goods to Indians. The barter (begun in 1700's) reached peak in 1864–1868, when Apaches, Comanches and Kiowas rustled horses and thousands of cattle "down in Texas," to use in trades.

Jose Tafoya, who had wagons as well as pack mules, sold guns to Indians until U.S. Army caught and threatened to hang him in 1874 unless he enlisted as a frontier scout. There were many other Comancheros. Tafoya is an example of one who helped rid Texas of Indian marauders.

(1969)

QUITMAN (Wood Co.)
Park Rd. 50, James S. Hogg Park

James Stephen Hogg
(March 24, 1851–March 3, 1906)
Texas statesman whose nationally-acclaimed public career began at this site. The third son of Gen. Joseph L. and Lucanda (McMath) Hogg was born near Rusk. Orphaned during troubled Civil War era, he began at age 14 to earn his own way as a farmhand, clerk, printer's devil, typesetter, country editor. At 22, he was elected Justice of the Peace, Precinct 1, and headed Commissioners' Court of Wood County, 1874–75. He was admitted to the bar in 1875 and soon held higher offices: county attorney (1879–81), district attorney (1881–85), Texas attorney general (1887–90). Inaugurated on Jan. 20, 1891, he was the first native Texan to become governor of the state.

He championed the common people. An intellectual and physical giant, personally fearless, he saw Texas as victim of Wall Street greed, and corrected many injustices. To equalize business opportunities among great and small, he led in creating Texas Railroad Commission, hailed as a model throughout the world.

Public office left him financially insecure. Later came wealth, which has been invested by his heirs in Texas mental health and culture. His wife was Sallie Stinson of Wood County. Their children—Will, Ima, Mike and Tom—were all philanthropists. (1971)

QUITMAN (Wood Co.)
SH 37, 1.7 mi. S

Wood County
Created February 5, 1850. Organized August 5, 1850. Named in honor of George T. Wood, 1795–1858. Member of Congress of the Republic of Texas. An officer in the Mexican War. Governor of Texas, 1847–1849. Quitman, county seat.

QUITMAN (Wood Co.)
Park Road 45
in Gov. Hogg Shrine State Park,
off SH 75

James A. Stinson Home
Constructed in 1869 of virgin pine and oak by James A. Stinson, a widower who came to Texas in 1868 from Georgia after having served as a colonel in the Confederate Army. He brought with him his daughter Sallie. He bought extensive timber and farm lands in the eastern area of Wood County; operated a large sawmill which sent lumber throughout the state. Was also known as an early-day scientific farmer.

Mrs. Nathan Jones, a widow with one daughter, Mary, became the second wife of Col. Stinson. They had two daughters, Lily and Cliffie, and one son, James F.

In the parlor of the house, on April 22, 1874, Sallie Stinson married James Stephen Hogg, who later became the first native-Texan governor of the state.

Col. Stinson was a Southern aristocrat, a progressive thinker and a great scholar of government. He probably had great influence on James S. Hogg's ideas on good government. Was a leader in the County and State Grange, an organization which strove to protect rural interests. He was also instrumental in getting enacted into law the bill creating experimental farm, Texas Agricultural and Mechanical College.

Stinson's home was always open to young and old. (1968)

QUITMAN (Wood Co.) FM 778, .5 mi. SE
Collins-Haines Home, 1860
First brick structure in Wood County. Erected by James A. and Harriet C. Collins, 1859 settlers from Mississippi.

Bricks were molded and burned nearby; furniture crafted in plantation shop by Collins and slaves. They also planted fine gardens and landscapes.

Past this home, 1861–1865, marched Confederate units, to Civil War.

Since 1870 owned by family of George W. Haines. Awarded Medallion Plate. (1965)

QUITMAN (Wood Co.) SH 37, Governor Hogg Shrine Historic Park
James Stephen Hogg's Early Home
Built in 1860s; bought Jan. 8, 1873, by James Stephen Hogg (1851–1906), who in 1874 married Sallie Stinson of Wood County. When the couple honeymooned in this cottage, young Hogg was editor-publisher of *Quitman News* and justice of the peace—start of a brilliant career which led to governorship of Texas, 1891–1895.

Local clubs bought the cottage and moved it here in 1946. It was restored in 1952 by Gov. and Mrs. Hogg's only daughter, Miss Ima. Awarded Medallion Plate. (1962)

RALLS (Crosby Co.) SH 207, 5.5 mi. SW
Site of Second County Seat of Crosby County
Emma
(1 mi. N)
Founded spring, 1891, by R. L. Stringfellow and H. E. Hume, merchants in nearby Estacado. Named in honor of Miss Emma Savior, who later became Mrs. Stringfellow.

The two men organized a general store and laid out a townsite, which opened with a picnic and town lot sale. In the fall of 1891, the county seat was moved from Estacado to Emma, and for 3 years the new town experienced a boom. Many businesses were opened and by 1910 population had reached 400.

In 1910 and 1911, however, the railroad came through the county, bypassing Emma; and in 1911, the county seat moved to Crosbyton. These events drew population away from Emma. Soon most of the residences and businesses were moved to Crosbyton and Ralls, being taken across the prairie by a caravan of 4 engines, 30 men, and 22 mules. The old courthouse was hauled to Cedric by 4 large tractors.

Thus Emma provides an example of the 119 cases of change of county seat that have occurred in Texas' 254 counties. (Two counties have each had 5 seats.) Shifts in travel routes (as in Crosby County), changes in boundaries, and trends from agrarian to industrial economy have all caused county seats to be relocated. Today, only cemetery shows town of Emma once existed. (1968)

RANDOLPH (Fannin Co.) SH 121 Bus., ½ mi. NE
Lindsey-Randolph Cemetery
Tennessee native Thomas Lindsey (b. 1794) brought his family to this part of Fannin County in 1837. In the late 1840s, Lindsey donated four acres of his farmland for a school and cemetery. The first burial in the cemetery was for one of Lindsey's slaves. The one-room schoolhouse built next to the graveyard served as a community church where funeral services were held.

Over the years, this cemetery has served residents of the surrounding area, including the community of Randolph, which was founded in 1887 on the Louisiana, Arkansas and Texas Railroad. The main street in Randolph was located about ¾ mile southwest of the Lindsey School and Cemetery, and a wooden sidewalk connected the two. In the middle 1890s, the Lindsey School was moved to Randolph, and the original school grounds were added to the cemetery.

Among those buried here are Thomas Lindsey and his wife, Rebecca, and their son-in-law, the Rev. Burwell Cox, who organized several Presbyterian churches in the area. Other graves located here include those of businessmen, farmers, doctors, pioneer citizens and their descendants, and veterans of several wars. (1984)

RANGER (Eastland Co.)
US 80, 3 mi. SW

Site of
First Oil Well Drilled
in Eastland County

The J. H. McClesky No. 1 Discovery Well of the Ranger Pool was drilled by Warren Wagner under the supervision of W. K. Gordon of the Texas Pacific Coal and Oil Company, July 2–October 27, 1917. Initial production was 1600 barrels with three million feet of gas. Abandoned May 30, 1930 after producing 275,000 barrels of oil. (1964)

RANGER (Eastland Co.)
Loop 254 & Main St.

Roaring Ranger

Boom of high excitement and strategic importance. When oil demand was high during World War I, Texas Pacific Coal Company General Manager W. K. Gordon, a believer in deep drilling, persuaded his company to make the venture that started Ranger's oil boom at McClesky No. 1 (1 mi. S). This blew in October 1917, as a 1700-barrels-a-day gusher. Later gushers yielded up to 7,000 and 11,000-barrels-a-day each.

Ten daily trains brought in prospectors packed in the aisles or on tops of coaches. Ranger's dozen or so houses became a city of drillers, suppliers, oil company offices. Living quarters were so scarce that not only were beds of day-tour men occupied by the graveyard-tour men, but overstuffed chairs were also rented for sleeping. Food was hard to get and prices were high. For two rainy years, Ranger was a sea of mud. A sled taxied people across streets, or a man in hip boots carried them piggyback. However, money was plentiful, and forces of vice moved in. After five murders occurred in one day, law officers arrested many criminals and expelled gamblers and vagrants.

Ranger's success overshadowed its troubles. It is said to have yielded in a year twice the wealth of best years in California and Klondike gold fields. (1967)

RANKIN (Upton Co.)
US 67, .5 mi. E

Upton County

Formed from Tom Green County. Created Feb. 26, 1887. Organized May 7, 1910. Named in honor of John Cunningham Upton, 1828–1862. A distinguished Confederate officer killed at Manassas Aug. 30, 1862. County seat, Upland 1910–1921, Rankin since.

A cattle and sheep raising country. Oil wells dot the county. (1936)

RANKIN (Upton Co.)
SH 349, 7 mi. N

The Benedum Oil Field and
Benedum Townsite
(About 9 mi. E)

Field named in 1950 by Texas Railroad Commission in honor of Michael Late (Mike) Benedum, 1869–1959, who devoted 69 of his 90 years to the oil business, and won fortune and fame as "The Great Wildcatter."

His work began in 1890. With a partner, Joe C. Trees, he discovered or developed oil fields in Illinois, West Virginia, Louisiana (the great Caddo Field); the Tuxpam in Mexico; deMares in Colombia, South America; and in Texas the Desdemona, Big Lake, Yates, East White Point, Susan Peak and Benavides.

Discovery of Big Lake Field (1923) on University of Texas land tapped the great wealth of the Permian Basin, which opened in 1920 with a small discovery. Alford No. 1, original well in Benedum Field (later reclassified as a gas field), was completed Jan. 4, 1948, at depth of 12,011 feet by Slick-Urschel Oil Co., under a partnership agreement. The field later benefited by dedication of Benedum Townsite.

The "Great Wildcatter" was an oil pioneer whose work enriched one of the world's large constitutional permanent university funds. Revenues from oil and gas operations give Texas the largest permanent public school fund in the world. (1965)

RANKIN (Upton Co.) *US 67, 5 mi. E*
Rankin
Made Upton County seat in 1921. Named for F. E. Rankin, who gave site for railway station—the center of community life over and above its business dealings; was scene of cowboy dances of Saturday nights, church services on Sundays.

Home of Rankin Museum and of World Champion Rodeo Stars Toots Mansfield and Allen Holder. (1964)

RANKIN (Upton Co.) *US 67, 8.4 mi. W*
Rattlesnake Butte
(¼ mi. S)
Named for wildlife seen here 1919 by University of Texas geology team of students and professors mapping county resources.

A meandering formation, 2,600 ft. elevation, this is part of an uplift in southern Permian Basin; associated with uplift are county's oil fields. (1967)

RANKIN (Upton Co.) *SH 349, 10 mi. N (now on courthouse grounds)*
Upland: First County Seat of Upton
Ghost town (3 mi. W), intended as station on railroad from St. Louis to Chihuahua, Mex., was located near old stage route of Butterfield Overland Mail. Townsite was mapped by ranch owners, M. Halff & Son, who sold lots at cost of notary fee.

By 1908, cowboys' families had moved in and built a school.

County was organized in 1910. Courthouse was built in 1911.

When old stage route was not followed, Upland was bypassed and homes and other buildings were placed on skids and moved to new town of Rankin, on railroad. Courthouse was abandoned. (1964)

RATCLIFF (Houston Co.) *On SH 7*
Ratcliff
About 1875, a 32-wagon train of settlers came here from Georgia. Jesse H. Ratcliff (1844–1920) built a sawmill about 1885, drawing more people. Post office opened 1889, with Ratcliff as postmaster, and town soon had several stores. Professional men included Drs. H. L. McCall and Jack Jackson.

Sold 1901 to Louisiana & Texas Lumber Co., then to Central Coal & Coke Co., sawmill became a vast complex, running until 1917, when it closed. Turning to logging or other enterprises, the community survived, although many residents moved away. The Ratcliff schools consolidated (1955) with Kennard. (1972)

RAYMONDVILLE (Willacy Co.) *SH 186, 8.4 mi. W*
Great Salt Lake
Here has existed, since the first Spanish chronicler traversed the region, a Great Salt Lake which supplied all Northern Mexico with salt.

RAYMONDVILLE (Willacy Co.) *SH 186 right-of-way, 12 mi. E*
San Juan de Carricitos Land Grant
The largest land grant in South Texas, the San Juan de Carricitos lands were awarded to Don Jose Narciso Cavazos in 1792 by the the king of Spain. Comprising over one-half million acres, the grant included virtually all of present Willacy County, including the sites of the towns of Sebastian, Lyford, Raymondville, Lasara, San Perlita, and Port Mansfield. In 1793, Cavazos took formal possession of the land grant seven miles north of this site. Most of the grant was later sold by Cavazos' heirs, although some descendants still live within its boundaries. (1988)

REAGOR SPRINGS (Ellis Co.) *US 287 at Old US 287 N*
Richardson Cemetery (1 Mi. SW)
John I. Richardson (1839–1922), county surveyor, mason, and veteran of the 12th Texas Confederate Cavalry, married Ann Elizabeth Reagor (1849–1923) in 1865. Both were descendants

of the family for which Reagor Springs was named. A cousin, Robert S. Reagor, was buried on the Richardsons' property in 1879. In 1890 the land was deeded for use as a cemetery. Also buried here are two of the Richardsons' six children. The Richardsons left Reagor Springs near the turn of the century. Other early area families also are buried in the cemetery, which contains thirty graves. Those interred in the Richardson Cemetery helped to forge Reagor Springs and early Ellis County.
(1998)

RED OAK (Ellis Co.)
SH 342, 1 mi. S
Red Oak Cemetery
Originally known as the Kemble Cemetery, this graveyard began as a family burial ground. Abraham Kemble acquired the land on which the cemetery is located about 1860. He and his wife Mary were both buried here in 1867. In 1892, Kemble descendants gave the land to Liberty Baptist Church, later renamed First Baptist Church, Red Oak. The cemetery became a public burial ground after the turn of the century. Those interred here include generations of Kemble family members, area pioneers, and veterans of several wars, beginning with the Civil War.   (1988)

REDWATER (Bowie Co.)
US 67 at FM 991
Redwater
The first community in this area was Mooresville (2 mi. E), settled in 1840 by the Charles Moores (1776–1852) family. It had disappeared before this town grew up near the Daniels and Spence sawmill in 1875. Because of mill workers' disregard for religion, the village was first named Ingersoll for the famous agnostic of that day, Robert Green Ingersoll (1833–1899).

A branch of the St. Louis Southwestern (Cotton Belt) Railway arrived here in the late 1870s, attracting more upstanding citizens. William Thomas Fagan built two more sawmills in the early 1880s. English-born Earnest Thomas Page (1860–1937) opened a general store, which also housed the town's first post office (1881). Church-going townspeople objected to the name Ingersoll and suggested changing it to Redwater, for the color of spring and well water in the area. A town vote in 1894 made Redwater the official name.

In 1914, a tornado destroyed many businesses here, but Redwater quickly rebuilt. The economy was based on farming and lumbering until 1941, when the Red River Army Ammunition Depot and Lone Star Ordnance Plant were built just north of town. The opening of the International Paper Mill in the 1970s has created new interest in lumbering and tree farming.
(1975)

REFUGIO (Refugio Co.)
US 77, .5 mi. S
The Urrea Oaks
By tradition, camping place in March 1836, during Texas War for Independence, of Gen. José Urrea of Mexico. Strategically located, this was Urrea's staging area.

Capt. Amon B. King came from Goliad with his Texas Volunteers to support the Refugio townsmen, who were taken into the safety of Mission Nuestra Señora del Refugio. Then Lt. Col. William Ward also arrived on March 13, and the "Battle of Refugio" began. Both King and Ward left protection of the mission, and Urrea won final victories over them, capturing King's command on March 15 and Ward's on March 22.   (1973)

REFUGIO (Refugio Co.)
US 183 at SH 202, 2 mi. N
Sally Scull
Woman rancher, horse trader, champion "cusser." Ranched NW of here. In Civil War Texas, Sally Scull (or Skull) freight wagons took cotton to Mexico to swap for guns, ammunition, medicines, coffee, shoes, clothing and other goods vital to the Confederacy.

Dressed in trousers, Mrs. Scull bossed armed employees; was sure shot with the rifle carried on her saddle or the two pistols strapped to her waist.

Of good family, she had children cared for in New Orleans school. Often visited them. Loved dancing. Yet during the war, did extremely hazardous "man's work."   (1964)

REFUGIO (Bee Co.)
SH 202, 10 mi. W
Blanconia (Old N2) Church
The First Baptist Church in Refugio County was organized on April 22, 1855, and met in the Doughty schoolhouse near Refugio. In 1865, the first sanctuary was erected (5 mi. W) and named

for the cattle brand of member and benefactor N. R. McDaniel. The Blanco Baptist Association was organized at the "N2" Church in 1873. In 1888, the fellowship moved to Blanconia where the first sanctuary on this site was built in 1891. One of the oldest Baptist churches in South Texas, Blanconia Church served as a nucleus for growth of area churches and has ordained several pastors. (1985)

RHOME (Wise Co.)   *US 287 bypass at SH 114*

First National Bank
in Rhome

Prominent area businessman Dan Waggoner began this financial institution in 1904 as a branch of his privately-owned bank in Decatur (15 mi. NW). His son, W. T., served for a time as its president. Rhome's first bank was given a national charter in 1914 and grew steadily through the years. Its sound financial policies enabled it to survive the period of the Great Depression. Headquartered downtown for more than seventy years, the First National Bank in Rhome has been located at this site since 1975. (1984)

RICHLAND SPRINGS (San Saba Co.)   *US 190 at FM 45*

John Duncan's Fort

A private, or settler's, fort, built 1858. Cabins of 4 families (30 people) formed a stockade for defense against Indians. Daily a hunting party would go out for meat; other men stood guard. Residents went home to farm in spring, but through 1865 "forted up each fall." (1968)

RICHMOND (Fort Bend Co.)   *US 90A, E in roadside park*

Mirabeau Buonaparte Lamar
President of the Republic of Texas

Born 1798 in Georgia. Came to Texas 1835. Became involved immediately in movement for independence from Mexico. Upon fall of the Alamo and news of Goliad massacre, joined Texas Army as a private, as Houston moved eastward toward San Jacinto.

In swiftly moving chain of events, Lamar was made a colonel on eve of Battle of San Jacinto. There he commanded cavalry with distinction and ten days later was named Secretary of War in the interim government. Elected vice-president in new nation's first government, was candidate of the Anti-Sam Houston faction for president in next election. He won, and took office in 1838 for 3-year term.

During his administration, the Republic of Texas was recognized by Great Britain and France. He was known for his forceful Indian policy and for his opposition to annexation. He laid the foundation for first system of public education in Texas. By his decision, Austin was made capital of Texas.

A poet and diplomat, he projected the writing of a history of Texas, but died in 1859, before book was well begun. His plantation was near Richmond. He is buried near here, in the Morton Cemetery. (1965)

RICHMOND (Fort Bend Co.)   *US 90A, W bank of Brazos River, S Bridge*

Site of Fort Bend

Built in November, 1821 by William Little, William Smithers, Charles Beard, Joseph Polly and Henry Holster. Its name was given to the county when created in 1837. (1965)

RICHMOND (Fort Bend Co.)   *Front St., .5 mi. on Ransom Road*
(By appointment only)

Site of the Home of
Mirabeau B. Lamar
1798-1859

Father of Texas education. President of the Republic of Texas, 1838–1841. He lived here from 1851 to 1859. (1965)

RICHMOND (Fort Bend Co.)   *US 90A in roadside park*

Dismounted Texas Cavalry

The 95,000 men of military age in Civil War Texas, unaccustomed to walking, preferred the daring and mobility of the cavalry used to scout the enemy, screen troop movements and make lightning attacks. 58,533 Texans joined it, riding their own horses or ones donated by citizens' groups. Many of Texas' 325,000 horses were sent to other states.

Yet footsoldiers were needed, too. The state set up camps of instruction, to teach Texans to walk and fight. By mid-1862 the need for infantry was so great that the following units were unhorsed under strong protest: 6th Texas Cavalry Battalion, 13th, 16th, 18th, 22nd, 24th, 25th and 28th Texas Cavalry Regiments.

On Aug. 15, 1863, a part of A. W. Terrell's Cavalry Regiment at Richmond was ordered to dismount and march to the defense of Galveston. On Sept. 11, an order to dismount still more men caused mutiny, and 91 rode their prized horses north to homes on the Indian frontier or to join other cavalry units. When 25 were tried later, only the officers were punished. Enlisted men returned to the regiment, and fought in such actions as the 1864 Red River Campaign to prevent a Federal invasion of Texas.

RICHMOND (Fort Bend Co.)   *FM 1093, 10 mi. NW*
Town of Fulshear
On July 16, 1824, land grant of Mexico to Churchill Fulshear, one of the "Old 300" settlers of Stephen F. Austin, Father of Texas. Churchill Fulshear, Jr., veteran of Texas War for Independence, built 4-story brick mansion in 1850s, bred and raced horses at Churchill Downs (at Pittsville, 2 mi. N). His pupil, John Huggins, won world fame by training first American horse to win the English Derby.

Town platted here 1890 by San Antonio & Aransas Pass Railroad, soon was trade center, with many facilities. The Rev. J. H. Holt was first (1894) pastor of the still existent Methodist church.

(1971)

RICHMOND (Fort Bend Co.)   *6th and Houston St.*
Erastus ("Deaf") Smith
(April 17, 1787–November 30, 1837)
Most famous scout in Texas War for Independence. Obeyed Gen. Sam Houston's strategic order, then raised San Jacinto battle cry: "Fight for your lives! Vince's Bridge has been cut down."

A native of New York, Smith settled here in 1821 in San Antonio. Trading in land and goods, he traveled Texas province, making him an invaluable guide for the army during the War for Independence.

He married Guadalupe Ruiz Duran, and they had three daughters.

Dying here in the home of Randall Jones (a friend), he was buried in Calvary Churchyard, Houston at 6th. His grave is now unidentified.

(1973)

RICHMOND (Ft. Bend Co.)   *200 block of 4th St.*
Jane Long Boarding House
Born in Maryland in 1798, Jane H. Wilkinson moved to Mississippi (1811) and became the ward of her famous relative, Gen. James Wilkinson, Field Commander of the United States Army. Jane married Dr. James Long in 1815 and later followed him on a filibustering expedition to free Texas from Spain. In 1821, Long led his forces into battle, leaving Jane alone with their daughter Ann and slave girl Kian at Point Bolivar, near Galveston. On Dec. 21, 1821, with snow falling, their food supply gone, and Kian ill, Jane gave birth to a daughter, then rose and got food and firewood for her family. Her heroism earned her the name "Mother of Texas." Later she learned of her husband's death in Mexico.

During the period Texas was a colony and a republic, Jane Long operated two well-known boarding houses. She started the first in Brazoria in 1832; her guests included William B. Travis, Sam Houston, and Mirabeau B. Lamar. In 1837, Jane moved to Richmond and on this site opened another boarding house which became a center for social and political activities as well as lodging for prominent Texans and European visitors. Jane ran this hotel until her plantation near town became prosperous in the 1840s. She died in 1880 and is buried in Richmond's Morton Cemetery.

(1975)

RINGGOLD (Montague Co.)   *US 81 at US 82*
Early Trails in Montague County
Lying on a direct line of travel from the United States to Mexico, California, and points west, the area now Montague County was once a network of trails.

One of the first area roads forged by white men was the Chihuahua Traders' Trail of 1840. Blazed by merchants hoping to open a trade route from Mexico to St. Louis, Mo., this road crossed present Montague County and left tracks for later travelers. In 1841 came the Texan-Santa Fe Expedition; though it failed to open regular commerce between the Republic of Texas and Northern Mexico, this delegation also left a road and enforced the claims of Texas to western territories. In 1849 U.S. Army Capt. Randolph B. Marcy charted a "California Trail," using parts of older routes. This soon grew into a thoroughfare for forty-niners and sturdy pioneers who came later.

In 1858 the famous Butterfield Overland Mail Line came across the county; and in the 1870s, as Texas was building her image as a cattle empire, Montague County was crossed by two feeder branches of the Chisholm Trail. In 1882, the county's first railroad followed much of the Texan-Santa Fe Trail.

Today Highway 82 partly traces Marcy's route and other roads parallel many of these early trails. (1969)

RINGGOLD (Montague Co.) *US 81, 5 mi. S in roadside park*
Highways Paved with Gold
From time immemorial man has searched for a land where streets were paved with gold. As early as the 16th century he was in Texas, lured by Indian reports of "seven cities of gold." They never were found. But they provided the basis for legends of untold riches—stories still spun by some Texans.

Surprisingly, perhaps, many of the "tall tales" are more fact than fiction. For instance, both this section of U.S. Highway 81 and a portion of adjacent U.S. Highway 287 are actually paved with gold!

The story began in 1936 when the Texas Highway Department was paving the two highways here in Montague County. Sand for the concrete was taken from a nearby pit, opened three years earlier. The grains glistened with such intensity as they were mixed that a closer examination seemed prudent. So a small supply was sent to a Fort Worth laboratory for assay.

Back came the report: the sand contained gold. The news sent the owner of the pit in feverish search of the mother lode. But in vain. Top assays on his extensive "soundings" came to no more than 54 cents per ton of ore. His ardor was cooled further when he learned the gold was not free but deeply imbedded in the sand.

Disheartened, he settled back into routine sand production. From his pit, however, eventually came $250,000 in gold—all part of the sand. It has been reckoned that as much as $31,000 is distributed along 39 miles of roadway, some $25,000 in U.S. Highway 81 and $6,000 in U.S. Highway 287. The remainder has gone into other construction in the region, including numerous buildings in which concrete has been used.

So it is that today's motorist has discovered the highways paved with gold and the "golden" cities which his predecessors sought in vain.

RIO FRIO (Real Co.) *FM 1120*
Lombardy Irrigation Ditch
Dug in 1868, in pick-and-shovel operation, by Lombardy Irrigation Company, whose officers were N. M. C. Patterson, W. F. Smith, and T. Watkins.

Besides channeling water to irrigate over 800 acres, the 2-mile ditch furnished power for a cotton gin, and shingle, grist, and flour mills.

The settlement which grew up in the area was known as "The Ditch" until a post office was established in 1875. It was then named "Rio Frio" ("Cold River").

For a century the ditch has irrigated lands of families of two original company officers. (1968)

RIO GRANDE CITY (Starr Co.) *US 83, 2.5 mi. W*
Site of the
Mission San Agustin de Laredo a Vista
Established in 1749 as a part of Jose de Escandon's project to settle the region and civilize and Christianize the Indians.

RIO GRANDE CITY (Starr Co.) *US 83, Business Route Loop 254*
Site of Cortina Battle
Dec. 27, 1859
Crushing defeat for partisan leader Juan Cortina who in late 1859 laid waste the Lower Rio Grande Valley. Cortina's band of 450 were surprised here at daybreak by Maj. S. B. Heintzelman

with U.S. Army troops, joined by Texas Rangers recruited by John S. ("Rip") Ford. Cortina fled to Mexico by horseback. Many of his men jumped into the Rio Grande.

Regarrisoning of Ringgold barracks ended partisan raids for a time. But with the American Civil War (1861–1865) and Cortina's rise to power in Tamaulipas, raids were renewed—until Cortina was removed, 1875. (1970)

RIO HONDO (Cameron Co.) *FM 508 at FM 1420, 1 mi. N*
Rogers Massacre
U.S. annexation of Texas in December 1845 intensified Mexico's asserted claim to Texas. In March 1846, U.S. Commander Zachary Taylor advanced his federal army beyond the Nueces River and established a supply base at Point Isabel and a garrison (Fort Brown) on the north bank of the Rio Grande. Roswell D. Denton, appointed by Taylor to transport supplies from New Orleans, enlisted Patterson Rogers and sons, Anderson W. and William L., to carry supplies from Corpus Christi to Point Isabel. The Rogerses, 9 other men, 3 women, and 4 children left Corpus Christi on April 25, 1846 with supplies bound for Point Isabel. Near this site on May 1, 1846, they were ambushed by Mexican bandits led by Juan Balli.

Outnumbered and outgunned, Rogers surrendered when Balli offered prisoner-of-war protections. Balli broke his pledge and had two men shot to death. The rest of the men were bound and led to a bluff overlooking the Arroyo Colorado where their throats were slit and their bodies tossed into the arroyo. The women and children were subsequently murdered.

William Long Rogers miraculously survived and though severely wounded made his way over 40 miles to a ranch near Fort Brown. Rogers lived for many years and became a prominent south Texas citizen. (1994)

RIO VISTA (Johnson Co.) *FM 916, 5 mi. W*
Bennett Home on the
Chisholm Trail
(500 yds. N)
In early days, grove here (a day's walk from Kimbell's Bend Crossing on Brazos River) was a guide point for cowboys driving cattle north on Chisholm trail. At the trees, crews made camp.

Water was obtained at home of Richard Bennett family, 1870 settlers from Kentucky. Bennett chose land here to be free of fences and neighbors. Sons soon were trail hands, and ranched this land for five generations.

As a Chisholm Trail campsite, this spot witnessed, 1866–1890, passage of greatest movement of animals under control of men in all of history. (1966)

RIO VISTA (Johnson Co.) *SH 174 on grounds of First State Bank*
Henry Briden Cabin
Henry Briden (1825–1908) came to Texas from his native Germany in 1845 and served for two years as a Texas Ranger. In 1849, he and his wife, Lucinda Sevier (1831–75), became first permanent white settlers in what is now Johnson County, when they built this cabin on the east bank of Nolan's River (2.5 mi. northwest). The one-room log structure was later used as a barn when Briden erected a larger home nearby. In 1974, it was restored and moved to this site. (1975)

RIO VISTA (Johnson Co.) *SH 174 on grounds of Rio Vista State Bank*
Early Cattle Trade
Famed for its beef since era of the Republic, Texas fed a great part of the Confederacy—both civilians and army—in the Civil War years, (1861–1865).

Routes for beef supplying were many: Shreveport Trail to Vicksburg, Miss.; Alexandria Trail to Natchez, Miss.; Opelousas Trail to Woodville, Miss., and on to Mobile, Ala.; Old Government Road to Little Rock, Ark.; Oliver Loving's 1859 Trail North, to Indian Territory; trails to all army depots and even to Mexico.

Cowboys had to swim cattle across rivers—even the Mississippi. After undergoing such hardships, one outfit was mistakenly arrested by Confederates. Lt. Col. J. F. Scurlock and son, from Johnson County, on a Texas beef drive into Southern Louisiana, were arrested by Federals and died in prison, of fever.

Meredith Hart (1811–1864), a leading beef supplier, came to Johnson County in 1855, after fighting for the Texas Republic in 1836. In the 1850s, he sold beef to the U.S. Army. During the Civil

War, he was one of the ranchers victimized by beef contractors using counterfeit money, but accepted losses in the faith that beef was feeding his sons and others on Confederate fighting fronts. Hart's home was 1½ miles west of Rio Vista. (1965)

RISING STAR (Eastland Co.) SH 36, City Park
Rising Star
First settlers—families of Andrew Agnew, Isaac Agnew, Fletcher Fields, David McKinley, Allis Smith, and W. W. Smith—arrived in a wagon train from Gregg County, Jan. 6, 1876. Area was known for hardships: Indian raids, vigilante activities, gunfights. But a stable community developed around log school-church building erected in 1876. First store was founded about 1879 by Thomas W. Anderson and son William.

Post office established 1880. The most credible story as to how the town got its name is that the settlers suggested the name Star for the post office but it was rejected by the U.S. postal authorities as another Texas town had that name. The settlers argued all night over the name selection, looked up and saw the morning star as they started home from their meeting and agreed to call it Rising Star.

The city was first incorporated in 1891. In a 1905 election, there was a vote to dissolve the corporation but the charter was restored later the same year.

Rising Star is the home of Texas (1939–1941) poet laureate Lexie Dean Robertson. Unique local structure is city hall built of stone from buried petrified forest.

Economy is based on ranching, farming (a chief crop is Spanish peanuts), commercial pecans, industry, oil. (1968)

RIVERSIDE (Walker Co.) FM 980, 1.8 mi. SE
Bethea Creek
A tributary of the Trinity River, Bethea Creek (pronounced buh-thay) is named for John and Elizabeth Bethea, pioneer settlers of the area. John settled in present-day Walker County in the 1830s and was an early gristmill operator and postmaster in the nearby riverport settlement of Newport, now a ghost town. Soon after Riverside was established along a rail line in the early 1870s, the Betheas moved to the town and operated a gristmill. This stream, which bears their name, remains as a symbol of the contributions made by the area's earliest settlers. (1983)

RIVERSIDE (Walker Co.) FM 980, .5 mi. E
Town of Riverside
Founded 1872 when Houston & Great Northern Railroad (later, International & Great Northern) was being built into the area. Walker County landowners gave earth, timber, and rock to the road in order to gain shipping facilities. Post office was moved here Feb. 23, 1872, from Newport (6 mi. SE), where wharves were idle when Trinity River was low.

Riverside developed churches, a 4-teacher school, and two blocks of businesses, including stores, blacksmith shop, livery stable, saloon, barber shop, 2-story hotel, cotton gin. In the 1920s, Fuller's Earth Refining Plants were built. (1972)

RIVIERA (Kleberg Co.) US 77, 4 mi. N at roadside park
Approximate Route of
U.S. Army March to Rio Grande, 1846
Battle Road of General Zachary Taylor and largest U.S. Army fielded in first half of the 19th century.

After annexation of former Republic of Texas was approved in 1845, the United States sent Taylor to occupy area below the Nueces—to support claim to all land east of the Rio Grande. In August, 1845, he reached Corpus Christi where he waited while U.S. and Mexico tried to reach boundary agreement. He also sent out engineers to map a road parallel to the gulf, where the U.S. Navy watched the crisis.

His army—including on its rosters two later U.S. presidents and many later statesmen and generals—drilled throughout a rainy winter. On orders from Washington, it moved toward Rio Grande in March, 1846. Along its path were few people but much game—wild cattle, antelope, deer, mustang horses, wild turkeys.

Although challenged about 70 miles south of here by a Mexican patrol, Taylor proceeded to occupy Rio Grande Valley. April attacks and May battles of Palo Alto and Resaca de la Palma caused the United States to declare war. Afterward many troops took this road and joined the fighting, which fixed the Rio Grande as boundary and gained for U.S. lands now in Arizona, California, Nevada and New Mexico. (1968)

RIVIERA (Kleberg Co.)

US 77, 1 mi. N

Federal Raid
from Camp Boveda, 1863

On Dec. 23, 1863, Capt. Jas. Speed of Gen. Napoleon J. T. Dana's Brownsville-based Federal Army force raided unguarded King Ranch. Objectives were to capture or kill Capt. Richard King and destroy the Confederate cotton trade. King, forewarned, evaded the enemy.

At King Ranch, the raiders killed Francisco Alvarado; captured C. S. A. captains John Brown, Alvin Dix, W. S. Gregory and Jas. McClearly and Chaplain Hiram Chamberlain; rifled all buildings; dispersed ranch employees; declared the slaves free; confiscated all horses and mules; impounded Confederate government cotton, promising that if it were moved or burned, King's life would be the forfeit; and threatened further raids from Boveda by Col. E. J. Davis, former South Texas attorney turned Federal officer.

Mrs. King and children moved to San Antonio for the war's duration; soon Col. J. S. "Rip" Ford's Confederate Cavalry came to protect the cotton road and ranch.

At Camp (Rancho) Boveda, near a ford on Los Olmos Creek, were seven cypress-walled water wells, possibly used by Gen. Zachary Taylor in 1846. Campsite 2½ miles east of this point, on lot 2, block 15, Koch Subdivision Number One, present Poteet Ranch. (1965)

RIVIERA (Kleberg Co.)

US 77 at FM 771

8 mi. E to
Indian Burial Ground
(Dietz Archeological Site)

Centuries old, this burial ground was once used by the primitive Karankawa Indians. A little-known group, this coastal tribe cared for Spanish Explorer Cabeza De Vaca when he was shipwrecked in Texas in 1528.

Although previously looted, the site produced over 20 skeletons when excavated by archeologists in 1927 and later. Also found were large quantities of burned human bones (suggesting ritual cannibalism), potsherds, arrowpoints, flint tools, fire implements, and shells.

European explorers found the Karankawas unusually tall and muscular, but were repelled by their habits of tattooing and painting their bodies and smearing themselves with alligator grease to keep off insects.

Much ritual attended Karankawa death, especially that of boys and young men, who were mourned for an entire year. Three times a day the family wept for the departed youth. After a year, the mourners purified themselves with smoke in a special rite.

Ordinary persons were buried in shallow graves with some tools and ornaments, but Shamans (medicine men) were cremated during a ceremonial dance.

Never very numerous, the Karankawas drifted into Mexico after the white man's diseases and enmity reduced them to a handful of survivors. (1970)

RIVIERA (Kleberg Co.)

US 77, 4.5 mi. N at roadside park

1766 Exploration of Diego Ortiz Parrilla

First expedition to give detailed descriptions of Texas' offshore islands and to refer to Corpus Christi bay by its present name.

The exploration was ordered by the viceroy of New Spain in the midst of rumors that the English planned to encroach on Spanish territory. Parrilla, who had fought the Moors for Spain before holding positions of civil and military leadership in the New World, was ordered to expel any intruders.

He began his trek at San Juan Bautista on the Rio Grande, September 13, 1766. At Corpus Christi Bay a detachment marched south to explore the coastal islands. Their report of uniformly bleak, treeless, waterless dunes (including this area) cast doubt on the feasibility of enemy occupation.

At this point; torrential rains and floods impeded the party's progress. At La Bahia (present Matagorda Bay) Parrilla was luckily about to interview some of the soldiers serving along the coast and thus he obtained knowledge of the geography of the area and its Indians as far north as Trinity Bay.

After several months Parrilla returned, having helped disprove rumors of the English intrusion and bearing vital information on the Texas Gulf Coast. (1970)

ROARING SPRINGS (Motley Co.) *End of Broadway St.*
Roaring Springs Depot
Under the leadership of Samuel Lazarus (1855–1926), the Quanah, Acme & Pacific Railroad contributed much to Motley County's economic development. One of the townsites along the line, Roaring Springs was platted in 1912, one year before the tracks reached this point. This brick mission revival style depot was completed within a year, and handled passenger and freight traffic until 1971. Roaring Springs' oldest structure, it was purchased by the city in 1972. (1977)

ROBERT LEE (Coke Co.) *SH 158, 1 mi. E in roadside park*
Coke County
Formed from Tom Green County. Created March 13, 1889. Organized April 23, 1889. Named in honor of Richard Coke, 1829–1896. Governor of Texas 1874–1876. Member of United States Senate 1878–1896.

County seat, Hayrick, 1889; Robert Lee, since 1890. (1964)

ROBERT LEE (Coke Co.) *SH 158, 9 mi. W*
Edith
Original Site 1 mi. N
Settled by cattlemen who ran herds on open range, and stock-farming homesteaders.

Development began in early 1880s after Winfield Scott, rancher, fenced his spread.

Area had three schools, lodge hall, tabernacle, general store, cotton gin and blacksmith shop.

The post office, established in 1890, was named for Edith Bonsall, an admired young lady of Ballinger. It closed in 1955. Dwindling schools combined, then consolidated with those of nearby Robert Lee.

As trend toward urban living increased, Edith declined. (1969)

ROBERT LEE (Coke Co.) *US 277, Near Tennyson Post Office*
Mule Creek Cemetery
(4.5 mi. SW)
Established by pioneers of Mule Creek community, a small frontier settlement founded in 19th century. Said to be named either for (1) an early horse and mule ranch, or (2) a stagecoach mule that died at a creek which runs nearby. The Abilene-Fort Concho Stage once served area.

For years principal building here was a combination school-church. Since 20th century, shift to urban living has diminished population of Mule Creek.

Inscriptions on tombstones chronicle history of community. In spring, grounds are covered with bluebonnets, state flower. (1971)

ROBERT LEE (Coke Co.) *SH 208, 13 mi. NW*
Panther Gap
Landmark on ancient Indian trail, and early route of travelers and military west of Fort Chadbourne (20 miles east) before the Civil War. After 1880, was used extensively to connect this area with the railroad at Colorado City. Named for panthers (cougars), which still roam the region. (1973)

ROBERT LEE (Coke Co.) *SH 208, ½ mi. E*
Robert Lee Cemetery
Established in 1891, two years after the founding of the city of Robert Lee. Developers L. B. Harris and Eugene Cartledge, as president and secretary of the Austin & Northern Land & Cattle Company, on Sept. 29, 1892, sold for $1.00 this 11.7-acre burial ground. Already site of several graves, it was deeded to Hayrick Lodge No. 696, A. F. & A. M., for "sole use as cemetery grounds for the members, relatives, and friends." Later it was named by the lodge.

Buried here are 34 civil war veterans, as well as soldiers of later wars and members of many of the families in Robert Lee. (1973)

ROBERT LEE (Coke Co.)   *SH 208, 9 mi. N, Sanco Loop, 6 mi. N*
Sanco
(Originally Located 1 mi. E)
On site of prehistoric Indian camps; in area where in 1850s Fort Chadbourne soldiers often skirmished with Indians.

One of the first settlements and second pioneer post office (established 1888) in county.

Named for the Comanche Chief Sanaco, who with Chief Yellow Wolf had regularly camped here. Yellow Wolf, killed in a fight with Lipans, is buried nearby.

In 1907, new site was surveyed; town relocated here on Yellow Wolf Creek. School, post office, store, blacksmith shop moved to this new site, where Methodist Church was already located.   (1966)

ROBERT LEE (Coke Co.)   *RR 2034, 16 mi. SW*
Natural Landmark Shelving Rock
(8 mi. W, on Private Land)
Archeological findings at an overhanging rock ledge on Walnut Creek show that the spot, midway between the Colorado and North Concho Rivers, was for hundreds of years campsite or village of nomadic Indians who sought the shelter, running water, wood, and high lookout point above ledge.

After 1850, campsite was used in turn by Fort Chadbourne and Fort Concho scouts, surveyors, and line riders of area ranches.

There rangers, state militia, and a posse of settlers hunting horses and Indians rendezvoused a few nights prior to disastrous Battle of Dove Creek, Jan. 8, 1865.   (1972)

ROBERT LEE (Coke Co.)   *US 277 at SH 70 E*
Southern Overland Mail, 1858–1861
(Butterfield Stage)
Passed near this site, providing for the first time combined passenger and mail service between Pacific and Atlantic coasts. Operating west from St. Louis and Memphis, John Butterfield's company used 1350 horses and mules and 90 Concord coaches and wagons.

Stage traveled at a run, despite lack of good roads. A signal given approaching a station would have fresh horses ready and food on the table for crew and passengers. Route had stations 12 to 113 miles apart, and was sometimes changed to get water. Crew and passengers wore guns; to reduce danger of Indian attacks, mules (less coveted than horses) were used west of Ft. Belknap. The trip one way took 25 days—seven spent crossing Texas, from Preston (now under Lake Texoma) to Jacksboro, Ft. Belknap, Ft. Chadbourne and El Paso. One way fare for the 2700 miles was $200. Passengers rarely stopped off, because they might not find seats on a later stage. Merchants in Jacksboro and other towns used Butterfield's light freight service to make mail order sales.

Greatest contribution of the overland stage was its carrying news; coaches also brought mail from the west one to 10 days faster than it came by ship.

Service was ended in 1861 by the Civil War.   (1966)

ROBSTOWN (Nueces Co.)   *SH 44 & South Violet Rd., 4 mi. E*
Old Saint Anthony's Catholic Church
In Nov. 1909, the Rev. J. Goebels called a meeting to organize St. Anthony's parish for the recently settled German Catholic farm families in the community of Land Siding, later known as Violet. Louis Petrus donated five acres for a church site, and five additional acres were purchased. The parishioners began construction of the building in 1910, with John W. Hoelscher (1866–1941), one of the earliest settlers here, as foreman of the project. Originally measuring 26 ft. by 40 ft., the frame structure served as a schoolhouse and church.

The congregation enlarged and extensively remodeled the building in 1919. Three towers were added at that time. A bell, purchased earlier from Spohn Sanitarium in Corpus Christi, was installed in one. The rectory, which served as a schoolhouse and living quarters for visiting priests, was attached to the church building in 1920. Members then fenced and landscaped the area.

In 1952, the parish built a larger church, and this structure was moved to the parish mission of Our Lady of Mount Carmel in nearby Clarkwood community. In 1975, after that congregation erected a new church facility, the old St. Anthony's building was relocated 200 ft. east of its original site and restored as a museum by the Violet Historical Society.   (1978)

ROBY (Fisher Co.)

US 180, 5 mi. E

Fisher County

Site of old Indian trail from Mexico to settlements on Texas frontier. In this region in 1856, Colonel Robert E. Lee, then commanding the famed U.S. Second Cavalry (and later General-in-chief of the Confederate Army), campaigned against the Indians.

County formed from Young and Bexar territories. Created 1876. Settled in 1877. Organized 1886. Named for Samuel Rhoads Fisher (1794–1839), a signer of the Texas Declaration of Independence, Secretary of the Navy in the Republic of Texas, 1836.

Roby, county seat, named for landowners. (1965)

ROBY (Fisher Co.)

US 180 at SH 70

Roby

Located on land originally included in a land grant to Texas War for Independence veteran Thomas H. Cosby, the town of Roby was first platted in 1885. The land was purchased by D. C. and M. L. Roby of Mississippi, relatives of Cosby's second wife, Martha.

The Robys hired Walton, Hill, and Walton, a Travis County law firm, to represent their interests, and instructed the attorneys to organize a town to be named county seat of Fisher County. On behalf of their clients, the attorneys donated land for churches, schools, a park, and a cemetery. Town lots were also given to settlers who would build homes within ninety days. In an election held in April 1886, Roby was declared the county seat.

The first county court was held in a shed behind the V. H. Anderson house, which served as the town's first post office. A frame courthouse was built on the southwest corner of the town square and was replaced over the years by a succession of other structures.

Schools, churches, and businesses were established as settlement in the town increased. Retaining its small town atmosphere, Roby remains a center of commerce for Fisher County. (1989)

ROBY (Fisher Co.)

SH 70 right-of-way, 1 mi. N

Roby Cemetery
(½ mi. E)

Settlers began arriving in this area in the late 19th century. The oldest grave marker in the Roby cemetery, that of Mable W. Deming, bears the date 1884, one year prior to the organization of Fisher County and the establishment of the town of Roby.

Brothers D. C. and M. L. Roby purchased over 4,000 acres of land in 1885. They had a townsite platted; donated sites for schools, churches, and a park; and designated the land containing Mable Deming's grave as a public cemetery. The original cemetery plot consisted of seven acres, and the brothers stipulated that no fee was to be levied for grave sites in that section.

The Roby Cemetery served as the principal burial ground for citizens of Fisher County. In the late 1950s the county deeded the cemetery lands to the city of Roby. In 1975, the Roby Cemetery Association was chartered and accepted the deed to the cemetery property from the city. Later land acquisitions increased the graveyard's size to twenty-one acres.

Those interred in the Roby cemetery include pioneer settlers of Fisher County, veterans of the Civil War, and one former slave, "Aunt" Abbie Alborn, who came to this area from Tennessee in 1886. The graveyard serves as a reminder of the area's early history. (1988)

ROBY (Fisher Co.)

FM 1224 at FM 2142, 9 mi. E

Royston Townsite

The town of Royston came into existence in 1906, when the Texas Central Railroad built a line through this area. In addition to the railroad depot, homes and businesses were soon established in the new town.

The Royston post office was established in 1907. Businesses included a 30-room hotel, the *Royston Record* weekly newspaper, the Royston Mercantile Company, the Royston State Bank, a cotton gin, tin shop, grocery and hardware store, drug store, restaurant, and two lumberyards. A public school was in operation until 1947, when it was consolidated with McCaulley School. Churches in the town included Methodist, Baptist, and Pentecostal.

The center of a rich agricultural area, Royston's economic base was broadened after the discovery of oil in the area in 1928. The railroad continued both freight and passenger service until 1972, and Royston was an important supply center for the surrounding agricultural area for a number of years.

The town of Royston gradually declined, and the rails were removed by the railroad company. This site marks the approximate southern boundary of the town square. Now a ghost town, it is nevertheless an important part of Fisher County history. (1988)

ROCHELLE (McCulloch Co.) US 190
Rochelle Depot
J. F. Crew of Ohio purchased land here in 1902 and later moved to McCulloch County and founded the settlement of Rochelle. When the Fort Worth and Rio Grande Railroad built a line from Brownwood to Brady in 1902–1903, he was successful in having it routed through Rochelle. Later part of the Sante Fe system, the railroad played an important role in the area's early growth and agricultural development. The town's first depot burned and was replaced about 1912 by this frame structure. In 1956, it was moved to this site for use as a community center. (1982)

ROCKDALE (Milam Co.) US 79, 2.5 mi. E
La Recluta and La Escuelita
Jose Leal received six leagues of land in this area in 1833. In 1867, coal was discovered, and the railroad reached Rockdale in 1874. Not until 1890 did the first coal mine, owned by Herman Vogel, begin operation. Others opened, and more settlers came looking for work. Many workers came from Mexico, leaving behind a revolution. These immigrants settled on land owned by E.A. Camp. They sharecropped, growing enough for themselves, and worked in the mines. They named their settlement, just north of the International–Great Northern Railroad tracks, La Recluta, or "recruitment." Family names represented here include Ruiz, Flores, Casarez, Zapata, Aldama, Montoya and Lumbreras. The men, like many other industry workers at the time, received their pay in tokens, which were redeemable only for mine commissary purchases and doctor visits. Several men were trapped in an International Mine Company cave-in in 1913. Eight men and one mule awaited rescue for six days; one man did not survive. Yards away from the collapsed mine entrance is La Escuelita, the small schoolhouse built for the children of the community. Classes were taught in English, although most students spoke Spanish at home. As part of the Talbott Ridge School District, the students transferred to Rockdale schools in 1944, when the districts consolidated. In 1946, Rockdale merchants donated benches to La Escuelita building. In 1953, the school was deeded to the St. Joseph's Cemetery Association, the support group for the community's cemetery, where nearly 300 gravestones tell the stories of La Recluta's families, many of whom remain in the area. (2002)

ROCKDALE (Milam Co.) FM 908, 8 mi. W
Site of the
Mission San Francisco Xavier de
Los Dolores
Established by Franciscan missionaries in 1746 with the hope of civilizing and Christianizing the Coco, Mayeye, Orcoquiza, Karankawa and other tribes of Indians. The martyrdom of Padre Jose Ganzabal and the circumstances connected therewith caused the departure of the Indians and the Friars and the removal of this mission to the San Marcos River in 1755. Re-established in 1757 on the San Saba River for the conversion of the Lipan Apaches with the new name of Mission Santa Cruz de San Saba.

ROCKNE (Bastrop Co.) FM 535 right-of-way, in front of Sacred Heart Church
Rockne
Rockne began as a small farming community. Phillip Goertz (1825–1900), considered to be the first German Catholic settler of the area, arrived from Germany in 1856 and purchased land along Walnut Creek. He was soon joined by more German Catholic immigrants who established family farms.

The first church built by the settlers, Ascension of Christ Church, was erected on Walnut Creek in 1876 but was destroyed by an arsonist's fire in 1891. A new structure was completed in 1892 and named Sacred Heart Church.

Rockne has been known by several names. First called Walnut Creek because of its proximity to the stream, it was known as Lehmanville when the Lehman post office was established in 1900, and as Hilbigville after William Hilbig opened a store here.

In 1931, the children of Sacred Heart School were given the opportunity to permanently name their town. A vote was taken, with the children electing to name the community Rockne in honor of Knute Rockne, the famous Notre Dame University football player and head coach who had died in a plane crash in 1931.

Rockne continues to be a rural community, with Sacred Heart Catholic Church at its center.

(1988)

ROCKNE (Bastrop Co.) — *FM 20, 2 mi. SW*
Samuel Wolfenberger
(1804–1860)

Early land grantee in this area. Of Dutch descent, he was born in Virginia. Came to Texas (then part of Mexico) in 1831 as a colonist of Stephen F. Austin, the "Father of Texas."

Received a Spanish league of land (4,444 acres) here. Active in Texas Revolution, he took part in storming of Bexar in 1835; served with Robert Coleman's Rangers in 1836. Lived in Bastrop many years, joining efforts to promote town as capital of the republic in 1839. Was collector same year; alderman 1845–1847.

Married Caroline Fliesart; had 7 children. Grave located 1 mi. E.   (1972)

ROCKPORT (Aransas Co.) — *2 mi. N on Fulton Beach*
Home of
George W. Fulton

Born at Philadelphia, June 8, 1810. Served in the Texan Army in 1836. A pioneer resident of Refugio County.

After an engineering career of distinction elsewhere, he returned to Texas and became a cattle baron. Died October 31, 1893. The town of Fulton bears his name.   (1964)

ROCKPORT (Aransas Co.) — *Orleans St., between N and S lanes of SH 35*
Rockport

The town of Rockport was founded by cattlemen J. M. and T. H. Mathis in 1867. Originally a part of Refugio County, it became county seat of newly formed Aransas County in 1871. Shipping and fishing provided the primary economic base of the town in its early years. The railroad arrived in 1888 and with it came a decline in the shipping industry, although shipyards were in operation during World War I and World War II. Rockport has been a popular recreation center over the years, and tourism continues to be important to the local economy.   (1988)

ROCKPORT (Aransas Co.) — *1800 S. Church St. (SH 70)*
Site of Heldenfels Shipyard

Shipping industries flourished on the Rockport waterfront by the 1880s. Heldenfels Shipyard was established here on 12.9 acres in October 1917. Four 281-foot wooden cargo vessels were to be built for military use in World War I; the *Baychester* was launched on July 31, 1919, and the *Zuniga* on September 9, 1919. At the height of construction, over 900 men were employed at the shipyard. The need for ships fell as the war ended.

Despite hurricane damage to the shipyard on September 14, 1919, the *Jasper* and the *Manchester* were completed as barges in 1920, ending this vital war contract.   (1996)

ROCKPORT (Aransas Co.) — *SH 35, 10 mi. N*
Site of the Town of Lamar

Named for Mirabeau B. Lamar, 1798–1859. President of the Republic of Texas 1838–1841.

Established in 1838. Made a port of entry in 1839. Sacked by Union troops Feb. 11, 1864. Survived until 1914 but never flourished.

ROCKPORT (Aransas Co.) — *SH 35, 6.5 mi. N*
Site of One of the Homes of
James Power

Born in Ireland, 1789. Died in Live Oak Point, Texas, 1852. With James Hewetson, he was granted authority January 11, 1828 to settle 200 families in Texas. Served Texas under three flags as empresario, soldier, statesman. Signed the Texas Declaration of Independence. Ever a loyal son of his adopted country, Honored and loved by his people.

ROCKPORT (Aransas Co.)

SH 35, .6 mi. N

Aransas County

Created September 18, 1871 from Refugio County. Organized in 1871 with Rockport as the county seat.

Named for the river Nuestra Señora de Aranzazu. (1964)

ROCKPORT (Aransas Co.)

SH 35, 2 mi. N on Fulton Beach

Fulton Mansion

This palatial Victorian house with Franco-Italianate details was erected 1871–1875 by George Fulton (1810–1898). An architect, surveyor, artist, and scholar, he had marble and ironwork made in Italy; lumber was precut in New Orleans. Tanks on roof held rain water for drinking, laundry, and plumbing (a modern feature for era). In small secret room Fulton kept cash from sales of cattle by the Coleman-Fulton Pasture Company, a great ranch. Awarded Medallion Plate. (1970)

ROCKSPRINGS (Edwards Co.)

SH 55, 26 mi. S

Camp Fawcett

Opened 1930. Named for E. K. Fawcett, president, Southwest Texas Council, Boy Scouts of America. That area—Dimmit, Edwards, Kinney, Maverick, Real, Uvalde, Val Verde, and Zavala counties—merged in 1943 with the Concho Valley Council. Main hall is named for 1930 camping chairman, V. A. Brown. (1967)

ROCKSPRINGS (Edwards Co.)

SH 55, NW 9½ mi.

Mackenzie Trail
(Merged at this point into SH 55)

When the U.S. Army built Forts Clark (70 mi. SW) and McKavett (90 mi. NE) this frontier trail connected the posts. After Fort Concho was established in 1867, the trail was extended farther north, to present San Angelo. It was later named for Col. Ranald S. Mackenzie, the commander of Fort Clark, who traveled it in his campaigns against hostile Indians. One of its landmarks was Mackenzie Lake (6.5 mi. N) which furnished water for the troops, for cattle drives up the trail, for settlers and for Texas Rangers on frontier patrols. (1977)

ROCKSPRINGS (Edwards Co.)

US 377 at Paint Rock Springs,
21 mi. NE of Rocksprings

Stopping Place on
Ft. Clark–Ft. McKavett
Military Road

One of many roads connecting U.S. Cavalry's frontier posts. This route led south to Ft. Clark and north to Ft. McKavett, 1852–1883.

This spot, Paint Rock Springs, at head of South Llano River, was a natural midway rest stop, as it had abundant water.

Here, too, Maj. John B. Jones' Frontier Battalion assembled in 1877 to begin the famous outlaw roundup, to make this area safe for settlement by ranchers.

Besides its army uses, this road was open to immigrants, cattle drovers, pioneer ranchers, mail carriers, and freighters. (1967)

ROCKSPRINGS (Edwards Co.)

US 377, ¼ mi. NE at park

The Rock Spring

Known to early Texans as one-inch flow of water out of rocks.

Site of a camp for travelers and freighters. Occupants of land around the spring included W. J. Greer, with a sheep camp, 1882; Francis Winans, with a cattle and sheep ranch, 1884; A. O. Burr, farming, about 1885. Cattlemen, including Frank Gray, camped here during roundups. Outlaws in 1880s frequented a hut nearby.

Rocksprings post office opened 1891 in townsite platted for a new county seat at center of Edwards County. The rock spring still seeps, in city and county historic park and playground. (1972)

ROCKSPRINGS (Edwards Co.)   *SH 55 & US 377*
Site of Rocksprings' First
School Building
First school session in new town of Rocksprings was held in a frame house surrounded by a strong rock wall, in winter of 1891–1892. Teachers were a Mr. Cole and a Mr. Vaughn (whose strong voice served instead of a bell to call "books"). Pupils came from families of Abner Benton, a Mr. Buswell, John Campbell, Charlie Cooper, Julian Gill, West Hill, O. W. Holmes, George Maul, J. R. Sanford, Reuben Stewart, J. R. Sweeten, and Ira Wheat.

This school was succeeded by the Gem City Academy, which had 111 students in its second term.   (1972)

ROCKSPRINGS (Edwards Co.)   *SH 55 at US 377/SH 41, .6 mi. E*
Rocksprings Cemetery
The town of Rocksprings traces its beginnings to 1889, when J. R. Sweeten dug the first water well in the area to serve new settlers. Three years later, in 1892, Sweeten donated two acres of land to be used as a community cemetery.

There were some burials at this site prior to its formal designation as a cemetery. Two children, Willie J. Blackwell and Ben Smith, were interred here in 1891. Many of the people buried in the Rocksprings Cemetery in the early years were travelers passing through the area. Among the more than one thousand graves are those of victims of a devastating tornado which struck the town on April 12, 1927.

Over the years, additional land acquisitions have increased the size of the cemetery. Iron fencing which once surrounded some grave sites was donated to scrap metal drives during World War II.

The Rocksprings Cemetery Association, which originated in 1897, was formally chartered by the state in 1967. Through such projects as surveys and landscaping, the association continues to maintain the historic graveyard, which remains as a visible link to the community's past.   (1989)

ROCKSPRINGS (Edwards Co.)   *FM 674, 32 mi. SW*
Site of Ranch of the
Thurmans of Kickapoo
(The Eugene Mayes Ranch, 1920–1966)
First (1882) permanent settlers on west prong of Nueces River: Joe Thurman and sons Bill, Sam, and Jess. Neighbors by 1895: the Barksdale, Chapman, Cox, Ellis, Haley, Justice, Silman, and Tabor families. Brush arbor sheltered first school, with Perry Ellis as teacher; first church, with Virgil Silman and A. J. Cox, preachers.

For primitive ranch community, Joe Thurman acted as physician, dentist, and coffin maker. His family raised fine horses for chief local amusement, racing. In 1895 matched favorite against horse of John Nance Garner (later United States Vice-President).   (1972)

ROCKWALL (Rockwall Co.)   *SH 66, .8 mi. NE (moved to courthouse)*
Rockwall County
First settled in the 1840s, this region was a part of Kaufman County until 1873, when Rockwall County was created. With an area of 147 square miles, this is the smallest of Texas' 254 counties. The county and city of Rockwall were named for an underground formation of rock discovered in the early 1850s. Crossed by the Missouri, Kansas & Texas Railroad, Rockwall County is an area of fertile farmland. The location here of the aluminum industry and the creation of Lake Ray Hubbard from the east fork of the Trinity River diversified the local economy in recent years.   (1976)

ROCKWALL (Rockwall Co.)   *IH 30 and FM 740*
Central National Road
of the Republic of Texas
In an effort to improve overland transportation, the Republic of Texas Congress authorized the Central National Road in Feb. 1844. The roadway was to be 30 feet wide and cleared of stumps over 12 inches high. A survey team led by Major George W. Stell platted the route from near the mouth of Elm Fork on the Trinity River in present downtown Dallas, northeast to Kiomatia on the Red River. The highway linked a road leading south to Austin and San Antonio with a U.S. military highway extending north to St. Louis from Fort Towson in present Oklahoma.

Running east from Dallas, the Central National Road turned northeast to cross the area that is now Rockwall County. Portions of FM 740, known locally was Ridge Road, follow the historic route. The earliest Rockwall County pioneers settled near the road about 1846. Sterling R. Barnes located his homestead about two miles south of the present site of Rockwall, and John O. Heath settled near the crossing of the east fork of the Trinity River. The towns of Heath, originally named "Black Hill" and later "Willow Springs," and Rockwall, the county seat, were founded along the highway. (1977)

ROCKWALL (Rockwall Co.) *SH 66, 104 S. Goliad St.*
East Trinity Lodge No. 157, A.F. & A.M.
A dispensation for the formation of the lodge was granted July 26, 1854, when Rockwall was part of Kaufman County. The Grand Lodge of Texas designated James Wilson as the first Master. John O. Heath served as Senior Warden and S. R. Barnes as Junior Warden. Barnes and Heath were among the earliest residents of the area to receive land grants in 1848. The lodge charter was issued January 18, 1855. The E. C. Heath Masonic Lodge, located six miles south, merged with East Trinity in 1968. (1980)

ROCKWALL (Rockwall Co.) *SH 205, 10 mi. SE in McLendon-Chisholm Community*
Chisholm Cemetery
Enoch P. Chisholm, a circuit-riding Methodist minister, brought his family to this area in the 1860s. The community which grew up here was named in his honor. Chisholm donated land for this graveyard in 1871, and in 1875 he became the first person interred in it. A chapel, also named for Chisholm, was built that same year on the cemetery grounds. At its peak, the town of Chisholm boasted a school, post office, Masonic lodge, cotton gin, and stores. Many early pioneers were interred in the Chisholm cemetery, and some of their descendants still reside in the area. (1990)

ROMA (Starr Co.) *US 83, 1 mi. W*
The Mier Expedition
A body of Texans intent on invading Mexico camped here on December 21, 1842. After being made prisoners at Salado, Mexico, they drew beans, white for life in prison, black for death. 17 members of the expedition were shot by order of General Santa Anna, March 25, 1843.

ROMA (Starr Co.) *US 83, 3.5 mi. NW*
Mission Mier A Vista
In the vicinity of this site was Mission Mier A Vista.
Established in 1750 as a part of Jose de Escandon's project to settle the region and civilize and Christianize the Indians.

ROMERO (Hartley Co.) *US 54, 3.5 mi. NE at roadside park (at Punta de Agua Park)*
Chief of the Pastores
Casimiro Romero
(1833–1912)
Moved to Texas, 1876, from New Mexico—wife and two children in a coach, goods in 14 wagons. Owned 6,000 sheep. A Castilian Spaniard by birth, Romero spoke for Pastores (sheep herders), who built eleven haciendas and plazas in Canadian River area. Cattle Rancher Chas. Goodnight in late 1876 made a pact with Romero to respect right of the Pastores to valley of Canadian River. But railroads and cattle ranchers in 1800s cut into sheep lands. Romero returned to New Mexico, selling Texas lands, 1897. He is memorialized in this area by town of Romero (3.5 mi SW of here). (1970)

ROPESVILLE (Hockley Co.) *US 82, .5 mi. S*
Site of
Primrose School
(About .5 mi. SW)
First public school in Hockley County; named for a wild prairie flower. In 1902 homesteaders had begun farming here. By 1909 their children needed education, so the parents hauled lumber by wagon from Big Spring (about 100 mi. S), donated labor, and built a one-room schoolhouse.

Classes began Dec. 13, 1909, with pupils from the Ardis, Baker, Blankenship, Brown, Carter, Cowan, Dixon, Perritt, Rose, and Witherspoon families. The schoolhouse served as polling place, church, and public meeting hall until 1917, when Ropesville was established about a mile away, with better facilities. (1974)

ROSENBERG (Fort Bend Co.) *1117 First Street (SH 36)*
First Baptist Church of Rosenberg
In 1896, three Baptist men organized this church. T.E. Muse served as the first pastor from 1898 to 1900. The 1900 Galveston hurricane destroyed an unfinished church building. Services were held in a nearby church and in a rail car until a schoolhouse was purchased in 1901. In 1912, a brick sanctuary was built, with the first electric lights in town. Some baptism services were held in the Brazos River until the 1930s. New facilities were added over the years as the congregation grew. The church continues to serve the Rosenberg community. (1996)

ROTAN (Fisher Co.) *SH 92 at CR 251, 15.1 miles E*
Site of Hitson Community
Ranchers John and William Hittson were among the first to settle in this area in about 1870; the area around their homes became known as Hittson or Hitson. Fisher County was created in 1876, and settlement began to increase. A post office opened in 1885. A school began operation in 1888 and by 1896 Hitson had a general store operated by C. W. Morris as well as a Methodist church. The Hittson brothers were the major landowners in the area, but the community included a number of large farming families who cleared the fertile land and planted crops. Though the post office was moved to Swedonia in 1906, the community of Hitson continued to grow. Oil was discovered in the area after World War I, providing an additional means of income for the townspeople as well as the Hitson School for a time. In 1925 there were 32 families with 120 school-age children living in the area. By 1940 the town had a school, a church, three businesses and scattered dwellings. As was the case in many small towns across Texas and the U.S. during World War II, most of the town's young people enlisted in the armed forces or moved to cities to take part in the war effort. With their labor force thus depleted, Hitson farmers were unable to survive. Small family farms were sold to larger enterprises. Most of the new owners lived in nearby Hamlin or Rotan. Hitson School was consolidated with Hamlin schools in 1947; the white frame church building used by the Hitson Baptist Church was moved to Roby in 1959 and by the end of the 20th century all that remained of the community were a few homes and a cemetery. (2000)

ROUND MOUNTAIN (Blanco Co.) *⅒ mile E of US 281 on RR 962*
Elitha Smith Martin
(Jan. 30, 1830–Aug. 10, 1899)
Prominent local businesswoman; born in Patrick County, Virginia, she married John Martin (1826–69) on June 27, 1848. The couple came to Texas in 1856 with 4 children and settled in Llano County, where 5 more children were born. After John Martin's death, Mrs. Martin and the younger children moved here and built a 2-story hotel (100 yards east), a livery stable, and a general mercantile store. On December 4, 1879, Mrs. Martin was appointed postmaster and served in that position until May 16, 1896, keeping the post office in the store. She was buried beside her husband in Llano County. (1974)

ROUND ROCK (Williamson Co.) *North Mays St. (US 81) at US 79, in the city*
In Memory of the Pioneer Builders
Greenwood Masonic Institute, 1867–1881, one quarter mile west and Round Rock Institute, one half mile south, 1881–1891, under auspices Cumberland Presbyterian Church, 1881–1887 and the Southern Presbyterian Church 1887–1891, "Built for the people by the people" of Round Rock and vicinity. Erected by the State of Texas. (1936)

ROUND ROCK (Williamson Co.) *SH 29, 2½ mi. E*
½ mi. S to the Site of Kenney Fort
First settlement in Williamson County. Erected as a home by Dr. Thomas Kenney and Joseph Barnhart in the spring of 1839 & served as a place of defense during Indian raids and rendezvous of the Santa Fe Expedition, 1841. Here the archives of the Republic of Texas enroute to Washington-on-the-Brazos were captured on Dec. 31, 1842 and returned to Austin. (1936)

ROUND ROCK (Williamson Co.)

US 79, 2.5 mi. E

Palm Valley Lutheran Church

In area first claimed in 1838 by white men. Valley bears name of the Anna Palm family, 1853 Swedish settlers. "Brushy," the first Lutheran Church (of logs), was built here by Andrew John Nelson and 3 hired men in 1861. This also housed early school.

Congregation was formally organized Nov. 27, 1870. Second church, built 1872, was used for sessions of Palm Valley School.

Present gothic revival style building was erected in 1894. (1970)

ROUND ROCK (Williamson Co.)

1 mi. W of Business District on Chisholm St.

The Round Rock

A guide for Indians and early settlers, this table-shaped stone in the middle of Brushy Creek once marked an important low-water wagon crossing. Hundred-year-old wheel ruts are still visible in the creek bottom. The rocky stream bed also provided building stone for pioneer homes. "Brushy Creek" post office was established in 1851 to serve the settlement that grew up near this natural ford. At the urging of Postmaster Thomas C. Oatts, it was renamed "Round Rock" in 1854. This name was retained when the town relocated along the railroad (1 mi. E) in 1877. (1975)

ROUND ROCK (Williamson Co.)

W. Main St. at Round Rock Ave.

Sam Bass' Death Site

An uneducated Indiana orphan who drifted to Texas as a youth, Sam Bass won fame racing his swift "Denton Mare," gambling, and robbing trains. A rich haul in Nebraska was followed by months of reckless spending. Bass liked to shower gold on people who fed or harbored him while he eluded law officers. In July 1878 he came to Round Rock to rob a bank, and was shot by Texas Rangers. Gallant to the last, refusing to name guilty partners, he became a hero to 19th century balladeers. His celebrated grave is situated in Old Round Rock Cemetery. (1981)

ROUND ROCK (Williamson Co.)

RR 1431 near Brushy Creek, 6 mi. W

Wilson-Leonard Brushy Creek Burial Site

In this vicinity is a prehistoric archeological site discovered in 1973 by a team of Texas Highway Department archeologists. Scientific excavations have produced evidence that the site was a major camping ground for prehistoric peoples, particularly during the Archaic Period (2,000–8,000 years ago). More than 150 fireplaces, numerous projectile Plainview points, and several types of spear points have been uncovered. In 1982, archeologists discovered the skeleton of a human female, 10,000 to 13,000 years old, that became known as the "Leanderthal Lady." (1985)

ROUND ROCK (Williamson Co.)

US 79, 2.5 mi. E

The Double File Trail

As the Delaware Indians moved from their home in the "Redlands" of East Texas in 1828 to near present Nuevo Laredo, Mexico, they laid out this trace. It was named Double File Trail because two horsemen could ride side by side. The first settlement in Williamson County, Kenney Fort, was built here at the Brushy Creek crossing in 1838. It served as a way station and for Indian protection. In 1841, members of the Santa Fe Expedition assembled here. Texas Rangers, early Anglo-American settlers, surveying parties, and explorers also used this important route. (1979)

ROUND TOP (Fayette Co.)

SH 237 & FM 1437

Early Texas Hotels and Inns

Two miles east, at Winedale, is the old "Sam Lewis Stopping Place" of the 1850s—a typical early Texas inn, now a University of Texas research center.

Built 1834, as a settler's 2-room log cabin of hand-hewn cedar; then enlarged twice and (with work of local German craftsmen) improved in style, it was home after 1848 to Lewis, his wife, eight children; also entertained guests from passing stagecoaches. It was near roads connecting major Texas cities.

Many roadside homes in early Texas were inns. The horseback traveler would shelter his pony in the barn, share family meals, get a room for the night. All stage lines depended on such accommodations—for changes of horses, for passengers' meals, and for overnight stops. With travel difficult at best, such inns rendered a service of great public necessity.

A frontier inn might even by a dugout, where the guests rolled up in blankets and slept on the floor. (Travelers sometimes had to sleep under a tree, so any sort of sheltering house was usually welcomed.)

Most stage stops dispatched and received U.S. mail for the community. Towns originated at many stops.

ROUND TOP (Fayette Co.)　　　　　　　*FM 1457 at Wolf Rd., 2½ mi. E*
.5 mi. S to Site of
Nassau Plantation

An extensive tract of land purchased in 1843 for colonization by German emigrants. Named for Duke Adolf of Nassau, protector of the emigration society, it was once one of the show places of Texas.

Although the 4,428 acres could have been a good half way station for German colonists on the long journey to western lands, this use was rejected by Prince Carl of Solms-Braunfels, the commissioner-general of the "Adelsverein," or German emigration society. He feared that the site, which was close to non-German settlements, would cause his people to lose their distinctive national culture.

Though never colonized, Nassau became a welcome place for relaxation during trying periods of the emigration movement. Here the prince enjoyed horse-racing and held feasts costing thousands of dollars. His successor as commissioner, John O. Meusebach, came to Nassau for less extravagant entertainment.

The main dwelling on the plantation was built of oak, two stories high. Even in frontier days it had two glass windows. Cotton was grown on the lands.

In 1848 the bankrupt Adelsverein sold Nassau. It was later divided into small farms, cultivated by descendants of the original German pioneers.　　　　　　　　(1968)

RUNGE (Karnes Co.)　　　　　　　*FM Road 81, Town Square*
Runge, Texas

Early Texas town. Near site where old ox-cart road from San Antonio to Indianola crossed the Ojo de Agua (Spanish name meaning "Eye of Water" or Spring) Creek. Here pioneer travelers found essentials of water, wood, and grass. Numerous Indian artifacts found nearby indicate that Karankawas, Tonkawas, Apaches, and Comanches camped or hunted in vicinity.

First Anglo-American settlement here, in early 1850s, was named Sulphur Spring; in the late 1850s and 1860s the place was called Mineral Spring. In 1886 a group of Cuero merchants known as H. Runge and Company bought a large tract of land on which they platted the townsite of Runge. The San Antonio & Aransas Pass Railroad, called the "Sap," extended its line from Kenedy toward Houston and built a depot, a switch, and stockpens at Runge. The first post office was established here September 20, 1887.

By 1890 Runge had grown to be the largest town in Karnes County. The public schools were organized in 1891 and Runge citizens engaged in many typical pioneer social and civic activities, including weekly band concerts held in the town square.

The economy of the region has been sustained by farming, ranching, dairying, and petroleum production.　　　　　　　　(1965)

RUSK (Cherokee Co.)　　　　　　　*Courthouse Square*
Cherokee County

Cherokee County has a rich and varied history. Spanish and French explorers of the seventeenth century found Tejas and Hasinai Indians living in this area, and Spanish missions were established in the region.

Driven out of the United States, the Cherokee Indians migrated to this area about 1822, and were here at the time of early Anglo-American colonization in the 1820s and 1830s. Under the administration of Republic of Texas President Mirabeau B. Lamar, the Cherokees were expelled from the area in 1839.

Following formal creation of Cherokee County from Nacogdoches County in 1846, settlement of the area increased rapidly. Family farms and towns soon sprung up throughout the county. The building of roads and the advancement of railroads and river navigation contributed further to settlement.

The chief economic base of the county from its beginning, agriculture remained a vital force as industrialization and business interests developed. The establishment of schools and churches formed the basis for the area's social history.

Cherokee County has been the birthplace of two Texas governors, one governor of Wyoming, and one speaker of the Texas House of Representatives.   (Texas Sesquicentennial 1836–1986)

RUSK (Cherokee Co.) US 69 and Avenue A
Rusk Penitentiary Building

The abundance of iron ore for use in manufacturing prompted a commission appointed by Gov. Richard Coke in 1875 to select this region for a state penitentiary. In 1877, this 19,000-acre tract was purchased from T. Y. T. Jamison and his wife. Contractors Kanmacher and Denig of Columbus, Ohio, built this structure the following year. The walls are of two-and-a-half foot thick sandstone. The administrative offices, a hospital, chapel, dining area, and cells were housed here.

The prisoners helped construct the Texas State Railroad from Rusk to Palestine. They built the "Old Alcalde" iron ore smelting furnace adjacent to this structure. The furnace produced iron products for construction throughout the United States and for use in the erection of many state buildings. Convict labor was used in the area at contract prices.

In 1917, the Texas Legislature changed the facility to a state hospital for the mentally ill.The building was renovated and ready for occupancy by 1919 and operated under the name of Rusk State Hospital.

The Department of Mental Health and Mental Retardation was designated as the governing body in 1963. This structure became the administrative center for the hospital.   (1979)

RUSK (Cherokee Co.) Rusk Terminus of Texas State Railroad, 2.5 mi. W
Texas State Railroad

In the late 1880s, the Texas prison system built a short rail line from the state penitentiary facility in North Rusk southwestward to hardwood timber stands, where charcoal was made for use in firing the prison's iron ore smelting furnaces. The line served as the foundation of the Texas State Railroad, which was organized in 1894 in an effort to make the prison more self-sufficient by providing new markets for prison products. Two Texas governors, James Stephen Hogg and Thomas M. Campbell, both natives of Cherokee County, were instrumental in the railroad's development.

Built by prisoners and supervised by the state prison system, the line was completed in 1909 to Palestine (30 mi. W), where it connected with existing routes. Setbacks, including the closing of the furnaces and the prison unit, limited the railroad's success; however, under a board of managers appointed by the legislature, the line was later leased to the Texas & New Orleans Railroad and the Texas & Southeastern Railroad. In 1972, control was transferred to the Texas Parks and Wildlife Commission for development as a state park. It now symbolizes the significant role the railroad industry played in Texas history.   (1982)

RUSK (Cherokee Co.) US 84, 1 mi. NE
Mountain Home

Birthplace of James Stephen Hogg, son of Lucanda McMath Hogg and Joseph Lewis Hogg. Born March 24, 1851. Died March 3, 1906. First native Texan to serve as governor.

Inspirer of the passage of the Railroad Commission Law, Stock and Bond Law, Alien Land Law.   (1964)

RUSK (Cherokee Co.) US 84, city limits
Site of Confederate Gun Factory

Built in 1862 by John L. Whitesarver, William H. Campbell and Benjamin F. Campbell. When unable to secure materials and tools for the manufacture of rifles, Colt-model pistols were made. A number of Negroes were employed.

RUSK (Cherokee Co.) US 84, 0.25 mi. W of courthouse on W. 6th St.
Site of Rusk Public School No. 2 For African Americans

By 1884, the Rusk Public School District maintained two schools: No. 1 for its Anglo students and No. 2 for its African American students. A yearly average of 50 students met in a small house built here about 1895 to house Rusk Public School No. 2. In 1939, the Rusk Independent School District erected a new school building southeast of downtown Rusk for its African American stu-

dents. Named after long-term principal G. W. Bradford, the facility was used until Rusk integrated its schools in the 1960s. Many graduates of this school became highly respected professionals.
(1993)

RUSK (Cherokee Co.)   *207 E. Sixth St. (US 84)*
Bachelor Girl's Library Club
Formed by 15 young single women in 1902 with fewer than 50 books, this library club would later donate to the City of Rusk a volume of books that greatly contributed to an inventory in excess of 23,000 books. The book club, originally housed in downtown Rusk at the Acme Hotel, is believed to be the first public library established in Cherokee County. In 1904 the club changed its name to "The Maids and Matrons Library Club" and rescinded its rule prohibiting married members in order that several of its original founders who had since married could continue in the organization. The name of the club was changed once more in 1916 to the "Library Study Club." In 1936 the members formed a club for younger women called "The Thalian Study Club." The size of the library's holdings continued to grow so that by 1966 the club had for some years required the services of a paid librarian. That year the club donated all of its books and furnishings to the City of Rusk. In 1969 they became part of the permanent collection at the newly constructed Singletary Memorial Library building. The Library Study Club and its offspring the Thalian Club continued to support the Rusk Community Library.   (1993)

RUSK (Cherokee Co.)   *US 69, 3 mi. S*
Site of Tassie Belle and Star and Crescent Iron Ore Furnaces
New Birmingham was a boomtown nearby in the late 1800s built around local iron ore operations. The furnaces, capable of producing 50 tons of iron daily, were named "Tassie Belle," after the wife of town founder A. B. Blevins, and the "Star and Crescent." About 275 work men were required to keep furnaces in continual operation. The town grew to over 3,000 people with a business district of 15 blocks including 32 mercantile houses, an ice plant, the spacious southern hotel, bottling works, and an early electric power plant. The 1893 panic bankrupted the industries and killed the town.   (1996)

SABINAL (Uvalde Co.)   *US 90*
Sabinal Methodist Church
This church began in 1876 as part of the Sabinal circuit assigned to the Rev. Henry T. Hill. Circuit ministers served the fellowship until 1900, when it became an organized congregation. Services were held in the Christian and Baptist Church buildings, until the present structure was completed in 1907. For a time pastors at Sabinal Methodist Church also served new rural congregations in Trio and Knippa. As the membership grew and church programs expanded to meet the needs of the community, additions were made to the church facility.   (1983)

SABINAL (Uvalde Co.)   *US 90, 1 mi. W on west side of Sabinal River*
Site of Camp Sabinal
Established July 12, 1856 by Captain Albert G. Brackett, Second U.S. Cavalry, as a protection to the San Antonio-El Paso road and frontier settlers. Occupied by Federal troops until November 1856. Later served as a Ranger camp.

SABINAL (Uvalde Co.)   *US 90, 3 mi. E*
Habermacher Home
A Medallion Home
The house was used as a stage coach stop and Indian fortress before stage stop or town of Sabinal was built. Many early pioneers of Texas were guests and visitors to this home.

SABINAL (Uvalde Co.)   *Old US 90 at SH 127/187, ½ mi. E*
John M. Davenport
(February 8, 1827–October 28, 1859)
Stock-raiser and captain of a company of volunteer Indian fighters. Killed near here by 30 Comanches. Inquest for him was first in area for Indian victim.

Settlers and soldiers from Fort Inge trailed the band 200 miles. After battle, found Davenport's gun on one of the Indians.   (1969)

SABINAL (Uvalde Co.) *US 90, west*
Sabinal
Named by Spanish for Rio Sabina and cypress trees along river.

Town founded in 1854 by Thomas B. Hammer, who operated a stage stop and was first postmaster.

Despite Indian depredations, town thrived as settlers built homes, and a railroad reached here in 1881.

In 1906, town was incorporated, telephone service started, city waterworks and volunteer fire department organized.

In 1907, Sabinal Christian College was founded. Closed in 1917.

Cotton industry was foremost in early 1900s. Today, farming and ranching flourish in community. (1967)

SABINE PASS (Jefferson Co.) *SH 87, 6.5 mi. W at roadside park*
Near Site of Confederate
Fort Manhassett
Coastal fortification installed to protect Texas against Federal invasion during the Civil War. Gen. John Bankhead Magruder ordered the construction of a fort at this site on Sept. 4, 1863—four days before the famous Confederate victory won by Dick Dowling and his 40-odd men against 22 ships and gunboats at Sabine Pass (7 mi. NE). After the Federal retreat, the Confederate coastal defense program continued, since Federal blockading vessels still patrolled these waters and other invasions might be planned. A storm on Sept. 19 sent the patrol steamers out to sea, but drove ashore their coaling ship, the *Mannahasset*. Confederate Commodore Leon Smith dismantled the ship, taking charge of her cargo. Apparently the builders adapted name of the prize as title for the fort.

Col. Valery Sulakowski, formerly of the Austrian Army, designed this fort. In charge of construction was Maj. Getulius Kellersberger, Swiss-born engineer who had settled in America some years earlier.

By Oct. 1863, five companies (comprising 500 men) garrisoned the five redoubts of the new fort and manned its 10 cannons. One action for men of Fort Manhassett was participation in capture of two Union ironclad ships at Calcasieu Pass, La., May 6, 1864. (1971)

SABINE PASS (Jefferson Co.) *SH 87 W*
Sabine Pass
Established in 1837 as Republic of Texas port of entry and customs office. In the Civil War had defenses of one cavalry, one artillery and three infantry companies. Guarded shipping against the Federal blockade, admitting to port vital factory goods, guns, gunpowder, medicines. Guarded access to upriver ports that loaded out cotton, received guns. Stood sentry over coastal troop movements by rail, wagon or horseback from Texas to eastern battles.

Was swept in 1862 by yellow fever brought in by ships from Havana. Ailing men had to spike their guns. Lost Sabine City to the Federals, who burned Taylor's Bayou railroad bridge and planned to make coastal plantations their commissary.

Recaptured in Jan. 1863 by Confederates, the pass made military history Sept. 8, 1863, when fewer than 50 men under Lt. Dick Dowling defeated large Federal fleet bringing in 5,000 troops to conquer Texas and cut her off from remainder of the Confederacy.

Battlefield park and monument open to public.

Now a commercial fishing and marine repair center. Entrance from the Gulf of Mexico of Sabine-Neches Waterway. Important because of the petrochemical and oil industry along the shores. (1969)

SABINE PASS (Jefferson Co.) *1 mi. SE, Sabine Pass Historical Park*
United States Forces
at the Battle of Sabine Pass
Federal forces in the Civil War failed in most of their early efforts to capture Texas. In the fall of 1863, after taking New Orleans and Vicksburg, their leaders attacked western Louisiana in a renewed effort. They wished to divert valuable stocks of cotton from Confederate to Federal uses, and to cut off French troops who might come from Mexico to aid the Confederacy. General

N. P. Banks, U.S.A., ordered 5,000 troops to go by sea, capture Sabine Pass, and establish a land base near the river. He wanted these men to rendezvous later with troops he was leading overland to the Red River for a sweep into Texas.

Federal ships carrying men and materiel converged beyond the sandbars, and on Sept. 8, 1863, began to run north through Sabine Pass. They saw a Confederate installation, Fort Griffin, sitting above the pass, but got no response when they fired upon it while advancing. When they came within 1200 yards of the fort, however, fire was returned, crippling the gunboats *Clifton* and *Sachem*. After the battle, at least 56 men were dead or missing. Both gunboats surrendered and the rest of the fleet retreated. (1980)

SABINE PASS (Jefferson Co.) *Dick Dowling Park*
Site of Fort Griffin
(1863–1865)

Renowned for brilliant Civil War victory, Sept. 8, 1863. Confederates in this fort repulsed a fleet seeking to land thousands of Federal soldiers.

Lt. Richard W. Dowling (1838–1867), in civilian life a Houston businessman, commanded the fort during the enemy assault. His men, mostly Irishmen from Galveston and Houston, had been comrades in arms since Feb. 1861.

Sabine Pass, where Dowling's men (Co. F, Texas Heavy Artillery) were assigned in 1863, was a center for blockade-running, whereby Confederacy exported cotton and obtained in exchange vital goods such as medicines and arms. Here Co. F built Fort Griffin, named in honor of Lt. Col. W. H. Griffin, Confederate commander at Sabine City, and designated by Col. Valery Sulakowski, formerly of the Austrian Army.

Fort Griffin was an earthwork strengthened with railroad iron and ship's timbers. It was unfinished when Confederates learned of the approach of 22 ships.

Dowling kept watch, but ordered no response to the early shelling by the Federals. When first ships entered range of Fort Griffin's guns, however, the battle began. Dowling himself served as one of the gunners. The fort sent 137 shells toward the targets. Dowling monument (near here) tells of the victory. (1969)

SADLER (Grayson Co.) *SH 901*
Sadler United
Methodist Church

First called Quillin's Chapel, this church was organized in Sept. 1876 in a schoolhouse just west of Sadler Cemetery. The Rev. William M. Robbins (1836–1898), then serving the Dexter Circuit, was the founding pastor. J. P. Collier, E. J. Craven, William Jones, James Mitchell, and W. S. Robinson were the original trustees. Renamed Salem Methodist Church in 1880, the congregation became Sadler Methodist when it moved to this site in 1895. Local contractor Joe Cariker erected the present church building in 1910. (1977)

SAINT JO (Montague Co.) *FM 677, at City Park*
Town of Saint Jo

One of oldest towns in Montague County. Founded in 1850s, during great California gold rush, by E. S. and Ithane Singletary (brothers) and John Hughes, who hoped to find gold here. The community they started became known as "Head of Elm" for its location at headwaters of Elm Fork of Trinity River. In 1858, Head of Elm ran—and lost—the race for county seat. A post office opened here (at site of marker) in 1859, with John Womble, another pioneer, as postmaster. An early store and saloon were owned by Dominick Burns.

The next spurt of growth for the town came with the Chisholm Cattle Trail about 1868. In 1871, village had a post office, blacksmith shop, and five stores. In 1872, I. H. Boggess (owner of the famous Stonewall Saloon) and Joe Howell bought 640 acres of land and laid out townsite, which Boggess named "Joe," for Howell. One story says he decided to add "Saint" because Joe was a staunch non-drinker; another version claims he added it to make the name longer.

In 1874, citizens built an all-faiths church, and in 1876, a newspaper was established. Saint Jo was organized as a town in 1880; incorporated in 1886. Population has remained about 1,000 since that time, and economy is still based on farming and ranching. (1972)

SALADO (Bell Co.)   *US 81, .8 mi. SW*
Site of Salado College
(Across from Stagecoach Inn)
Founded 1856 with a gift by Col. C. S. Robertson of 100 acres of land. The Athens of Texas from 1858 to 1884. This marker rests on ground where the college building stood.

SALADO (Bell Co.)   *¼ mi. SW of Salado Post Office*
Birthplace of White House Aide
Mary Elizabeth Carpenter
Great-granddaughter of builders. Daughter of Thomas S. and Mary Elizabeth (Robertson) Sutherland.

First woman vice president of student body, University of Texas. Married Leslie Carpenter; has 2 children. In 1954 was president Women's National Press Club.

First woman ever to serve as executive assistant to the vice president of the United States, 1961. First newswoman to be staff director and press secretary to a First Lady, Mrs. Lyndon B. Johnson. Outstanding Women of Texas series, 1967. Awarded Medallion Plate.

SALADO (Bell Co.)   *US 81*
Twelve Oaks, 1867–1869
Greek revival mansion built of stone from adjacent land, for B. D. McKie, Texas doctor who fought and was wounded in Mexican and Civil wars.

Restoration by parents of Lt. Henry Clay de Grummond, Jr., World War II combat hero, is dedicated to his memory. Awarded Medallion Plate.

SALADO (Bell Co.)   *US 81, across from the Stagecoach Inn*
Site of
Thomas Arnold High School
Dr. Samuel J. Jones (1857–1918) and his wife, Charlotte Hallaran Jones (d. 1904), established Thomas Arnold High School on this site in 1890. The school, which was actually a private academy, occupied the stone buildings vacated by Salado College, where Dr. Jones taught. Named for Thomas Arnold (1795–1842), noted headmaster of Rugby School in England, the academy provided quality education during a time when there were few public high schools. After it closed in 1913, the facilities were again operated as Salado College until 1918, and as a public school until 1924, when the buildings burned.   (1975)

SALADO (Bell Co.)   *US 81, Main Street*
Stagecoach Inn
Constructed during the 1860s, the Stagecoach Inn was known as Salado Hotel and as Shady Villa before the current name was adopted in 1943. Military figures George Armstrong Custer and Robert E. Lee, and cattle baron Shanghai Pierce are among those thought to have stayed here. A good example of frontier vernacular architecture, the Stagecoach Inn features a two-story galleried porch with a second-story balustrade.   (1962)

SALADO (Bell Co.)   *Stagecoach Rd. and IH 35*
Salado Church of Christ
Founded in March 1859, this congregation first met in a brush arbor on the north bank of Salado Creek. The first two elders were James Anderson and J. W. Vickrey, both of whom were instrumental in the organization of Salado College. A frame sanctuary, erected on North Main Street in 1875, was destroyed by fire in 1908. A second frame structure served the congregation until 1961, when it was replaced by a brick sanctuary. A new building was erected in 1988. This church has served the people of Salado for over a century.   (1988)

SALT FLAT (Hudspeth Co.)   *US 62, 1 mi. E*
Site of El Paso Salt War
Resentment over private control of the Salt Lakes in this region, often called Guadalupe Lakes, in 1877 led to the El Paso Salt War which entailed the loss of many lives and much property.

SALT FLAT (Hudspeth Co.)   *US 62/180, 4.5 mi. E of Salt Flats*
Crow Springs
(15 mi. N)
Named for birds habitually there in abundance, Crow Springs was an oasis for Indians for centuries. The Butterfield Overland Mail in 1858 built a stage relay station at the springs, but used it less than a year before shifting the route south, to go by Fort Davis.

During the Apache Wars of the early 1880s, Texas Rangers and the U.S. 10th Cavalry camped at Crow Springs occasionally, to prevent Indians in New Mexico from joining the war leaders, Victorio and Nana, in Mexico.

Today the springs are dry, the station has fallen to dust, and the crows have disappeared.   (1974)

SAN ANGELO (Tom Green Co.)   *US 87, 4 mi. SE*
Tom Green County
A part of the Miller and Fisher grant, 1842. Created a county March 13, 1874. Organized January 5, 1875.

Named in honor General Thomas Green, 1814–1864. A veteran of San Jacinto, member of the Somerall expedition. A Confederate officer. First mail routes to the Pacific converged here in 1858. County seat, Ben Ficklin, 1875. San Angelo since 1882.

SAN ANGELO (Tom Green Co.)   *US 277, 4 mi. S*
Site of Ben Ficklin
An early stage stand named in honor of Major Ben Ficklin, noted frontiersman, mail and stage contractor, who assisted in establishing the Pony Express. He carried the first message from the Governor of California to the Governor of Missouri. First county seat of Tom Green County, 1875–1882. Destroyed by flood, August 24, 1882.

Major Ben Ficklin, C.S.A.
(1827–1871)
Called mystery man of the Confederacy. Educated at Virginia Military Institute. At age 18 served as a corporal in Mexican War. In 1850s worked with stagecoach and mail lines from Missouri to San Francisco. Helped to start the Pony Express line in 1860. Promoted idea of the railroad that later was the Union Pacific—the first to span the U.S.

Was a soldier and state quartermaster in Virginia at start of Civil War. Appointed Confederate purchasing agent, his swagger and success in Europe excited Federal envy. Personally ran blockade and passed through New York and Washington on secret missions.

In 1867 was awarded U.S. contract for weekly mail run from Fort Smith, Ark., to San Antonio and El Paso. Had his operational headquarters 3 miles below Fort Concho. Owned 640 acres of land here. Built corrals, blacksmith shop, storage rooms, adobe house, kitchen and commissary. On a visit to Washington, died of swallowing fish bone. Was buried in Charlottesville, Va. Associates carried on the mail stage runs, later named town near Fort Concho for the late major.

"Ben Ficklin" was first county seat of Tom Green, serving until was destroyed by flood in 1882.   (1964)

SAN ANGELO (Tom Green Co.)   *US 87, 8 mi. NW*
The Butterfield or California Trail
Established 1849; crossed at this point. Marked by the Pocahontas Chapter DAR, 1928.

SAN ANGELO (Tom Green Co.)   *FM 584, 6 mi. SW, 100 yds.*
from Lake Nasworthy Bridge
John R. ("Sarge") Nasworthy
(September 12, 1849–November 4, 1924)
Colorful pioneer and Texas Ranger who helped to create civilization and institutions of West Texas. Owned ranch land on which today is situated Lake Nasworthy—first conservation lake in this area.

Born in Georgia. Served 1864–1865 in Confederate Army, during Civil War. Later came to Texas, living first at Bonham. After he moved west, he operated in Menard area as a buyer of beef cattle for United States Army mess halls at Fort Concho. In 1880s he was deputy county clerk and deputy sheriff of Tom Green County and the first treasurer of the City of San Angelo. He owned the first local brick kiln, a wagon yard, a livery stable, and the only hearse in town in the early days. He was second man to fence land, second man to grow cotton in the county. A county commissioner, 1910–1916, he promoted building of the old Chadbourne viaduct. A leader in church and philanthropic endeavors, he was a promoter of the Baptist Encampment at Christoval (then one of the largest religious gatherings in the South).

He married Dena Von Fisher. The family had homes on Beauregard Street, Knickerbocker Road, Ben Ficklin Road and at Nasworthy Lake site. His six children carry on family tradition of community leadership. (1970)

SAN ANGELO (Tom Green Co.) — *Irving and Beauregard Sts., Courthouse Lawn*
Original Tom Green County

On Transcontinental Trail of California Gold Rush. Until 1846 a part of Bexar Land District, Republic of Texas. Private tracts were surveyed as early as 1847. German emigration company colony (90 mi. SE) had grants here, but in 1840s found Indians blocking settlement. Butterfield Overland Mail managers lived at stands in area, 1858–1861. R. F. Tankersley family established a permanent home in 1864 in future Tom Green County. By 1874 there were five settlements here, including Bismarck Farm, colony of 15 German immigrants. The county (12,756 sq. mi., 10½ times as large as state of Rhode Island) was created in 1874 and named for heroic Gen. Green (1814–1864), a state official and gallant Texas soldier.

After a decade of progress, the original Tom Green County began losing outlying areas. Midland County—halfway between Fort Worth and El Paso on newly opened Texas & Pacific Railway—was created in 1885. Settlers remote from San Angelo petitioned for new counties in 1887, and the Texas Legislature created Crane, Loving, Upton, Ward and Winkler. Coke and Irion counties were cut out of Tom Green in 1889. Ector and Sterling were created in 1891. Last divisions—Glasscock (1893) and Reagan (1903)—gave Tom Green its present size. It remains influential in the region. (1972)

SAN ANGELO (Tom Green Co.) — *18 E. Avenue A*
Municipal Swimming Pool

In September 1936, a devastating flood swept down the South Concho River, inundating much of the city of San Angelo. Among the many properties lost or severely damaged were the city's parks and its public swimming pool.

Plans were made to rebuild the parks and construct a new municipal swimming pool, but a bond election held in 1937 to finance the project was defeated by the voters. Once it was determined that the federal government would assist with Works Progress Administration funds and labor for the project, a new bond election was held and passed by sixty-six votes.

Work on the project began in March 1938 and was completed in October. Opening ceremonies were held on April 29, 1939. During its first two days of operation, the pool hosted 795 swimmers.

Designed by John G. Becker, the Pueblo Revival complex features a two-story hexagonal stone structure flanked by one-story wings. Exposed vigas are symmetrically placed on the upper portion of the wings. The complex reflects the 1930s construction and planning activity of the Federal Works Progress Administration. (1989)

SAN ANGELO (Tom Green Co.) — *US 87, 3 mi. NW*
Sheep and Goat Industry in Texas

Spanish explorers introduced sheep to the Southwest in the 1500s, and Spanish missions depended on the animals for food and clothing. The first Angora goats, known for the beauty and strength of their mohair, were brought to Texas in 1853 by Col. W. W. Haupt. Pioneer of modern sheep ranching in Texas from 1857 to 1867 was George Wilkins Kendall, who encouraged others with glowing reports of the industry's future while improving his own flocks. Kendall was one of the first to crossbreed the coarse-wooled Mexican Churro sheep with the fine-wooled Merino variety brought by European settlers.

The land, climate, and vegetation of the Edwards Plateau area especially suited the raising of sheep and goats. After 1870, with new markets and abundant land, the industry boomed. Ranchers fought disease, predators, deadly plants, and drouths to build their flocks. Today Texas is the leading producer of sheep and goats in the nation, and San Angelo is the major market center for these animals and their wool. Research facilities such as the San Angelo Research and Extension Center, built in 1969 through the efforts of Gen. Earl Rudder, then president of the Texas A. & M. System, work for the industry's continued prosperity. (1974)

SAN ANGELO (Tom Green Co.)
*Oakes St. and Ave. D,
in front of Fort Concho Museum*
Fort Concho
The center of a line of forts extending from the northeastern border of Texas to El Paso. Was also northern point of southern chain of forts extending to Rio Grande, thence along that river to its mouth. Established 1867 (at then junction of Butterfield Trail, Goodnight Trail and road to San Antonio) by 4th Cavalry under Capt. George G. Huntt to protect frontier.

By March 1, 1870, fort buildings were (in order of their construction) a commissary and quartermaster storehouse, hospital, five officers' quarters, a magazine and two barracks—all built of sandstone.

Among those who commanded the post were: Gen. Wm. R. Shafter (later Major General of Volunteers, Spanish-American War and commanded troops at capture of Santiago de Cuba, July 1898); Maj. John P. Hatch (at one time fort was named in his honor); Gen. Wesley Merritt (first commander of Fort Davis after Civil War; was later superintendent of U.S. Military Academy at West Point); Gen. Ranald Slidell Mackenzie (who led attacks from this and other forts, credited with defeat of Indian resistance in Southwest); and Gen. Benjamin H. Grierson, commander of Negro troops of 10th Cavalry.

On June 20, 1889, fort was abandoned as a military post and property passed into private ownership. (1970)

SAN ANGELO (Tom Green Co.)
*Oakes St. and Ave. D,
Fort Concho Nat'l Historic Site*
The Tenth Cavalry
Following the Civil War, the United States Congress authorized the creation of six regiments of Black U.S. army troops. The Tenth Cavalry was organized in 1867 under the leadership of Col. Benjamin Grierson (1826–1911). The order creating black troops also specified that they would be commanded by white officers. Facing problems of racial discrimination at the regiment's headquarters in Fort Leavenworth, Kansas, Grierson wanted the Tenth Cavalry reassigned to the West, and they arrived at Fort Concho in the spring of 1875.

The contributions of the men of the Tenth Cavalry to the settlement of the American West are of major importance. They took part in grueling scouting and mapping expeditions and campaigns against hostile Indians, often facing days without proper supplies or water on the High Plains. They were instrumental in the defeat of the Mescalero Apache Indians led by Chief Victorio in 1880.

The men of the Tenth Cavalry were stationed at Fort Concho until 1882, when they were moved to Fort Davis. Transferred frequently after 1885, members of the unit eventually served throughout the world, including Cuba, North Africa, Germany, Korea, and Vietnam. (1987)

SAN ANTONIO (Bexar Co.)
Intersection W. W. White, Hildebrand, & Cacias Sts.
In this Vicinity the Battle of Rosalis
Was fought on March 28, 1813. Here the "Republican Army of the North" composed of Anglo-Americans, Mexicans and Indians defeated, with heavy loss of life, Spanish Royalist troops commanded by Manuel de Salcedo, governor of Texas. The prisoners of war were brutally murdered shortly afterwards by order of Colonel Bernardo Gutierrez.

SAN ANTONIO (Bexar Co.)
FM 1937 at Losoya, 14 mi. S off US 281 S
The Battle of The Medina
Was fought here on August 18, 1813 by an army of Spanish Royalists commanded by General Jose Joaquin Arredondo which defeated with terrific slaughter the Republican Army of the North composed of Anglo-Americans, Mexicans and Indians commanded by Jose Alvarez de Toledo. Thus ended an attempt to free Texas and Mexico from Spanish rule.

SAN ANTONIO (Bexar Co.)
Holbrook Rd., 1 blk. off Ritterman Rd., 6 mi. N
The Battle of the Salado
Decisive in Texas history, was fought here, September 18, 1842. Col. Mathew Caldwell and Capt. John C. Hays, commanding a force of Texas volunteers, opposed the Mexican Army under General Adrian Woll that had captured San Antonio, and, with the loss of only one man, checked

the last Mexican invasion of Texas and thereby prevented the capture of Austin, capital of the Republic of Texas.

SAN ANTONIO (Bexar Co.) *US 87, 3 mi. E*
Site of the Camp of Stephen F. Austin
October 20–26, 1835
While assembling troops preparatory to the attack on the Mexican garrison at San Antonio. After his appointment on November 12 as Commissioner to the United States, the Texans, under Colonels Ben Milam and Frank W. Johnson stormed and captured San Antonio, December 10, 1835.

SAN ANTONIO (Bexar Co.) *US 90 W, on E bank of San Lucas Creek*
"Battle" of Adams Hill
In San Antonio on Feb. 16, 1861, Federal armies in Confederate Texas were surrendered by Gen. David E. Twiggs. The soldiers were marched to the coast and sent north as soon as ships could be procured. In April, after war began, all Federals still in Texas were made prisoners of war. There was, however, one Federal unit still armed and not in Confederate custody. Marching southward from Forts Bliss, Davis and Quitman in far West Texas were 320 men of the Federal 8th Infantry, under Col. I. V. D. Reeves.

On May 9, here near San Lucas Creek, Col. Earl Van Dorn, Confederate Commander of Texas, drew up more than 1000 of his men and a 4-gun battery to meet Reeves. The Federals were on Adams Hill, half a mile in front, also drawn up for battle.

Van Dorn sent across the half-mile a demand for surrender. This was refused. A second flag of truce with the same demand was also refused. Van Dorn had his way, with his third request: that the Federal commander come over, see the Confederate strength and surrender without useless bloodshed. The move brought an end soon to the Battle of Adams Hill without the firing of a shot. Reeves' men were made prisoners of war, interned, and later exchanged. (1965)

SAN ANTONIO (Bexar Co.) *Acme at Castroville Road*
Chihuahua Trail
This is route of an old Indian road, often path for Apache and Comanche depredations in Texas. Passed Castroville, Uvalde, Horse-Head Crossing on the Pecos; went through Presidio into northern Mexico. In some stretches, water holes were 40 miles apart. Men chewed boots to slake thirst. At smell of water, oxen ran.

Texas' commercial use began in 1835. Leather, silver, other metals came here over the road in big-wheel Mexican carts. On south to seaports went some of the goods. In the Civil War, the route brought rope, hats, shoes, salt and other goods to Texas. (1965)

SAN ANTONIO (Bexar Co.) *Intersection of Ashley, Roosevelt &*
S Flores St. & US 82
Surrender of Federal Forces by
General David E. Twiggs
Brought about as Texas moved to expel 2600 Federal troops—a step necessary after secession. Frontier fighter Ben McCulloch with 400 volunteers forced surrender negotiated at headquarters of Gen. Twiggs a block and a half from here, by 4 representatives of the Texas Committee on Public Safety.

Talks began Feb. 8, 1861; were stalled by Feb. 15. That night 90 of McCulloch's men stole in, fixed guns on Federal sentries and garrison in Alamo Plaza. 300 more Texas troops entered the city. The 160 men of Twiggs' force were disarmed and held in quarters. On Feb. 16, Gen. Twiggs agreed to evacuate his troops with arms and personal gear. Further pressure was used and on Feb. 18 he surrendered over $3,000,000 worth of Federal property: ordnance, wagons, mules, horses, supplies, money and a chain of forts.

Gen. Twiggs, native of Georgia, career soldier, veteran of War of 1812 and Mexican War, was 70 and in poor health. He held sacred his oath as an officer. Since Dec. 27, 1860, he had written 4 times to his superior in Washington, General of the Army Winfield Scott, for orders to use in event Texas seceded. He had no reply. Nevertheless, surrender brought him dismissal for treachery—and personal heartbreak. (1965)

SAN ANTONIO (Bexar Co.)   *Alamo Plaza*
The Alamo
(Founding of the Mission and Origin of Name)
The San Antonio de Padua Mission was founded in San Antonio in 1716 by the Franciscan Father, Antonio Olivanes, and after merging with the San Francisco Solano Mission in 1718, it was officially founded as the San Antonio de Valero Mission. The present site was selected in 1724. It was named in honor of Saint Anthony de Padua and the Duke of Valero, a Spanish Viceroy. The cornerstone of this chapel was laid May 8, 1744. Founded for the purpose of Christianizing and educating the Indians, it later became a fortress and was the scene of many conflicts prior to the immortal siege of 1836. Its activity as a mission began to wane after 1765, and it was abandoned in 1793 and the mission archives were removed to San Fernando, the parish church. During Mexico's War for Independence from Spain, a company of Spanish soldiers from Alamo del Pamas Coahuila, Mexico, occupied the abandoned mission, using its buildings as barracks for a number of years. From this association probably originated the name, Alamo. According to some historians, the name "Alamo" was derived from a grove of cottonwood trees growing on the banks of the Acequia, "Alamo" being the Spanish word for cottonwood.

SAN ANTONIO (Bexar Co.)   *Alamo Plaza, in the Alamo*
The Defense of the Alamo
"Thermopylae had its messenger of defeat. The Alamo had none."
The Alamo in 1836 consisted of this church, the convent and a large rectangular area or plaza, an enclosure of about six acres surrounded by walls with barracks on the west side of the Plaza. On February 23, 1836 Colonel William Barret Travis entered the Alamo with an approximate force of two hundred men. The siege, commanded by General Santa Anna and an army of several thousand Mexican soldiers, lasted nearly two weeks. At dawn on Sunday, March 6, the final assault was made, and in less than an hour the defenders slain. Later the bodies were burned by order of General Santa Anna.

This victory in defeat was the means of uniting the colonists in a determined effort to resist further oppression and by armed force to secure permanent independence.

It was here that a gallant few, the bravest of the brave, threw themselves between the enemy and the settlements, determined never to surrender nor retreat. They redeemed their pledge to Texas with the forfeit of their lives. They fell the chosen sacrifice to Texas freedom.

SAN ANTONIO (Bexar Co.)   *Alamo Plaza*
Adina de Zavala (November 28, 1861–March 1, 1955)
As the granddaughter of Lorenzo de Zavala (1789–1836), first vice-president of the Republic of Texas, young Adina de Zavala was exposed to vivid accounts of Texas' revolutionary and republican past. She became a guiding force in the preservation of many of Texas' most revered historic structures and sites, including the Alamo, Mission San Francisco de los Tejas in east Texas, and San Antonio's Spanish Governor's Palace. The "De Zavala Daughters," a women's group formed by Miss Adina in 1889, erected Texas' first historical markers and helped preserve San Antonio's Spanish missions.

Her firm belief, later verified, was that remnants of Mission San Antonio de Valero, known in 1836 as the Alamo's long barracks, lay underneath the wooden exterior of buildings adjacent to the Alamo church. By 1893, as president of the De Zavala Chapter of the Daughters of Republic of Texas (DRT), Miss Adina had secured the adjacent property owner's commitment to give the chapter first purchase option. In 1907, upon hearing that the 2-story long barracks were about to be razed, Miss Adina barricaded herself inside the buildings for three days and nights in an effort that ultimately prevented their destruction.   (1994)

SAN ANTONIO (Bexar Co.)   *Alamo Plaza*
Alamo Low Barracks and Main Gateway
Mission San Antonio de Valero, established nearby in 1718, was relocated here in 1724; by 1762, the mission plaza was enclosed by thick stone and adobe walls. The 11 × 14-foot main gateway was located at this site along the south wall. In 1803, Spanish cavalry from San Carlos de Parras del Alamo, Mexico, occupied the secularized mission and built one-story (low) barracks inside the south wall on each side of the main gateway. The Alamo, as the complex came to be

known, was occupied in 1835 by Mexican soldiers led by Gen. Cos. They fortified the main gateway with artillery pieces and a defensive lunette, a semi-circular enclosure with deep trenches.

In December 1835, Texas patriots captured the Alamo, but by Feb. 23, 1836, were under siege by an armed force led by Gen. Santa Anna. Couriers departed the Alamo through the main gateway during the siege. On March 6, Mexican troops breached the main gateway and retook the Alamo. After the assault, some Mexican military observers and local residents stated that Col. James Bowie and others died in the low barracks. The low barracks and main gateway were leveled in 1871, melding Valero Plaza on the south with the Alamo's plaza to create an open space.

(1996)

SAN ANTONIO (Bexar Co.)   *204 Alamo Plaza, exterior wall of Menger Hotel*
Barbed Wire Demonstration

Once called "bobwire" by cowboys, barbed wire was a French invention first patented in the U.S. in 1867, but it did not gain favor with cattlemen until the late 1870s. Joseph Glidden of Dekalb, Illinois, received a patent for his barbed wire in 1874, and it was wire of his manufacture that was the first barbed wire fencing successfully demonstrated in Texas. In 1876, veteran salesman Pete McManus and his young partner, John Warne Gates, made their first demonstration of "the Glidden winner" barbed wire. Though speculation has placed this demonstration in San Antonio's bustling Military Plaza, it was here in the quiet "mudhole" of Alamo Plaza that McManus and Gates set up a barbed wire corral and then drove cattle into the pen. It is said that after the corral held the thundering animals under the astonished eyes of cowboys and cattlemen, the flamboyant Gates invited spectators into the Menger Hotel to place their orders. After the theatrical demonstration in Alamo Plaza, the market for barbed wire fencing suddenly exploded with large sales to Texas ranchers and others along the frontier. Pete McManus reportedly sold more barbed wire fencing than any salesman in the world. John W. "Bet-A-Million" Gates became the world's largest barbed wire manufacturer. He helped found the Texas Company (later Texaco) and developed the town of Port Arthur. Barbed wire fencing changed the landscape of the American West and with it the industries of ranching and agriculture. It made possible the introduction of cultivated cattle stock into the beef industry and opened up the fertile land to farmers and other homesteaders. Within 25 years nearly all the open range had become privately owned and was under fence.

(2000)

SAN ANTONIO (Bexar Co.)   *FM 1937, 6 mi. S to Mount Carmel Cemetery, Losoya*
Enrique Esparza
(September, 1824–December 20, 1917)

Son of Alamo Defender Gregorio Esparza, 11-year-old Enrique, his mother, two brothers, and sister were present at the siege by the Mexican Army (Feb. 23–Mar. 6, 1836).

Hidden in a pile of hay, the youth saw his father fall and witnessed the heroic death of James Bowie on his sick bed. He then watched the bodies of the Texans burn in two huge pyres.

Enrique Esparza's eye-witness story later became invaluable, for he was one of few survivors.

(1967)

SAN ANTONIO (Bexar Co.)   *S. Colorado, between Vera Cruz and Tampico at*
San Fernando Cemetery #1
Alejo de la Encarnación Pérez (March 23, 1835–October 10, 1918)

Alejo de la Encarnación Pérez, infant son of María Juana Navarro Pérez, was the youngest known survivor of the 1836 Battle of the Alamo. From 1861 to 1864 Alejo served in the Confederate Army. After the Civil War he served the city of San Antonio in a number of offices, including those of police officer and city marshall. Alejo's marriages, to María Antonia Rodríguez and Florencia Sappo Valdez, produced 11 children. At the time of his death he was the last known Alamo survivor.

(1998)

SAN ANTONIO (Bexar Co.)   *Mission Drive, near the aqueduct*
Mission San Francisco de la Espada
Dam, Ditch and Aqueduct

Since water was vital to the permanency of San Francisco de la Espada Mission, the Franciscan missionaries and their Indian followers built a dam, irrigation ditch, and aqueduct. The 270-foot dam, an engineering feat which "curved the wrong way," was built across the San Antonio River.

Lime salts in the water gradually cemented the dam's layers of brush, gravel, and rocks. Water transported by Espada ditch crossed Piedras Creek by way of the Espada Aqueduct. This, the only such structure in the United States, was built from 1740 to 1745.

The alluvial valley produced crops of maize, beans, melons, calabashes, and cotton; however, deterioration had set in at Espada before its secularization in 1794. Even so, the dam, ditch, and aqueduct survived a century of Indian attacks, ravaging floods, and controversy before the Espada Ditch Company repaired the dam in 1895.

In 1941, to help insure the preservation of this singular colonial aqueduct, the San Antonio Conservation Society purchased the adjacent lands. Further assurance came in 1965, when the United States Department of Interior designated Espada Aqueduct as a registered national historic landmark. (1970)

SAN ANTONIO (Bexar Co.) *US 181, at the mission*
Mission San Juan Capistrano
Founded in March, 1731, by Franciscan missionaries on the banks of the San Antonio River; named for St. John of Capistrano, who in 1456 led a European religious crusade that saved the city of Belgrade from infidels. Mission San Juan was a successor to Mission San Jose de los Nazonis, established in 1716 in East Texas. It moved here due to the difficulty of defense. One of a complex of missions, San Juan was devoted to the cultural and religious conversion of the Coahuiltcan-speaking Indians of South Texas.

During the uncertain early years, buildings were constructed, crops planted, and the Indians had to be continually persuaded to stay long enough to reap the benefits of civilization. Apache raids, cholera and smallpox epidemics, and harassment by the civil authorities also plagued the missions constantly.

By 1762, however, San Juan had surplus harvests of corn, cotton, beans, chili peppers, watermelons, and cantaloupes. It also owned numerous cattle, sheep, goats, and horses. The 203 resident Indians lived in thatched huts; the chapel and convent were of stone.

The mission was secularized in 1794. In 1967, when the buildings were restored, many artifacts relating to the three centuries of occupancy were unearthed. (1968)

SAN ANTONIO (Bexar Co.) *Randolph Air Force Base*
Building 100
"The Taj Mahal"
In 1928 the San Antonio Airport Company purchased 2300 acres of land near the city and donated it to the United States Army Air Corps for development of a consolidated flight training facility. Called "The West Point of the Air," Randolph Field was dedicated June 20, 1930. One month later, construction was begun on an administration building, designated as Building 100. Because of the structure's exotic appearance, student flyers nicknamed it "The Taj Mahal" soon after its completion in October 1931.

With its height and location, the building dominated Randolph Field and the surrounding countryside. It was also a prominent feature in several motion pictures filmed here. To many Americans, "The Taj Mahal" came to symbolize military aviation at a time when air power was becoming vital to military strength.

Building 100 was designed by San Antonio Architect Atlee B. Ayres. Its unusual 170-foot tower conceals a 500,000-gallon water storage tank. A powerful beacon atop the tower can be seen by aircraft up to fifty miles away. The building also contains an 1100-seat movie theater. Its administrative offices now (1975) house the command section of the 12th Flying Training Wing of the United States Air Force. (1975)

SAN ANTONIO (Bexar Co.) *646 S Main*
Arsenal Magazine
At the urging of United States Secretary of War Jefferson Davis, land was secured at San Antonio in 1858 for an arsenal. In 1859, the state of Texas added 16 acres, and the arsenal became headquarters for the U.S. Army's Department of Texas.

Under construction when the Civil War (1861–1865) began, this magazine was included in Federal property surrendered in 1861. The building was completed for Confederate Texas by local contractor J. H. Kampmann. Carefully spaced vents and cavities in the walls permitted air circulation and reduced the danger of sparks igniting stored gunpowder. The arsenal supplied arms for South Texas and frontier defense, as well as for the Sibley Expedition to New Mexico in 1862.

Reoccupied by Federal forces in 1865, this became the principal supply depot for the line of forts defending frontier settlements. It served the U.S. Army until 1947, when the arsenal was closed.

The long, narrow one-story structure features walls of extremely thick ashlar limestone construction. Details include end gables extended above the roofline, lintels which protrude as hood molds, and a date stone in relief over the side entry.   (1977)

SAN ANTONIO (Bexar Co.)   *N side of river level of Tower Life Building*
Bowen's Island
This tract of land is a natural peninsula in the San Antonio River. It once was bounded by the river on three sides and on the fourth by the Concepcion Acequia. In 1845, John Bowen, a native of Philadelphia, bought the property from Maria Josefa Rodriguez de Yturri for $300. Bowen and his wife, Mary Elizabeth, built a seven-room home on the island for their family of six children. Here they planted fruit trees and grapevines. On the east bank of the river, they built a waterwheel to irrigate their truck farm.

During the 1840s and 1850s John Bowen served San Antonio as United States postmaster and city treasurer. He was a staunch Unionist and, according to family tradition, protected fugitive slaves. John Bowen died on the island in 1867 and was buried here.

Bowen's Island was a well-known garden spot and a popular setting for social gatherings and celebrations. Here the first volksfest was held, and the Turnverein, a German athletic club, performed. During the 1870s, it was the site of Wolfram's Central Garden, a pleasure resort.

Mary Elizabeth Bowen died in 1903. During the 1920s, the river was diverted, and Bowen's Island became part of the San Antonio mainland.   (1985)

SAN ANTONIO (Bexar Co.)   *100 E. Houston St. at Soledad St.*
Site of De la Garza House, Gardens and Mint
Erected on this site in 1734 for prominent Bexar citizens Geronimo and Javiera Cantú de la Garza, the De la Garza family home was designed by Geronimo's brother-in-law Pedro Flores Valdez. The complex occupied an entire city block and was crafted with limestone and plaster walls three feet thick. Extensive gardens included cottonwood, pecan, fig and peach trees. The Spanish government granted the property to Javiera de la Garza in 1736 after her husband's death. Two generations later, José Antonio de la Garza used the home's vault to safeguard the valuables of local merchants. In 1818 the Spanish Crown granted him permission to mint coins which became known as "jolas," a Spanish slang term for small currency of local issue used in the northeastern provinces of New Spain. The "jolas" replaced scarce Spanish silver in the value of a half "real," making the De la Garza home what was probably the first mint in Texas. During the Siege of Bexar in 1835, Ben Milam's troops engaged in a two-day battle to commandeer the fortress-like compound as their headquarters. Milam died in the struggle to take the city. After the siege possession of the home returned to the family, in whose control it remained for the rest of the century. Six months of demolition were required to bring down the De la Garza home in 1912. At that time a large sum of money was found hidden in the house and a sixteen-pound cannonball was discovered embedded in the walls, inscribing another page in the De la Garza chapter of San Antonio history.   (1999)

SAN ANTONIO (Bexar Co.)   *County Courthouse*
Bexar County under Nine Governments
The administrative government of Bexar County, besides being the oldest in Texas, is distinguished by having served under nine governments.

The community served under Spanish rule from May, 1718, until January, 1811, when it was taken over by the revolutionary "Casas Regime." Only five weeks later, the "Counter-Revolutionary Junta of Bexar" overthrew the Casas government and eventually restored Spanish rule.

In April, 1812, however, the "Republican Army of the North" deposed the provincial Spanish government and declared independence from Spain. Five months later the Spanish regained control, holding Texas until 1821.

The fifth regime, "First Imperial Government of Mexico" was created when Mexico gained independence from Spain in 1821. The emperor relinquished control to army leaders within two years, however, and the "Republic of Mexico" was established.

Texas gained independence from Mexico in 1836, thereby establishing Bexar's seventh government, the "Republic of Texas." In 1845, Texas became the twenty-eighth state of the United States and remained in the Union until 1861, when the Southern States seceded to form the Confederacy. Following the Civil War, U.S. rule returned to Bexar County in 1865.   (1967)

SAN ANTONIO (Bexar Co.)   *Northwest corner of Courthouse Lawn*
The Canary Islanders
Earliest civilian colonists of San Antonio, this nucleus of pioneers from the Canary Islands formed the first organized civil government in Texas and founded the village of San Fernando de Bexar in 1731.

Following a sea and land voyage of over a year, these weary travelers arrived at the Presidio (fort) of San Antonio early on March 9, 1731. Totaling 56 persons, they had emigrated to Texas from the Spanish Canary Islands near Africa, by order of King Phillip V.

On July 2, they began to lay out a villa (village), choosing a site on the west side of the Plaza de las Yslas (present Main Plaza) for the church and a site on the east side for the Casa Real (government building). On July 9, the captain of the presidio, Juan Antonio de Almazan, read to the islanders the decree of the Viceroy naming them and their descendants "Hijos Dalgos," persons of nobility.

The heads of the 16 families who settled in San Antonio were Juan Leal Goraz, Juan Curbelo, Juan Leal, Antonio Santos, Jose Padron, Manuel de Nis, Vicente Alvarez Travieso, Salvador Rodriguez, Jose Leal, Juan Delgado, Jose Cabrera, Juan Rodriguez Granadillo, Francisco de Arocha, Antonio Rodriguez, Lorenzo and Martin de Armas, and Felipe and Jose Antonio Perez.
(1971)

SAN ANTONIO (Bexar Co.)   *IH 37, HemisFair Park, off hwy.,*
at the excavated Acequia Madre
Acequia Madre de Valero
(Main irrigation ditch of Valero Mission)
One in a network of ditches begun by the Spanish and their Indian charges at the founding of San Antonio in 1718.

Hand-dug and made of dressed limestone, the Acequia diverted water from San Antonio River through fields belonging to San Antonio de Valero Mission. Irrigation was the key to the growth of mission and town.

The ditch paralleled present Broadway by Brackenridge Park and Alamo Street, then fed back into the river southwest of this section. It became part of modern waterworks after 1877. This section was restored, 1968.   (1968)

SAN ANTONIO (Bexar Co.)   *IH 37 at Commerce St., Chamber of Commerce Bldg.*
250th Anniversary of the
Founding of San Antonio
Area was first explored and named by Spaniards in 1691. Colonial settlement began here May 1–5, 1718, with founding of Franciscan Mission San Antonio de Valero (later known as "The Alamo"). In vicinity of the mission was the Presidio San Antonio de Bexar, named for one of the great heroes of Spain, the Duc de Bexar, brother of the Viceroy of New Spain.

The place was renamed San Fernando de Bexar, 1731, when it became a municipality—the first in all of Texas. But the name "San Antonio" persisted. Today it is San Antonio in the County of Bexar.

In its lifetime it has given allegiance to nine governments, and from 1772 to 1824 it served as the provincial and territorial capital of Texas.

HemisFair '68—a world's fair held here April 6 to October 6, 1968, on the 250th anniversary of the birth of the City of San Antonio—had as its theme "The Confluence of Civilizations in the Americas." It originated as a tribute to the diverse peoples who have occupied the Western Hemisphere from pre-Columbian times: Indians who were the first known inhabitants; proud Spanish conquerors and devout padres; the pioneering American settlers; and the immigrants from many different lands.   (1968)

SAN ANTONIO (Bexar Co.)   *IH 35 frontage road near San Antonio stockyards*
The Grass Fight

Near this site on Nov. 26, 1835, occurred the Grass Fight, one of the least decisive but certainly most unusual battles of the Texas war for independence. For more than a month, the Texas forces, composed of both Anglo- and Mexican-Texans, had camped near San Antonio de Bexar waiting for an opportunity to engage the army of the Centralist Regime stationed in the city. Erastus "Deaf" Smith, a Texas scout, learned that a Mexican pack train carrying silver to pay the garrison would arrive in Bexar. On Nov. 26 Smith sighted an approaching caravan and alerted the Texas camp. Col. James Bowie led about 100 volunteers, while others followed Col. Edward Burleson. Near the junction of Alazan, Apache and San Pedro Creeks, the Texans overtook the pack train. Soldiers from the garrison in Bexar road to aid their comrades, but the Texans forced them to retreat and captured the pack animals. About 50 Mexican soldiers were killed in the clash; two Texans were wounded.

In the packs the Texans found not silver but hay that Mexican troops had foraged for their livestock. Two weeks later, supported by a contingent under Juan N. Seguin, Ben Milam led Texan volunteers in the storming of Bexar, expelling the Centralist Army and setting the stage for the siege of the Alamo, Feb. 23–March 6, 1836.   (1982)

SAN ANTONIO (Bexar Co.)   *Loop 410 and Nacogdoches Rd.*
Route of El Camino Real

The main thoroughfare of early Texas, the Camino Real, or "King's Highway," followed ancient Indian and buffalo trails. It stretched 1,000 miles from Mexico to present Louisiana. Domingo Terán de los Rios, first Governor of Texas, blazed the central section of the road in 1691. Called the "Trail of the Padres," it linked Monclova, Mexico with the Spanish missions of East Texas. Over the centuries, priests, soldiers, traders, and settlers used the Camino Real. The French adventurer St. Denis probably traveled the road from Louisiana to the Rio Grande in 1714.

San Antonio was a major stop on this frontier highway. Moses Austin followed the Camino Real to San Antonio in 1820 seeking colonization rights from Spain. Many Anglo-American settlers called it the "Old San Antonio Road." It joined this city with Nacogdoches, San Augustine, and other East Texas settlements.

In 1915, the Texas Legislature appropriated $5,000 to mark the historic roadway across the state. The Daughters of the American Revolution, along with other patriotic groups, endorsed the project. V. N. Zivley surveyed the route and indicated the spacing for granite markers every five miles. Today many modern highways follow the path of the Camino Real.   (1979)

SAN ANTONIO (Bexar Co.)   *IH-10 at Boerne Stage Road*
(in TxDOT park-and-ride parking lot)
First Officers Training Camp

The First World War came to America on April 6, 1917, when President Woodrow Wilson signed the declaration, passed by Congress, that a state of war existed between the United States of America and Germany. Immediately thereafter, eight camps were established in the U.S. to train officers for combat leadership. The first was at Leon Springs, Texas, and on May 8, 1917, three thousand volunteers assembled at Camp Funston on the Schasse Ranch (now a part of Camp Bullis near this site) for training in various branches of the army. They endured three months of intense training and 1,846 young men graduated on August 15, 1917, as second lieutenants. The length of their training resulted in the term "90-day wonders." Embodying their motto "Brave men shall not die because I faltered," the members of the first officers training camp served with distinction in the war, many of them highly decorated for valor in combat. Almost 300, many highly ranking colonels or generals, returned to active duty for service in World War II. Three of those trained here later became governors: Beauford Jester of Texas, James R. Beverley of Puerto Rico, and Charles H. Martin of Oregon. Many more "first campers" were prominent leaders in business, industry and government throughout Texas and the United States. Following their training and service, the former comrades in arms organized the "First Officers Training Camp Association" in 1931. Members residing in 30 states and several foreign countries gathered for annual meetings for more than fifty years. Now succeeded by generations of modern soldiers and officers, the First Officers Training Camp veterans leave a legacy of honor, courage and service to their country.   (1999)

SAN AUGUSTINE (San Augustine Co.)   SH 21, 7 mi. W
Home of Thomas S. McFarland
1810–1880
Surveyor, soldier and statesman. Aide-de-camp to Major Bullock in the Battle of Nacogdoches, 1832. Laid out the town of San Augustine in 1833. Soldier in the Texan Army, 1836. Member of the Congress of the Republic of Texas. Chief Justice, San Augustine County.

SAN AUGUSTINE (San Augustine Co.)   SH 147, .5 mi. S
Mission Nuestra Señora de los Dolores de los Ais
Established in 1716 by Padre Fray Antonio Margil de Jesus. Here faithful Franciscans labored for the purpose of civilizing and Christianizing the Ais Indians. Abandoned temporarily due to the French incursions from Louisiana in 1719. Restored by the Marquis of Aguayo in 1721. The mission also served to confirm the claim of the King of Spain to the Province of Texas.

SAN AUGUSTINE (San Augustine Co.)   SH 21, 4 mi. E
Site of the Home of Elisha Roberts
1774–1844
Early influential citizen. Important figure in the Fredonian Rebellion, Alcalde of San Augustine in 1831. A haven of hospitality to travelers.

SAN AUGUSTINE (San Augustine Co.)   SH 21, .4 mi. E of Carrizo Creek
Site of
Battle of Fredonia
Climax of first Anglo-American rebellion in East Texas. In 1826 colonizer Hayden Edwards defied expulsion orders of Mexico and founded Republic of Fredonia—raising flag of "Independence, Liberty, and Justice." When Ayish Bayou settlers refused to join, he ordered their banishment.

Fredonians, from log fort at this site, were ordered to take Ayish Bayou on Jan. 21, 1827. That day, however, without a shot, Stephen Prather's 9 white men and 60 Indians took the fort and 200 soldiers. At news of this, Edwards fled to the U.S., ending the Fredonian Rebellion.   (1966)

SAN AUGUSTINE (San Augustine Co.)   SH 147, 4 mi. N, then 2 mi. W
Bodine Place, (Medallion) Built 1886
This is the third Bodine house on this site. The original builder was with Commodore Perry on Lake Erie, and one son in each succeeding generation has been named Oliver Hazard Perry Bodine, the name of the builder of this house.

SAN AUGUSTINE (San Augustine Co.)   SH 147, 4 mi. N at cemetery entrance
Antioch Church of Christ
William P. Defee, a medical doctor, arrived in Texas in 1833 and began preaching in homes. In 1836, he began this congregation. They met in a dirt-floored, log building on Rhoddy Anthony's property. The name "Antioch" was chosen because the disciples were first called Christians in Antioch. Anthony was selected elder and served for 50 years. About 1870, a new sanctuary was built on this land belonging to Stephen Passmore. The building served as a school-house and community meeting place. This structure was completed in 1938.   (1979)

SAN AUGUSTINE (San Augustine Co.)   SH 147, 1.5 mi. N
Alexander Horton Cemetery
Pioneer, soldier, civic leader, and state legislator, Alexander Horton (1810–1894) came to Texas in 1824. He served as an aide-de-camp to Gen. Sam Houston at the Battle of San Jacinto, April 21, 1836. This cemetery is situated on property Horton bought in 1837. His home once stood adjacent to the plot. According to family tradition, the first grave here was that of Horton's brother William Wade, a Texas Ranger who died in 1849. Maintained by descendants, the cemetery contains about 20 graves, including those of Horton and other family members.   (1977)

SAN AUGUSTINE (San Augustine Co.)   Corner of Livingston and Goldenway
Jerusalem Memorial
Christian Methodist Episcopal Church
Blacks in San Augustine worshiped together as early as 1845, when two slaves known as Sutton and Bartlett were granted licenses to preach in the Methodist Episcopal Church, South.

They built a place of worship, referred to as the "Church on the Branch," on a lot thought to belong to local landholder George Teel. After the Civil War the fellowship declined invitations to join independent groups such as the African Methodist Episcopal Church, and remained part of the Methodist Episcopal Church, South.

In 1866, the Methodist Episcopal Church, South, formed a separate conference for its Black members, which was known as the Colored Methodist Episcopal (C.M.E.) Church. The San Augustine "Church on the Branch" joined the conference in 1870 under the pastorate of the Rev. Sam Horton, but was not officially known as Jerusalem C.M.E. Church until 1946. The name Christian Methodist Episcopal Church was adopted in 1954.

With its earliest history dating to the pre-Civil War era, Jerusalem Memorial C.M.E. Church is considered one of the oldest Black congregations in the state. For over a century it has played an important role in the growth of Methodism in San Augustine. (1983)

SAN AUGUSTINE (San Augustine Co.)   *128 E. Columbia (SH 21/147)*
Sam Houston in San Augustine

Sam Houston (March 2, 1793–July 26, 1863) left home in 1809 and lived among the Cherokees. After two years he returned to the Anglo world; he opened a school, fought the British under Andrew Jackson, and was Governor of Tennessee. After a three-week marriage, Houston left the governorship and returned to the Cherokees; three years later, he came to Texas. Upon his arrival in San Augustine, Sam Houston opened a legal practice on this site. For the next thirty years he used "The Redlands" as a place of business, residence, or refuge. Houston is said to have recuperated from the Battle of San Jacinto in the home of Colonel Phillip Sublett, issuing his report of the battle from San Augustine. Following Houston's term as President of the Republic of Texas, the people of San Augustine elected him to serve them in the Texas House of Representatives during the Fourth and Fifth Congresses. Houston's divorce from Eliza Allen took place in San Augustine in 1837. He married Margaret Lea in 1840; though her health would not permit her to live in San Augustine, she made frequent visits. The early and strong support of the people of "The Redlands" for Sam Houston and Houston's love for them is documented in the history and lore of San Augustine and its people. (1998)

SAN AUGUSTINE (San Augustine Co.)   *SH 147, .2 mi. S*
Columbus Cartwright House
(A Medallion House)

Built circa 1838. (Date reported on one chimney, now eroded).

Story and half house originally with back hall to stairway. Fine mantels, Columbus Cartwright, active in early Texas affairs. (1962)

SAN AUGUSTINE (San Augustine Co.)   *SH 21, west side*
¼ mi. N to Site of
Early Texas Sawmill

Texas' first million-dollar industry—lumbering—was born to recorded history with the building of two sawmills in 1819. One, located on Ironosa Creek in present San Augustine County, was run by pioneer Wm. Ward; the other was in Nacogdoches. In 1825 yet another mill (¼ mi. N) was turning out about 500 board feet of lumber a day. Wm. Quirk was miller.

In these times, trees were felled using an ax and a wedge. Then one end, of each huge log was slung under a heavy cart and dragged to a stream or road.

At the mill the logs were often stored in mill pond, to keep them from rotting, and then they were sawed by various methods. Two primitive ones—soon abandoned—were pit sawing (a slow, exhausting two-man process) and the Muley-mill powered by animals. A later improvement was the sash saw, which was so nearly effortless that one old-timer claimed the attendant "could read the Bible or the *Galveston News* while the saw was cutting."

In the mid-19th century, logging served as a pivot-point for dozens of subsidiary industries; railroad building and lumbering had a strong mutual influence and the gusto of loggers' lore is still alive in the rich heritage of the piney woods. (1969)

SAN AUGUSTINE (San Augustine Co.)
Norwood-Legrand House

SH 103/147, 7 mi. S

Unusual scalloped cornice at front porch. Free standing columns and front rail. Occupied by E. O. LeGrande, signer of the Texas Declaration of Independence. William C. Norwood, the builder of the house, and E. O. LeGrande were brothers-in-law. A Medallion Home.

SAN AUGUSTINE (San Augustine Co.)
William Garrett House

SH 21, 1 mi. W

William Garrett (1808–1884) purchased this land soon after coming to Texas in 1830. In 1861, he erected this two-story house using pine boards from his nearby sawmill. Built by slave labor, the structure had unusual free-standing columns in front and carved mantels over its six fireplaces. Garrett's home was often a stop for travelers on the Old San Antonio Road. The property was sold to Sam Parker in 1904. C. T. and Ruby (Parker) Dorsey are the current (1975) owners.   (1962)

SAN AUGUSTINE (San Augustine Co.)
Old Greer House
(A Medallion House)

US 96 at FM 1277

Built 1870. On original Charlton Paine place. Built by T. N. B. Greer.

SAN AUGUSTINE (San Augustine Co.)
Phillip A. Sublett House
(A Medallion House)

SH 21 (Camino Real), 4 mi. E

Built 1874 just SW of site of original Phillip A. Sublett house, circa, 1834.
Interesting entrance, stairway and mantels.
Phillip Sublett was a partner with Sam Houston on several land deals.   (1962)

SAN AUGUSTINE (San Augustine Co.)

SH 21, 7 mi. E in the
Chapel Hill Cemetery

The Thompson Family

Dr. Samuel (1765–1843) and Precious Wofford (d. 1841) Thompson and their sons were among the earliest settlers of this area. Samuel Thompson served as Alcalde of the San Augustine municipality and later organized area churches and schools.

Burrell J. Thompson (1790–1875), the eldest Thompson son, came to Texas in 1821 with Stephen F. Austin. He was involved in the Fredonian Rebellion, gave financial aid to the Texas Revolution, and later served three terms as justice of the peace in San Augustine.

William Alston Thompson (1795–1837) arrived in Texas with his brother Burrell in 1821. He served in the Texas Revolution and in 1837 was murdered by horse thieves near his home.

Napoleon B. Thompson served in a Ranger company during the Texas Revolution. He was district attorney of the San Augustine judicial district and died sometime before 1850.

Charleton W. Thompson (1809–1838) was alcalde at Anahuac, served in the Convention of 1833, and was a member of the Republic of Texas Congress in 1838.

John H. Thompson was a participant in the Battle of Nacogdoches. Descendants of the pioneer Thompson family still remain in San Augustine County.   (Texas Sesquicentennial 1836–1986)

SAN AUGUSTINE (San Augustine Co.)
San Augustine

US 96 and SH 21

An early eastern gate to Texas, in area claimed in 1600s by both France and Spain. To back her claim, Spain in 1691 charted from Mexico past this site El Camino Real (The King's Highway) and established nearby in 1717 Mission Dolores de los Aies.

Inhabited by Ayish Indians and Spaniards until the later 1790s, when Richard Sims came and was soon followed by John Quinalty, Edmond Quirk and families of Broocks, Cullens, Cartwrights, Hortons, Hustons, Prathers and others. By 1824 the settlement had a water mill to grind corn meal; in 1826, a cotton gin.

In the 1827 Battle of Ayish Bayou, Col. Prather and 69 men put down Fredonian uprising over land titles.

The town was laid off in 1833 by Thomas McFarland. In 1836 it sent as delegates to sign Declaration of Independence S. W. Blount and E. O. LeGrand; fielded 3 companies to fight in the War for Independence. Its Republic of Texas statesmen included vice-president K. L. Anderson; J. A. Greer, secretary of the treasury; Wm. Holman, congressman; J. Pinckney Henderson, minister to England and France, and later the first governor of the state. Oran M. Roberts was 16th governor.

Home of 1965 United States Ambassador to Australia Edward Clark. Many historic sites are marked. (1966)

SAN BENITO (Cameron Co.) US 77 Loop and SH 345
Spiderweb Railroad
Col. Sam A. Robertson, who founded the town of San Benito in 1907, promoted and built the San Benito & Rio Grande Valley Railway. It was designed to provide a more accessible and efficient transportation system for the shipping of area farm products. Because of the railroad's intricate network of lines and spurs, it was commonly known as the Spiderweb Railroad.

The first phases of the rail line were begun in 1911 under the supervision of Col. Robertson's brother Frank S. Robertson. Construction of the feeder rail lines brought trackside loading facilities to the remote farming areas of the valley and assured the continuing development of brushland into irrigated farms. Trains carrying freight and passengers were soon making two round trips daily over routes that eventually stretched 128 miles.

For many years the Spiderweb remained essential to the valley's development as one of the leading agricultural regions of the nation. Traffic on the line declined, however, because of improved roads, motor transportation and more centralized loading facilities. Today the history of the line serves as a reminder of the pioneer farmers and businessmen who were instrumental in the area's early growth. (1982)

SAN BENITO (Cameron Co.) 216 S. Sam Houston (SH 345)
Water District Building
Designed by Austin architects Endress and Walsh and built by contractor L. Fleming, the San Benito Land and Water Company building was completed in 1910 at a cost of $14,386. Thirty-foot pine beams and locally made brick were used to construct the home of the company. A fine example of the Mission Revival Style, the edifice features a red tile roof, wooden bracketed eaves, a stucco exterior, and curved gable parapets. The building has been home to many San Benito institutions, notably the irrigation and drainage districts. A beloved fixture of downtown San Benito, it stands as a memorial to the vital role of irrigation in valley life. (1997)

SAN BENITO (Cameron Co.) SH 281, 8 mi. S
The Landrum House
This house stands on the 1781 Concepcion de Carricitos grant from the king of Spain to Eugenio and Bartolome Fernandez. Acquiring a part of the grant as fee for his legal services to the heirs, Col. Stephen Powers of Brownsville gave the site to his daughter Frances and her husband, James Lambert Landrum. The Landrums, who completed the house in 1902, had daughters: Martha, Pauline and Frances. In 1978, Frances owns and lives in the house. (1978)

SAN DIEGO (Duval Co.) SH 359, 1 mi. SW
Duval County
Created February 1, 1858. Organized November 7, 1876. Named in honor of Burr H. Duval, 1809–1836. Captain of A Company of Fannin's command at Goliad. Murdered after the surrender, March 25, 1836. San Diego, county seat.

SAN DIEGO (Duval Co.) SH 44, 11 mi. W
Felipe Valerio Store and Garage (1.5 mi. SE)
Built in 1905 by Felipe Valerio (1878–1953) and his wife Jesusa (1886–1973), the Valerio store was an integral part of the small community of La Rosita. Located approximately halfway between San Diego and Freer, the store provided groceries and other goods for residents of this rural area, an increase in business from the area oil boom in the 1930s led to the addition of a gas station and garage. The store also served as a bus station, and Felipe Valerio was local postmaster from 1917 to 1929. Construction of State Highway 44 led to the closing of the store in 1956. (1994)

SAN ELIZARIO (El Paso Co.)

US 80

Los Portales
Awarded the Texas Historical Building Medallion

Served as first courthouse and as the San Elizario School.

SAN ELIZARIO (El Paso Co.)

US 80

Presidio Chapel of San Elizario

Site of the Presidio de Nuestra Señora del Pilar Y Glorioso Señor San Jose. Established by Don Domingo Jironza Petriz de Cruzate in 1683 near Mission de Nuestra Señora de Guadalupe in present Ciudad Juarez, Mexico. Located on this site 1773 and renamed Presidio de San Elizario. Its chapel was served by Franciscan missionaries.

SAN ELIZARIO (El Paso Co.)

San Elizario Plaza

San Elizario

San Elizario was established in 1789 on the former site of Hacienda de los Tiburcios as a Spanish colonial fort known as the Presidio de San Elceario. The Presidio was moved from its original location (approx. 37 mi. S) in response to requests from settlers for military protection from Indian raids. It operated as a Spanish post until 1814, when troops withdrew during the Mexican War for Independence (1810–1821).

During its years as a part of Mexico, the Presidio de San Elceario (now San Elizario) was occupied periodically by Mexican troops. A reduced military presence resulted in the fort's decline.

American control of the area began in 1848, with the treaty of Guadalupe Hidalgo, which established the Rio Grande as the border between the United States and Mexico. When the county of El Paso was organized in 1850, the town of San Elizario was chosen first county seat and served as such until 1873. In 1877, it was the scene of a crisis known as the Salt War, in which local businessmen attempted to control the salt market that had operated since colonial times.

Although San Elizario was bypassed by the railroad and has become a rural farming community, it remains an important element in the region's rich heritage. (1985)

SAN ELIZARIO (El Paso Co.)

FM 258, SE corner of Plaza San Elizario

Rodríguez-Chamuscado Expedition—1581

Inspired by Indian stories of settlements in present New Mexico and authorized by the Spanish Viceroy, Fray Agustín Rodríguez, a Franciscan priest, led a missionary expedition to the area. Accompanied by Fray Juan de Santa María, Fray Francisco López, nine soldiers, and nineteen Indian servants, he left Santa Barbara, Mexico, on June 5, 1581. The military escort was led by Francisco Sanchez, who, because of his red beard, was known as Chamuscado, "The Singed."

Following the Rio Grande, the expedition reached El Paso del Norte. Proceeding through the pass, they spent the remainder of 1581 exploring the vast region from present western New Mexico to the Texas Panhandle.

After Indians killed Fray Santa María in September 1581, plans were made to return for a report to the Spanish authorities. Despite the hostile environment, the two remaining missionaries chose to stay. Chamuscado led the others back through the Pass of the North, but died before reaching Santa Barbara.

Believed to have been the first Spanish expedition to use the Pass of the North, the Rodríguez-Chamuscado Expedition marked the beginning of Spanish influence in the area. Their exploration opened the region, now the American Southwest, to later colonization. (1981)

SAN ELIZARIO (El Paso Co.)

FM 258 (Socorro Rd.), San Elizario Plaza

Espejo-Beltran Expedition—1582–1583

Following the Rodríguez-Chamuscado Expedition of 1581, there was increased interest in the area now known as New Mexico and Texas. There was also concern for the safety of Fray Rodríguez and Fray López, who had stayed in the area. In 1582, a Franciscan priest from Santa Barbara, Mexico, Fray Bernardino Beltran, formed an expedition to find the missionaries. His military escort was led by Antonio de Espejo, a former Santa Barbara merchant and rancher living in voluntary exile over a legal dispute with the Spanish authorities.

The expedition departed the mining outpost of San Bartolome in November 1582. By the following January they had reached the El Paso area. In present New Mexico they learned that Fray Rodríguez and Fray López had been killed by Indians. Fray Beltran led a small party back to

Mexico, but Espejo and several companions stayed to check the Indian stories of silver mines and wealthy pueblos. On their journey the Spaniards became the first explorers in the region from the Pecos River Valley to the Junta de los Rios, the junction of the Concho River and the Rio Grande. The reports of their explorations further heightened the interest in the area. (1981)

SAN ELIZARIO (El Paso Co.)   *San Elizario Plaza*
Salt War
The Salt War rose from political conflicts in El Paso County and from controversies over control of the salt lakes east of El Paso, which for centuries had been a free source of salt for local residents. In 1877, Charles Howard, a former county judge who claimed ownership of the lakes, shot political adversary Luis Cardis over the issue of the salt beds. While under the protection of state troops in San Elizario, Howard and several of the troopers were killed by a riotous mob. Federal and state investigations of the Salt War led to the reestablishment of Ft. Bliss in 1878. (1984)

SAN FELIPE (Austin Co.)   *Historical Area, Stephen F. Austin State Park*
Replica of Stephen F. Austin's Cabin
Built in 1954, this structure is a replica of the only Texas home of Stephen F. Austin, "Father of Texas." The chimney contains bricks from the original (1828) cabin. Other materials were made as authentically as possible.

Austin (1793–1836) opened the Anglo-American colonization of Texas. His cabin, located in capital city of San Felipe, welcomed pioneers and statesman of era, and witnessed many crucial events leading to Texas Revolution. (1970)

SAN FELIPE (Austin Co.)   *FM 1458, 2 mi. N of IH 10 at roadside park*
San Felipe de Austin
First Anglo-American Capital of Texas. Came into being on July 26, 1823, as capital of the Austin Colony, by decree of the Mexican government. Father of Texas Stephen F. Austin had begun under the 1821 grant from Mexico the settlement of more than 1,000 families. The original colony ran from the coast on the south to the Old San Antonio Road on the north, and from the Lavaca River on the west to the San Jacinto River on the East. In this first American town in Texas lived Austin, William Barret Travis, Sam Houston, David G. Burnet and Jane Long. All settlers crossed its threshold for land grants.

After the organization of other colonies, this continued to be the recognized center of Texas. It was capital of the Mexican Department of Brazos, site of the conventions of 1832 and 1833 and the consultation of 1835 where Texans aired grievances and tried to reach understanding with Mexico. The provisional government created with Henry Smith as governor in 1835 functioned here until it gave way to the convention declaring Texas independent of Mexico on March 2, 1836.

Republic of Texas capitals were Columbia, Houston, Washington-on-the-Brazos and Austin.

SAN FELIPE (Austin Co.)   *IH 10, Stephen F. Austin State Park*
Stephen Fuller Austin
Father of Texas. November 3, 1793–December 27, 1836. He planted the first Anglo-American colony in Texas, "The Old Three Hundred." In his several colonies he settled more than a thousand families. He was from 1823 until 1828 the actual ruler of Texas and thereafter its most influential leader. His own words are a fitting epitaph. "The prosperity of Texas has been the object of my labors–the idol of my existence. It has assumed the character of a religion–for the guidance of my thoughts and actions," and he died in its service. No other state in the Union owes its existence more completely to one man than Texas does to Austin.

SAN FELIPE (Austin Co.)   *FM 1458 E at 6th St.*
San Felipe Town Hall
Successor to 1828 hall used by "Ayuntamiento" (town council). Conventions of 1832, 1833, and consultation of 1835—leading to Texas Revolution—met there. Burned during revolution in 1836.

Two-story section of present structure was built about 1842 and may have served as county courthouse until 1847. It was joined to a one-story school after 1900; moved to this site, 1915. By old custom, council meets each Saturday before full moon. Awarded Medallion Plate. (1970)

SAN FELIPE (Austin Co.)
IH 10, Stephen F. Austin State Park
Stephen F. Austin Home
On this site stood the only home owned in Texas by Stephen F. Austin.
It was burned, March 29, 1836, when San Felipe was set afire by Texans to prevent its falling into the hands of the advancing Mexican Army under General Santa Anna. (1964)

SAN FELIPE (Austin Co.)
Park Road 38, off FM 1458
in Stephen F. Austin State Park
Early Roads to San Felipe
During the mid-1820s, when Stephen F. Austin was founding this town, the only roads in the area were wagon ruts or beaten trails marked by notched trees. Within a decade, however, the village of San Felipe, one of the first Anglo settlements in Texas, had become a hub from which eight or more roads projected.

Many of these were small, intra-colony routes, but the main trails extended to major towns or joined "highways," such as the San Antonio Road (El Camino Real). A main route which passed through San Felipe was the Atascosita Road, connecting Goliad with the United States. It took its name from Atascosa (Spanish for "boggy") Spring near Liberty, which once was its main terminus. The Gotier Trace, another travel artery, was laid out about 1830 by pioneer James Gotier. It joined the northern and southern parts of Austin's colony and was used for decades. The San Felipe Road proper, which ran to Harrisburg, transported goods inland from the Gulf coast.

Even the main thoroughfares, however, were dusty trails in the summer and impassable quagmires in the winter, often flooded by knee-deep water. Not until well into the 20th century did Texas begin to develop her present, outstanding highway system. (1969)

SAN GABRIEL (Milam Co.)
FM 487, 6 mi. E
Site of the Mission San Ildefonso
Established by Franciscan missionaries in 1749 with the hope of civilizing and Christianizing the Coco, Mayeye, Orcoquiza, Karankawa, and other tribes of Indians. The martyrdom of Padre Jose Ganzabal and the circumstances connected therewith caused the departure of the Indians and the Friars and the removal of this mission to the San Marcos River in 1755. Reestablished in 1762 on the Nueces River for the conversion of the Lipan Apaches with the new name of Mission San Lorenzo de la Santa Cruz.

SAN GABRIEL (Milam Co.)
FM 487, 1.5 mi. E
Site of the Mission Nuestra Señora de la Candelaria
Established by Franciscan missionaries in 1749 with the hope of civilizing and Christianizing the Coco, Mayeye, Orocoquiza, Karankawa, and other tribes of Indians. The martyrdom of Padre Jose Ganzabal and the circumstances connected therewith caused the departure of the Indians and the Friars and the removal of this mission to the San Marcos River in 1755. Reestablished in 1762 on the Sabinal River for the conversion of the Lipan Apaches with the same name of Nuesta Señora de la Candelaria.

SAN JUAN (Hidalgo Co.)
FM 1426, 7.5 mi. S, then .5 mi. W
San Juan Plantation
Foreman's house. Built 1904 by John Closner; 1891–1912 Sheriff of Hidalgo County, who helped bring in and finance railroads and establish respect for law. Only reminder today of the 45,000 acre plantation complex that had sugar mill, post office, general store, pumping station, and produced sugar cane, cotton, potatoes, alfalfa and onions. Built the same year Closner's sugar won St. Louis World's Fair medal. Awarded Medallion Plate. (1964)

SAN MARCOS (Hays Co.)
US 81, 1.5 mi. N
Hays County
Formed from Travis County. Created March 1, 1848. Organized August 7, 1848. Named in honor of John Coffee (Jack) Hays, 1817–1883. Captain of Texas Rangers. Colonel in the Mexican War. County seat, San Marcos.

SAN MARCOS (Hays Co.)

SH 21, 3.7 mi. NE near the
San Marcos de Neve marker

Don Felipe Roque de la Portilla

At the request of Antonio Cordero, interim governor of the Province of Texas, Spanish born Felipe Roque de la Portilla (1768?–1841) established a colony here on El Camino Real. With his own family of eight, he brought 51 persons from the interior of Mexico and founded San Marcos de Neve in April 1808. Titles were issued to 13 lots, and homes were built, only to be washed away in June floods. Hardships plagued the colony: the defensive troops departed; no priest arrived; seed and a farm irrigation system did not materialize; horses and cattle were lost to Indians, and the people feared for their own lives. In 1809 new settlers brought the population to 81 without bettering living conditions. Portilla lost his health and fortune and was forced to lead his people back to Matamoros, Mexico, in 1812.

In 1829, however, he helped his son-in-law, James Power, and Power's associate, James Hewetson, plant their colony at Refugio, near Copano Bay. Portilla received land there in 1834, but left for Mexico in 1836. Because he invested his own fortune in the colonizing effort, he is sometimes called the first Empresario, and recognized as a forerunner of Stephen F. Austin, "The Father of Texas."   (1976)

SAN MARCOS (Hays Co.)

US 81, 2 mi. N in roadside park

Beef for the Confederacy

Throughout Hays County, 1861–1865, as in the rest of Texas, beef production for the Confederacy was a major patriotic service. Leading ranchers, called government stockraisers, had the duty of supplying the commissary department of the army.

Hays County, with its well-established cattle industry, had several men designated as C. S. A. beef raisers. These included James M. ("Doc") Day, John W. Day, Wm. H. Day, and their brothers-in-law, Jesse L. Driskill; Wm. Washington Moon; and Ezekiel Nance.

These men had hazardous work. They had either to fight or detour around Indians, rustlers and enemy patrols. Herds had to swim flooded streams, some with quicksand beds. Wm. H. Day once was almost drowned while swimming a herd across the flooding Brazos. At least two of the Day brothers were in military service as well as supply duty. Moon, a veteran of the Mexican War, and founder of the City of San Marcos, not only was a stockraiser but also joined the 32nd Texas Cavalry. He donated beef to soldiers' families and furnished leather and horse feed to his cavalry company. Besides supplying beef to the quartermasters, Nance manufactured cotton cloth for the Confederacy.   (1965)

SAN MARCOS (Hays Co.)

Loop 82, in Aquarena Park, N edge of city

Post San Marcos

The Republic of Texas Congress in Dec. 1838 called for military roads and forts from Red River to the Nueces. A road from Austin, joining El Camino Real near St. Mark's Springs, was designed for rapid communication between San Antonio and the capital. Post San Marcos was to be constructed at the springs, to safeguard travel.

Adj. Gen. Hugh McLeod (1814–62) laid out the fort, to be garrisoned by a company of 56 men. Capt. Joseph Wiehl's Co. H, 1st Inf. Regt., in Oct. 1840 completed the road and the fort. In 1841 the Republic of Texas Army disbanded for lack of funding, and the post was closed.   (1973)

SAN MARCOS (Hays Co.)

Aquarena Springs Dr. at entrance to park

San Marcos Springs

Pouring forth millions of gallons of clear, icy water daily, these springs feed the San Marcos River and the 1,380-square-mile area in which it drains. The immense springs rise at the Balcones Escarpment, a geologic fault line which slices across the state, separating upland from lowland Texas.

The abundance of fresh water made these springs a mecca for the Indians who inhabited Central Texas and later for the European explorers and settlers who followed. The name San Marcos was first given to a Texas river by the Alonso de Leon Expedition on April 26, 1689 (Saint Mark's Day). The name was not applied to the present river, however, until 1709. Other explorers inspected this area and in 1755 it became a temporary site for several Spanish missions.

Almost a century later, in 1845, pioneers William W. Moon and Mike Sessom made a permanent settlement here. In 1851 Gen. Edward Burleson, William Lindsey, and Eli T. Merriman bought the adjacent land and on it laid out the town of San Marcos.

Attracted by the scenic beauty of the area, A. B. Rogers started a park here in 1926. Over the years it has been developed into Aquarena Springs, one of Central Texas' most popular tourist attractions.　(1971)

SAN MARCOS (Hays Co.)　　　　　　*S on SH 80, 1 mi. past Blanco River*
McGehee Crossing

The Camino Real, also known as the Old San Antonio Road and the King's Highway, followed a route from Nacogdoches to the Rio Grande. Louis Juchereau de St. Denis (1676–1744) traveled the route to establish trade between the French in Louisiana and the Spanish of Coahuila province on the Rio Grande in 1714.

The first settlement at the San Marcos River crossing of the road was Villa San Marcos de Neve, established by the Spanish in 1808. It was abandoned by 1812 due to the brewing Mexican Revolution.

During their colonization efforts in 1820 and 1821, Moses Austin (1761–1821) and his son, Stephen F. Austin (1793–1836), very likely crossed the San Marcos River near this point.

Thomas Gilmer McGehee (1810–1890) settled on the east side of the river on a Mexican land grant about 1846. In 1859, his nephew, Charles L. McGehee, Jr. (1837–1929), acquired 1200 acres of land bordered by the Camino Real and the river. Ten years later he sold the land to his cousin, George T. McGehee (1836–1926). Due to the McGehee family's association with this historic site, it became known as McGehee Crossing.　(1987)

SAN MARCOS (Hays Co.)　　　*Aquarena Park at the San Marcos River*
General Edward Burleson House

Awarded the Texas Historical Building Medallion.

SAN PATRICIO (San Patricio Co.)　　　　　　　　*FM 666*
San Patricio de Hibernia

Founded in 1830 by John McMullen and James McGloin as the seat of their Irish colony under an Empresario contract dated August 17, 1828, which was fulfilled by the Empresarios 1830–1835.

Named in honor of Saint Patrick, the Patron Saint of Ireland. As the frontier outpost of Texas when the revolution began, San Patricio, 1835–1845, suffered all the miseries of that conflict with no compensating returns.

At and near San Patricio, on February 27, 1836, General Jose Urrea's division of Santa Anna's Army surprised and overwhelmed Johnson's Texan party of 35 men, 9 or 10 Texans were killed, 6 or 7 escaped, and 20 were sent to Matamoros as prisoners. After San Jacinto the town was destroyed and its inhabitants driven away.

SAN PERLITA (Willacy Co.).　　　　*FM 2209, Hollywood Park*
San Perlita
"Pearl of the Valley"

Part of the Carricitos Land Grant issued in 1790 by the King of Spain to Jose Narcisso Cavazos, this agricultural community and the surrounding farmland were developed soon after the Missouri Pacific Railroad extended a branch line to this area in 1926. The San Perlita Development Company cleared more than twenty thousand acres of land for growing staple, vegetable, and citrus crops and laid out the townsite of San Perlita. Since its development, the area has made significant contributions to the quality of life in this part of the Rio Grande Valley.　(1984)

SAN SABA (San Saba Co.)　　　　　　　*FM 2732, 16 mi. W*
Comanche Indian Treaty

On this site a treaty of peace was agreed upon March 1–2, 1847, between twenty Comanche chiefs and the German colonists represented by Otfried Hans Frieherr von Meusebach (1812–1897), who became a citizen of Texas under the name of John O. Meusebach. This treaty was never broken.　(1936)

SAN SABA (San Saba Co.)　　　　　*US 190, at city limits East*
San Saba County

On northeastern border of the Edwards Plateau. Created from Bexar County, Feb. 1, and organized May 3, of 1856. Named for San Saba River. County seat of same name.

Area first explored in 1732 by Juan Antonio Bustillo y Zevallos. Anglo-American settlement began in 1840s.

Economy based on ranching, farming and commercial quarrying of marble, sand and limestone. Principal crops are cotton, grains, peanuts, sorghums and clovers. Ranchers market wool and mohair. Known as "Pecan Capital of the World." (1966)

SAN SABA (San Saba Co.) US 190, corner of Wallace & Second
San Saba Church of Christ

San Saba County was organized in 1856, and in 1860 the commissioners court issued a block of land to each religious body; the Christian Church was one of these. The congregation traded their land for another block upon which they built a small frame structure.

The first documented preacher of the Christian Church in San Saba was J. A. Henderson. For many years, services were conducted by lay elders and by traveling ministers. Popular religious debates held in San Saba often involved members of the Christian Church.

The 20th century was ushered in by the 1904 division in the Christian Church, which led the San Saba congregation to choose the Church of Christ, despite the split and such lean years as those of the depression era, the San Saba Church of Christ thrived, popular activities such as summer revivals increased membership in the church, with new facilities erected as needed. A controversy over the support of mission work resulted in the founding of a separate congregation in 1957, but the original San Saba congregation carried on and quickly regained its strength, flourishing in the 1970s.

The San Saba Church of Christ upholds the unique traditions of its founders through worship, missionary, and community outreach programs in Texas and beyond. (1998)

SAN SABA (San Saba Co.) US 190, ¾ mi. E
San Saba Lodge No. 225, A. F. & A. M.

The history of San Saba is closely tied with the story of Freemasonry in the area, as many of those who helped organize San Saba County were Masons. Local Freemasons were already gathering as a group when the first county courthouse was erected in 1857 and the Commissioners Court allowed the Masons to meet in the new building. Twelve Master Masons petitioned the Grand Lodge of Texas for dispensation to form a lodge; their petition was granted in May 1858. A full charter for San Saba Lodge No. 225 was granted in June 1859. Members of the lodge were county officials, community leaders, frontier trailblazers, Texas Rangers, sheriffs and Confederate soldiers. The lodge first focused on the need for a public school in San Saba as members built a combination school and lodge hall. The Texas Legislature granted an official charter to the San Saba Masonic College in 1863. Freemasonry grew in popularity and in 1863 the Royal Arch Masons were granted a dispensation for a San Saba chapter, remaining active until 1869. Despite a membership of 84 in 1879, San Saba lodge suffered the same financial hardships as most of the Texas lodges during Reconstruction. San Saba Lodge No. 225 surrendered its charter in 1882, due in part to perceived association with the San Saba mob, an outlaw vigilante group that terrorized the county during that era. A new lodge was organized in 1884, however, allowing Freemasonry to survive in San Saba. (1999)

SAN SABA (San Saba Co.) US 190, 4 mi. E of San Saba
Site of
Barnett-Hamrick Settlement, 1855–1895

John W. Barnett and family with sons-in-law, Burrell L. and Tom P. C. Hamrick, settled large tract of land here. Founded community of Simpson Creek. Were first in area to farm as well as to irrigate crops. Were active in local commerce. Helped organize county. First camp meeting and one of first schools were held here. (1969)

SAN SABA (San Saba Co.) US 190, 3 mi. W
Harkeyville

A site once famous for its horses and racetrack. Riley Harkey (1832–1920) and Israel Harkey (1835–1914) were Indian scouts in Texas in 1850–1853. In 1855 they led their parents, Mathias and Catherine Harkey, to move here from Arkansas with other adult sons, daughters, in-laws, and grandchildren. The families ranched, and Mathias Harkey ran a country store for many years.

Riley Harkey brought to Texas a fine, fleetfooted mare, who with her racing progeny drew crowds of enthusiasts to this site for half a century. Other sons and grandsons of Mathias Harkey also joined in the breeding, training, and racing of horses. Stores, blacksmith shop, and other businesses all faced east on a single street overlooking the flat with its racetrack and baseball diamond. There was no post office, but the village was so well known that mail addressed to Harkeyville promptly arrived here.

On Nov. 26, 1873, George W. Barnett (1823–1885) gave land for the first school; the schoolhouse was used also for church services and public meetings.

The racetrack closed in 1970; the cotton gin burned in 1920, and was not rebuilt; school consolidated in 1929 with San Saba. The last store closed in 1954. A community hall, built 1973, marks site of the town. (1974)

SAN SABA (San Saba Co.)   *US 190, 5 mi. E*
Indian Signaling Grounds

Heights used from pre-settlement days to 1870s by Comanches and others to send messages over long distances. Smoke once rose from here (Five Mile Hill); Chappel Hill, 2 mi. south; and old community of Sloan in West San Saba County. Tribes wintered at main village near Sloan; burial ground is on Chappel Hill.

An early settler recalls Indians peering through cracks in cabin at night while she, children, and friend put ashes on fire and hid. She believed Indians would not enter a dark house. Another time she heard livestock being taken. Many pioneers saw signals on nearby hills.

Indians communicated by means of smoke, at times mirrors. Codes were used to confuse enemies. Messages sent news and could gather or disperse tribes. The Comanches had an excellent smoke signal system, also imitated animal cries. These often warned settlers to prepare for attack. In some areas, whites later pre-empted signal grounds for use against the Indians.

Mirabeau B. Lamar visited this area in 1837; later, as president of Republic of Texas, he had a forceful Indian policy. On banks of San Saba in 1847, German Emigration Company bought peace from the Comanches for $3,000 worth of beads, trinkets; and in 1850 at Wallace Creek, about 15 mi. southwest, the U.S. signed an Indian treaty. (1967)

SAN SABA (San Saba Co.)   *US 190, 10.7 mi. W on a boulder*
The John Robert Polk Ranch

Known as San Saba County property with history of longest continuous ownership by a single family. Texas settler Headley Polk, a kinsman of 1845–1849 United States President James K. Polk, bought from grantee Burke Trammel in 1849 a section of land a half-mile to the south of this marker. Headley's son, John Robert Polk (1853–1946), grew up in Lockhart and on the San Marcos River at the Mooney Mill, where he made fine furniture. In 1883, "Bob" and his wife Kate Word Polk moved to this property with their herd of cattle. Over the years they bought adjacent land until they had 2,000 acres with frontage of three and one-half miles on the San Saba River. The second tract of land in this county ever to be enclosed was fenced by Polk with the help of a man named Baker. Two schoolhouses were built at different times on this ranch, for the convenience of the Polk family and neighbors. In the early era, Polk trailed his Bar-P cattle to market; for years he belonged to the Texas Trail Drivers' Association.

John Robert and Kate Polk were parents of a son, Headley (who died at 17, in 1904) and five daughters: Annie (later Mrs. W. W. Holman), Eupha (Mrs. Louis J. Bryan), Ivor Mac, Katie (Mrs. J. A. Sloan), and Lex. (1971)

SAN SABA (San Saba Co.)   *SH 16, ¼ mi. N, San Saba Cemetery*
About 276 yds. W is Grave of Sion Record Bostick
(December 7, 1819–October 15, 1902)

A member of the party of young Texans who captured the escaping Mexican General Santa Anna after Battle of San Jacinto, during the Texas War for Independence.

Migrated from Alabama in 1828. Served in Texas Army at Gonzales and Bexar (San Antonio), 1835; at San Jacinto, 1836; and 1840 stand against Comanches, at Plum Creek.

An American soldier in Mexican War, 1846; a Confederate in Hood's Brigade in the Civil War, 1860s.

Married Susan Townsend; after her death, Mary Indiana Rhodes. Had several children. Became a leader in veterans' reunions. He is buried in San Saba Cemetery. (1973)

SAN SABA (San Saba Co.)   US 190, .20 mi. E
John H. "Shorty" Brown Cemetery
After living for a time in Arkansas, John H. "Shorty" Brown (1817–1896), his wife Jane Ann, and some of their children came here. Brown helped found San Saba in 1854 and became a civic leader. Although San Saba County provided a graveyard, Brown and his wife deeded this plot near their home for a family burial ground. Jane Ann, who bore 17 of Brown's 21 children, was probably the first burial here about 1874. Brown's son and a son-in-law who were murdered are buried here along with other family members and friends.   (1980)

SAN YGNACIO (Zapata Co.)   US 183 right-of-way, 5 mi. SE
                                               in the Ramireno Community
Old Ramireño
Old Ramireño was located on land granted to Don Jose Luis Ramirez by the King of Spain in 1784. Part of the colonization effort of Col. Jose de Escandon, Ramirez' grant was designated as porcion 5.

A resident of Revilla (now Guerrero), Nuevo Santander (now Tamaulipas) in Mexico, Don Jose Luis Ramirez, his wife Maria Bacilia Martinez, and their children moved across the Rio Grande and established a home on their land in present Zapata County. Don Jose Luis and Maria Bacilia Martinez Ramirez had ten children. Their families and descendants formed the nucleus of the community of Ramireño.

The men of the ill-fated Mier Expedition of 1842 camped at Ramireño during their march to Mexico, and the settlement was also the site of United States military activity during the Mexican Revolution and border raids of 1916–1917.

The construction of Falcon Reservoir on the Rio Grande caused the relocation of several area communities, including Ramireño. The settlement founded by Don Jose Luis Ramirez was moved in 1953 to a site two miles from the original Ramirez Ranch. The hand-cut sandstone Ramirez ranch home was covered by the waters of Falcon Reservoir.   (1988)

SANDERSON (Terrell Co.)   Courthouse Grounds
County Named for Texas Confederate
General Alexander W. Terrell
1827–1912
Born in Virginia. Came to Texas in 1852. Dist. Judge 1857–1863. Entered Confederate service 1863 as Lt. Col. Commanded Terrell's Texas Cavalry. Assigned special duty to try to keep open vital supply sources of cotton—lifeblood of South. Led his unit in Red River Campaign 1864 to prevent Union invasion of Texas, being wounded at the Battle of Mansfield. Promoted to Brigadier General 1865. Went to Mexico rather than surrender at war's end, soon returned to Texas. As state legislator authored present primary election law. Minister to Turkey 1893–1897. Outstanding lawyer and public servant.

SANDERSON (Terrell Co.)   US 90, 1 mi. W (now at Courthouse Square)
Terrell County
Formed from Pecos County. Created April 8, 1905. Organized September 19, 1905. Named in honor of Alexander Watkins Terrell, 1827–1912. A distinguished officer in the Confederate Army. Member of the Texas Legislature for sixteen years. Sanderson, the county seat.

SANDIA (Jim Wells Co.)   SH 359
Fort Casa Blanca, CSA
First building erected in area that is now Jim Wells County early as 1855. During the Civil War was on Confederate supply line that started in Corpus Christi, followed the Nueces here, went to Laredo, to Brownsville and back to Corpus Christi. When Federals were in Corpus Christi, Thomas Wright, the sutler, drove from here to other points.

Casa Blanca was supplied by small boats that out-maneuvered Federals on Nueces Bay, slipped into the Nueces River, and came up Penitos Creek. They hauled guns, ammunition, medicine, and other wartime goods and took out cotton, "Currency of the Confederacy."

The fort had walls 28" thick, an escape tunnel from its well led to the creek. Its one entryway, wide enough for a 2-wheel cart of 2 horses abreast, was closed with a heavy cypress door. Cypress shutters covered its few small windows. Corner parapets and portholes at 3 heights gave it emplacements for defense. It not only warehoused goods, but also provided shelter and water for drivers passing with wagons along the Cotton Road from San Antonio to Matamoros. For cotton wagons it meant safety from bandit chases and from killing thirsts. In the 20th century the fort has disappeared.

SANGER (Denton Co.) — FM 455, 7.5 mi. W at entrance to ranch
Forester Ranch
William S. Forester brought his family to Denton County from Tennessee in the early 1850s, and established a ranch about 1852. He was assisted in his ranching operation by his sons, one of whom, Sol, was killed by Indians at the age of sixteen while herding cattle on the ranch.

Following William Forester's death, the ranch was operated by his son, Lock S. Forester (1844–1913). A Confederate veteran, Lock Forester increased the size of the ranch to over 6,000 acres. Under his management the ranch's "Two I Jinglebob" brand became well known. He supervised the ranch interests until 1890, when he moved to Denton.

Ed W. Forester, son of Lock Forester, assumed management of the ranch in 1890. In 1913, the ranch was divided into sections, with Lock S. Forester's three children each receiving one-third of the ranch property. Ed Forester became a successful rancher in his own right, raising champion shorthorn cattle as well as quarter horses, sheep, and other livestock. He served two terms as Denton County commissioner.

The Forester Ranch has been an important part of the history of Denton County for over a century. (1987)

SANTA ANNA (Coleman Co.) — US 84, 3 mi. NE
Coleman County
Formed from Travis and Brown Counties. Created February 1, 1858, organized October 6, 1864. Named in honor of Robert M. Coleman, 1799–1837, a signer of the Declaration of Independence, a hero of San Jacinto, organizer of first company of Texas Rangers. Coleman approved as county seat April 28, 1876. (1936)

SANTA ANNA (Coleman Co.) — US 84 at US 67
Santa Anna, C.S.A.
Mountain and town named in honor of man in power here in 1840s, a Comanche chief friendly to Texans. Santa Anna in 1846 visited President Polk in Washington during U.S. negotiations to annex Texas. Also signed and kept until his death of cholera in 1849 peace treaties that allowed the German Emigration Company to settle lands north of the Llano River.

Comanches used Santa Anna peaks as signal points. Early surveyors, travelers, explorers and settlers took them as guide points. In 1857, nearby United States Cavalry at Camp Colorado kept lookouts here.

In the Civil War, 1861–1865, frontier rangers camped at foot of mountain, with sentries on height watching at the pass the military road from San Antonio northeastward to Fort Belknap, a strategic outpost guarding Texas from invasion by Indians and Federal troops. During the 1870s, thousands of longhorns went through the gap, over the western cattle trail.

In 1879, "The Gap" had a store and post office to supply the cattle drives. When Gulf, Colorado and Santa Fe built here in 1886, settlers moved from the gap to the railroad, starting the present town.

Quarries in the mountain yield fine sands for the manufacturing of glass. (1965)

SANTA ANNA (Coleman Co.) — US 67/84, 3 mi. E
Route of Old Military Road
Opened in 1850s for supply trains and cavalry travel along line of U.S. forts from Belknap on the Brazos to Fort Mason and to Fort Clark near the Rio Grande.

Along this road passed great men, including Col. Robert E. Lee, later (1861–1865) General of Confederate forces in the Civil War. (1972)

SANTA ANNA (Coleman Co.) — US 67, ½ mi. W
The Turner House
Built 1886 by an attorney from Mississippi. Colonial architecture. House was enlarged from 8 to 12 rooms after 1903 purchase by Fred W. Turner, rancher and oilman.

This was gathering place for area social and business leaders. Awarded Medallion Plate.

(1968)

SANTA ANNA (Coleman Co.)
US 84, 1 mi. NW of Santa Anna
Old Rock House
This site was claimed in 1857 under a Republic of Texas land certificate held by former State Representative Darwin Stapp of Victoria County. In 1869 he sold the tract to another absentee owner. By tradition, this house was built in the 1870s by John J. Brestow, a squatter who came to this area for his health. The one-room cabin was constructed of stone from the nearby Santa Anna mountains. Later owners, including Mrs. Sarah Himmins, rented the property to tenant farmers. Mr. and Mrs. C. D. Bruce, who purchased the land in 1947, restored the rock house and maintain it now as a museum. (1975)

SANTA ANNA (Coleman Co.)
FM 1176, SE edge of Santa Anna
John R. Banister
(May 24, 1854–Aug. 2, 1918)
Missouri native John Banister left home in 1867 and came to Texas. He received training as a cowboy and participated in several cattle drives to northern markets. Banister served with his brother, Will, as a Texas Ranger and participated in the capture of outlaw Sam Bass. Other contributions to the state included his service as a railway officer, inspector for the Cattle Raisers' Association, and Coleman County sheriff. (1984)

SANTA FE (Galveston Co.)
SH 6 at Jackson Ave.,
in roadside park
Dairy Industry in the Santa Fe Area
The railroad communities of Arcadia, Alta Loma, and Algoa, established in the 1890s, formed the nucleus of the Santa Fe area at the turn of the 20th century. Citrus and fig production, truck farming, and a burgeoning dairy industry dominated the local economy at that time. Creameries operating at Alta Loma and Arcadia produced and shipped large amounts of butter and milk to markets in Galveston and Houston by 1912.

Dairy farming, unlike the citrus and fig industry, emerged as a major economic base in the area during the 1920s. According to local tradition they became so prevalent during this time that most everyone had a dairy. Trucks had supplanted trains for transporting dairy products to markets in Galveston and Houston by this time. Local citizens recalled catching rides on milk trucks before community bus service was available.

Although able to recover from a crushing hoof and mouth epidemic in the mid-1920s, many small dairies were bought out by larger operations able to afford land leases for grazing purposes made necessary by stock laws of the 1930s restricting grazing on public lands. Though many dairies prospered with the introduction of automation in the 1950s, the gradual loss of workers to higher paying urban jobs resulted in the closing of all Santa Fe area dairies by the 1970s. (1993)

SANTA MARIA (Cameron Co.)
US 281, 8 mi. E at roadside park
Near Routes of
Alonso de Leon Expeditions
Some of the first systematic explorations of East Texas. Conducted by the Spanish between 1686 and 1690, de Leon's five expeditions were spurred by the fear that the French explorer La Salle, who had landed on the Texas coast in 1685, was claiming vast areas of the New World for France. Because Spain and France were bitter rivals, de Leon was directed to find and destroy any signs of French encroachment.

His first trip, originating in Mexico in 1686, took him to the mouth of the Rio Grande, where he sounded the river's depth and took latitude observations.

On the second expedition, begun in 1687, he crossed the river near present Roma and followed it to the mouth. Very likely his men traveled several miles away from the water to avoid mud, brush, and hidden Indians. He proceeded up the coast as far as a "Salt River," possibly Olmos Creek, which runs into Baffin Bay near the present town of Rivera.

On his three later expeditions, de Leon found and burned the ruins of La Salle's "Fort St. Louis." He also established the first Spanish mission in East Texas, "San Francisco de los Tejas."

Stimulated by both of these successes, Spain began her great enterprise of colonizing Texas. (1968)

SANTA MARIA (Cameron Co.)
US 281, 1 mi. E of town at ranch gate
Rancho de Santa María
Part of Spain's 1777 La Feria Grant (12.5 leagues), partitioned into 6 units 1843. Here in 1850s was a sub-post of Fort Brown (28 mi. SE) and Fort Ringgold (65 mi. NW). This was proposed site in 1860s for "Homeville," this locality's first small-acreage promotion.

Present compound, built 1870 by L. J. Hynes, has buildings for dairy, kitchen, ammunition. Hynes, first postmaster (1876), had stage depot, general store, telegraph office, shipping wharf on river. Chapel was built 1880. In 1892, Frank Rabb bought the ranch. In 1916 border troubles, U.S. Army established headquarters here. (1968)

SANTA MARIA (Cameron Co.)
US 281, .5 mi. E
Our Lady of Visitation Catholic Church
A rare South Texas snowstorm marked the cornerstone laying ceremonies for this church building, Dec. 29,1880. The gothic revival edifice was constructed of bricks made at nearby El Rancho de Santa Maria, owned by L. J. Hynes, who gave land for the church. Built from plans drawn by Father Peter I. Keralum, O. M. I., the structure was dedicated June 29, 1882. The wooden steeple was blown off during a 1933 hurricane. Residents of Bluetown, Santa Maria, and neighboring communities worshiped here. (1977)

SARGENT (Matagorda Co.)
FM 457, 5.1 mi. SE
Confederate Defenses at the Mouth of Caney Creek
During the Civil War (1861–1865), Federal forces tried several times to seize Texas ports. Galves-ton was taken on Oct. 5, 1862, but recaptured by a Confederate Army on Jan. 1, 1863. Lt. Dick Dowling's troops stopped a Federal invasion at Sabine Pass on Sept. 8, 1863.

Another thrust began on Nov. 7, 1863, when a Federal expedition under Maj. Gen. N. P. Banks seized Brownsville, then moved up the coast, capturing Corpus Christi, Aransas Pass, Pass Cavallo, and Port Lavaca (Dec. 26). Maj. Gen. John B. Magruder, Confederate commander of Texas, ordered fortification of the mouth of Caney Creek in an attempt to halt the invasion. In Jan. 1864, an earthen fortress, rifle pits, trench works, and four redoubts were erected near this site. Defended by 4000–6000 Confederates, the area was bombarded by Federal gunboats during January and February.

No ground combat occurred at Caney Creek, but the preparations deterred a further Federal advance. In March 1864, Gen. Banks moved most of his troops to Louisiana and launched an unsuccessful invasion along Texas' eastern border. Removal of Federal forces from key Texas ports allowed blockade runners to continue transporting needed materials to Civil War Texas. (1976)

SARITA (Kenedy Co.)
US 77, 3 mi. N
Kenedy County
Created April 2, 1921, out of Cameron, Willacy and Hidalgo counties. Named for Captain Mifflin Kenedy, 1818–1895, sent to Texas in 1846 on United States Army supply boats. Commercial navigator of the Rio Grande 1848–1860. Sarita is the county seat.

SARITA (Kenedy Co.)
US 77, 7 mi. S
Site of General Zachary Taylor Camp
Under this tree General Zachary Taylor, commanding the Expeditionary Army of the United States, sent to Texas in 1845, encamped on March 15, 1846, while enroute with his troops from Corpus Christi to the Rio Grande. (1936)

SARITA (Kenedy Co.)
US 77, 20 mi. S, entrance to Armstrong Ranch
The Armstrong Ranch
In 1852, James H. Durst, son of a leading Nacogdoches, Texas family, purchased 83,219 acres of land here, part of the "La Barreta" Spanish land grant. In 1878, Mary Helena "Mollie" Durst, daughter of James and Mary Josephine Atwood Durst, married the noted Texas Ranger John Barkley Armstrong. Armstrong had served with Captain Leander McNelly and played a major role in bringing law and order to South Texas. He participated in the arrest of King Fisher and gained national fame for his capture of the notorious Texas outlaw John Wesley Hardin.

Armstrong moved his family to the ranch home he built here. Their close friends and neighbors were the families of Captain Richard King and Captain Mifflin Kenedy. The ranch was an important site in the area; General Zachary Taylor had camped here prior to the Mexican War and for many years the ranch served as a stop on the stage route between Corpus Christi and Brownsville.

Under Armstrong's guidance, the Armstrong Ranch became one of the legendary cattle ranches of Texas. His descendants have continued the tradition of family enterprise here through the 20th century. (1983)

SARITA (Kenedy Co.)
US 77, 20 mi. S
The Armstrong Ranch House
This residence was begun in 1897, after John B. Armstrong moved the headquarters of his ranch from the Chicago pasture (7 mi. SE) to this site. Built in stages, the house was completed about 1900. The first portion was made of adobe and plastered over. Later a frame wing was added. Changes were made to the front porch after the destructive hurricane of 1919. This structure exemplifies the evolution of a South Texas ranch headquarters. (1982)

SAVOY (Fannin Co.)
US 82 at FM 1752, roadside park next to bridge
Fort Warren
(Site 6 mi. N)
First settlement and fort in Fannin County. Built in 1836 by Abel Warren, Indian trader from Arkansas, to protect his trading post. Constructed of Bois D'Arc wood, the structure had two-story guardhouses at all four corners. Kiowa, Tonkawa, Caddo, Wichita and other Indians came here to trade furs for paint, knives and trinkets.

In Civil War, Fort Warren was a transport and food supply center, where goods were sent to Confederate Indian refugees and troops in Indian territory (to the north) and to soldiers in Louisiana and Arkansas. (1968)

SAVOY (Fannin Co.)
US 82, 3 mi. E
Little Jordan Cemetery
Sid H. (1833–1914) and Suzan Brown Pierce (1845–1923) donated this burial ground, near the Little Jordan Baptist Church (active 1850–1893).

The Ector Baptist Church, organized by former Little Jordan members, deeded the cemetery to Savoy Baptist Church, 1953. Pioneers' heirs fenced the area in 1966. (1973)

SCHULENBURG (Fayette Co.)
US 90 right-of-way, E city limits
Schulenburg
German and Czech settlers used this gateway to the rolling hills of Fayette County. Settled by former residents of Lyons and High Hill in 1873, when the Galveston, Houston & San Antonio Railway reached here. Named for landowner Louis Schulenburg, town was incorporated in 1875. (1970)

SCHULENBURG (Fayette Co.)
SH 77, 1 mi. S
Site of Former Town of
Lyons
Early town of land grant of Keziah Cryer. Named for settler James Lyons, killed in 1837 by Indian raiders, who kidnapped his son Warren.

In 1860s town had stores, Masonic Lodge, school, post office; and was on "Cotton Road" to Mexico, but it died in 1870s when the Southern Pacific Railroad was built. (1972)

SCHULENBURG (Fayette Co.)
FM 1383, 2.5 mi. from US 90
intersection, 6 mi. NE
Dubina
Dubina, which derives its name from the Czech word for oak grove, was founded in 1856 by a group of Moravian immigrants, including the Marak, Kahlich, Sramek, Peter, Holub, Muzny, and Haidusek families. By 1900, the farming community had erected a church building, mill, cotton gin, blacksmith shop, store, and post office. A 1909 storm and a 1912 fire caused extensive damage from which the town never recovered. As the first settlement in Texas to be founded entirely by Czech-Moravians, Dubina remains an important part of the state's regional and cultural history. (1983)

SCOTLAND (Archer Co.)

US 281, West side

J. H. Meurer Home

German native John H. Meurer (b. 1850) settled his family in this area about 1900 when he became a land agent for H. J. Scott of the Clark and Plumb Company. In selling over 60,000 acres of land, Meurer helped to establish the towns of Windthorst (6 mi. S) and Scotland (named for H. J. Scott), both primarily German Catholic settlements. Meurer had this one-and-a-half story home built in 1911. The 11-room house with wraparound porch remained in the Meurer Family until 1941 when Saint Boniface Catholic Church purchased it to serve as a residence for parish priests. (1982)

SEABROOK (Harris Co.)

NASA Road 1, 3 mi. W, Harris County Park

Harris County Boys' School
Archeological Site

In this vicinity lies a prehistoric Indian campsite and burial ground that takes its name from the property on which it resided at the time of its discovery. It is classified as a Shell Midden Site because of the presence of a midden, or refuse pile, of oyster and rangia clam shell. The midden collected as the result of early inhabitants consuming shellfish and leaving the empty shells where they ate, which was usually at or near their campsite.

Archeological excavations revealed a variety of artifacts, including a Plainview dart point, which is associated with very early Indians. Its discovery supported radiocarbon testing that had dated part of the midden to 1476 B.C. Evidence of 32 burials was uncovered in another section of the site. Ceramics interred with the burials dated the cemetery from the first millenium A.D.

Scientific investigation of the Harris County Boys' School archeological site led to other studies of the cultural aspects of the prehistoric inhabitants of the area. The site remains as a significant example of the shell midden, once relatively common along the Texas coast, but now rarely found due to beach erosion and subsidence. (1985)

SEABROOK (Harris Co.)

Pine Gully Park

Prehistoric Indian Campsite

In this vicinity are the remains of a prehistoric Indian refuse pile, comprised mainly of clam shells. Archeologists call such sites "shell middens." They are the result of centuries of shellfish harvesting by early Indian groups. Shells found at this site have been identified as belonging to the *Rangia cuneata* (common *Rangia*) clam, a species once found in abundant numbers in Galveston Bay.

As the shell midden grew in size over the years, it became the foundation for a large Indian campsite. Stone tools and pottery uncovered here are evidence of the later occupation. Although the tribal origins of the Indians cannot be determined, it is known that both Orcoquisac and Karankawa once lived in the area in historic times.

Shell middens similar to this one were once more common along the streams feeding into the bay. Storms, subsidence, and natural erosion, however, have destroyed many, as have mining operations that used the shells for road construction projects. As a result, this is one of the best remaining examples of a prehistoric midden and campsite in Harris County. Because of its significance, the site has been afforded special protection as a state archeological landmark. (1988)

SEADRIFT (Calhoun Co.)

SH 185

Seadrift

Settlement here began in the 1840s when German immigrants disembarking at Indianola stayed in the vicinity. A post office was granted in 1888, its name inspired by debris that collected on the shore blown in by heavy storms from the Gulf of Mexico. In 1912, A. D. Powers founded the Seadrift Townsite Company, and the city was incorporated that December. By 1914, Seadrift had 3 churches, 2 banks, 4 hotels, factories, a telephone line, and a weekly newspaper called the *Seadrift Success*. Despite a severe 1919 hurricane, the city survived. Processing plants were established in the area beginning in the 1950s. The village of Seadrift continues to be a popular resort and recreation spot. (1998)

SEBASTIAN (Willacy Co.)

US 77 & FM 506, next to post office

Sebastian

Originally part of the San Juan de Carricitos land grant, this townsite later was part of South Texas' famed King Ranch. Sebastian was known as Stillman Town Tract until 1906, when it was renamed to honor an officer of the Rock Island Railroad. In 1914, the Sebastian Realty Company was promoting the town in the hope that it would become a major agricultural center. During the early 20th-century period of lawlessness in South Texas, Sebastian experienced a bandit raid in which two members of the Austin family were killed. (1985)

SEBASTIAN (Willacy Co.) *US 77 N near intersection with FM 1018*
Stagecoach to the Rio Grande C.S.A.
About ten miles east of this site during the Civil War was Paso Real ferry point on the Arroyo Colorado. As early as 1846 stage coaches had gone over Paso Real ferry (the name probably meant "The Kings Pass." It was a crossing for the Cotton Road, lifeline to the Confederacy. When Federal coastal blockades had cut off imports and exports for the entire South, this road moved cotton down to Matamoros so that it could be exchanged for guns, ammunition, medicines, cloth, shoes, blankets, and other vital goods.

Besides the prized cotton loads that went past Paso Real, the stage coach connection there was of importance to Confederate and foreign businessmen, government agents, diplomats, and army personnel. This was area of conflict and intrigue. Bandits and army deserters watched the road for stages and cotton wagons to pilfer. Mysterious travelers went this way—sometimes a pursuing sheriff on the next stage. Of thirty-one stagelines in Confederate Texas (hauling mail, soldiers, civilians) no other was more vital nor interesting to travel than this through Paso Real.

SEGUIN (Guadalupe Co.) *US 90A, 5 mi. E*
Battleground Prairie
Where 80 volunteers commanded by General Edward Burleson defeated Vicente Cordova and 75 Mexicans, Indians and Negroes, March 29, 1839, and drove them from Texas, ending the "Cordova Rebellion." 25 of the enemy were killed. Many volunteers were wounded, but none fatally. (1965)

SEGUIN (Guadalupe Co.) *US 90A, 3 mi. E*
Tiemann School
Named for Theodore Tiemann, who sold one acre of land to the county school district for $5.00, Tiemann School provided educational, cultural, and recreational opportunities for citizens in this area. Beginning in 1903 as a one-room, one-teacher facility, the school eventually was enlarged to accommodate two teachers and many students. A gathering place for many community events, Tiemann school closed in 1943. Along with other area schools, it was annexed by the Seguin school system in 1949. (1990)

SEGUIN (Guadalupe Co.) *US 90, 1.9 mi. W*
Guadalupe County
Formed from Gonzales and Bexar counties. Created March 30, 1846. Organized July 13, 1846. Named for the Guadalupe River, to which this name was given by Alonso de Leon in 1689. Seguin, the county seat, named in honor of Juan Nepomuceno Seguin 1806–1890. (1965)

SEGUIN (Guadalupe Co.) *US 90A, 11 mi. E*
Old Claiborne West Home
Awarded the Texas Historical Building Medallion.

SEGUIN (Guadalupe Co.) *US 90, .5 mi. W of courthouse*
Sebastopol
Named for Crimean war site. Built 1850–1855 by Col. Joshua W. Young (1811–1897), for his sister, Catherine LeGette. Nationally famed Seguin chemist Richard Parks patented the concrete used. Pool of water on roof cooled the house. A later owner was Mayor Joseph Zorn. Awarded Medallion Plate. (1964)

SEGUIN (Guadalupe Co.) *SH 123, edge of city, at Starcke Park*
The Guadalupe River
One of the earliest explored rivers in Texas. Named for our Lady of Guadalupe by Spaniard Alonso de Leon in 1689.

During 1691–1693, Domingo Teran de los Rios, Spanish governor of Texas, maintained a colony on the Guadalupe. An early Anglo-American settlement, 30 or 40 families located along its bank, which formed a boundary of the Power-Hewetson Irish Colony.

Near the mouth of the river, historic Victoria was founded, and 60 miles above was Gonzales, where the first shot for Texas freedom was fired, Oct. 2, 1835. The Guadalupe is 250 miles long.

(1969)

SEGUIN (Guadalupe Co.)   *SH 123, 1.5 mi. SW in Starcke Park*
Saffold Dam
Named for William Saffold, who owned land here in the mid-1800s, Saffold Dam is typical of many mill dams built during the late 19th and early 20th centuries. Originally a natural rock out-cropping, the dam was first improved by Henry Troell in the late 1800s when he added rock to the dam to raise the water level to power a cotton gin. The city of Seguin bought Troell's property in 1907 to further develop the river's hydroelectricity, and subsequent improvements have led to the establishment of a hydroelectric plant on the dam's south side.   (1991)

SEGUIN (Guadalupe Co.)   *SH 123, 1.5 mi. SW in Starcke Park*
Henry Troell (October 5, 1838–December 19, 1921)
A native of Wichmannshausen, Germany, Henry Troell moved to this area sometime prior to 1860. He served in the Confederate Army and in 1872 married area native Johanna Woehler. A successful freighting business enabled him to invest in several local properties and enterprises, including an innovative dam/gristmill operation at this site. He expanded the mill's water and hydroelectric generation capabilities and in the 1890s provided the city its first water and electric utility systems. His entrepreneurial and business legacy represent an important part of the city's development.   (1994)

SEGUIN (Guadalupe Co.)   *US 90A, 1.5 mi. E, San Geronimo Cemetery*
Andrew Jackson Sowell
Born in Tennessee, 1815. Came to Texas about 1829. Served in the Army of Texas. A courier from the Alamo, he left the fortress just before it fell to hurry reinforcements and supplies. Died about 1882. His wife, Lucinda Turner Sowell. Born 1827. Died 1883.   (1965)

SEGUIN (Guadalupe Co.)   *US 90A, 1.5 mi. E, San Geronimo Cemetery*
Elijah Valentine Dale
A San Jacinto veteran. Born in Georgia, February 14, 1807. Died December 14, 1890. His wife, Jane Johnson Dale. Born in Ohio, August 3, 1821. Died June 17, 1896.

John N. Sowell
Born in Tennessee. Came to Texas about 1829. Served in the Army of Texas, 1836. Brother of Andrew Jackson Sowell and son of John Sowell, who participated in the battle of Gonzales. Died in 1858.   (1956)

Star and Wreath
Robert D. McAnelly
Born in Kentucky, 1806. Came to Texas in 1835. Joined the Texas Army on its way to San Antonio. One of the storming party who entered Bexar, December 5, 1835. Died in Guadalupe County, Texas, 1888.   (1962)

SEGUIN (Guadalupe Co.)   *SH 46, Entrance to Texas Lutheran College*
Texas Lutheran College
The first German Evangelical Lutheran Synod in Texas authorized the establishment of a college in Brenham in 1890. Directed by the Rev. G. Langner, the Evangelical Lutheran College of Brenham opened in September 1891.

Modeled after the European gymnasium schools, the Brenham Academy offered elementary and secondary courses taught in both German and English. It continued as an academy until 1906. That year the Synod limited the focus of the school to prepare students for the ministry. In 1909, the name was changed to Evangelical Lutheran Proseminary.

The school remained in Brenham until 1912, when it moved to Seguin after citizens here offered land and improvements as a relocation incentive. Reestablished as a coeducational academy, it became known as the Lutheran College of Seguin and gained accreditation in 1928 from the Texas Association of Junior Colleges.

The Swedish Lutheran Trinity College at Round Rock merged with the Seguin school in 1929, and in 1932 the name was changed to Texas Lutheran College. It became a senior college in 1948 and attained accreditation in 1953. In 1954, the Norwegian Lutheran Clifton College merged with Texas Lutheran College.   (1991)

SEGUIN (Guadalupe Co.)   *SH 46, 7 mi. NW*
Site of Dietz Community
In 1851, Jamaica native Jacob de Cordova (1808–1868) settled here. He selected this spot for its beauty, rich soil and nearby springs. He built his first home, "Wanderer's Retreat." It served as a stage stop on the San Antonio Road and as a mail delivery station. De Cordova, acting as a land agent, sold over 90,000 acres of Texas land including this site. Nine German bachelors purchased the property and it became known as "Bachelor's Hall" and "Nine Men's House." Two brothers, Ferdinand Michael and J. August Dietz, cowboys for de Cordova, bought out the other men and the community became "Dietz."

Johann Phillip Stautzenberger (1838–1904) bought the land in 1861, built a substantial house and general store, and became the first postmaster.

Formal education began in a small room adjacent to Stautzenberger's store with Frankfort School starting later. "The Frohsinn Maennerchor," a singing group, was organized in the schoolhouse. Later they adopted the present name of "Frohsinn Mixed Chorus of Clear Springs." In 1895, a group of farmers founded present-day Friedens Church in the school building.

Consolidation of the schools, closing of the post office, and good roads and automobiles caused this early community to disappear.   (1978)

SEGUIN (Guadalupe Co.)   *SH 46 right-of-way, 8 mi. NW*
                                          in front of Clear Spring Restaurant
Clear Spring Hall and Store
This area was settled by German immigrants in the 1840s and 1850s. Named for a water source later inundated by Lake Dunlap, the Clear Spring community never evolved into a town, but remained a rural settlement. A store built at this site in the 1870s by Johann Andreas Breustedt became the commercial and social center for the surrounding area. A saloon and community hall were added to the building in later years, and the Clear Spring Gin Company located behind the store was important to the local cotton industry.   (1989)

SEMINOLE (Gaines Co.)   *US 180 at SH 214*
Gaines County
Named for James L. Gaines, a signer of the Texas Declaration of Independence, this county was formed out of Bexar County in 1876. Anglo settlement of the area began about 1895, and the county was formally organized in 1905. Seminole was established as the county seat that year, and a courthouse was built in 1906. Ranching and farming were the most prominent and profitable occupations until the mid-1930s, when they were eclipsed by oil production. Gaines County encompasses 1,479 square miles, and Seminole and Seagraves are its two largest cities.   (1989)

SEMINOLE (Gaines Co.)

US 385, 2 mi. S

Historic Hackberry Grove

Earliest known human habitation in Gaines County. This small, unique grove of hackberry trees has survived in this arid land because of sub-irrigation provided by a very shallow draw.

First officially reported by Col. W. R. ("Pecos Bill") Shafter, 24th Infantry, during his scouting of the north and western plains area in 1875. In this draw, Col. Shafter and his men found some 50 wells, 4 to 15 feet deep. Surrounding one well in the grove were evidences of use of roving bands of Indians as a seasonal campsite.

A Fourth of July gathering of settlers in this grove in 1905 planned local organization of Gaines County, which had been created in 1876. In election of October 24, 1905, the first officers were selected and Seminole was named the county seat.

Hackberry Grove and the shallow water well which is located here served Gaines Countians as an area for recreation and outdoor meetings until the early 1940s, when the discovery of oil and installation of a pump station caused the grove to be closed to the public. (1968)

SEMINOLE (Gaines Co.)

US 385, north edge

Seminole

Founded and designated county seat in 1905, same year county was organized. Took name from Seminole wells, Indian watering places to south and west.

First store and post office were established in 1905 by W. B. Austin of nearby Caput. The courthouse was built in 1906.

Seminole grew slowly, being chiefly important as a trading center. Arrival of the Midland & Northwestern Railroad (1918) and development of highways and oil resources all helped speed the town's later expansion. Today it is a business center for farming and petroleum industry. (1970)

SEMINOLE (Gaines Co.)

US 385, Gaines County Park

Oil Industry in Gaines County

The first oil lease in Gaines County was in 1912 and the first drilling occurred in 1925. Ten years later the Landreth Co. brought in the first producing well. In 1936, Amerada Oil Co. opened up the Seminole pool, a major field that yielded 350 wells within a decade. Less than 50 years after that discovery, Gaines County had produced over one billion barrels of crude oil. With several active fields, Gaines ranks as one of the top oil producing counties in Texas. The petroleum industry accounts for much of this area's prosperity. (1979)

SEMINOLE (Gaines Co.)

US 180, 20 mi. E

Lake Mackenzie
(¼ mi. N)

According to geologists, this dry salt lake may be the remains of an ancient river bed. Water from infrequent rains quickly evaporates, leaving a deposit of salt and alkali. The lake and nearby draw were named for Col. Ranald S. Mackenzie (1840–1889). During the 1870s, Col. Mackenzie led several U.S. Army expeditions across the Staked Plains and fought a series of Indian battles. He was instrumental in bringing hostile tribes under control and opening this area to settlement. West Texas pioneers named a number of natural landmarks in his honor. (1979)

SEVEN POINTS (Henderson Co.)

US 85, 3 mi. W at Reese Rd.
in Aley community

Buffalo

Before Henderson County was created by the Texas Legislature in 1846, a small community known as Buffalo had developed around a ferry that operated in this area on the Trinity River. Despite its location in the northwest section of the county, Buffalo served as the seat of government from 1847 until 1850.

Instrumental in the development of the small community were pioneer area landholder Henry Jeffries and surveyor and lawyer John H. Reagan. Reagan, who later became a United States congressman and served as Postmaster General of the Confederacy, was appointed road overseer, deputy sheriff, and first probate judge.

Few records have survived to tell the history of Buffalo. Although lots for a church and school were designated on the town plat, no other reference to their existence has been uncovered. The community was awarded a post office in 1847. Minutes of the commissioner's court indicate that the major work done during the county's formative years was the establishment and laying out of public roads, most of which began at Buffalo and extended in all directions. When Athens became the Henderson County seat in 1850, Buffalo began to decline and eventually disappeared, never realizing the expectations of its founders. (1984)

SEYMOUR (Baylor Co.) — *US 82 & US 277, 9 mi. NE*
Baylor County
Created February 1, 1858. Organized April 23, 1879. Named in honor of Dr. Henry W. Baylor, 1818–1854, Indian fighter and Ranger captain. Served in the Mexican War. Seymour, the county seat. (1964)

SEYMOUR (Baylor Co.) — *FM 2374, 15 mi. SE*
Round Timber Community
Named for round clumps of oaks. Pioneered by C. C. (Lum) Mills, 1863, but soon abandoned to Indians, site became the first permanent settlement in Baylor County when reopened in 1874 by T. K. Hamby, C. C. and W. B. Mills, John W. Stevens and Tom Whitworth. Post office opened in 1879 with A. C. Burnham as postmaster. In school built in 1879, first teacher was Eliza Mitchell. Town had stores, barber and blacksmith shops, 1880s. The church was built by Methodists, 1897, sold to Baptists, 1933. The burial ground, dating from 1870, was deeded 1962 by J. Hop Parker to the Cemetery Association. (1972)

SEYMOUR (Baylor Co.) — *US 87/277 in roadside park, at NE city limits*
Near Route of the Western Trail
Principal cattle trail from Texas to Kansas and beyond from 1876 to 1887; superseded the Chisholm Trail after Dodge City replaced Abilene as the main intermediate northern beef market.

As its name implies, the Western Trail ran west of the Chisholm Trail, by about 100 miles. Most of its feeder trails started in South Texas, although some made connections at San Antonio and Fort Griffin.

Here in Baylor County the trail crossed the Brazos River passing half a mile east of Seymour, a major supply center. The herds bedded near Seymour Creek, at the site of the present fair grounds. The Millett Ranch (established 1874) served as a watering spot, and the Millett brothers—Eugene, Alonzo, and Hiram—were among the first users of the trail.

From Seymour the route continued north, leaving Texas at Doan's Store on the Red River. It then ran through Oklahoma to Dodge City, lesser extensions proceeding to Nebraska, Wyoming, and Montana.

During its life, the Western Trail moved hundreds of thousands of cattle north to stock ranges, Indian reservations, and markets. But after the fencing of the open range and building of the Texas & Pacific Railroad, it ceased to be used by the cattle industry. (1972)

SEYMOUR (Baylor Co.) — *SH 114 and Hale Rd., 16 mi. SE*
Westover
Platted in 1910 on the Gulf, Texas and Western Railroad, Westover developed into a small market center providing goods and services for area farmers and ranchers. J. W. Stevens offered part of his ranchland for the townsite, which was given the maiden name of his mother-in-law. James H.B. Kyle served as first postmaster when the post office was established in 1910. Businesses, including a bank, barbershops, cotton gins and dry goods stores, as well as churches, a school and a cemetery were established to serve area residents. After the commercial area suffered a fire in 1921 and the rail line was abandoned in 1942, many settlers and businesses moved to Seymour. (2002)

SEYMOUR (Baylor Co.) — *SH 114 at Hale Rd., 16 mi. SE*
Westover School
One-half mile east of this site is the location of the former Westover School, which served students in this part of Baylor County from 1910 until 1950. School classes first met in the Church of Christ building in Westover until trustees constructed a frame schoolhouse in 1911. Six years later, that building was replaced by a two-story brick building, which held all eleven grades and included seven classrooms, a library and an auditorium. Enrollment reached 400 students by the 1930s, but with abandonment of the rail line in 1942 and the general movement of people from rural areas after World War II, the student population declined, and Westover School closed in

SHAFTER (Presidio Co.)
US 67, 4.5 mi. N
Milton Faver Ranches

Milton Faver (ca.1822–1889), a native of the midwest United States, moved to this area in the 1850s from Presidio Del Norte, where he owned a general store and operated a freighting business on the Chihuahua Trail. By the 1880s, Faver controlled vast acreage in this part of the county, including most of the best permanent water sources, which he built into a formidable cattle, sheep, and goat ranching empire.

Faver's three ranches—El Fortín Del Cibolo, El Fortín de la Cienega, and La Morita—comprised the largest single-owner landholdings in the county. Structures on the ranches, including dwellings, work rooms, fences, corrals, and irrigation systems, were built with traditional adobe and stone building methods. Census and tax records show that Faver owned the largest live stock herds in the county in the late 19th century.

Following the deaths of Milton Faver in 1889, his wife Francisca in 1893, and his son Juan in 1913, and after a lawsuit, the ranchlands were sold by the Faver heirs. Other pioneer ranching families in the area, including George and Juliana Dawson (niece of Francisca Faver), and J. A. Pool, Sr., J.W. Pool, and their heirs, the Greenwood family, operated ranches on the former Faver lands until the late 20th century. (1995)

SHAFTER (Presidio Co.)
SH 67, 5 mi. N
Milton Faver (ca. 1829–December 1889)

The earliest large-scale cattleman to settle in the Big Bend, Milton (Don Meliton) Faver prospered against seemingly impossible odds to become the first cattle baron west of the Pecos. While operating a freighting business on the Chihuahua Trail, he moved his family to Presidio Del Norte and opened a general store about 1855. After accumulating a large herd of cattle in Mexico he moved his family and vaqueros to the mountain country north of Presidio and made his headquarters on Cibolo Creek in 1857. He established two other ranches at nearby La Cienega and La Morita.

Springs flowed abundantly on all three ranches, providing water for livestock and agriculture. In the fertile fields surrounding the ranches, Faver devised and installed irrigation systems that supplied water for vegetables, grain, and large peach orchards. El Fortín del Cibolo, ranch headquarters, served as a supply station for the U.S. Army Quartermaster Division at Ft. Davis. Troops used the ranch as a point of departure for forays into Indian occupied regions to the west and north.

Celebrated for his hospitality, Faver was known as a gentleman of means who lived in style. He died in December 1889 and was buried on his ranch at Cibolo. (1992)

SHAMROCK (Wheeler Co.)
IH 40, 10 mi. E at roadside park
Greer County, Texas
(To the East in Present Oklahoma)

Created 1860; until 1896, one of largest counties in Texas. Organized at old Mobeetie, northwest of here. In 1880s settlement was rapid; by 1892 nearly 2,500 pupils were in county's schools. A post office, jail and many houses were built, and over 60,000 cattle grazed the 3,480 square miles of the county's area.

But for a half-century (1846–1896) the United States and Texas waged a heated dispute over Greer County. Controversy had origin in an 1819 treaty fixing the line between United States and Spanish territory. A map designating the Red River and 100th meridian as boundary lines was part of treaty; but map aroused dispute, for it incorrectly marked 100th meridian and showed only one fork of two-forked Red River.

Texas claimed the north fork and meridian shown on map defined territory, and legislation and occupancy by Texans decided sovereignty. United States contended south fork (larger of the two) and true 100th meridian marked boundaries. Three joint survey commissions failed to settle the issue.The U.S. Supreme Court in 1896 ruled that the region was in 1819 part of the Union and thus was actually a part of Oklahoma.

Named for John A. Greer, Senator, Secretary of State, Republic of Texas; Lieutenant Governor, 1847–1853. (1967)

SHEFFIELD (Pecos Co.)   *US 290, city park*
Sheffield
Spanish explorers traveled Indian trails here in the Pecos River Valley as early as 1590. Later, U.S. Cavalry, a camel train, and stage and mail lines between San Antonio and San Diego, California, used the route.

Nearby Pecos Spring attracted settlers to the area in the 1880s and '90s. Families lived in tents on the north side of the creek and hauled water from the spring. About 1890, a community water well was dug. Early residents were sheep and cattle ranchers. Mail and supplies had to be brought from San Angelo and Ozona. About 1901, Will Sheffield built a grocery and dry goods store approximately one mile from the spring. A post office opened with Will Sheffield as postmaster. Since he was the first to operate a store, the settlement was named for him. A saloon was opened, and in 1901 a school was begun with sixty-four pupils. After living for several years in tents, residents began building permanent homes.

Garrett Bean purchased a section of land from the state where the present townsite is located and drew off town lots in 1905.

Well-known Texas Ranger Frank Hamer got his start in law enforcement here. Sheffield offers churches and a trade center for area ranches.   (1980)

SHELBYVILLE (Shelby Co.)   *US 59, 3 mi. NW*
Site of Last Battle, August 14, 1844
Between Regulators and Moderators, warring factions in Shelby County, 1841–1844, who caused heavy sacrifice of life and property before General James Smith with Texas troops restored order.

SHELBYVILLE (Shelby Co.)   *FM 417 at SH 87*
First County Seat
Shelbyville, once known as Nashville, was the first county seat of government of the District of Tenaha or Shelby County. The first courthouse stood on this site. The settlement began before 1825. It became headquarters for the "Regulator-Moderator War." Troops were raised here to fight the Indians; for the Texas Army; and Confederate forces were organized here.

SHELBYVILLE (Shelby Co.)   *SH 147, 8 mi. S*
Roberts' Hill
A home-site of Col. Oran Milo Roberts, "Old Alcalde." He rose from district attorney to Chief Justice Texas Supreme Court; President Texas Secession Convention; Col. Confederate Infantry Regiment; selected U. S. Senator; Governor of Texas; author; first President Texas Historical Association; law professor University of Texas.

SHEPHERD (San Jacinto Co.)   *FM 223, 2 mi. E*
Near Site of Coushatta Indian Village
Inhabited from about 1835–1900 by members of the Coushatta tribe. Most of the Indians had small farms, but also worked for wages after crops were harvested. Burial pits excavated by archeologists (1968) revealed skeletal remains, ironstone dishes, glass beads (obtained in trade with Anglos), ornaments made from silver coins.   (1969)

SHEPHERD (San Jacinto Co.)   *SH 150*
Town of Shepherd
Originated in vicinity of old Drew's Landing, a Trinity River port for settlers bringing in goods and shipping cotton, tobacco, and other products to markets. An early nearby community was Big Creek.

Into these pioneer settlements came Houston East & West Texas Railroad investors, including Benjamin A. Shepherd (1814–1891) of Houston, who in 1875 platted townsite here, naming it for himself. The town square was on west side of H. E. & W. T., which was completed beyond this point in 1879. The Shepherd post office opened Dec. 22, 1879, with Jack B. Noble as postmaster.

A pioneer physician was Dr. William Herbert Beazley (1837–1919); Mrs. Jessie Fain operated an early hotel; Mrs. Jane Langham taught first public school session, in Methodist Church building. James Ephraim Tribe, a native of Canada, came here in 1895, was a carpenter, coffin maker, millwright, and wheelwright. A Baptist, he built a church edifice for that faith in 1896.

Distinguished native son Robert Scott Lovett (1860–1932), became president of Southern Pacific and Union Pacific railroads and rendered outstanding civilian service to the nation during World War I.

Once a center for the lumbering industry, Shepherd remains an important market town of Southeast Texas. (1972)

SHERMAN (Grayson Co.)

US 82, 4 mi. W then ½ mi.
N on Preston Rd. to Cherokee Trail

First Site of City of Sherman

When Grayson County was created on March 17, 1846, by the First Legislature of the State of Texas, the act named the county seat in honor of Sidney Sherman (1805–1873), an heroic leader at the Battle of San Jacinto and in the affairs of the Republic of Texas.

Commissioners to select possible courthouse sites within 3 miles of center of the county were Micajah Davis, George C. Dungan, Richard McIntire, James Shannon, and James G. Thompson. This site on the old Cherokee Trail and the road to important river crossing at Preston Bend won approval of the voters. Townsite lots were auctioned late in the year 1846.

Chief Justice James G. Thompson supervised building of courthouse under a contract awarded in Jan. 1847 to M. L. Webster. Completion of the structure called for special celebration in a Fourth of July picnic with barbecue, a barrel of whiskey, music, and dancing.

Water and wood for public use were scarce at this site, called "A Bald Prairie." State Representative James B. Shannon (one of the original county seat commissioners) secured new legislation; he and Samuel Blagg, his business partner, on Nov. 23, 1848, deeded from their holdings to the county commissioners an 80-acre Sherman townsite 5 miles to the east. (1972)

SHERMAN (Grayson Co.)

US 75, East access rd.

Sherman Manufacturing Company

Sherman Seamless Bag Mill was founded here in 1891, to serve the cotton industry of North Central Texas.

Elected to board of directors on March 18, 1891, were C. A. Andrews, Edward Eastburn, W. C. Eubank, Thomas Forbes, J. F. Jaques, J. C. Jones, Tom Randolph, Z. E. Raney, and J. C. Tassey to serve as chairman.

Elegant cornerstone was shipped from Cromwell, Mass., to go into the original structure. Suffering from financial problems during those early years, the plant operated and closed intermittently.

Acquired in 1906 by Wellington-Sears Company of New York, who added buildings and centered production upon single-filling flat duck. Purchased, 1946, by Ely Walker & Company of St. Louis, Missouri; wide sheeting became main product. Merged into Burlington Industries, Inc., 1955.

Cornerstone of original building opened 1956. Disclosed old coins, 1891 newspapers, timetable for trains to Indian territory (now State of Oklahoma), saloon tokens and menu from Binkley Hotel coffee shop.

A portion of the original structure remains as a useful part of this modern plant.

Through Burlington's international organization, products made here are sold in market places throughout the world. (1967)

SHERMAN-DENISON (Grayson Co.)

US 75 Bus (Texoma Parkway)
at Wood Lake Rd.

First Texas Interurban

Electric railways (trolleys) provided convenient travel between many Texas cities for more than forty years. The first interurban line was established in Grayson County, connecting the cities of Sherman and Denison. Founded in 1900 by Fred Fitch and John P. Crerar, the Denison and Sherman Railway began operations on May 1, 1901, with a single 10.5-mile track.

The company built a power plant, offices, and a car barn near this site halfway between its passenger stations in the two cities. In order to provide water for the power plant, they built a dam below Tanyard Springs, creating a small lake. Named Wood Lake, it provided recreational facilities for passengers on the line's excursion trains.

The Texas Traction Company, founded in 1906, began construction of a second interurban line from Dallas to McKinney in 1906. Merged with the Denison and Sherman Railway in 1908, the company expanded its operations, eventually connecting a number of North Texas cities and changing its name to the Texas Electric Railway in 1917. The advent of automobile travel signalled the decline of the Texas Interurbans by the 1930s. The last train passed this site on December 31, 1948, on its route from Denison to Dallas. (1965, 1990)

SHERMAN (Grayson Co.) *900 N Grand Ave.*
Austin College
Oldest college in Texas operating under original charter. Founded in 1849 by the Presbytery of Brazos under leadership of Daniel Baker. Named for Stephen F. Austin, Father of Texas. Opened in Huntsville, with Sam Houston, Anson Jones, and Henderson Yoakum—Texas statesmen—among original trustees. Bell donated by Houston hangs in present chapel. For years competence in Greek and Latin was required for admittance.

In 1855, opened the first law school in state, and became the first college in Texas to award graduate degrees in 1856. Had the first chapter in Texas of any national fraternity (Phi Delta Theta). Remained open during Civil War although most students joined Confederate Army. Postwar problems and epidemics caused move to Sherman in 1876. Oldest building is Luckett Hall (1908), the first building on this campus having been destroyed by arson in 1913.

Erected first college Y.M.C.A. building west of the Mississippi River, 1911. In World War I, cooperated with the student army training corps and admitted first coeds. In World War II, aided army air training corps.

Founded to serve youth pioneer families, college now enrolls students from all over the world and is a leader in creative Christian liberal arts education.

SHERMAN (Grayson Co.) *Grayson County Courthouse lawn, Lamar & Travis (SH 56)*
Butterfield Overland Mail Route through Grayson County
In the mid-19th century, mail traffic between the eastern United States and the western states and territories was accomplished via Panama and Cape Horn. In 1857, Congress authorized the postmaster to contract a new overland mail service. The successful bidder for the southern route was John Butterfield, who agreed to convey mail twice weekly in 25 days per run. The "Oxbow Trail" originated at St. Louis, Missouri, and Memphis, Tennessee, then merged at Fort Smith, Arkansas. The stagecoaches traveled through Indian Territory (later Oklahoma) and across northern Texas to Tucson, Arizona, and on to Los Angeles and San Francisco, California, traveling 2,795 miles from St. Louis. The trail entered Grayson County by crossing the Red River at Colbert's Ferry and proceeding into Sherman. It crossed the county toward Gainesville in Cooke County en route to Franklin (later El Paso). The citizens of Sherman are credited with especially courting the mail route to use Colbert's Ferry instead of entering Texas near Preston (8 mi. upriver). Sherman became a distribution point in 1858, bringing mail service to Texas settlements. Waterman L. Ormsby of "The New York Herald" was the first through passenger on the Butterfield Trail in September 1858. He described Sherman as "a pleasant little village of about six hundred inhabitants," and chronicled the remainder of his trip across Grayson County, writing "our course lay across a fine rolling prairie, covered with fine grass, . . . the beautiful moonlight lit up the vast prairies making its sameness appear like the boundless sea and its hills like the rolling waves." The southern route was terminated in March 1861. The course of the trail is still visible in a number of locations in Grayson County. (1999)

SHERWOOD (Irion Co.) *US 67 and FM 72*
Sherwood Courthouse
(Built 1900–1901)
First permanent courthouse for Irion County, locally organized 1889. Replaced temporary housing in several buildings. Site was gift of Mr. and Mrs. Frank Ripley. Contractors: Martin and Moody. Stone was quarried nearby.

Courthouse was used for dances, teachers' institutes, community events, yards for summer socials.

Enclosed to keep out grazing stock, approach was by a stile over fence beside which were water troughs and hitching posts for teams and saddle horses.

A 1936 election made Mertzon county seat. Once pride of area, this now is a community center. (1971)

SHINER (Lavaca Co.) *SH 95 at Ponton Creek, 4 mi. N*
Ponton Family
Virginians William (1772–1834) and Isabella (Moreland) Ponton came to Texas in 1829 from Missouri, with them were their children Andrew, Sarah Ann, and Mary Jane, and son-in-law James Patrick. Their son Joel Ponton arrived in 1834. The families received land in DeWitt's colony.

William Ponton was the first recorded settler killed by Comanche indians in the area that became Lavaca County, Joel Ponton and a companion were attacked in the same area in 1840; Joel survived with two arrows in his back. Ponton Creek was named for William.

The Pontons and their neighbors stood up against the Mexican Army in the Battle of Gonzales and later fled the area in "The Runaway Scrape" in the wake of Santa Anna's victory at the Alamo. After the Texan victory at the Battle of San Jacinto, they returned to rebuild their homes from almost nothing. They endured Indian attacks and lived through the eras of the Republic of Texas, statehood, the Civil War, and Reconstruction. Exemplary pioneers, they were mothers and fathers, alcaldes, judges, tax collectors, commissioners, doctors, preachers, storekeepers, farmers, ranchers, and official peacemakers.

The children and grandchildren of William and Isabella Ponton forged Lavaca County from a wilderness. The story of the Ponton family is a story of Texas. (1998)

SHINER (Lavaca Co.) *SH 95, ½ mi. N*
Kasper Wire Works
Founded as outgrowth of an 1895 invention that used smooth wire discarded when barbed wire fencing was introduced in this area. August Kaspar, son of a Swiss Lutheran missionary to Texas, salvaged some of the plain wire and made a corn shuck basket for home use. A neighbor saw and bought the basket. Soon Kaspar disposed of his baskets as rapidly as he could make and put them to use in his own barn.

In 1898 he began the full-time manufacture of wire baskets and horse muzzles. His backyard shop was equipped with little more than a pair of pliers and his inventive genius. A rented wagon was the original Kaspar show room.

Arthur H. Kaspar, son of the founder, purchased the business in 1924. In 1949 a grandson, Don A. Kaspar, joined the organization. Kaspar Wire Works has progressed to assembly-line manufacturing of nationally and internationally distributed goods—including display racks, baskets, newspaper racks, wire shelving and many other products.

The growth and success of Kaspar Wire Works was officially recognized in 1967 by the bestowal of The First Annual Governor's Expansion Award under the auspices of The Texas Industrial Commission. (1970)

SHINER (Lavaca Co.) *US 90A*
Shiner
Originated as German-Czech community of Half Moon, located west of present town. When the San Antonio & Aransas Pass Railroad came through in 1887, citizens moved to rail line, where H. B. Shiner, Victoria landowner, had given a townsite.

Shiner was developed by cattlemen. Industries include brewery, wire works. City has museum. (1969)

SHINER (Lavaca Co.) *US 90A, 1 mi. E*
Shiner-Welhausen Homestead
Henry B. Shiner purchased this land in 1875 for his cattle raising enterprise. In 1887, when the railroad was built through the area, he donated land for a townsite, which was later named in his honor. Although the homestead was sold to Charles Welhausen in 1884, the Shiner family continued to reside here until 1890. The Welhausens lived on the homestead until 1895, when they moved into the town of Shiner. Still owned by Welhausen descendants, this property has been the site of picnics, cattle round-ups, baseball games, and other community activities. (1989)

SIDNEY (Comanche Co.) *FM 1689 and FM 589*
Community of Sidney
Began about 1870 when William Yarborough and J. A. Wright, early settlers, located on Jimmie's Creek. As a community developed, the settlers built a log schoolhouse near a spring, in

1877. W. D. Cox was the first teacher. The Methodist Church was also founded in 1877 and a few years later the Baptist Church and Church of Christ were started. All denominations took turns using the log schoolhouse for worship.

In 1883 Tom Davis opened a store and soon J. C. Stapp bought an interest in it. In 1886 Stapp became the first postmaster, naming the post office after his young son Sidney. Holstein dairy cattle, basis of a major industry, were brought here in the 1880's.

Between 1890 and 1910 Sidney had several doctors' offices, drug stores, gins, a general store, barber shop, lodge hall, and telephone exchange. Reorganized in 1902, the school became an accredited high school.

Around the turn of the century, the town shared in the national attention focused on nearby Round Mountain—first field laboratory of the remarkable Dr. Robert T. Hill (1858–1941), world-famous geologist. His studies vastly increased knowledge of the geology of North America and Texas, and after his death, he had his ashes scattered atop the mountain.   (1969)

SIERRA BLANCA (Hudspeth Co.)   *Old US 80 and FM 1111*
Eagle Spring Stage Stand
A station (1854–1882) for the stage coaches and wagon trains of the Overland-Chihuahua Trails, which linked the east to the pioneer west, brought heartening mail and passengers, and supplies, and quickened the life of this remote region, then far out on the lonely fringes of frontier civilization.

SIERRA BLANCA (Hudspeth Co.)   *Old US 80 at FM 1111*
Hudspeth County
Formed from El Paso County. Created February 16, 1917. Organized August 25, 1917. Named in honor of Claude Benton Hudspeth. Born in 1877. A native Texan, holder of large ranching interests, member of the Texas Legislature and the United States Congress. Sierra Blanca, the county seat.

SIERRA BLANCA (Hudspeth Co.)   *Old US 80 at Sierra Blanca Ave., at Oval Park*
America's Second Transcontinental Railroad
(Joined Here in 1881)
Great achievement in American history. Victory for statesmen, including Henry Clay and John C. Calhoun, who early as 1845 had supported in the United States Congress the idea of a transcontinental railroad. This was effected in 1869, but a need remained—as advocated in the Congress—for a southern route.

In 1869 the Southern Pacific began constructing such a line eastward from the West Coast. In 1871 the Texas & Pacific began building a line, under a special act of Congress, from East Texas to Southern California.

They ran a dramatic race which reached its climax as construction crews for the two roads neared this site. Southern Pacific reached Sierra Blanca on Nov. 25, 1881—while crews of the T. & P. were 10 miles to the east of here.

On Nov. 26, 1881, an agreement was reached by Jay Gould, for the Texas & Pacific, and Collis P. Huntington, for the Southern Pacific, whereby in Sierra Blanca the roads would ". . . approach, . . . meet . . . and . . . form one continuous line to the Pacific Ocean . . ."

The lines were joined here on Dec. 15, 1881, and on Dec. 16 transcontinental service was inaugurated.   (1968)

SIERRA BLANCA (Hudspeth Co.)   *IH 10, 8½ mi. W in roadside park*
Claude Hudspeth
(1877–1941)
State senator and member of U.S. House of Representatives from whom Hudspeth County was named. Became a ranch worker at age 9 and editor-publisher of an Ozona newspaper at 16. Was largely self-educated.

Won seat in legislature in 1902—starting 29-year public career. He authored many bills to benefit working man. Served in Texas Senate 1907–1919. During this time, he studied law and was admitted to the bar, 1909.

Served in U.S. Congress 1919–1931. Upheld sending U.S. force to defend El Pasoans endangered by Mexican Revolution fighting.   (1969)

SIERRA BLANCA (Hudspeth Co.)   *Bus. IH 10 at FM 1111, off IH 10 at Oval Park*
The Killing of General J. J. Byrne
(Event Occurred 15 mi. S of Here in Quitman Canyon)
One of the final acts of violence in raiding led during 1880 by the feared Apache Chieftain, Victorio.

Just prior to this incident, Victorio's band—100 to 200 strong—had finished a sanguinary two years of raiding in Southwest Texas, New Mexico, and Mexico. His brilliant guerrilla tactics baffled his U.S. Army pursuers and earned their grudging admiration.

J. J. Byrne, a surveyor and retired military man, had fought in U.S. Army in the Civil War (1861–1865), having been cited both for gallantry and meritorious conduct. At the time of his death, he was the lone passenger on the stage bound for Fort Davis.

Drawn by small, swift Mexican mules, the coach left Fort Quitman, a former army post on the Rio Grande, August 13, 1880. As it entered a steep canyon Victorio's men attacked. Gen. Byrne was killed almost at once but the driver, Ed Walde, turned the stage and raced back to the fort for safety.

Later in 1880 the United States and Mexico fielded 5,000 soldiers to hunt down Victorio, who was finally killed in Mexico, thus ended the career of one of the most notable Indian chiefs in the Southwest.

Byrne, born in Ireland about 1842, was buried near Fort Quitman but later reinterred in Fort Worth.   (1973)

SILVER (Coke Co.)   *RR 1672 at SH 208*
First Producing Oil Well in Coke County
Sun Oil Company's well—No. 1 Allen Jameson—was staked in Sept. 1946 and struck oil Nov. 17.

Intermittent drilling had gone on in Coke County for 30 years, but this discovery began a county-wide oil boom.

Drilled by the Dallas firm of Roberts & Hawkins, the well hit pay dirt at 6,230 feet in fossil-bearing limestone 280 million years old. In a 24-hour test it flowed 168 barrels.

Coke County recently ranked among the top quarter of oil-producing counties in Texas, with its 18 fields exceeding 6.4 million barrels annually.   (1968)

SILVERTON (Briscoe Co.)   *SH 256, 10 mi. E at Sky High roadside rest area*
William E. Schott
Briscoe County pioneer William E. Schott (1870–1941) was born in Ohio and moved to North Texas in 1885. Still legally a minor, he came to this area in 1890 and filed to a claim for the first of his later extensive landholdings. In 1891, he overcame the caprock barrier by building the first wagon road to Silverton, where in 1892 he helped organize Briscoe County. A major factor in the settlement of this region, Schott Cap Road (1.5 mi. N) was improved when auto travel began. Schott supported local education and encouraged improvement of cattle herds. He married (1907) Tina Kitchen; they had four children.   (1975)

SILVERTON (Briscoe Co.)   *SH 207, 11 mi. NW*
Archeological Sites
At Mackenzie Reservoir and Tule Canyon
Before this area was covered by Mackenzie Reservoir, evidence of human occupancy was found at 77 recorded archeological sites. The earliest artifacts date back 10,000 years to a bison kill. Prehistoric occupancy is indicated by burial sites, shallow hearths, and stone tools. Gun flints, glass beads, and metal objects confirm 18th century European contact. By 1874, Col. Ranald S. Mackenzie's 4th Cavalry had driven the Indians from the Tule Canyon area, which had been a lush grazing ground for buffalo and antelope.   (1979)

SILVERTON (Briscoe Co.)   *SH 207, 8 mi. S*
Site of Reeves Post Office (.5 mi. E)
Since the railroad was 60 miles from this sparsely populated prairie, the establishment of Reeves post office opened a communication link for the early pioneers. Begun July 13, 1899, in the front room of postmaster Joseph H. Reeves' two-story frame home, the post office served 110 settlers. James U. Strickland bought the house and took over as postmaster August 24, 1905. He

served until the facility closed on March 30, 1907, and mail was delivered to Silverton (8 mi. N). After Strickland sold the home to Forrest Leonard Weast in 1909, it was destroyed by fire.

SKIDMORE (Bee Co.) US 181, 10 mi. S at roadside park
Papalote Creek
A few yards south passes Papalote Creek, crossed by the fierce Karankawa Indians who found kite-shaped pebbles and named it Papalote, which means "kite-shaped" or "wing-shaped." Along its banks came the leaders of the Power and Hewetson Colonists, holding Mexican land grants in the 1830's. On its Rata tributary there is evidence the Mexican Army camped on its way to suppress the Texas Revolution.

By 1857 the town of Papalote had emerged. It was the center of entertainment for the county, boasting of a circular dance hall built by cowboys trading steer yearlings at $3 a head for lumber. There were rooster fights, ring tournaments and horse races. In 1886, when the railroad came, the town was booming.

After the turn of the century, however, Papalote began to die away. A land company sold lots to settlers from as far away as Hawaii. Expecting to grow citrus fruits, they were disillusioned when the first killing frost doomed the project. Threats of Pancho Villa's raids continued as late as 1916, when women and children hid in a brick schoolhouse. Then dancing was banned, and the dance hall became a school house on a full-time basis. Today there is no post office, only a rural route for the few remaining households. (1965)

SLIDELL (Wise Co.) FM 455 (Main Street)
Slidell
Named for John Slidell, one of the Confederate diplomats in the "Trent Affair" (1861), this community was established to supply goods and services to nearby farmers. The post office was started in 1884. Garrett Fletcher, donor of land for a cemetery and church, gave lots to nearby businesses that moved here in 1885, including twenty-two-year-old Dr. Drury Young Stem's medical office and drugstore. George W. Durham gave land (1893) for the public square and the first school building, and Nathaniel Pruett began (1895) the telephone system. Today Slidell serves as a farm and ranch area. (1974)

SLIDELL (Wise Co.) SH 51, 2 mi. N
A. H. Fortenberry
(1829–1868)
In the 1850s, A. H. ("Sevier") Fortenberry and his second wife Jane (Odell) moved from Arkansas to the wilderness then existing in this section of Texas. Living as a farmer and stockraiser, Fortenberry joined neighbors in warding off Indian raids which endangered the settlements. On Oct. 30, 1868, at a site ¾ of a mile northwest of this marker, he was intercepted and killed by Indians while trying to join a defensive posse. He was buried in the Pollard Cemetery, Denton County. It is thought that he was the last fatality in the Indian Wars in this vicinity. (1976)

SMITH POINT (Chambers Co.) FM 562, .75 mi. N near McNeir Cemetery
Sarah Ridge Paschal Pix
Born on the family plantation in the Cherokee Nation near present Rome, Georgia, Sarah Ridge (1814–1891) attended mission schools and girls' seminary. Her father Major Ridge was a Cherokee leader and friend of Sam Houston. Major Ridge, Sarah's brother John, and cousin were later assassinated for supporting the treaty that traded Indian lands for acreage in the West. This treaty led to the infamous "Trail of Tears."

Sarah married a lawyer, George Washington Paschal, in 1837 and they settled in Arkansas. In 1847, the family and slaves moved to Galveston. During the 1850 yellow fever epidemic Sarah opened her home and treated many of the ill with an Indian remedy. After Sarah and Paschal were divorced, she married Charles C. Sisson Pix, an Englishman, in 1856 in the home of Republic of Texas President Mirabeau B. Lamar.

Sarah traded her Galveston home for this land at Smith Point soon after her marriage. Pix cattle ranged from here to present Liberty. While Pix served in the Confederate Army, Sarah built the ranch into a large operation. With the end of slavery, the ranch declined.

After Sarah divorced Pix in 1880, she remained on the ranch with her widowed daughter Agnes Paschal McNeir and two grandsons. Heirs still own the land. (1979)

SMITHLAND (Marion Co.)

SH 49, 4 mi. E near the intersection of FM 727

Potter's Point

(About 6 mi. S)

Site of one of most famous events in Texas. Robert Potter—a signer, Texas Declaration of Independence, a chief author of Republic's Constitution, first Secretary of Navy, Republic of Texas—settled 1837 on Caddo Lake. A former U.S. Congressman, he won election 1840 to Texas Senate. After Senate adjourned in 1842 he tried to arrest his political foe, William P. Rose. On night of March 1, 1842, Rose led armed men to Potter's home. At dawn Senator Potter jumped into the lake to swim for help, but was shot to death. He is buried in State Cemetery, Austin. (1969)

SMITHVILLE (Bastrop Co.)

SH 71, approx 3 mi. W

Site of Early Bastrop County Fort

In the late 1820s, a group of families settled in this area as a part of Stephen F. Austin's second colony. Included in this group were the Winslow Turner, Stephan Cottle, and Ahijah M. Highsmith families, who came to Texas from Lincoln County, Missouri. They were later joined by other families, including the Whites, Crafts, Grimeses, Ridgeways, and Parkers. For defense purposes, they built a log fort at the juncture of the Colorado River and Alum Creek (south of this site) and placed their cabins near the fort.

During the 1830s, settlers established churches, schools, and communities around the fort and in neighboring areas on land given to them in return for their colonization efforts. Alum Creek, Craft's Prairie, Yeupon, Cottletown, Antioch, and Mount Pleasant were some of the names given to these settlements. A post office was established, and a number of early sawmills in Bastrop County were located near the fort site.

It is not certain when the fort was razed. Though no physical evidence remains, the site is important as a reminder of early Bastrop County settlement and of the harshness of life during the early years of colonization in Texas. (1984)

SMITHVILLE (Bastrop Co.)

FM 2571, 7 mi. W

Stephen Scallorn

Maryland native Stephen Scallorn (1787–1887) lived in Kentucky and Tennessee, where he practiced medicine and was active in the Primitive Baptist Church, before moving to Texas. He was attracted to the Republic by the favorable accounts of his oldest son John Wesley Scallorn, who had served with the Texas Army at the Battle of San Jacinto.

Stephen Scallorn and his brother William came to Texas with their families in 1837–1838 and settled in the vicinity of Plum Creek in Fayette County. There they were instrumental in the formation of the Hopewell Baptist Church, an important early church in Texas. Later divided by doctrinal disagreements, the brothers helped form separate fellowships.

Two of Scallorn's sons, John Wesley and Elam, died in defense of the Republic. Members of Capt. Nicholas Dawson's outfit, they were attacked by Mexican forces near San Antonio in 1842 and killed.

Scallorn remained active in church organization and helped establish an Upton congregation at the age of 98. Twice married and the father of 14 children, he lived in Bastrop County with his son Francis. Stephen Scallorn died at the age of 100 and was buried in the nearby Scallorn family cemetery. (1981)

SNOOK (Burleson Co.)

FM 2155

Community of Snook

(Originally Located 1 mi. W)

Settled 1880s by Czech immigrants. First called "Sebesta's Corner." In 1895 named "Snook" for John Snook, who helped secure post office. Soon had a one-room school, a "masova schuza" (slaughterhouse), a cooperative store, and lodge for "Czechoslovak Benevolent Society." (1971)

SNYDER(Scurry Co.)

US 180, 12 mi. W in roadside park

Scurry County

Formed from Young and Bexar Territories. Created August 21, 1876. Organized June 28, 1884. Named in honor of General William R. Scurry, 1821–1864. Member of the last Texas Congress. A distinguished officer in the Confederate Army. Snyder, the county seat.

SNYDER (Scurry Co.)

FM 1614 at FM 1673, 10 mi. E

Old Town of Camp Springs

Named for W. H. Camp, an early settler who built a dugout in 1878 at springs, ½ mile northwest of here.

Petrified trees—one 300 feet tall—and bones of prehistoric animals have been found in area. Tools, pictographs in nearby cave indicate Indians camped here.

Emigrant trail to California blazed in 1849 by Army Captain R. B. Marcy, came through region. General Robert E. Lee followed part of same trail searching for hostile Comanches in 1856. Both men made camp at Green Springs, six miles southwest. Post office was established, 1891.

(1967)

SNYDER (Scurry Co.)

US 180, two blocks west of square, 100 ft. W of the bridge

Channel of Deep Creek

Once a spring-fed tributary of the Colorado River; heads and ends within Scurry County.

In 1870's it supplied buffalo hunters living in hide-covered half dugouts. "Pete" Snyder's Trading Post, which eventually grew into the county-seat town of Snyder, was located on bank.

Although state surveyors had officially named it Culvers Creek, famous buffalo hunters John and J. Wright Mooar called it Deep Creek in 1876, and soon the name became widely used.

Played central role in early town life as a scene of picnics, horse races, and baptisms.   (1969)

SNYDER (Scurry Co.)

US 84, 6 mi. N

Scurry County's Billionth Barrel of Oil

Petroleum discoveries in this county began in 1923, with recovery of oil in the San Andres Formation—eventually penetrated by over 2,000 shallow wells.

In late 1948, rigs drilling deeper than 6,000 feet tapped the Canyon Reef geological formation. Four exploratory wells—Sun Oil Company's Schattel; Magnolia's Winston; Standard Oil Company of Texas' Brown; Lion Oil Company's C. T. McLaughlin—and other extensive drilling defined a gigantic field covering 85,000 acres and containing oil reserves estimated to total at least four billion barrels.

The local economy and growth rate improved greatly. Many farmers and ranchers who had fought years of drouth and adversity paid off debts, modernized their homes, and continued to live on their land.

On Oct. 8, 1973, twenty-five years after the Canyon Reef discovery, Scurry County produced from that formation its billionth barrel of oil, and in a week of festivities paid tribute to the petroleum industry. The celebrated billionth barrel of oil came from the well near this marker. By 1973, Scurry County was producing 3.2 percent of all the oil recovered annually in the United States.

(1975)

SNYDER (Scurry Co.)

US 180, 3 mi. W

Von Roeder Cotton Breeding Farms

Pioneer cotton breeders; aides to world fiber market, economy.

Clemens Von Roeder, born 1888 in Austin County, moved 1907 to Scurry County. As farmer began use of mutations, 1923, produced a long staple, big boll cotton; later added strains to resist hail, windstorm, rust.

He was joined by his brother Nolan in 1934; Bentley Baize, an agricultural executive, 1940; and Nolan's son, Max, in 1957.

Von Roeder-marketed seeds are Texas Mammoth and Western Prolific, for hand-picking; and Western Stormproof, for modern mechanical harvesting.   (1967)

SNYDER (Scurry Co.)

US 180, 6 mi. W

The Block 97 Controversy

Notorious county land dispute arising from state practice of paying railroads in public land for trackage laid began in 1873 when Houston & Texas Central claimed, in error, some 300,000 acres of Block 97 which were in reserve for Texas & Pacific.

Found in 1882, the error voided all deeds from H. & T. C. for lots in the reserve. Much land was unscrupulously resold, causing a decade of conflict over claims.

Issue was decided only when 1899 Legislature, on authority of State Supreme Court, declared land to be state school land and gave settlers option to buy.   (1972)

SNYDER (Scurry Co.) *US 180, 12 mi. E, 1.5 mi. SW of springs in roadside park*
Greene Springs and
Site of Archeological Discoveries
(1.5 mi. SW)
Located at a place occupied by man for centuries, these springs compose the first live (running) water that flows into the south fork of the Clear Fork of the Brazos River. The waters, which collect in large potholes in a sandstone formation, have produced a constant flow since first discovered by settlers.

For many centuries before, they were also visited by Indians. Food grinding holes and petroglyphs (rock carvings) on the sandstone creek walls give evidence of this early use. Since 1964, explorations by the Scurry Chapter, South Plains Archeological Society, have produced many artifacts such as stone knives and scrapers, beads, potsherds, and arrow points.

In the 19th century, military units under Capt. R. B. Marcy (1849) and Gen. Robert E. Lee (1856) camped at Greene Springs. Somewhat later, buffalo hunters, freighters, and emigrants moving west and north stopped for water at this beautiful place.

The springs were named about 1881 for J. L. "Jim" Greene, a horse rancher who moved here at that time. Greene and his family lived in two dugouts until their first house was built in 1890. Remains of the dugouts are still visible today in a nearby hill. (1968)

SOCORRO (El Paso Co.) *US 80*
Socorro
Site of the mission and pueblo of Nuestra Señora de la Concepcion Del Pueblo de Socorro established by Don Antonio de Otermin and Father Fray Francisco Ayeta, O. F. M. in 1683. Maintained by Franciscan missionaries for the civilizing and christianizing of the Piro, Thano and Gemex Indians, refugees after the Pueblo Revolt in New Mexico. (1964)

SOCORRO (El Paso Co.) *10140 Socorro Rd.*
Casa Ortiz
Legend says this house was built before 1800. In 1840s, its owner was Jose Ortiz, whose cart train freighted salt from foot of Guadalupe Mountains to Durango; knives, sarapes, clothing to Santa Fe and Llano Estacado. There he traded with Comanches and other wild Indians for dried buffalo hides and meat. He was a "Comanchero, Salinero, Cibolero." Francisca Lujan, the widow of Epifanio Ortiz (1842?–1932), was last of family to live here, in 1940s.

A fine example of New Spain's frontier architecture: thick adobe walls; cottonwood and willow vigas and latias with dirt roof. (1973)

SOCORRO (El Paso Co.) *US 80*
Mission Nuestra Señora de las Purisima
Concepcion Del Socorro
Our Lady of the Immaculate Conception of Socorro
Established in 1680 by brother Antonio Guerra for Piros Indians, refugees from Old Socorro, N. M., this and 1682 mission at Ysleta (located 3.7 mi. W) are among oldest continuously occupied settlements in the Southwest. By 1750, town had 498 Indians and 54 Spaniards.

Present church, built about 1840, exhibits Indian influence on basic Spanish mission style. Adobe brick walls are several feet thick. (1963)

SOMERVILLE (Burleson Co.) *SH 36 at north city limits*
1906 Reunion of Hood's
Texas Brigade
In 1906, Somerville hosted the annual reunion of the Hood's Texas Brigade Association, a group established in 1872 for veterans of the celebrated Confederate unit. For two days, June 27–28, 74 veterans were honored with a celebration which included speeches, a baseball game, and a grand ball. The local events were planned under the direction of the association's president R. A. Brantley, Sr., and his daughter Mrs. Norton B. Wellborn, both of Somerville. Part of a tradition which ended in 1934, the reunion reflected the area's respect for the former Civil War soldiers. (1981)

SOMERVILLE (Burleson Co.)   *SH 36 right of way, near northern city limits*
Somerville

Located where two branches of the Gulf, Colorado & Santa Fe Railway joined, town was named for Albert Somerville, first president of the railroad. First settlers arrived after town was surveyed about 1883; the post office was permanently established in 1897. Somerville boomed in the 1890s when local citizens persuaded a railroad tie plant to locate here. Santa Fe Railroad bought the operation in 1905. This is still an important industry. Incorporated in 1913, the town has become a recreation center since Lake Somerville was created in the 1960s.   (1974)

SOMERVILLE (Burleson Co.)   *SH 36, about .25 mi. S of the bridge*
Yegua Creek

In 1690 the Spanish gave the name "San Francisco" to this 62-mile Brazos River tributary; but on an 1822 map, Stephen F. Austin, "Father of Texas," marked it "Yegua," Spanish for "mare." Mustang mares and foals then grazed among the Indians on the timbered creek. In 1826, Colonist John P. Coles built a mill on the stream. A measure signed in 1837 by Texas President Sam Houston made the Yegua a county boundary. Floods often devastated the area until Lake Somerville harnessed Yegua's waters in 1967. Now a recreation area, the lake and creek benefit crops, wild life, and vacationers.   (1976)

SOMERVILLE (Burleson Co.)   *SH 36 & CR 422*
Oaklawn Cemetery

Dating to 1900, this graveyard was first called the Somerville and Lyons Cemetery. Land was purchased by J.W. Lauderdale to establish a cemetery upon the death of his two-year-old son Charles on November 6, 1900. The name was changed to Oaklawn Cemetery in 1913. Among the more than 2000 burials are 22 Civil War veterans, 20 children between 1900–1905, and victims of a typhoid fever epidemic in 1903. The construction of the dam at Somerville in 1963 caused 16 people to be re-interred here from other graveyards. The cemetery is still in use.   (1996)

SONORA (Sutton Co.)   *IH 10 (US 290), 30 mi. E, 2 mi. N*
Site of Fort Terrett

Established February 5, 1852 by the United States Army as a protection to frontier settlers. Named in honor of Lieutenant John C. Terrett who fell at Monterrey, September 21, 1846. Abandoned February 26, 1854. Awarded Texas Historical Building Medallion.

SONORA (Sutton Co.)   *IH 10 (US 290), 4 mi. E*
Sutton County

Has traces of culture at least 20,000 years old. Occupied by Apache Indians up to founding of Fort Terrett, 1852. Anglo-Texan settlement began 1879 at Sonora, a trading post on San Antonio-El Paso Road.

Created April 1, 1887, from land then in Crockett County. Organized Nov. 4, 1890, with Sonora as the county seat.

Named in honor of John S. Sutton (1821–1862), a member of Santa Fe Expedition, Texas Ranger and Indian fighter, soldier in Mexican War and colonel of Mounted Volunteers, who died of wounds received in Civil War Battle of Val Verde.   (1965)

SONORA (Sutton Co.)   *US 277, 3 mi. S*
About 200 yds. W is Site of Ghost Town Wentworth

Situated in 1880s at water well of A. J. Winkler, who platted townsite, gave title bond, and named place for Fort Terrett area rancher P. H. Wentworth. The residents occupied tents and picket homes. Principal building was two-story school, church, and hall of Dee Ora Lodge No. 715, A. F. & A. M. Town had a post office Aug. 1890–Aug. 1891. Postmaster was Thomas Stevenson, uncle of a future Texas Governor. Losing 1891 county seat election to Sonora, Wentworth citizens moved away.

Lodge hall, relocated late 1891 in Sonora, served as school and community building until 1938.   (1972)

SOUR LAKE (Hardin Co.).

SH 105, .5 mi. NW

Sour Lake, C.S.A.

Early-day health resort, with baths that attracted such Texans as Gen. Sam Houston. The healing waters had been used for years by the Indians.

One spring's water, with high sulphuric acid content, primed telegraph batteries during the Civil War. This was of vital importance, for at best telegraph service was limited. Started in 1854, the 1861–1865 system went only from Shreveport to Marshall to Houston, and Houston to Galveston to Orange.

A 20-word telegram sent from Shreveport to Houston in February, 1865 cost $36.   (1964)

SOUR LAKE (Hardin Co.)

SH 326 & Crosby St.

Stephen Jackson
(1803–1860)

Born in South Carolina, Stephen Jackson moved to Lorenzo de Zavala's colony in Texas in 1831. He received a labor of land (177 acres) to establish a farm. In 1835 Jackson was granted a league of land (4,428 acres), which included the later community of Sour Lake. In 1836 Jackson served in Captain Logan's company of the Texas Army and was awarded 320 acres of land in Milam County as bounty. He married Susan Choate (1807–1873) in 1838 and established their home near here. They are buried along with their children—Ambrose, Sarah, James A., Minerva, Stephen, and W. J. in the family cemetery (.5 mi. NW).   (Texas Sesquicentennial 1836–1986)

SPANISH FORT (Montague Co.)

FM 103

Town of Spanish Fort

Named San Teodora by Spanish. Important trading-post between French and Indians. During 18th century, Spain, resenting this encroachment on her territory, sent expedition to drive them out, suffered defeat by Indians who had been supplied with weapons and trained in war tactics by French. A monument marks the site: Red River Station. A frontier post for state militia, most northwestern outpost of Confederacy. Became thriving settlement and main crossing on Red River for vast herds of Texas cattle "going up" the Chisolm Trail to Northern markets. Town abandoned 1887. Thus trail driving through this area marked the advance of American settlement westward.

SPANISH FORT (Montague Co.)

FM 103 across from general store

The Site of the 1759 Taovaya Victory Over Spain

Col. Diego Ortiz Parilla, Commandant of Presidio San Saba (near the later site of Menard) had grave Indian problems in 1759. Priests and others were killed in Comanche attacks on Mission San Saba. Comanches and their friends were allied to Frenchmen, who were trading deep in Spanish domain. Parilla wished to whip the Comanches and expel the French. With 380 soldiers and Indian support to a total of 600 men, he left San Antonio in August. A victory over some Tonkawas on the Brazos as he marched north gave him false confidence. When he arrived at this site in October, he saw Red River forming a moat around a fort. His Apaches tried in vain to span the river and invade the fortified Taovaya Village. He saw 14 or more Frenchmen; a French flag was flying. Indians played drum and fife and had plenty of guns and ammunition. He bombarded the fort with cannons, but after losing 52 men in a 4-hour battle he was glad that nightfall gave him a chance to withdraw. He was pursued for many days as he retreated to Presidio San Saba, which he reached on Oct. 25, 1759.

The Taovaya Indians were later known as Wichitas, and continued to resist white men until the 1870s.   (1976)

SPEARMAN (Hansford Co.)

SH 15, 3 mi. NE

Hansford County

Formed from Young and Bexar Territories. Created August 21, 1876. Organized March 11, 1889. Named in honor of John M. Hansford. Came to Texas in 1837. Member of the Texas Congress, judge of the Seventh Judicial District, 1840–1842. Died in 1844. Hansford, the county seat.   (1965)

SPEARMAN (Hansford Co.)   *SH 207, 6 mi. NW*
Hansford Cemetery
First burial ground set aside in this county earliest grave (1890) was that of Mrs. Alfie P. Magee, wife of the first sheriff. Also buried here: the Cator Brothers, founders of Zulu Stockade; and the Wright brothers, early ranchers.

Only official cemetery in county until 1928; is still in use.   (1967)

SPEARMAN (Hansford Co.)   *SH 207, in SW*
Spearman
Founded 1917; incorporated 1921. Named for Thomas C. Spearman, a vice-president and head of the land department of the Santa Fe Railway. The Santa Fe Line was completed to Spearman in 1920, making this the first railroad shipping point in the county.

Hansford County, created 1876 and organized 1889, relocated its county seat here in 1929. The courthouse was built 1931.

Center for agriculture, wheat storage, ranching, and petroleum industry. Early 1960s growth included 25 new businesses in two years. Streets paved with brick make city distinctive. (1967)

SPEARMAN (Hansford Co.)   *SH 207 right-of-way, .4 mi. S*
of intersection with 13th Ave.
Lindberghs Land at Spearman
At ten minutes before 11:00 a.m. on Monday, September 24, 1934, a small monocoupe airplane landed in a pasture about ¼ mile west of this site. The pilot taxied his craft to a stop near a windmill, deplaned, and asked the curious resident, "Lady, can I park my plane in your back yard?"

The day proved a momentous one for Spearman residents. The pilot was Charles Augustus Lindbergh (1902–1974), traveling from California to New York with his wife, Anne. With about one hundred miles' worth of fuel left in his plane, Lindbergh chose to stop in this small community to refuel in order to avoid the inevitable crowds his arrival would cause in a larger town. A passing motorist was sent into town to purchase fuel for the airplane while the Lindberghs rested, enjoyed refreshments, and gave their hostess a tour of the airplane.

As news of the Lindberghs' landing spread, school children were excused from classes to see the famous aviator and watch the plane depart two hours later. Although brief in duration, the visit by Charles and Anne Morrow Lindbergh to this small rural community was a significant local event.   (1989)

SPEARMAN (Hansford Co.)   *SH 207, 6.5 mi. W*
Dodge City–Tascosa Trail
This road was surveyed during the Civil War to haul military supplies to Ft. Bascom, New Mexico Territory. Then came the buffalo hunters using the trail going to Dodge City hauling hides and buying supplies. Tascosa became a town in the early 1880s. Ox teams and mule teams hauled freight for the cowboy capitol of the Panhandle and ranches that ran into hundreds of thousands of dollars annually. Herds from all the Panhandle trailed into Dodge over this route for a number of years. Kit Carson and his New Mexico volunteers came down this trail from Ft. Bascom in November, 1865 to fight a losing battle with the Indians at the first adobe walls site. Stage coaches ran weekly carrying mail and passengers over the 242 mile route. Post offices and stage stands out of Tascosa were Little Blue, Cator's Zula Stockade, Hardesty Ranch in "No Man's Land," Jim Lanes Beaver Creek, Hines Crossing, Cimarron, Hoodoo Brown, Crooked Creek, on into Dodge brick for the courthouse at nearby ghost town of Hansford was hauled from Dodge City. Later freight came over this trail from Liberal, Kansas. Ranchers continued to use portions of the old trail until 1920 when the railroad built across the county and Spearman was built. Thus another old historic trail was fenced and plowed under. Hansford County Historical Survey Committee Twentieth Century Club.   (1963)

SPRINGLAKE (Lamb Co.)   *US 385, 6.2 mi. S*
Lamb County Sand Hills
A natural landmark, this chain of sand dunes extends for 130 miles and is three to five miles wide. Archeological findings show that the area was inhabited 6,000 years ago. Comanches camped in the sand hills because of wild game, vegetation, protection from the wind, and the availability of water. Spanish explorers and later Anglo-Americans used the old Indian trails that

passed along the dunes. Early ranching did little damage to the area. However, in recent years, the sand hills have been destroyed by extensive farming and industrial operations.   (1979)

SPRINGTOWN (Parker Co.)   *SH 51 (Main St.) at First St.*
Eureka Lodge No. 371, A. F. & A. M.
The Eureka Masonic Lodge entered into an agreement with W. L. Hutcheson to build this two-story structure in 1897. Over the years, while the first floor housed a variety of businesses, including Hutcheson's hardware store, the lodge continued to occupy the second floor. Exhibiting influences of the Romanesque Revival style, the building features round-arch windows, a detailed keystone on the upper central window, and a red sandstone cornerstone.   (1987)

SPUR (Dickens Co.)   *SH 70, 6 mi. N*
Site of Anderson's Fort or Soldier's Mound
Here behind extensive breastworks Major Thomas M. Anderson, Tenth U.S. Infantry, maintained a supply camp for the cavalry under General Ranald S. Mackenzie, Fourth U.S. Cavalry, who in 1874–1875 forced the Indians of the region onto reservations and opened the plains to white settlement.

STAFFORD (Fort Bend Co.)   *US 90A*
Buffalo Bayou, Brazos & Colorado
First Railroad in Texas
Planned 1840 to benefit the Republic of Texas by moving rich sugar and cotton crops from plantation areas. Chartered 1841 by 5th Congress of the Republic, in name of Harrisburg Railroad & Trading Company.

H.R.&T.C. did not succeed in building a railroad. Its holdings were transferred in 1847 to Gen. Sidney Sherman, a hero of the Battle of San Jacinto, who was backed by eastern capital and leading Texans—W. J. Hutchins, Gen. Hugh McLeod, Wm. Marsh Rice (benefactor of Rice University), B. A. Shepherd, James H. Stevens, and John Grant Tod (a former Texas naval officer).

B. F. Terry (destined to lead Terry's Texas Rangers in the Civil War) and W. J. Kyle graded the roadbed. The first locomotive, "General Sherman," arrived 1852.

In August 1853, the tracks extended 20 miles from Harrisburg to Stafford's Point, early Texas center of trade and social life. On Sept. 1, with fanfare, a special train brought a load of honored guests to join planters here for a barbecue-jubilee. Regular schedules were soon in operation. Stafford's Point, end of the line for two years, did much business.

Buffalo Bayou, Brazos & Colorado in 1860 reached Alleyton—a distance of 80 miles from Harrisburg.   (1967)

STAIRTOWN (Caldwell Co.)   *SH 80 and FM 671, 2 mi. SE*
Rafael Rios No. 1
(Located .8 mi. N on Farm Road 671)
Discovery well of Luling Field, a major Texas oil area. Wildcatter E.B. Davis drilled on land owned by R. Rios. Well came in Aug. 10, 1922, after 3 dry holes had been drilled in same area. Magnolia (now Mobil) Oil Co. bought field 1926. By 1969, production was 135,000,000 barrels. Incise on back: Donated by Mobil Oil Corporation.   (1970)

STAMFORD (Jones Co.)   *US 277 Bus., 0.25 mi. E of US 277*
Stamford
Swedish native Swante Magnus Swenson and his two sons, Eric Pierson and Swen Albin Swenson, came to Texas in 1882 to establish the SMS ranches. In 1899, Eric P. and Swen A. Swenson donated a large section of land for a townsite on an extension of the Texas Central Railway. Railway president Henry McHarg named the new town Stamford for his hometown in Connecticut. A Cumberland Presbyterian Church was organized in members' homes and a post office was established in a railroad boxcar in 1899. The Bank of Stamford opened for business in January 1900 and the first train pulled out of the Stamford depot in February. Businesses, churches and utilities soon were established. The booming town was incorporated in January 1901 and P. P. Berthelot became the first mayor. Stamford relied primarily on agriculture for its economy. Cotton, Swenson's Herefords and other area livestock brought substantial income. The town also boasted a flour mill, cottonseed oil plant, iron foundry, gins, brick manufacturers and

a railroad roundhouse. Both passenger and freight trains brought business to town. Stamford Collegiate Institution (later Stamford College), a Methodist school, opened in 1907. Oil was discovered near Stamford in 1935 and broadened the town's economic base still further. U. S. Army pilots trained at nearby Arledge Field during World War II. The town of Stamford thrived throughout the 20th century. Though the Burlington Northern Railroad (final proprietor of the railway through Stamford) abandoned the track in the late 1990s, the Swenson Land and Cattle Company remained in operation, and cotton, cattle and wheat continued to be among Stamford's leading industries at the dawn of the 21st century.   (2000)

STAMFORD (Jones Co.)

US 277 and SH 92, ¾ mi. W
Stamford Square at Reunion Headquarters
Texas Cowboy Reunion Oldtimers' Association

Founded 1930, jointly with Texas Cowboy Reunion—to "hand down to posterity, customs and traditions" of early cattle people who lived in dugouts and fought drouths, die-outs, heat and freeze-ups, raising the longhorns that finally brought settlement to the Southwest. Here (1930) were 335 men who had been cowboys prior to 1895. Besides regular cowmen, early members included musician Paul Whiteman, Editor Amon Carter, Ranger Captain Tom Hichman and Will Rogers, ex-cowhand, internationally famous entertainer and columnist. Colonel R. L. Penick was first president.

In 1932, donation of a bull started building fund for bunkhouse and roundup hall standing nearby. Ranch donated site. The interior and exterior of the bunkhouse feature ranch brands of many members.

Oldtimers' Reunion and Rodeo held 3 days annually (including July 4th) features chuckwagon meals, square dancing, and oldtimers' memories and songs.

Town celebrates with cowboy parade and thousands come to see what is called "World's Largest Amateur Cowboy Show," with actual cowhands performing.

These oldtimers represent the end of the open range and beginning of the era of barbed wire. They opened Texas' last frontier.   (1969)

STANTON (Martin Co.)

US 80, .5 mi. N
Martin County

On lower great plains of West Texas. Formed from Young and Bexar territories. Created Aug. 21, 1876, and organized Nov. 4, 1884. Named for Wyly Martin, member of Austin's Colony and Texas patriot.

County seat established by the first commissioners court which authorized construction of courthouse in Stanton (then called Mariensfield).

Early C. C. Slaughter Ranch headquarters, 12 miles northwest of Stanton at Mustang Spring, best campsite west of Big Spring.

Economy based on grain sorghum, cotton farming; cattle ranching; petroleum.   (1966)

STANTON (Martin Co.)

FM road to Courtney, 12 mi. NW
Mustang Spring

Watering place known as early as 1849 when Capt. Randolph B. Marcy of the U.S. Army stopped here in route from Ft. Smith, Ark., to El Paso. Described in 1859 as "Mustang Pond, two miles north of Emigrant's Road." First water west of Big Spring. Erected by state of Texas 1936.

STANTON (Martin Co.)

US 80, .5 mi. E
The J. E. Millhollon Ranch House

About 1900, J. E. and Nettie (Bell) Millhollon trailed their cattle from Glasscock to Martin County, acquiring this homesite and 34 sections of land. Business and church leaders in Stanton, the couple had this house erected in 1907 by N. H. Hunt of Big Spring, who built many structures along the Texas & Pacific Railroad. The restoration, begun 1970 by Mr. and Mrs. Mike Hull, is being continued by Mr. and Mrs. Norman Wright, who bought the property in 1974. Awarded Historical Building Marker.   (1974)

STANTON (Martin Co.) *Courthouse Square*
Old Martin County Jail
The cell block of this jail was originally included in the 1885 Martin County Courthouse, built the year after the organization of Martin County when Stanton was known as Marienfeld. When the courthouse was torn down following a 1908 bond election, the cells were retained as the nucleus of this rock jail building. Completed that same year, it included living quarters for the sheriff's family. It later served as a library and museum. (1982)

STEPHENVILLE (Erath Co.) *US 281, 5.5 mi. S*
Wyatt-Boyd Ranch Complex
This is a rare example of a virtually complete 19th-century cross timbers farmstead. Thought to have been built in the early 1870s by James J. Wyatt, the Cumberland plan one-story rough limestone two-room ranch house was altered in the 1890s by J. H. Boyd and modified in the 1930s and 1940s. Other structures in the ranch complex include a single-room masonry dugout, two stone barns, and a rock base for an elevated cistern. (1987)

STEPHENVILLE (Erath Co.) *US 281 at FM 1188, 10 mi. NE*
Morgan Mill Tabernacle
The community of Morgan Mill, named for early settler George Bryan Morgan, traces its history to the mid-19th century. A post office was established in 1877. Several community church congregations shared a brush arbor in the summers for revivals and other meetings. In 1910, the brush arbor was replaced with this permanent structure, named the Morgan Mill Tabernacle.

In addition to serving the churches, the tabernacle also was used by the local school and other community organizations. It remains in use as a community gathering place. (1994)

STEPHENVILLE (Erath Co.) *US 80 and SH 108, 21 mi. N*
Thurber
Most important mine site in Texas for 30 years. Coal here, probably known to Indians, was "discovered" in 1886 by W. W. Johnson, who with his brother Harvey sold out to Texas & Pacific Coal Company in 1888. (T. & P. Coal Company provided fuel for the Texas & Pacific Railroad, but was independently owned.)

Town was named for H. K. Thurber, friend of T. & P. Coal Company founders. Most dynamic firm member was Robert D. Hunter (1833–1902), developer of 7 of 15 mines. Next president was E. L. Marston, Hunter's son-in-law, who left mining largely to William K. Gordon (1862–1949), an engineer who brought daily output to 3,000 tons.

Then in 1917, Gordon (backed by management of coal company) was primarily responsible for discovery of Ranger Oil Field, 20 miles west. Adoption of oil-burning railway locomotives cut demand for coal. Last mine here closed in 1921, and the 10,000 or more inhabitants of Thurber began to move away.

The coal firm changed its name to Texas Pacific Coal and Oil Company and was sold in 1963 to Joseph E. Seagram & Sons, Inc., for $277,000,000.00. Renamed Texas Pacific Oil Company, it is now one of the largest independent domestic energy suppliers. Much coal (by estimate 127,000,000 tons) remains underground. (1969)

STERLING CITY (Sterling Co.) *US 87, 9 mi. NW*
Site of Camp Elizabeth
Thought to have been established 1853. Used as an outpost hospital of Fort Concho, 1874–1886.

STERLING CITY (Sterling Co.) *US 87, 4 mi. E at Montvale Cemetery*
Dr. P. D. Coulson
(October 4, 1839–December 10, 1925)
Born near Morganton, Tenn. He enlisted, May 22, 1861, as private in 3rd Tenn. Inf., Confederate Army. Promoted to surgeon with rank of major, 1862, he saw much action—first Manassas, Shiloh, Corinth, Vicksburg, Atlanta, other battles. Was twice wounded.

Came to Texas after Civil War. Served as first county judge of Sterling County in 1890s. County Judge of Coke County, 1907–1910.

Married Etheldra Ann Johnson. Had four sons, four daughters. (1970)

STERLING CITY (Sterling Co.)

US 87, 4 mi. E at Montvale Cemetery

Montvale

The community of Montvale was established in 1884 when the pioneer settlement of St. Elmo was relocated here. Then a part of Tom Green County, Montvale was located on the Shafter Military Trail, an early road from Fort Concho.

A community school, the earliest in the area, was in operation by 1886. Three years later the town was platted by H. B. Tarver, the surveyor for Tom Green County. It is believed the settlement was named for a nearby hill referred to in Tarver's field notes at Mt. Vale.

Early businesses in Montvale included the saddle and harness shop of R. B. Cummins and the general store and blacksmith shop of B. Z. Cooper. The town was also the site of a Methodist Church, a hotel, a post office and a variety of stores. About 1889, R. B. Cummins started the town of Cummins (5.4 mi. NW) upriver from Montvale. Both settlements began to decline in 1891 with the establishment of Sterling City (3.5 mi. NW) as the seat of government for the newly created Sterling County.

A community cemetery is all that remains of the townsite of Montvale, a pioneer settlement that played an important role in the area's development. (1982)

STERLING CITY (Sterling Co.)

US 87, Public Square

Sterling County

This prairie region split by the North Concho River is old Comanche, Kickapoo, Kiowa, Lipan, and Wichita hunting ground. Possibly it was crossed by six or so Spanish explorations between 1540 and 1654. In the 1860s and 70s, Anglo-Americans hunted buffalo commercially in this area. An 1860s hunter, Capt. W. S. Sterling, had a dugout home on the creek that bears his name. In the 1870s, bandits Frank and Jesse James kept horse herds on a tributary of Sterling Creek. In 1874, the United States Army occupied Camp Elizabeth, a Fort Concho outpost hospital, about ten miles west of here. Ranchers from other counties began to bring in large cattle herds in the 1870s, to capitalize on free grass. After keeping out small herds for a time, they permitted actual settlers to share the range. Family men staked land claims, grew crops in the valleys, and opened stores, schools, and post offices. On March 4, 1891, on the petition of 150 citizens, the county was created out of part of Tom Green County, and named for its first regular resident. Sterling City became the county seat.

Petroleum production has been important to the economy since the 1950s; yet the land essentially remains range country, grazed by cattle and sheep. (1976)

STERLING CITY (Sterling Co.)

US 87, 1.9 mi. W

Site of Town of Cummins
(100 yds. SW)

The pioneer settlement of Cummins developed at this site about 1890 around the saddle and harness shop of the earliest permanent settler, Mississippi native Robert Benjamin Cummins (b. 1848). A post office opened here in 1890 with J. H. Kellis as postmaster. The following year the nearby town of Sterling City (1.9 mi. E) was founded.

The two towns became rivals for the designation of county seat when the Texas Legislature created Sterling County from Tom Green County on March 4, 1891. An intense publicity campaign developed, aided by the writings of the respective town newspaper editors: W. L. Thurman of the Cummins paper, the *North Concho News,* and S. R. Ezzell of the *Sterling Courier.* An election, conducted May 20, 1891, appeared to be a victory for Cummins until several voting boxes were dismissed for technical reasons, resulting in a tie. A second election on July 7 gave Sterling City a 13-vote margin and it was named the county seat.

Most Cummins businesses and residents had moved to Sterling City by the end of 1891. Nothing remains of the early townsite, which once included a school, saloon, meat market, mercantile, blacksmith shop, and grocery stores. (1981)

STINNETT (Hutchinson Co.)

SH 207, Courthouse Square

Hutchinson County Courthouse

Hutchinson County, named for prominent judge and writer Anderson Hutchinson, was one of 54 counties created out of the District of Bexar in 1876 by the Texas Legislature. It was not until 1901, however, that the county was officially organized. That year a temporary county court-

494

house was erected in the county seat of Plemons. A permanent courthouse was built in Plemons by contractor E. E. Ackers. Stinnett replaced Plemons as Hutchinson County seat in 1926.

The county courthouse was temporarily housed in an office building in downtown Stinnett in 1926 before this courthouse was erected in 1927 at a time of major oil discoveries in the area. Designed by Amarillo architect W. C. Townes and built by local contractor C. S. Lambie & Company, the Spanish renaissance revival style building also housed the county jail. It features brick construction with cut stone ornamentation, a 3-bay primary facade with grand entry bay, raised basement with end entries, metal sash windows and 2nd floor windows with round-arch stone lintels. Friezes at the east and west entrances of the court house depict the petroleum, farm and ranch, and cattle industries, historically the three principal commercial enterprises in the area.

(Recorded Texas Historic Landmark 1962)

STINNETT (Hutchison Co.)

SH 207 N, about 11.2 mi.; E on CR about 17 mi. to battle site

The Battle of Adobe Walls

Was fought here November 25, 1864, when Colonel Christopher (Kit) Carson (1809–1868) with a few companies of United States troops under the protection of the adobe walls attacked a band of hostile Kiowa and Comanche Indians and killed over 60 braves. This was "Kit" Carson's last fight. (1936)

STINNETT (Hutchinson Co.)

SH 15/FM 278, 5 mi. N

First Battle of Adobe Walls
(November 25, 1864)

Largest Indian battle in Civil War, 15 miles east, at ruins of Bent's old fort, on the Canadian.

3,000 Comanches and Kiowas, allies of the South, met 372 Federals under Col. Kit Carson, famous scout and mountain man. Though Carson made a brilliant defense—called greatest fight of his career —the Indians won.

Some of the same Indians lost in 1874 Battle of Adobe Walls, though they outnumbered 700 to 29 the buffalo hunters whose victory helped open the Panhandle to settlement. (1964)

STOCKDALE (Wilson Co.)

SH 87 bypass, on W side

Stockdale Cemetery

Before the Stockdale Cemetery was begun in the 1870s, most burials in the area took place in private, family graveyards. About 1873, however, a young man who was not related to any of the local settlers was thrown from his horse and killed. To provide a place for his burial, Dr. T. M. Batte gave one acre of land at this site, and the burial ground has been used by Stockdale citizens since that time. Additional acreage was purchased in 1881 and 1904, and in 1938, area resident Paul Ballard donated an acre of land for use by anyone who did not have a family plot and needed a place for burial.

The earliest marked grave in the Stockdale Cemetery, that of Sallie A. Pope, is dated 1873. Many early settlers are buried here, including the town's founder, John R. King, and the first schoolteacher, Martin West. The cemetery also contains the graves of numerous war veterans and victims of a post-World War I flu epidemic.

The women of Stockdale formed an organization in the early 1900s to care for the gravesites, and in 1965 the Stockdale Cemetery Association was formally organized.

In use for more than 100 years, the Stockdale cemetery continues to serve the residents of the Stockdale area. (1983)

STONEHAM (Grimes Co.)

SH 105, 1 mi. W at Stoneham Cemetery

Andrew Jackson Montgomery
(Apr. 4, 1801–Dec. 3, 1863)

Born in Blount County, Tennessee, Andrew Jackson Montgomery came to Texas in 1819 with the James Long Expedition. In 1823, as the first known settler in Montgomery County, he opened a trading post at the crossing of two Indian trails. From his post emerged the town of Montgomery from which Montgomery County took its name. A veteran of the Battle of San Jacinto, Montgomery married Mary Mahulda Farris at age 43, and they had nine children. (1986)

STONEHAM (Grimes Co.)
SH 105, 1 mi. W at Stoneham Cemetery
John Montgomery
Native of Alabama. Came to Texas in 1830 with his brother Andrew. Participated in the Battle of San Jacinto as a member of Captain James Gillaspie's Company. (1956)

STONEWALL (Gillespie Co.)
US 290, 3 mi. E in SH Dept. Park,
adjoining LBJ Park
Site of the Andreas Lindig Lime Kiln
First kiln, eastern Gillespie County. Built 1874 by Andreas Lindig, trained in his native Germany in quicklime making. On his homestead, he found rock to be hauled to this site by oxwagon, using 7 loads of rock for each "batch" of lime. Post oak wood, burned in a cooking bed, produced high heat which produced the lime. Besides that for his own use, he made lime commercially for neighbors.

Lindig's home (built 1874, about .5 mi. S) shows endurance of cement made from his lime. So does the 1963–1969 "Texas White House," built nearby in 1897 by Willie Meier. (1970)

STONEWALL (Gillespie Co.).
Stonewall Elementary School Campus
The 36th President of the
United States of America
Lyndon Baines Johnson
As a 12-year-old student attended classes of the 8th grade here at the old Stonewall school from October 1920 to June 1921. (1971)

STONEWALL (Gillespie Co.)
SH 1
Trinity Lutheran Church
Was organized in June, 1902. This corner stone and surrounding stones formed the foundation for the second church which was dedicated in June, 1904. (1904)

STONEWALL (Gillespie Co.)
US 290, 3 mi. E, at
Lower Albert, SW corner
Andreas and Frederike Lindig Farmstead
German immigrants Andreas and Frederike Lindig arrived in Texas in 1869. They established a farmstead here in 1874 on 448 acres that included a main farmhouse, summer kitchen, barn, water well, and commercial lime kiln. Lindig used native post oak timbers to build a log farmhouse to which he added limestone shed rooms. They grew cash crops of peanuts, sweet potatoes, and cotton. Their sons Friedrich, Karl, and Christian built homes nearby. Andreas (d. 1898) and Frederike (d.1913) are buried in the family cemetery (one-half mile SE). The property remained in the family until 1980. (1995)

STRATFORD (Sherman Co.)
US 54, 2.5 mi. NE at roadside park
County Named for Sidney Sherman, C.S.A.
Born in Massachusetts, 1805. Led his crack Kentucky Militia Company to join Texas Army in War for Independence. Commanded cavalry wing, Battle of San Jacinto. Major-General and Congressman, Republic of Texas.

Built second railroad west of Mississippi River. First engine to run in Texas was "General Sherman," named in his honor.

Put in command of fortifying Galveston, most valued seaport in Texas, at outbreak of Civil War. Set up marine guard and batteries of cannon. Lost eldest son in Galveston recapture, 1863. Gen. Sherman died in 1873.

STRATFORD (Sherman Co.)
US 287, 2 mi. N in roadside park
Early Settlers on Coldwater Creek
(Creek Located 6½ mi. S)
First area in Sherman County to be settled, and only live water for miles. First settler, buffalo hunter J. D. Rawlings, came 1870s. Later county judge.

W. B. Slaughter acquired the Rawlings Place about 1894. Later ran bank and store in Stratford.

John Lanners (arrived 1892) was a cowboy at Slaughter's ranch; acquired land and ran a mule-drawn supply line.

One of largest spreads was owned by Thomas Snyder (also arrived in 1892). Among other prominent early settlers were J. H. Williams, freighter, and Geo. Loomis, merchant.   (1971)

STRAWN (Palo Pinto Co.)   *SH 16, N city limits*
Bethel Strawn, C.S.A.

An 1858 settler and leading citizen of Palo Pinto County. Enlisted 1864 in Co. B, 1st Frontier District, Texas State Troops, in Maj. Wm. Quayle's command. Saw service mainly in keeping down Indian depredations and protecting settlements that were furnishing food, salt, hides, leather, and other goods to aid the Confederate cause during the Civil War.

In 1880, when Texas & Pacific Railroad built through western Palo Pinto County, a stop was named for Bethel Strawn, who owned land at that point. By 1885, Strawn settlement had grown into a town drawing off people from old Palo Pinto.

During 20th century oil developments, the name Strawn is used for petroleum bearing formations of rock that underlie this county and other areas. Strawn minerals include coal, once mined locally.

36 Texas counties were named for men prominent in the Confederacy during the Civil War. One county, Val Verde, was named for a Civil War battlefield on which Texas troops were victorious during the New Mexico-Arizona Campaign of 1861–1862.

41 Texas towns were named for men who figured in the Civil War. Strawn, however, is the one geographical name commemorating a Texan in the Civil War.   (1965)

STRAWN (Palo Pinto Co.)   *SH 16, 6 mi. N*
Robinson School

In 1937, Guy U. Robinson led his neighbors to petition the county for a new common school district, in part to protest high school taxes in Strawn. Leo Ankenbauer sold two acres of land to school trustees, and craftsmen Bill Roberson and W. Proctor of Strawn completed this one-room, red brick schoolhouse in time for classes to begin in September 1937. Darker brick at the corners and around the windows and the door provide some ornament to the simple vernacular structure. In use only until 1943, when the number of pupils declined to two, Robinson School is a unique reminder of the county's rural educational history.   (2001)

STRAWN (Palo Pinto Co.)   *715 Central Avenue (SH 16)*
Thomas House

Designed by Dallas architect Thomas J. Galbraith and completed in 1919, this house is an excellent regional example of the Prairie School style of architecture. Its strong historical associations with area ranches and with the Ranger Oil Boom lend additional significance to its place in the architectural history of Palo Pinto County. Rancher Randal Burton Thomas, Sr. (1886–1969), grew up in West Texas assisting his mother, Mary Ellen Satterfield Thomas, in running her family ranch. Having first arrived in Strawn from Bowling Green, Kentucky, by 1881, when railroads began to reach this area, their family was among the region's first settlers. The Ranger Oil Boom, begun in 1917 with McClesky No. 1 Well, brought new wealth to the family from the many producing wells on their properties. When Thomas began making plans to move into town, he designed this house with living quarters for his family on the north side and for Mary Ellen Satterfield Thomas on the south side. It remained their home until their deaths. The Thomas house features strong elements of the Prairie style, with its horizontality enhanced by the use of wide, projecting eaves. Designed to be heated with coal from the nearby mines in Thurber, the house features extensive use of concrete and a red metal roof. Still in the Thomas family at the turn of the 21st century, the house is an important reminder of West Texas history and culture.   (2002)

STREETMAN (Navarro Co.)   *FM 416, off US 75, 3 mi. NE*
Birdston Community and Cemetery
When V. I. Bird opened a general mercantile store about 2 miles to the northwest in the 1860s, Birdston Community was founded. As local economy then depended on cotton, a gin was soon built near the store. In a few years, store and gin were relocated a mile east of this cemetery, at halfway point on main road from Fairfield to Corsicana. The Birdston Post Office opened Dec. 11, 1866. By 1867 the community also had a school; by 1872 a church building, used by all faiths.

The cemetery was opened on land donated by Edd and Juliett Burleson for church and school purposes. The first grave, located near the church, was that of a child, Mary Rayburn, whose family had been traveling from Fairfield to Corsicana, stopping at Sherrard's boarding house in Birdston, where the child fell ill and died. A second grave was dug near the church when T. J. Gilbert died on Dec. 5, 1872. By 1888 additional cemetery land was sold to trustees by Mrs. Burleson.

When Birdston was bypassed in 1909 by Burlington Rock Island Railroad, it lost its post office and businesses; the school closed in 1920. The cemetery has continued in use through ensuing years, and in the 1950s had a new section annexed by purchase of acreage from the Charley Gregory Estate.

STREETMAN (Freestone Co.)   *FM 416, 11 mi. E*
The New Hope Baptist Church and St. Elmo Cemetery
This locality was settled about 1849 by pioneers from Alabama, Florida, and Georgia. Cotton and corn plantations thrived. A school was opened in the 1850s, but closed during the Civil War (1861–1865). A site on the centrally-situated Manning Land Grant became a public burial ground. Earliest documented grave is that of J. W. Darden, who died in 1869.

The Little Hope Baptist Church was organized in the community in Aug. 1872, by a Freestone county missionary, the Rev. J. M. Gambrell, who served as the first pastor, with R. B. Anderson as church clerk.

In 1875 a schoolhouse was built near the burial ground on the Manning Grant. The school was called "St. Elmo," probably for a popular 19th century novel. The Baptists held services in the schoolhouse until 1886; then they adopted "New Hope" as the church name, bought a 6-acre tract that included the cemetery and school grounds, and built a church. Present sanctuary, which replaced that original building, was remodeled in 1954. St. Elmo Cemetery Association administers the affairs of the cemetery, which now (1974) contains about 850 graves.   (1974)

SUDAN (Lamb Co.)   *US 84 at FM 298*
Old Watering Trough
One of Sudan's oldest structures. Built 1916, when Santa Fe Railway terminus here shipped out cattle of early ranches.

Here ranchers watered herds and horses, traded, told yarns, hired hands.

Trough also served mule teams, after the farming era began in the 1920's. (1966)

SUGAR LAND (Fort Bend Co.)   *US 90A, city limits marker*
Sugar Land
Founded 1853. Named by B. F. Terry and W. J. Kyle for sugar mill and plantation bought on their return with fortunes from California Gold Rush.

The town's founders organized Terry's Texas Rangers at the start of the Civil War.

Farming market. Site of Texas' only cane sugar refinery. Texas prison farms are located nearby.

SUGAR LAND (Fort Bend Co.)   *US 90A*
The Sugar Land Refinery
Stephen F. Austin's colonists brought sugar cane to Fort Bend County in the 1820s. The Sugar Land area was once part of Oakland Plantation, where Nathaniel (1800–1884) and Matthew

Williams (1805–1852) planted sugar cane about 1840. They began processing the cane in 1843 using a horse-powered mill and open-air cooking kettles.

In 1853, the plantation and mill were purchased by William J. Kyle (1803–1864) and Benjamin F. Terry (1821–1861). They improved the mill and promoted a railroad for the area, which they named Sugar Land. Terry later helped organize the famed Confederate cavalry unit, Terry's Texas Rangers, and was killed in the Civil War (1861–1865).

After the war, the operation was sold to Edward H. Cunningham (1835–1912), who expanded the sugar mill into a refinery. W. T. Eldridge (1862–1932) and Galveston businessman I. H. Kempner, Sr. (1873–1967) purchased the refinery in 1907. They began importing raw sugar to operate the refinery year-round because local cane was available only seasonally and in decreasing quantities in the early 1900s. Named by Kempner for the Imperial Hotel in New York City, the Imperial Sugar Company and the city of Sugar Land have grown steadily. During the 1970s, the Imperial Sugar Company produced more than three million pounds of refined cane sugar daily.   (1978)

SULPHUR BLUFF (Hopkins Co.)   *FM 71, ½ mi. E on SW*
corner of Sulphur Bluff Cemetery
Early Sulphur Bluff—First Settlement in Hopkins County
First known settlers in area were family of John Gregg. Their cemetery (2 mi. N) has marker dated 1837, from Republic of Texas era. Other early settlers were the brothers Hezekiah and Robert Hargrave, from Indiana. They built brush-roofed log homes (3 mi. N), on high bluff above Sulphur River, offering protection from Indians and providing abundant game.

Robert Hargrave, a mechanical genius, built a wood and iron shop, a blacksmith shop, and a grist mill that drew customers from Caddo Mills, 50 miles away.

A post office was built 1849; early school was founded 1852.   (1968)

SULPHUR SPRINGS (Hopkins Co.)   *SH 154, 1.1 mi. S*
Shooks Chapel Methodist Church
This church traces its history to 1886, when area settlers organized a congregation of the Methodist Episcopal Church, South. The church was named for the Rev. W. A. Shook, who held the first revival here. The congregation met in a brush arbor or a nearby schoolhouse until a sanctuary was built on land donated by B. P. Joiner. Early worship services were led by student pastors who were often paid in produce. Associated with the church is a community cemetery, begun in 1889. A second sanctuary, built in 1916, was replaced by a new structure in 1974.   (1988)

SULPHUR SPRINGS (Hopkins Co.)   *US 67/IH 30, 5 mi. E in roadside park*
Hopkins County
Formed from Lamar and Nacogdoches Counties. Created March 25, 1846. Organized July 13, 1846. Named in honor of the pioneer Hopkins family which came to Texas from Kentucky and Indiana. County Seat, Tarrant (1846–1858); Sulphur Springs since.

SULPHUR SPRINGS (Hopkins Co.)   *SH 19/154, 5 mi. N in roadside park*
Confederate Refugees in Texas, C.S.A
In the vicinity of Old Tarrant, south of here, the Civil War refugee family of Mrs. Amanda Stone, of Louisiana, was shown great kindness when rescued by Hopkins Countians after a road accident. The Stones saw the Texans share the little they had, even cooking the last tough old farm hen, to feed them.

The Stones were but one of many families to flee from war lines to the comparative safety of Texas. Here, though Federal invasion repeatedly threatened, only a few coastal towns were under fire from the enemy. The family of Gen. Stand Watie, from Indian Territory, visited relatives in Wood County. Gen. Kirby Smith, with headquarters in Shreveport, rented homes in Marshall or Hempstead for his wife and babies.

Like most refugees, the Stones when they visited in Hopkins County were heartbroken over loss of their old home to the enemy. In Texas they endured poverty, loneliness, and sorrow at deaths of two sons in the war. They had to lease farm land, to support the family and 90 slaves dependent upon them. Their young boys at one time carried pistols for safety when schoolmates resented their strange manners.

Yet eventually they and most other refugees were grateful to Texas for its many generosities.
(1965)

SULPHUR SPRINGS (Hopkins Co.)   *SH 19/154 right of way, 4.5 mi. N*
Townsite of Tarrant
Eldridge Hopkins, for whose family Hopkins County was named in 1846, donated this site for the county seat. Named for Gen. Edward H. Tarrant (1796–1858), Texas Ranger and Mexican War veteran, Tarrant Post Office was established in March, 1847. A two-story frame courthouse was begun in 1851, but lack of funds delayed completion for two years.

Tarrant quickly grew into a thriving frontier town with a tannery, steam mill, blacksmith shop, brick kiln, and hotel. After 1851, it had a Masonic Lodge and school. During the 1850s, a newspaper, the "Texas Star," began publication, and a Methodist college opened.

Encircled by creeks, the town was difficult to reach in bad weather. The inconvenience of travel to Tarrant led Capt. Thomas M. Tolman in 1868 to transfer county records to Sulphur Springs, where Federal troops under his command were stationed after the Civil War to enforce Reconstruction laws. Despite local protests, county government remained there until civilian rule was restored in 1870. The return to Tarrant was brief, because this State Legislature in 1870 named Sulphur Springs as permanent county seat. Soon Tarrant began to decline. A rural community and old cemetery now mark the site of the first Hopkins County Seat.   (1975)

SUNDOWN (Hockley Co.)   *FM 303, 1.5 mi. S*
First Oil Well in Hockley County—J. E. Guerry No. 1
(700 yds. SW)
On April 6, 1937, this well was completed by the Texas Company (Texaco, Inc.), flowing 502 barrels per day from a depth of 5,023 feet, on land owned by J. E. Guerry (1885–1956).

The Guerry family purchased surface and ⅛ mineral rights on 177 acres, in 1929, from R. L. (Bob) Slaughter (1870–1938), who inherited over 16,000 acres of the Lazy S Ranch after death of his father, Col. C. C. Slaughter (1837–1919).

Located in the vast Slaughter field, this well was the first of over 2,600 active wells in the county, which have produced over 400 million barrels of oil.   (1973)

SUTHERLAND SPRINGS (Wilson Co.)   *FM 539, 3 mi. N*
Whitehall
"White Hall," built 1847–1851 by Joseph H. Polley, first sheriff in Austin Colony, detailed in 1836 to guard "Runaway Scrape," exodus of settlers fleeing Santa Anna.

Cabinet work came by sea from New York. Bandera cypress framing.

House guest Robt. E. Lee wrote his last Texas letter from here. Awarded Medallion Plate.
(1965)

SWEETWATER (Nolan Co.)   *1 mi. N of Nolan County Courthouse at Fairgrounds*
Herefords in Sweetwater
Organized 1922, the Sweetwater Hereford Breeders Association and Auction Sale (now Sweetwater Area Hereford Association) is considered Texas' third oldest group formed to promote this fine beef breed. First officers: Walter L. Boothe, president; G. E. Bradford and J. D. Dulaney, vice presidents; E. P. Neblett, secretary.

The Texas Hereford Association assisted local breeders in early sales. First sale was held March 1, 1922. Then semi-annual events, sales are now held annually.

Some consignors to the Golden Anniversary Sale, Dec. 4, 1972, are from families of the organizers.   (1972)

SWEETWATER (Nolan Co.)   *IH 20 access road N, 4 mi. W*
W. A. S. P. Training Base: Avenger Field
(¼ mi. N)
Women's Airforce Service Pilots (WASP) trained here in military aircraft during World War II, from Feb. 21, 1943, through final graduation Day, Dec. 7, 1944.

Avenger Field first served as a training base for British Royal Air Force Cadets in 1942, then for U.S. Army Air Forces Cadets Aug. 1942–April 1943.

The WASP program was started under Gen. H. H. ("Hap") Arnold to train women to fly every kind of mission short of combat, releasing male pilots for overseas duty. Jacqueline Cochran was director of women pilots; Ethel A. Sheehy, WASP staff field executive; Nancy Harkness Love, WASP staff executive-ferrying division; and Leoti Clark Deaton, WASP staff executive-training bases. Of 25,000 girls who applied for WASP flight training, 1,830 were accepted; 1,074 won their silver wings. The WASPs flew 60 million miles on operational duty; 37 lost their lives serving their country. WASPs had civil service—not military—status, but were granted eligibility to apply for reserve commissions in the Air Corps after the WASP program ended when the Allies were winning the war in Europe and the U.S.A. pilot shortage was past.

Avenger Field was closed after a short post-WASP span of service as a missile base.   (1972)

SWEETWATER (Nolan) *SH 70, 3 mi. S of I-20 intersection*
Site of U. S. Army Air Corps Plane Crash
At 6:05 A.M. on Friday, April 20, 1945, twenty-five Army Air Corps officers and enlisted men left Midland Army Air Field in a C-47 transport plane en route to Berry Army Air Field in Nashville, Tennessee. The flight crew consisted of the pilot, First Lieutenant James A. Bailey; the co-pilot, Captain John R. Rawls; and the flight engineer, Sergeant William H. Edwards. It was Sergeant Edwards' 36th birthday. Included among the passengers were eight officers and fourteen enlisted men. Two Sweetwater cab drivers spotted the plane on fire in mid-air. They notified their dispatcher, who alerted authorities at nearby Avenger Field. A crash landing message came from the plane itself at 6:30 A.M. Another C-47 flying just a few minutes behind the doomed aircraft never encountered a problem. After the crash, parts of the plane were found on a straight line almost two miles from the crash site. By 10:00 A.M. most of the bodies of the victims had been recovered from the smoldering wreckage and taken to funeral homes in Abilene and Sweetwater. The soldiers, whose ages ranged from 20 to 37, were buried in Arkansas, Florida, Illinois, Iowa, Massachusetts, Michigan, New Jersey, New York, North Carolina, Ohio, Oklahoma, Pennsylvania, Texas and Washington, D. C. Ten days after the crash, the Army Air Corps Aircraft Accident Classification Board met to determine its cause. It was the opinion of the regional safety officer that the craft had encountered a thunderstorm with only one of its two engines running, putting the plane into a roll. The plane's 4,000 hours of flight time, mainly spent towing gliders, probably caused a weakness in the tail and contributed to its disintegration in severe turbulence.   (2000)

SYLVESTER (Fisher Co.) *FM 1812*
Adair-Steadman Site
In this vicinity is a prehistoric archeological site discovered in 1969 near the clear fork of the Brazos River. Archeologists have conducted extensive scientific excavations and attribute most of the cultural materials to the Paleo-Indian period. The Adair-Steadman site was a large base campsite for makers of fluted points, who were part of the distinctive Folsom culture between nine and eleven thousand years ago.

Prehistoric peoples chose to live here because of the availability of water at the time of occupation and the presence of a large stone resource area nearby. Stone tools and other material recovered include fluted point fragments, point preforms, channel flakes, scrapers, gravers, and large bifaces. Future archeological, geological, and paleontological studies of the site may yield sufficient data to reconstruct the physical appearance of the site during its period of occupation.

One of the most significant locations of Folsom artifacts in North America, the Adair-Steadman site is important as a valuable source of information on the prehistory of the state, the nation, and the entire continent. It is protected from disturbance by federal and state antiquities laws.   (1984)

TAHOKA (Lynn Co.) *US 87, 5 mi. N in roadside park*
Lynn County
Created 1876 from Bexar Territory. Name honors G. W. Lynn, "one of those who baptized the altar of Texas with life blood at the Alamo." Tahoka Lake and Double Lakes Springs were watering places on Indian, Spanish, U.S. Army and cattle-driving trails. This was home land of

nomadic Indians; visited by Spaniards, 1500s–1880s; used by New Mexicans grazing large herds of sheep in 1860s; site of last great buffalo hunts and the U.S. Cavalry's drive against Comanches, 1874–1877. Last cowboy-Indian skirmish occurred 1879 at Double Lakes. Earliest open-range cattlemen settled here in 1880s. First schools, Lynn and T-Bar, opened in 1902. In April 1903, county was organized, with Tahoka as county seat. The first officials: M. L. Elliott, county judge; S. N. McDaniel, county and district clerk; C. H. Doak, sheriff and tax collector; O. L. Miller, treasurer; A. S. Coughran, tax assessor; W. E. Porterfield, surveyor; J. E. Ketner, H. E. Baldridge, B. Humphries, and W. T. Petty, commissioners.

The Santa Fe Railroad built to this point in 1910. This has since become a major agricultural area, ranking among top ten cotton counties in Texas—and one of the top twenty in the United States.

(1970)

TAHOKA (Lynn Co.) *US 380 at FM 212, 10 mi. E*
Grasslands
(2 mi. S)

On one of first land patents in South Plains, lying along a well-marked Indian trail used by explorers, U.S. Army, and (after 1880) the stages and freighters northbound from Colorado City.

Grasslands Ranch (named for an estate of President Cleveland) was established 1888 by Enos L. Seeds, the 1889–1900 postmaster, who erected a fine frame house and first trading post on South Plains. Mrs. Seeds was the first permanent white woman resident in county. Nearby is grave of area's firstborn white child (a son of Mr. and Mrs. Todd Wilson). Community name is now Grassland.

(1970)

TASCOSA (Oldham Co.) *US 385*
Boot Hill Cemetery

Along with law-abiding, God-fearing men and women were buried here, often without benefit of clergy, men who "died with their boots on." The name was borrowed from a cemetery in Dodge City, Kansas, while it was a resort of buffalo hunters and trail drivers.

TAYLOR (Williamson Co.) *SH 95, 6 mi. N near San Gabriel River Bridge*
C.S.A Cotton Cards Factory

Near this site in 1862–65. Used power from the San Gabriel River. Chartered by Confederate Texas during re-tooling of agricultural economy to meet demands of the Civil War years. Because trade of bales of cotton for finished cloth was no longer practical, and textiles had to be made at home, Texas imported through neutral Mexico, at costs of $4 to $20 a pair, thousands of cotton cards—stiff brushes that made fluffy cotton into firm, smooth "batts" to be spun into yarn or thread, quilted or made into mattresses. The administration of Governor F. R. Lubbock (1861–1863) also acted to have cards made in Texas, in factories such as the one here, owned by Joseph Eubank, Jr.

Heavy military demands (90,000 Texas men under arms; a 2,000 mile coastline-frontier to guard) plus reduced imports, caused fast expansion of industry. Arms and munitions plants were built, land grants, were used to encourage production. Private effort met the need, and produced vital supplies for both the military and civilian populations. Confederate quartermasters set up depots and shops for military goods. Production of salt and "King Cotton" was hiked to trade for scarce items. The state of Texas became a storehouse for the Confederacy.

(1964)

TAYLOR (Williamson Co.) *FM 619, 15 mi. S*
Pioneer Publisher and Printer David Ervin Lawhon
(Buried ½ mi. NW of Here)

Born in Tennessee on June 15, 1811. While very young learned the printing trade and worked at it in some of the principal cities of the United States.

Came to Nacogdoches, Texas, in November, 1835, in answer to pleas for volunteers for Texas Army. Was pressed into service publishing *The Texean and the Emigrant's Guide,* with essential war proclamations. Also printed handbills, patriotic songs and legal documents. His newspaper was one of several printed in Texas during War for Independence, 1836.

In 1839, moved to what is now Jefferson County and engaged in cattle ranching. Served as captain of a Ranger company. Was county's chief justice during the days of the Republic of

Texas. Moved to Bastrop County in 1861, where he tried farming; then moved to Williamson County where he died February 14, 1884.

As a newspaper publisher and printer for the Army of the Revolution (1835–1836), an Indian fighter, frontiersman and judge, he contributed much to the early development of Texas.

In 1840, David Lawhon married Nancy Carr, a daughter of one of Stephen F. Austin's "Old Three Hundred" settlers. Their eleven children carried on their pioneering spirit and tradition.   (1967)

TAYLOR (Williamson Co,) SH 112, 15 mi. SE
Shiloh Baptist Church
Founded Nov. 2, 1854, by 18 charter members. Services and revivals were often held under brush arbors at two early meeting sites (located 3 mi. NE and 2 mi. S of here). Building retains its simple pioneer style even with modern interior and siding. Awarded Medallion Plate.   (1968)

TAYLOR (Williamson Co.) SH 29, 8 mi. NW
Sloan Home
Home built 1854 by David McCurdy Sloan (1827–1912) and wife, Mary Elizabeth Easley (1829–1890), who came to Texas from South Carolina.

Finished lumber was hauled from Houston; rest hand-hewn in nearby river bottom, by slave labor. Awarded Medallion Plate.   (1965)

TAYLOR (Williamson Co.) FM 973 at 1660, 8 mi. S
James O. Rice
(1815–About 1875)
South Carolina-born James O. Rice migrated to Texas by 1835 and served in the Texas Army during the War for Independence. In early days of the Republic of Texas, he protected frontier settlements as part of a Texas Ranger company. On May 17, 1839, in command of a volunteer force clashing with Mexican troops led by Manuel Flores on the North San Gabriel River, Rice captured vitally important documents related to the Cordova Rebellion against the Republic of Texas. He joined the Somervell and Mier Expeditions of 1842 and the Snively Expedition of 1843. He also served in the Mexican War (1846–1848). For military services, he received several bounties of land.

When Williamson County was created in 1848, Rice was one of the commissioners named to select a site for the county seat. One of the county's largest landowners. Rice built his home on Brushy Creek about one mile west of here at a site then known as Blue Hill and later call Rice's Crossing. He ran a store and was postmaster of Blue Hill Post Office, 1849–1857. For a short time, he had a tanyard in Georgetown.

Rice married Nancy D. Gilliland (d. 1860), of an early Texas family. The couple had four daughters. Rice is buried in the Sneed family cemetery near Austin.   (1977)

TEAGUE (Freestone Co.) FM 1365, 6 mi. W
1 mi. N to Birthplace of Harvey Means
(1868–1943)
Noted Negro civic leader and barber to two generations of prominent Texans. An adventurous youth, Means began work at age 18 as shoe-shine boy in a West Texas barber shop. When rowdy cowboys demanded haircuts one day, Means (though inexperienced) complied with their wishes, and thus began a 54-year career.

His last 31 years were spent in Fort Worth, where he helped establish a hospital and city park for black citizens. He led in civic, religious, and fraternal affairs and worked continually to improve race relations. His 10 children all attended college.   (1971)

TEHUACANA (Limestone Co.) US 84, .5 mi. S
Trinity University
One-half mile north to the site once occupied by Trinity University. Established by the Brazos Synod of the Cumberland Presbyterian Church. Opened its doors as a co-educational institution September 23, 1869. Chartered August 13, 1870. Included Schools of Law and Theology. Removed in 1902 to Waxahachie.

TEMPLE (Bell Co.)   *SH 36, 10 mi. W*

Moffat

Founded in 1857 by New York native Dr. Chauncy W. Moffet and his wife, Amelia, the town of Moffat came to be known by a misspelling of their name. A Union loyalist during the Civil War, Dr. Moffet was impressed into Confederate service, but later also served the Union. He disappeared mysteriously after returning to the Moffat community in 1868. The town was platted that year by D. F. and Calista Wiswell. Moffat soon had 3 churches, a school, a post office, stores, and small industries. The Moffat cemetery, begun before the Civil War, is still in use.   (1985)

TEMPLE (Bell Co.)   *SH 36, 1.5 mi. W*

½ mi. N to Bird Creek Battlefield

Named in honor of Captain John Bird, who lost his life here May 26, 1839.
With only 34 Texas Rangers, he met 240 Indians at this point, and routed them.   (1964)

TEMPLE (Bell Co.)   *SH 36, 2 mi. W*

Bird Creek Indian Battle
May 26, 1839

This marker commemorates the death of Captain John Bird, Sergeant William Weaver, Jesse E. Nash, H. M. C. Hall, Thomas Gay, and the heroic and successful battle of a Ranger force of 34 against 240 Indians.   (1964)

TEMPLE (Bell Co.)   *SH 95, 3 mi. E of Sparks Baptist Church*

Miriam A. Ferguson Birthplace
(800 ft. E)

A five-room log cabin on this land was the home of Miriam A. Wallace (1875–1961) from her birth until her marriage to James E. Ferguson in 1899.

After her husband had been twice elected governor, Mrs. Ferguson became the first woman elected governor of any state. She served two terms, from 1925 to 1927 and from 1933 to 1935.

The property was inherited by Mrs. Ferguson and about 1917 was mortgaged to support her husband's political career. The home was destroyed by fire in 1926.   (1967)

TEMPLE (Bell Co.)   *SH 320 right-of-way, 12 mi. E, just N of SH 320 at FM 2904*

Farmers Mutual Protective
Association of Texas (RVOS)

The Farmers Mutual Protective Association of Texas (Rolnick´y Vzájemne Ochranñy Spolek Státu Texasu) was organized in the community of Ocker (400 feet NW) by nine men of Czechoslovakian descent on February 27, 1901. Created as a means of providing farmers and rural citizens with insurance coverage, the association was a cooperative effort of neighbors ready to help each other in times of need.

By the rules of the non-profit organization, only rural property was insurable, and each member was obligated to pay a share of any losses sustained by fellow members. In 1933, city property became insurable.

Association officers worked from their homes until 1946, when offices were rented in Temple. A home office was built on South 4th Street in 1950, and replaced by a new building at 2301 South 37th Street in 1981.

Charter members of the association were: Joseph R. Marek (1856–1936), Martin Stepan (1859–1935), Joseph R. Schiller (1874–1918), Frank J. Wotipka (1847–1933), Josef Wentrcek (1860–1922), F. Vincenc Schiller (1849–1941), Jan Baletka (1858–1939), Joseph Schiller (1847–1929), and Jan Zabcik (1856–1916).   (Texas Sesquicentennial 1836–1986)

TEMPLE (Bell Co.)   *SH 53, 9 mi. E*

Ocker Brethren Church

A group of deeply devoted followers of the Unity of the Brethren Faith were among the Czech immigrant families who settled in this area of eastern Bell County in the late 1870s and established the farming community of Ocker. The group initially worshipped informally in their homes. Annual visits from 1884 to 1891 by the Rev. Henry Juren and the Rev. Bohuslav Emil Lacjak encouraged them to organize. The Evangelical Congregation of the Bohemian and Moravian Brethren of Ocker was established in 1892. The dedication of their first church building, erected in 1893, was conducted by the Rev. Juren and the Rev. Adolph Chlumsky, noted early-day Czech community preachers. The church cemetery was established later that year.

Membership in the church grew from 52 families in 1900 to 92 families in 1925. A new church/Sunday school building was erected at this site in 1931 to meet the spiritual needs of a growing congregation. By mid-1940, English had replaced Czech as the language used in Sunday School and worship services.

The congregation was served by part-time pastors until 1981 when a full-time pastor was called. The church continues to serve the local community with spiritual guidance and outreach programs. (1994)

TEMPLE (Bell Co.) *1901 SW H. K. Dodgen Loop*
King's Daughters Hospital
The Temple Charter of the International Order of the King's Daughters and Sons, a Protestant ecumenical group, was formed in 1893 to provide medical care to indigent citizens. The group, made up largely of educated women, rented rooms in a small house and opened King's Daughters Hospital in 1896. In 1898 a board of trustees was elected which appointed the first staff physicians; Cornelia Parsons became hospital superintendent. By 1920 the King's Daughters organization had discontinued support of the hospital facility. Considered ahead of its time from its earliest days, King's Daughters Hospital remains a major provider of affordable modern medical care. (1998)

TEMPLE (Bell Co.) *1901 SW H. K. Dodgen Loop*
King's Daughters Hospital School of Nursing
Nursing training was implemented at King's Daughters Hospital from as early as 1897, and formal two-year classes began in 1903. In 1906, the hospital revised its charter to officially include a nurses' training school and the curriculum expanded to three years about 1910. Mary Julia Putts provided outstanding leadership as director in the 1920s. In difficult Depression years, an expanded curriculum and facilities helped the school survive, but a shortage of enrollees caused it to close its doors in 1948. The hospital began its own vocational nursing program in 1954. School alumnae formed an association in 1921 and served with distinction in both world wars. (1998)

TENNESSEE COLONY (Anderson Co.) *FM 321 at Spur 324, off SH 287*
Tennessee Colony
Founded in 1838 by settlers who came from the Old South by wagons, seeking fertile, watered farm lands. Later their cotton shipped from Magnolia Ferry on the Trinity created great wealth. Early businesses were a general store, blacksmith shop, cabinet shop (which made furniture still found in area). Town was trade center for places as far away as Dallas. The plantation era reached a climax in grandeur on the properties of F. S. Jackson, a settler from Virginia.

Circuit riders held religious services in homes until a log cabin church could be built, probably in late 1838; a second log church succeeded this one.

Masons attended the lodge in Magnolia for years, but in 1857 obtained charter for Tyre Lodge No. 198, A. F. & A. M., in Tennessee Colony. They then worked to build a 2-story church-school-lodge hall, which was finished in 1860 (and was to be used until 1948). The schools were outstanding, especially those taught by a Mr. Hooker and by Professor Sidney Newsome. They drew patronage from Palestine and other area towns. Remembered students included Addison and Randolph Clark, later to become founders of a college that would be forerunner of Texas Christian University. Descendants of original colonists still live here. (1971)

TERRELL (Kaufman Co.) *FM 986, 1 mi. N*
Porter Farms
Birthplace of Agricultural (Cooperative) Extension, under lead of Dr. Seaman A. Knapp, U.S. Department of Agriculture.

On Feb. 26, 1903, from places offered, a special committee of citizens selected farm of Mr. and Mrs. Walter C. Porter for first "Farm Demonstration." The project was highly successful in demonstrating methods of farming.

Extension is now part of each state land-grant university and adapted in many foreign nations.

Porter sons still operate this pioneer farm, "where science and farmers first joined hands."

(1970)

TEXARKANA (Bowie Co.) — *901 State Line Avenue*
Scott Joplin
(November 24, 1868–April 1, 1917)

Black composer Scott Joplin, often called the "King of Ragtime Music," was born in Texarkana, Texas, five years before the townsite was platted in 1873. His family lived in this vicinity, and he attended nearby Orr School on Laurel Street. His early musical training came from his father, Giles Joplin, an ex-slave who played the fiddle, and mother, Florence Givens Joplin, who played the banjo. By tradition, a German music teacher realized Joplin's talent and gave him lessons.

Joplin left home at age 14 and wandered through the Midwest entertaining in saloons and honky-tonks. In the 1890s, he was one of the originators of ragtime, a rhythmic new musical form that combined black and white musical traditions. Joplin's "Maple Leaf Rag," published in 1899, launched ragtime as a national fad. Joplin defended ragtime against those who called it frivolous and worked constantly to refine his music, which included over 30 piano rags. Demand for ragtime had declined by 1917, when Joplin died in New York City.

Joplin's background is revealed in his most ambitious work, the black folk opera *Treemonisha*, set on a plantation "northeast of the town of Texarkana." It was not produced until the 1970s, when a revival of Joplin's music inspired public recognition of his genius.   (1976)

TEXARKANA (Bowie Co.) — *US 59/US 71, 2 mi. N*
Hatchel/Barkman
Caddo Indian Village

Near here for 1,000 years, A.D. 800–1800, lived civilized Caddoes, who thought they were the sole survivors of a prehistoric flood and ancestors of all Indians. Their ceremonial mounds stood high above Red River. They had a significant role in exchanges between Puebloan Indians and the Mound-Builders in the East. They domesticated food plants such as corn, squash and beans and manufactured fine pottery. Because of pressure from Euro-American settlers, they left this area, and descendants are found in Oklahoma. Their village site is now under state protection.   (1981)

TEXARKANA (Bowie Co.) — *US 71 and 59, 4½ mi. N*
First Disciples of Christ of Texas
(9 mi. NW)

Worshiped in 1831 at McKinney's landing, where the McKinney family and a small group of neighbors met together for informal services. During the winter of 1841–1842, a traveling preacher from Illinois, G. Gates, organized the congregation into a church. He later wrote, "I remained with the brethren about a week...gathered scattered sheep and constituted a church of 16 members, with fair prospects for more."

First leader of the group was Collin McKinney (1766–1861), who had come with his family from Kentucky to Texas in 1831, when Mexico governed the state. The worship services he started were in defiance of the laws of Mexico, which demanded the allegiance of each citizen to the Catholic religion. In 1836 he signed the Texas Declaration of Independence. Collin County and the city of McKinney bear his name.

Between 1844 and 1846, the McKinney families and neighbors moved their congregation to Mantua, near Van Alstyne, where they met in a wooden church with a four-foot wall separating men from women. Five slaves of the family were members of the Mantua group. When the railroad built past Van Alstyne, they moved there and organized the First Christian Church, a direct descendant of the 1831 congregation.   (1967)

TEXARKANA (Bowie Co.) — *SH 8 & FM 2149, 10 mi. W*
Old Boston

Established while part of Mexico; to serve plantations on Red River. Mail came horseback from Arkansas. Named for W. J. Boston, first storekeeper. A battalion was formed here to fight in Texas Revolution.

First Bowie County Seat, 1841. Large stores surrounded square and two-story brick courthouse. Became educational center with 3 fine private schools. Texas Governors Hardin R. Runnels and S. W. T. Lanham have lived here.

New Boston (4 mi. N) founded on railroad, 1877. Boston (1 mi. S), exact county center, made county seat 1890, and this became "Old" Boston. (1966)

TEXARKANA (Bowie Co.) *US 71/59, 4½ mi. N*
The French in Texas
Were explorers and traders for about a century. Claimed coastal Texas early as 1685, when La Salle established his Fort Saint Louis Colony.

Another Fort Saint Louis, among Nassonite Indians, a few miles northwest of this marker, was founded in 1719 by a French captain, Benard De La Harpe, who came up the Red River. This fort was a center for trade with the Cadodacho (Caddoes) of Northeast Texas and the Wichita, Tawakoni, Tonkawa and other tribes of North Texas. Over 250,000 French and Caddo Indian artifacts have been found near here—including two millstones used in a flour mill near the fort.

Although Spain claimed Texas earlier and during the time of La Harpe, this did not discourage the French; they traded as far south as the mouth of the Trinity until Louisiana was ceded to Spain in 1762.

The chief French influence in East Texas was the Cavalier Saint Denis (1676–1744), who controlled Red River area of Louisiana, frequently coming into Texas. At first he prospected for silver and gold, as Spain had done. Later he found trading with the Indians was very profitable. The French had no policy against trading guns to Indians; partly for that reason they were more popular than the Spaniards. (1966)

TEXARKANA (Bowie Co.) *US 59/71, 4.5 mi. N*
Trammel's Trace
Entered Texas at this point. The 1813 road from St. Louis. Brought in great numbers of pioneers: Stephen F. Austin, his settlers, Sam Houston, James Bowie, David Crockett and others who died in the Texas Revolution. From here pointed Southwest. Crossed the Sulphur at Epperson Ferry, going south to Nacogdoches, linking "Southwest Trail" with the King's Highway to Mexico.

Surveyed by Nicholas Trammel (born in Nashville, Tenn. 1780; died, LaGrange, Texas, 1852), one of a family of U.S. surveyors and scouts. Mapped many trails, but only this one bears his name. (1965)

TEXARKANA (Bowie Co.) *IH 30, near N State Line Ave.*
Wavell's Colony
Projected in 1826 by General Arthur G. Wavell, Scottish-born soldier of fortune. By terms of a Mexican grant, he agreed to introduce 400–500 families into an area on the Red River. Ben Milam, frontiersman, was agent.

Many pioneers were actually brought in, but because Mexico and the U.S. disputed part of the grant, no titles were ever issued by Wavell. Some settlers, however, later received titles from the Republic of Texas.

The colony included virtually all of present Bowie, Red River Counties (Tex.), Miller County (Ark.), and possibly others to the west. (1969)

TEXARKANA (Bowie Co.) *1121 South Lake Dr.*
Dr. A. H. A. and Ruby Jones House
Ruby Lee Williams (1900–1979) was born in Texarkana to George and Carrie Williams. In 1928, she wed Jamaica-born Austin Hervin Archibald Jones (1901–1962), a successful dentist with a degree from Howard University. Ruby designed this bungalow-style home, utilizing African American craftsmen to build it in 1938. The home features decorative brickwork and a unique cubical tower. The Jones family often opened its home to touring African American entertainers, including Louis Armstrong and Dinah Washington. (2002)

TEXAS CITY (Galveston Co.)   *29th St. at Loop 197*
Texas City Memorial Cemetery
On April 16 and 17, 1947, disastrous explosions aboard two ships docked at the Texas City port killed hundreds of people. In the weeks that followed, relief workers led by the American Red Cross and other volunteers labored to identify the victims.

Temporary morgues were set up in the Central High School gymnasium and at Camp Wallace, a former army post. Eventually, 444 people were confirmed dead, and an additional 143 were listed as missing. Sixty-three bodies were never identified.

There was no public cemetery in Texas City in 1947. A burial committee appointed by local officials used donated funds to purchase this two-acre tract of land and made plans to bury the unidentified victims on Sunday, June 22. An interfaith and inter-racial funeral service was conducted before an estimated 5,000 mourners. Funeral homes from 28 towns provided individual caskets and hearses, and florists from throughout Texas donated flowers.

The Texas City Memorial Cemetery is still reserved for the 63 people who, although unknown by name, are remembered each year at a memorial service on the 16th of April.   (1991)

TEXAS CITY (Galveston Co.)   *Dock Rd. at Loop 197*
The Texas City Disaster
On April 16, 1947, three ships—the *Grandcamp,* the *High Flyer,* and the *Wilson B. Keene*—were docked in the Texas City port. They were loaded with cargo, including ammonium nitrate fertilizer, bound for Europe to assist in the post-World War II recovery effort.

At 8:33 a.m. the Texas City fire department responded to a call for assistance with a fire on the *Grandcamp.* As smoke billowed from the ship, spectators gathered to watch. The *Grandcamp* exploded at 9:12 a.m. with a tremendous force that was felt for miles around. A second explosion came at 1:10 a.m. on April 17, when the *High Flyer*'s cargo caught fire, destroying the *Wilson B. Keene* as well.

More than 550 people, including 27 firemen, were killed; flying pieces of concrete, steel, and glass injured thousands more; resulting fires took days to extinguish. Response to the disaster came immediately, with the American Red Cross coordinating relief efforts.

Far-reaching effects of the Texas City disaster included the implementation of safety standards and revised emergency medical treatment procedures. Citizens determined to rebuild. By 1950, few physical reminders of the disaster remained, although the event retains a prominent place in state and national history.   (1990)

TEXAS CITY (Galveston Co.)   *Loop 197 & 29th Street near*
                                                1947 Explosion Cemetery

Old Bay Lake Ranch
(½ mi. NW)
Established by Guy M. Bryan (1821–1901), nephew of Stephen F. Austin, "Father of Texas." Bryan was one of couriers for Wm. B. Travis's Alamo letter. Served in state legislature (where he was a speaker of the house) and U.S. Congress. Aide to Confederate President Davis and a colonel in army in Civil War.   (1967)

TEXAS CITY (Galveston Co.)   *Loop 197, 1 mi. NE of intersection*
                                                SH 3 & SH 146 w/IH 45

Site of Landmark Campbell's Bayou
(1 mi. E)
Settled 1821 by Privateer James Campbell (1791–1856), U.S. Navy veteran, War of 1812, who after discharge was lieutenant and close friend of Buccaneer Jean Lafitte, operating out of Galveston (then called Campeche).

In Karankawa Indian rituals about 1817, Mary Sabinal (1795–1884) became Campbell's bride. When Lafitte left Texas in 1821, Campbell pleased his wife by settling here as a rancher.

Community remained until its second destruction by hurricane, 1915. Graves of the Campbells and many other early Texans are in cemetery at Campbell's Bayou.   (1968)

TEXON (Reagan Co.)   *SH 67 at FM 1675*
The Town of Texon
Early travelers along many historic trails in this area found the region arid and inhospitable. Given (1876) to the University of Texas, the lands around this marker were leased to cattlemen. The Kansas City, Mexico & Orient Railroad built its line here in 1911, but did little local hauling. Development came after Frank Pickrell and Haymon Krupp of Texon Oil & Land Company drilled for oil. Their driller, Carl Cromwell, brought in Santa Rita No. 1, the first gusher in the Permian Basin, on May 28, 1923.

Texon, first company town in the Permian Basin, was founded in 1924 by Big Lake Oil Company. Levi Smith, president of the firm, planned and supervised building of the town, and Ted Williams served as city manager for the company. Texon had stores, shops, a school, a physician, a dentist, a hospital, a theater, a park, a well-known baseball team, and many facilities for recreation. The post office opened in 1926. As many as 2,000 people lived here—boosters claimed up to 10,000—manning the drilling, a gasoline plant, an oil treating plant, and other operations. Plymouth Oil Company absorbed Big Lake Oil Company, then sold out to Marathon Oil Company. The company town was closed in 1962.   (1977)

THE COLONY (Denton Co.)   *SE corner of Blair Oaks and S. Colony Dr.*
The Hedgcoxe War
Distribution of land in the Peters Colony of North Texas triggered a dispute known as the Hedgcoxe War. The Texas Emigration and Land Co. organized the colony under an 1841 Republic of Texas law which allowed it to keep one-half of a settler's grant. After protests, this right was repealed, but in Feb. 1852 the company was compensated with 1,088,000 acres of vacant land within the colony. This action angered settlers and speculators with land certificates, who feared that the large grant would lower land values. At that time, the company's unpopular agent, English-born Henry O. Hedgcoxe, operated a land office on nearby Office Creek. On July 12 and 13, 1852, a group of Dallas men broke in and examined the land records. They reported to a meeting in Dallas on July 15 that the company was defrauding the colonists. John J. Good (1827–82), later mayor of Dallas, then led a band of armed men to Hedgcoxe's office. Hedgcoxe escaped, but most of his files were seized and the office burned. After the raid, tensions quickly cooled. The law was amended so that settlers obtained their grants from the state rather than from the company agent. The company kept its land grant, however, and Hedgcoxe returned to help survey the tract.   (1975)

THE GROVE (Coryell Co.)   *SH 236, 6 mi. NE on Park Road 14*
Mother Neff State Park
First official state park in Texas; suggested the idea for the state parks system.

Originated with a 6-acre plot willed to Texas in 1916 by Mrs. Isabella E. Neff, mother of Pat M. Neff, governor of Texas 1921–1925. Because Texas then had no state parks, Mrs. Neff stated the land was to be used for religious, fraternal, political, and educational activities.

Seeing the need for more such areas, 1923, the 39th Legislature created the State Parks Board. In 1934, Pat Neff deeded 250 acres, and other owners 3 acres, to enlarge the original tract.
                                               (1968)

THOMASTON (DeWitt Co.)   *US 87*
Thomaston
(Founded 1872)
DeWitt County's first railroad town. Absorbed Price's Creek, 1848 settlement of Republic of Texas patriot, Judge David Murphree (1811–1866). Thomaston was named for State Legislator Nathan Thomas (1809–1891), who sold south part of townsite (in Refugio Amador survey) to Gulf, Western Texas & Pacific Railroad. North part of plat was donated (from Charles Lockhart survey) by John P. and Mary (Lockhart) Wright. Schoolteacher J. H. Moore and wife Lou (Thomas) built first house and owned cotton gin and grist mill. James Pridgen was first railroad agent, postmaster, and merchant. At peak, town had 500 people.   (1973)

THORNTON (Limestone Co.)

SH 14, 2 mi. S

Eaton Cemetery

The Richard Eaton family came to Texas in 1833 as members of the Robertson Colony. They moved to this area about 1845 and established a home and farm. The oldest grave in this cemetery, which was established on the family farm, is that of Richard's first wife, Mary, who died about 1848. Also interred here are Richard Eaton and his second wife, Charity, as well as other members of their family and neighbors. There are both marked and unmarked graves in the Eaton Cemetery, the final resting place of many Texas pioneers. (1990)

THORNTON (Limestone Co.) *FM 1246, 12 mi. E on roadside at site of old shop*

Site of Old Potter's Shop

The fine, white clay mined near here was used at this shop from the 1840s to 1912 to make pitchers, jars, crocks, churns, flower pots, and ornamental urns, which were used locally and shipped out of county.

In the 1870s the shop, built by Alberry Johnson, was a major industry in Pottersville (later Oletha). Wm. C. Knox later bought the plant and hired J. L. Stone as the chief artisan. John Fowler then became owner and was joined by his son E. J. Fowler about 1900.

Men dug kaolin clay from pits and hauled it to the plant, where mules provided labor to grind the clay to powder and it was fashioned into ceramics.

Historically, kaolin—still mined today from the deposits nearby—has been used to make fine porcelain and china. It ranks with gas, oil, and stone as a major commercial resource in Limestone County.

During the 19th century, vast natural resources throughout the state were creating new enterprises. Cattle and cotton headed the list of products, which also included lumber, iron ore, stone and salt, as well as finished articles such as cloth, iron kettles, soap, flour, brick, and matches.

These businesses, although crude and not of the "luxury" type, initiated the industrial growth of Texas. (1967)

THORP SPRING (Hood Co.)

FM 4 and Caraway St.

Add-Ran Christian College

Here J. A. Clark and his two sons, Addison and Randolph began a private school chartered in 1873 under the name of Add-Ran Christian College. Removed to Waco on December 25, 1895. Reestablished at Fort Worth in 1909 as Texas Christian University.

THREE RIVERS (Live Oak Co.)

FM 72, 4 blks. W of US 281

Site of Three Rivers Glass Factory

Opened 1922 by company headed by Charles R. Tips (b. 1892), the founder of town of Three Rivers.

Powered by local natural gas, plant used quartzose sand mined in area to make glass bottles for milk and other beverages and jars for food and cosmetics, attaining annual gross sales of a million dollars. Sold in 1937 to Ball Glass Company, it was closed in 1938, but had shown Texas' potential in the industry.

In later years, factory site became location of a warehouse.

Glass with Three Rivers cipher is highly prized by collectors. (1973)

THREE RIVERS (Live Oak Co.)

US 281

Three Rivers

Founded March 1913 by Charles R. Tips, an investor. Chartered June 12, 1913, as Hamiltonburg—named for local family. Town lot sale began July 4, 1913.

Townsite renamed by U.S. Postal Department May 1, 1914, to Mark Fork of Three Rivers—Nueces, Atascosa and Frio.

Present interests are ranching, farming, gas, oil and recreation. (1967)

THROCKMORTON (Throckmorton Co.)

RR 2528, 17 mi. S

Site of Camp Cooper

Established by Major W. J. Hardee, 2nd U.S. Cavalry, on January 3, 1856 for the purpose of defending the frontier against the Comanche Indians. Named in honor of Samuel Cooper, adjutant general, U.S. Army. Home of General Robert E. Lee for nineteen months, 1856–1857. From this post the Cimarron Expedition set out October 1, 1859. Abandoned February 21, 1861.

THROCKMORTON (Throckmorton Co.)
US 283/183, N of city limits
Throckmorton Co.
Formed from Fannin and Bosque Counties. Created January 13, 1858. Organized March 18, 1879. Named in honor of Dr. William Edward Throckmorton, 1795–1843.

A Revolutionary soldier. Father of James Webb Throckmorton, who became Governor of Texas in 1866. County seat Throckmorton.

THURBER (Erath Co.)
IH 20 south frontage road, 1 mi. E of Thurber exit
Site of Thurber Big Lake and Dairy
In 1891, a 20-acre "little lake" was built south of the Thurber town site to supply water to the community. It soon proved inadequate, however, and five years later a 150-acre "big lake" was constructed here about a mile southeast of town. Texas and Pacific Coal Company president R. D. Hunter organized a hunting and fishing club at the Big Lake for company executives and staff. Water from the lake irrigated company-owned farmland in the valley below, and provided water for the nearby Thurber dairy. The dairy's twin silos were still visible decades later. (1995)

THURBER (Erath Co.)
IH 20 south frontage road, 1 mi. E of Thurber exit
Site of Thurber Brick Plant
Texas and Pacific Coal Company general manager W. K. Gordon, seeing potential in the shale mud found in Thurber, persuaded company president R. D. Hunter to build a brick plant here in 1897. Original machinery included 3 Ross-Keller brick presses powered by a Corliss steam engine nicknamed "Old Hunter." The operation covered 5 acres and employed 800 men. Brick manufactured here was used to pave roads throughout Texas, including Old Bankhead Highway (US 80), Austin's Congress Avenue, Fort Worth's Camp Bowie Boulevard, and the Galveston Sea Wall. The plant closed in 1931. (1995)

THURBER (Erath Co.)
IH 20 south frontage road, 1 mi. E of Thurber exit
Site of Thurber's First Coal Mine
Hundred yards southeast of this site, at the base of the hill and at a depth of 65 feet, the first coal mine in this area was placed in operation by brothers William W. and Harvey E. Johnson. After Harvey's death in 1888, and because of labor and financial difficulties, William Johnson sold his mining interest to R. D. Hunter's Texas and Pacific Coal Company.

Railroads provided a ready market for coal, and the company town of Thurber (named for investor H. K. Thurber) became completely unionized after a 1903 strike. The company employed 2,500 miners of 18 nationalities. (1995)

TILDEN (McMullen Co.)
SH 173, Martin Park
Camp Rio Frio, C.S.A.
A Civil War Home Guard Post, acting as buffer to protect older settlements from Apaches and bandits. Scattered local men were members of the 29th Brigade, Texas Militia.

Picket homes with dirt floors. Diet of prickly pear salad and fruit, Spanish dagger blooms, hominy, turkey, quail and deer meat. Homespun and linsey clothing dyed blue with Brazil root or gold with agarita. Such was local scene the home guard protected.

Camp Rio Frio was later Dogtown, then became Tilden. It proved itself in a rugged era.
(1964)

TILDEN (McMullen Co.)
SH 16, 10 mi. N
Cross
This community (earlier known as Nopal, San Miguel, Franklin) is one of area's first permanent settlements. Named for Samuel C. Cross, who opened grocery store, became first postmaster, 1924. Post office closed, 1934. Gas well completed nearby, 1953, was largest in state at that time. Ranching also is important to economy. (1967)

TILDEN (McMullen Co.)

SH 16, 10 mi. N

Franklin Ranch

Ranch Founder, Ralph S. "Rafe" Franklin, was born in Louisiana, April 4, 1848. He came to McMullen County in the early 1860s with his family.

He started this ranch about 1870, building it up until he owned 40,000 acres, one of the largest holdings in this area. On Nov. 4, 1870, he married Minerva Holland; their children were: Murray; Buddy; R. S. Jr.; Green; Felix; Chapman; Amy; Claude; Tom; John; Margaret; Sam; Julius.

The ranch headquartered on San Miguel Creek. In 1913, the present ranch home was built at the same location. It was a travelers' refuge; relatives and friends from near and far visited often to attend parties, dances, picnics and other social gatherings.

For a short time Franklin ran sheep and goats but changed to cattle. In 1902, he purchased a herd of Black Angus, the first in this part of the country.

The old "San Antonio-Laredo Stage Road" traverses ranch, crossing San Miguel Creek below ranch home. During the Civil War much cotton passed over this road headed for the Mexican border.

The Franklins were pioneers in truest sense—few were more dynamic than they in early McMullen County development. "Rafe" Franklin died March 14, 1913.   (1967)

TILDEN (McMullen Co.)

SH 72, 4.7 mi. W
at exact crossing of Old Road

Old San Antonio–Laredo Road

Shortly after the founding of Laredo, in 1755, the Spanish established a transportation-communication route across this site. The road provided necessary abundance of water and grass for travel across this arid region, and served as a vital link between San Antonio and Laredo for well over a century.

Although under constant surveillance by hostile Indian tribes, this route was traversed by numerous notable people. Fray Gaspar Jose de Solis passed this site on Aug. 21, 1768, on return from an inspection of Spanish Texas missions. Stephen F. Austin, en route to Mexico City to seek a colonization grant, crossed here about March 18, 1822. On Feb. 26, 1828, Manuel de Mier y Teran passed on his way to survey Anglo-American strength in Mexican Texas. The Somervell Expedition, in punitive retaliation for a Mexican invasion of Texas, crossed here on Dec. 1, 1842, bound for Laredo.

Before and after the Civil War the road was used as a military supply route from San Antonio to Forts Ewell (1852–1854), at Nueces River crossing, and McIntosh, at Laredo, and as a trade outlet for early settlers.

Although abandoned after ranches were fenced and a railroad from San Antonio to Laredo was built in 1881, the road is still visible on the open range.   (1973)

TILDEN (McMullen Co.)

SH 16, 7.8 mi. S

San Caja Hill
(Located 14 mi. S)

The name, originally "Sin Caja," means "without coffin" in Spanish and may refer to the grim aftermath of the Turkey Creek Indian Battle, which was fought a short distance west of the hill in December, 1872.

The fight developed after raiding Indians had stolen livestock, chased young rancher Andrew Tullis, and dragged a herder to death at the J. Campbell Place.

The day following the killing, 13 ranchers from Oakville overtook the band at Turkey (now "Hill") Creek. Five Indians were slain, while one white man, Sebastian Beall, had a tooth shot out. Others in the fight were Caleb Coker, Time Cude, John Edwards, Bob and Sam Nations, Tobe Odom, Cullen Sanders, Andrew and Woodie Tullis, Rans Tullos, Pleas Waller, John Wilson.

The bones of the warriors, put in a cave in San Caja Hill, later mysteriously disappeared. They were supposedly removed by members of the same tribe.

Legends of treasure also hinge upon the name of the hill, for "caja" can mean "box" or "chest." This is thought to refer to money hidden in boxes here by Mexican bandits who raided wagon trains and stages traveling on the nearby Laredo-Goliad Road. Other tales tell of silver from the rich San Saba mines once buried nearby, but now lost to history.   (1969)

TILDEN (McMullen Co.)   SH 173 at SH 16
Tilden
Settled 1858 as Rio Frio. Later called "Dog Town" because ranchers used many dogs to round up cattle. 1871 townsite was laid out as Colfax. Made county seat 1877. Renamed for S. J. Tilden, who won popular vote for U.S. President, 1876.

Ranching and petroleum center. Noted for fine rural high school, annual rodeo, historic sites.

(1966)

TILDEN (McMullen Co.)   SH 16 at SH 72
McMullen County
Created 1858. Organized 1862. Abandoned because of bandit activities in thicket area during the Civil War. Reorganized 1877, with Tilden as county seat.

Named for John McMullen (1785–1853), founder with James McGloin of the Irish Colony at San Patricio: president pro tempore of the general council which governed Texas in 1836, on the eve of the Republic.

Of the 254 Texas counties, 42 bear Indian, French or Spanish names. 10 commemorate such colonizers as McMullen and Stephen F. Austin, "Father of Texas." 12 honor Washington and other American patriots.

96 were named for men who fought in the Texas War for Independence (15 dying at the Alamo), signed the Declaration of Independence from Mexico, or served as statesmen in the Republic of Texas.

23 have the names of frontiersmen and pioneers.

11 honor American statesmen who worked for the annexation of Texas; 10, leaders in Texas since statehood, including jurists, ministers, educators, historians, statesmen; and 36, men prominent in the Confederacy during the Civil War.

Rockwall and 8 others have geographical names. San Jacinto and Val Verde were named for battles; Live Oak and Orange, for trees; and Mason for a fort.   (1964)

TILDEN (McMullen Co.)   SH 173, across from courthouse
Old Rock Store
Built about 1865 by Pat Cavanaugh, Irish stonemason, assisted by Dick Barker.

Site of gun battles in Dog Town (now Tilden), "wide open" during lawless era of the 1860s and 1870s.

Preserved since 1929 by Clifton Wheeler, owner.   (1966)

TILDEN (McMullen Co.)   SH 16 on School Campus
Old McMullen College
Established 1881 under leadership of Dr. John Van Epps Covey, founder of three Texas colleges—aided here by civic leaders S. F. Dixon, Dr. M. W. C. Frazier, C. F. H. Hiers, R. W. Johnson, M. F. Lowe and L. Wheeler.

A 3-acre site was bought from James Lowe, and S. D. Frazier constructed the building. Funds were raised by subscription to defray initial costs. Dr. Covey, his wife, and the Rev. Woodlief Thomas were teachers during the first year. Accommodations were planned for 100 students. The curriculum included spelling, mathematics, geography, surveying, bookkeeping, logic, history, reading, Latin, other liberal arts courses.

In September 1897, after 16 years of service, the college ended its career. Its building was turned over to the trustees of the newly-organized Tilden School District, and used as a public school until January 1926, when a new structure replaced it.

Texas had numerous early schools with similar histories. Like McMullen College, these were founded by dedicated civic groups eager to see that young Texans were offered sound education. Most of these small local colleges had primitive facilities and endured repeated financial crises, but they held to ideals they were never able to attain.   (1967)

TILDEN (McMullen Co.)   SH 72, 6 mi. E by Yarbrough Bend marker
5 mi. SE to Townsite of Wentz
Founded as market center for a 44,000-acre development. Thrived for 3 years, 1914–1916.

Wentz Townsite was named for C. C. Wentz (1872–1957), agent of the Two Rivers Ranch Co. He promoted the townsite for the absentee Kansas landlords and was also a well-known businessman in West Virginia before coming to Texas.

The town grew to have about 200 people by 1916. A limousine was hired to meet each train at Three Rivers and bring the mail to Wentz. A severe drouth in 1917, though, forced most citizens to move. The post office closed, 1921; the two schools in 1948. (1968)

TILDEN (McMullen Co.) *SH 72, 5 mi. NE*
Site of County's First Settlement Yarbrough Bend
(5 mi. NE, on Frio River)

Founded 1858. Named for John Swanson Yarbrough, an original settler. Town contained about 30 log "picket houses." Settlers were often harassed by Indians, cattle thieves and wild animals.

Other original settlers were: Dr. George Dilworth, John Moore, James Tope, N. H. Walker, Joe Walker and Benjamin Franklin Winters. (1968)

TILDEN (McMullen Co.) *SH 97, 22 mi. NW in front of Zella Hotel*
Townsite of Zella

Organized 1913, with 189 city blocks laid off along San Antonio, Uvalde & Gulf Railroad. Structures built included depot, store-post office, schoolhouse, hotel. A water well was drilled.

War and the 1917 drouth stifled growth. Few lots were sold; land ownership was retained by founders. (1968)

TIMPSON (Shelby Co.) *US 59/84 right-of-way, 4.5 mi. E*
George Washington Green
(December 22, 1858–December 14, 1937)

Georgia native George Washington Green grew up in Tennessee and in 1878 set out for Texas. He married Tempie Ann Fowler in Logansport, Louisiana, that year, and they settled in this part of Texas. Green worked first as a sharecropper, growing cotton and corn, before purchasing his first parcel of land in 1883. Two years later, as the Houston East & West Texas Railroad began to build its line through Shelby County, G. W. Green purchased more land on both sides of the rail line and soon became a prominent landowner in the area, operating a general store and cotton gin. The Bobo community, primarily a train stop, was established on Green's land and operated a post office from 1893 until 1898. The phrase "Tenaha, Timpson, Bobo and Blair," used by the railroad conductor to announce stops along the rail line, became very popular and was used as a cadence during World War I. In 1905, George Washington Green made a lasting contribution to the area when he developed Green's Lake as a recreational spot and water source for the railroad. From 1905 through the 1940s, families came to picnic, swim and fish, and churches held baptismal services in the lake. George and Tempie Green reared four children: Luther (1880–1956), R. H. "Cooter" (1889–1969), Inez (M. Drewery) (1895–1965) and Nubern (1900–1959). George died in 1937 and is buried in the Buena Vista Cemetery. His contributions to the development of the rail line and to the Bobo community remain a significant part of the history of Shelby County. (2001)

TIOGA (Grayson Co.) *FM 377*
Primitive Baptist Church of Tioga

Organized 1884, in Lone Star; moved to Tioga, 1893. Present church built, 1948. T. N. Cutler, first pastor.

Sam Rayburn, Speaker, U.S. House of Representatives was baptized here 1956, by H. G. Ball, elder.

Ball conducted Rayburn's funeral in Bonham, 1961. Four presidents attended. (1967)

TIVOLI (Refugio Co.) *SH 113, 7 mi. W*
Nicholas Fagan

Came to Texas and settled in Powers Colony in 1829. A private in Fraser's Refugio Company at the Battle of Coleto.

He was saved from the massacre through the intervention of Mexican colonial friends. (1956)

TIVOLI (Refugio Co.)   SH 113 at SH 35
Preston Rose Austin
(November 11, 1872–September 29, 1929)

A far-sighted businessman who contributed much to the development of South Texas, Preston Rose Austin was born in Harrison County and grew up in Victoria County. After achieving prominence as a stock raiser, Austin became a partner in the Refugio Land and Irrigation Company, which acquired large landholdings in this area in 1902. Austin conducted a series of agricultural experiments and determined that the land was best suited to raising cotton. The company divided the property into small cotton farms for sale to German and Bohemian farmers.

Austin then founded two market towns to serve the settlers. The townsite of Tivoli was platted in 1907 by J. W. Ward. Austwell, named for Austin and one of his partners, Jesse McDowell of Pennsylvania, was platted in 1912 by L. A. Gueringer. The company provided each community with a church, school, store, hotel, and cotton gin and mill, as well as modern conveniences such as electricity and a telephone system. Austin and his associates also financed a branch line of the Missouri Pacific Railroad, which connected Tivoli and Austwell with Victoria when it was completed in 1912. Austin's energetic ventures resulted in extensive settlement of northern Refugio County.   (1976)

TOM BEAN (Grayson Co.)   SH 11, 2 mi. W
First United Methodist Church

This congregation was organized in the mid-1880s, growing out of brush arbor meetings at the Cedar campground near Whitemound.

The original church building at Whitemound was moved, in 1906, to Tom Bean, where it burned in 1924. Methodists worshiped in the Presbyterian Church until it was destroyed by a tornado a short time later. A new edifice was built, serving both denominations until 1972. In 1974, the sanctuary was moved here, and the heritage of the old Perrin Air Force Base chapel was preserved when it was added to the facility.   (1975)

TORNILLO (El Paso Co.)   SH 20 at O. T. Smith Road
Tornillo

The town of Tornillo derives its name from the Spanish word for screw-bean bush, a hardy firewood once prevalent in the area. Efforts to establish this site as a major agricultural center began when the United States Reclamation Service announced plans to build dam and reservoir projects on the Rio Grande. The Tornillo Townsite Company, founded by an El Paso investment firm, mapped the townsite in 1909, and the Tornillo post office was established the same year.

After the Elephant Butte project north of El Paso was completed, agricultural speculation in the valley increased. In about 1917, three leading agriculturists, J. B. Dale, Will T. Owen, and Louis J. Ivey, planted 600 acres of cotton in Tornillo. They harvested a successful crop and built the town's first cotton gin. Other farmers and businessmen, attracted by their success, settled here, and by the late 1920s Tornillo boasted several corporations, packing plants, and a cattle feeding operation, as well as several stores and a modern school system.

The town's economy suffered during the Great Depression of the 1930s and never fully revived. Urban growth in nearby El Paso contributed to the decline of the settlement. Tornillo stands today as a symbol of early commercial development in El Paso County.   (1983)

TOYAH (Reeves Co.)   US 80 at FM 2903
Toyah

Began as division point, 1881 on T. & P. Railway, with shops, roundhouse, hotel, cafe. Water was hauled from Monahans and sold by the barrel. Stage took passengers and mail to Brogado. 1882 cattle shipping brought cowboy-detective Charles Siringo here to look for rustlers.   (1964)

TRENTON (Fannin Co.)   US 69 Bus. at Hamilton Street
Trenton

The earliest Anglo settlers in this area, drawn to the fertile farmlands, probably came to the locality known as Wildcat Thicket in the mid-1800s. By the 1870s a community had begun to form, and settler A. J. Russell reportedly named Trenton for a hospital in which he had been treated during the Civil War. The railroad arrived in Trenton in 1881, the same year a post office was established, and the town began to boom. By 1885 there were several thriving businesses in operation. Trenton was incorporated in 1890. Dr. W. C. Holmes, a former Trenton mayor and active citizen, began to publish the weekly "Trenton Tribune" in 1909. The town maintained its size during the 20th century, outlasting many of its neighbors. Trenton remains a bustling community. (1999)

TRENTON (Fannin Co.)   *SH 69, 5 mi. NW*
Old Kirkpatrick Home
Victorian architecture. Built 1899 by family of Rev. W. A. Kirkpatrick. Still has original cypress roof, Bois D'Arc foundation, some of first furnishings.

Center, social life old Grayson College, and Presbyterian community. Awarded Medallion Plate. (1967)

TRICKHAM (Coleman Co.)   *FM 1176, at site, near Community Center*
Town of Trickham
Oldest town in county; founded about 1855 as a cowboy trading post for ranching activities of cattle baron John Chisum. During 1860–1890, it was a boisterous community at a crossroads of cattle trails. Because of notorious jokes played at local general store, "Trick 'em" was suggested for name of post office here. (1969)

TRINIDAD (Henderson Co.)   *SH 31 W of SH 274 intersection*
The Malakoff Man
A sandstone image of a human head–carved by prehistoric men—was found near here in 1929 by workmen of Texas Clay Products Company. It was dug from gravel pit now under Cedar Creek Lake.

The carving weighed 98 pounds, was 16 by 14 inches, with eyes 2½ inches wide. First stone was found at depth of 16½ feet. Two similar images were unearthed in same area in 1935 and 1939.

Archaeologists date Malakoff "men" as many thousands of years old. Found near the images were fossil remains of extinct horse, elephant, camel species. Images now in Texas Memorial Museum. (1967)

TRINIDAD (Henderson Co.)   *SH 31 just W of SH 274 intersection*
The Trinity River
Three main tributaries—the West, Elm, and East Forks—feed the Trinity from headwaters in North Texas. Discovery of prehistoric Malakoff man carved stone heads near this site in the 20th century revealed that humans inhabited the Trinity valley thousands of years ago. Indian villages dotted the river banks when European exploration began. French explorer Robert Cavalier Sieur de la Salle called this waterway the River of Canoes in 1687. Spaniard Alonso de Leon is credited with first using the name "Trinity" in 1690.

The fertile Trinity flood plain drew Anglo-American settlers to this area during the Republic of Texas. Buffalo, first Henderson County seat, was founded a few miles upstream at a ferry crossing. Navigation of the Trinity has been proposed in a number of ambitious plans since the 1850s. Steamboats plied the river carrying cotton, cattle, and lumber to Galveston and other Gulf of Mexico ports until the 1870s. Arrival of the railroad ended the era of riverboat trade.

Founded in 1881 on the St. Louis Southwestern Railroad, also known as the Cotton Belt, the town of Trinidad had a pump station to draw water for the boilers of steam locomotives. A ferry crossed the Trinity here until a bridge was erected in 1900. (1977)

TUCKER (Anderson Co.)   *US 79/84 right-of-way at church*
Green Bay A.M.E. Church
This congregation traces its history to 1866, when a group of Black workers at the Long Lake Cotton Plantation gathered together informally to organize a church. The following year the owners of the plantation designated a plot of land on which the workers built a sanctuary, known as Green Bay Church. In 1868, the congregation was formally recognized by the African Methodist Episcopal (A.M.E.) denomination and was renamed Green Bay A.M.E. Church. It was the first church in the Long Lake area.

In 1870, members of the church organized a day school for their children which became known as Green Bay School. When the church was moved to this site in 1887, school classes were held in the church building until a new school facility was erected in 1899.

The church continued to grow in its new location. Missionary activities included the establishment of two new congregations in the Tucker vicinity: New Salem Church and Bailey Chapel.

Construction of a new sanctuary at this site began in 1956 and was completed in 1959. Still an active congregation, Green Bay A.M.E. Church continues to serve the community with worship and outreach. (1989)

TUCKER (Anderson Co.)   *US 79, Green Bay Community Center*
Green Bay High School
Green Bay High School traces its origin to October 11, 1899, when eleven black men of the community formed a board of trustees and organized a school for the area's black children. The first school facility was provided by Green Bay Methodist Church. New school buildings erected in the early 1900s also housed the Mt. Sinai Masonic Lodge. Many dedicated teachers served in the Green Bay School, and students from a large rural area attended the school from its creation until desegregation of area school systems was achieved in 1966. (Texas Sesquicentennial 1836–1986)

TUCKER (Anderson Co.)   *SH 294, 2 mi. SW*
Site of Woodhouse School
Woodhouse School began with the consolidation of the Long Lake, Tucker and Magnolia schools into Consolidated Common School District No. 7. These were all small schools, each with two teachers: one for grades one through four and another for grades five through eight. In December 1937, William Phillip Bishop Woodhouse (1864–1951) deeded a portion of his landholdings to the school district for the construction of Woodhouse School. Most of the teachers from Long Lake, Tucker and Magnolia returned to teach at Woodhouse for its opening session in the fall of 1938. Originally serving grades one through eight, the school added a grade each year until 1942, when the first senior class graduated and the first yearbook was published. First superintendent of the school district was J.P. Brookshire, who remained in that position until 1939. The Work Projects Administration (WPA) built additional facilities for Woodhouse School in 1941, including an agriculture building, a cafeteria and a home economics cottage. Athletic programs centered around basketball, and Woodhouse fielded competitive boys' and girls' basketball teams throughout much of its history. Consolidation with the Four Pines School to create Westwood School signaled the closing of Woodhouse. The class of 1960 was the last to graduate from Woodhouse, although its facilities continued in use until 1979. Woodhouse remains an important part of the history of rural education in Anderson County. (2001)

TULETA (Bee Co.)   *US 181 N*
Park Hotel
Reinhart C. M. Nelson, one of many midwesterners lured to the area by the promotional literature of land developers, moved his family here from Minnesota in 1905. He built this structure in 1910. Named for its park-like setting, it is an unusual example of standard 20th century hotel form. It features innovative concrete construction, distinctive cast concrete classical columns, and a wraparound porchs.

The building was converted for use as a private residence in 1920.
(Recorded Texas Historic Landmark 1995)

TULIA (Swisher Co.)   *SH 86, 17 mi. E*
Battle of Palo Duro Canyon
General Ranald S. Mackenzie, 4th U. S. Cavalry, ordered shot the 1,450 horses captured from Indians in Battle of Palo Duro Canyon Sept. 28, 1874 to prevent their possible recovery by the Indians and to force the Indians to return to their reservations on foot. (1936)

TULIA (Swisher Co.)   *US 87 and 6th Street*
Swisher County
Formed from Young and Bexar Territories. Created August 21, 1876. Organized July 17, 1890. Named in honor of James Gibson Swisher, 1794–1864, conspicuous for gallantry at the storming of Bexar, 1835, signer of the Texas Declaration of Independence, 1836. County seat, Tulia.
(1936)

TUSCOLA (Taylor Co.)
US 83 S, (city limits at bridge)
Jim Ned Creek
Probably named for Jim Ned, Delaware Indian chief. During Republic and early statehood of Texas (about 1840–1860), he was a scout for the Texas Militia on several campaigns against wild Indians in this area.

Dams near junction of two main forks of creek create Lake Brownwood.

Note: Marker has been vandalized. (1968)

TYLER (Smith Co.)
US 271, 2 mi. NE in roadside park
Camp Ford
On this site during the Civil War was located Camp Ford, the largest prisoner of war compound for Union troops west of the Mississippi River. Named in honor of Col. John S. "Rip" Ford, who originally established a training camp here in 1862. It was converted in the summer of 1863 to a prison camp.

It first consisted of four to five acres enclosed by a stockade sixteen feet high. In the spring of 1864 following the Confederate victories at Mansfield, Louisiana, and Mark's Mills, Arkansas, the enclosure was doubled to accommodate the large influx of prisoners. Approximately 4700 Federals were confined here during this period. This over-crowded condition was somewhat relieved through a series of prisoner of war exchanges between the North and the South.

Union soldiers representing nearly one hundred different regiments plus sailors from gunboats and transports were confined here. In addition there were imprisoned Union sympathizers, spies, and even Confederate deserters.

The prisoners constructed their own shelters ranging from log huts and burrows called "she-bangs" to brush arbors and tents made of blankets.

A spring located about 100 yards southwest of this marker furnished an ample supple of good water. Their meager rations, essentially the same as that of their guards, usually consisted of beef and corn meal and were sometimes supplemented by vegetables purchased from nearby farms.

Although escape attempts were frequent, very few were successful, due to the long distance to Union lines and the difficulty including the tracking hounds used by the Confederate guards.

Even though conditions were primitive, it compared favorably with the other Civil War prison camps. Camp Ford continued to serve as a prison until the surrender of the Trans-Mississippi Department in May, 1865. It was later destroyed by Federal occupation troops. (1962)

TYLER (Smith Co.)
US 271 right-of-way, 3.5 mi. NE
Camp Fannin
Numerous military bases were expanded or established throughout Texas during World War II. Originally planned as an air corps installation, construction of Camp Fannin began in late 1942. Named in honor of Texas Revolutionary hero James Walker Fannin, Jr., the camp opened in the spring of 1943 and was formally dedicated in September.

The main purpose of the camp was an Infantry Replacement Training Center (IRTC), and during its peak operation as many as 35,000 to 40,000 men were trained every four months to replace troops killed, wounded, or recalled from the war's battlefronts.

In addition to the Infantry Training Center, the camp also included a German prisoner of war facility from 1943 to 1946, and a Women's Army Corps (WAC) installation in 1944.

Camp Fannin had a tremendous impact on the local economy, employing about 3,000 civilian workers and giving rise to numerous new businesses catering to the military trade. Many of the camp's facilities were later acquired by business interests and are still in use. Soldiers stationed here, as well as at least one former German prisoner, returned to East Texas to settle after the war. (1989)

TYLER (Smith Co.)
US 69, ¼ mi. S of Sabine River
At this Site was the Camp of
the Army of the Republic of Texas
Under Generals Edward Burleson, Thomas J. Rusk, Albert Sidney Johnston, Hugh McLeod, Kelsey H. Douglass and Colonel Willis H. Landrum just before they engaged Chief Bowles of the Cherokees and associated tribes in the decisive battle of July 16, 1839, by which the Indians were forever driven from East Texas. (1936)

TYLER (Smith Co.) *US 271, 9 mi. NE in churchyard*
Scouts of Texas Army
In the vicinity of Harris Place, scouts from the Army of the Republic of Texas were dispatched from present county of Van Zandt after the battle with Cherokees and associate tribes July 16, 1839, in which Chief Bowles was killed.

TYLER (Smith Co.) *SH 64, 2 mi. W*
Smith County
Formed from Nacogdoches County. Created April 11, 1846. Organized July 13, 1846. Named in honor of General James Smith, pioneer soldier and statesman, friend of General Sam Houston, Thomas Rusk and J. Pinckney Henderson. Born September 10, 1792. Died December 25, 1855, buried with military honors at Henderson. Tyler, county seat.

TYLER (Smith Co.) *SH 64, 6 mi. E*
Headache Springs, C.S.A.
Medical Laboratory
A quarter mile north of this site is "Headache Springs," noted for its healing mineral waters.

During the Civil War, as sea blockades cut off imports, a Confederate medical laboratory operated here. One of nine, and only one west of Mississippi River. For the government it made medicines and whiskey. The army at this time was buying medicinal herbs, including poke root, snakeroot, mullein, jimson weed, Jerusalem oak, nightshade, mistletoe and cherry bark. With mineral salts, these were the medicines of desperation. (1965)

TYLER (Smith Co.) *SH 155 at FM 344, 16 mi. SW*
Neches Saline, C.S.A.
Now covered by the waters of Lake Palestine, the Neches Saline was the source of salt for early settlers from over a wide area of East Texas. As early as 1765, the Spanish missionary Calahorra recorded the presence of salines in the area.

An early manufacturing process for extracting salt from the saline involved drawing water from shallow wells and boiling it to the evaporation point, leaving the salt behind. The possibilities for commercial development of the Neches Saline became evident to the early settlers, and a small isolated settlement developed here before the Texas Revolution.

Local salt making declined throughout the South between 1850 and 1861 as salt began to be imported from England. With the Federal embargo during the Civil War, salt began to be made locally again. It was reported that James S. O. Brooks, who had come to Texas from West Virginia, had twelve furnaces operating at the Neches Saline during the war and manufactured 100 bushels of salt per day to meet the needs of the Confederacy. Brooks leased the salt works to his son, William Bradford, in 1865. W. B. Brooks, who purchased the operation in 1871, apparently was the last owner and operator of the salt works at the Neches Saline. (1965)

TYLER (Smith Co.) *FM 14 right-of-way, 17 mi. N*
Head of Navigation on the Sabine River: Belzora Landing
A thriving port for Tyler and East Texas, from 1850s until arrival of railroads in 1870s. One of many ports established when settlers (as in eastern states) turned to rivers for transportation. In Texas, river-freighting proved rather disappointing. The long, winding rivers were difficult for even small, shallow-draft steamers to navigate. Boats on the Sabine fared very well, however, because of abundant rainfall and favorable terrain.

For several months each year, light steamboats could ascend the river to Belzora. The *Galveston News* for that period included Belzora in listings of ports. In dry seasons it was local practice to load goods on barges, flatboats and other craft and wait for a freshet to send them downstream.

In addition to the boat landing, Belzora had a ferry used by travel on the Dallas-to-Shreveport Post Road. The town had a dozen businesses, a post office and a combination church-schoolhouse.

Ambitious plans for greater inland navigation, deepening of river channel, and building of locks and dams never materialized. Belzora, like many sister ports, became an historic relic—a ghost town. (1970)

TYLER (Smith Co.) *US 69, 22 mi. NW, N of Old 69 at CR 484*

On Burleson Lake, 3.5 mi. W of Here Was Last
Cherokee War Camp of the Army of the Republic of Texas

Under Gen. Kelsey H. Douglass, Gen. Thomas J. Rusk, Gen. Edward Burleson, and Col. Willis H. Landrum. Texas Secretary of War Albert Sidney Johnston ordered the army mustered out after its decisive victory in Battle of the Neches against Chief Bowles of the Cherokees and associated tribes on July 16, 1839, in Van Zandt County. From the Burleson Lake Camp, the soldiers departed for their homes on July 25, 1839. (1975)

TYLER (Smith Co.) *Tyler Rose Park, East Texas Fairgrounds*

Smith County Rose Industry and the Tyler Rose Garden

A combination of sandy soil, year-round rainfall, and a long growing season make the Tyler area ideal for rose propagation. First known commercial production began here in the 1870s when industry pioneers such as G. A. McKee and Mathew Shamburger (1827–1888) sold rosebushes along with other nursery stock.

Business expanded in the 1920s as more nurserymen began growing roses. Production was increased by new growing methods such as irrigation, introduced in 1924 by A. F. Watkins. The Texas Rose Festival was started in Oct. 1933 to publicize the industry. Scientific plant research, begun in the 1930s by J. C. Ratsek, Dr. E. W. Lyle, and others from the Tyler substation of the Texas Agricultural Experiment Station, was implemented by organization of the Texas Rose Foundation, Inc., in 1945.

The Tyler Rose Garden, a 22-acre municipal park, was created in 1952. Nurseries donate the many varieties of plants, which are cared for by the city.

Today the rose industry is vital to the economy of Smith County. In 1973 the value of bushes and flowers shipped around the world by local nurseries totaled $9,000,000. One-half of the rosebushes produced each year in the United States come from the Tyler area. (1975)

TYLER (Smith Co.) *SH 64, 13.5 mi. W in Van Zandt Co.*

On this site the Cherokee Chief Bowles was killed

On July 16, 1839 while leading 800 Indians of various tribes in battle against 500 Texans. The last engagement between Cherokees and whites in Texas.

UMBARGER (Randall Co.) *US 60 at Buffalo Lake Rd.*

Umbarger

On land settled 1895 by Civil War veteran S. G. Umbarger, who built on his farm a wagon yard and sheds for travelers bound for Amarillo from Southwest. When the Pecos Valley Railroad was built in 1898, his name was given to a switch here.

Post office was established in 1902. In that year a strong German-Catholic influence was introduced by Pius Friemel and family, whose close friends and relatives soon followed. Church and school were founded by 1908.

The parish church remains the center of religious, social and economic affairs of community. (1967)

UTOPIA (Uvalde Co.) *FM 187, 8 mi. S*

Captain John Coffee Hays

In this vicinity, June 24, 1841, Captain John Coffee Hays and his company of 16 Rangers, assisted by thirty Mexicans under Captain Flores, encountered ten Comanche Indians, killed eight and captured the other two. None of the Rangers were killed and but one wounded.

UTOPIA (Uvalde Co.) *FM 187, Main Street*

Old Rock Store

Utopia's first building. Erected 1873 of native rock for R. H. Kincheloe, owner, by Joe Hastler, stone mason. (1967)

UTOPIA (Uvalde Co.) *FM 187, 4 mi. N*

Site of Old Taylor School

Founded 1883, named for Henry Taylor. He, Cid Thompson and other early settlers gave land and founded school. First trustees were D. Harper, H. Kennedy, H. Taylor. First one-room frame building had homemade desks and recitation benches.

After it burned two more were built before consolidation with Utopia, 1937. Miss Sue Harper, Frank Robinson, and "Miss Mattie" Noel listed among outstanding teachers. This was community center; weekly literary society, Sunday school, church met here. This marker given by and in memory of former pupils. (1967)

UTOPIA (Uvalde Co.) *FM 187, Main Street*
Utopia
After an 1866 Indian raid on their nearby Little Creek home, R. H. Kincheloe and family moved here, built a home and in 1873 a 2-story rock store. They platted town as "Montana," giving land for churches, school, and community square. Post office moved from Waresville in 1883. Methodists had church here before town was founded. Baptists organized their church in 1883. Church of Christ congregation relocated here, 1902.

New name praising climate was chosen by Postmaster George Barker. Stores and shops were built. Town is now a center for ranching, retirement, vacationing. (1973)

UTOPIA (Uvalde Co.) *FM 187, in Utopia*
Utopia Methodist Church
Established in 1866 as part of the Uvalde-Kerrville Mission, later in the Uvalde Circuit.

Pecan grove behind present church was site of many pioneer camp meetings under brush arbors. The first was held in 1868 by the Rev. A. J. Potter, noted Civil War chaplain and circuit rider.

This Gothic sanctuary, built in early 1890s with members doing much of the work, is on a site given by the Rev. Irving Jones and R. H. Kincheloe. (1967)

UTOPIA (Uvalde Co.) *FM 187, 1 mi. S*
Old Waresville
(¼ mi. W)
First non-military colony in Uvalde County. Founded 1852 by Capt. Ware, veteran of Battle of San Jacinto. Ware built first log cabin home (still standing). Other early settlers included Gideon Thompson, whose wife was first Anglo-American woman in Sabinal Canyon.

Colony lost settlers in Indian raids, 1856–1866. Although the post office moved to Utopia in 1883, still here is the cemetery where Capt. Ware was buried in 1853; first store and post office built by Charles Durbon, 1856; homes of Joel Finley, John Ware, built of native stone, 1870s. (1966)

UVALDE (Uvalde Co.) *FM 140, 4.5 mi. SE*
Site of Fort Inge
Established by Captain Sidney Burbank, First U.S. Infantry, March 13, 1849, on east bank of Leona River in Uvalde County. Named for Lieutenant Zebulon M. P. Inge, killed in Battle of Resaca de la Palma, May 9, 1846, in the Mexican War.

Protected the Southern Overland Mail Route from Indian raids.

Visited by Robert E. Lee, 1856. At that time fort consisted of a dozen primitive but neatly kept buildings.

Occupied by Confederate soldiers in Civil War. Reoccupied 1866 by Federal troops until abandoned March 28, 1869. (1966)

UVALDE (Uvalde Co.) *US 90, 3.9 mi. E*
Uvalde County
Created 1850. Named for canyon which in turn had been named for the Spanish Army Captain Juan de Ugalde, who fought and routed Indians here in 1790. Over the years, "Ugalde" became "Uvalde."

Many cattle, sheep, goats are raised; and Uvalde honey is famous for its flavor. Noted for fine hunting and scenic drives.

Historic sites marked include 3 old forts, 2 Spanish missions, a Ranger camp.

Home of Southwest Texas Junior College, Garner State Park and home (now museum and library) of John Nance Garner, first Texan elected vice-president of United States. (1965)

UVALDE (Uvalde Co.)　　　　　　　　　　*SH 55 at Chalk Bluff Road, 15 mi. N*
Chalk Bluff Indian Massacre
(Site 1 mi. W)
Here on May 29, 1861, two of Southwest Texas' most feared Indian fighters were ambushed by a band of 20 hostile Indians.

Henry Robinson—tall and red-bearded—was so well known to the tribes that they had painted his picture on a rock near the Llano River. He and his companion, Henry Adams (also his daughter's fiance), were en route to Camp Wood when the attack came. The Indians, after they had killed the two men, took both their scalps and Robinson's beard, too; they then attacked Robinson's home, but his family fought them off successfully.　　　　　　(1970)

UVALDE (Uvalde Co.)　　　　　　　　　　*US 83 at US 90, Town Plaza*
Early Texas Wagon Yards
Places of shelter for drivers, teams and wagons. Here travelers could cook bacon, eggs, beans, coffee; talk with friends and strangers. For people from the country, a wagon yard was both a hotel and a social center. Usually it was an open area flanked by a shed, stalls and feed rooms. It might cover a city block, and charges were 25¢ to $1.00 a day.

Drivers pulled into yards, cared for teams, found cooking and sleeping space. Men or families might stay for weeks, await kin or goods coming by train or stage. Amusements were practical jokes, gossip, games, music by fiddle, guitar, harmonica. Young boys overcame bashfulness, learned to dance, roller skate, whip bullies. The yard was center for trading goods and horses; obtaining advice on travel, work, weather. Some yards were stops for stages and freighters.

A block west of this site was wagon yard of F. A. Piper Company (predecessor of Horner's Store). Like many Texas merchants, Piper built and ran the wagon yard to aid customers, who used it free of charge.

Modern transportation has made the wagon yard a relic of the past, but it has a secure place in the history of pioneer days in Texas.　　　　　　(1966)

UVALDE (Uvalde Co.)　　　　　　　　　　*300 N. Getty St. (US 83)*
First Presbyterian Church of Uvalde
The Western Texas Presbytery assigned the Rev. James R. Bridges to the Uvalde field in 1881. Serving Bandera, Brackettville, Del Rio, Montell and the Nueces and Frio Canyon areas, Bridges found Uvalde and especially its surrounding areas wild and often dangerous. However, he soon met Presbyterian families who were anxious to organize a new church. William and Mattie Jones and their six children, also new arrivals to the area, helped the young minister gather charter members and organize the church. In February 1882, the Rev. Mr. Bridges and eleven charter members met in Uvalde and organized the Uvalde Presbyterian Church. The Presbyterians met in the Methodist church building while funds were raised for a meeting house of their own. The new building was dedicated in 1883, the same year that Bridges was called to serve in Baltimore. A windstorm destroyed the church building early in the 20th century, and a new facility was built in 1907. In 1909, the Rev. Thomas Alexander Hardin of Tennessee became minister of the Uvalde church. His arrival ended years of uncertainty for the church and began an era of stability. The 1907 church building was moved to this site in 1914. A ladies' group, later called the Women's Auxiliary, was in operation by 1921. Ill health compelled the Rev. Mr. Hardin to retire in 1933; he was pastor emeritus until his death in 1946. The church grew in numbers despite the difficulties of World War II. A men's group began in 1947. In the 1950s and early 1960s a new church complex was completed. The church has remained active in community service and worship, growing steadily since that time.　　　　　　(1999)

UVALDE (Uvalde Co.)　　　　　　　　　　*301 N. Getty (US 83)*
Original Site of Uvalde High School
Four years after Uvalde became a railroad shipping point, the people of the city built their first school building. Completed in 1885, the facility served all grade levels. The picketed structure was constructed of cedar logs and erected on this site, which was donated by the town's founder, Reading W. Black. The demand for space quickly required a new four-room two-story structure. Four more rooms were added in 1891, the year of the first graduating class. Graduation cere-

monies, which took place after completion of the tenth grade, were sometimes held in the Uvalde Opera House. The school building burned to the ground in 1898. Determined to continue to meet the educational needs of their children, Uvalde citizens erected a new building on this site in 1900. The two-story edifice cost $10,000 to build, and there was some controversy over its size. By 1907, Uvalde had become an independent school district, and even the modern 1900 structure was no longer adequate for the rapidly growing area. Plans for a larger Uvalde High School on West Main Street were carried out in 1908. The educational investments of the early citizens of Uvalde have been multiplied in the graduates of Uvalde High School. For more than a century, Uvalde students have become valuable community members.   (1998)

UVALDE (Uvalde Co.)   *524 N Getty Street (US 83)*
Schwartz House
Built in 1927 as the home of Lee Schwartz, local merchant and city alderman, and his wife Agnes (Racer), this house was designed by San Antonio architect Will A. Noonan. Constructed on land formerly owned by Mrs. Schwartz's mother, the house was built on the site of an earlier home. Features of the modest colonial revival style house include a pedimented entry, single entry door with sidelights, and groupings of multi-light windows.   (Recorded Texas historic landmark 1997)

UVALDE (Uvalde Co.)   *US 90 W, at grave, old section of Uvalde Cemetery*
John Nance Garner
(November 22, 1868–November 7, 1967)
Vice President of U.S. 1933–1941. Began career as Uvalde County Judge 1893–1896. Served in Texas Legislature 1898–1902; in U.S. Congress 1904–1932, where he was, in last term, Speaker of House of Representatives. Also an able trial lawyer, rancher, banker, and benefactor of Southwest Texas Junior College. Married Ettie Rheiner. Had a son, Tully; one grandchild, Genevieve G. Currie.

Known as "Cactus Jack" for his unique Western individualism.

UVALDE (Uvalde Co.)   *US 90, on grounds of Texas Hwy. Dept. Bldg.*
⅓ mi. NE to Homesite of Pat Garrett
Pioneer law officer Patrick F. Garrett, renowned for killing outlaw Billy the Kid in 1881, lived in a house at this site during his residence in Uvalde.

He had come from Alabama to Texas in 1869; here he worked as a farmer, cowboy, and buffalo hunter. He served as sheriff in several cities and also dealt in ranching operations. He owned property here from 1891 to 1900.

In 1908 he was killed in New Mexico after an argument over land, but many people assumed that the quarrel was merely a ruse to force Garrett to fight or be murdered from ambush.   (1970)

UVALDE (Uvalde Co.)   *US 90 (E Main St.) & 4th St.*
USS Uvalde
Constructed and commissioned by the U.S. Navy in 1944, the *USS Uvalde* was a C-2 type cargo ship named to honor former United States Vice-President John Nance Garner and the county of his residence. The *Uvalde* was built by the Moore Drydock Company of Oakland, California, with an overall length of 459 feet.

The *Uvalde* served the United States Navy during World War II and was most active in the campaigns of the Pacific Theater. After the war ended, the ship provided troop and cargo transport to vital outposts in the Western Pacific and earned the Occupation Service Medal for operations in Chinese waters.

After service as part of the United Nations Force in the Korean Conflict, the *Uvalde* became part of the reserve fleet. In 1961, the ship was reactivated in response to the events of the Cold War, including the Berlin and Cuban missile crises.

After earning numerous service awards and citations, the *USS Uvalde* was decommissioned in 1968. The city of Uvalde, which had remained interested in the ship's service record over the years, gladly accepted the navy's offer of several items of the vessel's equipment. The anchor and bell displayed at this site are reminders of the history of the ship and her crew.

(Texas Sesquicentennial 1836–1986)

UVALDE (Uvalde Co.)
FM 140, 6 mi. S
Site of Early Settlement Known as The Ditch
Community established along waterway of Leona Irrigation and Agricultural Association, formed in 1874 by Greenville and W. B. Bowles, A. B. Dillard, Charles T. Rose, A. J. Spencer, and T. E. Taylor.

Irrigation produced rich crops; many families settled here. A schoolhouse doubled as church and community center. Settlers gathered in from a large area for dances, weddings and other festivities—often prolonged.

An 1894 flood ruined the farms, and people moved away—many to Uvalde, to become substantial citizens there. Only a cemetery remains (1 mi. W) of "Ditch" Settlement.   (1970)

VALERA (Coleman Co.)
US 67, .5 mi. W
Cleveland-Anson House
First fine house in area. Built in 1880 by George P. Cleveland, a sheep rancher. Structure of native stone and lumber hauled from Fort Worth by ox-wagon, has two-foot walls. Second owner was Englishman Billy Anson, son of the Earl of Litchfield. Awarded Medallion Plate.   (1970)

VALLEY MILLS (Bosque Co.)
SH 6 at 5th St.
First Methodist Church of Valley Mills
Methodists in this area trace their history to the 1840s, when circuit-riding preachers began holding camp meetings on a nearby farm. In 1889, after the railroad caused Valley Mills to relocate south of the Bosque River, the Methodists built their first church, located in a residential area. In 1915, the congregation voted to move downtown.

Brick structure, which features two inset temple-front entries with ionic columns, was completed by 1916. Art glass windows, corbelled brickwork, and a pressed metal roof that simulates tile are also prominent.   (1991)

VALLEY VIEW (Cooke Co.)
IH 35, 3 mi. N at rest area
Kiowa Raid of 1868
(SW Part of County)
On Jan. 5–6, 1868, Chief Big Tree and 150 to 200 Kiowas raided Willa Walla Valley, Clear Creek and Blocker Creek. Burned homes; killed 13 people; scalped one woman alive. Captured 10 women and children; 3 escaped, 2 were ransomed. Raiders reached Elm Creek at Gainesville before blizzard forced withdrawal.

More damage and deaths would have resulted if George Masoner had not become the "Paul Revere" of valleys and warned settlers of impending danger.

Indian raids such as this one were in retaliation for loss of hunting grounds to settlers.   (1968)

VAN (Van Zandt Co.)
IH 20, 1 mi. W at rest area
Park Dedicated to Memory of Texas State Highway Commission Chairman
Brady P. Gentry
(March 25, 1895–Nov. 9, 1966)
A man whose public service was of highest order. Born on a farm near this site in Van Zandt County. Educated at Cumberland University (Tennessee) and Tyler Commercial College, was county attorney and county judge of Smith County. As chairman of Texas Highway Commission, 1939–1945, he traveled almost every Texas highway to learn road needs of state. Aided long-range financial strength of highway program by supporting the reservation of road-use revenue for road building.

An authority on highway policy, Gentry served in 1943 as president of the American Association of State Highway Officials. In that capacity he aided post-war expansion in use of motor vehicles by implementing legislation to provide funds for farm-to-market roads and the first major expressways in the country.

Interested in education, Gentry helped to establish Tyler Junior College. He served as U.S. Congressman, 1953–1957, for Third Congressional District of Texas. A member of committees for public works and roads, he helped design legislation for interstate highway system. Refused to vote along merely political lines.

The preeminent position of the Texas Highway Department and the high quality of roads in Texas and the U.S. are a tribute to the ability of Brady P. Gentry.   (1967)

The Free State of Van Zandt

Pioneer nickname appropriate to this area's many freedoms—particularly from want and fear. (Food was obtained with little effort; and although the Indians fought white men here as late as 1842, the settlers by 1847 slept in the open with no dread of Indians or wild animals.) According to tradition, Van Zandt county (created 1848) also by a legal accident had freedom from sharing debts of its parent county, Henderson—and was proud of that unusual advantage.

Other parts of Texas share "free state" traditions. An 1826 "Republic of Fredonia" was proclaimed in Nacogdoches and endured for a few weeks. Along the Mexican border, citizens maintained in 1839–1840 the "Republic of The Rio Grande." Because it developed great self-reliance in recurring border troubles, Hidalgo County called itself a republic, 1852–1872. A Panhandle County formed the secessionist "Free State of Ochiltree" in the 1890s.

All secessions have been brief. When Texas in 1845 voted to become a part of the United States, it was given (but declined) the right to become five states. Such movements as "The Free State of Van Zandt" soon lost force. Ten proud years as the Republic of Texas invoke unusual loyalty to the state.   (1968)

VAN (Van Zandt Co.)   *SH 110, 3 mi. N*

Pruitt Baptist Church and Pruitt Community

Named for Adelia Pruitt, the first postmistress, the town of Pruitt began in the 1880s. It included a cotton gin, blacksmith shop, general store, barber shop, Woodmen of the World Lodge, drug store, school, Methodist Church, and Congregational Church. The Pruitt Baptist Church was organized in 1896 by Malinda Ashworth and E. R. Crocker. In 1912, a church building was erected for the Baptist congregation one mile west of this site. The sanctuary was moved in 1947 and replaced with a new structure in 1962. Many additions have been made to the building. The church continues to serve the area.   (1996)

VAN ALSTYNE (Grayson Co.)   *FM 121, 6 mi. E*

Old Town of Cannon

Founded 1852 by Elijah Cannon, who came from South Carolina with his children and slaves, to develop 700 acres of land. Family established a church, cotton gin, grist mill, wagon factory.

By 1885 town had an academy and 400 people. Bypassed by Houston & Texas Central Railroad, it declined rapidly in the 1890s.   (1967)

VAN HORN (Culberson Co.)   *IH 10, 1 mi. W*

Culberson County

Formed from El Paso County. Created March 10, 1911. Organized April 18, 1911. Named for David B. Culberson, 1830–1902, famous Constitutional lawyer, a Confederate officer, member of the Texas Legislature, member of the United States Congress. Van Horn, the county seat.   (1964)

VAN HORN (Culberson Co.)   *US 90, 12 mi. S*

Van Horn Wells
(½ mi. W)

Only dependable water supply in miles of arid terrain. Used by Indians for centuries. Named for either Maj. Jefferson Van Horne (who passed here en route to establish fort at El Paso, in 1849), or for Lt. J. J. Van Horn (stationed here to fight Indians, 1859). Wagon trains from South Texas welcomed the "seep-water" from wells, as did soldiers on San Antonio-El Paso Military Road. Riders for "Jackass Mail" (San Antonio-San Diego) stopped here and the Butterfield Mail Line built a stage stand at Wells, 1859. Town of Van Horn grew up (12 mi. N) in 1880s.   (1970)

VAN HORN (Culberson Co.)   *US 80, 3 mi. W at roadside park*

San Antonio–California Trail
(3 mi. S)

One of Texas' first cross-country wagon trails. The San Antonio-El Paso section of this route was surveyed in 1848 by a party under the intrepid Indian fighter Jack Hays. Used first by emigrants and gold-seekers, it became part of the San Antonio-San Diego Mail Line (1857), one of America's pioneer mail services.

Passengers on the line paid $200 (one-way) to share a swaying Concord coach with 600 pounds of mail and braved bandits, dust, floods, and Indians to spend 27 days traveling 1,500 miles. Service ended in 1861 at the outbreak of the Civil War. (1968)

VAN HORN (Culberson Co.) *SH 54, 32 mi. N*
Figure 2 Ranch

The lands which now lie within the boundaries of the Figure 2 Ranch were occupied in the 19th century by nomadic native American tribes. One of the last battles between Texas Rangers and Apache Indians occurred in the mountains west of this site in 1881.

James Monroe Daugherty (1850-1942), who came to Texas from Missouri as a small child in 1851, served as a Confederate express rider at age 14, following the Civil War he returned home to Denton County and became interested in the cattle business. He participated in numerous cattle drives and by 1872 purchased his first ranch. He was a charter member of the Texas and Southwestern Cattle Raisers Association.

As his empire grew, Daugherty acquired additional ranches in several states. In 1900, he purchased land here and founded the Figure 2 Ranch. Taking up residence here by 1905, he was active in local politics and served as one of Culberson County's first commissioners upon its creation in 1911.

Due to his failing health, Daugherty sold the Figure 2 Ranch in 1933 to legendary millionaire businessman James Marion West, Sr. (1871–1941) of Houston. Although West did not live at the ranch, he visited often and the property remained in his family until 1992. (1994)

VEGA (Oldham Co.) *US 66, 5 mi. SE in roadside park*
Oldham County

Formed from Young and Bexar Territories. Created August 21, 1876. Organized January 12, 1881.

Named in honor of Williamson Simpson Oldham, 1813–1868, Arkansas lawyer and jurist member of the Confederate Senate from Texas. County seat, Tascosa, 1881. Vega, since 1915. (1936)

VEGA (Oldham Co.) *US 66 at US 385*
Site of Old Tascosa
(23 mi. NE)

Contains one of the famous Boot Hill Cemeteries of Wild West days and was the gathering place for pleasure-seeking cowboys, gamblers and "bad men" of the Panhandle in the 1870s and '80s. Outlaws such as Billy the Kid and lawmen like Pat Garrett and Bat Masterson walked its streets.

At first an Indian camping place at a crossing on the Canadian River, then Mexican trading point and pastoral settlement, Atascosa (Boggy Place) rapidly became an open-range trading center and capital of a cattle empire from 1876 to 1877. Romero Plaza and Howard and Rinehart Store marked the boom in growth. Struggles between large ranch owners like Charles Goodnight and the "Little Men" of the plains were focused there. Became seat of Oldham County, 1880, and then legal capital of ten unorganized counties.

Progress spelled doom for the town. The railroad in 1887 created other important towns and barbed wire fences ended the vital trading routes and great roundups. The open ranges and cattle trails like the famous Dodge City Trail were gone. When county seat was moved to Vega in 1915, few residents remained.

Today "Old Tascosa" retains only the courthouse and Boot Hill. Cal Farley's Boy's Ranch is located there.

VERNON (Wilbarger Co.) *FM 2916, 3 mi. E of US 283, 13 mi. N*
Doan's Crossing

A major route for cattle drives known primarily as the Western Trail developed from far South Texas to Dodge City, Kansas, in the 1870s. About 1876, trail drivers along the route began crossing the Red River near this site. In 1878, Ohio native Jonathan Doan established a trading post near the crossing and became the first person to permanently settle in Wilbarger County (organized in 1881). In the early 1880s he and his partner/nephew Corwin F. Doan recorded the passage of hundreds of thousands of cattle along this river crossing which became known as Doan's Crossing. (1993)

VERNON (Wilbarger Co.)   *FM 2916, 3 mi. E of US 283, 13 mi. N*
Doan's Crossing on Red River
By herds on the Western Texas-Kansas Trail, 1876–1895. Six million cattle and horses crossed here. "You don't need much monument if the cause is good. It's only these monuments that are for no reason at all that has to be big. Good luck to you all anyhow.

Yours,
Will Rogers"

Dedicated to George W. Saunders, president of the Old Trail Drivers Ass'n. "who kept the Trail records straight."   (1936)

VERNON (Wilbarger Co.)   *US 370, 2 mi. E*
Early Wilbarger County
Organized 1858 and named in honor of Matthias and Josiah P. Wilbarger, early Texas settlers.

Josiah, a surveyor, had become famous as the man who lived 12 years after being scalped by Comanches, 1833, near Austin. He had saved his life by putting a wool sock on his head; he was rescued next day by neighbors.

An adobe house built 1878 by Jonathan and C. F. Doan, the first Wilbarger County settlers, marks the Red River crossing of the famous Western Cattle Trail.

Vernon (formerly Eagle Flat) became county seat in 1881. The first railroad reached town, 1886.   (1968)

VERNON (Wilbarger Co.)   *FM 2916, 15 mi. E via US 283*
The Doan's Adobe Building
Corwin F. Doan (1848–1929) settled here on Red River in 1878; erected this house in 1881. In his early picket store and later, permanent building, he had large stocks of goods to supply the cowboys who annually drove cattle in herds of thousands along the western trail. The village of "Doan's Crossing" had 14 or more buildings. Doan, his wife Lide (1850–1905), and their 3 children entertained people from all walks of life—English Lords to Indians—in this adobe house. Awarded Medallion Plate.   (1962)

VERNON (Wilbarger Co.)   *US 287, 3 mi. E, East View Cemetery*
Jonathan Doan
(May 20, 1837–November 6, 1902)
Frontier trader and merchant; a Quaker, peaceable on troubled frontiers. With nephew C. F. Doan, came from Ohio and entered hides trade in Indian Territory, 1874–1875.

In April 1878 opened trading post at Western Cattle Trail Crossing on Red River (12 mi. NE), C. F. Doan moved down that fall to run post. Jonathan Doan continued to trade on frontier. Doans' store and the family were famous and respected among the Indians, the cattlemen, and the frontiersmen.   (1972)

VICTORIA (Victoria Co.)   *US 59 at River Bridge*
Guadalupe River
Discovered in this vicinity on April 14, 1689 by Alonso de Leon. Named in honor of "Our Lady of Guadalupe" patron saint of Mexico. Here at a ford, used since Indian days, Empresario Martin de Leon founded the town of Victoria in 1824.

VICTORIA (Victoria Co.)   *US 59, 8 mi. SW in Coleto Creek roadside park*
Victoria County, C.S.A.
Transportation, military and supply center in the Civil War. On one branch of the Cotton Road, which moved crop to Mexico for exchange on foreign markets for vital guns, ammunition, medicines and other goods. The 1861 vote favored secession 313 to 88.

Troops furnished the Confederacy included 5 cavalry companies. County men were also in the 6th Texas Infantry, which trained at "Henry E. McCulloch," a camp of instruction 4 miles from Victoria. Local men in Hood's, Ross' and Sibley's Brigades, Terry's Texas Rangers and Buchel's Cavalry were among the 90,000 Texans noted for mobility and daring who fought on every battlefront. Fort Esperanza, on Matagorda Island, was garrisoned by 100 Victoria militia, who were captured by 1,900 Federals.

The people at home made cloth, tallow candles, shoe blacking from China berries, coffee substitutes from parched corn, dried potatoes or okra seeds.

To block 1863 threat of Federal invasion, Gen. John B. Magruder, commander of the Dept. of Texas, destroyed the railroad from Port Lavaca to Victoria. Citizens sacrificed their fine river harbor, one of the two busiest in Texas, by felling trees and sinking boats in the shipping lanes.

VICTORIA (Victoria Co.) *US 87, 1 mi. N*
Camp Henry E. McCulloch
At the suggestion of Confederate Col. Henry McCulloch, an area near this site north of Victoria, known as Nuner's Mott, was selected for the establishment of a military training camp in 1861. Troops from Bell, Bexar, Calhoun, Dewitt, Gonzales, Guadalupe, Matagorda, Travis, and Victoria counties began arriving that September. Col. Robert Garland of Virginia was appointed regimental commander. The entire regiment, now known as the Sixth Texas Infantry, trained at Camp McCulloch until May 1862. Captured at Arkansas Post in 1863, the regiment later fought in the battles of Missionary Ridge, Atlanta, Franklin, and Nashville before finally surrendering with the Army of Tennessee in North Carolina. (1998)

VICTORIA (Victoria Co.) *US 87, 4 mi. N*
C.S.A. Camp Henry E. McCulloch
October 1861, on this site in Nuner Mott, a valley extending southwest in Victoria County, several infantry and two cavalry companies of the 6th Regiment Texas Infantry trained in this camp of instruction commanded by Col. R. R. Garland.

Co. A, of Port Lavaca, under A. Ham Phillips, and Co. B, Victoria, under Jacob Rupley, were joined for eight months by troops from nearby towns. The 6th on May 22, 1862, was ordered to Gen. Van Dorn at Arkansas Post, where it was captured. Less than 100 of the 643 men survived the war. (1963)

VICTORIA (Victoria Co.) *US 87, 2 mi. N, City Park*
Tonkawa Bank Visita of Mission Espiritu Santo
Campsite for Franciscans from Mission Espiritu Santo (La Bahia) bringing Christian teachings to Indians associated with mission. Tonkawas and other tribes were in locality when first visited by the Spaniards, 1689. Indians were sought as converts after mission was founded in 1722. In turn, converts became mission's "cowboys"—herding horses and stock. Although nomadic, they left many occupational sites. Stone footings nearby indicate permanent structure for padres' use. Tonkawas were here in Anglo-American colonization era, 1800s. (1970)

VICTORIA (Victoria Co.) *SH 59 E*
Victoria County
Inhabited briefly by adventurer Cabeza De Vaca in 1530s and French explorer La Salle in 1680's. Site of 1720 Mission Espiritu Santo de Zuniga. Mission friars, sent here to Christianize and civilize the Karankawa Indians, laid foundation for the cattle industry of Texas, their stray stock forming nucleus for later vast herds of wild cattle. Presidio La Bahia, founded 1721 with present Victoria County, has been restored on a later site, in Goliad.

Civilian settlement began in 1824 with Martin De Leon's grant from the Mexican government to plant a colony on the Guadalupe River. Placido Benavides, son-in-law of De Leon, commanded Victoria militia, which as part of army of Gen. Sam Houston, opposed Mexican countrymen during the Texas Revolution.

After the establishment of the Republic of Texas, Victoria County was officially organized in 1837. Many settlers from the Old South immigrated to the area.

Navigation of Guadalupe River began 1854 with line of steamers between Victoria and Indianola. Kemper's Bluff was principal cotton loading point.

Known as "Cradle of the Cattle Industry in Texas," county remained principally agricultural and ranching area until oil was discovered in later 1930s. (1967)

WACO (McLennan Co.) *US 81, 2 mi. N*
McLennan County
Created January 22, 1850. Organized August 5, 1850. Named in honor of Neil McLennan, 1787–1867. Came to Texas in 1835. Located on the Bosque River in 1840. Built the first dwelling, a log cabin, in McLennan County. Waco, county seat.

WACO (McLennan Co.)

IH 35, 6 mi. SW in roadside park

General Richard Harrison
(1821–1876)

One of a trio of brothers—great grand-nephews of U.S. President Wm. Henry Harrison—who all gained rank of general in the Confederate Army during the Civil War. Richard Harrison was a physician and statesman prior to army service. Won his general's commission in Jan. 1865 in Mississippi.

Moved to Texas, 1866, settling near older brother, Gen. Jas. E., and younger brother, Gen. Thos. Harrison. Practiced medicine, farmed, helped rebuild Texas economy, was a church leader.

A trustee of Waco University, a forebear of Baylor University.   (1965)

WACO (McLennan Co.)

IH 35, #11 Lake Brazos Park North

Site of A. J. Moore High School

In 1875, Professor A. J. Moore of Paul Quinn College, concerned over the lack of quality education for Waco's Negro population, began teaching small groups of children in his home. He later founded the Second District Negro School. The first schoolhouse, a frame building that had been relocated east of this site, had formerly served as a hospital. In 1923, the frame schoolhouse was replaced with a brick building. The school was renamed for its founder, A. J. Moore, who served as principal from 1881 to 1905.

As the first school in Waco designated to educate the city's Negro youth, A. J. Moore High School was an important institution in the community. Until 1952, Moore High housed students from grades one through twelve. From 1952 to 1971 it served grades seven through twelve only. Moore High was closed in 1971.

More than 4,000 students were graduated from A. J. Moore High School during its nearly 100 years of service. Many of them have made significant contributions in the fields of education, medicine, religion, law, public health, business, engineering, law enforcement, social services, theater, sports, and military service.   (1985)

WACO (McLennan Co.)

US 84 at SH 31, 8 mi. E

Waco

Founded 1849. Named for Waco Indians. Sent men to state frontier defense and Confederate Army in Civil War. Home of five C.S.A. generals.

Center for medicine, recreation, financial institutions and manufacturing enterprises.

Home of Baylor University, Paul Quinn College, Cameron Park and Annual Heart O'Texas Fair.

WACO (McLennan Co.)

SH 6 at Harrison Switch Rd., 14 mi. SE

Torrey's Trading Post No. 2

Site of greatest Indian council in Republic of Texas. There President Sam Houston made famous 1844 peace talks to assembled chiefs. A "listening post" for frontier; aided in peacekeeping. Built 1844 and run by Geo. Barnard for the Torrey Brothers. In 1849 the post was moved to Waco by Barnard.   (1966)

WACO (McLennan Co.)

IH 35, Fort Fisher

The Texas Rangers and the Fence Cutters

Before 1875 in Texas, cattle roamed over thousands of acres of public land, and free grazing became a tradition. After 1875, however, an increasing farm populace tended to protect crops and other property with barbed wire fences which were resented by stockraisers. Cattle losses in drouths of the 1880s provoked such widespread cutting of fences that the Texas government recognized this as a crime and in 1884 enacted laws and measures to curb the practice.

Texas Rangers were dispatched by the governor at the call of county judges and sheriffs to apprehend the fence cutters. They operated from the Red River to the Rio Grande, and from the Panhandle to the pine woods of East Texas. Disguise and concealment were required, and one of the Rangers who won praise for his work pronounced it the most disagreeable duty in the world. The vigorous effort went on for some years. Finally, however, stockmen who had wanted to restore the open range were won over to fencing their own lands and using windmills to water their cattle herds. The Texas Rangers had in one more instance helped to stabilize life in the West.   (1976)

WACO (McLennan Co.)
Courthouse grounds
County Seat of McLennan County—Waco
Within sight of this spot March 1, 1849, occurred the first sale of town lots at Waco Village, former home of Waco Indians. Shapley P. Ross, first settler, started Brazos Ferry in 1850. McLennan County was created same year, named for Neil McLennan, pioneer Scot whose cabin on the South Bosque River became first Anglo-American home in the area (1845).

Waco, county seat, grew steadily as a center of trade, education, and industry for rich farm and ranch area. Completion of first Brazos River Bridge, 1870, and coming of first railroad, 1872, set city on the road to industrial expansion. At the turn of the century, Waco was one of Texas' major inland cotton exporters.

Three Texas governors have resided in the city: Richard Coke (1874–1876), Sul Ross (1887–1891), and Pat M. Neff (1912–1925). Baylor University moved to Waco, 1886, and Texas Christian University was located here 1896–1910.

Military training (1917–1918 and 1941–1966) made Waco famous in faraway places. Camp McArthur and aviation schools at Rich Field, Blackland, Waco Army Air Field, and Connally Air Force Base have been located here.

Flood control dams on Brazos Basin (built 1954–1965) assure future water supply of the area and have opened much land for development in metropolitan Waco.   (1967)

WACO (McLennan Co.)
US 77 right-of-way, 11 mi. S
Fletcher Cemetery
This cemetery began with the 1868 burial of early settler Sample Carrigan, who is interred in an unmarked grave. The first marked burial site is that of Clinton A. Mahoney (1860–1868). The graveyard was used chiefly by the Carrigan, Needham, and Harris families until Catherine Carrigan Fletcher set aside three acres as a public cemetery in 1873. The burial ground served residents of several McLennan and Falls County communities, including Golinda, Mooreville, Robinson, Rosenthal, and Satin. A number of Civil War veterans are buried here.   (1985)

WADSWORTH (Matagorda Co.)
SH 60 at Ave. F
Sacred Heart Catholic Church
Early residents of Wadsworth (est.1909) John H. and Anna Ottis received help from Galveston Bishop N.A. Gallagher, the Rev. George Montreuil, and other Catholics in the area to erect the 2-story Sacred Heart Catholic Church/School building in 1912 at the corner of 1st and Ave. H. Though the school closed after 2 years, Catholic services were continued. Road construction prompted the Rev. M.J. O'Regan and the congregation to reassemble the original sanctuary here in 1924. Sacred Heart continues to serve the community as a mission of Bay City's Holy Cross Catholic Church.   (1993)

WAELDER (Gonzales Co.)
US 90, on building
Miller's Store
Erected 1900–1901 by R. L. Miller and sons. Now owned by 4th generation of family. First store established 1866.

Unique bannister features wooden balls carved by the contractor "Cap" Smith.

Bullet holes in awning testify to rowdy early era. Awarded Medallion Plate.   (1968)

WAELDER (Gonzales Co.)
SH 97 at US 90
The Town of Waelder
In 1875 and 1876, when the Galveston, Harrisburg, and San Antonio Railroad built through Gonzales County, this town was laid out to serve as a shipping point for the surrounding agricultural and ranching area.

Hopkinsville, a thriving community five miles north, moved here to become the nucleus of Waelder. Because of valuable services rendered to railroad interests in the early days, the G. H. and S. A. named the new town for the company attorney, Frederick Jacob Waelder (1820–1887).

Born in Germany, Waelder spent most of his life in Texas where he was a lawyer, Representative in the State Legislature (1855–1859) and briefly an officer in the Confederate Army. He was also a leader of the German-Texas colonists in numerous undertakings.

The town of Waelder, which grew to be the second largest in the county by 1900, can trace the history of its populace back to the three waves of German immigrants who settled in Texas from 1831 to 1900.

Highly regarded by their neighbors, German citizens were considered frugal and industrious. Joining with Latin Americans and Old South Anglo-Americans, the two other largest ethnic groups in Texas, they have left a distinctive mark on the culture of the state. (1968)

WALLIS (Austin Co.)
SH 36 right-of-way, 4 mi. N
Martin Allen (November 28, 1780–December 30, 1837)

As a young man Martin Allen assisted his father, Benjamin, in surveying roads in their native state of Kentucky. He married Elizabeth Vice in 1804 and by 1810 they and their three children were living in Louisiana.

Martin joined the Gutierrez-Magee expedition's bid to rid Texas of Spanish rule in 1812–1813. His father and nephew were killed at the decisive battle of Medina. Martin, on a recruiting mission at the time, survived. After a brief stay in Arkansas Territory, the Allens moved back to northwest Louisiana about 1818 and settled in a community which shortly thereafter was named Allen's Settlement in Martin's honor.

In 1821, Martin traveled to nearby Wharton County as one of Stephen F. Austin's "Old 300" colonists and was among the first settlers on the Colorado River. About 1834, the Allens purchased land here at Eight Mile Point (so named for its distance from San Felipe de Austin) from their son, Miles N. The Allens lived on this property for the rest of their lives.

Allen family members operated a "public house" about ¼ mile east of here that was frequently visited by future hero of the Alamo, William B. Travis. Martin, a Texas War for Independence veteran, was buried near the "public house" in the Allen family cemetery. (1993)

WALLISVILLE (Chambers Co.)
IH 10 frontage road, .5 mi. S
at Wallisville Heritage Park
Joseph Blancpain's French Trading Post

French trader Joseph Blancpain established a trading post in this vicinity in August 1754. He had been living in Natchitoches, Louisiana, where he was the owner of a mercantile store.

With a small group of men, Blancpain arrived in August and soon opened trade with the Atakapan and related Indian tribes of this region. He had entered Spanish territory, and the Spanish soon received word of his presence. The Spanish governor ordered a detachment of soldiers to arrest the French. Aided by the Bidai Indians, the Spaniards located the settlement and attacked on October 10. The Frenchmen were imprisoned in Mexico City, where authorities concluded that Blancpain was an agent of the French government. He died in prison in Mexico on March 14, 1756, and the other members of his party were imprisoned in Spain for life.

The Spanish established Presidio San Augustin de Ahumada and Mission Nuestra Señora de la Luz on the site of Blancpain's trading post. The complex was destroyed in a 1766 hurricane. One hundred years later the archeological remains of both the French and Spanish settlements were uncovered and were later entered in the National Register of Historic Places.
(Texas Sesquicentennial 1836–1986)

WALNUT SPRINGS (Bosque Co.)
SH 144, Walnut Springs Park
Captain J. J. Cureton, C.S.A.
(1826–1881)

Indian fighter, lawman and rancher. Settled on the Palo Pinto County frontier, 1854. Led neighbors in defending homes during Indian raids.

In 1860 helped rescue Cynthia Ann Parker, who had been taken 24 years before by Comanches. Captain in frontier troops during Civil War, defending Northwest Texas from Indians and northern invasion. Camp Cureton, Archer County C.S.A. outpost, was named for him.

Sheriff of Bosque County, 1876–80. Grave is on Flat Top Ranch, near here.

WALNUT SPRINGS (Bosque Co.)
SH 144, Walnut Springs Park
James Buckner "Buck" Barry, C.S.A.
(1821–1906)

Came to Texas from North Carolina in 1845. Fought in Mexican War and Indian campaigns.

In the Civil War, commanded Confederate Cavalry Regiment in Texas outposts from Red River to Fort McKavett. Camps were a day's horseback ride apart. Patrols protected outer settlements and prevented Indian attacks and threatened Federal invasion from Indian Territory.

Elected to Texas Legislature 1883. Died on ranch near here. Left personal records of his years in frontier defenses.

WASHINGTON (Washington Co.) *SH 90, Washington State Pk*

Anson Jones
1798–1858

Last President of the Republic of Texas, surgeon in the army, soldier at San Jacinto, representative and senator in the Congress of Texas, minister to the United States.

Residence built in 1845 at Barrington, country home of Dr. and Mrs. Anson Jones, moved to this site in 1936.

George Campbell Childress

Born in Nashville, Tennessee, January 8, 1804. Died in Galveston, Texas, October 6, 1841. Before coming to Texas in December 1835, he assisted in raising funds and securing volunteers for the Army of Texas. Delegate from the municipality of Milam to the Constitutional Convention held here March 1 to 17, 1836.

Chairman of the committee of five which drafted the Texas Declaration of Independence, appointed by President Burnet March 19, 1836, agent of Texas at Washington to secure the recognition of the sovereignty and Independence of Texas by the United States.

Replica of Convention Hall

Replica of the house in which the Constitutional Convention was held March 1 to 17, 1836, and in which the Texas Declaration of Independence was signed.

Washington County

To the memory of those courageous souls, the delegates to the Constitutional Convention held here March 1–17, 1836, who declared Texas free. Organized a Republic, and framed its constitution.

Washington-on-the-Brazos

This village—site of the signing of the Texas Declaration of Independence and first capital of the Republic of Texas—began in 1822 as a ferry crossing. Here the historic La Bahia Road (now Ferry Street) spanned the Brazos River.

In 1834 a townsite was laid out and named, probably for Washington, Georgia, home of a leading settler.

In 1835, as political differences with Mexico led toward war, the General Council (the Insurgent Texas Government) met in the town. Enterprising citizens then promoted the place as a site for the Convention of 1836 and, as a "bonus," provided a free meeting hall. Thus Texas Declaration of Independence came to be signed in an unfinished building owned by a gunsmith.

The provisional government of the Republic was also organized in Washington, but was removed, March 17, as news of the advancing Mexican army caused a general panic throughout the region. The townspeople fled too on March 20, 1836, in the "runaway scrape."

After the Texan victory at San Jacinto, the town thrived for a period. It was again Capital of Texas, 1842–1845; and became center of Washington State Park, 1916. It now contains historic buildings and "Barrington," home of Anson Jones, the last president of Texas.   (1969)

Andrew Robinson, Sr.

First settler of Stephen F. Austin's "Old 300" colonists to arrive in Texas. Came November 1821 with his wife Nancy and 2 children. In 1824 he received title to over 9,000 acres of land and was made a captain in the Colonial Militia. The town of Washington was surveyed on his grant and he became a co-founder of it. By 1830 he was operating a ferry at La Bahia crossing as well as a hotel and saloon. In 1835 he fought in the Battle of Gonzales, where his unit first carried into battle the original Lone Star Flag made by Sarah Dodson. He died 1852.   (1965)

Asa Brigham

Alcalde of Brazoria Municipality, 1835. Signer of the Texas Declaration of Independence, 1836. Auditor of the Republic, 1836. Treasurer of the Republic 1836–1840 and 1841–1844. Born in Massachusetts, 1790. Died in Washington, Texas, July 2, 1844.

John William Smith
Soldier in the Army of the Republic. Member of Congress. First mayor of San Antonio. Born in Virginia, 1792. Died in Washington, Texas, January 13, 1845. (1936)

WASHINGTON (Washington Co.)   *SH 90 at FM 912, 2 mi. SW*
Washington-on-the-Brazos
This frontier village was the setting for the convention that on March 2, 1836, wrote and signed the immortal Texas Declaration of Independence. In this first capital of the Republic of Texas, the constitution was drawn, the government organized. However, Washington was a target for Santa Anna's army, and on March 17 the government had to flee.

After the Texas victory at San Jacinto, April 21, 1836, Washington was again proposed as capital but Houston was selected instead.

In 1842, the Republic's government returned to Washington and remained here during the term of Anson Jones, fourth and last President of Texas.

Anson Jones, native of Massachusetts, in 1833 had come to Texas, where he at once began the practice of his profession, medicine. At the Battle of San Jacinto in the Texas Revolution, he took the field as surgeon of the 2nd Regiment. Later he served in the Texas Congress, was minister to the United States, secretary of state, a senator, and finally the president from 1844 to 1846.

Upon annexation of Texas to the United States, Dr. Jones retired to Barrington, his plantation near Washington. He died in Houston on January 9, 1858. (1965)

WASKON (Harrison Co.)   *FM 134, 4 mi. NW, via IH 20*
Swanson's Landing
(Site 16 mi. NE; Historic Railroad Bed Here)
A key port on Caddo Lake for traffic to New Orleans, 1830s–1860s. Founded by Peter Swanson (1789–1849), a civil engineer and planter. Cotton, pelts and other products went out and settlers' goods came in at this landing.

1850s terminal of Southern Pacific (first railroad in East Texas), built to Marshall from the landing. During Civil War, 1861–1865, road was rerouted to haul troops between Marshall and Western Louisiana.

Later, port declined. Steamer "Mittie Stephens" on Feb. 11, 1869, burned near Swanson's Landing with loss of 69 lives. (1969)

WATER VALLEY (Tom Green Co.)   *US 87, in Water Valley Cemetery*
World War I Peace Monument
At the close of "The Great War," the citizens of Water Valley wanted to honor those of their community who had served overseas. They were inspired by a small family monument erected on the eastern ridge of Mount McLaughlin in 1902.

On Armistice Day, November 11, 1918, at least ten men and a burro named "Come on" climbed the 2,410-foot rise of Mount McLaughlin two miles south of this site. They built five tiers of native fieldstone on the western end of the peak. Designed by local mason Harry Howard, the monument stands 22 feet high and measures 8 feet wide at its base. It bears the names of the Water Valley men who served in World War I: Herschel Ditmore, John Gillespie, Webb Gillespie, Earl Hanson, Chester Harden, Mark Harden, Ollie McCrary, John Runnels, Boone Rainey, Ulysis Rainey, J. H. Ruth, and Mark Trotter. Important facts about the war also are listed. The builders of this monument were Frank Demere, George Demere, Houston Ditmore, Harve Earnest, Will Garner, Pablo Garza, Harry Howard, S. L. Tate, Stanley Turner, and R. R. Wade.

The monument continues to honor the heroes of Water Valley. Four of the veterans and five of the builders are interred in the Water Valley Cemetery. (1998)

WAXAHACHIE (Ellis Co.)   *US 77, 8 mi. N Sterrell*
Ellis County
Created December 20, 1849 from Navarro County. Organized August 5, 1850. Named in honor of Richard Ellis, 1781–1846. A Virginian by birth, and education jurist and statesman of Alabama, 1813–1825. Moved to Texas in 1825. President of the Constitutional Convention, March, 1836. Member, Congress of the Republic of Texas. Waxahachie, the county seat. (1964)

WAXAHACHIE (Ellis Co.)   US 77, 8 mi. N
Parsons' Cavalry, C.S.A.
Originally comprised of men from Ellis and surrounding counties. Organized for Civil War service at Rockett's Spring (4 mi. E of this site), Sept. 1861. Unit was trained and commanded by Col. William H. Parsons, Mexican War veteran, colorful duelist, editor, merchant, and lawyer.

In a Confederate Brigade, this unit was joined with 12th–19th, and 21st Texas Cavalry Regiments, Morgan's Battalion and Pratt's Battery, to scout and fight in Missouri, Arkansas, Louisiana, and Indian Territory. It was famous for attacks on Federal ironclad ships, Red River Campaign, 1864.   (1972)

WAXAHACHIE (Ellis Co.)   *US 77, Rogers St. Bridge over Waxahachie Creek*
Rogers Street Bridge
Located on an early Waxahachie Creek fording site that served pioneer settlers of the area, this truss bridge was built in 1889. It was manufactured by the Wrought Iron Bridge Company of Canton, Ohio, and was one of thirteen approved by Ellis County Commissioners from 1888 to 1890. The span provided an extension for Rogers Street, a road named for Emory Rogers, donor of the Waxahachie townsite. As part of an important early north-south commercial route, the Rogers Street Bridge was vital to the growth and development of the city.   (1981)

WAXAHACHIE (Ellis Co.)   *SH 287, 1203 W. Main*
Dunlap-Simpson House
A fine example of Queen Anne Revival architecture, this house has among its many rooms two hexagons, two octagons. It was built in 1890–1891 by Judge Oscar E. Dunlap (1849–1925), a banker, political leader, chairman of Texas Council of Defense in World War I, good roads advocate, industrialist, humanitarian, founder of the Sims Library, Waxahachie. Later owners have included Mr. and Mrs. E. B. Prince, Mrs. Sadie R. Hardesty, and Mr. and Mrs. Max H. Simpson.
                                                                         (1974)

WAXAHACHIE (Ellis Co.)   *SH 287, 604 W. Main*
The Mahoney-Thompson House
Constructed in 1904 by Dennis Mahoney, contractor and builder.

He came from Connecticut to Texas in late 1800s to build Trinity University in Waxahachie (now in San Antonio). Cornerstone was laid March 21, 1902.

He later moved to Waxahachie and erected this stately house, which later belonged to family of his son-in-law, W. B. Thompson.

The building is now restored by the Ellis County Historical Museum and Art Gallery, Inc.
                                                                         (1969)

WAXAHACHIE (Ellis Co.)   *E. Main and Clift Sts. (US 287)*
Bessie Coleman
(1892–1926)
Born in Atlanta, Texas, pioneer aviatrix Bessie Coleman grew up and went to school in a Waxahachie neighborhood a few blocks north of this site. At age 23 she moved to Chicago and first expressed her desire to fly. Since there were no flight schools in this country that would teach African American women, Coleman learned to fly in France and obtained her international pilot's license in 1921. Upon her return to the United States, she was hailed as the first Black woman pilot. Extremely popular, "Queen Bess," as she was known, performed as a barnstormer for integrated audiences at air shows and exhibitions around the country before her death in an air accident in Jacksonville, Florida.   (2001)

WAXAHACHIE (Ellis Co.)   *SH 287, courthouse square*
Richard Ellis
By birth and education, a Virginian; through residence, 1813–1825, an Alabaman jurist. In that year, Texas claimed him.

As president of the Constitutional Convention in 1836 and as a member of the Congress of the young Republic, he steered the helm of state through troubled waters.

Nurtured in the culture of the Old South, practiced in the application of the law, he exercised, in behalf of Texas, courage, vision, and leadership.

Born February 14, 1781—Died December 20, 1846.
"Leaving the old, both worlds at once they view, that stand upon the threshold of the new."
(1936)

WAXAHACHIE (Ellis Co.) US 287, 5 mi. NW
Sardis United Methodist Church
Methodist church activities in this area can be traced to 1845, when the Rev. Thomas Welch, a circuit-riding minister, preached a sermon at Sardis. Following a brush arbor meeting near this site in 1873, a formal congregation was organized. Services were held in a log schoolhouse until 1879, when a frame church was erected to serve the Methodist and Cumberland Presbyterian congregations. A separate Methodist church building was completed in 1904. The Sardis United Methodist Church has been a part of Ellis County history for over one hundred years.
(Texas Sesquicentennial 1836–1986)

WAXAHACHIE (Ellis Co.) US 287, 6 mi. NW next to school building
Sardis School
Children of the Sardis community attended school in the Methodist church building from the early 1870s until a small two-room schoolhouse was constructed near this site in 1897. By 1915, the school population had grown such that a larger facility was needed. Over the years, the Sardis school system served as a source of leadership for the community. As the population dwindled and school bus service became available, consolidation with the Waxahachie School District began in 1937 and was completed in 1952. The c. 1915 schoolhouse remains in use as a community center.
(Texas Sesquicentennial 1836–1986)

WAYSIDE (Armstrong Co.) SH 207, 8 mi. NE in roadside park
Roadside Park on Hamblen Drive
Named for Will H. Hamblen (1878–1952), who in 1890s pioneered a crude road (about 6 mi. N) into Palo Duro Canyon along old Indian trails. This cut 120 miles off settlers' trips to courthouse in Claude, but was steep and dangerous.

Hamblem and his wife, Ada (1883–1955) ranched near Wayside after 1905. He worked unceasingly to get a passable road through Palo Duro. Elected county commissioner in 1928, he at last had a graded road built. By decision of the commissioners' court, this was dedicated in 1930 as Hamblem Drive. With its paving in 1954, a dream of a lifetime was realized. (1968)

WAYSIDE (Roberts Co.) SH 70, 6 mi. N of Pampa
Wayside Community
Settlers came to this locality in 1876. The county was organized in 1889. Pioneer School District No. 5 originated by court order in 1890 to serve this area with schools known as Tallahone, Poole, and Wayside, taught usually in homes. In 1914, Frederic Foster of New York gave this 2-acre school site to the county. The district bought materials, and patrons erected this 28 by 36-foot schoolhouse, painting it red. It soon became the focus for the community—site for elections, church services, and other activities, as well as housing the Wayside School. The trustees in 1914 were James A. Poole, J. M. Story, and Early Talley.

Despite enrollment fluctuations caused by drouths, oil booms, and other economic factors, Wayside prided itself on scholastic excellence. Beginning in 1929, high school students were transferred by bus into Pampa, Wayside District paying their tuition. In 1933–1934, all grades were transferred—an arrangement used until 1950, when Wayside consolidated with Pampa.

White Deer Land Co., successor to original donor Frederic Foster, then deeded the red schoolhouse for continuing community use to trustees Paul Caylor, R. E. Montgomery, and J. T. Roberts. Current trustees are C. W. Osborne, J. T. Rogers, and Jack Sloan. (1974)

WEATHERFORD (Parker Co.) US 80, 15 mi. E in Willow Park Community
The Dean of Texas Trail Drivers, Oliver Loving
(1812–1867)
Founder of three major cattle trails, Oliver Loving came from Kentucky to Texas in 1845 and to Parker County about 1855. During the Civil War (1861-65), he supplied beef to Confederate forces. With Charles Goodnight as partner on a drive to New Mexico, Loving scouted ahead of the cattle, was badly wounded by Indians, lay five days without food before his rescue, and died

of gangrene on Sept. 25, 1867. His dying wish was fulfilled when his son Joseph joined Goodnight to bring the body 600 miles by wagon for burial in this county. Recorded (1977).

WEATHERFORD (Parker Co.)   *Thrush St. at Soldier Spring Park*
Soldier Spring Park
Confederate soldiers are said to have camped here in the 1860s because of the inviting spring. In 1890, veterans used the site for their 25th reunion. During the next year, 55 acres were set aside as "Soldier Spring Park." Chautauqua programs (1910–1928), circuses, town gatherings, other reunions, and the public hanging of a criminal (1908) occurred here before the park fell into disuse. The city dump, 1934–1953, and then a caliche mine, the area reverted to park use in 1973. Civic groups joined to develop recreational facilities and restore natural beauty with native plantings.

(1976)

WEATHERFORD (Parker Co.)   *US 180, 10 mi. W*
Porter Cemetery
(.4 mi. N)
Robert Scott Porter (1795–1877), first Parker County judge, dedicated this land near his cabin as a family cemetery in 1867 after the death of his 3-year-old granddaughter Syrene E. Newberry. Judge Porter's grandson Elbert T. Doss (1847–1869) and the judge's daughter Mary, her husband W. G. Light, and the child were killed by Indians and buried here. This site may contain about 50 burials, but only 28 are identified. The graves of Judge Porter and his wife Nancy Ann (Pearce) (1806–1901) are here. Their daughter Elizabeth Jane Doss Upton (1826–1908) was the last burial. Porter family descendants restored this cemetery in 1976.   (1978)

WEBSTER (Harris Co.)   *100 block of S Galveston Rd. at 300 block of E Nasa Blvd., E of SH 3*
Contributions to the Texas Rice Industry by
Seito and Kiyoaki Saibara
Seito Saibara (1861–1939), former president of Doshisha University in Kyoto, Japan, and first Christian member of the Japanese Diet (parliament), arrived in the United States in 1901 to study theology, and with the desire to establish a Japanese colony in America. Saibara came to Texas in August 1903 at the invitation of the Houston Chamber of Commerce to advise farmers on the cultivation of rice, which was emerging as a major cash crop. He decided rice farming was the ideal business for a colony, leased this tract of land (which he later purchased), and sent for his family.

The oldest son, Kiyoaki Saibara (1884–1972), brought from Japan 300 pounds of Shinriki seed, a variety superior to native rice; and together, father and son planted a field near the canal (½ mile NE). Their first crops were utilized primarily for distribution as seed in Texas and Louisiana. The Saibaras built a house (250 yards S), and several families soon moved here from Japan, but the colonization effort failed because of disillusionment and homesickness of the new colonists.

Seito Saibara aided the growth of the Texas rice industry with improved rice strains and agricultural techniques until his death, and Kiyoaki Saibara continued new development until his retirement in 1964.   (1974)

WECHES (Houston Co.)   *1 mi. from Mission State Park gate*
Mission San Francisco de Los Tejas
Was founded near this marker May 24, 1690, at the Nabedache (Tejas) Indian Village. (1934)

WECHES (Houston Co.)   *SH 21, 1 mi. W, Tejas Mission State Park*
The Joseph R. Rice Log Cabin
Joseph Redmond Rice (1805–1866) cut timber, then his young wife, Willie Masters Rice (1809–1881), snaked the logs to a homesite 16 miles southwest of here. The cabin they built was a noted way-station on the San Antonio Road. They brought up nine children, enlarging their cabin several times. After a grandson built a frame home in 1919, the old cabin became a farm storage shed. The Texas Centennial Commission in 1936 marked its history, and in 1973 it was given to the state of Texas and moved here for restoration and exhibition.   (1976)

WECHES (Houston Co.)
SH 21, 4 mi. E
Mission Santissimo Nombre de Maria
Was founded in this vicinity summer 1690 on the banks of El San Miguel (Neches) River. Erected A. D. 1934 by De Zavala Chapter Texas Historical and Landmarks Association.

WECHES (Houston Co.)
SH 21, at entrance to Weches Cemetery
Community of Weches
Located near the site of 17th-century Spanish missionary activity, this farming community had its beginnings with the settlement of the McLean, Conners, Patton, and Gregg families, who had all arrived in the area by 1840. Originally known as Neches for the nearby river, the similar name Weches was adopted in 1887 when post office officials informed residents that "Neches" had been assigned to another community. The following year Alfred Monroe Gregg set aside land for a church, school, and cemetery. The Weches post office closed in 1939.

(Texas Sesquicentennial 1836–1986)

WEIMAR (Colorado Co.)
US 90, 6 mi. E across Southern Pacific tracks
Site of the Beef Canning Plant and Residence, Built in 1872, by
Gail Borden
1801–1874
Pioneer surveyor, newspaper editor and inventor of the process of condensing milk, who operated this plant until his death. Demolished in 1885.

(1964)

WEIMAR (Colorado Co.)
CR 208 and CR 205
Old Osage
Site of 1820 trading post of Jesse Burnam. His ferry on the Colorado River helped Gen. Sam Houston reach San Jacinto, 1836. To cut off Santa Anna, Houston then burned post and ferry.

Town started in 1850s was named for Osage orange trees.

In 1861, Civil War recruiting center. Furnished most of Co. A, 5th Texas Cav., Green's Brigade.

This park, on land deeded by Edward Austin for school and churches, includes cemetery and graves of many Civil War veterans. Was also burial site, Wm. B. Scates, signer of the Texas Declaration of Independence.

(1965)

WEIMAR (Colorado Co.)
US 90, Post Office
Town of Weimar
This land—once part of first Anglo-American Colony in Texas—grew into a townsite in 1873 with coming of the Galveston, Harrisburg, & San Antonio Rail Line. D. W. Jackson donated half of land for town, which was named for Weimar, Germany.

Post office was established in 1873. Town incorporated 1875. By 1887 Weimar was enjoying a prosperous cotton economy, had many stores and 2 newspapers. Local opera house (150 yds. S), built about 1880, was one of the first between Houston and San Antonio.

Present economy is based on agriculture. Population is 2,050.

(1970)

WELLINGTON (Collingsworth Co.)
US 83, 2 mi. N
Collingsworth County
Formed from Young and Bexar Territories. Created August 21, 1876. Organized November 4, 1890. Named in honor of James Collinsworth, 1806–1838, the first Chief Justice of the Republic of Texas. Signer of the Declaration of Independence at the Battle of San Jacinto. Secretary of State in Burnet's Cabinet.Wellington, the County Seat.

(1964)

WELLINGTON (Collingsworth Co.)
US 83, about 8 mi. N in roadside park
Rocking Chair "Ranche"
(1883–1893)
Owned by Scottish Earls of Aberdeen and Tweedmouth. The headquarters were at Aberdeen (about 7 mi. NE). Starting with 14,745 cattle, the Rocking Chair made profits for a few years, then failed. In north part of county are hills bearing its name. Also, town of Wellington was given that name at wish of Rocking Chair owners, who had a kinsman die at Waterloo where he was aide to the Duke of Wellington.

537

W. E. Hughes in 1893 bought the land and added it to Mill Iron Ranch. Later the 235 sections were sold to others, to convert to farms and smaller ranches. (1970)

WELLINGTON (Collingsworth Co.)   *US 83, 7 mi. N, South of Salt Fork Bridge*
The Red River Plunge of Bonnie and Clyde
On June 10, 1933, Mr. and Mrs. Sam Pritchard and family saw from their home on the bluff (west) the plunge of an auto into Red River. Rescuing the victims, unrecognized as Bonnie Parker and Clyde and Buck Barrow, they sent for help. Upon their arrival, the local sheriff and police chief were disarmed by Bonnie Parker. Buck Barrow shot Pritchard's daughter while crippling the family car to halt pursuit. Kidnapping the officers, the gangsters fled. Bonnie and Clyde were fated to meet death in 1934. In this quiet region, the escapade is now legend. (1975)

WELLS (Cherokee Co.)   *US 69, in Wells*
Falvey Memorial United Methodist Church
In the late 1860s or early 1870s, Republic of Texas Army veteran James H. Bowman offered one hundred acres of land to the Rev. W. D. Lewis, Sr., of nearby Barsola, on the condition that he move to the Mt. Hope community for the purpose of establishing a Methodist church. The Rev. Mr. Lewis accepted the offer, and the Mt. Hope Methodist Episcopal Church, South, was organized by 1875. The Wells community was established in 1885 as the Kansas and Gulf Short Line Railroad was built through the area to the south of Mt. Hope. It was named for Major E. H. Wells, a railroad engineer. Dr. J. C. Falvey and his wife, Matilda Falvey, settled in Wells that year. They joined the Mt. Hope Methodist congregation after it relocated to Wells in 1888. The congregation soon built a parsonage behind the new church. The church was a focal point for area Methodist pioneers. This congregation prospered for the remainder of the 19th century and well into the 20th. From 1948 to 1950 a new church building was constructed on this site in honor of Dr. J. C. and Mrs. Matilda Falvey by their son. The Falvey Memorial Methodist Church was dedicated in 1951. Active in the Mt. Hope and Wells communities from its earliest days, Falvey Memorial United Methodist Church continues to serve the area with programs of worship and service. These include ecumenical gatherings, such as a Bible reading marathon and Easter sunrise services at Mt. Hope Cemetery Tabernacle, as well as community outreach. Falvey Memorial United Methodist Church continues in the traditions of its founders. (2000)

WESLACO (Hidalgo Co.)   *US 83 Bus. at S. Texas Blvd.*
Weslaco
Located on part of a Spanish land grant known as Llano Grande, Weslaco was founded in 1919 by a partnership composed of R. C., Dan, and Ed Couch and Robert L. Reeves. The city's name is taken from the initials of the W. E. Stewart Land Co., which held title to the site from 1917 to 1919. Weslaco had a post office by 1920 and was incorporated in 1921. Founded nearly ten years after most other valley cities in the area, Weslaco depends on a wide variety of businesses for its economic base. Descendants of some of the early settlers still live here. (1985)

WESLACO (Hidalgo Co.)   *2415 E. US 83 Bus.*
Camp Llano Grande
Occupied in 1916–1917 by Indiana, Nebraska, Minnesota, and North Dakota National Guard units, Camp Llano Grande was one of a line of encampments established along the Rio Grande in response to Mexican bandit raids into the U.S. Covering over 200 acres, it included a headquarters building, commissary, and recreational facilities. South of the railroad tracks were parade grounds, tent encampments, and stock pens. The camp was abandoned in March 1917, one month before the U.S. entered World War I, and former Llano Grande troops were called for war service in France. (Texas Sesquicentennial 1836–1986)

WESLACO (Hidalgo Co.)   *US 83, 1.5 mi. E, A&M Experiment Station*
Citrus Fruit Developed in Rio Grande Valley
Red-Meat Grapefruit
Unique and colorful product of saline-alkaline soil of Rio Grande Valley of Texas. Bred of Thompson pink wood budded on sour orange rootstock.

Two nurserymen, A. E. Henninger of Mission and Dr. J. R. Webb of Donna, discovered red fruit in their orchards in 1929. They cast lots and Henninger won right to get a patent. He named his variety "Ruby Red," and was issued U.S. Plant Patent No. 53.

Dr. Webb's new strain, "Red Blush," is equally popular. Both varieties, with rose-colored meat and red-tinged rinds, are sweet, early, delectable fruits.   (1966)

WEST (McLennan Co.)   *IH 35, 3.5 mi. S access road*
The Crash at Crush
(.5 mi. E)

A head-on collision between two locomotives was staged on Sept. 15, 1896, as a publicity stunt for the Missouri, Kansas & Texas Railroad. Over 30,000 spectators gathered at the crash site, named "Crush" for MKT passenger agent William G. Crush, who conceived the idea. About 4 p.m. the trains were sent speeding toward each other. Contrary to mechanics' predictions, the steam boilers exploded on impact, propelling pieces of metal into the crowd. Two persons were killed and many others injured, including Jarvis Deane of Waco, who was photographing the event.   (1976)

WEST COLUMBIA (Brazoria Co.)   *1 mi. NW near Varner Hogg*
Plantation State Park
Home of George B. McKinstry
1802–1837

A member of Austin's Colony, 1829. Soldier in the Battle of Velasco. Delegate to the General Convention, 1832. Chief Justice of Brazoria County, 1836. In this home, built about 1830, Stephen F. Austin died, December 27, 1836.   (1964)

WEST COLUMBIA (Brazoria Co.)   *SH 36, .5 mi. S*
Site of the Home of Josiah Hughes Bell
1791–1838

One of the "Old Three Hundred" who came to Texas with Stephen F. Austin in 1821. First Alcalde of Austin's Colony. On this tract of 6,642 acres, granted him in 1824, was later built the Town of Columbia, first Capital of the Republic.   (1964)

WEST COLUMBIA (Brazoria Co.)   *Varner Hogg Plantation State Park*
The "Varner," 1835

Last home of James Stephen Hogg, first native Texan to be elected governor.

Located on an 1824 Spanish land grant made to Martin Varner. House built by sugar planter C. R. Patton.

Restored 1920. Given to the state, 1958, by Miss Ima Hogg. Awarded Medallion Plate.
(1964)

WEST COLUMBIA (Brazoria Co.)   *SH 36, 1 mi. NW*
W. H. Abrams Well No. 1

In 1920, Texas & Pacific Railway official William H. Abrams (1843–1926) of Dallas owned this old plantation land, then considered fit only for pasture. He leased minerals rights to the Texas Company (now Texaco, Inc.), whose drilling reached a climax on July 20, 1920. At 7:45 that evening a massive jet of oil and gas erupted from a 2,754-foot depth, heralding a major discovery now known as West Columbia Field.

W. H. Abrams No. 1 was a gusher. Three pipe lines were laid at once to draw the oil to earthen tanks, filled by powerful steam pumps with over 20,000 barrels daily. For Abrams, this wildcat well was a second bonus, as land he owned in Mitchell County produced the first oil in the Permian Basin in June 1920.

Locally, land that sold for 10¢ an acre in 1840 and $5 an acre in 1888 now brought $96,000 an acre for mineral rights, irrespective of surface values. Yet the boom days were hazardous. Brazoria County oldtimers suffered along with oilfield workers, all living precariously and dangerously until the flow of oil money led to better schools, roads and general social conditions. Half a century later, the socio-economic significance of the West Columbia discovery could be acknowledged as a nationwide contribution.   (1977)

WEST COLUMBIA (Brazoria Co.)

125 N. Fourteenth St.

Near Site of the
First Capitol of the Republic of Texas

About 1833 Leman Kelsey built a story-and-a-half clapboard structure near this location. When Columbia became capital of the Republic of Texas in 1836, the building was one of two which housed the newly formed government. The first Republic of Texas Congress convened in Columbia. Here Sam Houston took office as President and Stephen F. Austin as Secretary of State. In 1837, the government moved to Houston. The 1900 storm destroyed the original capitol. The replica at this site was built in 1976–1977.

(1979)

WEST POINT (Fayette Co.)

SH 71, 1.5 mi. W

Site of Wood's Fort

Used by Colonists of this vicinity as a protection against Indian attacks, 1828–1842.

Fortified residence of Zadock Woods, veteran of the War of 1812. One of the old "Three Hundred" of Austin's Colonists. Oldest man killed in the Dawson Massacre," September 18, 1842.

WESTBROOK (Mitchell Co.)

IH 20, 1 mi. W

Discovery Well for the Permian Basin
No. 1 T. & P.–W. H. Abrams
(2 mi. N)

Drilled 1920 by Steve Owen, a wildcatter, or oil prospector, in Sec. 33, Block 28, T. & P. Survey. Now owned by Standard Oil Co. of Texas. The well, extended to 2,978 ft. from strike depth of 442 ft., is still producing.

From this well, H. L. Lockhart in 1922 constructed the first pipeline in the Permian Basin. Additional discoveries led to the building in Colorado City of Basin's first refinery, 1924.

The Permian Basin—one of the richest petroleum areas in the world—covers 88,160 sq. mi. Mitchell County now has 22 oil fields.

(1967)

WESTHOFF (DeWitt Co.)

SH 87 right-of-way

Westhoff

Founded 1906 as Bello ("Beautiful View"), tent city of workers building Texas & New Orleans Railroad. Renamed 1909 for Wm. Westhoff (Aug. 8, 1831–March 19, 1911), local merchant and political leader.

For a time town had 3 cotton gins, 13 stores. It remains a farming-ranching-uranium leasing center, inhabited by many ethnic groups.

(1970)

WHARTON (Wharton Co.)

US 59, 3.2 mi. N

Wharton County

Created April 3, 1846 from Matagorda, Jackson and Colorado Counties, organized same year. Named for William H. Wharton, 1806–1839, Texas Minister to the United States, 1836–1837, and his brother, John A. Wharton, 1809–1838, Adjutant at San Jacinto. Member of Congress of the Republic of Texas, 1837–1838. Wharton, the county seat.

WHARTON (Wharton Co.)

FM 1301, 7 mi. SE

G. C. and Clara Mick Home, 1909

Oldest in town, founded 1900, on new Wharton-Palacios Rail Line. Mick, Missouri wheat grower and stock farmer, entered Texas on a "Rice Special," 1903. First home of land was a hurricane victim.

Eldest son, A. C. Mick, laid out Iago, was architect of this house. Used Cuban carpenters.

Mansard roof. Cistern on porch. First electric plant in area. Bell rung only in emergencies. Often a shelter in hurricanes. Awarded Medallion Plate.

(1965)

WHEELER (Wheeler Co.)

US 83, 1.7 mi. N

Wheeler County

Formed from Young and Bexar Territories. Created August 21, 1876. Organized April 12, 1879. Named in honor of Royal T. Wheeler, 1810–1864.

Associate Justice of the Supreme Court of Texas, 1844–1858; Chief Justice, 1858–1864. County seat, Mobeetie, 1879–1906. Wheeler since.

WHEELOCK (Robertson Co.)   *FM 391*
Wheelock
Founded in 1833 by Colonel E. L. R. Wheelock, soldier, lawyer, and educator. One of the organizers of Robertson's Colony. Captain of Texas Rangers. Died in Edwardsville, Ill., in 1846 while visiting the place of his birth.

WHITE DEER (Carson Co.)   *US 60, city limits*
Last Great Panhandle Cattle Drive to Montana
Each spring and summer after 1880, many Texas herds went up the trail to northern states for fattening. For the cowboys, trail drives meant hard work. They had to turn stampedes, ford rivers and quicksand streams, and fight Indians and cattle thieves. They endured hunger, thirst, and other physical hardships.

The last great Texas Panhandle drive was organized here at N Bar N (N-N) headquarters. Ranch manager was J.L. Harrison; trail boss, T.L. (Tom) Coffee. 100 cowboys drove 10 herds, each with 2500 cattle, or a total of 25,000 beeves, to Montana from April to September 1892. The cattle belonged to Niedringhaus brothers, German tinsmiths of St. Louis, who put into ranching a fortune made in enamel granite household wares.

From 1882 to 1886, N Bar N leased range in Carson and neighboring counties from the Francklyn Land & Cattle Company, a British syndicate backed by Cunard Steamship Line. Afterward this range belonged to White Deer Land Company. The N Bar N outfit left here because White Deer Land Company wanted the range cleared of large herds. By 1907, the 650,000 acres of its land was offered for sale to small ranchers and farmers. It was fenced and the steam plow introduced to turn the rich, grassy sod.   (1965)

WHITE DEER (Carson Co.)   *US 60 NE*
N-Bar-N Headquarters
Carson County's oldest house. Built 1887 by a British syndicate, White Deer Land Co. Site first North Plains water well. Awarded Medallion Plate.   (1965)

WHITE DEER (Carson Co.)   *SH 60 at Main*
Jackson General Store
This commercial structure was built at the original townsite of White Deer (0.5 mi. E). It was moved here in 1908, when the present townsite was established. It housed the general merchandise business of J. C. Jackson (d. 1966), a prominent leader in the development of White Deer. In his career as a public servant, Jackson was mayor, postmaster, county judge (1935-41), and precinct commissioner (1947-66). In addition, he and his wife Dolly (d. 1957) were founders of the First Presbyterian Church. The Jacksons maintained their home in the general store building for many years.   (Texas Sesquicentennial 1836–1986)

WHITEFLAT (Motley Co.)   *SH 70 right-of-way*
Whiteflat
This area of Motley County was first called "White Flat" due to the tall white needlegrass which covered the flat prairie land. A post office, named Whiteflat, was established for the rural settlement in 1890 at the request of W. R. Tilson.

At its height, the community boasted four grocery stores, three service stations, three garages, two cafes, a hardware store, two gins, and three churches. A school, first housed in a one-room schoolhouse built by volunteers, opened in 1890. It was replaced by a four-room school in 1908, and in 1922 a new two-story brick structure was erected. It also served as a community gathering place.

Dependent on an economy based on agriculture and small family farms, the community began to decline as a result of the depression and dust bowl years of the 1930s. The Whiteflat school closed in 1946, when it was consolidated with Matador Schools. The local churches disbanded in the 1960s; The post office closed in 1966 following the death of the last postmaster, Ida Morris; and the last remaining retail business, a grocery store and service station, closed in 1968.   (1991)

WHITESBORO (Grayson Co.)

US 82, 1 mi. W

Diamond Horse Ranch

Diamond Horse Ranch, founded 1850 by James R. and John Diamond. Joined later by their brother, George, who had founded paper that today is *Houston Post*. Station 1858–1861, on Butterfield Stage Line. The Diamond brothers were political leaders and active in Texas frontier defense and Masonry. James is buried here.

WHITESBORO (Grayson Co.)

US 82 5 mi. E

Sanborn Ranch

Established in late 1870's by H. B. Sanborn, one of the major promoters of barbed wire. Ranch (a showplace) was first large area in Texas to be fenced with barbed wire—a model demonstration project, contributing to decline of open-range West. In 1888, Sanborn founded City of Amarillo and thereafter sold ranch.

(1967)

WHITESBORO (Grayson Co.)

SH 56, near water well, Main St.

Whitesboro

Settlers moved to this site after Ambrose B. White (1811–1883) camped here on his way west from Illinois in 1848. His inn here was on the Butterfield Stage Route after 1858. The post office, opened in 1860, was named for White, who surveyed (1869) the townsite with Dr. W. H. Trolinger (1827–1895), donor of land for a park. When Whitesboro incorporated in 1873, White was elected its first mayor. The Denison & Pacific Railroad, later part of the Missouri, Kansas, & Texas, arrived in 1879; The Texas & Pacific in 1881. Today the area's economy is based on recreational facilities and peanut production.

(1975)

WHITEWRIGHT (Grayson Co.)

SH 160, 3.5 mi. S

Bethel Baptist Church

This congregation grew from an early prayer group, established in the Bethel Community in 1875. A small group met in the schoolhouse, which also served as a community center, for weekly prayer and Bible study. On April 16, 1884, nine men and women met to organize the Bethel Baptist Church. These charter members were Mr. and Mrs. J. P. Autrey, Mr. and Mrs. B. F. Blanton, Mr. and Mrs. J. F. Holland, Mr. and Mrs. E. F. Jones, and Mrs. Sarah Miller. The Rev. Bob Thomas served as first pastor. The small congregation grew rapidly and soon had more than 150 members.

In 1897, this property was deeded to Bethel Baptist Church by Mr. and Mrs. J. P. Autrey. In the same year, during the pastorate of J. M. Harder, a one-room sanctuary was constructed. A 1918 storm damaged the building, but it was repaired and the congregation continued to worship there until another was constructed in 1937.

Throughout its history, Bethel Baptist Church has served as a focal point for the small community. The congregation continues to maintain the ideals and traditions of its pioneer founders.

(1984)

WHITEWRIGHT (Grayson Co.)

SH 11, 3 mi. W

Kentucky Town

When first settled in 1830s was known as Annaliza. Renamed by Kentucky emigrants in 1858. Unique layout gave town protection against Indian attacks. On freight and stage routes. "Sacred Harp," a robust frontier gospel style of singing and composition, began here. During Civil War was Quantrill Gang rendezvous.

(1965)

WHITEWRIGHT (Grayson Co.)

SH 11, 3 mi. W

Vittitoe Cemetery

This graveyard was begun as a family burial plot by Samuel and Ellen Vittitoe, who settled on land surrounding this site in 1852. Their son, Frank, probably was the first to be buried here sometime before the outbreak of the Civil War, although his headstone is undated. The Vittitoes made it known to the residents of Kentucky Town (1 mi. N) that their plot was open for burials outside the family, but the cemetery was not used as a public burial ground until it was legally established as such in 1885.

More than 700 graves have been recorded in the Vittitoe Cemetery. Most of them bear tombstones with legible inscriptions, but others are marked only by stakes or pieces of stone or rock.

Included among those buried here are early settlers such as Andrew Thomas, who brought his family to the area in 1837; numerous Civil War veterans; the Rev. Isaac Teague, pastor of the Kentucky Town Baptist Church during the early 1900s; and Benjamin Earnest, who helped establish a general store soon after settling in Kentucky Town in 1859.

Vittitoe Cemetery, which is cared for by the Vittitoe Cemetery Association, is an important reminder of the early history of this part of Grayson County. (1985)

WHITSETT (Live Oak Co.) *US 281*
Town of Whitsett

Situated on 1835 land grant of Mexico to John Houlihan. At this site in 1800s was water and a camp for cross-country drives of cattle hogs. Town arose in 1913 when San Antonio, Uvalde & Gulf Railroad was built and post office opened. Named for ranch family donating right-of-way and townsite. Soon shipped steers by thousands to Northern markets.

International fame began 1924 when H. A. Coffey acquired 125 bee colonies, bred and sold queens. Besides beekeeping, area has oil and uranium production, farming, horse and cattle ranching, rock-gems and game hunting, fishing. (1973)

WICHITA FALLS (Wichita Co.) *US 281, 1.7 mi. S*
Wichita County

Formed from Young Land District. Created February 1, 1858. Organized June 21, 1882. Named for the Wichita Indians who formerly resided here. County seat, Wichita Falls.

WICHITA FALLS (Wichita Co.) *Call Field Road, Call Field sub-station*
Call Field

When the United States entered World War I, April 1917, the Aviation Section, Signal Corps, U.S. Army, had only 112 pilots. Yet the allies, relying heavily on the U.S., planned the greatest of all aerial fleets, and the U.S. moved at once to meet the expectations. In August, Wichita Falls was chosen, because of good winter weather, as location for a new aviation field for pilot training programs. Through efforts of local citizens, this 640-acre site was leased and named for Lt. Loren H. Call, a pilot killed on duty in Texas, 1913.

Construction began Sept. 4, 1917, on primary flight training school; 50 to 60 buildings went up north of this spot on Call Field Road; runways and 12 hangars were situated south of the road. Planes used included the standard JL and Curtiss JN4.

Maj. John Brooks (later Maj. Gen. Brooks) was the first commanding officer. (His horse stable, 360 north, is only surviving Call Field building). With him came 15 enlisted men from 6th Aero Sqn., Hawaiian Terr., and five flying cadets from San Diego, Calif. In time, over 3,000 officers, cadets and enlisted men were based here. Before Call Field closed in July 1919, the school gave commissions and wings to some 500 men and sent two aero squadrons overseas for combat duty. (1973)

WILLIS (Montgomery Co.) *Old US 75, 3 mi. N*
Esperanza

When the I. and G. N. Railroad came through the county, the town of Willis was established, and most of the citizens of Danville, where the Spillers then lived, moved to the new town to be on the railroad. In 1897 W. F. Spiller moved his home and store over nearer the railroad and named it Esperanza.

WILLIS (Montgomery Co.) *US 75, south edge of Willis*
Willis

Founded in 1870. Named for P. J. and R. S. Willis (large land and timber owners who formerly were merchants in area). They gave townsite, on the Houston & Great Northern Railroad. With the line came prosperity, and in 1874 Willis and Montgomery vied for county seat, but both eventually lost to Conroe.

Willis boasted a college, opera house, numerous stores; and by 1895 had vast tobacco fields supporting 7 cigar factories. This industry faded when tariff on Cuban tobacco was lifted. Present industries are timber and livestock. (1970)

WILLS POINT (Van Zandt Co.)
Wills Point Schools
US 80E and 101 School St.

Wills Point city officials under Mayor Thomas J. McKain established a public school system in 1886. Classes began in a rented building on North Fourth Street with Professor W. I. Cowles as superintendent. In 1891, trustees purchased 6.1 acres, the homesite of pioneer area settler John O'Neal, that became the nucleus of the district's later growth. Over 20 early rural schools have consolidated with Wills Point, an independent school district since 1913. For over a century, the local schools have been a focal point and a source of pride for the community.

(Texas Sesquicentennial 1836–1986)

WILLS POINT (Van Zandt Co.)
Dallas-Shreveport Road
SH 64 at Dallas-Shreveport Road

A trail established by Caddoan Native Americans and later used by French traders who traversed this area is known today as the Dallas-Shreveport Road. The trail emerged in the mid-1830s as a main route into North Texas for emigrants and cargo from the river port of Shreveport, Louisiana. Van Zandt County's first courthouse was built along the route at Jordan's Saline in 1848. Used extensively for troop movements during the Civil War, the route remained active with emigrants and ox teams into the 1900s. The route has greatly influenced settlement patterns in this area.

(1995)

WILLS POINT (Van Zandt Co.)
County Seat War
SH 64 and CR 3415

Due to a surveyor's error, the county seat of Van Zandt County was located on private property in 1850. An election was called 27 years later because of discontent with the site. On May 28, 1877, County Judge Cadwell Walton Raines ordered court records moved to Wills Point from Canton. Many citizens objected, and about 200 armed men from around Canton marched on Wills Point. Governor R.B. Hubbard assigned militia troops to maintain order and fighting was averted. The records were returned in October 1878 and the county seat ultimately remained in Canton.   (1997)

WILLS POINT (Van Zandt Co.)
US 80 at Post Oak Road,
0.4 mi. NW of the intersection
White Rose Cemetery

The town of Wills Point was established in the early 1870s on the Texas and Pacific Railroad. It was named for the log cabin/trading post established at a nearby site on the Dallas-Shreveport road by early settler William Wills. This cemetery began with the burial of Wills on family land in 1864. Wills' widow, Mary Ann (Phillips), set aside eight acres here in a grid pattern and sold lots for community burials.

Although the graveyard was known as the Wills Point Cemetery in 1874, the White Rose Cemetery Association was formed that year to maintain the grounds. In 1886, Mary Wills retained the family burial plot and deeded the remainder of the 8 acre graveyard to the Wills Point Cemetery.

The White Rose Cemetery Association fenced the grounds and erected a gate with a connecting archway at the graveyard's west entrance in 1901. In 1909, the association obtained a state charter and officially renamed the graveyard White Rose Cemetery. The cemetery was enlarged over the years and by 1964 covered about 45 acres. Among the cemetery's approximately 31,500 burials are many of the area's pioneer settlers and their descendants and veterans of conflicts ranging from the Civil War to the Vietnam War.

(Sesquicentennial of Texas Statehood 1845–1995)

WILSON (Lynn Co.)
SH 211, West edge of city
Site of Mackenzie Cavalry Camp

At or near this spot, Colonel Ranald S. Mackenzie, with two companies of United States 4th Cavalry, was overtaken on Dec. 4, 1874, by a snowstorm. Forced to spend the night here without wood or water, or grass for the horses, troops called this the most miserable night of their duty in the Southwest. Several horses froze to death.

Mackenzie was hunting here for straggling Indians, during last weeks of 1874 campaign to confine tribes to reservations.

On Dec. 5 his troops reached Tahoka Lake, where they found shelter under a cliff.   (1967)

WILSON (Lynn Co.)
SH 211, at East edge of city
Spanish Explorers' Route
A prehistoric road discovered and used by Indians, Spaniards, United States Army units, and cattle drovers. It crossed the Llano Estacado from Gholson Spring (7 mi. E of present-day Slaton), to Tahoka Lake (3 mi. S of Wilson), then to Tobacco Creek, Big Spring, and the North Concho.

Here passed many 17th century Spanish visitors: Father Salas, coming from New Mexico in 1629 on pleas of Jumano Indians to preach to them; Captains Hernan Martin and Diego del Castillo, exploring in 1650; Captain Diego de Guadalajara, seeking pearls and other treasure, in 1654. (1967)

WIMBERLEY (Hays Co.)
FM 12 at River Road
Wimberley Mills
In 1848 William C. Winters (1809–1864), a veteran of San Jacinto, came to this valley and built a grist mill and sawmill on Cypress Creek. A settlement called Winters' Mill soon emerged from the wilderness. After a flood destroyed the millhouse about 1856, Winters moved to higher ground across the creek and built a new 2-story millhouse with a long millrace and tailrace. After Winters' death in 1864, his son-in-law, John M. Cude operated the mill successfully and the village came to be called Cude's Mill.

Pleasant Wimberley (1823–1919) in 1874 bought the mill complex which included a stone flour mill, French buhrstone grist mill, sawmill, shingle mill, and a one-stand cotton gin, powered by a 21-inch turbine type waterwheel. The "Wimberley Mills" Post Office, opened in 1880, soon was renamed "Wimberley."

A short supply of cypress wood in the early 1880s caused the shingle mill to close. In 1893 the flour mill shut down. Because of the diminishing flow of Cypress Creek, the operation was converted to steam power in 1900 and the millhouse was rebuilt in order to continue in operation.

The milling enterprise was abandoned in 1934, after over 85 years of service on Cypress Creek. (1974)

WINDOM (Fannin Co.)
US 82 at railroad crossing
Old Baldwin Home
Mid-Victorian architecture, built 1890s by John Baldwin. His cotton gin patrons, 70 or 80 per day, were guests at meals in the home.

During the early 1940s, many legislators, two governors, Coke Stevenson and W. Lee O'Daniel, were entertained here.

WINDOM (Fannin Co.)
FM 1743, 3 mi. S
The Sam Rayburn Homesite
Samual Taliaferro Rayburn (1882–1961), son of William Marion and Martha (Waller) Rayburn, was born in Tennessee; moved to Texas, 1887.

Educated at East Texas State University and the University of Texas Law School, became lawmaker: Texas House of Representatives, 1906–1913 (House Speaker, 1911–1913), United States Congress, 1913–1961. World famous as Speaker, United States House of Representatives, 17 years, in terms of Presidents F. D. Roosevelt, Harry S Truman, Dwight Eisenhower, J. F. Kennedy.

His homesite (1887–1912) was half a mile south of this marker. (1972)

WINDTHORST (Archer Co.)
SH 16 at Prideaux Rd., 9 mi. S
West Fork School
Begun in the early 1880s as the Baggett School, taught by landowner Silas Baggett, the West Fork School served students in this rural region for more than 60 years. In order to remain in the center of a dispersed agricultural community, the two-room school building was moved twice: once in 1886, when it was renamed New Hope, and again in the 1920s to this site, where it was called West Fork. By 1944, enrollment had declined to six children, and the school was closed. Students were reassigned to school in Antelope. The building was relocated to Archer City, where it served as a residence until it burned some years later. (2002)

WINDTHORST (Archer Co.)   *SH 16, 10 mi. S*
The Stone Houses
Named for shapes resembling teepees; an Indian ceremonial ground, yielding war paint. In famed "Battle of Stone Houses," Nov. 10, 1837, Lt. A. Van Benthousen and 18 Rangers (hunting stolen horses) were attacked 1.5 miles west of here by 150 Keechis. Ten Rangers and 50 Indians died in 3-hour battle. Indians fired the grass. Rangers lost their horses but escaped through a ravine and walked back to settlements.

In 1874, area's first permanent home was built near the stone houses (and 5 mi. W of here) by English-born Dr. R. O. Prideaux (1884–1930), who helped organize this county.   (1970)

WINDTHORST (Archer Co.)   *US 281, 4½ mi. S*
Marcy Trail
Mapped 1849 by U.S. Army Capt. Randolph B. Marcy. Used for California gold rush; export of buffalo hides; West Texas settlers; cattle drives; 1859 Indian exodus from Texas. Route connected Texas Ranger frontier posts.

Wagon ruts, water stops visible 3 miles to west.   (1967)

WINK (Winkler Co.)   *SH 115 at FM 1232*
Wink
On land ruled up to 1874 by Comanche Indians, later part of famed "W" Cattle Ranch. Town "born" in 1926 when Roy Westbrook's Permian Basin oil discovery 1.5 miles to the north brought in 10,000 to 20,000 people, initiated area's conversion to industrialization. Named for Col. C. M. Winkler, famed Texas Confederate soldier.

WINK (Winkler Co.)   *SH 115, 1.5 mi. NE opposite city hall*
Winkler County Discovery Well
"Hendrick No. 1"; site 1.5 mi. NE
First of 612 wells in Hendrick Field, a very prolific, 10,000-acre West Texas oil pool.

This area, called "Wildcatters' Graveyard," lay on the 30,000-acre T. G. Hendrick Ranch. Drillers Roy A. Westbrook & Associates leased land at 10 cents an acre.

Well arrived dramatically, in great blasts of oil and rock, about midnight, Sept. 3, 1926. Its eventual depth was 3,049 feet. Total production when plugged in 1939 was 235,000 barrels.

Data gathered here was vital in future drilling of El Capitan reef lime, a major oil-bearing geologic formation.   (1972)

WINNSBORO (Wood Co.)   *SH 37, 1.5 mi. S*
Lee Cemetery
North Carolina natives Benjamin Lee, his wife Alice, and their family came to this area about 1853, and soon acquired over 1,230 acres of land. The Lees operated a large cotton plantation with the help of their ten children and slave labor. Benjamin Lee became a community leader and was elected county commissioner one year after his arrival in the area.

Currently covering over thirteen acres, this cemetery began as a small family burial ground in 1856, upon the death of Benjamin Lee. Alice Lee was the second person to be buried here, and their graves are included in the Lee family plot in the oldest section, surrounded by an iron fence. The graves of the four Lee sons, all of whom served in the Confederate Army, are also in the family plot.

Although established as a family graveyard, the Lee Cemetery was expanded to include graves of neighbors and gradually became a public community cemetery. Many types of stones and grave markers can be seen here, including one above-ground brick vault burial. Members of the community interred here include banker Charles H. Morris; mayor and state legislator William D. Suiter; Doctor John B. Goldsmith; and newspaper publishers Homer R. and Mae O. Weir.

(Texas Sesquicentennial 1836–1986)

WINONA (Smith Co.)   *SH 16 at FM 757, about 4 mi. SE*
Starrville Community
In 1852 the Rev. Joshua Starr, a Methodist minister from Alabama, bought 640 acres of land here on the Dallas-Shreveport Road. Platting Starrville, one of the earliest towns in Smith County, he sold lots with deed covenants against gambling and liquor. In 1853 he helped organize Starr Lodge

No. 118, A. F. & A. M.; Methodists and Masons shared a 2-story building which the church bought from Starr in 1854. The post office was moved from nearby Gum Spring to Starrville in 1857. The town thrived with stores and overnight lodgings for freighters. It had grist mills, sawmills, foundries, and a wagon factory; music teachers, dentists, physicians, photographers. Its churches and schools were highly influential. The Methodists supported a female high school; the Baptists founded Ann Judson Female School. A union academy, male high school, and female college also existed before the Civil War (1861–1865).

Bypassing Starrville by the Tyler Tap Railroad in the 1870s brought population losses. In 1907 the post office and the Masonic Lodge were removed to Winona. The schools of Starrville and Baker Springs were consolidated in 1924, and later were merged with the Winona Public School System. (1977)

WINONA (Smith Co.)
SH 155, 1 mi. N
The Kay House

South Carolina planter Francis Lemuel Kay (1814–1867) settled in Smith County in 1856. Between 1856 and 1860, Kay bought 640 acres of land and built this two-story home for his wife Mary Ellen (Black) (1826–1896) and their eleven children. By 1860, Kay owned and operated 1,300 acres of farm and ranchland. The Kay family sold the property to the Combination Orchard Company in 1909, and the house became the headquarters for the company's pecan orchards. In 1937, the Hunt Oil Company bought the house and land and has continued to operate the pecan business. (1983)

WINONA (Smith Co.)
SH 155 right-of-way, 2 mi. S
Elisha Everett Lott
(February 24, 1820–January 17, 1864)

Elisha Everett Lott moved to Harrison County, Texas in 1840. Elected to the Republic of Texas Congress in 1842, he helped open this area of Texas for settlement. He moved here in 1845, and in 1846 was instrumental in the organization of Smith County and the selection of Tyler as the county seat. He helped promote steamboat navigation of the Sabine River and in 1853 was elected to the state senate. A Confederate veteran of the Civil War, Lott died at his Starrville home in 1864 and is buried near this site in the Lott family cemetery. (1991)

WINTERS (Runnels Co.)
SH 153, 12 mi. E
Crews

Settled in 1880s. Named for C. R. Crews, Ballinger businessman. Mrs. Betty Sims was earliest voluntary teacher-mail carrier. School was built 1890 (with the Rev. Mr. Lockhart, first teacher); post office established 1892 in Wise & Broughten Store; first postmaster, J. D. Wise. Methodist Church was organized in 1890; Baptist Church in 1894. Later 11 businesses were in operation; by 1930 school had 7 teachers. The doctors serving longest were F. M. Hale, C. A. Watson, R. E. Burrus.

Post office closed 1922; school consolidated with others 1948. The churches are still active. (1968)

WINTERS (Runnels Co.)
FM 2405 and FM 2595 in Drasco
Drasco Community

Originally called County Line. Name changed when general store owner R. O. Kerr applied for a post office and was granted one under name Drasco on Dec. 16, 1904. (Post office is across street, south.) Kerr was postmaster until 1909.

First school house was built in 1902 on land donated by Tom Puckett. School consolidated with Winters School in 1947.

During Drasco's thriving years, there were 2 stores, a cotton gin, a blacksmith shop, a 5-room school building and 2 churches—Baptist Church is still active. Population never exceeded 30. (1968)

WINTERS (Runnels Co.)
SH 153 at junction of FM 384 and FM 2111
Poe Chapel

Named in honor of William Wyatt Poe, who came to Texas from his native Alabama in late 1870. Married Jerusha Evaline Cline in 1885; had ten children.

Moved family to Runnels County, 1904. Gave land for school and church buildings. Was school trustee. Three sons were later on school board.

Family active in farming, civic and church affairs. Son, Howard, introduced 4-row tractor farming to area in 1930. Upon W. W. Poe's death, 1945, each child inherited a farm. Land is still farmed, mainly by his grandsons. (1967)

WOLFE CITY (Hunt Co.)
SH 11, .7 mi. SE
Mt. Carmel Cemetery
(.9 mi. S)
William J. ("Uncle Billy") Williams (1826–1918), whose family settled this area in 1844, set aside 3.5 acres of this cemetery in 1852 for burial of his two-year-old niece, Angelina Williams. Oldest gravestones are those of his parents, Elizabeth (1789–1861) and George Williams (1786–1863). First called Williams Cemetery, it became known as Mt. Carmel after a Methodist church by that name was built nearby in 1883. An open chapel was added to the property in 1891; another erected in 1920 still stands. Maintained by Mt. Carmel Cemetery Association, the site has grown to 37.6 acres and contains about 10,000 graves. (1975)

WOODLAWN (Harrison Co.)
US 59, 1 mi. S
Woodlawn Baptist Church
Organized as Bethesda Baptist Church on July 21, 1850, with 13 charter members, most of whom had come from Mississippi or Alabama. Bethesda church building, erected in 1850, was moved in 1877 to a site donated by Capt. Henry L. Berry. For 95 years, until 1945, services were held only on the fourth Sunday of each month, sometimes furnishing an occasion for "dinner on the ground." In 1958, the congregation adopted its present name and completed this modern building on a site given by Mr. and Mrs. George C. Ives. (1974)

WOODVILLE (Tyler Co.)
FM 2097, Kirby Museum
Alabama-Coushattas of Texas
Two tribes, welded into one in their wanderings, visited Texas briefly in 1816, at Peach Tree Village, Tyler County, before swinging back into Louisiana.

Seeking land to call their own, however, returned and made first home in Texas on this site, from 1836 to 1844, under leadership of First Chief Colabe Sylestine and Second Chief Antone Sylestine. Tribe built log cabins for chiefs and lean-tos of bark and wood for rest of the people.

Settlement locations had to be carefully selected. As place for important tribal gatherings, an open field of deep sand had to be situated at center of every village. Here were held tribal pow-wows and ceremonial dancing, but the field's really popular function was as the ball park.

Ball playing among the Alabama-Coushattas was a form of lacrosse, in which a long-handled racquet was used to catch, carry or throw a hard ball past the goalee. Women of the tribe, when they played, used no racquet—only their hands.

Known as migrants, rather than agricultural Indians, the Alabama-Coushattas nevertheless were Texas settlers who contributed to the culture of the state. (1964)

WOODVILLE (Tyler Co.)
FM 2097, Kirby Memorial Museum
Site of Old Peach Tree Village
In the early 19th century, the Alabama Indians—then a large tribe—made their headquarters on this site, and called their village "Ta-Ku-La," which meant "Peach Tree."

Two trails blazed by early pioneers crossed here. A north-south trail came from Anahuac on the Gulf of Mexico, over the Neches River, leading onward to Nacogdoches; the other ran east-west from Opelousas, Louisiana, through what is now Moscow, to present Huntsville, then west to San Antonio. Other trails diverged from this: to the Galveston Bay area, San Felipe de Austin, and Goliad. The crossing of the trails made this a trading center of importance.

With the coming of white settlers, the Alabama Indians withdrew, and the remnant of that tribe is now located about 15 miles south—occupying the only Indian reservation in Texas.

In old Peach Tree Village, some historic homes are marked. It is also site of the Kirby Museum, founded by John Henry Kirby (1860–1940), who was born here, and whose career included service as a legislator, as well as leadership in lumbering, banking, oil development and railroad building. (1966)

WOODVILLE (Tyler Co.) *Shivers Library and Museum*
Texas Statesman Allan Shivers
One of Texas' strongest governors, a progressive, colorful, dynamic leader. Administration (1949–1957)—longest in state's history—was marked by winning fight for restoration of the Tidelands to Texas.

In state Senate, 1935, where he was youngest man ever seated up to that time, he was author of Texas old-age pension and unemployment compensation laws.

In 1947–1949 he served as Lieutenant Governor.

As governor he made reforms in state hospitals, prisons, schools for deaf and exceptional children; created agencies for higher education, historical preservation, water resources, studies of alcoholism. In his administration highway mileage doubled. He had a moderate tax policy and a balanced budget.

He was Chairman, National and Southern Governors Conferences, and Interstate Oil Compact Commission; President of the Council of State Governments.

Born Oct. 5, 1907, in Lufkin, of pioneer East Texas family. Son of Robert A. and Easter Creasy Shivers. Attended Woodville schools; graduate of Port Arthur High School; University of Texas, B.A., 1931, LL.B., 1933.

Married Marialice Shary, 1937. Has four children. Served in Europe in World War II. Is a Baptist and a Mason; lawyer, rancher, farmer, investor, civic leader. (1966)

WOODVILLE (Tyler Co.) *US 190, 1 mi. W*
Tolar Kitchen
Built as home south of town in 1866 by Robert Tolar. Logs cut, squared and notched on site. Has "mud cat" chimney, roof of hand-rived shakes. Converted to "Cook House." Here 3 meals every day were cooked over open fireplace until 1960. Pots were cooked "full" for travelers who "dropped in." (1964)

WOODVILLE (Tyler Co.) *US 190, 25 mi. NE on SH 92*
Town Bluff
County seat of Menard County which was created in 1842. Original seat of government for Tyler County created in 1846.

A ferry has been operated at this point continuously since 1833. Was commercial center of this section and important river port until railroads were constructed through the county. (1936)

WORTHAM (Freestone Co.) *SH 14, North at Wortham Negro Cemetery*
Blind Lemon Jefferson
(1897–1929)
Born near Wortham. As a young street musician, played a guitar and sang spirituals and blues. Composed many of his songs, and had a distinctive vocal style.

From Dallas' Deep Ellum District went to Chicago in 1920s with a talent scout: made 70 great jazz and blues recordings.

One of America's outstanding, original musicians. Influenced Louis Armstrong, Bix Beiderbecke, Tommy Dorsey, Harry James, Bessie Smith, and other great artists. (1967)

WORTHAM (Freestone Co.) *SH 14, City Park*
City of Wortham
Situated on grant given 1834 by Mexico to Robert B. Longbotham (1797–1883), a Texas colonist from England who settled here in 1839. Years later, in 1871, when Houston & Texas Central Railway was planned through the area, R. B. Longbotham sold right of way through his land for token sum of $5, and townsite was bought from him by investors. Although town was platted as "Tehuacana," post office was established Nov. 10, 1871, as Longbotham, for original landowner. In 1874 name again changed, to honor Col. Luther Rice Wortham, a merchant instrumental in securing railway for area.

Wortham was incorporated in 1910, but remained a modest market town until the 1920s, when rumors of oil attracted such prospectors as hotel man Conrad Hilton, who soon left when wells yielded salt water.

A Thanksgiving Day gusher in 1924 opened the boom. Population leaped from 1,000 to over 30,000 at once. Law enforcement was impossible, housing inadequate, but in time the town met its obligations. Churches and schools prospered. The Municipal Band was the official band of 1926 United Confederate Veterans' Convention in Birmingham, Ala. Intensive drilling had ended the boom by later 1927. In 1972 a few wells are still pumping, and new horizons are being explored.

(1972)

WORTHAM (Freestone Co.) *SH 14, City Park*
The Wortham Oil Boom
The City of Wortham rejected a well drilled by C. L. Witherspoon in 1912 when it produced gas, not water. However, oil and gas wells in 1919–1923 gave prosperity to neighbors north and south, and petroleum exploration began here.

Discovery well for the Wortham Field, Roy Simmons No. 1(1 mi. S), came in as a gusher on Nov. 27, 1924. Within three weeks over 300 drilling rigs were in the field.

3,509,768 barrels of oil were produced in Jan. 1925; total for the year was 16,838,150 barrels.

Wasteful drilling slowed yield to 3,000 barrels a day by Sept. 1927, and the boom was concluded.

(1972)

YOAKUM (Lavaca Co.) *US 77, N city limits*
In Memory of the Trail Drivers
Of Southwest Texas who passed this way, 1867–1887.

YOAKUM (DeWitt Co.) *US 77A at SH 111*
Holy Cross Lutheran Church
Lutheran missionaries began serving settlers in the Yoakum area about 1888. The Rev. Cornelius Ziesmer and about ten families organized Holy Cross Lutheran Church on January 27, 1891. Early worship services were held in homes, the city hall, the old community opera house, and the Cumberland Presbyterian Church.

The First Lutheran sanctuary, completed in October 1893 at the corner of Hochheim and Schwab Streets, was destroyed by a tornado the following month. The members worked together to build a new structure on the same site, and it was completed in January 1894. The Rev. W. C. Wolfsdorf became the congregation's first resident pastor that same year.

Serving a predominantly German membership, the church grew quickly. Its activities have included worship, civic, and missionary endeavors. The congregation purchased property at this site in 1948, and a new sanctuary was built in 1951–1952 to serve the growing membership.

An important part of local history for generations, Holy Cross Lutheran Church continues to be an integral part of the Yoakum community, still counting among its members descendants of its founding families.

(1991)

YOAKUM (DeWitt Co.) *SH 111, 3.2 mi. W*
Von Hugo–Von Clausewitz Family Cemetery
(1,000 ft. S.)
The nearby oak grove served as a family cemetery from the 1870s, originally for two Prussian families immigrating to Texas in the 1850s. They sailed to the port of Indianola and settled here, close to Hochheim Prairie (3 mi. W).

Carl Ottomar Gunther Theodor Von Hugo (1805–1875) originally owned the property; his is the oldest marked grave in the cemetery. He was born in Prussia and married Albertine Amalie Elise Elenore, Countess Zu Dohna (1813–1890), also a Prussian native.

Gustav Adolph Frederick Von Clausewitz (1802–1874) owned the land adjacent to the cemetery. He was born at Berg, Prussia, and his passport for immigration was dated 1858. He married Elise Elenore Wilhelmine, Countess Zu Dohna (1817–1870), sister of Albertine Von Hugo. Both Von Clausewitz graves are now unmarked but are recorded in the family cemetery.

The cemetery has some 14 known graves, and possibly others from before the turn of the century. Other family names represented in the cemetery by record are Barth, Bulwer, Nelson, Petering, and Stablefeld.

Burials ceased evidently after the completion of nearby St. Ann's Church in 1906 and the location there of a church cemetery.

(Texas Sesquicentennial 1836–1986)

YOAKUM (Lavaca Co.) *SH 111 at FM 318, .6 mi. E*
Ruins of Brushy Creek Church
(Several Hundred Yards North)
On 50-acre site donated 1868 for church and school purposes by John H. and Stephen Dunn. In large Irish and Czech Catholic area near the Post Road Trading Station of Bovine it was 1876–1912 Church of St. Joseph's Parish, founded in 1860s by Father John Anthony Forest (1838-1911), third Bishop (1895–1911), Diocese of San Antonio. Parishioners built church 1869–1876 of stone from muldoon, East Texas milled pine, and hand-hewn logs. Blacksmiths made nails and hinges on the site. Floor was of hard-packed, mortared clay.

On Aug. 26, 1912, last mass was said here; church burned in 1932. (1973)

YOAKUM (Lavaca Co.) *US 77, N city limits*
Yoakum
Located on DeWitt-Lavaca county line on land granted by Mexico in 1835 to settler John May. Cattle gathering area for Chisholm Trail. With coming of San Antonio & Aransas Pass Railroad in 1887, became transportation center. Named for rail official B. F. Yoakum, incorporated in 1889. Industries: beef, leather, canning plant. (1971)

YORKTOWN (Dewitt Co.) *SH 72, .3 mi. NW*
DeWitt County
Created March 24, 1846, from Gonzales, Victoria and Goliad Counties. Organized July 13, 1846, with Cameron as the county seat. Named in honor of Green De Witt, a Texas empresario. Born in Kentucky February 12, 1787. Died in Mexico May 18, 1835. (1964)

YORKTOWN (DeWitt Co.) *FM 237 at SH 72, E edge of city*
County's Oldest Incorporated Town
Founded 1848 as way station on Old Indianola Trail. Chartered Aug. 2, 1854. Incorporated 1871. San Antonio & Aransas Pass Railroad reached here 1886. Town's first school organized 1853.

Prospered as center of farming and ranching; later, of oil and gas. Pioneer strains are German, American, Pole, Czech, Spaniard, Mexican, Negro. (1968)

YSLETA (El Paso Co.) *US 80, 2 mi. NW*
Approximate Site of the Mission and Pueblo of
San Antonio De Senecu
Established by Don Antonio De Otermin and Father Fray Francisco Ayeta, O. F. M. in 1682. Maintained by Franciscan missionaries for the civilizing and Christianizing of the Piro and Tompiro Indians. (1964)

YSLETA (El Paso Co.) *US 80*
First Mission and Pueblo in Texas, Corpus Christi de la Ysleta
Established by Don Antonio De Otermin and Fray Francisco Ayeta O. F. M. in 1682. Maintained by Franciscan missionaries for the civilizing and Christianizing of the Tigua Indians, Pueblo Revolt refugees. (1964)

ZAPATA (Zapata Co.) *US 83, Courthouse Plaza*
Mission Revilla a Visita
In the vicinity of this site was Mission Revilla a Visita; established in 1750 as a part of José de Escandón's project to settle the region and civilize and Christianize the Indians. (1936)

ZAPATA (Zapata Co.) *US 83, 5 mi. NW*
Zapata County
Formed from Webb and Starr Counties. Created January 22, 1858. Organized April 26, 1858. Named in honor of Antonio Zapata, a pioneer stockman of the region, supporter of the Republic of the Rio Grande. County seat, Carrizo, 1858. Name later changed to Zapata.

ZAPATA (Zapata Co.)

US 83 right-of-way, 4 mi. N

Site of Uribeño

One of five Zapata County settlements inundated by the waters of Falcon Reservoir in the 1950s, Uribeño traces its origin to 1803, when Porción 41 was granted to José Nicolás Clemente Gutiérrez de Lara (1770–1805) for his service in the Spanish army. As required by the terms of the grant, José Nicolás Clemente worked to establish a ranch on his property against the odds of Indian raids, scorching heat, drought and periodic river flooding. He returned to his hometown of Revilla in Mexico just prior to his death, leaving behind his widow, María Josefa Martínez, and six children. Development of the ranch on Porción 41 was delayed until after Mexico won its independence from Spain in 1821. After the war, some of José Nicolás Clemente's sons returned to the ranch; by 1826 all of his children had married and moved to the ranch, which was named Uribeño. By 1860, the population of the Uribeño community, which took its name from the Gutiérrez ranch, was 152. Located about two miles west of this site, it was a small, poor community, comprised primarily of farmers, herdsmen and laborers. Although no permanent church existed, visiting priests periodically held worship services. A cemetery, a schoolhouse and a small grocery store existed to serve the residents. When the United States government built Falcon Dam, Uribeño met the same fate as its neighboring towns, but its residents chose not to move the community to another site before the waters flooded the town. Only the cemetery was relocated to serve as a physical reminder of this early border community.   (2001)

ZEPHYR (Brown Co.)

US 84/183 at CR 259, .5 mi. SE

Zephyr Cemetery

The unincorporated town of Zephyr, located on land granted to early settlers Benjamin Head and Felix Wardziski, was established in the 1860s. As the settlement grew, a school was opened in the 1870s, and churches and businesses were established. Mail was delivered weekly from Brownwood.

This cemetery has served the residents of Zephyr and the surrounding area since the 1870s. The earliest known burials in the graveyard are those of three children of the Staggs family, who died in 1878 and 1879. Another early grave is that of Ann Catherine Sewell Ward (1843–1879).

The first official deed of cemetery property took place in 1899, although it was in use prior to that time. Subsequent land acquisitions have increased the size of the graveyard to more than seven acres.

Among those buried here are thirty-three victims of the devastating tornado of May 29, 1909, which almost completely destroyed the town, and veterans of six wars: the Mexican War, the Civil War, World War I, World War II, Korea, and Vietnam.

The Zephyr cemetery stands as a reminder of the pioneer spirit of the area's early settlers. It is maintained by the Zephyr Cemetery Association.   (1988)

ZEPHYR (Brown Co.)

SH 218, 1 block E of US 183

Zephyr Gospel Tabernacle

In 1898 John N. Coffey (1847–1919) and John Schwalm (1825–1900) deeded this site for a community tabernacle. Townspeople donated labor and material to erect this open air shelter and to rebuild it after damage from a 1909 cyclone that devastated Zephyr. Many towns in Texas once had tabernacles like this for summer church revivals, political rallies, and social events. The Zephyr home demonstration club led community restoration of this structure in 1976.   (1976)

ZION HILL (Jasper Co.)

US 96 about 7 mi. S, in Zion Hill

Zion Hill Missionary Baptist Church and Cemetery

Local tradition and Baptist church records indicate that the Zion Hill Missionary Baptist Church was organized in 1852 with the Rev. John Bean as first pastor. The first church building on this site is thought to have been a small log house. On August 15, 1853, Aurin Goodgame Horn donated 3 acres including the graveyard to the Zion Hill Baptist Church. The oldest marked grave is that of Joseph Wood, who was born in 1792 in North Carolina and died in Jasper County on September 16, 1854. The original church building was quickly replaced by a board-and-batten structure and in the 1880s, a large frame building. This stood until 1967, when it was demolished and replaced by a modern brick edifice outside the cemetery's north fence. Of over 1,186 graves in Zion Hill Cemetery, 36 are unmarked or unknown. Several were citizens of the Republic of Texas; 75 war veterans are interred on this site. The graves of 102 young children bear witness to the high infant mortality rate among pioneers. Another notable grave is that of the Rev. A. C. Sims (1845-1920), who was born in the Republic of Texas, served in the Confederate Army, and was a pastor of Zion Hill Baptist Church.   (1998)

Index

Cherokee Trace, 305, 399
Cherokee war camp, 520
Chicago, 28
Chihuahua Road, Trail, 144, 286, 380, 448
Childress, George Campbell, 532
Childress County, 96
Chillicothe First Methodist Church, 96
Chimney Park, 343
Chinese farmers, home of, 82
Chisholm, Jesse, 181
Chisholm Cattle Trail, 49, 67, 80, 130, 213,
  348, 426
  Kimball Crossing, 49, 348
Chisholm Cemetery, 436
Chisum, John S., 381
Chocolate Bayou and Oyster Creek, 9
Choctaw Robinson Tree, 223
Chriesman, 97
Christoval, 98
Church & Fields oil discovery well, 121
Church of the Ascension, 345
Church of the Visitation, 307
Cibolo, 98
Citrus fruit in Rio Grande Valley, 538
Civil War bombardment, of Port Lavaca, 408
Civil War frontier defense, 367
Civil War Indian trouble, 336
Civil War Secession Convention, 25
Clairette Cemetery, 98
Clairette Schoolhouse, 98, 235
Clara, ghost town, 73
Clarendon Cemetery, 98
Clark's Ferry and Cemetery, 150
Clarksville, 99
Claude Cemetery, 101
Clay County, 72, 234
Clayco No.1 Oil Well, 164
Clear Creek Confederate War Camps, 231
Clear Spring Hall and Store, 474
Cleveland-Anson House, 524
Cline, 104
Clinton, 131
  cemetery, 128
Coalson, Nick and family, The Pioneer, 32
Coalson-Pullen Colony, 265
Cochran County, 48, 348
Coffeeville, C.S.A., 201
Coffman Cemetery, 16
Coke County, 65, 429–30, 483
  first producing oil well, 483
Colbert's ferry, 145
Coldwater Creek, early settlers of, 496
Coleman, Bessie, 24, 534
Coleman, Robert M., 105
Coleman County, 105, 467–68, 516, 524

Coleto, Battle of, 208
Collier, John, residence, 30
Collin County, 5, 16–17, 170, 189, 328–30,
  416
  Courthouse of 1927, 329
  old Courthouse, 330
Collingsworth County, 312, 537–38
Collins, James L., 119
Collins-Haines Home, 419
Colmesneil–Mount Zion Cemetery, 106
Colonial Capital, Sarahville de Viesca, 320
Colony Cemetery, 172
Colony Line Road, near Greenville, 221
Colorado City Standpipe, 106
Colorado County, 107–9, 156, 188, 195, 205,
  356, 537
  site of camp, 108
Colorado River, navigation of, 156
Coltharp community, 271
Columbus, Texas Meat and Ice Co., 108
Comal County, 16, 56, 360–61
Comanche County, 109–10, 140, 223, 288,
  415, 481
  first courthouse, 223
Comanche Exodus, route of, 20
Comanche Indian Treaty, 463
Comanche Peak, 218
Comanche Trail, 315
Comanche War Trail, 47, 372
Comanchero Trail, 300
Comfort, first pharmacy, 110
Compressor transmission engine, first of
  El Paso Natural Gas Co., 372
Comstock-Ozona Stage Stand, 379
Concho County, 158–59, 341, 381
Concord, site of, 281, 304
Concord Baptist Church of Liberty County,
  349
Concord Baptist Church of Morris County,
  375
Concrete College, 130
Cone, 112
Confederate defenses at the mouth of Caney
Creek, 469
Confederate fort, at Gonzales, 214
Confederate gun factory, 440
Confederate Hero General "Stonewall"
  Jackson, 22
Confederate Lady Paul Revere, 413
Confederate refugees in Texas, C.S.A., 499
Confederate Veterans and Old Settlers
  Reunion Grounds of Hill County, 237
Conroe Oil Field, 113
Constitution Bend, 244
Convention Hall, replica of, 532

Conway Community Church, 387
Cook Ranch Oil Field, 4
Cook Springs Baptist Church, 249
Cooke County, 81, 190–91, 299, 351, 524
  C.S.A., 191
  first oil well, 81
Cooks Point, 113
Cooks Point United Methodist Church, 80
Copper mines of Archer County, 19
Copperas Methodist Church, 265
Cordier-Tschirhart-Seal House, 92
Corn Trail, 109
Corpus Christi, port of, 117
Coronado, Francisco Vasquez de, 88
Coronado Expedition, route of, 170
Coronado in Blanco Canyon, 173
Coronado's Camp, 2
Cortina Battle, 425
Coryell County, 115, 168, 196, 509
Cottle County, 381
Cottle No. 1, gas well, 347
Cotton cards factory, C.S.A., 502
Cottondale, 390
Cottonwood Spring, 375
Cottonwood Springs, 120
Cotulla Cemetery, 120
Coulson, P. D., 493
County Line Baptist Church and Cemetery,
  197
Coushatta Indian village, 478
Cove, 344
Cowboy strike, 234
Cowden F. Bar Ranch, 371
Cox's Point, site of, 402
Coyote Lake, 351
Crabb, Hillary Mercer, 249
Craft, 258
Crandall, 120
Crane County, 120–21
  one hundred million barrels of oil, 121
Crash at Crush, 539
Crater Hill, 113
Crawford, 122
Crawford, Simpson, 215
Cree, Thomas, 388
Crews, 547
Crockett, Elizabeth, grave of, 3, 122
  home, 217
Crockett County, 378–80
  first producing oil well, 378
Crosby Cemetery, 322
Crosby County, 112, 126–27, 419
Cross, 511
Cross Mountain, 183
Cross Timbers, 190

Crow Springs, 445
Crownover Chapel, 317
Crowther Ranch, 81
Cuero, 130
Cuero I Archeological District, 239
Culberson County, 398, 525–26
Culbertson, John James, 391
Cummins, site of, 494
Cuney, Norris Wright, 231
Cunningham, James, home, 109
Cunningham family reunion, 110
Cureton, J. J., C.S.A., 531
Curry, Charles Booth, 121
Curtis Airfield, 58
Cypress Creek, Indian sites, 273
Czech immigrants in Texas, 1
  first immigrants, 359
  Hill County, 1
  oldest settlement in Texas, 283

Daingerfield, C.S.A., 131
Dairy Industry in the Santa Fe Area, 468
Dale, Elijah Valentine, 473
Dale-Rugeley-Sisk Home, 324
Dallam County, 132
Dallas, 133
  first ferry and bridge, site of, 136
Dallas County, 93, 133–37, 195, 218, 250,
  255, 290, 336
Dallas-Shreveport road, 544
Danevang, ("Danish Meadow"), 137
Daniel McLean Claim, 122
Davenport, John M., 441
Davidson, Isaiah, site of homestead, 227–28
Davis, George Washington, 129
Dawdy's Ferry, 250
Dawn, 137
Dawson County, 288
De Berry, 139
De Kalb, 139
De la Garza, Geronimo and Javiera Cantú,
  site of home, 452
De Leon Peanut Company, 140
De Zavala, Adina, 449
De Zavala, Lorenzo, 242
  home, 242
Dead Man's Hill, 157
Deaf Smith County, 137, 234–35
  ghost towns, 234
Del Rio canal system, 144–45
Delaware Indian Village site, 7
Delhi, 331
Della Plain, 173
Dellwood Park, 349
Delta County, 43, 114–15

Great Salt Lake, 421
Great Spanish Road, 12
Green, George Washington, 514
Green Bay A.M.E. Church, 516
Green Bay High School, 517
Green Lake, 409
Greenville, 220
Greenville, fourth-Sunday Singing, 220
Greenville County, 220
Greenvine gas discovery, 221
Greenwood Baptist Church, 339
Greenwood Masonic Institute, 437
Greer County, Texas, 477
Greer House, 457
Gregg County, 204, 274, 305–6
Gregg Route, 1840, 11
Griffin, site of, 363
Grigsby's Bluff, 409
Grimes, Rosanna Ward Britton and Jesse, home, 357
Grimes County, 14, 39–40, 357–58, 495–96
Grinninger Fence, 24
Groce, Jared E., family plantation, 231
Groveton, 223
Guadalupe County, 98, 200, 312, 318, 472–74
Guadalupe Peak, 398
Guadalupe River, 472, 527
Gudeblye School, 124
Guenther's Live Oak Mill, 185
Gulf, Colorado and Santa Fe Railway Planing Mill, 42
Gulf Burnett No. 2, 388
Gulf Intracoastal Waterway, 186
Gulf Prairie Cemetery, 187
Gunter, 223
  ranch, 223

Habermacher Home, 441
Hackberry Grove in Gaines County, 475
Hagerville community, 271
Hale County, 1, 160, 224, 400
  ranching and farming, 224
Half Moon Reef Lighthouse, 408
Halfway, 400
Halfway House, 97
Hall County, 331
Hallettsville, 224
Hamblen, S. P., family, 101
Hamblen, Will H., 535
Hamilton County, 226, 235
  C.S.A., 226
Hamlin, 226
Hammond, site of, 81
Hancock Springs, 290
Hansford Cemetery, 490

Hansford County, 223, 489–90
Happy, Old, site of, 90
Hardeman County, 96–97, 417
  railroad depot, 417
Hardin, 281
Hardin County, 281–82, 304, 489
Hardin-Concord Road, 281
Hargus Farm, 158
Harkeyville, 464
Harleton, 227
Harman, Lewis Given, 315
Harman-Toles Elevator, 227
Harmonson Rancho, 366
Harper Presbyterian Church, 228
Harrell Camp Ground, 276
Harris Cemetery, 333
Harris County, 32, 37–38, 41–42, 125, 241–46, 247, 392, 471, 536
Harrison County, 227–28, 268–69, 320–21, 533, 548
Harrison, Richard, 529
Harrison, Thomas, 319
Hartley County, 94, 228, 436
  Courthouse, 94
Harvey Massacre, 82
Haskell County, 229
Hasse community, 109
Havana, 285
Hawkins, Joseph H., 287
Hawkins, William Alden, 340
Hawkins Spring, 340
Hawley Cemetery, 49
Hawn Lumber Company, site of, 23
Hayden Baptist Church, 352
Hayes Park, 24
Haynie Chapel Methodist Church, 195
Hays County, 154, 283, 461–63, 545
Hays, John Coffee, 520
Headache Springs, 519
Hedgcoxe War, 509
Heldenfels Shipyard, 433
Helena, 230
Helium plant at Amarillo, 10
Heller, W. F., homesite, 90
Hemphill County, 84–86
Henderson, 232
Henderson, Homer Robert, 372
Henderson, John Barry, home, 321
Henderson Cemetery, 254
Henderson County, 22–23, 67, 94, 127, 167, 414, 475, 516
Henderson, C.S.A., 22
Hendrick No. 1, 546
Henry and Emerson Colleges, 84
Herefords in Sweetwater, 500

About the Editor

Betty Dooley Awbrey is a retired educator from San Antonio, where she was involved in educating gifted and bilingual children for nearly thirty years. She holds an M.A. degree from the University of Texas at San Antonio. Her father, Claude Dooley, a Texas history enthusiast and retired businessman from Odessa, Texas, compiled the original edition of *Why Stop?* more than twenty-five years ago. Mrs. Awbrey began working with her father to update new editions until his death in 1997.

FIFTH EDITION

Why Stop?

TAYLOR TRADE PUBLISHING
Lanham • New York • Boulder • Toronto • Oxford